T0189851

Lecture Notes in Computer Science 2993

Edited by G. Goos, J. Hartmanis, and J. van Leeuwen

Springer

Berlin
Heidelberg
New York
Hong Kong
London
Milan
Paris
Tokyo

Rajeev Alur   George J. Pappas (Eds.)

Hybrid Systems: Computation and Control

7th International Workshop, HSCC 2004
Philadelphia, PA, USA, March 25-27, 2004
Proceedings

Springer

Series Editors

Gerhard Goos, Karlsruhe University, Germany
Juris Hartmanis, Cornell University, NY, USA
Jan van Leeuwen, Utrecht University, The Netherlands

Volume Editors

Rajeev Alur
University of Pennsylvania, Department of Computer and Information Science
3330 Walnut Street, Philadelphia, PA 19104, USA
E-mail: alur@cis.upenn.edu

George J. Pappas
University of Pennsylvania, Department of Electrical and Systems Engineering
200 South 33rd Street, Philadelphia, PA 19104, USA
E-mail: pappasg@ee.upenn.edu

Cataloging-in-Publication Data applied for

A catalog record for this book is available from the Library of Congress.

Bibliographic information published by Die Deutsche Bibliothek
Die Deutsche Bibliothek lists this publication in the Deutsche Nationalbibliografie;
detailed bibliographic data is available in the Internet at <http://dnb.ddb.de>.

CR Subject Classification (1998): C.3, C.1.m, F.3, D.2, F.1.2, J.2, I.6

ISSN 0302-9743
ISBN 3-540-21259-0 Springer-Verlag Berlin Heidelberg New York

Springer-Verlag is a part of Springer Science+Business Media

springeronline.com

© Springer-Verlag Berlin Heidelberg 2004
Printed in Germany

Typesetting: Camera-ready by author, data conversion by PTP-Berlin, Protago-TeX-Production GmbH
Printed on acid-free paper   SPIN: 10993194   06/3142   5 4 3 2 1 0

Preface

This volume contains the proceedings of the 7th Workshop on *Hybrid Systems: Computation and Control* (HSCC 2004) held in Philadelphia, USA, from March 25 to 27, 2004. The annual workshop on hybrid systems attracts researchers from academia and industry interested in modeling, analysis, and implementation of dynamic and reactive systems involving both discrete and continuous behaviors. The previous workshops in the HSCC series were held in Berkeley, USA (1998), Nijmegen, The Netherlands (1999), Pittsburgh, USA (2000), Rome, Italy (2001), Palo Alto, USA (2002), and Prague, Czech Republic (2003). This year's HSCC was organized in cooperation with ACM SIGBED (Special Interest Group on Embedded Systems) and was technically co-sponsored by the IEEE Control Systems Society.

The program consisted of 4 invited talks and 43 regular papers selected from 117 regular submissions. The program covered topics such as tools for analysis and verification, control and optimization, modeling, and engineering applications, as in past years, and emerging directions in programming language support and implementation. The program also contained one special session focusing on the interplay between biomolecular networks, systems biology, formal methods, and the control of hybrid systems.

We would like to thank the program committee members and reviewers for an excellent job of evaluating the submissions and participating in the on-line program committee discussions. Special thanks go to Edmund M. Clarke (Carnegie Mellon University, USA), John Doyle (California Institute of Technology, USA), Patrick Lincoln (SRI, USA), and Harvey Rubin (University of Pennsylvania, USA) for their participation as invited speakers. We are also grateful to the Steering Committee for helpful guidance and support. Many other people worked hard to make HSCC 2004 a success. We would like to thank T. John Koo for publicity, Janean Williams for local arrangements, and Valya Sokolsky for putting together the proceedings. We would like to express our gratitude to the US National Science Foundation and the University of Pennsylvania for financial support. Their support helped us to reduce the registration fee for graduate students.

January 2004   Rajeev Alur and George J. Pappas

Organization

Organizing Committee

Program Co-chairs   Rajeev Alur (University of Pennsylvania)
         George J. Pappas (University of Pennsylvania)
Publicity   T. John Koo (Vanderbilt University)

Program Committee

Rajeev Alur, Co-chair (University of Pennsylvania, USA)
Alberto Bemporad (University of Siena, Italy)
Paul Caspi (Verimag, France)
Edmund M. Clarke (Carnegie Mellon University, USA)
Thao Dang (Verimag, France)
Jennifer Davoren (University of Melbourne, Australia)
David L. Dill (Stanford University, USA)
Magnus Egerstedt (Georgia Institute of Technology, USA)
Emilio Frazzoli (University of Illinois at Urbana-Champaign, USA)
Thomas A. Henzinger (University of California at Berkeley, USA)
Benjamin Kuipers (University of Texas at Austin, USA)
John Lygeros (University of Patras, Greece)
Manfred Morari (ETH Zurich, Switzerland)
George J. Pappas, Co-chair (University of Pennsylvania, USA)
William Rounds (University of Michigan, USA)
Alberto Sangiovanni-Vincentelli (University of California at Berkeley, USA)
A.J. (Arjan) van der Schaft (University of Twente, The Netherlands)
Jan H. van Schuppen (CWI, The Netherlands)
Claire J. Tomlin (Stanford University, USA)
Frits W. Vaandrager (University of Nijmegen, The Netherlands)

Steering Committee

Rajeev Alur (University of Pennsylvania, USA)
Bruce H. Krogh (Carnegie Mellon University, USA)
Oded Maler (Verimag, France)
Manfred Morari (ETH Zurich, Switzerland)
George J. Pappas (University of Pennsylvania, USA)
Anders P. Ravn (Aalborg University, Denmark)

Sponsors

US National Science Foundation
School of Engineering and Applied Science, University of Pennsylvania

Referees

Mazen Alamir
Keith Amonlirdviman
Eugene Asarin
Hamsa Balakrishnan
Andrea Balluchi
Mato Baotic
Alexandre Bayen
Calin Belta
Luca Benvenuti
Amit Bhatia
George Biros
Francesco Borrelli
Manuela Bujorianu
Francesco Bullo
Benoît Caillaud
Panagiotis Christofides
Frank Christophersen
P. Collins
Daniele Corona
Jorge Cortes
Vaughan Coulthard
Gregory Detweiler
Alexandre Donze
Nicola Elia
Ansgar Fehnker
Yan Gao
Tobias Geyer
Ronojoy Ghosh
Nicolò Giorgetti
Antoine Girard
Alain Girault

Gregor Goessler
Pascal Grieder
L.C.G.J.M. Habets
Inseok Hwang
Jianghai Hu
Hideaki Ishii
Franjo Ivancic
Radha Jagadeesan
Jung Soon Jang
A.A. Julius
Jim Kapinski
Eric Kerrigan
T. John Koo
Michal Kvasnica
Kostas Kyriakopoulos
Yassine Lakhnech
Savvas Loizou
Rupak Majumdar
Oded Maler
Laurent Mazaré
P. Madhusudan
Natasha Neogi
Xavier Nicollin
Kristian Nolde
Meeko Oishi
Joel Ouaknine
Lucia Pallottino
Stefania Pancanti
David Muñoz de la Peña
M. Petreczky
Bruno Picasso

Vinayak Prabhu
Maria Prandini
Robin Raffard
Dev Rajnarayan
S. Ramamoorthy
Chris Rao
Aude Rondepierre
Marco Sanvido
Klaus Schmidt
Sriram Shankaran
Vikrant Sharma
Miguel P. Silva
Slobodan Simic
Michel Sorine
Dusan Stipanovic
Olaf Stursberg
Stuart Swift
Paulo Tabuada
Herbert Tanner
Petter Tøndel
Rodney Teo
Michael Theobald
Stavros Tripakis
M.H. Vellekoop
R. Travis Wendt
Sergio Yovine
Chenggui Yuan
Sandro Zampieri
Eleonora Zanderigo

Table of Contents

Regular Papers

Invited Contribution

Lazy Rectangular Hybrid Automata

Manindra Agrawal[1] and P.S. Thiagarajan[2]

[1] Department of Computer Science and Engineering
Indian Institute of Technology, Kanpur
manindra@cse.iitk.ac.in
[2] School of Computing
National University of Singapore
thiagu@comp.nus.edu.sg

Abstract. We introduce the class of lazy rectangular hybrid automata. The key feature of this class is that both the observation of the continuous state and the rate changes associated with mode switchings take place with bounded delays. We show that the discrete time dynamics of this class of automata can be effectively analyzed without requiring resetting of the continuous variables during mode changes.

1 Introduction

We introduce here a class of linear rectangular hybrid automata called *lazy hybrid automata* and study its discrete time behavior. A central feature of this class is that the sensors report the current values of the variables and the actuators effect changes in the rates of evolution of the variables with bounded delays. More specifically, the state observed at T_k is a state that held at some time in a bounded interval contained in (T_{k-1}, T_k). Further, if an instantaneous mode change has taken place at T_k, then any necessary change in the rate of a variable will not kick in immediately. Rather, it will do so at some time in a bounded interval contained in (T_k, T_{k+1}). A final restriction is that each variable's allowed range of values is bounded. For convenience, we study the case where there is a single rate vector associated with each control state instead of a bounded rectangular region of vectors as is customary for rectangular hybrid automata [2].

Since both sensors and actuators have delays associated with them, a single symbolic trajectory of the automaton can correspond to uncountably many concrete trajectories; even in a discrete time setting with the initial region being a singleton. Hence computing the discrete time behavior of a lazy hybrid automaton is non-trivial. Our main result is that this can be carried out effectively. It then follows that the discrete time behavior of a network of lazy hybrid automata that communicate by synchronizing on common actions can also be effectively computed.

As is well known, the continuous variables available to an hybrid automaton and the fact that their rates of evolution can change instantaneously during a mode switch endows them with a great deal of expressive power. As a result, in a variety of settings, the control state reachability problem becomes undecidable,

R. Alur and G.J. Pappas (Eds.): HSCC 2004, LNCS 2993, pp. 1–15, 2004.

as reported for instance, in [3]. A sharp characterization of the boundary between decidable and undecidable features of hybrid automata is provided in [8] as well as [2]. These results, as also the positive results reported elsewhere - for example, [5,13,11,10] - make it clear that except under very restrictive settings, one can not expect to get decidability if the continuous variables don't get reset during mode changes; particularly in case their rates change as a result of the mode change. Viewed as a model of digital control systems that interact with physical plants through sensors and actuators, the resetting requirement severely restricts the modeling power of the automaton. Our results show that by introducing bounded delays into the functioning of the sensors and actuators, we can allow the variables to retain their values during mode changes. Admittedly, our positive results are obtained in the restricted setting of rectangular hybrid automata but the wealth of research concerning this setting (for instance, [6,8,5,7]) suggests that this is a natural and well motivated starting point.

We study the discrete time semantics of lazy hybrid automata. From a technical standpoint, our work is a generalization of [7] where the discrete time behavior of rectangular hybrid automata is studied with the requirement that all instantaneous transitions should take place only at integer-valued instances of time. In our terms, [7] further assumes that the sensors and actuators function with zero delays which simplifies their analysis problem. In our setting, things are more complicated due to the non-zero delays associated with the sensing of values and actuating rate changes. Further, we feel that the approach proposed here is of some independent interest from a modeling point of view. It may also lead to the tractable analysis of larger classes of hybrid automata. Finally, our focus on discrete time semantics is relevant -as also argued in [7]- in that, as a model of digital controllers for continuous plants, the discrete time semantics of hybrid automata is more natural and useful than the continuous time semantics.

Our work is, at least conceptually, in line with previous attempts to reduce the expressive power of timed and rectangular automata by taking away their ability to define trajectories with infinite precision [4,9,12]. Typically one demands the set of admitted trajectories to be "fuzzy"; if a trajectory is admitted by the automaton then it should also admit trajectories that are sufficiently close to the trajectory where "closeness" is captured using a natural topology over the trajectories. Surprisingly enough, this idea does not lead to more tractability as detailed in [9] and [12]. The key difference between our work and these previous works is that in lazy hybrid automata, the fuzziness is introduced into the *dynamics*; the observed continuous state based on which a mode change takes place at an instant is different from the actual continuous state that holds at that instant. Similarly, the actual rate at which a variable may be evolving at an instant may be different from the rate demanded by the current mode of the automaton.

In the next section, we formulate the model of lazy hybrid automata. In section 3 we prove our main result, namely, the language of state sequences and action sequences generated by a lazy hybrid automaton are regular. Moreover, finite state automata representing these languages can be effectively computed. In section 4 we discuss the restrictions placed on lazy automata and point out that many of them can be easily relaxed. We also sketch how our main result can be easily extended to networks of automata which communicate by performing common actions together. In the concluding section we summarize and point to some possible future work.

2 Lazy Hybrid Automata

Fix a positive integer n and one function symbol x_i for each i in $\{1, 2, \ldots, n\}$. We will view each x_i as a function $x_i : \mathbb{R}_{\geq 0} \mapsto \mathbb{R}$ with $\mathbb{R}$ being the set of reals and $\mathbb{R}_{\geq 0}$, the set of non-negative reals. We let $\mathbb{Q}$ denote the set of rationals and $\mathcal{I}$ denote the set of closed intervals of the form $[l, r]$ with $l, r \in \mathbb{Q}$ and $l < r$. We view $[l, r]$ as the subset of $\mathbb{R}$ given by $\{z \mid l \leq z \leq r\}$.

A *lazy hybrid automaton* is a structure
$\mathcal{A} = (Q, Act, q_{in}, V_{in}, D, \{\rho_q\}_{q \in Q}, \mathrm{B}, \longrightarrow)$ where:

- Q is a finite set of *control states*.
- Act is a finite set of *actions*.
- $q_{in} \in Q$ is the initial control state.
- $V_{in} \in \mathbb{Q}^n$ is the initial valuation.
- $D = \{g, \delta_g, h, \delta_h\} \subseteq \mathbb{Q}$ is the *set of delay parameters* such that $0 < g < g + \delta_g < h < h + \delta_h < 1$.
- $\rho_q \in \mathbb{Q}^n$ is a rate vector which specifies the rate $\rho_q(i)$ at which each x_i evolves when the system is in the control state q.
- $\mathrm{B} = [B_{min}, B_{max}] \in \mathcal{I}$ is the *allowed range*.
- $\longrightarrow \subseteq Q \times Act \times \mathcal{I}^n \times Q$ is a transition relation such that $q \neq q'$ for every (q, a, I, q') in $\longrightarrow$. Furthermore, if $(q, a, I, q'), (q, a, I', q') \in \longrightarrow$ then $I = I'$.

We shall study the discrete time behavior of our automata. At each time instant T_k, the automaton receives a measurement regarding the current values of the x_i's. However, the value of x_i that is observed at T_k is the value that held at some $t \in [T_{k-1} + h, T_{k-1} + h + \delta_h]$. If at T_k, the automaton is in control state q and observed n-tuple of values $(v_1, v_2, \ldots, v_n)$ is in I with (q, a, I, q') being a transition, then the automaton may perform this transition instantaneously by executing the action a and move to the control state q'. Thus as usual, the x_i's will cease to evolve at the rates ρ_q and instead start evolving at the rates $\rho_{q'}$. However, this change in the rate of evolution will not kick in at T_k but at some time $t \in [T_k + g, T_k + g + \delta_g]$. In this sense, both the sensing of the values of the x_i's and the rate changes associated with mode switching take place in a lazy fashion but with bounded delays.. We expect g to be close to 0, h to be close to 1 and both δ_g and δ_h to be small compared to 1 so that in the idealized setting, the change in rates due to mode switching would kick in immediately $(g = 0 = \delta_g)$ and the value observed at T_k is the value that holds at exactly T_k $(h = 1$ and $\delta_h = 0)$. Indeed, this is the setting considered in [7].

B specifies the range of values within which the automaton's dynamics are valid. The automaton gets stuck if any of the x_i's ever assume a value outside the allowed range $[B_{min}, B_{max}]$. A number of the restrictions that we have imposed are mainly for ease of presentation. Later, we will discuss how these restrictions can be relaxed. Our main result is that the control state and action sequence languages generated by a lazy hybrid automaton are both regular. Furthermore, these language can be computed effectively.

2.1   The Transition System Semantics

Through the rest of this section we fix a lazy hybrid automaton $\mathcal{A}$ as defined above and assume its associated notations and terminology. The behavior of $\mathcal{A}$ will be defined in terms of an associated transition system.

A *valuation* is just a member of $\mathbb{R}^n$. We let i range over $\{1, 2, \ldots, n\}$. The valuation V will be viewed as prescribing the value $V(i)$ to each variable x_i. A *configuration* is a triple (q, V, q') where q, q' are control states and V is a valuation. q is the control state holding at the current time instant and q' is the control state that held at the previous time instant. V captures the *actual* values of the variables at the current instance. The configuration (q, V, q') is *feasible* iff $V(i) \in [B_{min}, B_{max}]$ for every i. The initial configuration is, by convention, the triple (q_{in}, V_{in}, q_{in}). We assume without loss of generality that the initial configuration is feasible. We let $C_{\mathcal{A}}$ denote the set of configurations. Since $\mathcal{A}$ will be clear from the context, we will often write C instead of $C_{\mathcal{A}}$.

As in the case of timed automata [1], a convenient way to understand the dynamics is to break up each move of the automaton into a time-passage move followed by an instantaneous transition. At T_0, the automaton will be in its initial configuration. Suppose the automaton is in the configuration (q_k, V_k, q'_k) at T_k. Then one unit of time will pass[1] and at time instant T_{k+1}, the automaton will make an instantaneous move by performing an action a or the silent action τ and move to a configuration $(q_{k+1}, V_{k+1}, q'_{k+1})$. The silent action will be used to record that no mode change has taken place during this move. Again, as often done in the case of timed automata, we will collapse the two sub-steps of a move (unit-time-passage followed by an instantaneous transition) into one "time-abstract" transition labeled by a member of Act or by τ.

With this intuition in mind, we now define the transition relation $\Longrightarrow \subseteq C \times Act \cup \{\tau\} \times C$ as follows.

- Let (q, V, q') and $(q1, V1, q1')$ be configurations and $a \in Act$. Then $(q, V, q') \overset{a}{\Longrightarrow} (q1, V1, q1')$ iff $q1' = q$ and there exists in $\mathcal{A}$ a transition of the form $q \overset{a, I}{\longrightarrow} q1$ and there exist $\widehat{t1} \in [g, g + \delta_g]^n$ and $\widehat{t2} \in [h, h + \delta_h]^n$ such that the following conditions are satisfied for each i.
  (1) $V1(i) = V(i) + \rho_{q'}(i) \cdot \widehat{t1}(i) + \rho_q(i) \cdot (1 - \widehat{t1}(i))$.
  (2) $V(i) + \rho_{q'}(i) \cdot \widehat{t1}(i) + \rho_q(i) \cdot (\widehat{t2}(i) - \widehat{t1}(i)) \in I(i)$ for each i.
- Let (q, V, q') and $(q1, V1, q1')$ be configurations. Then $(q, V, q') \overset{\tau}{\Longrightarrow} (q1, V1, q1')$ iff $q1 = q1' = q$ and there exists $\widehat{t1} \in [g, g + \delta_g]^n$ such that $V1(i) = V(i) + \rho_{q'}(i) \cdot \widehat{t1}(i) + \rho_q(i) \cdot (1 - \widehat{t1}(i))$ for each i.

---

[1] We assume that the unit of time has been fixed at some suitable level of granularity and that the rate vectors $\{\rho_q\}$ have been scaled accordingly.

Basically there are four possible transition types depending on whether $q = q'$ and $\alpha \in Act$. Suppose $(q, V, q') \overset{a}{\Longrightarrow} (q1, V1, q1')$ with $a \in Act$. Assume that $q \overset{a,I}{\longrightarrow} q1$ in $\mathcal{A}$ and $\hat{t1} \in [g, g + \delta_g]^n$ and $\hat{t2} \in [h, h + \delta_h]^n$ are as specified above. We first note that $q1 \neq q$ by the definition of the transition relation of $\mathcal{A}$. The requirement $q1' = q$ captures follows from our convention that $q1'$ is the control state that held in the previous instant and we know this was q.

First consider the case $q \neq q'$ and let us suppose that the configuration (q, V, q') holds at T_k. We take $q \neq q'$ to mean that a change of mode from q' to q has just taken place (instantaneously) at T_k based on the observations that were made available at T_k. However, at T_k, the automaton will continue to evolve at the rate dictated by ρ'_q. Indeed, each x_i will, starting from T_k, evolve at rate $\rho'_q(i)$ until some $T_k + t_1$ with $t_1 \in [g, g + \delta_g]$. It will then start to evolve at rate $\rho_q(i)$ until T_{k+1}. Consequently, at T_{k+1}, the value of x_i will be $V1(i) = V(i) + \rho'_q(i) \cdot t_1 + \rho_q(i) \cdot (1 - t_1)$. On the other hand, $q1 \neq q$ implies that another instantaneous mode change has taken place at T_{k+1} based on the measurements made in the interval $[T_k + h, T_k + h + \delta_h]$. Suppose x_i was measured at $T_k + t_2$ with $t_2 \in [T_k + h, T_k + h + \delta_h]$. Then in order for the transition $q \overset{a,I}{\longrightarrow} q1$ of $\mathcal{A}$ to be enabled at T_{k+1}, it must be the case that the observed value of x_i at $T_k + t_2$ falls in $I(i)$. But then this value is $V(i) + \rho'_q(i) \cdot t_1 + \rho_q(i) \cdot (t_2 - t_1)$. This explains the demands placed on the transition $(q, V, q') \overset{a}{\Longrightarrow} (q1, V1, q1')$. It is worth noting that in case $q = q'$ (i.e. no mode change has taken place at T_k) then $V1(i) = V(i) + \rho_q(i) \cdot t_1 + \rho_q(i) \cdot (1 - t_1) = V(i) + \rho_q$ as it should be. Furthermore, $V(i) + \rho_q(i) \cdot t_1 + \rho_q(i) \cdot (t_2 - t_1) = V(i) + \rho_q(i) \cdot t_2$ and this must fall in $I(i)$ as to be expected.

Similar (and simpler) considerations motivate the demands placed on transitions of the form $(q, V, q') \overset{\tau}{\Longrightarrow} (q1, V1, q1')$. Here again, it is worth noting that, in case $q = q'$, $V1(i)$ is determined uniquely, namely, $V1(i) = V(i) + \rho_q(i)$.

We now define the transition system $TS_{\mathcal{A}} = (RC_{\mathcal{A}}, (q_{in}, V_{in}, q_{in}), Act \cup \{\tau\}, \Longrightarrow_{\mathcal{A}})$ via:

- $RC_{\mathcal{A}}$, the set of *reachable configurations* of $\mathcal{A}$ is the least subset of C that contains the initial configuration (q_{in}, V_{in}, q_{in}) and satisfies:
  Suppose (q, V, q') is in $RC_{\mathcal{A}}$ and is a feasible configuration. Suppose further, $(q, V, q') \overset{\alpha}{\Longrightarrow} (q1, V1, q)$ for some $\alpha \in Act \cup \{\tau\}$. Then $(q1, V1, q) \in RC_{\mathcal{A}}$.
- $\Longrightarrow_{\mathcal{A}}$ is $\Longrightarrow$ restricted to $RC_{\mathcal{A}} \times Act \cup \{\tau\} \times RC_{\mathcal{A}}$.

We will often write RC instead of $RC_{\mathcal{A}}$ and write $\Longrightarrow$ instead of $\Longrightarrow_{\mathcal{A}}$. We note that a reachable configuration can be the source of a transition in $TS_{\mathcal{A}}$ only if it is feasible. Thus infeasible reachable configurations will be deadlocked in $TS_{\mathcal{A}}$.

A *run* of $TS_{\mathcal{A}}$ is a finite sequence of the form
$$\sigma = (q_0, V_0, q'_0) \alpha_0 (q_1, V_1, q'_1) \alpha_1 (q_2, V_2, q'_2) \ldots (q_k, V_k, q'_k)$$ where (q_0, V_0, q'_0) is the initial configuration and $(q_m, V_m, q'_m) \overset{\alpha_m}{\Longrightarrow} (q_{m+1}, V_{m+1}, q'_{m+1})$ for $0 \leq m < k$. The *st-sequence (state sequence)* induced by the run σ above is denoted as $st(\sigma)$ and it is the the sequence $q_0 q_1 \ldots q_n$. On the other hand, the *act-sequence* induced

by σ is denoted as $act(\sigma)$ and it is the sequence $\alpha_0\alpha_1 \dots \alpha_n$. We now define the languages $\mathcal{L}_{st}(\mathcal{A})$ and $\mathcal{L}_{act}(\mathcal{A})$ as :

- $\mathcal{L}_{st}(\mathcal{A}) = \{st(\sigma) \mid \sigma \text{ is a run of } \mathcal{A}\}$.
- $\mathcal{L}_{act}(\mathcal{A}) = \{act(\sigma) \mid \sigma \text{ is a run of } \mathcal{A}\}$.

Our main result is that $\mathcal{L}_{st}(\mathcal{A})$ is a regular subset of Q^* while $\mathcal{L}_{act}(\mathcal{A})$ is a regular subset of $(Act \cup \{\tau\})^*$. Moreover, we can effectively construct finite state automata representing these languages. As a consequence, a variety of verification problems for lazy hybrid automata can be effectively solved.

3   Proof of the Main Result

We shall first establish the main result for the one dimensional case. As is often the case with rectangular hybrid automata [5], it will then be easy to lift the proof to the n-dimensional case with the help of a (Cartesian) product operation.

3.1   The One Dimensional Case

Let $\mathcal{A} = (Q, Act, q_{in}, V_{in}, D, \{\rho_q\}_{q \in Q}, B, \longrightarrow)$ be a lazy automaton. We assume for $\mathcal{A}$, the terminology and notations defined in the previous section. Until further notice , we set $n = 1$ and we will write x instead of x_i and ρ_q instead of $\rho_q(i)$ for $q \in Q$. The key idea is quantize the unit time interval and correspondingly the phase interval $[B_{min}, B_{max}]$. We first define Δ to be the largest positive rational number that *integrally* divides every number in the finite set of rational numbers $\{g, \delta_g, h, \delta_h, 1\}$. We next define Γ to be the largest positive rational number that *integrally* divides each number in the finite set of rational numbers $\{\rho_q \cdot \Delta \mid q \in Q\} \cup \{B_{min}, B_{max}\} \cup \{l, r \mid (q, a, [l, r], q') \text{ is a transition in } \mathcal{A}\}$.

Let $\mathbb{Z}$ denote the set of integers. We now define the map $\|\cdot\| : \mathbb{R} \to \mathbb{Z} \times (\{0, 1\} \cup \{\bot\})$ as follows.

- If $v \in (-\infty, B_{min})$, then $\|v\| = (k_{min} - 1, \bot)$ where $k_{min} \cdot \Gamma = B_{min}$. If $v \in (B_{max}, \infty)$ then $\|v\| = (k_{max}, \bot)$ where $k_{max} \cdot \Gamma = B_{max}$.
- Suppose $v \in [B_{min}, B_{max}]$ and $k \in \mathbb{Z}$ and $\widehat{v} \in [0, \Gamma)$ such that $v = k \cdot \Gamma + \widehat{v}$. Then $\|v\| = (k, 0)$ if $\widehat{v} = 0$ and $\|v\| = (k, 1)$ if $\widehat{v} \neq 0$.

The map $\|\cdot\|$ can be extended in a natural way to configurations. Denoting this extension also as $\|\cdot\|$, we define $\|(q, v, q')\|$ to be $(q, \|v\|, q')$. Let $\mathcal{D}_{\mathcal{A}} = \{\|c\| \mid c \in C_{\mathcal{A}}\}$. Clearly $\mathcal{D}_{\mathcal{A}}$ is a finite set and we will often write $\mathcal{D}$ instead of $\mathcal{D}_{\mathcal{A}}$. Our goal is to show that the equivalence relation over the reachable configurations RC of $\mathcal{A}$ induced by the map $\|\cdot\|$ in turn induces a right congruence of finite index over Q^*. The proof will make use of the following simple observation. In stating the observation and elsewhere, we will use the following notations. For $q, q' \in Q$ we let N_q and $N_{qq'}$ be the positive integers such that $|\rho_q \cdot \Delta| = N_q \cdot \Gamma$ and $|(\rho_q - \rho'_q) \cdot \Delta| = N_{qq'} \cdot \Gamma$. Clearly, N_q and $N_{qq'}$ exist because of the choice of Δ and Γ.

Lemma 1. *Let* $q, q' \in Q$. *Define the functions* f_q *and* $f_{qq'}$ *as:*

(1) $f_q : [0, \Delta/N_q] \to [0, \Gamma]$ *and is given by* $f_q(\theta) = \lfloor \rho_q \cdot \theta \rfloor$.
(2) $f_{qq'} : [0, \Delta/N_{qq'}] \to [0, \Gamma]$ *and is given by* $f_{qq'}(\theta) = \lfloor (\rho_q - \rho_{q'}) \cdot \theta \rfloor$.

Then both f_q *and* $f_{qq'}$ *are well-defined, continuous and onto.*

Proof. Follows easily from the definitions and the basic property of monotonic real valued functions over bounded domains.   □

We are now ready to tackle the main part of the proof.

Theorem 1. *Let* $c1$ *and* $c2$ *be two reachable configurations such that* $\|c1\| = \|c2\|$. *Suppose* $\alpha \in Act \cup \{\tau\}$ *and* $c1'$ *is a reachable configuration such that* $c1 \overset{\alpha}{\Longrightarrow}_{\mathcal{A}} c1'$. *Then there exists a reachable configuration* $c2'$ *such that* $c2 \overset{\alpha}{\Longrightarrow}_{\mathcal{A}} c2'$ *and* $\|c1'\| = \|c2'\|$.

Proof. Clearly $c1$ is feasible and since $\|c1\| = \|c2\|$, it follows that $c2$ is also feasible.

   Assume that $c1 = (q1, V1, q1')$ and $c2 = (q2, V2, q2')$ and that $\|V1\| = (K1, z1)$ and $\|V2\| = (K2, z2)$. Since $\|c1\| = \|c2\|$, we can set $q = q1 = q2$, $q' = q1' = q2'$ and $(K, z) = (K1, z1) = (K2, z2)$. If $z = 0$ then $V1 = V2$ and hence $c1 = c2$ and the result follows.

   So assume that $z = 1$ and $V1 \neq V2$. Hence $V1, V2 \in (K.\Gamma, (K+1).\Gamma)$ and hence $\|(q, V1, q')\| = \|(q, V2, q')\| = (q, (K, 1), q')$. Furthermore, there exist $v1, v2 \in (0, \Gamma)$ such that $v1 \neq v2$ and $V1 = K \cdot \Gamma + v1$ and $V2 = K \cdot \Gamma + v2$. In what follows, for the sake of convenience, we will assume that $0 \leq \rho_{q'} \leq \rho_q$ and that $v2 < v1$. From the structure of the proof it will be obvious that this involves no loss of generality.

   Let $c1' = (s, V1', q)$. Then we have $(q, V1, q') \overset{\alpha}{\Longrightarrow} (s, V1', q)$. We are required to show that there exists $V2'$ such that $(q, V2, q') \overset{\alpha}{\Longrightarrow} (s, V2', q)$ with $\|V1'\| = \|V2'\|$. We shall do this by considering four cases.

Case 1: $q = q'$ **and** $\alpha = \tau$.

   Since $q = q'$, no mode change has taken place in the previous time interval. Hence the automaton will evolve at rate ρ_q during the current unit interval. On the other hand, $\alpha = \tau$ implies that $s = q$ and hence no mode change takes place at the end of this unit interval either. Consequently, we must have $V1' = V1 + \rho_q$. We now set $V2' = V2 + \rho_q$. Then it follows that $(q, V2, q') \overset{\alpha}{\Longrightarrow} (q, V2', q)$. We need to argue that $\|V1'\| = \|V2'\|$.

   In what follows, we define for $\zeta \in \{g, \delta_g, h, \delta_h, 1\}$, N_ζ to be the positive integer satisfying $\zeta = N_\zeta \cdot \Delta$. These positive integers must exist by the choice of Δ.

   Now $\rho_q = \rho_q \cdot 1 = \rho_q \cdot N_1 \cdot \Delta = N_q \cdot N_1 \cdot \Gamma$. (Recall that $\rho_q \cdot \Delta = N_q \cdot \Gamma$). But then $V1, V2 \in (K \cdot \Gamma, (K+1) \cdot \Gamma)$ and hence $V1', V2' \in ((K + N_q \cdot N_1) \cdot \Gamma, (K + 1 + N_q \cdot N_1) \cdot \Gamma)$. This at once leads to $\|V1'\| = \|V2'\|$.

Case 2: $q = q'$ **and** $\alpha \in Act$.

   Since $q = q'$ we again have that no mode change has taken place in the previous interval and hence the automaton will evolve at rate ρ_q in the current interval. Hence, as in the previous case, we must have $V1' = V1 + \rho_q$. Again, we set $V2' = V2 + \rho_q$. Consequently as shown in the previous case, $\|V1'\| = \|V2'\|$. So if we show that $(q, V2, q') \stackrel{\alpha}{\Longrightarrow} (s, V2', q)$, then we are done.

We are given that $(q, V1, q') \stackrel{\alpha}{\Longrightarrow} (s, V1', q)$. Hence there exists a transition of the form (q, α, I, s) in $\mathcal{A}$ and there exists $t1 \in [h, h+\delta_h]$ such that $V1 + \rho_q \cdot t1 \in I$. We just need to show that there exists $t2 \in [h, h+\delta_h]$ such that $V2 + \rho_q \cdot t2 \in I$.

In order to fix $t2$, recall that $h = N_h \cdot \Delta$ and $\delta_h = N_{\delta_h} \cdot \Delta$. We first note that $t1 \in [N_h \cdot \Delta, (N_h + N_{\delta_h}) \cdot \Delta]$. Noticing that $\rho_q \cdot \Delta = N_q \cdot \Gamma$ and hence $\rho_q \cdot (\Delta/N_q) = \Gamma$ we set $\Delta_q = \Delta/N_q$, and observe that $t1 \in [N_h \cdot N_q \cdot \Delta_q, (N_h + N_{\delta_h}) \cdot N_q \cdot \Delta_q]$. Let N be the least integer in the interval $[N_h \cdot N_q, (N_h + N_{\delta_h}) \cdot N_q]$ such that $t1 \in [N \cdot \Delta_q, (N + 1) \cdot \Delta_q]$. Let $\theta 1 = t1 - N \cdot \Delta_q$. Clearly $\theta 1 \in [0, \Delta_q]$.

Suppose $\theta 1 = 0$. Then $\rho_q \cdot t1 = \rho_q \cdot N \cdot \Delta_q = N \cdot \Gamma$ and hence $\widehat{V1} = V1 + \rho_q \cdot t1 \in ((K + N) \cdot \Gamma, (K + 1 + N) \cdot \Gamma)$. Set $t2 = t1$. Then $\widehat{V2} = V2 + \rho_q \cdot t1 \in ((K + N) \cdot \Gamma, (K + 1 + N) \cdot \Gamma)$ too. Now assume that $I = [l, r]$. Then there exist integers N_l and and N_r such that $l = N_l \cdot \Gamma$ and $r = N_r \cdot \Gamma$ with $N_l < N_r$. Since $\widehat{V1} \in [l, r]$, we must have $N_l \leq (K + N) < (K + N + 1) \leq N_r$. But this implies that $\widehat{V2} = V2 + \rho_q \cdot t1 \in [l, r]$ too. Hence $(q, V2, q') \stackrel{\alpha}{\Longrightarrow} (s, V2', q)$.

The case $\theta 1 = \Delta_q$ can be dealt with in a similar manner by again setting $t2 = t1$.

So now assume that $\theta 1 \in (0, \Delta/N_q)$. Then clearly $\widehat{V1} = V1 + \rho_q \cdot t1 \in [v1 + (K + N) \cdot \Gamma, v1 + (K + N + 1) \cdot \Gamma]$. (Recall that $v1 = V1 - K \cdot \Gamma$ and $v2 = V2 - K \cdot \Gamma$.) There are three possibilities to consider.

Firstly, suppose $\widehat{V1} \in [v1 + (K + N) \cdot \Gamma, (K + N + 1) \cdot \Gamma)$. Then we set $t2 = N \cdot \Delta_q$. Clearly $\widehat{V2} = V2 + \rho_q \cdot N \cdot \Delta_q \in ((K+N) \cdot \Gamma, (K+N+1) \cdot \Gamma)$. But then $\widehat{V1} \in [v1 + (K+N) \cdot \Gamma, (K+N+1) \cdot \Gamma)$ implies $\widehat{V1} \in ((K+N) \cdot \Gamma, (K+N+1) \cdot \Gamma)$. Consequently $\widehat{V1} \in [l, r]$ implies $N_l \leq (K + N) < (K + N + 1) \leq N_r$ as before and this in turn implies $\widehat{V2} \in [l, r]$. This leads to $(q, V2, q') \stackrel{\alpha}{\Longrightarrow} (s, V2', q)$.

Secondly, suppose $v1 = (K + N + 1) \cdot \Gamma$. Then, $(K + N + 1) \cdot \Gamma \in (v2 + (K + N) \cdot \Gamma, v2 + (K + N + 1) \cdot \Gamma)$. From Lemma 1, it follows that there exists θ_2 in $[0, \Delta_q]$ such that $v2 + (K+N) \cdot \Gamma + \rho_q \cdot \theta_2 = (K+N+1) \cdot \Gamma$. Set $t2 = N \cdot \Delta_q + \theta_2$. Clearly, $\widehat{V2} = V2 + \rho_q \cdot t2 = \widehat{V1} = (K + N + 1) \cdot \Gamma$. Again, $\widehat{V1} \in [l, r]$ implies $\widehat{V2} \in [l, r]$ as required.

Thirdly, suppose $\widehat{V1} \in ((K + N + 1) \cdot \Gamma, v1 + (K + N + 1) \cdot \Gamma]$. Then we set $t2 = (N + 1) \cdot \Delta_q$. Clearly $\widehat{V2} = V2 + \rho_q \cdot (N + 1) \cdot \Delta_q \in ((K + N + 1) \cdot \Gamma, (K + N + 2) \cdot \Gamma)$. But then $\widehat{V1} \in ((K + N + 1) \cdot \Gamma, v1 + (K + N + 1) \cdot \Gamma]$ implies $v1 \in ((K + N + 1) \cdot \Gamma, (K + N + 2) \cdot \Gamma)$. Thus again, $\widehat{V1} \in [l, r]$ implies $\widehat{V2} \in [l, r]$.

Case 3: $q \neq q'$ and $\alpha = \tau$.

Since $q \neq q'$, an instantaneous transition has taken place at the end of the time-passage move leading to $(q, V1, q')$. Hence the automaton will continue to evolve at rate $\rho_{q'}$ until some $t1 \in [g, g+\delta_g]$ and then will evolve at the rate ρ_q for the rest of the period $1-t1$. Moreover $t1$ is such that $V1' = V1 + \rho'_q \cdot t1 + \rho_q \cdot (1 - t1)$. We need to find $t2 \in [g, g + \delta_g]$ such that $V2' = V2 + \rho_{q'} \cdot t2 + \rho_q \cdot (1 - t2)$ and $\|V1'\| = \|V2'\|$. In order to fix $t2$, let $g = N_g \cdot \Delta$ and $\delta_g = N_{\delta_g} \cdot \Delta$.

Noticing that $(\rho_q - \rho_{q'}) \cdot \Delta = N_{qq'} \cdot \Gamma$ and hence $(\rho_q - \rho_{q'}) \cdot (\Delta / N_{qq'}) = \Gamma$ we set $\Delta_{qq'} = \Delta / N_{qq'}$, and observe that $t1 \in [N_g \cdot N_{qq'} \cdot \Delta_{qq'}, (N_g + N_{\delta_g}) \cdot N_{qq'} \cdot \Delta_{qq'}]$. Let N be the least integer in the interval $[N_g \cdot N_{qq'}, (N_g + N_{\delta_g}) \cdot N_{qq'}]$ such that $t1 \in [N \cdot \Delta_{qq'}, (N + 1) \cdot \Delta_{qq'}]$. Let $\theta 1 = t1 - N \cdot \Delta_{qq'}$. Clearly $\theta 1 \in [0, \Delta_{qq'}]$.

We now have $V1' = V1 + \rho_{q'} \cdot N \cdot \Delta_{qq'} + \rho_{q'} \cdot \theta 1 + \rho_q \cdot (\Delta_{qq'} - \theta 1) + \rho_q \cdot (N_1 \cdot N_{qq'} - N - 1) \cdot \Delta_{qq'}$. (Recall that $N_1 \cdot \Delta = 1$.) Expanding this expression and simplifying using the definitions of N_q, $N_{q'}$, $N_{qq'}$ and $\Delta_{qq'}$, we get: $V1' = V1 + (N_1 \cdot N_q - N) \cdot \Gamma - (\rho_q - \rho_{q'}) \cdot \theta 1$. We recall that $v1 = V1 - K \cdot \Gamma$ and $v2 = V2 - K \cdot \Gamma$. Since $\theta 1$ ranges over $[0, \Delta_{qq'}]$, we have that $(\rho_q - \rho_{q'}) \cdot \theta 1$ ranges over $[0, \Gamma]$. Hence $V1' \in [v1 + (K + N_1 \cdot N_q - N)\Gamma, v1 + (K + N_1 \cdot N_q - N + 1) \cdot \Gamma]$. Again there are three situations to consider. For convenience, let $K' = N_1 \cdot N_q - N$.

Suppose $V1' \in [v1 + (K + K') \cdot \Gamma, (K + K' + 1) \cdot \Gamma)$. Then we set $t2 = N \cdot \Delta_{qq'}$. Then it is easy to see that $t2 \in [g, g + \delta_g]$. Now let $V2' = V2 + \rho_{q'} \cdot t2 + \rho_q \cdot (1 - t2)$. Then by our choice of $t2$, we have, $V2' = V2 + \rho_{q'} \cdot N \cdot \Delta_{qq'} + \rho_q \cdot (N_1 \cdot N_{qq'} - N) \cdot \Delta_{qq'}$. Simplifying this expression, we get $V2' = V2 + K' \cdot \Gamma$. Since $V2 = v2 + K \cdot \Gamma$, we then get $V2' \in ((K + K') \cdot \Gamma, (K + K' + 1) \cdot \Gamma)$. As a result, $\|V1'\| = \|V2'\|$. By the choice of $t2$, it is also clear that $(q, V2, q') \stackrel{\tau}{\Longrightarrow} (s, V2', q)$.

The case $V1' \in ((K + K' + 1) \cdot \Gamma, v1 + (k + K + 1) \cdot \Gamma]$ is handled in a similar manner by setting $t2 = (N + 1) \cdot \Delta_{qq'}$.

So suppose that $V1' = (K + K' + 1) \cdot \Gamma$. Then by Lemma 1 we can find $\theta 2 \in (0, \Delta_{qq'})$ such that with $t2 = N \cdot \Delta_{qq'} + \theta 2$, and $V2' = V2 + \rho_{q'} \cdot t2 + \rho_q \cdot (1 - t2)$, we can obtain $V2' = (K + K' + 1) \cdot \Gamma$. This follows from the fact that as $\theta 2$ ranges over $[0, \Delta_{qq'}]$, we will have $V2'$ ranging continuously over $[v2 + (K + K') \cdot \Gamma, v2 + (K + K' + 1) \cdot \Gamma]$ and surely $(K + K' + 1) \cdot \Gamma$ lies within this range. Clearly by the choice of $t2$ and $V2'$, we have $(q, V2, q') \stackrel{\tau}{\Longrightarrow} (s, V2', q)$. It also follows at once that $\|V1'\| = \|V2'\|$.

Case 4: $q \neq q'$ **and** $\alpha \in Act$.

This is the most general case where the rate will change during the current period *and* the time-pass move will be followed by an instantaneous execution of a transition of $\mathcal{A}$.

Since $(q, V1, q') \stackrel{\alpha}{\Longrightarrow} (s, V1', q)$, there exist $t1 \in [g, g + \delta_g]$ and $t1' \in [h, h + \delta_h]$ and a transition $q \stackrel{(\alpha, I)}{\longrightarrow} s$ in $\mathcal{A}$ such that $V1' = V1 + \rho_{q'} \cdot t1 + (1 - t1) \cdot \rho_q$ and $V1 + \rho_{q'} \cdot t1 + \rho_q \cdot (t1' - t1) \in I$. We need to find $t2 \in [g, g + \delta_g]$ and $t2' \in [h, h + \delta_h]$ such that $V2 + \rho_{q'} \cdot t2 + \rho_q \cdot (t2' - t2) \in I$ and $\|V1'\| = \|V2'\|$ where $V2' = V2 + \rho_{q'} \cdot t2 + (1 - t2) \cdot \rho_q$.

As before, we set $\Delta_{qq'} = \Delta / N_{qq'}$ and let N be the least integer in the interval $[N_g \cdot N_{qq'}, (N_g + N_{\delta_g}) \cdot N_{qq'}]$ such that $t1 \in [N \cdot \Delta_{qq'}, (N + 1) \cdot \Delta_{qq'}]$. Let $\theta 1 = t1 - N \cdot \Delta_{qq'}$. Clearly $\theta 1 \in [0, \Delta_{qq'}]$. Using the argument developed to settle the previous case, we can conclude that $V1' = V1 + (N_1 \cdot N_q - N) \cdot \Gamma - (\rho_q - \rho_{q'}) \cdot \theta 1$. As before, we set $K' = N_1 \cdot N_q - N$. We need to examine two cases. (It is worth recalling here that we are operating under the assumptions $0 \leq \rho_q' < \rho_q$ and $v2 < v1$).

Suppose $V1' \in [v1 + (K + K') \cdot \Gamma, v2 + (K + K' + 1) \cdot \Gamma]$. Consider $t2 = (N + 1) \cdot \Delta_{qq'} + \theta 2$ for some $\theta 2 \in [0, \Delta_{qq'}]$. Define $V2' = v2 + (K' + K + 1) \cdot \Gamma - \theta 2 \cdot (\rho_q - \rho_{q'})$.

As $\theta 2$ ranges over $[0, \Delta_{qq'}]$, $V2'$ will range over $[v2 + (K' + K) \cdot \Gamma, v2 + (K + K' + 1) \cdot \Gamma]$. Hence, by Lemma 1, we can fix a $\theta 2$ such that $V2' = V1'$.

Suppose on the other hand, $V1' \in (v2 + (K + K' + 1) \cdot \Gamma, v1 + (K + K' + 1) \cdot \Gamma]$. Then we set $\theta 2 = 0$ so that $t2 = (N+1) \cdot \Delta_{qq'}$ and hence $V2' = v2 + (K + K' + 1) \cdot \Gamma$. Clearly both $V1'$ and $V2'$ lie in $((K + K' + 1) \cdot \Gamma, (K + K' + 2) \cdot \Gamma)$. Hence $\|V1'\| = \|V2'\|$.

We note that in either case, our choice of $\theta 2$ guarantees that $V1' = V2'$ or $V2' < V1'$ with $V1' - V2' \le v1 - v2$.

Turning to the choice of $t2'$, we define as before, $\Delta_q = \Delta/N_q$. Let J be the least integer in the interval $[N_h \cdot N_q, (N_h + N_{\delta_h} - 1) \cdot N_q]$ such that $t1' \in [J \cdot \Delta_q, (J + 1) \cdot \Delta_q]$. Let $\theta 1' = t1' - (J \cdot \Delta_q)$. Clearly $\theta 1' \in [0, \Delta_q]$.

Let $V1'' = V1 + \rho_{q'} .t1 + \rho_q \cdot (t1' - t1)$. Then $V1'' = V1 + \rho_{q'} \cdot N \cdot \Delta_{qq'} + \rho_{q'} \cdot \theta 1 + \rho_q \cdot (\Delta_{qq'} - \theta 1) + \rho_q \cdot (J \cdot N_q \cdot \Delta_q - (N + 1) \cdot \Delta_{qq'}) + \rho_q \cdot \theta 1'$. Again expanding and simplifying this expression, we get $V1'' = V1 + (N_q \cdot J - N) \cdot \Gamma - (\rho_q - \rho_{q'}) \cdot \theta 1 + \rho_q \cdot \theta 1'$. Let $L = N_q \cdot J - N$. Then $V1'' = v1 + (K + L) \cdot \Gamma - (\rho_q - \rho_{q'}) \cdot \theta 1 + \rho_q \cdot \theta 1'$.

Now $V1''' = v1 + (K+L) \cdot \Gamma - (\rho_q - \rho_{q'}) \cdot \theta 1$ must lie in $[v1 + (K+L) \cdot \Gamma, v1 + (K + L + 1) \cdot \Gamma]$. Suppose $V1'''$ lies in $[v1 + (k+L) \cdot \Gamma, v2 + (K + L + 1) \cdot \Gamma]$. Then our choice of $\theta 2$ ensures that $v2 + (K + L) \cdot \Gamma - (\rho_q - \rho_{q'}) \cdot \theta 2 = v1 + (K + L) \cdot \Gamma - (\rho_q - \rho_{q'}) \cdot \theta 1$. We now set $\theta 2' = \theta 1'$ and $t2' = J \cdot \Delta_q + \theta 2'$. Clearly $t2' \in [h, h + \delta_h]$ and $V2'' = V2 + \rho_{q'} \cdot t2 + \rho_q \cdot (t2' - t2) = V1'' \in I$ and hence we have, as required, $(q, V2, q') \overset{\alpha}{\Longrightarrow} (s, V2', q)$ with $\|V1'\| = \|V2'\|$.

Finally, assume that $V1''' = v1 + (K + L) \cdot \Gamma - (\rho_q - \rho_{q'}) \cdot \theta 1$ lies in $(v2 + (K + L + 1) \cdot \Gamma, v1 + (K + L + 1) \cdot \Gamma]$ Then our choice of $\theta 2$ ensures that $V2''' = v2 + (K + L) . \Gamma - (\rho_q - \rho_{q'}) \cdot \theta 2 = v2 + (K + L + 1) \cdot \Gamma$ and thus $V1''' - V2''' \le v1 - v2$. Now depending on $\theta 1'$, the value of $V1''$ must lie in $(v2 + (K + L + 1) \cdot \Gamma, v1 + (K + L + 2) \cdot \Gamma]$. If $V1''$ lies in $(v2 + (k + L + 1) \cdot \Gamma, v2 + (k + L + 2) \cdot \Gamma]$ then we can, by lemma 1, pick $\theta 2' \in [0, \Delta_q]$ so that $V2'' = V1''$ where $V2'' = V2 + \rho_{q'} \cdot t2 + \rho_q \cdot (t2' - t2)$ with $t2' = J \cdot \Delta_q + \theta 2'$. If on the other hand, $V1''$ lies in $(v2 + (K + L + 2) \cdot \Gamma, v1 + (k + L + 2) \cdot \Gamma]$ we can set $\theta 2' = \Delta_q$ and $t2' = J \cdot \Delta + \theta 2'$ so that $V2'' = v2 + (K + L + 2) \cdot \Gamma$. In either case, we have $t2' \in [h, h + \delta_h]$ and $V2'' \in I$ so that $(q, V2, q') \overset{\alpha}{\Longrightarrow} (s, V2', q)$ with $\|V1'\| = \|V2'\|$.   □

We now define the finite state automaton $\mathcal{Z}_{\mathcal{A}} = (\mathcal{D}, (q_{in}, (k_0, 0), q_{in}), Act \cup \{\tau\}, \rightsquigarrow, \mathcal{D})$ where $k_0 \cdot \Gamma = V_{in}$ and the transition relation $\rightsquigarrow \subseteq \mathcal{D} \times (Act \cup \{\tau\}) \times \mathcal{D}$ is given by: $(q, (k, d), q') \overset{\alpha}{\rightsquigarrow} (q1, (k1, d1), q1')$ iff there exist configurations (q, V, q') and $(q1, V1, q1')$ such that $(q, V, q') \overset{\alpha}{\Longrightarrow} (q1, V1, q1')$ and $\|V\| = (k, d)$ and $\|V1\| = (k1, d1)$. In what follows, we will often write $\mathcal{Z}_{\mathcal{A}}$ as just $\mathcal{Z}$. Note that, we are setting all the states of $\mathcal{Z}$ to be its final states.

We define $\mathcal{L}_{st}(\mathcal{Z})$ to be the subset of Q^* as follows. A *run* of $\mathcal{Z}$ is a sequence of the form $(q_0, (l_0, d_0), q_0') \alpha_0 (q_1, (l_1, d_1), q_1') \alpha_1 \ldots (q_m, (l_m, d_m), q_m')$ where $(q_0, (l_0, d_0), q_0') = (q_{in}, (k_0, 0), q_{in})$ and $(q_j, (l_j, d_j), q_j') \overset{\alpha_j}{\rightsquigarrow} (q_{j+1}, (l_{j+1}, d_{j+1}), q_{j+1}')$ for $0 \le j < m$. Next we define $q_0 q_1 \ldots q_m \in \mathcal{L}_{st}(\mathcal{Z})$ iff there exists a run of $\mathcal{Z}$ of the form $(q_0, (l_0, d_0), q_0') \alpha_0 (q_1, (l_1, d_1), q_1') \alpha_1 \ldots (q_m, (l_m, d_m), q_m')$. Clearly $\mathcal{L}_{st}(\mathcal{Z})$ is a regular subset of $Q^\star$ and it does not involve any loss of generality to view $\mathcal{Z}_\mathcal{A}$ itself as a representation of this regular language.

Theorem 2. *The automaton $\mathcal{Z}_\mathcal{A}$ can be computed effectively. Moreover $\mathcal{L}_{st}(\mathcal{A}) = \mathcal{L}_{st}(\mathcal{Z}_\mathcal{A})$ and $\mathcal{L}_{act}(\mathcal{A}) = \mathcal{L}(\mathcal{Z}_\mathcal{A})$ where $\mathcal{L}(\mathcal{Z}_\mathcal{A})$ is the regular subset of $(Act \cup \{\tau\})^\star$ accepted by $\mathcal{Z}_\mathcal{A}$ in the usual sense. (Note that all the states of $\mathcal{Z}_\mathcal{A}$ are final states.)*

Proof. Clearly the finite set of states $\mathcal{D}$ and the initial state $(q_{in}, (k_0, 0), q_{in})$ can be computed easily. The transition relation $\rightsquigarrow$ is expressible in the first order theory of the real ordered field which is a decidable theory [14] .[2]. For instance, to determine if $(q, (k, 1), q') \overset{a}{\rightsquigarrow} (q1, (k1, 1), q)$, with $a \in Act$, we first check if there is a transition tr in $\mathcal{A}$ of the form $(q, a, I, q1)$. If there is no such transition then we conclude that $(q, (k, 1), q') \overset{a}{\rightsquigarrow} (q1, (k1, d1), q)$ is *not* a transition in $\mathcal{Z}_\mathcal{A}$. If there is such a transition then for each such transition tr we construct the formula φ_{tr}, take the disjunction of all such formulas and check for its satisfiability.

Suppose $tr = (q, a, I, q1)$. Then φ_{tr} will conjunctively assert the following:

- There exists V such that $k \cdot \Gamma < V < (k+1) \cdot \Gamma$.
- There exists $t1$ such that $g \leq t1 \leq g + \delta_g$ and $k1 \cdot \Gamma < V + \rho_{q'} \cdot t1 + \rho_q \cdot (1-t1) < (k1+1) \cdot \Gamma$.
- There exists $t2$ such that $h \leq t2 \leq h + \delta_h$ and $l \leq V + \rho_{q'} \cdot t1 + \rho_q \cdot (t2 - t1) \leq r$ (where $I = [l, r]$).

To see that $\mathcal{L}_{st}(\mathcal{A}) = \mathcal{L}_{st}(\mathcal{Z})$ we first note that $\mathcal{L}_{st}(\mathcal{A}) \subseteq \mathcal{L}_{st}(\mathcal{Z})$ follows from the definition of $\mathcal{Z}_\mathcal{A}$. To conclude inclusion in the other direction, we will argue that for each run $(q_0, (l_0, d_0), q'_0) \alpha_0 (q_1, (l_1, d_1), q'_1) \alpha_1 \ldots (q_m, (l_m, d_m), q'_m)$ of $\mathcal{Z}$ there exist $V_0, V_1 \ldots V_m \in \mathbb{R}$ such that $(q_0, V_0, q'_0) \alpha_0 (q_1, V_1, q'_1) \alpha_1 \ldots (q_m, V_m, q'_m)$ is a run of $TS_\mathcal{A}$. And furthermore, $\|V_j\| = (l_j, d_j)$ for $0 \leq j \leq m$. The required inclusion will then follow at once. For $m = 1$, it is clear from the definitions and so suppose that $\quad (q_0, (l_0, d_0), q'_0) \alpha_0 (q_1, (l_1, d_1), q'_1) \alpha_1 \ldots (q_m, (l_m, d_m), q'_m)$ $\alpha_m (q_{m+1}, (l_{m+1}, d_{m+1}), q'_{m+1})$ is a run of $\mathcal{Z}$. By the induction hypothesis, there exists a run $(q_0, V_0, q'_0) \alpha_0 (q_1, V_1, q'_1) \alpha_1 \ldots (q_m, V_m, q'_m)$ of $TS_\mathcal{A}$ with the property, $\|V_j\| = (l_j, d_j)$ for $0 \leq j \leq m$.

Now $(q_m, (l_m, d_m), q'_m) \overset{\alpha_m}{\rightsquigarrow} (q_{m+1}, (l_{m+1}, d_{m+1}), q'_{m+1})$ implies that there exist V'_m and V'_{m+1} such that $(q_m, V'_m, q'_m) \overset{\alpha_m}{\rightsquigarrow} (q_{m+1}, V'_{m+1}, q'_{m+1})$ and $\|V'_m\| = (l_m, d_m)$ and $\|V'_{m+1}\| = (l_{m+1}, d_{m+1})$. But this implies that $\|V'_m\| = \|V_m\|$. Hence by Theorem 1, there exists V_{m+1} such that $(q_m, V_m, q'_m) \overset{\alpha_m}{\rightsquigarrow} (q_{m+1}, V_{m+1}, q'_{m+1})$ and moreover $\|V'_{m+1}\| = \|V_{m+1}\|$. Thus $\mathcal{L}_{st}(\mathcal{A}) = \mathcal{L}_{st}(\mathcal{Z}_\mathcal{A})$. It now also follows easily that $\mathcal{L}_{act}(\mathcal{A}) = \mathcal{L}(\mathcal{Z}_\mathcal{A})$. □

In what follows, we will refer to $\mathcal{Z}$ as the *zone version* of $\mathcal{A}$.

---

[2] This is an overkill as detailed later

3.2   The n-Dimensional Case

We now consider an n-dimensional hybrid automaton $\mathcal{A}$ defined as in the previous section with the associated terminology and notations. Our goal is to show that $\mathcal{L}_{st}(\mathcal{A})$ is a regular subset of $Q^\star$ while $\mathcal{L}_{act}(\mathcal{A})$ is a regular subset of $(Act \cup \{\tau\})^\star$.

To do so, we first define the family of one dimensional automata $\{\mathcal{A}^i\} = (Q, Act, q_{in}^i, V_{in}^i, D, \{\rho_q^i\}_{q \in Q}, B, \longrightarrow_i)$ where:

- $V_{in}^i(i)$ is $V_{in}(i)$, the i-th component of V_{in}.
- $\rho_q^i = \rho_q(i)$
- $q \xrightarrow{(a, I^i)}_i q'$ iff there exists $q \xrightarrow{(a, I)} q'$ in $\mathcal{A}$ with $I^i = I(i)$. Again, $I(i)$ denotes the i-th component of I.

Let $\mathcal{Z}^i$ be the zone version of $\mathcal{A}^i$ with $\mathcal{Z}^i = (\mathcal{D}^i, (q_{in}, (k_0^i, 0), q_{in}), Act \cup \{\tau\}, \leadsto_i)$. We now define the finite state automaton $\mathcal{Z}_{\mathcal{A}} = (\mathcal{D}, (q_{in}, \kappa_0, q_{in}), Act \cup \{\tau\}, \leadsto, \mathcal{D})$ which will constitute the zone version of the n-dimensional automaton $\mathcal{A}$ as follows.

- $\mathcal{D}$, the states of this automaton, will be of the form (q, κ, q') with $q, q' \in Q$ and $\kappa \in ((\mathbb{Z} \times \{0, 1\})^n$. Let $\kappa = ((k_1, d_1), (k_2, d_2) \ldots, (k_n, d_n))$. Then $(q, \kappa, q') \in \mathcal{D}$ iff there $(q, (k_i, d_i), q') \in \mathcal{D}^i$ for each i in $\{1, 2, \ldots, n\}$.
- $\kappa_0 = ((k_0^1, 0), (k_0^2, 0), \ldots, (k_0^n, 0)$
- $\leadsto \subseteq \mathcal{D} \times (Act \cup \{\tau\}) \times \mathcal{D}$ is given by:
  Let $(q, \kappa, q'), (q1, \kappa 1, q1') \in \mathcal{D}$ with $\kappa = ((k_1, d_1), (k_2, d_2) \ldots, (k_n, d_n))$ and $\kappa 1 = ((k1_1, d1_1), (k1_2, d1_2) \ldots, (k1_n, d1_n))$. Then $(q, \kappa, q') \xrightarrow{\alpha} ((q1, \kappa 1, q1')$ iff $(q, (k_i, d_i), q') \xrightarrow{\alpha}_i (q1, (k1_i, d1_i), q)$ for each $i \in \{1, 2, \ldots, n\}$.

As before, we will often write $\mathcal{Z}$ instead of $\mathcal{Z}_{\mathcal{A}}$ and refer to it as the zone version of $\mathcal{A}$. We denote by $\mathcal{L}_{st}(\mathcal{Z})$ the state sequence language of $\mathcal{Z}$ and define it in the obvious way. We also define $\mathcal{L}(\mathcal{Z})$ to be the subset of $(Act \cup \{\tau\})^\star$ accepted by the finite state automaton $\mathcal{Z}$.

Theorem 3. *The automaton $\mathcal{Z}_{\mathcal{A}}$ can be computed effectively. Moreover $\mathcal{L}_{st}(\mathcal{A}) = \mathcal{L}_{st}(\mathcal{Z}_{\mathcal{A}})$ and $\mathcal{L}_{act}(\mathcal{A}) = \mathcal{L}(\mathcal{Z}_{\mathcal{A}})$.*

Proof. Since, by Theorem 2, each of the finite state automata $\mathcal{Z}^i$ can be computed effectively, so can $\mathcal{Z}$ be. The proof of the facts $\mathcal{L}_{st}(\mathcal{A}) = \mathcal{L}_{st}(\mathcal{Z}_{\mathcal{A}})$ and $\mathcal{L}_{act}(\mathcal{A}) = \mathcal{L}(\mathcal{Z}_{\mathcal{A}})$ is routine and we omit the details. $\qquad \square$

As for the complexity of our decision procedure, we first estimate the size of the automaton and the time complexity of constructing the automaton for the one dimensional case. Let I be the total number of relevant intervals on $\mathbb{R}$. In other words, $I = (B_{max} - B_{min})/\Gamma + 2$. Then the number of states is $O(m^2 \cdot I)$ where $m = | Q |$ is the number of control states of the lazy automaton. For constructing the transitions, we need to check if there is a transition from $(q, (k, 1), q')$ to $(q1, (k1, 1), q)$ labeled with the action α. It is clear that the most complex case is when $\alpha \in Act$ and $q \neq q'$ and we need to check for the existence of at most

$O(m^4 \cdot I^2 \cdot |Act|)$ such possible transitions. To decide if such a transition exists for a given pair of states $(q, (k, 1), q')$ to $(q1, (k1, 1), q)$ and a given symbolic transition in the lazy automaton of the form $(q, a, [l, r], q1)$ we need to check if there exists V and $t1$ and $t2$ such that:

- $k \cdot \Gamma < V < (k+1) \cdot \Gamma$
- $g \leq t1 \leq g + \delta_g$
- $k1 \cdot \Gamma < V + \rho_{q'} \cdot t1 + \rho_q \cdot (1 - t1) < (k1 + 1) \cdot \Gamma$
- $h \leq t2 \leq h + \delta_h$
- $l \leq V + \rho_{q'} \cdot t1 + \rho_q \cdot (t2 - t1) \leq r.$

The above are 10 linear inequalities in three variables V, $t1$, and $t2$. Linear programming allows us to check if they all can be satisfied. This can be done in time proportional to the length of the constraints as there are a constant number of variables and constraints. Therefore, the time to check each inequality is $O(\log(\frac{1}{\Gamma}))$ since Γ requires the largest number of bits to represent of all the quantities in the inequalities. Thus the time complexity of building the automata in the one dimensional case is $O(m^4 \cdot I^2 \cdot |Act| \cdot \log(\frac{1}{\Gamma}))$.

For the n dimensional case, the number of states is $O(m^2 \cdot I^n)$. So the number of possible transitions is $O(m^4 \cdot I^{2n} \cdot |Act|)$. Now there are n groups of 10 inequalities with each group involving 3 variables. Hence overall time complexity of constructing the automata is $O(m^4 \cdot I^{2n} \cdot |Act| \cdot n \cdot \log(\frac{1}{\Gamma}))$.

4   Some Extensions

In order to simplify the initial presentation, we placed a number of restrictions on our automata. Here we first examine which of these can be relaxed so that, with minor overhead, our main results go through smoothly. We then formulate a composition operation for lazy hybrid automata in a standard way using which large automata can be presented in a succinct fashion. These networks of lazy hybrid automata can also be analyzed effectively.

Let $\mathcal{A} = (Q, Act, q_{in}, V_{in}, D, \{\rho_q\}_{q \in Q}, \mathrm{B}, \longrightarrow)$ be a lazy hybrid automaton. We could permit a set of initial control states and a set of initial valuations for each initial control state, provided they can be specified using rectangular constraints. Our results will go through with minor modifications. It is also clear that our demand $0 < g < g + \delta_g < h < h + \delta_h < 1$ is only for convenience. We could have different delay parameters for different variables and these delays could spill over more than one time unit.

The restriction that there is at most one a-labeled transition between a pair of control states is mainly for convenience. If this condition is violated we could use renaming to enforce this property, construct the zone automaton and then restore the old names.

State invariants can be introduced in the expected manner and we could allow resets of the variables during a mode switch. Finally, we have avoided the customary use of differential inclusions to specify the rates mainly to avoid clutter. Our results will still go through, with some additional notational overhead, if we permit these extensions.

The boundedness restriction on the allowed range $B = [B_{min}, B_{max}]$ is crucial though, from a modeling point of view, it is not crippling. The fact that we have *linear rates* is crucial. Our proof idea breaks down for non-linear rates. The fact that non-empty closed intervals are used for specifying the transitions of $\mathcal{A}$ is not important. However, the fact that we have rectangular constraints is important.

We now wish to argue that we can easily cope with networks of lazy hybrid automata in which the component automata communicate by synchronizing on common actions.

Let $\mathcal{P}$ be a finite set of agent names with u, v ranging over $\mathcal{P}$. We define a *product* lazy hybrid automaton to be a structure $\mathcal{A}_\mathcal{P} = \prod_{u \in \mathcal{P}} \mathcal{A}_u$ where $\mathcal{A}_u = (Q_u, Act_u, q_{in}^u, V_{in}^u, D, \{\rho_q^u\}_{q \in Q_u}, \mathrm{B}, \longrightarrow_u)$ for each u in $\mathcal{P}$. For convenience, we will write TS_u instead of $TS_{\mathcal{A}_u}$ to denote the transition system over the reachable configurations of $\mathcal{A}_u$ as defined in section 2. The operational behavior of $\prod_{u \in \mathcal{P}} \mathcal{A}_u$ is given by the transition system denoted as $TS_\mathcal{P}$ and is defined in the obvious way; it is just the usual synchronized product of the transition systems $\{TS_u\}$. The only twist is, in line with our discrete time semantics, *all* the components must move during a transition. If it is an a-move, then all the components that have $a \in Act_u$ must make an a-move while the remaining components must make a τ-move. In a τ-move, all the compoents must make a τ-move.

It is a routine exercise to establish that $\mathcal{L}_{st}(Aut_\mathcal{P})$ and $\mathcal{L}_{act}(\mathcal{A}_\mathcal{P})$ can be computed effectively.

5   Conclusion

We have formulated here the class of lazy hybrid rectangular automata. These are basically linear rectangular hybrid automata but where each automaton is accompanied by the delay parameters $\{g, \delta_g, h, \delta_h\}$. Our main result is that the discrete time behavior of these automata can be effectively computed if the allowed ranges of values for the variables are bounded. We have not outlined the verification problems for lazy rectangular hybrid automata that can be settled effectively. It should be clear however that we can model-check the discrete time behavior of our automata against a variety of linear time and branching time temporal logic specifications.

We believe that associating non-zero bounded delays with the sensors and actuators is a natural assumption and it cuts down the the expressive power of hybrid automata. We also feel that it is useful to focus on the discrete time behavior of hybrid automata. Finally, there is some hope that larger classes of lazy hybrid automata may turn out to be tractable in terms of their discrete time behaviors. A related intersting problem is to determine the border between the decidable and undecidable in the context of lazy hybrid automata.

References

[1] R. Alur and D.L. Dill. A theory of timed automata. *Theoretical Comp. Sci.*, 126(2):183–235, 1994.

[2] R. Alur, T.A. Henzinger, G. Lafferriere, and G.J. Pappas. Discrete abstractions of hybrid systems. *Proc. of the IEEE*, 88:971–984, 2000.

[3] E. Asarin, O. Bournez, T. Dang, and O. Maler. Reachability analysis of piecewise-linear dynamical systems. In *Hybrid Systems: Comp. and Control, LNCS 1790*, pages 20–31. Springer-Verlag, 2000.

[4] V. Gupta, T.A. Henzinger, and R. Jagadeesan. Robust timed automata. In *HART 97, LNCS 1201*, pages 331–345. Springer-Verlag, 1997.

[5] T.A. Henzinger. Hybrid automata with finite bisimulations. In *22nd ICALP, LNCS 944*, pages 324–335. Springer-Verlag, 1995.

[6] T.A. Henzinger. The theory of hybrid automata. In *Proc. of the 11th Ann. Symp. on Logic in Comp. Sci.*, pages 278–292. IEEE Comp. Society Press, 1996.

[7] T.A. Henzinger and P.W. Kopke. Discrete-time control for rectangular hybrid automata. *Theoretical Comp. Sci.*, 221:369–392, 1999.

[8] T.A. Henzinger, P.W. Kopke, A. Puri, and P. Varaiya. What's decidable about hybrid automata? *J. of Comp. and Sys. Sci.*, 57:94–124, 1998.

[9] T.A. Henzinger and J.-F. Raskin. Robust undecidability of timed and hybrid systems. In *HSCC 00, LNCS 1790*, pages 145–159. Springer-Verlag, 2000.

[10] Y. Kesten, A. Pnueli, J. Sifakis, and S. Yovine. Integration graphs: A class of decidable hybrid systems. In R.L. Grossman, A. Nerode, A. Ravn, and H. Rischel, editors, *Hybrid Systems, LNCS 736*, pages 179–208. Springer-Verlag, 1993.

[11] J. McManis and P. Varaiya. Suspension automata: A decidable class of hybrid automata. In *6th CAV, LNCS 818*, pages 105–117. Springer-Verlag, 1994.

[12] J. Ouaknine and J. Worrell. Revisiting digitization, robustness and decidability for timed automata. In *25th LICS*, pages 198–207. IEEE Press, 2003.

[13] A. Puri and P. Varaiya. Decidability of hybrid systems with rectangular differential inclusions. In *6th CAV, LNCS 818*, pages 95–104. Springer-Verlag, 1994.

[14] A. Tarski. *A Decision Method for Elementary Algebra and Geometry*. University of California Press, 1951.

Affine Hybrid Systems

Aaron D. Ames and Shankar Sastry

University of California, Berkeley CA 94720, USA
{adames,sastry}@eecs.berkeley.edu

Abstract. Affine hybrid systems are hybrid systems in which the discrete domains are affine sets and the transition maps between discrete domains are affine transformations. The simple structure of these systems results in interesting geometric properties; one of these is the notion of *spatial equivalence*. In this paper, a formal framework for describing affine hybrid systems is introduced. As an application, it is proven that every compact hybrid system $\mathbf{H}$ is spatially equivalent to a hybrid system $\mathbf{H}_{\mathrm{id}}$ in which all the transition maps are the identity. An explicit and computable construction for $\mathbf{H}_{\mathrm{id}}$ is given.

1 Introduction

This paper introduces affine hybrid systems. Affine hybrid systems are hybrid systems where the discrete domains are affine sets, and the transition maps between discrete domains are affine transformations. This definition differs from other definitions of hybrid systems that have been proposed [9], but the underlying ideas involved in the definition of affine hybrid systems have been seen in the literature [6,7]. We give a formal framework to these ideas.

Affine hybrid systems are simple, and it is this simplicity that allows us to say some useful things about them. The structure of affine hybrid systems contains a wealth of intrinsic information. Affine sets can be described in terms of matrix inequalities, and affine transformations are characterized by elements of $SE(n)$. In this paper, we use the geometric information intrinsic in affine hybrid systems to develop the idea of *spatial equivalence* between an affine hybrid system $\mathbf{H}$ and an affine hybrid system $\mathbf{G}$.

In the literature on hybrid systems, it typically is assumed that all of the transition maps of a hybrid system are the identity; all switched systems are essentially hybrid systems where the transition maps are the identity [4,10]. This assumption is very restrictive; some of the simplest hybrid systems do not satisfy this assumption, e.g., the hybrid system $\mathbb{T}^2$ constructed in Example 2.1 of this paper. For this reason, it is desirable to find a way to bridge the gap between hybrid systems where all the transition maps are the identity and hybrid systems where this is not the case.

Given an affine hybrid system $\mathbf{H}$, we would like to construct an affine hybrid system $\mathbf{H}_{\mathrm{id}}$ such that all of the transition maps are the identity. We also would like this affine hybrid system $\mathbf{H}_{\mathrm{id}}$ to be as similar to $\mathbf{H}$ as possible. In what way should these two affine hybrid systems be considered similar? Spatial equivalence

R. Alur and G.J. Pappas (Eds.): HSCC 2004, LNCS 2993, pp. 16–31, 2004.
© Springer-Verlag Berlin Heidelberg 2004

is introduced as a way to consider an affine hybrid system $\mathbf{H}$ as similar to an affine hybrid system $\mathbf{G}$. Spatial equivalence can be thought of in an intuitive manner (see Figure 4 for a visual interpretation). Replace each edge of $\mathbf{H}$ by a sequence of edges and domains with vector fields such that if we "start" at the source of the edge, the target of the edge will be reached in some time. If the affine hybrid system obtained by appending these edges, domains and vector fields to $\mathbf{H}$ is $\mathbf{G}$, then $\mathbf{H}$ is spatially equivalent to $\mathbf{G}$. A formal definition of spatial equivalence will be given in Section 5, but having this intuitive picture in mind will be helpful.

An affine hybrid system $\mathbf{H}$ is compact if each of its domains is compact. The main theorem of this paper is:

Main Theorem. *Every compact affine hybrid system* $\mathbf{H}$ *is spatially equivalent to an affine hybrid system* $\mathbf{H}_{\mathrm{id}}$ *in which every transition map is the identity. Moreover,* $\mathbf{H}_{\mathrm{id}}$ *is computable.*

This paper begins by introducing, in Section 2, the definition of an affine hybrid system. Sections 3 and 4 present some results in affine geometry that are necessary for the proof of the Main Theorem. In Section 3, given two $(n-1)$-dimensional affine sets X and $Y = RX + p$, for $(R, p) \in SE(n)$, we determine conditions on X, R and p such that there exists an n-dimensional affine set with X and Y as faces. When these conditions are satisfied, we find a closed form solution for a set S which has X and Y as faces. This closed form solution allows us later to compute $\mathbf{H}_{\mathrm{id}}$. When there does not exist an affine set S with X and Y as faces, an admissible sequence of faces, $X = Z_0, Z_1, ..., Z_k = Y$, is introduced; it is used to construct a sequence of affine sets, $S_1, S_2, ..., S_k$, where X is a face of S_1 and Y is a face of S_k. Admissible sequences of faces are used in Section 4 to generalize the results of Section 3 by showing that if $Y = RX + p$, for $(R, p) \in SE(n)$, there is an admissible sequence of faces

$$Z_0 = X, Z_1, ..., Z_{\frac{11}{2}n(n-1)+1}, Z_{\frac{11}{2}n(n-1)+2} = Y.$$

In Section 5, the results in affine geometry that were introduced in Sections 3 and 4 are used to prove the Main Theorem and give an explicit construction for $\mathbf{H}_{\mathrm{id}}$. This is done by using the admissible sequence of faces found in Section 4 to define the domains of the hybrid system $\mathbf{H}_{\mathrm{id}}$.

2   Affine Hybrid Systems

This section introduces the notion of an affine hybrid system. An affine hybrid system consists of the following data: a set of discrete states, domains, edges and vector fields. The discrete states provide a way to index the domains. The domains are affine sets, i.e., sets that are affinely constrained. The edges provide a relationship between two faces of two domains; each edge has a source which is the face of a domain and a target which is also the face of a domain. It is required that there exists an affine transformation between the source and the target of each edge; thus each edge gives rise to a transition map, which is an affine transformation from the source of the edge to the target of the edge. The set of vector fields is a collection of vector fields that are Lipschitz on each domain.

Before we formally introduce the definition of an affine hybrid system, we will describe each of the components of its definition. This section is concluded by solidifying the concepts introduced through an example: the torus $\mathbb{T}^2$. This example also will be important later in the paper.

2.1 (Discrete states). Let $Q \subset \mathbb{Z}$ denote the set of *discrete states*. This set is finite, and the number of discrete states is given by $|Q|$. For simplicity, typically we let $Q = \{1, ..., m\}$.

2.2 (Domains). The set of *domains* is the set $D = \{D_i\}_{i \in Q}$, where each $D_i \subset \mathbb{R}^n$ is an n-dimensional affine set, i.e., a set that is affinely constrained. For each set D_i, there exists a matrix $A_i \in \mathbb{R}^{k_i \times n}$ and a vector $a_i \in \mathbb{R}^{k_i}$ such that

$$x \in D_i \qquad \Leftrightarrow \qquad A_i x + a_i \geq 0.$$

We say that D_i is *determined* by the affine constraints $A_i x + a_i$.

The boundary of D_i can be written as the union of k_i affine sets of dimension $n - 1$ called the *faces* of D_i. The faces of D_i can be indexed by introducing the indexing set,

$$F_i = \{1, ..., k_i\}, \qquad i \in Q.$$

The jth face of D_i is denoted by $\mathrm{Face}_j(D_i)$, where $j \in F_i$. We can pick an indexing of the faces of D_i by letting $\mathrm{Face}_j(D_i)$ be the affine set determined by the jth row of A_i. More precisely, if $(A_i)_{j*}$ is the jth row of A_i and $(a_i)_j$ is the jth entry of a_i, then

$$x \in \mathrm{Face}_j(D_i) \qquad \Leftrightarrow \qquad \begin{pmatrix} A_i \\ -(A_i)_{j*} \end{pmatrix} x + \begin{pmatrix} a_i \\ -(a_i)_j \end{pmatrix} \geq 0. \qquad (1)$$

We can define

$$A_{ij} = \begin{pmatrix} A_i \\ -(A_i)_{j*} \end{pmatrix}, \qquad a_{ij} = \begin{pmatrix} a_i \\ -(a_i)_j \end{pmatrix},$$

so $x \in \mathrm{Face}_j(D_i)$ if and only if $A_{ij}x + a_{ij} \geq 0$. Therefore, $\mathrm{Face}_j(D_i)$ is determined by the affine constraints $A_{ij}x + a_{ij}$.

2.3. For a set U with $U = \prod_{i=1}^n U_i$, denote the projections on each of the factors of U by $\pi_i : U \to U_i$.

2.4 (Edges). Define the set of *edges* as a set

$$E \subseteq \{((i,j),(k,l))\}_{(i,j) \in Q \times Q, \ (k,l) \in F_i \times F_j},$$

satisfying the condition that for each $e \in E$, there exists a map $T_e(x) = R_e x + p_e$, with $(R_e, p_e) \in SE(n)$, such that

$$T_e(\mathrm{Face}_{\pi_3(e)}(D_{\pi_1(e)})) = \mathrm{Face}_{\pi_4(e)}(D_{\pi_2(e)}). \qquad (2)$$

In other words, an edge defines a relationship between two faces of two affine sets and an affine transformation between these faces.

More concretely, an element $e \in E$ then has the form

$$e = ((i, j), (k, l)), \qquad (i, j) \in Q \times Q, \qquad (k, l) \in F_i \times F_j,$$

so $\pi_1(e) = i$, $\pi_2(e) = j$, $\pi_3(e) = k$ and $\pi_4(e) = l$. Condition (2) allows us to write

$$T_e(\text{Face}_k(D_i)) = R_e \text{Face}_k(D_i) + p_e = \text{Face}_l(D_j).$$

2.5. Given an edge $e \in E$, the affine transformation $T_e(x) = R_e x + p_e$ from $\text{Face}_{\pi_3(e)}(D_{\pi_1(e)})$ to $\text{Face}_{\pi_4(e)}(D_{\pi_2(e)})$ is called the *transition map*. The set of transition maps is the set $T = \{T_e\}_{e \in E}$.

2.6 (Vector field). A set of vector fields is a set $V = \{V_i\}_{i \in Q}$ where V_i is a Lipschitz vector field when restricted to the domain D_i. The flow of V_i on D_i is denoted by $\phi_i(t, x)$ for $x \in D_i$.

Definition 2.1. *An* affine hybrid system *is a tuple* $\mathbf{H} = (Q, D, E, V)$.

Note 2.1. From this point on, for the sake of brevity, we will refer to "affine hybrid systems" as "hybrid systems".

2.7. If for some $e \in E$, $T_e(x) = x$, then we say that the transition map associated to the edge e is the identity map. This implies that

$$\text{Face}_{\pi_3(e)}(D_{\pi_1(e)}) = \text{Face}_{\pi_4(e)}(D_{\pi_2(e)}).$$

A very special class of hybrid systems are hybrid systems in which every transition map is the identity, and we denote such hybrid systems as $\mathbf{H}_{\text{id}}$.

Example 2.1 (The torus: $\mathbb{T}^2$). We will construct a hybrid system called the torus, which we will denote by $\mathbb{T}^2$ (see Figure 1). The torus is given by one discrete state $Q^{\mathbb{T}^2} = \{1\}$. The domain $D_1^{\mathbb{T}^2} = \{(x, y) : x \in [0, 1], \ y \in [0, 1]\}$ is given by the affine constraints

$$A_1^{\mathbb{T}^2} \begin{pmatrix} x \\ y \end{pmatrix} + a_1^{\mathbb{T}^2} = \begin{pmatrix} 1 & 0 \\ -1 & 0 \\ 0 & -1 \\ 0 & 1 \end{pmatrix} \begin{pmatrix} x \\ y \end{pmatrix} + \begin{pmatrix} 0 \\ 1 \\ 1 \\ 0 \end{pmatrix}.$$

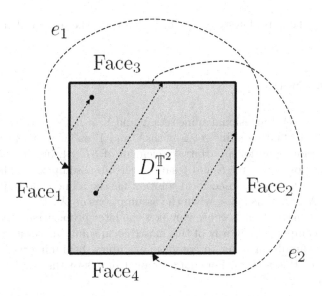

Fig. 1. The torus: $\mathbb{T}^2$.

Applying (1), the affine constraints for $\text{Face}_1(D_1^{\mathbb{T}^2})$, $\text{Face}_2(D_1^{\mathbb{T}^2})$, $\text{Face}_3(D_1^{\mathbb{T}^2})$ and $\text{Face}_4(D_1^{\mathbb{T}^2})$ are given, respectively, by

$$A_{11}^{\mathbb{T}^2}\begin{pmatrix} x \\ y \end{pmatrix} + a_{11}^{\mathbb{T}^2} = \begin{pmatrix} A_1^{\mathbb{T}^2} \\ -1 \quad 0 \end{pmatrix}\begin{pmatrix} x \\ y \end{pmatrix} + \begin{pmatrix} a_1^{\mathbb{T}^2} \\ 0 \end{pmatrix}, \tag{3}$$

$$A_{12}^{\mathbb{T}^2}\begin{pmatrix} x \\ y \end{pmatrix} + a_{12}^{\mathbb{T}^2} = \begin{pmatrix} A_1^{\mathbb{T}^2} \\ 1 \quad 0 \end{pmatrix}\begin{pmatrix} x \\ y \end{pmatrix} + \begin{pmatrix} a_1^{\mathbb{T}^2} \\ -1 \end{pmatrix},$$

$$A_{13}^{\mathbb{T}^2}\begin{pmatrix} x \\ y \end{pmatrix} + a_{13}^{\mathbb{T}^2} = \begin{pmatrix} A_1^{\mathbb{T}^2} \\ 0 \quad 1 \end{pmatrix}\begin{pmatrix} x \\ y \end{pmatrix} + \begin{pmatrix} a_1^{\mathbb{T}^2} \\ -1 \end{pmatrix},$$

$$A_{14}^{\mathbb{T}^2}\begin{pmatrix} x \\ y \end{pmatrix} + a_{14}^{\mathbb{T}^2} = \begin{pmatrix} A_1^{\mathbb{T}^2} \\ 0 \quad -1 \end{pmatrix}\begin{pmatrix} x \\ y \end{pmatrix} + \begin{pmatrix} a_1^{\mathbb{T}^2} \\ 0 \end{pmatrix}. \tag{4}$$

$E^{\mathbb{T}^2}$ consists of two edges: $e_1 = ((1,1),(2,1))$ and $e_2 = ((1,1),(3,4))$. In other words, e_1 is a relation between the top and bottom of the square and e_2 is a relation between the right and left side of the square. The associated transition maps are

$$T_{e_1}(x,y) = \begin{pmatrix} x \\ y \end{pmatrix} + \begin{pmatrix} -1 \\ 0 \end{pmatrix}, \qquad T_{e_2}(x,y) = \begin{pmatrix} x \\ y \end{pmatrix} + \begin{pmatrix} 0 \\ -1 \end{pmatrix}.$$

Finally, $V_1^{\mathbb{T}^2}$ is any vector field, Lipshitz on $D_1^{\mathbb{T}^2}$.

The advantage of defining the edges as a relationship between the faces rather than a relationship between the domains can be seen in this example. Although the expression for the edges is more complicated, the end result is a simpler definition of the hybrid system; in other references, the torus is defined with two discrete states [9].

3   Affine Sets

Given two $(n-1)$-dimensional affine sets X and $Y = RX + p$, for $(R, p) \in SE(n)$, is it possible to find an affine set S with X and Y as faces? Clearly the answer to this question is no for an arbitrary element of $SE(n)$, but it is yes if X is in the "proper position" and R and p satisfy certain assumptions. The purpose of this section is to find a closed form solution for the affine constraints defining a set S with X and Y as faces, when the assumptions on X, R and p are satisfied. This result is important because it makes the later propositions and theorem of this paper computable by way of this closed form solution. We also will use this formula repeatedly in order to compute examples, beginning with an example at the end of this section. For more detailed proofs of the results presented in this section, see [1,2].

3.1. First, recall some important facts and terminology regarding affinely con-strained sets. We define a *face* of an n-dimensional affine set X, denoted by $\text{Face}_i(X)$ for $i = 1, ..., k$ (where k is the number of faces), as a subset ∂X such that there exists a hyperplane H_i where $H_i \cap \partial X = \text{Face}_i(X)$. This hyperplane is called the hyperplane defining $\text{Face}_i(X)$. If X is determined by the affine con-straints $Ax + a$, and if we define the $\text{Face}_i(X)$ as the set determined by the affine constraints

$$A_i x + a_i = \begin{pmatrix} A \\ -A_{i*} \end{pmatrix} x + \begin{pmatrix} a \\ -a_i \end{pmatrix},$$

then the defining hyperplane, H_i, is given by $H_i = \{\sum_{j=1}^n a_{ij} x_j + a_i = 0\}$. If the smallest number of affine constraints that determine X is k, then X has k faces. Note that in this case it is always possible to define X in terms of more that k affine constraints, but never less.

Proposition 3.1. *Let X be an affine set of dimension $n - 1$ in $\mathbb{R}^n$, and assume that $X \subseteq \{x_i = 0\}$. If $Y = X + p$, with $p_i \neq 0$, then there exists an affine set S such that X and Y are both faces of S. Moreover, there is a closed form solution for the affine constraints that determine S.*

Proof. If $X \subseteq \{x_i = 0\}$ is an $(n-1)$-dimensional affine set with k faces, then the affine constraints defining X can be put in the form

$$\begin{pmatrix} a_{11} & \cdots & a_{1,i-1} & 0 & a_{1,i+1} & \cdots & a_{1n} \\ \vdots & \ddots & \vdots & \vdots & \vdots & \ddots & \vdots \\ a_{k1} & \cdots & a_{k,i-1} & 0 & a_{k,i+1} & \cdots & a_{kn} \\ 0 & \cdots & 0 & 1 & 0 & \cdots & 0 \\ 0 & \cdots & 0 & -1 & 0 & \cdots & 0 \end{pmatrix} \begin{pmatrix} x_1 \\ \vdots \\ \vdots \\ x_n \end{pmatrix} + \begin{pmatrix} a_1 \\ \vdots \\ a_k \\ 0 \\ 0 \end{pmatrix}.$$

Since $p_i \neq 0$, if we define

$$c_k = -\frac{1}{p_i} \sum_{\substack{j=1 \\ j \neq i}}^{n} p_j a_{kj},$$

the affine constraints for the set S are given by

$$\begin{pmatrix} a_{11} & \cdots & a_{1,i-1} & c_1 & a_{1,i+1} & \cdots & a_{1n} \\ \vdots & \ddots & \vdots & \vdots & \vdots & \ddots & \vdots \\ a_{k1} & \cdots & a_{k,i-1} & c_k & a_{k,i+1} & \cdots & a_{kn} \\ 0 & \cdots & 0 & \text{sign}(p_i) & 0 & \cdots & 0 \\ 0 & \cdots & 0 & -\text{sign}(p_i) & 0 & \cdots & 0 \end{pmatrix} \begin{pmatrix} x_1 \\ \vdots \\ \\ x_n \end{pmatrix} + \begin{pmatrix} a_1 \\ \vdots \\ a_k \\ 0 \\ \text{sign}(p_i)p_i \end{pmatrix}. \tag{5}$$

It can be verified easily that X is the face of S given by intersecting S with the hyperplane $\{x_i = 0\}$. Similarly, Y is the face of S given by intersecting S with the hyperplane $\{x_i - p_i = 0\}$. □

3.2. Throughout this paper, we will use *angle* to refer to a scaler with values in $[-\pi, \pi)$. For $n \geq 2$, *Givens rotations* (see [5,8]) are $n \times n$ matrices of the form

$$P_{ij}(\theta) = \begin{pmatrix} 1 & & & & & & \\ & \ddots & & & & & \\ & & \cos\theta & & -\sin\theta & & \\ & & & 1 & & & \\ & & & & \ddots & & \\ & & \sin\theta & & \cos\theta & & \\ & & & & & \ddots & \\ & & & & & & 1 \end{pmatrix} \begin{matrix} \\ \\ \leftarrow \text{row } i \\ \\ \\ \leftarrow \text{row } j \\ \\ \end{matrix}$$

with $\text{column } i$ and $\text{column } j$ indicated.

Givens rotations are important because, for every $R \in SO(n)$ with $n \geq 2$, there exists $n(n-1)/2$ angles $\theta_{ij} \in [-\pi, \pi)$ such that $R = \prod_{i=1}^{n-1} \prod_{j=i+1}^{n} P_{ij}(\theta_{ij})$ (cf. [3]). Moreover, there is a closed form solution for θ_{ij}. Therefore, understanding the effect of applying an element of $SO(n)$ to an affine set is equivalent to understanding the effect of applying a Givens rotation.

Proposition 3.2. *Let X be an affine set of dimension $n-1$ in $\mathbb{R}^n$, and assume that $X \subseteq \{x_i = 0\} \cap \{x_j \geq 0\}$. If $Y = P_{ij}(\theta)X$, with $\theta \in (0, \pi)$, then there exists an affine set S such that X and Y are both faces of S. Moreover, there is a closed form solution for the affine constraints that determine S.*

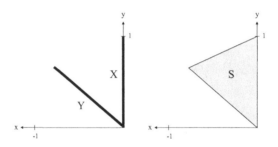

Fig. 2. Left: The sets X and Y in Example 3.1. Right: The set S with X and Y as faces.

Proof. If $X \subseteq \{x_i = 0\} \cap \{x_j \geq 0\}$ is an $(n-1)$-dimensional affine set with k faces, the affine constraints defining X can be written as

$$
\begin{array}{cc}
\text{column } i & \text{column } j \\
\downarrow & \downarrow
\end{array}
$$

$$
\begin{pmatrix}
a_{11} & \cdots & a_{1,i-1} & 0 & a_{1,i+1} & \cdots & a_{1,j-1} & a_{1j} & a_{1,j+1} & \cdots & a_{1n} \\
\vdots & \ddots & \vdots & \vdots & \vdots & \ddots & \vdots & \vdots & \vdots & \ddots & \vdots \\
a_{k1} & \cdots & a_{k,i-1} & 0 & a_{k,i+1} & \cdots & a_{k,j-1} & a_{kj} & a_{k,j+1} & \cdots & a_{kn} \\
0 & \cdots & 0 & 1 & 0 & \cdots & 0 & 0 & 0 & \cdots & 0 \\
0 & \cdots & 0 & -1 & 0 & \cdots & 0 & 0 & 0 & \cdots & 0 \\
0 & \cdots & 0 & 0 & 0 & \cdots & 0 & 1 & 0 & \cdots & 0
\end{pmatrix}
\begin{pmatrix} x_1 \\ \vdots \\ \\ x_n \end{pmatrix}
+
\begin{pmatrix} a_1 \\ \vdots \\ a_k \\ 0 \\ 0 \\ 0 \end{pmatrix}. \quad (6)
$$

The affine constraints for the set S with X and Y as faces are given by

$$
\begin{array}{cc}
\text{column } i & \text{column } j \\
\downarrow & \downarrow
\end{array}
$$

$$
\begin{pmatrix}
a_{11} & \cdots & a_{1,i-1} & a_{1j}(\cot\theta - \csc\theta) & a_{1,i+1} & \cdots & a_{1j} & \cdots & a_{1n} \\
\vdots & \ddots & \vdots & \vdots & \vdots & \ddots & \vdots & \ddots & \vdots \\
a_{k1} & \cdots & a_{k,i-1} & a_{kj}(\cot\theta - \csc\theta) & a_{k,i+1} & \cdots & a_{kj} & \cdots & a_{kn} \\
0 & \cdots & 0 & \cos\theta & 0 & \cdots & \sin\theta & \cdots & 0 \\
0 & \cdots & 0 & -1 & 0 & \cdots & 0 & \cdots & 0
\end{pmatrix}
\begin{pmatrix} x_1 \\ \vdots \\ x_n \end{pmatrix}
+
\begin{pmatrix} a_1 \\ \vdots \\ a_k \\ 0 \\ 0 \end{pmatrix}. \quad (7)
$$

It can be verified easily that X is the face of S given by intersecting S with the hyperplane $\{x_i = 0\}$. Similarly, Y is the face of S given by intersecting S with the hyperplane $\{\cos\theta x_i + \sin\theta x_j = 0\}$. $\qquad \square$

Example 3.1. Consider the set $X = \{(x,y) : x = 0, y \in [0,1]\}$ and $Y = P_{12}(\frac{\pi}{4})X$. Since $X \subset \{x = 0\} \cap \{y \geq 0\}$, we can apply Proposition 3.2 to determine an affine set S with X and Y as faces. The affine constraints for X are given by

$$
\begin{pmatrix}
0 & 1 \\
0 & -1 \\
1 & 0 \\
-1 & 0 \\
0 & 1
\end{pmatrix}
\begin{pmatrix} x \\ y \end{pmatrix}
+
\begin{pmatrix} 0 \\ 1 \\ 0 \\ 0 \\ 0 \end{pmatrix},
$$

where these affine constraints are in the same form as (6). Applying (7) gives the affine constraints for S as

$$
\begin{pmatrix} (1-\sqrt{2}) & 1 \\ -(1-\sqrt{2}) & -1 \\ \frac{1}{\sqrt{2}} & \frac{1}{\sqrt{2}} \\ -1 & 0 \end{pmatrix} \begin{pmatrix} x \\ y \end{pmatrix} + \begin{pmatrix} 0 \\ 1 \\ 0 \\ 0 \end{pmatrix}.
$$

Or this set is given by the constraints that $y \leq -(1-\sqrt{2})x + 1$, $y \geq -x$ and $x \leq 0$. The remaining constraint, that $y \geq -(1-\sqrt{2})x$, is satisfied when the other three constraints are satisfied. The set S is exactly the set that we would have hoped for (see Figure 2).

4   Admissible Sequences

For two $(n-1)$-dimensional affine sets X and $Y = RX + p$, in general it is not true that there exists an n-dimensional affine set with X and Y as faces. When there is not an affine set with X and Y as faces, the question is: does there exist a sequence of affine sets where the first affine set has X as a face, the last affine set has Y as a face, and any two adjacent affine sets in the sequence share a common face? In this section, it will be shown that for any set X and $Y = RX + p$, there exists a sequence of affine sets of this form; these sequences will be essential to the proof of the Main Theorem. The results of the previous section allow each of the affine sets in the sequence to be computed. Detailed proofs of the results of this section can be found in [1,2].

Definition 4.1. *Two $(n-1)$-dimensional affine sets, X and Y, are* admissible faces *if there exists an n-dimensional affine set $\Xi(X,Y)$ with X and Y as faces.*

4.1. If $\Xi(X,Y)$ is an affine set, for $(R,p) \in SE(n)$, there are the following properties

$$
\Xi(X,Y) = \Xi(Y,X),
$$
$$
R\Xi(X,Y) + p = \Xi(RX + p, RY + p),
$$

where $\Xi(RX + p, RY + p)$ is an affine set with $RX + p$ and $RY + p$ as faces.

4.2. We have shown in Proposition 3.1 that if $X \subset \{x_i = 0\}$ and $Y = X + p$ with $p_i \neq 0$, then X and Y are admissible faces; we can take $\Xi(X,Y)$ to be the affine set given by the affine constraints in (5). Similarly, by Proposition 3.2, if $X \subset \{x_i = 0\} \cap \{x_j \geq 0\}$ and $Y = P_{ij}(\theta)X$, for $\theta \in (0,\pi)$, then X and Y are admissible faces; we can take $\Xi(X,Y)$ to be the affine set given by the affine constraints in (7).

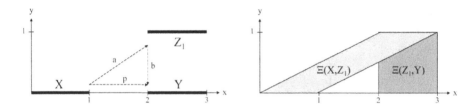

Fig. 3. Left: the sets X, Z_1 and Y in Example 4.1. Right: the affine sets $S_1 = \Xi(X, Z_1)$ and $S_2 = \Xi(Z_1, Y)$.

Definition 4.2. *A sequence* $Z_0, Z_1, ..., Z_k$ *of* $(n-1)$-*dimensional affine sets is an* admissible sequence of faces *if there exists affine sets,*

$$\Xi(Z_0, Z_1), \quad \Xi(Z_1, Z_2), \quad ..., \quad \Xi(Z_{k-1}, Z_k).$$

Proposition 4.1. *Let* X *be an* $(n-1)$-*dimensional affine set and* $Y = X + p$. *Then there exists an admissible sequence of faces* $Z_0 = X, Z_1, Z_2 = Y$.

Proposition 4.2. *Let* X *be a compact* $(n-1)$-*dimensional affine set with* $n \geq 3$, *and* $Y = P_{ij}(\theta)X$. *Then there exists an admissible sequence of faces*

$$Z_0 = X, Z_1, ..., Z_9, Z_{11} = Y.$$

Remark 4.1. In the case where $n = 2$, an obvious modification of Proposition 4.2 gives an admissible sequence of faces $Z_0 = X$, Z_1, ..., Z_4, $Z_5 = Y$. Throughout the rest of the paper, we will assume that $n \geq 3$. All of the results are applicable to the case where $n = 2$, with the obvious modifications.

Theorem 4.1. *Let* X *be a compact* $(n-1)$-*dimensional affine set, and* $Y = RX + p$, *with* $(R, p) \in SE(n)$. *Then there exists an admissible sequence of faces*

$$Z_0 = X, Z_1, ..., Z_{\frac{11}{2}n(n-1)+1}, Z_{\frac{11}{2}n(n-1)+2} = Y.$$

Example 4.1. Let $X = \{(x, y) : x \in [0, 1], \ y = 0\}$, $p = (2, 0)$, and $Y = X + p$, i.e., $Y = \{(x, y) : x \in [2, 3], \ y = 0\}$. Therefore, X and Y are given by the affine constraints:

$$\begin{pmatrix} 1 & 0 \\ -1 & 0 \\ 0 & 1 \\ 0 & -1 \end{pmatrix} \begin{pmatrix} x \\ y \end{pmatrix} + \begin{pmatrix} 0 \\ 1 \\ 0 \\ 0 \end{pmatrix}, \qquad \begin{pmatrix} 1 & 0 \\ -1 & 0 \\ 0 & 1 \\ 0 & -1 \end{pmatrix} \begin{pmatrix} x \\ y \end{pmatrix} + \begin{pmatrix} -2 \\ 3 \\ 0 \\ 0 \end{pmatrix},$$

respectively. It is clear that there is not a single n-dimensional affine set with X and Y as faces. This is evident in the fact that the assumptions of Proposition

3.1 are not satisfied; $X \subset \{y = 0\}$, but $p_2 = 0$. By Proposition 4.1, we can find a sequence of admissible faces $Z_0 = X, Z_1, Z_2 = Y$, and the corresponding affine sets $S_1 = \Xi(X, Z_1)$ and $S_2 = \Xi(Z_1, Y)$.

Define $a = (2, 1)$ and $b = (0, -1)$, then $a + b = p$ and $Z_1 = X + a = \{(x, y) : x \in [2, 3], y = 1\}$. We can let $S_1 = \Xi(X, Z_1)$, which is given by the affine constraints in (5). Since $Z_1 = Y - b$, $S_2 = \Xi(Z_1, Y) = \Xi(Y - b, Y) = \Xi(Y, Y - b)$. Because $Y \subset \{y = 0\}$ and $b_2 \neq 0$, applying Proposition 3.1 gives the affine constraints for S_2. Therefore, applying (5) to the affine constraints defining X and Y gives the affine constraints defining S_1 and S_2 as:

$$
\begin{pmatrix} 1 & -2 \\ -1 & 2 \\ 0 & 1 \\ 0 & -1 \end{pmatrix} \begin{pmatrix} x \\ y \end{pmatrix} + \begin{pmatrix} 0 \\ 1 \\ 0 \\ 1 \end{pmatrix}, \qquad
\begin{pmatrix} 1 & 0 \\ -1 & 0 \\ 0 & 1 \\ 0 & -1 \end{pmatrix} \begin{pmatrix} x \\ y \end{pmatrix} + \begin{pmatrix} -2 \\ 3 \\ 0 \\ 1 \end{pmatrix},
$$

respectively. For a visual interpretation of these results, see Figure 3.

5 Spatial Equivalence

In this section we use the sequence of admissible faces found in Section 4 to prove the Main Theorem of this paper. In the proof of this theorem, the hybrid system $\mathbf{H}_{\mathrm{id}}$ is constructed. This allows $\mathbf{H}_{\mathrm{id}}$ to be explicitly computed, as will be seen through an example following the proof of the Main Theorem.

5.1. A hybrid system $\mathbf{H} = (Q^{\mathbf{H}}, D^{\mathbf{H}}, E^{\mathbf{H}}, V^{\mathbf{H}})$ is said to be *spatially equivalent* to a hybrid system $\mathbf{G} = (Q^{\mathbf{G}}, D^{\mathbf{G}}, E^{\mathbf{G}}, V^{\mathbf{G}})$ if the following conditions hold:

1. $|Q^{\mathbf{G}}| \geq |Q^{\mathbf{H}}| = m$.
2. For every $i \leq m$, $D_i^{\mathbf{H}} = D_i^{\mathbf{G}}$ and for $i > m$, there exist admissible faces X_i and Y_i such that $D_i^{\mathbf{G}} = \Xi(X_i, Y_i)$.
3. For every edge $e \in E^{\mathbf{H}}$ there exists a sequence of k discrete states $\nu(1), ..., \nu(k) > m$ and edges $\eta_1, ..., \eta_{k+1} \in E^{\mathbf{G}}$ such that

$$
T_{\eta_1}(\mathrm{Face}_{\pi_3(e)}(D_{\pi_1(e)}^{\mathbf{H}})) = X_{\nu(1)},
$$
$$
T_{\eta_2}(Y_{\nu(1)}) = X_{\nu(2)},
$$
$$
\vdots
$$
$$
T_{\eta_{k+1}}(Y_{\nu(k)}) = \mathrm{Face}_{\pi_4(e)}(D_{\pi_2(e)}^{\mathbf{H}}).
$$

In the special case where $k = 0$, we require η_1 to be an edge such that

$$
T_{\eta_1}(\mathrm{Face}_{\pi_3(e)}(D_{\pi_1(e)}^{\mathbf{H}})) = \mathrm{Face}_{\pi_4(e)}(D_{\pi_2(e)}^{\mathbf{H}}).
$$

4. For $i \leq m$, $V_i^{\mathbf{H}} = V_i^{\mathbf{G}}$, and for $i > m$, $V_i^{\mathbf{G}}$ is a vector field such that $\phi_i^{\mathbf{G}}(1, X_i) = Y_i$, where $\phi_i^{\mathbf{G}}(t, x)$ is the solution to $V_i^{\mathbf{G}}$.

Remark 5.1. Note that spatial equivalence is not an equivalence relation. The term "equivalence" is used in order to stress the equivalence of the qualitative behavior of **H** and **G**, when **H** is spatially equivalent to **G**. Although it might be appropriate to replace "spatial equivalence" by a term such as "spatial embedding", the authors are concerned that this term would not stress the behavioral similarities of the two hybrid systems.

Definition 5.1. *A hybrid system* **H** *is* compact *if each of its domains is compact.*

Theorem 5.1. *If* **H** *is a compact hybrid system, then* **H** *is spatially equivalent to a hybrid system* $\mathbf{H}_{\mathrm{id}}$ *such that every transition map is the identity, i.e.,* $T_\eta = \mathrm{id}$ *for every* $\eta \in E^{\mathbf{H}_{\mathrm{id}}}$*. Moreover,* $\mathbf{H}_{\mathrm{id}}$ *is computable.*

Proof. In order to prove this theorem, we will explicitly construct the hybrid system $\mathbf{H}_{\mathrm{id}}$. First, we define

$$E_{\mathrm{id}}^{\mathbf{H}} := \{e \in E^{\mathbf{H}} : \ T_e \neq \mathrm{id}\},$$

which is the set of edges such that the associated transition map is not the identity. If $|E_{\mathrm{id}}^{\mathbf{H}}| = k$, then we can write the elements of $E_{\mathrm{id}}^{\mathbf{H}}$ as $e_1, ..., e_k$ (by arbitrarily indexing them). For simplicity of notation, define the functions

$$f(n) = \frac{11}{2}n(n-1) + 2,$$
$$g(m,n,i) = (i-1)f(n) + m + 1,$$

which will be used throughout the course of the construction.

CONSTRUCTION OF $\mathbf{H}_{\mathrm{id}}$

$\underline{Q^{\mathbf{H}_{\mathrm{id}}}}$: If $Q^{\mathbf{H}} = \{1, ..., m\}$, then define $Q^{\mathbf{H}_{\mathrm{id}}} = \{1, ..., m + kf(n)\}$, with $k = |E_{\mathrm{id}}^{\mathbf{H}}|$.

$\underline{D^{\mathbf{H}_{\mathrm{id}}}}$: For $i \leq m$, define $D_i^{\mathbf{H}_{\mathrm{id}}} = D_i^{\mathbf{H}}$. If $A_i x + a_i$ are the affine constraints determining $D_i^{\mathbf{H}}$, then we also let $A_i x + a_i$ (with the order of the rows maintained) be the affine constraints determining $D_i^{\mathbf{H}_{\mathrm{id}}}$. In particular, this implies that $\mathrm{Face}_j(D_i^{\mathbf{H}_{\mathrm{id}}}) = \mathrm{Face}_j(D_i^{\mathbf{H}})$.

Now we can construct the other domains of $\mathbf{H}_{\mathrm{id}}$. For every edge $e_i \in E_{\mathrm{id}}^{\mathbf{H}}$, $1 \leq i \leq k$, the transition map is given by $T_{e_i}(x) = R_{e_i}x + p_{e_i}$, or we have

$$\mathrm{Face}_{\pi_4(e_i)}(D_{\pi_2(e_i)}^{\mathbf{H}}) = R_{e_i}\mathrm{Face}_{\pi_3(e_i)}(D_{\pi_1(e_i)}^{\mathbf{H}}) + p_{e_i}.$$

Now by Theorem 4.1 we have the following admissible sequence of faces

$$Z_0^i = \mathrm{Face}_{\pi_3(e_i)}(D_{\pi_1(e_i)}^{\mathbf{H}}), \ Z_1^i, \ ..., \ Z_{f(n)-1}^i, \ Z_{f(n)}^i = \mathrm{Face}_{\pi_4(e_i)}(D_{\pi_2(e_i)}^{\mathbf{H}}).$$

Setting

$$X_{g(m,n,i)} = Z_0^i,$$
$$X_{g(m,n,i)+1} = Z_1^i = Y_{g(m,n,i)},$$

$$\vdots$$

$$X_{g(m,n,i)+f(n)-1} = Z_{f(n)-1}^i = Y_{g(m,n,i)+f(n)-2},$$
$$Z_{f(n)}^i = Y_{g(m,n,i)+f(n)-1},$$

define the domains

$$D_{g(m,n,i)+j}^{\mathbf{H}_{\mathrm{id}}} = \Xi(X_{g(m,n,i)+j}, Y_{g(m,n,i)+j}), \qquad 1 \le i \le k, \qquad 0 \le j \le f(n)-1.$$

It can be verified that for these values of i and j, $g(m,n,i)+j$ takes all values from $m+1$ to $m+kf(n)$, inclusive, and with no repeats.

$\underline{E^{\mathbf{H}_{\mathrm{id}}}}$: If $e \in E^{\mathbf{H}}$ and $e \notin E_{iA}^{\mathbf{H}}$, then the associated transition map is $T_e = \mathrm{id}$. So define an edge $\eta(e) \in E^{\mathbf{H}_{\mathrm{id}}}$ to be $\eta(e) = e$. It follows that $T_{\eta(e)} = \mathrm{id}$. If $e \in E_{iA}^{\mathbf{H}}$, then $e = e_i$ for $i \in \{1,...,k\}$. We can now define a set of edges $\eta_1(e_i), \eta_2(e_i), ..., \eta_{f(n)+1}(e_i) \in E^{\mathbf{H}_{\mathrm{id}}}$ as follows: if we index the faces of $D_{g(m,n,i)+j}^{\mathbf{H}_{\mathrm{id}}}$ such that

$$X_{g(m,n,i)+j} = \mathrm{Face}_1(D_{g(m,n,i)+j}^{\mathbf{H}_{\mathrm{id}}}), \qquad Y_{g(m,n,i)+j} = \mathrm{Face}_2(D_{g(m,n,i)+j}^{\mathbf{H}_{\mathrm{id}}}),$$

then we define

$$\eta_1(e_i) = ((\pi_1(e_i), g(m,n,i)), (\pi_3(e_i), 1),$$
$$\eta_2(e_i) = ((g(m,n,i), g(m,n,i)+1), (2,1)),$$

$$\vdots$$

$$\eta_j(e_i) = ((g(m,n,i)+j-2, g(m,n,i)+j-1), (2,1)),$$

$$\vdots$$

$$\eta_{f(n)}(e_i) = ((g(m,n,i)+f(n)-2, g(m,n,i)+f(n)-1), (2,1)),$$
$$\eta_{f(n)+1}(e_i) = ((g(m,n,i)+f(n)-1, \pi_2(e_i)), (2, \pi_4(e_i)).$$

The associated transition maps are

$$T_{\eta_1(e_i)} : \mathrm{Face}_{\pi_3(e_i)}(D_{\pi_1(e_i)}^{\mathbf{H}}) \to X_{g(m,n,i)},$$
$$T_{\eta_j(e_i)} : Y_{g(m,n,i)+j-2} \to X_{g(m,n,i)+j-1}, \qquad 1 < j \le f(n),$$
$$T_{\eta_{f(n)+1}(e_i)} : Y_{g(m,n,i)+f(n)-1} \to \mathrm{Face}_{\pi_4(e_i)}(D_{\pi_2(e_i)}^{\mathbf{H}}),$$

so

$$\mathrm{Face}_{\pi_3(e_i)}(D_{\pi_1(e_i)}^{\mathbf{H}}) = X_{g(m,n,i)},$$
$$Y_{g(m,n,i)+j-2} = X_{g(m,n,i)+j-1}, \qquad 1 < j \le f(n),$$
$$Y_{g(m,n,i)+f(n)-1} = \mathrm{Face}_{\pi_4(e_i)}(D_{\pi_2(e_i)}^{\mathbf{H}}).$$

By definition, it follows that

$$T_{\eta_1(e_i)} = T_{\eta_2(e_i)} = \cdots = T_{\eta_{f(n)+1}(e_i)} = \mathrm{id}.$$

If we apply this construction to every edge in $E^{\mathbf{H}}$ the result is the set $E^{\mathbf{H}_{\mathrm{id}}}$. It is clear that for every edge in $\eta \in E^{\mathbf{H}_{\mathrm{id}}}$, $T_\eta = \mathrm{id}$. It also follows that $|E^{\mathbf{H}_{\mathrm{id}}}| = |E^{\mathbf{H}}| + 2f(n)$.

$\underline{V^{\mathbf{H}_{\mathrm{id}}}}$: If $i \leq m$, define $V_i^{\mathbf{H}_{\mathrm{id}}} = V_i^{\mathbf{H}}$. If $i > m$, then $D_i^{\mathbf{H}_{\mathrm{id}}} = \Xi(X_i, Y_i)$, where X_i and Y_i differ by an element of $SE(n)$, i.e., $Y_i = Q_i X_i + q_i$. Using this, we define

$$\phi_i^{\mathbf{H}_{\mathrm{id}}}(t, x) = (1 - t)x + t(Q_i x + q_i), \qquad V_i^{\mathbf{H}_{\mathrm{id}}}(x) = \frac{d}{dt}(\phi_i^{\mathbf{H}_{\mathrm{id}}}(t, x)),$$

and we have the property that $\phi_i^{\mathbf{H}_{\mathrm{id}}}(1, X_i) = Q_i X_i + q_i = Y_i$.

To conclude the proof we note that in the process of constructing $\mathbf{H}_{\mathrm{id}}$ we have shown that $\mathbf{H}$ and $\mathbf{H}_{\mathrm{id}}$ satisfy properties 1-4 of Paragraph 5.1, hence $\mathbf{H}$ is spatially equivalent to $\mathbf{H}_{\mathrm{id}}$. □

Remark 5.2. Note that the hybrid system we constructed in the proof of Theorem 5.1 is not unique. Moreover, the number of discrete states given in the construction is not necessarily the smallest number of discrete states needed to construct a spatially equivalent hybrid system. For example, if for every edge $e \in E^{\mathbf{H}}$, the faces $\mathrm{Face}_{\pi_3(e)}(D_{\pi_1(e)}^{\mathbf{H}})$ and $\mathrm{Face}_{\pi_4(e)}(D_{\pi_2(e)}^{\mathbf{H}})$ are admissible (see Definition 4.1), then we can construct a hybrid system $\mathbf{H}_{\mathrm{id}}$, spatially equivalent to $\mathbf{H}$, with $Q^{\mathbf{H}_{\mathrm{id}}} = \{1, ..., m+k\}$. This will be the case in the following example.

Example 5.1. We will construct $\mathbb{T}_{\mathrm{id}}^2$, or a hybrid system spatially equivalent to $\mathbb{T}^2$ (see Example 2.1) where every transition map is the identity. In this case we have two edges, $e_1, e_2 \in E^{\mathbb{T}^2}$, and $|E_{\mathrm{id}}^{\mathbb{T}^2}| = 2$. First, note that we can define $\mathbb{T}_{\mathrm{id}}^2$ in terms of fewer than the number of discrete states given in the proof of Theorem 5.1 because $\mathrm{Face}_{\pi_3(e_i)}(D_{\pi_1(e_i)}^{\mathbf{H}})$ and $\mathrm{Face}_{\pi_4(e_i)}(D_{\pi_2(e_i)}^{\mathbf{H}})$ are admissible faces for $i = 1, 2$ (see Remark 5.2).

Set $Q^{\mathbb{T}_{\mathrm{id}}^2} = \{1, 2, 3\}$, and let $D_1^{\mathbb{T}_{\mathrm{id}}^2} = D_1^{\mathbb{T}^2}$, which we defined in Example 2.1. To construct $D_2^{\mathbb{T}_{\mathrm{id}}^2}$ and $D_3^{\mathbb{T}_{\mathrm{id}}^2}$, note that

$$\mathrm{Face}_2(D_1^{\mathbb{T}^2}) = \mathrm{Face}_1(D_1^{\mathbb{T}^2}) + \begin{pmatrix} 1 \\ 0 \end{pmatrix}, \qquad \mathrm{Face}_3(D_1^{\mathbb{T}^2}) = \mathrm{Face}_4(D_1^{\mathbb{T}^2}) + \begin{pmatrix} 0 \\ 1 \end{pmatrix}.$$

Since $\mathrm{Face}_1(D_1^{\mathbb{T}^2}) \subset \{x = 0\}$ and $\mathrm{Face}_4(D_1^{\mathbb{T}^2}) \subset \{y = 0\}$, by applying Proposition 3.1 to the affine constraints $A_{11}^{\mathbb{T}^2} x + a_{11}^{\mathbb{T}^2}$ and $A_{14}^{\mathbb{T}^2} x + a_{14}^{\mathbb{T}^2}$, given in equations (3) and (4), it can be verified that

$$\Xi(\mathrm{Face}_1(D_1^{\mathbb{T}^2}), \mathrm{Face}_2(D_1^{\mathbb{T}^2})) = \Xi(\mathrm{Face}_4(D_1^{\mathbb{T}^2}), \mathrm{Face}_3(D_1^{\mathbb{T}^2})) = D_1^{\mathbb{T}^2}.$$

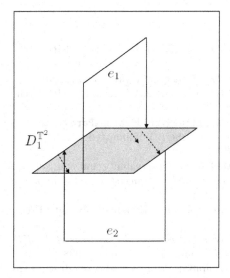 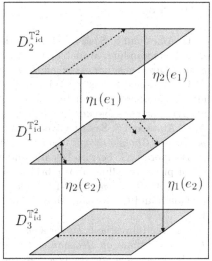

Fig. 4. Left: $\mathbb{T}^2$. Right: $\mathbb{T}^2_{\mathrm{id}}$.

Now as in the proof of Theorem 5.1, define

$$X_2 = \mathrm{Face}_2(D_1^{\mathbb{T}^2}), \qquad Y_2 = \mathrm{Face}_1(D_1^{\mathbb{T}^2}),$$
$$X_3 = \mathrm{Face}_3(D_1^{\mathbb{T}^2}), \qquad Y_3 = \mathrm{Face}_4(D_1^{\mathbb{T}^2}),$$

then

$$D_2^{\mathbb{T}^2_{\mathrm{id}}} = \Xi(X_2, Y_2) = D_1^{\mathbb{T}^2}, \qquad D_3^{\mathbb{T}^2_{\mathrm{id}}} = \Xi(X_3, Y_3) = D_1^{\mathbb{T}^2},$$

and $D^{\mathbb{T}^2_{\mathrm{id}}} = \{D_1^{\mathbb{T}^2_{\mathrm{id}}}, D_2^{\mathbb{T}^2_{\mathrm{id}}}, D_3^{\mathbb{T}^2_{\mathrm{id}}}\}$.

Now we will determine the edges of $\mathbb{T}^2_{\mathrm{id}}$. As in the proof of Theorem 5.1, index the faces of $D_2^{\mathbb{T}^2_{\mathrm{id}}}$ and $D_3^{\mathbb{T}^2_{\mathrm{id}}}$ such that

$$X_2 = \mathrm{Face}_1(D_2^{\mathbb{T}^2_{\mathrm{id}}}), \qquad Y_2 = \mathrm{Face}_2(D_2^{\mathbb{T}^2_{\mathrm{id}}}),$$
$$X_3 = \mathrm{Face}_1(D_3^{\mathbb{T}^2_{\mathrm{id}}}), \qquad Y_3 = \mathrm{Face}_2(D_3^{\mathbb{T}^2_{\mathrm{id}}}),$$

and for the two edges $e_1, e_2 \in E^{\mathbb{T}^2}$, define

$$\eta_1(e_1) = ((1,2),(2,1)), \qquad \eta_1(e_2) = ((1,3),(4,1)),$$
$$\eta_2(e_1) = ((2,1),(2,1)), \qquad \eta_2(e_2) = ((3,1),(2,3)).$$

Set $E^{\mathbb{T}^2_{\mathrm{id}}} = \{\eta_1(e_1), \eta_2(e_1), \eta_1(e_2), \eta_2(e_2)\}$, and note that the corresponding transition maps $T_{\eta_1(e_1)} = T_{\eta_2(e_1)} = T_{\eta_1(e_2)} = T_{\eta_2(e_2)} = \mathrm{id}$ (see Figure 4).

Finally, define $V_1^{\mathbb{T}^2_{\mathrm{id}}} = V_1^{\mathbb{T}^2}$ and

$$V_2^{\mathbb{T}^2_{\mathrm{id}}}(x) = \begin{pmatrix} -1 \\ 0 \end{pmatrix}, \qquad V_3^{\mathbb{T}^2_{\mathrm{id}}}(x) = \begin{pmatrix} 0 \\ -1 \end{pmatrix},$$

So, $V^{\mathbb{T}^2_{\mathrm{id}}} = \{V_1^{\mathbb{T}^2_{\mathrm{id}}}, V_2^{\mathbb{T}^2_{\mathrm{id}}}, V_3^{\mathbb{T}^2_{\mathrm{id}}}\}$. This completes the construction of $\mathbb{T}^2_{\mathrm{id}}$.

References

1. A. D. Ames and S. Sastry. Affine hybrid systems: part 1. UC Berkeley ERL Technical Memorandum, available at
   http://www.eecs.berkeley.edu/~adames/AffineHybridSystemsPart1.pdf.
2. A. D. Ames and S. Sastry. Affine hybrid systems: part 2. UC Berkeley ERL Technical Memorandum, available at
   http://www.eecs.berkeley.edu/~adames/AffineHybridSystemsPart2.pdf.
3. A. D. Ames and S. Sastry. Givens Rotations and $SO(n)$. Submitted to *ACM Symposium on Computational Geometry*, 2004.
4. A. Bemporad, G. Ferrari-Trecate, and M. Morari. Observability and controllability of piecewise affine and hybrid systems. In *IEEE Transactions on Automatic Control*, 45(10): pages 1864-1876, October 2000.
5. G. Golub and C.V. Loan, *Matrix Computation*, Johns Hopkins University Press, 1996.
6. M. Jirstrand. Invariant sets for a class of hybrid systems. In *Proceedings of the 37th IEEE Conference on Decision and Control*. Tampa, FL, December 1998.
7. M. Johansson and A. Rantzer. On the computation of piecewise quadratic Lyapunov functions. In *Proceedings of the 36th IEEE Conference on Decision and Control*. San Diego, CA, December 1997.
8. C. Meyer. *Matrix analysis and applied linear algebra*. SIAM, 2000.
9. S. N. Simic, K. H. Johansson, J. Lygeros, and S. Sastry. Towards a Geometric Theory of Hybrid Systems. In *Hybrid Systems: Computation and Control*, number 1790 in LNCS, pages 421-436. Springer-Verlag, 2000.
10. Z. Sun and D. Zheng. On reachability and stabilization of switched linear systems. In *IEEE Transactions on Automatic Control*, 46(2): pages 291-295, February 2001.

Abstraction by Projection and Application to Multi-affine Systems

Eugene Asarin[1] and Thao Dang[2]

[1] LIAFA,
Université Paris 7, Case 7014, 2 place Jussieu, 75251 Paris 5, France
`Eugene.Asarin@liafa.jussieu.fr`
[2] VERIMAG,
Centre Equation, 2 av de Vignate, 38610 Gières, France
`Thao.Dang@imag.fr`

Abstract. In this paper we present an abstraction method for nonlinear continuous systems. The main idea of our method is to project out some continuous variables, say z, and treat them in the dynamics of the remaining variables x as uncertain input. Therefore, the dynamics of x is then described by a differential inclusion. In addition, in order to avoid excessively conservative abstractions, the domains of the projected variables are divided into smaller regions corresponding to different differential inclusions. The final result of our abstraction procedure is a hybrid system of lower dimension with some important properties that guarantee convergence results. The applicability of this abstraction approach depends on the ability to deal with differential inclusions. We then focus on uncertain bilinear systems, a simple yet useful class of nonlinear differential inclusions, and develop a reachability technique using optimal control. The combination of the abstraction method and the reachability analysis technique for bilinear systems allows to treat multi-affine systems, which is illustrated with a biological system.

1 Introduction

Recent developments in embedded control systems have motivated much research on automated verification of continuous and hybrid systems. For systems involving non-trivial continuous dynamics (described by differential equations), exact and approximate reachability analysis methods have been developed [16,22,9,3, 20,24]. Even though these methods have been used to treat interesting case studies, the complexity of reachability computations currently limits the application to small size systems. In order to scale to larger systems, abstraction methods have been investigated (see [9,32,2,31,26]). Roughly speaking, abstraction is a general approach allowing to deduce properties of a system by analyzing a more abstract and, in general, smaller system (see [10,8] and references therein). Some of the abstraction methods for hybrid systems, inspired by techniques from program analysis, aim at extracting (exactly or approximately) a finite-state model from a continuous/hybrid system while the other exploit the structure of the

R. Alur and G.J. Pappas (Eds.): HSCC 2004, LNCS 2993, pp. 32–47, 2004.

system in order to reduce it into a system of smaller dimension which preserves the properties of interest. In addition, the methods based on approximating continuous systems by hybrid systems with simpler continuous dynamics [28,18,4], that we call 'hybridization-based' methods, can also be viewed as an abstraction approach.

In this work, we propose an abstraction method for dimension reduction, which is along the lines of the hybridization-based approach. Our first observation is that in many practical systems, the properties to verify involve only a subset of variables, and the other variables may not need to be analyzed with great accuracy. The main idea of our method is to project out some continuous variables, say z, and treat them in the dynamics of the remaining variables x as uncertain input. Therefore, the dynamics of x is then described by a differential inclusion. In addition, in order to avoid excessively conservative abstractions, the domains of the projected variables are divided into smaller regions corresponding to different differential inclusions. The final result of our abstraction procedure is a hybrid system of lower dimension with some important properties that guarantee convergence results. However, this abstraction method does not solve the verification problem by itself. The success depends on the ability to deal with differential inclusions. We thus focus on the reachability problem for uncertain bilinear systems, a simple yet useful class of nonlinear differential inclusions. The combination of the abstraction method and the reachability analysis method for bilinear systems allows to treat multi-affine systems, which can be found in numerous applications in engineering, biology and economics.

The rest of the paper is organized as follows. In Section 2 we present our abstraction method and the convergence results. Section 3 is devoted to a reachability analysis method for uncertain bilinear systems, which is motivated by the application to multi-affine systems. This reachability technique uses results from optimal control. Section 4 contains an example of a biological system illustrating the theoretical results of the paper.

2 Abstraction by Projection

2.1 Basic Idea

We consider a continuous system

$$\begin{cases} \dot{x} = f(x, z) \\ \dot{z} = g(x, z) \end{cases} \tag{1}$$

where $x \in \mathcal{X} \subseteq \mathbb{R}^n$, $z \in \mathcal{Z} \subseteq \mathbb{R}^m$. We assume that the state space of the system is compact and the functions f, g are Lipschitz continuous. Given a vector x we use the notation x_i to denote the ith component of x.

Suppose that we want to reduce the dimension of the system (1) from $n + m$ to n by projecting out the variables z. As in qualitative simulation, the first step of the abstraction is to partition the domain of z into disjoint regions, and in each region the dynamics of x is approximated by a *differential inclusion* which is obtained from $f(x, z)$ by letting z to take any value in the region. In other words, the effect of z in the dynamics of x is modeled as uncertain external input. Let us now formalize this idea.

We suppose that the domain of variable z_i is an interval $\mathcal{I}_i = [\underline{z}_i, \bar{z}_i]$, and the domain of z is thus a box $\mathcal{B} = \mathcal{I}_1 \times \mathcal{I}_2 \times \ldots \times \mathcal{I}_m$. We partition each interval $\mathcal{I}_i$ into k disjoint intervals[1] of the form $\{\mathcal{I}_i^1 = [\underline{z}_i^1, \bar{z}_i^1), \mathcal{I}_i^2 = [\underline{z}_i^2, \bar{z}_i^2), \ldots, \mathcal{I}_i^k = [\underline{z}_i^k, \bar{z}_i^k]\}$ such that $\underline{z}_i^1 = \underline{z}_i$, $\bar{z}_i^k = \bar{z}_i$ and for all $j \in \{1, \ldots, k-1\}$ $\bar{z}_i^j = \underline{z}_i^{j+1}$. Therefore, the box $\mathcal{B}$ is partitioned into k^m boxes, and we denote by $\mathcal{B}^{\mathbf{i}}$ with $\mathbf{i} \in \mathbb{N}^m$ the box $\mathcal{I}_1^{\mathbf{i}_1} \times \ldots \times \mathcal{I}_m^{\mathbf{i}_m}$. In the following we shall approximate the $(n + m)$-dimensional continuous system (1), referred to as the original system, by a *hybrid automaton* with n continuous variables.

Each box $\mathcal{B}^{\mathbf{i}}$ corresponds to a location $loc^{\mathbf{i}}$ of the approximating hybrid automaton where the dynamics of x is approximated by the following differential inclusion: $\dot{x} \in F^{\mathbf{i}}(x) = \{f(x, z) \mid z \in \mathcal{B}^{\mathbf{i}}\}$. The transitions of this hybrid automaton correspond to the reachability relation between the boxes $\mathcal{B}^{\mathbf{i}}$ of the original system (1), which can be abstracted as follows. Note that since (1) is continuous, only transitions between adjacent boxes need to be considered. For our further developments, we need to introduce some additional notations. The boxes $\mathcal{B}^{\mathbf{i}}$ and $\mathcal{B}^{\mathbf{j}}$ are called *adjacent* if $|\mathbf{j}_i - \mathbf{i}_i| \leq 1$ for all i and $\mathbf{i} \neq \mathbf{j}$. We denote by $d(\mathbf{i}, \mathbf{j}) = \{i \mid 1 \leq i \leq m \wedge \mathbf{j}_i \neq \mathbf{i}_i\}$ the set of indices at which the components of $\mathbf{i}$ and $\mathbf{j}$ differ. We use $\partial(\mathcal{B}^{\mathbf{i}}, \mathcal{B}^{\mathbf{j}})$ to denote the common boundary of the boxes. Given two adjacent boxes $\mathcal{B}^{\mathbf{i}}$ and $\mathcal{B}^{\mathbf{j}}$, the condition for the transition from $\mathcal{B}^{\mathbf{i}}$ to $\mathcal{B}^{\mathbf{j}}$, denoted by $\mathcal{B}^{\mathbf{i}} \rightarrow \mathcal{B}^{\mathbf{j}}$, is:

$$\exists z \in \partial(\mathcal{B}^{\mathbf{i}}, \mathcal{B}^{\mathbf{j}}) \; \forall i \in d(\mathbf{i}, \mathbf{j}) : (\mathbf{j}_i - \mathbf{i}_i)g_i(x, z) \geq 0 \tag{2}$$

where g_i denotes the ith component of g. The above condition says that the transition from a box to one of its adjacent boxes is possible if there exists at least one point on the common boundary of the two boxes at which the derivative of z points into the arrival box. As an example, for two adjacent boxes $\mathcal{B}^{\mathbf{i}}$ and $\mathcal{B}^{\mathbf{j}}$ such that $\mathbf{j}_i = \mathbf{i}_i + 1$ and $\mathbf{j}_j = \mathbf{i}_j$ for all other $j \neq i$, the condition for the transition $\mathcal{B}^{\mathbf{i}} \rightarrow \mathcal{B}^{\mathbf{j}}$ is $g_i(x, \bar{z}^i) \geq 0$. Similarly, the condition for the transition $\mathcal{B}^{\mathbf{j}} \rightarrow \mathcal{B}^{\mathbf{i}}$ is $g_i(x, \bar{z}^i) \leq 0$. Obviously, the condition (2) is not sufficient since it only implies that there exists a trajectory of the original system that goes from one box to an adjacent box. Hence, the resulting hybrid system is an over-approximation of the original continuous system. The approximating system where z is scalar is shown in Figure 1.

2.2   Remedy Discontinuities

It should be noted that the way we project out the variables z introduces discontinuities in the derivative of the remaining variables x. For the sake of well-posedness, as in the sliding mode[2] approaches, we shall "convexify" the dynamics

---

[1] For simplicity of notation, we choose the same number of intervals for all z_i.

[2] The literature of sliding mode control is vast, see for example [34,1].

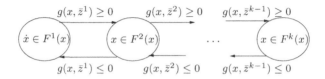

Fig. 1. Hybrid automaton obtained after projecting out the variables z.

of the abstract system in order to guarantee the existence of solutions [14] as well as an error bound of the approximation of the solution set.

Let $\mathcal{B}^{\mathbf{i}}$ and $\mathcal{B}^{\mathbf{j}}$ be two adjacent boxes. Between the locations $loc^{\mathbf{i}}$ and $loc^{\mathbf{j}}$, we add a location $loc^{\mathbf{ij}}$ whose continuous dynamics is defined as: $\dot{x} \in F^{\mathbf{ij}}(x) = co\{F^{\mathbf{i}}(x), F^{\mathbf{j}}(x)\}$ where co denotes the closed convex hull. The resulting system is illustrated in Figure 2. For brevity, we denote the approximating system of Figure 2 by

$$\dot{x} \in \mathcal{F}(x). \tag{3}$$

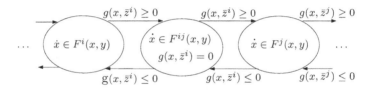

Fig. 2. Approximating hybrid system with upper semi-continuous dynamics.

The above "convexification" provides the system (3) with an important property stated in the following lemma.

Lemma 1. *The multifunction $\mathcal{F}$ in (3) is one-sided Lipschitz and upper semi-continuous.*

The concepts of one-sided Lipschitz and upper semi-continuity are recalled in the proof of the lemma, presented in Appendix.

To quantify the error between the original and approximating systems, we first define the size of the discretization of z. The diameter of the box $\mathcal{B}^{\mathbf{i}}$ is $diam(\mathcal{B}^{\mathbf{i}}) = \max\{|z - z'| : z \in \mathcal{B}^{\mathbf{i}} \wedge z' \in \mathcal{B}^{\mathbf{i}}\}$ where $|\cdot|$ is the Euclidean norm. Then, the size of the discretization of z is $\delta_z = \max_{\mathbf{i}}\{diam(\mathcal{B}^{\mathbf{i}})\}$.

Lemma 2. *Let δ_z be the size of the discretization of z and L_f be the Lipschitz constant of the function f in (1). Let $(x(\cdot), z(\cdot))$ be a solution of (1). Then, for all $t \geq 0\ d_H(\dot{x}(t), \mathcal{F}(x(t)) \leq L_f \delta_z$ where d_H is the Haussdorf distance.*

The above lemma gives a bound on the distance between the derivatives of the original system and the approximating system. Using the one-sided Lipschitz and upper semi-continuity properties of the approximating system, we can establish the following convergence result.

Theorem 1. *Let $x(\cdot)$ and $z(\cdot)$ be absolutely continuous functions satisfying (1). Then, there exists a solution $\tilde{x}(\cdot)$ of (3) such that for all $t \geq 0$*

$$|x(t) - \tilde{x}(t)| \leq |x(0) - \tilde{x}(0)|e^{\mathcal{L}t} + \frac{\Delta}{\mathcal{L}}(e^{\mathcal{L}t} - 1)$$

where $\mathcal{L}$ is the Lipschitz constant of $\mathcal{F}$, and $\Delta = L_f \delta_z$ is the bound on the distance between the derivatives estimated in Lemma 2.

This theorem is proved in Appendix. The proof uses the assumption that $\mathcal{F}(x)$ is nonempty and takes closed convex values.

2.3   Abstraction with Timing Information

So far we have used only the sign of the derivative of z to determine the switching conditions of the hybrid system. However, the time for the system to move from one box to its adjacent boxes is omitted, in other words, in the approximating system this time can be anything between 0 and $+\infty$. To obtain a more precise abstraction, we can include information about the time the system can stay in a location, which we call *staying time*. In order to see how the information about staying time can improve the abstraction precision, we notice that in the original system a point (x, z) satisfying the condition for the transition from $\mathcal{B}^i$ to $\mathcal{B}^j$, such as $g(x, \bar{z}^i) \geq 0$, does not necessarily lie on the switching surface $\partial(\mathcal{B}^i, \mathcal{B}^j)$ and thus from there the system can either continue with the dynamics of $\mathcal{B}^i$ or switch to the dynamics of $\mathcal{B}^j$. Consequently, for soundness, the transitions in the approximating hybrid automaton in Figures 1 and 2 are not urgent, and it is possible to stay at the same location indefinitely (i.e. no staying condition is imposed). It is clear that there may be boxes in which the original system can stay for only a finite time; hence, adding constraints on staying time at each location allows to reduce approximation error.

For a general nonlinear dynamics of z, it is not easy to estimate the staying time. A method to approximate the smallest time a linear systems with constant input can stay inside a convex polyhedron is developed in [15] and extended to uncertain linear systems in [11]. However, its generalization to nonlinear systems requires solving a nonlinear optimization problem. Here, we propose a simple method to exploit timing information by considering not only the sign but also the values of $\dot{z}$. More concretely, we additionally discretize the derivative of z into a finite number of disjoint boxes, as it is done for z. Each location of the approximating hybrid automaton now corresponds to a box $\mathcal{B}^i$ of z and a box β^j of $\dot{z}$, and we label it with loc^{ij}. Then, based on the intervals of the derivative of each component z_i, we can estimate the bounds on the staying time and then embed this information in the transition guards.

To facilitate the discussion, we introduce some definitions and notations. Location $loc^{\mathbf{ij}}$ is called a *neighbor* of location $loc^{\mathbf{pq}}$ if either the corresponding boxes $\mathcal{B}^{\mathbf{i}}$ and $\mathcal{B}^{\mathbf{p}}$ or the boxes $\beta^{\mathbf{j}}$ and $\beta^{\mathbf{q}}$ are adjacent. Location $loc^{\mathbf{ij}}$ is called the *left z_i-neighbor* of $loc^{\mathbf{pq}}$ if $\mathbf{p}_i - \mathbf{i}_i = 1$ and the *right z_i-neighbor* if $\mathbf{i}_i - \mathbf{p}_i = 1$. The *left* and *right $\dot{z}_i$-neighbors* are defined similarly.

We first specify the staying conditions of the approximating hybrid system. The staying condition of location $loc^{\mathbf{ij}}$ is simply $\dot{z} \in \beta^{\mathbf{j}}$, which can be rewritten as $G^{\mathbf{j}}(x) \cap \beta^{\mathbf{j}} \neq \emptyset$ where $G^{\mathbf{j}}(x) = \{g(x,z) \mid z \in \mathcal{B}^{\mathbf{i}}\}$. Since $g(x,z)$ is continuous[3], only transitions between neighbor locations are possible. However, we do not know the evolution of the derivative of g, therefore we let the guards of the transitions between $\dot{z}$-neighbors be *true*, meaning that the switchings between $\dot{z}$-neighbors are only restricted by the staying conditions of the locations. To define the guards of the transitions between z-neighbors, we shall use the bounds on $\dot{z}$ to estimate the time $t_{\mathbf{ij}}$ the system can stay within a location $loc^{\mathbf{ij}}$. Again, we illustrate the idea with the case where z is scalar, i.e. $m = 1$. Consider location $loc^{\mathbf{ij}}$ which corresponds to intervals $[\underline{z}^i, \bar{z}^i)$ of z and $[\underline{\xi}^j, \bar{\xi}^j)$ of $\dot{z}$. We distinghuish the following 3 cases: (1) If $\bar{\xi}^j < 0$, then a transition from $loc^{\mathbf{ij}}$ to its right z-neighbor is impossible. The staying time is $t_{\mathbf{ij}} \in [(\bar{z}^i - \underline{z}^i)/|\underline{\xi}^j|, (\bar{z}^i - \underline{z}^i)/|\bar{\xi}^j|)$ if $\underline{\xi}^j \neq -\infty$ and $t_{\mathbf{ij}} < (\bar{z}^i - \underline{z}^i)/|\bar{\xi}^j|$ otherwise; (2) If $\underline{\xi}^j > 0$, then a transition from $loc^{\mathbf{ij}}$ to its left z-neighbor is impossible and the bounds on $t_{\mathbf{ij}}$ are defined similarly; (3) If $\bar{\xi}^j \geq 0 \wedge \underline{\xi}^j \leq 0$, then the transitions from $loc^{\mathbf{ij}}$ to its both left and right z-neighbors are possible. However, unlike in the two previous cases, the staying time $t_{\mathbf{ij}}$ may range from 0 to $+\infty$.

2.4   Application to Multi-affine Systems

We have presented an abstraction method for nonlinear continuous systems. The resulting abstract system is simpler than the original system in terms of dimensionality, however it requires the ability to deal with nonlinear differential inclusions. In the remainder of the paper we focus on the reachability problem for a class of differential inclusions which are *uncertain bilinear control systems*. The study of such systems is motivated by our interest in applying the abstraction approach to a large class of biological systems which are modeled as multi-affine systems [19,23]. Indeed, by projecting out some variables of a *multi-affine system*, one can obtain an uncertain bilinear system, as illustrated in Section 4 where we study a simplified model of a biological system.

Before proceeding with the reachability problem for bilinear systems, we mention that besides the interest of bilinear systems for effective applications of our abstraction approach, these systems have received much attention over the past decades since they could represent a variety of important physical processes in engineering. A number of results related to the control of such systems can

---

[3] In more general cases, the discontinuities in g can be modeled explicitly by discrete transitions with resets.

be found in [25]. On the other hand, it should be noted that the problem of approximating viability kernels of differential inclusions, which is closely related to the reachability problem, was studied in [29].

3   Reachability Analysis of Bilinear Control Systems

In this section, we present a method for solving the reachability problem for uncertain bilinear systems with both multiplicative and additive control input:

$$\dot{x}(t) = f(x(t), u(t)) = Ax(t) + \sum_{j=1}^{l} u_j(t) B_j x(t) + Cu(t) \qquad (4)$$

where $x \in \mathbb{R}^n$ is the state variables; $u(\cdot) \in \mathcal{U}$, the set of admissible inputs consisting of piecewise continuous functions u of the form $u : \mathbb{R}^+ \to U$, U is a bounded convex polyhedron in $\mathbb{R}^l$. The matrices A, B_j and C are of appropriate dimension.

The reachability problem for a system with uncertain input can be formulated as an optimal control. The essential idea of our reachability method is to use the Pontryagin Maximum Principle to find the inputs allowing to derive a conservative approximation of the reachable set.

3.1   Approximating the Reachable Set Using Optimal Control

Let $\varphi(t, x, u(\cdot))$ denote the trajectory of (4) starting from x under input $u(\cdot)$. For a set of initial points $X_0 \subseteq \mathbb{R}^n$ and $t > 0$, the reachable set at time t is defined as: $\mathcal{R}(t, X_0) = \{ y \mid \exists u(\cdot) \in \mathcal{U} \; \exists x \in X_0 \; : \; y = \varphi(t, x, u(\cdot)) \}$. Indeed, we can show that $\mathcal{R}(t, X_0) = \{ x \in \mathbb{R}^n \mid V(t, x) \leq 0 \}$ where $V(t, x)$ is the value function: $V(t, x) = \min_{u(\cdot) \in \mathcal{U}} \{ d^2(x_0, X_0) \mid x = \varphi(t, x_0, u(\cdot)) \}$ where $d(x_0, X_0)$ is the distance from x_0 to X_0. For nonlinear systems, the exact solution $V(t, x)$ can be determined by solving a rather complicated HJB equation [20,21]. Reachability methods based on solving the partial differential equations have been developed (see e.g. [33,24]). As mentioned earlier, our approach is to use the results from optimal control to overapproximate the reachable set. More concretely, the idea is to track the evolution of the supporting hyperplanes of the initial set under some (optimal) input. This idea has been explored in [35,5] to compute polyhedral approximations of the reachable set of linear control systems.

Let $\mathcal{H}$ be a hyperplane with the normal vector v that supports the initial set X_0 at point p. Then, for all points $x \in X_0$ we have

$$\langle v, x \rangle - \langle v, p \rangle \leq 0 \qquad (5)$$

where $\langle \cdot, \cdot \rangle$ is the scalar product. The following result is obtained by applying the Pontryagin Maximum Principle (see [27]).

Theorem 2. *Let $S(t)$ be the halfspace defined as $S(t) = \{x \in \mathbb{R}^n \mid \rho(t, x) \leq 0\}$ where $\rho(t, x) = \langle \tilde{q}(t), x \rangle - \langle \tilde{q}(t), \tilde{x}(t) \rangle$ such that $\tilde{q}(t)$ and $\tilde{x}(t)$ are solutions of the following Hamiltonian system with the maximality condition:*

$$\dot{\tilde{x}} = A\tilde{x} + \sum_{j=1}^{l} \tilde{u}_j B_j \tilde{x} + C\tilde{u} \tag{6}$$

$$\dot{\tilde{q}} = -\frac{\partial H}{\partial x}(\tilde{x}, \tilde{q}, \tilde{u}) \quad \text{where } H(q, x, u) = \langle q, Ax + \sum_{j=1}^{l} u_j B_j x + Cu \rangle \tag{7}$$

$$\tilde{u}(t) \in \text{argmax}\{\langle \tilde{q}(t), \sum_{j=1}^{l} u_j B_j \tilde{x}(t) + Cu \rangle \mid u \in U\} \tag{8}$$

with initial conditions: $\tilde{q}(0) = v$, $\tilde{x}(0) = p$. Then, $\forall t > 0 : \mathcal{R}(t, X_0) \subseteq S(t)$, and $\mathcal{H}(t) = \{x \in \mathbb{R}^n \mid \rho(t, x) = 0\}$ is a supporting hyperplane of $\mathcal{R}(t, X_0)$.

The proof of the theorem can be found in Appendix. We note that the Hamiltonian H in (7) is affine with respect to u, therefore the input $\tilde{u}$ takes its values in the boundary of the polyhedron U. Furthermore, we assume the optimality of $\tilde{u}$, and for a bilinear system this assumption can be effectively verified using sufficient optimality conditions in [30].

Theorem 2 provides a method to overapproximate the reachable set of (4). Indeed, by the theorem, for every face of the initial polyhedron X_0 there exists an input such that tracking the evolution of the face under this input is sufficient to derive a polyhedral overapproximation of the reachable set. However, solving the optimal control problem (6)-(8) for a bilinear system under a general class of input functions is difficult, we therefore restrict to piecewise constant inputs. This allows more tractable solutions and, in addition, the error inherent to the restriction can be estimated and controled, as we shall show in the next section.

3.2   Reachability Algorithm for Uncertain Bilinear Control Systems

Suppose that the initial polyhedron X_0 can be represented as intersection of a finite number n_f of halfspaces: $X_0 = \bigcap_{\nu=1}^{n_f} S^\nu$ where $S^\nu = \{x \mid \langle v^\nu, x \rangle \leq \langle v^\nu, p^\nu \rangle\}$, v^ν is the outward normal vector and p^ν is a point on the face of S^ν.

Let us recall that for tractability purposes, we shall solve the optimal problem (6)-(8) in Theorem 2 for a class of piecewise constant inputs. Given the set of admissible inputs $\mathcal{U}$ and a time step $h > 0$, we define a set $\mathcal{U}_h$ of piecewise constant inputs:

$$\mathcal{U}_h = \{u(\cdot) \in \mathcal{U} \mid u(\cdot) \text{ is constant on } (t^k, t^{k+1}), t^k = kh, k > 0\}. \tag{9}$$

We consider the following bilinear equations with $\nu = 1, \ldots, n_f$ which describe the evolution of the normal vectors v^ν and supporting points p^ν of the faces of the initial set X_0:

$$\begin{cases} \dot{q}^\nu(t) = -(A + \sum_{j=1}^l u_j^\nu(t)B_j)^T q^\nu(t), \\ \dot{x}^\nu(t) = Ax^\nu(t) + \sum_{j=1}^l u_j^\nu(t)B_j x^\nu(t) + Cu^\nu(t), \\ u^\nu(t) \in \arg\max \ \{\langle q^\nu(t), \sum_{j=1}^l u_j B_j x_i(t) + Cu \rangle \mid u \in U\}, \\ q^\nu(0) = v^\nu; \ x^\nu(0) = p^\nu \ \text{(initial condition)}. \end{cases} \tag{10}$$

The superscript T denotes the transpose of a matrix. We denote by $\hat{\mathcal{P}}(\cdot)$ the polyhedron constructed from the solution $(x^\nu(\cdot), q^\nu(\cdot), u^\nu(\cdot))$ of (10) under the set $\mathcal{U}$ of admissible inputs: $\hat{\mathcal{P}}(t) = \bigcap_{\nu=1}^{n_f} \{x \mid \langle q^\nu(t), x \rangle \leq \langle q^\nu(t), x^\nu(t) \rangle\}$. If the set of admissible inputs is $\mathcal{U}_h$ defined in (9), we denote the corresponding polyhedron by $\hat{\mathcal{P}}_h(t)$. Note that by Theorem 2, $\mathcal{R}(t, X_0) \subseteq \hat{\mathcal{P}}(t)$.

Theorem 3. *For all $t > 0$ the Haussdorf distance between $\hat{\mathcal{P}}(t)$ and $\hat{\mathcal{P}}_h(t)$ satisfies: $d_H(\hat{\mathcal{P}}(t), \hat{\mathcal{P}}_h(t)) \leq Ch^2$, where C is a constant depending only on $|U|$ and the norm of the matrices A, B and C of (4).*

The above theorem shows that the error due to the restriction to piecewise constant inputs is quadratic in the discretization time step h. This bound is proved by using arguments similar to those in the paper [36], which investigated the problem of second order time-discretization of control systems. The proof (together with a formula describing the relation between the constant C, $|U|$ and the norm of the matrices) is omitted due to space limitation and it can be found in [11]. In the remainder of this section, we assume that we are provided with a scheme to solve the bilinear system (4) under a fixed piecewise constant input $u(\cdot) \in \mathcal{U}_h$, which has the form:

$$\begin{cases} x^\nu(t^{k+1}) = \alpha^\nu(x^\nu(t^k), u(t^k)), \\ q^\nu(t^{k+1}) = \beta^\nu(q^\nu(t^k), u(t^k)), \\ t^k = kh, \ \nu = 1, \dots, n_f. \end{cases} \tag{11}$$

where $u(t^k)$ is the value of input $u(t)$ for all $t \in [t^k, t^{k+1})$. The development of such a scheme is defered to Section 3.3.

The procedure for overapproximating the reachable set of uncertain control bilinear systems is summarized in Algorithm 1. Each iteration k produces a polyhedral approximation $\hat{\mathcal{P}}_h(t^{k+1})$ of the reachable set at time $t^k = kh$. First, for each halfspace $S^\nu(t^k)$ represented by normal vector $\tilde{q}^\nu(t^k)$ and supporting point $\tilde{x}^\nu(t^k)$, the value $\tilde{u}^\nu(t^k)$ of the optimal piecewise constant input for the time interval $[t^k, t^{k+1})$ is computed using the maximality condition. Note that this can be done by solving a linear programming problem. Once $\tilde{u}^\nu(t^k)$ is determined, the new normal vector $\tilde{q}^\nu(t^{k+1})$ and supporting point $\tilde{x}^\nu(t^{k+1})$ are then computed using (11). Finally, the polyhedron $\hat{\mathcal{P}}_h(t^{k+1})$ is the intersection of the new halfspaces. Algorithm 1 produces indeed an overapproximation of the reachable set of the system (4) with the set $\mathcal{U}_h$ of admissible inputs. Using Theorem 3, we can enlarge the sets $\hat{\mathcal{P}}_h(t^{k+1})$ by the error bound to obtain an overapproximation of the reachable set of the original system.

Algorithm 1 Reachability algorithm for uncertain bilinear systems

---

for all $\nu \in \{1, \dots, n_f\}$ $\tilde{x}^\nu(0) = v^\nu$, $\tilde{q}^\nu(0) = p^\nu$
$k = 0$ /* (k_{max} is the maximal number of iterations) */
while $k \leq k_{max}$ **do**
  $t^{k+1} = (k+1)h$
  for all $\nu \in \{1, \dots, n_f\}$ **do**
    $\tilde{u}^\nu(t^k) \in \arg \max \; \{\langle \tilde{q}^\nu(t^k), \sum_{j=1}^l u_j B_j \tilde{x}^\nu(t^k) + Cu \rangle \mid u \in U\}$
    $\tilde{x}^\nu(t^{k+1}) = \alpha^\nu(\tilde{x}^\nu(t^k), \tilde{u}^\nu(t^k)); \;\; \tilde{q}^\nu(t^{k+1}) = \beta^\nu(\tilde{q}^\nu(t^k), \tilde{u}^\nu(t^k))$
    $S^\nu(t^{k+1}) = \{x \mid \langle \tilde{q}^\nu(t^{k+1}), x \rangle \leq \langle \tilde{q}^\nu(t^{k+1}), \tilde{x}^\nu(t^{k+1}) \rangle\}$
  end for
  $\hat{\mathcal{P}}_h(t^{k+1}) = \bigcap_{\nu=1}^{n_f} S^\nu(t^{k+1}), \;\; k = k+1$
end while

3.3 Approximate Solution of Bilinear Systems with Piecewise Constant Input

In this section, we present a method to solve a bilinear system with piecewise constant input, which is used as the scheme (11) in Algorithm 1.

We assume a fixed input $u(\cdot) \in \mathcal{U}_h$ such that $\forall k \geq 0 \; \forall t \in [t^k, t^{k+1}) \; u(t) = u^k \in U$ where $t^k = kh$. For simplicity, we denote by $x^k = x(t^k)$ the reachable state at time t^k under such input $u(\cdot)$. The problem now is to determine the reachable state x^{k+1} from x^k. In all the formulas that follow, the superscript k of a term is used to indicate that its value depends on the interval k.

Since the input remains constant during $[kh, (k+1)h)$, given x^k one can compute x^{k+1} using the flow of affine vector field $A^k x + Cu^k$ where $A^k = A + \sum_{j=1}^l u_j^k B_j$, that is, $x^{k+1} = e^{hA^k}(x^k + \int_0^h e^{-\tau A^k} Cu^k d\tau)$. However, to do so, the transition matrix needs to be evaluated for each time interval since A^k depends on u^k. We present in the following an efficient computation scheme which requires matrix exponential computation only once.

The main idea is to consider the bilinear term in (4) during each time interval $[kh, (k+1)h]$ as independent input, in other words, the bilinear system is treated as a time invariant linear system with input $\sum_{j=1}^l u_j(t) B_j x(t) + C u(t)$. For brevity, we denote $W^k = \sum_{j=1}^l u_j^k B_j$. Then,

$$x^{k+1} = e^{Ah} x^k + \int_0^h e^{A(h-\tau)} W^k x(\tau) \, d\tau + \int_0^h e^{A(h-\tau)} Cu^k \, d\tau. \qquad (12)$$

The second integral has a closed form. As for the first integral, we shall approximate it by replacing the exact solution $x(\tau)$ for $\tau \in [0, h)$ with a polynomial $\pi^k(\tau) = p_3^k \tau^3 + p_2^k \tau^2 + p_1^k \tau + p_0^k$ where $p_i^k \in \mathbb{R}^n$ satisfying the following Hermite interpolation conditions: $\pi^k(0) = x^k, \;\; \dot{\pi}^k(0) = \dot{x}(t^k), \;\; \pi^k(h) = x^{k+1}, \;\; \dot{\pi}^k(h) = \dot{x}(t^{k+1})$. It is well-known that the coefficients of Hermite interpolating polynomials are uniquely determined [17]. After some straightforward calculations, the coefficient p_i^k can be written in the following form:

$$p_i^k = (M_i u^k + N_i) x^k + (P_i u^k + Q_i) x^{k+1} + r_i^k, \ i \in \{0, 1, 2, 3\}. \qquad (13)$$

Then, developing the first integral with $x(\tau)$ replaced by $\pi(\tau)$ gives:

$$x^{k+1} = e^{Ah} x^k + \sum_{i=0}^{3} \Gamma_i W^k p_i^k + \Gamma_0 C u^k. \qquad (14)$$

where $\Gamma_i = \int_0^h e^{A(h-\tau)} \tau^i \, d\tau$, which can also be written in a closed form. Combining (13) and (14), we obtain an affine relation between x^k and x^{k+1} of the form:

$$R^k x^{k+1} = D^k x^k + d^k, \qquad (15)$$

One can see from (14) and (13) that all the terms dependent of u^k (i.e. W^k and p_i^k) do not involve matrix exponentials. Therefore, using (15) to compute reachable states x^{k+1}, we only need to compute the matrix exponential e^{Ah}.

Lemma 3. *Let $x(\cdot)$ be a solution of (4) under a fixed input $u(\cdot) \in \mathcal{U}_h$ and $\bar{x}^k$ be the approximate solution obtained by the scheme (15) with the same input $u(\cdot)$ such that $x(0) = \bar{x}^0$. If the derivative $x^{(4)}(t)$ is bounded by $\mathcal{M}$, then for all $k > 0$ $|x^k - \bar{x}^k| \leq \mathcal{M} h^4 / (4!)$.*

The proof of the lemma uses standard results on the remainder term of Hermite interpolating polynomials [17], and it is omitted here. The lemma shows that the error of the scheme (15) is of order $O(h^4)$. As shown earlier, the error due to the restriction to piecewise constant inputs is quadratic; hence, this additional error does not change the order of the method.

4   Application to a Biological System

In this section, we illustrate our approach with a multi-affine system, used to model the gene transcription control in the *Vibrio fischeri* bacteria. The results are obtained using an experimental implementation of the abstraction method and the reachability technique for bilinear systems presented in the previous sections. This bioregulatory network problem has been studied in [7]. The following brief description of the model is borrowed from [7]. The differential equations describing the dynamics of a mode of the system are as follows:

$$\begin{cases} \dot{x}_1 = k_2 x_2 - k_1 x_1 x_3 + u_1 \\ \dot{x}_2 = k_1 x_1 x_3 - k_2 x_2 \\ \dot{x}_3 = k_2 x_2 - k_1 x_1 x_3 - n x_3 + n u_2 \end{cases} \qquad (16)$$

The state variables x_1, x_2, x_3 represent cellular concentration of different species, and the parameters k_1, k_2, n are binding, dissociation and diffusion constants. The variables u_1 and u_2 are control variables (plasmid and external source of autoinducer). We abstract away the variable x_1 by discretizing its range and construct a hybrid automaton using the abstraction method of Section 2. The influence of x_1 in the dynamics of the variables x_2 and x_3 is modeled as an uncertain input u_x, and the resulting system is a hybrid system with uncertain bilinear dynamics. As an example, the dynamics of x_2 and x_3 of the location corresponding to the interval I^i of the values of x_1 are:

$$\begin{cases} \dot{x}_2 = k_1 u_x x_3 - k_2 x_2 \\ \dot{x}_3 = k_2 x_2 - k_1 u_x x_3 - n x_3 + n u_2 \\ u_x \in I^i \end{cases} \tag{17}$$

The reachability analysis results for this system are shown in Figure 3. The left figure is the reachable set of the approximate hybrid system when the control in unactivated ($u = 0$). The initial set is the rectangle X_0 where $x_2 \in [1.05, 1.55]$ and $x_3 \in [1.25, 1.95]$. We can see that the uncontrolled system can exit the rectangle $R = [1,2] \times [1,2]$ via the face $x_3 = 1$ while the control objective is to steer the system through the face $x_2 = 2$. In [7] the following feedback control law for this objective is designed: $u_2 = 6$ and u_1 is a multi-affine function of the state variables x. The reachability computation result for the system under this control law from the same initial set X_0 is shown in Figure 3 where on the left we can see the reachable set of the location corresponding to the interval $x_1 \in [1.0, 1.5]$ and on the right the reachable set of the location corresponding to $x_1 \in [1.5, 2]$. This result shows that indeed the controlled system is driven to the face $x_2 = 2$, as desired.

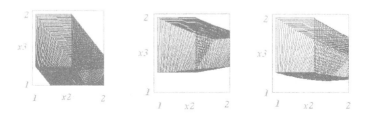

Fig. 3. Left: Reachable set of the uncontrolled system, i.e. when $u = 0$. Middle and right: Reachable set of the controlled system: location $u_x \in [1.0, 1.5]$ (middle); location $u_x \in [1.5, 2.0]$ (right), the input u_x represents the variable x_1 that is projected out.

5 Concluding Remarks

In this paper, we proposed a framework for abstraction of continuous nonlinear systems by means of hybridization. We also developed a reachability algorithm for uncertain bilinear systems, necessary for an effective application of the approach to multi-affine systems. Experimental results are encouraging and various interesting research directions need to be explored. One important issue is the choice of variables to project out which still allows to prove the properties of interest. In addition, the assume-guarantee ideas from model-checking could be useful in this framework. Indeed, one can assume a reachable set for some variables z which is used as a set of input values in the computation for the remaining variables x. The reachable set of x is in turn used as the set of input values for the computation on z, which allows to verify the initial assumption. On the other hand, we intend to apply our approach to more problems in biological systems.

References

1. J.C. Alexander and T.I. Seidman. Sliding modes in intersecting switching surfaces, *Houston J. Math.*, 24:545-569, 1994.
2. R. Alur, T. Dang, and F. Ivancic. Reachability Analysis Via Predicate Abstraction. In *HSCC*, LNCS 2289, Springer, 2002.
3. E. Asarin, O. Bournez, T. Dang, and O. Maler. Approximate Reachability Analysis of Piecewise-Linear Dynamical Systems. In *HSCC*, LNCS 1790, Springer, 2000.
4. E. Asarin, T. Dang, and A. Girard. Reachability Analysis of Nonlinear Systems Using Conservative Approximation. In *HSCC*, LNCS 2623, Springer, 2003.
5. E. Asarin, T. Dang, and O. Maler. d/dt: A tool for Verification of Hybrid Systems. *Computer Aided Verification*, Springer, LNCS, 2002.
6. J.P. Aubin and A. Cellina. Differential Inclusions: Set-valued Maps and Viability Theory, Springer, 1984.
7. C. Belta, L. C. G. J. M. Habets, and V. Kumar. Control of multi-affine systems on rectangles with an application to gene transcription control. *Proc. of CDC*, 2003.
8. S. Bensalem, Y. Lakhnech,and S. Owre. Computing Abstractions of Infinite State Systems Compositionally and Automatically. In *Computer Aided Verification*, LNCS 1427, Springer, 1998.
9. A. Chutinan and B.H. Krogh. Verification of Polyhedral Invariant Hybrid Automata Using Polygonal F low Pipe Approximations. In *HSCC*, LNCS 1569, Springer, 1999.
10. P. Cousot and R. Cousot. Abstract Interpretation and Application to Logic Programs. *Journal of Logic Programming*, 103-179, 1992.
11. T. Dang. Reachability Analysis of Bilinear Systems. Tech. report IMAG, 2003.
12. K. Deimling. Multivalued Differential Equations. De Gruyter, 1992.
13. T. Donchev and E. Farkhi. Stability and Euler approximation of one-sided Lipschitz differential inclusions. *SIAM Journal of Control and Optimization*, 36(2):780-796, 2000.
14. A.F. Filippov. Diff. Equations with Discontinuous Righthand Sides. Kluwer, 1988.
15. A. Girard. Detection of Event Occurence in Piecewise Linear Hybrid Systems, *Proc. RASC'02*, December 2002, Nottingham, UK.
16. M.R. Greenstreet and I. Mitchell. Reachability Analysis Using Polygonal Projections. In *HSCC*, LNCS 1569 Springer, 1999.
17. G. Hämmerlin and K. Hoffmann. Numerical Mathematics, Springer, 1991.
18. T.A. Henzinger, P.-H. Ho, and H. Wong-Toi. Analysis of Nonlinear Hybrid Systems. *IEEE Transactions on Automatic Control* 43, 540-554, 1998.
19. D. Kirschner, S. Lenhart, and S. Serbin. Optimal control of the chemotherapy of HIV. *Journal of Mathematival Biology*, 35:775-792, 1997.

20. A. Kurzhanski and P. Varaiya. Ellipsoidal Techniques for Reachability Analysis. In *HSCC*, LNCS 1790, Springer, 2000.
21. A. Kurzhanski and P. Varaiya. Dynamic optimization for reachability problems. *JOTA*, 108(2):227-251, 2001.
22. G. Lafferriere, G. Pappas, and S. Yovine. Reachability computation for linear systems. *Proc. of the 14th IFAC World Congress*, 7-12 E, 1999.
23. U. Ledzewicz and H. Schättler. Optimal control for 3-compartment model for cancer chemotherapy with quadratic objective. *Proc. of the 4th Int Conf on Dynamical Systems and Differential Equations*, Wilmington, NC, 2002.
24. I. Mitchell and C. Tomlin. Level Set Method for Computation in Hybrid Systems. In *HSCC*, LNCS 1790, Spinger-Verlag, 2000.
25. R.R. Mohler. Nonlinear Systems, 2, Prentice-Hall, Inc., Englewood Cliffs, 1991.
26. George J. Pappas. Bisimilar linear systems, in *Automatica*, 2003.
27. L. S. Pontryagin, V. G. Boltyanskii, R. V. Gamkrelidze, and E. F. Mischenko. The Mathematical Theory of Optimal Processes. *Pergamon Press*, Oxford, 1964.
28. A. Puri and P. Varaiya. Verification of Hybrid Systems using Abstraction. In *Hybrid Systems II*, LNCS 999, Springer, 1995.
29. P. Saint-Pierre. Approximation of Viability Kernels and Capture Basin for Hybrid Systems. *Proc. of European Control Conf. ECC'01*, 2776-2783, 2001.
30. A. Sarychev. Time-optimality of bang-bang controls for chained systems. *Proc. of 2nd IFAC Workshop on Lagrangian and Hamiltonian Methods for Nonlinear Control*, 2003.
31. P. Tabuada and G. Pappas, Model-Checking LTL over controllable linear systems is decidable. In *HSCC*, LNCS 2623, Springer, 2003.
32. A. Tiwari and G. Khanna. Series of Abstractions for Hybrid Automata. In *HSCC*, LNCS 2289, Springer, 2002.
33. C. Tomlin, J. Lygeros, and S. Sastry. A Game-Theoretic Approach to Controller Design for Hybrid Systems. *Proc. of the IEEE*, 88:940-970, 2000.
34. V.I. Utkin. Sliding Modes and their Application in Variable Structure Systems. *Mir, Moscow*, 1978.
35. P. Varaiya. Reach Set Computation using Optimal Control. *Proc. KIT Workshop*, Grenoble, 1998.
36. V. Veliov. On the time-discretization of control systems. *SIAM journal on Control and Optimization*, 35(5):1470-1468, 1997.

Appendix

Proof of Lemma 1. We first recall some basic definitions and notations (see [6, 13] for more details). We denote by B the open unit ball centered at the origin. Let $\mathcal{F} : \mathbb{R}^n \to \mathcal{X}$ be a multifunction where $\mathcal{X}$ is the set of all nonempty compact subsets of $\mathbb{R}^n$. $\mathcal{F}$ is called *upper semi-continuous* (respectively *lower semi-continuous*) at $x \in \mathbb{R}^n$ if for every $\varepsilon > 0$ there exists $\delta > 0$ such that $\forall x' \in x + \delta B \; \mathcal{F}(x') \subseteq \mathcal{F}(x) + \varepsilon B$ (respectively $\mathcal{F}(x) \subseteq \mathcal{F}(x') + \varepsilon B$). $\mathcal{F}$ is called *one-sided Lipschitz* (OSL) with a constant $\mathcal{L}$ if and only if for all $x, x' \in \mathbb{R}^n$, $f \in \mathcal{F}(x)$ there exists $f' \in \mathcal{F}(x')$ such that $\langle x - x', f - f' \rangle \leq \mathcal{L}|x - x'|^2$.

We proceed to prove Lemma 1. The condition that $\mathcal{F}$ is one-sided Lipschitz is easy to verify. To prove that $\mathcal{F}$ is upper semi-continuous, it suffices to prove that it is upper semi-continuous at the switching surfaces. Let x be a point on the switching surface S^{ij}, hence $\mathcal{F}(x) = F^{ij}(x)$. For a point $x' \in (x+\delta B)\setminus S^{ij}$ (in the δ-neighborhood of x but not on the switching surface), either $\mathcal{F}(x') = F^i(x')$ or $\mathcal{F}(x') = F^j(x')$. Since all F^i are Lipschitz continuous, there exists $\varepsilon > 0$ $F^i(x') \subseteq F^i(x) + \varepsilon B$. Therefore, $\mathcal{F}(x') \subseteq \mathcal{F}(x) + \varepsilon B$. Obviously, this also holds for a point $x' \in (x + \delta B) \cap S^{ij}$; hence, $\mathcal{F}$ is upper semi-continuous at x. $\square$

Proof of Theorem 1. To prove the theorem we suppose that the multifunction $\mathcal{F}$ in (3) is one-sided Lipschitz with a constant $\mathcal{L}$ and bounded on bounded sets. We also assume that $\mathcal{F}$ is upper semi-continuous and takes closed convex values. By Lemma 2, $x(\cdot)$ is absolutely continuous and satisfies $d_H(\dot{x}(t), \mathcal{F}(x(t))) \leq \Delta$ for all $t > 0$. We shall prove that there exists a solution $\tilde{x}(\cdot)$ of $\frac{d\tilde{x}(t)}{dt} \in \mathcal{F}(\tilde{x}(t))$; $\tilde{x}(0) = \tilde{x}_0$ such that for all $t > 0$

$$|\tilde{x}(t) - x(t)| \leq |\tilde{x}(0) - x(0)|e^{\mathcal{L}t} + \frac{\Delta}{\mathcal{L}}(e^{\mathcal{L}t} - 1). \tag{18}$$

To do so, we consider the differential inclusion

$$\frac{\tilde{x}(t)}{dt} \in \mathcal{G}(\tilde{x}(t)); \quad \tilde{x}(0) = \tilde{x}_0 \tag{19}$$

where $\mathcal{G}(\tilde{x}) = \{v \in \mathcal{F}(\tilde{x}) \mid \langle x(t) - \tilde{x}, \dot{x}(t) - v \rangle \leq \mathcal{L}|x(t) - \tilde{x}|^2 + \Delta|x(t) - \tilde{x}|\}$. We shall use a well-known existence theorem for upper semi-continuous differential inclusions from [12] to prove that (19) has a solution that satisfies (18). To do so, we need to verify that $\mathcal{G}(\tilde{x})$ is nonempty, convex, closed-valued and satisfies the condition of boundedness of the solution set. We first prove that $\mathcal{G}(\tilde{x})$ is nonempty for each $\tilde{x}$. Let $w \in \mathcal{F}(x)$ be such that $|\dot{x}(t) - w| = d_H(\dot{x}(t), \mathcal{F}(x(t))) \leq \Delta$. By the OSL condition, given $\tilde{x}$, we can choose $v \in \mathcal{F}(\tilde{x})$ such that $\langle x(t) - \tilde{x}, w - v \rangle \leq \mathcal{L}|x(t) - \tilde{x}|^2$. Hence,

$$\langle x(t) - \tilde{x}, \dot{x}(t) - v \rangle = \langle x(t) - \tilde{x}, \dot{x}(t) - w \rangle + \langle x(t) - \tilde{x}, w - v \rangle$$
$$\leq |x(t) - \tilde{x}|\Delta + \mathcal{L}|x(t) - \tilde{x}|^2 \tag{20}$$

The above implies that $v \in \mathcal{G}(\tilde{x})$. It is not hard to see that $\mathcal{G}(\tilde{x})$ is convex, closed-valued and satisfies the condition of boundedness of the solution set since $\mathcal{F}$ does. From Theorem 5.2 of [12] we conclude that there exists a solution $\tilde{x}(\cdot)$ of (19). Denoting $\sigma(t) = |x(t) - \tilde{x}(t)|$, σ is an absolutely continuous function. Furthermore, if $\dot{\sigma}(t)$ exists, then $\sigma(t)\dot{\sigma}(t) = \frac{1}{2}\frac{d}{dt}\sigma^2(t) = \langle x(t)-\tilde{x}(t), \dot{x}(t)-\dot{\tilde{x}}(t) \rangle \leq \mathcal{L}\sigma^2(t)+\Delta\sigma(t)$, by (20). From this, it can be shown that $\dot{\sigma}(t) \leq \mathcal{L}\sigma(t)+\Delta$ for all $t > 0$, and combining with $\sigma(0) = |x(0)-\tilde{x}(0)|$ we obtain the inequality (18). $\square$

Proof of Theorem 2. The equation (7) can be rewritten as $\dot{\tilde{q}} = -\frac{\partial H}{\partial x}(\tilde{q}, \tilde{x}, \tilde{u}) = -(A+\sum_{j=1}^l \tilde{u}_j B_j)^T \tilde{q}$. For brevity, we use $x(t)$ to denote a trajectory $\varphi(t, x_0, u(\cdot))$ of (4) starting from some point $x_0 \in X_0$ under an arbitrary admissible input $u(\cdot)$. Then, $\frac{d\langle \tilde{q}(t), x(t) \rangle}{dt} = \langle \dot{\tilde{q}}(t), x(t) \rangle + \langle \tilde{q}(t), \dot{x}(t) \rangle = \langle \tilde{q}(t), -(A + \sum_{j=1}^l \tilde{u}_j B_j)x(t) \rangle + \langle \tilde{q}, Ax(t)+\sum_{j=1}^l u_j B_j x(t)+Cu(t) \rangle = \langle \tilde{q}, -\sum_{j=1}^l \tilde{u}_j B_j x(t) + \sum_{j=1}^l u_j B_j x(t) +$

$Cu(t)\rangle$. By the maximality condition (8), for all admissible inputs $u(\cdot)$ and all $t > 0$, $\langle \tilde{q}(t), \sum_{j=1}^{l} u_j(t) B_j \tilde{x}(t) + Cu(t)\rangle \leq \langle \tilde{q}(t), \sum_{j=1}^{l} \tilde{u}_j(t) B_j \tilde{x}(t) + C\tilde{u}(t)\rangle$. Therefore, $\frac{d\langle \tilde{q}(t), x(t)\rangle}{dt} \leq \frac{d\langle \tilde{q}(t), \tilde{x}(t)\rangle}{dt}$. In addition, from the initial condition and (5), $\langle \tilde{q}(0), x(0)\rangle \leq \langle \tilde{q}(0), \tilde{x}(0)\rangle$. Thus, we have $\forall t > 0$ $\langle \tilde{q}(t), x(t)\rangle \leq \langle \tilde{q}(t), \tilde{x}(t)\rangle$. It then follows that every point x reachable by (4) from X_0 at time $t > 0$ satisfies $\rho(t, x) \leq 0$. □

Observability of Switched Linear Systems

Mohamed Babaali and Magnus Egerstedt

Electrical and Computer Engineering, Georgia Institute of Technology,
Atlanta, GA 30332, USA
{babaali,magnus}@ece.gatech.edu

Abstract. The observability of deterministic, discrete-time, switched, linear systems is considered. Depending on whether or not the modes are observed, and on whether the continuous state or the mode sequence is to be recovered, several observability concepts are defined, characterized through linear algebraic tests, and their decidability assessed.

1 Introduction

By switched linear systems (SLS), we refer to discrete-time systems that can be modeled as follows:

$$\begin{aligned}
x_{k+1} &= A(\theta_k)x_k + B(\theta_k)u_k \\
y_k &= C(\theta_k)x_k,
\end{aligned} \tag{1}$$

where $x_k \in \mathbb{R}^n$, $u_k \in \mathbb{R}^m$, and $y_k \in \mathbb{R}^p$ are the states, the inputs and the measurements, respectively. θ_k, which we refer to as the mode at time k, assumes its values in the set $\{1, \ldots, s\}$, so that the system parameter matrices $A(\theta_k)$, $B(\theta_k)$, and $C(\theta_k)$ switch among s different known matrices. We assume that the mode sequence $\{\theta_k\}_{k=1}^{\infty}$, whether known or unknown, is arbitrary and independent of the initial state and inputs. In particular, we impose no constraints on the time separation between two consecutive switches, and we assume that the switches are not triggered by state space based events.

By observability, we mean the ability to infer the initial state x_1, and possibly a finite portion of the mode sequence (when unobserved), from a finite number of measurements $y_1, \ldots, y_N$. While the concept of observability has a simple well-known characterization in classical linear systems, it has been associated with several notions in the SLS literature. Indeed, the fact that the mode sequence may or may not be observed, and, in the latter case, that one may or may not wish to recover it along with the state, makes for the need to consider several different problems, thus different definitions and characterizations. In this paper, our aim is to introduce and define several different concepts of observability in SLS's, to characterize them, and to assess their main properties, among which decidability is of special importance.

While we are concerned with the deterministic case, the first attempts at defining observability for SLS were motivated by stochastic optimal control and optimal estimation problems [7,8,9,11], and are therefore of limited relevance to

R. Alur and G.J. Pappas (Eds.): HSCC 2004, LNCS 2993, pp. 48–63, 2004.
© Springer-Verlag Berlin Heidelberg 2004

the present paper. In parallel with those works, the continuous-time case [5], and a special discrete-time class [6] were studied, both assuming observed modes. The recent surge of interest in hybrid systems expressed by the control and computer science communities has motivated renewed research efforts towards the SLS observability problem under unobserved modes. Particularly, the work in [3] concerned piece-wise affine systems, in which the future mode depends on the current state. In [2], two routes were proposed for recovering the modes: the first through a finite automaton formalism (which uses extra sources of information, beside the measurements, that we, in this paper, assume to be unavailable), and the second through failure detection techniques, which require the mode sequence to be slowly-varying. Finally, in [10], a systematic attempt at carefully defining observability for SLS under unobserved modes was made, from which some results in this paper draw inspiration. In the observed modes case, observability was characterized and its decidability proven in [1].

The outline of this paper is as follows. In Section 2, the autonomous case is studied. In Section 3, we discuss the non-autonomous case.

2   Autonomous Systems

We restrict our attention, for now, to autonomous systems of the form:

$$\begin{aligned} x_{k+1} &= A(\theta_k)x_k \\ y_k &= C(\theta_k)x_k, \end{aligned} \tag{2}$$

obtained simply by removing the $B(\theta_k)u_k$ term from (1). Before going any further, we need a few definitions. Since we are dealing with finite-time problems, we abandon the mode sequence notation and we define a path θ as a finite sequence (or string) of modes $\theta = \theta_1\theta_2\ldots\theta_N$, where N is the path length denoted by $|\theta|$. We also define Θ_N as the set of all paths of length N. Moreover, we denote by $\theta_{[i,j]}$ the infix of θ between i and j, i.e. $\theta_{[i,j]} = \theta_i\theta_{i+1}\ldots\theta_j$, we use $\theta\theta'$ to denote the concatenation of θ with θ', and we let $\Phi(\theta) \triangleq A(\theta_N)\cdots A(\theta_1)$ denote the transition matrix of a path θ. By convention, we let $\theta_{[i,i-1]} = \epsilon$, the empty word, and $\Phi(\epsilon) = I$. We next define the observability matrix $\mathcal{O}(\theta)$ of a path θ as:

$$\mathcal{O}(\theta) \triangleq \begin{pmatrix} C(\theta_1) \\ \vdots \\ C(\theta_N)A(\theta_{N-1})\cdots A(\theta_1) \end{pmatrix}. \tag{3}$$

Finally, we define:

$$Y(\theta, x) \triangleq \mathcal{O}(\theta)x, \tag{4}$$

and we then get that if $x = x_1$ and $\theta = \theta_1\theta_2\ldots\theta_N$ in (2), then $Y(\theta, x) = (y_1^T \ \ldots \ y_N^T)^T$. Therefore, throughout the remainder of this section, we will use (4) to describe (2) in a more compact way.

In this section, we will define and characterize several concepts of observability for autonomous SLS (2). The observed modes case is considered in Section 2.1, and the unobserved modes case in Section 2.2.

2.1   The Observed Modes Case

We assume that both the mode path θ and $Y(\theta, x)$ are available, and we wish to recover the state x uniquely. More precisely, we study the existence of an integer N such that the map $(x, \theta) \mapsto (Y(\theta, x), \theta)$ is injective or, in other words, that

$$x \neq x' \Rightarrow Y(\theta, x) \neq Y(\theta, x') \tag{5}$$

for every path θ of length N. Since $Y(\theta, x) = \mathcal{O}(\theta)x$, this clearly amounts to requiring that $\mathcal{O}(\theta)$ be of full column rank (i.e. that $\rho(\mathcal{O}(\theta)) = n$, where $\rho(\cdot)$ denotes the rank function, and we then say θ is *observable*), in which case, letting $\mathcal{O}(\theta)^{\{1\}}$ be a $\{1\}$-inverse of $\mathcal{O}(\theta)$ (see Appendix A), we get

$$x = \mathcal{O}(\theta)^{\{1\}} Y(\theta, x). \tag{6}$$

The existence of such an integer N was defined in [1] as *pathwise observability*:

Definition 1 (Pathwise Observability (PWO)). *The SLS (2) is pathwise observable (PWO) if there exists an integer N such that every path θ of length N is observable, i.e. satisfies $\rho(\mathcal{O}(\theta)) = n$. We refer to the smallest such integer N as the index of PWO.* ◊

PWO was moreover shown to be decidable. More precisely, the index of pathwise observability was shown to be bounded above by numbers $\mathcal{N}(s, n)$ (actually, $\mathcal{N}(s, n, n)$ in [1]) depending only on s, the number of modes (or pairs) of the system, and n. Even though the numbers $\mathcal{N}(s, n)$ were not given explicitly, they were shown to be smaller than numbers $N(s, n)$ (again, $N(s, n, n)$ in [1]) that, moreover, satisfy (we let $\mathcal{R}(M)$ denote the row range space of a matrix M):

Theorem 1 *If θ is a path of length $N(s, n)$, then there exists a prefix θ^0 of θ (i.e. $\theta = \theta^0 \theta^1$ for some θ^1) and a path θ' of arbitrary length such that*

$$\mathcal{R}(\mathcal{O}(\theta^0 \theta')) \subset \mathcal{R}(\mathcal{O}(\theta^0)), \tag{7}$$

and thus $\rho(\mathcal{O}(\theta^0 \theta')) = \rho(\mathcal{O}(\theta^0)) \leq \rho(\mathcal{O}(\theta))$. ◊

Even though this theorem was not explicitly stated in [1], its proof can easily be derived from that of [1, Theorem 1].

2.2   The Unobserved Modes Case: Mode Observability

In this section, we assume that only the continuous measurements $Y(\theta, x)$ are available, and we investigate the possibility to infer a prefix of the path θ (i.e. $\theta_{[1, N']}$ for some $N' < |\theta|$) from the successive measurements $Y(\theta, x)$ only. But first, noting that when $x = 0$, $Y(\theta, x) = 0$ for any path θ, we observe that it is *impossible* to distinguish between paths whenever $x = 0$. As it turns out, this happens in general for all states in a union of subspaces of $\mathbb{R}^n$. Moreover, this issue is closely related to false alarms in failure detection, as pointed out in [2]. We therefore have to consider the problem from a looser point of view, which leads us to the following definition, in which *a.e.* x stands for "for almost every x", by which we mean for all $x \in \mathbb{R}^n$ but a union of proper subspaces, thus for all x but a set of Lebesgue measure 0:

Definition 2 (Mode Observability (MO)). *The SLS (2) is MO at N if there exists an integer N' such that for all $\theta \in \Theta_{N+N'}$ and for a.e. $x \in \mathbb{R}^n$,*

$$\theta_{[1,N]} \neq \theta'_{[1,N]} \Rightarrow Y(\theta, x) \neq Y(\theta', x') \ \forall \ x' \in \mathbb{R}^n. \tag{8}$$

The index of MO at N is the smallest such N'. ◇

In other words, we require the possibility to recover the first N modes (i.e. $\theta_{[1,N]}$) uniquely whenever $N + N'$ measurements (i.e. $Y(\theta, x)$) are available, and for a.e. state x. To this end, we need a way to discern between the paths θ using the measurements $Y(\theta, x)$ they produce through $Y(\theta, x) = \mathcal{O}(\theta)x$. As we are about to show, the only way to achieve that without any information other than the available measurement $Y(\theta, x)$ is by taking advantage of the following inclusion, immediate from $Y(\theta, x) = \mathcal{O}(\theta)x$:

$$Y(\theta, x) \in \Re(\mathcal{O}(\theta)), \tag{9}$$

where $\Re(M)$ denotes the column range space of the matrix M. The question is then whether $\theta' \neq \theta \ \Rightarrow \ Y(\theta, x) \notin \Re(\mathcal{O}(\theta'))$, which would provide us with a simple procedure for recovering a path from the measurements (using the range inclusion test, see Appendix A):

$$\theta = \arg_{\theta' \in \Theta_N} \{Y(\theta, x) \in \Re(\mathcal{O}(\theta'))\} \tag{10}$$

The main issue lies in whether the test (10) has a unique solution. In order to analyze this, we introduce the concept of *discernibility*:

Definition 3 (Discernibility). *A path θ is discernible from another path θ' of the same length if*

$$\rho([\mathcal{O}(\theta)\mathcal{O}(\theta')]) > \rho(\mathcal{O}(\theta')), \tag{11}$$

where $[\mathcal{O}(\theta)\mathcal{O}(\theta')]$ denotes the horizontal concatenation of $\mathcal{O}(\theta)$ and $\mathcal{O}(\theta')$, and where the degree d of discernibility is defined as

$$d = \rho([\mathcal{O}(\theta)\mathcal{O}(\theta')]) - \rho(\mathcal{O}(\theta')). \tag{12}$$

We then say that θ is d-discernible from θ'. ◇

The following proposition is now in order:

Proposition 1 *$Y(\theta, x) \notin \Re(\mathcal{O}(\theta'))$ for almost any $x \in \mathbb{R}^n$ iff θ is discernible from θ'.* ◇

Proof: We have $Y(\theta, x) \in \Re(\mathcal{O}(\theta'))$ iff $Y(\theta, x)$ also lies in the the *output subspace of conflict of θ and θ'*, defined as:

$$C(\theta, \theta') \triangleq \Re(\mathcal{O}(\theta)) \cap \Re(\mathcal{O}(\theta')). \tag{13}$$

We therefore need to show that the dimension of the inverse image of $C(\theta, \theta')$ by $\mathcal{O}(\theta)$, $c(\theta, \theta') \triangleq \mathcal{O}(\theta)^{-1}(C(\theta, \theta'))$, which we refer to as the *input subspace of conflict of θ with θ'*, is smaller than n (which implies that its Lebesgue measure is 0) if and only if θ is discernible from θ'. We have:

$$\dim(C(\theta, \theta')) = \rho(\mathcal{O}(\theta)) + \rho(\mathcal{O}(\theta')) - \rho([\mathcal{O}(\theta)\mathcal{O}(\theta')]). \tag{14}$$

Noting that $\dim(c(\theta, \theta')) = \dim(C(\theta, \theta')) + \dim\ker(\mathcal{O}(\theta))$, and then recalling that $\rho(\mathcal{O}(\theta)) + \dim\ker(\mathcal{O}(\theta)) = n$, we get

$$\dim(c(\theta, \theta')) = n - \rho([\mathcal{O}(\theta)\mathcal{O}(\theta')]) + \rho(\mathcal{O}(\theta')). \tag{15}$$

Therefore, by definition of discernibility, we see that $\dim(c(\theta, \theta')) < n$ if and only if θ is discernible from θ', in which case we moreover have

$$\dim(c(\theta, \theta')) = n - d, \tag{16}$$

where d is the degree of discernibility defined in (12). $\qquad\square$

Remarks 1

- *Discernibility does not imply that either path is observable (see Example 1).*
- *From (16), the degree of discernibility appears as a measure of separation between the two paths θ and θ': the larger the degree d, the smaller the dimension of the input subspace of conflict. It is clear that the maximum value for d is n, in which case the input subspace of conflict is trivial.*
- *Note that, as we have defined it, discernibility is not symmetric.*
- *If $\theta_{[1,N-1]} = \theta'_{[1,N-1]}$, i.e. if the two paths only differ by their last value, then their index of discernibility is bounded by p.* $\diamond$

The last remark raises the question of whether an upper bound (p, the size of each measurement y_k) is imposed on the maximum degree of discernibility that can be guaranteed for all pairs of paths of a certain length. A related limitation was pointed out in [10], where p had to equal n, since the criterion considered for "switch detection" was similar to n-discernibility. It turns out that this limitation can be overcome, provided one can use further measurements in order to discern the paths, which leads us to the idea of *forward discernibility*:

Definition 4 (Forward Discernibility (FD)). *Given an integer $d > 0$, a path θ is forward d-discernible (d-FD) from another path θ' of the same length if there exists an integer N_d such that for any pair of paths λ and λ' of length N_d, $\theta\lambda$ and $\theta'\lambda'$ are discernible with degree at least d. The smallest such integer N_d is the index of d-FD of θ from θ'.* $\diamond$

Proposition 2 $Y(\theta\lambda, x) \notin \Re(\mathcal{O}(\theta'\lambda'))$ *for all* $\lambda, \lambda' \in \Theta_{N'}$ *and for almost any* $x \in \mathbb{R}^n$ *iff* θ *is FD (i.e. 1-FD) from* θ' *with an index no larger than* N'. $\diamond$

Proof: Clearly, the set $\{x \in \mathbb{R}^n \mid \exists \lambda, \lambda' \in \Theta_{N'}, \, Y(\theta\lambda, x) \in \Re(\mathcal{O}(\theta'\lambda'))\}$ equals $\bigcup_{\lambda,\lambda'} c(\theta\lambda, \theta'\lambda')$, which, by Proposition 1 and by virtue of the fact that a finite union of null sets is a null set, has measure 0 iff θ is FD from θ'. $\square$

We now turn to showing that forward discernibility is decidable. We first establish the following lemma, which indicates that the indexes of d-FD increase with d, which is not an obvious fact.

Lemma 1 *Let* θ *and* θ' *be two different paths of length* N, *and* λ *and* λ' *be any paths of length* N'. *The degree of discernibility of* $\theta\lambda$ *from* $\theta'\lambda'$ *is greater than or equal to the degree of discernibility of* θ *from* θ'. *In other words, the degree of discernibility is nondecreasing as the length increases.* $\diamond$

Proof: It is easily shown, by elementary linear algebra, that

$$\rho([\mathcal{O}(\theta\lambda)\mathcal{O}(\theta'\lambda')]) - \rho([\mathcal{O}(\theta)\mathcal{O}(\theta')]) \geq \rho(\mathcal{O}(\theta\lambda)) - \rho(\mathcal{O}(\theta)). \tag{17}$$

In other words, the rank of the concatenation must increase by at least the increase of each path. $\square$

Theorem 2 (Decidability of Forward Discernibility) *FD is decidable for any degree, as the index of d-FD, where d is the maximum degree of FD between some pair of paths, is smaller than or equal to* $N(s^2, 2n)$. $\diamond$

Proof: Fix θ and θ', and let λ and λ' be such that the degree of discernibility of $\theta\lambda$ from $\theta'\lambda'$ is minimal over all pairs of paths λ and λ' of length $N(s^2, 2n)$.

First, note that the matrices $[\mathcal{O}(\lambda)\mathcal{O}(\lambda')]$ are produced by the following set of s^2 pairs:

$$\begin{pmatrix} A(i) & 0 \\ 0 & A(j) \end{pmatrix} \qquad \begin{pmatrix} C(i) \, C(j) \end{pmatrix} \qquad (i,j) \in \{1, \ldots, s\}^2. \tag{18}$$

Therefore, by Theorem 1, there exist λ^0 and λ'^0, respective prefixes of λ and λ' of the same length, and two paths μ and μ' of the same, arbitrary, length, such that $\mathcal{R}([\mathcal{O}(\lambda^0\mu)\mathcal{O}(\lambda'^0\mu')]) \subset \mathcal{R}([\mathcal{O}(\lambda^0)\mathcal{O}(\lambda'^0)])$, which, by [1, Lemma 4] and upon some manipulation, implies that

$$\mathcal{R}([\mathcal{O}(\theta\lambda^0\mu)\mathcal{O}(\theta'\lambda'^0\mu')]) \subset \mathcal{R}([\mathcal{O}(\theta\lambda^0)\mathcal{O}(\theta'\lambda'^0)]). \tag{19}$$

By Lemma 1, Equation (19) implies that the degree of discernibility of $\theta\lambda^0\mu$ from $\theta'\lambda'^0\mu'$ is equal to that of $\theta\lambda^0$ from $\theta'\lambda'^0$, which, again by Lemma 1, is smaller than that of $\theta\lambda$ from $\theta'\lambda'$, which completes the proof since μ and μ' are of arbitrary length. $\square$

Before establishing the main result of this section characterizing mode observability, we need the following definition:

Definition 5 (Complete Forward Discernibility (CFD)). *Given an integer $d > 0$, a path θ is completely forward d-discernible (d-CFD) if it is d-FD from every other path θ' of the same length. The index of d-CFD of θ is the maximum index of d-FD, over all $\theta' \neq \theta$, of θ from θ'.* ◇

Theorem 3 *The SLS (2) is MO at N iff every path of length N is CFD, (i.e. 1-CFD). Moreover, the index of MO is the largest index of CFD, over all paths of length N.* ◇

Proof: Clearly, the set $\{x \in \mathbb{R}^n \mid \exists \theta, \theta' \in \Theta_N, \exists \lambda, \lambda' \in \Theta_{N'}, Y(\theta\lambda, x) \in \Re(\mathcal{O}(\theta'\lambda'))\}$ equals $\bigcup_{\theta,\theta'} \bigcup_{\lambda,\lambda'} c(\theta\lambda, \theta'\lambda')$. Therefore, by Proposition 2, and by virtue of the fact that a finite union of null sets is a null set, it has measure 0 iff every θ is CFD with index at most N'. □

We now complete our study of mode observability in autonomous systems by answering the following two questions:

- what effect does N have on MO? In other words, is MO at larger N stronger or weaker?
- Is MO decidable?

The following proposition answers the first question:

Proposition 3 *If a system is MO at N, then it is MO at any $M \leq N$.* ◇

Proof: Let N' be the index of MO at N. Then for every pair of paths θ, θ' of length $N + N'$ with a switch at or before N (i.e. such that $\theta_i \neq \theta'_i$ for some $i \leq N$), θ must be discernible from θ'. But, since $M \leq N$, this implies the same whenever a switch occurs at or before M, which implies MO at M with an index smaller than or equal to $N' + (N - M)$. □

The converse is unfortunately not true, unless the A matrices are all invertible (a counterexample is given next):

Proposition 4 *If $A(1), \ldots, A(s)$ are all invertible, then MO at 1 implies MO at any positive integer N.* ◇

Proof: Let θ and θ' be two different paths of length N, and assume that the maximum index of FD over all pairs of different modes (i.e. paths of length 1) is N'. It suffices to show that θ is FD from θ' with index at most N'. Let λ and λ' be any two paths of length N'. It is easy to show that

$$c(\theta\lambda, \theta'\lambda') = \bigcap_{i=1}^{N} \phi(\theta_{[1,i-1]})^{-1} c(\theta_{[i,N]}\lambda, \theta'_{[i,N]}\lambda'). \tag{20}$$

Since $\theta \neq \theta'$, there exists $i \leq n$ such that $\theta_i \neq \theta'_i$. Note that $c(\theta_{[i,N]}\lambda, \theta'_{[i,N]}\lambda') = c(\theta_i\mu, \theta'_i\mu')$ with $\mu = \theta_{[i+1,N]}\lambda$, $\mu' = \theta'_{[i+1,N]}\lambda'$ and $|\mu| = |\mu'| \geq N'$. Therefore, since, by assumption, θ_i is FD from θ_i' with index at most N', $\dim(c(\theta_{[i,N]}\lambda, \theta_{[i,N]}'$ $\lambda')) < n$, and since all the A matrices, and thus $\phi(\theta_{[1,i-1]})$, are invertible, and using (20), we finally get $\dim(c(\theta\lambda, \theta'\lambda')) < n$, which completes the proof.   □

Example 1. Consider

$$A(1) = \begin{pmatrix} 0 & 0 \\ 0 & 0 \end{pmatrix} A(2) = \begin{pmatrix} 1 & 0 \\ 0 & 1 \end{pmatrix}$$
$$C(1) = \begin{pmatrix} 1 & 0 \end{pmatrix} \quad C(2) = \begin{pmatrix} 1 & 0 \end{pmatrix}. \tag{21}$$

The paths 1 and 2 (of length 1) are mutually FD with index 1, but the paths $1 \cdot 1$ and $1 \cdot 2$ are not, because they are not discernible and $A(1) = 0$, which prevents further measurements from increasing their discernibility.   △

And finally,

Theorem 4 *MO at any index N is decidable.*   ◇

Proof: Since the number of paths of length N is finite, and since, by Theorem 2, FD is decidable, it follows that CFD is decidable, and thus that MO is decidable as well.   □

Note that more precise versions of these last 3 results can be obtained, provided one extends the notion of *degree* to MO.

2.3   The Unobserved Modes Case: State Observability

In this section, we are concerned with whether the continuous state x only is recoverable. From the previous results, we know that if a system is PWO (with index N_{pwo}) and MO at N_{pwo} with index N_{mo}, then one can recover the state x uniquely from $Y(\theta, x)$ for all θ of length $N_{pwo} + N_{mo}$ and for almost any x. But if we do not need θ (which is the primary reason behind the "a.e."), is this still the best we can do? It turns out that we can do better, in that we can sometimes recover *all* states x uniquely, for all paths θ of a certain length. For now, we define our concept of *state observability*:

Definition 6 (State Observability (SO)). *The SLS (2) is SO if there exists an integer N (the smallest being the index) such that $\forall x \in \mathbb{R}^n$ and $\forall \theta \in \Theta_N$,*

$$x \neq x' \Rightarrow Y(\theta, x) \neq Y(\theta', x') \ \forall \ \theta' \in \Theta_N \tag{22}$$

In other words, a system is SO if any N consecutive measurements $Y(\theta, x)$ yield x uniquely without knowledge of θ, i.e. if the map $(x, \theta) \mapsto Y(\theta, x)$ is injective in its first coordinate. We first establish a sufficient condition.

Proposition 5 *If a system is PWO with index N_{pwo}, and if every path of length N_{pwo} is n-CFD, then it is SO.*   ◇

Proof: Let N_{cfd} be the maximum index of n-CFD, and $N = N_{pwo} + N_{cfd}$. This implies that the dimension of the input subspaces of conflict of any two paths of length N satisfying $\theta_{[1,N_{PWO}]} \neq \theta'_{[1,N_{PWO}]}$ is 0: 0 is therefore the only state whose measurements $Y(\theta, x)$ do not yield $\theta_{[1,N_{PWO}]}$ unambiguously. We then have two cases:

- $x \neq 0$, in which case the range inclusion test yields $\theta_{[1,N_{PWO}]}$, which can then be used in $x = \mathcal{O}(\theta_{[1,N_{PWO}]})^{\{1\}} Y(\theta, x)$.
- $x = 0$, in which case $Y(\theta, x) = 0$. By pathwise observability, we then know that $x = 0$.   □

Example 2. As an example, here is a system satisfying the conditions of Proposition 5:

$$A(1) = \begin{pmatrix} 1 & 2 \\ 0 & 1 \end{pmatrix} \ A(2) = \begin{pmatrix} 1 & 3 \\ 1 & 1 \end{pmatrix}$$
$$C(1) = \begin{pmatrix} 3 & 0 \end{pmatrix} \ C(2) = \begin{pmatrix} 2 & 0 \end{pmatrix},$$
(23)

Here, $N_{pwo} = 2$ and $N_{cfd} = 2$, and it is easy to check that the rank of $[\mathcal{O}(\theta\lambda)\mathcal{O}(\theta'\lambda')]$ equals 4 for any pair θ, θ' of different paths of length 2 and any pair λ, λ' of paths of length 2.   △

It turns out that the conditions given in Proposition 5 are not necessary (we will later give a counterexample). In order to study SO further, we introduce the concept of *joint observability*:

Definition 7 (Joint Observability (JO)). *Two different paths θ and θ' of the same length are jointly observable (JO) if they are both observable, and if their left inverses agree on $C(\theta, \theta')$, i.e.*[1]

$$(\mathcal{O}(\theta)^{\{1\}} - \mathcal{O}(\theta')^{\{1\}}) P_{C(\theta,\theta')} = 0,$$
(24)

or equivalently,

$$(\mathcal{O}(\theta) - \mathcal{O}(\theta')) P_{c(\theta,\theta')} = 0 \ and \ (\mathcal{O}(\theta) - \mathcal{O}(\theta')) P_{c(\theta',\theta)} = 0.$$
(25)

Note that, as opposed to discernibility, joint observability is symmetric. A direct consequence of this definition is:

Proposition 6 *θ and θ' are JO iff for all $x, x' \in \mathbb{R}^n$,*

$$x \neq x' \Rightarrow Y(\theta, x) \neq Y(\theta', x').$$
(26)

We also need to define *forward joint observability*:

Definition 8 (Forward Joint Observability (FJO)). *Two different observable paths θ and θ' of the same length are forward jointly observable (FJO) if there exists an integer N such that for all λ and λ' of length N, $\theta\lambda$ and $\theta'\lambda'$ are JO. The index of FJO is the smallest such integer.*   ◇

[.] Given a subspace V, we let P_V denote the matrix of a linear projection on V.

Before characterizing SO, we next show that FJO is decidable.

Theorem 5 *FJO is decidable, as the index of JO is bounded by* $N(s^2, 2n)$.   ◊

Proof: Suppose that θ and θ' are observable and that there exist λ and λ' of length $N(s^2, 2n)$ such that $\theta\lambda$ and $\theta'\lambda'$ are not JO. Similarly as in the proof of Theorem 2, we can find λ^0 and λ'^0, respective prefixes of λ and λ' of the same length, and two paths μ and μ' of the same, arbitrary, length, such that

$$\mathcal{R}([\mathcal{O}(\theta\lambda^0\mu)\mathcal{O}(\theta'\lambda'^0\mu')]) \subset \mathcal{R}([\mathcal{O}(\theta\lambda^0)\mathcal{O}(\theta'\lambda'^0)]). \tag{27}$$

Now, since $\theta\lambda$ and $\theta'\lambda'$ are not JO, neither can be $\theta\lambda^0$ and $\theta'\lambda'^0$, since $Y(\theta\lambda, x) = Y(\theta'\lambda', x')$ implies $Y(\theta\lambda^0, x) = Y(\theta'\lambda'^0, x')$.

Moreover, by Lemma 1, Equation (27) implies that the degree of discernibility of $\theta\lambda^0\mu$ from $\theta'\lambda'^0\mu'$ equals that of $\theta\lambda^0$ from $\theta'\lambda'^0 0$, which furthermore implies that $c(\theta\lambda^0\mu, \theta'\lambda'^0\mu') = c(\theta\lambda^0, \theta'\lambda'^0)$, thus that $(\mathcal{O}(\theta\lambda^0\mu) - \mathcal{O}(\theta'\lambda'^0\mu'))P_{c(\theta\lambda^0\mu,\theta'\lambda'^0\mu')}$ equals $(\mathcal{O}(\theta\lambda^0) - \mathcal{O}(\theta'\lambda'^0))P_{c(\theta\lambda^0,\theta'\lambda'^0)}$ and cannot equal zero since its submatrix $(\mathcal{O}(\theta\lambda^0) - \mathcal{O}(\theta'\lambda'^0))P_{c(\theta\lambda^0,\theta'\lambda'^0)}$ is not, because, as we have just shown, $\theta\lambda^0$ and $\theta'\lambda'^0$ are not JO. Therefore, $\theta\lambda^0\mu$ and $\theta'\lambda'^0\mu'$ are not JO, which completes the proof since μ and μ' are of arbitrary length.   □

We now characterize SO:

Theorem 6 *The following are equivalent.*

1. *The SLS (2) is SO.*
2. *The SLS (2) is PWO with index* N_{pwo}, *and every pair of different paths of length* N_{pwo} *is FJO.*
3. *The SLS (2) is PWO, and every* minimally observable *path (i.e. a path with no observable prefix) is FJO with every other observable path of the same length.*   ◊

Proof:

$2 \Rightarrow 1$: Let N_{fjo} be be the largest index of FJO over all pairs of paths of length N_{pwo}. Let us show that the system is SO with index at most $N = N_{pwo} + N_{fjo}$. Fix a path θ of length N, and suppose that θ' is such that $Y(\theta, x) = Y(\theta', x')$. Let $\theta_{[1,k]}$ be the minimally observable prefix of θ. First, if $\theta'_{[1,k]} = \theta_{[1,k]}$, then $x = x'$ by observability of $\theta_{[1,k]}$, since $Y(\theta, x) = Y(\theta', x')$ implies $Y(\theta_{[1,k]}, x) = Y(\theta'_{[1,k]}, x') = Y(\theta_{[1,k]}, x')$. On the other hand, if $\theta'_{[1,k]} \neq \theta_{[1,k]}$, then since $k \leq N_{pwo}$, it is easy to show that $\theta'_{[1,k]}$ and $\theta_{[1,k]}$ are FJO with index at most $N - k$. Proposition 6 then concludes that $x = x'$.

$3 \Rightarrow 2$: It is easily seen that the only pairs of paths of length N_{pwo} left to check for FJO are those sharing the same minimally observable prefix. Let θ and θ' be two paths of length N_{pwo}, and let $\theta'_{[1,k]} = \theta_{[1,k]}$ be their minimally observable prefix. $Y(\theta, x) = Y(\theta', x')$, which implies $Y(\theta_{[1,k]}, x) = Y(\theta'_{[1,k]}, x') = Y(\theta_{[1,k]}, x')$, implies that $x = x'$ by observability of $\theta_{[1,k]}$. θ and θ' are therefore JO, thus FJO.

1 $\Rightarrow$ 3: Necessity of PWO to SO is obvious. Suppose that a minimally observable path is not FJO with another observable path, i.e. that there exist λ, λ' of arbitrary length such that $\theta\lambda$ and $\theta\lambda'$ are not JO, which, by proposition 6, implies the existence of $x \neq x'$ such that $Y(\theta\lambda, x) = Y(\theta'\lambda', x')$, which contradicts SO. $\square$

The reason we give two characterizations is that their equivalence is not obvious, and because the second one is easier to check, since the number of minimally observable paths is in general smaller than $s^{N_{pwo}}$. Moreover, it is, in a sense, much tighter, since two paths can be non FJO only if they do not share the same minimally observable path. Finally,

Theorem 7 *SO is decidable.* $\Diamond$

Proof: PWO is decidable. Since FJO is decidable, and since there is a finite number of paths of length N_{pwo}, the first characterization of Theorem 6 concludes. $\square$

We now give an example of an SO system that does not satisfy the requirements of Proposition 5:

Example 3. Let

$$A(1) = \begin{pmatrix} 1 & 1 \\ 0 & 1 \end{pmatrix} A(2) = \begin{pmatrix} 1 & 2 \\ 0 & 3 \end{pmatrix}$$
$$C(1) = \begin{pmatrix} 1 & 0 \end{pmatrix} C(2) = \begin{pmatrix} 1 & 0 \end{pmatrix}, \tag{28}$$

This system is PWO with index 2, and any paths of length 2 are FJO with index 1. For instance, letting $\theta = 11$, $\theta' = 22$, and $\lambda = \lambda' = 1$, one gets

$$\mathcal{O}(\theta\lambda) = \begin{pmatrix} 1 & 0 \\ 1 & 1 \\ 1 & 2 \end{pmatrix}, \mathcal{O}(\theta'\lambda') = \begin{pmatrix} 1 & 0 \\ 1 & 2 \\ 1 & 8 \end{pmatrix}, \tag{29}$$

hence that $\theta\lambda$ and $\theta'\lambda'$ are JO because the first columns of their observability matrices, which span $C(\theta, \theta')$, are equal. Thus if we measure $Y(\mu, x) = (\alpha\ \alpha\ \alpha)^T$, then the initial state can only be $(\alpha\ 0)^T$, regardless of the path μ. $\triangle$

3   Non-autonomous Systems

We now return to the general non-autonomous case, and recall our model:

$$\begin{aligned} x_{k+1} &= A(\theta_k)x_k + B(\theta_k)u_k \\ y_k &= C(\theta_k)x_k. \end{aligned} \tag{30}$$

Our aim here is to extend some of the previous analysis to the system in (30). We thus first define, for a path θ of length N:

$$\Gamma(\theta) \triangleq \begin{pmatrix} 0 & \cdots & 0 & 0 \\ C(\theta_2)B(\theta_1) & \cdots & 0 & 0 \\ C(\theta_3)A(\theta_2)B(\theta_1) & \cdots & \vdots & 0 \\ \vdots & & 0 & \vdots \\ C(\theta_N)\Phi(\theta_{[2,N]})B(\theta_1) & \cdots & C(\theta_N)B(\theta_{N-1}) & 0 \end{pmatrix},$$

which enables us to further define:

$$Y(\theta, x, U) \triangleq \mathcal{O}(\theta)x + \Gamma(\theta)U, \tag{31}$$

where U is a control vector in $\mathbb{R}^{mN}$. Again, if $x = x_1$, $\theta = \theta_1 \cdots \theta_N$, and $U = (u_1^T \ \ldots \ u_N^T)^T$ in (30), then $Y(\theta, x, U) = (y_1^T \ \ldots \ y_N^T)^T$, and we can concentrate on equation (31). Now, by the separation principle for linear time-varying systems, it turns out that we do not need to repeat the analysis of the known modes case, and pathwise observability remains necessary and sufficient for state observability in finite time. In this section, we will instead begin directly by taking a first look at mode observability.

Given θ and θ', our objective in the autonomous case has been, roughly speaking, to make the intersection $C(\theta, \theta')$ of $\Re(\mathcal{O}(\theta))$ with $\Re(\mathcal{O}(\theta'))$ as small as possible. Here, Equation (31) suggests that we should rather consider the intersection of the affine subspaces $\Re(\mathcal{O}(\theta)) + \Gamma(\theta)U$ and $\Re(\mathcal{O}(\theta')) + \Gamma(\theta')U$ ($V + v$, where V is a subspace and v a vector of $\mathbb{R}^n$, denotes the affine subspace $\{x + v \mid x \in V\}$), and study what effect U has on it. Recalling the following classic theorem,

Theorem 8 *The intersection of $V + v$ and $V' + v'$ is either empty or equal to $V \cap V' + w$ for some w, in which case it has the dimension of $V \cap V'$.* ◇

we realize that, while the $\Gamma(\theta)U$ terms cannot increase the degree of discernibility, they can achieve something impossible in the non-autonomous case: they can render the output affine subspaces of θ and θ', i.e. $\Re(\mathcal{O}(\theta)) + \Gamma(\theta)U$ and $\Re(\mathcal{O}(\theta')) + \Gamma(\theta')U$, totally disjoint, which motivates the following definition:

Definition 9 (Strong Mode Observability (SMO)). *The SLS (30) is strongly mode observable (SMO) at N if there exists an integer N' and a vector U such that for all $x \in \mathbb{R}^n$ and all $\theta \in \Theta_{N+N'}$,*

$$\theta_{[1,N]} \neq \theta'_{[1,N]} \Rightarrow Y(\theta, x, U) \neq Y(\theta', x', U) \ \forall \ x' \in \mathbb{R}^n \tag{32}$$

We refer to such a vector U as a discerning control. ◇

Note that the difference lies in the replacement of "a.e. x" with "$\forall \ x$", which is a stronger statement. In order to characterize SMO, we unfortunately need a few more definitions:

Definition 10 (Controlled-Discernibility (CD)). *Two different paths θ and θ' of length N are controlled-discernible (CD) if*

$$(I - P)\big(\Gamma(\theta) - \Gamma(\theta')\big) \neq 0, \tag{33}$$

where P is the matrix of any projection on $\Re([O(\theta)\ \mathcal{O}(\theta')])$.

It can be verified that CD is well-defined, even though P is not unique. However, to fix the ideas, we let $P(\theta, \theta')$ be the matrix of the orthogonal projection on $\Re([O(\theta)\ \mathcal{O}(\theta')])$, throughout the remainder of this section. Furthermore, note that CD is also symmetric. We can now establish the following:

Proposition 7 *If θ and θ' are CD, then there exists a vector U such that*

$$\forall x \in \mathbb{R}^n, \ Y(\theta, x, U) \notin \Re(\mathcal{O}(\theta')) + \Gamma(\theta')U. \tag{34}$$

Even though $\Re(\mathcal{O}(\theta')) + \Gamma(\theta')U$ is an affine subspace, we can still use the range inclusion test, by testing whether $Y(\theta, x, U)) - \Gamma(\theta')U$ is in $\Re(\mathcal{O}(\theta'))$. The proof of Proposition 7 is as follows:

Proof: Let U satisfy $(I - P(\theta, \theta'))(\Gamma(\theta) - \Gamma(\theta'))U \neq 0$. Then, by elementary linear algebra, $\Re(\mathcal{O}(\theta)) + \Gamma(\theta)U$ and $\Re(\mathcal{O}(\theta')) + \Gamma(\theta')U$ are totally disjoint as affine subspaces of $\mathbb{R}^{pN}$, which completes the proof, since $Y(\theta, x, U) \in \Re(\mathcal{O}(\theta)) + \Gamma(\theta)U$. $\qquad\square$

Finally, we define:

Definition 11 (Forward Controlled-Discernibility (FCD)). *Two different paths θ and θ' of length N are forward controlled-discernible (FCD) if there exists an integer N' such that $\theta\lambda$ and $\theta'\lambda'$ are controlled discernible for any pair of paths λ and λ' of length N'. The smallest such integer is the index of FCD.* $\Diamond$

Unfortunately, we do not know whether or not FCD is decidable. This is in part due to the fact that, as opposed to $\mathcal{O}(\theta)$, we know little about the structure of $\Gamma(\theta)$. Nevertheless, we can characterize SMO as follows:

Theorem 9 *The SLS (30) is SMO at N iff any two different paths θ and θ' of length N are FCD.* $\Diamond$

Proof: Suppose the system is SMO at N with index N'. It follows that there exists a control vector U such that for all $\theta, \theta' \in \Theta_N$, $\theta \neq \theta'$, and $\lambda, \lambda' \in \Theta_{N'}$, $\Re(\mathcal{O}(\theta\lambda)) + \Gamma(\theta\lambda)U$ and $\Re(\mathcal{O}(\theta'\lambda')) + \Gamma(\theta'\lambda')U$ are totally disjoint, which implies that $(I - P(\theta\lambda, \theta'\lambda'))(\Gamma(\theta\lambda) - \Gamma(\theta'\lambda'))U \neq 0$, thus that $(I - P(\theta\lambda, \theta'\lambda'))(\Gamma(\theta\lambda) - \Gamma(\theta'\lambda')) \neq 0$, hence FCD of θ and θ' with index at most N'.

Now, let N' be the maximum index of FCD, over all pairs of different paths of length N, and let us show that the system is SMO with index at most N'. We need to show the existence of a vector U in $\mathbb{R}^{m(N+N')}$ such that

$$(I - P(\theta\lambda, \theta'\lambda'))(\Gamma(\theta\lambda) - \Gamma(\theta'\lambda'))U \neq 0 \tag{35}$$

for all $\theta, \theta' \in \Theta_N$, $\theta \neq \theta'$, and $\lambda, \lambda' \in \Theta_{N'}$. Since every pair θ and θ' of different paths of length N is FCD with index at most N', we get

$$(I - P(\theta\lambda, \theta'\lambda'))(\Gamma(\theta\lambda) - \Gamma(\theta'\lambda')) \neq 0. \tag{36}$$

Therefore,

$$K = \bigcup_{\theta, \theta', \lambda, \lambda'} \ker\left((I - P(\theta\lambda, \theta'\lambda'))(\Gamma(\theta\lambda) - \Gamma(\theta'\lambda'))\right) \neq \mathbb{R}^{m(N+N')}, \tag{37}$$

since it is a finite union of proper subspaces of $\mathbb{R}^{m(N+N')}$, by (36). Any control vector $U \in \mathbb{R}^{m(N+N')} \backslash K$ will work in (35), and is therefore discerning. $\square$

It should be noted that the existence of a single discerning control U implies that "almost" any vector of the same length is discerning, as established by (37). Finally, we describe an SMO system in the next example.

Example 4. Let

$$A(1) = A(2) = \begin{pmatrix} 1 & 1 \\ 0 & 1 \end{pmatrix}, \quad C(1) = C(2) = \begin{pmatrix} 1 & 0 \end{pmatrix} \tag{38}$$

$$B(1) = \begin{pmatrix} 1 \\ 0 \end{pmatrix} \quad B(1) = \begin{pmatrix} 2 \\ 1 \end{pmatrix} \tag{39}$$

Since the observability pairs $(A(1), C(1))$ and $(A(2), C(2))$ are equal, no two paths can be discernible, because all paths of the same length share the exact same observability matrix. However, this system is SMO at $N = 2$, with index $N' = 1$. To see this, it suffices to use Theorem 9 and to establish that $(I - P(\theta\lambda, \theta'\lambda'))(\Gamma(\theta\lambda) - \Gamma(\theta'\lambda')) \neq 0$ for any two different paths θ and θ' of length 2, and any pair of paths λ and λ' of length 1. $\triangle$

4   Conclusion

We have characterized several concepts of observability in switched linear systems through simple linear algebraic tests, and we have shown their decidability in the autonomous case. An assumption underlying all criteria studied was that the mode sequences were arbitrary, which is novel in the sense that most (if not all) previous work assumed constraints on the mode sequences, usually in the form of minimum "dwell times" between switches.

This paper is intended as an intermediate step towards a better understanding of the observability of switched systems. Indeed, some results need to be refined, some problems still need to be solved, and many extensions are in view. To mention a few, the decidability of *forward controlled-discernibility* (FCD), which seems to be a challenging problem, and the characterization and study of state observability in the non-autonomous case, still need to be addressed. Finally, the investigation of the application of the concept of *discernibility* to asymptotic observer design promises to be fruitful, and we leave it to a future endeavor.

References

1. M. Babaali and M. Egerstedt, "Pathwise observability and controllability are decidable," in *Proceedings of the 42nd IEEE Conference on Decision and Control*, (Maui, HW), December 2003.
2. A. Balluchi, L. Benvenuti, M. D. Di Benedetto, and A. L. Sangiovanni-Vincentelli, "Design of observers for hybrid systems," vol. 2289 of *Lect. Notes Comp. Sc.*, pp. 76–89, 2002.
3. A. Bemporad, G. Ferrari-Trecate, and M. Morari, "Observability and controllability of piecewise affine and hybrid systems," *IEEE Transactions on Automatic Control*, vol. 45, pp. 1864–1876, October 2000.
4. S. L. Campbell and C. D. J. Meyer, *Generalized Inverses of Linear Transformations*. New York, NY: Dover, 1991.
5. J. Ezzine and A. H. Haddad, "Controllability and observability of hybrid systems," *Int. J. Control*, vol. 49, no. 6, pp. 2045–2055, 1989.
6. D. Goshen-Meskin and I. Y. Bar-Itzhack, "Observability analysis of piece-wise constant systems - part I: Theory," *IEEE Trans. Aerospace & Electronic Systems*, vol. 28, no. 4, pp. 1056–1067, 1992.
7. I. Hwang, H. Balakrishnan, and C. Tomlin, "Observability criteria and estimator design for stochastic linear hybrid systems," in *Proceedings of the IEE European Control Conference*, (Cambridge, UK), September 2003.
8. Y. Ji and H. Chizeck, "Controllability, observability and discrete-time jump linear quadratic control," *Int. J. Control*, vol. 48, no. 2, pp. 481–498, 1988.
9. M. Mariton, "Stochastic observability of linear systems with markovian jumps," in *Proceedings of the 25th IEEE Conference on Decision and Control*, (Athens, Greece), pp. 2208–2209, December 1986.
10. R. Vidal, A. Chiuso, and S. Soatto, "Observability and identifiability of jump linear systems," in *Proceedings of the 41st IEEE Conference on Decision and Control*, (Las Vegas, NV), pp. 3614–3619, December 2002.
11. P. D. West and A. H. Haddad, "On the observability of linear stochastic switching systems," in *Proceedings of the 1994 American Control Conf.*, (Baltimore, MD), pp. 1846–1847, 1994.

A   Some Generalized Matrix Inversion Theory

We now present some definitions and results from matrix inversion theory (see, e.g., [4]). We first recall that $\mathcal{O}^{\{1\}}$ is a {1}-inverse of $\mathcal{O}$ if

$$\mathcal{O}\mathcal{O}^{\{1\}}\mathcal{O} = \mathcal{O}, \qquad (40)$$

and that the (Moore-Penrose) pseudo-inverse of $\mathcal{O}$ is defined as

$$\mathcal{O}\mathcal{O}^{\dagger}\mathcal{O} = \mathcal{O}, \ \mathcal{O}^{\dagger}\mathcal{O}\mathcal{O}^{\dagger} = \mathcal{O}^{\dagger}, \ \mathcal{O}^{\dagger}\mathcal{O} = (\mathcal{O}^{\dagger}\mathcal{O})', \ \text{and} \ \mathcal{O}\mathcal{O}^{\dagger} = (\mathcal{O}\mathcal{O}^{\dagger})'. \quad (41)$$

Note that the pseudo-inverse $\mathcal{O}^{\dagger}$ of $\mathcal{O}$ always satisfies (40), and is therefore a {1}-inverse. If furthermore $\mathcal{O}$ has full column rank, then any {1}-inverse $\mathcal{O}^{\{1\}}$ of $\mathcal{O}$ is a left inverse of $\mathcal{O}$, in the sense that $\mathcal{O}^{\{1\}}\mathcal{O} = I$, the identity matrix. We next consider the following equation:

$$Y = \mathcal{O}x, \qquad (42)$$

where $x \in \mathbb{R}^n$ and $Y \in \mathbb{R}^N$, and we examine the conditions on Y for (42) to have a solution in x, and how to compute that solution. Note that

$$\exists\, x \mid Y = \mathcal{O}x \iff Y \in \mathcal{R}(\mathcal{O}), \tag{43}$$

which is why we refer to the following test as the range inclusion test:

Proposition 8 (Range Inclusion Test) *If $\mathcal{O}^{\{1\}}$ is a $\{1\}$-inverse of $\mathcal{O}$, then*

$$Y \in \mathcal{R}(\mathcal{O}) \Leftrightarrow (\mathcal{O}\mathcal{O}^{\{1\}} - I)Y = 0. \tag{44}$$

Proof:

$\Leftarrow$ Let $x = \mathcal{O}^{\{1\}}Y$. Then $Y = \mathcal{O}x$, which concludes the proof.

$\Rightarrow$ We have $Y \in \mathcal{R}(\mathcal{O}) \Rightarrow \exists\, x$ s.t. $Y = \mathcal{O}x$. By definition of a left inverse, we have that $\mathcal{O}\mathcal{O}^{\{1\}}\mathcal{O}x = \mathcal{O}x$, which implies that $\mathcal{O}\mathcal{O}^{\{1\}}Y = Y$, which concludes the proof. $\qquad\square$

In words, equation (42) has a solution if and only if $(\mathcal{O}\mathcal{O}^{\{1\}} - I)Y = 0$ holds for some $\{1\}$-inverse (it then holds for *any* $\{1\}$-inverse). Note that if (42) admits a solution, then $x = \mathcal{O}^{\{1\}}Y$ is a solution to (42) for any $\{1\}$-inverse $\mathcal{O}^{\{1\}}$ of $\mathcal{O}$.

Inference Methods for Autonomous Stochastic Linear Hybrid Systems*

Hamsa Balakrishnan, Inseok Hwang, Jung Soon Jang, and Claire J. Tomlin

Hybrid Systems Laboratory
Department of Aeronautics and Astronautics
Stanford University, Stanford, CA 94305, U.S.A.
{hamsa,ishwang,jsjang,tomlin}@stanford.edu

Abstract. We present a parameter inference algorithm for autonomous stochastic linear hybrid systems, which computes a maximum-likelihood model, given only a set of continuous output data of the system. We overcome the potentially intractable problem of identifying the sequence of discrete modes by using dynamic programming; we then compute the maximum-likelihood continuous models using an Expectation Maximization technique. This allows us to find a maximum-likelihood model in time that is polynomial in the number of discrete modes as well as in the length of the data series. We prove local convergence of the algorithm. We also propose a novel initialization technique to derive good initial conditions for the model parameters. Finally, we demonstrate our algorithm on some examples - two simple one-dimensional examples with simulated data, and an application to real flight test data from a dual-vehicle demonstration of the Stanford DragonFly Unmanned Aerial Vehicles.

1   Introduction

The modeling of systems as stochastic hybrid systems has applications in fields such as target-tracking, the statistical analysis of time-series data, and systems biology. These systems frequently exhibit behavior that is a combination of discrete switches and continuous evolution; in addition, the data available in these applications is usually corrupted by noise. Most target-tracking algorithms for maneuvering targets, as well as estimators for hybrid systems, depend on the prior knowledge of a good model for the plant dynamics and noise characteristics, as well as knowledge of the transition probabilities between the discrete modes [1,2]. In this paper, we formulate an algorithm that finds the maximum-likelihood values of parameters for both the continuous dynamics in each mode, and the transition probabilities between the modes. We draw broadly on several techniques from data association and target tracking [3], motion-capture and synthesis methods in computer graphics [4,5] and statistical time series

---

* This work is supported by ONR under MURI contract N00014-02-1-0720, by DARPA under Software Enabled Control (AFRL contract F33615-99-C-3014) and by an NSF Career Award. H. Balakrishnan is supported by a Stanford Graduate Fellowship.

R. Alur and G.J. Pappas (Eds.): HSCC 2004, LNCS 2993, pp. 64–79, 2004.
© Springer-Verlag Berlin Heidelberg 2004

analysis [6]. While these techniques are related to classical methods of system identification for continuous- and discrete-time systems [7,8], we use them to develop a method to identify the parameters of a hybrid system. Given only the continuous- or discrete-time output of the system, our algorithm iteratively computes the maximum-likelihood parameters for the discrete and continuous models, and converges to a local maximum-likelihood autonomous stochastic linear hybrid system model. We propose methods to derive good initial conditions, so that the local maximum converged to is a suitable model for tracking the future behavior of the system.

2   Model Structure

We consider a class of hybrid systems, with linear stochastic dynamics in each discrete mode. An autonomous discrete-time stochastic linear hybrid system [9] is defined to be:

$$H : \begin{cases} x(k+1) = A_i x(k) + w_i(k) \\ y(k) \quad = C x(k) + v_i(k) \end{cases} , \quad k \in \mathbb{N} \tag{1}$$

where $x \in \mathbb{R}^n$ and $y \in \mathbb{R}^p$ are the continuous state and output variables respectively. The index $i \in \{1, 2, \cdots, N\}$ represents the discrete state, where N is the (unknown, but finite) number of discrete modes in the model. The system matrices are $A_i \in \mathbb{R}^{n \times n}$ for $i \in \{1, 2, \cdots, N\}$ (assumed unknown), and $C \in \mathbb{R}^{p \times n}$ is the measurement matrix (n and C can be determined using a Singular Value Decomposition (SVD) on the output data, and are therefore assumed to be known). We denote the covariance of the initial state $x(k_0)$ as $\pi_0 \in \mathbb{R}^N$, and assume that the process noise $w_i(k)$ and the measurement noise $v_i(k)$ are uncorrelated, zero-mean white Gaussian sequences with the unknown covariance matrices $\mathrm{E}[w_i(k)w_i(k)'] = Q_i \in \mathbb{R}^{n \times n}$ and $\mathrm{E}[v_i(k)v_i(k)'] = R_i \in \mathbb{R}^{p \times p}$ respectively, where $\mathrm{E}[\cdot]$ and $(\cdot)'$ denote expectation and matrix transpose. It is assumed that $w_i(k)$ and $v_i(k)$ are both uncorrelated with the initial state, i.e., $\mathrm{E}[x(k_0)w_i(k)'] = \mathrm{E}[x(k_0)v_i(k)'] = 0$. $Y_{1:T} \in \mathbb{R}^{p \times T}$ is used to represent the given data series, that is, the sequence of $p-$vectors $[y(1), y(2), \cdots, y(T)]$. We use similar notation for other sequences of vectors; for example, the sequence of state vectors $[x(1), x(2), \cdots x(t)]$ is denoted by $X_{1:t} \in \mathbb{R}^{n \times t}$. We denote the set of parameters which defines the dynamics for each discrete mode i by $\theta_i = \{A_i, Q_i, R_i\}$ and the entire continuous model by $\Theta = \{\theta_1, \theta_2, \cdots, \theta_N\}$.

Given only $Y_{1:T}$, we would like to find a model that maximizes the likelihood ($\mathcal{L}$ that the data was generated by this model. To do this, we segment $[1, T]$ into the *best* N_S ($\geq N$) segments, such that each segment corresponds to a single discrete mode, allowing for modes to be repeated in the data sequence. We label segment k as l_k, representing its discrete mode, ($l_k \in \{1 \cdots N\}, k = 1 \cdots N_S$). We impose the condition that the system stays in a mode for a given minimum *dwell time*, T_d: this constraint reflects the observation that physical systems do not exhibit infinitely fast switching; additionally, we have shown in [10] that a minimum dwell time is necessary to estimate the state of a hybrid system, once the model is given. We also compute the switching times between modes, denoted s_k, such that segment k spans the time interval $[s_k, s_{k+1} - 1]$, and in this segment, the system is in mode l_k. The minimum dwell time constraint can be expressed as $s_{k+1} - s_k \geq T_d$. We denote the switching time sequence by $S = \{s_1, s_2, \cdots s_{N_S}\}$, and the labeling sequence by $L = \{l_1, l_2, \cdots l_{N_S}\}$ (see Figure 1). We assume in this paper that the discrete transitions are independent of the continuous state of the system, the relaxation of this assumption will be the subject of future work. We also assume that the discrete transitions are Markovian, and we define the Markovian switching matrix M, whose elements are $M_{ij} = \text{prob}(l_k = j | l_{k-1} = i)$. M gives the probability of transition to any mode at the switching time. The Markovian assumption is reasonable, since systems frequently exhibit probabilistic patterns in their switching behavior - for example, a civilian aircraft is more likely to transition from a turn maneuver mode to a straight mode than to another maneuver mode. The optimal segmentation of the data sequence into N_S segments can also provide us with the maximum likelihood value of M, so we represent our discrete model by $D = \{S, L, M\}$. We use $\Omega_{(\cdot)}$ to denote the parameter space of $(\cdot)$, for example, Ω_y represents the parameter space of y, and is equal to $\mathbb{R}^p$. Finally, we define the function $\delta(statement)$ to be 1, if $statement$ is true; 0, otherwise. In summary, given a data series (of length T) denoted by $Y_{1:T}$, and knowing the measurement matrix (C), we would like to find the system parameters, continuous $(\{A_i, Q_i, R_i\}, i = 1 \cdots N)$ as well as discrete $(\{S, L, M\})$, such that the resultant model maximizes the likelihood that the data series was generated by the model.

For a stochastic linear hybrid system, there are an infinite number of continuous models that can realize a given output sequence. Since the main problem of interest to us is the design of hybrid estimators, we restrict ourselves to the class of systems which satisfy the following conditions: (1) We consider the innovations form of the model [7,11], given by $\hat{x}(k + 1) = A_i\hat{x}(k) + K_i(k)e_i(k)$; $y(k) = C_i\hat{x}(k) + e_i(k)$, where the innovations $e_i(k) = y(k) - C_i\hat{x}(k)$, $K_i(k)$ is the Kalman filter gain and $\hat{x}$ is the state estimate, and we assume $A_i - K_iC_i$ is stable [11]. (2) We require that the stochastic linear hybrid system be *identifiable*. This condition, while not overly restrictive, roughly ensures that the models are distinct enough so as to be distinguished from each other using their continuous outputs. This would also give us a class of transformations for the continuous model which would explain the given output. The conditions for identifiability for a deterministic linear hybrid system have been derived in [12], these can be extended quite naturally to stochastic linear hybrid systems.

3   Parameter Inference Algorithm for Stochastic Linear Hybrid Systems

In this section, we propose an algorithm for hybrid system model inference, assess its complexity, and prove its convergence to a local optimum. The structure of the algorithm (for one iteration) is given in Figure 2.

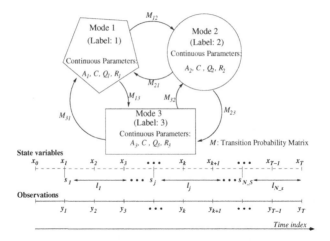

Fig. 1. Example of a three mode hybrid model, showing model parameters.

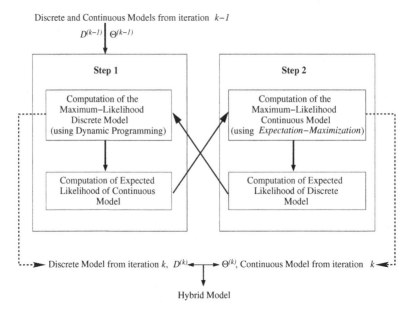

Fig. 2. Structure of the Parameter Inference Algorithm for Stochastic Linear Hybrid Systems.

3.1 Expectation Maximization

For the sake of clarity, we first briefly describe the traditional Expectation-Maximization (EM) algorithm [13]. Given general observed data $Y \in \Omega_Y$, we could postulate probability density functions (pdfs) $g(Y|\psi)$, which depend on parameters ψ. The Expectation-Maximization algorithm is a method of finding a valuation of ψ that maximizes $g(Y|\psi)$ given the observed Y. Suppose we knew that the observations were in fact *incomplete* data, for which the underlying *complete* data $Z \in \Omega_Z$ had corresponding pdfs $f(Z|\psi)$. (For example, in the case of a stochastic linear system, the observations form the incomplete data, while the observations together with the state variables form the complete data). Denoting the vector of parameters by $\Psi = (\psi_1, \cdots \psi_d)$, if the mapping from $\Omega_Z \mapsto \Omega_Y$ were many to one, we could write

$$g(Y|\Psi) = \int_{\Omega_Z(y)} f(Z|\Psi)dZ \qquad (2)$$

To find the model that is most likely to have generated the data, the EM algorithm iteratively computes $\log \mathcal{L}(\Psi) \triangleq \log f(Z|\Psi)$, updating the parameter fit (Ψ) at every step. We compute $\log \mathcal{L}(\Psi)$ instead of $\mathcal{L}(\Psi)$, because for many exponential families, including systems which are Gaussian, the logarithm of the likelihood is easier to compute than the likelihood itself; and since the logarithm is a monotonic function, maximizing the log-likelihood is equivalent to maximizing the likelihood. However the complete data Z is not available in practice (we only have the data we actually measure), and so we use the expectation of the log-likelihood, *i.e.*, $E_\Psi\{\log \mathcal{L}(\Psi)|Y\}$, derived using the current fit for Ψ. For example, in the case of stochastic linear systems, these expectations can be computed using Kalman recursions. Therefore it is the expectation of the likelihood that is maximized; hence the name *Expectation-Maximization*.

Algorithm 1 (Classical (G)EM Algorithm [13])
Let $\Psi^{(0)}$ be some initial value of Ψ.
Repeat:

1. ***E-* Step:** *Compute*

$$\mathcal{Q}(\Psi|\Psi^{(k)}) \triangleq E_{\Psi^{(k)}}\{\log \mathcal{L}(\Psi)|Y\} = E_{\Psi^{(k)}}\{\log f(Z|\Psi)|Y\}, \qquad (3)$$

   where $E_\Psi(\cdot)$ denotes the expectation derived using the parameter set Ψ.
2. ***M-* Step:** *Choose $\Psi^{(k+1)}$ to be any value of $\Psi \in \Omega_\Psi$ which maximizes $\mathcal{Q}(\Psi|\Psi^{(k)})$, i.e.,*

$$\mathcal{Q}(\Psi^{(k+1)}|\Psi^{(k)}) \geq \mathcal{Q}(\Psi|\Psi^{(k)}), \text{ for all } \Psi \in \Omega_\Psi \text{ (denoted EM)}; \qquad (4)$$

   or any value that satisfies the less restrictive condition:

$$\mathcal{Q}(\Psi^{(k+1)}|\Psi^{(k)}) \geq \mathcal{Q}(\Psi^{(k)}|\Psi^{(k)}) \text{ (denoted Generalized EM (GEM))}. \qquad (5)$$

until $\mathcal{L}(\Psi^{(k+1)}) - \mathcal{L}(\Psi^{(k)})$ *converges to ϵ, where $\epsilon \in \mathbb{R}$ is arbitrarily small.*

The EM algorithm is a special case of the GEM algorithm (5). The EM algorithm maximizes the conditional expectation at every iteration, while the GEM only ensures its increase. Under fairly general conditions, such as the boundedness of the likelihood functions, several properties of the EM and GEM algorithms, including convergence, have been proved in [13,14]. In particular, it can be shown that a sequence of likelihoods obtained using the GEM algorithm will converge to a local optimum [14]. We will use this property to prove the convergence of the algorithm that we propose for stochastic linear hybrid systems, which have Gaussian and bounded likelihoods.

The two main issues with the implementation of any version of the Expectation-Maximization algorithm are: (1) the pdf $f(Z|\Psi)$ (or its conditional expectation) is sometimes difficult to compute; (2) since the convergence is to a local maximum, a good choice of initial conditions is necessary. We develop methods to alleviate both of these problems in the application of EM to the inference of stochastic linear hybrid systems.

3.2   Parameter Inference Algorithm for Stochastic Hybrid Systems

In order to fit into the form of the standard EM algorithm [13], we note that we wish to find the maximum likelihood solution to our model parameters, $i.e.$,

$$\{\overline{D}, \overline{\Theta}\} = \arg \max_{\{D, \Theta\}} \mathcal{L}(Y_{1:T}|D, \Theta) \tag{6}$$

$\mathcal{L}(Y_{1:T}|D, \Theta)$ is analogous to the function $g(Y|\psi)$ in (2). As in the case of the classical EM algorithm, rather than work with this density function, we define the *complete* data as the combination of the sequence of state variables (X) and the observations (Y), from system (1), and denote it by Z. In other words, $z(k) = \{x(k), y(k)\} \in \mathbb{R}^n \times \mathbb{R}^p$. The algorithm can be written as follows:

Algorithm 2 (Parameter Inference Algorithm for Stochastic Linear Hybrid Systems)
Assume an initial continuous model $\Theta^{(0)}$ and an initial discrete model $D^{(0)}$. Iterate the following until the convergence of the likelihood to a local maximum:

1. **Step 1:** *Find the globally optimal segmentation points (S) and their respective labels (L), assuming the model parameters of the current iteration (k). Then, update the switching probability matrix M, using:*
   $M_{ij} = \sum_{k=2}^{N_S} \delta(l_{k-1} = i)\delta(l_k = j)$, *normalized such that $\sum_{j=1}^{N_S} M_{ij} = 1$. This gives us the maximum-likelihood discrete model, $D^{(k+1)}$.*
2. **Step 2:** *Fit new maximum-likelihood models into the segmented time sequences; i.e., for the computed $\{S, L\}$ fit the best $\Theta^{(k+1)}$.*

Drawing an analogy to the classical EM algorithm (Algorithm 1): $\Psi = \{D, \Theta\}$. Then, we would like to maximize the expectation

$$\mathcal{Q}(\Psi|\Psi^{(k)}) = \mathrm{E}_{\Psi^{(k)}}\{\log \mathcal{L}(\Psi)|Y\} = \mathrm{E}_{D^{(k)}, \Theta^{(k)}}\{\log f(Z|D, \Theta)|Y\}.$$

We may rewrite Algorithm 2 in terms of the different conditional likelihoods maximized in each step. The algorithm begins with an initialization of $D^{(0)}$ and $\Theta^{(0)}$. Then, we iterate the following until the convergence of $\mathrm{E}_{D^{(k)}, \Theta^{(k)}}\{\log f(Z|\Psi)|Y\}$ to a local maximum:

In Step 1, we maximize $\mathrm{E}_{D^{(k)},\Theta^{(k)}}\{\log f(Z|D,\Theta^{(k)})|Y\}$; this allows us to compute the conditional expectation $\mathrm{E}_{D^{(k+1)},\Theta^{(k)}}\{\log f(Z|\Theta,D^{(k+1)})|Y\}$.

In Step 2, we maximize $\mathrm{E}_{D^{(k+1)},\Theta^{(k)}}\{\log f(Z|\Theta,D^{(k+1)})|Y\}$, and compute the conditional expectation $\mathrm{E}_{D^{(k+1)},\Theta^{(k+1)}}\{\log f(Z|D,\Theta^{(k+1)})|Y\}$.

Algorithm 2 no longer falls into the classical EM framework, since we do not compute the expectation in one step and maximize it in the next. In Algorithm 2, in Step 1, we assume a continuous model and compute the best discrete model for this continuous model. In Step 2, we assume this discrete model, and compute the maximum-likelihood continuous model. While both steps correspond to either an E-step or an M-step, the expectation computed in one step is maximized in the next, and vice versa. Since the likelihood function is changed at every step, it is not clear that the convergence properties of classical EM or GEM hold in this case, and thus the convergence of Algorithm 2 must be analyzed.

Theorem 1. *Algorithm 2 iteratively generates a sequence of models, whose likelihoods satisfy the model-likelihood sequence conditions (5) of the Generalized Expectation-Maximization Algorithm [13,14]. Therefore the algorithm is guaranteed to converge to a local maximum.*

Proof. Let us consider the likelihood sequence generated. For iteration $k+1$, we would like to prove that the model parameters $\{D^{(k+1)},\Theta^{(k+1)}\}$ satisfy (5), *i.e.*,

$$\mathcal{Q}(D^{(k+1)},\Theta^{(k+1)}|D^{(k)},\Theta^{(k)}) \geq \mathcal{Q}(D^{(k)},\Theta^{(k)}|D^{(k)},\Theta^{(k)}). \tag{7}$$

We can rewrite Algorithm 2 as follows:

Step 1: Maximize $\mathrm{E}_{D^{(k)},\Theta^{(k)}}\{\log f(z|D,\Theta^{(k)})|Y_{1:T}\}$: compute $D^{(k+1)}$ such that

$$\mathcal{Q}(D^{(k+1)},\Theta^{(k)}|D^{(k)},\Theta^{(k)}) \geq \mathcal{Q}(D,\Theta^{(k)}|D^{(k)},\Theta^{(k)}), \text{ for all } D \in \Omega_D. \tag{8}$$

Step 2: Maximize $\mathrm{E}_{D^{(k+1)},\Theta^{(k)}}\{\log f(z|\Theta,D^{(k+1)})|y\}$: compute $\Theta^{(k+1)}$ such that

$$\mathcal{Q}(D^{(k+1)},\Theta^{(k+1)}|D^{(k)},\Theta^{(k)}) \geq \mathcal{Q}(D^{(k+1)},\Theta|D^{(k)},\Theta^{(k)}), \text{ for all } \Theta \in \Omega_\Theta \tag{9}$$

Combining (8) and (9), we get

$$\begin{aligned}
\mathcal{Q}(D^{(k+1)},\Theta^{(k+1)}|D^{(k)},\Theta^{(k)}) &\geq \mathcal{Q}(D^{(k+1)},\Theta|D^{(k)},\Theta^{(k)}), \text{ for all } \Theta \in \Omega_\Theta \\
&\geq \mathcal{Q}(D^{(k+1)},\Theta^{(k)}|D^{(k)},\Theta^{(k)}) \\
&\geq \mathcal{Q}(D^{(k)},\Theta^{(k)}|D^{(k)},\Theta^{(k)}),
\end{aligned} \tag{10}$$

thus proving (7). Since in the case of stochastic models with Gaussian noise, the likelihood functions are bounded, the sequence will converge to either a stationary point (saddle surface) or a local maximum. Such a convergence to a saddle surface can only occur in the continuous step (Step 2). However, in the case of linear Gaussian systems, we can show that the Hessian is always negative definite, ruling out convergence to a stationary point. Therefore the sequence converges to a local maximum, proving the convergence of the parameter inference algorithm for hybrid systems. (Note that the convergence criterion is the convergence of the likelihood, and not the model parameters [14]. However, we prevent oscillations between different discrete models with identical likelihoods by updating the discrete model only when the likelihood increases.) ∎

4 Implementation of Parameter Inference Algorithm for Hybrid Systems

Algorithm 2 is of little use if we cannot efficiently compute the likelihoods. In this section, we describe the actual likelihood functions chosen, as well as the procedures used to maximize them. The problem of maximizing the likelihood in Step 1 is potentially intractable, since we need to find the maximum likelihood hypothesis from $\mathcal{O}(N^T)$ potential segmentations. However, it is fortunately possible in this case to compute the solution, by formulating a dynamic program of polynomial complexity [4]. In Step 2, we need to iteratively compute the model parameters to maximize the likelihood of the dynamics in each of the modes. We use an algorithm which iteratively maximizes this likelihood using a form of the EM algorithm [15].

4.1 Step 1: Maximizing the Likelihood of the Discrete Model

Suppose we have initial values of Θ and D (we leave the discussion of details of the initialization for Section 4.3). We want to find globally optimal segmentation points (S) and labels (L). To achieve this purpose, we employ the following **dynamic programming** algorithm [4]:

Let us define a reward function $\mathcal{L}max_n(t)$ as the maximum value of likelihood that can be derived from dividing $Y_{1:t}$ into n segments. $\mathcal{L}max_n(t)$ is achieved by the optimal segmentation of $Y_{1:t}$ into n parts. Let us define $LastMode_n(t)$ and $LastStart_n(t)$ to be the label (mode) and start time of the final segment in this optimal segmentation.

Clearly, the optimal segmentation is the one that maximizes the likelihood of the entire data set, *i.e.*, has likelihood $\max_{1 \leq n \leq \lfloor \frac{T}{T_d} \rfloor} \mathcal{L}max_n(T)$, and N_S is the number of segments in this "optimal" segmentation. Then, for $T_d \leq t \leq T$,

$$\mathcal{L}max_1(t) = \max_{1 \leq i \leq N} \mathcal{L}(Y_{1:T}|\theta_i), \text{ and } LastMode_1(t) = \arg\max_i \mathcal{L}(Y_{1:T}|\theta_i) \quad (11)$$

Also, while $1 \leq n \leq \lfloor \frac{T}{T_d} \rfloor$, and $nT_d \leq t \leq T$,

$$\mathcal{L}max_n(t) = \max_{\substack{1 \leq i \leq N \\ (n-1)T_d < b \leq t - T_d}} [\mathcal{L}max_{n-1}(b-1)M_{li}\mathcal{L}(Y_{b:t}|\theta_i)]$$

$$[LastMode_n(t), LastStart_n(t)] = \arg\max_{i,b} [\mathcal{L}max_{n-1}(b-1)M_{li}\mathcal{L}(Y_{b:t}|\theta_i)] \quad (12)$$

where $l = LastMode_{n-1}(b-1)$. In other words, the maximum likelihood derived from segmenting a sequence into n parts is the maximum product of the likelihood resulting from segmenting a smaller sequence into $n-1$ parts in the best manner, multiplied by the likelihood of the new sequence, multiplied by the probability of the corresponding mode switch. A schematic representation of this dynamic programming algorithm is given in Figure 3. Therefore, the required optimal solution to the segmentation is

$$\mathcal{L}max(T) = \max_{1 \leq n \leq \lfloor \frac{T}{T_d} \rfloor} \mathcal{L}max_n(T) \tag{13}$$

and the optimal number of segments is $N_S = \arg\max_n \mathcal{L}max(T)$. We can also find the optimal segmentation ($\{S, L\}$) corresponding to this solution. We note that

$$s_1 = 1; \ s_{N_S+1} = T + 1; \ s_n = LastStart_n(s_{n+1} - 1), \text{ for } N_S \geq n > 1 \tag{14}$$
$$l_{N_S} = LastMode_{N_S}(T); \ l_{n-1} = LastMode_{n-1}(s_n - 1), \text{ for } N_S \geq n > 1 \tag{15}$$

We now also update the switching matrix, using the labels from the optimal segmentation
$M_{ij} = \sum_{k=2}^{N_S} \delta(l_{k-1} = i)\delta(l_k = j)$, normalized such that $\sum_{j=1}^{N_S} M_{ij} = 1$.
This algorithm solves the optimal segmentation problem with a complexity of $\mathcal{O}(NT^3)$, if we know the likelihood function $\mathcal{L}(Y_{1:t}|\theta_i)$. In the case of stochastic linear systems with Gaussian noise, it is possible to simply express the likelihood function in terms of the residuals of a Kalman filter. Given θ_i, we can design an optimal estimator for the continuous dynamics in the form of a Kalman filter. Given the predictions for the continuous state variables $E(x(k)|Y_{1:k-1}) = x(k|k-1)$, and their covariances $P(k|k-1)$, we can express the likelihood as :

$$\log \mathcal{L}(Y_{1:t}|\theta_i) = -\frac{1}{2} \sum_{k=1}^{t} \log |\Sigma_{ki}| - \frac{1}{2} \sum_{k=1}^{t} (r_i(k))' \Sigma_{ki}^{-1} r_i(k) \tag{16}$$

where $r_i(k) = y(k) - C_i x(k|k-1)$ is the residual at time k, with a covariance $\Sigma_{ki} = C_i P(k|k-1)C_i' + R_i$. It can be shown ([13,14]) that maximizing $\mathcal{L}(Y_{1:t}|\Theta, M)$ over $\{\Theta, M\}$ is equivalent to maximizing $E[\log \mathcal{L}(Z|\{\Theta, M\})|Y]$, where Z is the "complete" data, i.e., the joint likelihood of the observed variables ($Y_{1:t}$, and the state variables $X_{1:t}$). Given the optimal segmentation (S, L), the function we would like to maximize is the sum of the conditional likelihood functions for the data in each segment. To do this, we update the models in Step 2 to be the maximum (conditional) likelihood values for the data of each of the segments.

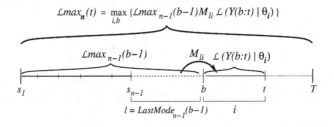

Fig. 3. Dynamic Programming Algorithm for Step 1.

4.2 Step 2: Finding the Maximum Likelihood Continuous Model

For each mode, we fit the maximum likelihood model, using a form of the EM algorithm proposed in [15,6]. We demonstrate this for one of the segments which we (in Step 1) have labeled as mode i. Suppose the data output of this sequence is $Y_{b+1:b+n}$, where $b + 1 < b + n < T$, $n > T_d$. Then, the desired log-likelihood for this segment can be written as

$$\log \mathcal{L}(Z_{b+1:b+n}|\theta_i) = -\frac{1}{2}\log|\Sigma| - \frac{1}{2}(x(b) - \mu)'\Sigma^{-1}(x(b) - \mu) - \frac{n}{2}\log|Q_i|$$

$$-\frac{1}{2}\sum_{k=b+1}^{b+n}(x(k) - A_i x(k-1))'Q_i^{-1}(x(k) - A_i x(k-1)) \quad (17)$$

$$-\frac{n}{2}\log|R_i| - \frac{1}{2}\sum_{k=b+1}^{b+n}(y(k) - C_i x(k))'R_i^{-1}(y(k) - C_i x(k))$$

where, as before, $Z_{b+1:b+n}$ is the joint ("complete") data, namely, the observed variables $Y_{b+1:b+n}$, and the continuous state variables, $X_{b+1:b+n}$; μ and Σ are the mean and covariance of the initial values in that segment of the continuous state variable, *i.e.*, $x(b)$. Then, as explained earlier, the maximum likelihood solution is the one that maximizes the function

$$\mathcal{Q}(\mu, \Sigma, A_i, Q_i, R_i) = \mathrm{E}[\log \mathcal{L}(Z_{b+1:b+n-1}|\theta_i)|Y_{b+1:b+n}] \quad (18)$$

In computing the conditional expectation in (17), we need to compute the following conditional means and covariances, which are easily obtained using Kalman recursions [16]: $x^b(k|s) = \mathrm{E}[x(k)|Y_{b+1:b+s}]$, $P^b(k|s) = \mathrm{cov}(x(k)|Y_{b+1:b+s})$, and $P^b(k, k-1|s) = \mathrm{cov}(x(k), x(k-1)|Y_{b+1:b+s})$. We define the following quantities:

$$\mathcal{A} \triangleq \sum_{k=b+1}^{b+n}\left(P^b(k-1|n) + x^b(k-1|n)x^b(k-1|n)'\right)$$
$$\mathcal{B} \triangleq \sum_{k=b+1}^{b+n}\left(P^b(k, k-1|n) + x^b(k|n)x^b(k-1|n)'\right)$$
$$\mathcal{C} \triangleq \sum_{k=b+1}^{b+n}\left(P^b(k|n) + x^b(k|n)x^b(k|n)'\right)$$

As shown in [15], taking conditional expectations on (17), we get:

$$\mathcal{Q}(\mu, \Sigma, A_i, Q_i, R_i) = -\frac{1}{2}\log|\Sigma| - \frac{1}{2}\mathrm{tr}\left\{\Sigma^{-1}\left(P^b(b|n) + (x(b) - \mu)(x(b) - \mu)'\right)\right\}$$
$$-\frac{n}{2}\log|Q_i| - \frac{1}{2}\mathrm{tr}\{Q_i^{-1}(\mathcal{C} - \mathcal{B}A_i' - A_i\mathcal{B}' + A_i\mathcal{A}A_i')\}$$
$$-\frac{n}{2}\log|R_i|$$
$$-\frac{1}{2}\mathrm{tr}\Big\{R_i^{-1}\sum_{k=b+1}^{b+n}\begin{matrix}[(y(k) - C_i x^b(k|n))(y(k) - C_i x^b(k|n))' \\ + C_i P^b(k|n)C_i']\end{matrix}\Big\}$$

where tr denotes the trace of a matrix. It can be shown, as in ([15]), that at iteration r, the choice of parameters that maximizes $\mathcal{Q}(A_i, Q_i, R_i)$ is:

$$A_i(r+1) = \mathcal{B}\mathcal{A}^{-1} \tag{19}$$

$$Q_i(r+1) = \frac{1}{n}\{\mathcal{C} - \mathcal{B}\mathcal{A}^{-1}\mathcal{B}'\} \tag{20}$$

$$R_i(r+1) = \frac{1}{n}\sum_{k=b+1}^{b+n} \begin{matrix}[(y(k) - C_i x^b(k|n))(y(k) - C_i x^b(k|n))' \\ +C_i P^b(k|n)C_i']\end{matrix} \tag{21}$$

Therefore Step 2 consists of the following EM algorithm: For each of the models, for the corresponding optimal segment(s) from the E-step, we repeat the following until the estimates and the log-likelihood converge to a local maximum.

1. Compute the means and covariances of the continuous state estimates using a Kalman filter.
2. Find the new iterates of parameters using (19), (20) and (21).

The converged values of the (continuous) model parameters (Θ) are the maximum likelihood model parameter fits to the segmented data sequence.
As shown in [17,7], for a large number of samples, the difference between the estimate and the true model (local maximum it converges to) tends in distribution to a zero-mean Gaussian with a covariance given by $-\left[\frac{\partial^2 \mathcal{L}}{\partial \Theta^2}\right]^{-1}$. Therefore, the inverse of the Hessian of the likelihood function gives us a measure of the uncertainty of our parameter estimates.

4.3   Initialization

We have already mentioned that the EM algorithm is only guaranteed to converge to a local minimum. The optimal solution is a function of how "good" the initial guesses of the parameters are. We present here a novel method of initializing the continuous parameters. Since we know that the system stays in a mode for at least a time T_d, we fit in the maximum likelihood model for mode 1 by applying the method of the Step 2 described earlier, to $Y_{1:T_d}$. Given a state estimate and measurement for the current time step, and a model for the dynamics, the Kalman filter gives us a prediction for the measurement at the next time step, as well as a region of uncertainty around it, in the form of a covariance matrix. We call the ellipsoidal region defined by the predicted estimate and the covariance, the validation-gate. We iteratively proceed, one time step at a time, and compare the measurement at every time step with the validation-gate from the Kalman filter prediction from the previous time step. If the measurement falls outside the validation gates of all previously identified modes propagated from the previous time step, we initiate a new mode into the system. Doing this repeatedly, we estimate the number of modes (N), the initial segmentation (S, L), and the initial M. If the stochastic hybrid system is identifiable, then the Kalman filter validation gates will be distinguishable, and the algorithm will find the correct number of modes; if not, it will only give us a possible model that would explain the output data.

5   Examples

Examples 1 and 2: We first present two illustrative 1-D examples to explain the proposed algorithm. We use simulated data generated from the stochastic linear hybrid system $x(k+1) = a_i x(k) + v(k); y(k) = c_i x(k) + w(k)$ [9] where $i \in \{1, 2, 3\}$, $a_1 = 0.5$, $a_2 = 1.0$, $a_3 = 1.1$, and $c_i = 1$, for $i = 1, 2, 3$. The noise covariances are 1.0 and 0.1 respectively. The switching times in the original system are at 39s., 56s., and 79s. The results of the parameter inference algorithm for hybrid systems for this 1-D example are given in Figure 4. The algorithm correctly identifies three discrete modes, and correctly detects the switching times. It also converges to a model consistent with the actual model. This is illustrated by the following extracts from the algorithm output:

Parameter	$a.$	$a.$	$a.$	$Q.$	$Q.$	$Q.$	$R.$	$R.$	$R.$	Transitions
True Value	0.5	1.0	1.1	1.0	1.0	1.0	0.1	0.1	0.1	[39 56 79]
Estimate	0.5014	1.0564	1.1023	1.547	1.2547	1.436	0.0939	0.0455	0.156	[39 56 79]

We realize that the estimates of the dynamical parameters (a_i) are more critical to this method than the noise covariances, which are statistical, and therefore whose values will depend on the number of trials of data available. Clearly, there is a very good match in the actual and inferred values of the system dynamics and switching times. This is further illustrated by another example, this time with data generated by a system with parameters $a_1 = 1.3$, $a_2 = 1.5$, $a_3 = 0.6666$, and $c_i = 1$, for $i = 1 \cdots 3$. In this case, with the same switching times as before, the system parameters are identified correctly.

System Parameter	$a.$	$a.$	$a.$	Switching Times
True Value	1.3	1.5	0.6666	[39 56 79]
Estimated Value	1.3	1.5	0.6666	[39 56 79]

The training data and the results of the mode-detection are shown in Figure 5, along with the error plots. The error is the difference between the estimate of the continuous state from the inferred model, and the actual continuous state.

Example 3: We apply the algorithm to data obtained from the DragonFly Testbed at the Hybrid Systems Laboratory, at Stanford University. These are Unmanned Aerial Vehicles (UAVs), and the data we use are the position and velocity estimates. The data shown in this paper corresponds to a Dual-vehicle Flight Test. Aircraft 1 is referred to as the *evader*, and Aircraft 2 as the *blunderer*. The purpose of this experiment that produced this data was to demonstrate algorithms for provably safe closely-spaced parallel approaches [18]. However, we now use this data for a different purpose: given only the $x-$ and $y-$ position and velocity measurements, *i.e.*, no discrete or continuous state information, we build a model of the system which estimates the different modes of flight and the continuous states. While applying Algorithm 2 to Aircraft 1, we identify three discrete modes, with four distinct segments in the data. The switching times are estimated to be at $t = 9, 20$ and 39 seconds. Comparing this to the times when the autopilot actions were initiated, we find that the system mode-transition commands were issued at $t = 21$ and $t = 39$ seconds. This further

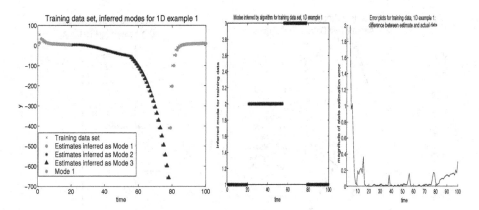

Fig. 4. Training data, with output of proposed algorithm for hybrid systems, for 1D Example (1). Left: Data sets, as a function of time. The different markers correspond to different identified discrete modes. Center: Mode transitions inferred from data set. Right: Estimation error plot.

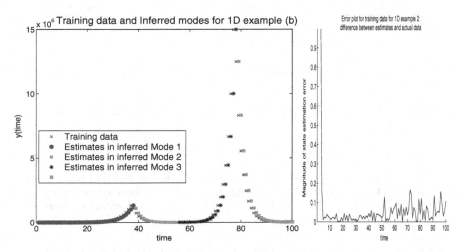

Fig. 5. Left: Training data, with output of Algorithm 2, for 1D Example (2). The different markers correspond to different identified discrete modes. Right: Estimation error plot.

validates the performance of the algorithm we have proposed. We are also able to identify the other segments (and their modes) in the data sequence. In both aircraft trajectories, the initial segment (Mode 1) corresponds to the localizer-capture segment in which the aircraft first moves into autopilot, and attempts to capture the localizer trajectory (straight line). Mode 2 corresponds to the localizer-tracking segment. Now that the two aircraft are flying parallel to each other, at $t = 18$ seconds, the blunderer (Aircraft 2) transitions to a mode that causes a potential conflict with the evader. Detecting this potential conflict, at $t = 21$ seconds, the evader initiates a maneuver command to avoid the blunderer.

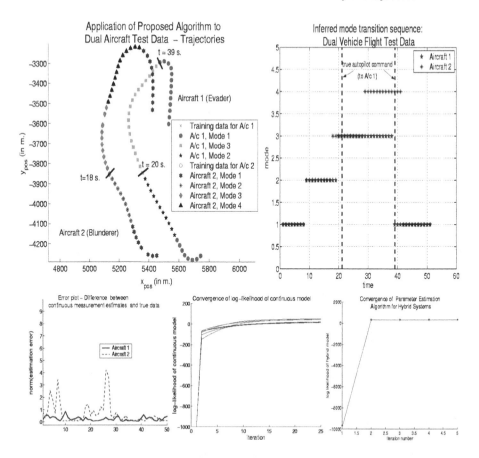

Fig. 6. Parameter Inference Algorithm for Stochastic Linear Hybrid Systems, applied to Dual-Vehicle Flight Test data. Top: (right) Training data, inferred modes, estimates. (left) Mode transition sequence. Bottom (left) Error plots. (center) Convergence of continuous model. (right) Convergence of hybrid model.

At $t = 39$ seconds, the manual pilot takes over from the autopilot and flies the aircraft back. The trajectories are plotted in Figure 5, along with the norm error of the smoothed estimates compared to the true data, the convergence plots, and the mode transition sequences.

6   Conclusions

We have proposed an algorithm that determines a maximum-likelihood hybrid system model, given only the continuous output of the system. With an intelligent choice of initial conditions, we also compute physically realistic models. We have applied these methods to the analysis of flight data from our UAV testbed (DragonFly) and obtained models that allow us to track the vehicles. These methods will have a wide-range of applications ranging from system identification for the many modes of an aircraft, to the problems of modeling biological systems as hybrid systems for the purpose of analysis. These techniques also provide a means of determining the parameters of a system that are required for the efficient design of hybrid estimators, as well as algorithms for multiple-target tracking and identity management [2].

Acknowledgments. The authors would like to thank Rodney Teo for providing the data from the CSPA algorithm verification, as well as for invaluable discussions on the same.

References

1. Y. Bar-Shalom and T.F. Fortmann. *Tracking and Data Association.* Academic Press, 1988.
2. I. Hwang, H. Balakrishnan, K. Roy, and C.J. Tomlin. Multiple-target Tracking and Identity Management in Clutter for Air Traffic Control. Submitted to the American Control Conference, 2004.
3. Y. Bar-Shalom and X.R. Li. *Estimation and Tracking: Principles, Techniques, and Software.* Artech House, Boston, 1993.
4. Y. Li, T. Wang, and H.-Y. Shum. Motion texture: A two-level statistical model for character motion synthesis. In *ACM SIGGRAPH2002*, pages 465–472, 2002.
5. S. Soatto, G. Doretto, and Y.-N. Wu. Dynamic textures. In *Proceedings of the International Conference on Computer Vision*, volume 2, pages 439–446, July 2001.
6. R.H. Shumway and D.S. Stoffer. *Time Series Analysis and Its Applications.* Springer-Verlag, New York, 2000.
7. L. Ljung. *System Identification: Theory for the User.* Prentice-Hall Inc., New Jersey, 1987.
8. B. De Moor and P. Van Overschee. Numerical algorithms for subspace state space system identification. In A. Isidori, editor, *Trends in Control: A European Perspective, The European Control Conference*, pages 385–422, 1995.
9. H.A.P. Blom and Y. Bar-Shalom. The Interacting Multiple Model algorithm for systems with Markovian switching coefficients. *IEEE Transactions on Automatic Control*, 33(8):780–783, 1988.
10. I. Hwang, H. Balakrishnan, and C.J. Tomlin. Observability criteria and estimator design for stochastic linear hybrid systems. In *Proceedings of the European Control Conference*, September 2003.
11. T. Kailath, A.H. Sayed, and B. Hassibi. *Linear Estimation.* Prentice Hall, New Jersey, 2000.
12. R. Vidal, A. Chiuso, and S. Soatto. Observability and identifiability of jump linear systems. In *Proceedings of the 41th IEEE Conference on Decision and Control*, December 2002.
13. A.P. Dempster, N.M. Laird, and D.B. Rubin. Maximum likelihood from incomplete data via the EM algorithm. *Journal of the Royal Statistical Society, Series B*, 39:185–197, 1977.
14. C.F.J. Wu. On the convergence properties of the EM algorithm. *The Annals of Statistics*, 11(1):95–103, 1983.
15. R.H. Shumway and D.S. Stoffer. An approach to time series smoothing and forecasting using the EM algorithm. *Journal of Time Series Analysis*, 3(4):253–264, 1982.

16. A.H. Jazwinski. *Stochastic Processes and Filtering Theory*. Academic Press, New York, 1970.
17. E.J. Hannan and M. Deistler. *The Statistical Theory of Linear Systems*. Wiley Series in Probability and Mathematical Statistics. John Wiley and Sons, 1988.
18. R. Teo and C.J. Tomlin. Computing danger zones for provably safe parallel approaches. *Journal of Guidance, Control and Dynamics*, 26(3):434–442, May-June 2003.

Synthesis for Idle Speed Control of an Automotive Engine[*]

Andrea Balluchi[1], Federico Di Natale[1],
Alberto Sangiovanni-Vincentelli[1,2], and Jan H. van Schuppen[3]

[1] PARADES, Via di S.Pantaleo, 66, 00186 Roma, Italy.
{balluchi,alberto}@parades.rm.cnr.it, http://www.parades.rm.cnr.it
[2] Dept. of EECS, University of California at Berkeley, CA 94720, USA.
alberto@eecs.berkeley.edu, http://www.eecs.berkeley.edu
[3] CWI, P.O. Box 94079, 1090 GB Amsterdam, The Netherlands.
J.H.van.Schuppen@cwi.nl, http://www.cwi.nl/~schuppen

Abstract. The problem of maintaining the crankshaft speed of an automotive engine within a given set interval (*idle speed control*), is formalized as a constrained control problem using a hybrid model of the engine. The control problem is difficult because the system has delays and a large number of constraints. The approach for the synthesis of a controller for this system is based on the theory developed for affine systems on polytopes. A structured control synthesis procedure is applied in which constraints for state and input variables are backward propagated from the controlled output (the crankshaft speed) across successive subsystems.

1 Introduction

In the automotive industry, increased performance, safety and time-to-market pressure require the use of complex control algorithms with guaranteed properties. Best practices in this industry are based on extensive experimentation and tuning of parameters for the control algorithm and for the engine model. This procedure needs a substantial overhaul to eliminate long re-design cycles and potential safety problems after the car is introduced in the market. Using more accurate models and control algorithms with guaranteed properties reduces greatly the need for extensive experimentation and points to potential problems early in the design cycle. In this paper, we investigate this strategy for the idle control problem of a four-cylinder engine.

In particular, we address the problem by proposing

- a hybrid piecewise affine model of a four cylinder in–line engine that represents more faithfully the dynamical behavior of the engine than the traditional *mean-value models*;
- the theory of control of affine systems on polytopes.

---

[*] This research has been partially supported by the E.C. project *Control and Computation* IST-2001-33520.

R. Alur and G.J. Pappas (Eds.): HSCC 2004, LNCS 2993, pp. 80–94, 2004.

The hybrid model for the four–cylinder automotive engine was developed by PARADES in close cooperation with Magneti Marelli Powertrain (see ([1, 2]). The model consists of the series connection of three sub–models: the intake manifold, the cylinders, and the crankshaft.

The difficulty of the problem lies in the load variations coming from the intermittent use of devices powered by the engine, such as the air conditioning system and the steering wheel servo-mechanism, which may cause engine stalls. The reformulation of the hybrid model as a piecewise affine hybrid system allows to derive an efficient synthesis procedure for a controller that satisfies the specifications.

The paper is organized as follows: the model is formulated as a piecewise-affine hybrid system in Section 2. Section 3 contains concepts and results for control of affine systems on polytopes. A control law is formulated for maintaining the crankshaft speed at a set interval even in the presence of disturbances in Section 4.

2   Hybrid Model of the Engine

In this section, to set the stage for our control synthesis strategy, the hybrid model of the engine described in [1] is cast in the framework of piecewise-affine hybrid systems. Piecewise-affine hybrid systems[1] have been proposed in [5,6] and are based on piecewise-linear systems as introduced by E.D. Sontag, see [8].

Definition 1. *A (time-invariant continuous-time) piecewise-affine hybrid system (PAHS) consists of an automaton $(Q, E_{in} \cup E_{cd}, f)$ in combination with a $|Q|$-tuple of affine systems on polytopes parametrized by $q \in Q$ that interact in the following way. At a discrete state $q \in Q$, the continuous state x_q evolves according to the affine dynamical system,*

$$\dot{x}_q(t) = A(q)x_q(t) + B(q)u(t) + a(q), \ x_q(t_0) = x_q^+, \tag{1}$$
$$y(t) = C(q)x_q(t) + D(q)u(t) + c(q), \tag{2}$$

with $x_q \in X_q$ and $u \in U$. The state set X_q for all $q \in Q$, the input set U, and the output set Y are assumed to be polyhedral sets. As soon as a discrete input event $e \in E_{in}$ is applied, or an event generated by the continuous dynamics occurs, $e \in E_{cd}$, because the continuous state has reached the guard $G_q(e) \subseteq \partial X_q$, a discrete transition takes place according to the transition map f and the reset map is applied to the continuous state at the past discrete state to yield the initial condition at the new discrete state:

$$\text{if } x_{q^-}^- = \lim_{s \uparrow t} x_{q^-}(s) \in G_{q^-}(e) \text{ or if } e \in E_{in} \text{ occurs, then}$$

$$q^+ = f(q^-, x_{q^-}, e),$$
$$x_{q^+}^+ = A_r(q^-, e, q^+)x_{q^-}^- + b_r(q^-, e, q^+).$$

---

[1] The class of piecewise-affine hybrid systems has been proven to be equivalent with that of mixed logic-dynamical systems in discrete-time and with linear complementary systems, see [3].

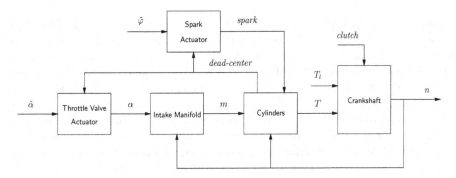

Fig. 1. Engine hybrid model for idle speed control.

At the new discrete state q^+, the evolution of the new continuous state x_{q^+} is described by differential equation (1), with q replaced by q^+, and with initial value $x_{q^+}^+$.

We recall also the notions of invariant, robust invariant, and controlled robust invariant sets that will be used in the rest of the paper.

Definition 2. *A subset of the state set of an autonomous dynamic system is said to be* forward invariant *(or* positively invariant*) if for any initial state in the subset the state trajectory for all future times remains inside the state set. A subset of a dynamic system with input is said to be* controlled forward invariant *if there exists an input function such that the closed-loop system has a forward invariant set.*

A subset of the state set of an autonomous dynamic system is said to be a robust (forward) invariant *subset with respect to a set of disturbance signals if for any initial condition in the subset and for any disturbance signal the resulting state trajectory remains inside the subset. A subset of a dynamic system with input is said to be a* controlled robust (forward) invariant *subset with respect to disturbances if there exists an input function such that the closed-loop system has a robust (forward) invariant subset.*

As shown in Figure 1, the engine hybrid model is composed of three interacting subsystems, namely the *intake manifold*, the *cylinders* and the *crankshaft*, plus the spark and throttle valve actuators. In idle speed control, the output of interest is the crankshaft speed n, whose evolution depends on the engine torque T, the load torque T_l acting on the crankshaft, and the state of the clutch (either open or closed). The engine torque T is a function of the spark ignition timing and the mass m of air-fuel mixture loaded in the cylinder during the intake stroke (the mixture is assumed to be stoichiometric):

$$T = \eta(\varphi)(Gm + T_0) \tag{3}$$

where φ denotes the spark advance[2] and $\eta(\varphi)$ denotes the spark ignition efficiency. The latter is a strictly increasing function defined on the interval of

---

[2] The spark advance is defined as the difference between the angular position of the crankshaft at the end of the compression stroke and its value at ignition time.

feasible spark advances $[-15, 20]$, with $\eta(-15) = 0.6$ and $\eta(20) = 1$. The spark advance is positive if ignition occurs during the compression stroke and negative if it occurs during the expansion stroke. The *spark actuator* models the delay of the spark actuation system. Due to this delay, the engine control has to issue the desired value of spark advance $\tilde{\varphi}$ at the beginning of the compression stroke, for each engine cycle.

The mass m of air-fuel mixture is controlled by the throttle plate position α and is subject to the dynamics of the cylinder filling due to the intake manifold.

The *throttle valve actuator* describes the synchronization of throttle control with the engine cycle. The throttle valve is driven by sequences of commands $\tilde{\alpha}$, with a time separation of 5 msec, and synchronized with dead–center events[3]: each sequence starts with the first command triggered by a dead–center event, the number of commands in the sequences depend on the time between two consecutive dead–center events, i.e. on the crankshaft speed. Throttle valve commands $\tilde{\alpha}$ are nonnegative and bounded from above by 20 degrees.

Due to the necessary synchronization between the engine cycle and throttle valve and spark ignition actuators, the *cylinders* model returns the dead–center event signals to both actuators.

The hybrid model of the engine has 6 discrete states and a 10–dimensional continuous state, i.e.

$$Q = \{S_-, S, S_+, S_-^L, S^L, S_+^L\} \quad \text{and} \quad x = (\alpha, \tau, p, m_C, m_E, \varphi, \varphi_N, T, n, \theta)$$

with: α the throttle valve angular position, τ a timer introduced to generate throttle valve command events, p the intake manifold pressure, m_C the mass of air-fuel mixture in the cylinder currently in compression stroke, m_E the mass of air-fuel mixture in the cylinder currently in expansion stroke, φ the spark advance, φ_N the spark advance in the next expansion, T the engine torque, n the crankshaft speed, and θ the crankshaft angle.

The discrete behavior of the hybrid system, namely the transitions between the discrete states and the reset maps, is represented in Figure 2. Transitions are triggered by

- input events in $E_{in} = \{on, off\}$, modeling opening and closing of the clutch, respectively;
- events generated by the continuous dynamics in $E_{cd} = \{\theta = 180, \theta = 180 - \varphi, \theta = -\varphi, \tau = 5\}$ and modeling, respectively, the reaching of a dead–center, the actuation of a positive spark advance, the actuation of a negative spark advance, and the reading of a throttle valve command.

Variables $\alpha, m_C, m_E, \varphi, \varphi_N, T$ evolve as piecewise constant signals (i.e. according to the dynamic $\dot{x} = 0$) and are updated by the reset maps defined in Figure 2. Note that variables m_E and φ_N are used only to model negative spark advance.

---

[3] In 4–stroke 4–cylinder in–line engines, at any time each cylinder is in a different stroke (intake, compression, expansion, exhaust). Stroke transitions, occurring when pistons reach either a top or a bottom dead–center, are synchronous.

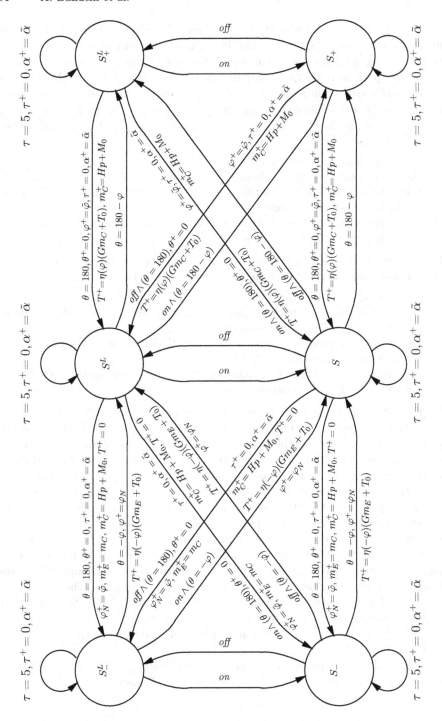

Fig. 2. Model of the discrete behavior of the engine.

Consider first the discrete states S, S_+ and S_-, corresponding to the clutch in open state. In state S, the cylinder in expansion is generating torque, and the cylinder in compression has not received the spark command yet.

If the spark advance φ is positive then, when $\theta = 180 - \varphi$ the spark is ignited and a transition to S_+ takes place. In state S_+ the spark command has been given for the cylinder in compression, while the cylinder in expansion is generating torque. At the next dead-center, i.e. when $\theta = 180$, a transition from S_+ to S occurs:

- the crankshaft angle θ is reset;
- the desired value of spark advance φ for the next cylinder is received;
- the value of the engine torque T produced by the cylinder entering the expansion stroke is computed $(T^+ = \eta(\varphi)(Gm_C + T_0))$;
- the mass of mixture m_C loaded by the cylinder at the end of the intake stroke is determined $(m_C^+ = Hp + M_0)$.

From state S, if a negative spark advance φ is applied then, when the next dead–center event is generated (i.e. $\theta = 180$), a transition to S_- takes place:

- the crankshaft angle θ is reset;
- the desired value of spark advance φ_N for the next cycle (related to the cylinder currently in compression stroke) is received;
- the mass of mixture m_C loaded by the cylinder at the end of the intake stroke is determined $(m_C^+ = Hp + M_0)$;
- the engine torque T is reset, since spark has not been ignited yet for the cylinder currently in expansion stroke.

In phase S_-, the cylinder in expansion is waiting for the spark command and the cylinder in compression has not received the spark command yet. No torque is generated in this case. When the specified value φ of negative spark advance is reached, spark ignition occurs with the transition from S_- to S and the corresponding value of engine torque is produced $(T^+ = \eta(-\varphi)(Gm_E + T_0))$.

A timer τ, assuming values in the interval $[0, 5]$, is introduced to model the higher frequency of throttle valve commands. In all transitions produced by the dead–center event $\theta = 180$, the timer is reset and the first value of a new sequence of commands is received from the input $\tilde{\alpha}$. Then, the timer τ evolves with dynamic $\dot{\tau} = 1000$. The self–loop transitions in Figure 2 detect when τ reaches the value 5. When they are activated, 5 msec have been elapsed from the last timer reset and a new throttle valve command is read from the input $\tilde{\alpha}$.

The behavior of the system for the discrete states S_-^L, S^L, S_+^L, related to clutch closed, is analogous. Transitions between states S_-, S, S_+ and states S_-^L, S^L, S_+^L are due to clutch switching, which are modeled by the input events in $E_{in} = \{on, off\}$.

The model is completed by the continuous dynamics of the p, n and θ. The dynamic of the manifold pressure p is identical in all discrete states:

$$\dot{p}(t) = a_p(p(t) - p_0) + b_p(\alpha(t) - \alpha_0) , \qquad (4)$$

where p_0, α_0 is the equilibrium point around which the linear model has been obtained.

The dynamic of the crankshaft depends on the clutch state:

$$\dot{n}(t) = \begin{cases} a_n n(t) + b_n [T(t) - T_p - T_l(t)] & \text{if } q \in \{S_-, S, S_+\} \\ a_n^L n(t) + b_n^L [T(t) - T_p - T_l(t)] & \text{if } q \in \{S_-^L, S^L, S_+^L\} \end{cases} \qquad (5)$$

$$\dot{\theta}(t) = 6n(t) \qquad (6)$$

where T_p is a constant term modeling pumping work and friction, $T_l(t) \in [0, T^M]$ is a bounded disturbance modeling variable friction and the action of subsystems powered by the crankshaft, n is in rpm and θ is in degrees.

Finally, since all the continuous state variables are nonnegative and bounded from above, then in each discrete state q the continuous input $(\tilde{\varphi}, \tilde{\alpha})$, state x and output $y = n$ evolve in polyhedral sets U, X_q, Y, respectively. However, the boundaries of X_q that can be reached, causing an internal event which trigger a discrete state transition, are only those defined by $\theta = 180$, for $q \in \{S, S_+, S^L, S_+^L\}$, $\theta = 180 - \varphi$, for $q \in \{S, S^L\}$, $\theta = -\varphi$, for $q \in \{S_-, S_-^L\}$, and $\tau = 5$ in any $q \in Q$.

3   Control Synthesis for Affine Systems on Polytopes

Our approach to synthesis for idle speed control is based on concepts and theorems derived for affine systems on polytopes. An important role is played by the so called *control-to-facet* problem. The problem is to guide the closed–loop trajectory of the system from a given point to a particular facet without first crossing or touching any other facet of the polytope. Necessary and sufficient conditions for the existence of a control law that solve the control-to-facet problem exist [5,7]. We report below some extensions of these results to the case of discrete-time affine systems on simplices.

Problem 1. Consider a discrete-time affine system on a simplex,

$$x(t+1) = Ax(t) + Bu(t) + a, \qquad x(t_0) = x_0$$
$$X_1 = \text{convh}(\{v_1, \ldots, v_{n+1}\})$$

with $A \in \mathbb{R}^{n \times n}$, $B \in \mathbb{R}^{n \times m}$, $a \in \mathbb{R}^n$, and a polytope

$$X_2 = \text{convh}(\{w_1, \ldots, w_m\}) = \{x \in \mathbb{R}^n | n_j^T x \le k_j, \ \forall j \in \{1, 2, \ldots, m\}\}$$

with $m \ge n+1$, normal $n_j \in \mathbb{R}^n$ pointing out of the polytope, and w_j opposite vertex of normal $n_j \in \mathbb{R}^n$. Determine a control law $g : X_1 \to U$ such that the closed-loop system,

$$x(t+1) = Ax(t) + Bg(x(t)) + a, \ x(t_0) = x_0,$$

is such that for all $t \in T$, $x(t) \in X_1$ implies that $x(t+1) \in X_2$.

A special case of the above problem is that with $X_2 = X_1$, and then the closed-loop system leaves the set X_1 invariant or X_1 is a controlled invariant set.

Proposition 1. *Assume that the polytope X_2 is a simplex, i.e. $m = n + 1$. If there exist vectors $u_1, \ldots, u_{n+1} \in U = \mathbb{R}^m$ such that*

$$n_j^T (Aw_i + Bu_i + a) \leq k_j, \quad \forall i, j \in \{1, 2, \ldots, n + 1\}, \tag{7}$$

then the matrix $\begin{pmatrix} w_1^T & 1 \\ \vdots & \vdots \\ w_{n+1}^T & 1 \end{pmatrix}$ *is invertible and the affine control law $g(x) = Fx + h$,*

$$\text{with} \quad \begin{pmatrix} F^T \\ h^T \end{pmatrix} = \begin{pmatrix} w_1^T & 1 \\ \vdots & \vdots \\ w_{n+1}^T & 1 \end{pmatrix}^{-1} \begin{pmatrix} u_1^T \\ \vdots \\ u_{n+1}^T \end{pmatrix} \in \mathbb{R}^{(n+1) \times m}, \tag{8}$$

solves Problem 1.

Proof. Since X_2 is a simplex, then the matrix with parameters w_j in (8) is invertible, see [7] for a proof. Note that, by (8), for all $j \in \{1, 2, \ldots, n + 1\}$, $Fw_j + h = u_j$. The closed-loop system is,

$$x(t + 1) = Ax(t) + Bu(t) + a = (A + BF)x(t) + (a + Bh).$$

Because X_2 is a simplex,

$$\exists c \in \mathbb{R}_+^{n+1}, \ \sum_{i=1}^{n+1} c_i = 1, \text{ such that, } x \in X_2 \Rightarrow x = \sum_{i=1}^{n+1} c_i w_i.$$

$$u(t) = Fx(t) + h = \sum_{i=1}^{n+1} c_i (Fw_i + h) = \sum_{i=1}^{n+1} c_i u_i.$$

$$n_j^T x(k + 1) = n_j^T [Ax(t) + Bu(t) + a]$$

$$= \sum_{i=1}^{n+1} c_i n_j^T (Aw_i + Bu_i + a) \leq \sum c_i k_j = k_j, \ \forall j \in \{1, 2, \ldots, n + 1\}$$

$$\Rightarrow x(t + 1) \in X_2.$$

Note that if $X_2 = X_1 = X$, then X is a forward invariant $=$ subset. If $X_2 \subset X_1$ then $x(t + 1) \in X_2 \subset X_1$, hence $x(t + 2) \in X_2 \subset X_1$ and X_2 is forward invariant.

Proposition 2. *Problem 1 admits a solution for polytope X_2 not a simplex, if there exists a feasible solution for F and h to the problem*

$$n_j^T (Av_i + B(Fv_i + h) + a) \leq k_j, \ \forall j \in \{1, 2, \ldots, m\}, \ \forall i \in \{1, 2, \ldots, n + 1\}.$$

A technique for computing feedback parameters F and h, based on a partitioning of the set X_1 is presented in [7].

4   Control Synthesis for Idle Speed Control

In this section, we use a structured synthesis method analogous to back–stepping to synthesize a hybrid idle speed control algorithm. In general, the idle speed control problem can be formalized as follows:

Problem 2. Given a set point for the crankshaft speed $n^0 \in (0, \infty)$ and an interval $I_n \subset (0, \infty)$, such that n^0 belongs to the interior of I_n, determine a control law such that the closed-loop system satisfies the following control objectives:

(1) *Bounding the crankshaft speed.* There exists a non trivial robust invariant set $X_{ri} \subseteq \{x \in X | n \in I_n\}$. Thus, if $x_0 \in X_{ri}$ then, for any disturbance signals, $x(t) \in X_{ri}$ and $n(t) \in I_n$ for all $t \geq 0$.
(2) *Asymptotic stability.* In the absence of disturbances, $\lim_{t \to \infty} n(t) = n^0$.
(3) *Attraction.* For any disturbance signals, $\lim_{t \to \infty} x(t) \in X_{ri}$.
(4) *Rejection of disturbances.* For stepwise disturbances, $\lim_{t \to \infty} n(t) = n^0$.

We focus on the control objective (1) formulated above, with $I_n = [750, 850]$ rpm. The problem is difficult because the dynamic system for the crankshaft speed is a system with delays, where the duration of the delays depends on the full dynamics. Our approach to controller synthesis makes use of the structure of the dynamic system. The system consists of a series connection of
    1. the intake manifold system,
    2. the cylinder system, and
    3. the crankshaft system.
First, we synthesize a control law for the torque, which is the input to the crankshaft system. Then, proceeding backward in the system, we produce a control law for the cylinder system with as input the gas mixture and the spark advance angle such that the control objectives are met for the torque. Finally, we devise a control law for the throttle valve, which is the input to the intake manifold system.

Step 1 - Controller synthesis for the crankshaft system. By specification the crankshaft speed n is bounded between 750 rpm and 850 rpm. Furthermore, for idle speed control it is reasonable to bound the engine torque to the range $[0, 30]$ Nm. Then, consider an extended model of the crankshaft with state variables (n, θ, T), defined on the multi-variable box

$$B^c = \{(n, \theta, T) | n \in [750, 850], \theta \in [0, 180], T \in [0, 30]\}$$
$$= [750, 850] \times [0, 180] \times [0, 30] .$$

Let F^o and F^e be the facets of B^c lying on the subspaces $\theta = 0$ and $\theta = 180$, respectively, i.e.

$$F^o = [750, 850] \times \{0\} \times [0, 30] \text{ and } F^e = [750, 850] \times \{180\} \times [0, 30] .$$

Consider the *control-to-facet* problem of determining a subset of B^c such that F^e is the unique exit facet. Since θ monotonically increases in B^c, this problem can be stated as follows:

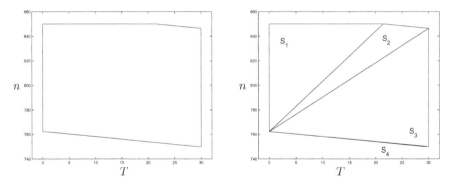

Fig. 3. Set S^c (on the left) and its partition $S_1 \cup S_2 \cup S_3 \cup S_4$ (on the right).

Problem 3. Find a subset $S^c \subset [750, 850] \times [0, 30]$ such that, under any action of the disturbances *clutch* $\in \{on, off\}$ and $T_l(t) \in [0, T^M]$, all trajectories starting from $(n(0), \theta(0), T(0)) = (n_0, 0, T_0) \in F^o$, with $(n_0, T_0) \in S^c$, reach in finite time the exit facet F^e and $(n(t), \theta(t), T(t)) \in B^c$, until F^e has been reached.

Note that the time required to reach the target set F^e depends on the evolution of the crankshaft angle θ, which is affected by both the engine torque $T(t)$ and the disturbances *clutch* and $T_l(t)$. A polyhedral set S^c for which the following proposition holds has been computed:

Proposition 3. *If the initial state (n_0, θ_0, T_0) of crankshaft system satisfies $\theta_0 = 0$ and $(n_0, T_0) \in S^c$, with S^c as in Figure 3, then F^e is the unique exit facet from B^c. Furthermore, the worst torque disturbance $T_l(t)$ is constant and equal either to 0 or T^M and the worst clutch signal is clutch constant and open.*

Let t_k denote the sequence of times at which dead–center events are produced. From the above proposition it follows that

Corollary 1. *If the engine torque is controlled in such a way that*

$$(n^+(t_k), T^+(t_k)) \in S^c, \quad \forall k \in \mathbb{Z}_+^0 \tag{9}$$

then $(n(t), \theta(t), T(t)) \in B^c$ for all $t \geq t_0$ and the control objective (1) of Problem 2 is met.

To ensure that condition (9) is verified at each dead–center, the crankshaft system is represented by a discretized model that expresses the evolution of the system at dead–center times. The discretized model is obtained by assuming that the engine torque T and the disturbance torque T_l are constant between dead–center times. While assuming T_l constant between dead–center times is justified by Proposition 3, this assumption is actually not verified for T in the case of negative spark advance. In fact, according to the engine hybrid model, the expansion stroke starts in the state S_- (or S_-^L) associated to a zero engine torque and proceeds in the state S (or S^L) with the generation of a constant engine torque. However, since assuming T constant greatly simplify the developments, then this assumption will be kept for the moment and the particular behavior in case of negative spark advance will be handled in Step 2 below. To model the compression delay, we introduce a virtual input $u(k)$ corresponding to the next value of the engine torque. The discretized crankshaft model is

$$n(k+1) = a_d(k)n(k) + b_d(k)(T(k) - T_p - T_l(k)) \tag{10}$$
$$T(k+1) = u(k) \tag{11}$$

where $n(k) = n^+(t_k)$, $T(k) = T^+(t_k)$, and $T_l(k) \in \{0, T^M\}$ models the worst torque disturbance. Model (10-11) is time–varying since its parameters

$$a_d(k) = e^{a_n(t_{k+1}-t_k)} \quad \text{and} \quad b_d(k) = -[1 - e^{a_n(t_{k+1}-t_k)}]b_n/a_n \tag{12}$$

depend on the dead–center time interval length $t_{k+1} - t_k$, which is assumed unknown. However, since the crankshaft speed is bounded by specification, then

$$\frac{30}{850} = \frac{30}{\max n(t)} = t_{min} \le t_{k+1} - t_k \le t_{max} = \frac{30}{\min n(t)} = \frac{30}{750}, \tag{13}$$

and parameters $a_d(k), b_d(k)$ are bounded as follows

$$e^{a_n t_{max}} = \underline{a}_d \le a_d(k) \le \bar{a}_d = e^{a_n t_{min}} \tag{14}$$
$$-[1 - e^{a_n t_{min}}]b_n/a_n = \underline{b}_d \le b_d(k) \le \bar{b}_d = -[1 - e^{a_n t_{max}}]b_n/a_n . \tag{15}$$

Then, condition (9) of Corollary 1 is verified once the following problem is solved:

Problem 4. Find a feedback $u(k) = g(n(k), T(k))$ and a set $X \subseteq S^c$ such that

(1) X is a robust invariant set for the crankshaft discretized model (10–11), with time–varying parameters (12) bounded as in (14–15), under feedback $u(k) = g(n(k), T(k))$ and for any action of the disturbances $clutch \in \{on, off\}$ and $T_l(t) \in [0, T^M]$;
(2) the feedback $g(n(k), T(k))$ can be implemented by the cylinder model using appropriate values of spark advance φ and mass of gas mixture m.

The design of a feasible feedback $u(k) = g(n(k), T(k))$ and its implementation will be addressed in the next step.

Step 2 - Controller synthesis for the cylinder system. In general, it is not easy to determine a non trivial controlled robust invariant subset X contained in some polyhedral set S^c as specified in point (1) of Problem 4. Therefore an indirect method will be used:

1. Partition the polytope S^c into a finite number of simplices, denoted by $\Pi = \{S_1, \ldots, S_N\}$. This procedure is called *triangulation* (see [7]).
2. Select a subset of these simplices $\Pi^I = \{S_{\ell_1}, \ldots, S_{\ell_M}\} \subseteq \Pi$, which defines a candidate set $X = \cup_{S_p \in \Pi^I} S_p$ on which robust controlled invariance will be tested.

3. Split the set of simplices Π^I into Π^I_1 and Π^I_2, with $\Pi^I_1 \cup \Pi^I_2 = \Pi^I$ and $\Pi^I_1 \cap \Pi^I_2 = \emptyset$, and determine for each simplex $S_p \in \Pi^I$ whether there exists an affine control law $g_p(x) = F_p x + h_p$ such that the closed-loop system maps robustly in one step S_p to a subset of $\cup_{S_p \in \Pi^I_2} S_p$.

4. If it fails, either choose a different partition Π^I_1, Π^I_2, or a different subset of simplices Π^I, or change[4] the triangulation of S^c.

The set S^c has been partitioned in the subsets $\Pi = \{S_1, S_2, S_3, S_4\}$, represented in Fig. 3. Furthermore, robust controlled invariance has been enforced on $\Pi^I = \{S_1, S_2, S_3\}$, by choosing $\Pi^I_1 = \{S_1\}$ and $\Pi^I_2 = \{S_2, S_3\}$, so that the robust controlled invariant set $X = S_1 \cup S_2 \cup S_3$ has been determined.

By a result of Benvenuti and Farina (see [4]), due to the boundness (14–15) of the time–varying parameters $a_d(k), b_d(k)$ and the linearity of (12) with respect to the term $e^{a_p(t_{k+1}-t_k)}$, the closed–loop system, obtained by (10-11) and an piecewise affine feedback $g_p(\cdot)$, maps robustly each $S_p \in \Pi^I$ inside $\cup_{S_p \in \Pi^I_2} S_p$ if this is verified for the two systems obtained by replacing $a_d(k), b_d(k)$ with $\underline{a}_d, \overline{b}_d$ and $\overline{a}_d, \underline{b}_d$. For each simplex S_p in $\Pi^I = \{S_1, S_2, S_3\}$, the parameters F_p and h_p of the affine control law

$$g_p(n(k), T(k)) = F_p \begin{bmatrix} n(k) \\ T(k) \end{bmatrix} + h_p \tag{16}$$

are obtained from Proposition 2, where:

- v_i define the simplex $S_p = X_1 = \mathrm{convh}(\{v_1, v_2, v_3\})$
- n_j, k_j define the target polyhedron

$$X_2 = S_2 \cup S_3 = \{x \in \mathbb{R}^2 | n_j^T x \le k_j, \; \forall j \in \{1, \dots, 4\}\}$$

- A, B and a model the dynamics corresponding to the extreme values of the uncertain parameters and the worst case actions of disturbances

$$A = \begin{bmatrix} A' \\ A' \\ A'^L \\ A'^L \end{bmatrix}, \quad B = \begin{bmatrix} B' \\ B' \\ B' \\ B' \end{bmatrix}, \quad a = \begin{bmatrix} -a'T_p \\ -a'(T_p + T^M) \\ -a'^L T_p \\ -a'^L (T_p + T^M) \end{bmatrix},$$

$$A' = \begin{bmatrix} 0 & 0 \\ \underline{a}_d & \overline{b}_d \\ 0 & 0 \\ \overline{a}_d & \underline{b}_d \end{bmatrix}, \quad A'^L = \begin{bmatrix} 0 & 0 \\ \underline{a}_d^L & \overline{b}_d^L \\ 0 & 0 \\ \overline{a}_d^L & \underline{b}_d^L \end{bmatrix}, \quad B' = \begin{bmatrix} 0 \\ 1 \\ 0 \\ 1 \end{bmatrix}, \quad a' = \begin{bmatrix} 0 \\ \overline{b}_d \\ 0 \\ \underline{b}_d \end{bmatrix} \quad a'^L = \begin{bmatrix} 0 \\ \overline{b}_d^L \\ 0 \\ \underline{b}_d^L \end{bmatrix}$$

where $\underline{a}_d^L, \overline{a}_d^L, \underline{b}_d^L, \overline{b}_d^L$ are defined as in (14–15), with the closed clutch parameters a_n^L, b_n^L in place of the open clutch parameters a_n, b_n.

The envelopes P_1, P_2, P_3 of the one–step ahead projections of simplices S_1, S_2 and S_3, under the proposed piecewise affine feedbacks (16) and considering parameter uncertainties and disturbances, are represented in Figure 4.

---

[4] A methodology for defining triangulations of S^c suitable for robust controlled invariant set computation is currently under investigation.

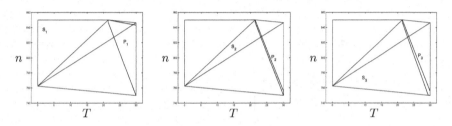

Fig. 4. Envelopes P_1, P_2, P_3 of one–step ahead projections of simplices S_1, S_2, S_3.

The cylinder system has to produce engine torques that implement feedbacks (16), using appropriate values of spark advance φ and mass of gas mixture m. Since the spark ignition efficiency $\eta(\varphi)$ is bounded between 0.6 and 1, then to guarantee feasibility (see point (2) of Problem 4), the amount of mass m loaded during intake has to satisfy

$$0.6(Gm + T_0) \leq g_p(n, T) \leq (Gm + T_0) \qquad \forall (n, T) \in S_1 \cup S_2 \cup S_3 . \quad (17)$$

Then, the mass of mixture is controlled to the interval $[m_{min}, m_{max}]$, with

$$m_{min} = \frac{1}{G}\left[\left(\max_{v_i \in S_1, S_2, S_3} F_p v_i + h_p\right) - T_0\right], \qquad m_{max} = \frac{1}{0.6}m_{min} . \quad (18)$$

Feedbacks (16) are implemented by a modulation of the spark advance efficiency computed at the dead–center time t_k as follows

$$\tilde{\varphi} = \begin{cases} \phi_1 & \text{if } \phi_1 \geq 0 \\ \phi_2 & \text{if } \phi_1 < 0 \end{cases}$$

with ϕ_1 and ϕ_2 obtained for $[n(t_k), T(t_k)]^T \in S_p$ from the following expressions[5]

$$\phi_1 = \eta^{-1}\left(\frac{F_p[n(t_k) \quad T(t_k)]^T + h_p}{Gm_C(t_k) + T_0}\right) \quad (19)$$

$$\eta(\phi_2)(Gm_C(t_k) + T_0) = \frac{1 - e^{an\frac{30}{n(t_k)}}}{1 - e^{an\left[\frac{30}{n(t_k)}\left(1 - \frac{\phi_2}{180}\right)\right]}}\left[F_p\left(\frac{n(t_k)}{T(t_k)}\right) + h_p\right] . \quad (20)$$

Step 3 - Controller synthesis for the intake manifold system. From the target interval for the mass of mixture (18), the corresponding interval $[p_{min}, p_{max}]$, with

$$p_{min} = \frac{m_{min} - M_0}{H} \quad \text{and} \quad p_{max} = \frac{m_{max} - M_0}{H},$$

for the intake manifold pressure is derived. An intake manifold controller that keeps the value of the intake manifold pressure inside the interval $[p_{min}, p_{max}]$

---

[5] The fraction on the right–hand side of (20) takes into account that, for negative spark advance, the engine torque is produced only in the second part of the expansion stroke, its value is then appropriately increased to achieve the same result on $n(t_{k+1})$.

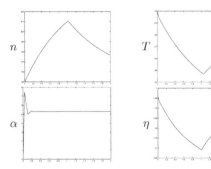

Fig. 5. Simulation results with a torque load T_l acting at time $t = 1\,\mathrm{sec}$.

at each dead center is designed using the control-to-facet approach. The intake manifold controller is an affine feedback

$$\alpha(k) = f_1 p(k) + h_1 \tag{21}$$

obtained by applying the results of Proposition 2 with

- $X_1 = \mathrm{convh}(\{v_1, v_2\})$, with $v_1 = p_{min}$ and $v_2 = p_{max}$
- $X_1 = X_2$, with $n_1 = -n_2 = 1$, $k_1 = p_{max}$ and $k_2 = -p_{min}$
- dynamic parameters

$$A = \begin{bmatrix} \underline{a}_p \\ \overline{a}_p \end{bmatrix}, \quad B = \begin{bmatrix} \overline{b}_p \\ \underline{b}_p \end{bmatrix}, \quad a = \begin{bmatrix} (1 - \underline{a}_p)p_0 - \overline{b}_p \alpha_0 \\ (1 - \overline{a}_p)p_0 - \underline{b}_p \alpha_0 \end{bmatrix}, \qquad \text{with}$$

$$\underline{a}_p = e^{a_p t_{max}}, \overline{a}_p = e^{a_p t_{min}}, \underline{b}_p = [e^{a_p t_{min}} - 1]\frac{b_p}{a_p}, \overline{b}_p = [e^{a_p t_{max}} - 1]\frac{b_p}{a_p}.$$

The implementation of the intake manifold controller (21) exploits the fact that the throttle valve is actuated with a frequency higher than the dead–center event frequency. In fact, the throttle valve is driven by sequences of commands, with a time separation of 5 msec, and synchronized with dead–center events. Since $t_{min} = \frac{30}{850} > 30\,\mathrm{msec}$ and $t_{max} = \frac{30}{750} = 40\,\mathrm{msec}$, then for each intake stroke a sequence of 8 commands is applied.

The sequence of throttle valve commands for the k–th intake stroke, lasting from time t_k to time t_{k+1}, is obtained as follows:

- the first command at time t_k, synchronized with the dead–center event at the beginning of the intake stroke, is given by (21) with $p(k) = p(t_k)$;
- the following 7 commands, given at times $t_h = t_k + \ell 5\,\mathrm{msec}$, with $\ell = 1 : 7$, are computed with a feedback of the most recent value of intake manifold pressure measurement $p(t_h)$, on the basis of the updated information on the time to the $(k+1)$-th dead–center:

$$\alpha(t_h) = \frac{\overline{p}(k+1) - e^{a_p \tau} p(t_h) + (1 - e^{a_p \tau})p_0 + [1 - e^{a_p \tau}]b_p/a_p\,\alpha_0}{-[1 - e^{a_p \tau}]b_p/a_p}$$

with $\tau = \frac{30}{n(t_h)} \left(1 - \frac{\theta}{180}\right)$ the estimated time to the end of the intake stroke and

$$\bar{p}(k+1) = e^{a_p \frac{30}{n(t_k)}} p(t_k) - \left[1 - e^{a_p \frac{30}{n(t_k)}}\right] \frac{b_p}{a_p} \left(f_1 p(t_k) + h_1\right) \qquad (22)$$

the target intake manifold pressure value given by feedback (21).

Some simulation results of the proposed controller are reported in Figure 5.

5 Concluding Remarks

We presented a control synthesis procedure for idle speed control. The procedure is based on the formulation of the problem as an affine hybrid system control problem on polytopes. The control synthesis uses a novel combination of the back–stepping procedure, control for affine systems on polytopes, the theory of controlled invariant sets, and interactive control design. In the proposed approach, input and state constraints are handled by partitioning the continuous–state space in polytopes and designing feedback laws for each polytope such that, in the evolution of the controlled system, the continuous state is driven only on those polytopes for which the constraints are verified.

References

1. A. Balluchi, L. Benvenuti, M. D. Di Benedetto, C. Pinello, and A. L. Sangiovanni-Vincentelli. Automotive engine control and hybrid systems: challenges and opportunities. *Proceedings of the IEEE*, 88:888–912, 2000.
2. A. Balluchi, L. Benvenuti, M. D. Di Benedetto, and A. L. Sangiovanni-Vincentelli. *Nonlinear and Hybrid Systems in Automotive Control*, ch. Idle speed control synthesis using an assume–guarantee approach. pp. 229–243. London, UK: Springer-Verlag, 2002.
3. A. Bemporad and M. Morari. Control of systems integrating logic, dynamics, and constraints. *Automatica*, 35:407–427, 1999.
4. L. Benvenuti and L. Farina. Constrained control for uncertain discrete-time linear systems. *International Journal on Robust and Nonlinear Control*, 8:555-565, 1998.
5. L.C.G.J.M. Habets and J.H. van Schuppen. Control of piecewise-linear hybrid system on simplices and rectangles. In M.D. Di Benedetto and A. Sangiovanni-Vincentelli, editors, *Hybrid Systems; Computation and Control, 4th Int. Workshop, Rome, Italy, March 2001*, pages 261–274, Berlin, 2001. Springer.
6. Luc C.G.J.M. Habets and Jan H. van Schuppen. A controllability result for piecewise-linear hybrid systems. In *Proceedings of European Control Conference (ECC2001)*, pages 3870–3873, Porto, 2001.
7. L.C.G.J.M. Habets and J.H. van Schuppen. A control problem for affine dynamical systems on a full-dimensional polytope. *Automatica*, 40:21–35, 2004.
8. E.D. Sontag. Nonlinear regulation: the piecewise linear approach. *IEEE Trans. Automatic Control*, 26:346–358, 1981.
9. G.M. Ziegler. *Lectures on polytopes*. Number 152 in Graduate Texts in Mathematics. Springer, Berlin, 1995.

Network Congestion Alleviation Using Adjoint Hybrid Control: Application to Highways*

Alexandre M. Bayen**, Robin L. Raffard, and Claire J. Tomlin

Hybrid Systems Laboratory, Department of Aeronautics and Astronautics
Stanford University, Stanford, CA 94305-4035
{bayen,rraffard,tomlin}@stanford.edu

Abstract. This paper derives an optimization-based control methodology for networks of switched and hybrid systems in which each mode is governed by a *partial differential equation* (PDE). We pose the continuous controller synthesis problem as an optimization program with PDEs in the constraints. The proposed algorithm relies on an explicit formulation of the gradient of the cost function, obtained via the adjoint of the PDE operator. First, we show how to use the result of the optimization to synthesize on/off control strategies. Then, we generalize the method to optimal switching control of hybrid systems over PDEs: the system is allowed to switch from one mode (or PDE) to another at times which we synthesize to minimize a given cost. We derive an explicit expression of the gradient of the cost with respect to the switching times. We implement our techniques on a highway congestion control problem using *Performance Measurement System* (PeMS) data for the California I210 for a 9 mile long strip with 26 on-ramps (controllable with red/green metering lights) and off-ramps (uncontrollable).

1 Introduction

Physical systems governed by *partial differential equations* (PDEs) abound in science and engineering: fluid mechanics, biology, control of processes, and integrated circuits are four examples. Within the realm of PDE driven systems, we are interested in the class of systems governed by one dimensional networked PDEs; this class includes highway networks [6], the air traffic control system [15], and irrigation networks [14]. One common feature of these networked PDE systems is that the governing PDE for each portion of the network is linked to neighboring PDEs through boundary conditions. However, the actuation available to control these systems depends on the problem: for irrigation channels, one controls the boundary conditions (water inflow), using dams; in air traffic control, the control is the velocity field prescribed by air traffic controllers. For the

---

* Research supported by NASA under Grant NCC 2-5422, by ONR under MURI contract N00014-02-1-0720, by DARPA under the Software Enabled Control Program (AFRL contract F33615-99-C-3014), and by a Graduate Fellowship of the Délégation Générale pour l'Armement (France).
** Corresponding author

R. Alur and G.J. Pappas (Eds.): HSCC 2004, LNCS 2993, pp. 95–110, 2004.
© Springer-Verlag Berlin Heidelberg 2004

present case, in which we are interested in controlling congestion on the highway, a standard actuation scheme consists of controlling boundary conditions with *metering lights* which delay the entrance of cars onto the highway [16]. An alternate control scheme [9] uses time varying speed limits which prevent the creation of traffic jams in congested areas.

Numerous approaches which attempt to control highway systems rely on the well-known *Lighthill-Whitham-Richards* (LWR) model [13,17], which describes the evolution of the car density on the highway using a PDE. This PDE relates the time derivative of the car density to the space derivative of the *flux function*, where the flux function is an empirically determined function which relates the number of cars traveling through a given section of the highway per unit of time to the local car density. To our best knowledge, no approach has ever tackled the problem of controlling the LWR PDE directly. Rather, most of the research focuses on controlling the discretized LWR PDE [6,16] using classical optimal control techniques for discrete time dynamical systems; the technique is easier, but the underlying discrete time dynamical system sometimes exhibits discrepancies from the original continuous model [13,17].

Recent mathematical results have enabled the characterization of the entropy solution [8] as the correct weak solution of the LWR PDE for non-convex flux functions [1]. Modern numerical analysis techniques have enabled accurate computations of this solution [11]. Finally, recent development of adjoint-based techniques have enabled the control of nonlinear first order PDEs [10,3].

A mathematical difficulty appears naturally in the treatment of the highway control mentioned above: it is by its nature a hybrid problem. The metering lights are a set of on/off systems, which one tries to regulate. Determining the on/off sequences of actuators for distributed systems is a difficult task in general. For the alternate control scheme, realistic time dependent speed limits require the system to switch between modes in which the maximum allowable speed is one of three possible values (typically 45mph, 55mph and 65mph). As will be seen, in each of the modes (45, 55 or 65), the governing equation of the system is a different PDE. Other approaches [16] have also characterized the highway system as hybrid by nature and modeled different modes of the highway (congested mode, free flow mode, etc.), each of them governed by a discrete time dynamical system. These approaches make the problem easier to control. However, we are interested in deriving control based on the continuous PDE directly, before performing any discretization. This paper contains contributions pertinent to several different aspects of the problem.

1. Concerning the model and the numerical simulations, this work is to the best of our knowledge the first to attack the problem of accurate simulations of the continuous LWR PDE. We demonstrate the efficiency of numerical schemes against analytically constructed entropy solutions [1,8]. In particular, we show excellent performance of the *Jameson-Schmidt-Turkel* (JST) [11] and the *Daganzo* [6] schemes, which are both nonlinear. An important advantage of the JST scheme is that it works for any flux function as well as for the adjoint problem, which we will demonstrate here. We also show that linear

numerical schemes such as Lax-Friedrichs, by contrast, exhibit extremely poor performance, which raises questions about the use of these schemes.

2. We construct an adjoint based method to solve an optimization program formulation of the control problem, which is applicable to highway networks. We have already applied this approach successfully to air traffic control [2], here we show how to apply this method to on/off systems.

3. We generalize the notion of optimal control to hybrid systems for which the modes are governed by PDEs. We show how to compute gradients with respect to the switching times between the different PDEs.

4. We apply our results to actual highway data obtained from the *Performance Measurement System* (PeMS) [12] database to I210 in Los Angeles. We successfully control a highway portion containing 26 on- and off-ramps.

This paper is organized as follows. In Section 2, we derive the network model and validate the computational tools we will use against an analytically derived entropy solution of the LWR PDE. In Section 3, we set up the optimal control problem as an optimization program with PDE constraints, and derive an explicit expression of the gradient through the adjoint problem (Formula 1). We embed this result into a gradient descent algorithm to solve the optimization problem. We explain how to use the result to synthesize on/off switching sequences and apply it to the I210 example. In Section 4, we generalize these results and compute a gradient with respect to the switching times (Formula 2).

2 Eulerian Highway Network Model

2.1 PDE Model

We consider a network of N connected highway segments, indexed by i. The density of cars on link i is denoted ρ_i. We call L_i the length of link i, and $x_i \in [0, L_i]$ the coordinate on this link. Several models exist for describing the evolution of car density on the highway. We use the *Lighthill-Whitham-Richards* (LWR) model in the present study. In this model, the density obeys the LWR *partial differential equation* (PDE):

$$\mathcal{N}_i(\rho_i) \triangleq \frac{\partial \rho_i}{\partial t} + \frac{\partial q_i(\rho_i)}{\partial x_i} = 0 \qquad (1)$$

in which $q_i(\cdot)$ represents a flux function relating the flux of cars (number of cars through a given section of the highway during a time unit) to the car density at that location. This equation expresses that the local rate of change of car density is equal to the space derivative of the flux of cars, i.e. conservation of mass. $q_i(\cdot)$ is identified empirically from highway data. Several models have been proposed for $q_i(\cdot)$, such as the Greenshield model [1], trapezoidal or triangular models [6, 16]. As will be seen in the next section, the computational method that we use can handle any $q_i(\cdot)$.

The links can merge and can diverge, have on- and off-ramps. In the context of the present work, we will be interested in a highway portion connecting two

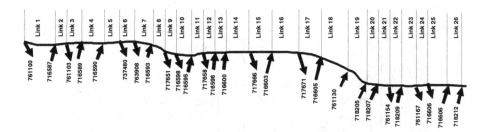

Fig. 1. Example of interest for this study: portion of highway I210 East between I5 and I605 in Pasadena, decomposed into 26 links. Each of the arrows denotes an on- or off-ramp. The numbers refer to the link detectors [12], which measure the flow through the on- or off-ramps. The total length of this strip is 9 miles. The loop detector labeled 761100 is at mile 26 (from a given reference point upstream); the loop detector labeled 718212 is at mile 35. The flow is going East (in increasing order of the links).

highways, with a total of N on- or off-ramps (see Figure 1). The governing equations for this system are given by:

$$
\begin{cases}
\mathcal{N}_i(\rho_i) = \frac{\partial \rho_i}{\partial t} + \frac{\partial q_i(\rho_i)}{\partial x_i} = 0 & 1 \leq i \leq N \\
\rho_i(x_i, 0) = \rho_i^\circ(x_i) & 1 \leq i \leq N \\
q_i(\rho_i(0,t)) = q_{i-1}(\rho_{i-1}(L_{i-1}, t)) + q_i^{on}(t) & \forall i \in \mathcal{ON} \\
q_i(\rho_i(0,t)) = (1 - \beta_{i-1}(t))q_{i-1}(\rho_{i-1}(L_{i-1}, t)) & \forall i \in \mathcal{OFF}
\end{cases}
\tag{2}
$$

In the previous equation, $\rho_i^\circ(x_i)$ denotes the density of cars at time 0. $\mathcal{ON}$ denotes the set of links with merging on-ramps (in Figure 1, $\mathcal{ON} = \{2, 4, 5, \cdots\}$); $\mathcal{OFF}$ denotes the set of links with diverging off-ramps ($\mathcal{OFF} = \{1, 3, 6, \cdots\}$). $q_i^{on}(t)$ denotes the inflow of cars into link i, $\beta_i(t) \in [0, 1]$ denotes the proportion of cars leaving link i through an off-ramp. Every x_i ranges in $[0, L_i]$, and $t \in [0, T]$. The interpretation of the two last equations in (2) is as follows: the third equation in (2) expresses the conservation of flow at an on-ramp location (the flow into link i is the flow from link $i - 1$ plus the additional flow from the ramp); and the last equation (2) expresses the same with off-ramps. In this last equation, $\beta_i(t)$ represents the proportion of flow leaving link i. For the rest of this article, we will use the first order approximation that $\beta_i(t) = \beta_i$ does not depend on time. In order for (2) to be consistent with Figure 1, we need to set $q_0(\rho_0(L_0, t)$ equal to the inflow into the highway, and β_0 to the portion of this flow leaving the highway through link 761100. Note that this framework encapsulates more general network topologies, as was successfully done in the context of Air Traffic Control [2] (time dependent β_i and a more general network).

2.2   Numerical Schemes

In this section, we briefly demonstrate the performance of the numerical scheme which will be used for the rest of the article to solve various forms of the PDE model (2). The LWR PDE is a first order hyperbolic PDE, which admits several

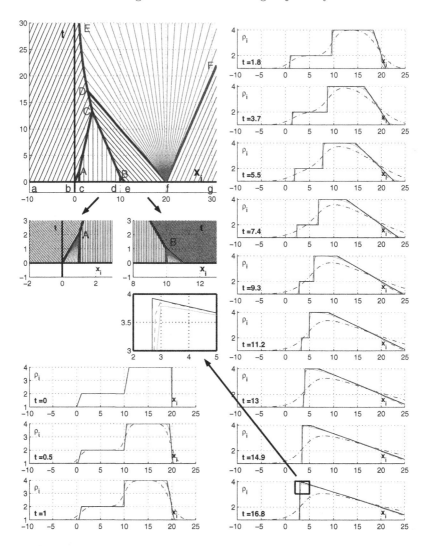

Fig. 2. Subplots indexed by time: entropy solution of the LWR PDE (1) with Green-shield flux function [1] and initial condition shown for $t = 0$. Comparisons of the results provided by the different numerical schemes: analytical solution constructed with the method of characteristics (solid, sharp), Daganzo (solid, lightly shaded), JST $(--)$, visually almost not differentiable from the analytical solution, Lax Friedrichs scheme $(-\cdot)$. As can be seen, there is a traffic jam initially between 11 and 20 (flow is going to the right). It dissolves on the right, because of low density downstream. The low density upstream piles up into the region of medium density, generating a compression wave, which becomes a shock wave. The same happens with the medium density into the region of high density. The two shock waves collapse into a single shock wave after $t = 13$, as the traffic jam further dissolves (which is known as the "N-wave" because of its shape). The upper left plot represents the characteristics [8] in the (x_i, t) plane used to obtain the analytical solution. The two little subplots below are magnified plots of the characteristics around A and B.

weak solutions [8]. These solutions can exhibit features which hinder numerical computation, such as shocks. Among these solutions, [8] shows the existence and uniqueness of a particular solution called the *entropy solution*, which was identified in [1] as the correct solution to the highway problem. We use the *Jameson-Schmidt-Turkel* (JST) scheme [11] to compute the entropy solution numerically. We show convergence of this scheme for a benchmark problem by comparing the numerical results to an analytically computed entropy solution obtained with the method of characteristics [8], and we compute the error as a function of the number of gridpoints.

Numerical validation example: We consider one link ($i = 1$). We use the Greenshield model: $q_i(\rho_i) = v_i\rho_i\left(1 - \rho_i/\rho_i^{\max}\right)$, where the speed v_i is a constant and $\rho_i^{\max}$ is called *jam density* (above which cars stop on the highway). In the experiment, $v_i = 1$ [unit of length / unit of time] and $\rho_i^{\max} = 4$ [cars / unit length]. These numbers are nondimensional, but for the applications presented later, we will use highway data. The initial conditions $\rho_i(x_i, 0)$, which are prescribed (infinite domain), and solution $\rho_i(x_i, t)$, which we computed, are outlined below:

$$
\begin{cases}
\rho_i(x_i,0) = 1 & \text{if } x_i \leq 0 \\
\rho_i(x_i,0) = 1 + x_i & \text{if } x_i \in [0,1] \\
\rho_i(x_i,0) = 2 & \text{if } x_i \in [1,10] \\
\rho_i(x_i,0) = 2 + 2(x_i - 10) & \text{if } x_i \in [10,11] \\
\rho_i(x_i,0) = 4 & \text{if } x_i \in [11,20] \\
\rho_i(x_i,0) = 1 & x_i \geq 20
\end{cases}
$$

$$
\begin{cases}
abACDE & \rho_i(x_i,t) = 1 \\
bAc & \rho_i(x_i,t) = \frac{1 + x_i - v_i t}{1 - \frac{v_i t}{2}} \\
cACBd & \rho_i(x_i,t) = 2 \\
dBe & \rho_i(x_i,t) = 2(1 + \frac{x_i - 10}{1 - v_i t}) \\
eBCDf & \rho_i(x_i,t) = 4 \\
EDfF & \rho(x_i,t) = 2(1 - \frac{x_i - 20}{v_i t}) \\
Ffg & \rho_i(x_i,t) = 1
\end{cases}
$$

where the polygons of the previous formula are shown in Figure 2; we computed this solution analytically using Rankine-Hugoniot jump conditions and self similar expansion waves [8]. This scenario represents the backwards propagation of a traffic jam into a medium density portion of the highway and its dissolution. Figure 2 shows three different numerical schemes: Lax-Friedrichs (LxF), Daganzo (Dag) and Jameson-Schmidt-Turkel (JST). The numerical validation is summarized in the following array:

$N_{\text{gridpoints}}$	L_2 rel. error (LxF)	L_2 rel. error (JST)	L_2 rel. error (Dag)
40	0.2404	0.1088	0.0981
80	0.1804	0.0729	0.0641
160	0.1376	0.0474	0.0430
320	0.1049	0.0299	0.0291
640	0.0787	0.0187	0.0198

As can be seen, linear numerical schemes such as LxF perform relatively poorly at low resolutions. The excellent performance of JST and Dag (less than 2% relative error) enables us to use them for the rest of this article. We will use the JST, because it not only applies to the problem of interest, but also to the adjoint, which we construct later.

2.3   Validation of the Model against PeMS Data

Even though the LWR PDE model is not new and is acknowledged as a valid model of highway traffic [13,17,6,16], we want to demonstrate its accuracy and thus the accuracy of our direct numerical solutions by simulating highway traffic using real data from the PeMS website [12]. From the PeMS database, we can get data sampled at a 5 minute rate for the I210 East in Los Angeles. We simulate a 9 mile long section between I5 and I605, with 26 on- and off-ramps (see Figure 1). The highway has 5 lanes and a carpool lane, which become 4 lanes and a carpool lane at Link 14. We can compute the flux functions $q_i(\cdot)$ empirically from the PeMS data. We have access to both flux and density at the on- and off-ramps as well as on the highway, using algorithms available in [12]. At the on-ramps, we can use this data to compute the $q_i^{on}(t)$ directly. At the off-ramps, we can evaluate the β_i as the ratio of the exiting flow over the flow on the highway. We perform a validation over four hours of traffic. The results are shown in Figure 3 for 35 minutes, and are available in movie format at [19]. The simulation starts at 14:00, captures the increase in density until its peak around 17:00. After 17:00, it stays at the peak and captures an almost steady state car density, jammed upstream. The discrepancies between measurements and simulations observed in Figure 3 have several causes we list: exact location of the sensors on the highway, noise in the data, lack of data, sensor malfunctions, and highway configuration. Despite these discrepancies, we are able to capture the propagation of congestion on the highway, which is our goal; this comparison thus demonstrates the validity of the model for our purposes.

3   Gradient Computation via the Adjoint Problem

We can now use the framework presented in the previous section to design a control methodology for the network problem. For this section, the control variables are the $q_i^{on}(t)$, which we can adjust in order to prevent the density on the highway from becoming too high. We first explain how to synthesize a set of continuous $q_i^{on}(t)$, and then how to use it to regulate the metering lights on the highway with an on/off control strategy.

3.1   PDE Constrained Optimization Formulation of Control Problems

We want to optimize a cost function subject to the constraints inherent to the problem and imposed by the available control. The framework presented below is very general and allows any cost function. We will illustrate this by maximizing the *Vehicle Miles Traveled* (VMT), as defined in [5], which represents the sum of distances driven by cars on a highway section over a time interval. The VMT is very easily expressed as a function of $q_i(\rho_i(\cdot))$, as can be seen in the cost function of the following optimization program:

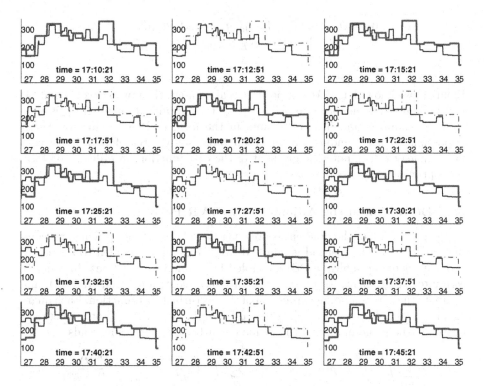

Fig. 3. Simulation for 35 minutes of traffic for I210 East. The horizontal axis is the distance (in miles, see Figure 1); the vertical axis is the density (in vehicles per mile). The solid thin curve is the result of the simulation. It is obtained with the JST scheme. The time step is on the order of 0.25 sec., i.e. we compute the (simulated) data every 0.25 sec.; it is displayed every 150 sec., and compared to the measured data. The measured data is available every 5 minutes. It is displayed when measured (thick line), and does not change until the next measurement (therefore the dash-dotted curves are just copies of the previous thick curve). This data is extracted from a movie obtained for four hours of traffic, available at [19].

$$\textbf{max:} \ \sum_{i=1}^{N} \int_0^{L_i} \int_0^T q_i(\rho_i(x_i, t)) dx_i dt$$
$$\textbf{s.t.:} \ (2)$$
$$0 \le q_i^{\text{on}}(t) \le q_{\text{max},i}(t) \tag{3}$$

The constraints in the previous optimization program are (2), which are the governing equations of the system, and $0 \le q_i^{\text{on}}(t) \le q_{\text{max},i}(t)$, which sets a bound on the number of cars that can be let into the highway ($q_i^{\text{on}}(t)$ is the control variable which we want to compute for this study, and from which we want to extract the on/off sequence for the switching metering light at on-ramp i). Using a standard log barrier technique [4] to avoid constraints in the control, we can transform the problem into:

$$\textbf{min: } \mathcal{J} \overset{\triangle}{=} -\sum_{i=1}^{N} \int_{0}^{L_i} \int_{0}^{T} q_i(\rho_i(x_i,t))dx_i dt$$
$$-\frac{1}{M} \sum_{i \in \mathcal{ON}} \int_{0}^{T} \log(q_i^{\text{on}}(t)(q_{\max,i}(t) - q_i^{\text{on}}(t))) \tag{4}$$
$$\textbf{s.t.: } (2)$$

From [4], we know that if M is a positive real number, then problems (3) and (4) will be equivalent in the limit $M \to +\infty$. This optimization program is non-convex, nonlinear and has constraints in the form of PDEs, which makes it impossible to use standard optimization tools [4]. We therefore will derive a methodology to compute the gradient of the cost function, in order to perform this optimization.

3.2   Derivation of the Adjoint of the LWR Problem

The computation of the gradient is done via the adjoint problem, which we compute as follows. The method is adapted from [10,3] and extended to a network problem involving multiple PDEs coupled by boundary conditions. In order to compute the gradient, we perturb the variables (control q_i^{on} and state ρ_i), and compute the corresponding expression of the perturbed cost function. Each quantity is written as $\rho_i = \bar{\rho}_i + \rho_i'$, $q_i^{\text{on}} = \bar{q}_i^{\text{on}} + q_i^{\text{on}\prime}$, $\mathcal{J} = \bar{\mathcal{J}} + \mathcal{J}'$ etc, where the overline denotes nominal and the prime perturbation. The result reads:

$$\mathcal{J}' = -\sum_{i=1}^{N} \int_{0}^{L_i} \int_{0}^{T} c_i(\bar{\rho}_i)\rho_i' dx_i dt - \frac{1}{M} \sum_{i \in \mathcal{ON}} \int_{0}^{T} \left(\frac{q_i^{\text{on}\prime}(t)}{\bar{q}_i^{\text{on}}(t)} - \frac{q_i^{\text{on}\prime}(t)}{q_{\max,i}(t) - \bar{q}_i^{\text{on}}(t)} \right) dt$$

In the previous formula, c_i denotes the first derivative of the flux function $dq_i(\rho_i)/d\rho_i$, called the *celerity*. Written as such, this expression cannot be used practically, since it depends on the state ρ_i' which cannot be controlled directly. We compute the linearized differential operator $\mathcal{N}_i'(\cdot)$ associated with the LWR operator $\mathcal{N}_i(\cdot)$ from (2), and appropriate perturbed boundary and initial conditions:

$$\begin{cases} \mathcal{N}_i'(\bar{\rho}_i)\rho_i' := \frac{\partial \rho_i'}{\partial t} + \frac{\partial}{\partial x_i}(c_i(\bar{\rho}_i)\rho_i') = 0 & 1 \leq i \leq N \\ \rho_i'(0, x_i) = 0 & 1 \leq i \leq N \\ c_i(\bar{\rho}_i(0,t))\rho_i'(0,t) = c_{i-1}(\bar{\rho}_{i-1}(L_{i-1},t))\rho_{i-1}'(L_{i-1},t) + q_i^{\text{on}\prime}(t) & \forall i \in \mathcal{ON} \\ c_i(\bar{\rho}_i(0,t))\rho_i'(0,t) = (1-\beta_{i-1}(t))c_{i-1}(\bar{\rho}_{i-1}(L_{i-1},t))\rho_{i-1}'(L_{i-1},t) & \forall i \in \mathcal{OFF} \end{cases}$$

where dependencies in x_i and t are omitted when trivial. As usual [10,3], the linearized operator depends on the nominal flow $\bar{\rho}_i$. We denote by $\langle \cdot | \cdot \rangle_i$ the inner product, defined for any two functions ρ_i^* and ρ_i' by:

$$\langle \rho_i^* | \rho_i \rangle_i := \int_{0}^{T} \int_{0}^{L_i} \rho_i^*(x_i,t)\rho_i(x_i,t)dx_i dt \tag{5}$$

We denote by ρ_i^* the adjoint variable of ρ_i', and by $\mathcal{N}_i^*(\bar{\rho}_i)$ the adjoint operator of $\mathcal{N}_i'(\bar{\rho}_i)$, defined algebraically by the adjoint identity:

$$\langle \rho_i^* | \mathcal{N}_i' \rho_i' \rangle_i \overset{\triangle}{=} \langle \mathcal{N}_i^* \rho_i^* | \rho_i' \rangle_i + b_i \tag{6}$$

where b_i denotes the boundary conditions. The adjoint operator and the boundary conditions can be computed explicitly:

$$\begin{cases} \mathcal{N}_i^* = -\frac{\partial(.)}{\partial t} - c_i(\bar{\rho}_i)\frac{\partial(.)}{\partial x_i} \\ b_i = \int_0^{L_i} \rho_i^* \rho_i'\big|_0^T \, dx_i + \int_0^T \rho_i^* c_i(\bar{\rho}_i)\rho_i'\big|_0^{L_i} \, dt \end{cases} \tag{7}$$

Note that the adjoint depends on $\bar{\rho}_i$. Let ρ_i^* be the solution of the following PDE:

$$\mathcal{N}_i^*(\rho_i^*) = c_i(\bar{\rho}_i(x_i, t)) \tag{8}$$

Then, using the adjoint identity, we can plug $\mathcal{N}_i^*(\rho_i^*)$ into $\mathcal{J}'$; using the boundary conditions of (7), we can eliminate all perturbed states from $\mathcal{J}'$ provided:

$$\begin{cases} \rho_i^*(x_i, T) = 0 & 1 \le i \le N \\ \rho_i^*(L_i, t) = 0 & i = N \\ \rho_{i-1}^*(L_{i-1}, t) = \rho_i^*(0, t) & i \in \mathcal{ON} \\ \rho_{i-1}^*(L_{i-1}, t) = (1 - \beta_{i-1})\rho_i^*(0, t) & i \in \mathcal{OFF} \end{cases} \tag{9}$$

which provides the following formula:

Formula 1 (Reduced gradient formulation): The perturbation of the cost function can be expressed as the inner product of the gradient and the control variable as follows

$$\mathcal{J}' = \sum_{i \in \mathcal{ON}} \left\langle -\rho_i^*(0, \cdot) - \frac{1}{M}\left(\frac{1}{\bar{q}_i^{\text{on}}(\cdot)} - \frac{1}{q_{\max,i}(\cdot) - \bar{q}_i^{\text{on}}(\cdot)} \right) \middle| q_i^{\text{on}'}(\cdot) \right\rangle_{[0,T]} \tag{10}$$

where $\langle \cdot | \cdot \rangle_{[0,T]}$ denotes the inner product w.r.t. t only.

We can now use Formula 1 to embed the gradient computation into an algorithm to solve the control problem through the optimization program (4):

Algorithm 1 (adjoint based gradient optimization): The following algorithm converges to a minimum of the optimization program (4):

0 Start with a guess $q_i^{\text{on}} \le q_{\max,i}$;
1 Compute the $\bar{\rho}_i$ with JST from the known ρ_i° for all i, for a small M;
2 Compute the solution $\bar{\rho}_i^*$ of (8)-(9) using $\bar{\rho}_i$ computed in 1, for all i;
3 Compute the optimal update $\{q_i^{\text{on}'}\}_{i \in \{1, \cdots, N\}}$ using (10) from Formula 1;
4 Use steepest descent with backtracking to update q_i^{on} for all i;
5 Compute $\bar{\rho}_i$ with updated q_i^{on}. Unless converged, go back to 2;
6 Unless log term is negligible, increase M and go back to 2.

The solution of this algorithm converges [4] to a solution of the initial optimization problem (3) in the limit $M \to \infty$. The backtracking procedure is sometimes referred to by the name of the more general *Armijo condition* [7,4].

The entropy solution of the LWR equation is known to be discontinuous (as was shown in the validation example). The gradient derivation however is only

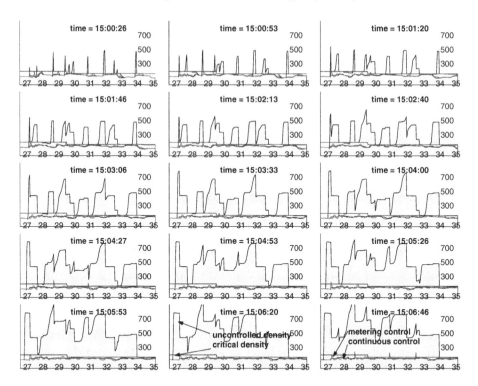

Fig. 4. Congestion control results for the highway portion shown in Figure 1. The horizontal axis is the distance (in miles, see Figure 1); the vertical axis is the density (in vehicles per mile). The critical density, above which q_i is the horizontal line with one step (its value decreases when the highway becomes 4 lanes between mile 29 and 30). The uncontrolled density is the solid line enclosing the shaded area. The density controlled with continuous control is the dark solid line below the critical density; the density controlled with metering control is the bright solid below the critical density, with small wiggles. The full simulation is available as a movie at [19].

valid for infinitesimal ρ', which we know is not true in presence of shocks. In our simulations, we add a logarithmic barrier to the density, in order to avoid exceeding the critical density. Given the triangular expression of our fit of q_i, we can prove very easily that this will prevent the appearance of shocks. We will also show that this method works in practice in presence of shocks, even though a more careful analysis of the first order perturbation is necessary to mathematically validate this approach.

3.3   Application to On/Off Switching for Metering Traffic

From the previous section, we now can compute the continuous q_i^{on} in order to prevent congestion of the network. We call the corresponding control input *continuous control*. Because these continuous functions must be implemented as on/off metering lights, we can construct a set of t_n from these continuous functions defined by $\int_{t_n}^{t_{n+1}} q_i^{on}(t)dt = q_{max,i}T_{green}$. Here, T_{green} is the duration of the green light metering, which, after satisfying a minimum practical requirement, we choose arbitrarily (in practice five seconds); t_0 is the time at which we want to start the metering, t_{n+1} can be solved recursively from t_n, knowing q_i^{on}. We set the light to red in $[t_n, t_{n+1} - T_{green}]$ and to green in $[t_{n+1} - T_{green}, t_{n+1}]$. By construction, $t_n \leq t_{n+1} - T_{green}$. We call *metering control* the resulting control. It is clear that the same amount of flow is released into the network over a time interval of $[t_n, t_{n+1}]$ as with the continuous control, but the corresponding solution is suboptimal, since it does not release all the flow according to q_i^{on}. Figure 4 shows the results of the simulations obtained for the highway system shown in Figure 1, for 10 minutes of traffic. The goal of this simulation is to demonstrate the capability of maintaining the density below the critical density. For this, we take real on-ramp flows (from PeMS data), and multiply them by 10. As can be seen, in absence of control, the density (solid lines above the critical density) almost immediately exceeds the critical density (thick horizontal line) at the on-ramps. Within less than one minute, this density spreads out and progressively jams the rest of the highway (the jam density for this portion of the highway is on the order of 1000 cars / mile). The result of the continuous control can be seen to always remain below the critical density. The metering control only exceeds the critical density for very small amounts of time at locations dispersed over the highway strip. The effect of the continuous control is to increase the VMT by 42% with respect to traffic without metering; in presence of sampling (metering control), the VMT is increased by 41%. If the inflows were only multiplied by 2 or 3, we might be able to get similar results by running longer experiments (it takes a significant amount of time for the highway to become saturated), and the benefit of the metering control only appears once the highway is jammed.

4   Hybrid PDE Switching

In the previous section, we derived adjoint-based control for a continuous problem, and implemented it as a discrete approximation in order to use metering lights; in this section, we consider a true hybrid problem, which is based on regulation of car speed limits [9]. In this context, each link i can be in one of finitely many modes, indexed by j, and can switch between these modes. The goal of this section is to derive a counterpart to Formula 1 for the case in which the control variables are switching times instead of boundary conditions. Mode j is represented by an LWR PDE which incorporates the speed limit in that mode for link i. Consider an infinitely long road, with density ρ. Let $T > 0$ be given, and consider $0 = \tau_0 < \tau_1 < \cdots < \tau_M < \tau_{M+1} = T$, where the τ_j, $j \in \{1, \cdots, M\}$ are not known a priori. Assume that the car density on the highway is governed by the following PDE:

$$\mathcal{N}_\tau(\rho) \overset{\triangle}{=} \frac{\partial \rho}{\partial t} + \sum_{j=0}^{M} \chi_{[\tau_j, \tau_{j+1}]}(t)\frac{\partial q_j(\rho)}{\partial x} - \epsilon\frac{\partial^2 \rho}{\partial x^2} = 0 \qquad (11)$$

In the previous formula, $\chi_{[\tau_j,\tau_{j+1}]}(t) = 1$ for $t \in [\tau_j, \tau_{j+1}]$, and 0 otherwise; the $q_j(\cdot)$ are functions indexed by j, representing the flux function of the road in different modes (i.e. with different speed limits). Finally, ϵ is a small diffusion coefficient, which enables us to eliminate shocks, while preserving the large scale shape of the solution. As a result, we expect the solution of (11) to be smooth.[1] The interpretation of (11) is as follows: for $t \in [\tau_j, \tau_{j+1}]$, ρ is governed by the LWR PDE corresponding to $q_j(\cdot)$ (flux function incorporating maximum allowable speed for mode j) augmented by a small diffusion operator to smooth the solution. Note that the order of the switching problem is known a priori.

This problem falls into the class of hybrid systems, where each mode is modeled by a different PDE governing the state. The application of adjoint-based optimization to this problem is, to our best knowledge, new. A counterpart for the conventional hybrid system case in which each mode is governed by an ODE is the problem of optimal control of switching times, for which recent results are presented in [18,7]. In the context of discrete linear hybrid dynamical systems for the same highway problem, observability and controllability results are available in [16].

The control problem consists in maximizing the following cost function: $\sum_{j=0}^{M} \int_{\mathbb{R}} \int_{\tau_j}^{\tau_{j+1}} p(x)q(\rho(x,t))dxdt$, where the control variables are the τ_j, $j \in \{1, \cdots, M\}$, and $p(x)$ is a penalty function, which is arbitrary (for example we might penalize more heavily locations in which we would like fewer cars). In mathematical terms,

$$\begin{aligned}
&\textbf{min: } \mathcal{J} \triangleq -\sum_{j=1}^{M} \int_{\mathbb{R}} \int_{\tau_j}^{\tau_{j+1}} p(x)q_j(\rho(x,t))dxdt \\
&\textbf{s.t.: } (11), \text{ with } \rho(x,0) = \rho^{\circ}(x) \text{ given} \\
&\quad 0 = \tau_0 < \tau_1 < \cdots < \tau_M < \tau_{M+1} = T
\end{aligned} \tag{12}$$

We apply the same technique as before: we compute the first variation of $\mathcal{J}$, obtained by perturbation of the τ_j: call ρ the solution of $\mathcal{N}_\tau(\rho) = 0$, and $\bar{\rho}$ the solution of $\mathcal{N}_{\bar{\tau}}(\bar{\rho}) = 0$ (nominal flow). Let $\rho' \triangleq \rho - \bar{\rho}$. Defining

$$\mathcal{N}'_{\bar{\tau}}(\bar{\rho})\rho' \triangleq \frac{\partial \rho'}{\partial t} + \sum_{j=0}^{M} \chi_{[\bar{\tau}_j,\bar{\tau}_{j+1}]}(t)\frac{\partial c_j(\bar{\rho})\rho'}{\partial x} - \epsilon\frac{\partial^2 \rho'}{\partial x^2}$$

it can be shown that ρ' satisfies the following relation:

$$\mathcal{N}'_{\bar{\tau}}(\bar{\rho})\rho' = -\sum_{j=0}^{M} \left(\sigma_{[\tau_j,\bar{\tau}_j]}(t) + \sigma_{[\bar{\tau}_{j+1},\tau_{j+1}]}(t)\right)\frac{\partial q_j(\rho)}{\partial x} \tag{13}$$

---

[1] Analytical solutions computed for benchmark examples with three links and one switch, available at [19] have shown that numerous undesirable phenomena occur at boundaries of the links and switching surfaces (shocks and expansion waves are generated). In order to cast this problem in a mathematically sound framework, it is necessary to add this diffusion operator to the PDE, which "smooths" the solution and avoids problems of differentiability of the solution.

where $\sigma_{[\tau_j,\bar{\tau}_j]} = \chi_{[\tau_j,\bar{\tau}_j]}$ if $\tau_j < \bar{\tau}_j$ and $\sigma_{[\tau_j,\bar{\tau}_j]} = -\chi_{[\tau_j,\bar{\tau}_j]}$ otherwise. The first variation of $\mathcal{J}$ can be computed in terms of the nominal, perturbed, and perturbation variables: calling $\tau_j' \triangleq \tau_j - \bar{\tau}_j$, we have

$$\mathcal{J}' = \sum_{j=1}^{M} \tau_j' \int_{\mathbb{R}} p(x)[q_j(\bar{\rho}) - q_{j-1}(\bar{\rho})]dx - \sum_{j=1}^{M} \int_{\mathbb{R}} \int_{\bar{\tau}_j}^{\bar{\tau}_{j+1}} p(x)c_j(\bar{\rho})\rho' dx dt$$

Following the steps of the previous section, we can define the adjoint of $\mathcal{N}_{\bar{\tau}}'(\bar{\rho})$ by the identity

$$\langle \rho^* | \mathcal{N}_{\bar{\tau}}'(\bar{\rho})\rho' \rangle \triangleq \langle \mathcal{N}_{\bar{\tau}}^*(\bar{\rho})\rho^* | \rho' \rangle + b$$

A double integration by parts provides the following explicit form of the adjoint:

$$\mathcal{N}_{\bar{\tau}}^*(\bar{\rho})\rho^* = -\frac{\partial \rho^*}{\partial t} - \sum_{j=1}^{M} \chi_{[\bar{\tau}_j,\bar{\tau}_{j+1}]} q_j(\bar{\rho}) \frac{\partial \rho^*}{\partial x} - \epsilon \frac{\partial^2 \rho^*}{\partial x^2}$$

Using the continuity of ρ' and ρ^* at $t = \bar{\tau}_j$, the fact that $\rho'(x,0) = 0$, the "good choice" $\rho^*(x,T) = 0$, and the assumption that $\lim_{x \to \pm\infty} \rho(x,t) = 0$, as well as its derivatives, we get $b = 0$. Now making the "good choice" $\mathcal{N}_{\bar{\tau}}^*(\bar{\rho})\rho^* = -p(x)c_j(\bar{\rho})$, we can substitute $\langle \mathcal{N}_{\bar{\tau}}^*(\bar{\rho})\rho^* | \rho' \rangle$ into $\mathcal{J}'$. After using the adjoint identity, we obtain:

$$\mathcal{J}' = \sum_{j=1}^{M} \tau_j' \int_{\mathbb{R}} p(x)[q_j(\bar{\rho}) - q_{j-1}(\bar{\rho})]dx + \langle \rho^* | \mathcal{N}_{\bar{\tau}}'(\bar{\rho})\rho' \rangle$$

which we can evaluate using (13). The result provides us with the following expression of the first variation of $\mathcal{J}$.

Formula 2 (Gradient with respect to switching): The perturbation of the cost function can be expressed as the inner product of the gradient and the control variables as follows

$$\mathcal{J}' = \sum_{j=1}^{M} \tau_j' \int_{\mathbb{R}} \left\{ p(x)[q_j(\bar{\rho}) - q_{j-1}(\bar{\rho})] + \rho^*(x,\bar{\tau}_j) \left\{ \frac{\partial q_j(\bar{\rho})}{\partial x} - \frac{\partial q_{j-1}(\bar{\rho})}{\partial x} \right\} \right\}_{t=\bar{\tau}_j} dx$$

Formula 2 is a first step towards computing the gradient with respect to switching for the network problem of Section 2. For this, one major difficulty inherent to the network needs to be overcome: the discontinuities of the solutions generated by boundary conditions and perturbation of the inflows (which do not appear in the infinite road problem). This is to our best knowledge a known open problem in fluid mechanics, whose solution will enable the computation of the first variation of the cost function.

5   Conclusion

We have shown how to synthesize hybrid controllers for systems governed by PDEs, via an adjoint-based computation of the gradient, which we have embedded in an optimization algorithm. We have shown how to make use of very efficient numerical schemes to compute these gradients accurately, and have performed simulations on a highway congestion problem with PeMS data. We also are interested in computing the Hessian of the optimization problem via the adjoint, in order to avoid the use of steepest descent, for obvious efficiency reasons. We are still in the process of determining when this is possible. We are also interested in higher order models of highway traffic (using second order PDEs). Finally, we will apply these techniques to other networks of PDEs, such as irrigation channels [14], in order to demonstrate the generality of the method.

Acknowledgments. We are grateful to Prof. Tom Bewley for useful conversations regaring the application of the adjoint method to flow control, and his help in the original formulation of the control problem. We thank Dr. Sriram Shankaran for letting us using his JST code, and Prof. Antony Jameson for his help on the JST scheme.

References

1. R. ANSORGE. What does the entropy condition mean in traffic flow theory? *Transportation Research*, 24B(2):133–143, 1990.
2. A. M. BAYEN, R. RAFFARD, and C. J. TOMLIN. Adjoint-based constrained control of Eulerian transportation networks: application to Air Traffic Control. Submitted to the *2004 American Control Conference*.
3. T. R. BEWLEY. Flow control: new challenges for a new renaissance. *Progress in Aerospace Science*, 37:21–58, 2001.
4. S. BOYD and L. VANDENBERGHE. *Convex Optimization.* Cambridge University Press, Cambridge, UK, 2004.
5. C. CHEN, Z. JIA, and P. VARAIYA. Causes and cures of highway congestion. *IEEE Control Systems Magazine*, 21(4):26–33, 2001.
6. C. DAGANZO. The cell transmission model, part II: network traffic. *Transportation Research*, 29B(2):79–93, 1995.
7. M. EGERSTEDT, Y. WARDI, and F. DELMOTTE. Optimal control of switching times in switched dynamical systems. In *Proceedings of the IEEE Conference on Decision and Control*, Maui, HI, Dec. 2003.
8. L. C. EVANS. *Partial Differential Equations.* American Mathematical Society, Providence, Rhode Island, 1998.
9. A. HEGYI, B. DE SCHUTTER, and J. HELLENDOORN. MPC-based optimal coordination of variable speed limits to suppress shock waves in freeway traffic. In *Proceedings of the 2003 American Control Conference*, pages 4083–4088, Denver, CO, June 2003.
10. A. JAMESON. Aerodynamic design via control theory. *Journal of Scientific Computing*, 3(3):233–260, 1988.

11. A. JAMESON. Analysis and design of numerical schemes for gas dynamics 2: Artificial diffusion and discrete shock structure. *International Journal of Computational Fluid Dynamics*, 4:1–38, 1995.

12. Z. JIA, C. CHEN, B. COIFMAN, and P. VARAIYA. The PeMS algorithms for accurate, real time estimates of g-factors and speeds from single loop detectors. In *IEEE Intelligent Transportation Systems Conference Proceedings*, pages 536–541, Oakland, CA, Aug. 2001.

13. M. J. LIGHTHILL and G. B. WHITHAM. On kinematic waves. II. A theory of traffic flow on long crowded roads. *Proceedings of the Royal Society of London*, 229(1178):317–345, 1956.

14. X. LITRICO. Robust IMC flow control of SIMO dam-river open-channel systems. *IEEE Transactions on Control Systems Technology*, 10(5):432–437, 2002.

15. P. K. MENON, G. D. SWERIDUK, and K. BILIMORIA. A new approach for modeling, analysis and control of air traffic flow. In *Proceedings of the AIAA Conference on Guidance, Navigation and Control*, Monterey, CA, Aug. 2002. Paper 2002-5012.

16. L. MUNOZ, X. SUN, R. HOROWITZ, and L. ALVAREZ. Traffic density estimation with the cell transmission model. In *Proceedings of the American Control Conference*, Denver, CO, June 2003.

17. P. I. RICHARDS. Shock waves on the highway. *Operations Research*, 4(1):42–51, 1956.

18. X. XU and P. J. ANTSAKLIS. Results and perspectives on computational methods for optimal control of switched system. In *Sixth International Workshop on Hybrid Systems: Computation and Control*, Prague, The Czech Republic, Apr. 2003.

19. http://cherokee.stanford.edu/~bayen/HSCC04.html.

Understanding the Bacterial Stringent Response Using Reachability Analysis of Hybrid Systems

Călin Belta[1], Peter Finin[2], Luc C.G.J.M. Habets[5], Ádám M. Halász[2], Marcin Imieliǹski[3], R. Vijay Kumar[2], and Harvey Rubin[4]

[1] Department of Mechanical Engineering
Drexel University, Philadelphia, PA 19101, USA
[2] General Robotics, Automation, Sensing and Perception Laboratory,
[3] Graduate Group in Computational Biology and Genomics
University of Pennsylvania, Philadelphia, PA 19101, USA
[4] Department of Medicine
University of Pennsylvania, Philadelphia, PA 19101, USA
[5] Department of Mathematics and Computer Science
Eindhoven University of Technology, Eindhoven, The Netherlands

Abstract. In this paper we model coupled genetic and metabolic networks as hybrid systems. The vector fields are *multi - affine, i.e.,* have only product - type nonlinearities to accommodate chemical reactions, and are defined in rectangular invariants, whose facets correspond to changes in the behavior of a gene or enzyme. For such systems, we showed that reachability and safety verification problems can be formulated and solved (conservatively) in an elegant and computationally inexpensive way, based on the fact that multi-affine functions on rectangular regions of the space are determined at the vertices. Using these techniques, we study the stringent response system, which is the transition of bacterial organisms from growth phase to a metabolically suppressed phase when subjected to an environment with limited nutrients.

1   Introduction

The traditional approach to modeling of genetic and metabolic networks leads to highly nonlinear systems of differential equations for which analytical solutions are not normally possible. The only alternative for analysis is numerical simulation. One way to work around the difficulties of the nonlinearities is to use simplified, approximate models. Existing work focuses on very low dimensional networks. Decoupled piecewise linear differential equations (PLDE) are considered in [1,2], where gene regulation is modeled as a discontinuous step function and chemical reactions are ignored. This (over)simplified approach to modeling allows for interesting qualitative analysis [3] . An even more radical idealization is obtained if the state of a gene is abstracted to a Boolean variable and the interaction among elements to Boolean functions, as in Boolean networks [4]. Other types of simplified approaches combining logical and continuous aspects include generalized logical formalisms [5] and qualitative differential equations [6]. The

R. Alur and G.J. Pappas (Eds.): HSCC 2004, LNCS 2993, pp. 111–125, 2004.
© Springer-Verlag Berlin Heidelberg 2004

highest level of abstraction is achieved in the knowledge-based, or rule-based formalism [7]. While amenable for interesting analysis, the methods mentioned above are based on assumptions which disregard important biochemical phenomena. Most of them only capture protein dynamics but cannot accommodate chemical reactions [4]. When the regulatory systems are not spatially homogeneous, partial differential equations and other spatially distributed models such as reaction-diffusion equations [8] and the gene circuit method [9] can be used. The modeling approach based on differential equations implicitly assumes that the concentrations of the species in the network vary continuously and deterministically. The continuity assumption is compromised in cases when the number of molecules of a certain species is small or due to fluctuations in the timing of cellular events. The use of discrete stochastic models is proposed in [10,11,12]. However, these methods are computationally expensive and cannot handle high dimensional systems.

Our modeling approach is deterministic and based on *hybrid systems* [13, 14,15,16], *i.e.,* systems in which discrete events are combined with continuous differential equations to capture the switching behavior that is observed in phenomena such as transcription [17], protein-protein interactions, and cell division and growth. We also propose the use of hybrid system as the natural framework giving a global description of a biological system described locally around operating points by simpler dynamics, which are easier to approach for analysis. We successfully used hybrid systems to model, simulate and perform preliminary analysis on small dimensional genetic networks for the quorum sensing system in the marine bacterium *Vibrio fischeri* [18,19,20,21,22]. More specifically, as in [1,3], we assume a simplified model of regulation, but, in addition to step functions, we allow for piece-wise linear activation functions, which seem more realistic. Moreover, we dramatically enlarge the class of regulatory systems by allowing for coupling and product type nonlinearities in the vector field. Consequently, chemical reactions among the species involved in the regulation can be included. The vector fields are *multi - affine*, *i.e.,* have only product - type nonlinearities to accommodate chemical reactions, and are defined in rectangular partitions of the state space, called *invariants*. The facets of the rectangles correspond to changes in the behavior of a gene or enzyme. For such systems, we show that reachability and safety verification problems can be formulated and solved (conservatively) in an elegant and computationally inexpensive way, based on some interesting properties of multi-affine functions on rectangular regions of the Euclidean space of arbitrary dimension: a multi-affine function is uniquely determined everywhere in a rectangle by its value at the vertices.

We apply this method to the stringent response system, namely, to the question of the existence of an upper limit to the concentration of (p)ppGpp and to the number of stalled translational complexes following a nutritional downshift.

The paper is organized as follows. In the following section we describe our model. We give a brief biological background. We then describe the basic reaction groups and substances that we included in our model, and we formulate the model as a hybrid system. In Section 3 we present the reachability algorithm we use in this paper. Section 4 gives our analytical and numerical results. We identify the steady states of the model, analytically and numerically. We present results of simulations in a setting similar to what triggers the stringent response in nature. We use reachability analysis to investigate the existence of an upper limit for one of the biologically interesting variables of the model. Finally we summarize our results and outline directions for future work.

2   Biological Background and Model Definition

The stringent response has become an important area of study in *M. tuberculosis* (*M.tb*), where it is has been found to be crucial for latent survival in the infected host [23]. The stringent response occurs in the setting of nutrient deprivation. It is characterized by reduced amino acid consumption and protein production, suppression of anabolic processes, and rerouting of metabolic pathways towards those most essential for survival [24]. Bacteria which lack the stringent response are unable to survive in nutrient deprived media and die from either unrestrained growth or accumulation of misfolded proteins.

In *M.tb*, as in many other bacteria, the stringent response is mediated via the level of (p)ppGpp. In the setting of amino acid deprivation, the levels of (p)ppGpp increase, resulting in a set of genetic regulatory events which trigger cell-wide metabolic changes. The level of (p)ppGpp in the cell is set by the equlibrium of two reactions, synthesis and hydrolysis, which synthesize and destroy (p)ppGpp, respectively. In *M.tb*, both of these functions are performed by the enzyme RelMtb [25]. The rate of the synthesis reaction increases dramatically in the presence of the Rel Activating Complex (RAC) [26]. This complex is formed when the translation machinery of the cell, the ribosome, encounters an uncharged tRNA during protein synthesis. The level of uncharged tRNA is thought to be the mechanism through which *M.tb* senses the abundance of amino acids in its environment. The increase in (p)ppGpp levels has several effects on transcription, which results in a dramatic downregulation of stable RNA and a less dramatic downregulation of mRNA [27]. Downregulation of stable RNA results in the reduction of ribosome concentration, and thus protein synthesis. Though global mRNA levels decrease in the stringent response, a small subset of genes are upregulated [28]. These include genes coding for proteins involved in amino acid biosynthesis and antigen production.

2.1   Model Equations

A map of the reactions accounted for in our model is shown in Figure 1. Our *dynamical variables* are: the concentrations of two species of promoters P_u and P_d, free RNA polymerase R, four intermediate complexes RP_u, RP_d, R_u^*, R_d^*, the ribosomes Rib, and the number of translational complexes Q_{tot}. Several other substances (including two species of mRNA and the signaling substance (p)ppGpp, denoted by diamonds in Figure 1) are calculated at steady state so they are algebraic functions of the former. We follow two *observables*, one proportional to the concentration of (p)ppGpp, g, and one which gives a measure

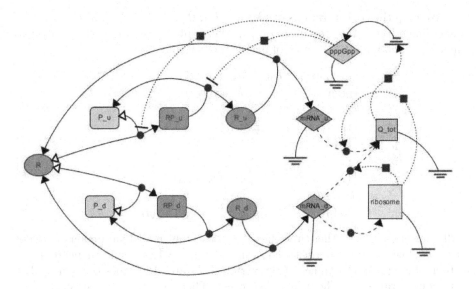

Fig. 1. Screenshot from Charon's model design interface with the schematic of the model.

of the transcriptional activity in the cell, q. We distinguish an *external parameter* r which is defined as the ratio of uncharged versus charged tRNA, a measure of the availability of resources. The lower r, the more nutrients are available. There is a significant number of fixed parameters that control the reaction kinetics.

We distinguish two generic species of mRNA, 'upregulated' (u) and 'downregulated' (d), each with its own species of promoter P_x ($x = u, d$) and intermediate complexes. Free RNA polymerase binds to the promoters to form the RP_x complexes. The eventual liberation of the promoter site results in the respective transcriptional complexes, R_x^*. The RNAP is regained at the end of the ensuing elongation process, which results in the transcript $mRNA_x$. The total amount of mRNA and the concentration of ribosomes (which is in equilibrium with the 'd' transcript concentration) determine the rate of translation initiation. The number of translational complexes Q_{tot} is controlled by the initiation rate and the average elongation time. The latter varies with the outside parameter r, proportionally to $1 + r$ (elongation slows down when nutrients are scarce). The number of stalled complexes is a fraction of Q_{tot}, in a ratio of $r/(1 + r)$. Finally, the concentration of stalled complexes determines the equlibrium concentration of (p)ppGpp, which increases linearly with it, up to a saturation value. The feedback loop is closed by the influence of (p)ppGpp on the kinetics of transcription. The transcription of the 'd' species is inhibited when the (p)ppGpp concentration is high, leading to a decrease in ribosomes which in turn reduces the translation initiation rate.

We map the concentrations of $\{RPu, RPd, R_u^*, R_d^*, Rib, Q_{tot}, R, P_u, P_d\}$ on a nine-dimensional state space $\{x_k\}_{k=\overline{1,9}}$. The result is a hybrid system with two modes, depending on the value of one of the variables, x_6.

$$
\begin{aligned}
\frac{dx_1}{dt} &= k_{1u}\, x_7 x_8 \;-\; (k_{3u} + k_{2u})\, x_1 \\
\frac{dx_2}{dt} &= \bar{k}_{1d}(g(x_6))\, x_7 x_9 \;-\; (\bar{k}_{3d}(g(x_6)) \;+\; \bar{k}_{2d}(g(x_6)))\, x_2 \\
\frac{dx_3}{dt} &= k_{3u}\, x_1 \;-\; \frac{1}{\tau} x_3 \\
\frac{dx_4}{dt} &= \bar{k}_{3d}(g(x_6))\, x_2 \;-\; \frac{1}{\tau} x_4 \\
\frac{dx_5}{dt} &= \frac{\ell}{\tau}\, x_4 \;-\; \frac{1}{C_{rib}} x_5 \\
\frac{dx_6}{dt} &= k_4 \frac{1}{\tau \lambda_{mRNA}} x_5(x_3 + x_4) \;-\; \frac{1}{\theta(1+r)} x_6 \\
\frac{dx_7}{dt} &= \frac{1}{\tau}(x_3 + x_4) - x_7(k_{1u}\, x_8 + k_{1d}\, x_9) \\
\frac{dx_8}{dt} &= (k_{3u} + k_{2u})\, x_1 - k_{1u}\, x_7 x_8 \\
\frac{dx_9}{dt} &= (\bar{k}_{3d}(g(x_6)) + \bar{k}_{2d}(g(x_6)))\, x_2 - \bar{k}_{1d}(g(x_6))\, x_7 x_9 \;.
\end{aligned}
\tag{1}
$$

All quantities in (1), other than the x_k, are constant model parameters[1], except for the 'down-regulated' kinetic constants, $\{\bar{k}_{xd}, x = \overline{1,3}\}$, which depend on the observable $g(x_6)$. The values of the variables x_k are always positive (since they are concentrations of chemical substances). There are three conservation laws which are automatically satisfied, giving the conservation of the total RNAP, $R_{tot} = x_1 + x_2 + x_3 + x_4 + x_7$, and the promoters, $P_u^{tot} = x_1 + x_8$, and $P_d^{tot} = x_2 + x_9$.

The observable $g(x_6)$ is a dimensionless quantity defined as the concentration of the signaling substance (p)ppGpp times a kinetic constant. The latter is a function of x_6, and it increases linearly with it from a basal value g_{low} (at $x_6 = 0$) to a saturation value g_{high}, corresponding to a reference value of $x_6^{ref} = (1 + r)Q_{ref}/r$. The kinetic constants $\bar{k}_{xd}$ that depend on g have a similar dependence. Their value changes linearly from the one at $g = 0$, k_x, to that at $g = 1$, k_x', and stays there for $g > 1$. The upper value g_{high} for the parameter set used in this calculation is larger than 1, so the true threshold for the x_6-dependence is the value that gives $g(x_6^0) = 1$. Below the threshold, the constants $\bar{k}_{xd}$ ($x = \overline{1,3}$) depend linearly on x_6, and above they are simply equal to k_x':

$$
\bar{k}_{xd} =
\begin{cases}
k_x^{min} + \Delta_x x_6 & ; \quad x_6 < x_6^0 \\
k_x' & ; \quad x_6 \geq x_6^0
\end{cases}
\tag{2}
$$

where k_x^{min} and Δ_x are appropriate functions of k_x, k_x', x_6 and the limiting values of g. Our other observable, q, is a measure of transcriptional activity, or rather, the rate at which translations are initiated. We define it as the first term in the r.h.s. of the equation for x_6 in (1), normalized so that it is comparable to x_6/x_6^{ref},

$$
q = \frac{k_4 \theta}{\tau \lambda_{mRNA}} \frac{1}{Q_{ref}} x_5(x_3 + x_4) \quad ; y \equiv \frac{x_6}{r x_6^{ref}} = \frac{1}{1+r} \frac{x_6}{Q_{ref}} \;.
\tag{3}
$$

This rather cumbersome definition has the advantage that it does not depend explicitly on r. At equilibrium we have $q = y$.

---

[1] For a definition of all the constants refer to a detailed description of the model [29]

In summary, the model has two modes defined by the values of x_6, with the mode transitions occur at $x_6 = x_6^0$, corresponding to $g = 1$. The equations in both modes are obtained from (1) with the 'up-regulated' kinetic constants $k_{xu}, x = \overline{1, 2, 3}$ replaced by k_x, and the 'down-regulated' constants given by (2). The transition map is trivial, i.e., all of the dynamical variables continue on with the same values they had just before the transition.

3   Algorithm for Analysis of Hybrid Multi-affine Systems with Rectangular Invariants

The model described above is defined in rectangular regions of the state space and it is affine in each of the state variables x_i, i.e., it is multi-affine. This section formally introduces the definition of a multi-affine rectangular hybrid system and extends some results presented in [19].

3.1   Hybrid Rectangular Multi-affine Systems

Definition 1 (Multi-affine function). *A multi-affine function $f : \mathbb{R}^N \longrightarrow \mathbb{R}^N$ is a polynomial in the indeterminates $x_1, \ldots, x_N$ with the property that the degree of f in any of the indeterminates $x_1, \ldots, x_N$ is less than or equal to 1. Stated differently, f has the form*

$$f(x_1, \ldots, x_N) = \sum_{i_1, \ldots, i_N \in \{0,1\}} c_{i_1, \ldots, i_N} x_1^{i_1} \cdots x_N^{i_N}, \tag{4}$$

with $c_{i_1, \ldots, i_N} \in \mathbb{R}^m$ for all $i_1, \ldots, i_N \in \{0,1\}$ and using the convention that if $i_k = 0$, then $x_k^{i_k} = 1$.

An N-dimensional rectangle in $\mathbb{R}^N$ is characterized by two vectors $a = (a_1, \ldots, a_N) \in \mathbb{R}^N$ and $b = (b_1, \ldots, b_N) \in \mathbb{R}^N$, with the property that $a_i < b_i$ for all $i \in \{1, \ldots, N\}$:

$$R_N(a, b) = \{x = (x_1, \ldots, x_N) \in \mathbb{R}^N \mid \forall i \in \{1, \ldots, N\} : a_i \leq x_i \leq b_i\}. \tag{5}$$

The set of vertices of $R_N(a, b)$ is denoted by $V_N(a, b)$, and may be characterized as

$$V_N(a, b) = \prod_{i=1}^{N} \{a_i, b_i\} \tag{6}$$

Let $\xi : \{a_1, \ldots, a_N, b_1, \ldots, b_N\} \longrightarrow \{0, 1\}$ be defined by

$$\xi(a_k) = 0, \quad \xi(b_k) = 1, \quad k = 1, \ldots, N \tag{7}$$

Then $R_N(a, b)$ has $2N$ facets described by

$$F_N^{j\xi(w_j)}(a, b) = R_N(a, b) \cap \{x \in \mathbb{R}^N \mid x_j = w_j\}, \ w_j \in \{a_j, b_j\}, \ j = \overline{1, N} \tag{8}$$

The outer normal of facet $F_N^{j\xi(w_j)}(a,b)$ is given by

$$n_N^{j\xi(w_j)} = (-1)^{\xi(w_j)+1}e_j, \; w_j \in \{a_j, b_j\}, \; j = \overline{1, N} \tag{9}$$

where e_j, $j = 1, \ldots, N$ denote the Euclidean basis of $\mathbb{R}^N$.

A rectangular partition of the state space $(x_1, \ldots, x_N)$ is defined as follows. Each axis Ox_i, $i = 1, \ldots, N$ is divided into $n_i \geq 1$ intervals by the thresholds $0 = \theta_0^i < \theta_1^i < \ldots < \theta_{n_i}^i$. The jth interval on the Ox_i, $i = \overline{1, N}$ axis is therefore defined as $\theta_{j-1}^i \leq x_i < \theta_j^i$, $j = \overline{1, n_i}$. By convention, $\theta_0^i = 0$ and $\theta_{n_i}^i$ is an upper bound giving a physical limit of x_i. The division of the axes determines a partition of the state space into $\prod_{i=1}^{N} n_i$ rectangles. If we let

$$a_{k_1 \ldots k_N} = (\theta_{k_1-1}^1, \ldots, \theta_{k_N-1}^N) \in \mathbb{R}^N, \; b_{k_1 \ldots k_N} = (\theta_{k_1}^1, \ldots, \theta_{k_N}^N) \in \mathbb{R}^N \tag{10}$$

then following the notation in (5), (6), and (8), an arbitrary rectangle from the partition is given by $R_N(a_{k_1 \ldots k_N}, b_{k_1, \ldots k_N})$, the corresponding set of vertices by $V_N(a_{k_1 \ldots k_N}, b_{k_1, \ldots k_N})$, and the facets by $F_N^{j\xi_j(w_j)}(a_{k_1 \ldots k_N}, b_{k_1, \ldots k_N})$. Explicitly,

$$R_N(a_{k_1 \ldots k_N}, b_{k_1, \ldots k_N}) = \{(x_1, \ldots, x_N) \in \mathbb{R}^N | \theta_{k_i-1}^i \leq x_i \leq \theta_{k_i}^i, \; i = \overline{1, N}\} \tag{11}$$

In each rectangle $R_N(a_{k_1 \ldots k_N}, b_{k_1, \ldots k_N})$, the system evolves along specific dynamics described by

$$\dot{x} = f_{k_1 \ldots k_N}(x), \; x \in R_N(a_{k_1 \ldots k_N}, b_{k_1, \ldots k_N}) \tag{12}$$

Remark 1. A convenient way of representing a hybrid multi-affine system with rectangular invariants (12), (11) is as a *simple graph* with $\prod_{i=1}^{N} n_i$ nodes. Node $(k_1 \ldots k_N)$ corresponds to rectangle $R_N(a_{k_1 \ldots k_N}, b_{k_1, \ldots k_N})$ and has associated dynamics (12). An edge in the graph connects nodes corresponding to adjacent rectangles, *i.e.*, there is an edge between any pair of nodes that differ by a Hamming distance of 1.

3.2   Multi-affine Functions on Rectangles

Let $R_N(a,b)$ denote an arbitrary rectangle as defined by (5) and $f : R_N(a,b) \longrightarrow \mathbb{R}^N$ a multi-affine function as in (4).

Proposition 1. *A multi-affine function $f : R_N(a,b) \longrightarrow \mathbb{R}^N$ is a convex combination of its values at the vertices of $R_N(a,b)$.*

$$f(x_1, \ldots, x_N) = \sum_{(v_1, \ldots, v_N) \in V_N(a,b)} \prod_{k=1}^{N} \left(\frac{x_k - a_k}{b_k - a_k} \right)^{\xi(v_k)} \left(\frac{b_k - x_k}{b_k - a_k} \right)^{1-\xi(v_k)} f(v_1, \ldots, v_N),$$

$$\tag{13}$$

and

$$1 = \sum_{(v_1, \ldots, v_N) \in V_N(a,b)} \prod_{k=1}^{N} \left(\frac{x_k - a_k}{b_k - a_k} \right)^{\xi(v_k)} \left(\frac{b_k - x_k}{b_k - a_k} \right)^{1-\xi(v_k)}. \tag{14}$$

The proof of this proposition can be found in [19].

Corollary 1. *The projection of a multi-affine vector field defined on a rectangle along a given direction is positive (negative) everywhere in the rectangle if and only if its projection along that direction is positive (negative) at the vertices.*

3.3 Analysis

We assume that the piecewise defined vector field (12) (possibly non-differentiable), is continuous everywhere, *i.e.*, the vector fields in adjacent rectangles coincide on the common facet. A simple consequence of Corollary 1 can be used to qualitatively analyze the system.

Problem 1 (Safety verification). Consider a rectangular partition of the state space (11) with specific dynamics (12) in each rectangle. For a given target rectangle, determine a set of rectangles with the property that if the system starts from arbitrary initial states in any of these rectangles, it will never reach the target rectangle.

The target rectangle in the above Problem can be thought of as a collection of "bad" states. The goal of Problem 1 is to determine collections of initial states which are "safe" to start from.

Corollary 1 is applied to the facets of the N - rectangles (11), which are, of course, $N - 1$ - rectangles. A simple and elegant solution to Problem 1 can be described by defining an orientation for the simple graph of the network defined in Remark 1. We allow for both unidirectional and bidirectional edges in the oriented graph. The semantics of the orientation are defined as follows. Let r and p be two adjacent nodes in the graph and R and P the corresponding adjacent rectangles. A unidirectional edge from r to p means that there exists at least one trajectory originating in R that penetrates into P through the separating facet, and there is no trajectory starting in P going to R through that facet. A bidirectional edge insures the existence of both trajectories originating in R penetrating in P and originating in P penetrating into R.

Note that, in the oversimplified description above, Algorithm 1 seems inefficient. Indeed, if we apply it to all the rectangles in the partition, most of the vertices are visited more than ones, and this is not necessary because the vector fields in adjacent rectangles match on the separating facet. A more efficient description would require more complicated notation which is beyond the scope of this paper.

Using the oriented graph, we can now provide a solution to Problem 1. Let T denote the target rectangle, or, equivalently, the target node in the graph. The following algorithm constructs a set $\mathcal{R}$ of nodes with the property that if the system starts in any of the corresponding rectangles, then it is possible to reach T. The complement of $\mathcal{R}$ with respect to the set of all nodes is a safe set $\mathcal{S}$.

Remark 2. Algorithm 2 for the construction of a safe set $\mathcal{S}$ might be too conservative, *i.e.*, the set $\mathcal{S}$ might be unecessarily small. Indeed, the theory developed

---

Algorithm 1 Define an oriented graph

---

for each node $(k_1 \ldots k_N)$, $k_i = \overline{1, n_i}$, $i = \overline{1, N}$ **do**
  for each incident edge **do**
    for each vertex of the corresponding facet **do**
      calculate the projection of $f_{k_1 \ldots k_N}$ along the outer normal of the facet
    end for
    if the projections are positive at all vertices **then**
      the edge is unidirectional oriented out of $(k_1 \ldots k_N)$
    end if
    if the projections are negative at all vertices **then**
      the edge is unidirectional oriented towards $(k_1 \ldots k_N)$
    end if
    if there is a sign change among the projections at the vertices **then**
      the edge is bidirectional
    end if
  end for
end for

Algorithm 2 Construct a safe set $\mathcal{S}$

---

intialize $\mathcal{R}$ with T
repeat
  for each element R of $\mathcal{R}$ **do**
    for all incident nodes P connected with an edge (uni or bi-directional) oriented
    towards R **do**
      if P is not already in $\mathcal{R}$ **then**
        add P to $\mathcal{R}$
      end if
    end for
  end for
until cardinality of $\mathcal{R}$ increases
$\mathcal{S}$ is the complement of $\mathcal{R}$ with respect to the set of all nodes

---

in this paper guarantees the existence of a trajectory from a reactangle R to an adjacent rectangles P if the (unidirectional or bidirectional) edge between the corresponding nodes in the oriented graph has an arrow from R to P. But if there is an edge from R to P and also an edge from P to T, we cannot guarantee that there is a trajectory of the system from R to T. In our analysis, we simply say that there might be a trajectory from R to T, and so R is classified as "unsafe" for T.

4   Results

4.1   Steady States and Dynamical Simulations

The steady-state equations of (1) together with the three conservation laws imply[2]

$$R^{tot} = x_7 \left(1 + P_u^{tot} \frac{(1 + \tau \bar{k}_{3u}(g))\alpha_u}{1 + \alpha_u x_7} + [P_d^{tot}] \frac{(1 + \tau \bar{k}_{3d})(g)\alpha_d(g)}{1 + \alpha_d(g)x_7}\right) \quad , (15)$$

where we solved for x_1, x_2, x_3, x_4 and used the conservation laws for x_8, x_9. The r.h.s. of this equality is a monotonic function of x_7. It is zero for $x_7 = 0$ and exceeds R_{tot} for $x_7 = R_{tot}$. Therefore, *independently of g* , this equation has exactly one solution for x_7 in the interval $[0, R_{tot}]$. With this result we can solve uniquely for x_5 and finally, for x_6.

We can hence determine the quantity q (as defined in (3)), as a function of only g (or x_6). We illustrate this in Figure 4, where we plot $q(g)$ that results from the above derivation (thick line). On the other hand, from the steady-state condition on x_6, q should also be equal to $y = x_6/Q_{ref}(1 + r)$. The patterned lines in Fig. 4 represent the values of $q^{equilibrium} = y(g)$ as determined by the dependence of g on x_6, for two different r values. The steady states (for the respective r values) are at the intersection of the two types of lines.

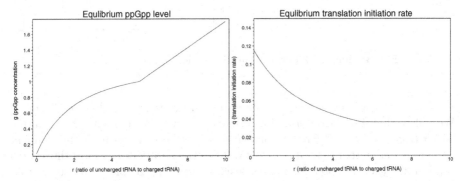

Fig. 2. Steady state values of the normalized ppGpp concentration (left) and of the normalized translation initiation rate (right), as a function of the outside quantity r.

We have verified the steady states described above numerically. The calculations have been performed in part by the software package Charon. Finding steady states in a hybrid system can be accomplished by finding steady states for each set of dynamics and discarding those that fall outside of the region that their dynamics hold over. Charon does this using the NLEQ package, which uses a damped Newton's method to search for roots of systems of equations. For each

---

[2] α_u, α_d are notations for $(k_{2u} + k_{3u})/k_{1u}$ and $(\bar{k}_{2d}(g) + \bar{k}_{3d}(g))/\bar{k}_{1d}(g)$, respectively.

set of dynamics, Charon selects several initial guesses in the appropriate region, looks for equilibrium points, and compares any results to the region in question.

There is only one valid steady state for a given value of the parameter r and conserved quantities $R^{tot}, P_d^{tot}, P_u^{tot}$. It follows the thick line in Figure 4. For $r < r_{trans}$[3] the steady state lies in the 'low' mode and then it crosses over to the 'high' mode. In fact both modes have their own steady state, but both lie on the same side of the mode dividing line $g = 1$. The dependence of our two observables (the (p)ppGpp concentration g and the transcription rate q) on the outside parameter r is given in Figure 2. As r increases, so does g and the transcription rate q decreases accordingly. The higher r, the fewer nutrients are available to the bacterium. This illustrates the main function of the switching mechanism. (p)ppGpp is a signalling substance, its concentration increases as an indicator of an adverse condition. The result of the adjustment is a decrease in transcriptional activity, to match the reduced availability of nutrients.

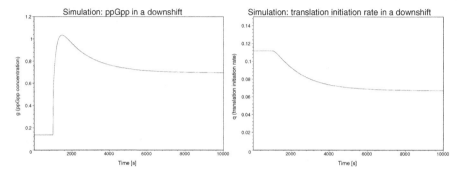

Fig. 3. Simulation output from the model. See text for details.

Outputs of a time-dependent simulation are presented in Figures 3 and 4. We follow the observables g and q discussed earlier. We emulate the situation which triggers the stringent response in nature. We start with an environment rich in nutrients, represented by a low value of the parameter r. After the system equilibrates (i.e., the steady state is reached), we change the parameter r to a high value, corresponding to a sudden downshift in the available nutrients[4]

In Figure 3 we plot our two observables as a function of time. At the downshift g increases very fast, then tapers off to stabilize at the equilibrium level. By contrast, q slowly decreases to reach the equilibrium value on the same timescale as g. This illustrates how the signal is immediately triggered by the sudden change in the outside conditions, while the state of the system (the transcription rate) lags behind, changing to the new value over a longer timescale. The pairs

---

[3] r_{trans} is the value of r for which $g^{equilibrium} = 1$.

[4] From here on the system evolves entirely in the dynamics determined by the higher r value, with the steady-state corresponding to the low r as initial condition. Hence all the following discussion refers to the dynamics with r fixed at the higher value.

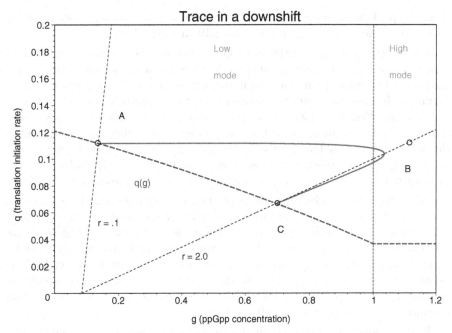

Fig. 4. A trace of the states of the simulation shown in Figures 2 and 3. The initial state is A and the final state is C. See text for details.

of (g, q) values for the same simulation are traced out in Figure 4, where we also indicated the locations of the equilibria. The initial and final states correspond to the points A and C respectively. In the course of the simulation the system crosses the mode boundary, when g briefly exceeds the threshold value of 1. There are no qualitative consequences of this transition. This should not be surprising since the model has been designed to seamlessly match the two modes.

4.2   Reachability Analysis

The role of the stringent response mechanism is to adjust the cell's transcriptional output to the level of available nutrients. This dependence is illustrated in Figure 2 for our model. The real cell has a similar characteristic. Nature constrains the bacterium very tightly to the optimal output: if the output is too high, stalled translational complexes will pile up and will eventually poison it; if it is too low, competitor species will gain an edge by using the nutrients more efficiently. Furthermore, the speed with which the adjustment takes place may also be a matter of life and death.

In *E.coli* the onset of the stringent response is accompanied by a surge in the intracellular level of (p)ppGpp. This high level persists for a relatively short time and then decreases to the equilibrium level for the new conditions. The final (p)ppGpp concentration is higher than the original one, but significantly lower than the peak value immediately following the onset. The surge of (p)ppGpp may have a role in achieving a fast downshift in transcription.

We are interested in how the surge in (p)ppGpp is determined in our model, which lacks an explicit mechanism that completely shuts down the transcription machinery (as can be seen from the horizontal section of the equilibrium line in Figure 4). Is our model capable of preventing the uncontrolled accumulation of stalled translational complexes? The number of stalled complexes is proportional to our variable x_6, the same as the one g is linked to. Therefore the height of the surge observed x_6 has a dual significance. It links to a directly measurable quantity (p)ppGpp which can serve as an experimental check, and it is also a measure of the potentially lethal (if too high) amount of translational complexes.

In applying the reachability algorithm to our model, we posed the following question: *given a value of r and an initial state of the system, is there a value of the variable x_6 which can not be reached in its subsequent evolution?* In the simulation described in Figure 3 the system is initially in the steady state for $r = 0.1$, and in the second part of the simulation the value of r is set to 2. So we are interested in the dynamics of the system at $r = 2$, and we would like to determine the upper limit for x_6 for various initial states, in a range that includes the steady state for $r = 0.1$.

We implemented various rectangular partitions of the nine-dimensional state space. Typically we used a small number, 2 or 3, of partitions for the variables other than x_6, and a large number of partitions (up to 16) for x_6. In a larger run, we used a set of $3^5 \times 6^2 \times 2^3 \times 17 = 1189728$ rectangular boxes, but only half of them were accessible because of a diagonal conservation law constraint (see below). With the boundaries chosen restrictively, only 30239 of these were reachable, or 'unsafe', yielding an upper limit of approximately $g^{max} = 1.4$. This should be compared to the actual maximum hit by the simulation, close to $g = 1.05$, and the built-in maximum close to $g^{hi} = 4.6$. Unconstrained calculations would lead to either full reachability, or exceed the limit of 100000 'unsafe' hyper-rectangles imposed by memory constraints. We conclude that the model does provide a significant limitation to the height of the surge in x_6 which is in reasonable agreement with the results of traditional simulations.

We found that limits imposed on the other variables have a strong influence on the outcome of the highest-value reachability analysis. In fact, a lack of such limits (i.e., lower limit zero and upper limits beyond those imposed by the conservation laws) leads to practically all points being reachable, hence no upper limit on x_6. This should not be surprising since a limitation on x_6, if it exists, can probably be traced back to a limitation on the other variables. The calculations that yielded reasonable upper limits had the allowed ranges for every variable set based on the initial equilibrium state (i.e., $0.2, 0.6, 1.2$ of the initial value). Furthermore, constraints on the variables that feed into x_6, that is x_3, x_4, x_5, had dramatic effects. In imposing the limits derived from a conservation law, $x_3 + x_4 < R_{tot}$, we had to limit the set of allowed rectangles to a set bounded by the 'discrete diagonal', i.e., the sum of the labels in the 3 and 4 directions were constrained to be less than a fixed integer.

5   Conclusions

We have built a model for the stringent response in bacteria such as $M.tb$ and $E.coli$. Analytical and numerical study shows that it indeed reproduces the main features of the stringent response. One striking feature is an upsurge in the concentration of (p)ppGpp following a nutritional downshift. This raises the question of an upper limit for the number of translational complexes, which is one of the dynamical variables in our model. In our framework, this question can be answered by performing a (conservative) reachability analysis of the switched rectangular multi-affine system. We plan to expand the capabilities of our software tools to perform series of reachability analyses targeted at refining a limiting extremal value. Also, we will examine further the issue of conservation laws which are characteristic to networks of chemical reactions.

Acknowledgement. This work was supported by the DARPA Biocomp grant, AF F30602-01-2-0563, and NSF grant EIA01-30797.

References

1. Glass L. Classification of biological networks by their qualitative dynamics. *Journal of Theoretical Biology*, 54:85–107, 1975.
2. Mestl T., E. Plathe, and S. W. Omholt. Periodic solutions in systems of piecewise-linear differential equations. *Dynamics and stability of systems*, 10(2):179–193, 1995.
3. de Jong H., J. L. Gouze, C. Hernandez, M. Page, T. Sari, and J. Geiselmann. Hybrid modeling and simulation of genetic regulatory networks: a qualitative approach. In *Hybrid Systems: Computation and Control*, 2003.
4. Kauffmann S. A. Metabolic stability and epigenesis in randomly constructed genetic nets. *Journal of Theoretical Biology*, 22:437–467, 1969.
5. Thomas R. Regulatory networks seen as asynchronous automata: a logical description. *Journal of Theoretical Biology*, 153:1–23, 1991.
6. Kuipers B. Qualitative simulation. *Artificial intelligence*, 29:289–388, 1981.
7. Brutlag D. L., A. R. Galper, and D. H. Millis. Knowledge-based simulation of *dna* metabolism: prediction of enzyme action. *Computer Applications in the Biosciences*, 7(1):9–19, 1991.
8. Kauffmann S. A. *The origins of order: self-organization and selection in evolution.* Oxford University Press, New York, 1993.
9. Mjolsness E., D. H. Sharp, and J. Reinitz. A connectionist model of development. *Journal of Theoretical Biology*, 152:429–453, 1991.
10. Gillespie D. T. Exact stochastic simulation of coupled chemical reactions. *J. Phys. Chem.*, 81:2340–2361, 1977.
11. McAdams H. M. and A. Arkin. Stochastic mechanisms in gene expression. *Proceedings of the National Academy of Science of the USA*, 94:814–819, 1997.
12. Gillespie D. T. Fluctuation and Dissipation in Brownian Motion. *Am. J. Phys*, 61():1077–1083, 1993.
13. R. Alur, T.A. Henzinger, and E.D. Sontag, editors. *Hybrid Systems III: Verification and Control.* LNCS 1066. Springer-Verlag, 1996.

14. T. Henzinger and S. Sastry, editors. *Hybrid Systems: Computation and Control.* LNCS 1386. Springer, 1998.
15. F. Vaandrager and J. van Schuppen, editors. *Hybrid Systems: Computation and Control.* LNCS 1569. Springer, 1999.
16. N. Lynch and B.H. Krogh, editors. *Hybrid Systems: Computation and Control.* LNCS 1790. Springer, 2000.
17. Tomlin C. and R. Ghosh. Lateral inhibition through delta-notch signaling: A piecewise affine hybrid model. *LNCS vol. 2034, Springer Verlag*, 2001.
18. R. Alur, C. Belta, F. Ivancic, V. Kumar, H. Rubin, J. Schug, O. Sokolsky, and J. Webb. Visual programming for modeling and simulation of bioregulatory networks. In *International Conference on High Performance Computing*, Bangalore, India, 2002.
19. C. Belta, L. Habets, and V. Kumar. Control of multi-affine systems on rectangles with applications to hybrid biomolecular networks. In *41st IEEE Conference on Decision and Control*, Los Angeles, NV, 2002.
20. C. Belta, J. Schug, T. Dang, V. Kumar, G. J. Pappas, H. Rubin, and P. V. Dunlap. Stability and reachability analysis of a hybrid model of luminescence in the marine bacterium vibrio fischeri. In *40th IEEE Conference on Decision and Control*, Orlando, FL, 2001.
21. R. Alur, C. Belta, V. Kumar, M. Mintz, G. J. Pappas, H. Rubin, and J. Schug. Modeling and analyzing biomolecular networks. *Computing in Science and Engineering*, pages 20–30, Jan/Feb 2002.
22. R. Alur, C. Belta, F. Ivancic, V. Kumar, M. Mintz, G. Pappas, and J. Schug. Hybrid modelling and simulation of biomolecular networks. In *Lecture Notes in Computer Science*, volume 2034, pages 19–32. 2001.
23. Primm T. P., S. J. Andersen, V. Mizrahi, D. Avarbock, H. Rubin, and C. E. Barry 3rd. The stringent response of *Mycobacterium tuberculosis* is required for long-term survival. *J. Bacteriol. Sep;182(17):4889-98*, 2000.
24. Gourse R. L., Gaal T., Bartlett M. S., Appleman J.A., and Ross W. rrna transcription and growth rate-dependent regulation of ribosome synthesis in *Escherichia coli. Annu. Rev. Microbiol., 50:645-77*, 1996.
25. Avarbock D., J. Salem, L. Li, Z. Wang, and H. Rubin. Cloning and characterization of a bifunctional *RelA/SpoT* homologue from *Mycobacterium tuberculosis. Gene 233, 261-269.*, 1999.
26. Avarbock D., A. Avarbock, and H. Rubin. Differential regulation of opposing activities by the amino-acylation state of a $tRNA \cdot Ribosome \cdot mRNA \cdot Rel_{Mtb}$ complex. *Biochemistry 39, 11640-11648.*, 2000.
27. Barker M. M., T. Gaal, C. A. Josaitis, and R. L. Gourse. Mechanism of regulation of transcription initiation by ppgpp. i. effects of (p)ppGpp on transcription initiation in vivo and in vitro. *J. Mol. Biol. Jan 26;305(4):673-88*, 2001.
28. Betts J. C., P. T. Lukey, L. C. Robb, R. A. McAdam, and K. Duncan. Evaluation of a nutrient starvation model of mycobacterium tuberculosis persistence by gene and protein expression profiling. *Mol Microbiol Feb;43(3):717-31*, 2002.
29. C. Belta, P. Finin, Á. Halász, M. Imieliñski, V. Kumar, and H. Rubin. Stringent Response in *Mycobacterium tuberculosis*, in preparation. A technical document is available upon request.

A SAT-Based Hybrid Solver
for Optimal Control of Hybrid Systems

Alberto Bemporad and Nicolò Giorgetti

Dip. Ingegneria dell'Informazione, University of Siena,
via Roma 56, 53100 Siena, Italy
{bemporad,giorgetti}@dii.unisi.it

Abstract. Combinatorial optimization over continuous and integer
variables was proposed recently as a useful tool for solving complex optimal control problems for linear hybrid dynamical systems formulated in
discrete-time. Current approaches are based on mixed-integer linear or
quadratic programming (MIP), which provides the solution after solving
a sequence of relaxed standard linear (or quadratic) programs (LP, QP).
An MIP formulation has the drawback of requiring conversion of the
discrete/logic part of the hybrid problem into mixed-integer inequalities.
Although this operation can be done automatically, most of the original
discrete structure of the problem is lost during the conversion. Moreover,
the efficiency of the MIP solver mainly relies upon the tightness of the
continuous LP/QP relaxations. In this paper we attempt to overcome
such difficulties by combining MIP and techniques for solving constraint
satisfaction problems into a "hybrid" solver, taking advantage of SAT
solvers for dealing efficiently with satisfiability of logic constraints. We
detail how to model the hybrid dynamics so that the optimal control
problem can be solved by the hybrid MIP+SAT solver, and show that
the achieved performance is superior to the one achieved by commercial
MIP solvers.

1 Introduction

Over the last few years we have witnessed a growing interest in the study of dynamical processes of a mixed continuous and discrete nature, denoted as hybrid
systems, both in academia and in industry. Hybrid systems are characterized by
the interaction of continuous models governed by differential or difference equations, and of logic rules, automata, and other discrete components (switches, se-
lectors, etc.). Hybrid systems can switch between many operating modes where
each mode is governed by its own characteristic continuous dynamical laws. Mode
transitions may be triggered internally (variables crossing specific thresholds),
or externally (discrete commands directly given to the system). The interest
in hybrid systems is mainly motivated by the large variety of practical situations where physical processes interact with digital controllers, as for instance
in embedded control systems.

Despite the fact that the first paper on hybrid systems appeared in the sixties [1], only in very recent years several modelling frameworks for hybrid systems

R. Alur and G.J. Pappas (Eds.): HSCC 2004, LNCS 2993, pp. 126–141, 2004.

have been proposed, we refer the interested reader to [2, 3] and the references therein. Several authors focused on the problem of solving optimal control problems for hybrid systems. For continuous-time hybrid systems, most of the literature either studied necessary conditions for a trajectory to be optimal, or focused on the computation of optimal/suboptimal solutions by means of dynamic programming or the maximum principle [4, 5, 6].

The hybrid optimal control problem becomes less complex when the dynamics is expressed in discrete-time, as the main source of complexity becomes the combinatorial (yet finite) number of possible switching sequences. In particular, in [7, 8, 9] the authors have solved optimal control problems for discrete-time hybrid systems by transforming the hybrid model into a set of linear equalities and inequalities involving both real and (0-1) variables, so that the optimal control problem can be solved by a mixed-integer programming (MIP) solver.

An MIP solver provides the solution after solving a sequence of relaxed standard linear (or quadratic) programs (LP, QP). A potential drawback of MIP is (1) the need for converting the discrete/logic part of the hybrid problem into mixed-integer inequalities, therefore losing most of the original discrete structure, and (2) the fact that its efficiency mainly relies upon the tightness of the continuous LP/QP relaxations.

Such a drawback is not suffered by techniques for solving constraint satisfaction problems (CSP), i.e., the problem of determining whether a set of constraints over discrete variables can be satisfied. Under the class of CSP solvers we mention constraint logic programming (CLP) [10] and SAT solvers [11], the latter specialized for the satisfiability of Boolean formulas.

While CSP methods are superior to MIP approaches for determining if a given problem has a feasible (integer) solution, the main drawback is their inefficiency for solving optimization, as they do not have the ability of MIP approaches to solve continuous relaxations (e.g., linear programming relaxations) of the problem in order to get upper and lower bounds to the optimum value.

For this reason, it seems extremely interesting to integrate the two approaches into one single solver. Some efforts have been done in this direction [12, 13, 14, 15, 16], showing that such mixed methods have a tremendous performance in solving mathematical programs with continuous (quantitative) and discrete (logical/symbolic) components, compared to MIP or CSP individually. Such successful results have stimulated also industrial interest: ILOG Inc., which is on of the worldwide leaders in software for combinatorial optimization, is currently distributing OPL (Optimization Programming Language), a modeling and programming language which allows the formulation and solution of optimization problems, using both MIP and CSP techniques, combining to some extent the advantages of both approaches.

At the light of the benefits and drawbacks of the previous work in [7,8,9] for solving control and stability/safety analysis problems for hybrid systems using MIP techniques, in this paper we follow a different route that uses a combined approach of MIP and CSP techniques. In particular, we focus on combinations of convex programming (e.g., linear, quadratic, etc.) for optimization over real

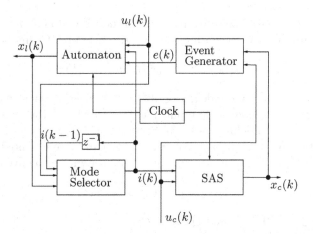

Fig. 1. Discrete-time hybrid system

variables, and of SAT-solvers for determining the satisfiability of Boolean formulas.

We build up a new modeling approach directly tailored to the use of a "hybrid" MIP+SAT solver for solving optimal control problems, and show its computational advantages over pure MIP methods. A preliminary work in this direction appeared in [17], where generic constraint logic programming (CLP) was used for handling the discrete part of the problem.

The paper is organized as follows. Discrete-time hybrid models are introduced in Section 2. In Section 3 the optimal control problem is formulated and in Section 4 it is reformulated in a suitable way for the combined MIP-CSP approach. Section 5 introduces the new solution algorithm and an example showing the benefits of this technique, compared to pure MIP approaches [7,9] is shown in section 6.

2   Discrete-Time Hybrid Systems

Following the ideas of [9], a hybrid system can be modeled as the interconnection of an automaton (AUT) and a switched affine system (SAS) through an event generator (EG) and a mode selector (MS) (see Figure 1). The automaton describes the logic dynamics of the hybrid system, the SAS describes the continuous dynamics, the EG and MS describe the interactions between these dynamics.

2.1   Automaton

The discrete dynamics of a hybrid system can be modeled as an automaton (or finite state machine). We will only refer to "synchronous automata", where transitions are clocked and synchronous with the sampling time of the continuous dynamical equations. The adjective "synchronous" will be omitted for brevity. The automaton evolves according to the logic state update function

$$x_l(k+1) = f_l(x_l(k), u_l(k), e(k)), \tag{1a}$$

where $k \in \mathbb{Z}^+$ is the time index, $x_l \in \mathcal{X}_l \subseteq \{0,1\}^{n_l}$ is the logic state, $u_l \in \mathcal{U}_l \subseteq \{0,1\}^{m_l}$ is the exogenous logic input, $e \in \mathcal{E} \subseteq \{0,1\}^{n_e}$ is the endogenous input coming from the EG defined below in Section 2.3, and $f_l : \mathcal{X}_l \times \mathcal{U}_l \times \mathcal{E} \rightarrow \mathcal{X}_l$ is a deterministic Boolean function. An automaton can be represented as a directed graph (as in Figure 2, for instance). An automaton may also have a logic output

$$y_l(k) = g_l(x_l(k), u_l(k), e(k)), \tag{1b}$$

where $y_l \in \mathcal{Y}_l \subseteq \{0,1\}^{p_l}$, and $g_l : \mathcal{X}_l \times \mathcal{U}_l \times \mathcal{E} \rightarrow \mathcal{Y}_l$ is also a Boolean function. In the sequel, with a slight abuse of notation, we will refer to the codomain of Boolean functions both as $\{0,1\}$ and as $\{\text{FALSE}, \text{TRUE}\}$. In the context of Boolean functions and formulas, the equal sign $(=)$ should be interpreted as an if-and-only-if condition $(\longleftrightarrow)$.

2.2   Switched Affine System

The continuous dynamics can be modeled by a switched affine system (SAS). A SAS is a collection of affine systems:

$$x_c(k+1) = A_{i(k)} x_c(k) + B_{i(k)} u_c(k) + f_{i(k)} \tag{2a}$$
$$y_c(k) = C_{i(k)} x_c(k) + D_{i(k)} u_c(k) + g_{i(k)}, \tag{2b}$$

where $x_c \in \mathcal{X}_c \subseteq \mathbb{R}^{n_c}$ is the continuous state vector, $u_c \in \mathcal{U}_c \subseteq \mathbb{R}^{m_c}$ is the exogenous continuous input vector, $y_c \in \mathcal{Y}_c \subseteq \mathbb{R}^{p_c}$ is the continuous output vector, $i(k) \in \mathcal{I} \triangleq \left\{ [1\,0\cdots0]^T, \cdots, [0\cdots0\,1]^T \right\} \subseteq \{0,1\}^s$ SAS is operating, $|\mathcal{I}| = s$ is the number of elements of $\mathcal{I}$, and $\{A_i, B_i, f_i, C_i, D_i, g_i\}_{i \in \mathcal{I}}$ is a collection of matrices of opportune dimensions. The mode $i(k)$ is generated by the mode selector, as described below in Section 2.4. A SAS of the form (2) preserves the value of the state when a switch occurs. However, resets can be modeled in the present discrete-time setting as detailed in [9].

2.3   Event Generator

An event generator is a mathematical object that generates a logic signal according to the satisfaction of a linear affine constraint:

$$[e_j(k) = 1] \longleftrightarrow [a_j^T x_c(k) + b_j^T u_c(k) \le c_j], \tag{3}$$

where the subscript j denotes the jth component of the vector, and $a_j \in \mathbb{R}^{n_c}$, $b_j \in \mathbb{R}^{m_c}$, $c_j \in \mathbb{R}$ define a linear guard (i.e., an hyperplane) in the space of continuous states and inputs.

2.4   Mode Selector

The dynamic mode $i(k)$ of the SAS, that we will also call the *active mode*, is selected through a *mode selector*

$$i(k) = f_{\text{MS}}(x_l(k), u_l(k), i(k-1)), \tag{4}$$

where $f_{MS} : \mathcal{X}_l \times \mathcal{U}_l \times \mathcal{I} \to \mathcal{I}$ is a Boolean function of the logic state $x_l(k)$, of the logic input $u_l(k)$, and of the active mode $i(k-1)$ at the previous sampling instant. We say that a *mode switch* occurs at step k if $i(k) \neq i(k-1)$. Note that contrarily to continuous time hybrid models, where switches can occur at any time, in our discrete-time setting a mode switch can only occur at sampling instants.

3   Optimal Control

A finite-time optimal control problem for the class of hybrid systems introduced in the previous section can be formulated as follows:

$$\min_{\{x(k+1), u(k)\}_{k=0}^{T-1}} \sum_{k=0}^{T-1} \ell_k(x(k+1) - r_x(k+1), u(k) - r_u(k)) \tag{5a}$$

$$\text{s.t. dynamics } (1), (2), (3), (4) \tag{5b}$$

$$h_D(x(0), \{x(k+1), u(k), e(k), i(k)\}_0^{T-1}) \leq 0 \tag{5c}$$

$$h_A(x(0), \{x(k+1), u(k), e(k), i(k)\}_0^{T-1}) \leq 0 \tag{5d}$$

where T is the control horizon, $\ell_k : \mathbb{R}^{n \times m} \to \mathbb{R}$ is a nonnegative convex function, $n = n_c + n_l$, $m = m_c + m_l$, $r_x \in \mathbb{R}^n$, $r_u \in \mathbb{R}^m$ are given reference trajectories to be tracked by the state and input vectors, respectively.

The constraints of the optimal control problem can be classified in three different categories:

Dynamical constraints (5b) . These constraints represent the discrete-time hybrid system dynamics. They may also include other constraints such as saturation constraints on continuous input variables, that are embodied in the variable domain $\mathcal{U}_c$.

Design constraints (5c) . These are artificial constraints imposed by the designer to fulfill the required specifications. Examples of such constraints may be state limits

$$x_{min}(k) \leq x_c(k) \leq x_{max}(k), \ k = 1, \ldots, T,$$

where $x_{min}(k)$, $x_{max}(k)$ are bounds that the designer wants to impose on continuous states.

Ancillary constraints (5d). These constraints provide an a priori additional and auxiliary information for determining the optimal solution. They do not change the solution itself, rather help the solver by restricting the set of feasible combinations, and therefore the size of the decision tree in a branch a bound strategy. For example, one may pre-compute all possible mode transitions of the SAS dynamics using reachability analysis, and impose *reachability constraints* of the form $[\delta_h(k) = 1] \rightarrow [\delta_j(k+1) = 0]$ (or equivalently $\delta_h(k) + \delta_j(k+1) \leq 1$) for all $k = 0, \dots, T-2$ whenever a transition from the hth mode to the jth mode is not possible.

4   Problem Reformulation

Problem (5) can be solved via MILP when the costs ℓ_k are convex piecewise linear functions, for instance $\ell_k(x, u) = \|Q_x x\|_\infty + \|Q_u u\|_\infty$, where Q_x, Q_u are full-rank matrices and $\|\cdot\|_\infty$ denotes the infinity-norm ($\|Qx\|_\infty = \max_{j=1,\dots,n} |Q^j x|$, where Q^j is the j-th row of Q) [8], or via MIQP (mixed integer quadratic programming) when $\ell_k(x, u) = x'Q_x x + u'Q_u u$, where Q_x, Q_u are positive (semi)definite matrices [7].

Following a different route, in this paper we wish to solve problem (5) by using MIP and SAT techniques in a combined approach, taking advantage of SAT for dealing with the purely logic part of the problem. In order to do this, we need to reformulate the problem in a suitable way.

The automaton and mode selector parts of the hybrid system are described as a set of Boolean constraints so they do not require transformations. The event generator (2.3) can be equivalently expressed, by adopting the so-called "big-M" technique, as

$$(a_j^T x_c(k) + b_j^T u_c(k) - c_j) \leq M_j(1 - e_j(k)), \tag{6a}$$

$$(a_j^T x_c(k) + b_j^T u_c(k) - c_j) > m_j e_j(k), \tag{6b}$$

where $j = 1, \dots, n_e$, M_j, m_j are upper and lower bounds, respectively, on $a_j^T x_c(k) + b_j^T u_c(k) - c_j$, and $e_j(k) \in \{0, 1\}$. From a computational viewpoint, it may be convenient to have a set of inequalities without strict inequalities. In this case we will follow the common practice [18] of replacing the strict inequality (6) as

$$(a_j^T x_c(k) + b_j^T u_c(k) - c_j) \geq \epsilon + (m_j - \epsilon) e_j(k), \tag{6c}$$

where ϵ is a small positive scalar, e.g., the machine precision, although the equivalence does not hold for $0 < (a_j^T x_c(k) + b_j^T u_c(k) - c_j) < \epsilon$ (i.e., for the numbers in the interval $(0, \epsilon)$ that cannot be represented in the machine). The continuous state update equation of the SAS dynamics (2) can be equivalently written as the combination of linear terms and *if-then-else* rules:

$$w_i(k) = \begin{cases} A_i x_c(k) + B_i u_c(k) + f_i & \text{if } (\delta_i = 1) \\ 0 & \text{otherwise} \end{cases} \tag{7a}$$

$$x_c(k+1) = \sum_{i=1}^{s} w_i(k) \tag{7b}$$

where $w_i(k) \in \mathbb{R}^{n_c}$, $i = 1, \ldots, s$. The output y_c of the SAS dynamics admits a similar transformation. The SAS representation (7) can be translated into a set of constraints by also using the big-M technique [18]:

$$-M_i^j \delta_i(k) + w_i(k) \leq 0, \tag{8a}$$

$$m_i^j \delta_i(k) - w_i(k) \leq 0, \tag{8b}$$

$$m_i^j(1 - \delta_i(k)) + w_i(k) \leq A_i^j x_c(k) + B_i^j u_c(k) + f_i^j, \tag{8c}$$

$$-M_i^j(1 - \delta_i(k)) - w_i(k) \leq -A_i^j x_c(k) - B_i^j u_c(k) - f_i^j, \tag{8d}$$

where M_i^j, m_i^j are upper and lower bounds on $A_i^j x_c(k) + B_i^j u_c(k) + f_i^j$, $\delta_i(k) \in \{0,1\}$, $w_i(k) \in \mathbb{R}^{n_c}$, $x_c \in \mathbb{R}^n$, $u \in \mathbb{R}^m$, j denotes the jth component or row, $j = 1, \ldots, n_c$, $i = 1, \ldots, s$, and k is the time index. Note that the vector of (0-1) variables $i(k) = [\delta_1(k) \ \ldots \ \delta_s(k)]' \in \{0,1\}^s$ is subject to the exclusive or condition

$$\delta_1(k) \oplus \delta_2(k) \oplus \ldots \oplus \delta_s(k) = \text{TRUE}. \tag{9}$$

By using the transformations into mixed integer inequalities described earlier, problem (5) can be cast as the mixed-integer convex program

$$\min_{\substack{\{x(k+1), u(k), \\ w(k), \delta(k)\} \\ k = 0, \ldots, T-1}} \sum_{k=0}^{T-1} \ell_k(x(k+1) - r_x(k+1), u(k) - r_u(k)) \tag{10a}$$

$$\text{s.t. } A x_c(k) \leq b, \ x_c(k+1) = \sum_{i=1}^{s} w_i(k) \tag{10b}$$

$$M_1 x_c(k) + M_2 u_c(k) + M_3 w(k) \leq M_4 e(k) + M_5 \delta(k) + M_6 \tag{10c}$$

$$g(x_l(k+1), x_l(k), u_l(k), e(k), \delta(k)) = \text{TRUE} \tag{10d}$$

$$w(k) = [w_1(k) \ldots w_s(k)]', \ w_i(k) \in \mathbb{R}^{n_c}, \ \delta(k) \in \{0,1\}^s,$$

where $\{x_c(k+1), u_c(k), w(k)\}_{k=0}^{T-1}$ are the continuous optimization variables, $\{x_l(k+1), u_l(k), \delta(k), e(k)\}_{k=0}^{T-1}$ are the binary optimization variables, $x_c(0)$, $x_l(0)$ is a given initial state, constraints (10b), (10c) represent the EG and SAS parts (6a), (6c), (7b), (8), and the purely continuous or mixed constraints from (5c), (5d), while (10d) represents the automaton (1a), the mode selector (4), possible purely Boolean constraints from (5c), (5d), as well as the exclusive or condition (9). Matrices M_i, $i = 1 \ldots 6$, are obtained by the big-M representations (6) and (8).

Problem (10) belongs to the following general class of *mixed logical/convex* problems:

$$\min_{z,\nu,\mu} f(z) \tag{11a}$$

$$\text{s.t. } g_c(x_c(0), z) \leq 0, \ h_c(x_c(0), z) = 0 \qquad \text{(Continuous constraints)} \tag{11b}$$

$$g_m(x_c(0), x_l(0), z, \mu) \leq 0, \ h_m(x_c(0), x_l(0), z, \mu) = 0 \qquad \text{(Mixed constraints)} \tag{11c}$$

$$g_L(x_l(0), \nu, \mu) = \text{TRUE} \qquad \text{(Logic constraints)} \tag{11d}$$

$$z \in \mathbb{R}^{n_z}, \ \nu \in \{0,1\}^{n_\nu}, \ \mu \in \{0,1\}^{n_\mu}$$

where $g_c : \mathbb{R}^{n_z} \rightarrow \mathbb{R}^{q_{gc}}$, $g_m : \mathbb{R}^{n_z+n_\mu} \rightarrow \mathbb{R}^{q_{gm}}$ are convex functions, $h_c : \mathbb{R}^{n_z} \rightarrow \mathbb{R}^{q_{hc}}$, $h_m : \mathbb{R}^{n_z+n_\mu} \rightarrow \mathbb{R}^{q_{hm}}$ are affine functions, and $g_L : \{0,1\}^{n_\nu \times n_\mu} \rightarrow \{0,1\}^{n_{CP}}$ is a Boolean function. In the hybrid optimal control problem at hand, z collects all the continuous variables ($x_c(k+1)$, $u_c(k)$, $k = 0, \ldots, T-1$), the auxiliary variables needed for expressing the SAS dynamics, possibly slack variables for upper bounding the cost function in (10a) [8], μ collects the integer variables that appear in mixed constraints ($e(k)$, $\delta_i(k)$, $k = 0, \ldots, T-1$, $i = 1, \ldots, s$), and ν collects the integer variables such as $x_l(k)$, $u_l(k)$ that only appear in logic constraints. Note that in general if the objective function in the the form $f(z, \mu)$ we could consider the new objective function ϵ, $\epsilon \in \mathbb{R}$, and an additional constraint $f(z, \mu) \leq \epsilon$ which is a mixed convex constraint that could be included in (11c).

5   SAT-Based Branch and Bound

5.1   Constraint Satisfaction and Optimization

CSP and optimization are similar enough to make their combination possible, and yet different enough to make it profitable. Optimization is primarily associated with mathematics and engineering, while CSP was developed (more recently) in the computer science and artificial intelligence communities. The two fields evolved more or less independently until a few years ago. Yet they have much in common and are applied to solve similar problems. Most importantly for the purposes of this paper, they have complementary strengths, and the last few years have seen growing efforts to combine them [13, 12, 19, 14, 20].

The recent interaction between CSP and optimization promises to affect both fields. In the following subsections we illustrate an approach for merging them into a single problem-solving technology, in particular by combining convex optimization and satisfiability of Boolean formulas (SAT).

Convex Optimization. Convex optimization is very popular in engineering, economics, and other application domains for solving nontrivial decision problems. Convex optimization includes linear, quadratic, and semidefinite programming, for which several extremely efficient commercial and public domain solvers are nowadays available. An excellent reference to convex optimization is the book by Boyd and Vandenberghe [21].

SAT Problems. An instance of a satisfiability (SAT) problem is a Boolean formula that has three components:

- A set of n variables: $x_1, x_2, \ldots, x_n$.
- A set of literals. A literal is a variable $(Q = x)$ or a negation of a variable $(Q = \neg x)$.
- A set of m distinct clauses: $C_1, C_2, \ldots, C_m$. Each clause consists of only literals combined by just logical *or* $(\vee)$ connectives.

The goal of the satisfiability problem is to determine whether there exists an assignment of truth values to variables that makes the following Conjunctive Normal Form (*CNF*) formula satisfiable:

$$C_1 \wedge C_2 \wedge \ldots \wedge C_m,$$

where $\wedge$ is a logical *and* connective. For a survey on SAT problems and related solvers the reader is referred to [11].

5.2   A SAT-Based "Hybrid" Algorithm

The basic ingredients for an integrated approach are (1) a solver for convex problems obtained from relaxations over continuous variables of mixed integer convex programming problems, and (2) a SAT solver for testing the satisfiability of Boolean formulas. The relaxed model is used to obtain a solution that satisfies the constraint sets (11b) and (11c) and optimizes the objective function (11a). The optimal solution of the relaxation may fix some of the (0-1) variables to either 0 or 1. If all the (0-1) variables in the relaxed problem have been assigned (0-1) values, the solution of the relaxation is also a feasible solution of the mixed integer problem. More often, however, some of the (0-1) variables have fractional parts, so that further "branching" and solution of further relaxations is necessary. To accelerate the search of feasible solutions one may use the fixed (0-1) variables to "infer" new information on the other (0-1) variables by solving a SAT problem obtained by constraint (11d). In particular, when an integer solution of μ is found from convex programming, a SAT problem then verifies whether this solution can be completed with an assignment of ν that satisfies (11d).

The basic branch&bound (B&B) strategy for solving mixed integer problems can be extended to the present "hybrid" setting where both convex optimization and SAT solvers are used. In a B&B algorithm, the current best integer solution is updated whenever an integer solution with an even better value of the objective function is found. In the hybrid algorithm at hand an additional SAT problem is solved to ensure that the integer solution obtained for the relaxed problem is feasible for the constraints (11d) and to find an assignment for the other logic variables ν that appear in (11d). It is only in this case that the current best integer solution is updated.

The B&B method requires the solution of a series of convex subproblems obtained by branching on integer variables. Here, the non-integer variable to branch on is chosen by selecting the variable with the largest fractional part (i.e., the one closest to 0.5), and two new convex subproblems are formed with that variable fixed at 0 and at 1, respectively. When an integer feasible solution of the relaxed problem is obtained, a satisfiability problem is solved to complete the solution. The value of the objective function for an integer feasible solution of the whole problem is an upper bound (UB) of the objective function, which may be used to rule out branches where the optimum value attained by the relaxation is larger than the current upper bound.

Let P denote the set of convex and SAT subproblems to be solved. The proposed SAT-based B&B method can be summarized as follows:

1. **Initialization.** $UB = \infty$, $P = \{(p^0, SAT^0)\}$. The convex subproblem p^0 is generated by using (11a),(11b), (11c) along with the relaxation $\mu \in [0, 1]^{n_\mu}$, and the SAT subproblem SAT^0 is generated by using (11d).
2. **Node selection.** If $P = \emptyset$ then go to 7.; otherwise select and remove a (p, SAT) problem from the set P; The criterion for selecting a problem is called *node selection rule*.
3. **Logic inference.** Solve problem SAT. If it is infeasible go to step 2.
4. **Convex reasoning**. Solve the convex problem p, and:
   4.1. If the problem is infeasible or the optimal value of the objective function is greater than UB then go to step 2.
   4.2. If the solution is not integer feasible then go to step 6.
5. **Bounding.** Let $\mu^* \in \{0, 1\}^{n_\mu}$ be the integer part of the optimal solution found at step 4.; to extend this partial solution, solve the SAT problem finding ν such that $g(\nu, \mu^*)$ =TRUE. If the SAT problem is feasible then update UB; otherwise add to the LP problems of the set P the "no-good" cut [12]

$$\sum_{i \in T^*} \mu_i - \sum_{j \in F^*} \mu_j \leq B^* - 1,$$

   where $T^* = \{i | \mu_i^* = 1\}$, $F^* = \{j | \mu_j^* = 0\}$, and $B^* = |T^*|$. Go to step 2.
6. **Branching.** Among all variables that have fractional values, select the one closest to 0.5. Let μ_i be the selected non-integer variable, and generate two subproblems $(p \cup \{\mu_i = 0\}, SAT\&\{\neg\mu\})$, $(p \cup \{\mu_i = 1\}, SAT\&\{\mu\})$ and add them to set P; go to step 2.
7. **Termination.** If $UB = \infty$, then the problem is infeasible. Otherwise, the optimal solution is the current value UB.

Remark 1. At each node of the search tree the algorithm executes a three-step procedure: logic inference, solution of the convex relaxation, and branching. The first step and the attempted completion of the solution do not occur in MIP approaches but they are introduced here by the distinction of mixed (0-1) variables μ and pure (0-1) variables ν. The logic inference and the attempted completion steps do not change the correctness and the termination of the algorithm but

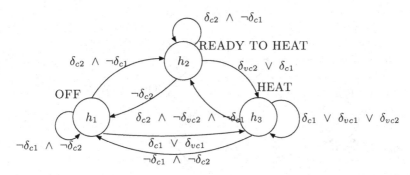

Fig. 2. Automaton regulating the heater

they improve the performance of the algorithm because of the efficiency of the SAT solver in finding a feasible integer solution.

6   Numerical Results

In this section we show on an example of hybrid optimal control problem that the hybrid solution technique described in the previous sections has a better performance compared to commercial MIP solvers.

6.1   Hybrid Model

Consider a room with two bodies with temperatures T_1, T_2 and let T_{amb} be the room temperature (this example is an extension of the example reported in [22]). The room is equipped with a heater, close to body 1, delivering thermal power u_{hot} and an air conditioning system, close to body 2, draining thermal power u_{cold}. These are turned on/off according to some rules dictated by the closeness of the two bodies to each device. We want guarantee that the bodies are not cold or hot.

The discrete-time continuous dynamics of each body is described by the difference equation

$$\frac{T_i(k+1) - T_i(k)}{T_s} = -\alpha_i(T_i(k) - T_{amb}) + k_i(u_{hot}(k) - u_{cold}(k)) + cu_e(k), \tag{12}$$

where $i = 1, 2$, α_i, k_i, c are suitable constants, T_s is the sampling time, and $u_e(k)$ is an exogenous input that can be used to deliver or drain thermal power manually (e.g. by opening a window or by changing the water flow from a centralized heating system).

The automaton part of the system is described by the two automata represented in Figures 2 and 3, where $\delta_{ci}, \delta_{vci}, \gamma_{hi}$ and γ_{vhi}, for $i = 1, 2$, are logic variables defined as follows

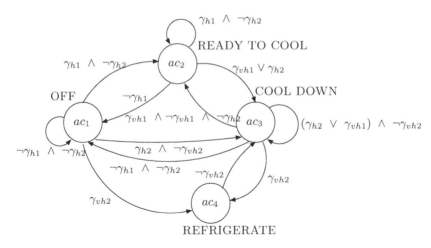

Fig. 3. Air conditioning system automaton

$$[\delta_{vci}(k) = 1] \longleftrightarrow [T_i(k) \leq T_{vci}], \tag{13a}$$

$$[\delta_{ci}(k) = 1] \longleftrightarrow [T_i(k) \leq T_{ci}], \tag{13b}$$

$$[\gamma_{hi}(k) = 1] \longleftrightarrow [T_i(k) \geq T_{hi}], \tag{13c}$$

$$[\gamma_{vhi}(k) = 1] \longleftrightarrow [T_i(k) \geq T_{vhi}], \tag{13d}$$

and where $T_{vci} \leq T_{ci} \leq T_{hi} \leq T_{vhi}$ are constant thresholds. The automaton for the heater (Figure 2) sets the heater in the "ready to heat" state if body 2 is cold, and will go in "heat" state if body 2 is very cold. If body 1 is cold or very cold the heater is turned on immediately. The automaton of the air conditioning (A/C) system (Figure 3) sets the air conditioning system in the "ready to cool" state if body 1 is hot, unless body 2 is cold, in other words, the A/C system is turned on only when body 1 is very hot. However, the draining thermal power is half of the full power. The A/C system is set to the maximum power if the body 2 is very hot but it is immediately switched to half power as soon as body 2 is only hot (due to energy consumptions of the A/C system).

The heater delivers thermal power and the A/C system drains thermal power according to the following rules:

$$u_{\text{hot}} = \begin{cases} u_H & \text{if } h_3 = 1 \\ 0 & \text{otherwise} \end{cases} \qquad u_{\text{cold}} = \begin{cases} u_C & \text{if } ac_4 = 1 \\ \frac{u_C}{2} & \text{if } ac_3 = 1 \\ 0 & \text{otherwise} \end{cases} . \tag{14}$$

By following the notation of (1), we have $x_l = [h_1 \ h_2 \ h_3 \ ac_1 \ ac_2 \ ac_3 \ ac_4]' \in \{0,1\}^7$, $u_l = \emptyset$ and $e(k) = [\delta_{vc1} \ \delta_{vc2} \ \delta_{c1} \ \delta_{c2} \ \gamma_{h1} \ \gamma_{h2} \ \gamma_{vh1} \ \gamma_{vh2}]' \in \{0,1\}^8$.

The system has six modes: $(u_{\text{hot}}, u_{\text{cold}}) \in \{(0,0), (u_H, 0), (0, u_C), (0, u_C/2),$ $(u_H, u_C), (u_H, u_C/2)\}$. The mode selector function is defined as follows

$$
i(k) = \begin{bmatrix} \neg h_3(k) \wedge \neg ac_4(k) \wedge \neg ac_3(k) \\ h_3(k) \wedge \neg ac_4(k) \wedge \neg ac_3(k) \\ \neg h_3(k) \wedge ac_4(k) \wedge \neg ac_3(k) \\ \neg h_3(k) \wedge \neg ac_4(k) \wedge ac_3(k) \\ h_3(k) \wedge ac_4(k) \wedge \neg ac_3(k) \\ h_3(k) \wedge \neg ac_4(k) \wedge ac_3(k) \end{bmatrix} \in \{0,1\}^6,
$$

which only depends on logic states.

The SAS dynamics (12), i.e., the continuous part of the hybrid system, is translated into a set of inequalities using (8), which provides the set of constraints

$$
Ax_c(k) + Bu_c(k) + Cw(k) \leq D\delta(k) + E, \tag{15}
$$

where $x_c = [T_1\ T_2]'$, $u_c = u_e$, $w(k) \in \mathbb{R}^3$ contains the auxiliary continuous variables needed to represent the conditions $u_{\text{hot}} = u_H$, $u_{\text{cold}} = u_C$, $u_{\text{cold}} = u_C/2$, and $\delta(k) = [h_3(k)\ ac_3(k)\ ac_4(k)] \in \{0,1\}^3$. Constraints (15) are obtained by employing the HYSDEL compiler [9].

Finally, the event generator is represented by (13a) and (13b). These are translated by HYSDEL into a set of linear inequalities using (6):

$$
G'_x x_c(k) + G'_u u_c(k) + D'e(k) \leq E', \tag{16}
$$

where $e(k) = [\delta_{vc1}\ \delta_{vc2}\ \delta_{c1}\ \delta_{c2}\ \gamma_{h1}\ \gamma_{h2}\ \gamma_{vh1}\ \gamma_{vh2}]' \in \{0,1\}^8$.

6.2   Optimal Control Problem

The goal is to design an optimal control profile for the continuous input u_e that minimizes $\sum_{k=0}^{T} |T_i(k) - T_{amb}|$ subject to the hybrid dynamics and the following additional constraints:

– Continuous constraints on temperatures to avoid that they assume unacceptable values

$$
-10 \leq T_1(k) \leq 50 \qquad\qquad -10 \leq T_2(k) \leq 50. \tag{17a}
$$

These constraints may be interpreted as dynamical constraints due to physical limitations of the bodies.

– A continuous constraint on exogenous input to avoid excessive variations:

$$
-10 \leq u_e(k) \leq 10. \tag{18}
$$

This constraint may be interpreted as a design constraint of the form (5c).

The above dynamics and constraints are also modeled in HYSDEL [9] to obtain an MLD model of the hybrid system in order to compare the performance achieved by the hybrid solver with the one obtained by employing a pure MILP approach.

The optimal control problem is defined over horizon of T steps as:

$$\min_{\{x,u,z,\delta,\epsilon_T\}} \sum_{k=0}^{T-1} \epsilon_T(k) \tag{19a}$$

$$\text{s.t. } \epsilon_T(k) \begin{bmatrix} 1 \\ \vdots \\ 1 \end{bmatrix} \geq \pm(T_i(k) - T_{amb}), \tag{19b}$$

$$\text{automata Figures 2, 3,} \tag{19c}$$

$$(15), (16) \tag{19d}$$

$$(17), (18) \tag{19e}$$

where $\{x, u, z, \delta, \epsilon_T\} = \{x(k), u(k), z(k), \delta(k), \epsilon_T(k)\}_{k=0}^{T-1}$, $\epsilon_T = [\epsilon_{T1}(0), \epsilon_{T2}(0), \ldots, \epsilon_{T1}(T-1), \epsilon_{T2}(T-1)]' \in \mathbb{R}^{2T}$.

Each part of the optimal control problem is managed by either the SAT solver or the LP solver: the cost function (19a), the inequalities (19b), (19d), and the additional constraints (19e) are managed by the LP solver, the logic part (19c) is managed by the SAT solver. In our simulations we have used, respectively, zCHAFF [23] for SAT and CPLEX [24] for LP.

In all our simulations we have adopted depth first search as the *node selection rule*, to reduce the amount of memory used during the search.

For the initial condition $T_1(0) = 5°$ C, $T_2(0) = 2°$ C and for $T_{amb} = 25°$ C we have done simulations for different horizons (the obtained optimal solution is clearly the same both using the SAT-based B&B and the MILP), reported in Table 1.

We can see that the performance of the SAT-based B&B is always better than the one obtained via MILP. The main reason is that the SAT B&B algorithm solves a much smaller number of LPs than the MILP solver. The "cuts" performed by the SAT solver, i.e. the infeasible SAT problems, obtained at step 3 of the algorithm turn out very useful to exclude subtrees containing no integer feasible solution. Moreover, the time spent for solving an integer feasibility problem described as SAT problem is much smaller than solving a pure integer problem, see Table 2. We can also see from Table 1 that the number of feasible SAT solved equals the number of LP solved plus one. This one more SAT is used to complete a feasible solution and it turns out very useful to further reduce the computation time.

The results were simulated on a PC Pentium IV 1.8 GHz running CPLEX 8.1 and zCHAFF 2003.07.22.

7   Conclusions

In this paper we have proposed a new unifying framework for MIP and CSP techniques based on the integration of convex programming and SAT solvers for

Table 1. Optimal control solution: comparison between pure MILP (CPLEX) and SAT-based B&B

T	Int Vars	MILP (s)	LPs	SATbB&B (s)	LPs	SATs	"cuts"
5	75	0.04	60	0.04	15	16	0
10	150	0.22	119	0.38	15	16	0
15	225	0.61	152	0.66	17	18	2
20	300	1.452	248	1.011	17	18	3
25	375	2.594	301	1.512	19	20	2
30	450	4.307	363	2.093	20	21	4
35	525	5.729	367	2.844	20	21	5
40	600	12.058	486	3.505	27	28	9
45	675	13.479	534	4.367	31	32	7
50	750	19.108	607	5.368	43	44	8

Table 2. Computation time for solving a pure integer feasibility problem: comparison between the SAT (zCHAFF) and MILP (CPLEX)

T	Int. Vars	Constraints	SAT (s)	MILP (s)
5	75	460	0	0.03
10	150	920	0.01	0.03
15	225	1380	0.02	0.04
20	300	1840	0.03	0.04
25	375	2300	0.04	0.05
30	450	2760	0.05	0.06
35	525	3220	0.06	0.08
40	600	3680	0.08	0.11
45	675	4140	0.08	0.15
50	750	4600	0.08	0.18

solving optimal control problems for discrete-time hybrid systems. The approach consists of a logic-based branch and bound algorithm, whose performance in terms of computation time is superior in comparison to more standard mixed-integer programming techniques, as we have illustrated on an example.

Ongoing research is devoted to the improvement of the logic-based method by including relaxations of the automaton and MS parts of the hybrid system in the convex programming part, to the investigation of alternative relaxations of the SAS dynamics that are tighter than the big-M method, to the use of SAT solvers for also performing domain reduction (cutting planes), and to the use of the SAT-based B&B algorithm for reachability analysis and for efficiently converting discrete-time hybrid systems to an equivalent piecewise affine form.

Acknowledgment. This research was supported by the European Union through project IST-2001-33520 "CC-Computation and Control".

References

1. H. Witsenhausen. A class of hybrid-state continuous-time dynamic systems. *IEEE Trans. Automatic Control*, 11(2):161–167, 1966.
2. P.J. Antsaklis. A brief introduction to the theory and applications of hybrid systems. *Proc. IEEE, Special Issue on Hybrid Systems: Theory and Applications*, 88(7):879–886, July 2000.
3. C.G. Cassandras, D.L. Pepyne, and Y.Wardi. Optimal control of a class of hybrid systems. *IEEE Trans. Automatic Control*, 46(3):3981–415, 2001.
4. X. Xu and P.J. Antsaklis. An approach to switched systems optimal control based on parameterization of the switching instants. In *Proc. IFAC World Congress*, Barcelona, Spain, 2002.
5. B. Lincoln and A. Rantzer. Optimizing linear system switching. In *Proc. 40th IEEE Conf. on Decision and Control*, pages 2063–2068, 2001.
6. F. Borrelli, M. Baotic, A. Bemporad, and M. Morari. An efficient algorithm for computing the state feedback optimal control law for discrete time hybrid systems. In *Proc. American Contr. Conf.*, Denver, Colorado, 2003.

7. A. Bemporad and M. Morari. Control of systems integrating logic, dynamics, and constraints. *Automatica*, 35(3):407–427, March 1999.
8. A. Bemporad, F. Borrelli, and M. Morari. Piecewise linear optimal controllers for hybrid systems. In *Proc. American Contr. Conf.*, pages 1190–1194, Chicago, IL, June 2000.
9. F.D. Torrisi and A. Bemporad. HYSDEL - A tool for generating computational hybrid models. *IEEE Transactions on Control Systems Technology*, 2003. To appear.
10. K. Marriot and P.J. Stuckey. *Programming with constraints: an introduction.* MIT Press, 1998.
11. J. Gu, P.W. Purdom, J. Franco, and B. Wah. Algorithms for the satisfiability (SAT) problem: A survey. In *DIMACS Series on Discrete Mathematics and Theoretical Computer Science*, number 35, pages 19–151. American Mathematical Society, 1997.
12. J. Hooker. *Logic-based methods for Optimization*. Wiley-Interscience Series, 2000.
13. A. Bockmayr and T. Kasper. Branch and infer: A unifying framework for integer and finite domain constraint programming. *INFORMS Journal on Computing*, 10(3):287–300, Summer 1998.
14. R. Rodosek, M. Wallace, , and M. Hajian. A new approach to integrating mixed integer programming and constraint logic programming. *Annals of Oper. Res.*, 86:63–87, 1997.
15. F. Focacci, A. Lodi, and M. Milano. Cost-based domain filtering. In *J. Jaffar, editor, Principle and Practice of Constraint Programming*, volume 1713 of *Lecture Notes in Computer Science*, pages 189–203. Springer Verlag, 2001.
16. I. Harjunkoski, V. Jain, , and I.E. Grossmann. Hybrid mixed-integer/constraint logic programming strategies for solving scheduling and combinatorial optimization problems. *Comp. Chem. Eng.*, 24:337–343, 2000.
17. A. Bemporad and N. Giorgetti. A logic-based hybrid solver for optimal control of hybrid systems. In *Proc. 43th IEEE Conf. On Decision and Control*, Maui, Hawaii, USA, Dec. 2003.
18. H.P. Williams. *Model Building in Mathematical Programming*. John Wiley & Sons, Third Edition, 1993.
19. G. Ottosson. *Integration of Constraint Programming and Integer Programming for Combinatorial Optimization*. PhD thesis, Computing Science Department, Information Technology, Uppsala University, Sweden, 2000.
20. E. Tsang. *Foundations of Constraint Satisfaction*. Academic Press, 1993.
21. S. Boyd and L. Vandenberghe. *Convex Optimization*. In press., 2003. http://www.stanford.edu/\char126\relaxboyd/cvxbook.html.
22. A. Bemporad. Efficient conversion of mixed logical dynamical systems into an equivalent piecewise affine form. *IEEE Trans. Automatic Control*, 2003. In Press.
23. M. Moskewicz, C. Madigan, Y. Zhao, L. Zhang, and S. Malik. Chaff: Engineering an efficient sat solver. In *39th Design Automation Conference*, June 2001. http://www.ee.princeton.edu/\char126\relaxchaff/zchaff.php.
24. ILOG, Inc. *CPLEX 8.1 User Manual*. Gentilly Cedex, France, 2002.

Incremental Search Methods for Reachability Analysis of Continuous and Hybrid Systems*

Amit Bhatia and Emilio Frazzoli

Coordinated Science Laboratory
University of Illinois at Urbana-Champaign, Urbana, IL 61801
{bhatia2,frazzoli}@uiuc.edu

Abstract. In this paper we present algorithms and tools for fast and efficient reachability analysis, applicable to continuous and hybrid systems. Most of the work on reachability analysis and safety verification concentrates on conservative representations of the set of reachable states, and consequently on the generation of safety certificates; however, inability to prove safety with these tools does not necessarily result in a proof of unsafety. In this paper, we propose an alternative approach, which aims at the fast falsification of safety properties; this approach provides the designer with a complementary set of tools to the ones based on conservative analysis, providing additional insight into the characteristics of the system under analysis. Our algorithms are based on algorithms originally proposed for robotic motion planning; the key idea is to incrementally grow a set of feasible trajectories by exploring the state space in an efficient way. The ability of the proposed algorithms to analyze the reachability and safety properties of general continuous and hybrid systems is demonstrated on examples from the literature.

1   Introduction

The analysis of reachable sets of discrete, continuous and hybrid systems—i.e., systems exhibiting both discrete and continuous dynamics—plays a fundamental role in many important engineering problems, such as the verification of the correctness and safety of embedded controllers for aircraft, automobiles, medical devices, energy production and distribution plants, and other safety-critical applications [1]. As a consequence, an intense research activity has been devoted to the formal analysis of reachability properties and safety characteristics of such systems [2]. Verification of a system entails proving that a certain property, called a *specification*, is true for all possible behaviors of the system, irrespective of initial conditions and inputs from the user or from the environment. An important class of specifications include *safety properties*, which ensure that the state of the

---

* The research leading to this work was supported by the NSF Embedded and Hybrid Systems program, under the direction of Dr. Helen Gill, through grant CCR-0208891 (with Branicky and LaValle). Any opinions, findings, conclusions or recommendations expressed in this publication are those of the authors and do not necessarily reflect the views of the National Science Foundation.

R. Alur and G.J. Pappas (Eds.): HSCC 2004, LNCS 2993, pp. 142–156, 2004.

system never enters an unsafe of otherwise "bad" set. Most of the approaches developed for safety verification of hybrid systems (e.g., [2,3,4,5,6,7]) suffer from a common drawback, that is, their liability to spurious counterexamples. In other words, while these techniques provide strong safety guarantees when they terminate with a safety certificate, they are not able, in the general case, to prove unsafety. While refinements are possible [8,9], the successive refinement procedure might fail to terminate, either because of the inherent undecidability of the problem [10], or because of the structure of the approximation used. Very limited classes of hybrid systems, for which exact, computable representations of reachable sets can can be found, have been identified in [11,12,13].

As an additional analysis tool to complement established techniques, we propose an efficient *safety falsification* tool aiming at the *fast generation of* feasible counterexamples, i.e., state trajectories for the hybrid system that violate the safety property. In other words, we aim at the generation of a growing sequence of under-approximations of the reachable set, converging, in an appropriate sense, to the reachable set as the number of iterations increases. If the system is unsafe, the proposed technique will be able to generate quickly a feasible counter-example, with high probability. The proposed techniques adapt recently-developed algorithms for robotic motion planning, characterized by a demonstrated ability to explore the reachable set in a very efficient manner. As the prime example of such algorithms, to which we will collectively refer to as Sampling-based Incremental Search (SIS) algorithms, we will consider the Rapidly-exploring Random Trees (RRTs), introduced in [14,15]. The first example of application of RRTs to hybrid systems is [16]; to the authors' best knowledge, the present paper represents the first instance of the usage of RRTs for reachability analysis and verification of hybrid systems.

The paper is organized as follows. In Section 2 we introduce a modelling formalism for hybrid systems, and formulate the problems we wish to address. In Section 3 we present the basic RRT algorithm, and discuss several extensions and modifications to adapt it to reachability and safety falsification problems. In Section 4 we present results from examples taken from the literature. In Section 5, we draw some conclusions and make some remarks towards possible future efforts.

2   Problem Formulation

In this paper we consider the problems of reachability analysis and verification for continuous and hybrid systems, subject to uncertain, bounded, exogenous inputs. Below we explain the problem we wish to address in more detail.

Definition 1 (Hybrid System). *We define a (time-invariant) hybrid system H as a tuple $H = (Q, X, U, \Phi, \Delta, I, S, T)$, where:*

- *Q is a finite set of locations. (In other words, Q is the discrete state space.)*
- *$X \subseteq \mathbb{R}^n$ is the continuous state space, of dimension n. The product $Q \times X$ defines the hybrid state space of H, and states are represented by couples of*

the form $z = (q, x)$, with q and x representing the discrete and continuous states, respectively.

- *$\mathcal{U} \subset \mathbb{R}^m$ is a compact set of dimension m, representing all possible values of an exogenous input u. The exogenous input is used to model uncertainty or non-determinism in the dynamics of the hybrid system. The function $t \mapsto u(t)$ is assumed piecewise continuous. For simplicity, we will consider $\mathcal{U}$ as the ∞-norm unit ball in $\mathbb{R}^m$, i.e., $\mathcal{U} = \{u \in \mathbb{R}^m : \|u\|_\infty \leq 1\}$. The extension of the treatment in this paper to general polytopes is straightforward.*

- *$\Phi : \mathcal{Q} \times \mathcal{X} \times \mathcal{U} \to \mathbb{R}^n$ is a function describing the continuous evolution of the hybrid state, governed by an ordinary differential equation of the form $\dot{x} = \Phi(q, x, u) = f_q(x, u)$. The function Φ is assumed to be uniformly continuous in its second and third arguments.*

- *$\Delta \subset (\mathcal{Q} \times \mathcal{X})^2$, a relation describing discrete transitions in the hybrid states. Discrete transitions can occur on location-specific subsets $G(q, q') \subseteq \mathcal{X}$, called guards, and result in jump relations of the form $(q, x) \mapsto (q', r(x))$, where r is a continuous reset map, assumed to be unique for each pair of discrete states q, q'. (In cases in which we wish to simulate trajectories backwards in time, we require that the reset maps be invertible, that is, if $(q, x, q', r(x)) \in \Delta$, then $(q, r^{-1}(x'), q', x') \in \Delta$.) In order to rule out Zeno phenomena, we assume that there are no sequences $(q_1, q_2, \ldots, q_L) \in \mathcal{Q}^L$, with $L > 2$, $q_L = q_1$, such that $G(q_{i-1}, q_i) \cap G(q_i, q_{i+1}) \neq \emptyset$ for all $i = 2 \ldots L - 1$.*

- *$\mathcal{I}, \mathcal{S}, \mathcal{T} \subseteq \mathcal{Q} \times \mathcal{X}$ are, respectively, the invariant set, the initial condition set, and a target set.*

The *semantics* of our model are defined as follows. When the discrete state is in location q, the continuous state evolves according to the ODE $\dot{x}(t) = f_q(x(t), u(t))$, for some value of the input $u(t) \in \mathcal{U}$, with $(q(0), x(0)) \in \mathcal{S}$. In addition, whenever $x(t) \in G(q(t), q')$ for some q', the system has the option to perform one of the discrete transitions modeled by the relation Δ, and be instantaneously reset to the new discrete state q', and continuous state $r(x(t))$. (An alternative model for this source of undeterminism would include a discrete exogenous input, but is not necessary for our purposes.) The system will always remain within $\mathcal{I}$, for example by appropriately constraining the allowable u and forcing discrete jumps: we implicitly assume that $\mathcal{I}$ is specified in such a way that this is always possible. The *reachability problem* can be synthetically stated as the problem of finding the set $\mathcal{R} \subseteq \mathcal{Q} \times \mathcal{X}$ of all states that can be reached by the hybrid system H, for initial conditions in $\mathcal{S}$, under the action of the exogenous input u, and for some switching sequence in 2^Δ. The *safety falsification problem* is a weaker version of the reachability problem, which only aims at proving that an unsafe set $\mathcal{T}$ is reachable, i.e., $\mathcal{R} \cap \mathcal{T} \neq \emptyset$, and providing a state and control trajectory $[0, t_f] \ni t \mapsto (q(t), x(t), u(t))$ that is feasible with respect to the given semantics of H, with $(q(t_f), x(t_f)) \in \mathcal{T}$.

3   Incremental Search Algorithms for Reachability Analysis

The main idea we wish to push in this paper is that efficient methods recently developed for robotic motion planning can be profitably used for reachability analysis and safety verification, both for continuous and hybrid systems. In robotics, the motion planning problem requires the computation of a feasible path for a robot, to move from an initial configuration to a target set, in an obstacle-cluttered environment. The problem is in general very hard; the so-called piano mover's problem is known to be PSPACE-hard [17]. In recent years, a class of planners based on the incremental construction of graphs of feasible trajectories (roadmaps), through random sampling of the workspace, has established itself as a powerful and flexible tool for solving rapidly previously intractable problems. We will refer to these algorithms as Sampling-based Incremental Search (SIS) planners. Initially, a strong emphasis had been placed on the probabilistic nature of SIS planners; however, recent results indicate that certain deterministic sampling strategies can in fact outperform purely random methods [18,19]. Among the methods proposed in the literature, we mention [20,21,22,23,24]; one of the most popular approaches for incremental roadmap construction is the Rapidly-Exploring Random Tree (RRT) algorithm first introduced in [14,15]. In the remainder of the paper we will present extensions and adaptations of the basic RRT algorithm to reachability analysis and verification of hybrid systems.

3.1   Rapidly-Exploring Random Trees

In this section, we will briefly present the RRT algorithm and some of its main properties. For a more thorough treatment, we refer the reader to [14,15].

The basic form of the RRT algorithm is outlined in Fig. 1; in the following discussion we will use a notation consistent with Section 2. The algorithm works by incrementally building a tree—i.e., an acyclic directed graph $G(V, E)$—of feasible trajectories, for a nonlinear, time-invariant system $\dot{x} = f(x, u)$. The vertices V of the graph G correspond to the endpoints of feasible trajectories, and are called *milestones*; the edges E are labeled with the (constant) control input $u \in \mathcal{U}$ necessary to transfer the state of the system from the source to the target milestone, in a given time interval Δt. The graph G is initialized with only one vertex—i.e., the root of the tree—corresponding to the initial conditions of the system x_{initial}.

At each iteration, `generate_sample` outputs a sample $x_{\text{sample}} \in \mathcal{X}$; this function can have different forms, and can be based either on pseudo-random number generators, or—as discussed in [18,19]—on deterministic sequences with certain desirable properties; the only requirement on this function is that the probability of sampling a point in any non-zero measure subset of $\mathcal{X}$ must be strictly positive. As each sample is generated, the nearest milestone $x_{\text{near}} \in V$— e.g., according to some metric ρ—is selected by the function `nearest_neighbor`. Starting from x_{near}, a candidate milestone x_{new} is computed by the function `extend` by applying, over a time interval ΔT, the control input u_{new}, selected in

Algorithm RRT(x_{initial}, x_{target}, Δt, ϵ)

> $V \leftarrow \{x_{\text{initial}}\}$
> $E \leftarrow \emptyset$
> **while** $\min_{x \in V} \rho(x, x_{\text{target}}) > \epsilon$ **do**
>> $x_{\text{sample}} \leftarrow$ generate_sample()
>> $x_{\text{near}} \leftarrow$ nearest_neighbor(V, x_{sample})
>> $(x_{\text{new}}, u_{\text{new}}) \leftarrow$ extend(x_{near}, x_{sample}, Δt)
>> **if** feasible(x_{near}, u_{new}) **then**
>>> $V \leftarrow V \cup \{x_{\text{new}}\}$
>>> $E \leftarrow E \cup \{(x_{\text{near}}, x_{\text{new}}, u_{\text{new}})\}$
>> **end if**
> **end while**
> **return** $G(V, E)$

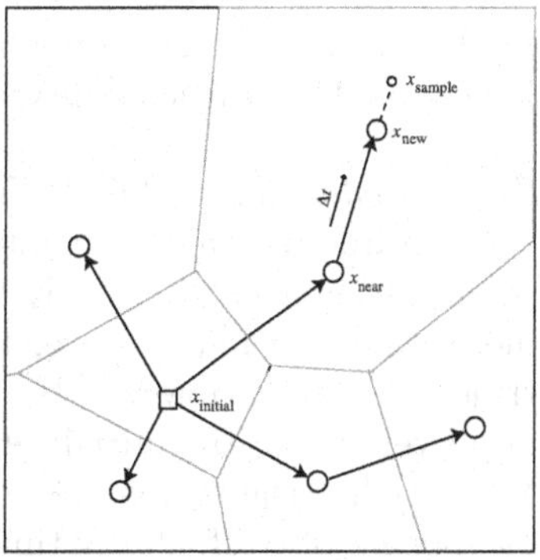

Fig. 1. The basic RRT algorithm: pseudo-code (left) and illustration (right); the light lines show the Voronoi regions associated to the vertices in the trees before the addition of x_{new}. The vertex labeled x_{near} was the most likely candidate for further exploration, since it was the generator of the largest Voronoi region.

order to minimize the distance between x_{new} and x_{sample}. If the trajectory from x_{near} to x_{new} satisfies certain global constraints, such as collision avoidance, the candidate milestone x_{new} is added to the set of vertices V; furthermore, the edge from x_{near} to x_{new}, with control input u_{new}, is added to the set of edges E. This procedure is repeated until a milestone is discovered within some distance ϵ from the target point x_{target}.

The soundness of motion planning algorithms is measured in terms of completeness. A motion planning algorithm is said *complete* if it terminates with a feasible trajectory from the initial condition x_{start} to the target x_{target}, if one exists, or terminates with failure otherwise. A probabilistically complete algorithm relaxes the completeness requirement by allowing the probability of successful termination to approach one asymptotically; probabilistic completeness for the RRT algorithm, applied to a discrete-time, discrete-input system, was established in [25]. These results were extended in [26] to a deterministic guarantee, through the notion of resolution completeness; in other words, the algorithm is guaranteed to terminate correctly if the state and input spaces are discretized finely enough. The above mentioned results, while establishing the theoretical soundness of the algorithm, do not provide details on the rate at which the probability of success approaches one. In fact, some attempts in that direction were made in [25,22], but rely on parameters that are difficult to compute in practice. However, the RRT heuristic does provide a very efficient exploration technique for many problems; an intuitive explanation for this is that at each step the new milestone tends to be selected in such a way that the volume of the largest Voronoi region generated by the old milestones is reduced (see Fig. 1).

3.2   RRTs for Reachability Analysis

In this section, we give details about the main modifications needed for using RRTs to address reachability problems for continuous and hybrid systems.

Tree initialization. While RRTs were originally devised to generate trajectories starting from a common point in the state space, it is possible to handle initial conditions in a set $\mathcal{S}$. Strictly speaking, when allowing trajectories to grow from more than one initial state, the RRT algorithm produces a *forest* of feasible trajectories [16]. However, by defining a dummy root vertex, acting as a parent of all vertices in the initial set, we can maintain the single-tree data structure. We initialize the search tree by selecting at least one point in each connected component of $\mathcal{S}$. If, at any time during the execution of the algorithm, a sample is generated in the initial set, it is immediately considered for addition to the search tree.

Time discretization. Incremental search algorithms are based on an incremental simulator, i.e., every new milestone is created by integrating the system's ODE for a time Δt, assuming a constant control input u, starting from an old milestone. In order to ensure that the set of points reachable after one propagation step has a non-zero measure, we split the interval Δt into $k \geq \lfloor n/m \rfloor$ segments. In each of these segments the control input is kept constant; the control input signal is parameterized by a km-dimensional vector $v = (v_1, \dots, v_k)$, with $u(t) = v_i$ for $t \in [(i-1)/k\Delta t, i/k\Delta t)$. New milestones are created through continuous dynamics by updating the continuous state according to $x_{\text{new}} = \phi(x_{\text{old}}, v_{\text{new}}, \Delta t)$, where the state flow ϕ, as a function of the time increment t, satisfies $\phi(x, v, t) = \int_0^t f(\phi(x, v, \tau), u(\tau)) \, d\tau$ for constant x and v. We assume that the state flow can be computed either exactly, e.g., through symbolic integration of the ODE, or to any arbitrary precision, through numerical methods. We will also make use of the following quantities:

$$\alpha_q(x,t) := \phi_q(x,0,t), \quad \beta_q(x,t) := \left. \frac{\partial \phi_q(x,v,t)}{\partial v} \right|_{v=0} .$$

In the remainder of the paper, we will assume that β_q has full rank; a necessary condition for this to be true is that the continuous dynamics be accessible [27]. A suitable k can always be found for several classes of accessible systems, including controllable linear systems, nilpotent systems, and systems in chained form [28].

Notions of distance. Given two points $z_1 = (q, x_1)$ and $z_2 = (q, x_2)$ in the same discrete location, we define their distance as:

$$\text{dist}(z_1, z_2) := \|v^*\|_\infty, \text{ with } v^* = \arg \min_{v \in \mathbb{R}^{km}} \|\phi(x_1, v, \Delta t) - x_2\|_\infty . \quad (1)$$

In other words, the distance between two points is measured as the effort required to take z_1 closest to z_2, in one propagation step; if $\text{dist}(z_1, z_2) \leq 1$ then z_2 is reachable from z_1 in one step. The distance (1) is parameterized by the time increment Δt, and is not necessarily a metric. Given, in the same location, two sets $Z_1, Z_2 \subset \{q\} \times \mathcal{X}$, we define $\mathrm{dist}(Z_1, Z_2) := \min_{z_1 \in Z_1, z_2 \in Z_2} \mathrm{dist}(z_1, z_2)$. If the sets Z_1 and Z_2 on $\mathcal{X}$ are polyhedra, the distance between them can be computed by solving a Linear Program (LP).

To handle distances between states in different discrete locations, we construct a directed graph $G_d(\mathcal{Q}, E_d)$ of discrete transitions, in which each vertex corresponds to a discrete location, and each edge corresponds to one of the transition guards, i.e., two states q_1 and q_2 are connected by an edge if $\mathcal{G}(q_1, q_2) \neq \emptyset$. (This is the usual representation of the discrete dynamics of H as a hybrid automaton.) Let $\delta : \mathcal{Q} \times \mathcal{Q} \to \mathbb{N}_+$ be the topological distance between two vertices on G_d, i.e., the minimum number of vertices on a path between them. Given two states $z_1 = (q_1, x_1)$ and $z_2 = (q_2, z_2)$, we will consider the composite distance

$$
\mathrm{Dist}(z_1, z_2) = \begin{cases} (0, \mathrm{dist}(z_1, z_2)) & \text{if } q_1 = q_2 \\ (\delta(q_1, q_2), \min_{q \in \mathcal{Q}_{\mathrm{next}}} \mathrm{dist}(z_1, G(q_1, q))) & \text{otherwise,} \end{cases} \tag{2}
$$

with the lexicographic ordering, as a measure of distance between them. In the above, $\mathcal{Q}_{\mathrm{next}} = \{q \in \mathcal{Q} : \delta(q, q_2) < \delta(q_1, q_2)\}$.

Tree extension. Given a sample z_{sample}, the nearest neighbor z_{near} in the tree can be found through the lexicographic ordering on the composite distance (2). The extend function tries to minimize (the second component of) the composite distance, by applying the control v_{new} over a time Δt. In general, this might be a difficult non-convex program; we found that, when all sets in the specification of H are convex polyhedra, it is in practice more efficient to determine v_{new} by solving the LP obtained through the approximation $x_{\mathrm{new}} \approx \alpha_{q_{\mathrm{near}}}(x_{\mathrm{near}}, \Delta t) + \beta_{q_{\mathrm{near}}}(x_{\mathrm{near}}, \Delta t)v$ in eq.(1).

Discrete resets. Every time a milestone (q, x) is generated, checks are made to determine whether it lies within a transition guard, and all points (q', x') such that $(q, x, q', x') \in \Delta$—i.e., the images of (q, x) under the discrete transitions—are added as additional milestones to the tree [16]. The number of discrete resets for each new milestone is bounded, because of the assumption we made on the jump relations.

3.3   RRTs for Safety Falsification

In cases in which it is desired to falsify a safety property, i.e., the set $\mathcal{T}$ is not empty, it is possible to introduce heuristics to speed up the search for feasible trajectories that violate the property.

Greedy tree expansion. For example, it is possible to add a bias to the growth of the tree, in the direction of the failure set. This can be done by interleaving sampling-based tree extension steps with *greedy* steps. In a greedy step, the tree extension is determined by aiming at minimizing the composite distance between the tree vertices and the target set $\mathcal{T}$, as opposed to a sampled state. The frequency of greedy steps can be set a priori, or can be adaptively adjusted on-line.

Dual tree techniques. All the remarks made up to this point, for building a tree of feasible trajectories for the hybrid system $H = (\mathcal{Q}, \mathcal{X}, \mathcal{U}, \Phi, \Delta, \mathcal{I}, \mathcal{S}, \mathcal{T})$, can be applied to building a tree of feasible trajectories for the backward-time counterpart of H, that is, $H^- = (\mathcal{Q}, \mathcal{X}, \mathcal{U}, \Phi^-, \Delta^-, \mathcal{I}, \mathcal{T}, \mathcal{S})$. In other words, the backward-time system H^- is obtained from H by (i) reversing the role of the initial and target sets, (ii) reversing the direction of Φ, setting $f_q^-(x, u) = -f_q(x, u)$ for all $q \in \mathcal{Q}$, and (iii) commuting the order of terms in the relation Δ, i.e., $(z_1, z_2) \in \Delta \Leftrightarrow (z_2, z_1) \in \Delta^-$ (for this operation to be well defined the reset maps must be invertible). Two trees can be grown, one for each direction of time; if at any iteration milestones from each tree can be joined in one step by a feasible control input, a trajectory connecting $\mathcal{S}$ and $\mathcal{T}$ has been found.

3.4 R4T: Recursively-Refined RRT

A difficulty that is often encountered when computing reachable sets incrementally is that, given a fixed time increment Δt, states which can only be reached after a time $t >> \Delta t$ require an excessive numbers of iterations to be found. This problem is exacerbated by the fact that methods based on over-approximations of the reachable set typically require Δt to be small in order to reduce conservatism; similarly, in motion planning, small time steps are chosen in order to ensure feasibility of the trajectory with respect to collision avoidance constraints. However, as long as the system is guaranteed to stay within the invariant set, nothing prevents us from using very large—possibly infinite—time increments at the initial stages of the search, and subsequently refine them. The Recursively Refined RRT (R4T) algorithm, described in this section, and illustrated in Figure 2, is based on this idea.

Given a time t_e, define $\bar{\mathcal{I}}(t_e) \subseteq \mathcal{I}$ as the set of initial conditions, such that no continuous trajectory will escape the invariant set $\mathcal{I}$ within time t_e; indicate by $\bar{\mathcal{I}}(\infty)$ the set of initial conditions for which continuous trajectories will never escape $\mathcal{I}$. Obviously, $\bar{\mathcal{I}}(0) = \mathcal{I}$, and $t_1 \leq t_2 \Rightarrow \bar{\mathcal{I}}(t_1) \supseteq \bar{\mathcal{I}}(t_2)$. Define $\bar{\mathcal{S}}(t) = \mathcal{S} \cap \bar{\mathcal{I}}(t)$. If $\bar{\mathcal{S}}(\infty)$ is not empty, and $\lim_{t->\infty} \phi_q(x, \upsilon, t)$ exists for all $x \in \bar{\mathcal{S}}(\infty)$ and for all $\upsilon \in \mathcal{U}^k$, then the tree is initialized with the vertices of a polytopic representation of the initial set $\bar{\mathcal{S}}_p(\infty)$, and of its image under the infinite-time state flow (which will be reached asymptotically).

Once the tree is initialized, pick Δt_0 such that $\bar{\mathcal{S}}(\Delta t_0)$ is not empty, and execute the *RRT* algorithm, with the following two main modifications: First, the nearest neighbor is sought only among the vertices in $\bar{\mathcal{I}}(\Delta t)$. Second, a new milestone x_{new} is added to the tree only if $\min_{x \in V} \|x - x_{\text{new}}\|_\infty > \epsilon(\Delta t) > 0$, where $\epsilon(\Delta t)$ is a given tolerance level.

A count of consecutive milestone candidate rejections is kept; if this number exceeds a preset threshold $N_{\text{fail}}(\Delta t)$ we proceed to a refinement of the tree. Every edge $(z_\text{s}, z_\text{t}, \upsilon_c)$, whose source and targets are in the same discrete location, is

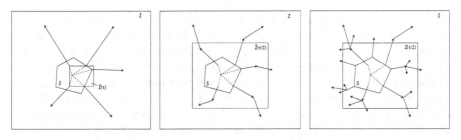

Fig. 2. Illustration of the main steps in the R4T algorithm: Initialization (left), tree refinement (center), tree expansion (right).

split in $2k$ segments of equal time duration, and replaced by $2k - 1$ new nodes at intermediate points on the trajectory from z_s to z_t, and $2k$ edges with the appropriate controls v. To conclude the tree refinement procedure, the time increment is updated as $\Delta t \leftarrow \Delta t/(2k)$. After the refinement, the exploration is resumed with the modified RRT search. This process is repeated until either a milestone is discovered within the target set, or until the quality of the approximation of the reachable set is deemed satisfactory (e.g., by specifying a minimum time resolution, and a maximum number of rejections at that resolution).

All trajectories generated by R4T are feasible trajectories for H, regardless of the time interval ΔT. At each stage of the refinement, the standard RRT algorithm is applied, and existing results on probabilistic and resolution completeness hold [25,26].

The advantage of the R4T algorithm is that it allows quick exploration of the reachable states even on very long time horizon (with mostly constant control input), while retaining the ability to discover states reachable only through control input signals with a richer structure. The refinement step is automatically invoked when new milestones cannot be added to the tree at the current resolution level.

3.5   Co-RRT: A LP Relaxation of RRTs

As the search tree grows, the number of distance computations to be done in `nearest_neighbor` increases, as does the amount of memory required to store the tree. However, it is often the case that only the milestones lying at the outer edges of the search tree are actually selected for expansion, and contribute to the exploration of the reachable set. Hence, an idea for a more efficient implementation of the RRT algorithm would limit the milestones kept in memory and considered for expansions to the ones on the boundary of the tree. Finding such vertices is not easy in general, but efficient methods exist to compute the convex hull of a finite set of points [29]. With this in mind, the question that needs to be answered is the following: given a set V of endpoints of feasible trajectories, under what conditions all points of the convex hull of V are themselves feasible? An answer to this question is given in the following observation, based on the concept of Viability Kernel [30].

In short, given a set $\mathcal{K} \subset \mathcal{X}$, and a system S, a trajectory $\xi : [0, t] \to \mathcal{X}$ of S is viable in $\mathcal{K}$ if $\xi(t) \in \mathcal{K}$ for all $t \geq 0$. The set $\mathcal{K}$ is said a viability domain if, for every $x \in \mathcal{K}$, there exists at least one viable trajectory ξ of S, with $\xi(0) = x$. Finally, the viability kernel of $\mathcal{K}$, denoted by $\mathrm{Viab}(\mathcal{K})$, is the largest viability domain contained in $\mathcal{K}$. We will indicate with $\mathrm{Viab}^-(\mathcal{K})$ the backward-time version of the viability kernel, i.e., the largest subset of $\mathcal{K}$ such that all of its points are endpoints of at least one trajectory of S, extending for an arbitrarily long time in the past, entirely contained in $\mathcal{K}$.

Proposition 1. *Given a time-invariant linear system $\dot{x} = Ax + Bu$, with initial conditions in a convex set $\mathcal{S}$, and with a convex input set $\mathcal{U}$, consider two feasible trajectories $[0, t_1] \ni t \mapsto (x_1(t), u_1(t))$, and $[0, t_2] \ni t \mapsto (x_2(t), u_2(t))$. Any convex combination of the endpoints $x_1(t_1)$ and $x_2(t_2)$ is reachable if $\mathcal{S} = \mathrm{Viab}^-(\mathcal{S})$.*

Proof. In order to prove this statement, observe that, if $t_1 = t_2$, then the result is easily obtained: in this case, for any $\lambda \in [0, 1]$,

$$
\begin{aligned}
x_\lambda(t_1) &= (\lambda x_1(t_1) + (1 - \lambda)x_2(t_1)) = \\
&\quad \exp(At_1)(\lambda x_1(0) + (1 - \lambda)x_2(0)) + \\
&\quad \int_0^{t_1} \exp(A(t - \tau))B(\lambda u_1(\tau) + (1 - \lambda)u_2(\tau)) \, d\tau = \\
&\quad \exp(At_1)x_\lambda(0) + \int_0^{t_1} \exp(A(t - \tau)Bu_\lambda(\tau)) \, d\tau \ ,
\end{aligned}
\tag{3}
$$

with $x_\lambda(0) \in \mathcal{S}$, and $u_\lambda(t) \in \mathcal{U}$, for all $t \in [0, t_1]$. The same cannot be said in general if $t_1 \neq t_2$. Assume, without loss of generality, that $t_1 > t_2$; if $\mathcal{S} = \mathrm{Viab}^-(\mathcal{S})$, one can find a trajectory $[t_2 - t_1, 0] \ni t \mapsto x_2'(t)$ which is entirely contained in $\mathcal{S}$, with $x_2'(0) = x_2(0)$. The concatenation of the two trajectories x_2', x_2 is a trajectory with initial conditions in $\mathcal{S}$, and total duration t_1; on the basis of (3) the desired result is proven. $\square$

A trivial case in which $\mathcal{S} = \mathrm{Viab}^-(\mathcal{S})$ is when $\mathcal{S}$ is an equilibrium point for the system. This result let us concentrate solely on points on the convex hull of a search tree, if the continuous dynamics are linear, and the initial set is (backward-time) viable.

Note that, if H is a continuous system—i.e., if $|\mathcal{Q}| = 1$— the co-RRT algorithm is the LP-relaxation of RRT. At each step, when a new state z_{sample} is sampled, nearest_neighbor and extend find the milestone $z_{\mathrm{opt}} \in V$, and the control v_{opt}, that solve the following program:

$$
\begin{aligned}
(z_{\mathrm{opt}}, v_{\mathrm{opt}}) &= \underset{(z,v)}{\arg \min} \, \|\phi(z, v, \Delta t), z_{\mathrm{sample}}\|_\infty \\
\text{s.t.:} \ z &\in V \ .
\end{aligned}
\tag{4}
$$

If H has only one discrete location, relaxing the constraint $z \in V$ to $z \in \mathrm{co}(V)$ makes (4) a linear program. The same holds true when the target is a set of states.

In the case in which H contains more than one discrete location, the set of reachable states in one location will be given by the union of several convex hulls, each one originating at the image of a transition guard.

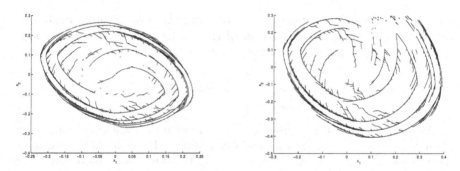

Fig. 3. Linear systems with bounded inputs: reachable sets for the linear system for different initial conditions.

4   Examples

Due to space limitations, we will only discuss two examples of application of the proposed techniques. More information and demos will be made available upon release of the software package.

4.1   Linear Systems Subject to Bounded Input

In Figure 3 we show the output of the R4T (and of its convex-hull version co-R4T), applied to the linear system

$$\dot{x} = \begin{bmatrix} 0 & 1 \\ -2 & -1 \end{bmatrix} x + \begin{bmatrix} 1 & 0 \\ 1 & 1 \end{bmatrix},$$

subject to a bounded input u, $\|u(t)\|_\infty \leq 1$, $\forall t$, with initial conditions in $\mathcal{S}_1 = \{(x_1, x_2) \in \mathbb{R}^2 : x_1, x_2 \in [-0.1, 0.1]\}$ (left) and $\mathcal{S}_2 = \{(x_1, x_2) \in \mathbb{R}^2 : x_1, x_2 \in [0.1, 0.2]\}$ (right). The shape of the reachable sets in both these cases cannot be computed exactly (unlike the case of energy-bounded inputs), but the trees grown in the figure present a good approximation. The convex-hull version of the R4T algorithm was applied only in the first case, since the initial set in the second case is not backward-time viable. The figures were obtained in about 1.5 minutes on an Apple Powerbook 867 MHz G4, running Mac OS X. All algorithms have been implemented in C++.

4.2   Aircraft Collision Avoidance

This example is based on a general aircraft collision avoidance problem, introduced in [31], and subsequently analyzed in [32].

Consider two airplanes, the evader and the pursuer, moving at velocity v_e, v_p, respectively. The aircraft can either fly straight, or turn with a bounded heading rate ω_e, ω_p, with $|\omega_e|, |\omega_p| \leq 1$. The relative configuration of the aircraft is expressed by the state vector $z = [x, y, \psi]$, in which x and y are the components of the relative position of the pursuer with respect to the evader, respectively along the longitudinal and transversal axes of the evader airplane; ψ is the relative heading angle. The kinematics of the system are given by:

$$\dot{z} := \frac{d}{dt} \begin{bmatrix} x \\ y \\ \psi \end{bmatrix} = \begin{bmatrix} -v_e + v_p c_\psi + \omega_e y \\ v_e s_\psi - \omega_e x \\ \omega_p - \omega_e) \end{bmatrix}. \tag{5}$$

Assume that the pursuer intends to collide with the evader; collision occurs when $r^2 := x^2 + y^2 \leq d^2$, for some collision radius d. The evader adopts a simple control law, aiming at maximizing the instantaneous second derivative of the relative distance r. Simple calculations yield that $\omega_e = -\text{sign}(y)$ achieves this goal; hence the evader can be modeled as a hybrid system, switching between two escape modes (break left/right). In order to analyze the performance of the proposed control law, we wish to determine the corresponding unsafe set, i.e., the set of relative configuration for which the pursuer might be able to force a collision, if the evader acts as specified.

While our algorithms can be applied to any general combination of paremeters in the problem, we select $v_e = v_p$, since an analytical characterization of the smallest unsafe set (i.e., the unsafe set for the best possible collision avoidance policy for the evader) is available [33,34]. In order to compute the unsafe set, we perform a reachability analysis on the system, in backward time: in other words, given the starting set as the collision set $\mathcal{T} : \{z \in \mathbb{R}^4 : z_1^2 + z_2^2 \leq d^2\}$, we propagate trajectories backwards in time. The evader's actions ω_e are determined by the stated control law, and the pursuer's actions ω_p constitute the input to the RRT-based reachability analysis (in other words, ω_p is trying to find all trajectories which will ultimately lead to collision).

In Figure 4, we show the projections on the (x, y) and (y, ψ) planes of the trajectories in the search tree after 30 seconds of computation, along with the boundary of the projection of the minimal unsafe set according to the analysis in [33,32]. As it can be seen, the unsafe set for the simple control law $\omega_e = -\text{sign}(y)$ seems to be very close to the smallest unsafe set achievable with the optimal control law. The analysis of the reachable set was carried out rapidly—95% of the reachable set was found in about 10 minutes— on a relatively modest laptop and gave results that match very well with analytic results. It is interesting to consider the second plot shown in Figure 4: the volume of the set reachable in one step from the tree grows much faster than the number of milestones during the first stages of the algorithm execution. In other words, the first few vertices in the tree do most of the exploration; the subsequent vertices only achieve minor improvements in the approximation of the reachable set. Accordingly, safety is falsified very quickly (computation times are in the order of a few seconds) for all instances in which the initial conditions are chosen inside the computed unsafe set.

5   Conclusions

In this paper we have presented extensions of an algorithm developed for motion planning, suitable for reachability analysis and safety verification (or, more

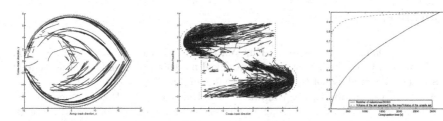

Fig. 4. Results from the aircraft collision avoidance example. Projection of the unsafe set on the (x, y) and (x, θ) planes, compared to the analytically computed boundary (left, center) and history of the number of vertices in the tree and volume of the set reachable in one step from the tree, as a function of computation time (right).

correctly, falsification), for continuous and hybrid systems, and demonstrated its capabilities on a few examples. The main advantage of our approach is that is can very quickly declare that a system is unsafe, without a systematic or otherwise massive exploration of all possible combinations of initial conditions and external inputs. Moreover, we have minimal requirements on the nature of the system, beside uniform continuity of the continuous state dynamics: as a consequence, the proposed algorithms can be applied to a very large class of problems. We see the benefits of the proposed approach as twofold. First of all, the fast generation of feasible trajectories showing the possible safety violations in a system can allow designers to detect fallacies in the control logic at an early stage, with minimal impact on the development schedule and costs. Second, the availability of a tool generating "large" under-approximations of the reachable set, can provide important complementary information to those provided by tools based on abstraction or on over-approximation methods. In particular, it can guide the refinement process by providing additional insight on the behaviors of the system. Furthermore, the availability of both under-approximations and over-approximations of the reachable set, and a measure of the gap between them, can provide the user with valuable information about the quality of the approximations.

Future work will include both a further investigation of the role of sampling-based incremental search algorithms in reachability analysis, and the development of a set of software tools for the analysis of complex, continuous and hybrid systems. For example, the proposed algorithms can be used to reduce the conservatism of methods based on predicate abstraction, determining feasible transitions between abstract states. In addition, work is currently under way to study the applicability of these methods to differential game problems.

Acknowledgments. The authors are grateful to Professors Steven LaValle (U. of Illinois at Urbana-Champaign) and Michael Branicky (Case Western Reserve U.) for stimulating discussion on the subject of this paper, and to Dr. Thao Dang (Verimag, France) for providing the d/dt verification software and examples.

References

1. Alur, R., Dang, T., Esposito, J., Hur, Y., Ivančić, F., Kumar, V., Lee, I., Mishra, P., Pappas, G.J., , Sokolsky, O.: Hierarchical modeling and analysis of embedded systems. Proceedings of the IEEE **91** (2003) 11–28
2. Alur, R., Courcoubetis, C., Halbwachs, N., Henzinger, T., Ho, P., Nicollin, X., Olivero, A., Sifakis, J., Yovine, S.: The algorithmic analysis of hybrid systems. Theoretical Computer Science **138** (1995) 3–34
3. Henzinger, T., Ho, P.H., Wong-Toi, H.: Algorithmic analysis of nonlinear hybrid systems. IEEE Transactions on Automatic Control **43** (1998) 540–554
4. Daws, C., Olivero, A., Tripakis, S., Yovine, S.: The tool KRONOS. In Alur, R., Henzinger, T.A., Sontag, E.D., eds.: Hybrid Systems III: Verification and Control. Volume 1066 of Lecture Notes in Computer Science. Springer-Verlag (1996)
5. Chutinan, A., Krogh, B.H.: Verification of polyhedral-invariant hybrid automata using polygonal flow pipe approximations. In: Hybrid Systems: Computation and Control. Springer (1999)
6. Kurzhanski, A.B., Varaiya, P.: Ellipsoidal techniques for reachability analysis. In: Hybrid Systems: Control and Computation. Volume 1790 of Lecture Notes in Computer Science. Springer-Verlag (2000)
7. Alur, R., Dang, T., Ivančić, F.: Reachability analysis of hybrid systems via predicate abstraction. In Tomlin, C.J., Greenstreet, M.R., eds.: Hybrid Systems: Computation and Control. Lecture Notes in Computer Sciences. Springer (2002) 35–48
8. Grumberg, O., Jha, S., Lu, Y., , Veith, H.: Counterexample-guided abstraction refinement. In: Computer Aided Verification. Lecture Notes in Computer Science. Springer (2000) 154–169
9. Alur, R., Dang, T., Ivančić, F.: Counter-example guided predicate abstraction of hybrid systems. In: 9th International Conference on Tools and Algorithms for the Construction and Analysis of Systems. (2003)
10. Blondel, V., Tsitsiklis, J.N.: The boundedness of all products of a pair of matrices is undecidable. Systems and Control Letters **41** (2000) 135–140
11. Alur, R., Dill, D.: A theory of timed automata. Theoretical Computer Science **126** (1994) 183–235
12. Henzinger, T.A., Kopke, P.W., Puri, A., Varaiya, P.: What's decidable about hybrid automata? In: Proceedings of the 27th ACM Symposium on Theory of Computing (STOC). (1995) 373–382
13. Lafferriere, G., Pappas, G.J., Yovine, S.: Symbolic reachability computation for families of linear vector fields. Journal of Symbolic Computation **32** (2001) 231–253
14. LaValle, S.M.: Rapidly-exploring random trees: A new tool for path planning. Technical Report 98-11, Iowa State University, Ames, IA (1998)
15. LaValle, S., Kuffner, J.: Randomized kinodynamic planning. In: Proceedings of the 1999 IEEE International Conference on Robotics and Automation. (1999)
16. Branicky, M.S., Curtiss, M.M., Levine, J., Morgan, S.: Sampling-based planning and control. In: Proceedings of the 12th Yale Workshop on Adaptive and Learning Systems, New Haven, CT (2003)
17. Reif, J.: Complexity of the mover's problem and generalizations. In: FOCS. (1979) 421–427
18. LaValle, S.M., Branicky, M.S.: On the relationship between classical grid search and probabilistic roadmaps. In: Workshop on the Algorithmic Foundation of Robotics (WAFR), Nice, France (2002)

19. LaValle, S.M., Branicky, M.S., Lindemann, S.R.: On the relationship between classical grid search and probabilistic roadmaps. International Journal of Robotics Research (2003) To appear.

20. Kavraki, L., Svestka, P., Latombe, J., Overmars, M.: Probabilistic roadmaps for path planning in high-dimensional configuration spaces. IEEE Transactions on Robotics and Automation **12** (1996) 566–580

21. Hsu, D., Kavraki, L., Latombe, J., Motwani, R., Sorkin, S.: On finding narrow passages with probabilistic roadmap planners. In: Proceedings of the 1998 Workshop on Algorithmic Foundations of Robotics, Houston, TX (March 1998)

22. Hsu, D., Latombe, J.C., Motwani, R.: Path planning in expansive configuration spaces. Int. J. Comp. Geometry and Applications **9** (1999) 495–512

23. Hsu, D., Kindel, J., Latombe, J.C., Rock, S.: Randomized kinodynamic motion planning with moving obstacles. In: Proc. Workshop on Algorithmic Foundations of Robotics (WAFR'00), Hanover, NH (2000)

24. Bohlin, R., Kavraki, L.: Path planning using lazy PRM. In: Proceedings of the International Conference on Robotics and Automation. (2000) 521–528

25. LaValle, S.M., Kuffner, J.J.: Randomized kinodynamic planning. International Journal of Robotics Research **20** (2001) 378–400

26. Cheng, P., LaValle, S.M.: Resolution complete rapidly-exploring random trees. In: Proc. IEEE Int'l Conf. on Robotics and Automation. (2002)

27. Nijmeijer, H., Van der Schaft, A.J.: Nonlinear Dynamical Control Systems. Springer-Verlag (1990)

28. Sastry, S.: Nonlinear Systems: Analysis, Stability, and Control. Volume 10 of IAM. Springer Verlag, New York, NY (1999)

29. Barber, C.B., Dobkin, D.P., Huhdanpaa, H.T.: The Quickhull algorithm for convex hulls. ACM Transactions on Mathematical Software (1996)

30. Aubin, J.P.: A survey on viability theory. SIAM Journal of Control and Optimization **28** (1990) 749–789

31. Tomlin, C., Lygeros, J., Sastry, S.: A game theoretic approach to controller design for hybrid systems. Proceedings of the IEEE **88** (2000) 949–970

32. Mitchell, I., Tomlin, C.: Level set methods for computation in hybrid systems. In: Hybrid Systems: Computation and Control. Volume 1790. Springer (2000) 310–323

33. Merz, A.W.: The game of two identical cars. Journal of Optimization Theory and Applications **9** (1972) 324–343

34. Mitchell, I.: Games of two identical vehicles. SUDAAR 740, Department of Aeronautics and Astronautics, Stanford University, Stanford, CA (2001)

Discrete and Hybrid Nonholonomy*

Antonio Bicchi[1], Alessia Marigo[2], and Benedetto Piccoli[3]

[1] Centro "E. Piaggio", Universitá di Pisa
bicchi@ing.unipi.it
[2] Dip. Matematica, Universita di Roma "La Sapienza"
marigo@iac.rm.cnr.it
[3] Ist. per le Appl. del Calcolo "M.Picone" C.N.R., Roma
piccoli@iac.rm.cnr.it

Abstract. In this paper we consider the generalization of the classical notion of nonholonomy of smooth constraints in analytical mechanics, to a substantially wider set of systems, allowing for discrete and hybrid (mixed continuous and discrete) configurations and transitions. We show that the general notion of nonholonomy can be captured by the definition of two different types of nonholonomic behaviours, which we call *internal* and *external*, respectively. Examples are reported of systems exhibiting either the former only, or the latter only, or both. For some classes of systems, we provide equivalent or sufficient characterizations of such definitions, which allow for practical tests.

1 Introduction

Although nonholonomic mechanics has a long history, dating back at least to the work of Hertz and Hölder towards the end of the 19th century, it is still today a very active domain of research, both for its theoretical interest and its applications, e.g. in wheeled vehicles, robotics, and motion generation. In the past decade or so, a flurry of activity has concerned the study of nonholonomic systems as nonlinear dynamic systems to which control theory methods could be profitably applied. As a result, the control of classical nonholonomic mechanical systems such as cars, trucks with trailers, rolling 3D objects, underactuated mechanisms, satellites, etc., has made a definite progress, and often met a satisfactory level.

Systems considered in classical nonholonomic mechanics are smooth, continuous time systems, i.e., they can be described by ODEs on a smooth manifold of configurations, on which smooth (most often, analytic) constraints apply. However, nonholonomic-like behaviours can be recognized in more general systems, some of great practical relevance, which may present for instance discontinuities of the dynamics, discreteness of the time axis, and discreteness (e.g., quantization) of the input space. For these systems, some very basic control problems

---

* Partial support by contracts EC-IST 2001-37170 "RECSYS" and MIUR PRIN 095297-002/2002.

R. Alur and G.J. Pappas (Eds.): HSCC 2004, LNCS 2993, pp. 157–172, 2004.

such as the analysis of reachability and the synthesis of steering control sequences
still pose quite challenging problems.

This paper attempts at providing a general conceptual framework capable of
capturing the notion of nonholonomy for a broad class of systems, allowing for
discrete and hybrid (mixed continuous and discrete) configurations and transitions. Upon the analysis of few simple but significant examples, a unique definition encompassing all "intuitively nonholonomic" behaviours in hybrid systems,
does not appear to be feasible, or practical. Hence we propose the definition
of two different types of nonholonomic behaviours, which we call *internal* and
external, respectively. These two types are not obviously reducible to a single
one, and indeed we show examples of simple mechanical systems exhibiting only
internal, only external, or both internal and external nonholonomy, respectively.
Although our definitions are not always directly computable, we provide equivalent, or sufficient conditions for some specific classes of systems, which allow for
practical tests to be applied.

2   Nonholonomic Behaviours in Nonsmooth Systems

In general, classical nonholonomic constraints come in two varieties, kinematic
constraints (often due to contact kinematics, as e.g. in rolling), and dynamic
constraints (due to symmetries induced by conservation laws, for instance, of
angular momentum) [1,2]. In this paper we focus on the former type. Recall
the definition of a (smooth) nonholonomic constraint that is familiar from elementary mechanics textbooks: a mechanical system described by coordinates
$q \in \mathcal{Q}$, with $\mathcal{Q}$ a smooth n-dimensional manifold, subject to m smooth constraints $A(q)\dot{q} = 0$, is nonholonomic if $A(\cdot)$ is not integrable.

An equivalent description of such systems is often useful, which uses a basis
$G(q)$ of the distribution that annihilates $A(q)$ to describe allowable velocities
$\dot{q} \in T_q\mathcal{Q}$ as

$$\dot{q} = G(q)u. \tag{1}$$

Thanks to Frobenius' theorem, nonholonomy can thus be investigated by studying the Lie algebra generated by the vector fields in $G(q)$, or, in other terms, by
analyzing the geometry of the reachability set of (1). Such simple formulation
of kinematic nonholonomic systems is sufficient to illustrate two fundamental
aspects of nonholonomy:

1) elements of $u \in \mathbb{R}^{n-m}$ in (1) play the role of control inputs in a nonlinear, affine–in–control, driftless dynamic system. If the original constraint is
nonholonomic, the dimension of the reachable manifold is larger than the number of inputs. This has motivated purposeful introduction of nonholonomy in
the design of mechanical devices, to spare actuator hardware while maintaining
steerability (see e.g. [3,4]). Notice explicitly that for driftless systems, reachability on a manifold with dimension larger than the dimension of the input
space is an essentially nonlinear phenomenon, which is altogether destroyed by
linearization, and can be considered as a synonim of nonholonomy;

2) the effects of different consecutive inputs in nonholonomic systems do not commute. Moreover, such noncommutative inputs may produce net motions of the system in directions not belonging to the input distribution evaluated at the starting point. This observation is crucial in the interpretation of the role of Lie–brackets in deciding integrability of the system[5].

Behaviors that, by similarity, could well be termed "nonholonomic", may actually occur in a much wider class of systems than mechanical systems with smooth contact constraints or symmetries. Let us refer to general time-invariant dynamic systems as a quintuple $\Sigma = (\mathcal{Q}, \mathcal{U}, \Omega, \mathcal{A})$, with $\mathcal{Q}$ denoting the configuration set, $\mathcal{U}$ a set of admissible input symbols, Ω a set of admissible input streams (continuous functions, or discrete sequences) formed by symbols in $\mathcal{U}$, and $\mathcal{A}$ a state–transition map $\mathcal{A}: \mathcal{Q} \times \Omega \rightarrow \mathcal{Q}$. In many cases $\mathcal{U}$ is determined by a set of controls defined on an ordered time set, $\mathcal{T}$.

It has been observed that in piecewise smooth (p.s.) systems (where time is continuous, $\mathcal{Q}$ is a p.s. manifold, and $\mathcal{A}$ is a p.s. map) with holonomic dynamics within each smooth region, nonholonomic behaviours can be introduced by switching among different smooth regions of the configuration space. Piecewise holonomic systems have been studied rather extensively (see e.g. [6,7,8,9,10]). A prominent role in the study of p.s. nonholonomic systems is played by tools from differential geometric control theory (cf. [1,2]) and from the theory of stratified manifolds ([11]).

Nonholonomic behaviors may also be exhibited by discrete–time systems ($\mathcal{T} = \mathbb{N}$). Consider that, if $\mathcal{Q}$ and $\mathcal{U}$ in the system quintuple represent continuous sets, a classical discrete–time control system is described. For such systems, the reachability problem has been already clarified in the literature (see e.g. [12,13, 14,15]). On the other hand, if $\mathcal{Q}$ and $\mathcal{U}$ are assumed to be discrete sets, then the system essentially represents a sequential machine (automaton). Reachability questions for such systems are fundamentally equivalent to graph connectivity analysis, an extensively studied topic.

A particularly stimulating problem arises when $\mathcal{Q}$ has the cardinality of a continuum, but $\mathcal{U}$ is quantized (i.e. finite, or discrete with values on a regular mesh). Such systems, which will be referred to as quantized control systems (QCS), are encountered in many applications, due e.g. to the need of using finite–capacity digital channels to convey information through an embedded control loop, or to abstract symbolic information from too complex sensorial sources (such as video images in visual servoing applications). As a consequence, several researchers devoted their attention to this type of systems (see e.g. [16,17,6,18]). It is important to notice that, while inputs are quantized, the system configurations are not a priori restricted to any finite or discrete set: thus, it may happen that the reachable set has accumulation points, or is dense in the whole space, or in some subsets, or nowhere ([19]).

Chitour and Piccoli [20] have studied a quantized control synthesis problem for the linear case $x^+ = Ax + Bu$, providing sufficient conditions and a constructive technique to find a finite input set $\mathcal{U}$ to achieve a reachability set which is dense in $\mathcal{Q}$. The analysis of the reachability set of a QCS with a given quantized

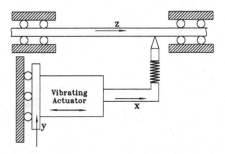

Fig. 1. A micro-electro-mechanical (M.E.M.) motion rectifier illustrating the definition of external nonholonomy in a piecewise holonomic system.

input set $\mathcal{U}$, has been considered in [21,19]. In these papers, a complete analysis is achieved for driftless linear systems (while it is pointed out that the problem for general linear systems is as though as some reputedly hard problems in number theory), and for a particular class of driftless nonlinear systems, namely the exact sampled models of n-dimensional chained–form systems ([22]), which can be considered as the simplest nonholonomic system model.

3 A Set of Examples

To motivate and drive our discussion, we start by illustrating few basic examples of systems whose behaviour we should like any definition of hybrid nonholonomy to be able to capture.

Example 1. A first set of elementary examples is obtained by considering the Heisenberg-Brockett nonholonomic integrator ([6])

$$Dq = \begin{bmatrix} 1 \\ 0 \\ -y \end{bmatrix} u_1 + \begin{bmatrix} 0 \\ 1 \\ x \end{bmatrix} u_2, \quad q \in \mathcal{Q} = \mathbb{R}^3, \tag{2}$$

in four different settings:

1-i)   Continuous time ($t \in \mathcal{T} = \mathbb{R}^+$, $Dq := \frac{d}{dt}q(t)$), continuous control ($u \in \mathcal{U} = \mathbb{R}^2$). The system is nonholonomic in the classical sense.

1-ii) Discrete time ($t \in \mathcal{T} = \mathbb{N}$, $Dq := q(t+1) - q(t)$), continuous control;

1-iii) Continuous time, quantized control ($u \in \mathcal{U}$, Card $(\mathcal{U}) \in \mathbb{N}$, Ω = piecewise-constant functions with values in $\mathcal{U}$. For instance, take $\mathcal{U} = \{(u_1, u_2)^T |\ u_1 \in \{0, a, -a\},\ u_2 \in \{0, b, -b\}\}$, for some constant $a, b \in \mathbb{R}$;

1-iv) Discrete time, quantized control.

Example 2. As an example of a piecewise holonomic system, we will consider the simplified version of one of Brockett's rectifiers ([23]) in figure 1. The tip of a piezoelectric or electrostrictive element oscillates in the x–direction, while an

Fig. 2. Three discrete approximations of the plate-ball systems.

actuator drives the oscillator support along the y–direction. When y reaches a threshold y_0, dry friction is sufficient to push the rod in the z–direction. Disregarding dynamics, the rectifier can be modeled by a continuous–time system with configurations $q = (x, y, z) \in \mathcal{Q} = \mathbb{R}^3$. Assuming that the velocity of the support $(\dot{y})$, and of the oscillator tip $(\dot{x})$ can be freely chosen, a model for this system congruent with the definitions above would be

$$\begin{bmatrix} \dot{x} \\ \dot{y} \\ \dot{z} \end{bmatrix} = \begin{bmatrix} 0 \\ 1 \\ 0 \end{bmatrix} u_1 + \begin{bmatrix} 1 \\ 0 \\ 0 \end{bmatrix} u_2 + \begin{bmatrix} 1 \\ 0 \\ 1 \end{bmatrix} u_3$$

with the input restrictions

$$\begin{cases} u_3 = 0 \ y < y_0 \\ u_2 = 0 \ y \geq y_0 \end{cases}.$$

Example 3. As a third example, we consider a system comprised of a polyhedron with one face lying on a plane, which is rolled by control actions which place one of the adjacent faces on the plane (i.e., by rotating the polyhedron about one of the edges of the face currently in contact by the exact amount that brings an adjacent face onto the plane). This can be regarded as a discrete approximation of the plate-ball system (see fig. 2), a standard example in nonholonomic textbooks. Although it may seem intuitive that "nonholonomy" is conserved by at least the finest approximations, no current definition of "nonholonomy" would be applicable to this example.

4   Discrete Nonholonomy

From consideration of examples 2 and 3, it follows directly that to afford the generality we aim at, the input set in the system quintuple Σ should be state–dependent. In other words, different sets of input actions may be available at different states, as it is clearly the case for the polyhedron when lying with different states on the plane. To deal with this problem, let us be more specific on the definition of the input set $\mathcal{U}$, and assume that there exists a multivalued function $\phi : \mathcal{Q} \to \mathcal{U}$ where $\phi(q) = \mathcal{U}_q \subset \mathcal{U}$ is the set of admissible inputs at q. Consider an input equivalence relation on $\mathcal{Q}$ given by $q_1 \overset{\mathcal{U}}{\equiv} q_2$ iff $\phi(q_1) = \phi(q_2)$, and denote $\mathcal{Q}/\phi$ the set of input equivalence classes, $[q]$ the input equivalence class of q.

Further, let Ω_q be the language over $\mathcal{U}$ consisting of admissible input streams for the system being currently in configuration q. For each $q \in \mathcal{Q}$ and $\omega \in \Omega_q$, let the end-point map, i.e. the state that the system reaches from q under $\omega \in \Omega_q$, be denoted as $\mathcal{A}(q, \cdot) : \Omega_q \to \mathcal{Q}$, or simply as $\mathcal{A}_q(\omega)$.

Two configurations q_1, q_2 are stream equivalent (denoted $q_1 \overset{\Omega}{\equiv} q_2$) iff $\Omega_{q_1} = \Omega_{q_2}$. Accordingly, $\mathcal{Q}/\Omega$ denotes the set of stream equivalence classes, and $[q]_\Omega$ is the stream equivalence class of q. Clearly, input and stream equivalence classes coincide if the following compatibility condition of the map $\mathcal{A}$ with the equivalence relation $\overset{\mathcal{U}}{\equiv}$ holds (see [24]):

[H1] $\forall q_1 \overset{\mathcal{U}}{\equiv} q_2$ and $\forall u \in \mathcal{U}_{q_1} (= \mathcal{U}_{q_2})$, $\mathcal{A}_{q_1}(u) \overset{\mathcal{U}}{\equiv} \mathcal{A}_{q_2}(u)$.

We assume in the following that $\mathcal{Q}$ is a manifold and that each input and stream equivalence classes are connected submanifolds of $\mathcal{Q}$.

Denote by $\widetilde{\Omega}_q = \{\omega \in \Omega_q : \mathcal{A}_q(\omega) \in [q]\}$ the sublanguage consisting of those input streams which steer the system eventually back to the same equivalence class of the initial point. For $\omega_1, \omega_2 \in \widetilde{\Omega}_q$, the stream concatenation $\omega_1 \omega_2$ is well defined. The notion of kinematic (i.e., driftless) systems of the form (1) can be extended in this context by the assumption that $\widetilde{\Omega}_q$ contains an identity element, $0 \in \widetilde{\Omega}_q$, such that $\mathcal{A}_q(0) = q$, for all $q \in [q]$. In general, the language $\widetilde{\Omega}_q$ is not prefix-closed. However, we will also consider the *orbit* of $q \in [q]$ under $\widetilde{\Omega}_q$ (denoted as $\mathcal{R}_q(\overline{\widetilde{\Omega}}_q)$) as the reachable set from q under words in the prefix-closure $\overline{\widetilde{\Omega}}_q$ of $\widetilde{\Omega}_q$, in other words $\mathcal{R}_q(\overline{\widetilde{\Omega}}_q) := \left\{ p \in \mathcal{Q} : p = \mathcal{A}_q(\omega_s), \omega_s \in \overline{\widetilde{\Omega}}_q \right\}$ with $\overline{\widetilde{\Omega}}_q := \left\{ \omega_s \in \mathcal{U}^* : \exists \omega_t \in \mathcal{U}^*, (\omega_s \omega_t \in \widetilde{\Omega}_q) \right\}$.

Consideration of the examples above, and the introduction of input equivalence classes and orbits, induces us to consider two different types of behaviours which may be termed "nonholonomic" by analogy with observations made in paragraph 2 about the increased reachability afforded by cyclic controls. Loosely speaking, we will refer to the case where cyclic switchings that temporarily "get out" of an equivalence class add to reachability more than what availed by paths "staying in", as to an "external" type of nonholonomy. On the other hand, when there exist reachability-generating cycles which keep the configuration always within the same equivalence class, or orbit, then we will speak of an "internal" type of nonholonomy.

4.1   External Nonholonomy

More precisely, consider the maximal sublanguage $\widehat{\Omega}_q \subseteq \widetilde{\Omega}_q$ of words that always keep the configuration within the same equivalence class, and compare the corresponding orbit $\mathcal{R}_q(\widehat{\Omega}_q) = \mathcal{R}_q(\widehat{\Omega}_q) \subseteq [q]$ with the set reachable from q under $\widetilde{\Omega}_q$, $\mathcal{R}_q(\widetilde{\Omega}_q) = \{\mathcal{A}_q(\omega) : \ \omega \in \widetilde{\Omega}_q\}$.

Definition 1. *A system* $(\mathcal{Q}, \mathcal{U}, \Omega, \mathcal{A})$ *is said to be externally nonholonomic at* $q \in \mathcal{Q}$ *if* $\mathcal{R}_q(\widetilde{\Omega}_q) \supsetneq \mathcal{R}_q(\widehat{\Omega}_q)$.

Checking for external nonholonomy directly from its definitions is clearly not feasible in general. However, under some mild conditions, we can replace the set comparison in the definition with a comparison of groups, which can be easily computed in many cases, for instance comparing sets of generators for the groups themselves.

Let $\mathcal{Q}^{\mathcal{Q}}$ be the set of mappings of $\mathcal{Q}$ into itself. The action of words in Ω on $\mathcal{Q}$ $a : \Omega \to \mathcal{Q}^{\mathcal{Q}}$, $a(\omega) \mapsto \mathcal{A}(\cdot, \omega)$, with a null element $\varepsilon \in \Omega$ such that $a(\varepsilon) = \mathcal{A}(\cdot, \varepsilon) = Id$, and with the natural composition law on $\mathcal{Q}^{\mathcal{Q}}$, is a monoid homomorphism. Let $\widetilde{S} \subset \mathcal{Q}^{\mathcal{Q}}$ be the subset of bijective, hence invertible, maps of $\mathcal{Q}$ into itself. Then $\widetilde{S}$ is a group for the composition operation. Under the further assumption that the system is *invertible*, i.e. that

[(H2)] $\forall q \in \mathcal{Q}$, $a(\widetilde{\Omega}_q) \subset \widetilde{S}$ and $\forall \omega \in \widetilde{\Omega}_q$, $\exists \, \bar{\omega} \in \widetilde{\Omega}_q$ such that $a(\omega) = (a(\bar{\omega}))^{-1}$,

we have that $\widetilde{\Omega}_q$ and $\widehat{\Omega}_q$ can be both endowed with a group structure. Under this hypothesis, we write $\omega\bar{\omega} = \bar{\omega}\omega = \varepsilon$, so that $\mathcal{A}_q(\omega\bar{\omega}) = \mathcal{A}_q(\varepsilon) = q$. Hence $\widetilde{\Omega}_q$ (or the quotient of $\widetilde{\Omega}_q$ over the corresponding equivalence relation among multiple possible inverses), is a group. We therefore have that $a : \widetilde{\Omega}_q \to \widetilde{S}$ is a group homomorphism, and the following holds:

Proposition 1. *If a system* $(\mathcal{Q}, \mathcal{U}, \Omega, \mathcal{A})$ *is externally nonholonomic at* $q \in \mathcal{Q}$ *then* $a(\widetilde{\Omega}_q) \subsetneq a(\widehat{\Omega}_q)$, *where the inclusion is a group inclusion.*

Notice that the converse of proposition 1 does not hold in general, as shown in this example, where $a(\widehat{\Omega}_q) \subsetneq a(\widetilde{\Omega}_q)$ but $\mathcal{R}(\widetilde{\Omega}_q) = \mathcal{R}(\widehat{\Omega}_q)$:

Example 4. Consider a quantized system defined on $\mathbb{R}^2$ by the following control sets: $\mathcal{U}_1 = \{e, u, \bar{u}, v\}$ for $q \in \mathcal{Q}_1 = \{(q_1, q_2) : q_1 \in \mathbb{R}, \ -1 < q_2 \le 0\}$ and $\mathcal{U}_2 = \{e, w, \bar{w}, \bar{v}\}$, for $q \in \mathcal{Q}_2 = \{(q_1, q_2) : q_1 \in \mathbb{R}, \ 0 < q_2 \le 1\}$, with $\mathcal{A}_{(q_1, q_2)}(\varepsilon) = (q_1, q_2)$, $\mathcal{A}_{(q_1, q_2)}(u) = (q_1 + 1, q_2)$, $\mathcal{A}_{(q_1, q_2)}(\bar{u}) = (q_1 - 1, q_2)$, $\mathcal{A}_{(q_1, q_2)}(v) = (q_1, q_1 + 1)$, $\mathcal{A}_{(q_1, q_2)}(\bar{v}) = (q_1, q_2 - 1)$, $\mathcal{A}_{(q_1, q_2)}(w) = (-q_1, q_2) = \mathcal{A}_{(q_1, q_2)}(\bar{w})$. Set $q = (0, -1/2)$, then $\widehat{\Omega}_q = \{u^{k_1}\bar{u}^{k_2}, \ k_1, k_2 \in \mathbb{Z}\}$ and $\widetilde{\Omega}_q = \widehat{\Omega}_1 \cup \{u^{k_1}vw^{k_2}\bar{v}\bar{u}^{k_3}, \ k_1, k_2, k_3 \in \mathbb{Z}\}$, hence $a(\widehat{\Omega}_q) \subsetneq a(\widetilde{\Omega}_q)$, but $\mathcal{R}(\widetilde{\Omega}_q) = \mathcal{R}(\widehat{\Omega}_q) = \{q + (k, 0), \ k \in \mathbb{Z}\}$. The above holds true also for the choice $q = (k, \alpha)$, $k \in \mathbb{Z}$ and $-1 < \alpha \le 0$. However, the following holds:

Proposition 2. *Assume that on* $[q]$ *it is defined an operation* "$\cdot$", *so that* $([q], \cdot)$ *is a group, and* "$\cdot$" *is compatible with the action of* $\widetilde{\Omega}_q$, *in the sense that* $a(\widetilde{\Omega}_q) \subset$

$\{\varphi : [q] \mapsto [q] : \exists q_1 \in [q]\ s.t. \forall q_2 \in [q],\ \varphi(q_2) = q_1 \cdot q_2\}$. *Assume also that the empty word* ε *in* $\widetilde{\Omega}$ *is the unique element of the isotropy group at* q, *i.e.* $\{\omega \in \widetilde{\Omega}_q :\ \mathcal{A}_q(\omega) = q\} = \{\varepsilon\}$, *Then, the system* $(\mathcal{Q}, \mathcal{U}, \Omega, \mathcal{A})$ *is externally nonholonomic at* $q \in \mathcal{Q}$ *if and only if* $a(\widetilde{\Omega}_q) \subsetneqq a(\widehat{\Omega}_q)$, *where the inclusion is a group inclusion.*

Proof. By the hypothesis we can identify $a(\widetilde{\Omega}_q)$ with a subgroup of $([q], \cdot)$ and write $\mathcal{R}_q(\widetilde{\Omega}_q) = a(\widetilde{\Omega}_q) \cdot q$. Then $a(\widetilde{\Omega}_q) \supsetneqq a(\widehat{\Omega}_q)$ if and only if $\mathcal{R}_q(\widetilde{\Omega}_q) \supsetneqq \mathcal{R}_q(\widehat{\Omega}_q)$.

4.2   Internal Nonholonomy

We restrict to driftless invertible systems where the inverse is defined uniquely, which is tantamount to assuming that $\widetilde{\Omega}_q$ is a group. Assume also that $\widetilde{\Omega}_q$ is finitely generated and denote by $S = \{s_1, \dots, s_n\}$ a set of generators.

Consider now the subset Ω_q^S of *simple* input words over S, i.e. those strings that either include a generator, or its inverse, but not both. More precisely, let

$$\widetilde{\Omega}_q^S = \{s_{\sigma(1)}^{k_{\sigma(1)}} s_{\sigma(2)}^{k_{\sigma(2)}} \dots s_{\sigma(n)}^{k_{\sigma(n)}} :\ \sigma \in \mathcal{P}(n), k_{\sigma(j)} \in \mathbf{Z},\ j = 1, \dots, n\}$$

where $k_{\sigma(i)}$ is the number of times the symbol $s_{\sigma(i)}$ is used (negative values meaning that $\bar{s}_{\sigma(i)}$ is used instead), and $\mathcal{P}(n)$ is the set of permutations of $(1, 2, \dots, n)$. Let $\mathcal{R}_q(\widetilde{\Omega}_q)$ and $\mathcal{R}_q(\widetilde{\Omega}_q^S)$ denote the reachable set from q under input streams in $\widetilde{\Omega}_q$ and in $\widetilde{\Omega}_q^S$, respectively. Definitions we propose to capture the second type of nonholonomy are then as follows:

Definition 2. *A system* $(\mathcal{Q}, \mathcal{U}, \Omega, \mathcal{A})$ *is said to be noncommutative at* $q \in \mathcal{Q}$ *if* $\widetilde{\Omega}_q$ *contains at least two elements* ω_1 *and* ω_2 *such that for their commutator* $[\omega_1, \omega_2] := \omega_1 \omega_2 \bar{\omega}_1 \bar{\omega}_2$ *it holds* $\mathcal{A}_q([\omega_1, \omega_2]) \neq q$. *A system is* internally nonholonomic *at* q *if there exists a set of generators* S *and* $\omega_1, \omega_2 \in \widetilde{\Omega}_q^S$ *such that* $\mathcal{A}_q([\omega_1, \omega_2]) \notin \mathcal{R}_q(\widetilde{\Omega}_q^S)$.

Clearly, this definition tends to generalize upon the second observation made in the introduction about classic nonholonomic systems, i.e. noncommutativity of vector fields.

The two notions of nonholonomy have a suggestive geometric interpretation (see fig.3), which is reminiscent of Berry's phase in quantum mechanics [25]. Berry noticed that if a quantum system evolves in a closed path in its parameter space, after one period the system would return to its initial state, however with a multiplicative phase containing a term depending only upon the geometry of the path the system traced out, or Berry's Phase. In our setting, consider a local decomposition of $\mathcal{Q}$ in a *base* space $\mathcal{B}$ and a *fiber* space $\mathcal{F}$, with $\mathcal{B} \times \mathcal{F} = \mathcal{Q}$. Choosing coordinates $q = (q_B, q_F)$ and denoting the canonical projections $\Pi_B(q) = q_B$, $\Pi_F(q) = q_F$, let $\mathcal{B}$ be a maximal codimension set such that $\Pi_F(\mathcal{R}_q(\widetilde{\Omega}_q^{[q]}))$ (for external nonholonomy), or $\Pi_F(\mathcal{R}_q(\widetilde{\Omega}_q^S))$ (for internal nonholonomy), are constant. If there exists an input stream which would steer the system from q to $q^\star$ with

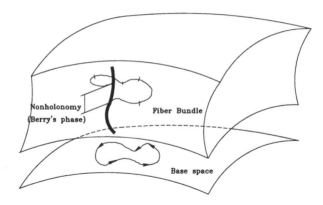

Fig. 3. Illustrating the definition of nonholonomic systems

$\Pi_B(q) = \Pi_B(q^\star)$ but $q \neq q^\star$, then the system is nonholonomic at q, and the difference between $\Pi_F(q^\star)$ and $\Pi_F(q)$ is the corresponding holonomy phase.

As regards tests for checking internal nonholonomy, we notice explicitly that an equivalent statement of internal nonholonomy is $\mathcal{R}_q(\widetilde{\Omega}_q^S) \subsetneq \mathcal{R}_q(\widetilde{\Omega}_q)$. The situation is quite different from external nonholonomy, though, because the comparison among such reachable sets can not be lifted to a comparison among groups. Indeed, $\widetilde{\Omega}_q^S$ lacks a group structure (the composition of simple words is not simple in general), and, by definition, the group generated by $\widetilde{\Omega}_q^S$ is the whole $\widetilde{\Omega}_q$. In the following, we provide a characterization of internal nonholonomy for systems of type (3).

We should like first to compare the traditional notions of nonholonomy with our more general definitions, showing that the former are particular cases of the latter. In particular, recall that the smooth, continuous time system

$$\dot{q} = G(q)u, \quad q \in \mathcal{Q} = \mathbb{R}^n, \ \mathbf{u} \in \mathcal{U} = \mathbb{R}^m \tag{3}$$

is nonholonomic in the classic sense iff $\dim(Lie_q) > \dim(\Delta_q)$, where $\Delta_q :=$ span $\{G(q)u : u \in \mathcal{U}\}$ denotes the distribution generated by $G(q, u)$, while Lie_q is the Lie Algebra of system (3) evaluated at q.

Remark 1. Notice that the classic concept of nonholonomy is intrinsically local, being indeed equivalent to a notion of small-time local (or local-local) controllability. Such local character of classical nonholonomy is not reflected in the above definition of internal nonholonomy, as shown by the example below.

Example 5. Consider the system

$$\begin{bmatrix} \dot{x}_1 \\ \dot{x}_2 \end{bmatrix} = \begin{bmatrix} v \ w \end{bmatrix} \begin{bmatrix} u_1 \\ u_2 \end{bmatrix} = \begin{bmatrix} 1 \\ \alpha \end{bmatrix} u_1 + \begin{bmatrix} 1 \\ \alpha + \varphi(q - \bar{q}) \end{bmatrix} u_2$$

with $(u_1, u_2) \in \mathbb{R}^2$ and $(x_1, x_2) \in T^2$, the two dimensional torus identified with $\mathbb{R}^2$ quotient the equivalence relation $(x_1, x_2) \sim (x_1 + k_1, x_2 + k_2)$, $k_1, k_2 \in \mathbb{Z}$.

Fix $\bar{q} \in T^2$, take α a constant $\alpha \notin \mathbb{Q}$, and $\varphi(\cdot)$ a function with $\varphi(0) = 0$ and $\nabla\varphi(0) = (0,1)$. Observe that $[v,w](\bar{q}) = (0,\alpha)$, thus $\dim(\Delta_{\bar{q}}) = 1$, $\dim(Lie_{\bar{q}}) = 2$, so the system is classically nonholonomic at $\bar{q}$.

However the system is not internally nonholonomic. Indeed, taking two generators that make the system flow along the vector fields v and w respectively, the set

$$\mathcal{R}_{\bar{q}}(\widetilde{\Omega}_{\bar{q}}^S) = \left\{ e^{tv}e^{sw}\bar{q} : t,s \in \mathbb{R} \right\}$$

coincide with T^2.

With such a motivation, consider a neighborhood $R \subseteq [q]$ of q, and the set $\mathcal{R}_q^R(\widetilde{\Omega}_q^S)$ of configurations reachable from q under input streams in $\widetilde{\Omega}_q^S$, restricted so that the trajectory from q does not leave R. A system will be said internally nonholonomic at q *with respect to* R, if $A_q([\omega_1,\omega_2]) \notin \mathcal{R}_q^R(\widetilde{\Omega}_q^S)$. When this holds for arbitrarily small R, the system is said to be *locally* internally nonholonomic.

Proposition 3. *A smooth, continuous time system (3) which is nonholonomic in the classic sense, is locally internally nonholonomic.*

Proof. Clearly, there is only one equivalence class $[q] = \mathcal{Q}$ in this case, and $\widetilde{\Omega}$ contains all input functions. We assume, without loss of generality (cf. [26]), that the columns of G are independent and that $\widetilde{\Omega}$ is comprised of actions corresponding to piecewise constant functions $\mathbb{R}^+ \mapsto \mathbb{R}^m$.

A set of generators for $\widetilde{\Omega}$ can be written as $S = (s_1, \ldots, s_m)$, $s_i = w_i e_i$, where e_i denotes the i–th column of the $m \times m$ identity matrix, and w_i is the (δ, τ) window function,

$$w_i(t) = \begin{cases} 0, & t < 0 \\ \delta_i, & 0 \le t < \tau_i \\ 0, & \tau_i \le t. \end{cases}$$

Notice that both the amplitude $\delta_i \in \mathbb{R}$ and duration $\tau_i \in \mathbb{R}^+$ of the window functions in the generators are considered free, hence each generator is a two-parameter family of finite-support, constant functions. The corresponding actions are given by

$$a(\widetilde{\Omega}_q^S) = \{ e^{F_{\sigma(1)}}e^{F_{\sigma(2)}}\ldots e^{F_{\sigma(n)}}, \sigma \in \mathcal{P}(n), F_i = \tau_i\delta_i Ge_i, \\ \delta_i \in \mathbb{R}, \tau_i \in \mathbb{R}^+, \ i = 1, \ldots, n \},$$

where $e^{F_j} = e^{\tau_j\delta_j Ge_j}$ is the formal exponential flow along the j-th control vector field. Therefore, the tangent space to the set of points locally reachable from q by simple words is given by Δ_q. Since there exists a bracket $[Ge_i, Ge_j](q)$ not contained in Δ_q, then the action of the commutator $(s_i s_j \bar{s}_i \bar{s}_j)$ generating this bracket proves the desired result.

Remark 2. The definition of internal nonholonomy requires the existence of a set of generators for which the action of commutators can not be obtained by simple actions. In general, not all sets of generators are suitable to show internal nonholonomy for a system, as is in general required that the generator set satisfies a minimality condition (this is illustrated in the example 1-iii) in the next section). We therefore introduce the following

Definition 3. *A system of generators S is minimal if $\#(S) = \dim(\Delta_q)$, where $\#(S)$ is the cardinality of S.*

Define a matrix $W = \begin{bmatrix} W_1 | \cdots | W_p \end{bmatrix} \in \mathbb{R}^{m \times p}$, with $rank(W) = m$, and consider a quantized input set

$$\mathcal{U} = \{0, \pm W_1, \ldots, \pm W_p\} \subset \mathbb{R}^m. \tag{4}$$

Proposition 4. *The system*

$$\dot{q} = G(q)u, \quad q \in \mathcal{Q} = \mathbb{R}^n, \; u \in \mathcal{U} \subset \mathbb{R}^m \tag{5}$$

with $\dim(Lie_q) > \dim(\Delta_q)$, and $\mathcal{U}$ a final set as in (4) is locally internally nonholonomic.

Proof. Again $[q] = \mathcal{Q}$ here, and $\widetilde{\Omega} = \mathcal{U}^*$. Let $S = (s_1, \ldots, s_m)$, $s_j = W_{i_j}$, $j = 1, \ldots, m$, $i_j \in \{1, \ldots, p\}$, be a minimal set of generators. Recall the Baker-Campbell-Hausdorff formula:

$$e^{t_n GW_{\sigma(n)}} \cdots e^{t_1 GW_{\sigma(1)}} =$$
$$\exp \left(\sum_{i=1}^{n} t_i GW_{\sigma(i)} + \tfrac{1}{2} \sum_{i<j} t_i t_j [GW_{\sigma(i)}, GW_{\sigma(j)}] + o(t^4) \right).$$

Since the set of generators is minimal, we have that $G(q)W_i$ are independent vectors. Hence the term $\sum_i t_i G(q)W_i$ vanishes only for all t_i equal to zero. We obtain that simple word actions can locally reach points only along the directions of $\Delta(q)$. Since the system is classically nonholonomic there exists a bracket $[GW_i, GW_j](q)$ not contained in Δ_q, hence the commutator action generating this bracket gives the desired result.

We now give some definition and results to provide a partial converse of Propositions 3, 4. Consider a system described by the dynamics in (5), with quantized input set.

We need to introduce the following

Definition 4. *A system of type (3),(5) is strongly internally nonholonomic if $T_q \mathcal{R}_q^R(\widetilde{\Omega}) \supsetneq T_q \mathcal{R}_q^R(\widetilde{\Omega}^S)$, where by $T_q \mathcal{R}_q^R(\widetilde{\Omega})$ (resp. $T_q \mathcal{R}_q^R(\widetilde{\Omega}^S)$) we denote the tangent space at q to the set of reachable points from q using controls in $\widetilde{\Omega}$ (resp. $\widetilde{\Omega}_q^S$) so that the trajectory from q does not leave a small neighborhood R of q.*

We immediately have

Proposition 5. *If a system of type (3),(5) is strongly internally nonholonomic, then it is internally nonholonomic.*

Proposition 6. *A strongly internally nonholonomic system of type (3) or (5) is classically nonholonomic.*

Proof. The above proposition follows directly from the definition. Indeed, by absurd, consider a holonomic system, then the flow along any bracket of any order is given by the flow along some direction in the vector space generated by the columns of $G(q)$. Then $T_q \mathcal{R}_q^R(\widetilde{\Omega}) = T_q \mathcal{R}_q^R(\widetilde{\Omega}^S)$.

5 Examples Revisited

Example 1 - i). Internal nonholonomy of this system follows directly shown by proposition 3. It is interesting however to report a direct constructive proof in this case, obtained by taking the input construction commonly used in textbooks to illustrate "lie-bracket motions" (see e.g. [5]). Namely, let $S = (s_1, s_2)$ with $s_1(t) = (\delta_1\ 0)$, $t \in [0, \tau_1)$ and $s_2(t) = (0\ \delta_2)$, $t \in [0, \tau_2)$ (hence $\bar{s}_i = -s_i$, $i = 1, 2$). One easily gets $\mathcal{R}_{q_0}(\widetilde{\Omega}^S) = (x_0 + \alpha,\ y_0 + \beta,\ z_0 - y_0\alpha + x_0\beta + \alpha\beta)$, $\alpha, \beta \in \mathbb{R}$, while $\mathcal{A}_{q_0}(s_1 s_2 \bar{s}_1 \bar{s}_2) = (x_0, y_0, z_0 + 2\delta_1\delta_2\tau_1\tau_2)$. Hence $\mathcal{A}_{q_0}([s_1, s_2]) \notin \mathcal{R}_{q_0}(\widetilde{\Omega}^S)$.

Example 1 - ii). Definition (2) equally applies in discrete time. This can be shown by taking e.g. $s_1 = (\delta_1\ 0)$, $s_2 = (0\ \delta_2)$, so that $\mathcal{A}_{q_0}([s_1, s_2]) = (x_0, y_0, z_0 + 2\delta_1\delta_2)$, while $\mathcal{R}_{q_0}$ is as before. The continuity of the control set guarantees complete reachability for this system in both the continuous and discrete time cases.

Example 1 - iii). The restriction on controls does not substantially change the analysis under continuous time. Indeed, considering $s_1(t) = (a\ 0)$, $t \in [t_1, t_1 + \tau_1]$, $s_2(t) = (0\ b)$, $t \in [t_2, t_2 + \tau_2]$, one gets $\mathcal{A}_{q_0}([s_1, s_2]) = (x_0, y_0, z_0 + 2ab\tau_1\tau_2)$, and both nonholonomy and complete reachability easily follow from arbitrarity of τ_1, τ_2.

We want to underscore here how a non-minimal choice of generators would not lead to a conclusion. Take for instance

$$\mathcal{U} = \{0, \pm(1, 0), \pm(-1/2, 1/2),\ \pm(-1/2, -1/2)\} .$$

The actions corresponding to the above controls give the flows along the vector fields: $v_1 = (1, 0, -y)$, $v_2 = \frac{1}{2}(-1, 1, x + y)$, $v_3 = \frac{1}{2}(-1, -1, y - x)$. Moreover the action corresponding to a simple input stream is given by

$$e^{t_3 v_{\sigma(3)}} e^{t_2 v_{\sigma(2)}} e^{t_1 v_{\sigma(1)}} = \exp\left(\sum_{i=1}^{3} t_i v_{\sigma(i)} + \frac{1}{2}\sum_{i<j} t_i t_j [v_{\sigma(i)}, v_{\sigma(j)}] + o(t^4)\right)$$

where the above equivalence is given by the Campbell-Baker-Hausdorff formula. Computing the Lie brackets $[v_i, v_j]$, $i, j = 1, 2, 3$ gives

$$[v_1, v_2] = (0, 0, 1),\ [v_1, v_3] = (0, 0, -1),\ [v_2, v_3] = (0, 0, 1),$$

hence the system is classically nonholonomic. However, this set of generators does not show internal nonholonomy, since it is possible to reach any point (p_1, p_2, p_3) in a neighborhood of the origin by the action of a simple input stream. Indeed, up to higher order terms, it is enough to solve one of the two systems

$$\begin{cases} (p_1, p_2, 0) = t_1 v_1 + t_2 v_2 + t_3 v_3 \\ (0, 0, p_3) = t_1 t_2 [v_1, v_2] + t_1 t_3 [v_1, v_3] + t_2 t_3 [v_2, v_3] \end{cases}$$

or

$$\begin{cases} (p_1, p_2, 0) = t_1 v_1 + t_2 v_3 + t_3 v_2 \\ (0, 0, p_3) = t_1 t_2 [v_1, v_3] + t_1 t_3 [v_1, v_2] + t_2 t_3 [v_3, v_2] \end{cases}$$

obtained via simple stream actions for the choice $\sigma = (1)$ and $\sigma = (23)$ respectively. From the first system we get

$$t_1 = t_3 + p_1 + p_2$$
$$t_2 = t_3 + 2p_2$$
$$t_3^2 + 4p_2 t_3 - \gamma = 0$$
$$\gamma = 2p_3 - 2p_2(p_1 + p_2)$$

while from the second we obtain:

$$t_1 = t_3 + p_1 - p_2$$
$$t_2 = t_3 - 2p_2$$
$$t_3^2 - 4p_2 t_3 + \gamma = 0$$
$$\gamma = 2p_3 - 2p_2(p_1 + p_2).$$

Hence at least one of the two systems has a real solution.

Example 1 - iv). In the discrete input, discrete time case, the input commutator $[s_1, s_2]$ with $s_1 = (a,\ 0)$, $s_2 = (0\ b)$, produces $\mathcal{A}_{q_0}([s_1, s_2]) = (x_0, y_0, z_0 + 2ab)$. Internal nonholonomy is maintained. However, the reachable set from the origin is only comprised of configurations in a discrete set, $\mathcal{R}_0 = \{q\ :\ x = \ell a,\ y = mb,\ z = nab,\ \ell, m, n \in \mathbb{Z}\}$. The situation is completely different, and density of the reachable set is guaranteed, if e.g. $\mathcal{U} = \{(u_1, u_2)|\ u_1 \in \{0, a, -a, c, -c\}$, $u_2 \in \{0, b, -b, d, -d\}$, $a, b, c, d \in \mathbb{R}\}$ with $\frac{a}{c}, \frac{b}{d} \notin \mathbb{Q}$.

The interpretation of nonholonomy given in fig.3 applies to all cases above, using coordinates x, y to describe the base space, while z parameterizes the fiber.

Example 2. Two input equivalence classes are defined in $\mathcal{Q}$ as $[q]_{free} = \{q \in \mathcal{Q} : y < y_0\}$ and $[q]_{engaged} = \{q \in \mathcal{Q} : y \geq y_0\}$. Clearly, $\mathcal{R}_{q_0}(\widehat{\Omega}_{q_0}) = \{(x, y, z) \in \mathcal{Q} : z = z_0\}$, for all $q_0 = (x_0, y_0, z_0) \in [q]_{free}$, while $\mathcal{R}_{q_0}(\Omega_{q_0}) = \mathbb{R}^3$. The system is thus externally nonholonomic according to definition (1).

Interestingly enough, the system is not internally nonholonomic as per definition (2). Indeed, to generate the set $\widetilde{\Omega}_{q_0}$, at least two types of streams must be considered: an internal type e.g. $s_i : (x_0, y_0, z_0) \mapsto (x, y, z_0)$, and an external type (taking the state out of $[q]_{free}$ temporarily), e.g. $s_e : (x_0, y_0, z_0) \mapsto (x', y', z')$. Clearly, simple streams over this set of generators are sufficient to reach any configuration of the system ($\mathcal{R}_q(\widetilde{\Omega}_q^S) = \mathbb{R}^3$), hence internal nonholonomy does not apply.

Base variables for this example would be x and y, while z represents the fiber variable. Rectification of motion is obtained by holonomic phase accumulation in succesive cycles. By changing frequency and phase of the inputs, different directions and velocities of the rod motion can be achieved. Note in particular that input u_2 need not actually to be finely tuned, as long as it is periodic, and it could be chosen as a resonant mode of the vibrating actuator: tuning only u_2 still guarantees in this case the (non-local) reachability of the system (cf. [27,11]).

Example 3. In the rolling polyhedron system let a configuration be described by the index, position and orientation of the face currently on the plane, as $q = (F, x, \theta) \in \mathcal{F} \times \mathbb{R}^2 \times S^1$, with $\mathcal{F} = \{F_1, \dots, F_n\}$ the set of faces. For each face is associated to a finite set of adjacent faces, there are n input equivalence classes given by $[q] = \{F = F_i, x \in \mathbb{R}^2, \theta \in S^1\}$. This system verifies the hypothesis of proposition 2, because we can identify a class $[q]$ with a subgroup of isometries of the plane $\mathbb{R}^2 \oplus S^1$. External nonholonomy can be proved quite straightforwardly in this case by comparing the action of the group $\mathcal{R}_q(\widehat{\Omega}_q)$ of sequences of faces starting and ending with F_i, with $\mathcal{R}_q(\widehat{\Omega}_q) = \emptyset$.

Internal nonholonomy according to definition 2 also holds: indeed, $\widetilde{\Omega}_q$, the set of words that bring back the polyhedron on the same face lying on the plane, is generated (see [28]) by the finite set $S = \{R_\lambda, \ \lambda = 1, \dots, h - 1\}$, where R_λ is a planar rotation of an angle equal to the polyhedron defect angle β_λ at the λ–th vertex, centered at the point corresponding with that vertex in the planar development of the polyhedron. If $\beta_\lambda/\pi \in \mathbb{Q}$ for all $\lambda = 1, \dots, h - 1$, then $\widetilde{\Omega}_q^S$ is a finite set because, if $\beta_\lambda = 2\pi \frac{m_\lambda}{p_\lambda}$, $R_\lambda^{p_\lambda} = (0,0)$. Therefore $\mathcal{R}_q(\widetilde{\Omega}_q^S)$ is a finite set. Since $\mathcal{R}_q(\widetilde{\Omega}_q)$ is an infinite countable set, nonholonomy immediately follows. If, otherwise, there exists λ such that $\beta_\lambda/\pi \notin \mathbb{Q}$ then there exists another index λ', $\lambda' \neq \lambda$ for which it also holds $\beta_{\lambda'}/\pi \notin \mathbb{Q}$. Without loss of generality we can assume $\lambda = 1$ and $\lambda' = 2$ and choose the set of $h - 1$ generators given by $\beta_2, \dots \beta_h$. In order to prove nonholonmy we have to compare commutators with translations in $\widetilde{\Omega}_q^S$. Translations in $\widetilde{\Omega}_q^S$ are written as $R_{\sigma(2)}^{k_{\sigma(2)}} R_{\sigma(3)}^{k_{\sigma(3)}} \cdots R_{\sigma(h)}^{k_{\sigma(h)}}$, with $k_{\sigma(j)} = 0$ if $\beta_{\sigma(j)}/\pi \notin \mathbb{Q}$. In other words translations in $\widetilde{\Omega}_q^S$ have to be generated only by those generators with λ such that β_λ is irrational with π. Now, let t be any translation in $\widetilde{\Omega}_q^S$. Then the commutator $[R_2, t]$ gives a translation of $t(e^{-\jmath\beta_2} - 1)$ which cannot be generated by simple words.

6   Conclusions

The notions of nonholonomy and reachability are conventionally related to differentiable control systems, and are defined in terms of their differential geometric properties. However, these notions apply also to more general systems, including discrete and hybrid systems. In this paper, we have given a generalization of the concept of nonholonomy to such classes of systems. By studying the intimate nature of a few carefully chosen examples, we observed two different aspects of the hybrid nonholonomic phenomenon, which have been captured in the notions of internal and external nonholonomy. We also provided some tools for investigating the applicability of definitions to given systems. However, much work remains to be done in that direction.

Acknowledgments. Authors should like to thank Yacine Chitour for many useful discussions on the nonholonomy of rolling polyhedra.

References

1. A. M. Bloch and P. E. Crouch, "Nonholonomic control systems on Riemannian manifolds," *SIAM Journal on Control and Optimization*, vol. 33, no. 1, pp. 126–148, 1995.
2. A. Bloch, P. Krishnaprasad, J. Marsden, and R. Murray, "Nonholonomic mechanical systems with symmetry," *Archive for Rational Mechanics and Analysis*, vol. 136, pp. 21–29, December 1996.
3. O.J. Sordalen and Y. Nakamura, "Design of a nonholonomic manipulator," in *Proc. IEEE Int. Conf. on Robotics and Automation*, 1994, pp. 8–13.
4. A.Marigo and A.Bicchi, "Rolling bodies with regular surface: Controllability theory and applications," *IEEE Trans. on Automatic Control*, vol. 45, no. 9, pp. 1586–1599, September 2000.
5. R.M. Murray, Z. Li, and S.S. Sastry, *A mathematical introduction to robotic manipulation*, CRC Press, Boca Raton, 1994.
6. R.W. Brockett, "Asymptotic stability and feedback stabilization," in *Differential Geometric Control Theory*, Millmann Brockett and Sussmann, Eds., pp. 181–191. Birkhauser, Boston, U.S., 1983.
7. M. J. Coleman and P. Holmes, "Motions and stability of a piecewise holonomic system: the discrete Chaplygin sleigh," *Regular and Chaotic Dynamics*, vol. 4, no. 2, pp. 1–23, 1999.
8. K.M. Lynch and M.T. Mason, "Controllability of pushing," in *Proc. IEEE Int. Conf. on Robotics and Automation*, 1995, pp. 112–119.
9. J. Ostrowski and J. Burdick, "Geometric perspectives on the mechanics and control of robotic locomotion," in *Robotics Research: The Seventh International Symposium*, G. Giralt and G. Hirzinger, Eds. Springer Verlag, 1995.
10. S.D. Kelly and R.M.Murray, "Geometric phases and robotic locomotion," *Journal of Robotic Systems*, vol. 12, no. 6, pp. 417–431, 1995.
11. B. Goodwine and J. Burdick, "Controllability of kinematic control systems on stratified configuration spaces," *IEEE Trans. on Automatic Control*, vol. 46, no. 3, pp. 358–368, 2001.
12. M. Fliess and D. Normand-Cyrot, "A group theoretic approach to discrete-time nonlinear controllability," in *Proc. IEEE Int. Conf. on Decision and Control*, 1981, pp. 551–557.
13. S. Monaco and D. Normand-Cyrot, "An introduction to motion planning under multirate digital control," in *Proc. IEEE Int. Conf. on Decision and Control*, 1992.
14. B. Jakubczyk and E. D. Sontag, "Controllability of nonlinear discrete time systems: A lie-algebraic approach," *SIAM J. Control and Optimization*, vol. 28, pp. 1–33, 1990.
15. V. Jurdjevic, *Geometric control theory*, Cambridge University Press, 1997.
16. D. F. Delchamps, "Extracting state information from a quantized output record," *Systems and Control Letters*, vol. 13, pp. 365–371, 1989.
17. D. F. Delchamps, "Stabilizing a linear system with quantized state feedback," *IEEE Trans. Autom. Control*, vol. 35, no. 8, pp. 916–926, 1990.
18. N. Elia and S. K. Mitter, "Quantization of linear systems," in *Proc. 38th Conf. Decision & Control*. IEEE, 1999, pp. 3428–3433.
19. A. Bicchi, A. Marigo, and B. Piccoli, "On the reachability of quantized control systems," *IEEE Trans. on Automatic Control*, vol. 47, no. 4, pp. 546–563, April 2002.
20. Y. Chitour and B. Piccoli, "Controllability for discrete systems with a finite control set," *Math. Control Signals Systems*, vol. 14, no. 2, pp. 173–193, 2001.

21. A. Marigo, B. Piccoli, and A. Bicchi, "Reachability analysis for a class of quantized control systems," in *Proc. IEEE Int. Conf. on Decision and Control*, 2000, pp. 3963–3968.

22. S. S. Sastry R. M. Murray, "Nonholonomic motion planning: Steering using sinusoids," *IEEE Trans. on Automatic Control*, vol. 38, pp. 700–716, 1993.

23. R.W. Brockett, "On the rectification of vibratory motion," *Sensors and Actuators*, vol. 20, pp. 91–96, 1989.

24. A. Marigo, B. Piccoli, and A. Bicchi, "A group-theoretic characterization of quantized control systems," in *Proc. IEEE Int. Conf. on Decision and Control*, 2002, pp. 811–816.

25. M. V. Berry, "Quantal phase factors accompanying adiabatic changes," *Proc. Roy. Soc. A*, vol. 392:45, 1984.

26. R. Hermann and A. Krener, "Nonlinear controllability and observability," *IEEE Trans. on Automatic Control*, vol. 22, no. 5, 1977.

27. R. W. Brockett, "Smooth multimode control systems," in *Proc. Berkeley-Ames Conference on Nonlinear Problems in Control and Fluid Dynamics*, L. Hunt and C. Martin, Eds., 1984, pp. 103–110.

28. A. Marigo, Y. Chitour, and A. Bicchi, "Manipulation of polyhedral parts by rolling," in *Proc. IEEE Int. Conf. on Robotics and Automation*, 1997, vol. 4, pp. 2992–2997.

Approximations of the Rate of Growth of Switched Linear Systems[*]

Vincent D. Blondel, Yurii Nesterov, and Jacques Theys[**]

Université catholique de Louvain, CESAME
Department of Mathematical Engineering
4-6, avenue Georges Lemaître, B-1348 Louvain-la-Neuve
{blondel,nesterov,theys}@inma.ucl.ac.be

Abstract. The joint spectral radius of a set of matrices is a measure of the maximal asymptotic growth rate that can be obtained by forming long products of matrices taken from the set. This quantity appears in a number of application contexts, in particular it characterizes the growth rate of switched linear systems. The joint spectral radius is notoriously difficult to compute and to approximate. We introduce in this paper the first polynomial time approximations of guaranteed precision. We provide an approximation $\hat{\rho}$ that is based on ellipsoid norms that can be computed by convex optimization and that is such that the joint spectral radius belongs to the interval $[\hat{\rho}/\sqrt{n}, \hat{\rho}]$ where n is the dimension of the matrices. We also provide a simple approximation for the special case where the entries of all the matrices are non-negative; in this case the approximation is proved to be within a factor at most m (m is the number of matrices) of the exact value.

1 Introduction

Let M be a set of square real matrices. The *trajectories* associated to the discrete-time *switched linear system* generated by the set M are given by the vector sequences defined by the discrete linear inclusion:

$$x_{k+1} \in \{A_i x_k : A_i \in M\} \quad k = 0, 1, \ldots.$$

A switched linear system is said to be *stable* if all its trajectories converge to the origin. This condition is equivalent to the condition that all infinite products of matrices taken from the set M converge to zero. Stability can be equivalently expressed by requiring the joint spectral radius of the set M to be less than one. The *joint spectral radius* of a set of matrices is a quantity, introduced by Rota and Strang in the early 60's, that measures the maximal asymptotic growth rate

---

[*] This paper presents research results of the Belgian Program on Interuniversity Attraction Poles, initiated by the Belgian State, Prime Minister's Office for Science, Technology and Culture. The scientific responsibility rests with its authors.

[**] JT holds a FNRS fellowship (Belgian National Research Fund).

R. Alur and G.J. Pappas (Eds.): HSCC 2004, LNCS 2993, pp. 173–186, 2004.

that can be obtained by forming long products of matrices taken from the set; see [17]. More formally, the joint spectral radius of the set M is defined by:

$$\rho(M) := \limsup_{k \to \infty} \rho_k(M),$$

where

$$\rho_k(M) = \sup_{A_1,\dots,A_k \in M} \|A_k \cdots A_1\|^{1/k}.$$

The values of $\rho_k(M)$ do in general depend on the chosen norm but one can show that the limit value $\rho(M)$ does not. When the set M consists of only one matrix A, the joint spectral radius coincides with the usual notion of spectral radius of a single matrix which is equal to the maximum magnitude of the eigenvalues of the matrix. If in the previous definition we had used the spectral radius instead of the norm, we would have obtained the *generalized spectral radius*:

$$\rho'(M) = \limsup_{k \to \infty} \rho'_k(M),$$

where

$$\rho'_k(M) = \sup_{A_1,\dots,A_k \in M} \rho(A_k \cdots A_1)^{1/k}.$$

This quantity appears for the first time in [6], where it is also conjectured that in the case of bounded sets of matrices (and in particular for finite sets of matrices), the joint and generalized spectral radii are equal. This conjecture is proved to be correct in [2].

Questions related to the computability of the joint spectral radius of sets of matrices have been posed in [20] and [14]. The joint spectral radius can easily be approximated to any desired accuracy. Indeed, the following bounds, proved in [14],

$$\rho'_k(M) \le \rho(M) \le \rho_k(M)$$

can be evaluated for increasing values of k and lead to arbitrary close approximations of ρ. These are however expensive calculations. It is proved in [21] that, unless $P = NP$, there is in fact no polynomial-time approximation algorithm for the joint spectral radius of two matrices.

In this paper, we provide two easily computable approximations of the joint spectral radius for finite sets of matrices. The first approximation that we provide, $\hat{\rho}$, is based on the computation of a common quadratic Lyapunov function, or, equivalently, on the computation of an ellipsoid norm. This approximation has the advantage that it can be expressed as a convex optimization problem for which efficient algorithms exist. This first approximation satisfies

$$\frac{1}{\sqrt{n}} \, \hat{\rho} \le \rho \le \hat{\rho}$$

where n is the dimension of the matrices. For the special case of symmetric matrices, triangular matrices, or for sets of matrices that have a solvable Lie algebra, we prove equality between the joint spectral radius and its approximation, $\rho = \hat{\rho}$.

We then prove a result of independent interest: the largest spectral radius of the matrices in the convex hull of $M = \{A_1, \ldots, A_m\}$ is a lower bound for the joint spectral radius of M:

$$\max_{0 \leq \lambda_i \leq 1, \sum \lambda_i = 1} \rho\left(\sum_i \lambda_i A_i\right) \leq \rho(M).$$

By using this inequality, we prove a simple bound for the joint spectral radius of sets of matrices that have *non-negative entries*. The spectral radius of the matrix S whose entries are the componentwise maximum of the entries of the matrices in M satisfies

$$\frac{\rho(S)}{m} \leq \rho(M) \leq \rho(S)$$

where m is the number of matrices in the set. In this expression, M is a set of matrices, whereas S is a single matrix.

The problem of computing approximations of the joint spectral radius is raised and analyzed in a number of recent contributions. In [16], the exponential number of products that appear in the computation of ρ_k' based on its definition is reduced by avoiding duplicate computation of cyclic permutations; the total number of product to consider remains however exponential. In [8], an algorithm based on the above idea is presented. The algorithm gives arbitrarily small intervals for the joint spectral radius, but no rate of convergence is proved.

This paper gives the first polynomial-time approximations of guaranteed precision. The paper is organized as follows. In the next section, we define the joint spectral radius approximation based on ellipsoid norms. In Section 3, we describe situations for which this approximation is exact, and situations for which it is not. In Section 4, we prove the inequality $\hat{\rho}(M)/\sqrt{n} \leq \rho$ by using a geometrical property of ellipsoids known as John's ellipsoid theorem. Finally, in Section 5 we provide an under-approximation of the joint spectral radius based on the spectral radius of all convex combinations of the matrices in the set M and use this result to prove an approximation for sets of non-negative matrices.

2   The Ellipsoid Norm Approximation

The joint spectral radius can be defined by an extremal norm property. The statement of the following theorem is compiled from results in [13] and also [1].

Theorem 1. *Let $\rho(M)$ be the joint spectral radius of the finite set of matrices M. Then:*

1. *There exists a vector norm $\|.\|_*$ for which $\|A_i x\|_* \leq \rho(M)\, \|x\|_*$, $\forall x$ and $\forall A_i \in M$;*
2. $\rho(M) = \inf_{\|.\|} \left(\max_{A_i \in M} \|A_i\|\right)$.

The joint spectral radius is thus given by the infimum over all possible matrix norms of the largest norm of the matrices in the set. A norm achieving this infimum is said to be *extremal* for the set (not every set of matrices possesses an extremal norm, see [22] for a discussion of this issue). In [13], Kozyakin describes the theoretical construction of such an extremal norm. This method is not explicit and partly relies on the a-priori knowledge of the numerical value of the joint spectral radius. One can of course not hope enumerating all possible matrix norms for computing the joint spectral radius, but we can enumerate particular sets of norms. Our first approximation of the joint spectral radius is obtained by finding, among all ellipsoid norms $\| \cdot \|_P$, one that minimizes $\max_i \|A_i\|_P$.

Let us briefly recall the definition of the ellipsoid norm. Let P be a positive definite matrix[1]; the vector P-norm is defined as $\|x\|_P = \sqrt{x^T P x}$. Associated to this vector norm, there is an induced matrix norm which we call *ellipsoid norm*:

$$|||A_i|||_P = \sup_{x \neq 0} \frac{\|A_i x\|_P}{\|x\|_P} = \sup_{x \neq 0} \frac{\sqrt{x^T A_i^T P A_i x}}{\sqrt{x^T P x}} . \tag{1}$$

Further on, we will use the notation $\|.\|_P$ for both the vector and matrix norms. Let us now define the *ellipsoid norm approximation* of the joint spectral radius by:

$$\hat{\rho}(M) = \inf_{P \succ 0} \max_{A_i \in M} \|A_i\|_P.$$

The infimum on all ellipsoid norms cannot be lower than the infimum on all possible norms and so it immediately follows from Theorem 1 that $\rho(M) \leq \hat{\rho}(M)$. The ellipsoid norm approximation can be computed as follows. Notice first that the definition implies that

$$\forall x, \; \sqrt{x^T A_i^T P A_i x} \leq \|A_i\|_P \sqrt{x^T P x}$$
$$\forall x, \; x^T (A_i^T P A_i - \|A_i\|_P^2 P)x \leq 0$$
$$A_i^T P A_i - \|A_i\|_P^2 P \preceq 0 .$$

One can therefore think of $\|A_i\|_P$ as the smallest scalar value γ for which $A_i^T P A_i \preceq \gamma^2 P$ for some $P \succ 0$. The ellipsoid norm approximation of a set $M = \{A_1, \ldots, A_m\}$ is thus equal to the smallest scalar γ for which there is a solution $P \succ 0$ to $A_i^T P A_i \preceq \gamma^2 P, \forall i$. This problem can be solved efficiently by convex optimization; see, e.g., [5].

A natural question to ask is how good this approximation is in the general case. In the next section, we describe situations for which the approximation is equal to the joint spectral radius, and we provide an example for which the approximation is larger than the joint spectral radius.

3   The Joint Spectral Radius and Its Approximation

We prove in this section that the joint spectral radius and the ellipsoid norm approximation are equal (and are equal to the largest spectral radius of the

---

[1] Positive definiteness is denoted $\succ 0$ and positive semi-definiteness is denoted $\succeq 0$.

matrices in the set) in the following situations: all matrices are symmetric, all matrices are triangular or, more generally, the Lie algebra associated to the matrices is solvable. We close the section with an example for which the joint spectral radius and its approximation are different. We start with the case of symmetric matrices:

Proposition 1. *For a set of symmetric matrices, the joint spectral radius and its ellipsoid norm approximation are equal and are equal to the largest spectral radius of the matrices in the set.*

Proof. Using the identity I as matrix P, we get $A_i^2 \preceq \|A_i\|_I^2 I$, so that $\rho(A_i) = \|A_i\|_I$. Knowing that $\rho(A_i) \leq \inf_{P \succ 0} \|A_i\|_P$, we have actually $\rho(A_i) = \inf_{P \succ 0} \|A_i\|_P$, which finally yields $\max_i \rho(A_i) = \hat{\rho}(M)$. $\square$

In order to derive our result for triangular matrices, we first establish a discrete-time analog to a continuous-time result established in [15] on the existence of a common quadratic Lyapunov function for switched linear systems.

Lemma 1. *Let $M = \{A_1, \dots, A_m\}$ and consider the discrete-time switched linear system*

$$x_{k+1} = A_{i_k} x_k \quad A_{i_k} \in M.$$

If the switched system is stable and the matrices are upper-triangular, then there exists a common quadratic Lyapunov function in the form of a diagonal matrix.

Proof. Let $\{A_i, \dots, A_m\}$ be a set of upper-triangular (possibly complex) matrices and P the candidate Lyapunov function (diagonal, real):

$$A_i = \begin{pmatrix} a_{11}^i & a_{12}^i & \cdots & a_{1n}^i \\ 0 & a_{22}^i & \cdots & a_{2n}^i \\ \vdots & \vdots & \ddots & \vdots \\ 0 & 0 & \cdots & a_{nn}^i \end{pmatrix}, P = \begin{pmatrix} p_1 & 0 & \cdots & 0 \\ 0 & p_2 & \cdots & 0 \\ \vdots & \vdots & \ddots & \vdots \\ 0 & 0 & \cdots & p_n \end{pmatrix}, p_k > 0, \forall k .$$

For P to be a Lyapunov function of $x_{k+1} = A_i x_k$ (fixed A_i), the following relation has to hold:

$$P - A_i^* P A_i \succ 0 .$$

Developing $P - A_i^* P A_i$, we get:

$$\begin{pmatrix} p_1 & 0 & \cdots & 0 \\ 0 & p_2 & \cdots & 0 \\ \vdots & \vdots & \ddots & \vdots \\ 0 & 0 & \cdots & p_n \end{pmatrix} - \begin{pmatrix} {a_{11}^i}^* & 0 & \cdots & 0 \\ {a_{12}^i}^* & {a_{22}^i}^* & \cdots & 0 \\ \vdots & \vdots & \ddots & \vdots \\ {a_{1n}^i}^* & {a_{2n}^i}^* & \cdots & {a_{nn}^i}^* \end{pmatrix} \begin{pmatrix} p_1 & 0 & \cdots & 0 \\ 0 & p_2 & \cdots & 0 \\ \vdots & \vdots & \ddots & \vdots \\ 0 & 0 & \cdots & p_n \end{pmatrix} \begin{pmatrix} a_{11}^i & a_{12}^i & \cdots & a_{1n}^i \\ 0 & a_{22}^i & \cdots & a_{2n}^i \\ \vdots & \vdots & \ddots & \vdots \\ 0 & 0 & \cdots & a_{nn}^i \end{pmatrix}$$

$$= \begin{pmatrix} p_1 & 0 & \cdots & 0 \\ 0 & p_2 & \cdots & 0 \\ \vdots & \vdots & \ddots & \vdots \\ 0 & 0 & \cdots & p_n \end{pmatrix} - \begin{pmatrix} {a_{11}^i}^* p_1 & 0 & \cdots & 0 \\ {a_{12}^i}^* p_1 & {a_{22}^i}^* p_2 & \cdots & 0 \\ \vdots & \vdots & \ddots & \vdots \\ {a_{1n}^i}^* p_1 & {a_{2n}^i}^* p_2 & \cdots & {a_{nn}^i}^* p_n \end{pmatrix} \begin{pmatrix} a_{11}^i & a_{12}^i & \cdots & a_{1n}^i \\ 0 & a_{22}^i & \cdots & a_{2n}^i \\ \vdots & \vdots & \ddots & \vdots \\ 0 & 0 & \cdots & a_{nn}^i \end{pmatrix}$$

which yields

$$
\begin{pmatrix}
(1 - |a^i{}_{11}|^2)p_1 & -a^i{}_{11}{}^* a^i{}_{12}p_1 & \cdots \\
-a^i{}_{11}a^i{}_{12}{}^* p_1 & -|a^i{}_{12}|^2 p_1 + (1 - |a^i{}_{22}|^2)p_2 & \cdots \\
\vdots & \vdots & \ddots \\
-a^i{}_{11}a^i{}_{1n}{}^* p_1 & -a^i{}_{12}a^i{}_{1n}{}^* p_1 - a^i{}_{22}a^i{}_{2n}{}^* p_2 & \cdots
\end{pmatrix}
\succ 0 .
\tag{2}
$$

The first thing to note is that this matrix is Hermitian, and so its leading principal minors are real (see [10]).

As A_i is assumed to be stable, $a^i_{jj} < 1, \forall j$. The first diagonal element in (2) is therefore positive, for any value of p_1. Let it be chosen as 1. Moreover, the value of p_2 can be chosen in such a way that the (2×2) leading principal minor is positive. Indeed, p_2 only appears in its last diagonal element, and its coefficient $(1 - |a^i_{22}|^2)$ is positive, as $a^i_{22} < 1$. So, taking p_2 such that

$$
\begin{vmatrix}
(1 - |a^i{}_{11}|^2) & -a^i{}_{11}{}^* a^i{}_{12} \\
-a^i{}_{11}a^i{}_{12}{}^* & -|a^i{}_{12}|^2 + (1 - |a^i{}_{22}|^2)p_2
\end{vmatrix} > 0
$$

is possible, and simple developments give the following condition:

$$
p_2 > \frac{1}{(1 - |a^i{}_{22}|^2)} \left[\frac{(|a^i{}_{11}||a^i{}_{12}|)^2}{(1 - |a^i{}_{11}|^2)} + |a^i{}_{12}|^2 \right] .
$$

We can define in this way a p_2 that satisfies this for all matrices A_i of the set by choosing

$$
p_2 > \max_i \frac{1}{(1 - |a^i{}_{22}|^2)} \left[\frac{(|a^i{}_{11}||a^i{}_{12}|)^2}{(1 - |a^i{}_{11}|^2)} + |a^i{}_{12}|^2 \right] .
$$

The same argument shows that we can successively choose the values of $p_3, \dots, p_n$ in a way such that the leading principal minors of (2) are all positive, and this for any matrix A_i of the set. Indeed, let the leading principal minor of order k be > 0. Then, the leading principal minor of order $k + 1$ can be made > 0 too, because p_{k+1} only appears in its last diagonal term, with a strictly positive coefficient. So, taking p_{k+1} large enough is sufficient. The finiteness of the elements of A_i guarantees us that such a value p_{k+1} exists and is finite.

A Hermitian matrix H is positive definite if and only if all its leading principal minors are positive ([10]), and so we can deduce that the Hermitian matrix appearing in (2) is indeed positive definite, for any i. So, the P matrix built in this way is a common quadratic Lyapunov function for the set M. □

Corollary 1. *For a set of triangular matrices, the joint spectral radius and its ellipsoid norm approximation are equal and are equal to the largest spectral radius of the matrices in the set.*

Proof. From lemma 1, it turns out that, for a set of stable upper-triangular matrices A_i, there exists a positive definite P_* such that $\|A_i\|_{P_*} < 1, \forall i$. This is equivalent to expressing

$$\max_i \rho(A_i) < 1 \Rightarrow \exists P_* \succ 0 : \max_i \|A_i\|_{P_*} < 1 \ .$$

By linearity, this implies that $\max_i \rho(A_i) \geq \max_i \|A_i\|_{P_*}$. Indeed, let us pose $\max_i \rho(A_i) = r$, so that $\forall y > r$, $\max_i \rho\left(\frac{A_i}{y}\right) < 1$. This implies that $\forall y > r, \exists P_* : \max_i \frac{\|A_i\|_{P_*}}{y} < 1$ or again, $\forall y > \max_i \rho(A_i), \exists P_* : \max_i \|A_i\|_{P_*} < y$. So, $\max_i \|A_i\|_{P_*}$ is arbitrarily close (from above) to $\max_i \rho(A_i)$ and the announced inequality $\max_i \rho(A_i) \geq \max_i \|A_i\|_{P_*}$ holds.

On the other hand, we know that the joint spectral radius is greater or equal to the largest spectral radius of the matrices in the set, that is $\rho(M) \geq \max_i \rho(A_i)$. So, summing up, we have

$$\rho(M) \geq \max_i \rho(A_i) \geq \max_i \|A_i\|_P \geq \hat{\rho}(M) \ .$$

As $\hat{\rho}$ is an over-approximation of $\rho(M)$, this yields $\rho(M) = \max_i \rho(A_i)$ and $\hat{\rho}(M) = \rho(M)$. $\qquad\square$

We now generalize the previous result to a more general class of sets of matrices. This development is very similar to the one presented in [15]. Let us recall the following notations and definitions. The Lie bracket stands for the commutator of two operators :

$$[A, B] = AB - BA \quad .$$

The Lie algebra $\{A_0, A_1\}_{LA}$ is the linear span of

$$\{A_0, A_1, [A_0, A_1], [A_0, [A_0, A_1]], [A_1, [A_0, A_1]], \dots\}.$$

The *commutator series* of a Lie algebra $\mathfrak{g}$ is the sequence of subalgebras recursively defined by $\mathfrak{g}^{k+1} = [\mathfrak{g}^k, \mathfrak{g}^k]$, and $\mathfrak{g}^0 = \mathfrak{g}$. Noting $[a, b]$ the linear span of elements of the form $[A, B]$, where $A \in a, B \in b$, we have

$$\mathfrak{g}^1 = [\mathfrak{g}^0, \mathfrak{g}^0] = \mathrm{span}\{[A_0, A_1], [A_0, [A_0, A_1]], [A_1, [A_0, A_1]], \dots\} \ ,$$
$$\mathfrak{g}^2 = [\mathfrak{g}^1, \mathfrak{g}^1] = \mathrm{span}\{[[A_0, A_1], [A_0, [A_0, A_1]]], [[A_0, A_1], [A_1, [A_0, A_1]]], \dots\},$$
$$\mathfrak{g}^3 = [\mathfrak{g}^2, \mathfrak{g}^2] = \dots \ .$$

These sets are such that $\mathfrak{g}^0 \supseteq \mathfrak{g}^1 \supseteq \mathfrak{g}^2 \supseteq \dots$, and if $\mathfrak{g}^k = \mathfrak{g}^{k+1}$ then all subsequent $\mathfrak{g}^{k+p}$ $(p \in \mathbb{N})$ are also equal to $\mathfrak{g}^k$. A Lie Algebra is *solvable* if its commutator series $\mathfrak{g}^k$ vanishes for some k.

An often used example of solvable Lie algebra is the vector space of upper-triangular matrices. It is easy to check that the sequence of subalgebras $\mathfrak{g}^k$ is the set of upper-triangular matrices whose elements on the diagonal at distance less than k from the main diagonal are all zero.

We make use of the following result (cited in [15], referring to [18]):

Lemma 2. *Let $\mathfrak{g}$ be a solvable Lie algebra over an algebraically closed field, and let ρ be a representation of $\mathfrak{g}$ on a vector space V of finite dimension n. Then there exists a basis $\{v_1, \ldots, v_n\}$ of V such that for each $X \in \mathfrak{g}$ the matrix of $\rho(X)$ in that basis takes the upper-triangular form*

$$\begin{pmatrix} \lambda_1(X) & \cdots & * \\ \vdots & \ddots & \vdots \\ 0 & \cdots & \lambda_n(X) \end{pmatrix},$$

where the $\lambda_1, \ldots, \lambda_n$ denote the eigenvalues of the matrix $\rho(X)$.

Theorem 2. *Let $M = \{A_1, \ldots, A_m\}$ and consider the switched linear system*

$$x_{k+1} = A_{i_k} x_k, \ A_{i_k} \in M.$$

If all matrices in M have a spectral radius less than 1 and the Lie algebra associated to M is solvable, then the system has a common quadratic Lyapunov function.

Proof. So, if $\{A_i : A_i \in M\}_{LA}$ is solvable, then there exists a (possibly complex) invertible matrix T such that

$$A_i = T^{-1} \tilde{A}_i T, \text{ with } \tilde{A}_i \text{ upper-triangular}, \forall i \ .$$

This introduction of complex values does not change the main argument.

Lemma 1 shows that there exists a real common quadratic Lyapunov function $\tilde{P}$ in diagonal form for such a set of matrices $\tilde{M} = \{\tilde{A}_1, \ldots, \tilde{A}_n\}$. From this $\tilde{P}$, we can deduce the form of the corresponding P for the non-upper-triangular set $M = \{A_1, \ldots, A_n\}$:

$$\tilde{A}_i^* \tilde{P} \tilde{A}_i - \tilde{P} \prec 0$$
$$(T A_i T^{-1})^* \tilde{P} T A_i T^{-1} - \tilde{P} \prec 0$$
$$T^{*-1} A_i^* T^* \tilde{P} T A_i T^{-1} - \tilde{P} \prec 0$$
$$A_i^* (T^* \tilde{P} T) A_i - (T^* \tilde{P} T) \prec 0 \ .$$

And we get $P = T^* \tilde{P} T$. As $\tilde{P}$ is positive definite, so is P. Moreover, $\tilde{P}$ being diagonal, $T^* \tilde{P} T$ is actually Hermitian, but is not guaranteed to be real. Let us then denote

$$-R := A_i^* (T^* \tilde{P} T) A_i - (T^* \tilde{P} T)$$

where R is, by construction, Hermitian positive definite. We can write, by separating the real and imaginary parts,

$$P = \mathbb{R}(P) + i\mathbb{I}(P) \text{ and } R = \mathbb{R}(R) + i\mathbb{I}(R) \ .$$

As P and R are Hermitian, $\mathbb{R}(P)$, $\mathbb{R}(R)$ are symmetric positive definite and $\mathbb{I}(P)$, $\mathbb{I}(R)$ are skew-symmetric. We can rewrite

$$A_i^* (\mathbb{R}(P) + i\mathbb{I}(P)) A_i - (\mathbb{R}(P) + i\mathbb{I}(P)) = -(\mathbb{R}(R) + i\mathbb{I}(R))$$

and taking the real part,

$$A_i^* \mathbb{R}(P) A_i - \mathbb{R}(P) = -\mathbb{R}(R) \ .$$

As a consequence, $\mathbb{R}(P)$ is a real common quadratic Lyapunov function for the solvable Lie algebra $\{A_i : A_i \in M\}_{LA}$. $\qquad\square$

Corollary 2. *If the Lie algebra associated to the set* $M = \{A_1, \dots, A_m\}$ *is solvable, then the joint spectral radius of* M *is equal to* $\max_i \rho(A_i)$ *and also to its ellipsoid norm approximation.*

Proof. Indeed, Theorem 2 allows us to deduce that $\rho(M) < 1 \Rightarrow \hat{\rho}(M) < 1$, which yields $\rho(M) \geq \hat{\rho}(M)$, allowing to deduce the strict equality, thanks to the already known $\rho(M) \leq \hat{\rho}(M)$. Here again, we already know that $\rho(M) \geq \max_i \rho(A_i)$, and Theorem 2 teaches us that $\max_i \rho(A_i) < 1 \Rightarrow \rho(M) < 1$, so $\max_i \rho(A_i) \geq \rho(M)$. And we deduce $\rho(M) = \max_i \rho(A_i)$. $\qquad\square$

We have equality between the joint spectral radius and its ellipsoid norm approximation when the Lie algebra is solvable. One could wonder whether the solvability of the Lie algebra is necessary for this equality to hold. This is not the case. In order to exhibit a counter-example, we first prove a property of independent interest.

Proposition 2. *The joint spectral radius of* $\{A, A^T\}$ *is equal to its ellipsoid norm approximation and to the largest singular value of* A.

Proof. In such a particular case, we use the inequalities $\rho(A, A^T) \leq \hat{\rho}(A, A^T) \leq \sigma(A)$, which can be seen by using $P = I$ in the definition of $\hat{\rho}$, so that we get $A^T I A \leq \gamma^2 I$, holding for $\gamma \geq \sigma(A)$. And finally,

$$\rho(A, A^T) \geq \rho(AA^T)^{1/2} = \sigma(A)$$

yields

$$\rho(A, A^T) = \hat{\rho}(A, A^T) = \sigma(A) \ .$$

$\qquad\square$

Consider now the matrices

$$A = \begin{pmatrix} 1 & 1 \\ 0 & 1 \end{pmatrix}, \ A^T = \begin{pmatrix} 1 & 0 \\ 1 & 1 \end{pmatrix}$$

It is easy to check that the Lie algebra associated to these matrices is not solvable. On the other hand it follows from the above proposition that for this pair of matrices the joint spectral radius and its ellipsoid norm approximation are equal (and are equal to $\sigma(A) = \frac{1+\sqrt{5}}{2} \simeq 1.618$).

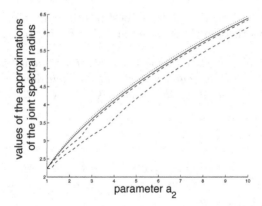

Fig. 1. The spectral radius and its ellipsoid norm approximation as functions of the real parameter a_2 (a_1 is fixed to 1). The two dashed curves represent upper and lower bounds on the exact value of the spectral radius (computed with products of length 6). The solid curve represents $\sqrt{1 + 4a_2}$. The two dotted curves are indistinguishable and represent upper and lower bounds on the approximation $\hat{\rho}$.

We close this section with a numerical example of two matrices for which we do not have equality between the joint spectral radius and its ellipsoid norm approximation. Let us consider the following matrices (inspired by [7]):

$$A_1 = \begin{pmatrix} 1 & 2\,a_1 \\ -2/a_1 & 1 \end{pmatrix}, A_2 = \begin{pmatrix} 1 & 2\,a_2 \\ -2/a_2 & 1 \end{pmatrix} .$$

Assuming that $a_2 \geq a_1 \geq 1$, extensive calculations that are not reproduced here (see the Technical Report [19] for more details) show that the approximation $\hat{\rho}$ is such that

$$\hat{\rho}(A_1, A_2) \geq \sqrt{1 + 4\,a_2/a_1} .$$

For $a_1 = 1, a_2 = 2$, the joint spectral radius can be shown to be less than 2.8584 by using an exhaustive calculation of all the products of length 5 or less than 2.783 when considering all products of length 16. This is less than $\sqrt{1 + 4 \times 2/1} = 3$, so here $\rho < \hat{\rho}$. The gap between the joint spectral radius and its approximation can be seen on figure 1 for $a_1 = 1$ and varying a_2.

4   Guaranteed Precision of the Approximation

The ellipsoid norm approximation of the joint spectral radius can be shown to have a guaranteed precision. The argument for this is simple: Let ρ be the joint spectral radius of the set $\{A_1, \ldots, A_m\}$; we know by Theorem 1 that there exists a vector norm $\|.\|_*$ for which $\|A_i x\|_* \leq \rho \|x\|_*$ for all x and i. The level curves of this norm define closed convex set that can be approximated by ellipsoids, the quality of these approximations can be measured and provides a guaranteed precision for the approximation.

We start by describing the quality of best possible ellipsoids (the result below is known as John's theorem; it is stated in [11], referring to [12]).

Theorem 3. *Let $K \subset \mathbb{R}^n$ be a compact convex set with nonempty interior. Then there is an ellipsoid E with center c such that the inclusions $E \subseteq K \subseteq n(E - c)$ hold. If K is symmetric about the origin $(K = -K)$, the constant n can be changed into $\sqrt{n}$.*

Knowing this, we can now prove:

Theorem 4. *Let ρ be the joint spectral radius of a finite set of matrices of dimension n. Let $\hat{\rho}$ be the ellipsoid norm approximation of the joint spectral radius. Then $\hat{\rho}/\sqrt{n} \leq \rho \leq \hat{\rho}$.*

Proof. The norm mentioned above is symmetric about the center, as $\|x\|_* = \|-x\|_*, \forall x$. So, the above theorem guarantees us that, whatever the norm $\|.\|_*$ is, there exists a quadratic norm $\|x\|_P = x^T P x$ (of which level curves are ellipsoids) such that

$$\|x\|_P \leq \|x\|_* \leq \sqrt{n}\|x\|_P .$$

As, $\forall q > \rho(M)$, the norm $\|.\|_*$ satisfies $\|A_i x\|_* \leq q\|x\|_*, \forall x, \forall i$, we can now write

$$\forall x, \forall i, \|A_i x\|_P \leq \|A_i x\|_* \leq q\|x\|_* \leq q\|x\|_P \sqrt{n}$$
$$\forall x, \forall i, \ \|A_i x\|_P \leq q\|x\|_P \sqrt{n}$$
$$\forall x, \forall i, \ x^T A_i^T P A_i x \leq q^2 n \ x^T P x$$
$$\forall i, A_i^T P A_i - q^2 n P \preceq 0 .$$

Thus, the approximation $\hat{\rho}$ defined by $\hat{\rho}(M) = \inf_{P \succ 0} \max_{A_i \in M} \|A_i\|_P$ is $\leq q\sqrt{n}$. So, at worst, the approximation will result in the value $\rho(M)\sqrt{n}$. Summing up, this gives:

$$\rho(M) \leq \hat{\rho}(M) \leq \rho(M)\sqrt{n} .$$

$\square$

5   Matrices with Non-negative Entries

In this section, we introduce an approximation of the joint spectral radius for matrices with non-negative entries. We first provide a result for general matrices that is of independent interest.

Proposition 3. *Let $M = \{A_1, \ldots, A_m\}$. Then*

$$\max_{\sum_{i=0}^{m} \alpha_i = 1, \ \alpha_i \geq 0} \rho\left(\sum \alpha_i A_i\right) \leq \rho(M).$$

Proof. We have, using the inequality $\rho(.) \leq \|.\|$ (for any valid matrix norm $\|.\|$) and the subadditivity of the norm,

$$\tilde{\rho}(M) := \rho\left(\sum_i \alpha_i A_i\right) \leq \left\|\sum_i \alpha_i A_i\right\|$$

$$\leq \sum_i \|\alpha_i A_i\| = \sum_i \alpha_i \|A_i\|$$

$$\leq \max_i (\|A_i\|) \quad , \text{ as } \sum_i \alpha_i = 1 \ .$$

Now, if $\rho(M) < 1$, we know that there exists a norm $\|.\|_*$ such that $\forall i, \|A_i\|_* < 1$ (see [13]). We can then deduce from the previous inequality that $\tilde{\rho}(M) < 1$. So,

$$\rho(M) < 1 \Rightarrow \tilde{\rho}(M) < 1 \ ,$$

and we deduce, using linearity, that $\tilde{\rho}(M) \leq \rho(M)$.   □

For deriving the approximation of this section we need one more property.

Lemma 3. *Let M_1 and M_2 be matrices with non-negative entries. If $(M_2)_{ij} \geq (M_1)_{ij}$, then $\rho(M_2) \geq \rho(M_1)$.*

We are now ready to prove:

Theorem 5. *Let $M = \{A_1, \ldots, A_m\}$ be a set of matrices with non-negative entries and define $S_{ij} = \max_{1 \leq k \leq m}(A_k)_{ij}$. We have*

$$\frac{\rho(S)}{m} \leq \rho(M) \leq \rho(S). \tag{3}$$

Proof. For the first inequality of (3), non-negativity, Lemma 3 and Proposition 3 give

$$S \leq \sum_{k=1}^m A_k \Rightarrow \rho(S) \leq \rho\left(\sum_{k=1}^m A_k\right) = m\rho\left(\frac{\sum_{k=1}^m A_k}{m}\right) \leq m\rho(M) \ .$$

To prove the second inequality of (3), we may note that, as the elements are non-negative, for any sequence ω of k indices, the product A_ω satisfies $(S^k)_{ij} \geq (A_\omega)_{ij}$. Lemma 3 allows us to deduce, $\forall \omega : |\omega| = k$,

$$S^k \geq A_\omega \Rightarrow \limsup_{k\to\infty} \|S^k\|^{1/k} \geq \limsup_{k\to\infty} \left(\max_{|\omega|=k} \|A_\omega\|^{1/k}\right) \Rightarrow \rho(S) \geq \rho(M) \ .$$

□

For all set cardinalities m, the equality $\rho(S)/m = \rho(M)$ is achieved for some particular matrices. For $m = 2$ consider the following pair:

$$\left\{ A = \begin{pmatrix} 1 & 0 \\ 1 & 0 \end{pmatrix}, B = \begin{pmatrix} 0 & 1 \\ 0 & 1 \end{pmatrix} \right\}$$

for which $\rho(S) = 2$. On the other hand, we see that $A^2 = A$, $B^2 = B$, $AB = B$ and $BA = A$. Any product generated by $\{A, B\}$ is either equal to A or to B, so $\rho(A, B) = 1$ and we indeed have $\hat{\rho}/2 = \rho$. A similar construction is immediate for the cases $m \geq 3$.

6   Conclusion

We introduce in this paper a polynomial-time approximation of the joint spectral radius that is easy to compute and that is guaranteed to be within a factor $\sqrt{n}$ of the exact value, where n is the dimension of the matrices. We describe particular classes of matrices for which our approximation is equal to the joint spectral radius. The problem of characterizing exactly the sets of matrices for which equality holds is a question that remains open. We also provide an easy way of approximating the joint spectral radius of matrices with non-negative entries, and show that this approximation is within a factor at most n of the exact value, where n is the number of matrices in the set. This last result does not depend on the size of the matrices. The question remains open to find better approximations at a reasonable computational cost. In particular, both approximations presented in this paper have relative errors that increase with the size or number of the matrices. It is yet unclear if a polynomial time approximation is possible that gives a fixed guaranteed relative error.

Acknowledgements. We wish to thank Professor Alexander Megretski for suggesting the proof of Theorem 4 during a discussion at the Mittag-Leffler Institute (Stockholm, Sweden). Thanks are also due to Professor Alexander Vladimirov for numerous discussions during his visits at CESAME in Belgium.

References

1. N. E. Barabanov, Lyapunov indicators of discrete inclusions, part I, II and III, Translation from Avtomatika i Telemekhanika, 2, pp.40-46, 3, pp.24-29 and 5, pp.17-24, 1988.
2. M. A. Berger and Y. Wang, Bounded Semigroups of Matrices, Journal of Linear Algebra and its Applications, vol.166, pp.21-27, 1992.
3. P.-A. Bliman and G. Ferrari-Trecate. Stability analysis of discrete-time switched systems through lyapunov functions with nonminimal state. IFAC Conference on the Analysis and Design of Hybrid Systems (ADHS 03), 2003.
4. V.D. Blondel, J.N. Tsitsiklis, The boundedness of all products of a pair of matrices is undecidable, Systems and Control Letters, 41:2, pp. 135-140, 2000.
5. Linear Matrix Inequalities in System and Control Theory, S. Boyd, L. El Ghaoui, E. Feron, and V. Balakrishnan, SIAM, 1994.
6. I. Daubechies and J. C. Lagarias, Sets of Matrices All Infinite Products of Which Converge, Journal of Linear Algebra and its Applications, vol.161, pp.227-263, 1992.
7. W. P. Dayawansa and C.F. Martin, A Converse Lyapunov Theorem for a Class of Dynamical Systems which Undergo Switching, IEEE Transactions on Automatic Control, Vol.44, 4, pp.751-760, 1999.
8. G. Gripenberg, Computing the Joint Spectral Radius, Linear Algebra and its Applications, 234, pp.43-60, 1996.
9. Leonid Gurvits, Stability of Discrete Linear Inclusion, Linear Algebra and its Applications, 85, pp.231-47, 1995.
10. R.A. Horn, C.R. Johnson, Matrix Analysis, Cambridge University Press, 1993.

11. Ralph Howard, The John Ellipsoid Theorem, University of South Carolina.
12. F.John, Extremum problems with inequalities as subsidiary conditions, Studies and Essays Presented to R.Courant on his 60th birthday, January 8, 1948, Interscience Publishers, Inc., New-York, N.Y., pp.187-204, 1948.
13. V.S. Kozyakin, Algebraic unsolvability of problem of absolute stability of desynchronized systems, Automation and Remote Control, 51, 754-759, 1990.
14. J.C. Lagarias and Y. Wang, The finiteness conjecture for the generalized spectral radius of a set of matrices, Linear Algebra Appl., 214, 17-42, 1995.
15. D. Liberzon, J. P. Hespanha and A. S. Morse, Stability of switched systems: a Lie-algebraic condition, Systems ans Control Letters, volume 37, 3, pp.117-122, 1999.
16. M. Maesumi, An Efficient Lower Bound for the Generalized Spectral Radius, Linear Algebra and its Applications, 240, pp.1-7, 1996.
17. G.-C. Rota and G. Strang, A note on the joint spectral radius, Indag. Math., 22, pp.379-381, 1960.
18. H. Samelson, Notes on Lie Algebras, Van Nostrand Reinhold Co., New York, 1969.
19. J. Theys, Note on upper and lower bounds for the joint spectral radius,Technical Report 2003.88, CESAME / UCL, Belgium.
20. J.N. Tsitsiklis, The Stability of the Products of a Finite Set of Matrices, Open Problems in Communication and Computation, T.M. Cover and B. Gopinath (Eds.), Springer–Verlag, New York, 161–163, 1987.
21. J. Tsitsiklis, V. Blondel, The Lyapunov exponent and joint spectral radius of pairs of matrices are hard – when not impossible – to compute and to approximate, Mathematics of Control, Signals, and Systems, 10, pp. 31-40, 1997. (Correction in 10, pp. 381, 1997)
22. F. Wirth, The generalized spectral radius and extremal norms, Linear Algebra Appl., 342, pp. 17-40, 2002.

The Hybrid Guaranteed Capture Basin Algorithm in Economics

Noël Bonneuil[1] and Patrick Saint-Pierre[2]

[1] Institut national d'études démographiques,
133 bd Davout, 75980 Paris cedex 20,
École des hautes études en sciences sociales,
54, Bld Raspail, 75006, Paris, France
[2] Centre de Recherche Viabilité, Jeux, Contrôle,
Université Paris IX-Dauphine,
Place du Maréchal de Lattre de Tassigny,
F-75775 Paris cedex 16, France

Abstract. Reaching a target while remaining in a given set for impulse dynamics can be characterized by a non deterministic controlled differential equation and a controlled instantaneous reset equation. The set of initial conditions from which a given objective can be reached is calculated using the Hybrid Guaranteed Capture Basin Algorithm. This algorithm was developed in finance to evaluate options in absence of impulse but in the presence of uncertainty and in control to evaluate minimal time functions to reach a target, in the presence of impulse but in absence of uncertainty. We study the problem of reaching a target in the presence of both impulse and uncertainty and present two applications in economics.

1 Introduction

Consider a two-level system describing the evolution of a state variable $x \in \mathbb{R}^n$ regulated by two non cooperative controllers. The first controller longs at reaching a given objective. The second controller can represent an exogenous event. The question is to determine a feedback regulation $x \to \widetilde{u}(x)$ so that the evolution remains viable in a given closed set $K \subset \mathbb{R}^n$ until the state variable reaches the target in finite time.

The lower level evolution corresponds to a continuous dynamics given by:

$$x'(t) = f(x(t), u(t), v(t)), \ \ u(t) \in U(x(t)), \ \ v(t) \in V(x(t)), \text{ for almost all } t \geq 0 \tag{1}$$

where sets $U(x) \subset U$ and $V(x) \subset V$ are closed for any x.

The upper level evolution corresponds to an impulse dynamics driven by instantaneous events. The state x can be reset according to the following equation

$$x_{i+1} = \varphi(x_i, \pi_i), \ \ \pi_i \in P(x_i) \tag{2}$$

R. Alur and G.J. Pappas (Eds.): HSCC 2004, LNCS 2993, pp. 187–202, 2004.

Resetting is possible when x belongs to a prescribed subset $D(\Phi)$ of $\mathbb{R}^n$.

Mathematical and numerical tools developed in the framework of hybrid dynamical systems make it possible to solve various control problems in presence of uncertainty. In Differential Games Theory, P. Bernhard in [12, Bernhard] introduced robust control to evaluate options in finance while independently J.-P. Aubin, D. Pujal and P. Saint-Pierre evaluated options in presence of transaction costs [25, Pujal & Saint-Pierre] and [6, Aubin, Pujal & Saint-Pierre].

Stochastic modelling is a marvellous tool in situations of repeated events. However, with non seriable events, in an environment of decision and not of risk such as in differential games the concept of "Tyche[1]" is more adequate: We are content with saying that the perturbation $v(t)$ belongs to a closed set V. the point is less to reveal an underlying probabilistic law than to be able to react to any misfortune in store for us. Tyches correspond in Control Theory to the concept of "disturbances" - against which one have to find "robust" control - and in Dynamical Games against Nature to the concept of "perturbation" against which one have to seek "guaranteed strategies".

Recent results bridge the gap between stochastic and tychastic systems. Thanks to the equivalence formula between Itô and Stratonovitch's stochastic integrals and the "Support Theorem" of Strook and Varadhan ([23, Doss]), stochastic viability and capturability problems are equivalent to tychastic invariant systems ([4, Aubin & Doss]). Stochastic viability was addressed in mathematical finance [13, Björk], [31, Zabczyk] and [21,22, Da Prato & Frankowska].

These results were strengthened by the fact that the Guaranteed Viable Capture Basin algorithm works for stochastic as well as for tychastic systems as shown in [25, Pujal & Saint-Pierre], [28, Saint-Pierre] for applications to Finance.

Geometric characterizations of the Guaranteed Viable Capture Basin and of the minimal time function were studied in ([18, Crück], [16, Cardaliaguet, Quincampoix & Saint-Pierre], [19, Crück, Quincampoix & Saint-Pierre] and numerically in [27, Saint-Pierre] and [20, Crück & Saint-Pierre].

We also mention other works dealing with capture basins or with reachable sets (which are capture basins associated with backward dynamic) but in absence of constraints, using Hamilton-Jacobi approximation, level sets methods [24, Mitchell, Bayen & Tomlin], [10, Bayen, Crück & Tomlin], [30, Sethian & Vladimirsky] or tychastic differential games [11, Bayen].

Here we integrate uncertainty and impulse thanks to the Capture Basin algorithm applied to evolutionary systems. This was developed in [19, Crück, Quincampoix & Saint-Pierre] in the context of non anticipative strategies. We use this algorithm to solve two concrete questions in economics: how to evaluate replicating portfolios in the presence of barriers and how to manage patrimony in term of wealth and children over the life course. In both cases the problem is to reach a target while remaining within constraints under a tychastic uncertain environment and in presence of impulse changes of the dynamic.

---

[1] from the Greek "$\tau\acute{\upsilon}\chi\eta$": Chance, fate, luck.

The mathematical formulation, definitions and numerical methods are presented in the first section. The second and the third sections are devoted to these two models and we present numerical results.

2 Viability of Hybrid Tychastic Dynamical Systems

Let $K \subset \mathbb{R}^n$ be a closed set in which the impulse system should stay and $\mathcal{T} \subset K$ a target. The objective of the controller is to reach $\mathcal{T}$ before leaving K, or to stay in K forever if $\mathcal{T}$ cannot be reached.

Consider the impulse system described by the set-valued maps

$$\begin{cases} F(x,u) := \{f(x,u,v) : v \in V(x)\} \text{ where } u \in U(x), \\ \Phi(x) \quad := \begin{cases} \{\varphi(x,\pi) : \pi \in \Pi(x)\} \text{ if } x \in D(\Phi), \\ \emptyset \qquad\qquad\qquad \text{otherwise,} \end{cases} \end{cases} \tag{3}$$

so that for a given evolution $u(\cdot)$ of the control, the continuous-time evolution of the system is a solution to the differential inclusion

$$x'(t) \in F(x(t), u(t)), \tag{4}$$

and the discrete-time evolution is described by the inclusion

$$x^+ \in \Phi(x^-). \tag{5}$$

where $\Phi(x^-)$ is the set of all available states x^+ attainable from the position x^-. Set-valued maps $(x,u) \mapsto F(x,u)$, $x \mapsto \Phi(x)$, $x \mapsto U(x)$ and $x \mapsto V(x)$ satisfy several assumptions specified in appendix.

We denote $\mathcal{U}$ and $\mathcal{V}$ the sets of measurable functions $t \to u(t) \in U$ and $t \to v(t) \in V$, and $\mathcal{P}$ the set of sequences $i \to \pi_i \in P$. We assume that

Assumption 1

(i) F is $\begin{cases} \diamond \text{ upper semicontinuous with nonempty compact, convex values} \\ \quad \textit{and linear growth,} \\ \diamond \text{ bounded on } K, \textit{ i.e. } \exists M > 0, \ \forall x \in K, \ \forall y \in F(x), \ \|y\| \leq M. \end{cases}$

(ii) Φ is $\begin{cases} \diamond \textit{ upper semicontinuous with compact domain and compact values,} \\ \diamond \textit{ such that } \forall x \in D(\Phi), \ \Phi(x) \cap D(\Phi) = \emptyset. \end{cases}$

Definition 1 *We call* **run** *of impulse system* (F, Φ) *with initial condition* x_0 *and given pair* $(u(\cdot), v(\cdot))$ *a collection of finite or infinite sequences* $\{\tau_i, x_i, x_i(\cdot)\}_{i \in I}$ *in* $\mathbb{R}^+ \times \mathbb{R}^n \times S_F(\mathbb{R}^n)$, *where* $\{\tau_i\}_{i \in I}$ *is a sequence of durations such that for all* $i \in I$

$$x_i'(t) = f(x_i(t), u(t), v(t)), \ \ x_i(0) = x_i.$$
$$x_i(\tau_i) \in D(\Phi), \ \ x_{i+1} \in \Phi(x_i(\tau_i))$$

A **trajectory** *is a function* $x(\cdot)$ *associated with a run as*

$$x(t) = \begin{cases} x_0 & \textit{if } t < 0 \\ x_i(t - \sum_{j<i} \tau_i) & \textit{if } t \in \left(\sum_{j<i} \tau_j\right) + [0, \tau_i[\end{cases} \tag{6}$$

2.1   Guaranteed Viability Kernels

Consider the impulse dynamical system (F, Φ) defined on $\mathbb{R}^n$, a closed set $K \subset \mathbb{R}^n$ of constraints and a closed target set $\mathcal{T} \subset \mathbb{R}^n$. We are interested in runs that remain in K forever or at least until the associated trajectory reaches the target $\mathcal{T}$ in spite of uncertainty $v(\cdot)$.

Definition 2 *For a given feedback $x \to \widetilde{u}(x)$ and a given rule for jumps $x \to \widetilde{\pi}(x)$ we denote $\mathrm{Inv}_{(F,\Phi)}(K, \mathcal{T}, \widetilde{u}(\cdot), \widetilde{\pi}(\cdot))$ the **Invariance Kernel** of (F, Φ) which is the set of initial states $x_0 \in K$ such that for any open loop $v(\cdot) \in \mathcal{V}$, the solution to*

$$x_i'(t) \in f(x_i(t), \widetilde{u}(x_i(t)), v(t)), \quad x_i(0) = x_i,$$

$$x_i(\tau_i) \in D(\Phi), \quad x_{i+1} \in \varphi(x_i(\tau_i), \widetilde{\pi}(x_i(\tau_i)))$$

remains in K forever or at least until the associated trajectory reaches $\mathcal{T}$.

For a prescribed pair of feedback controls $(\widetilde{u}(\cdot), \widetilde{\pi}(\cdot))$ the Invariance Kernel can be empty.

Definition 3 *Let $\widetilde{\mathcal{U}}$ and $\widetilde{\mathcal{P}}$ be two families of feedbacks $x \to \widetilde{u}(x) \in U(x)$ and $x \to \widetilde{p}(x) \in P(x)$. The **Guaranteed Viability Kernel** of (F, Φ) is the set*

$$\mathrm{Viab}^g_{(F,\Phi)}(K, \mathcal{T}) := \bigcup_{(\widetilde{u}, \widetilde{\pi}) \in \widetilde{\mathcal{U}} \times \widetilde{\mathcal{P}}} \mathrm{Inv}_{(F,\Phi)}(K, \mathcal{T}, \widetilde{u}, \widetilde{\pi})$$

J.P. Aubin and F. Catté [2] proved that, if f and φ are Lipschitz, the Guaranteed Viability Kernel enjoys the viability property in the sense that, under adequate assumptions, there exists feedbacks $\widetilde{u}$ and $\widetilde{p}$ such that discrete/digitalized approximations converge to the Guaranteed Hybrid Viability Kernel.

2.2   The Guaranteed Capture Basin Algorithm

In order to approximate the Guaranteed Viability Kernel or the Guaranteed Capture Basin we discretize the impulse dynamical system as in [20, Crück & Saint-Pierre] for control hybrid systems.

Discretization of Impulse Systems. Let M be an upper bound of the velocity set F: $M := \max_{y \in F(x)} |y|$. We fix a time step ρ and $h = \rho(M + \phi(\rho))$ and replace the derivative $x'(t)$ of x at time t by the difference $\frac{x^{p+1} - x^p}{\rho}$ where x^p stands for $x(p\rho)$ with $x^0 = x(0)$.

Let us set $\mathcal{D}_h := D(\Phi) + h\mathcal{B}$ where $\mathcal{B}$ denotes the unit ball and let us define the approximate reset map $\Phi_h(y) := \cup_{y' \in \mathcal{B}(y,h)} \Phi(y')$. We set

$$S_\rho(y) = \begin{cases} y & \text{if } y \notin \mathcal{D}_h \\ y \cup \Phi_h(y) & \text{if } y \in \mathcal{D}_h \end{cases}$$

$$G_\rho(x, u) = \{ S_\rho(x + \rho\varphi) \mid \varphi \in F_\rho(x, u) \text{ and } u \in U(x) \} \tag{7}$$

As the graph of Φ_h is closed, the graph of the set-valued map S_ρ is also closed by construction. We consider the discrete dynamical system

$$x^{p+1} \in G_\rho(x^p, u^p) \tag{8}$$

Proposition 1 *If the graphs of $F(\cdot, v(\cdot))$ and Φ are closed and if F is compact valued, then for all $\rho > 0$, the graphs of G_ρ and $\widetilde{G}_\rho$ are closed.*

To the discrete dynamical system (8) we add two equations to evaluate a time t and the total number of resets r.

Either x^{p+1} comes from the continuous part of the evolution so that, from assumption (1-i)), $d(x^{p+1}, x^p) \leq \rho M$ or x^{p+1} comes from the impulse part of the evolution so that, from assumption (1-ii)) and the compactness of K, there exists $m > 0$ such that $d(x^{p+1}, x^p) \leq \inf_{x \in K} d(x, \Phi(x)) > m$ and choosing $\rho \leq \frac{m}{2M}$ we have $d(x^{p+1}, x^p) \geq 2\rho M$.

Then we define the discrete map $\Gamma_\rho(x^p, r^p) =$
$\begin{cases} r^p & \text{if } d(x^{p+1}, x^p) \leq \rho M \\ r^p + 1 & \text{if } d(x^{p+1}, x^p) \geq 2\rho M \end{cases}$ and obtain an extended discrete dynamical system

$$(x^{p+1}, r^{p+1}, t^{p+1}) \in (G_\rho(x^p), \Gamma_\rho(x^p, r^p), t^p + \rho) \tag{9}$$

Impulse Guaranteed Viability Algorithm. Let $K_\rho^0 = K$. We define the sequence K_ρ^p by

$$K_\rho^{p+1} = \{x \in K_\rho^p \mid \exists u \in U(x), \ G_\rho(x) \subset K_\rho^p\} \tag{10}$$

An element $x \in K_\rho^{p+1}$ if and only if $x \in K_\rho^p$ and if there exists a control $u \in U(x)$ such that for any $v \in V_\rho(x)$, $S_\rho(x + \rho f(x, u, v)) \in K_\rho^p$.

The size of the domain $V_\rho(x)$ depends[2] on the time step ρ.

The graphs of S_ρ and of $Id + \rho F_\rho$ are closed and K is compact so that K_ρ^p is compact. The decreasing sequence K_ρ^p converges in the sense of Painlevé-Kuratowski to the limit set $K_\rho^* = \overrightarrow{\text{Viab}}_{G_\rho}(K)$. The proof of the convergence is out of the scope of this paper (see [27, Saint-Pierre] for approximate Viability Kernels, [16, Cardaliaguet, Quincampoix & Saint-Pierre] for approximate Discriminating Kernels, [29, Saint-Pierre] for hybrid control systems and [19, Crück, Quincampoix & Saint-Pierre] for hybrid differential games).

---

[2] The Impulse Guaranteed Viability Algorithm gives Guaranteed Kernels for systems where uncertainty is tychastic and for systems where uncertainty is stochastic. The Guaranteed Kernel is obtained for tychastic systems with choosing $V_\rho(x) = V(x)$ and, for stochastic systems, with choosing $V_\rho(x) = \frac{\sigma}{\sqrt{\rho}} V(x)$.

3   Application to Finance: Evaluation of Barrier Options

The viability/capturability algorithm constitutes a helpful tool to evaluate and manage a portfolio. The usual framework of stochastic control is superseded by dynamical game, where the concept of guaranteed viable-capture basin plays a prior role in selecting the appropriate portfolio on due time.

In the Cox, Ross and Rubinstein model, even with large time steps, we know how to extend numerical algorithms to evaluate of options and determine optimal strategies where uncertainty is stochastic or tychastic. The Capture Basin Algorithm is calibrated in the particular case of Black and Scholes valuation.

3.1   Evaluation of Options

A put or a call is a contract giving the right to buy (call) or to sell (put) a quantity of an asset at a given date (European put or call) or at any date before a fixed date T (American put or call). The point is to determine the value of the contract at the start. This value is the price the seller should ask for in order to secure herself against risk. An evaluation model consists in evaluating the cost for risk covering. Facing the risks inherent in her position, the seller builds up a theoretical portfolio in investing into the underlying asset by self-financing. This permanently adjusted portfolio yields the same losses and profits as the put or call. It is said to duplicate the put or call. The knowledge of this profit at maturity dictates the initial investment.

3.2   Constraints and "Target"

Constraints and targets are formalized by a couple of cost functions $(\mathbf{b}, \mathbf{c})$. In the case of $n = 2$:

1) $\forall (t, S) \in \mathbb{R}_+ \times \mathbb{R}_+^2$, $\mathbf{b}(t, S) \geq 0$ describes the "floor" constraints.
2) $\forall (t, S) \in \mathbb{R}_+ \times \mathbb{R}_+^2$, $0 \leq \mathbf{b}(t, S) \leq \mathbf{c}(t, S)$ describes the targets on maturity.

The intrinsic value of a call plays an important role for risk managers, so that the payoff function U reads: $U(S_0, S_1) = (S_1 - K)^+$. Let $\mathcal{E}pi(U)$ denote the epigraph of U. We express the two functions $\mathbf{b}$ and $\mathbf{c}$ in terms of U from now on. These functions associate a number, possibly infinite, to each period t and each price S. Consider:

$$\mathbf{c} : (t, S) \to \mathbf{c}(t, S) = \begin{cases} U(S_0, S_1) & \text{if } t = 0 \\ +\infty & \text{otherwise} \end{cases} \tag{11}$$

for common puts and calls, $\mathbf{b} : (t, S) \mapsto \mathbf{b}(t, S) = U(S_0, S_1)$ for American puts and calls, and $\mathbf{b} = 0$ for European puts and calls.

The question is to determine the set of portfolio strategies $S \to \widetilde{\pi}(S)$ such that, whatever the variations of capital $S(\cdot)$, the following conditions hold true:

$$\begin{aligned} &i) \ \ \forall t \in [0,], \ W_{\widetilde{\pi}(\cdot)}(t)) \geq \mathbf{b}(T - t, S(t)) \\ &ii) \ W_{\widetilde{\pi}(\cdot)}(T) \geq \mathbf{c}(0, S(T)) \end{aligned} \tag{12}$$

and, amongst them, select the portfolio strategy such that, for all predictable variations, the initial value of the portfolio corresponds to the cheapest capital $V(T, S(0))$ which we identify as the evaluation function of the put or call. The evaluation function $V : \mathbb{R}_+ \times \mathbb{R}_+^2 \mapsto \mathbb{R}_+$ associates the cheapest value $V(T, S(0))$ of the initial capital to each couple $(T, S(0))$ made of maturity T and initial prices of assets, and satisfying conditions (12).

3.3   The Dynamical Game Describing the Replicating Process

Consider a riskless asset and an underlying risky asset of respective prices S_0 and S_1. Let $S = (S_0, S_1) \in \mathbb{R}^2$ and $\pi = (\pi_0, \pi_1)\mathbb{R}^2$ the array of which each component is the total number of assets in a portfolio of value:

$$W_\pi = \pi_0 S_0 + \pi_1 S_1$$

The riskless and the risky assets are governed by a deterministic and a non deterministic differential equation

$$\begin{cases} S_0'(t) = S_0(t)\gamma_0(S_0(t)) \\ S_1'(t) = S_1(t)\gamma_1(S_1(t), v(t)) \end{cases}$$

The variations of price $S(t)$ of assets at date t help find the variations $W_{\pi(\cdot)}(t)$ of capital as a function of a strategy $\pi(\cdot)$ of the replicating portfolio. Indeed, the value of the replicating portfolio is given by $W_\pi(t) := \pi_0(t)S_0(t) + \pi_1(t)S_1(t)$. The self-financing principle of the portfolio reads

$$\forall\, t \geq 0, \quad \langle \pi'(t), S(t) \rangle = \pi_0'(t)S_0(t) + \pi_1'(t)S_1(t) = 0$$

so that the value of the portfolio satisfies

$$W'(t) = \langle \pi(t), S'(t) \rangle = \pi_0(t)S_0(t)\gamma_0(S(t)) + \pi_1(t)S_1(t)\gamma_1(S_1(t), v(t))$$

which is $W'(t) = W(t)\gamma_0(S(t)) - \pi_1(t)S_1(t)(\gamma_0(S_0(t)) - \gamma_1(S_1(t), v(t)))$.
  Let $\tau(t) := T - t$, then $S(t)$ and $W(t)$ change according to:

$$\begin{cases} \tau'(t) = -1 \\ S_0'(t) = S_0(t)\gamma_0(S_0(t)) \\ S_1'(t) = S_1(t)\gamma_1(S_1(t), v(t)) \\ W'(t) = W(t)\gamma_0(S(t)) - \pi_1(t)S_1(t)(\gamma_0(S_0(t)) - \gamma_1(S_1(t), v(t))) \end{cases} \tag{13}$$

where $\pi(t) \in \Pi(S(t))$ and $v(t) \in Q(S(t))$.

Example: Guaranteed Evaluation of a Standard European Call. Figure 1 shows the graph of the Evaluation Function and the optimal strategy π_1 which represents the amount of risky asset necessary to replicate the portfolio. The riskless asset was taken as $\gamma_0 = 5\%$, the maturity price $K = 100$.

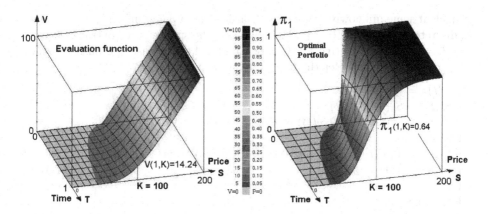

Fig. 1. Guaranteed Evaluation Function of an European call with uncertainty of Cox, Ross and Rubinstein type and the optimal portfolio: π_1

Table 1. Values of a call using the Guaranteed Capture Basin Method

value of S_1	Value of the Call	π_0	π_1
80	4.53	-22.10	0.3332
90	8.61	-34.94	0.4844
100	14.24	-48.17	0.6240
110	21.04	-59.94	0.7363
120	28.84	-69.63	0.8207

3.4   The Barrier Mechanism

Barriers complicate the evaluation of the replicating portfolio. A barrier is a particular value S^* for the price $S(t)$ beyond which the contract changes. There are four types of options with barriers:
"up and in": the contract becomes effective at the first time t^* when

$$S(t) < S^*, \forall t < t^*, S(t^*) = S^*$$

"down and in": the contract becomes effective at the first time t^* when

$$S(t) > S^*, \forall t < t^*, S(t^*) = S^*$$

"up and out": the contract ceases at the first time t^* when

$$S(t) < S^*, \forall t < t^*, S(t^*) = S^*$$

"down and out": the contract ceases at the first time t^* when

$$S(t) > S^*, \forall t < t^*, S(t^*) = S^*.$$

The celebrated Black and Scholes formula is inappropriate to evaluate options in presence of barriers. The challenge is to evaluate today a contract which will vanish at some unknown future date. Consider an "up and in" call and introduce a discrete variable $L \in \{0,1\}$ which "labels " the state of the contract: effective for $L = 1$ or non effective for $L = 0$. The label L increases because we study "in" options. We consider the hybrid dynamical system

$$
\begin{cases}
\tau'(t) & = -1 \\
S_0'(t) & = S_0(t)\gamma_0(S_0(t)) \\
S_1'(t) & = S_1(t)\gamma_1(S_1(t), v(t)) \\
L'(t) & = 0 \\
W'(t) & = \begin{cases} W(t)\gamma_0(S(t)) - \pi_1(t)S_1(t)(\gamma_0(S_0(t)) - \gamma_1(S_1(t), v(t))) & \text{if } L(t) = 1 \\ 0 & \text{if } L(t) = 0 \end{cases} \\
\tau^+ & = \tau^- \\
S_0^+ & = S_0^- \\
S_1^+ & = S_1^- \\
L^+ & = \begin{cases} 1 & \text{if } S_1^- \geq S^* \\ L^- & \text{if } S_1^- < S^* \end{cases} \\
W^+ & = W^-
\end{cases}
$$

We wish to determine the Guaranteed Capture Basins of the epigraph of $\mathbf{c}$ while remaining in the epigraph of $\mathbf{b}$ and $\tau > 0$.

The continuous level of the dynamic is approximated by the discrete system

$$
\begin{cases}
\tau^{p+1} & = \tau^p - \rho \\
S_0^{p+1} & = S_0^p(1 + \rho\gamma_0(S_0^p)) \\
S_1^{p+1} & = S_1^p(1 + \rho\gamma_1(S_1^p, v^p)) \\
L^{p+1} & = L^p \\
W^{p+1} & = \begin{cases} W^p + \rho\pi_0^p S_0^p \gamma_0(S_0^p) + \rho\pi_1^p S_1^p \gamma_1(S_1^p, v^p) & \text{if } L^p = 1 \text{ or } S_1^p \geq S^* \\ W^p & \text{if } L^p = 0 \text{ and } S_1^p < S^* \end{cases}
\end{cases}
$$

under the constraints $b(p\rho, S_1^p) \leq W^p(p\rho, S_1^p) \leq c(p\rho, S_1^p)$ and $p \leq N = \frac{T}{\rho}$.

At each step, $W^p = \pi_0^p S_0^p + \pi_1^p S_1^p$, π_0^p is expressed in terms of π_1^p and W^p : $\pi_0^p S_0^p = W^p - \pi_1^p S_1^p$, hence

$$ W^{p+1} = W^p(1 + \rho L^p \gamma_0(S_0^p)) + \rho L^p \pi_1^p S_1^p(\gamma_1(S_1^p, v^p) - \gamma_0(S_0^p)) $$

The seller of an option looks after securing herself at the best. She can always cover the risk in buying the asset in choosing $\pi_0 = 0$ and $\pi_1 = 1$ but any better covering will be π_1 less than 1. Also the set of available controls is $P(S) = \{(\pi_0, \pi_1) \in (-\infty, 0] \times [0,1]\}$. The upper and lower bounds between which v varies over each interval of length ρ are denoted $v_m(\rho)$ and $v_M(\rho)$. Control and uncertainty are from now on assumed to vary within: $\pi_1 \in [0,1]$ and $v \in [v_m, v_M]$. We denote:

$$ g_\rho(t, S_1, L, W, \pi_1, v) := (t - \rho, S_1(1 + \rho\gamma_1(S_1, v)), $$
$$ W(1 + \rho L\gamma_0(t)) + \rho L\pi_1 S_1(\gamma_1(S_1, v) - \gamma_0(t)) $$

The Guaranteed Hybrid Capture Basin Algorithm leads to the construction of a decreasing sequence of subsets K_ρ^p as in (10). These subsets can be rewritten as epigraphs of functions $(\tau, S_1, L) \rightarrow V_{g_\rho}^p(\tau, S_1, L)$ defined recursively by:

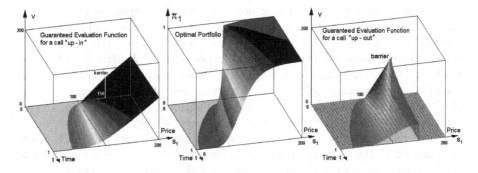

Fig. 2. Guaranteed Evaluation Function of an European call with barrier "up in" with uncertainty of Cox & Rubinstein type and the corresponding Optimal strategy: π_1. On the right, the case of an "up out" call.

$$V_{g_\rho}^0(t, S_1, L) = \begin{cases} \mathbf{b}(t, S_1) & \text{if } t \in]0, T] \\ \mathbf{c}(0, S_1) & \text{if } t \in]-\rho, 0] \end{cases} \text{ if } L = 1 \text{ and } 0 \text{ if not}$$
$$\mathcal{E}pi(V_{g_\rho}^{p+1}) = \{(t, S_1, L, W) \in \mathcal{E}pi(V_{g_\rho}^p) \mid \exists \pi_1 \in [0, 1], \, \forall v \in [v_m, v_M], \quad (14)$$
$$g_\rho(t, S_1, W, L, \pi_1, v) \in \mathcal{E}p(V_{g_\rho}^p)\}$$

Hence the rule to build the sequence of functions $V_{g_\rho}^{p+1}$ for $L = 0$ and for $L = 1$:

$$V_{g_\rho}^{p+1}(t, S_1, L) := \max \left(V_{g_\rho}^p(t, S_1, L), \right.$$
$$\inf_{\pi_1 \in [0,1]} \sup_{v \in [v_m, v_M]} \frac{V_{g_\rho}^p(t - \rho, S_1(1 + \rho\gamma_1(S_1, v)), \Lambda) - \rho\Lambda\pi_1 S_1(\gamma_1(S_1, v) - \gamma_0(t))}{1 + \rho\gamma_0(t)}$$

with $\Lambda = 1$ if $S_1(1 + \rho\gamma_1(S_1, v)) \geq S^*$ and $\Lambda = L$ if not, and the approximated Guaranteed Evaluation Function:

$$V_{g_\rho}(t, S, L) = V_{g_\rho}^p(p\rho, S_1, L), \, \forall t \in](p-1)\rho, p\rho]$$

For $L = 1$ the approximated Guaranteed Evaluation Function coincides with the case of a plain call without barrier. Also the true function holds for $L = 0$ and for $S < S^*$.

Figure 2 shows the graph of the Evaluation Function $V_{g_\rho}(t, S)$ of a call "up in" with $s^* = 150$, the optimal strategy π_1 and, on the right, the graph of the Evaluation Function of a call "up out" with $s^* = 150$.

4   Application to the Economics of the Life Cycle

This application is taken from [15, Bonneuil & Saint-Pierre]. The life cycle hypothesis says that people save during their lives, then dissave after retirement to consume. Most dynamic models are built on the maximization of an intertemporal utility function, indicating how couples decide how to consume and how they devote their time between leisure, work and children. These models tell specific stories, which permit or not a certain achievement in life. The viability approach offers to look at the life cycle the other way round: to sustain a certain way of life, make a certain total number of children and retire with a certain capital, while adapting to uncertainties on the job market and on the stock exchange, where should a couple start from, and which decisions in consumption and savings should be taken at each time of the life cycle? The fact that the birth of a child changes consumption abruptly (notably lodging or car) is seldom fully taken into account. Impulse differential equations are specifically suited to reflect abrupt changes. One remarquable feature of this study is the combination of the capture-viability problematic with the impulsive aspect of the dynamics, inherent in the discrete nature of the arrival of new borns (parity) and its abrupt consequence on consumption and standard of living.

4.1 The Life Cycle as an Hybrid Differential Inclusion under Constraints

We consider a family where both spouses take part to a same utility function. A couple receives a salary $S(t)$ at the age t of the woman, changes in time with an expected growth rate r_S and the exogenous perturbations on the labor market $v_1(t)$ varying in a closed set V_1, with range given by σ_1, reflecting the uncertainty linked to income, notably the risk of unemployment:

$$S'(t) = r_S(1 + \sigma_1 v_1(t))S(t) \tag{15}$$

This couple spends $C(t)$) in consumption and $N(t)$ is the total number of living children at t. Their wealth $W(t)$ has a return $r(t)$ on the financial market:

$$W'(t) = -C(t) + S(t) + (\gamma_0 \pi_0(t) + (1 - \pi_0(t))(\gamma_2 + \sigma_2 v_2(t)))W(t) \tag{16}$$

where γ_0 is the mean interest rate of the riskless asset, γ_2 the mean interest rate of the risky asset, $\pi_0(t) \in [0, 1]$ the part of the riskless portfolio, σ_2 the volatility and $v_2(t)$ a measurable perturbation varying in a closed set V_2, whose range reflects the degree of asset uncertainty. Couples have then to decide when and how many children to have, they can reduce or increase their consumption, and are faced to the uncertainties $v_1(t)$ on the labor market, as well as those $v_2(t)$ on the stock exchange. All children born alive remain so until the retirement of the mother. Each new birth starts a new way of life. There remains a room of personal decision reflected by a growth rate $u_1(t)$ varying within a closed set U_1 of admissible values corresponding to habit and taste:

$$C'(t) = u_1(t)C(t) \tag{17}$$

When a child is born, at age n of the mother, the system is started again at a different way of life, with an additional cost for the birth. Finally, the system is described by five differential equations in continuous time and five impulsional equations, the whole constituting a hybrid differential game:

$$
\text{Continuous level} \quad
\begin{cases}
S'(t) = r_S(1 + \sigma_1 v_1(t))S(t) \\
C'(t) = u_1(t)C(t) \\
W'(t) = -C(t) + S(t) + (\gamma_0 \pi_0(t) \\
\qquad\qquad + (1 - \pi_0(t))(\gamma_2 + \sigma_2 v_2(t)))W(t) \\
N'(t) = 0 \\
\tau'(t) = 0 \text{ if } \tau(t) - t > 0 \; ; \; 1 \text{ if } \tau(t) - t > 0 \qquad (18) \\
S^+ = S^- + a_S(N^-) \\
C^+ = C^- + a_B(N^-) \\
W^+ = W^- - a_B(N^-) \\
N^+ = N^- + 1 \\
\tau^+ = \tau^- + i(N^-, \tau^-)
\end{cases}
$$

$$\text{Impulse level}$$

where $i(N, t)$ is the minimum biological birth interval after the Nth birth, at age t of the woman. a_S^N is a birth allowance, $a_B^{(n)}$ the cost of the nth birth.

The constraints are:

$$
\begin{cases}
C(t) \geq \underline{C}(N(t), t) = a_1 + a_2 N(t) + a_3 \ln(S(t)) \\
W(t) \geq \underline{W}(t) \\
t \in [0, T]
\end{cases}
\qquad (19)
$$

The reset set is $\{t \in [\alpha, \beta]\}$, the interval of fertile ages, intersected with the set $\{t \mid \tau(t) = t\}$ of dates when pregnancy is biologically possible.

We considered that the total number of children and a minimal capital at the age of retirement constitute a "target", ex ante (people fix objectives to themselves) or ex post (the achievement at the moment of retirement):

$$
\begin{cases}
N(\beta) = N_\beta \\
W(T) \geq W_T
\end{cases}
\qquad (20)
$$

where T is the age of retirement, N_β is the parity, born during the fertile span $[\alpha, \beta]$ of the woman, W_T is the capital gathered at the moment of retirement.

Before reaching $N(\beta)$ and W_T, the family consumed at least $(\underline{C}(N(t), t))$ and could not borrow more than $(\underline{W}(t))$: households are liquidity and loan constrained. To achieve this objective while satisfying constraints, the couple has the freedom to consume more or less in time and to switch between risky and riskless assets:

$$
u_1(t) \in U_1 \text{ and } \pi_2(t) \in [0, 1]
$$

notably in order to adapt to unpredictable perturbations varying abruptly within closed sets:

$$
v_1(t) \in V_1 \text{ and } v_2(t) \in V_2
$$

The point is, given perturbations $v_1(t)$ and $v_2(t)$, to find a strategy $(u_1(t), \pi_2(t))$ safeguarding the standard of living and the objectives in terms of family, in terms of consumption during the life cycle, and in terms of capital at retirement.

Results: The viable hybrid capture basin is obtained thanks to the capture basin algorithm extended to hybrid dynamics. An example is represented on Figure 3 for a final parity $N_\beta = 5$ children. From all states in the bottom set (no children yet), there exist solutions satisfying the constraints of consumption and loan during the life cycle and reaching the "target" of capital at retirement and parity. This solution must successively belong to the sets with growing parity. If not, then parity or standard of consumption must be changed. For each perturbation on wage or on assets, there exists at least one change in consumption to safeguard the solution within the set of constraints and capable of reaching the "target" in capital and children.

Numerical values chosen for the example are:

$T = 65$ years old, $r_S = 0.03$, $\sigma_1 = 0.2$, $\sigma_2 = 0.1$, $\gamma_0 = 0.03$, $\gamma_1 = 0.03$, $a_1 = 1$, $a_2 = 0.8$, $a_3 = 2.1$, $\underline{W} = -10$ k euros, $\alpha = 18$ years old, $\beta = 45$ years old, $S(0) = 10$ k euros, $a_B^{(n)} = 10$ k euros, $a_S^{(n)} = 0$ euros, $W_T = 12$ k euros, $U_1 = [-0.5, 0.5]$, $V_1 = [-1, 0]$, $V_2 = [-1, 1]$.

The hybrid capture-viability kernel then represents the room to manoeuvre so as to "stay in the game" in terms of the economics of the life cycle. The three trajectories represented on Figure 3 remain in the capture-viability kernel.

Figure 3 (on the left hand side) shows that different trajectories can start from initial states close to each other, reflecting the trade-off between consuming young and having children late or beginning fertility earlier and consuming later in life. Each trajectory remains in each successive viable set for parity $n = 1, 2, 3, 4, 5$ at least during the biological birth interval $i(t^{(n)})$, but must leave the viable set for n at least before the end of the fertile age of the woman minus the predictable coming birth intervals. The actual birth interval between n and $n + 1$ children corresponds to the part of the trajectory spent in the viable set of order n. From all states in the bottom set (no children yet) starts at least one solution satisfying the constraints of consumption and loan during the life cycle and reaching a given capital at retirement and a given parity.

This solution must successively "jump" to the sets with growing parity. If not, then parity or the standard of consumption must be changed. For each perturbation on wage or on assets, there exists at least one change in consumption to safeguard the solution within the set of constraints and capable of reaching the "target" in capital and children.

The three diagrams on the right show three solutions starting from different initial positions viable in the guaranteed hybrid viability kernel. Each lower curve corresponds to the evolution of the parity $t \rightarrow N(t)$ and each upper curve corresponds to the evolution of the wealth $t \rightarrow W(t)$.

The trajectory starting from A corresponds to a couple having an initial consumption of 25 k€ and a wealth of 45 k€. This couple has the five children after gathering sufficient capital in the very last possibility of the woman (children born when the woman is respectively 35, 36, 38, 41 and 45 years old).

The trajectory starting from B corresponds to a couple having an initial consumption of 25 k€ and a wealth of 75 k€. The births of children are distributed when the mother is 18, 22, 27, 34 and 44 years old respectively.

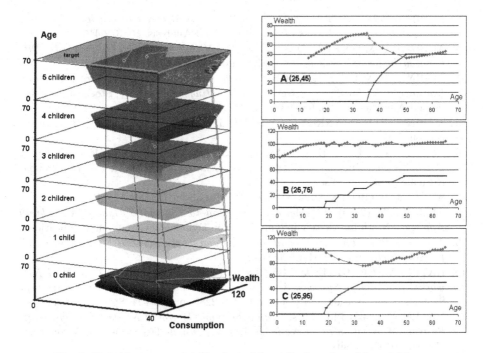

Fig. 3. Hybrid capture-viability kernel for a final parity of five children.

The trajectory starting from C corresponds to a couple having an initial consumption of 25 k€ and a wealth of 95 k€. This couple has its children relatively early when the mother is 18, 19, 21, 24 and 28 years old respectively.

4.2   Conclusion

The viability approach renders financial, demographic and economic diversity, which we can observe in every day life, where actions on consumption or on portfolio management can be taken continuously and combined with exogenous perturbations. These perturbations may generate abrupt changes, so that a specific treatment is necessary, which was done thanks to impulse dynamics. Instead of focusing on all possible trajectories, which is impossible to represent, we delineated the set of all initial states from which a solution can be regulated against all perturbations. This is a way to characterize the complexity of a set-valued dynamics.

References

1. AUBIN J.-P., BAYEN A., BONNEUIL N. & SAINT-PIERRE P. (in preparation) VIABILITY, CONTROL AND GAME THEORIES: REGULATION OF COMPLEX EVOLUTIONARY SYSTEMS UNDER UNCERTAINTY, Springer-Verlag.

2. AUBIN J.-P. & CATTE F. (2002) *Fixed-Point and Algebraic Properties of Viability Kernels and Capture Basins of Sets*, Set-Valued Analysis, 10, 379-416.

3. AUBIN J.-P. & DA PRATO G. (1998) *The Viability Theorem for Stochastic Differential Inclusions*, Stochastic Analysis and Applications, 16, 1-15.

4. AUBIN J.-P. & DOSS H. (2003) *Characterization of Stochastic Viability of any Nonsmooth Set Involving its Generalized Contingent Curvature*, Stochastic Analysis and Applications, 25, 951-981.

5. AUBIN J.-P. & FRANKOWSKA H. (1990) SET-VALUED ANALYSIS, Birkhäuser, Boston, Basel.

6. AUBIN J.-P., PUJAL D. & SAINT-PIERRE P. (2001) *Dynamic Management of Portfolios with Transaction Costs under Tychastic Uncertainty*, Preprint, Scuola Normale Superiore, Pisa.

7. AUBIN J.-P. (1991) VIABILITY THEORY Birkhäuser, Boston, Basel.

8. AUBIN J.-P. (2000) *A Concise Introduction to Dynamical Games: A Viability Approach*, Ninth International Symposium on Dynamical Games and Applications.

9. AUBIN J.-P. (to appear) *Viability Kernels and Capture Basins of Sets under Differential Inclusions*, SIAM J. Control.

10. BAYEN A., CRÜCK E. & TOMLIN C. (2002) *Computational Control of Networks of Dynamical Systems: Application to the National Airspace System*, Hybrid Systems: Computation and Control, LNCS 2289, pp. 90-104, Springer-Verlag.

11. BAYEN A. (2003) PhD Thesis *Computational Control of Networks of Dynamical Systems: Application to the National Airspace System*, Department of Aeronautics of Stanford University.

12. BERNHARD P. (2001) *Robust control approach to option pricing, including transaction costs*, Annals of Dynamic Games.

13. BJORK T. (1998) ARBITRAGE THEORY IN CONTINUOUS TIME, Oxford University Press.

14. BLACK F. & SCHOLES M. (1972) *The Valuation of Option Contracts and a Test of Market Efficiency*, Journal of Finance, 27, 399-418.

15. BONNEUIL N. & SAINT-PIERRE P. (2004) *Beyond Optimality: Managing Children, Assets and Consumption over the Life Cycle* (preprint).

16. CARDALIAGUET P., QUINCAMPOIX M. & SAINT-PIERRE P. (1999) *Set-valued numerical methods for optimal control and differential games*, In STOCHASTIC AND DIFFERENTIAL GAMES. THEORY AND NUMERICAL METHODS, Annals of the Intern. Soc. of Dynamical Games, 177-247, Birkhäuser.

17. COX J., ROSS S. & RUBINSTEIN M. (1985) OPTIONS MARKET, Prentice Hall.

18. CRÜCK E. (2002) (to appear) *Target Problems under State Constraint for Non linear Impulsive Systems*, Journal of Mathematical Analysis and Applications, 270(2):636-656.

19. CRÜCK E., QUINCAMPOIX, M. & SAINT-PIERRE P., (2003) *Values for Pursuit-Evasion Games with Impulsive Dynamics* (preprint).

20. CRÜCK E. & SAINT-PIERRE P. (2002) (to appear) *Non linear Impulse Target Problems under State Constraint: A Numerical Analysis based on Viability Theory*.

21. DA PRATO & FRANKOWSKA (1994) *A stochastic Filippov Theorem*, Stochastic Calculus, 12, 409-426.

22. DA PRATO & FRANKOWSKA (submitted) *Invariance of stochastic control systems with deterministic arguments*.

23. DOSS H. (1977) *Liens entre équations différentielles stochastiques et ordinaires*, Ann. Inst. Henri Poincaré, Calcul des Probabilités et Statistique, 23, 99-125-345.

24. MITCHELL I., BAYEN A. & TOMLIN C. (2001) *Validating a Hamilton-Jacobi Approximation to Hybrid System Reacheable Sets*, Hybrid Systems: Computation and Control, LNCS 2034, pp. 418-432, Springer-Verlag.
25. PUJAL D. & SAINT-PIERRE (2004) *Evaluation et Gestion Dynamiques de Porte-feuilles d'Actifs Conditionnels par l'Algorithme du Bassin de Capture*, (to appear) Revue FINANCE, Paris.
26. QUINCAMPOIX M. & VELIOV V. (1998) *Viability with a target: theory and applications*, Applications of mathematics in engineering, 47-54, Heron Press.
27. SAINT-PIERRE P. (1994) *Approximation of the viability kernel*, Applied Mathematics & Optimisation, 29, 187-209
28. SAINT-PIERRE P. (2003) *Viable Capture Basin for Studying Differential and Hybrid Games*, (to appear) International Game Theory Review, World Scientific Publishing Company.
29. SAINT-PIERRE P. (2003) *Hybrid Kernels and Capture Basins for Impulse Constrained Systems*, Proceedings of Hybrid Systems: Computation and Control, HSCC 2002,C. Tomlin, M. Greenstreet Editors, Lecture Notes in Computer Science, 2289, Springer-Verlag.
30. SETHIAN J.& VLADIMIRSKY A. (2002) PhD Thesis *Ordered Upwind Methods for Hybrid Control*, Hybrid Systems: Computation and Control, LNCS 2289, pp. 90-104, Springer-Verlag.
31. ZABCZYK J. (1996) CHANCE AND DECISION: STOCHASTIC CONTROL IN DISCRETE TIME, Quaderni, Scuola Normale di Pisa

Staying Alive as Cheaply as Possible

Patricia Bouyer[1]*, Ed Brinksma[2], and Kim G. Larsen[3]

[1] LSV – CNRS & ENS de Cachan – UMR 8643 – France
bouyer@lsv.ens-cachan.fr
[2] Department of Computer Science – University of Twente – The Netherlands
brinksma@cs.utwente.nl
[3] BRICS – Aalborg University – Denmark
kgl@cs.auc.dk

Abstract. This paper is concerned with the derivation of infinite schedules for timed automata that are in some sense optimal. To cover a wide class of optimality criteria we start out by introducing an extension of the (priced) timed automata model that includes both costs and rewards as separate modelling features. A precise definition is then given of what constitutes optimal infinite behaviours for this class of models. We subsequently show that the derivation of optimal non-terminating schedules for such double-priced timed automata is computable. This is done by a reduction of the problem to the determination of optimal mean-cycles in finite graphs with weighted edges. This reduction is obtained by introducing the so-called corner-point abstraction, a powerful abstraction technique of which we show that it preserves optimal schedules.

1   Introduction

In the past years the application of model-checking techniques to scheduling problems has become an established line of research. Scheduling problems can often be reformulated in terms of reachability, viz. as the (im)possibility to reach a state that improves on a given optimality criterion. Although there exists a wide body of literature and established results on (optimal) scheduling in the fields of real-time systems and operations research, the model-checking approach is interesting on two accounts. First of all, it serves as a benchmarking activity in which the effectivity and efficiency of model-checking can be compared to the best known results obtained by other techniques. Second, most classical scheduling solutions have good properties only in the context of additional assumptions that may or, quite often, may not apply in actual practical circumstances. Here model-checking techniques have the advantage of offering a generic approach for finding solutions in a model, in much the same way that, say, numerical integration techniques may succeed where symbolic methods fail.

Of course, model-checking comes with its own restrictions and stumbling blocks, the most notorious being the state-space explosion. A lot of research, therefore, is devoted to the containment of this problem by sophisticated techniques, such as data structures for compact state space representation, smart state space search strategies, etc.

---

* This work has been mostly done while visiting CISS at Aalborg University in Denmark and has been supported by CISS and by ACI Cortos, a program of the french ministry of research.

An interesting idea for the model-checking of reachability properties that has received more attention recently is to somehow "guide" the exploration of the (symbolic) state space such that "promising" sets of states are visited first. In a number of applications [Feh99,HLP00,NY01,BMF02] model-checkers have been used to solve a number of non-trivial scheduling problems. Such approaches are different from classical, full state space exploration model-checking algorithms. They are used together with, for example, branch-and-bound techniques [AC91] to prune parts of the search tree that are guaranteed not to contain optimal solutions. This development has motivated research into the extension of model checking algorithms with optimality criteria. They provide a basis for the guided exploration of state spaces, and improve the potential of model-checking techniques for the resolution of scheduling problems. Work on extensions for application of the real-time model-checker Uppaal [LPY97,BLL+98] to optimal scheduling problems is reported in [BFH+01b,BFH+01a,LBB+01]; related work is reported in [AM99, ALTP01]. A closely related activity is reported in [AM01,AM02], where specific search algorithms on timed automata models are defined to solve classes of scheduling problems, such as job-shop and task graph scheduling.

The formulation of scheduling synthesis as a reachability problem is not accurate in cases of reactive behaviours, where actually an infinite (optimal) schedule must be determined in case of reactive behaviours. In this case, not the (optimal) reachability of a good *final* state, but the reachability of good (optimal) infinite behaviours is relevant. Borrowing terminology from performance analysis, we can say that we are interested in the *stationary* behaviours of the system. In the discrete case, stationary behaviours are cyclic behaviours. Assuming cyclic behaviour the cost of reaching a cycle will be insignificant compared to the infinite cost related to non-terminating cyclic behaviours (assuming a single cycle execution has some positive cost). Approximating infinite behaviours by finite ones can yield good and even optimal solutions if it is possible to search sufficiently "deep", but costly pre-ambles may also obscure limit optimal behaviours [Mad03].

In this paper we study optimal infinite behaviour in the context of *priced* timed automata[1]. In a discrete setting the detection of optimal behaviours goes back to Karp's algorithm [Kar78], which determines the minimal mean cost of the cycles in a finite graph with weighted edges. Our contribution in this paper is that we show the computability of the corresponding symbolic question for priced timed automata using a reduction to a discrete problem *à la* Karp based on the so-called *corner-point abstraction*.

A second contribution is that we will not only establish computability of the problem in the original setting of priced timed automata [BFH+01b,BFH+01a,ALTP01], but also in an extension that features two price parameters, viz. *costs* and *rewards*. This is motivated by the fact that the optimality of infinite behaviours is usually expressed as a limit ratio between accumulated costs and rewards. In practical terms they may involve measures such as units of money, production, consumption, time, energy, etc., as in throughput (units/time), production cost (units/money), efficiency (units/energy), etc. In principle all of such measures could count both as cost and reward depending on the particular problem. In this paper the difference between cost and reward is merely a

---

[1] Called *linearly priced timed automata* in [BFH+01b,BFH+01a,LBB+01] and *weighted timed automata* in [ALTP01].

technical one: for infinite behaviour we insist that accumulated rewards diverge (tend to positive infinity), whereas the accumulation of cost has no such constraint. Optimality is then interpreted as maximizing or minimizing the cost/reward ratio.

The structure of the rest of this paper is as follows. In section 2 we define double-priced transition systems, and on that basis introduce the model of double-priced timed automata. Section 3 states the main technical result of the paper together with the assumptions that must be made. Section 4 introduces the central notion of corner-point abstraction related to the region automaton construction for timed automata. Section 5 contains the proof of a necessary result, which states that quotients of affine functions over regions (and more generally zones) attain their extreme values in corner points. In section 6 we show the corner-point abstraction to be sound, and in section 7 to be complete w.r.t. optimal behaviours. In section 8, finally, we draw our conclusions and give indications for future work.

For lack of space, proofs are not detailed in this article, but can be found in [BBL04].

2   Models and Problems

Double-Priced Transition Systems. A *Double-Priced Transition System* (DPTS for short) is a tuple $(S, s_0, T, \text{cost}, \text{reward})$ where S is a set of states, $s_0 \in S$ is the initial state, $T \subseteq S \times S$ is the set of transitions, and cost, reward : $T \to \mathbb{R}$ are price functions. If (s, s') is a transition then $\text{cost}(s, s')$ and $\text{reward}(s, s')$ are two *prices* (the cost and the reward) associated with the transition (s, s'). We shall use the notation $s \to s'$ whenever $(s, s') \in T$, and $s \xrightarrow{c,r} s'$ whenever $(s, s') \in T$ with $\text{cost}(s, s') = c$ and $\text{reward}(s, s') = r$.

Let $\gamma = s_0 \to s_1 \cdots \to s_n$ be a finite execution of a DPTS $(S, s_0, T, \text{cost}, \text{reward})$. The price functions extend to γ in a natural way:

$$\text{Cost}(\gamma) = \sum_{k=1}^{n} \text{cost}(s_{k-1}, s_k) \quad \text{and} \quad \text{Reward}(\gamma) = \sum_{k=1}^{n} \text{reward}(s_{k-1}, s_k) \ .$$

Moreover, for a finite execution γ the *ratio* $\text{Ratio}(\gamma)$ is defined as

$$\text{Ratio}(\gamma) = \frac{\text{Cost}(\gamma)}{\text{Reward}(\gamma)}$$

if this quotient does exist (*i.e.* if $\text{Reward}(\gamma) \neq 0$). Now consider an infinite execution Γ. Denote by Γ_n the finite prefix of length n of Γ. The *ratio* of Γ is defined as

$$\text{Ratio}(\Gamma) = \lim_{n \to +\infty} \text{Ratio}(\Gamma_n)$$

provided this limit exists. Otherwise, we consider the *infimum ratio* and the *supremum ratio* (denoted respectively as $\underline{\text{Ratio}}$ and $\overline{\text{Ratio}}$) defined by

$$\underline{\text{Ratio}}(\Gamma) = \liminf_{n \to +\infty} (\text{Ratio}(\Gamma_n)) \quad \text{and} \quad \overline{\text{Ratio}}(\Gamma) = \limsup_{n \to +\infty} (\text{Ratio}(\Gamma_n)) \ .$$

Given a DPTS $\mathcal{A}$, we define the *optimal ratio* $\mu_{\mathcal{A}}^*$ as

$$\mu_{\mathcal{A}}^* = \inf\{\, \underline{\text{Ratio}}(\Gamma) \mid \Gamma \text{ is an infinite execution of } \mathcal{A} \,\}$$

An infinite execution (also called *schedule*) $\Gamma_\mathcal{A}^*$ of $\mathcal{A}$ is *ratio-optimal* if $\mathsf{Ratio}(\Gamma_\mathcal{A}^*) = \mu_\mathcal{A}^*$. Note that (for infinite-state DPTSs) a ratio-optimal run may not exist. In this case, we will say that $\left(\Gamma_\mathcal{A}^{*,\varepsilon}\right)_{\varepsilon>0}$ is a ratio-optimal family of runs whenever for every $\varepsilon > 0$, $|\underline{\mathsf{Ratio}}(\Gamma_\mathcal{A}^{*,\varepsilon}) - \mu_\mathcal{A}^*| < \varepsilon$.

The *optimal ratio problem* consists then in computing $\mu_\mathcal{A}^*$ and, if it does exist, $\Gamma_\mathcal{A}^*$, or a family $\left(\Gamma_\mathcal{A}^{*,\varepsilon}\right)_{\varepsilon>0}$.

Example 1. Consider a DPTS with states $\{A, B, C\}$ and transitions $A \xrightarrow{1,1} B$, $B \xrightarrow{1,0} B$, $B \xrightarrow{2,1} C$, $C \xrightarrow{1,0} B$, $C \xrightarrow{2,1} C$ and $C \xrightarrow{1,1} A$, and with A initial state. To see that the ratio is not always defined consider the execution $B \to C \to B^2 \to C^2 \to B^4 \to C^4 \to \cdots \to B^{2^n} \to C^{2^n} \cdots$. Computing ratios of finite prefixes, we get respectively

$$\mathsf{Ratio}(B \to C \to B^2 \to C^2 \to \cdots \to B^{2^n}) = 3$$

whereas $\quad \mathsf{Ratio}(B \to C \to B^2 \to C^2 \to \cdots \to B^{2^n} \to C^{2^n}) = 5$

On the other hand, the execution consisting in an infinite repetition of the cycle $A \to B \to C \to A$ has a well-defined ratio, $\frac{4}{3}$, which is in fact the optimum ratio of the given DPTS. $\qquad\square$

Double-Priced Timed Automata. For *finite-state* DPTSs the optimal ratio μ^* is obviously computable. Karp's Theorem [Kar78] provides an algorithm with time complexity $\mathcal{O}(V.E)$ (V being the number of states and E the number of edges) in the case that the reward of each transition is 1. Extensions of Karp's algorithm have been proposed for computing μ^* in the general case, see for example [DG98,DIG99]. In the remainder of this paper we shall settle the computability of μ^* for *infinite-state* DPTS derived from so-called double-priced timed automata being timed automata extended with price(-*rates*) for determining cost and reward of discrete and delay transitions.

Given a set of clocks X, the set of clock constraints $\mathcal{C}(X)$ is defined inductively by the following rules:

$$g ::= x \bowtie c \mid g \wedge g$$

where $x \in X$, $c \in \mathbb{N}$ and $\bowtie \in \{<, \leq, =, \geq, >\}$.

Definition 1. *A Double-Priced Timed Automaton (DPTA for short) over a set of clocks X is a tuple $(L, \ell_0, E, I, \mathsf{c}, \mathsf{r})$, where L is a finite set of locations, ℓ_0 is the initial location, $E \subseteq L \times \mathcal{C}(X) \times 2^X \times L$ is the set of edges[2], $I : L \longrightarrow \mathcal{C}(X)$ assigns invariants to locations and $\mathsf{c}, \mathsf{r} : (L \cup E) \longrightarrow \mathbb{Z}$ assign price-rates to locations and prices to edges.*

Example 2. Consider a production system consisting of a number of machines $M_1, \ldots M_n$ all attended to by a single operator O. Each machine M_i has two production modes: a *high* (H) and a *low* (L) mode, characterized by the amount of goods produced per time-unit (G respectively g) and the amount of power consumed per time-unit (P respectively p). From the producers point of view the *high* production mode is preferable as it has a better (*i.e.* smaller) P/G-ratio than the *low* production mode. Unfortunately, each

---

[2] In case $(\ell, g, r, \ell') \in E$, we write $\ell \xrightarrow{g,r} \ell'$.

machine can only operate in the *high* production mode for a certain amount of time (D) without being attended to by the operator. The operator, in turn, needs a minimum time-seperation (S) between attending machines. The figure on the right provides DPTA's for a typical machine and an operator.[3] In Fig. 1 we consider a production system obtained as the product of a machine M_1 with parameters $D = 3, P = 3, G = 4, p = 5, g = 2$, a machine M_2 with parameters $D = 6, P = 3, G = 2, p = 5, g = 2$ and a single operator with seperation time $S = 4$. In the product construction a cost (reward) rate of a composite location is obtained as sum of the cost (reward) rates of the corresponding component locations.   □

The semantics of a DPTA is given as a DPTS. Intuitively, there are two types of transitions: delay transitions with cost and reward obtained by applying the rates c and r of the source location, and discrete transitions with cost and reward given by the values of c and r of the corresponding edge. Before formally stating the semantics, we introduce a few definitions. A clock valuation $u \in R_{\geq 0}^X$ is a function which assigns values to clocks. If $d \in R_{>0}$ is a delay, then $u + d$ denotes the clock valuation such that for each clock x, $(u + d)(x) = u(x) + d$. If r is a set of clocks then $[r \leftarrow 0]u$ is the clock valuation u' with $u'(x) = 0$ if $x \in r$ and $u'(x) = u(x)$ otherwise. Finally we write $u \models g$ if and only if the clock valuation u satisfies the guard g (defined in the natural way).

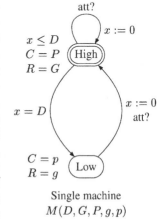

Single machine
$M(D, G, P, g, p)$

Operator $O(S)$

Definition 2. *The semantics of a DPTA* $\mathcal{A} = (L, \ell_0, T, I, \mathsf{c}, \mathsf{r})$ *over set of clocks* X *is the DPTS* $(S, s_0, \longrightarrow, \mathrm{cost}, \mathrm{reward})$ *over* X, *where* $S = L \times R_{\geq 0}^X$, $s_0 = (\ell_0, \mathbf{0})$ *(where* $\mathbf{0}$ *assigns* 0 *to each clock of* $\overline{X}$*), and* $\longrightarrow$ *is defined as follows:*

- $(\ell, u) \xrightarrow{c,r} (\ell, u + d)$ *if* $u + t \models I(\ell)$ *for every* $0 \leq t \leq d$, $c = \mathsf{c}(\ell) \cdot d$ *and* $r = \mathsf{r}(\ell) \cdot d$
- $(\ell, u) \xrightarrow{c,r} (\ell', u')$ *if there exists a transition* $\ell \xrightarrow{g,r} \ell'$ *in* T *such that* $u \models g$, $u' = [r \leftarrow 0]u$, $u' \models I(\ell')$, $c = \mathsf{c}\left(\ell \xrightarrow{g,r} \ell'\right)$, *and* $r = \mathsf{r}\left(\ell \xrightarrow{g,r} \ell'\right)$.

Example 3. Reconsider the Production System from Fig. 1. The following is an infinite execution providing a scheduling policy for the operator with the cost-reward ratio $96/66 \approx 1,455$:

---

[3] The cost and reward rates are both zero in the single location of the Operator.

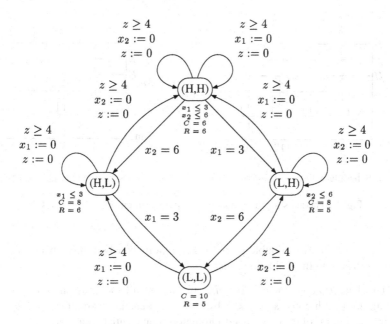

Fig. 1. Production System with Two Machines $M(D = 3, P = 3, G = 4, p = 5, g = 3)$ and $M(D = 6, P = 3, G = 2, p = 5, g = 2)$ and an Operator $O(4)$.

$$((H, H), x_1 = x_2 = z = 0) \xrightarrow{18,18} ((L, H), x_1 = x_2 = z = 3) \xrightarrow{8,5}$$
$$((L, H), x_1 = x_2 = z = 4) \longrightarrow ((H, H), x_1 = z = 0, x_2 = 4) \quad (*) \xrightarrow{12,12}$$
$$((H, L), x_1 = z = 2, x_2 = 6) \xrightarrow{8,6} ((L, L), x_1 = z = 3, x_2 = 7) \xrightarrow{10,5}$$
$$((L, L), x_1 = z = 4, x_2 = 8) \longrightarrow ((H, L), x_1 = z = 0, x_2 = 8) \xrightarrow{24,18}$$
$$((L, L), x_1 = z = 3, x_2 = 11) \xrightarrow{10,5} ((L, L), x_1 = z = 4, x_2 = 12) \longrightarrow$$
$$((L, H), x_1 = 4, x_2 = z = 0) \xrightarrow{32,20} ((L, H), x_1 = 8, x_2 = z = 4)$$
$$\longrightarrow ((H, H), x_1 = z = 0, x_2 = 4) \quad (*)$$

Fig. 2(a) illustrates this schedule as a Gantt chart. An other execution providing a scheduling policy with the cost-reward ratio $68/46 \approx 1,478$ is given in Fig. 2(b).   □

Remark. Let us point out several interesting subclasses of DPTAs. The reward will be said *impulse-based* whenever all reward-rates in locations are zero. This class corresponds roughly to the *mean* ratio as in classical finite-state systems [DIG99]. An other interesting class is the one where the reward corresponds to the elapsing of time, that is when all location reward-rates are 1 and all transition rewards are 0. This last class corresponds to the usual intuitive notion of stationary behaviours where the measure is the cost by unit of time.

3   Result

Restrictions. In the remainder of this paper, we do several restrictions on the models we consider. We first restrict ourselves to reward functions that are non-negative. We

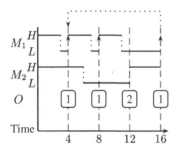 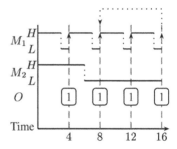

(a) Schedule with ratio 1,455   (b) Schedule with ratio 1,478

Fig. 2. Schedules for the Production System with ratios 1,455 and 1,478.

also restrict ourselves to double-priced timed automata where the reward is *strongly reward-diverging* in the following sense:

A DPTA $\mathcal{A}$ is *strongly reward-diverging* if, closing all the constraints of $\mathcal{A}$ (that is replacing in $\mathcal{A}$ each constraint $x < c$ by $x \leq c$ and each constraint $x > c$ by $x \geq c$), every infinite path Γ of the new *closed* automaton should satisfy that $\mathsf{Reward}(\Gamma) = +\infty$.

Example 4. The following DPTA does not meet the previous restriction. Indeed consider the path $\gamma_{n,d}$ that takes the first transition at date d and then takes n times the loop. We have that $\mathsf{Reward}(\gamma_{n,d}) = 2 + d.n$. Thus, the ratio of any real infinite path is $+\infty$ (because for those states d is positive). Now, if we consider the infinite path where d is 0 (this path is a path of the automaton where all constraints have been closed), we get that $\mathsf{Reward}(\gamma_{n,0}) = 2 \neq +\infty$.

Notice that this restriction implies in particular that all executions in timed automata we consider are *non-zeno* because the reward is in $\mathcal{O}(\text{time elapsed})$. As we will see later, this assumption will have an other important implication, see Proposition 2.

Assumption for the following. We assume that timed automata are *bounded*, that is there exists a constant M such that for every reachable extended state (ℓ, v), for every clock x, $v(x) \leq M$. This is not a restriction as every DPTA can be transformed into an "equivalent" bounded timed automaton (strongly bisimilar and with the same costs and rewards).

We can now state the main result of this paper.

Theorem 1. *The optimal ratio problem is computable for strongly reward-diverging DPTAs with non-negative rewards.*

A more precise statement of the above theorem is obtained by notions of *soundness* and *completeness*. Given two DPTSs $\mathcal{S}$ and $\mathcal{S}'$ we say that $\mathcal{S}'$ is *sound* w.r.t $\mathcal{S}$ whenever $\mu_{\mathcal{S}'}^* \leq \mu_{\mathcal{S}}^*$ and we say that $\mathcal{S}'$ is *complete* w.r.t. $\mathcal{S}$ whenever $\mu_{\mathcal{S}}^* \leq \mu_{\mathcal{S}'}^*$. Theorem 1 is now a corollary of the following Proposition:

Proposition 1. *Let $\mathcal{A}$ be a bounded and strongly reward-diverging DPTA with non-negative rewards. Then there exists a finite-state DPTS $\mathcal{S}$ which is sound and complete w.r.t. the DPTS defined by $\mathcal{A}$.*

The finite-state DPTS we will prove sound and complete w.r.t. to a bounded DPTA $\mathcal{A}$ is the so-called *corner-point abstraction* of $\mathcal{A}$ that we define in the next section.

4   Regions and Corner-Point Abstraction

The aim of this section is to propose a discretization of timed automata behaviours based on an extension of the region automaton construction [AD90,AD94]. We fix a DPTA $\mathcal{A}$ and we assume that it is bounded by M. Moreover, we denote by k its number of clocks.

Regions and Corner-Points. In this paper, we will use the standard notion of regions, as initially defined by Alur and Dill [AD90]. As we consider only bounded timed automata, we only need bounded regions. A *region* (bounded by M) over a (finite) set of clocks X is a tuple $r = (h, [X_0, ..., X_p])$ where $h : X \longrightarrow \mathbb{N} \cap [0, M]$ assigns to each clock an integer value between 0 and M, p is some integer, and $(X_i)_{i=0,...,p}$ forms a partition of X such that for all $i > 0$, $X_i \neq \emptyset$ and $h(x) = M$ implies $x \in X_0$.

Given a valuation v, we say that v is in the region r whenever:

 - for any clock $x \in X$, the integer part of $v(x)$ is $h(x)$,
 - for any clock x, $x \in X_0 \iff v(x) = h(x)$,
 - for all clocks (x, y), $\{v(x)\} \leq \{v(y)\} \iff x \in X_i$ and $y \in X_j$ with $i \leq j$.

where $\{\cdot\}$ represents the fractional part.

A(n M-)*corner-point* is an element $\alpha = (a_j)_{1 \leq j \leq k}$ of $\mathbb{N}^k$ such that for every $1 \leq j \leq k$, $0 \leq a_j \leq M$. Let R be a region. A corner-point α is associated with R whenever it is in the closure of R (for the usual topology of $\mathbb{R}^k$). Let $r = (h, [X_0, ..., X_p])$ be a region. It has $p + 1$ corner-points, $(\alpha_i)_{0 \leq i \leq p}$, such that:

$$\alpha_i(x) = \begin{cases} h(x) & \text{if } x \in X_j \text{ with } j \leq i \\ h(x) + 1 & \text{if } x \in X_j \text{ with } j > i \end{cases}$$

Corner-Point Abstraction. We will construct a finite state DPTS $\mathcal{A}_{\mathsf{cp}}$ called the *corner-point abstraction* of $\mathcal{A}$ where states are of the form (ℓ, R, α) with ℓ being a location, R a region and α a corner-point of R. Transitions of $\mathcal{A}_{\mathsf{cp}}$ are defined in the following manner:

Discrete transitions. If $e = \ell \xrightarrow{g,r} \ell'$ is a transition of $\mathcal{A}$, there will be transitions $e' = (\ell, R, \alpha) \longrightarrow (\ell', R', \alpha')$ in $\mathcal{A}_{\mathsf{cp}}$ with $R \subseteq g$, $R' = [r \leftarrow 0]R$, α corner-point associated with R, α' corner-point associated with R' and $\alpha' = [r \leftarrow 0]\alpha$. We set $\mathsf{cost}(e') = \mathsf{cost}(e)$ and $\mathsf{reward}(e') = \mathsf{reward}(e)$.

Idling transitions. There are two types of idling transitions.

- There are transitions $e' = (\ell, R, \alpha) \longrightarrow (\ell, R, \alpha')$ whenever α and α' are distinct corner-points of R and α' is the time successor of α (in which case, $\alpha' = \alpha + 1$). We set $\mathsf{cost}(e') = \mathsf{cost}(\ell)$ and $\mathsf{reward}(e') = \mathsf{reward}(\ell)$ (intuitively the delay between the corner-points is precisely one time unit).

- There are transitions $e' = (\ell, R, \alpha) \longrightarrow (\ell, R', \alpha)$ whenever R' is the time successor region of R and α is a corner-point associated with both R and R'. We set $\mathsf{cost}(e') = 0$ and $\mathsf{reward}(e') = 0$

The following proposition is an important consequence of the strongly reward-divergence hypothesis.

Proposition 2. *Let $\mathcal{A}$ be a bounded, strongly reward-diverging DPTA with non-negative rewards. Then there exist two constants $\lambda > 0$ and $\mu \geq 0$ such that for any infinite path Π of $\mathcal{A}_{\mathsf{cp}}$*

$$\mathsf{Reward}(\Pi_n) \geq \lambda.n - \mu$$

where Π_n denotes the prefix of length n of Π.

Note that the above λ and μ only depend on the automaton $\mathcal{A}$, not on the paths.

Let $\gamma : (\ell_0, u_0) \longrightarrow (\ell_1, u_1) \longrightarrow \ldots$ be a real (finite or infinite) path in $\mathcal{A}$. The set of all paths

$$\pi : (\ell_0, R_0, \alpha_{0,0}) \longrightarrow (\ell_0, R_0, \alpha_{0,1}) \ldots (\ell_0, R_0, \alpha_{0,p_0}) \longrightarrow (\ell_1, R_1, \alpha_{1,0}) \ldots$$

in $\mathcal{A}_{\mathsf{cp}}$ such that for every i, $u_i \in R_i$ and for every j, $\alpha_{i,j}$ is a corner-point associated with R_i is denoted $\mathsf{proj}_{\mathsf{cp}}(\gamma)$. Note that if $\gamma : (\ell_0, u_0) \longrightarrow (\ell_1, u_1) \longrightarrow \ldots$ and $\gamma' : (\ell_0, v_0) \longrightarrow (\ell_1, v_1) \longrightarrow \ldots$ are two "region-equivalent" real-paths (*i.e.* for every i, u_i and v_i are region-equivalent), then $\mathsf{proj}_{\mathsf{cp}}(\gamma) = \mathsf{proj}_{\mathsf{cp}}(\gamma')$.

In the remainder of the paper, we will prove that the optimal ratio of the corner-point abstraction is the same as the optimal ratio of the original DPTA. As the corner-point abstraction can be effectively constructed and as computing optimal ratios in finite-state DPTSs (the corner-point abstraction is a finite-state DPTS) is effective (see for example [Kar78,DG98,DIG99]), we get that $\mu_{\mathcal{A}}^*$ is effectively computable for DPTAs $\mathcal{A}$ satisfying the strongly reward-divergence hypothesis.

Example 5. If we come back to the automaton of Example 4, as we have already seen, it does not meet the strongly reward-divergence restriction. It is easy to compute that for any real infinite path Γ_d (where d denotes the date the first transition is taken), $\mathsf{Ratio}(\Gamma_d) = 11$. However if we consider the path Π of the corner-point abstraction where d would be 0, we get that $\mathsf{Ratio}(\Pi) = \frac{3}{2}$. We see that we could change the costs and rewards on the transitions, and we would get that there is no relation between the ratio of paths in the original automaton and ratio of paths in the corner-point abstraction. This shows that strongly reward-divergence is necessary.

5   Quotient of Affine Functions

This section contains technical results that will be useful in the following. Let A be a closed set. The *border* of A is denoted by $\mathsf{Border}_n(A)$ and is defined as $A \setminus \mathring{A}$ where $\mathring{A}$ denotes the interior of A. Let A be a closed set and x a point in R^n. The following statements are equivalent and characterize the border of A:

 - $x \in \mathsf{Border}_n(A)$
 - $x \in A$ and for every $\varepsilon > 0$, there exists $y \notin A$ such that $\|x - y\|_\infty < \varepsilon$. [4]

The proofs of the two following lemmas can be found in the appendix.

Lemma 1. *Let f be a function defined on a compact convex set $A \subset \mathrm{R}^n$ (where $n \geq 1$) such that*

$$f(x_1, ..., x_n) = \frac{\sum_{i=1}^n c_i x_i + c}{\sum_{i=1}^n r_i x_i + r}$$

We assume in addition that A is included in the definition set of f. Then the minimum of f on A is obtained on the border of A.

In the remainder of the section, we will use the standard notion of zone. A *zone* over the set of clocks X is a **convex** set of valuations defined by constraints of the forms $x \bowtie c$ and $x - y \bowtie c$ where x and y are in X, $\bowtie \in \{\leq, <, =, >, \geq\}$ and c is an integer. For example, the constraints $\{x \leq 3, y \geq 4, x - y < -5\}$ represent the set of valuations v such that $v(x) \leq 3$, $v(y) \geq 4$ and $v(x) - v(y) < -5$.

Lemma 2. *Let f be a function defined on a bounded zone $Z \subset \mathrm{R}^n$ (where $n \geq 1$) by*

$$f(x_1, ..., x_n) = \frac{\sum_{i=1}^n c_i x_i + c}{\sum_{i=1}^n r_i x_i + r}$$

We assume in addition that $\overline{Z}$ (the closure of Z for the usual topology) is included in the definition set of f. Then the infimum of f on Z is obtained on a point of $\overline{Z}$ with integer coordinates.

The two lemmas above together imply that the infimum of such a function f on a bounded zone Z is obtained in one of the corner-points of the zone. The result could be easily generalized to general bounded convex polyhedra, and not only bounded zones. The result would then be that the function f is minimized in one of the corner-points of the polyhedron, a corner-point representing intuitively an extremal point .

6   Soundness of the Corner-Point Abstraction

The aim of this section is to prove that the corner-point abstraction is sound, that is for all the infinite paths in the timed automaton, we can find an infinite path in the corner-point abstract automaton with a smaller ratio. The proof will be done in two steps: first, we will consider **finite** paths, and then we will extend the result to **infinite** paths.

Theorem 2. *Let $\mathcal{A}$ be a bounded, strongly reward-diverging DPTA with non-negative rewards. Then, $\mu^*_{\mathcal{A}_{cp}} \leq \mu^*_{\mathcal{A}}$.*

---

[4] Note that $\| \cdot \|_\infty$ denotes the infinite norm in every dimension.

Considering Finite Paths

Proposition 3. *Let $\mathcal{A}$ be a bounded, stronly reward-diverging DPTA and let γ be a **finite** execution in $\mathcal{A}$. Then there exists an execution $\pi \in \text{proj}_{\text{cp}}(\gamma)$ such that*

$$\text{Ratio}(\pi) \leq \text{Ratio}(\gamma) .$$

The special case where the reward is impulse-based may be obtained as a direct consequence of previous works on cost-optimality in timed automata (*cf* for example [BFH+01b,BFH+01a,LBB+01]). The general case however requires a new proof. It will require the technical results developed in section 5.

Proof. Let $\gamma = (\ell_0, u_0) \longrightarrow (\ell_0, u_0 + d_0) \longrightarrow (\ell_1, u_1) \longrightarrow (\ell_1, u_1 + d_1) \cdots \longrightarrow (\ell_n, u_n)$ be a finite execution in $\mathcal{A}$ (with alternating delay and discrete transitions). We set for any $1 \leq i \leq n, t_i = \sum_{0 \leq j < i} d_j$. We moreover assume that this execution is read on the sequence of transitions $\ell_0 \xrightarrow{g_1, C_1} \ell_1 \cdots \xrightarrow{g_n, C_n} \ell_n$ in $\mathcal{A}$. The ratio of γ is:

$$f(t_1, ..., t_n) = \frac{\sum_{i=1}^{n} c_i(t_i - t_{i-1}) + c}{\sum_{i=1}^{n} r_i(t_i - t_{i-1}) + r}$$

where c_i, r_i are the cost and reward of the transition $\ell_{i-1} \xrightarrow{g_i, C_i} \ell_i$ and c, r are the sum of all the discrete costs and rewards along γ.

We want to minimize this function with the constraints that for all i, $v_i' \in R_i$ where:

- $v_i'(x) = t_i - t_j$ where $j = \max\{k \leq i \mid x \in C_k\}$
- R_i is the region to which belongs v_i

The set of constraints $\{v_i' \in R_i \mid i = 1...n\}$ defines a zone Z on the variables $(t_i)_{i=1...n}$. We can apply Lemma 2 and we get that the infimum of f on Z is obtained in (at least) a point with integer coordinates, say $(\alpha_i)_{i=1...n}$. Note that this point is in the closure of Z, and thus that it satisfies in particular the set of constraints $\{v_i' \in \overline{R_i} \mid i = 1...n\}$.

We define the valuations $(\sigma_i)_{i=1...n}$ by $\sigma_i(x) = \alpha_i - \alpha_j$ where $j = \max\{k \leq i \mid x \in C_k\}$. Each valuation σ_i is in $\overline{R_i}$ and has integer coordinates. It is thus a corner-point of R_i. Moreover, the sequence of valuations $(\sigma_i)_i$ would be an accepted sequence if we replace the constraints R_i by $\overline{R_i}$. In addition, the time elapsed in each state ℓ_i would then be $\alpha_{i+1} - \alpha_i$.

It is now easy to build a path π in $\text{proj}_{\text{cp}}(\gamma)$ (see associated research report) which goes through the states $(\ell_i, \alpha_{i+1} - \alpha_i)$ and whose ratio is:

$$\text{Ratio}(\pi) = \frac{\sum_{i=1}^{n} c_i(\alpha_i - \alpha_{i-1}) + c}{\sum_{i=1}^{n} r_i(\alpha_i - \alpha_{i-1}) + r}$$

We thus get that $\text{Ratio}(\pi) \leq \text{Ratio}(\gamma)$ and we are done. $\qquad\square$

Extension to Infinite Paths. We will now prove that the previous property, restricted to finite executions, can be extended to infinite executions.

Proposition 4. *Let $\mathcal{A}$ be a bounded, strictly reward-diverging DPTA with non-negative rewards, and let Γ be a **non-zeno** infinite real path in $\mathcal{A}$. Then, there exists an infinite path Π in $\mathcal{A}_{\mathsf{cp}}$ such that*

$$\mathsf{Ratio}(\Pi) \leq \underline{\mathsf{Ratio}}(\Gamma) \ . \tag{$\star$}$$

Notice that, on the contrary to Proposition 3 the path Π may not be in $\mathsf{proj}_{\mathsf{cp}}(\Gamma)$. In addition, for any finite prefix γ of Γ, it may happen that no finite prefix of Π satisfies the property described in Proposition 3, which means that we will not solve the problem just by extending paths given by Proposition 3.

Proof. Let $\Gamma : (\ell_0, u_0) \longrightarrow (\ell_1, u_1) \ldots$ be an infinite path in $\mathcal{A}$. In the following, we will denote by Γ_n the prefix of length n of Γ.

Let α be the value of the minimal ratio for a reachable cycle in $\mathcal{A}_{\mathsf{cp}}$. Let n be an integer. From Proposition 3, there exists a path Π_n in $\mathsf{proj}_{\mathsf{cp}}(\Gamma_n)$ such that $\mathsf{Ratio}(\Pi_n) \leq \mathsf{Ratio}(\Gamma_n)$. Using Proposition 2, we get that $\mathsf{Reward}(\Pi_n) \in \Omega(n)$, which implies in particular that $\lim_{n \to +\infty} \mathsf{Reward}(\Pi_n) = +\infty$.

We decompose Π_n into cycles, *i.e.* we write $\Pi_n = \pi_{0,n}.C_{1,n}.\pi_{1,n} \ldots C_{p_n,n}.\pi_{p_n,n}$ where $\pi_{i,n}$ are simple paths and $C_{i,n}$ are cycles. We assume in addition that this decomposition is maximal in the sense that the path $\pi_{0,n}.\pi_{1,n} \ldots \pi_{p_n,n}$ is acyclic. The maximality property of our decomposition implies that the total length of $\pi_{0,n}.\pi_{1,n} \ldots \pi_{p_n,n}$ is less than the number of nodes in $\mathcal{A}_{\mathsf{cp}}$.

We set $C(n) = \sum_{i=0}^{p_n} \mathsf{Cost}(\pi_{i,n})$ and $R(n) = \sum_{i=0}^{p_n} \mathsf{Reward}(\pi_{i,n})$ and we compute now the difference between $\mathsf{Ratio}(\Pi_n)$ and α:

$$
\begin{aligned}
\mathsf{Ratio}(\Pi_n) - \alpha &= \frac{\sum_{i=1}^{p_n} \mathsf{Cost}(C_{i,n}) + C(n)}{\sum_{i=1}^{p_n} \mathsf{Reward}(C_{i,n}) + R(n)} - \alpha \\[2mm]
&= \frac{\frac{\sum_{i=1}^{p_n} \mathsf{Cost}(C_{i,n})}{\sum_{i=1}^{p_n} \mathsf{Reward}(C_{i,n})} + \frac{C(n)}{\sum_{i=1}^{p_n} \mathsf{Reward}(C_{i,n})}}{1 + \frac{R(n)}{\sum_{i=1}^{p_n} \mathsf{Reward}(C_{i,n})}} - \alpha
\end{aligned}
$$

We set $\beta(n) = \frac{\sum_{i=1}^{p_n} \mathsf{Cost}(C_{i,n})}{\sum_{i=1}^{p_n} \mathsf{Reward}(C_{i,n})}$ and we have that $\beta(n) \geq \alpha$ because α is the ratio of the minimal reachable cycle.[5] We get that

$$\mathsf{Ratio}(\Gamma_n) - \alpha \ \geq \ \mathsf{Ratio}(\Pi_n) - \alpha \ = \ \frac{\beta(n) - \alpha + \frac{C(n) - \alpha R(n)}{\sum_{i=1}^{p_n} \mathsf{Reward}(C_{i,n})}}{1 + \frac{R(n)}{\sum_{i=1}^{p_n} \mathsf{Reward}(C_{i,n})}} \tag{$\star\star$}$$

Observe now that $R(n)$ and $C(n)$ are bounded and that $\lim_{n \to +\infty} \sum_{i=0}^{p_n} \mathsf{Reward}(C_{i,n}) = +\infty$. We can now take the infimum limit of Equation $(\star\star)$, and we get:

$$\underline{\lim}_{n \to +\infty} (\mathsf{Ratio}(\Gamma_n)) - \alpha \geq \underline{\lim}_{n \to +\infty} \beta(n) - \alpha \geq 0$$

Hence, the infimum ratio of Γ is greater than the ratio of the optimal reachable cycle in $\mathcal{A}_{\mathsf{cp}}$. $\qquad\square$

---

[5] Remind the property that if $b > 0$ and $d > 0$, then $\min\left(\frac{a}{b}, \frac{c}{d}\right) \leq \frac{a+c}{b+d} \leq \max\left(\frac{a}{b}, \frac{c}{d}\right)$.

7 Completeness of the Corner-Point Abstraction

The aim of this section is to state the completeness of the corner-point abstraction. More precisely, we will prove that for every infinite path of the corner-point abstraction, there are real paths in the original automaton whose ratio is as close as we want to the ratio of the given path in the corner-point abstraction.

Theorem 3. *Let A be a bounded, strongly reward-diverging DPTA with non-negative rewards. Then, $\mu_A^* \leq \mu_{A_{cp}}^*$.*

The proof of this theorem will be done in two steps: we will first prove that we can approximate paths in A_{cp} by paths in A which are as close as we want to the original path (proposition 5). It will be sufficient to prove that for each infinite path in A_{cp}, under the strongly reward-divergence assumptions, we can find a real path in A whose ratio is as close as we want to the ratio of the given path in A_{cp} (proposition 6).

Proposition 5. *Let A be a bounded DPTA. Let π : (ℓ_0, R_0, α_0) $\longrightarrow$ $\cdots (\ell_n, R_n, \alpha_n) \cdots$ be a (possibly infinite) path in A_{cp}. Let $0 < \varepsilon < \frac{1}{2}$. There exists a real path $\gamma_\varepsilon : (\ell_0, u_0) \longrightarrow \cdots (\ell_n, u_n) \cdots$ in A such that $u_i \in R_i$ and $\|u_i - \alpha_i\|_\infty < \varepsilon$ for every i*[6].

Proof. Let v be a valuation. For any clock x, we define $\mu_v(x) = \min\{|v(x) - p| \mid p \text{ integer}\}$ and for any pair of clocks (x, y), $\nu_v(x, y) = \min\{|v(x) - v(y) - p| \mid p \text{ integer}\}$. We define the *diameter* of v as

$$\delta(v) = \max\left(\{\mu_v(x) \mid x \text{ clock}\} \cup \{\nu_v(x, y) \mid x, y \text{ clocks}\}\right)$$

Proposition 5 will be a direct consequence of the following technical lemma.

Lemma 3. *Consider a transition $(\ell, R, \alpha) \longrightarrow (\ell', R', \alpha')$ in A_{cp}, take a valuation $v \in R$ such that $\delta(v) < \varepsilon$ and $|v(x) - \alpha(x)| = \mu_v(x)$. There exists a valuation $v' \in R'$ such that $(\ell, v) \longrightarrow (\ell', v')$ in A, $\delta(v') < \varepsilon$ and $|v'(x) - \alpha'(x)| = \mu_{v'}(x)$.*

Using this lemma, we construct inductively a path γ_ε as described above, at each step of the construction we have that $\|v_i - \alpha_i\|_\infty \leq \delta(v_i)$. This concludes the proof. $\square$

We now use this result on paths to prove the following proposition on ratios.

Proposition 6. *Let A be a bounded, strongly reward-diverging DPTA with non-negative rewards. Let Π be an infinite path in A_{cp} such that $\mathsf{Ratio}(\Pi)$ is defined. Then the following holds: for any $\varepsilon > 0$, there exists a real path Γ^ε such that $|\mathsf{Ratio}(\Pi) - \mathsf{Ratio}(\Gamma^\varepsilon)| < \varepsilon$.*

---

[6] $\|.\|_\infty$ represents the usual infinite norm defined as $\|(x_i)_{i=1\ldots n}\|_\infty = \max\{|x_i| \mid i = 1\ldots n\}$.

Note that in case we have only non-strict constraints along the path accepting Γ in $\mathcal{A}$, Π corresponds to a real path in $\mathcal{A}$, it thus corresponds to $\Gamma_{\mathcal{A}}^*$. Otherwise, the paths constructed in the following will give us a family $\left(\Gamma_{\mathcal{A}}^{*,\varepsilon}\right)_{\varepsilon>0}$ of optimal schedules.

Note also that in $\mathcal{A}_{cp}$ (which is a finite automaton), optimal schedules are cycles for which the ratio is defined [Kar78,DG98,DIG99]. The previous proposition thus proves the completeness of the corner-point abstraction and concludes this section.

8   Future Work and Conclusion

In this paper, we have shown that the optimal infinite scheduling problem is computable for double-priced timed automata (and PSPACE-complete, see [BBL04]). We have reduced the problem to the computation of optimal infinite schedules in (weighted) finite-state graphs. This problem is equivalent to finding optimal cycles in finite-state graphs, which can be done using algorithms like Karp's algorithm [Kar78] and some of its extensions and improvements [DG98,DIG99].

However, there is still a number of issues which are open for future work. The proof of computability, based on regions and corner-points, does not provide a realistic implementation strategy. We would like to obtain an efficient implementation based on zones and on-the-fly exploration of the symbolic state-space. A restriction to a setting where one of the prices (cost or reward) is uniform (same rate in all locations) may be particularly useful. Implementations for this specific case could be much more efficient than those for the general problem. An idea would then be to approximate optimal infinite schedules by working with (repeated) cost horizons or by applying partitioning and refinement techniques, as done in the tool Rapture [DJJL01,DJJL02].

An extension of our present work would be to address the problem in the presence of adversaries, even if it seems very difficult, more difficult than that of cost-optimal winning strategies for (single-)priced timed automata with adversaries [LTMM02]. In the finite-state setting, however, the problem has been solved [ZP96].

References

[AC91]   D. Applegate and W. Cook. *A Computational Study of the Job-Shop Scheduling Problem*. OSRA Journal on Computing, vol. 3:pp. 149–156, 1991.

[AD90]   R. Alur and D. Dill. *Automata for Modeling Real-Time Systems*. In Proc. 17th Int. Coll. Automata, Languages and Programming (ICALP'90), vol. 443 of LNCS, pp. 322–335. Springer, 1990.

[AD94]   R. Alur and D. Dill. *A Theory of Timed Automata*. Theoretical Computer Science (TCS), vol. 126(2):pp. 183–235, 1994.

[ALTP01]   R. Alur, S. La Torre, and G. J. Pappas. *Optimal Paths in Weighted Timed Automata*. In Proc. 4th Int. Work. Hybrid Systems: Computation and Control (HSCC'01), vol. 2034 of LNCS, pp. 49–62. Springer, 2001.

[AM99]   E. Asarin and O. Maler. *As Soon as Possible: Time Optimal Control for Timed Automata*. In Proc. 2nd Int. Work. Hybrid Systems: Computation and Control (HSCC'99), vol. 1569 of LNCS, pp. 19–30. Springer, 1999.

[AM01]   Y. Abdeddaim and O. Maler. *Job-Shop Scheduling using Timed Automata*. In Proc. 13th Int. Conf. Computer Aided Verification (CAV'01), vol. 2102 of LNCS, pp. 478–492. Springer, 2001.

[AM02]   Y. Abdeddaïm and O. Maler. *Preemptive Job-Shop Scheduling using Stopwatch Automata*. In Proc. 8th Int. Conf. Tools and Algorithms for the Construction and Analysis of Systems (TACAS'02), vol. 2280 of LNCS, pp. 113–126. Springer, 2002.

[BBL04]   P. Bouyer, E. Brinksma, and K. G. Larsen. *Staying Alive as Cheaply as Possible*. Research Report LSV–04–2, LSV, ENS de Cachan, France, 2004.

[BFH⁺01a]   G. Behrmann, A. Fehnker, T. Hune, K. G. Larsen, P. Pettersson, J. Romijn, and F. Vaandrager. *Efficient Guiding Towards Cost-Optimality in* UPPAAL. In Proc. 7th Int. Conf. Tools and Algorithms for the Construction and Analysis of Systems (TACAS'01), vol. 2031 of LNCS, pp. 174–188. Springer, 2001.

[BFH⁺01b]   G. Behrmann, A. Fehnker, T. Hune, K. G. Larsen, P. Pettersson, J. Romijn, and F. Vaandrager. *Minimum-Cost Reachability for Priced Timed Automata*. In Proc. 4th Int. Work. Hybrid Systems: Computation and Control (HSCC'01), vol. 2034 of LNCS, pp. 147–161. Springer, 2001.

[BLL⁺98]   J. Bengtsson, K. G. Larsen, F. Larsson, P. Pettersson, W. Yi, and C. Weise. *New Generation of* UPPAAL. In Proc. Int. Work. Software Tools for Technology Transfer (STTT'98), BRICS Notes Series, pp. 43–52. 1998.

[BMF02]   E. Brinksma, A. Mader, and A. Fehnker. *Verification and Optimization of a PLC Control Schedule*. Journal of Software Tools for Technology Transfer (STTT), vol. 4(1):pp. 21–33, 2002.

[DG98]   A. Dasdan and R. K. Gupta. *Faster Maximum and Minimum Mean Cycle Algorithms for System Performance Analysis*. IEEE Transactions on Computer-Aided Design of Integrated Circuits and Systems, vol. 17(10):pp. 889–899, 1998.

[DIG99]   A. Dasdan, S. Irani, and R. K. Gupta. *Efficient Algorithms for Optimum Cycle Mean and Optimum Cost to Time Ratio Problems*. In Proc. 36th ACM/IEEE Design Automation Conf. (DAC'99), pp. 47–42. ACM, 1999.

[DJJL01]   P. R. D'Argenio, B. Jeannet, H. E. Jensen, and K. G. Larsen. *Reachability Analysis of Probabilistic Systems by Successive Refinements*. In Proc. 1st Int. Work. Process Algebra and Probabilistic Methods, Performance Modeling and Verification (PAPM-PROBMIV'01), vol. 2165 of LNCS, pp. 39–56. Springer, 2001.

[DJJL02]   P. R. D'Argenio, B. Jeannet, H. E. Jensen, and K. G. Larsen. *Reduction and Refinement Strategies for Probabilistic Analysis*. In Proc. 2nd Int. Work. Process Algebra and Probabilistic Methods, Performance Modeling and Verification (PAPM-PROBMIV'02), vol. 2399 of LNCS, pp. 57–76. Springer, 2002.

[Feh99]   A. Fehnker. *Scheduling a Steel Plant with Timed Automata*. In Proc. 6th Int. Conf. Real-Time Computing Systems and Applications (RTCSA'99), pp. 280–286. IEEE Computer Society Press, 1999.

[HLP00]   T. Hune, K. G. Larsen, and P. Pettersson. *Guided Synthesis of Control Programs Using* UPPAAL. In Proc. IEEE ICDS Int. Work. Distributed Systems Verification and Validation, pp. E15–E22. IEEE Computer Society Press, 2000.

[Kar78]   R. M. Karp. *A Characterization of the Minimum Mean-Cycle in a Digraph*. Discrete Mathematics, vol. 23(3):pp. 309–311, 1978.

[LBB⁺01]   K. G. Larsen, G. Behrmann, E. Brinksma, A. Fehnker, T. Hune, P. Pettersson, and J. Romijn. *As Cheap as Possible: Efficient Cost-Optimal Reachability for Priced Timed Automata*. In Proc. 13th Int. Conf. Computer Aided Verification (CAV'01), vol. 2102 of LNCS, pp. 493–505. Springer, 2001.

[LPY97]   K. G. Larsen, P. Pettersson, and W. Yi. UPPAAL *in a Nutshell*. Journal of Software Tools for Technology Transfer (STTT), vol. 1(1–2):pp. 134–152, 1997.

[LTMM02]   S. La Torre, S. Mukhopadhyay, and A. Murano. *Optimal-Reachability and Control for Acyclic Weighted Timed Automata*. In Proc. 2nd IFIP Int. Conf. Theoretical Computer Science (TCS 2002), vol. 223 of IFIP Conf. Proc., pp. 485–497. Kluwer, 2002.

[Mad03]   A. Mader. *Deriving Schedules for a Smart Card Personalisation System*, 2003. Submitted.

[NY01]   P. Niebert and S. Yovine. *Computing Efficient Operations Schemes for Chemical Plants in Multi-batch Mode*. European Journal of Control, vol. 7(4):pp. 440–453, 2001.

[ZP96]   U. Zwick and M. Paterson. *The Complexity of Mean Payoff Games on Graphs*. Theoretical Computer Science (TCS), vol. 158(1–2):pp. 343–359, 1996.

On O-Minimal Hybrid Systems*

Thomas Brihaye[†], Christian Michaux, Cédric Rivière[‡], and
Christophe Troestler

Université de Mons-Hainaut
Institut de Mathématique
6, Avenue du Champ de Mars
7000 Mons, Belgique
{thomas.brihaye,christian.michaux}@umh.ac.be
{cedric.riviere,christophe.troestler}@umh.ac.be

Abstract. This paper is driven by a general motto: bisimulate a
hybrid system by a finite symbolic dynamical system. In the case of
o-minimal hybrid systems, the continuous and discrete components
can be decoupled, and hence, the problem reduces in building a finite
symbolic dynamical system for the continuous dynamics of each location. We show that this can be done for a quite general class of hybrid
systems defined on o-minimal structures. In particular, we recover the
main result of a paper by Lafferriere G., Pappas G.J. and Sastry S. on
o-minimal hybrid systems.

Mathematics Subject Classification: 68Q60, 03C64.

1 Introduction

Hybrid systems consist of finite state machines equipped with a continuous dynamics. This notion has been intensively studied [ACH+,HKPV,Hen95] (see
[Hen96] for a survey), and is a generalization of timed automata [AD]. Hybrid
systems encompass many interesting applications such as air traffic management
[TPS] and highway systems [LGS].

Given a hybrid system, a natural question is to know whether the system
can reach some prohibited states. This question is known as *the reachability
problem*. Since the state space is usually uncountable it is necessary to have
an algorithmic approach to this problem. The main difficulty is the richness
of continuous dynamics and its interaction with a discrete dynamics. Several
results on decidability and undecidability of the reachability problem have been
developed in [ACH+,HKPV].

One approach to solve the reachability problem is to study equivalence relations preserving reachability and to find finite state systems equivalent to the
original one. Building *bisimulations* is a way to achieve this goal. This is the

* This work has been supported by a grant from the National Bank of Belgium.
† This author is supported by a FRFC grant: 2.4530.02.
‡ This author is supported by a FRIA grant and INTAS project 2000-447.

R. Alur and G.J. Pappas (Eds.): HSCC 2004, LNCS 2993, pp. 219–233, 2004.
© Springer-Verlag Berlin Heidelberg 2004

point of view adopted in this paper. Bisimulations have many other interesting properties (e.g. they preserve CTL, [AHLP]).

In [LPS], the notion of *o-minimal hybrid system* is defined. This class of hybrid systems have a particularly rich continuous dynamics, in particular it may be non-linear. Through this paper, we adopt the conventions introduced in [LPS, p. 6] for the discrete transitions. This allows to decouple the discrete and continuous components of the hybrid system. Hence the problem to find a finite bisimulation of such a hybrid system is equivalent to find a finite bisimulation, on each location, which respects some initial partition induced by resets, guards, initial and final regions. In [LPS, p. 12], the continuous dynamics of an o-minimal hybrid system is given by a smooth complete vector field F from $\mathbb{R}^n$ to $\mathbb{R}^n$ and the flow is assumed to be definable in an o-minimal extension of $\langle \mathbb{R}, <, +, - \rangle$. In particular, the system is time-invariant, the flow is injective w.r.t. the time and thus the trajectories are non self-intersecting. We relax these assumptions by permitting the system to be time-varying and to have self-intersecting trajectories, which are natural features of many real systems. The continuous transition relation of such systems is therefore much richer (see Section 2.3). Moreover the generalization allows for general dynamics instead of flow, for an output space M^{k_2} distinct from the input space M^{k_1} and for linearly ordered structures over spaces other than the reals.

In Section 3 of this paper, we present a general construction to associate words with trajectories of a continuous dynamics w.r.t. an initial partition of the space. By using this general tool, a finite symbolic dynamical system is associated with any *o-minimal dynamical system*, the states of which are represented by words (see Section 4). Let us mention that this kind of idea already appears in the literature (see for example [ASY]).

Under the extra assumption that there is a unique trajectory passing through a point, we show that this finite symbolic dynamical system bisimulates the original one. As a byproduct of this result, we obtain a simple proof of the main result of [LPS] which asserts that every o-minimal hybrid system admits a finite bisimulation.

In the last section, we give an example of an o-minimal dynamical system which does not admit a finite bisimulation w.r.t. some initial partition, setting in this way some limits to our results.

We do not address the effectiveness of our constructions, this question will be studied in subsequent papers, in which the techniques developed here will be applied to a wider class of hybrid systems.

2 Preliminaries

In this section, we recall some basic definitions and results. However we do not recall classical definitions about hybrid systems, they can be found for example in [Hen96]. For o-minimal hybrid systems and their extensions treated in the paper, we refer to [LPS].

2.1   Transition Systems and Bisimulation

Definition 2.1. A *transition system* $T = (Q, \Sigma, \rightarrow)$ consists of a set of states Q (which may be uncountable), Σ an alphabet of events, and $\rightarrow \subseteq Q \times \Sigma \times Q$ a transition relation.

A transition $(q_1, a, q_2) \in \rightarrow$ is denoted by $q_1 \xrightarrow{a} q_2$. A transition system is finite if Q is finite. If the alphabet of events is reduced to a singleton, $\Sigma = \{a\}$, we will denote the transition system $(Q, \rightarrow)$ and omit the event a.

Definition 2.2. Given two transition systems on the same alphabet of events, $T_1 = (Q_1, \Sigma, \rightarrow_1)$ and $T_2 = (Q_2, \Sigma, \rightarrow_2)$, a *partial simulation of T_1 by T_2* is a binary relation $\sim \subseteq Q_1 \times Q_2$ which satisfies the following condition:

$$\forall q_1, q_1' \in Q_1, \ \forall q_2 \in Q_2, \ \forall a \in \Sigma,$$
$$\left(q_1 \sim q_2 \text{ and } q_1 \xrightarrow{a}_1 q_1' \right) \Rightarrow \left(\exists q_2', \ q_1' \sim q_2' \text{ and } q_2 \xrightarrow{a}_2 q_2' \right)$$

This condition is read T_2 *simulates* T_1.

Definition 2.3. Given $\sim$ a partial simulation of T_1 by T_2, we say that $\sim$ is a *simulation of T_1 by T_2* if, for each $q_1 \in Q_1$, there exists $q_2 \in Q_2$ such that $q_1 \sim q_2$.

Definition 2.4. Given two transition systems on the same alphabet of events, $T_1 = (Q_1, \Sigma, \rightarrow_1)$ and $T_2 = (Q_2, \Sigma, \rightarrow_2)$, a *bisimulation between T_1 and T_2* is a relation $\sim \subseteq Q_1 \times Q_2$ such that $\sim$ is a simulation of T_1 by T_2 and the *inverse relation*[1] $\sim^{-1}$ is a simulation of T_2 by T_1.

Definition 2.5. Given $\sim$ a bisimulation between T_1 and T_2 if $\sim$ is a function from Q_1 to Q_2, we call it a *functional bisimulation*.

Remarks 2.6. – Given a transition system $T = (Q, \Sigma, \rightarrow)$, we can look at bisimulations on $Q \times Q$; they are called *bisimulations on T*.
 – Given T_1, T_2 two transition systems and $\sim \subseteq Q_1 \times Q_2$ a bisimulation between T_1 and T_2, the kernel[2] $\mathrm{Ker}(\sim)$ is a bisimulation on T_1.
 – Given $\sim$ a functional bisimulation between T_1 and T_2, we have that $\mathrm{Ker}(\sim)$ is an equivalence relation on Q_1; moreover there is a bisimulation between $T_1/\mathrm{Ker}(\sim)$ and T_2 (these statements and their proofs can be found in [Cau]).

Definition 2.7. Given T a transition system, $\mathcal{P}$ a partition of Q and $\sim \in Q \times Q$ a bisimulation which is an equivalence relation on Q, we say that the bisimulation $\sim$ *respects the partition* $\mathcal{P}$ if any $P \in \mathcal{P}$ is an union of equivalence classes for $\sim$. We will speak of *bisimulations w.r.t.* $\mathcal{P}$.

---

[1] If $\sim = \{(q_1, q_2) \in Q_1 \times Q_2 | q_1 \sim q_2\}$, then $\sim^{-1} = \{(q_2, q_1) \in Q_2 \times Q_1 | q_1 \sim q_2\}$.
[2] $\mathrm{Ker}(\sim) = \sim \circ \sim^{-1} = \{(p, q) \in Q_1 \times Q_1 \mid \exists r \in Q_2, \ p \sim r \text{ and } q \sim r\}$.

2.2   O-Minimality and Definability

Let $\mathcal{M}$ be a structure. In this paper when we say that some relation, subset, function is definable, we mean it is first-order definable (possibly with parameters) in the sense of the structure $\mathcal{M}$. A general reference for first-order logic is [Ho]. All the notions related to o-minimality and an extensive bibliography can be found in [vdD98]. Let us recall the definition of an o-minimal structure:

Definition 2.8. An extension of an ordered structure $\mathcal{M} = \langle M, <, ... \rangle$ is *o-minimal* if every definable subset of M is a finite union of points and open intervals (possibly unbounded).

In other words the definable subsets of M are the simplest possible: the ones which are definable with parameters in $\langle M, < \rangle$. This assumption implies that definable subsets of M^n (in the sense of M) admit very nice structure theorems (like *Cell decomposition*) or Theorem 2.10. The following are examples of o-minimal structures.

Example 2.9. The field of reals $\langle \mathbb{R}, <, +, \cdot, 0, 1 \rangle$, the group of rationals $\langle \mathbb{Q}, <, +, \cdot, 0, 1 \rangle$, the field of reals with exponential function, the field of reals expanded by restricted pfaffian functions and the exponential function, and many more interesting structures.

The main result we use on o-minimal structures is (see [vdD98, Corollary 3.6, p. 60]):

Theorem 2.10 (Uniform Finiteness). *Let $S \subseteq M^m \times M^n$ be definable, we denote by S_a the fiber $\{y \in M^n | (a, y) \in S\}$. Then there is a number $N_S \in \mathbb{N}$ such that for each $a \in M^m$ the set $S_a \subseteq M^n$ has at most N_S definably connected components.*

2.3   Dynamics

Definition 2.11. A *dynamical system* is a pair $(\mathcal{M}, \gamma)$ where:

- $\mathcal{M} = \langle M, <, ... \rangle$ is a totally ordered structure,
- $\gamma : M^{k_1} \times M \to M^{k_2}$ is a definable function of $\mathcal{M}$.

The function γ is called the *dynamics* of the dynamical system [3]. More generally, we can consider the case where γ is defined on definable subsets of $\mathcal{M}$ that is $\gamma : V_1 \times V \to V_2$ with $V_1 \subseteq M^{k_1}$, $V \subseteq M$ and $V_2 \subseteq M^{k_2}$.

Classically, when $M = \mathbb{R}$ is the field of the reals, we see M as the time, $M^{k_1} \times M$ as the space-time, M^{k_2} as the (output) space and M^{k_1} as the input space. We keep this terminology in the more general context of a structure $\mathcal{M}$.

Definition 2.12. If we fix a point $x \in M^{k_1}$, the set $\Gamma_x = \{\gamma(x, t) \mid t \in M\} \subseteq M^{k_2}$ is called the trajectory determined by x.

---

[3] Since we do not assume that the dynamics is given by a flow, this allows quite more general behavior than in the vector field case.

Fig. 1. A simple loop

Definition 2.13. Given $(\mathcal{M}, \gamma)$ a dynamical system, we define a *transition system* $T_\gamma = (Q, \to_\gamma)$ *associated with the dynamical system* by:

- the set Q of states is M^{k_2};
- the transition relation $y_1 \to_\gamma y_2$ is defined by:

$$\exists x \in M^{k_1}, \ \exists t_1, t_2 \in M, \ \left(t_1 \leqslant t_2 \text{ and } \gamma(x, t_1) = y_1 \text{ and } \gamma(x, t_2) = y_2\right)$$

Let us make an *important* observation. Given a transition $y_1 \to_\gamma y_2$, we denote the couple of instants of time corresponding to the positions y_1, y_2 by (t_1, t_2). If there exists a position y and different times $t < t'$ such that $\gamma(x, t) = \gamma(x, t') = y$ (see Figures 1 and 3 for example), then the transition relation $\to_\gamma$ allows the following sequence of transitions: $y_1 \to_\gamma y \to_\gamma y_2$ with couples of time (t_1, t') and (t, t_2). Let us look at a simple example of this behavior, in Figure 1, there clearly exists $t < t'$ such that $\gamma(x, t) = \gamma(x, t') = y$. The composition of transitions as explained above allows an arbitrary large number of passages in the loop.

3 Encoding Trajectories by Words

In this section, we describe the general tools that we use further on.

Given a dynamical system $(\mathcal{M}, \gamma)$ and $\mathcal{P}$ a finite definable partition of the space M^{k_2}, $\mathcal{P} = \{P_1, \ldots, P_s\}$, we want to encode the trajectories on M^{k_2} as words[4] on the finite alphabet $\mathcal{P}$.

Let us first remark that the partition $\mathcal{P}$ of the space M^{k_2} induces a partition $\tilde{\mathcal{P}}$ on the space-time $M^{k_1} \times M$ defined by the preimages of the P_i's under γ. The preimage of trajectory Γ_x is the line $\{x\} \times M$ in the space-time $M^{k_1} \times M$. This line crosses the regions $\tilde{P}_i$'s and looking to this crossing, when time is increasing, naturally gives a word on the alphabet $\tilde{\mathcal{P}}$. Replacing each letter $\tilde{P}_i$ by its corresponding letter P_i gives the word ω_x on the alphabet $\mathcal{P}$ we want to associate with Γ_x. For the sake of completeness, we mathematically formalize this idea.

---

[4] In this general (possibly uncountable) context, a word is a function from M (or from a quotient of M induced by a partition on M) to $\mathcal{P}$.

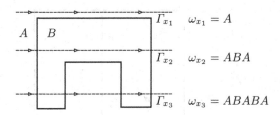

Fig. 2. Encoding trajectories by words

Given $x \in M^{k_1}$, we consider the sets $\{t \mid \gamma(x,t) \in P_i\}$ for $i = 1, \ldots, s$. This gives a partition of the time M. We associate a word on $\mathcal{P}$ with the trajectory determined by x such that two consecutive letters are different. Let $\mathcal{F}_x$ be the set of intervals defined by:

$$\mathcal{F}_x = \big\{ I \mid I \text{ is a time interval and is maximal for the property}$$
$$\exists i \in \{1, \ldots, s\}, \ \forall t \in I, \ \gamma(x,t) \in P_i \big\}.$$

For each x, the set $\mathcal{F}_x$ is totally ordered by the order induced from M. By analogy with the work of [Tr], we introduce a family of functions of *coloration* $\mathcal{C}_x : \mathcal{F}_x \to \mathcal{P}$ defined by:

$$\mathcal{C}_x(I) = P_i \quad \Leftrightarrow \quad \exists t \in I, \ \gamma(x,t) \in P_i \ .$$

The word ω_x is defined by:

$$\omega_x \text{ is the sequence } (\mathcal{C}_x(I))_{I \in \mathcal{F}_x} \ .$$

We denote by Ω the set of words associated with $(\mathcal{M}, \gamma)$ w.r.t. $\mathcal{P}$. In the sequel we will have to consider this construction w.r.t. different partitions.

Example 3.1. Consider the dynamical system and the partition $\mathcal{P} = \{A, B\}$ described in Figure 2. In this situation, we have $\Omega = \{A, ABA, ABABA\}$.

By encoding trajectories by words, we give a description of the "support" of the dynamical system. But, in order to recover the dynamics of a point in the trajectory, we need to encode more information: given a point (x,t) of the space-time, we want to know what the "position of $\gamma(x,t)$" in ω_x is. Given $(x,t) \in M^{k_1} \times M$, we associate a unique *dotted word* $\dot{\omega}_{(x,t)}$ in the following way: let $I \in \mathcal{F}_x$ be the unique interval such that $t \in I$, we add a dot on $\mathcal{C}_x(I)$ in ω_x. The set of dotted words associated with $(\mathcal{M}, \gamma)$ w.r.t. $\mathcal{P}$ is denoted by $\dot{\Omega}$.

Example 3.2. If we now consider the dotted words associated with Figure 2, we have $\dot{\Omega} = \{\dot{A}, \dot{A}BA, A\dot{B}A, AB\dot{A}, \dot{A}BABA, \ldots, ABAB\dot{A}\}$.

Remark 3.3. In general, γ is not injective and so a point y of the space M^{k_2} has more than one preimage (x,t). So several words ω_x and dotted words $\dot{\omega}_{(x,t)}$ are associated with y.

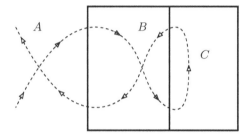

Fig. 3. Double loop

In view to describe this general situation, we introduce the notion of *dynamical type* W_y, for $y \in M^{k_2}$:

$$W_y = \big\{ \dot\omega_{(x,t)} \mid \exists (x,t) \in M^{k_1} \times M, \ \gamma(x,t) = y \big\}.$$

We denote by Δ the set of dynamical types associated with $(\mathcal{M}, \gamma)$ with respect to $\mathcal{P}$. Let us consider the partition given by the equivalence relation on the space M^{k_2} "*to have same dynamical type*". We can now repeat the previous construction w.r.t. this new partition (we will also denote it by Δ). So, we naturally obtain a set of words on Δ, denoted Ω_Δ. Let us notice that Δ is a refinement of $\mathcal{P}$. Given $x \in M^{k_1}$, we denote u_x the word on Δ associated with Γ_x, $\mathcal{F}_x^\Delta$ the ordered set of intervals induced on M and $\mathcal{C}_x^\Delta : \mathcal{F}_x^\Delta \to \Delta$ the coloration function.

Example 3.4. Figure 3 represents the trajectory Γ_x of some dynamical system through the partition $\mathcal{P} = \{A, B, C\}$, the word ω_x associated with the trajectory is $ABCBA$. For $y \in \Gamma_x$, there exists seven different dynamical types: $W_1 = \{\dot{A}BCBA\}, \ldots, W_5 = \{ABCB\dot{A}\}$, $W_6 = \{\dot{A}BCBA, ABCB\dot{A}\}$ and $W_7 = \{A\dot{B}CBA, ABC\dot{B}A\}$. The word u_x associated with the trajectory is $W_1 W_6 W_1 W_2 W_7 W_2 W_3 W_4 W_7 W_4 W_5 W_6 W_5$.

Given a trajectory Γ_x for some $x \in M^{k_1}$ and $y \in \Gamma_x$, we want to know "the position of y" in u_x. But by Remark 3.3 this position is not necessarily unique. We introduce a unique *multidotted word* $\ddot{u}_{(x,y)}$ in the following way: we add dots on $\mathcal{C}_x^\Delta(I)$ for all interval $I \in \mathcal{F}_x^\Delta$ such that there exists $t \in I$ with $\gamma(x,t) = y$.

We denote by $\ddot{\Omega}_\Delta$ the set of multidotted words associated with $(\mathcal{M}, \gamma)$ w.r.t. Δ.

4   O-Minimal Dynamical System

We have just described the general framework. Now we will be interested by *o-minimal dynamical systems*. In particular, we discuss two special and interesting cases in Sections 4.2 and 4.3. We freely use the notations introduced in the previous sections.

Definition 4.1. An *o-minimal dynamical system* $(\mathcal{M}, \gamma)$ is a dynamical system where $\mathcal{M}$ is an o-minimal structure.

4.1 Symbolic Dynamical System

In Section 3 we gave a description of the trajectories of any dynamical system in term of words. In the case of an o-minimal dynamical system, finitely many finite words are enough to describe the trajectories. This will allow us to define *finite* transition systems on the words.

Lemma 4.2. *Given* $(\mathcal{M}, \gamma)$ *an o-minimal dynamical system and a finite definable partition* $\mathcal{P}$, *the set of words* Ω *is a finite set of finite words.*

Proof. Let us recall from Section 3 that the partition $\mathcal{P}$ of the space induces a definable partition of the space-time whose regions are the $\tilde{P}_i$'s. Given $x \in M^{k_1}$, we have that $\mathcal{F}_x$ exactly consists in the connected components of the fibers of the $\tilde{P}_i$'s: $(\tilde{P}_i)_x = \{t \in M \mid \gamma(x, t) \in P_i\}$. By the Uniform Finiteness Theorem 2.10, we have that the number of connected components of the $(\tilde{P}_i)_x$'s is uniformly finite w.r.t. x, this implies that the length of the ω_x's is uniformly bounded. So since the number of P_i's is finite, we have that Ω is finite. □

The next result is a trivial consequence of Lemma 4.2 and the definition of $\dot{\Omega}$.

Corollary 4.3. $\dot{\Omega}$ *is finite.*

Remark 4.4. Let us remark that in the proof of Lemma 4.2, we just used the Uniform Finiteness Theorem 2.10. So this result holds in all the structures admitting the Uniform Finiteness Theorem 2.10.

We define $T_{\dot{\Omega}}$, a finite transition system on the dotted words. In order to mathematically formalize $T_{\dot{\Omega}}$, we need to introduce two functions: UNDOT : $\dot{\Omega} \to \Omega$ which gives the word ω corresponding to $\dot{\omega}$ without dot; DOT : $\dot{\Omega} \to \mathbb{N}$ which gives the position of the dot on $\dot{\omega}$. Given $x \in M^{k_1}$, the set $\mathcal{F}_x$ can be described as a finite ordered sequence of intervals $I_0 < I_1 < \cdots < I_k$ with $k < N_S$. If we consider $\dot{\omega}_x$ a dotted word constructed from ω_x, we have the following relation: the dot of $\dot{\omega}_x$ is on $\mathcal{C}_x(I_i)$ with $I_i \in \mathcal{F}_x$ if and only if DOT$(\dot{\omega}_x) = i$. We can now define $T_{\dot{\Omega}} = (\dot{\Omega}, \to_{\dot{\Omega}})$:

- the set of states Q is $\dot{\Omega}$
- the transition relation $\dot{\omega}_1 \to_{\dot{\Omega}} \dot{\omega}_2$ is defined by: the undotted words $\dot{\omega}_1$ and $\dot{\omega}_2$ are equal and the dot on $\dot{\omega}_2$ is on a righter (or on the same) position as the dot on $\dot{\omega}_1$. This can be formalized by:

$$\dot{\omega}_1 \to_{\dot{\Omega}} \dot{\omega}_2$$
$$\Updownarrow$$
$$\text{UNDOT}(\dot{\omega}_1) = \text{UNDOT}(\dot{\omega}_2) \text{ and } \text{DOT}(\dot{\omega}_1) \leqslant \text{DOT}(\dot{\omega}_2)$$

Example 4.5. Here is an example of transition on the dotted words w.r.t. Figure 2: $A\dot{B}ABAB \to_{\dot{\Omega}} ABAB\dot{A}B$

Lemma 4.6. *Given* $(\mathcal{M}, \gamma)$ *an o-minimal dynamical system and a finite definable partition* $\mathcal{P}$, *the set of words* Ω_Δ *is a finite set of finite words.*

Proof. We first notice that the number of dynamical types is finite since $|\Delta| \leqslant 2^{|\dot{\Omega}|}$ and $\dot{\Omega}$ is finite by Corollary 4.3. Since *being of dynamical type* W_y for some $W_y \in \Delta$ is definable, this induces a finite definable partition Δ of the space M^{k_2} and so we can use the same argument as in the proof of Lemma 4.2. $\square$

The next result is a trivial consequence of Lemma 4.6 and the definition of $\ddot{\Omega}_\Delta$.

Corollary 4.7. $\ddot{\Omega}_\Delta$ *is finite.*

We define also $T_{\ddot{\Omega}_\Delta}$, a finite transition system on the multidotted words. To mathematically formalize $T_{\ddot{\Omega}_\Delta}$, we need to introduce three functions: UNDOT : $\ddot{\Omega}_\Delta \to \Omega_\Delta$ gives the word u corresponding to $\ddot{u}$ without dot; MINDOT : $\ddot{\Omega}_\Delta \to \mathbb{N}$ gives the position of the left most dot on $\ddot{u}$ and MAXDOT : $\ddot{\Omega}_\Delta \to \mathbb{N}$ gives the position of the right most dot on $\ddot{u}$.

Given $x \in M^{k_1}$, the set $\mathcal{F}_x^\Delta$ can be described as a finite ordered sequence of intervals $I_0 < I_1 < \cdots < I_k$ with $k < N_S^\Delta$. If we consider a multidotted word $\ddot{u}_{(x,y)}$, constructed from u_x and y on the trajectory Γ_x, let W be the element of Δ such that $y \in W$. Those letters W correspond to some intervals $I_i \in \mathcal{F}_x^\Delta$ such that MINDOT$(\ddot{u}_{(x,y)}) \leqslant i \leqslant$ MAXDOT$(\ddot{u}_{(x,y)})$. We can now define $T_{\ddot{\Omega}_\Delta} = (\ddot{\Omega}_\Delta, \to_{\ddot{\Omega}_\Delta})$:

- the set of states is $\ddot{\Omega}_\Delta$
- the transition relation $\ddot{u}_1 \to_{\ddot{\Omega}_\Delta} \ddot{u}_2$ is defined by: the undotted words $\dot{u}_1$ and $\dot{u}_2$ are equal and the right most dot on $\ddot{u}_2$ is on a righter (or the same) position than the left most dot on $\dot{\omega}_1$. This can be formalized by:

$$\ddot{u}_1 \to_{\ddot{\Omega}_\Delta} \ddot{u}_2$$
$$\Updownarrow$$
$$\text{UNDOT}(\ddot{u}_1) = \text{UNDOT}(\ddot{u}_2) \quad \text{and} \quad \text{MINDOT}(\ddot{u}_1) \leqslant \text{MAXDOT}(\ddot{u}_2)$$

Example 4.8. Here is an example of transition on multidotted words w.r.t. Figure 3:

$$W_1\dot{W}_6W_1W_2W_7W_2W_3W_4W_7W_4W_5\dot{W}_6W_5$$
$$\to_{\ddot{\Omega}_\Delta} W_1W_6W_1W_2\dot{W}_7W_2W_3W_4\dot{W}_7W_4W_5W_6W_5$$

4.2   The Injective Case

The first situation that we will be interested in is the following: we suppose that there is a unique trajectory going through each point of the space M^{k_2} and that each trajectory does not self-intersect. In this situation, given $y \in M^{k_2}$, there exists a unique $(x,t) \in M^{k_1} \times M$ such that $\gamma(x,t) = y$. So the dotted words will encode enough information; precisely we can state the following theorem.

Theorem 4.9. *Let $(\mathcal{M}, \gamma)$ be an o-minimal dynamical system, let T_γ be the associated transition system on M^{k_2}, and let $\mathcal{P}$ be a finite definable partition of M^{k_2}. If from every $y \in M^{k_2}$ there exists a unique trajectory, which does not self-intersect, then there exists a finite bisimulation of T_γ that respects $\mathcal{P}$.*

Proof. To prove this theorem, we will show that there exists a bisimulation between the transition systems T_γ and $T_{\dot{\Omega}}$. Let us first recall that $T_{\dot{\Omega}}$ is a finite transition system by Corollary 4.3. We define a binary relation $\sim \, \subseteq M^{k_2} \times \dot{\Omega}$ as follow:

$$y \sim \dot{w} \quad \Leftrightarrow \quad \exists (x,t) \in M^{k_1} \times M, \ \left(\dot{w}_{(x,t)} = \dot{w} \text{ and } \gamma(x,t) = y \right).$$

Under the assumption of Theorem 4.9, given $y \in M^{k_2}$, there exists a unique $(x,t) \in M^{k_1} \times M$ such that $\gamma(x,t) = y$.

We begin by showing that $T_{\dot{\Omega}}$ simulates T_γ. Given $y_1, y_2 \in M^{k_2}$ and $\dot{w}_1 \in \dot{\Omega}$ such that $y_1 \to_\gamma y_2$ and $y_1 \sim \dot{w}_1$, we have to find $\dot{w}_2 \in \dot{\Omega}$ such that $\dot{w}_1 \to_{\dot{\Omega}} \dot{w}_2$ and $y_2 \sim \dot{w}_2$. By definition of $\to_\gamma$, there exists $x \in M^{k_1}$ and $t_1 \leqslant t_2 \in M$ such that $\gamma(x,t_1) = y_1$ and $\gamma(x,t_2) = y_2$. Since there exists a unique trajectory going though y_1, we have that $\dot{w}_1 = \dot{w}_{(x,t_1)}$. We set that $\dot{w}_2 = \dot{w}_{(x,t_2)}$. We have clearly that $y_2 \sim \dot{w}_2$. To prove that $\dot{w}_1 \to_{\dot{\Omega}} \dot{w}_2$, we first remark that $\text{UNDOT}(\dot{w}_1) = \text{UNDOT}(\dot{w}_2) = w_x$. Since $t_1 \leqslant t_2$, we have that $t_1 \in I_i$ an $t_2 \in I_j$, for some $I_i, I_j \in \mathcal{F}_x$, with $i \leqslant j$, so $\text{DOT}(\dot{w}_1) \leqslant \text{DOT}(\dot{w}_2)$.

Conversely let us prove that T_γ simulates $T_{\dot{\Omega}}$. Given $y_1 \in M^{k_2}$ and $\dot{w}_1$, $\dot{w}_2 \in \dot{\Omega}$ such that $\dot{w}_1 \to_{\dot{\Omega}} \dot{w}_2$ and $\dot{w}_1 \sim^{-1} y_1$, we have to find $y_2 \in M^{k_2}$ such that $y_1 \to_\gamma y_2$ and $\dot{w}_2 \sim^{-1} y_2$. Since $\dot{w}_1 \in \dot{\Omega}$, there exists $(x,t_1) \in M^{k_1} \times M$ such that $\dot{w}_1 = \dot{w}_{(x,t_1)}$ and $t_1 \in I_i$ for some $I_i \in \mathcal{F}_x$. We can find $I_j \in \mathcal{F}_x$ with $I_i \leqslant I_j$ such that if we add the dot corresponding to I_j on w_x we obtain $\dot{w}_2$. We take $t_2 \in I_j$, and set $y_2 = \gamma(x,t_2)$, we clearly have that $y_1 \to_\gamma y_2$ and $\dot{w}_2 \sim^{-1} y_2$.

We have proved that $\sim \, \subseteq M^{k_2} \times \dot{\Omega}$ is a bisimulation. Since a unique word is associated with each $y \in M^{k_2}$, it is a functional bisimulation. By Remark 2.6, $\sim$ induces a finite bisimulation on $M^{k_2} \times M^{k_2}$ given by $\text{Ker}(\sim)$; moreover, by definition of $\sim$ and $\text{Ker}(\sim)$, this bisimulation is an equivalence relation which respects $\mathcal{P}$. □

Remarks 4.10. By Theorem 4.9, we can recover the main result of [LPS, Theorem (4.3), p.11]. First by the argument that decouples the continuous and discrete components of the hybrid system given in [LPS, p. 6], we only need to prove that there exists a finite bisimulation on each location which respects the finite partition given by the resets, guards which are definable in the o-minimal structure we are working in, by assumption. In the assumptions of [LPS, Theorem (4.3), p.11], $\gamma(.,.)$ is the definable flow of a vector field $F : \mathbb{R}^n \to \mathbb{R}^n$ which does not depend of the time [LPS, p. 12], so in particular $\gamma(x,.)$ is injective [LPS, p. 13], therefore we are in situation of Theorem 4.9.

We can remark that in the proof of Theorem 4.9, we only use the Uniform Finiteness Theorem 2.10. In the proof of [LPS] *Cell decomposition* and the fact that *connectedness and arc-connectedness are equivalent* are used. If we were interested in bisimulations on the space-time, the proof of Theorem 4.9 shows that there always exists a finite bisimulation of $(\mathcal{M}, \gamma)$ that respects $\mathcal{P}$.

4.3 Self-Intersecting Curves

In this section, we consider a second situation: an o-minimal dynamical system such that with each point of the space is associated a unique trajectory but the trajectory can self-intersect (Figure 3 is an example of this situation). Let us remark that the self intersection set can be an arbitrary definable set.

In this context, given $y \in M^{k_2}$, there are different $(x,t) \in M^{k_1} \times M$ such that $\gamma(x,t) = y$. So the simple dotted words are no longer sufficient to encode the whole information. We will need the multidotted words.

Theorem 4.11. *Let $(\mathcal{M}, \gamma)$ be an o-minimal dynamical system, let T_γ be the associated transition system on M^{k_2}, and let $\mathcal{P}$ be a finite definable partition of M^{k_2}. If from every $y \in M^{k_2}$ there exists a unique trajectory then there exists a finite bisimulation of T_γ that respects $\mathcal{P}$.*

Proof. As in the proof of Theorem 4.9, we show that there exists a bisimulation between T_γ and $T_{\ddot{\Omega}_\Delta}$, which is a finite transition system by Corollary 4.7. We define a binary relation $\sim \subseteq M^{k_2} \times \ddot{\Omega}_\Delta$ in the following way:

$$y \sim \ddot{u} \quad \Leftrightarrow \quad \exists (x,t) \in M^{k_1} \times M, \ \left(\ddot{u}_{(x,y)} = \ddot{u} \text{ and } \gamma(x,t) = y \right).$$

Let us recall that there exists a unique multidotted word associated with each y (see last paragraph of Section 3).

First, we prove that $T_{\ddot{\Omega}_\Delta}$ simulates T_γ. Given $y_1, y_2 \in M^{k_2}$ and $\ddot{u}_1 \in \ddot{\Omega}_\Delta$ such that $y_1 \to_\gamma y_2$ and $y_1 \sim \ddot{u}_1$, we have to find $\ddot{u}_2 \in \ddot{\Omega}_\Delta$ such that $\ddot{u}_1 \to_{\ddot{\Omega}_\Delta} \ddot{u}_2$ and $y_2 \sim \ddot{u}_2$. By definition of $\to_\gamma$, there exists $x \in M^{k_1}$ and $t_1 \leqslant t_2 \in M$ such that $\gamma(x,t_1) = y_1$ and $\gamma(x,t_2) = y_2$. Since there is a unique trajectory going through y_1, we have that $\ddot{u}_1 = \ddot{u}_{(x,y_1)}$. By choosing $\ddot{u}_2 = \ddot{u}_{(x,y_2)}$, we have clearly that $y_2 \sim \ddot{u}_2$. Moreover we have that $\text{UNDOT}(\ddot{u}_1) = \text{UNDOT}(\ddot{u}_2)$. Since $t_1 \leqslant t_2$, $t_1 \in I_i$ and $t_2 \in I_j$ for some $I_i, I_j \in \mathcal{F}_x^\Delta$ with $i \leqslant j$ and so $\text{MINDOT}(\ddot{u}_1) \leqslant i \leqslant j \leqslant \text{MAXDOT}(\ddot{u}_2)$.

Conversely let us prove that T_γ simulates $T_{\ddot{\Omega}_\Delta}$. Given $y_1 \in M^{k_2}$ and $\ddot{u}_1$, $\ddot{u}_2 \in \ddot{\Omega}_\Delta$ such that $\ddot{u}_1 \to_{\ddot{\Omega}_\Delta} \ddot{u}_2$ and $\ddot{u}_1 \sim^{-1} y_1$, we have to find $y_2 \in M^{k_2}$ such that $y_1 \to_\gamma y_2$ and $\ddot{u}_2 \sim^{-1} y_2$. Since $\ddot{u}_1 \sim^{-1} y_1$, we have that $\ddot{u}_1 = \ddot{u}_{(x,y_1)}$ for some $x \in M^{k_1}$ and $y_1 = \gamma(x,t_1)$ for some $t_1 \in M$. We take $t_0 \in I_{\text{MINDOT}(\ddot{u}_1)} \in \mathcal{F}_x^\Delta$ such that $\gamma(x,t_0) = y_1$. Since $\text{MINDOT}(\ddot{u}_1) \leqslant \text{MAXDOT}(\ddot{u}_2)$, it is always possible to choose $t_2 \in I_{\text{MAXDOT}(\ddot{u}_2)} \in \mathcal{F}_x^\Delta$ such that $t_0 \leqslant t_2$. We now set $y_2 = \gamma(x,t_2)$.

All this construction respects the rules given for the composition of transitions (see the observation mentioned after Definition 2.13) .

We have proved that $\sim \subseteq M^{k_2} \times \ddot{\Omega}_\Delta$ is a bisimulation. Since there exists a unique multidotted word associated with each y, it is a functional bisimulation. By Remark 2.6, $\sim$ induces a finite bisimulation on $M^{k_2} \times M^{k_2}$ given by $\mathrm{Ker}(\sim)$. Moreover this bisimulation is an equivalence and clearly respects Δ, and so $\mathcal{P}$ since Δ is finer than $\mathcal{P}$.   □

Remark 4.12. In Theorems 4.9 and 4.11 the assumption that "there exists a unique trajectory going through $y \in M^{k_2}$" can be relaxed by requiring the uniqueness of the (multi)dotted word associated with each point y, as it can be seen by slight modifications of the proofs.

Remark 4.13. If we look at a different transition system on $(\mathcal{M}, \gamma)$ where the set of states Q is given by $M^{k_1} \times M^{k_2}$ and the transition relation $(x_1, y_1) \to_{\tilde{\gamma}} (x_2, y_2)$ is defined by: $(x_1 = x_2) \wedge \exists t_1 \leqslant t_2 \in M \; ((\gamma(x_1, t_1) = y_1) \wedge (\gamma(x_2, t_2) = y_2))$, the proof of Theorem 4.11 shows that any such o-minimal dynamical system admits a finite bisimulation which respects a given finite definable partition $\mathcal{P}$.

4.4   Counter-Example on the Torus

We proved that in particular situations (see Sections 4.2 and 4.3) we can obtain a finite bisimulation of the space w.r.t. a given partition. Unfortunately, we cannot hope to extend this result to any o-minimal dynamical system. This will be illustrated in this section by the study of a dynamical system on the torus. To establish the lack of finite bisimulation w.r.t. a given partition, it is sufficient to show the non-termination of the *bisimulation algorithm* appearing in [BFH, Hen95].

Given a transition system $T = (Q, \Sigma, \to)$ and $\mathcal{P}$ a finite transition of Q, the bisimulation algorithm iterates the computation of predecessors,[5] let us recall this algorithm:

Initialization: $Q/\sim := \mathcal{P}$
While $\exists P, P' \in Q/\sim$ such that $\varnothing \neq P \cap \mathrm{Pre}(P') \neq P$
   Set $P_1 = P \cap \mathrm{Pre}(P')$ and $P_2 = P \setminus \mathrm{Pre}(P')$
      Refine $Q/\sim := (Q/\sim \setminus \{P\}) \cup \{P_1, P_2\}$
End while

We work in the structure $\mathcal{M} = \langle \mathbb{R}, <, +, \cdot, 0, 1, \sin\lceil_{[0,4\pi]}\rangle$ which is o-minimal, as it can be seen from [vdD96]. A torus is a definable set of $\mathcal{M}$ since it is given by the following equations:

$$\begin{pmatrix} x \\ y \\ z \end{pmatrix} = \begin{pmatrix} (R + r\cos u)\cos v \\ (R + r\cos u)\sin v \\ r\sin u \end{pmatrix} =: \varphi(u, v)$$

with $u, v \in [0, 2\pi[$.

---

[5] Given T a transition system and $q \in Q$, the set of predecessors of q, denoted $\mathrm{Pre}(q)$, is defined by $\mathrm{Pre}(q) = \{q' \in Q | \exists a \in \Sigma, \; q' \xrightarrow{a} q\}$.

We define a dynamics $\gamma : [0, 2\pi[^2 \times \mathbb{R} \times \mathbb{R} \to \mathbb{R}^3$ on the torus : for all $t \in [0, 2\pi[$,

$$\gamma(u_0, v_0, a, t) = \begin{cases} \varphi(u_0 + t, v_0 + t) & \text{if } a = 1, \\ \varphi(u_0 + t, v_0 + 2t) & \text{if } a = 2, \\ \varphi(u_0, v_0) & \text{otherwise.} \end{cases}$$

The dynamics is definable in $\mathcal{M}$, so $(\mathcal{M}, \gamma)$ is an o-minimal dynamical system and the transition relation is the one given in Definition 2.13. The torus can be represented by a *square of length 2π where the opposite sides are identified*. We adopt this description in order to study the dynamics on the torus. Therefore the trajectories on the torus are given by pieces of lines on the square. We note that trajectories are closed curves. In this context, the equation of the dynamics $\gamma : [0, 2\pi[^2 \times \mathbb{R} \times \mathbb{R} \to [0, 2\pi[^2$ becomes :

$$\gamma(u_0, v_0, a, t) = \begin{cases} (u_0 + t, v_0 + t) \bmod 2\pi & \text{if } a = 1 \text{ and } t \in [0, 2\pi[, \\ (u_0 + t, v_0 + 2t) \bmod 2\pi & \text{if } a = 2 \text{ and } t \in [0, 2\pi[, \\ (u_0, v_0) & \text{otherwise.} \end{cases}$$

Given a point $(u_0, v_0) \in [0, 2\pi[^2$, three behaviors of the dynamics are possible: it can follow a line of slope 1 or 2, or it can remain stationary (see Figure 4).

We consider the following initial partition of the square $\mathcal{P} = \{P_0, P_1, P_2, P_3\}$ where:

$$P_0 = \{(0,0)\}, \qquad\qquad P_1 = \{(0, v) \mid v \in]0, 2\pi[\},$$
$$P_2 = \{(u, 0) \mid u \in]0, 2\pi[\}, \qquad P_3 = [0, 2\pi[^2 \backslash (P_0 \cup P_1 \cup P_2).$$

This induces a definable (in the sense of the structure $\mathcal{M}$) partition of the torus.

We will now apply the bisimulation algorithm and show that it does not terminate when we take this initial partition.

To formalize the non-termination of the algorithm we need to compute the set of predecessors of a given point (y_1, y_2) of the space. By the previous observation, we have that :

$$\mathrm{Pre}(y_1, y_2) = \{(y_1 + t, y_2 + t) \bmod 2\pi \mid t \in [0, 2\pi]\} \cup$$
$$\{(y_1 + t, y_2 + 2t) \bmod 2\pi \mid t \in [0, 2\pi]\}$$

We observe that the sets $\mathrm{Pre}(y_1, y_2) \cap P_1$ and $\mathrm{Pre}(y_1, y_2) \cap P_2$ are finite. The iterations of the **While** instruction of the bisimulation algorithm isolates[6] an infinite number of points. The next lemma formalizes this :

Lemma 4.14. *For each $n \geqslant 0$, there exists odd integers k, k' such that the algorithm isolates the points $(k\pi/2^n, 0)$ and $(0, k'\pi/2^n)$.*

Proof. We proceed by induction on n.

(1) In the case $n = 0$, we isolate $(\pi, 0)$ starting from $\{(0,0)\}$ and then we isolate $(0, \pi)$ by using the new isolated point $\{(\pi, 0)\}$, as shown on Figure 6.

---

[6] By "isolating a point q" we mean that the algorithm has constructed $P \in Q/\sim$ such that $P = \{q\}$.

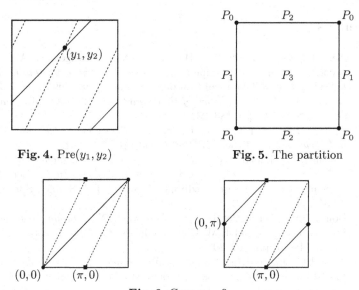

Fig. 4. Pre(y_1, y_2)　　　　　**Fig. 5.** The partition

Fig. 6. Case $n = 0$

(2) Suppose now that we have isolated the points $(0, k\pi/2^n)$ and $(k'\pi/2^n, 0)$ with k, k' satisfying the required conditions, we show how to obtain the new isolated points:

- Consider first the intersection $A = \text{Pre}(0, k\pi/2^n) \cap (X \times \{0\})$ where $X \times \{0\}$ is an element of a sub-partition of P_2; by the characterization of the predecessors above, we have that

$$(x, 0) \in A$$
$$\Leftrightarrow \exists t \in [0, 2\pi], \ \big(t = x \bmod 2\pi \ \text{ and } \ k\pi/2^n = -t \bmod 2\pi\big) \ \text{ or }$$
$$\big(t = x \bmod 2\pi \ \text{ and } \ k\pi/2^n = -2t \bmod 2\pi\big)$$
$$\Leftrightarrow x = 2\pi - k\pi/2^n \ \text{ or } \ x = 2\pi - k\pi/2^{n+1}$$

The second part of this disjunction permits to isolate the new point $(2^{n+2} - k)\pi/2^{n+1}$ with $2^{n+2} - k = 1 \pmod 2$.
- Using the same argument when considering $B = \text{Pre}(k'n/2^n) \cap (\{0\} \times Y)$, we obtain the second isolated point of the lemma. □

Remark 4.15. Maybe the discussion above does not enlighten where the assumptions of Theorems 4.9 and 4.11 are not satisfied by the dynamics. In fact there are points y of the torus with several trajectories going through and even several multidotted words associated with y. For example the multidotted words $\dot{P}_0$, $\dot{P}_0 P_3$ and $\dot{P}_0 P_3 P_2$ are associated with $(0, 0)$.

Acknowledgments. The authors would like to thank Véronique Bruyère for careful reading of drafts of this paper and relevant comments. They want also to thank the referees for their remarks.

References

[ACH+]   Alur R., Courcoubetis C., Halbwachs N., Henzinger T. A., Ho P.-H., Nicollin X., Olivero A., Sifakis J., Yovine S., *The algorithmic analysis of hybrid systems*, Theoretical Computer Science, **138** (1995), pp. 3–34.

[AD]   Alur R., Dill D. L., *A theory of timed automata*, Theoretical Computer Science, **126** (1994), pp. 183–235.

[AHLP]   Alur R., Henzinger T. A., Lafferriere G., Pappas G. J., *Discrete abstractions of hybrid systems*, Proc. IEEE **88** (2000), pp. 971–984.

[ASY]   Asarin E., Schneider G., Yovine S., *On the Decidability of the Reachability Problem for Planar Differential Inclusions*, In Di Benedetto and A. Sangiovanni-Vincentelli, editors, HSCC 01, LNCS 2034, Springer-Verlag (2001), pp. 89–104.

[BFH]   Bouajjani A., Fernandez J.-C., and Halbwachs N., *Minimal model generation*, In R.P. Kurshan and E.M. Clarke, editors, CAV 90, LNCS 531, Springer-Verlag (1990), pp. 197–203.

[Cau]   Caucal D., *Bisimulation of context-free grammars and push-down automata*, In Modal logic and process algebra, CSLI Lecture Notes, Stanford (1995), Vol. **53**, pp. 85–106.

[vdD96] van den Dries L., *o-Minimal Structures*, In Logic: from Foundations to Applications, European Logic Colloquium, Oxford University Press (1996) pp. 137–185.

[vdD98] van den Dries L., *Tame Topology and O-minimal Structures*, Cambridge University Press, Cambridge (1998).

[Hen95] Henzinger T. A., *Hybrid automata with finite bisimulations*, In ICALP'95, LNCS 944, Springer-Verlag (1995), pp. 324–335.

[Hen96] Henzinger T. A., *The Theory of Hybrid Automata*, Proceedings of the 11th Annual Symposium on Logic in Computer Science, IEEE Computer Society Press (1996), pp. 278–292.

[HKPV]   Henzinger T. A., Kopke P. W., Puri A., and Varaiya P., *What's decidable about hybrid automata?*, Journal of Computer and System Sciences, **57** (1998), pp. 94–124.

[Ho]   Hodges W., *A Shorter Model Theory*, Cambridge University Press, Cambridge (1997).

[LGS]   Lygeros J., Godbole D. N., Sastry S., *Verified hybrid controllers for automated vehicles*, IEEE Transactions on Automatic Control, **43**, 4 (1998), pp. 522–539.

[LPS]   Lafferriere G., Pappas G. J., Sastry S., *O-Minimal Hybrid Systems*, Mathematics of control, signals and systems, **13** (2000), pp. 1–21.

[TPS]   Tomlin C., Pappas G. J., and Sastry S., *Conflict resolution for air traffic management : A study in multi-agent hybrid systems*, IEEE Transactions on Automatic Control, **43**, 4 (1998), pp. 509–521.

[Tr]   Truss J., *Infinite permutation groups II - subgroups of small index* J. Algebra, **120** (1989), pp. 494–515.

Extended Stochastic Hybrid Systems and Their Reachability Problem*

Manuela L. Bujorianu

Department of Engineering,
University of Cambridge,
Cambridge, CB2 1PZ, UK
lmb56@eng.cam.ac.uk

Abstract. In this paper we generalize a model for stochastic hybrid systems. First, we prove that this model is a right Markov process and it satisfies some mathematical properties. Second, we propose a method based on the theory of Dirichlet forms to study the reachability problem associated with these systems.

Keywords: stochastic hybrid systems, reachability problem, extended automata, Markov processes, Dirichlet forms.

1 Introduction

In this paper we extend the stochastic hybrid system (SHS) model introduced by Lygeros et. al. in [15]. We call this new model *extended stochastic hybrid systems* (ESHS) (see section 2). In the first step we prove that this model is a Borel right process with the CADLAG property (section 3). In a second step we mainly study the reachability problem for ESHS (section 4). In a probabilistic framework, the reachability problem consists in determining the probability that the system trajectories enter some prespecified set starting from a certain set of initial conditions with a given probability distribution. Our investigation begins with a simple observation, namely, an ESHS is interleaving between a jump process and some diffusion processes. Therefore, studying the reachability problem for this model requires two reachability problems to be solved: one for the jump process and another one for the diffusion processes. Dealing with the standard apparatus of Markov processes (hitting times, hitting probability, harmonic measure), solving the reachability problem seems to be quite difficult.

This work promotes a new method, based on the theory of Dirichlet forms [14, 17], for the reachability problem. It has already been proved in the literature that Dirichlet forms constitute a powerful tool for studying Markov processes (see, for example, [1,17] and the references therein). Dirichlet form techniques have found striking applications in the study of stochastic partial differential equations [1, 8]. This is mainly due to the fact that they allow to develop a highly nontrivial stochastic analysis under some minimal regularity hypothesis, for instance, on

---

* Work Supported by European Comission under COLUMBUSIST-2001-38314.

R. Alur and G.J. Pappas (Eds.): HSCC 2004, LNCS 2993, pp. 234–249, 2004.

very irregular spaces without differentiable structure like fractals, or on infinite dimensional spaces like path spaces or spaces of measures.

For Dirichlet forms, a lot of work was carried out on axiomatizations and representation results. This provides a mathematical vehicle for zooming in and out at different levels of abstraction in a consistent way. For example, in the most abstract view, the Dirichlet spaces can be seen as mixing a linear space structure with a partial order structure, by providing simple compatibility axioms. In more concrete applications a Dirichlet space defines a logical type of functions with an inner product given explicitly by a logical expression. The advantage of Dirichlet forms which derives from this is that they can be easily implemented. There are two main streams: one is symbolic (like using a model-checker or a theorem prover or their combination like PVS [13]) and another one is numerical [10]. For the reachability problem the symbolic approach has been intensively applied (see e.g. the papers in [18]), especially because the accessible states can be generated. In the case of PVS, we can link these techniques with the huge mathematical libraries made available by the theorem provers.

The basic idea of the reachability method proposed here is to employ the correspondence between some 'nice' Markov processes (like our process) and some quadratic forms, called *Dirichlet forms*, defined using the process generator. Each (quasi-regular) Dirichlet form can be expressed as the sum of its parts: continuous, jumping and killing corresponding to the same parts of the Markov process considered. A Dirichlet form comes with the so-called notion of *capacity*, which is, roughly speaking, a nonlinear extension of a measure. The capacity associated with a Dirichlet form is in a very close connection with the hitting times of the corresponding Markov process. We investigate the possible benefits of applying a Dirichlet form based method to study the reachability problem of ESHS. Developing a reachability analysis methodology for this model will involve dealing with its two characteristics: forced jumps and diffusion segments between two consecutive jumps. In what follows, we will work with the corresponding jumping and continuous Dirichlet forms. Usually a target set E in the state space is a level set for a given function F, i.e. $E = \{\alpha | F(\alpha) > l\}$ (F can be chosen as the Euclidean norm or as the distance to the boundary of E). The probability of the set of trajectories which hit E until time horizon $T > 0$ can be expressed as $P\{ \sup_{t \in [0,T]} F(\alpha_t) > l\}$. An upper estimation for this probability will be given in terms of the Dirichlet form induced by F on $\mathbb{R}$. This form corresponds to the process $F(\alpha_t)$. One might, for instance, use the small induced processes rather then the huge original process to deal with the reachability problem. The induced Dirichlet form capacity (of $E^* = (l, \infty)$) plays an essential role in obtaining the reach event probability estimation. Intuitively, this capacity is the Laplace transform of the hitting time of the target set. If the model H is discretized then the induced process is a one-dimensional jump process and therefore the computation of Laplace transform and the mean level-crossing time is feasible. It is interesting to note that the capacity of the target set is subadditive. So even if the target set were very complex, then the capacity of target set is at most the sum of capacities of its parts.

2   Stochastic Hybrid Model

Stochastic Hybrid Systems (SHS) introduced in [15] are a class of non-linear, continuous-time stochastic hybrid processes. In this section we give a generalization of SHS called extended stochastic hybrid systems (ESHS). ESHS will be object for the reachability problem studied in section 4. ESHS can be considered, as well, a generalization of the model used in [4].

2.1   Model Description

ESHS involve a hybrid state space, with both continuous and discrete states. The continuous and the discrete parts of the state variable have their own natural dynamics, but the main point is to capture the interaction between them.

The time t is measured continuously. The state of the system is represented by a continuous variable x and a discrete variable i. The continuous variable evolves in some 'cells' X_i (open sets in the Euclidean space) and the discrete variable belongs to a countable set Q. The intrinsic difference between the discrete and continuous variables, consists of the way that they evolve through time. The continuous state is governed by an SDE that depends on the hybrid state. The discrete dynamics produces transitions in both (continuous and discrete) state variables x, i. Transitions occur when the continuous state hits a predefined set of the state space (forced transitions). Whenever a transition occurs the hybrid state is reset instantly to a new value. The value of the discrete state after the transition is determined uniquely by the hybrid state before the transition. On the other hand, the new value of the continuous state obeys a probability law which depends on the last hybrid state. Thus, a sample trajectory has the form $(q(t), x(t), t \geq 0)$, where $(x(t), t \geq 0)$ is piecewise continuous and $q(t) \in Q$ is piecewise constant. Let $(0 \leq T_1 \leq T_2 \leq ... \leq T_i \leq T_{i+1} \leq ...)$ be the sequence of jump times at which the continuous and the discrete part of the system interact. This time sequence is generated when the state of the system passes through a set of 'marked states' called set-interface.

2.2   Mathematical Model

Definition 1 (Extended Stochastic Hybrid System). *An ESHS is an extended automaton* $H = (Q, X, Dom, D, b, \sigma, Init, G, R)$ *where*

- *Q is a countable set of discrete variables[1];*
- *$X = \mathbb{R}^n$ is the continuous state space and $\mathcal{B}(\mathbb{R}^n)$ its σ-algebra Borel;*
- *$Dom : Q \to 2^X$, $Q \ni i \mapsto X_i \subset X$, with X_i a relatively compact open set;*
- *$D : Q \to 2^X$ assigns to each $i \in Q$ a measurable subset (an interface set) D_i of X such that $\partial X_i \subset D_i$.*
- *$b : Q \times X \to \mathbb{R}^n$, $\sigma : Q \times X \to \mathbb{R}^{n \times n}$;*
- *$Init : \mathcal{B}(Q \times X) \to [0, 1]$ is an initial probability measure on $(Q \times X, \mathcal{B}(Q \times X))$ concentrated on $\cup_{i \in Q} \{i\} \times X_i$;*

---

[1] Q can be taken as the set of natural numbers.

- $G : Q \times Q \to 2^X$ maps each $(i,j) \in Q \times Q$ into $G(i,j) \subset X$ such that
  $(\forall)$ $(i,j) \in Q \times Q$, $G(i,j)$ is a measurable subset of D_i (possibly empty);
  $(\forall)$ $i \in Q$, the family $\{G(i,j) \mid j \in Q\}$ is a disjoint partition of D_i;
- $R : Q \times Q \times X \to \mathcal{P}(X)$ assigns to each $(i,j) \in Q \times Q$ and $x \in G(i,j)$ a
  reset probability kernel on X concentrated on X_j.

To describe the dynamics, we need to consider an n-dimensional standard Wiener process $(W(t), t \geq 0)$ in a complete probability space $(\Omega, \mathcal{F}, P)$.

Assumption 1 *The functions $b(i,x)$ and $\sigma(i,x)$ are bounded and Lipschitz continuous in x. For all $i, j \in Q$ and for any measurable set $A \subset X_j$, $R(i,j,x)(A)$ is a measurable function in x.*

The first part of the Assumption 1 ensures, for any $i \in Q$, the existence and uniqueness (Theorem 6.2.2. in [2]) of the solution for the following SDE

$$dx(t) = b(i, x(t))dt + \sigma(i, x(t))dW_t,$$

where W_t is a n-dimensional standard Wiener process. Moreover, the assumption on R ensures that events we encounter later are measurable w.r.t. the underlying σ-field, hence their probabilities make sense.

We can introduce the ESHS execution.

Definition 2 (ESHS Execution). *A stochastic process $\alpha_t = (q(t), x(t))$ is called a ESHS execution if there exists a sequence of stopping times $T_0 = 0 \leq T_1 \leq T_2 \leq \ldots$ such that for each $j \in \mathbb{N}$,*

- $\alpha_0 = (q(0), x(0))$ is a $Q \times X$-valued random variable extracted according to the probability measure Init;
- For $t \in [T_j, T_{j+1})$, $q(t) = q(T_j)$ is constant and $x(t)$ is a (continuous) solution of the SDE:

$$dx(t) = b(q(T_j), x(t))dt + \sigma(q(T_j), x(t))dW_t \tag{1}$$

  where W_t is a n-dimensional standard Wiener process;
- $T_{j+1} = \inf \left\{ t \geq T_j : x(t-) \in D_{q(T_j)} \right\}$ (which is equal to $+\infty$ if the process never hits the target $D_{q(T_j)}$);
- $x(T_{j+1}^-) \in G(q(T_j), q(T_{j+1}))$, where $x(T_{j+1}^-)$ denotes $\lim_{t \uparrow T_{j+1}} x(t)$;
- The probability distribution of $x(T_{j+1})$ is governed by the law
  $R\left(q(T_j), q(T_{j+1}), x(T_{j+1}^-)\right)$.

Remark 1. The continuous post jump location $x(T_{j+1})$ is given by R and the hybrid state before jump, but the discrete post jump location $q(T_{j+1})$ depends only on the hybrid state before jump. In the stochastic model from [4], both continuous and discrete post jump locations depend on the hybrid state before jump and some i.i.d. random variables, which are independent of W_t.

3   Model Summary

3.1   Hybrid State Space

Let us define the hybrid state space and its 'boundary' as follows:

$$\mathbb{S} = \bigcup_{i \in Q} \{i\} \times X_i; \quad \overline{\mathbb{S}} = \mathbb{S} \cup \overline{\partial}\mathbb{S};$$

$$\overline{\partial}\mathbb{S} = \bigcup_{i \in Q} \{i\} \times D_i = \bigcup_{i \in Q} \left(\{i\} \times \bigcup_{j \in Q, j \neq i} G(i,j) \right).$$

Let us denote $\mathbb{S}_i = \{i\} \times X_i$, $\overline{\partial}\mathbb{S}_i = \{i\} \times D_i$ for every $i \in Q$. We can refine the last notation as follows: $\overline{\partial}\mathbb{S}_i = \bigcup_{j \in Q, j \neq i} \overline{\partial}\mathbb{S}_{ij}$ where $\overline{\partial}\mathbb{S}_{ij} = \{i\} \times G(i,j)$ for $i \neq j$. Define $\mathcal{B}(\widetilde{\mathbb{S}})$ as the σ-algebra on the set $\widetilde{\mathbb{S}} = Q \times \mathbb{R}^n$ generated by the sets $\{2^Q \times \mathcal{B}(\mathbb{R}^n)\}$. Let $\mathcal{B}(\overline{\mathbb{S}})$ be the σ-algebra on $\overline{\mathbb{S}}$ induced by $\mathcal{B}(\widetilde{\mathbb{S}})$. It is possible to define a metric ρ on $\overline{\mathbb{S}}$ in such a way that $\rho(\alpha_n, \alpha) \to 0$ as $n \to \infty$ with $\alpha_n = (i_n, x_n)$, $\alpha = (i, x)$ if and only if there exists m such that $i_n = i$ for all $n \geq m$ and $x_{m+k} \to x$ as $k \to \infty$. The metric ρ restricted to any component X_i is equivalent to the usual Euclidean metric [12]. Then $(\overline{\mathbb{S}}, \mathcal{B}(\overline{\mathbb{S}}))$ is a Borel space[2]. A cemetery point $\Delta \notin \overline{\mathbb{S}}$ is adjoined to $\overline{\mathbb{S}}$ as an isolated point, $\overline{\mathbb{S}}_\Delta \equiv \overline{\mathbb{S}} \cup \{\Delta\}$. Using the Lebesgue measure λ on $\mathbb{R}^n$, we define a measure m on $\mathcal{B}(\overline{\mathbb{S}})$ such that for each $i \in Q$ the projection of m to X_i is exactly $\lambda|_{X_i}$.

$$m(Q' \times A) := cardQ' \cdot \lambda(A), \quad Q' \subset Q, \ A \in \mathcal{B}(\mathbb{R}^n).$$

One can then consider the reset probability kernel of an ESHS as a transition measure $R : \overline{\mathbb{S}} \times \mathcal{B}(\overline{\mathbb{S}}) \to [0,1]$ such that: (i) $R((i,x), \cdot) = 0$, for all $(i,x) \in \overline{\mathbb{S}} \backslash \overline{\partial}\mathbb{S}$; (ii) for all $A \in \mathcal{B}(\overline{\mathbb{S}})$, $R(\cdot, A)$ is measurable; (iii) for all $(i,x) \in \overline{\partial}\mathbb{S}$ the function $R((i,x), \cdot)$ is a probability measure concentrated on $\{j\} \times X_j$ where j is the unique value of the discrete state such that $x \in G(i,j)$.

In short we have, the stochastic execution is given by

$$dx(t) = \{b(q(t), x(t)) + \sum_{j=0}^{\infty} [x(T_j) - x(T_j^-)]\delta_{(t-T_i)}\}dt + \sigma(q(t), x(t))dW_t;$$

$$q(t) = \sum_{j=0}^{\infty} [q(T_j) - q(T_j^-)]1_{(T_j \leq t)}$$

where δ is the Dirac measure and

$$x(T_j)(\omega) = \Psi(\omega, (q(T_j^-), x(T_j^-)(\omega))); \quad q(T_j)(\omega) = \sum_{i \in Q} i1_{G(q(T_j^-), i)}(x(T_j^-)(\omega))$$

---

[2] Recall that a Borel space is a topological space which is homeomorphic to a Borel subset of a complete separable metric space.

3.2   Markov Property

In this subsection we prove that any ESHS is a Borel right process (i.e. a right Markov process whose semigroup maps $\mathcal{B}(\overline{\mathbb{S}})^3$ into itself). A *right process* was originally defined by P. A. Meyer [19] as a process satisfying two *hypothèses droites* HD1 and HD2. A right process is a strong Markov process with the following properties: (i) The state space is Lusin[4] (i.e. it is isomorphic to a Borel subset of a compact metrizable space); (ii) It is right continuous; (iii) The p-excessive functions ($p > 0$) of the process are almost surely right continuous (If P_t is a Markov semigroup then a function f is p-excessive if it non-negative and $e^{-pt}P_t f \leq f$ for all $t \geq 0$ and $e^{-pt}P_t f \nearrow f$ as $t \searrow 0$).

Let H be an ESHS. We use the same notations as in the subsection 3.1.

Proposition 1. *Under the standard Assumption 1, any Extended Stochastic Hybrid System, H is a Borel right process.*

Proof. First we prove that H is a right Markov process. Clear, the state space $\overline{\mathbb{S}}$ is Lusin space (it is a Borel space and its closure can be embedded in a compact space). We have a countable number of state spaces $(\overline{\mathbb{S}}_i)_{i \in Q}$ provided with the *Feller semigroups*[5] $(P_t^i)_{i \in Q}$ associated with the diffusion processes defined by (1). Δ can be considered adjoined to all these spaces. The spaces Ω, Ω_i are taken as the canonical realizations with values in $\overline{\mathbb{S}}$, $\overline{\mathbb{S}}_i$ (see the remark below). We provide Ω with the measures P^α, $\alpha \in \overline{\mathbb{S}}$ such that if $\alpha \in \overline{\mathbb{S}}_i$ the measure P^α is equal to P^α corresponding to Ω_i (P^α is a measure on Ω supported by Ω_i). Since $\overline{\mathbb{S}}$ is a Borel space, then $\overline{\mathbb{S}}$ is homeomorphic to a subset of the Hilbert cube, $\mathcal{H}$[6] (Urysohn's theorem, Prop. 7.2 [6]). Moreover, X is a homeomorphic with a Borel subset of a compact metric space (Lusin space) because it is a locally compact Hausdorff space with countable base (see [12] and the references therein). The ESHP model is obtained by 'melange' operation [20] of the diffusion processes $(i, x(t))_{i \in Q}$, each one defined on $\overline{\mathbb{S}}_i$. Since each diffusion is, in particular, a right process, then the whole process is a right Markov process (Th.1 in [20]). The 'renaissance' kernel Ψ [20] used to mix the diffusion processes is given by

$$\Psi(\omega^i, A) = R((i, x(T_i^-)), A), \quad A \in \mathcal{B}(\mathbb{S})$$

where ω^i is a diffusion trajectory and $x(T_i^-)$ is its boundary hitting point.

Secondly, we prove that H is a Borel right process. Let (P_t) be the transition semigroup of (α_t) i.e. $P_t f(\alpha) = \mathbf{E}^\alpha[f(\alpha_t)]$, $\alpha \in \overline{\mathbb{S}}$, where $\mathbf{E}^\alpha$ is the expectation w.r.t. P^α, for all functions f for which the right-hand sides make sense. Let be f a bounded Borel function on $\overline{\mathbb{S}}$ and f_j the restriction of f to $\overline{\mathbb{S}}_i$. Let $t > 0$. Then $t \in [T_i, T_{i+1})$ where $(T_j)_{j \in \mathbb{N}}$ is the sequence of stopping times from definition 2. The construction of H implies the following equality

$$P_t f(\alpha) = \mathbf{E}^\alpha[f(\alpha_t)] = \mathbf{E}^\alpha[f(\alpha_t^{q(T_i)})|T_i \leq t < T_{i+1}] = P_t^{q(T_i)} f_{q(T_i)}(\alpha)$$

---

[3] here $\mathcal{B}(\overline{\mathbb{S}})$ is understood as the set of all real Borel functions defined on $\overline{\mathbb{S}}$.

[4] This condition is missing in other Markov process monographs, see e.g. [7].

[5] i.e. the function $\alpha \rightarrow P_t^i f(\alpha)$ is continuous for each $t \in \mathbb{R}_+$ if f is a bounded continuous function.

[6] $\mathcal{H}$ is the product of countable many copies of $[0, 1]$.

where $(\alpha_t^{q(T_i)})$ is the restriction of (α_t) to $[T_i, T_{i+1})$. Note that if $\alpha \notin \overline{\mathbb{S}}_{q(T_i)}$ then $P_t f(\alpha) = 0$. Therefore $P_t f$ is supported by $\overline{\mathbb{S}}_{q(T_i)}$ where it is a Borel function $(P_t^{q(T_i)}$ is Feller). Then $P_t f$ is a Borel function.

Remark 2. It is clear from the construction, that an ESHS has the CADLAG property (i.e. its trajectories are right continuous with left limits). Then the underlying probability space Ω can be taken, in a canonical way, equal to $D_{[0,\infty)}(\overline{\mathbb{S}})^7$.

3.3   Process Generator

We denote by $\mathcal{B}_b(\overline{\mathbb{S}})$ the set of all bounded measurable functions $f : \overline{\mathbb{S}} \to \mathbb{R}$. This is a Banach space under the norm $\|f\| = \sup_{\alpha \in \overline{\mathbb{S}}} |f(\alpha)|$. Associated with the semigroup (P_t) is its *strong generator* which, loosely speaking, is the derivative of P_t at $t = 0$. Let $D(L) \subset \mathcal{B}_b(X)$ be the set of functions f for which the following limit exists

$$\lim_{t \searrow 0} \frac{1}{t}(P_t f - f) \tag{2}$$

and denote this limit Lf. The limit refers to convergence in the norm $\|\cdot\|$, i.e. for $f \in D(L)$ we have

$$\lim_{t \searrow 0} \left\| \frac{1}{t}(P_t f - f) - Lf \right\| = 0.$$

The results from [3] give us the possibility to write the generator of any process as the sum of its corresponding continuous and jump parts. For $f \in C^2(Q \times \mathbb{R}^n) = \{f : Q \times \mathbb{R}^n \to \mathbb{R} | f(i, \cdot) \in C^2(\mathbb{R}^n)$ for all $i \in Q\}$ the expression of the ESHS generator [21] is

$$Lf(\alpha) = L^c f(\alpha) + L^j f(\alpha)$$

where

$$L^c f(\alpha) = \frac{1}{2} \sum_{k,m,l=1}^{n} \sigma_{kl}(\alpha)\sigma_{ml}(\alpha)\frac{\partial^2 f}{\partial \alpha_k \partial \alpha_m} + \sum_{k=1}^{n} b_k(\alpha)\frac{\partial f}{\partial \alpha_k}$$

and L^j is the *Lévy operator*, given by

$$L^j f(\alpha) = \int_{\overline{\partial \mathbb{S}}} (f(\beta) - f(\alpha))R(\alpha, d\beta).$$

Since any ESHS is a right Markov process, according to [5], there exists a Lévy system associated to the process. Recall that a Lévy system (n, dH_t) for a process (α_t) is a kernel $n(\alpha, d\beta)$ and a perfect continuous additive functional H_t (see the definition in [7]) such that such that for all α in the state space $\overline{\mathbb{S}}$, for

---

[7] $D_{[0,\infty)}(\overline{\mathbb{S}})$ is the space of all right continuous functions on $[0,\infty)$ with left limits taking values in $\overline{\mathbb{S}}$.

all stopping times T, and for all positive Borel measurable functions f on $\overline{\mathbb{S}} \times \overline{\mathbb{S}}$ that are 0 on the diagonal, the *Lévy system identity* holds:

$$\mathbf{E}^\alpha \sum_{0<t\le T} f(\alpha_{t-},\alpha_t) = \mathbf{E}^\alpha \int_0^T \int f(\alpha_t,\beta)n(\alpha_t,d\beta)dH_t \tag{3}$$

where both sides may be infinite. We will assume without loss of generality that $H_t(\omega) = t$ for all t and all ω, since one can always perform a time change on α_t [3]. For our process the Lévy kernel n can be chosen to be equal with R.

Remark 3. [17] Let $D[L]$ be the domain of the generator L. Under the assumptions 1, since (α_t) is a right Markov process[8], there exists a *quasi-regular Dirichlet form*[9] $(\mathcal{E}, D[\mathcal{E}])$ on $L^2(\overline{\mathbb{S}}, m)$ associated with the process, given by

$$\begin{cases} D[L] \subset D[\mathcal{E}] \\ \mathcal{E}(u,v) = (-Lu,v), \ u \in D[L], \ v \in D[\mathcal{E}]. \end{cases}$$

We can think of a Dirichlet form $\mathcal{E}$ as a recipe for a Markov process $(\alpha_t)_{t\ge 0}$, in the sense that $\mathcal{E}$ describes the behavior of the composed process $u(\alpha_t)$ for every u in the domain of $\mathcal{E}$. There is no guarantee that the 'coordinates' $(u(\alpha_t))_u$ can be put together in a consistent way to form a process with reasonable sample paths.

3.4 Jump Measures

Assumption 2 *For any $\varepsilon > 0$, $x \in \mathbb{S}$, $j(\cdot, \mathbb{S}\backslash B_\varepsilon(x))$ is a locally integrable function w.r.t. m.*

For each $\mathcal{B}(\overline{\mathbb{S}})$-measurable function u, let us define $Ru(\alpha) := \int_{\overline{\mathbb{S}}} u(\beta)R(\alpha,d\beta)$, $\alpha \in \overline{\mathbb{S}}$. It is clear that Ru satisfies some properties as below: (i) Ru is a $\mathcal{B}(\overline{\mathbb{S}})$-measurable function. (ii) If $\alpha \in \overline{\partial \mathbb{S}}$ (there exist $i \ne j$ such that $\alpha = (i,x)$ and $x \in G(i,j)$) then $Ru(i,x) = \int_{\mathbb{S}_j} u(j,y)R((i,x),(j,dy))$. Moreover, if $supp(u)\cap \mathbb{S}_j = \emptyset$ then $Ru(i,x) = 0$. If $u = 1_A$, $A \in \mathcal{B}(\mathbb{S})$ then $R1_A(i,x) = R((i,x),A\cap\{j\}\times X_j)$. (iii) $Ru(\alpha) = 0$ if $\alpha \in \overline{\mathbb{S}}\backslash\overline{\partial\mathbb{S}}$ or $supp(u) \cap \mathbb{S} = \emptyset$.

Let us define for any $u,v \in \mathcal{B}(\overline{\mathbb{S}})$, the following energies

$$\overrightarrow{\mathcal{E}}_R(u,v) = \int_{\overline{\mathbb{S}}} u(\alpha)Rv(\alpha)m(d\alpha) \tag{4}$$

$$\overleftarrow{\mathcal{E}}_R(u,v) = \int_{\overline{\mathbb{S}}} Ru(\alpha)v(\alpha)m(d\alpha) \tag{5}$$

Some simple computations give

$$\overrightarrow{\mathcal{E}}_R(u,v) = \int_{\overline{\mathbb{S}}} u(\alpha)\{\int_{\overline{\mathbb{S}}} v(\beta)R(\alpha,d\beta)\}m(d\alpha) = \int_{\overline{\partial\mathbb{S}}} u(\alpha)\{\int_{\mathbb{S}} v(\beta)R(\alpha,d\beta)\}m(d\alpha)$$

---

[8] In Meyer's sense, i.e. the state space $\overline{\mathbb{S}}$ is Lusin.
[9] See the definition 3.1 from [17]

$$= \sum_{i \in Q} \int_{\overline{\partial S}_i} u(i,x) \{ \sum_{j \in Q} \int_{S_j} v(j,y) R((i,x),(j,dy)) \}(i,\lambda(dx))$$

$$= \sum_{i \in Q} \sum_{l \in Q, l \neq i} \int_{\overline{\partial S}_{il}} u(i,x) \{ \sum_{j \in Q} \int_{S_j} v(j,y) R((i,x),(j,dy)) \}(i,\lambda(dx))$$

$$= \sum_{i \in Q} \sum_{j \in Q, j \neq i} \int_{\overline{\partial S}_{ij}} u(i,x) \int_{S_j} v(j,y) R((i,x),(j,dy))(i,\lambda(dx))$$

$$= \sum_{i \in Q} \sum_{j \in Q, j \neq i} \int_{\overline{\partial S}_{ij}} \int_{S_j} u(i,x) v(j,y) R((i,x),(j,dy))(i,\lambda(dx)). \tag{6}$$

$$\overleftarrow{\mathcal{E}}_R(u,v) = \sum_{i \in Q} \sum_{j \in Q, j \neq i} \int_{\overline{\partial S}_{ij}} \int_{S_j} v(i,y) u(j,x) R((i,y),(j,dx))(i,\lambda(dy)). \tag{7}$$

Letting in (6) $u = 1_{\overline{\partial S}_{ij}}$, $v = 1_{S_j}$ for $i \neq j$, we get $\int_{\overline{S}} u(\alpha) Rv(\alpha) m(d\alpha) = \lambda(G(i,j))$. Therefore, if $u = 1_{\overline{\partial S}_i}$, $v = 1_S$ then $\int_{\overline{S}} u(\alpha) Rv(\alpha) m(d\alpha) = \sum_{j \neq i} \lambda(G(i,j)) = \lambda(D_i)$. In the last, if $u = 1_{\overline{\partial S}}$, $v = 1_S$ then $\int_{\overline{S}} u(\alpha) Rv(\alpha) m(d\alpha) = \sum_{i \in Q} \lambda(D_i)$. Analogously, letting in (7) $u = 1_{\overline{\partial S}}$, $v = 1_S$ then $\int_{\overline{S}} Ru(\alpha) v(\alpha) m(d\alpha) = 0$.

Remark 4. If the energy $\overrightarrow{\mathcal{E}}_R(u,v)$ (resp. $\overleftarrow{\mathcal{E}}_R(u,v)$) is nonzero then $supp(u) \cap \overline{\partial S} \neq \emptyset$ and $supp(v) \cap S \neq \emptyset$ (resp. $supp(v) \cap \overline{\partial S} \neq \emptyset$ and $supp(u) \cap S \neq \emptyset$).

R induces a *positive jump measure* J and a *positive symmetric jump measure* $\tilde{J}$[10] on $\overline{S} \times \overline{S} \backslash d$ (d is the diagonal set) by

$$\int_{\overline{S} \times \overline{S} \backslash d} f(\alpha,\beta) J(d\alpha,d\beta) = \int_{\overline{S}} \int_{\overline{S}} f(\alpha,\beta) R(\alpha,d\beta) m(d\alpha); \ f \in C_0(\overline{S} \times \overline{S} \backslash d); \tag{8}$$

$$\int_{\overline{S} \times \overline{S} \backslash d} f(\alpha,\beta) \tilde{J}(d\alpha,d\beta) = \frac{1}{2} \left\{ \int_{\overline{S}} \int_{\overline{S}} f(\alpha,\beta) R(\alpha,d\beta) m(d\alpha) \right.$$

$$\left. + \int_{\overline{S}} \int_{\overline{S}} f(\alpha,\beta) R(\beta,d\alpha) m(d\beta) \right\}.$$

Remark 5. In the theory of stochastic processes the most frequently used jump measures are defined by means of symmetric transition kernels R (i.e. the energies defined by (4) and (5) are equal). In our case the computations (6) and (7) show

---

[10] The symmetric *Dirichlet form* associated with $\tilde{J}$ on $L^2(\overline{S}, m)$ is given by the following formula

$$\mathcal{E}(u,v) = \int_{\overline{S} \times \overline{S} \backslash d} (u(\alpha) - u(\beta))(v(\alpha) - v(\beta)) \tilde{J}(d\alpha, d\beta)$$

$$\mathcal{D}[\mathcal{E}] = \{ u \in L^2(\overline{S}, m), \ \mathcal{E}(u,u) < \infty \}.$$

where $\mathcal{D}[\mathcal{E}]$ is called the domain of $\mathcal{E}$.

that we can have equality between the two above energies only in some special cases. Necessarily this kind of equality implies that the Lesbesgue measure of the interface sets must be zero. But, this will sequentially imply that the energy should be zero, which is a very trivial case.

Remark 6. A simple computation gives the following:

$$
\int_{\overline{\mathbb{S}} \times \overline{\mathbb{S}} \backslash d} f(\alpha, \beta) \widetilde{J}(d\alpha, d\beta) = \frac{1}{2} \left\{ \int_{\overline{\partial \mathbb{S}}} \int_{\overline{\mathbb{S}}} f(\alpha, \beta) R(\alpha, d\beta) m(d\alpha) \right.
$$
$$
\left. + \int_{\overline{\partial \mathbb{S}}} \int_{\overline{\mathbb{S}}} f(\alpha, \beta) R(\beta, d\alpha) m(d\beta) \right\}
$$
$$
= \frac{1}{2} \left\{ \int_{\overline{\partial \mathbb{S}}} \int_{\mathbb{S}} f(\alpha, \beta) R(\alpha, d\beta) m(d\alpha) \right.
$$
$$
\left. + \int_{\overline{\partial \mathbb{S}}} \int_{\overline{\mathbb{S}}} f(\alpha, \beta) R(\beta, d\alpha) m(d\beta) \right\}
$$
$$
= \int_{\overline{\partial \mathbb{S}}} \int_{\mathbb{S}} \frac{f(\alpha, \beta) + f(\beta, \alpha)}{2} R(\alpha, d\beta) m(d\alpha).
$$

4   Reachability Problem

In this section we study the reachability problem for ESHS. Recall from our paper [9] the reachability definitions in the stochastic framework. Let E be a Borel set of the state space $\overline{\mathbb{S}}$. Define the reachable "events" associated to E:

$$
Reach_T(E) = \{\omega \in \Omega \mid \exists t \in [0, T] : \alpha_t(\omega) \in E\}
$$
$$
Reach_\infty(E) = \{\omega \in \Omega \mid \exists t \geq 0 : \alpha_t(\omega) \in E\}.
$$

where $T > 0$ is a finite positive time horizon. The measurability of these events can be easily obtained using the CADLAG property of the process and the fact that the underlying probability space is a Borel space. We deal in this section with the issue of the computation of reach set probabilities.

To compute the reach set probabilities, we propose a Dirichlet form based approach, which takes into consideration the two main features of the hybrid executions: (1) forced jumps; (2) diffusion segments between consecutive jumps.

First we summarize the main ideas of the computation method of the reach event probabilities. Let B, E be two Borel sets, where B is the initial condition set and E is the reachability target set. We can suppose that $E \subset \mathbb{S}_i$, $i \in Q$ (otherwise E can be written as a partition $\bigcup_{i \in Q} (E \cap \mathbb{S}_i)$). Then the reachable event associated to E is the intersection of two other events:

1. the set of all trajectories which jump in $\mathbb{S}_i$, i.e. the 'jump' reachable event, denoted by $Reach_T^j(\mathbb{S}_i)$;
2. the set of all diffusion paths (corresponding to $\mathbb{S}_i$) which reach E, i.e. the 'continuous' reachable event, denoted by $Reach_T^c(E)$.

Let be $\mathcal{E}$ the quasi-regular Dirichlet form associated to (α_t) (see remark 3). Each quasi-regular Dirichlet form[11] can be expressed as the sum of three parts: diffusion $\mathcal{E}^c$, jumping $\mathcal{E}^j$ and killing $\mathcal{E}^k$: $\mathcal{E} = \mathcal{E}^c + \mathcal{E}^j + \mathcal{E}^k$ (Beurling-Deny Formulae). The continuous part is used to study the continuous part of the process (i.e. it corresponds to the continuous pieces of process trajectories). The jumping part corresponds to the trajectory discontinuities of the process and finally, the killing part is connected with those trajectories which go the cemetery point.

We employ the first two parts of $\mathcal{E}$ to solve the reachability problem:

(i) the jump part $\mathcal{E}^j$ given by the jump measure (8) is used to compute $P[Reach_T^j(\mathbb{S}_i)]$.

(ii) the diffusion part $\mathcal{E}^c$ is employed to compute $P[Reach_T^c(E)]$.

Intuitively, the probability of the reachable event $P(Reach_T(E))$, $E \subset \mathbb{S}_i$, is a conditional probability, which is equal to the probability of $Reach_T^c(E)$ conditioned by the event $Reach_T^j(\mathbb{S}_i)$. It is clear that the probability to jump in $\mathbb{S}_i$ is given by the reset probability kernel of ESHS, R. Since R also defines the jump measure $\tilde{J}$, then the above jump probability should be related with the the jump component of the associated Dirichlet form. To compute $P[Reach_T^c(E)]$ we use the function F (which gives E as a level set) to obtain the induced Dirichlet form of $\mathcal{E}^c|_{\mathbb{S}_i}$. The induced Dirichlet forms are easy to deal with because their state space is $\mathbb{R}$. The Dirichlet form expression associated to different kind of diffusion is well known in the literature [14,17]. Therefore, the induced Dirichlet forms have nice representation formula [16], which allow to translate the computation problem of the 'continuous' reachable event probability from the initial state space to the 'induced' state space.

Suppose that B and $\overline{\mathbb{S}}_i$ are disjoint. More exactly, the computation steps are:

(A) compute the probability that the process, started in B, jumps in $\mathbb{S}_i$, using the estimation (11) of the Prop. 3 from below;

(B) give an upper bound for the probability that the process, arrived in $\mathbb{S}_i$, hits E, using the estimation (13) of Prop. 4 from below.

4.1   Computation of 'Jump' Reachable Event Probabilities

For $A \in \mathcal{B}(\overline{\mathbb{S}})$ define processes p, p^* and $\tilde{p}$ as follows:

$$p(t, A) = \sum_{k=1}^{\infty} I_{(t \geq T_k)} I_{(\alpha_{T_k} \in A)}; \quad p^*(t) = \sum_{k=1}^{\infty} I_{(t \geq T_k)};$$

$$\tilde{p}(t, A) = \int_0^t R(\alpha_{s-}, A) dp^*(s) = \sum_{T_k \leq t} R(\alpha_{T_k-}, A).$$

Note that p, p^* are counting processes and $p^*(t) = k$ if $t \in [T_k, T_{k+1})$, $k = 0, 1, 2, \ldots$ where $T_0 = 0$. $\tilde{p}(t, A)$ is the compensator of $p(t, A)$ (see [12] for more explanations). The following process is a local martingale.

$$q(t, A) = p(t, A) - \tilde{p}(t, A). \tag{9}$$

---

[11] See [14,17] for the theory of symmetric and non-symmetric Dirichlet forms.

Proposition 2. *For each $\alpha \in \overline{\mathbb{S}}$ we have*

$$P^{\alpha}(Reach_T^j(\mathbb{S}_i)) = \mathbf{E}^{\alpha}\widetilde{p}(T, \mathbb{S}_i)$$

Proof. If in the Lévy system identity (3) we take $f(\alpha, \beta) = 1_{\mathbb{S}_i^c}(\alpha) \cdot 1_{\mathbb{S}_i}(\beta)$ then the first member will give the expectation of the set of all trajectories which jump in $\mathbb{S}_i$ in the time interval $[0, T]$, i.e. $P^{\alpha}(Reach_T^j(\mathbb{S}_i))$

$$P^{\alpha}(Reach_T^j(\mathbb{S}_i)) = \mathbf{E}^{\alpha} \int_0^T \int f(\alpha_t, \beta) R(\alpha_t, d\beta) dt$$

$$= \mathbf{E}^{\alpha} \int_0^T \int_{\mathbb{S}_i} 1_{\mathbb{S}_i^c}(\alpha_t) R(\alpha_t, d\beta) dt = \mathbf{E}^{\alpha} \int_0^T 1_{\mathbb{S}_i^c}(\alpha_t) R(\alpha_t, \mathbb{S}_i) dt$$

$$= \mathbf{E}^{\alpha} \sum_{T_i \le T} R(\alpha_{T_i^-}, \mathbb{S}_i) = \mathbf{E}^{\alpha}\widetilde{p}(T, \mathbb{S}_i).$$

Remark 7. The proof of the Prop. 2 can be derived using the martingale property of q defined by (9).

For a Borel set G of state space we define the first hitting time $T_G := \inf\{t > 0 | \alpha_t \in G\}$. Let τ_G denote the first leaving time from G, i.e. $\tau_G = T_{\overline{\mathbb{S}} \backslash G}$ is the first hitting time of $\overline{\mathbb{S}} \backslash G$. Let p_t^G be the transition function of the restriction of the process (α_t) to G. Dealing with the jump times we use the following result:

Lemma 1. *[14] Let G be a relatively compact open set. For any h, f, g bounded positive Borel functions on $\overline{\mathbb{S}}$ such that $supp[h] \subset G$, $supp[f] \subset G$ and $supp[g] \subset \overline{\mathbb{S}} \backslash \overline{G}$ we have*

$$\mathbf{E}^{h \cdot m}(f(\alpha_{\tau_G^-})g(\alpha_{\tau_G}); \ \tau_G \le T) = 2 \int_0^T \left[\int \int p_t^G h(\alpha) f(\alpha) g(\beta) \widetilde{J}(d\alpha, d\beta) \right] dt \quad (10)$$

where , $\mathbf{E}^{h \cdot m}$ is the expectation given by the probability $P^{h \cdot m}(A) = \int_{\overline{\mathbb{S}}} P^{\alpha}(A) h(\alpha) m(d\alpha)$.

Proposition 3. *Let $\overline{\partial \mathbb{S}}_{\to i}$ be the subset of $\overline{\partial \mathbb{S}}$ from where the process (α_t) can jump in $\mathbb{S}_i$ ($i \in Q$). For any Borel set $B \subset \mathbb{S}_i$ (resp. $B \subset \overline{\mathbb{S}}_i^c$), $h = 1_B$, we have*

$$P^{h \cdot m}(\tau_{\mathbb{S}_i} \le T) = \int_0^T \left[\int_{\overline{\partial \mathbb{S}}_{\to i}} \int_{\mathbb{S}_i} p(\beta, t, B) R(\alpha, d\beta) m(d\alpha) \right] dt$$

$$(resp. \ P^{h \cdot m}(T_{\mathbb{S}_i} \le T) = \int_0^T \left[\int_{\overline{\partial \mathbb{S}}_{\to i}} p(\alpha, t, B) m(d\alpha) \right] dt). \quad (11)$$

Proof. By setting $f = 1_{\mathbb{S}_i}$, $h = 1_B$, $B \subset \mathbb{S}_i$, $g = 1_{\overline{\mathbb{S}} \backslash \mathbb{S}_i}$ in (10) we get the probability to remain in $\mathbb{S}_i$ until time horizon T, if the process has started in $\mathbb{S}_i$

$$P^{h\cdot m}(\tau_{\mathbb{S}_i} \le T) = \int_0^T \left[\int_{\overline{\partial \mathbb{S}}} \int_{\mathbb{S}} \{ p_t^{\mathbb{S}_i} h(\alpha) f(\alpha) g(\beta) \right.$$

$$\left. + p_t^{\mathbb{S}_i} h(\beta) f(\beta) g(\alpha) \} R(\alpha, d\beta) m(d\alpha) \right] dt$$

$$= \int_0^T \left[\int_{\overline{\partial \mathbb{S}} \setminus \overline{\partial \mathbb{S}}_i} \int_{\mathbb{S}_i} p_t^{\mathbb{S}_i} h(\beta) R(\alpha, d\beta) m(d\alpha) \right] dt$$

$$= \int_0^T \left[\int_{\overline{\partial \mathbb{S}}_{\to i}} \int_{\mathbb{S}_i} p_t^{\mathbb{S}_i} h(\beta) R(\alpha, d\beta) m(d\alpha) \right] dt$$

$$= \int_0^T \left[\int_{\overline{\partial \mathbb{S}}_{\to i}} \int_{\mathbb{S}_i} p(\beta, t, B) R(\alpha, d\beta) m(d\alpha) \right] dt.$$

Letting $f = 1_{\overline{\mathbb{S}}_i^c}$, $h = 1_B$, $B \subset \overline{\mathbb{S}}_i^c$, $g = 1_{\overline{\mathbb{S}}_i}$ the probability to hit $\mathbb{S}_i$ until T is

$$P^{h\cdot m}(T_{\mathbb{S}_i} \le T) = \int_0^T \left[\int_{\overline{\partial \mathbb{S}}} \int_{\mathbb{S}} \{ p_t^{\overline{\mathbb{S}}_i^c} h(\alpha) f(\alpha) g(\beta) \right.$$

$$\left. + p_t^{\overline{\mathbb{S}}_i^c} h(\beta) f(\beta) g(\alpha) \} R(\alpha, d\beta) m(d\alpha) \right] dt$$

$$= \int_0^T \left[\int_{\overline{\partial \mathbb{S}} \setminus \overline{\partial \mathbb{S}}_i} \int_{\overline{\mathbb{S}}_i^c} p_t^{\overline{\mathbb{S}}_i^c} h(\alpha) R(\alpha, d\beta) m(d\alpha) \right] dt$$

$$= \int_0^T \left[\int_{\overline{\partial \mathbb{S}}_{\to i}} p_t^{\overline{\mathbb{S}}_i^c} h(\alpha) R(\alpha, \overline{\mathbb{S}}_i) m(d\alpha) \right] dt$$

$$= \int_0^T \left[\int_{\overline{\partial \mathbb{S}}_{\to i}} p_t^{\overline{\mathbb{S}}_i^c} h(\alpha) m(d\alpha) \right] dt$$

$$= \int_0^T \left[\int_{\overline{\partial \mathbb{S}}_{\to i}} p(\alpha, t, B) m(d\alpha) \right] dt.$$

Remark 8. (11) gives the probability of hitting $\mathbb{S}_i$ through the Borel set B. Similar arguments as those used in the Prop. 3 lead to $P^{h\cdot m}(\tau_G \le T) = \int_0^T \left[\int_{\overline{\partial \mathbb{S}}_{\to i}} \int_G p(\beta, t, B) R(\alpha, d\beta) m(d\alpha) \right] dt$ for any open set $G \subset \mathbb{S}_i$, $h = 1_B$, $B \subset \mathbb{S}_i$. This estimation can be useful when G is known as a safety set of the state space. An interesting problem would be to find h or B maximizing the above probability. It is known that the transition probabilities $p(\beta, t, \cdot)$ for the diffusion[12] are the solutions of Kolmogorov backward equations [2].

4.2   Computation of 'Continuous' Reachable Event Probabilities

Suppose that the given Borel set $E \subset \mathbb{S}_i$ can be written as a level set $\{\alpha \in \mathbb{S}_i | F(\alpha) > l\}$, where $F : \mathbb{S}_i \to \mathbb{R}$ is a given function. Note that, in general,

---

[12] The restriction of the process to G is a diffusion process.

$F(\alpha_t)$ is not itself a Markov process (see [22]). The computation of probability of $Reach^c_T(E)$ means, in fact, the computation of $P^m(\sup\limits_{t\in[0,T]} F(\alpha_t) > l)$.

We consider the restriction (α^i_t) of our process to $\overline{\mathbb{S}}_i$. This is a diffusion process and the properties of the corresponding Dirichlet form $\mathcal{E}_i$ are well known [14,17]. Moreover, we can suppose that $\mathcal{E}_i$ is a regular symmetric Dirichlet form [11]. Let $\mathcal{B}^*$ denote the σ-algebra Borel of $\mathbb{R}$ and let m^* denote the image of m under F. We construct a form $\mathcal{E}^*_i$ on $D[\mathcal{E}^*_i] \times D[\mathcal{E}^*_i] \subset L^2(\mathbb{R}, m^*) \times L^2(\mathbb{R}, m^*)$ by

$$\mathcal{E}^*_i(u^*, v^*) \; : \; = \mathcal{E}_i(u^* \circ F, v^* \circ F), \; u^*, v^* \in D[\mathcal{E}^*_i],$$
$$D[\mathcal{E}^*_i] = \{u^* \in L^2(\mathbb{R}, m^*) | u^* \circ F \in D[\mathcal{E}_i].$$

Suppose that F is chosen such that $\mathcal{E}^*_i$ is a regular Dirichlet form [16]. Then there exists a certain $\mathbb{R}$-valued Markov process, (α^{i*}_t) associated with $\mathcal{E}^*_i$. Note if E^* is open in $\mathbb{R}$ and $E = F^{-1}(E^*)$ then we can consider the two first hitting times T_E and T_{E^*}. We define for $p > 0$, the p-capacity of E^*

$$Cap^*_p(E^*) = \inf\{\mathcal{E}^*_i(u^*, u^*) + p(u^*, u^*)_{m^*} | u^* \in D[\mathcal{E}^*_i], \; u^* \geq 1 \; m^* - a.e. \text{ on } E^*\}$$

where $(u^*, u^*)_{m^*}$ is the inner product of $L^2(\mathbb{R}, m^*)$. To give an upper estimate on $P^m(T_E \leq T)$ we need the following assumption:

Assumption 3 *We suppose that $m(\overline{\mathbb{S}}_i) < \infty$, $1 \in D[\mathcal{E}_i]$ and $E^* \subset \mathbb{R}$ is an open subset of finite Cap^*-capacity such that $E = F^{-1}(E^*)$.*

The Prop. 1.24 from [16] becomes in our case as follows:

Proposition 4. *For all $p > 0$, we have:*

$$P^m(T_E \leq T) \leq e^p\{\mathbf{E}^{m^*} e^{-pT^*_{E^*}/T} + Tp^{-1} \int_{\mathbb{R}} \mathbf{E}^r e^{-pT^*_{E^*}/T} k^*(dr)\}; \quad (12)$$
$$P^m(T_E \leq T) \leq p^{-1}e^p \min\{T\mathcal{E}^*_i(u^*, u^*) + p(u^*, u^*)_{m^*} | u^* \in D[\mathcal{E}^*_i], \quad (13)$$
$$u^* \geq 1, \; m^* - a.e. \text{ on } E^*\}.$$

where k^* is the killing measure associated with the killing part of $\mathcal{E}^*_i$.

Since we deal with the restriction of the process to $\overline{\mathbb{S}}_i$, the estimations (12), (13) still remain true if we replace P^m with $P^{g\cdot m}$, where $g = 1_{\mathbb{S}_i}$.

5 Conclusions and Further Work

In this paper we have extended and developed a stochastic hybrid system model introduced in [15]. The contributions of the paper are twofold: to prove correctness of this model (existence of the solution process which is a Borel right process), and to build mathematical tools for computing the probability of reaching a given set. The first contribution is necessary for any kind of mathematical exploration and serves as foundations for the development of the results. The second contribution can be viewed as a stochastic version of reachability. The method suggested is based on computation of so-called Dirichlet forms (already used for this purpose in stochastic analysis).

The possibility of implementation of the Dirichlet forms in a theorem prover leads to new directions in the stochastic hybrid system reachability study. On the other hand, for a stochastic hybrid system H with the Markov property, endowed with the corresponding Dirichlet form $\mathcal{E}$, using an appropriate proper map Φ from the state space $\mathbb{S}$ onto a 'smaller' space $\mathbb{S}^*$, one can construct the induced Dirichlet form $\mathcal{E}^*$ associated to a simpler system H^* (the image of H through Φ). The reachability problem for H and the target set $E \subset \mathbb{S}$ can be reduced to the reachability problem for H^* and the target set $\Phi(E)$. Therefore, it is possible to introduce a notion of *bisimulation of stochastic hybrid systems via Dirichlet forms*, which is a relatively new issue in the probabilistic framework.

One of the possible approaches which derives from this work is to study the reachability problem for ESHS with control. To solve this problem, it could be possible to use a cross-fertilization method which combines the Dirichlet form theory with the dynamic programming. For example, we intend to combine the results connected with the 'jumping' Dirichlet forms with the representations of reachable sets for the diffusion paths by means of viscosity solutions for some partial differential equations [23].

Acknowledgments. The author gratefully acknowledges the contribution of John Lygeros to this work and the constructive observations of the anonymous referees.

References

1. Albeverio, S., Ma, M.: A General Correspondence Between Dirichlet Forms and Right Processes. Bull.Amer.Math.Soc. **26**, No.2 (1992), 245-252, .
2. Arnold, L.: *Stochastic Differential Equations: Theory and Applications.* Wiley - Interscience, New York-London-Sydney (1974).
3. Bass, R.F.: Adding and Substracting Jumps from Markov Processes. Trans. of Amer. Math. Soc. **255** (1979), 363-376.
4. Bensoussan, A., Menaldi, J. L.: Stochastic Hybrid Control. Journal of Mathematical Analysis and Applications **249** (2000), 261-288.
5. Benveniste, A., Jacod, J.: Systèmes de Lévy de Processus de Markov. Invent. Math. **21** (1973), 183-198.
6. Bertsekas, D.P., Shreve, S.E.: *Stochastic Optimal Control: The Discrete-Time Case.* Athena Scientific, 1996.
7. Blumenthal, R.M., Getoor, R.K.: *Markov Processes and Potential Theory,* Academic Press, New York and London (1968).
8. Bouleau, N., Hirsch, F.: *Propriétés d'Absolue Continuité dans les Espaces de Dirichlet et Applications aux Equations Différentielles Stochastiques.* Sém. de Probabilités, LNM **20** (1986), Springer-Verlag.
9. Bujorianu, M.L., Lygeros, J.: Reachability Questions in Piecewise Deterministic Markov Processes, In [18], 126-140.
10. Chaffin, M.S., Berry, J.D.: Navier-Stokes and Potential Theory Solutions for a Helicopter Fuselage. NASA TM-4566 ATCOM-TR-94-A-013 (1994).

11. Chen, Z.Q., Ma, Z.-M., Rockner, M.: Quasi-Homeomorphisms of Dirichlet Forms. Nagoya Math. J. **136** (1994), 1-15.
12. Davis, M.H.A.: *Markov Models and Optimization*, Chapman & Hall, London, 1993.
13. Dutertre, B.: *Elements of Mathematical Analysis in PVS*. TPHOLs'96, Turku, Finland (1996).
14. Fukushima, M.: *Dirichlet Forms and Markov Processes*, N. Holland (1980).
15. Hu, J., Lygeros, J., Sastry, S.: Towards a Theory of Stochastic Hybrid Systems. LNCS **1790** (2000), *Hybrid Systems: Computation and Control*, N. Lynch and B. Krogh (Eds.), 160-173.
16. Iscoe, I., McDonald, D.: Induced Dirichlet Forms and Capacitary Inequalities, Ann. Prob. **18**, No.3 (1990), 1195-1221.
17. Ma, M., Rockner, M.: *The Theory of (Non-Symmetric) Dirichlet Forms and Markov Processes*, Springer Verlag, Berlin (1990).
18. Maler,O., Pnueli, A. Eds.: Proceedings *Hybrid Systems: Computation and Control*, 6th International Workshop, HSCC 2003, LNCS 2623, (2003).
19. Meyer, P.A.: *Probability and Potentials*. Blaisdell, Waltham Mass (1966).
20. Meyer, P.A.: Renaissance, Recollectments, Mélanges, Ralentissement de Processus de Markov. Ann. Inst. Fourier **25** (1975), 465-497.
21. Pola, G., Bujorianu, M.L., Lygeros, J., Di Benedetto, M. D.: Stochastic Hybrid Models: An Overview with applications to Air Traffic Management. ADHS, Analysis and Design of Hybrid System, Saint-Malo, 2003.
22. Rogers, L.C.G., Pitman, J.W.: Markov Functions. Ann. Prob. **9**, No.4 (1981), 573-582.
23. Soner, H.M., Touzi N.: A stochastic Representation for the Level Set Equations. Comm. Partial Diff. Eq. **27**, No.**9-10** (2002) 2031-2053.

On the Controllability of Bimodal Piecewise Linear Systems*

M.K. Çamlıbel[1,2,3], W.P.M.H. Heemels[2], and J.M. Schumacher[1]

[1] Dept. of Econometrics and Operations Research, Tilburg University,
P.O. Box 90153, 5000 LE Tilburg, The Netherlands
{k.camlibel,j.m.schumacher}@uvt.nl
[2] Dept. of Electrical Engineering, Eindhoven University of Technology,
P.O. Box 513, 5600 MB Eindhoven, The Netherlands
w.p.m.h.heemels@tue.nl
[3] Dept. of Electronics and Communication Eng., Dogus University,
Acibadem 81010, Kadikoy-Istanbul, Turkey

Abstract. This paper studies controllability of bimodal systems that consist of two linear dynamics on each side of a given hyperplane. We show that the controllability properties of these systems can be inferred from those of linear systems for which the inputs are constrained in a certain way. Inspired by the earlier work on constrained controllability of linear systems, we derive necessary and sufficient conditions for a bimodal piecewise linear system to be controllable.

1 Introduction

One of the most basic concepts in control theory is the notion of controllability. This concept has been studied extensively for linear systems, nonlinear systems, infinite-dimensional systems and so on. The notion of controllability plays a role for instance in stability theory and in realization theory; more recently it has also been used in safety studies where it is important to know whether certain regions of the state space are reachable or not under the influence of an external input. While the algebraic characterization of controllability of finite-dimensional linear systems is among the classical results of systems theory, global controllability results for nonlinear systems have been hard to come by. In this paper we consider global controllability for two related classes of piecewise linear systems, and obtain a complete characterization.

One class of switched linear systems that we consider consists of controlled systems whose dynamics depends on the sign of one of the state variables. Such systems have two modes, and the switching between these modes is determined by the zero crossings of the designated state variable or more generally of some linear function of the state variables. The evolution of the state variables is influenced not only by the internal dynamics, but also by an external input

---

* Sponsored by the EU project "SICONOS" (IST-2001-37172) and STW grant "Analysis and synthesis of systems with discrete and continuous control" (EES 5173)

which indirectly affects the switching behavior of the system. In the second class of switched systems that we study here, it is the input vector that may switch between two possible values, and the switching is determined directly by the sign of the input variable itself. Models of this type may be used to describe situations where "pushing" and "pulling" have different effects (besides a sign change). It turns out that the controllability problems for these two classes are closely related; we establish this relation by means of a special state representation akin to the strict feedback form that is used in backstepping control design.

The controllability problems that we consider are specified more precisely in the next section, in which we also present the main results of the paper along with some discussion of how these results relate to the existing literature. Most of the proofs are in the Appendix which follows after the conclusions section.

The following notational conventions will be in force throughout the paper. The symbol $\mathbb{R}$ denotes the set of real numbers, $\mathbb{R}^n$ n-tuples of real numbers, and $\mathbb{R}^{n \times m}$ $n \times m$ real matrices. The set of complex numbers is denoted by $\mathbb{C}$, natural numbers by $\mathbb{N}$. The set of locally integrable functions is denoted by $\mathcal{L}_1^{\mathrm{loc}}$, absolutely continuous functions by $\mathcal{AC}$, and infinitely differentiable functions by $\mathfrak{C}^\infty$. For a matrix $A \in \mathbb{R}^{n \times m}$, A^T stands for its transpose, $\ker A$ for its kernel, i.e. the set $\{x \in \mathbb{R}^m \mid Ax = 0\}$, $\mathrm{im}\, A$ for its image, i.e. the set $\{y \in \mathbb{R}^n \mid y = Ax \text{ for some } x \in \mathbb{R}^m\}$, $\exp(A)$ for its exponential. If B has also m columns then $\mathrm{col}(A, B)$ denotes the matrix obtained by stacking A over B. If $B \in \mathbb{R}^{p \times q}$ then $\mathrm{blockdiag}(A, B)$ denotes the block diagonal $(n + p) \times (m + q)$ matrix for which the left upper $n \times m$ block is A, the right lower $p \times q$ block is B, and the rest of the entries are zero.

2   Main Results

Consider the bimodal piecewise linear system given by

$$\dot{x}(t) = \begin{cases} A_1 x(t) + bu(t) & \text{if } c^T x(t) \leqslant 0, \\ A_2 x(t) + bu(t) & \text{if } c^T x(t) \geqslant 0 \end{cases} \tag{1}$$

where A_1, $A_2 \in \mathbb{R}^{n \times n}$ and b, $c \in \mathbb{R}^{n \times 1}$. We assume that the dynamics is continuous along the hyperplane $\{x \mid c^T x = 0\}$, i.e.

$$c^T x = 0 \Rightarrow A_1 x = A_2 x. \tag{2}$$

As the right hand side of (1) is Lipschitz continuous in the x variable, one can show that for each initial state $x_0 \in \mathbb{R}^n$ and input $u \in \mathcal{L}_1^{\mathrm{loc}}$ there exists a unique absolutely continuous function x satisfying (1) almost everywhere.

The system (1) is a special case of a family of hybrid systems that are called *linear complementarity systems* (LCSs). Lying in the intersection of the mathematical programming and systems theory, LCSs find applications in various engineering fields as well as economical sciences. We refer to [3] and the references therein for an account of the previous work on LCSs. An LCS is a system of the form

$$\dot{x}(t) = Ax(t) + Ez(t) + Bu(t) \tag{3a}$$

$$w(t) = Cx(t) + Dz(t) \tag{3b}$$

$$0 \leqslant z(t) \perp w(t) \geqslant 0. \tag{3c}$$

Here $A \in \mathbb{R}^{n \times n}$, $B \in \mathbb{R}^{n \times m}$, $C \in \mathbb{R}^{k \times n}$, $D \in \mathbb{R}^{k \times k}$, $E \in \mathbb{R}^{n \times k}$, the inequalities are componentwise, and $z \perp w$ means that $z^T w = 0$. The relation (3c) is known as the *complementarity condition* and the pair (z, w) as *complementarity variables*. Note that the complementarity conditions require, at least, one of the complementarity variables to be zero at a given time instant.

To see that (1) is a type of LCS, note that the condition (2) implies that the difference $A_2 - A_1$ is, at most, of rank one and its kernel contains the kernel of c^T. Therefore, one can find a vector $e \in \mathbb{R}^{n \times 1}$ such that $A_2 - A_1 = ec^T$. Consider the LCS

$$\dot{x}(t) = A_2 x(t) + ez(t) + bu(t) \tag{4a}$$

$$w(t) = c^T x(t) + z(t) \tag{4b}$$

$$0 \leqslant z(t) \perp w(t) \geqslant 0 \tag{4c}$$

where there is only one pair of complementarity variables. As a consequence, the overall system has two 'modes' (i.e. it is bimodal). Indeed, if the variable z is zero on an interval of time, then $c^T x$ is nonnegative on that interval and the system follows the dynamics of $\dot{x} = A_2 x + bu$. Alternatively, if the variable w is zero on an interval then $c^T x$ is nonpositive on that interval and the system follows the dynamics of $\dot{x} = (A_2 - ec^T)x + bu$. Note that $A_2 - ec^T = A_1$ by the construction of the vector e and hence (4) is equivalent to (1) in the obvious sense.

2.1   Controllability of Linear Systems

From a control theory point of view, one of the very immediate issues is the controllability of the system at hand. More precisely, the question is whether an arbitrary initial state x_0 can be steered to an arbitrary final state x_f. Following the classical literature, we say that the system (1) is *completely controllable* if for any pair of states (x_0, x_f) there exists an input $u \in \mathcal{L}_1^{\mathrm{loc}}$ such that the solution of (1) with $x(0) = x_0$ passes through x_f, i.e. $x(\tau) = x_f$ for some $\tau > 0$.

Before studying the controllability of (1), we want to discuss some of the available results on the controllability of linear systems. Note that the system (1) is nothing but a single-input linear system when $A_1 = A_2 = A$. In this case, (1) can be written as

$$\dot{x} = Ax + bu. \tag{5}$$

Ever since Kalman's seminal work [5] introduced the notion of controllability (and also observability) in the state space framework, it has been one of the central notions in systems and control theory. Tests for controllability were given by Kalman himself and many others (see e.g. [4] for historical details). The following theorem summarizes the classical results on the controllability of linear systems for the single input case.

Theorem 1. *The following statements are equivalent.*

1. *The system* (5) *is completely controllable.*
2. *The matrix* $\begin{bmatrix} b & Ab & \cdots & A^{n-1}b \end{bmatrix}$ *is of rank* n.
3. *For any eigenpair* (λ, z) *of* A^T *(i.e.,* $z^T A = \lambda z^T$*),* $z^T b \neq 0$.
4. *The rank of the matrix* $\begin{bmatrix} sI - A & b \end{bmatrix}$ *is equal to* n *for all* $s \in \mathbb{C}$.

In practice, one may encounter controllability problems for which the input may only take values from a set $\Omega \subset \mathbb{R}$. A typical example of such constrained controllability problems would be a (linear) system that may admit only positive controls. Study of constrained controllability goes back to the sixties (see for instance [6]). Early results consider only restraint sets Ω which contain the origin in their interior. The following theorem can be proven with the help of [6, Thm. 8, p. 92].

Theorem 2. *Consider the system* (5) *for which the input function is constrained as* $u(t) \in \Omega$ *where* Ω *is a compact set which contains zero in its interior. Then,* (5) *is completely controllable if and only if* (A, b) *is controllable and all eigenvalues of* A *lie on the imaginary axis.*

When only positive controls are allowed, the set Ω does not contain the origin in its interior. Saperstone and Yorke [7] were the first to consider such constraint sets. In particular, they considered the case $\Omega = [0, 1]$. More general restraint sets were studied by Brammer [2]. All these results were obtained for the multi-input case. For the single-input case, Brammer's contribution can be stated as follows.

Theorem 3. *Consider the system* (5) *for which the input function is constrained as* $u(t) \in \Omega$ *where the restraint set* Ω *has the following properties.*

i. $0 \in \Omega$,
ii. *convex hull of* Ω *has nonempty interior.*

Then, (5) *is completely controllable if and only if the following conditions hold.*

1. *The pair* (A, b) *is controllable.*
2. *There is no real eigenvector* w *of* A^T *satisfying* $w^T bv \leqslant 0$ *for all* $v \in \Omega$.

As a consequence of the above theorem, necessary and sufficient conditions for the complete controllability of the system (5) with a nonnegative input are i) the pair (A, b) is controllable, and ii) A has no real eigenvalue.

The main goal of the present paper is to investigate controllability properties of a piecewise linear system of the form (1). Although none of the above results are directly applicable, we will see that they will play a crucial role in studying controllability of piecewise linear systems.

2.2   Controllability of Bimodal Piecewise Linear Systems

For the moment, we focus on systems of the form

$$\dot{\zeta}(t) = K\zeta(t) + \begin{cases} N\eta(t) & \text{if } \eta(t) \leqslant 0 \\ P\eta(t) & \text{if } \eta(t) \geqslant 0, \end{cases} \tag{6}$$

where $K \in \mathbb{R}^{k \times k}$, $N \in \mathbb{R}^k$, $P \in \mathbb{R}^k$. As we shall see later, controllability of (6) is closely related to that of (1).

For (6), unlike the standard controllability problems, we will consider absolutely continuous inputs η. The following theorem presents necessary and sufficient conditions for the controllability of (6).

Theorem 4. *The following statements are equivalent.*

1. *For each ζ_0, $\zeta_f \in \mathbb{R}^k$ and η_0, $\eta_f \in \mathbb{R}$, there exist a real number $T > 0$ and a solution $(\zeta, \eta) \in \mathcal{AC}^{k+1}$ of (6) such that*

$$\zeta(0) = \zeta_0, \qquad \zeta(T) = \zeta_f \tag{7}$$
$$\eta(0) = \eta_0, \qquad \eta(T) = \eta_f. \tag{8}$$

2. *There exists no nonzero w such that*

$$w^T \exp(Kt)N \leqslant 0 \text{ and } w^T \exp(Kt)P \geqslant 0 \tag{9}$$

   for all $t \geqslant 0$.
3. *$(K, [N\ P])$ is controllable and $K^T z = \lambda z, \lambda \in \mathbb{R}, z \neq 0 \Rightarrow (z^T N)(z^T P) > 0$.*

Remark 1. When $N = P$, the system (6) is nothing but a linear system given by $\dot{\zeta} = K\zeta + P\eta$. As $N = P$, the condition $(z^T N)(z^T P) > 0$ is satisfied for any nonzero vector z. Hence, the third condition is equivalent to saying that (K, P) is a controllable pair.

Remark 2. Another special case that is captured by our theorem is the controllability of linear systems with positive controls. Indeed, if we take $N = 0$ controllability properties of the system (6) must be equivalent to those of the system $\dot{\zeta} = K\zeta + P\eta$ where η is restricted to be pointwise nonnegative. In this case, $(z^T N)(z^T P)$ is always zero. Therefore, the third condition of the above theorem is equivalent to saying that (K, P) is a controllable pair and K has no real eigenvalues. In other words, Theorem 3 is a special case of Theorem 4 when Ω is the set of nonnegative real numbers.

Now, we turn to the system (1). Define the transfer functions $G_i(s) = c^T(sI - A_i)^{-1}b$ for $i = 1, 2$. It follows from (2) that $G_1(s) \equiv 0$ if and only if $G_2(s) \equiv 0$. If $G_i(s) \equiv 0$ then the system (1) is not completely controllable. In the rest of the paper, we assume that $G_i(s) \not\equiv 0$ for $i = 1, 2$. Let $\mathcal{V}_i^\star$ be the largest (A_i, b)-controlled invariant subspace that is contained in $\ker c^T$. In other words, $\mathcal{V}_i^\star$ is the largest of the subspaces $\mathcal{V}_i$ such that $(A - bf^T)\mathcal{V}_i \subseteq \mathcal{V}_i$ for some $f \in \mathbb{R}^n$ and $\mathcal{V}_i \subseteq \ker c^T$. Also let $\mathcal{S}_i^\star$ be the smallest (c^T, A_i)-conditioned invariant subspace that contains $\operatorname{im} b$. Equivalently, $\mathcal{S}_i^\star$ is the smallest of the subspaces $\mathcal{S}_i$ such that $(A - gc^T)\mathcal{S}_i \subseteq \mathcal{S}_i$ for some $g \in \mathbb{R}^n$ and $\operatorname{im} b \subseteq \mathcal{S}_i$. We refer to [1] for a more detailed discussion on the controlled and conditioned invariant subspaces. Since $G_i(s) \not\equiv 0$, it is invertible. As a consequence, a well-known result of the geometric control theory states that $\mathcal{V}_i^\star \oplus \mathcal{S}_i^\star = \mathbb{R}^n$. By using (2), one can show that

1. $\mathcal{V}_1^\star = \mathcal{V}_2^\star =: \mathcal{V}^\star$,
2. $A_1 \mid_{\mathcal{V}_1^\star} = A_2 \mid_{\mathcal{V}_2^\star}$,
3. $\mathcal{S}_1^\star = \mathcal{S}_2^\star =: \mathcal{S}^\star$.

This means that we can rewrite (1) as

$$\dot{x} = \begin{cases} \begin{bmatrix} H & g_1 c_2^T \\ b_2 f^T & J_1 \end{bmatrix} x + \begin{bmatrix} 0 \\ b_2 \end{bmatrix} u & \text{if } c_2^T x_2 \leqslant 0 \\[4mm] \begin{bmatrix} H & g_2 c_2^T \\ b_2 f^T & J_2 \end{bmatrix} x + \begin{bmatrix} 0 \\ b_2 \end{bmatrix} u & \text{if } c_2^T x_2 \geqslant 0 \end{cases} \tag{10}$$

by choosing a basis for $\mathbb{R}^n$ which is adopted to $\mathcal{V}^\star$ and $\mathcal{S}^\star$. Here, $b_2 \in \mathbb{R}^{n_2}$, $c_2 \in \mathbb{R}^{n_2}$, $f \in \mathbb{R}^{n_1}$, $g_i \in \mathbb{R}^{n_1}$, $H \in \mathbb{R}^{n_1 \times n_1}$, and $J_i \in \mathbb{R}^{n_2 \times n_2}$ where $n_1 = \dim(\mathcal{V}^\star)$ and $n_2 = \dim(\mathcal{S}^\star)$. Let $e = \operatorname{col}(e_1, e_2)$ where $e_1 \in \mathbb{R}^{n_1}$ and $e_2 \in \mathbb{R}^{n_2}$ in this new coordinates. Note that

$$e_1 = g_2 - g_1. \tag{11}$$

Furthermore, the transfer functions $c_2^T (sI - J_i)^{-1} b_2$ do not have any finite zeros and the pairs (J_i, b_2) are controllable.

At this point, we claim that the system (10) is completely controllable if and only if for each x_0 and x_f there exist a real number $T > 0$ and $x = \operatorname{col}(x_1, x_2) \in \mathcal{AC}^n$ such that

$$\dot{x}_1 = Hx_1 + \begin{cases} g_1 c_2^T x_2 & \text{if } c_2^T x_2 \leqslant 0 \\ g_2 c_2^T x_2 & \text{if } c_2^T x_2 \geqslant 0 \end{cases} \tag{12}$$

with $x(0) = x_0$ and $x(T) = x_f$. The 'only if' part is evident. For the 'if' part, let x_0 and x_f be given arbitrary states. Let T and $x = \operatorname{col}(x_1, x_2)$ be such that (12) is satisfied with $x(0) = x_0$ and $x(T) = x_f$. Note that $c_2^T (sI - J_i)^{-1} b_2$ have polynomial inverses, say $L_i(s)$, as they both have no finite zeros. Now, it can be verified that the input

$$u = -f^T x_1 + \begin{cases} L_1(\frac{d}{dt}) c_2^T x_2 & \text{if } c_2^T x_2 \leqslant 0 \\ L_2(\frac{d}{dt}) c_2^T x_2 & \text{if } c_2^T x_2 \geqslant 0 \end{cases}$$

steers the initial state x_0 of the system (10) to the final state x_f in T units of time.

Hence, in view of Theorem 4, we proved that the system (10) (equivalently (1)) is completely controllable if and only if

1. $(H, [g_1 \ g_2])$ is controllable, and
2. The implication

$$H^T z = \lambda z, \ \lambda \in \mathbb{R}, \ z \neq 0 \Rightarrow (z^T g_1)(z^T g_2) > 0 \tag{13}$$

holds.

We claim that $(H, [g_1 \ g_2])$ is controllable if and only if so is $(A_1, [b \ e])$. To see this, we will use the Hautus test. Note that

$$\text{rank}([sI - A_1 \ b \ e]) = \text{rank}(\begin{bmatrix} sI - H & -g_1 c_2^T & 0 & e_1 \\ -b_2 f^T & sI - J_1 & b_2 & e_2 \end{bmatrix}). \tag{14}$$

After performing elementary column operations, we obtain

$$\text{rank}([sI - A_1 \ b \ e]) = \text{rank}(\begin{bmatrix} sI - H & -g_1 c_2^T & 0 & e_1 \\ 0 & sI - J_1 & b_2 & e_2 \end{bmatrix}) \tag{15}$$

$$= \text{rank}([sI - H \ -g_1 c_2^T \ e_1]) + \text{rank}([sI - J_1 \ b_2 \ e_2]). \tag{16}$$

As the pair (J_1, b_2) is controllable, the last summand equals to n_2. Note that the first one is equal to $\text{rank}([sI - H \ g_1 \ g_2])$ in view of (11). Consequently, $(H, [g_1 \ g_2])$ is controllable if and only if $(A_1, [b \ e])$ is controllable.

On the other hand, straightforward calculations show that (13) is equivalent to the implication

$$[v^T \ \mu_i] \begin{bmatrix} \lambda I - A_i & b \\ c^T & 0 \end{bmatrix} = 0, \ \lambda \in \mathbb{R}, \ v \neq 0, \ i = 1, 2 \Rightarrow \mu_1 \mu_2 > 0. \tag{17}$$

Thus, we proved the following theorem.

Theorem 5. *Let e be such that $A_2 - A_1 = ec^T$. The bimodal piecewise linear system (1) is completely controllable if and only if the following conditions hold.*

1. *The pair $(A_1, [b \ e])$ is controllable.*
2. *The implication*

$$[v^T \ \mu_i] \begin{bmatrix} \lambda I - A_i & b \\ c^T & 0 \end{bmatrix} = 0, \ \lambda \in \mathbb{R}, \ v \neq 0, \ i = 1, 2 \Rightarrow \mu_1 \mu_2 > 0. \tag{18}$$

holds.

3   Conclusions

We have obtained algebraic characterizations of controllability for two related classes of bimodal piecewise linear systems. These characterizations generalize classical results for single-mode linear systems as well as controllability results for systems subject to positive control. An interesting problem for further research is the characterization of controllability for similar systems with multiple inputs or outputs whose signs determine mode changes. Such systems may have many modes. Another question of interest would be to establish the relation between controllability and stabilizability in the context of the classes of switching linear systems considered here.

References

1. G.B. Basile and G. Marro. *Controlled and Conditioned Invariants in Linear System Theory*. Prentice Hall, Englewood Cliffs, NJ, 1992.
2. R.F. Brammer. Controllability in linear autonomous systems with positive controllers. *SIAM J. Control*, 10(2):329–353, 1972.
3. M.K. Çamlıbel, W.P.M.H. Heemels, A.J. van der Schaft, and J.M. Schumacher. Switched networks and complementarity. *IEEE Transactions on Circuits and Systems I*, 50(8):1036–1046, 2003.
4. T. Kailath. *Linear Systems*. Prentice-Hall, Englewood Cliffs, NJ, 1980.
5. R.E. Kalman. On the general theory of control systems. In *Proceedings of the 1st World Congress of the International Federation of Automatic Control*, pages 481–493, 1960.
6. E.B. Lee and L. Markus. *Foundations of Optimal Control Theory*. John Wiley& Sons, New York, 1967.
7. S.H. Saperstone and J.A. Yorke. Controllability of linear oscillatory systems using positive controls. *SIAM J. Control*, 9(2):253–262, 1971.

Appendix: Proof of Theorem 4

First we need some preparations. The following proposition will simplify the analysis of the controllability properties of (6).

Proposition 1. *The following statements are equivalent.*

1. *For each ζ_0, $\zeta_f \in \mathbb{R}^k$ and η_0, $\eta_f \in \mathbb{R}$, there exist a real number $T > 0$ and a solution $(\zeta, \eta) \in \mathcal{AC}^{k+1}$ of (6) such that*

$$\zeta(0) = \zeta_0, \qquad \zeta(T) = \zeta_f \qquad (19)$$
$$\eta(0) = \eta_0, \qquad \eta(T) = \eta_f. \qquad (20)$$

2. *For each ζ_0, $\zeta_f \in \mathbb{R}^k$, there exist a real number $T > 0$ and a solution $(\zeta, \eta) \in \mathcal{AC}^{k+1}$ of (6) such that*

$$\zeta(0) = \zeta_0, \quad \zeta(T) = \zeta_f \qquad (21)$$
$$\eta(0) = \eta(T) = 0. \qquad (22)$$

3. *For each $\zeta_m \in \mathbb{R}^k$, there exist real numbers $T_-, T_+ > 0$ and two solutions $(\zeta_-, \eta_-) \in \mathcal{AC}^{k+1}$ and $(\zeta_+, \eta_+) \in \mathcal{AC}^{k+1}$ of (6) such that*

$$\zeta_-(0) = \zeta_m, \zeta_-(T_-) = 0 \qquad \zeta_+(0) = 0, \zeta_+(T_+) = \zeta_m \qquad (23)$$
$$\eta_-(0) = \eta_-(T_-) = 0 \qquad \eta_+(0) = \eta_+(T_+) = 0. \qquad (24)$$

Proof. 1⇒2: Evident.

2⇒3: Evident.

3⇒1: Suppose that the statement 3 holds. We claim that for any $\zeta_0, \zeta_f \in \mathbb{R}^k$ and $\eta_0, \eta_f \in \mathbb{R}$, there exist a real number $T > 0$ and a solution $(\zeta, \eta) \in \mathcal{AC}^{k+1}$ of (6) such that

$$\zeta(0) = \zeta_0, \qquad \zeta(T) = \zeta_f \tag{25a}$$
$$\eta(0) = \eta_0, \qquad \eta(T) = \eta_f. \tag{25b}$$

In what follows we construct such a solution.

i. Let η_{pre} be a $\mathcal{C}^\infty$-function such that

$$\eta_{\mathrm{pre}}(0) = \eta_0 \text{ and } \eta_{\mathrm{pre}}(1) = 0.$$

Let $(\zeta_{\mathrm{pre}}, \eta_{\mathrm{pre}})$ be the solution of (6) with $\zeta_{\mathrm{pre}}(0) = \zeta_0$. Define $\zeta_0' := \zeta_{\mathrm{pre}}(1)$.

ii. Let η_{post} be a $\mathcal{C}^\infty$-function such that

$$\eta_{\mathrm{post}}(0) = 0 \text{ and } \eta_{\mathrm{post}}(1) = \eta_f.$$

Let $(\zeta_{\mathrm{post}}, \eta_{\mathrm{post}})$ be the solution of (6) with $\zeta_{\mathrm{post}}(1) = \zeta_f$. Define $\zeta_f' := \zeta_{\mathrm{post}}(0)$.

iii. The statement 3 guarantees the existence of the solutions $(\zeta_-, \eta_-) \in \mathcal{AC}^{k+1}$ and $(\zeta_+, \eta_+) \in \mathcal{AC}^{k+1}$ of (6) such that

$$\zeta_-(0) = \zeta_0', \zeta_-(T_-) = 0 \qquad \zeta_+(0) = 0, \zeta_+(T_+) = \zeta_f' \tag{26}$$
$$\eta_-(0) = \eta_-(T_-) = 0 \qquad \eta_+(0) = \eta_+(T_+) = 0. \tag{27}$$

Consider a $\mathcal{C}^\infty$-function η satisfying

$$\eta(t) = \begin{cases} \eta_{\mathrm{pre}}(t) & \text{if } 0 \leqslant t \leqslant 1, \\ \eta_-(t - 1) & \text{if } 1 \leqslant t \leqslant 1 + T_-, \\ \eta_+(t - 1 - T_-) & \text{if } 1 + T_- \leqslant t \leqslant 1 + T_- + T_+, \\ \eta_{\mathrm{post}}(t - 1 - T_- - T_+) & \text{if } 1 + T_- + T_+ \leqslant t \leqslant 2 + T_- + T_+. \end{cases}$$

Let ζ be the concatenation of the functions ζ_{pre}, ζ_-, ζ_+, and ζ_{post} in the same manner. By construction, (ζ, η) is a solution of (6) satisfying (25). ∎

The next lemma provides necessary and sufficient conditions for the system (6) to be controllable from the origin.

Lemma 1. *The following statements are equivalent.*

1. *For each $\zeta_m \in \mathbb{R}^k$, there exist a real number $T > 0$ and a solution $(\zeta, \eta) \in \mathcal{AC}^{k+1}$ of (6) such that*

$$\zeta(0) = 0, \zeta(T) = \zeta_m \tag{28}$$
$$\eta(0) = \eta(T) = 0. \tag{29}$$

2. *There exists no nonzero w such that*

$$w^T \exp(Kt)N \leqslant 0 \text{ and } w^T \exp(Kt)P \geqslant 0 \qquad (30)$$

for all $t \geqslant 0$.

Proof. 1⇒2: Suppose that 1 holds but 2 does not. Let w be such that

$$w^T \exp(Kt)N \leqslant 0 \text{ and } w^T \exp(Kt)P \geqslant 0 \qquad (31)$$

for all $t \geqslant 0$. Then, for any $\eta \in \mathcal{AC}$ the solution of (6) with $\zeta(0) = 0$ satisfies

$$w^T \zeta(T) = w^T \int_0^T \exp(K(T-s))(-N\eta^-(s) + P\eta^+(s)) \, ds \geqslant 0. \qquad (32)$$

In other words, 1 fails for any ζ_m with $w^T \zeta_m < 0$. Contradiction!

2⇒1: Consider for each $\Delta > 0$ a nonnegative valued $\mathfrak{C}^\infty$-function η^Δ with $\text{supp}(\eta^\Delta) \subseteq (\frac{\Delta}{4}, 3\frac{\Delta}{4})$ and

$$\int_{\Delta/4}^{3\Delta/4} \eta^\Delta(t) \, dt = 1.$$

It is a standard fact from distribution theory that η^Δ converges to a Dirac impulse as Δ tends to zero. Now, consider the input

$$\eta(t) = a_0 \eta^\Delta(t) - a_1 \eta^\Delta(t - \Delta) + - \cdots - a_{2q-1} \eta^\Delta(t - (2q-1)\Delta). \qquad (33)$$

where $0 \leqslant t \leqslant 2q\Delta$ and all a_is are nonnegative. Note that η is a $\mathfrak{C}^\infty$-function. Obviously, $\eta \in \mathcal{AC}$ for $T = 2q\Delta$. Let $M(\Delta)$ be defined as the integral

$$\int_0^\Delta \exp(K(\Delta - s))\eta^\Delta(s) \, ds.$$

Note that $M(\Delta)$ commutes with K and hence with $\exp(K\cdot)$. The input given by (33) steers the origin to the state

$$\zeta(T) = M(\Delta) \sum_{i=1}^{2q-1} \exp(K(2q - 1 - i)\Delta)L_i a_i \qquad (34)$$

under the dynamics of (6). Here $L_i = P$ if i is even and $L_i = -N$ if i is odd. Therefore, if ζ_m is a nonnegative linear combination of the columns of a matrix of the form

$$Q(\Delta, q) := M(\Delta) \left[-N \exp(K\Delta)P \cdots \exp(K(2q-1)\Delta)P\right] \qquad (35)$$

then there exists a solution of (6) which satisfies the properties (28). Now, suppose that 2 holds but 1 does not. Then, there should exist a ζ_m such that it cannot be written as a nonnegative linear combination of the columns of a matrix $Q(\Delta, q)$ for any pair (Δ, q). It follows from Farkas' lemma that for each Δ and q there exists $w_{\Delta, q}$ such that

$$w_{\Delta, q}^T \zeta_m < 0 \tag{36a}$$

$$w_{\Delta, q}^T Q(\Delta, q) \geqslant 0. \tag{36b}$$

Obviously, we can take $\| w_{\Delta, q} \| = 1$ without loss of generality. Take a sequence of real numbers Δ_i that converges to zero. Choose a positive real number T. Let q_i be the smallest integer such that $T \leqslant 2q_i \Delta_i$. As w_{Δ_i, q_i} is bounded, it admits a convergent subsequence due to the well-known Bolzano-Weierstrass theorem. Therefore, we can assume, without loss of generality, that the sequence w_{Δ_i, q_i} itself is convergent. Let w_T denote its limit. Note that, in view of (36b), one has

$$w_{\Delta_i, q_i}^T M(\Delta_i) \exp(K(2j)\Delta_i) N \leqslant 0 \tag{37a}$$

$$w_{\Delta_i, q_i}^T M(\Delta_i) \exp(K(2j+1)\Delta_i) P \geqslant 0 \tag{37b}$$

for all $j = 0, 1, \dots, q_i - 1$. Let j_i be the smallest integer such that $t \leqslant (2j_i + 1)\Delta_i$ for a fixed $t \in [0, T]$. Obviously, $2j_i \Delta_i$ and $(2j_i + 1)\Delta_i$ both converge to t. Note that $M(\Delta)$ converges to the identity matrix as Δ tends to zero. By taking the limit of (37), one has

$$w_T^T \exp(Kt) N \leqslant 0 \tag{38a}$$

$$w_T^T \exp(Kt) P \geqslant 0 \tag{38b}$$

for all $t \in [0, T]$ since $M(\Delta)$ converges to the identity matrix as Δ tends to zero. Note that $\| w_T \| = 1$. The Bolzano-Weierstrass theorem asserts that there exists a convergent subsequence within the set $\{w_T \mid T \in \mathbb{N}\}$, say w_{T_i}. Let w denote the limit of w_{T_i} as T_i tends to infinity. We claim that

$$w^T \exp(Kt) N \leqslant 0 \tag{39a}$$

$$w^T \exp(Kt) P \geqslant 0 \tag{39b}$$

for all $t \geqslant 0$. To show this, suppose that $w^T \exp(Kt') N > 0$ for some t'. Then, for some sufficiently large T', one has $w_{T'}^T \exp(Kt') N > 0$ and $t' < T'$. However, this cannot happen due to (38a). In a similar fashion, one can conclude that (39b) holds. As $w \neq 0$, (39) contradicts the statement 2. ∎

The condition (30) is existential in nature and as such it cannot be verified easily. Our next aim is to provide an alternative characterization of (30). First, we focus on the case for which K has no real eigenvalues. The following lemma can be found in [2, proof of Theorem 1.4].

Lemma 2. *Let* $K \in \mathbb{R}^{k \times k}$ *and* $R \in \mathbb{R}^{n \times m}$. *If* K *has no real eigenvalues and* (K, R) *is controllable then there exists no nonzero* w *such that* $w^T \exp(Kt) R \leqslant 0$ *for all* $t \geqslant 0$.

When (K, R) is not controllable, a similar result can be stated as follows.

Lemma 3. *Let $K \in \mathbb{R}^{k \times k}$ and $R \in \mathbb{R}^{n \times m}$. If K has no real eigenvalues then the implication*

$$w^T \exp(Kt)R \leqslant 0 \text{ for all } t \geqslant 0 \Rightarrow w^T \exp(Kt)R = 0 \text{ for all } t = 0 \quad (40)$$

holds.

Proof. With no loss of generality, one may assume that the pair (K, R) is in the following canonical form

$$K = \begin{bmatrix} K_{11} & K_{12} \\ 0 & K_{22} \end{bmatrix}, \quad R = \begin{bmatrix} R_1 \\ 0 \end{bmatrix} \quad (41)$$

where (K_{11}, R_1) is controllable. Note that

$$\exp(Kt) = \begin{bmatrix} \exp(K_{11}t) & * \\ 0 & \exp(K_{22}) \end{bmatrix}. \quad (42)$$

Hence, $w^T \exp(Kt)R = w_1^T \exp(K_{11}t)R_1$ for any w with a partition $w = \mathrm{col}(w_1, w_2)$ that conforms to the partition (41). Let w be such that $w^T \exp(Kt)R \leqslant 0$ for all $t \geqslant 0$. This would mean that $w_1^T \exp(K_{11}t)R_1 \leqslant 0$ for all $t \geqslant 0$. As (K_{11}, R_1) is controllable, however, Lemma 2 implies that $w_1 = 0$. Consequently, $w^T \exp(Kt)R = 0$ for all $t \geqslant 0$. $\blacksquare$

At the other extreme, the case for which K has only real eigenvalues stands. The following lemma presents an alternative characterization of the condition (30) for this case.

Lemma 4. *Let $K \in \mathbb{R}^{k \times k}$, $N \in \mathbb{R}^k$, and $P \in \mathbb{R}^k$. Suppose that K has only real eigenvalues. Then, the following conditions are equivalent.*

1. *There exists no nonzero w such that $w^T \exp(Kt)N \leqslant 0$ and $w^T \exp(Kt)P \geqslant 0$ for all $t \geqslant 0$.*
2. *Any eigenvector z of K^T satisfies $(z^T N)(z^T P) > 0$.*

Proof. 1$\Rightarrow$2: Suppose that 1 holds but 2 does not. Then, for an eigenvector of z of K^T one has $z^T N \leqslant 0$ and $z^T P \geqslant 0$. Obviously, $z^T \exp(Kt)N \leqslant 0$ and $z^T \exp(Kt)P \geqslant 0$ for all $t \geqslant 0$. Contradiction!

2$\Rightarrow$1: Suppose that 2 holds but 1 does not. Let $w \neq 0$ be such that

$$w^T \exp(Kt)N \leqslant 0 \text{ and } w^T \exp(Kt)P \geqslant 0 \text{ for all } t \geqslant 0.$$

It follows from [2, Lemma 2.4] that

$$w^T \exp(Kt) = \sum_{i=1}^{q} t^{j_i} \exp(\lambda_i t)[z_i^T + f_i^T(t)] \quad (43)$$

where

i. $\lambda_1 > \lambda_2 > \cdots > \lambda_q$ are the q distinct eigenvalues of the matrix K,
ii. $K^T z_i = \lambda_i z_i$,
iii. if $z_i = 0$ then $f_i^T(t) \equiv 0$,
iv. j_is are nonnegative integers, and
v. the functions f_i vanish as t tends to infinity.

Let q' be the smallest integer such that $z_{q'} \neq 0$. Note that the sign of $w^T \exp(Kt)N$ for all sufficiently large t is the same as the sign of $z_{q'}^T N$. Similarly, the sign of $w^T \exp(Kt)P$ for all sufficiently large t is the same as the sign of $z_{q'}^T P$. Therefore, $(w^T \exp(Kt)N)(w^T \exp(Kt)P) > 0$ for all sufficiently large t. Contradiction!   ∎

The above proof has the following side result that will be used later.

Corollary 1. *Let $K \in \mathbb{R}^{k \times k}$, $N \in \mathbb{R}^k$, and $P \in \mathbb{R}^k$. Suppose that K has only real eigenvalues and for any eigenvector z of K^T there holds that $(z^T N)(z^T P) > 0$. Then, for any vector w*

$$(w^T \exp(Kt)N)(w^T \exp(Kt)P) > 0 \tag{44}$$

for all sufficiently large t.

Lemma 5. *Let $K \in \mathbb{R}^{k \times k}$, $N \in \mathbb{R}^k$, and $P \in \mathbb{R}^k$. The following statements are equivalent.*

1. *There exists no nonzero w such that $w^T \exp(Kt)N \leqslant 0$ and $w^T \exp(Kt)P \geqslant 0$ for all $t \geqslant 0$.*
2. *The pair $(K, [N\ P])$ is controllable and $(z^T N)(z^T P) > 0$ for any real eigenvector z of K^T.*

Proof. $1 \Rightarrow 2$: Suppose that $(K, [N\ P])$ is not controllable. Then, the matrix $[s'I - K\ N\ P]$ is not of full row rank for some $s' \in \mathbb{C}$, i.e. there should exists a nonzero complex vector v such that $v^* [s'I - K\ N\ P] = 0$. Let $v = v_1 + iv_2$ where v_1 and v_2 are real vectors, and also let $s' = \sigma + i\omega$ where σ and ω are real numbers. Clearly, $v_i^T N = v_i^T P = 0$ for $i = 1, 2$. Note that

$$\begin{bmatrix} v_1^T \\ v_2^T \end{bmatrix} K = \begin{bmatrix} \sigma & \omega \\ -\omega & \sigma \end{bmatrix} \begin{bmatrix} v_1^T \\ v_2^T \end{bmatrix}. \tag{45}$$

This would result in

$$\begin{bmatrix} v_1^T \\ v_2^T \end{bmatrix} \exp(Kt) = \exp\left(\begin{bmatrix} \sigma & \omega \\ -\omega & \sigma \end{bmatrix} t \right) \begin{bmatrix} v_1^T \\ v_2^T \end{bmatrix}. \tag{46}$$

Therefore, we have $w^T \exp(Kt)N = w^T \exp(Kt)P = 0$ for any linear combination w of the vectors v_1 and v_2. We reach a contradiction. Consequently, the matrix $[sI - K\ N\ P]$ must have full row rank for all $s \in \mathbb{C}$. Suppose, now, that there exists a real eigenvector of K^T such that $(z^T N)(z^T P) \leqslant 0$. Without loss of generality, we can assume that $z^T N \leqslant 0$ and $z^T P \geqslant 0$. This, however, would mean that $z^T \exp(Kt)N \leqslant 0$ and $z^T \exp(Kt)P \geqslant 0$ for all $t \geqslant 0$. Contradiction! Therefore, $(z^T N)(z^T P)$ must be positive for any real eigenvector of K^T.

$2 \Rightarrow 1$: Suppose that 2 holds but 1 does not. Let the nonzero vector w satisfy $w^T \exp(Kt)N \leqslant 0$ and $w^T \exp(Kt)P \geqslant 0$ for all $t \geqslant 0$. We can assume that the matrix K has the form $K = \text{blockdiag}(K_1, K_2)$ (with possibly empty blocks) where K_1 has only real eigenvectors and K_2 has no real eigenvectors. Clearly, $\exp(Kt) = \text{blockdiag}(\exp(K_1 t), \exp(K_2 t))$. Let the partitions $N = \text{col}(N_1, N_2)$, $P = \text{col}(P_1, P_2)$, and $w = \text{col}(w_1, w_2)$ conform to the above partition of K. Then, we have

$$w_1^T \exp(K_1 t)N_1 + w_2^T \exp(K_2 t)N_2 \leqslant 0 \tag{47a}$$

$$w_1^T \exp(K_1 t)P_1 + w_2^T \exp(K_2 t)P_2 \geqslant 0 \tag{47b}$$

for all $t \geqslant 0$. It follows from Corollary 1 that $w_1^T \exp(K_1 t)N_1$ and $w_1^T \exp(K_1 t)P_1$ have the same sign for all sufficiently large t as every real eigenvector z of K^T satisfies $(z^T N)(z^T P) > 0$. Then, in order the relations (47) to hold, either

$$w_2^T \exp(K_2 t)N_2 \leqslant 0 \tag{48}$$

or

$$w_2^T \exp(K_2 t)P_2 \geqslant 0 \tag{49}$$

should be satisfied for all $t \geqslant t_0 \geqslant 0$ for some t_0. Therefore, either

$$\tilde{w}_2^T \exp(K_2 t)N_2 \leqslant 0 \tag{50}$$

or

$$\tilde{w}_2^T \exp(K_2 t)P_2 \geqslant 0 \tag{51}$$

is satisfied for all $t \geqslant 0$ where $\tilde{w}_2 := \exp(K^T t_0)w_2$. This means that either (50) or (51) should be satisfied as equality for all $t \geqslant 0$ in view of Lemma 3. We claim that in fact both are satisfied as equality. To see this, first suppose that (50) is satisfied as equality. From (48) and (47a), we get $w_1^T \exp(K_1 t)N_1 \leqslant 0$ for all $t \geqslant 0$. As a consequence of Corollary 1 and (47b), we get $w_2^T \exp(K_2 t)P_2 \geqslant 0$ for all $t \geqslant 0$. Due to Lemma 2 this would mean that (51) is also satisfied as equality for all $t \geqslant 0$. Now, suppose that (51) is satisfied as equality. Similar analysis as above would show that (50) should be satisfied as equality in this case. Since both (50) and (51) are satisfied as equality, the vector $\tilde{w}_2$ should lie in the intersection of the uncontrollable spaces of the pairs (K_2, N_2) and (K_2, P_2). By hypothesis, therefore, $\tilde{w}_2 = w_2 = 0$. From (47) and Lemma 4, we conclude that $w_1 = 0$. Hence, $w = 0$. Contradiction! ∎

After all these preparations, we are in a position to prove Theorem 6. Lemma 5 proves the equivalence of the second and third statements. Note that the conditions in 3 are satisfied by a triple (K, N, P) if and only if they are satisfied by $(-K, -N, -P)$. Therefore, the third statement is equivalent to the third statement in Proposition 1 due to Lemma 1. This concludes the proof.

Observability of
Piecewise-Affine Hybrid Systems

Pieter Collins and Jan H. van Schuppen

Centrum voor Wiskunde en Informatica,
P.O. Box 94079, 1090 GB Amsterdam, The Netherlands.
{Pieter.Collins,J.H.van.Schuppen}@cwi.nl

Abstract. We consider observability for a class of piecewise-affine hybrid systems without inputs. The aim is to give verifiable conditions for observability in terms of linear equations and inequalities. We first discuss a number of important concepts, such as discrete-event detectability and trajectory observability. We give sufficient conditions for observability, observability in infinitesimal time, and observability after a single discrete event. The former conditions are used to construct an observer for the system, the latter are applied to deduce observability for an example system.

1 Introduction

Observability of a systems is a sufficient condition for the proper operation of an observer. Observability is also one of the conditions needed to characterise minimality of a realization of an input-output map. Of these two uses of the concept of observability, the first is the most practically useful while the second is of primary theoretical significance. For each new class of dynamic systems the concept of observability has to be explored and conditions for it derived.

A piecewise-affine hybrid system (PAHS) can be considered as a product of a finite state automaton and a family of finite-dimensional affine systems on polytopes. A formal definition is given in Sect. 2. Attention will be restricted to piecewise-affine hybrid systems without input function. Observability will be formulated as injectiveness of the map from the initial state to the future output trajectory, as is generally done in system theory, see for example, [1,2]. The concept of final-state observability or reconstructability, in which one wishes to determine the final state from an output trajectory defined up to the current time, will not be considered. Observability of piecewise-affine hybrid systems is dual to reachability as developed in [3].

It was stated by E. Sontag [4] that observability is undecidable for a class of piecewise-linear hybrid systems, and this suggests that observability is also undecidable for the class of piecewise-affine systems considered here. We therefore concentrate on finding sufficient conditions for observability.

Observing a piecewise-affine hybrid system involves determining both the discrete state and the associated continuous state. Of critical importance is detecting the times of the discrete events. The interplay between the discrete and

R. Alur and G.J. Pappas (Eds.): HSCC 2004, LNCS 2993, pp. 265–279, 2004.

continuous dynamics means that the system may be observable even if the affine system associated with a particular discrete state is unobservable, since enough information may be available using a combination of outputs in different states to determine the initial state. Unlike linear systems, observability of piecewise-affine hybrid systems may be possible only after a finite time trajectory has been observed. As well as giving sufficient conditions for observability, we will also give a construction of an initial state observer.

An exponentially-stable observer for piecewise-affine hybrid systems was given by A. Balluchi et al in [5]. One of the conditions for the existence of the observer is that the affine system associated to each discrete state is observable. Due to this assumption, observability reduces to recovering the current discrete state, for which algorithms were provided in the paper. Sufficient conditions for final-state observability were given in [6]. Observability of piecewise-affine hybrid systems is also discussed in the paper [7]. During the Workshop Hybrid Systems—Computation and Control held in April 2003 in Prague [8], several papers on observability were presented. Of these papers, observability in the case of multiple discrete states was only explicitly discussed by R. Vidal et al [9], who gave necessary and sufficient conditions for observability of a restricted class of hybrid systems called *jump-linear systems*. This paper extends the results of [9] for jump-linear systems by considering affine systems, discontinuous jumps in the systems state, and switches induced by guard conditions.

An overview of this paper follows. Section 2 contains a definition of the class of piecewise-affine hybrid systems and of the concept of observability. The problem of characterising observability is formulated. In Sect. 3 a theorem is stated on how to recover the discrete state from the observed output, and results are formulated of how to recover the continuous state from the output functions. In Sect. 4 sufficient conditions are stated and proven for the observability of these systems. Procedures for the construction of the initial state are presented in Sect. 5. Examples of observable and of unobservable systems are presented in Sect. 6. The paper ends with concluding remarks.

2   Problem Formulation

We now give a formal definition of piecewise-affine hybrid systems, and discuss various concepts related to the observability of such systems.

2.1   Piecewise-Affine Hybrid Systems

Definition 1 (Piecewise-affine hybrid system).
A continuous-time piecewise-affine hybrid system consists of

- *A closed convex polyhedral input set $U \subset \mathbb{R}^m$.*
- *An observation set $Y \subset \mathbb{R}^p$.*
- *A finite discrete state set Q.*
- *A set E of discrete events, comprising a set E_{in} of input events and a set E_{ct} of dynamically generated events.*

– A discrete state transition function ρ, *which is a partial function* $Q \times E \to Q$.

– *For each discrete state* $q \in Q$,
  - *a convex polyhedral* continuous state space $X_q \subset \mathbb{R}^{n_q}$
  - *a convex polyhedral* initial state set $X_q^{\text{init}} \subset X_q$
  - *an* affine system $\mathcal{A}_q$ *given by*

$$\dot{x}(t) = a_q + A_q x(t) + B_q u(t)$$

  - *an affine* output map $\mathcal{C}_q : X_q \times U \to Y$ *given by*

$$y(t) = c_q + C_q x(t) + D_q u(t)$$

– *For each event* $e \in E$, *and each discrete state* $q \in Q$ *such that* $\rho(q,e)$ *is defined,*
  - *a closed convex polyhedral* guard set $X_{(q,e)}^{\text{guard}} \subset X_q$.
  - *an affine* continuous state transition function $\mathcal{F}_{(q,e)} : X_{(q,e)}^{\text{guard}} \to X_{\rho(q,e)}$ *given by*

$$\mathcal{F}_{(q,e)}(x) = f_{(q,e)} + F_{(q,e)} x.$$

The *state space* X of a PAHS is the set $\bigcup_{q \in Q} \{q\} \times X_q$. We can assume that each X_q has full dimension n_q, and so can be represented as the solution set of a system of linear inequalities. The initial sets X_q^{init} and the guard sets $X_{(q,e)}^{\text{guard}}$ can be represented by a combination of linear equations and linear inequalities. Since we shall be mostly interested in the linear equations for the initial and guard sets, we give explicit formulae:

- The linear equations for X_q^{init} are

$$\mathcal{J}_q(x) = j_q + J_q x = 0.$$

- The linear equations for $X_{(q,e)}^{\text{guard}}$ are

$$\mathcal{G}_{(q,e)}(x) = g_{(q,e)} + G_{(q,e)} x = 0.$$

However, the results in this paper extend easily to the case of mixed linear equations and inequalities defining polyhedral sets for X_q, X_q^{init} and $X_{(q,e)}^{\text{guard}}$.

Definition 2. *An* trajectory *of the PAHS system* $\mathcal{H}$ *on the time index set* $[t_0, t_1) \subset \mathbb{R}$ *with continuous input* $u : [t_0, t_1) \to U$ *is a right-continuous function* $(q, x) : [t_0, t_1) \to X$ *such that*

1. $x(t_0) \in X_{q(t_0)}^{\text{init}}$.
2. *If an event* $e \in E$ *occurs at time* t, *then*

$$x^-(t) \in X_{(q^-(t),e)}^{\text{guard}}, \qquad q(t) = \rho(q^-(t), e) \quad and \quad x(t) = \mathcal{F}_{(q^-(t),e)}(x^-(t)).$$

3. *If no event occurs at time t, then x is continuous at t, and*

$$\frac{d}{dt}x(t) = a_{q(t)} + A_{q(t)}x(t) + B_{q(t)}u(t).$$

Here we use $q^-(t)$ and $x^-(t)$ to denote, respectively, $\lim_{\tau \nearrow t} q(\tau)$ and $\lim_{\tau \nearrow t} x(\tau)$. Events in E_{ct} model events driven by the continuous dynamics, while events in E_{in} model user input events. If a event in E_{ct} is enabled at time t, then an event in E_{ct} must occur.

We further assume that every trajectory can be continued for infinite time (non-blocking), and only finitely many events occur on any finite time interval (non-Zenoness). Note that the non-blocking condition requires that each point of the boundary of X_q at which the continuous evolution leaves X_q must be contained in some guard set $X^{guard}_{(q,e)}$. For simplicity of exposition, we assume (unless otherwise stated) that no event occurs at the initial time t_0, and that at most one event occurs at any other subsequent time. The case of more than one event at a given time is a fairly straightforward extension.

For most of this paper we shall restrict to the class of PAHS *without inputs*. For such systems, there are no input events (i.e. $E = E_{ct}$) and the continuous dynamics in discrete state q reduces to

$$\dot{x}(t) = a_q + A_q x(t), \qquad y(t) = c_q + C_q x(t).$$

To simplify much of the notation, for each discrete state q and each time t we construct a *time-evolution map* $\mathcal{S}_{(q,t)}$ such that for any $x \in X_q$,

$$\frac{d}{dt}\mathcal{S}_{(q,t)}(x) = a_q + A_q \mathcal{S}_{(q,t)}(x).$$

By solving the continuous evolution equations, we find $\mathcal{S}_{(q,t)}$ is the affine map

$$\mathcal{S}_{(q,t)}(x) = s_{(q,t)} + S_{(q,t)}x = (\exp(A_q t) - I) A_q^{-1} a_q + \exp(A_q t)x. \qquad (1)$$

Note that $(\exp(A_q t) - I)A_q^{-1}$ is well-defined by its power series even if A_q is not invertible.

In examples, we will usually label states by integers i, and events e_{ij}, with $\rho(i, e_{ij}) = j$

2.2   Observability and Observers

The concept of observability is best formulated in terms of the *state-output* map of a system. The state-output map of a deterministic system on the time interval $[t_0, t_1)$ is the functional $\lambda : X \times U^{[t_0, t_1)} \to Y^{[t_0, t_1)}$ assigning to each initial state $x_0 \in X$ and each admissible input function $u(t)$ the output function $y(t)$ for the trajectory $x(t)$ giving the response of the system to the input function $u(t)$ with $x(t_0) = x_0$.

As proposed by Sontag [1,2], there are many different notions of observability, each relating to the degree to which the state can be determined from the state-output map. For systems without inputs, these observability concepts reduce to determining either the initial state $x(t_0)$ or the final state $x(t_1)$. A system is *(initial-state) observable* if the initial state can be determined from the output function $y(t) \in Y^{[t_0,t_1)}$, and *final-state observable* if the final state can be determined from the output function. Final-state observability is sometimes referred to as *current-state observability* or *reconstructability* in the literature [10, 6]. Some observability concepts for discrete event systems are given in [11]

We can further distinguish observability concepts by considering the dependence on the time domain.

Definition 3. *A system is* observable in time T *if the initial state can be determined from the output function η restricted to $[0, T)$.*

- *If the system is observable in time ϵ for all $\epsilon > 0$, then the system is observable in infinitesimal time.*
- *If the system is observable in time T for some finite T, it is observable in finite time.*
- *If the system is observable in time ∞, it is observable in infinite time.*

Unlike linear systems, which are either unobservable, or are observable in infinitesimal time, observable PAHS may be observable in infinitesimal, finite or infinite time.

By an *observer* for a system, we mean a dynamic system driven by the output $y(t)$ which produces an estimate of the state of the plant system. Just as for notions of observability we can consider *initial-state observers*, which estimate the initial state of the plant, $x(t_0)$, and *current-state observers*, which estimate the current state $x(t)$. A number of different classes of observer can be considered, including

- *point estimates* $\widehat{x}(t)$ satisfying $\lim_{t \to \infty} d(\widehat{x}(t), x(t)) = 0$,
- *set estimates* $\widehat{X}(t)$ such that $x(t) \in \widehat{X}(t)$, and
- *probabilistic estimates* which give a probability distribution for $x(t)$.

For linear systems, observers are usually constructed as point estimates evolving under a differential equation, and observability implies convergence of the estimate. For discrete-event systems, observers are usually constructed as set estimates [12]. For stochastic systems, probabilistic estimates such as Kalman filters are used.

For the theory of observability, the most natural concept of observer is an initial-state set estimator. We construct such an observer for PAHS in Sect. 5. A current-state point estimator for PAHS has been considered by Balluchi et al. [5]

2.3   Observability of PAHS

The main problem we shall consider is to determine necessary and sufficient conditions for observability of a PAHS without inputs, and the construction of observers. We shall see that the determination of the times of the discrete events is of critical importance. We say an event is *detectable* at a point x if it produces a measurable change in output, otherwise it is *undetectable at x*. An event may be detectable at certain points and not at others, even in the same discrete state. An event is *detectable* in a state q if it is detectable at all points in the guard set $X_{(q,e)}^{\text{guard}}$, and a system is *event detectable* if all events are detectable in all states. We shall see that conditions for event detectability can be expressed in affine form, and so is possible to determine whether an event is detectable.

Notice that by detectability we only require that the *time* that an event occurs can be determined; we do not require that actual event is known. Indeed, the determination of the event depends upon knowledge of the continuous state, and so may be possible at some points in the guard set but not others. The situation for hybrid systems is therefore more complicated than that of discrete-event systems, in which an event is either observable or unobservable.

The *event-time sequence* of a trajectory is the sequence (t_i) of event times. It is possible to compute the event-time sequence for an event-detectable hybrid system. The *timed event sequence* of a trajectory is the sequence of pairs (e_i, t_i) of events and event times. Since there are only finitely many events, for any event-time sequence of finite length, there are only a finite number of possible timed event sequences.

Under certain conditions, we can actually determine the discrete state completely from the continuous-time dynamics. We say discrete states q and q' are *distinguishable* if for any $x \in X_q$ and $x' \in X_{q'}$ the observations $y(t)$ for the trajectory through x and $y'(t)$ for the trajectory through x' are different on any interval $[0, \epsilon)$.

However, it is possible to obtain more information by considering events which have *not occurred* on some time interval (t_i, t_{i+1}) between consecutive events. These conditions take the form that $x(t)$ cannot satisfy the guard conditions for any $e \in E_{\text{ct}}$. Unfortunately, since $x(t)$ does not depend in an affine way on t, these conditions cannot be expressed as linear equations and inequalities. This means that while it is possible to give sufficient conditions for observability, the formulation of necessary conditions requires non-linear conditions. Some theoretical progress can be made by considering o-minimal systems [13], but these conditions do not seem particularly amenable to analysis. We shall therefore restrict attention to finding sufficient conditions for observability which can be expressed in terms of affine equations and inequalities.

3   Observability Equations

Rather than immediately give necessary or sufficient conditions for observability of PAHS, we consider important sub-problems for which we can formulate conditions in terms of linear equations. We give conditions for deducing the continuous state given the discrete state, detecting the occurrence of discrete events and determining the discrete state of the system. We then formulate equations which must be satisfied if the initial discrete state and the timed event sequence are known. Most of these equations follow in a straightforward way from the definitions, and are similar to those of [9], which are formulated in terms of *joint observability matrices* and *switching observability matrices*.

If it is not possible to detect an event, it is possible to formulate linear equations which hold between the continuous state after the previous detected event and before the next detected event. We shall not discuss the construction here.

3.1   Observability Equations for Affine Systems

Consider the affine system with state $x \in \mathbb{R}^n$ evolving by $\dot{x} = a + Ax$, and observations $y \in \mathbb{R}^p$ given by $y = c + Cx$. Computing derivatives of y, we obtain the general formula

$$\frac{d^k y}{dt^k} = CA^{k-1}a + CA^k x \quad \text{for } k \geqslant 1.$$

The linear terms are the same as for linear systems, and give the *observability matrix* O of linear systems theory. The constant expressions give rise to an *observability vector* o, and the derivatives give the *output derivative vector* $\mathcal{Y}(t)$. We have

$$O = \begin{pmatrix} C \\ CA \\ CA^2 \\ \vdots \end{pmatrix}, \qquad o = \begin{pmatrix} c \\ Ca \\ CAa \\ \vdots \end{pmatrix} \quad \text{and} \quad \mathcal{Y}(t) = \begin{pmatrix} y(t) \\ \dot{y}(t) \\ \ddot{y}(t) \\ \vdots \end{pmatrix}. \tag{2}$$

If we further define the *observability map* $\mathcal{O}$ by $\mathcal{O}\big(x(t)\big) = o + Ox(t)$ we obtain the following *observability equation*

$$\mathcal{Y}(t) = \mathcal{O}\big(x(t)\big) = o + Ox(t) \tag{3}$$

which is satisfied at all points on the trajectory. Further, if $\mathcal{Y}(t_0) = \mathcal{O}\left(x(t_0)\right)$ for some t_0, then $\mathcal{Y}(t) = \mathcal{O}\left(x(t)\right)$ for all t.

Recall that a linear system is observable if and only if $\mathrm{rank}(O) = n$, or equivalently, if $\mathrm{nullity}(O) = 0$. (The *nullity* of a matrix is the dimension of the null space.) An observable linear system is necessarily observable in infinitesimal time.

Remark 1. As defined here, the observability matrices have infinitely many rows. However, as is standard in systems theory for linear systems, we can restrict to matrices with pn rows, since CA^n can be expressed as a linear combination of the CA^k for $k < n$. In examples, we shall always consider enough rows to obtain the strongest available conditions.

3.2   Determining the Discrete Dynamics

The main difficulty in the observability analysis of hybrid systems is in determining the discrete state and events. We first aim to find conditions under which we can deduce that a discrete event has occurred. Since the system output is analytic, we can deduce the presence of a discrete event by the non-smoothness of the output function.

The following result gives necessary and sufficient conditions for event detectability, as discussed in Subsection 2.3.

Proposition 1 (Event detection). *The event e is detectable in $q \in Q$ if and only if the linear equations*

$$\mathcal{G}_{(q,e)}(x) = 0 \quad and \quad \mathcal{O}_q(x) = \mathcal{O}_{\rho(q,e)}\left(\mathcal{F}_{(q,e)}(x)\right) \tag{4}$$

have no solutions with $x \in X_q$.

The condition $\mathcal{O}_q(x) = \mathcal{O}_{\rho(q,e)}\left(\mathcal{F}_{(q,e)}(x)\right)$ is obtained by equating the vectors $\mathcal{Y}^-(t)$ and $\mathcal{Y}(t)$, and the condition $\mathcal{G}_{(q,e)}(x) = 0$ is simply the guard condition in X_q.

The following result gives a criterion for discrete states q and q' to be distinguishable, and follows immediately by considering $\mathcal{Y}(t)$.

Proposition 2 (Discrete state distinguishability). *If the linear equations*

$$\mathcal{O}_q(x) = \mathcal{O}_{q'}(x') \tag{5}$$

have no solution with $(x, x') \in X_q \times X_{q'}$, then the discrete states q and q' are distinguishable.

Clearly, if $c_q + C_q x \neq c_{q'} + C_{q'} x'$ for all $(x, x') \in X_q \times X_{q'}$, then q and q' are distinguishable; indeed, they can be distinguished by a single observation value without computing derivatives. Distinguishability of discrete states is a very strong condition.

Event detection is of critical importance in finding affine equations for observability, since the set of all initial points x_0 with a first discrete transition at time t_1 is an affine space, since $x^-(t_1) = \mathcal{S}_{(q_0, t_1 - t_0)}(x(t_0))$ is an affine function of $x(t_0)$, but the set of all points in X_q with a discrete transition e at *some* time $t \geqslant 0$ is *not* an affine space, as $x(t) = \mathcal{S}_{(q, t - t_0)}(x(t_0))$ does not depend in an affine way on t.

3.3   Determining the Continuous State

If the timed event sequence of the system is known, it is easy to write down equations for the continuous state. The system evolution can be written as

$$x(t_{n+1}) = \mathcal{F}_{(q_n, e_{n+1})} \mathcal{S}_{(q_n, t_{n+1} - t_n)} x(t_n) \tag{6}$$

Combining this with the guard equations and observability equations we obtain the following result.

Proposition 3. *Let $\mathcal{H}$ be a PAHS system, and suppose the initial time t_0, the initial state q_0, the timed event sequence (t_i, e_i) and the output function $y(t)$ are known. Let q_i be the state immediately after the ith event. Then the initial state $x = x(t_0)$ satisfies the following linear equations, the* trajectory equations

$$
\begin{aligned}
\mathcal{J}_{q_0} x(t_0) &= 0 \\
\mathcal{O}_{q_0} x(t_0) &= \mathcal{Y}(t_0) \\
\mathcal{G}_{(q_0,e_1)} \mathcal{S}_{(q_0,t_1-t_0)} x(t_0) &= 0 \\
\mathcal{O}_{q_1} \mathcal{F}_{(q_0,e_1)} \mathcal{S}_{(q_0,t_1-t_0)} x(t_0) &= \mathcal{Y}(t_1) \\
\mathcal{G}_{(q_1,e_2)} \mathcal{S}_{(q_1,t_2-t_1)} \mathcal{F}_{(q_0,e_1)} \mathcal{S}_{(q_0,t_1-t_0)} x(t_0) &= 0 \\
\mathcal{O}_{q_2} \mathcal{F}_{(q_1,e_2)} \mathcal{S}_{(q_1,t_2-t_1)} \mathcal{F}_{(q_0,e_1)} \mathcal{S}_{(q_0,t_1-t_0)} x(t_0) &= \mathcal{Y}(t_2) \\
&\vdots
\end{aligned}
\tag{7}
$$

Remark 2. If $t_{i+1} = t_i$ for some i, then we remove the equations containing $\mathcal{O}_{q_i}$, since no output is observed in state q_i.

4   Conditions for Observability of PAHS

We now present several sufficient conditions for observability of a PAHS. The conditions given in Theorem 1 are the sharpest, but cannot be verified since they contain nonlinear dependencies on the event times. However, these conditions can be used to construct an observer for the system. The conditions in Theorems 2 and 3 are expressed purely in terms of linear equations, and hence can be solved for a given system.

4.1   Sufficient Conditions for Observability

Unfortunately, it is not possible to give necessary and sufficient conditions for the observability of a PAHS purely in terms of linear equations involving the initial state and event times. The following conditions are sufficient for observability, and are expressed as equations which are linear in the initial state, but depend in a nonlinear way on the possible event times.

Theorem 1. *A PAHS $\mathcal{H}$ is observable if:*

1. *All events e of $\mathcal{H}$ are detectable.*
2. *For all possible event-time sequences (t_i), there exists at most one value (q_0, x_0) which is a solution of the trajectory equations (7) for any possible event sequence.*

Proof. Since all events are detectable, the event time sequence can be uniquely determined. Any possible initial state (q_0, x_0) must satisfy the trajectory equations (7) for some event sequence. Hence if there is only one such initial state which satisfies these equations for any event sequence, this must be the initial state of the system given the output, hence $\mathcal{H}$ is observable.

Remark 3. If for some initial state q_0 and timed event sequence (t_i, e_i) there are two initial points x_0 and x'_0 with the same output, we can eliminate the constant terms in the trajectory equations (7). Hence the conditions under which this occur reduce to a nullity (or rank) condition on the matrix giving the linear part of equations (7). Hence a necessary condition for the system to be observable is

$$\text{nullity} \begin{pmatrix} J_{q_0} \\ O_{q_0} \\ G_{(q_0,e_1)} S_{(q_0,t_1-t_0)} \\ O_{q_1} F_{(q_0,e_1)} S_{(q_0,t_1-t_0)} \\ \vdots \end{pmatrix} = 0. \tag{8}$$

4.2   Observability in Infinitesimal Time

Unfortunately, since the sufficient conditions for observability given in Theorem 1 include nonlinear dependencies on the event times t_i, which are not known a priori, they do not give checkable conditions. A simple checkable condition, which is akin to the observability conditions for linear systems, are the following necessary and sufficient conditions for observability in infinitesimal time.

Theorem 2 (Conditions for observability in infinitesimal time).
A PAHS $\mathcal{H}$ without inputs is observable in infinitesimal time if, and only if, for initial conditions in X^{init}:

1. *All discrete states are distinguishable, and*
2. *For all discrete states, the corresponding affine system is observable.*

Proof. If all discrete states are distinguishable, then the initial discrete state q_0 can be determined from the initial trajectory. The initial condition x_0 can then be determined since the continuous dynamics in the discrete state discrete state is observable.

Conversely, if the system $\mathcal{H}$ is observable in infinitesimal time, then it must be possible to determine the initial condition without seeing any discrete events. Hence the discrete states must be distinguishable, since it must be possible to determine the initial discrete state, and the affine systems must be observable, or else it is impossible to determine the initial continuous state.

In terms of linear equations, the conditions for observability in infinitesimal time become $\mathcal{J}_q(x) = \mathcal{J}_{q'}(x')$ and $\mathcal{O}_q(x) = \mathcal{O}_{q'}(x')$ has no solutions in $X_q \times X_{q'}$ if $q \neq q'$, and $J_q x = 0$ and $O_q x = 0$ has a single solution for all q.

4.3   Single-Event Observability

A second condition under which a hybrid system is observable using only linear equations is the following *single-event observability*.

Definition 4 (Single-event observability). *A hybrid system is single-event observable if any two trajectories are distinguishable for any time after their first discrete event.*

Conditions for single-event observability can be formulated in terms of linear equations if we ignore the dependence on the initial condition, since then the time-evolution map $\mathcal{S}_{(q_0, t_1 - t_0)}$ which has nonlinear dependence on t_1 does not enter into the equations.

Theorem 3 (Conditions for single-event observability). *A PAHS $\mathcal{H}$ is single-event observable if:*

1. *All events e of $\mathcal{H}$ are detectable.*
2. *If q and q' are discrete states for which there exist initial conditions for which no discrete events occur, then q and q' are distinguishable and the corresponding affine systems are observable.*
3. *For every pair of events e, e', the only solutions of the linear equations*

$$\mathcal{O}_q(x) = \mathcal{O}_{q'}(x') \qquad \mathcal{G}_{(q,e)}(x) = \mathcal{G}_{(q',e')}(x') = 0$$

$$\mathcal{O}_{\rho(q,e)}\left(\mathcal{F}_{(q,e)}(x)\right) = \mathcal{O}_{\rho(q',e')}\left(\mathcal{F}_{(q',e')}(x')\right)$$

(9)

are $(q, x) = (q', x')$.

If the initial conditions for $\mathcal{H}$ are $X_q^{\text{init}} = \mathbb{R}^{n_q}$ for all q, and every trajectory undergoes a discrete event, then these conditions are also necessary.

Proof. Since all events are detectable, it is possible to distinguish trajectories which have a discrete event from those which do not, and it is possible to distinguish trajectories which do not contain a discrete event by Theorem 2.

If the first event e_1 takes place at time t_1, let $x = x^-(t_1) \in X_{q_0}$. Then $x(t_0) = \mathcal{S}_{(q_0, t_1 - t_0)}^{-1}(x)$, so $x(t_0)$ can be reconstructed from x. The guard conditions give $\mathcal{G}_{(q_0, e_1)}(x) = 0$, and the observations give $\mathcal{O}_{q_0}(x) = \mathcal{Y}^-(t_1)$ and $\mathcal{O}_{(q_1, e_1)}\left(\mathcal{F}_{(q_0, e_1)}(x)\right) = \mathcal{Y}(t_1)$.

If $\mathcal{H}$ is single-event observable, then the initial discrete state must be uniquely determined, so there can be no solutions of (9) for $q \neq q'$ and $(x, x') \in X_q \times X_{q'}$. Hence the discrete state q can be determined from $y(t)$. Then there can be no solutions of (9) with $q = q'$ and $x \neq x'$.

The results of this section give sufficient conditions for observability of a PAHS. The main thrust of these results is that events should be detectable, and for all possible timed event sequences, there should be a single solution to the trajectory equation. The main difficulty with applying this result is determining the possible timed-event sequences. We therefore have stronger conditions for instantaneous observability and single-event observability.

5   Observers for PAHS

We now consider the construction of observers for an event-detectable PAHS. From the previous discussions of observability it is clear that an observer must contain a discrete-state estimate and some estimate of the (initial or current) continuous state. Since the initial conditions X_q^{init} and guard sets $X_{(q,e)}^{\text{guard}}$ polyhedra, it is natural to consider polyhedral estimates for the initial state, which can be given in terms of mixed linear equations and inequalities, and to update the estimate whenever an event is detected. This does not result in much loss of information; the only information that is lost is whether a state estimate is impossible due to some guard condition being met.

It is also possible to consider only the linear equations for the initial conditions and guard sets. This has the advantage that instead of considering systems of equations and inequalities defining polyhedra, which may contain arbitrarily many equations, an estimate of the initial state in X_q in terms of linear equations can be reduced to at most n_q equations. However, the loss of information may result in more discrete states than necessary being considered.

We remark that while our observers will be constructed based on the computation of derivatives of the output function, similar observers can be constructed by sampling $y(t)$ at discrete times; for generic sampling times and error-free sampling, the same information is obtained from n samples as from n derivatives of $y(t)$. See [14] for sampling of continuous-time linear systems.

5.1   Affine Observers

We now construct an affine observer for a PAHS.

Definition 5. *An* affine observer *is a pair* $(\tau, \mathbf{O})$ *where* τ *is the last event time, and* $\mathbf{O}$ *is a set of tuples* $(q^{\text{init}}, q, \Lambda, \Sigma)$ *where*

- $q^{\text{init}} \in Q$ *is the* initial state
- $q \in Q$ *is the* current discrete state
- Λ *is a system of linear equations and inequalities with domain* $\mathbb{R}^{n_{q_{\text{init}}}}$
- Σ *is an affine map from* $X_{q_{\text{init}}}$ *to* X_q.

The observer dynamics are given by the procedure below.

Procedure 4.

0. Set Obs $= (\tau, \mathbf{O})$ where τ is the initial time t_0 and $\mathbf{O} = \{O^{\text{init}}(q) : q \in Q\}$ where $O^{\text{init}}(q) = (q, q, \mathcal{J}_q, I)$. Here, $\mathcal{J}_q$ is a set of linear equations defining X_q^{init} and I is the identity on $\mathbb{R}^{n_q}$. Go to step 3.
1. Set $\delta t = t - \tau$, the time since the last event, and set $\tau = t$.
2. Replace each $O \in \mathbf{O}$ with a copy of itself for each $e \in E$ for which $\rho(q, e)$ is defined, and modify these copies as follows:
   a) Set $\Sigma = \mathcal{S}_{(q, \delta t)} \circ \Sigma$.
   b) Append the equations $(\mathcal{G}_{(q,e)} \circ \Sigma)(x) = 0$ to Λ.
   c) Set $\Sigma = \mathcal{F}_{(q,e)} \circ \Sigma$.
   d) Set $q = \rho(q, e)$.

3. After time ϵ update each $O \in \mathbf{O}$ by appending the equations $(\mathcal{O}_q \circ \Sigma)(x) = 0$ to Λ.
4. For each $O \in \mathbf{O}$, reduce the system of equations Λ.
5. If for any $O \in \mathbf{O}$, the system Λ is inconsistent, discard O.
6. If there exists $q \in Q$ and $x \in X_q$ such that for all $O \in \mathbf{O}$, the state q_{init} of O is q, and x is the only solution of $\Lambda x = 0$, the algorithm terminates. The initial state is (q, x).
7. Wait for a discrete event to be detected, then go to step 1.

This observer is a generalisation of an observer for a discrete-event system, which keeps a set of possible current states for each initial state. For PAHS, we also need to store the equations satisfied by the continuous state, and the time evolution map from the initial continuous state to the current continuous state given the discrete-event sequence the observer models. Note that not all the information obtained about the system needs to be stored. In particular, it is not necessary to store the complete time sequence, nor the discrete-event sequence modelled by each element of the observer array.

The observer given above only considers the linear equations for X^{init} and X^{guard}, but it is straightforward to include linear inequalities to Λ. At every stage, Λ therefore defines a closed convex polyhedral set of possible initial points.

6 Examples

Example 1. Let $\mathcal{H}$ be the PAHS with two states $Q = \{1, 2\}$ with $X_1 = X_2 = \mathbb{R}^2$, and events $E = \{e_{12}, e_{21}\}$ for which

$$X_1^{\text{init}} = \{(x_1, x_2) : x_1 = 5\}, \quad X_2^{\text{init}} = \{(x_1, x_2) : x_1 = 1\},$$

$$A_1 = \begin{pmatrix} -1 & 0 \\ 0 & -2 \end{pmatrix}, \quad A_2 = \begin{pmatrix} 3 & 0 \\ 0 & 4 \end{pmatrix}, \quad C_1 = \begin{pmatrix} 1 & 0 \end{pmatrix}, \quad C_2 = \begin{pmatrix} 5 & 6 \end{pmatrix},$$

$$X_{12}^{\text{guard}} = \{(x_1, x_2) : x_1 \leqslant 1\}, \quad X_{21}^{\text{guard}} = \{(x_1, x_2) : x_1 \geqslant 5\},$$

$$F_{12} = \begin{pmatrix} 1 & 0 \\ 0 & 1 \end{pmatrix}, \quad F_{21} = \begin{pmatrix} 1 & 0 \\ 0 & 1 \end{pmatrix}.$$

The observability matrices are

$$O_1 = \begin{pmatrix} 1 & 0 \\ -1 & 0 \\ 1 & 0 \end{pmatrix}, \quad O_2 = \begin{pmatrix} 5 & 6 \\ 15 & 24 \\ 45 & 96 \end{pmatrix}.$$

The transition observability matrix and joint observability matrix are

$$O_{12} = -O_{21} = \begin{pmatrix} 4 & 6 \\ 16 & 24 \\ 44 & 96 \end{pmatrix} \quad \text{and} \quad O_{(1,2)} = \begin{pmatrix} -1 & 0 & 5 & 6 \\ 1 & 0 & 15 & 24 \\ -1 & 0 & 45 & 96 \end{pmatrix},$$

Both events e_{12} and e_{21} are detectable since the transition observability matrices are nonsingular. However, the only solution to $O_1 x = O_2 x'$ has $x' = 0$, which is not a possible state of X_2, hence the discrete states are distinguishable. The system is therefore observable since the system is observable in discrete state 2, and every initial state is either in 2 or enters 2 in a detectable event. The trajectory observability matrix for any trajectory entering 2 is the full-rank matrix

$$\begin{pmatrix} O_1 \\ O_2 S_{1,t_1-t_0} \end{pmatrix} = \begin{pmatrix} 1 & 0 \\ 5 & 6 \\ 15 & 24 \end{pmatrix}.$$

Example 2. Consider the jump-linear system with $Q = \{1,2,3\}$, $X_1 = X_2 = X_3 = \mathbb{R}^2$,

$$A_1 = \begin{pmatrix} 0 & 0 \\ 0 & 0 \end{pmatrix}, \quad A_2 = \begin{pmatrix} 0 & 0 \\ 0 & 2 \end{pmatrix}, \quad A_3 = \begin{pmatrix} 1 & 0 \\ 0 & 1 \end{pmatrix},$$

$$C_1 = \begin{pmatrix} 1 & 0 \end{pmatrix}, \quad C_2 = \begin{pmatrix} 0 & 1 \end{pmatrix}, \quad C_3 = \begin{pmatrix} 1 & 1 \end{pmatrix}.$$

The observability matrices are given by

$$O_1 = \begin{pmatrix} 1 & 0 \\ 0 & 0 \end{pmatrix}, \quad O_2 = \begin{pmatrix} 0 & 0 \\ 0 & 2 \end{pmatrix}, \quad O_3 = \begin{pmatrix} 1 & 1 \\ 1 & 1 \end{pmatrix},$$

and the difference between any two observability matrices has full rank 2.

Suppose the output trajectory is given by

$$\eta(t) = \begin{cases} 0 & \text{if } t < t_1, \\ e^{t-t_1} & \text{if } t \geq t_1. \end{cases}$$

Then from the output on $[t_1, \infty)$ we deduce that for $t \geq t_1$ the system is in state 3, so for $t = t_1$ we have $x_1 + x_2 = 1$. This is consistent both with $q_0 = 1$, $x_0 = (0,1)$ and $q_0 = 2$ and $x_0 = (1,0)$, so the system not observable.

This is a counterexample to a claim of Vidal et al given in Item 4 in Sect. 3 of [9], which states that if a *jump linear system* with n-dimensional state space satisfies $\text{rank}(O_q - O_{q'}) = n$ for all states q, q', then the initial state is reconstructible from the output after the first even time t_1 if the output on $[t_0, t_1)$ is zero. For this system, although all switching times are observable, and the observability subspaces for each discrete state have empty intersection, the discrete states themselves are not observable, since (32) of [9] is satisfied by both states q_1 and q_2.

7   Concluding Remarks

The results of the paper are concepts for the observability of piecewise-affine hybrid systems. The case where one or more continuous-space systems at different discrete states are unobservable is explicitly treated. Sufficient conditions for observability of piecewise-affine hybrid systems are stated and proven. Open issues remain concerning the decidability of observability.

Acknowledgements. The authors gratefully acknowledge the financial support of the European Commission through the project Control and Computation (IST-2001-33520) of the Program Information Societies and Technologies.

References

1. Sontag, E.: Realization theory of discrete-time nonlinear systems: I. the bounded case. IEEE Trans. Circuits & Systems **26** (1979) 342–356
2. Sontag, E.D.: Mathematical Control Theory. Springer-Verlag, Berlin (1998)
3. van Schuppen, J.: A sufficient condition for controllability of a class of hybrid systems. In Henzinger, T., Sastry, S., eds.: Hybrid systems: Computation and control. Number 1386 in Lecture Notes in Computer Science, Berlin, Springer (1998) 374–383
4. Sontag, E.D.: From linear to nonlinear: Some complexity questions. In: Proceedings of the 34th IEEE Conference on Decision and Control, New York, IEEE Press (1995) 2916–2920
5. Balluchi, A., Benvenuti, L., Di Benedetto, M.D., Sangiovanni-Vincentelli, A.L.: Design of observers for hybrid systems. In Tomlin, C.J., Greenstreet, M.R., eds.: Hybrid Systems: Computation and Control. Volume 2289 of Lecture Notes in Computer Science. Springer-Verlag, Berlin Heidelberg New York (2002) 76–89
6. Balluchi, A., Benvenuti, L., Di Benedetto, M.D., Sangiovanni-Vincentelli, A.L.: Observability for hybrid systems. In: Proc. 42nd IEEE Conference on Decision and Control, Maui, Hawaii, USA (2003)
7. Bemporad, A., Ferrari-Trecate, G., Morari, M.: Observability and controllability of piecewise affine and hybrid systems. IEEE Trans. Automatic Control **45** (2000) 1864–1876
8. Maler, O., Pnueli, A., eds.: Hybrid Systems: Computation and Control. Number 2623 in Lecture Notes in Computer Science. Springer, Berlin (2003) jhvsb.
9. Vidal, R., Chiuso, A., Soatto, S., Sastry, S.: Observability of linear hybrid systems. In Maler, O., Pnueli, A., eds.: Hybrid Systems: Computation and Control (Prague). Number 2623 in Lecture Notes in Computer Science, Springer (2003) 527–539
10. Kalman, R.E., Falb, P.L., Arbib, M.A.: Topics in mathematical systems theory. McGraw-Hill, New York (1969)
11. Özveren, C., Willsky, A.: Observability of discrete event systems. IEEE Trans. Automatic Control **35** (1990) 797–806
12. Cassandras, C., Lafortune, S.: Introduction to discrete event systems. Kluwer Academic Publishers, Boston (1999)
13. Lafferiere, G., Pappas, G.J., Sastry, S.: O-minimal hybrid systems. Math. Control Signals Systems **13** (2000) 1–21
14. Åström, K.J., Wittenmark, B.: Computer-Controlled Systems. Prentice Hall (1997)

Non-deterministic Temporal Logics
for General Flow Systems[*]

Jennifer M. Davoren[1], Vangham Coulthard[1,2], Nicolas Markey[3], and Thomas Moor[4]

[1] Department of Electrical & Electronic Engineering
The University of Melbourne, VIC 3010 AUSTRALIA
davoren@unimelb.edu.au
[2] Computer Sciences Laboratory, RSISE
The Australian National University, Canberra ACT 0200 AUSTRALIA
vaughan@discus.anu.edu.au
[3] Département d'Informatique
Université Libre de Bruxelles, 1050 BELGIUM
markey@lsv.ens-cachan.fr
[4] Lehrstuhl für Regelungstechnik
Friedrich-Alexander-Universität, Erlangen D-91058 GERMANY
thomas.moor@rt.eei.uni-erlangen.de

Abstract. In this paper, we use the constructs of branching temporal logic to formalize reasoning about a class of general flow systems, including discrete-time transition systems, continuous-time differential inclusions, and hybrid-time systems such as hybrid automata. We introduce Full General Flow Logic, **GFL***, which has essentially the same syntax as the well-known Full Computation Tree Logic, **CTL***, but generalizes the semantics to general flow systems over arbitrary time-lines. We propose an axiomatic proof system for **GFL*** and establish its soundness w.r.t. the general flow semantics.

1 Introduction

Recent work in set-valued dynamical systems [4,5], investigates a general class known as *evolutionary systems*. These are described by a set-valued map $\mathcal{S}$ which maps each state $x \in X$ to the *set* $\mathcal{S}(x)$ of all possible *future evolutions* γ from initial state x, where $\gamma : [0, \infty) \to X$, $\gamma(0) = x$. These systems are *non-deterministic*: from an initial state, there may be none, exactly one, or many possible futures. The defining condition of these systems is that the family of sets $\mathcal{S}(x)$ must be closed under the operations of taking a *suffix* of an evolution, and of taking the *fusion* of the two evolutions at a common state. It includes as examples the solution maps over real time of differential equations with inputs, and of differential inclusions and their impulse/hybrid extensions [4,7]. In the discrete time case, these same closure properties come up in the study of sets *computation sequences*, in automata theory and the semantics of branching temporal

---

[*] Research support from Australian Research Council, Grants DP0208553 & LX0242359, and CNRS France, Embassy of France in Australia, & Aust. Academy of Science, Grant DEM-RIX236. The work has benefited from discussions with participants of the Logic Seminar at the University of Melbourne, particularly B. Humberstone, L. Humberstone and G. Restall.

R. Alur and G.J. Pappas (Eds.): HSCC 2004, LNCS 2993, pp. 280–295, 2004.
© Springer-Verlag Berlin Heidelberg 2004

logics such as **CTL*** [1,17,16]. The same closure properties appear again in Willems' *Behavioural Systems theory* [18], under the names *time invariance* and *axiom of state*, with the time domain the reals *or* the integers. In the analysis of evolutionary systems, there is particular interest in the area of *Viability Theory* [7,4], where a central concept is that of an evolution being *"viable in K until capturing target C"*, which means that the path starts at a state in K, and *either* remains in K for all time, *or* it reaches C in finite time, and remains within K until it does so. From a computer science perspective, this concept corresponds to the *Until* construct on paths in temporal logic.

The purpose of this paper is to generalize the class of evolutionary systems to give an adequate semantics for non-deterministic temporal logic that is uniform for discrete-time transition systems, continuous-time differential inclusions, and hybrid systems, where the time domains of evolutions lie in the lexicographically ordered $L = \mathbb{N} \times \mathbb{R}_0^+$. There are three novelties in our work. **First**, we take a minimalist approach to the notion of a time-line: for the suffix and fusion-closure properties, the minimal structure needed on a linear order are translation or shift maps, which is weaker than a semi-group. **Second**, we don't take as primitive objects evolutions or paths defined on the entire time line; that perspective gives something of a "god's eye" view of the system, looking forward from now to eternity. Instead, our basic object of a *path* describes a *bounded-time* segment of a possible evolution of or signal within a system; it *starts somewhere*, at relative time 0 with some value $x \in X$, and then progresses with an ordering given by the underlying time-line L to *end somewhere*, at some time-point $\tau \geqslant 0$, with a value $x' \in X$. We then build up a theory of infinitary extensions with unbounded time domains. **Third**, we don't restrict to paths $\gamma : T \to X$ with bounded *interval* time domains $T = [0, \tau] \subseteq L$, but rather allow "gaps" in T. Over $L = \mathbb{N} \times \mathbb{R}_0^+$, finite hybrid trajectories are functions taking values in some X, with time domains $T \subseteq L$ of the form $T = \bigcup_{i < N} [\,(i, 0),\, (i, \Delta_i)\,]$, with $\Delta_i \in \mathbb{R}_0^+$ the duration of the i-th interval. Within T, time $(i + 1, 0)$ is the immediate *discrete successor* of time (i, Δ_i), but in the underlying line L, there is a continuum-length open interval "gap" in between.

The body of the paper is as follows. Section 2 covers preliminaries on set-valued maps and linear orders, and develops some basic theory of paths with "gappy" time domains. We introduce general flow systems in Section 3, and give examples in discrete, continuous and hybrid time. In Section 4, we give an infinitary completion construction, and relate our model class to evolutionary systems and behavioural systems. Section 5 introduces Full General Flow Logic, **GFL***, with basically the same syntax as the well-known Full Computation Tree Logic, **CTL***, developed for discrete-time models, but semantics w.r.t. general flow systems over arbitrary time. In Section 6, we propose an axiomatic proof system for **GFL*** and sketch soundness w.r.t. general flow semantics.

2   Preliminaries: Set-Valued Maps, Time-Lines, and Paths

When we write $Y \subset X$ for sets X, Y, we will mean Y is a *proper* subset of X, and so $Y \subseteq X$ iff $Y \subset X$ or $Y = X$. We write $r : X \rightsquigarrow Y$ to mean $r : X \to 2^Y$ is a *set-valued map*, with set-values $r(x) \subseteq Y$ for every $x \in X$ (possibly $r(x) = \varnothing$); equivalently, $r \subseteq X \times Y$ is a *relation*. Let $[\,X \rightsquigarrow Y\,] := 2^{X \times Y}$ denote the set of all maps, partially ordered by $\subseteq$, so $r \subseteq r'$ iff $r(x) \subseteq r'(x)$ for all $x \in X$, with least element the empty map $\varnothing$. Every map $r : X \rightsquigarrow Y$ has a *converse* $r^{-1} : Y \rightsquigarrow X$ given by $x \in r^{-1}(y)$ iff $y \in r(x)$. The *domain* of a set-valued map is $dom(r) := \{x \in X \mid r(x) \neq \varnothing\}$, and the *range* is $ran(r) := dom(r^{-1}) \subseteq Y$. A map $r : X \rightsquigarrow Y$ is *total on* X if $dom(r) = X$. We distinguish several sub-classes of maps. We write $r : X \rightarrow Y$ to mean r is a (total) *function*, with values written $r(x) = y$. We also distinguish *partial functions*, and write $r : X \dashrightarrow Y$ to mean that r is single-valued on its domain $dom(r) \subseteq X$, and write $r(x) = y$ when $x \in dom(r)$, and $r(x) = $ UNDEF when $x \notin dom(r)$.

Let $(L, <, 0)$ be a *linear order* with least element 0 and no largest element, and $\leqslant$ the reflexive closure of $<$. For elements $a, b \in L$, the set $[a, b] := \{l \in L \mid a \leqslant l \leqslant b\}$ is a *closed, bounded interval* in L, and $(a, b) := \{l \in L \mid a < l < b\}$ is an *open bounded interval*; similarly for half-open/half-closed bounded intervals $[a, b)$ and $(a, b]$. For right *unbounded intervals*, we write $[a, \infty) := \{l \in L \mid a \leqslant l\}$. Any subset $T \subseteq L$ gives a linear order $(T, <_T)$, where $<_T := < \cap (T \times T)$. Define a partial function $\mathbf{succ}_L : L \dashrightarrow L$, for $a, b \in L$, by $\mathbf{succ}_L(a) := b$ iff $a < b$ and there does *not* exists an $l \in L$ such that $a < l < b$. A linear order L is called *discrete* if $\mathbf{succ}_L$ is a *total* function $(dom(\mathbf{succ}_L) = L)$, and is *dense* if $\mathbf{succ}_L$ if $dom(\mathbf{succ}_L) = \varnothing$. Given two linear orders $(L, <)$ and $(L', <')$, a function $g : L \rightarrow L'$ is called: *strictly order-preserving* if $(\forall l, k \in L)$, $l < k$ implies $g(l) <' g(k)$; and an *order isomorphism* if it bijective and both g and g^{-1} are strictly order-preserving.

Definition 1. *Let* $(L, <, 0)$ *be a* linear order *with least element* 0 *and no largest element. We call* L *a* (future) time line *if* L *is* shift invariant, *in the sense that if for each* $a \in L$, *there exists an order isomorphism* $\sigma^{-a} : [a, \infty) \rightarrow L$, *with inverse* $\sigma^{+a} := (\sigma^{-a})^{-1} : L \rightarrow [a, \infty)$, *and* $\sigma^{-0} = id_L$. *We call the functions* σ^{-a} left a-shift maps, *and the inverses* σ^{+a} right a-shift maps.

The discrete time line $\mathbb{N}$, and the dense continuum time line $\mathbb{R}_0^+ := [0, \infty)$, are considered with their usual orderings. The hybrid time space $\mathbb{N} \times \mathbb{R}_0^+$ is linearly ordered *lexicographically*: i.e. $(i, t) <_{\text{lex}} (j, s)$ iff $i < j$ or $i = j$ and $t < s$. The least element is $\mathbf{0} := (0, 0)$. This ordering does not admit any natural addition operation to make it a linearly ordered semi-group, but its shift invariance is witnessed by the following order isomorphisms: for each $a = (k, r) \in L$, define $\sigma^{-a} : [a, \infty) \rightarrow L$ by $\sigma^{-a}(i, t) := (0, t - r)$ if $i = k$ and $\sigma^{-a}(i, t) := (i - k, t)$ if $i > k$, for $l = (i, t) \in [a, \infty)$. Then $\sigma^{+a} : L \rightarrow [a, \infty)$ satisfies $\sigma^{+a}(i, t) = (k, t + r)$ if $i = 0$ and $\sigma^{+a}(i, t) = (i + k, t)$ if $i > 0$. The full hybrid time line $\mathbb{N} \times \mathbb{R}_0^+$ is everywhere dense. In the "gappy" time domains $T \subset L$ considered below, the partial function $\mathbf{succ}_T$ may be defined at some time points in T and not at others, so T is a "hybrid" of discrete and dense.

Definition 2. *Let* $(L, <, 0)$ *be a* time line. *A* bounded time domain *in* L *is a proper subset* $T \subset L$ *with least element* 0 *and a largest element* b_T *such that* T *is a finite union of closed intervals in* L, *of the form* $T = \bigcup_{i<N} [a_i, b_i]$, *where* $N \in \mathbb{N}$ *and* $a_0 = 0$ *and* $a_i \leqslant b_i < a_{i+1}$ *for* $i < N - 1$, *and* $b_{N-1} = b_T$. *Let* $\mathsf{BT}(L) \subset 2^L$ *denote the set of all bounded time domains in* L. *Also define* $\mathsf{BI}(L) := \{T \in \mathsf{BT}(L) \mid (\exists b \in L) \, T = [0, b]\}$ *to be the subset of* interval time domains. *Over any set (signal space)* $X \neq \varnothing$, *define the set of* L-paths *in* X, *by* $\mathsf{Path}(L, X) := \{\gamma : L \dashrightarrow X \mid dom(\gamma) \in \mathsf{BT}(L)\}$, *and define* $\mathsf{IPath}(L, X)$ *to be the subset* interval paths *with* $dom(\gamma) \in \mathsf{BI}(L)$. *For* $\gamma \in \mathsf{Path}(L, X)$, *define* $b_\gamma := b_{dom(\gamma)}$ *to be the largest element in* $dom(\gamma)$, *so that* $\gamma(0) \in X$ *is the* start-value *of* γ *and* $\gamma(b_\gamma) \in X$ *is the* end-value *of* γ.

Proposition 1. *For L any time line, the set* $\mathsf{BT}(L)$ *is closed under the following operations: for* $T, T' \in \mathsf{BT}(L)$ *and* $t \in L$,
- *intersection:* $T \cap T' \in \mathsf{BT}(L)$; *in particular,* $[0, t] \cap T \in \mathsf{BT}(L)$ *if* $t \in T$;
- *left t-shift:* $\sigma^{-t}([t, b_T] \cap T) \in \mathsf{BT}(L)$ *if* $t \in T$;
- *union with right t-shift:* $T \cup \sigma^{+t}(T) \in \mathsf{BT}(L)$ *if* $t \geqslant b_T$.

The subset $\mathsf{BI}(L)$ *of bounded initial closed intervals is closed under the first two operations, and is also closed under union with right shift restricted to* $t = b_T$.

For X any value space, the following operations are well-defined in $\mathsf{Path}(L, X)$: *for* $\gamma, \gamma' \in \mathsf{Path}(L, X)$ *and* $t \in dom(\gamma)$,
- *t-end prefix:* $\gamma|_t \in \mathsf{Path}(L, X)$, *where* $\gamma|_t := \gamma \upharpoonright_{[0,t] \cap dom(\gamma)}$
- *t-start suffix:* $_t|\gamma \in \mathsf{Path}(L, X)$, *where* $(_t|\gamma)(l) := \gamma(\sigma^{+t}(l))$ *for all* $l \in dom(_t|\gamma) := \sigma^{-t}([t, b_\gamma] \cap dom(\gamma))$
- *fusion:* $\gamma * \gamma' \in \mathsf{Path}(L, X)$, *provided that* $\gamma'(0) = \gamma(b_\gamma)$, *where*
  $(\gamma * \gamma')(l) := \gamma(l)$ *for* $l \in dom(\gamma)$ *and*
  $(\gamma * \gamma')(l) := \gamma'(\sigma^{-b_\gamma}(l))$ *for* $l \in \sigma^{+b_\gamma}(dom(\gamma'))$.

For each value $x \in X$, define the *trivial path* $\theta_x : [0, 0] \to X$ by $\theta_x(0) = x$. In $\mathsf{Path}(L, X)$, the trivial path θ_x functions as a point-wise identity with respect to fusion: $\theta_x * \gamma = \gamma$ iff γ starts at value $x = \gamma(0)$, and $\gamma * \theta_x = \gamma$ iff γ ends at value $x = \gamma(b_\gamma)$.

Definition 3. *Let* $(L, <, 0)$ *be a time line and X a value space. Define a partial order on* $\mathsf{Path}(L, X)$ *from the underlying linear order on L (re-using notation) by:* $\gamma < \gamma'$ *iff* $\gamma \subset \gamma'$ *and* $t < t'$ *for all* $t \in dom(\gamma)$ *and* $t' \in dom(\gamma') - dom(\gamma)$. *If* $\gamma < \gamma'$, *we say the path* γ' *is a (proper) extension of* γ, *or* γ *is a proper prefix of* γ'.

In general, the path extension ordering $<$ is a proper subordering of the subset relation, but when restricted to the set $\mathsf{IPath}(L, X)$, it collapses to the subset relation. The following proposition characterizes the path extension partial order in terms of the fusion operation.

Proposition 2. *For L a time line, X a value space, and for all* $\gamma, \gamma' \in \mathsf{Path}(L, X)$, $\gamma < \gamma'$ *iff* $\gamma' = \gamma * \gamma''$ *for some* $\gamma'' \in \mathsf{Path}(L, X)$ *with* $\gamma'' \neq \theta_x$ *and* $\gamma''(0) = \gamma(b_\gamma)$.

We now return to the hybrid time line $L = \mathbb{N} \times \mathbb{R}_\circ^+$ for a more detailed discussion of some of its paths. Define $DS := \mathsf{IPath}(\mathbb{N}, \mathbb{R}_\circ^+)$ to be the set of all (finite) *duration sequences*; i.e. $\Delta \in DS$ is a finite sequence of values $\Delta_i := \Delta(i) \in \mathbb{R}_\circ^+$ for $i < N$ for $N = \text{length}(\Delta) \in \mathbb{N}$. For duration sequences $\Delta \in DS$, define $HT(\Delta)$ to be the *hybrid time domain* determined by Δ:

$$\begin{aligned}
HT(\Delta) &:= \bigcup_{i < \text{length}(\Delta)} [(i, 0), (i, \Delta_i)] \\
\mathsf{HT} &:= \{ HT(\Delta) \in \mathsf{BT}(L) \mid \Delta \in DS \} \\
\mathsf{HPath}(X) &:= \{ \gamma \in \mathsf{Path}(\mathbb{N} \times \mathbb{R}_\circ^+, X) \mid dom(\gamma) \in \mathsf{HT} \}
\end{aligned} \tag{1}$$

For hybrid paths $\gamma \in \mathsf{HPath}(X)$, define the *duration sequence* of γ by $\text{ds}(\gamma) = \Delta$ iff $dom(\gamma) = HT(\Delta)$ for $\Delta \in DS$, and define the *discrete length* of γ by $\text{dl}(\gamma) := \text{length}(\text{ds}(\gamma)) \in \mathbb{N}$. Also define the *total duration* of γ by $\text{td}(\gamma) := \sum_{i < \text{dl}(\gamma)} \Delta_i$.

Proposition 3. *For all* $\gamma, \gamma' \in \mathsf{HPath}(X)$,

$$\gamma \leqslant_{\mathrm{lex}} \gamma' \text{ iff } \mathrm{dl}(\gamma) \leqslant \mathrm{dl}(\gamma') \text{ and } (\forall i < N := \mathrm{dl}(\gamma) - 1) \, \gamma_i = \gamma'_i \text{ and } \gamma_N \leqslant \gamma'_N$$

With hybrid paths, we have to deal with the product structure on the time line. We also encounter product structure on the value space. Let $\pi_X : (X \times Y) \rightarrow X$ and $\pi_Y : (X \times Y) \rightarrow Y$ be the standard coordinate projection functions on a product of sets $X \times Y$. These can be lifted to give projection functions on paths $\pi_X : \mathsf{Path}(L, X \times Y) \rightarrow \mathsf{Path}(L, X)$ and to projections on functions $\pi_X : [L \rightarrow (X \times Y)] \rightarrow [L \rightarrow X]$, by defining $(\pi_X \zeta)(t) := \pi_X(\zeta(t))$ for $t \in dom(\zeta)$ and $\zeta \in \mathsf{Path}(L, X \times Y)$ or $\zeta : L \rightarrow (X \times Y)$; and symmetrically for π_Y in the other coordinate.

3   General Flow Systems

The general dynamical system model we develop here is essentially Aubin's model of an evolutionary system, generalized to arbitrary time lines L, and "deconstructed", so that the basic objects are bounded length paths, having $dom(\gamma) \subseteq [0, b_\gamma]$.

Definition 4. *Let* $(L, <, 0)$ *be a time line, and let* $X \neq \varnothing$ *be an arbitrary value space. A* general flow system *over* X *with time line* L *is a map* $\Phi : X \rightsquigarrow \mathsf{Path}(L, X)$ *satisfying, for all* $x \in dom(\Phi)$, *for all* $\gamma \in \Phi(x)$, *and for all* $t \in dom(\gamma)$:

(GF0) initialization: $\gamma(0) = x$
(GF1) suffix-closure: $_t|\gamma \in \Phi(\gamma(t))$
(GF2) fusion-closure: $\gamma|_t * \gamma' \in \Phi(x)$ *for all* $\gamma' \in \Phi(\gamma(t))$

- Φ *has* interval paths *if* $ran(\Phi) \subseteq \mathsf{IPath}(L, X)$;
- Φ *has* hybrid paths *if* $ran(\Phi) \subseteq \mathsf{HPath}(X)$ *and* $L = \mathbb{N} \times \mathbb{R}_{\circ}^{+}$;
- Φ *is* reflexive *if* $\theta_x \in \Phi(x)$ *for all* $x \in dom(\Phi)$;
- Φ *is* blocked at x if $\Phi(x) = \{\theta_x\}$, *and* non-blocking *if not blocked at any* $x \in X$;
- Φ *is* prefix-closed *if* $\gamma|_t \in \Phi(x)$ *for all* $x \in dom(\Phi)$, $\gamma \in \Phi(x)$ *and* $t \in dom(\gamma)$;
- Φ *is* deterministic *if   for all* $x \in \mathrm{dom}(\Phi)$, *the set* $\Phi(x)$ *is linearly ordered by* $<$.

In terms of *Behavioural Systems theory* [18], the suffix-closure condition **(GF1)** corresponds to the *time invariance* property, while the fusion-closure condition **(GF2)** corresponds to the so-called *"axiom of state"* principle, that *"the state should contain sufficient information about the past so as to determine the future behaviour"*, because the various possible extensions of a trajectory at time t are exactly those which would have been possible if we had observed only the state at time t, and not the past of the trajectory prior to that point.

Proposition 4. *Let* $(L, <, 0)$ *be a time line, let* $X \neq \varnothing$ *be a value space, and let* $\Phi : X \rightsquigarrow \mathsf{Path}(L, X)$ *be a general flow system over* X *with respect to* L. *Then:*
(1.) *The set* $dom(\Phi) \subseteq X$ *is closed under reachability by* Φ-*paths:*
     if $x \in dom(\Phi)$ *and* $\gamma \in \Phi(x)$, *and* $t \in dom(\gamma)$, *then* $\gamma(t) \in dom(\Phi)$.
(2.) Φ *is reflexive iff* Φ *is prefix-closed.*
(3.) Φ *is non-blocking iff for all* $x \in dom(\Phi)$, $\gamma \in \Phi(x)$, *there is a* $\gamma' \in \Phi(x) : \gamma < \gamma'$.

Example 1. If $g : L_1 \to L_2$ is an order embedding, and $\Phi : X \rightsquigarrow \mathsf{Path}(L_1, X)$ is a general flow system, then the map $\Phi_g : X \rightsquigarrow \mathsf{Path}(L_2, X)$ is also a general flow, where for $x \in dom(\Phi_g) := dom(\Phi)$, define $\Phi_g(x) := \{\eta \in \mathsf{Path}(L_2, X) \mid \exists \gamma \in \Phi(x) : dom(\eta) = g(dom(\gamma)) \wedge (\forall t \in dom(\eta)) \, \eta(t) = \gamma(g^{-1}(t)) \}$.

Example 2. A (basic) *state transition system* is a structure (X, R) where $X \neq \varnothing$ is the state space, and $R : X \rightsquigarrow X$ is any set-valued map (the one-step transition relation). The map R determines a general flow system with interval paths over time-line $L = \mathbb{N}$:
$\Phi_R(x) := \{\gamma \in \mathrm{IPath}(\mathbb{N}, X) \mid \gamma(0) = x \wedge (\forall i < b_\gamma - 1) \, \gamma(i+1) \in R(\gamma(i)) \}$. It is easily verified that $\Phi_R(x) = \{\theta_x\}$ iff $x \notin dom(R)$. Hence Φ_R is non-blocking iff the map R is total on X, and Φ_R is deterministic iff the map R is a partial function.

Example 3. A *differential inclusion* is a structure (X, F) where $X \subseteq \mathbb{R}^n$ is a finite dimensional vector space with the Euclidean norm, and $F : X \rightsquigarrow \mathbb{R}^n$ is a set-valued map. Define $\mathsf{AC}(X) := \{\gamma \in \mathrm{IPath}(\mathbb{R}_\circ^+, X) \mid \gamma \text{ absolutely continuous on } [0, b_\gamma] \}$. Solutions to the inclusion $\dot{x}(t) \in F(x(t))$ starting at a state x are defined by: $\mathsf{Sol}_F(x) := \{\gamma \in \mathsf{AC}(X) \mid \gamma(0) = x \wedge (\frac{d}{dt}\gamma)(l) \in F(\gamma(l)) \text{ a.e. for } l \in [0, b_\gamma] \}$. It is immediate that Sol_F is reflexive and is suffix-closed and fusion, hence is a general flow system with interval paths over $L = \mathbb{R}_\circ^+$. For the non-blocking property, to ensure the existence of non-trivial solutions from each $x \in cl(dom(F))$, one needs to impose some regularity assumptions (e.g. *Lipschitz* or *Marchaud* conditions) on the map F [7,3,6]. If $F : X \to \mathbb{R}^n$ is actually a function and the differential equation $\dot{x}(t) = F(x(t))$ has a unique maximal solution $\eta : [0, c_x) \to X$ starting from each $x \in X$, with $c_x \in \mathbb{R}_\circ^+ \cup \{\infty\}$, then $\mathsf{Sol}_F(x) = \{\eta|_t \mid t \in [0, c_x) \}$ is linearly ordered, hence deterministic at every $x \in X$.

Example 4. A *hybrid automaton* [15,2,14,1] is a structure $H = (Q, E, X, F, D, R)$:
- Q is a finite set of control modes;
- $E : Q \rightsquigarrow Q$ is the discrete transition relation;
- $X \subseteq \mathbb{R}^n$ is the continuous state space;
- $F : Q \to [X \rightsquigarrow \mathbb{R}^n]$ maps each $q \in Q$ to a set-valued vector field $F(q) : X \rightsquigarrow \mathbb{R}^n$
    with differential inclusion solution map $\mathsf{Sol}_q := \mathsf{Sol}_{F(q)} : X \rightsquigarrow \mathrm{IPath}(\mathbb{R}_\circ^+, X)$;
- $D : Q \rightsquigarrow X$ maps each $q \in Q$ to a set $D_q := D(q) \subseteq X$, the domain of mode q;
- $R : E \to [X \rightsquigarrow X]$ maps $(q, q') \in E$ to a reset map $R_{q,q'} := R(q, q') : X \rightsquigarrow X$.

Define a map $\mathsf{Traj}_H : (Q \times X) \rightsquigarrow \mathsf{HPath}(Q \times X)$ by:

$\mathsf{Traj}_H (q, x) := \{\gamma \in \mathsf{HPath}(Q \times X) \mid$
(0) $\gamma(0, 0) = (q, x) \wedge (\forall i < \mathrm{dl}(\gamma)) \big[\text{ for } \Delta_i := \mathrm{ds}(\gamma)(i) \wedge q_i := \pi_Q \gamma_i(0)$
(1) $\pi_X \gamma_i \in \mathsf{Sol}_{q_i}(\pi_X \gamma_i(0)) \wedge ran(\gamma_i) \subseteq \{q_i\} \times D_{q_i} \wedge$
(2) $(q_i, q_{i+1}) \in E \wedge \pi_X \gamma_{i+1}(0) \in R_{q_i, q_{i+1}}(\pi_X \gamma_i(\Delta_i))$ if $i < \mathrm{dl}(\gamma) - 1 \big] \}$

Paths in Traj_H are called *(finite) trajectories* of H. Direct from the definition, we can see that $dom(\mathsf{Traj}_H) = D = \{(q, x) \in Q \times X \mid x \in D_q\}$.

We will say a hybrid automaton H is *well-constituted* if all of the following hold:

(A) $Q \neq \varnothing$, and $E : Q \rightsquigarrow Q$ is total;

(B) $X \subseteq \mathbb{R}^n$ is a non-empty finite dimensional vector space with the Euclidean norm;

(C) $D : Q \rightsquigarrow X$ is total, so $D_q \neq \varnothing$ for each $q \in Q$;

(D) for each $q \in Q$, domain $D_q \subset dom(\mathsf{Sol}_q)$ and Sol_q is not blocked at any $x \in D_q$;

(E) for each transition pair $(q, q') \in E$, the reset relation $R_{q,q'} : X \rightsquigarrow X$ satisfies the constraints $dom(R_{q,q'}) \neq \varnothing$ and $dom(R_{q,q'}) \subseteq D_q$ and $ran(R_{q,q'}) \subseteq D_{q'}$.

Any assumptions will do on the set-valued vector fields $F(q) : X \rightsquigarrow \mathbb{R}^n$, provided they give non-trivial solution paths in Sol_q on the mode domains D_q.

Proposition 5. *Let $H = (Q, E, X, F, D, R)$ be a hybrid automaton. Then the trajectory map $\mathsf{Traj}_H : (Q \times X) \rightsquigarrow \mathsf{HPath}(Q \times X)$ is a general flow system over $Q \times X$ with time line $\mathbb{N} \times \mathbb{R}_\circ^+$. If H is well-constituted then Traj_H is also prefix-closed.*

The conditions on H being well-constituted rule out all "trivial" ways that Traj_H may become blocked: Sol_q is not blocked at any $x \in D_q \subseteq dom(\mathsf{Sol}_q)$; since E is total, every $q \in Q$ has a discrete successor; and for each discrete transition $(q, q') \in E$, the *transition guard* set $dom(R_{q,q'})$ is non-empty and contained in D_q, and under the reset relation, the image set $ran(R_{q,q'})$ lies in $D_{q'}$. So in attending to the possibility of blocking, we need to focus only on states $x \in D_q$ that are not in any transition guard set, so no discrete transition is possible from (q, x), and states $x \in D_q$ from which every non-trivial q-solution leaves D_q "immediately after now", so there are no hybrid trajectories from (q, x) with non-trivial continuous evolution in mode q.

Proposition 6. *If a hybrid automaton H is well-constituted, and*

$$Out_q := \{ x \in D_q \mid (\forall \gamma \in \mathsf{Sol}_q(x))(\forall t \in dom(\gamma), t > 0)(\exists s < t) \ \gamma(s) \notin D_q \}$$
$$Grd_q := \bigcup_{q' \in E(q)} dom(R_{q,q'})$$

then Traj_H is non-blocking on its domain D iff $Out_q \subseteq Grd_q$ for each $q \in Q$.

The sets Out_q and the condition $Out_q \subseteq Grd_q$ are identified in [15], for systems with deterministic continuous dynamics. In virtue of the continuity of paths in $\mathsf{Sol}_q(x)$, the set Out_q is contained in the topological boundary: $Out_q \subseteq \mathrm{bd}(D_q) := \mathrm{cl}(D_q) - \mathrm{int}(D_q)$. An immediate corollary is that for well-constituted systems H, Traj_H will be non-blocking on D if for all $q \in Q$, either $(\mathrm{bd}(D_q) \cap D_q) \subseteq Grd_q$, or D_q is open.

We can also show the *impulse differential inclusion* model of hybrid systems from [7] to be an example of a general flow system over the hybrid time line; this example and others will be discussed in a separate paper.

4   Infinitary Extensions of General Flow Systems

From Proposition 4, we know that if a general flow Φ is non-blocking, then for each $x \in dom(\Phi)$ and $\gamma \in \Phi(x)$, there exists an infinite sequence of paths $\{\gamma_n\}$ with $\gamma_0 = \gamma$ and $\gamma_n \in \Phi(x)$ and $\gamma_n < \gamma_{n+1}$ for all n. Motivated by this fact, we view "maximal extensions" or "completions" of paths as infinitary objects, arising as limits of infinite ordered sequences of finitary bounded paths. In this paper, we take limits over ordered sequences of order type (ordinal) ω, the order type of $\mathbb{N}$, but we want to leave open the possibility, for later work, of dealing with sequences of transfinite length, with ordinals greater than ω (for formalizing the notion of a continuation of a Zeno hybrid trajectory that has discrete stages $\omega, \omega + 1, \omega + 2, \ldots$ up to some limit ordinal $\nu > \omega$). We need access to maximal length paths in order to formalize the *Until* construct in temporal logic, but we also want to "go to infinity" in order to be able to directly compare our class of dynamical systems with those developed in terms of functions over the whole time line $L = \mathbb{N}$ or $L = \mathbb{R}_\circ^+$; in particular, Aubin's model of an *evolutionary system* [5, 4], and also Willem's *behavioural systems* model [18].

Definition 5. *For any path set $\mathcal{P} \subseteq \mathsf{Path}(L, X)$, define the ω-extension of $\mathcal{P}$ by:*

$$\mathsf{Ext}^\omega(\mathcal{P}) := \{\, \eta : L \dashrightarrow X \mid (\exists \overline{\gamma} : \omega \to \mathsf{Path}(L, X))\,(\forall k < \omega)\,[\; \gamma_k := \overline{\gamma}(k) \;\wedge$$
$$\gamma_k \in \mathcal{P} \;\wedge\; \gamma_k < \gamma_{k+1} \;\wedge\; \eta = \textstyle\bigcup_{k<\omega} \gamma_k \;]\,\}$$

Define $\mathsf{EPath}^\omega(L, X) := \mathsf{Ext}^\omega(\mathsf{Path}(L, X))$; $\mathsf{EIPath}^\omega(L, X) := \mathsf{Ext}^\omega(\mathsf{IPath}(L, X))$. *Paths* $\eta \in \mathsf{Ext}^\omega(\mathcal{P})$ *will be called ω-paths of $\mathcal{P}$.*

Thus the ω-extension $\mathsf{Ext}^\omega(\mathcal{P})$ contains all the partial functions $\eta : L \dashrightarrow X$ that can arise as the union or limit of an ω-length strictly extending sequence of paths in the set $\mathcal{P}$. The path extension ordering $<$ on bounded paths induced by the linear order on L can be lifted to ω-paths. For paths $\eta, \eta' \in \mathsf{Path}(L, X) \cup \mathsf{EPath}^\omega(L, X)$, we extend Definition 3 to define $\eta < \eta'$ if $\eta \subset \eta'$ and $t < t'$ for all $t \in dom(\eta)$ and $t' \in dom(\eta') - dom(\eta)$. If $\eta < \eta'$ then $dom(\eta)$ must be a *bounded* subset of L.

For a general flow system, we want to pick out the ω-paths $\eta \in \mathsf{Ext}^\omega(\Phi(x))$ that are *maximal* in the sense that there are no real paths of the system in $\Phi(x)$ extending η.

Definition 6. *Given a general flow system $\Phi \colon X \rightsquigarrow \mathsf{Path}(L, X)$, define the maximized ω-extension of Φ to be the set-valued map $\mathsf{E}^\omega\Phi \colon X \rightsquigarrow \mathsf{EPath}^\omega(L, X)$ given by:*

$$(\mathsf{E}^\omega\Phi)(x) := \{\, \eta \in \mathsf{Ext}^\omega(\Phi(x)) \mid (\forall \gamma \in \Phi(x))\; \eta \not< \gamma \,\}$$

A system Φ will be called ω-extendible if for every $x \in dom(\Phi)$ and every $\gamma \in \Phi(x)$, there exists $\eta \in (\mathsf{E}^\omega\Phi)(x)$ such that $\gamma < \eta$.

In general, $dom(\mathsf{E}^\omega\Phi) \subseteq dom(\Phi)$; Φ is ω-extendible iff $dom(\mathsf{E}^\omega\Phi) = dom(\Phi)$. In reasoning about the behaviour of an ω-extendible system Φ, we can safely replace quantification over all possible paths in $\Phi(x)$, with quantification over $(\mathsf{E}^\omega\Phi)(x)$, the maximal ω-paths; this is crucial for the semantics of the temporal *Until* construct.

Proposition 7. *For any general flow $\Phi \colon X \rightsquigarrow \mathsf{Path}(L, X)$,*

(1.) *Φ is ω-extendible iff Φ is non-blocking.*

(2.) *If Φ non-blocking, then Φ is deterministic iff $\mathsf{E}^\omega\Phi$ is a partial function.*

The non-trivial direction is: Φ is non-blocking implies Φ is ω-extendible; the proof uses Zorn's Lemma to obtain a maximum of any strictly extending sequence of ω-paths.

We are now in a position to formalize the relationship between Aubin's model of an *evolutionary system* [5,4], and the general flow systems defined here. An evolutionary system, over time lines $L = \mathbb{R}_o^+$ or $L = \mathbb{N}$, is a map $\Psi : X \rightsquigarrow [L \to X]$ such that, for whole line paths $\eta : L \to X, \eta(0) = x$ for all $\eta \in \Psi(x)$ and Ψ is closed under the suffix and fusion operations (the natural extensions to unbounded paths of the operations in Proposition 1), in the same sense as which general flow systems with bounded paths are closed under these operations, as required by clauses **(GF1)** and **(GF2)** of Definition 4.

Proposition 8. *Let the time line be either $L = \mathbb{N}$ or $L = \mathbb{R}_o^+$, and $X \neq \varnothing$.*

$\Psi : X \rightsquigarrow [L \to X]$ *is an evolutionary system in the sense of Aubin*

iff *there exists an interval path general flow system $\Phi : X \rightsquigarrow \mathsf{IPath}(L, X)$ that is non-blocking and satisfies $\Psi = \mathsf{E}^\omega \Phi$.*

Thus evolutionary systems are a subclass of non-blocking general flow systems. In Willem's *Behavioural Systems* model [18], with time lines $L = \mathbb{N}$ or $L = \mathbb{R}_o^+$, a *behaviour* is a set of functions $\mathfrak{B} \subseteq [L \to X]$. It can also be established that $\mathfrak{B}$ is a time-invariant and complete state behaviour iff there exists an interval path, non-blocking general flow system $\Phi : X \rightsquigarrow \mathsf{IPath}(L, X)$ such that $\mathfrak{B} = ran(\mathsf{E}^\omega \Phi)$.

When $L = \mathbb{N}$, then all ω-paths $\eta \in \mathsf{EPath}^\omega(\mathbb{N}, X)$ have infinite time domain, so we will always have $(\mathsf{E}^\omega \Phi)(x) = \mathsf{Ext}^\omega(\Phi(x))$ for any non-blocking general flow Φ.

When $L = \mathbb{R}_o^+$, we know that every ω-path $\eta \in \mathsf{EIPath}^\omega(\mathbb{R}_o^+, X)$ must have $dom(\eta) = [0, c)$ for some $c \in \mathbb{R}_o^+ \cup \{\infty\}$. For a non-blocking flow Φ, suppose $\eta \in \mathsf{Ext}^\omega(\Phi(x))$ is any ω-path. Then $c = \infty$ automatically gives $\eta \in (\mathsf{E}^\omega \Phi)(x)$. If $c < \infty$, then we will have a maximally extended ω-path $\eta \in (\mathsf{E}^\omega \Phi)(x)$ exactly when $\eta|_t \in \Phi(x)$ for all $t \in [0, c)$ but the limit as $t \to c$ of $\eta(t)$ does not exist, or does exist but is not in $dom(\Phi)$; i.e. η has *finite escape time*. The analysis for the ω-extensions of general bounded paths $\eta \in \mathsf{EPath}^\omega(\mathbb{R}_o^+, X)$ is similar. For the differential inclusion systems in *Example 3*, the Marchaud conditions on F in [3,7] constitute a property stronger than non-blocking: they imply that $dom(\eta) = [0, \infty)$ for all $\eta \in (\mathsf{E}^\omega \mathsf{Sol}_F)(x)$, so there are no ω-paths with finite escape time.

When $L = \mathbb{N} \times \mathbb{R}_o^+$ is the hybrid time line, we can characterize the maximal ω-paths of a non-blocking system as follows.

Proposition 9. *For any $X \neq \varnothing$ and non-blocking general flow $\Phi : X \rightsquigarrow \mathsf{HPath}(X)$, every ω-path $\eta \in (\mathsf{E}^\omega \Phi)(x)$ is of one of two forms:*
(i) $\eta = \gamma * \upsilon$ *where $\gamma \in \Phi(x)$ and $\upsilon : \{0\} \times [0, c) \to X$ with $c \in \mathbb{R}_o^+ \cup \{\infty\}$ and $\upsilon = \bigcup_{n < \omega} \gamma_n$ and each $\gamma_n \in \Phi(\upsilon(0,0))$ has $\mathrm{dl}(\gamma_n) = 1$, hence η has finite discrete length $\mathrm{dl}(\eta) = \mathrm{dl}(\gamma) \in \mathbb{N}$, and total duration $\mathrm{td}(\eta) = \mathrm{td}(\gamma) + c$, which may be finite or infinite, depending on c; or*
(ii) $\eta = \bigcup_{n < \omega} \gamma_n$ *where $\mathrm{dl}(\gamma_n) < \mathrm{dl}(\gamma_{n+1})$, hence η has infinite discrete length, and total duration $\mathrm{td}(\eta) = \sum_{n < \omega} \mathrm{td}(\gamma_n)$, which may be finite or infinite;*

The non-blocking/ω-extendibility property here allows for two cases among extensions of hybrid paths that are typically considered "pathological": *Zeno* extended hybrid paths $\eta \in (\mathsf{E}^\omega \Phi)(x)$ that have infinite discrete length but finite total duration $\mathrm{td}(\eta) < \infty$; and *livelocked* extended hybrid paths $\eta \in (\mathsf{E}^\omega \Phi)(x)$ that have finite discrete length $\mathrm{dl}(\eta) = k + 1$ *and* finite total duration. Livelocked η are maximal with the last path segment having $dom(\eta_k) = [0, c)$; this Φ path would "die" at k-local time $t = c$ (hybrid time (k, c)) if it ever got there, but it never can, as for every extension of η_k to domain $[0, c]$, the resulting hybrid path is not in $\Phi(x)$. For a non-blocking hybrid automaton H, the general flow Traj_H will exhibit livelock on an extended trajectory $\eta \in (\mathsf{E}^\omega \mathsf{Traj}_H)(x)$ with $\mathrm{dl}(\eta) = k + 1$ iff the last path segment $\eta_k : [0, c) \to (Q \times X)$ is such that, for $q_k := \pi_Q \eta_k(0)$ and $x_k := \pi_X \eta_k(0)$, there exists a solution path $\gamma \in \mathsf{Sol}_{q_k}(x_k)$ such that $dom(\gamma) = [0, b_\gamma]$, with $b_\gamma > c$ and $\gamma \restriction_{[0,c)} = \pi_X \eta_k$, that eventually leaves the mode domain D_q, but never passes through Grd_q on the way: $\gamma(c) \notin D_q$ and $\gamma(t) \in D_q - Grd_q$ for all $t \in [0, c)$.

5 Full General Flow Logic GFL*: Syntax and Semantics

We now turn to the syntax and semantics of a logic we call *Full General Flow Logic*, **GFL***, which generalizes to general flow models the semantics of *Full Computation Tree Logic*, **CTL***, introduced by Emerson and Halpern in 1983 [10] for formalizing reasoning about executions of concurrent programs in discrete time. The syntax here is a labelled variant of that of **CTL***, allowing for semantic models consisting of a finite family of non-blocking general flow systems.

Definition 7. *A* signature *is a pair $\Sigma = (\mathrm{Sys}, \mathrm{Prp})$, where* Sys *is a finite set of system labels, and* Prp *is a countable set of atomic propositions. The temporal logic language $\mathcal{L}(\Sigma)$ consists of the set of all formulae φ generated by the grammar:*

$$\varphi ::= p \mid \neg\varphi \mid \varphi_1 \vee \varphi_2 \mid \varphi_1 \mathcal{U}_a \varphi_2 \mid \forall_a \varphi$$

for atomic propositions $p \in \mathrm{Prp}$, and system labels $a \in \mathrm{Sys}$.

The other propositional (Boolean) connectives and logical constants *true*, $\top$, and *false*, $\bot$, are defined in a standard way, and the path quantifiers $\forall_a$ have classical negation duals $\exists_a$, as follows:

$$\varphi_1 \wedge \varphi_2 \stackrel{\mathrm{def}}{=} \neg(\neg\varphi_1 \vee \neg\varphi_2) \qquad\qquad \varphi_1 \to \varphi_2 \stackrel{\mathrm{def}}{=} \neg\varphi_1 \vee \varphi_2$$
$$\varphi_1 \leftrightarrow \varphi_2 \stackrel{\mathrm{def}}{=} (\varphi_1 \to \varphi_2) \wedge (\varphi_2 \to \varphi_1) \qquad\qquad \exists_a \varphi \stackrel{\mathrm{def}}{=} \neg\forall_a \neg\varphi \qquad (2)$$
$$\top \stackrel{\mathrm{def}}{=} p \vee \neg p \quad \text{for any } p \in \mathrm{Prp} \qquad\qquad \bot \stackrel{\mathrm{def}}{=} \neg\top$$

The temporal operators, $\mathcal{U}_a$, for $a \in \mathrm{Sys}$, refer to the ω-path space of a non-blocking general flow system Φ_a. The formula $\varphi \mathcal{U}_a \psi$, read "$\varphi$ *until* ψ, for a-type paths", will hold along any ω-path η of type a if at some time in the future (along η) the formula ψ holds, and at all intermediate times (along η) between now and then, φ holds. The universal quantifier $\forall_a$ applied to a path formula produces a state formula, and $\forall_a(\varphi \mathcal{U}_a \psi)$ holds at a state x if *every* ω-path $\eta \in (\mathsf{E}^\omega \Phi_a)(x)$ satisfies the path formula $\varphi \mathcal{U}_a \psi$. Dually, $\exists_a(\varphi \mathcal{U}_a \psi)$ holds at a state x if *there exists* an ω-path $\eta \in (\mathsf{E}^\omega \Phi_a)(x)$ which satisfies the path formula $\varphi \mathcal{U}_a \psi$. The *until* construct on paths can be formulated in several distinct ways; we shall take as primitive the *strictest* version of *until*, and then define weaker variants in terms of it. In particular, an important *difference* between the logic here, and the usual presentation of **CTL*** developed for discrete time paths, is that instead of taking the *next-time* discrete successor operator as a syntactic and semantic primitive, we use a known method to *define* next-time in terms of the strictest *until* [8,13]. Our semantics covers arbitrary time lines, so in general the immediate successor map is only a partial function on the domain of a path, and in the case of interval paths in a dense time line, may be everywhere undefined.

Definition 8. *A* general flow logic model *(logic model, for short) of signature* $\Sigma =$ $(\mathrm{Sys}, \mathrm{Prp})$ *is a structure* $\mathfrak{M} = (X, \mathcal{L}, \mathcal{S}, \mathcal{P})$, *where:*

- $X \neq \varnothing$ *is the state space, of arbitrary cardinality;*
- $\mathcal{L}$ *is a function mapping each symbol* $a \in \mathrm{Sys}$ *to a time line* $L_a := \mathcal{L}(a)$;
- $\mathcal{S}$ *is a function mapping each symbol* $a \in \mathrm{Sys}$ *to an non-blocking general flow system* $\Phi_a := \mathcal{S}(a) : X \rightsquigarrow \mathsf{Path}(L_a, X)$ *over the space* X, *with time line* L_a;
- $\mathcal{P} : \mathrm{Prp} \rightsquigarrow X$ *maps each* $p \in \mathrm{Prp}$ *to a set* $\mathcal{P}(p) \subseteq X$ *of states.*

The ω-path space *of a model* $\mathfrak{M}$ *is defined by* $\mathsf{EPath}(\mathfrak{M}) := \bigcup_{a \in \mathrm{Sys}} \mathsf{EPath}^\omega(L_a, X)$.

Let $\mathbb{GF}(\Sigma)$ denote the class of all general flow logic models of signature Σ, and for the case of a single time line L, let $\mathbb{GF}(L, \Sigma)$ denote the subclass of all logic models $\mathfrak{M}$ such that $\mathcal{L}(a) = L$ for all $a \in \mathrm{Sys}$. For the further special case where $|\mathrm{Sys}| = 1$ and Prp is countably infinite, let $\mathbb{TR}(\mathbb{N})$ denote the subclass of all discrete time logic models $\mathfrak{M}$ with one general flow $\Phi_R : X \rightsquigarrow \mathsf{IPath}(\mathbb{N}, X)$ from a total transition relation $R : X \rightsquigarrow X$ (also called *R-generable models* [12,10,16]). For the case of deterministic systems, let $\mathbb{DF}(L)$ denote the subclass of all logic models where the time line L is the non-negative half of a linearly ordered abelian group, and the one general flow $\Phi : X \rightsquigarrow \mathsf{IPath}(L, X)$ is deterministic, total, interval path, and non-blocking [9].

Definition 9. *For* $\varphi \in \mathcal{L}(\Sigma)$ *and* ω-path $\eta \in \mathsf{EPath}(\mathfrak{M})$, *the relation "$\psi$ is satisfied along path η in model $\mathfrak{M}$", written* $\mathfrak{M}, \eta \models \psi$, *is defined by induction on the structure of formulae, with* $p \in \mathrm{Prp}$ *and* $a \in \mathrm{Sys}$:

$$\mathfrak{M}, \eta \models p \qquad \text{iff} \quad \eta(0) \in \mathcal{P}(p)$$
$$\mathfrak{M}, \eta \models \neg\psi \qquad \text{iff} \quad \mathfrak{M}, \eta \not\models \psi$$
$$\mathfrak{M}, \eta \models \psi_1 \vee \psi_2 \quad \text{iff} \quad \mathfrak{M}, \eta \models \psi_1 \ \text{or} \ \mathfrak{M}, \eta \models \psi_2$$
$$\mathfrak{M}, \eta \models \psi_1 \, \mathcal{U}_a \, \psi_2 \quad \text{iff} \quad \eta \in \mathsf{EPath}^\omega(L_a, X) \ \text{and} \ \exists t \in dom(\eta) \ \text{with} \ t > 0 :$$
$$\mathfrak{M}, {}_t|\eta \models \psi_2 \ \text{and} \ \forall s \in (0, t) \cap dom(\eta) : \mathfrak{M}, {}_s|\eta \models \psi_1$$
$$\mathfrak{M}, \eta \models \forall_a \psi \qquad \text{iff} \quad \forall \xi \in (\mathsf{E}^\omega \Phi_a)(\eta(0)) : \mathfrak{M}, \xi \models \psi$$

For formulas $\varphi \in \mathcal{L}(\Sigma)$, *the* ω-path denotation set $[\![\varphi]\!]^{\mathfrak{M}} \subseteq \mathsf{EPath}(\mathfrak{M})$, *and the* state denotation set $[\![\varphi]\!]_{\mathsf{st}}^{\mathfrak{M}} \subseteq X$, *are defined by:*

$$[\![\varphi]\!]^{\mathfrak{M}} := \{\, \eta \in \mathsf{EPath}(\mathfrak{M}) \mid \mathfrak{M}, \eta \models \varphi \,\}$$
$$[\![\varphi]\!]_{\mathsf{st}}^{\mathfrak{M}} := \{\, x \in X \mid \exists \eta \in \mathsf{EPath}(\mathfrak{M}) : \mathfrak{M}, \eta \models \varphi \ \text{and} \ x = \eta(0) \,\}$$

For a logic model $\mathfrak{M} \in \mathbb{GF}(\Sigma)$, *class of logic models* $C \subseteq \mathbb{GF}(\Sigma)$, *and for formulas* $\varphi \in \mathcal{L}(\Sigma)$, *we say:*

- φ *is* satisfiable *in* $\mathfrak{M}$, *if* $[\![\varphi]\!]_{\mathsf{st}}^{\mathfrak{M}} \neq \varnothing$;
- φ *is* true *in* $\mathfrak{M}$, *written* $\mathfrak{M} \models \varphi$, *if* $\mathfrak{M}, \eta \models \varphi$ *for every* $\eta \in \mathsf{EPath}(\mathfrak{M})$;
- φ *is* C-valid, *written* $\models_C \varphi$, *if* $\mathfrak{M} \models \varphi$ *for every* $\mathfrak{M} \in C$.

Define **Valid**$(C) := \{\psi \in \mathcal{L}(\Sigma) \mid \ \models_C \psi\}$ *to be the set of all C-valid formulas, and define* **CTL*** $:=$ **Valid**$(\mathbb{TR}(\mathbb{N}))$ *and* **GFL*** $:=$ **Valid**$(\mathbb{GF}(\Sigma))$.

The *while...always* operator is a negation dual of *until*: $\varphi \mathcal{A}_a \psi \overset{\text{def}}{=} \neg(\varphi \mathcal{U}_a (\neg \psi))$, which can be read as "if a type-a path, then *while φ, always ψ*". The semantics are:

$$\mathfrak{M}, \eta \models \varphi \mathcal{A}_a \psi \quad \textit{iff} \quad \text{if } \eta \in \mathsf{EPath}^\omega(L_a, X) \text{ then } \forall t \in dom(\eta) \text{ with } t > 0,$$
$$\text{if } (\forall s \in (0,t) \cap dom(\eta)) \; \mathfrak{M}, {}_s|\eta \models \varphi \quad \text{then} \quad \mathfrak{M}, {}_t|\eta \models \psi$$

Other one-place operators are defined as $\Diamond_a \varphi \overset{\text{def}}{=} \top \mathcal{U}_a \varphi$, $\Box_a \varphi \overset{\text{def}}{=} \top \mathcal{A}_a \varphi$, $\odot_a \varphi \overset{\text{def}}{=} \bot \mathcal{U}_a \varphi$, and $\circledcirc_a \varphi \overset{\text{def}}{=} \neg \varphi \mathcal{A}_a \bot$, where

$\Diamond_a \varphi$ type-a paths along which φ will *eventually* be true in the *future*;

$\Box_a \varphi$ type-a paths along which φ will *always* be true in the *future*, plus non-type-a paths;

$\odot_a \varphi$ type-a paths along which time 0 has a discrete successor, and φ is true *then*;

$\circledcirc_a \varphi$ type a-paths along which φ is true *immediately after now*, plus non-type-a paths.

In particular, the *next-time* operators, $\odot_a$, come out as: $\mathfrak{M}, \eta \models \odot_a \varphi$ *iff*

for $T := dom(\eta)$ and $0 \in dom(\mathbf{succ}_T)$ and $k := \mathbf{succ}_T(0)$ and $\mathfrak{M}, {}_k|\eta \models \varphi$

Different versions of *until* come by varying the constraints on end-values of the bounded paths that satisfy φ until they satisfy ψ:

$$\varphi \mathcal{U}_a^{\bullet\bullet} \psi \overset{\text{def}}{=} \varphi \wedge \varphi \mathcal{U}_a(\varphi \wedge \psi) \qquad\qquad \varphi \mathcal{U}_a^{\bullet\circ} \psi \overset{\text{def}}{=} \varphi \wedge \varphi \mathcal{U}_a \psi \qquad (3)$$

We briefly illustrate the expressivity of the logic in two areas.

***Viability Theory*:** In the recent work of Aubin and co-workers in *Viability Theory* [3,7, 4], the key concept is of paths being "*viable in K until capturing target C*". Define:

$$\varphi \mathcal{V}_a \psi \overset{\text{def}}{=} (\top \mathcal{U}_a \top \wedge \varphi \wedge \Box_a \varphi \wedge \Box_a \Diamond_a \top) \vee \varphi \mathcal{U}_a^{\bullet\bullet} \psi \qquad (4)$$

The formula $\varphi \mathcal{V}_a \psi$ is satisfied by an ω-path $\eta \in \mathsf{EPath}^\omega(L_a, X)$ iff *either* φ is true now and at all times in the future along η, and the time domain of η is unbounded, *or* there is a finite time along η at which ψ becomes true, and φ is true at all times between now and then (inclusive). Thus η is either *viable forever in the set* $[\![\varphi]\!]^{\mathfrak{M}}$ or *viable in* $[\![\varphi]\!]^{\mathfrak{M}}$ *until it captures the target set* $[\![\psi]\!]^{\mathfrak{M}}$ in finite time. Applying the path quantifiers $\exists_a$ and $\forall_a$ restricts to ω-paths of the system $\mathsf{E}^\omega \Phi_a$, and this can be used to formalize in the logic the two-place state set operators known as the *viability kernel with target* and the *invariance kernel with target*.

***Dynamical properties of hybrid automata*:** Given a hybrid automaton H, assume that H is well- constituted, and define a logic model $\mathfrak{M}_X^H$ with state space $X \subseteq \mathbb{R}^n$ the continuous state space of H. Let the system label set $\mathsf{Sys}_X^H := Q$, and for each $q \in Q$, the time line is $\mathcal{L}(q) := \mathbb{R}_\circ^+$ and the general flow systems are $\mathcal{S}(q) = \Phi_q := \mathsf{Sol}_q$.

Assume the atomic proposition set Prp^H includes constants D_q and G_q for each $q \in Q$, and the valuation $\mathcal{P} : \mathrm{Prp}^H \rightsquigarrow X$ satisfies $\mathcal{P}(\mathsf{D}_q) = D_q$, and $\mathcal{P}(\mathsf{G}_q) = Grd_q$.

- Traj_H is non-blocking $\quad$ iff $\quad$ $\mathfrak{M}_X^H \models \bigwedge_{q \in Q} ((\odot_q \neg \mathsf{D}_q) \rightarrow \mathsf{G}_q)$

- If Traj_H is non-blocking, $\quad$ then $\quad$ Traj_H has no livelock $\quad$ iff
$$\mathfrak{M}_X^H \models \bigwedge_{q \in Q} \forall_q ((\mathsf{D}_q \wedge \Diamond_q \neg \mathsf{D}_q) \rightarrow (\mathsf{D}_q \mathcal{U}_q (\mathsf{G}_q \wedge \Diamond_q \neg \mathsf{D}_q)))$$

We can, of course, also form a logic model $\mathfrak{M}^H$ with state space $Q \times X$, and have a single system label $\mathsf{Sys}^H := \{0\}$ with the general flow system $\Phi_0 := \mathsf{Traj}_H$, and formalize with the operators $\mathcal{U}_0$ and $\forall_0$ quite sophisticated temporal and dynamic properties of H as a single system. We can also reason about multiple systems over a common state space, and express comparative properties.

Definition 10. *Given a class of logic models $C \subseteq \mathbb{GF}(\Sigma)$, the* validity problem *for C is to determine, for any given formula $\varphi \in \mathcal{L}(\Sigma)$, whether or not $\varphi \in \mathbf{Valid}(C)$. The validity problem for C is* decidable *if there is a recursive procedure for determining membership of $\mathbf{Valid}(C)$ that finitely terminates on all input formulae $\varphi \in \mathcal{L}(\Sigma)$.*

Proposition 10. [12,11] *The validity problem is decidable $\mathbf{CTL}^\star$ (the class $\mathbb{TR}(\mathbb{N})$ of discrete time models), with complexity double exponential time in the length of the formula.*

We conjecture that the validity problem is decidable for the class $\mathbb{DF}(\mathbb{R}_0^+)$ of deterministic, total, interval path, non-blocking flows described by functions $\phi : X \times \mathbb{R} \rightarrow X$ satisfying the group action laws. These models are studied in [9], where they are used to give semantics for *until* and *since* (the time-reversal or past tense correlate) in the language of *Linear Temporal Logic* (**LTL**), with no path quantifiers, and the validity problem for that logic is decidable.

6   Axiomatisation and Soundness

We seek formal deductive proof systems for $\mathbf{GFL}^\star := \mathbf{Valid}(\mathbb{GF}(\Sigma))$, or for the validity set of distinguished subclasses of general flow models. The *soundness* or *adequacy* of a proof system Λ for a semantically characterized formula set such as $\mathbf{GFL}^\star$, is the property that if φ is provable in Λ, then $\varphi \in \mathbf{GFL}^\star$. For soundness proofs, the larger the class of semantic models, the stronger the result (so we do rather well here on that score). The technically much more challenging task is to establish *completeness* of a proof system Λ, which in our case is the property: if $\varphi \in \mathbf{GFL}^\star$, then φ is provable in Λ. Proofs of completeness proceed via the contrapositive, and in that form, are essentially a *model realization problem*: if φ is *Λ-consistent* (i.e. the formula $\neg \varphi$ is *not* provable in Λ), then there exists a logic model $\mathfrak{M} \in \mathbb{GF}(\Sigma)$ in which φ is satisfiable. Generally speaking, the smaller the class from which the realization models are drawn, the stronger or tighter the completeness result.

An axiomatic proof system Λ consists of a recursive list of *axioms*, usually given by taking all instances in the language of some finite set of *formula schemes*, together with a finite list of *inference rules*, of the form: **if** φ is provable in Λ, **then** ψ is provable in Λ.

A formula is provable in Λ if it is an axiom of Λ or is derivable from provable formulas by a finite sequence of applications of inference rules. We write $\vdash_\Lambda \varphi$ to mean that φ is provable in the system Λ.

A sound and complete axiomatic proof system for the logic $\mathbf{CTL}^\star$ remained an open problem for almost 20 years, and was solved by Reynolds quite recently [16]. That axiomatization lays side by side a list of axioms for path formulae, obtained from axiomatizing $\mathbf{LTL}$ together with a list of axioms for universal quantification over paths. In addition, Reynolds' proof system includes the axiom $\bot\mathcal{U}\top$, which asserts that the underlying time line is discrete, or equivalently, that the discrete successor map is total. It also includes an additional inference rule, which is an *induction rule* for "recursively unwinding" *Until* formulae in terms of the *next-time* operator. The axiomatic proof system we present for $\mathbf{GFL}^\star$ consists of Reynolds' system for $\mathbf{CTL}^\star$, *minus* those last two "discrete" items, the axiom and rule.

Let Λ be the proof system having as axioms all formulae of $\mathcal{L}(\mathrm{Sig})$ that are instances of propositional tautologies, or are instances of the schemes **(P1)** – **(P6)** and **(Q1)** – **(Q5)** below, and having as rules of inference the propositional rule of *Modus Ponens* (**MP**) along with three monotonicity rules:

$$(\text{Mono}\mathcal{U}\text{-1}): \quad \textbf{if} \ \vdash_\Lambda \varphi_1 \to \varphi_2 \ \textbf{then} \ \vdash_\Lambda \varphi_1\mathcal{U}_a\psi \to \varphi_2\mathcal{U}_a\psi$$

$$(\text{Mono}\mathcal{U}\text{-2}): \quad \textbf{if} \ \vdash_\Lambda \psi_1 \to \psi_2 \ \textbf{then} \ \vdash_\Lambda \varphi\mathcal{U}_a\psi_1 \to \varphi\mathcal{U}_a\psi_2$$

$$(\text{Mono}\forall): \qquad \textbf{if} \ \vdash_\Lambda \varphi \to \psi \qquad \textbf{then} \ \vdash_\Lambda \forall_a\varphi \to \forall_a\psi$$

(P1):
$$\bigvee_a(\top\mathcal{U}_a\top)$$

(P2):
$$\neg(\top\mathcal{U}_a\bot)$$

(P3):
$$(\varphi\mathcal{U}_a\psi_1 \wedge \neg(\varphi\mathcal{U}_a\psi_2)) \to \varphi\mathcal{U}_a(\psi_1 \wedge \neg\psi_2)$$

(P4):
$$(\varphi_1\mathcal{U}_a\psi \wedge \neg(\varphi_2\mathcal{U}_a\psi)) \to \varphi_1\mathcal{U}_a(\varphi_1 \wedge \neg\varphi_2 \wedge \varphi_1\mathcal{U}_a\psi)$$

(P5):
$$\varphi\mathcal{U}_a\psi \to (\varphi \wedge \varphi\mathcal{U}_a\psi)\mathcal{U}_a\psi$$

(P6):
$$\varphi\mathcal{U}_a(\varphi \wedge \varphi\mathcal{U}_a\psi) \to \varphi\mathcal{U}_a\psi$$

(P7):
$$(\varphi_1\mathcal{U}_a\psi_1 \wedge \varphi_2\mathcal{U}_a\psi_2) \to ((\varphi_1 \wedge \varphi_2)\mathcal{U}_a(\psi_1 \wedge \psi_2)$$
$$\vee (\varphi_1 \wedge \varphi_2)\mathcal{U}_a(\varphi_2 \wedge \psi_1)$$
$$\vee (\varphi_1 \wedge \varphi_2)\mathcal{U}_a(\varphi_1 \wedge \psi_2))$$

(Q1):
$$\forall_a\top$$

(Q2):
$$\forall_a(\varphi \wedge \psi) \to (\forall_a\varphi \wedge \forall_a\psi)$$

(Q3):
$$\forall_a\varphi \to \forall_a\forall_a\varphi$$

(Q4):
$$\forall_a\varphi \to \varphi$$

(Q5):
$$\varphi \to \forall_a\exists_a\varphi$$

Proposition 11. (Soundness of Axiomatisation) *For every formula $\varphi \in \mathcal{L}(\mathrm{Sig})$,*

$$\vdash_\Lambda \varphi \qquad \Rightarrow \qquad \varphi \in \mathbf{GFL}^\star$$

The verification of soundness of an axiom scheme φ consists of showing that $\mathfrak{M} \models \varphi$ for every model $\mathfrak{M} \in \mathbb{GF}(\Sigma)$, and for an inference rule of the form **if** $\vdash_\Lambda \varphi$ **then** $\vdash_\Lambda \psi$, one needs to show that if $\mathfrak{M} \models \varphi$, then $\mathfrak{M} \models \psi$, for all models $\mathfrak{M} \in \mathbb{GF}(\Sigma)$.

We give some verbal explanation for a selection of the axioms. The first axiom, **(P1)**, asserts that the union over a of all type-a paths is equal to the whole ω-path space of the model. To understand **(P5)**, suppose γ is an a-path satisfying $\varphi \mathcal{U}_a \psi$. Then there must be some positive time t along γ at which the suffix path $_t|\gamma$ satisfies ψ and at all strictly intermediate points along γ the suffix paths satisfy φ. In particular at all those strictly intermediate points, the suffix paths satisfy φ and $\varphi \mathcal{U}_a \psi$, meaning that γ satisfies $(\varphi \wedge \varphi \mathcal{U}_a \psi) \mathcal{U}_a \psi$. The axiom **(P6)** is sound because of the fusion closure of the ω-path space since the antecedent contains embedded *Until* operators. The axioms **(Q1-Q5)** all follow directly from the meaning of the universal (and existential) quantification. The three rules all express the monotonicity of the operators with respect to subset inclusion.

7 Summary and Discussion

In this paper, we propose and develop a quite general class of dynamical system models we call *general flow systems* which include and extend the broad class of evolutionary systems identified by Aubin, and the complete state behaviours of Willems. The advance specifically consists in modelling *hybrid time paths* as entities in their own right. We take the syntactic constructs of the non-deterministic and branching temporal logic **CTL*** originally developed for discrete time models, and re-interpret them in a semantics over general flow systems and with respect to arbitrary time lines. We propose a first candidate for an axiomatic proof system for the class of general flow models, and establish the soundness or adequacy of the proof system.

References

1. R. Alur, T.A. Henzinger, and P.-H. Ho. Automatic symbolic verification of embedded systems. *IEEE Transactions on Software Engineering*, 22:181–201, 1996.
2. R. Alur, T.A. Henzinger, G. Lafferriere, and G. Pappas. Discrete abstractions of hybrid systems. *Proceedings of the IEEE*, 88, July 2000.
3. J.-P. Aubin. Viability kernels and capture basins of sets under differential inclusions. *Siam Journal of Control*, 40:853–881, 2001.
4. J.-P. Aubin. Viability kernels and capture basins: Lecture notes. Technical report, Universidad Politecnica de Cartagena, Spain, April-May 2002.
5. J.-P. Aubin and O. Dordan. Dynamical qualitative analysis of evolutionary systems. In *Hybrid Systems: Computation and Control*, LNCS 2289, pages 62–75. Springer-Verlag, 2002.
6. J.-P. Aubin and H. Frankowska. *Set-Valued Analysis*. Birkhauser, Boston, 1990.
7. J.-P. Aubin, J. Lygeros, M. Quincampoix, S. Sastry, and N. Seube. Impulse differential inclusions: A viability approach to hybrid systems. *IEEE Transactions on Automatic Control*, 47:2–20, 2002.
8. J.P. Burgess. Axioms for tense logic I: "Since" and "Until". *Notre Dame Journal of Formal Logic*, 23:367–374, 1982.
9. V. Coulthard. *Temporal Logics of Dynamical Systems in Discrete and Dense Time*. PhD thesis, RSISE, The Australian National University, 2004. In preparation.
10. E.A. Emerson and J.Y. Halpern. "Sometimes" and "Not Never" revisited: on branching versus linear time. *Journal of the Association of Computing Machinery*, 33:151–178, 1986.
11. E.A. Emerson and C. Jutla. Complexity of tree automata and modal logics of programs. In *Proc. 29th IEEE Foundations of Computer Science (FOCS'88)*. IEEE, 1988.

12. E.A. Emerson and A. Sistla. Deciding Full Branching Time Logic. *Information and Control*, 61:175–201, 1984.
13. D.M. Gabbay, I. Hodkinson, and M. Reynolds. *Temporal Logic: Mathematical Foundations and Computational Aspects, Volume 1*. Clarendon Press, Oxford, 1994.
14. T.A. Henzinger. The theory of hybrid automata. In *Proc. of 11th Annual IEEE Symposium on Logic in Computer Science*, pages 278–292, 1996.
15. J. Lygeros, K.H. Henrik, S.N. Simić, and S.S. Sastry. Dynamical properties of hybrid automata. *IEEE Transactions on Automatic Control*, 48:2–17, 2003.
16. M. Reynolds. An Axiomatization of Full Computation Tree Logic. *J. Symbolic Logic*, 66:1011–1057, 2001.
17. C. Stirling. Modal and temporal logics. In *Handbook of Logic in Computer Science*, volume 2, pages 477–563. Oxford University Press, 1992.
18. J.C. Willems. Paradigms and puzzles in the theory of dynamical systems. *IEEE Transactions on Automatic Control*, 36:259–294, 1991.

Almost **ASAP** Semantics: From Timed Models to Timed Implementations[*]

Martin De Wulf, Laurent Doyen[**], and Jean-François Raskin

Computer Science Department, Université Libre de Bruxelles, Belgium

Abstract. In this paper, we introduce a parametric semantics for timed controllers called the *Almost* **ASAP** *semantics*. This semantics is a relaxation of the usual **ASAP** semantics (also called the *maximal progress semantics*) which is a mathematical idealization that can not be implemented by any physical device no matter how fast it is. On the contrary, any correct Almost **ASAP** controller can be implemented by a program on a hardware if this hardware is fast enough. We study the properties of this semantics, show how it can be analyzed using the tool HyTech, and illustrate its practical use on examples.

1 Introduction

Timed and hybrid systems are dynamical systems with both discrete and continuous components. A paradigmatic example of a hybrid system is a digital embedded control program for an analog plant environment, like a furnace or an airplane: the controller state moves discretely between control modes, and in each control mode, the plant state evolves continuously according to physical laws. A natural model for hybrid systems is the *hybrid automaton*, which represents discrete components using finite-state machines and continuous components using real-numbered variables which evolution is governed by differential equations or differential inclusions. Several verification and control problems have been studied for hybrid automata or interesting subclasses (see for example [HKPV98]). Tools like HyTech [HHWT95] have proven useful to analyze high-level descriptions of embedded controllers in continuous environments.

When a high level description of a controller has been proven *correct* it would be valuable to ensure that an implementation of that design can be obtained in a systematic way in order to ensure the *conservation of correctness*. This is often called program refinement: given a high-level description P_1 of a program, refine that description into another description P_2 such that the "important" properties of P_1 are maintained. Usually, P_2 is obtained from P_1 by reducing nondeterminism. To reason about the correctness of P_2 w.r.t. P_1, we often use a notion of simulation [Mil80] which is powerful enough to ensure conservation of LTL properties for example.

---

[*] Supported by the FRFC project "Centre Fédéré en Vérification" funded by the Belgian National Science Fundation (FNRS) under grant nr 2.4530.02

[**] Research fellow supported by the Belgian National Science Fundation (FNRS)

R. Alur and G.J. Pappas (Eds.): HSCC 2004, LNCS 2993, pp. 296–310, 2004.
© Springer-Verlag Berlin Heidelberg 2004

In this paper, we show how to adapt this elegant schema in the context of real-time embedded controllers. To reach this goal, there are several difficulties to overcome. First, the notion of time used by hybrid automata is based on a dense set of values (usually the real numbers). This is unarguably an interesting notion of time at the modeling level but when implemented, a digital controller manipulates timers that are digital clocks. Digital clocks have finite precision and take their values in a discrete domain. As a consequence, any control strategy that requires clocks with infinite precision can not be implemented. Second, hybrid automata can be called *"instantaneous devices"* in that they are capable of instantaneously react to time-outs or incoming events by taking discrete transitions without any delay. Again, while this is a convenient way to see reactivity and synchronization at the modeling level, any control strategy that relies for its correctness on that instantaneity can not be implemented by any physical device no matter how fast it is. Those problems are known and have already attracted some attention from our research community. For example, it is well-known that timed automata may describe controllers that control their environment by playing a so called zeno strategy, that is, by taking an infinite number of actions in a finite amount of time. This is widely considered as unacceptable even by authors making the synchrony hypothesis [AFP+03]. But even if we prove our controller model non-zeno, that does not mean that it can be implemented. In fact, we recently showed in [CHR02] that there are (very simple) timed automata that respect a syntactic criterion that ensures nonzenoness but requiring faster and faster reactions, say at times $0, \frac{1}{2}, 1, 1\frac{1}{4}, 2, 2\frac{1}{8}, 3, 3\frac{1}{16}, \ldots$. So, timed automata may model control strategies that can not be implemented because the control strategy does not maintain a minimal bound between two control actions. A direct consequence is that we can not hope to define for the entire class of timed automata a notion of refinement such that if a model of a real-time controller has been proven correct then it can be systematically implemented in a way that preserves its correctness.

The infinite precision and instantaneity characteristics of the traditional semantics given to timed automata is very closely related to the *synchrony hypothesis* that is commonly adopted in the community of synchronous languages [Ber00]. Roughly speaking, the synchrony hypothesis can be stated as follows: *"the program reacts to inputs of the environment by emitting outputs instantaneously"*. The rationale behind the synchrony hypothesis is that the speed at which a digital controller reacts is usually so high w.r.t. the speed of the environment that the reaction time of the controller can be neglected and considered as nil. This hypothesis *greatly simplifies* the work of the designer of an embedded controller: he/she does not have to take into account the performances of the platform on which the system will be implemented. We agree with this view at the modeling level. But as any hypothesis, the synchrony hypothesis *should be validated* not only by informal arguments but formally if we want to transfer correctness properties from models to implementations. We show in this paper how this can be done *formally* and *elegantly* using a semantics called the Almost ASAP semantics (AASAP-semantics).

The AASAP-semantics is a parametric semantics that leaves as a parameter the *reaction time* of the controller. This semantics relaxes the synchrony hypothesis in that it does not impose the controller to react instantaneously but imposes on the controller to react *within Δ time units* when a synchronization or a control action has to take place (is urgent). The designer acts as if the synchrony hypothesis was true, i.e. he/she models the environment and the controller strategy without referring to the reaction delay. This reaction delay is taken into account during the *verification phase*: we compute the largest Δ for which the controller is still receptive w.r.t. to the environment in which it will be embedded and for which the controller is still correct w.r.t. to the properties that it has to enforce (to avoid the environment to enter bad states for example).

We show that the AASAP semantics has several important and interesting properties. First, the semantics is such that "faster is better". That is, if the controller is correct for a reaction delay bounded by Δ then it is correct for any smaller Δ'. Second, any controller which is correct for a reaction delay bounded by $\Delta > 0$ can be implemented by a program on a hardware provided that the hardware is *fast enough* and provides *sufficiently precise digital clocks*. Third, the semantics can be analyzed using existing tools like HYTECH.

Structure of the paper. The paper is organized as follows. In section 2, we recall the notions of *timed transition systems*, *receptiveness* and *safety control*. We also define a notion of *simulation* that will ensure the conservation of receptiveness and safety properties imposed by the controller. In section 3, we review the syntax and *classical semantics* of timed automata. In section 4, we define formally the AASAP semantics and study some of its properties. In section 5, we introduce a *very simple and naive notion of real-time program* to make clear that any correct real-time controller for the AASAP semantics can be implemented. In section 6, we explain how the AASAP semantics can be *analyzed* and *used in practice*. Proofs and other examples can be found in a longer version of this paper at the following web page: http://www.ulb.ac.be/di/ssd/jfr.

2   Preliminaries

In this section, we recall the definition of timed transition systems and extend them with structured sets of labels. We define a notion of freedom of receptiveness problem and a compatible notion of simulation. This notion of simulation will be the formal basis for our notion of refinement. Finally, we introduce the problem of safety control and show how our notion of simulation can be used in that context.

Definition 1 [TTS] A *timed transition system* $\mathcal{T}$ is a tuple $\langle S, \iota, \Sigma, \rightarrow \rangle$ where S is a (possibly infinite) set of states, $\iota \in S$ is the initial state, Σ is a finite set of labels, and $\rightarrow \subseteq S \times \Sigma \cup \mathbb{R}^{\geq 0} \times S$ is the transition relation where $\mathbb{R}^{\geq 0}$ is the set of positive real numbers.

A state s of a TTS $\mathcal{T} = \langle S, \iota, \Sigma, \rightarrow \rangle$ is *reachable* if there exists a finite sequence $s_0 s_1 \ldots s_n$ of states such that $s_0 = \iota$, $s_n = s$ and for any i, $0 \leq i < n$, there exists $\sigma \in \Sigma \cup \mathbb{R}^{\geq 0}$ such that $(s_i, \sigma, s_{i+1}) \in \rightarrow$. The set of reachable states of $\mathcal{T}$ is noted $\mathsf{Reach}(\mathcal{T})$.

We need to compose TTS. For that purpose, we need TTS with structured set of labels. We say that a finite set of labels Σ is *structured* if it is partitioned into three subsets: Σ_{in} the set of input labels, Σ_{out} the set of output labels, and Σ_τ the set of internal labels. Let Σ be a structured alphabet and $\Sigma' \subseteq \Sigma$ be a subset of labels, then we note $\overline{\Sigma'}$ for the set $\{\bar{\sigma} \mid \sigma \in \Sigma'\}$, and assume this set is such that $\overline{\Sigma'} \cap \Sigma = \emptyset$.

Definition 2 [STTS] A *structured timed transition system* $\mathcal{T}$ is a tuple $\langle S, \iota, \Sigma_{\text{in}}, \Sigma_{\text{out}}, \Sigma_\tau, \rightarrow \rangle$, where S is a (possibly infinite) set of states, $\iota \in S$ is the initial state, the set of labels is partitioned into three subsets: Σ_{in} is the finite set of incoming labels, Σ_{out} is the finite set of outgoing labels, Σ_τ is the finite set of internal labels, and $\rightarrow \subseteq S \times \Sigma_{\text{in}} \cup \Sigma_{\text{out}} \cup \Sigma_\tau \cup \mathbb{R}^{\geq 0} \times S$ is the transition relation.

In the sequel, we use one STTS to model a timed controller and one to model the environment in which the controller has to be embedded. We model the communication between the two STTS using the mechanism of synchronization on common labels. This is a blocking communication mechanism. But we want to verify that the controller does not control the environment by refusing to synchronize on its output, and on the other hand, we do not want our controller to issue outputs that can not be accepted by the environment. To verify the absence of those synchronization problems, we make their potential presence explicit by introducing the notion of refusal function.

Definition 3 [Refusal function of a STTS] Given a STTS $\mathcal{T} = \langle S, \iota, \Sigma_{\text{in}}, \Sigma_{\text{out}}, \Sigma_\tau, \rightarrow \rangle$, we define its *refusal function* $\mathsf{Ref}_\mathcal{T} : S \rightarrow 2^{\Sigma_{\text{in}}}$ as follows :

$$\mathsf{Ref}_\mathcal{T}(s) = \{\sigma \in \Sigma_{\text{in}} \mid \neg \exists s' \in S : (s, \sigma, s') \in \rightarrow\}$$

We now define when and how two STTS can be composed to define a timed transition system.

Definition 4 [Composition of STTS] Two STTS $\mathcal{T}^1 = \langle S^1, \iota^1, \Sigma_{\text{in}}^1, \Sigma_{\text{out}}^1, \Sigma_\tau^1, \rightarrow^1 \rangle$ and $\mathcal{T}^2 = \langle S^2, \iota^2, \Sigma_{\text{in}}^2, \Sigma_{\text{out}}^2, \Sigma_\tau^2, \rightarrow^2 \rangle$ are *composable* if $\Sigma_{\text{in}}^1 = \Sigma_{\text{out}}^2$ and $\Sigma_{\text{in}}^2 = \Sigma_{\text{out}}^1$. Their composition, noted $\mathcal{T}^1 \| \mathcal{T}^2$ is the TTS $\mathcal{T} = \langle S, \iota, \Sigma, \rightarrow \rangle$ such that $S = \{(s^1, s^2) \mid s^1 \in S^1 \text{ and } s^2 \in S^2\}$, $\iota = (\iota^1, \iota^2)$, $\Sigma = \Sigma_{\text{out}}^1 \cup \Sigma_{\text{out}}^2 \cup \Sigma_\tau^1 \cup \Sigma_\tau^2$, and $\rightarrow$ is such that for any $\sigma \in \Sigma \cup \mathbb{R}^{\geq 0}$, we have that $((s_1^1, s_1^2), \sigma, (s_2^1, s_2^2)) \in \rightarrow$ iff one of the following three assertions holds:

- $\sigma \in \Sigma_{\text{out}}^1 \cup \Sigma_{\text{out}}^2 \cup \mathbb{R}^{\geq 0}$ and $(s_1^1, \sigma, s_2^1) \in \rightarrow^1$ and $(s_1^2, \sigma, s_2^2) \in \rightarrow^2$
- $\sigma \in \Sigma_\tau^1$ and $(s_1^1, \sigma, s_2^1) \in \rightarrow^1$ and $s_1^2 = s_2^2$
- $\sigma \in \Sigma_\tau^2$ and $(s_1^2, \sigma, s_2^2) \in \rightarrow^2$ and $s_1^1 = s_2^1$

When composing two STTS, we say that the result is free of receptiveness problem if there is no reachable state in the product where one STTS wants to issue an output that is not accepted by the other one.

Definition 5 [Freedom of receptiveness problems] The composition of two composable STTS $\mathcal{T}^1 = \langle S^1, \iota^1, \Sigma_{in}^1, \Sigma_{out}^1, \Sigma_\tau^1, \rightarrow^1 \rangle$ and $\mathcal{T}^2 = \langle S^2, \iota^2, \Sigma_{in}^2, \Sigma_{out}^2, \Sigma_\tau^2, \rightarrow^2 \rangle$ is *free of receptiveness problems* if their composition $\mathcal{T}^1 \| \mathcal{T}^2 = \langle S, \iota, \Sigma, \rightarrow \rangle$ is such that there does not exist $(s_1^1, s_1^2) \in \mathsf{Reach}(\mathcal{T}^1 \| \mathcal{T}^2)$, such that either:

- there exist $\sigma \in \Sigma_{out}^1$, $s_2^1 \in S^1$ such that $(s_1^1, \sigma, s_2^1) \in \rightarrow^1$ and $\sigma \in \mathsf{Ref}_{\mathcal{T}^2}(s_1^2)$
- there exist $\sigma \in \Sigma_{out}^2$, $s_2^2 \in S^2$ such that $(s_1^2, \sigma, s_2^2) \in \rightarrow^2$ and $\sigma \in \mathsf{Ref}_{\mathcal{T}^1}(s_1^1)$

Implementations of controllers are also formalized using STTS. To reason about the correctness of implementations w.r.t. higher level models, we use a notion of *simulation*. That notion of simulation makes explicit the notion of refusal in order to preserve the potential freedom of receptiveness problem property of the model.

Definition 6 [Simulation relation for STTS] Given two STTS $\mathcal{T}^1 = \langle S^1, \iota^1, \Sigma_{in}^1, \Sigma_{out}^1, \Sigma_\tau^1, \rightarrow^1 \rangle$ and $\mathcal{T}^2 = \langle S^2, \iota^2, \Sigma_{in}^2, \Sigma_{out}^2, \Sigma_\tau^2, \rightarrow^2 \rangle$, let $\Sigma = \Sigma_{out}^1 \cup \Sigma_{in}^1 \cup \Sigma_\tau^1$, we say that $\mathcal{T}^1$ is *simulable* by $\mathcal{T}^2$ and *as receptive* as $\mathcal{T}^2$, noted $\mathcal{T}^1 \sqsubseteq^r \mathcal{T}^2$, if there exists a relation $R \subseteq S^1 \times S^2$ (called a *simulation relation*) such that:

- $(\iota^1, \iota^2) \in R$
- for any $(s_1^1, s_1^2) \in R$, we have that:
  - for any $\sigma \in \Sigma \cup \mathbb{R}^{\geq 0}$, for any s_2^1 such that $(s_1^1, \sigma, s_2^1) \in \rightarrow^1$, there exists $s_2^2 \in S^2$ such that $(s_1^2, \sigma, s_2^2) \in \rightarrow^2$ and $(s_2^1, s_2^2) \in R$;
  - $\mathsf{Ref}_{\mathcal{T}^1}(s_1^1) = \mathsf{Ref}_{\mathcal{T}^2}(s_1^2)$.

The notion of simulation we have defined can be used to define a notion of refinement. We say that the STTS $\mathcal{T}^2$ *refines* the STTS $\mathcal{T}^1$, if $\mathcal{T}^1 \sqsubseteq^r \mathcal{T}^2$. The following theorem shows that our notion of refinement ensures that if a STTS $\mathcal{T}^1$ is free of receptiveness problems when composed with a STTS $\mathcal{T}^2$, then we can conclude the same for any STTS $\mathcal{T}^3$ that refines $\mathcal{T}^1$.

Theorem 1 *Let $\mathcal{T}^1$ and $\mathcal{T}^2$ be two composable STTS, let $\mathcal{T}^3$ be an STTS such that $\mathcal{T}^3 \sqsubseteq^r \mathcal{T}^1$, if $\mathcal{T}^1 \| \mathcal{T}^2$ is free of receptiveness problems then $\mathcal{T}^3 \| \mathcal{T}^2$ is free of receptiveness problems.*

We are now equipped to define the notion of safety control. This notion together with the notion of refinement we have introduced above allow us to formalize in section 4 and 5, the notion of correct implementation of an embedded timed controller.

Definition 7 [Safety Control] Let $\mathcal{T}^1 = \langle S^1, \iota^1, \Sigma_{in}^1, \Sigma_{out}^1, \Sigma_\tau^1, \rightarrow^1 \rangle$ and $\mathcal{T}^2 = \langle S^2, \iota^2, \Sigma_{in}^2, \Sigma_{out}^2, \Sigma_\tau^2, \rightarrow^2 \rangle$ be two composable STTS. Let $B \subseteq S^2$, we say that $\mathcal{T}^1$ *controls* $\mathcal{T}^2$ to avoid B if the following two conditions hold:

- $\mathcal{T}^1 \| \mathcal{T}^2$ is free of receptiveness problems;
- $\mathsf{Reach}(\mathcal{T}^1 \| \mathcal{T}^2) \cap \{(s^1, s^2) \mid s^1 \in S^1 \wedge s^2 \in B\}$ is empty.

We can now state a theorem linking our notion of refinement with the notion of safety control.

Theorem 2 *Let $\mathcal{T}^1 = \langle S^1, \iota^1, \Sigma_{in}^1, \Sigma_{out}^1, \Sigma_\tau^1, \rightarrow^1 \rangle$ and $\mathcal{T}^2 = \langle S^2, \iota^2, \Sigma_{in}^2, \Sigma_{out}^2, \Sigma_\tau^2, \rightarrow^2 \rangle$ be two composable STTS, let $\mathcal{T}^3$ be a STTS such that $\mathcal{T}^3 \sqsubseteq^r \mathcal{T}^1$, and let $B \subseteq S^2$, if $\mathcal{T}^1$ controls $\mathcal{T}^2$ to avoid B then $\mathcal{T}^3$ controls $\mathcal{T}^2$ to avoid B.*

3 Timed Automata

The STTS of previous section are specified using the formalism of timed automata. We recall their definition in this section.

Let X be a finite set of real-valued variables. A valuation for X is a function $v : X \rightarrow \mathbb{R}^{\geq 0}$. We write $[Y \rightarrow E]$ for the set of all valuations of set of variables Y to domain E. For a set $V \subseteq [X \rightarrow \mathbb{R}^{\geq 0}]$ of valuations, and $x \in X$, define $V(x) = \{v(x) \mid v \in V\}$. A *rectangular constraint* over X is a formula of the form "$x \in I$" where x belongs to X, and I is one of the intervals $(a, b), [a, b), (a, b]$ or $[a, b]$ where $a, b \in \mathbb{Q}^{\geq 0} \cup \{+\infty\}$, and $a \leq b$. $\mathbb{Q}^{\geq 0}$ denotes the positive rational numbers and, in the sequel, we also use $\mathbb{Q}^{>0}$ to denote the strictly positive rational numbers. A *rectangular predicate* is a finite set of rectangular constraints. For a rectangular predicate p and a valuation v, we write $v \models p$ if $v(x) \in I$ for all "$x \in I$" appearing in p. For a rectangular predicate p, $[\![p]\!]$ denotes the set $\{v \mid v \models p\}$. We say that a rectangular predicate is in normal form if it contains at most one rectangular constraint for any variable "$x \in X$"; any rectangular predicate can be put in that normal form. Let g be a rectangular predicate in normal form, then $g(x)$ denotes the rectangular constraint $x \in I$ if "$x \in I$" is the constraint over x in g and true if there is no constraint over x in g. We note $\mathsf{Rect}(X)$ the set of rectangular predicates built using variables in X. $\mathsf{Rect}_c(X)$ is the subset of rectangular predicates containing only closed rectangular constraints. Let $g(x)$ denote the closed rectangular constraints "$x \in [a, b]$", $lb(g(x))$ denotes the value a and $rb(g(x))$ denotes the value b. Let $v : E_1 \rightarrow E_2$ be a valuation, let $E_3 \subseteq E_1$, and $c \in E_2$, then $v[E_3 := c]$ denotes the valuation v' such that

$$v'(e) = \begin{cases} c & \text{if } e \in E_3 \\ v(e) & \text{if } e \notin E_3 \end{cases}$$

In the sequel, we sometimes write $v[e := c]$ instead of $v[\{e\} := c]$. Let $v : X \rightarrow \mathbb{R}^{\geq 0}$ be a valuation, for any $t \in \mathbb{R}^{\geq 0}$, $v - t$ is a valuation in $[X \rightarrow \mathbb{R}]$ such that for any $x \in X$, $(v - t)(x) = v(x) - t$. We define $v + t$ in a similar way. We extend this definition to valuation v in $[X \rightarrow \mathbb{R}^{\geq 0} \cup \{\bot\}]$ as follows: $(v + t)(x) = v(x) + t$, if $v(x) \in \mathbb{R}^{\geq 0}$, and $(v + t)(x) = \bot$ otherwise. We are now equipped to define timed automata and their *classical* semantics.

Definition 8 [Timed automata - syntax] A timed automaton is a tuple $\langle \mathsf{Loc}, l_0, \mathsf{Var}, \mathsf{Inv}, \mathsf{Lab}, \mathsf{Edg} \rangle$ where **(i)**Loc is a finite set of locations representing the discrete states of the automaton. **(ii)**$l_0 \in \mathsf{Loc}$ is the initial location. **(iii)**$\mathsf{Var} = \{x_1, \ldots, x_n\}$ is a finite set of real-valued clocks which value continuously increase as time passes with first derivative equal to one. **(iv)**$\mathsf{Inv} : \mathsf{Loc} \rightarrow \mathsf{Rect}(\mathsf{Var})$ is the invariant condition. The automaton can stay in location l as long as each variable x has a value in the interval $[\![\mathsf{Inv}(l)(x)]\!]$. We require that for any $x \in \mathsf{Var}$, $0 \in [\![\mathsf{Inv}(l_0)(x)]\!]$, to ensure the existence of an initial state. **(v)**$\mathsf{Lab} = \mathsf{Lab}_{\mathsf{in}} \cup \mathsf{Lab}_{\mathsf{out}} \cup \mathsf{Lab}_\tau$ is a structured finite alphabet of labels, partitioned into input labels $\mathsf{Lab}_{\mathsf{in}}$, output labels $\mathsf{Lab}_{\mathsf{out}}$, and internal labels Lab_τ. **(vi)**$\mathsf{Edg} \subseteq \mathsf{Loc} \times \mathsf{Loc} \times \mathsf{Rect}(\mathsf{Var}) \times \mathsf{Lab} \times 2^{\mathsf{Var}}$ is a set of edges. Every edge (l, l', g, σ, R) represents a discrete transition from location l to location l' with guard g, event σ and a subset $R \subseteq \mathsf{Var}$ of the variables to be reset.

Definition 9 [Timed automata - semantics] Let $A = \langle \text{Loc}, l_0, \text{Var}, \text{Inv}, \text{Lab}, \text{Edg} \rangle$ be a timed automaton, the semantics of A, noted $[\![A]\!]$, is the STTS $\mathcal{T} = (S, \iota, \Sigma_{\text{in}}, \Sigma_{\text{out}}, \Sigma_\tau, \rightarrow)$ where: **(i)** $S = \{(l, v) \mid l \in \text{Loc} \land v \in [\![\text{Inv}(l)]\!]\}$. **(ii)** $\iota = (l_0, v_0)$ such that for any $x \in \text{Var} : v_0(x) = 0$. **(iii)** $\Sigma_{\text{in}} = \text{Lab}_{\text{in}}$, $\Sigma_{\text{out}} = \text{Lab}_{\text{out}}$, and $\Sigma_\tau = \text{Lab}_\tau$. **(iv)** the transition relation $\rightarrow$ is defined as follows: (a) For the discrete transitions, $((l, v), \sigma, (l', v')) \in \rightarrow$ iff there exists an edge $(l, l', g, \sigma, R) \in \text{Edg}$ such that $v \models g$, $v' = v[R := 0]$. (b) For the continuous transitions, $((l, v), t, (l', v')) \in \rightarrow$ iff $l = l'$ and for each variable $x \in \text{Var}$ we have the two following conditions satisfied : $v'(x) = v(x) + t$ and $\forall t' \in [0, t] : v + t' \in [\![\text{Inv}(l)]\!]$.

For simplicity, we restrict ourselves in this paper to environments modeled as timed automata. Nevertheless, all the results presented below hold if hte environment is modeled using any class of hybrid automata.

Running example. Consider Fig. 1. The timed automaton of Fig. 1 (b) models a simple environment (a plant): when a request A is received, the response B is emitted before $y = 1$, and then the event C is accepted but it should occur at least one half time unit after A was received. Moreover, the event A *must* occur at least every α time units. If it was not the case, the environment would enter the location Bad modeling a fatal error. We will try to control the environment for $\alpha = 1$ and $\alpha = 2$.

The role of the controller is to produce an event A at least every α time units, to accept the subsequent event B and to output C respecting the timing constraint. An example of such a controller is given in Fig. 1 (a). The designer has chosen here to react to the event B only after three quarter time unit. Given this controller for the system, we must verify that it gives orders in such a way that any resulting behavior of the environment avoids to enter the bad state. We must additionally verify that the controller is receptive to the event B from the environment (otherwise it could simply control the environment to avoid Bad by refusing to synchronize with B). We must also verify that the environment is ready to receive the orders (A and C) when emitted by the controller. The reader can check that, with the classical semantics of timed automata, the controller controls the environment such that the location Bad is not reachable for $\alpha = 1$ and $\alpha = 2$. Later, we will see that if $\alpha = 1$ then the controller is not implementable, on the other hand, if $\alpha = 2$ then the controller can be implemented and control the environment to avoid Bad.

As we already pointed out in the introduction, the classical semantics given in definition 9 is problematic for the controller part if our goal is to transfer the properties verified on the model to an implementation. Below, we illustrate the properties of the classical semantics that makes it impossible to both implement the controller and ensure formally that the properties of the model are preserved.

First, note that invariants (grayed constraints in Fig. 1 (a)) are used to force the controller to take actions. Invariants can be removed if we assume a ASAP semantics for the controller: any action is taken as soon as possible, this is also called the *maximal progress assumption*. So the transition labeled with A! proceeds exactly when $z = 0$, *i.e.* instantaneously. Clearly, no hardware can

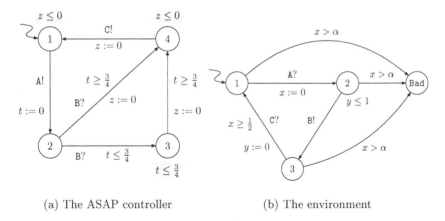

(a) The ASAP controller   (b) The environment

Fig. 1. Running example.

guarantee that the transition will always proceed without any delay. Second, synchronizations between the environment and the controller (*e.g.* transitions labeled B) cannot be implemented as instantaneous: some time is needed by the hardware to detect the incoming event B and for the software that implements the control strategy to take this event into account. Third, the use of real-valued clocks is only possible in the model: implementations use digital clocks with finite precision. It is then necessary to show that a digital clock can replace the real-valued clocks while preserving the verified safety properties.

These three problems illustrates that even if we have formally verified our control strategy, we can not conclude that an implementation will conserve any of the properties that we have proven on the model. This is unfortunate. If we simplify, there are two options to get out of this situation: (*i*) we ask the designer to give up the synchrony hypothesis and ask the designer to model the platform on which the control strategy will be implemented, as in [IKL$^+$00], or (*ii*) we let the designer go on with the synchrony hypothesis at the modeling level but relax the ASAP semantics during the verification phase in order to *formally validate the synchrony hypothesis*.

We think that the second option is *much more appealing* and we propose in the next section a framework that makes the second option possible *theoretically* but also feasible *practically*. The framework we propose is centered on a relaxation of the ASAP semantics that we call the AASAP semantics. The main characteristics of this semantics are summarized below:

– any transition that can be taken by the controller becomes urgent only after a small delay Δ (which may be left as a parameter);
– a distinction is made between the occurrence of an event in the environment (sent) and in the controller (received), however the time difference between the two events is bounded by Δ;
– guards are enlarged by some small amount depending on Δ.

We define formally this semantics in the next section and show in section 5 that it is *robust* in the sense that it defines a *tube of strategies* (instead of a unique strategy as in the ASAP semantics) which can be refined in a formal way into an implementation while preserving the safety properties imposed by this tube of strategies.

4   ELASTIC **Controllers and AASAP Semantics**

As explained in the previous section, invariants are useful when modeling controllers with the classical semantics in order to force the controller to take actions but they are useless with an ASAP semantics. This is also true with the semantics we define in this section. So, we restrict our attention to the subclass of timed automata without invariants. In the rest of the paper, we call the controller specified by this subclass ELASTIC[1] controllers.

Definition 10 [ELASTIC Controllers] An ELASTIC controller A is a tuple $\langle$Loc, l_0, Var, Lab, Edg$\rangle$ where Loc is a finite set of locations, $l_0 \in$ Loc is the initial location, Var $= \{x_1, \ldots, x_n\}$ is a finite set of clocks, Lab is a finite structured alphabet of labels, partitioned into input labels $\mathsf{Lab_{in}}$, output labels $\mathsf{Lab_{out}}$, and internal labels $\mathsf{Lab_\tau}$, Edg is a set of edges of the form (l, l', σ, g, R) where $l, l' \in$ Loc are locations, $\sigma \in$ Lab is a label, $g \in \mathsf{Rect_c}(\mathsf{Var})$ is a guard and $R \subseteq$ Var is a set of clocks to be reset.

Before defining the AASAP semantics we need some more notations:

Definition 11 [True Since] We define the function "True Since", noted TS : $[\mathsf{Var} \to \mathbb{R}^{\geq 0}] \times \mathsf{Rect_c}(\mathsf{Var}) \to \mathbb{R}^{\geq 0} \cup \{-\infty\}$, as follows:

$$\mathsf{TS}(v, g) = \begin{cases} t & \text{if } v \models g \wedge v - t \models g \wedge \forall t' > t : v - t' \not\models g \\ -\infty & \text{otherwise} \end{cases}.$$

Definition 12 [Guard Enlargement] Let $g(x)$ be the rectangular constraint "$x \in [a, b]$", the rectangular constraint $_\Delta g(x)_\Delta$ with $\Delta \in \mathbb{Q}^{\geq 0}$ is the formula "$x \in [a - \Delta, b + \Delta]$" if $a - \Delta \geq 0$ and "$x \in [0, b + \Delta]$" otherwise. If g is a closed rectangular predicate then $_\Delta g_\Delta$ is the set of closed rectangular constraints $\{_\Delta g(x)_\Delta \mid g(x) \in g\}$.

We are now ready to define the AASAP semantics. Intuitions are given right after the definition.

Definition 13 [AASAP semantics] Given an ELASTIC controller

$$A = \langle \mathsf{Loc}, l_0, \mathsf{Var}, \mathsf{Lab}, \mathsf{Edg} \rangle$$

---

[1] ELASTIC stands for Event-based LAnguage for Simple TImed Controllers; we also give to those timed controllers a semantics which is elastic in a sense that will be clear to the reader soon.

and $\Delta \in \mathbb{Q}^{\geq 0}$, the AASAP semantics of A, noted $[\![A]\!]_{\Delta}^{\mathsf{AAsap}}$ is the STTS

$$\mathcal{T} = \langle S, \iota, \Sigma_{\mathsf{in}}, \Sigma_{\mathsf{out}}, \Sigma_{\tau}, \rightarrow \rangle$$

where:

(A1) S is the set of tuples (l, v, I, d) where $l \in \mathsf{Loc}$, $v \in [\mathsf{Var} \to \mathbb{R}^{\geq 0}]$, $I \in [\Sigma_{\mathsf{in}} \to \mathbb{R}^{\geq 0} \cup \{\bot\}]$ and $d \in \mathbb{R}^{\geq 0}$;

(A2) $\iota = (l_0, v, I, 0)$ where v is such that for any $x \in \mathsf{Var} : v(x) = 0$, and I is such that for any $\sigma \in \Sigma_{\mathsf{in}}, I(\sigma) = \bot$;

(A3) $\Sigma_{\mathsf{in}} = \mathsf{Lab}_{\mathsf{in}}, \Sigma_{\mathsf{out}} = \mathsf{Lab}_{\mathsf{out}}$, and $\Sigma_{\tau} = \mathsf{Lab}_{\tau} \cup \overline{\mathsf{Lab}_{\mathsf{in}}} \cup \{\epsilon\}$;

(A4) The transition relation is defined as follows:
- for the discrete transitions, we distinguish five cases:

(A4.1) let $\sigma \in \mathsf{Lab}_{\mathsf{out}}$. We have $((l, v, I, d), \sigma, (l', v', I, 0)) \in \rightarrow$ iff there exists $(l, l', g, \sigma, R) \in \mathsf{Edg}$ such that $v \models_{\Delta} g_{\Delta}$ and $v' = v[R := 0]$;

(A4.2) let $\sigma \in \mathsf{Lab}_{\mathsf{in}}$. We have $((l, v, I, d), \sigma, (l, v, I', d)) \in \rightarrow$ iff $I(\sigma) = \bot$ and $I' = I[\sigma := 0]$;

(A4.3) let $\bar{\sigma} \in \overline{\mathsf{Lab}_{\mathsf{in}}}$. We have $((l, v, I, d), \bar{\sigma}, (l', v', I', 0)) \in \rightarrow$ iff there exists $(l, l', g, \sigma, R) \in \mathsf{Edg}$, $v \models_{\Delta} g_{\Delta}$, $I(\sigma) \neq \bot$, $v' = v[R := 0]$ and $I' = I[\sigma := \bot]$;

(A4.4) let $\sigma \in \mathsf{Lab}_{\tau}$. We have $((l, v, I, d), \sigma, (l', v', I, 0)) \in \rightarrow$ iff there exists $(l, l', g, \sigma, R) \in \mathsf{Edg}$, $v \models_{\Delta} g_{\Delta}$, and $v' = v[R := 0]$;

(A4.5) let $\sigma = \epsilon$. We have for any $(l, v, I, d) \in S : ((l, v, I, d), \epsilon, (l, v, I, d)) \in \rightarrow$.

- for the continuous transitions:

(A4.6) for any $t \in \mathbb{R}^{\geq 0}$, we have $((l, v, I, d), t, (l, v + t, I + t, d + t)) \in \rightarrow$ iff the two following conditions are satisfied:
  - for any edge $(l, l', g, \sigma, R) \in \mathsf{Edg}$ with $\sigma \in \mathsf{Lab}_{\mathsf{out}} \cup \mathsf{Lab}_{\tau}$, we have that:
  $$\forall t' : 0 \leq t' \leq t : (d + t' \leq \Delta \vee \mathsf{TS}(v + t', g) \leq \Delta)$$
  - for any edge $(l, l', g, \sigma, R) \in \mathsf{Edg}$ with $\sigma \in \mathsf{Lab}_{\mathsf{in}}$, we have that:
  $$\forall t' : 0 \leq t' \leq t : (d + t' \leq \Delta \vee \mathsf{TS}(v + t', g) \leq \Delta \vee (I + t')(\sigma) \leq \Delta)$$

Comments on the AASAP *semantics.* Rule $(A1)$ defines the states that are tuples of the form $\langle l, v, I, d \rangle$. The first two components, location l and valuation v, are the same as in the classical semantics; I and d are new. The function I records, for each input event σ, the time elapsed since its last occurrence if this occurrence has not been "treated" yet, otherwise the function returns the special value $\bot$. The time elapsed since the last location change in the controller is recorded by d. Rule $(A2)$ and $(A3)$ are straightforward. Rules $(A4.1 - 6)$ require more explanations. Rule $(A4.1)$ defines when it is allowed for the controller to emit an output event. The only difference with the classical semantics is that we enlarge the guard by the parameter Δ. Rules $(A4.2 - 3)$ defines how inputs from the environment are received $(A4.2)$ and treated $(A4.3)$ by the controller. First, the controller maintains, through the function I, a list of events that have occurred and are not yet treated. An input event σ can be received by the controller if no occurrence of σ is already present. An input event σ can be treated if $I(\sigma)$ is different of $\bot$. Once treated, the value of I for that event goes back to $\bot$. Rule $(A4.4)$ is similar to $(A4.1)$. Rule $(A4.5)$ expresses that the ϵ event can always be emitted. Rule $(A4.6)$ specifies how much time can elapse. Intuitively, time can pass as long as no transition starting from the current location is *urgent*. A transition labeled with an output or an internal event is urgent in a location l when the control has been in l for more than Δ time units $(d + t' > \Delta)$ and the guard of the transition has been true for more than Δ time units $(\mathsf{TS}(v + t', g) > \Delta)$. A transition labeled with an input event σ is urgent in a location l when the control has been in l for more than Δ time units $(d + t' > \Delta)$, the guard of the transition has been true for more that Δ time units $(\mathsf{TS}(v + t', g) > \Delta)$, the last occurrence of σ event has not been treated yet and has been emitted by the environment at least Δ time units ago $(I + t'(\sigma) > \Delta)$. This notion of urgency parameterized by Δ is the main difference between the AASAP semantics and the usual ASAP semantics.

We now state a first property of the AASAP semantics. The following theorem and corollary state formally the informal statement "faster is better", that is if an environment is controllable with an ELASTIC controller reacting within the bound Δ_1 then this environment is controllable by the same controller for any reaction time $\Delta_2 \leq \Delta_1$. This is clearly a desirable property.

Theorem 3 *Let A be an* ELASTIC *controller, for any $\Delta_1, \Delta_2 \in \mathbb{Q}^{\geq 0}$ such that $\Delta_1 \geq \Delta_2$ we have that $[\![A]\!]^{\mathsf{AAsap}}_{\Delta_2} \sqsubseteq^r [\![A]\!]^{\mathsf{AAsap}}_{\Delta_1}$.*

Theorem 2 and theorem 3 allow us to state the following corollary:

Corollary 1 *Let E be a timed automaton, $[\![E]\!]$ be an STTS with set of states S^E, $B \subseteq S^E$ be a set of bad states, and A be an* ELASTIC *controller. For any $\Delta_1, \Delta_2 \in \mathbb{Q}^{\geq 0}$, such that $\Delta_1 \geq \Delta_2$, if $[\![A]\!]^{\mathsf{AAsap}}_{\Delta_1}$ controls $[\![E]\!]$ to avoid B then $[\![A]\!]^{\mathsf{AAsap}}_{\Delta_2}$ controls $[\![E]\!]$ to avoid B.*

We say that an ELASTIC controller is able to control an environment modeled as a timed automaton E for a safety property modeled by a set of bad states B if there exists $\Delta > 0$ such that $[\![A]\!]^{\mathsf{AAsap}}_{\Delta}$ controls $[\![E]\!]$ to avoid B.

5   Implementability of the AASAP Semantics

In this section, we show that any ELASTIC controller which controls an environment E for a safety property modeled by a set of bad states B can be implemented provided there exists a hardware sufficiently fast and providing sufficiently precise digital clocks.

To establish this result, we proceed as follows. First, we define what we call the program semantics of an ELASTIC controller. The so-called program semantics can be seen as a formal semantics for the following procedure interpreting ELASTIC controllers. This procedure repeatedly executes what we call *execution rounds*. An execution round is defined as follows:

- first, the current time is read in the clock register of the CPU and stored in a variable, say T;

- the list of input events to treat is updated: the input sensors are checked for new events issued by the environment;
- guards of the edges of the current locations are evaluated with the value stored in T. If at least one guard evaluates to true then take nondeterministically one of the enabled transitions;
- the next round is started.

All we require from the hardware is to respect the following two requirements: (i) the clock register of the CPU is incremented every Δ_P time units and (ii) the time spent in one loop is bounded by a certain fixed value Δ_L. We choose this semantics for its simplicity and also because it is obviously implementable. There are more efficient ways to interpret ELASTIC controllers but as the AASAP semantics is such that "faster is better", this semantics is good enough for our purpose. In section 6, we show how to use this semantics in the context of the LEGO MINDSTORMS™ platform.

We proceed now with the definition of the program semantics. This semantics manipulates digital clocks, so we need the following definition:

Definition 14 [Clock Rounding] Let $T \in \mathbb{R}, \Delta \in \mathbb{Q}^{>0}, \lfloor T \rfloor_\Delta = \lfloor \frac{T}{\Delta} \rfloor \Delta.$

We are now ready to define the program semantics. Intuitions are given right after the definition.

Definition 15 [Program Semantics] Let A be an ELASTIC controller and Δ_L, $\Delta_P \in \mathbb{Q}^{>0}$. We define $\Delta_S = \Delta_L + 2\Delta_P$. The (Δ_L, Δ_P) program semantics of A, noted $[\![A]\!]^{Prg}_{\Delta_L, \Delta_P}$ is the structured timed transition system $\mathcal{T} = \langle S, \iota, \Sigma_{in}, \Sigma_{out}, \Sigma_\tau, \rightarrow \rangle$ where:

($P1$) S is the set of tuples (l, r, T, I, u, d, f) such that $l \in \mathsf{Loc}$, r is a function from Var into $\mathbb{R}^{\geq 0}$, $T \in \mathbb{R}^{\geq 0}$, I is a function from Lab_{in} into $\mathbb{R}^{\geq 0} \cup \{\bot\}$, $u \in \mathbb{R}^{\geq 0}$, $d \in \mathbb{R}^{\geq 0}$, and $f \in \{\top, \bot\}$;
($P2$) $\iota = (l_0, r, 0, I, 0, 0, \bot)$ where r is such that for any $x \in \mathsf{Var}$, $r(x) = 0$, I is such that for any $\sigma \in \mathsf{Lab}_{in}$, $I(\sigma) = \bot$;
($P3$) $\Sigma_{in} = \mathsf{Lab}_{in}$, $\Sigma_{out} = \mathsf{Lab}_{out}$, $\Sigma_\tau = \mathsf{Lab}_\tau \cup \overline{\mathsf{Lab}_{in}} \cup \{\epsilon\}$;
($P4$) the transition relation $\rightarrow$ is defined as follows:
- for the discrete transitions:
  ($P4.1$) let $\sigma \in \mathsf{Lab}_{out}$. $((l, r, T, I, u, d, \bot), \sigma, (l', r', T, I, u, 0, \top)) \in \rightarrow$ iff there exists $(l, l', g, \sigma, R) \in \mathsf{Edg}$ such that $\lfloor T \rfloor_{\Delta_P} - r \models_{\Delta_S} g_{\Delta_S}$ and $r' = r[R := \lfloor T \rfloor_{\Delta_P}]$.
  ($P4.2$) let $\sigma \in \mathsf{Lab}_{in}$. $((l, r, T, I, u, d, f), \sigma, (l, r, T, I', u, d, f)) \in \rightarrow$ iff $I(\sigma) = \bot$ and $I' = I[\sigma := 0]$;
  ($P4.3$) let $\bar{\sigma} \in \overline{\mathsf{Lab}_{in}}$. $((l, r, T, I, u, d, \bot), \bar{\sigma}, (l', r', T, I', u, 0, \top)) \in \rightarrow$ iff there exists $(l, l', g, \sigma, R) \in \mathsf{Edg}$ such that $\lfloor T \rfloor_{\Delta_P} - r \models_{\Delta_S} g_{\Delta_S}$, $I(\sigma) > u$, $r' = r[R := \lfloor T \rfloor_{\Delta_P}]$ and $I' = I[\sigma := \bot]$;
  ($P4.4$) let $\sigma \in \mathsf{Lab}_\tau$. $((l, r, T, I, u, d, \bot), \sigma, (l', r', T, I, u, 0, \top)) \in \rightarrow$ iff there exists $(l, l', g, \sigma, R) \in \mathsf{Edg}$ such that $\lfloor T \rfloor_{\Delta_P} - r \models_{\Delta_S} g_{\Delta_S}$ and $r' = r[R := \lfloor T \rfloor_{\Delta_P}]$.

$(P4.5)$ let $\sigma = \epsilon$. $((l, r, T, I, u, d, f), \sigma, (l, r, T + u, I, 0, d, \bot)) \in\to$ iff either $f = \top$ or the two following conditions hold:

- for any $\bar{\sigma}$ such that $\sigma \in \mathsf{Lab_{in}}$, for any $(l, l', g, \sigma, R) \in \mathsf{Edg}$, we have that either $\lfloor T \rfloor_{\Delta_P} - r \not\models_{\Delta_S} g_{\Delta_S}$ or $I(\sigma) \leq u$
- for any $\sigma \in \mathsf{Lab_{out}} \cup \mathsf{Lab_\tau}$, for any $(l, l', g, \sigma, R) \in \mathsf{Edg}$, we have that $\lfloor T \rfloor_{\Delta_P} - r \not\models_{\Delta_S} g_{\Delta_S}$

- for the continuous transitions:

$(P4.6)$ $((l, r, T, I, u, d, f), t, (l, r, T, I + t, u + t, d + t, f)) \in\to$ iff $u + t \leq \Delta_L$.

Comments on the program semantics. Rule $(P1)$ defines the states which are tuples (l, r, T, I, u, d, f), where l is the current location, r maps each clock to the digital time when it has last been reset, T records the (exact) time at which the last round has started; I, as in the AASAP semantics, records the time elapsed since the last arrival of each input event not yet treated, u records the time elapsed since the last round was started (so that $T + u$ is the exact current time), d records the time elapsed since the last location change, and f is a flag which is set to $\top$ if a location change has occurred in the current round. Rules $(P2)$ and $(P3)$ should be clear. We comment rules $(P4.1 - 6)$. First, we make some general comments on digital clocks and guards of discrete transitions of the controller. Note that in those rules, we evaluate the guards with the valuation $\lfloor T \rfloor_{\Delta_P} - r$ for the clocks, that is, for variable x, the difference between the digital value of the variable T at the beginning of the current round and the digital value of x at the beginning of the round when x was last reset. This value approximates the real time difference between the exact time at which the guard is evaluated and the exact time at which the clock x has been reset. Let t be this exact time difference, then we know that: $\lfloor T \rfloor_{\Delta_P} - r(x) - \Delta_L - \Delta_P \leq t \leq \lfloor T \rfloor_{\Delta_P} - r(x) + \Delta_L + \Delta_P$. Also note that the guard g has been enlarged by the value $\Delta_S = \Delta_L + 2\Delta_P$, this ensures that any event enabled at some point will be enabled sufficiently long so that the change can be detected by the procedure. Rule $(P4.1)$ expresses when transitions labeled with output events can be taken. Note that variables are reset to the digital time of the current round. Rule $(P4.2)$ simply records the exact time at which input event from the environment occurred. This rule simply ensures that the function I is updated when a new event is issued by the environment. Rule $(P4.3)$ says when an input of the environment can be treated by the controller: it has to be present at the beginning of the current round and the enlargement of the guard labelling the transition has to be true for digital values of the clocks at the beginning of the round, and no other discrete transitions should have been taken in the current round. Rule $(P4.4)$ is similar to rule $(P4.1)$ but applies to internal events. Rule $(P4.5)$ expresses that the event ϵ is issued when the current round is finished and the system starts a new round. Note that this is only possible if the program has taken a discrete transition or there were no discrete transition to take. This ensures that the program always takes discrete transitions when possible. Rule $(P4.6)$ expresses that the program can always let time elapse unless it violates the maximal time spent in one round.

The following simulation theorem expresses formally that if the hardware on which the program is implemented is fast enough (parameter Δ_L) and precise enough (parameter Δ_P) then the program semantics can be simulated by the AASAP semantics.

Theorem 4 (Simulation) *Let A be an* ELASTIC *controller, for any $\Delta, \Delta_L, \Delta_P$ $\in \mathbb{Q}^{\geq 0}$ be such that $\Delta > 3\Delta_L + 4\Delta_P$, we have $[\![A]\!]^{\mathsf{Prg}}_{\Delta_L, \Delta_P} \sqsubseteq^r [\![A]\!]^{\mathsf{AAsap}}_{\Delta}$.*

Theorem 5 (Simulability) *For any* ELASTIC *controller A, for any $\Delta \in \mathbb{Q}^{>0}$, there exists $\Delta_L, \Delta_P \in \mathbb{Q}^{>0}$ such that $[\![A]\!]^{\mathsf{Prg}}_{\Delta_L, \Delta_P} \sqsubseteq^r [\![A]\!]^{\mathsf{AAsap}}_{\Delta}$.*

And so, given a sufficiently fast hardware with a sufficiently precise digital clock, we can implement any controller that have been proved correct. This is expressed by the following corollary:

Corollary 2 (Implementability) *Let E be a timed automaton , let $[\![E]\!]$ be a STTS with set of states S^E, $B \subseteq S^E$ be a set of bad states. For any* ELASTIC *controller A, for any $\Delta \in \mathbb{Q}^{>0}$, such that $[\![A]\!]^{\mathsf{AAsap}}_{\Delta}$ controls $[\![E]\!]$ to avoid B, there exist $\Delta_L, \Delta_P \in \mathbb{Q}^{>0}$ such that $[\![A]\!]^{\mathsf{Prg}}_{\Delta_L, \Delta_P}$ controls $[\![E]\!]$ to avoid B.*

6   In Practice

In this section, we show that the AASAP semantics can be analyzed automatically using the tool HYTECH [HHWT95]. This is a direct corollary of the next theorem: for any $\Delta \in \mathbb{Q}^{\geq 0}$, for any ELASTIC controller A, the AASAP semantics of A can be encoded using the classical semantics of a timed automaton $\mathcal{A}^{\Delta}$ constructed from A and Δ.

Theorem 6 *For any* ELASTIC *controller A, for any $\Delta \in \mathbb{Q}^{>0}$, we can construct effectively a timed automaton $\mathcal{A}^{\Delta} = \mathcal{F}(A, \Delta)$ such that $[\![A]\!]^{\mathsf{AAsap}}_{\Delta} \sqsubseteq^r [\![\mathcal{A}^{\Delta}]\!]$ and $[\![\mathcal{A}^{\Delta}]\!] \sqsubseteq^r [\![A]\!]^{\mathsf{AAsap}}_{\Delta}$.*

Corollary 3 *For any* ELASTIC *controller A, for any $\Delta \in \mathbb{Q}^{>0}$, for any timed automaton E with state space S^E, for any set of states $B \subseteq S^E$, we have that $[\![A]\!]^{\mathsf{AAsap}}_{\Delta}$ controls $[\![E]\!]$ to avoid B iff $[\![\mathcal{F}(A, \Delta)]\!]$ controls $[\![E]\!]$ to avoid B.*

In practice, we use theorem 6 to reduce the controllability problem to a reachability problem:

- we construct $\mathcal{F}(A, \Delta)$ (where we can leave Δ as a parameter);
- we construct a HYTECH file with a description of $\mathcal{F}(A, \Delta)$ and E;
- we ask for which parameter value $reach([\![\mathcal{F}(A, \Delta)]\!] \parallel [\![E]\!]) \cap Bad = \emptyset$ (where Bad is a set of bad states) and the system is free of receptiveness problems.

If we apply the construction of theorem 6 to our running example (Fig. 1), we can ask HYTECH to establish for which value of Δ, the tube of control strategies defined by the timed automaton obtained by the construction of theorem 6 is valid.

In the case $\alpha = 1$, the result is $\Delta = 0$. We can interpret this as follows: we have a correct model w.r.t to the classical ASAP semantics but it is nevertheless not guaranteed to be correct when implemented on a real hardware. In fact, the condition $\Delta = 0$ means that some transitions in the controller are required to be taken instantaneously, which is impossible in the real world. It must be admitted that the synchrony hypothesis was not realistic in that case. The second case ($\alpha = 2$) is more useful: the model is correct for any $\Delta \leq \frac{1}{4}$. If we assume that the unit of time is the second, theorem 4 then tells us that, to preserve the desired property with a systematic implementation of the ELASTIC controller, we should have a platform with loop time Δ_L and clock precision Δ_P such that $3\Delta_L + 4\Delta_P < 250ms$. For instance, we can implement the controller on the LEGO MINDSTORMS™ platform, since it allows Δ_L to be as low as 6ms and offers a digital clock with $\Delta_P = 1$ms which is thus ample enough.

References

[AFP⁺03]   Tobias Amnell, Elena Fersman, Paul Pettersson, Hongyan Sun, and Wang Yi. Code synthesis for timed automata. *Nordic Journal of Computing(NJC)*, 9, 2003.

[Ber00]   G. Berry. *The Foundations of Esterel*. MIT Press, 2000.

[CHR02]   F. Cassez, T.A. Henzinger, and J.-F. Raskin. A comparison of control problems for timed and hybrid systems. In *HSCC 02: Hybrid Systems—Computation and Control*, Lecture Notes in Computer Science 2289, pages 134–148. Springer-Verlag, 2002.

[HHWT95]   T.A. Henzinger, P.-H. Ho, and H. Wong-Toi. A user guide to HYTECH. In E. Brinksma, W.R. Cleaveland, K.G. Larsen, T. Margaria, and B. Steffen, editors, *TACAS 95: Tools and Algorithms for the Construction and Analysis of Systems*, Lecture Notes in Computer Science 1019, pages 41–71. Springer-Verlag, 1995.

[HKPV98]   T.A. Henzinger, P.W. Kopke, A. Puri, and P. Varaiya. What's decidable about hybrid automata? *Journal of Computer and System Sciences*, 57:94–124, 1998.

[IKL⁺00]   T. Iversen, K. Kristoffersen, K. Larsen, M. Laursen, R. Madsen, S. Mortensen, P. Petterson, and C. Thomasen. Model-checking real-time control programs – verifying LEGO mindstorms systems using UPPAAL. In *Proc. 12th Euromicro Conf. on Real-Time Systems (ECRTS'00).*, 2000.

[Mil80]   R. Milner. *A Calculus of Communicating Systems*. Lecture Notes in Computer Science 92. Springer-Verlag, 1980.

Discrete State Estimators for a Class of Hybrid Systems on a Lattice

Domitilla Del Vecchio and Richard M. Murray

Control and Dynamical Systems
California Institute of Technology
1200 E California Boulevard, Mail Stop 107-81
Pasadena, CA 91125
{ddomitilla, murray}@cds.caltech.edu

Abstract. In this paper we consider the problem of estimating discrete variables in a class of hybrid systems where we assume that the continuous variables are available for measurement. Using lattice and order theory we develop a framework for constructing a discrete state estimator on an enlarged space of variables with lattice structure, which updates only two variables at each step. We apply our ideas to a multi-robot system example, the RoboFlag Drill.

1   Introduction

In the last decade hybrid systems models have become very popular in the control community. Some of the systems under study have been changing from systems governed by continuous differential equations, to systems characterized by very large numbers of discrete and continuous variables whose evolution is determined by both continuous dynamics and logics. Examples include internet systems, continuous plants controlled by digital controllers, and multi-agent systems. The interplay of continuous dynamics and decision protocols renders these systems interesting and complicated enough that new mathematical tools are needed for the sake of analysis and control. Issues like controllability and observability arise naturally when trying to analyze the properties of these systems for control.

The problem of estimating and tracking the values of non-measurable variables in hybrid systems with computational effort comparable to the one needed for simulating the hybrid system itself is a challenging one. Bemporad et al. [2] show that observability properties are hard to check for hybrid systems and an observer is proposed that requires large amounts of computation. A wealth of research has been done on designing observers for discrete event systems both deterministic and non-deterministic. For non-deterministic systems, [11] studies observability conditions for exact reconstruction of the current state after each system event, and [4] consider the problem of finding optimal control strategies for partially observable Markov-decision processes. In the deterministic case, [3] and [6] show that the complexity of the observer often arises from the need to compute maps on large sets of values, corresponding to the set of all possible internal states compatible with the observed output sequence. These same difficulties are encountered in [12], where the proposed observer fails to be applicable for large problem sizes.

R. Alur and G.J. Pappas (Eds.): HSCC 2004, LNCS 2993, pp. 311–325, 2004.
© Springer-Verlag Berlin Heidelberg 2004

In this paper we consider the problem of estimation and tracking of non-measurable discrete variables in deterministic hybrid systems. As a starting point for our study, we assume that among all the system's variables the continuous variables are available for measurement. This simplified scenario has already practical interest as in the case, for example, of decentralized multi-robot systems. In these systems the continuous variables may represent physical quantities such as positions and velocities, while discrete variables may represent the state of the logical system that is used for control and coordination. In these systems, the discrete and continuous variables are heavily coupled through logical operations and continuous dynamics, rendering difficult the estimation task. Therefore discrete state estimation strategies where the analysis of the continuous signal is enough for determining the discrete state, such as the ones proposed by [1], are not applicable.

Our point of view is that some of the complexity issues, such as those encountered in [12] or [3, 6], can be avoided by finding a good way of representing the sets of interest and of computing maps on them. As a naive example consider the set S of all natural numbers between one and one thousand. This set can be represented as $S = [1, 1000]$, without the need of listing all its elements. Suppose we want to know what set S is mapped to by a map ϕ. We can either compute such a map on all the elements of S, or we can compute it on the least and greatest elements of S. In this case if the map ϕ has some properties, the set $\phi(S)$ can be deduced by $\phi(1)$ and $\phi(1000)$ without additional computation. This simplification is possible thanks to the order structure naturally associated to $\mathbb{N}$ and thanks to the structure of the map ϕ.

In this paper we formalize these ideas using lattice theory. In particular given a system Σ defined on its space of variables, we extend it to a larger space of variables that has lattice structure so as to obtain the extended system $\tilde{\Sigma}$. Under certain properties verified by the extension $\tilde{\Sigma}$, discrete state estimator for system Σ can be constructed, which updates at each step only two variables. Namely it updates the least and greatest element of the set of all values of discrete variables compatible with the output sequence and with the dynamics of Σ. Throughout the paper we will refer to discrete estimator as observer, implicitly assuming that only the discrete variables are estimated.

The contents of this paper is as follows. In Section 2 we review some basic definitions and results on lattice theory, and some basic terminology of transition systems. The main result is given in Section 3, where we provide an explicit construction for the observer that updates least and maximum elements on a proper lattice structure. In Section 4 we introduce a multi-robot system, the RoboFlag Drill, and in Section 5 we show how to apply our ideas to this example. We then conclude the paper with some simulation results on the RoboFlag Drill system in Section 6.

2   Basic Concepts

In this section we give first some background on lattice theory as it can be found in [5]. Then we recall basic definitions on transition systems (see [10] for more details). Finally we recall some basic observability definitions as they can be found in many references (see [12] for example).

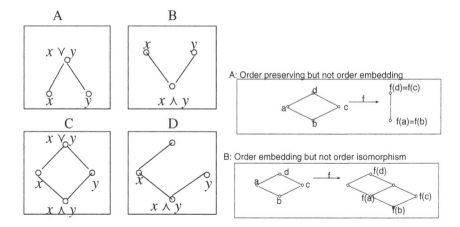

Fig. 1. (Left) In diagram A and B x and y are not related, but they have a join and a meet. In diagram C we show a complete lattice, and in diagram D we show an ordered set that is not a lattice, since the elements x and y have a meet, but not a join. (Right) In diagram A we show a map that is order preserving but not order embedding. In diagram B we show an order embedding map that is not order isomorphism: any two elements maintain the same order relation, but in between c and d there is nothing, while in between $f(c)$ and $f(d)$ some other elements appears (i.e. it is not onto).

2.1 Lattice Theory

Given a set χ with an order relation "$\leq$", we define the *join* "$\vee$" and the *meet* "$\wedge$" of two elements x and w in χ as

1. $x \vee w = \sup\{x, w\}$ and $x \wedge w = \inf\{x, w\}$;
2. if $S \subseteq \chi$, $\bigvee S = \sup S$ and $S \subseteq \chi$, $\bigwedge S = \inf S$;

where by $\sup\{x, w\}$ we denote the smallest element in χ that is bigger than both x and w, and we denote by $\inf\{x, w\}$ the biggest element in χ that is smaller than both x and w. In analogous way we denote by $\sup S$ the smallest element in χ that is bigger than all the elements in S, and we denote by $\inf S$ the biggest element in χ that is smaller than all the elements in S.

Let χ be a non-empty ordered set. If $x \wedge w$ and $x \vee w$ exist for any $x, w \in \chi$, then χ is a *lattice*. If $\bigvee S$ and $\bigwedge S$ exist for all $S \subseteq \chi$, then χ is a *complete lattice*. Notice that any finite lattice is complete. In Figure 1 (left) we report diagrams showing ordered sets. From the diagram it is easy to tell when one element is less than another: $x < w$ if and only if there is a sequence of connected line segments moving upward from x to w. Let χ be an ordered set. Then χ is a *chain* if for all $x, w \in \chi$, either $x \leq w$ or $w \leq x$, that is any two elements are comparable. At the opposite extreme of a chain is an anti-chain. The ordered set χ is an *anti-chain* if $x \leq y$ if and only if $x = y$. Let χ be a lattice and let $\emptyset \neq S \subseteq \chi$ be a subset of χ. Then S is a *sublattice* of χ if $a, b \in S$ implies that $a \vee b \in S$ and $a \wedge b \in S$.

Definition 1. Let P and Q be ordered sets. A map $f : P \to Q$ is said to be

(i)   *order preserving* if $x \leq w \implies f(x) \leq f(w)$;
(ii) *order embedding* if $x \leq w \iff f(x) \leq f(w)$;
(iii) *order isomorphic* if it is order embedding and it maps P *onto* Q.

Definition 2. If P and Q are lattices, then a map $f : P \to Q$ is said to be an *homomorphism* if f is *join-preserving* and *meet-preserving*, that is for all $x, w \in P$ we have that $f(x \vee w) = f(x) \vee f(w)$ and $f(x \wedge w) = f(x) \wedge f(w)$. A bijective homomorphism is a *(lattice) isomorphism.*

Every order isomorphic map faithfully mirrors the structure of P onto Q. In Figure 1 (right) we show some examples.

Lemma 1. *Let P and Q be ordered sets and $f : P \to Q$ be an order isomorphism. Then f preserves all joins and meets, that is for any $S \subseteq P$ whenever $\bigvee S$ ($\bigwedge S$) exists in P then $\bigvee f(S)$ ($\bigwedge f(S)$) exists in Q and*

$$f\left(\bigvee S\right) = \bigvee f(S), \quad \text{and} \quad f\left(\bigwedge S\right) = \bigwedge f(S).$$

2.2   State Transition Systems

For completeness, we review the basic definitions used in transition systems as described more completely in other work [10]. Consider a set of variable symbols V with types $type(v)$ for each $v \in V$. A *state* s is a function from V into U where $U = \bigcup_{v \in V} type(v)$. The set of all states is denoted S. A *transition relation* on S is a relation $R \subseteq S \times S$. If sRs' and $v \in V$, we will write v to refer to $s(v)$. The set of all states is denoted S. For a subset W of V, we denote by $s|_W$ the restriction of s to W, so that we have that $S|_W = \{s|_W : s \in S\}$.

Given a transition relation R, an *execution* of R is a sequence $\sigma = \{s_k\}_{k \in \mathbb{N}}$ such that $s_k R s_{k+1}$ for all $k \in \mathbb{N}$. The set of all executions of R is denoted $\mathcal{E}(R)$. If $\sigma \in \mathcal{E}(R)$ is fixed and $v \in V$ we denote by $v(k)$ the value $\sigma(k)(v)$. The *trajectory* of $v \in V$ with respect to σ is the sequence $\{\sigma(k)(v)\}_{k \in \mathbb{N}}$.

We now recall the notion of observability for transition systems as it can be found in [12].

Definition 3. Given a transition relation R on S and an output map $g : S \to U$, for some U, two executions $\sigma_1, \sigma_2 \in \mathcal{E}(R)$ are *distinguishable* if there exists a k such that $g(\sigma_1(k)) \neq g(\sigma_2(k))$.

Definition 4. (Observability) The transition relation R is said to be *observable* with respect to the output function $g : S \to U$ if any two executions $\sigma_1, \sigma_2 \in \mathcal{E}(R)$ are distinguishable.

We will consider state transition systems with both discrete and continuous variables. V_C is the set of continuous variables that we denote with z with $type(z) = \mathbb{R}^N$ for all $z \in V_C$, and V_D is the set of discrete variables that we denote with α with $type(\alpha) = \mathcal{U}$ for all $\alpha \in V_D$. In this paper we assume that $V = V_C \cup V_D$, with $V_C \cap V_D = \emptyset$. We will consider deterministic transition systems, as a consequence the transition relation becomes a function. In particular we denote by $h : \mathcal{U} \times \mathbb{R}^N \to \mathbb{R}^N$ and $f : \mathcal{U} \times \mathbb{R}^N \to \mathcal{U}$ the functions that update the values of the continuous variables and the values of the discrete variables respectively. In what follows we will denote a transition system Σ by the couple (f, h) assuming that V_C is the set of measurable variables, that is the output function is $g : S \to S|_{V_C}$.

3 Observer Construction

In this section we show that if we can extend the space $\mathcal{U}$ to a space χ with lattice structure, and if we can extend the maps f and g to the whole χ such that f is order isomorphic on suitable subsets of χ, then in the case in which Σ is observable we can construct a system that at each step updates only two variables. These variables are the join and the meet of the set of all possible α's values compatible with the output sequence; moreover the set that they define converges asymptotically to a set whose intersection with $\mathcal{U}$ is the current value of α. This is stated formally in the following theorem

Theorem 1. *Consider the system $\Sigma = (f, h)$ with $h : \mathcal{U} \times \mathbb{R}^N \to \mathbb{R}^N$ and $f : \mathcal{U} \times \mathbb{R}^N \to \mathcal{U}$. Let $z \in \mathbb{R}^N$ denote the continuous variables and $\alpha \in \mathcal{U}$ the discrete variables. Assume that variables z are measurable, that is $y = z$. Assume that*

(i) *There exist a lattice χ such that $\mathcal{U} \subseteq \chi$;*
(ii) *The map $h : \mathcal{U} \times \mathbb{R}^N \to \mathbb{R}^N$ can be extended to the whole χ as $\tilde{h} : \chi \times \mathbb{R}^N \to \mathbb{R}^N$, such that $\tilde{h}|_{\mathcal{U} \times \mathbb{R}^N} = h$ and*

$$A_y(k) := \{x \in \chi : y(k+1) = \tilde{h}(y(k), x)\} = [\bigwedge A_y(k), \bigvee A_y(k)],$$

  which means that $A_y \subseteq \chi$ is a lattice and is equal to $\{x : x \ge \bigwedge A_y \wedge x \le \bigvee A_y\}$;
(iii) *The map $f : \mathcal{U} \times \mathbb{R}^N \to \mathcal{U}$ can be extended to the whole χ as $\tilde{f} : \chi \times \mathbb{R}^N \to \chi$, such that $\tilde{f}|_{\mathcal{U} \times \mathbb{R}^N} = f$ and $\tilde{f} : A_y \to [\tilde{f}(\bigwedge A_y), \tilde{f}(\bigvee A_y)]$ is an order isomorphism;*
(iv) *System Σ is observable.*

Then the following system

$$L(k) = \tilde{f}(L(k-1)) \vee \left(\bigwedge A_y(k) \right), \tag{1}$$

$$U(k) = \tilde{f}(U(k-1)) \wedge \left(\bigvee A_y(k) \right), \tag{2}$$

with $L(0) = \bigwedge A_y(0)$ and $U(0) = \bigvee A_y(0)$, is such that

(a) *$\alpha(k) \in [L(k), U(k)] \cap \mathcal{U}$ for all k (correctness);*
(b) *$|[L(k+1), U(k+1)]| \le |[L(k), U(k)]|$ (non-increasing error);*
(c) *$|[L(k), U(k)] \cap \mathcal{U} - \alpha| \to 0$ as $k \to \infty$ (convergence),*

where $|S|$ denotes the cardinality of the set S. Moreover, if the extended system $\tilde{\Sigma} = (\tilde{f}, \tilde{h})$ defined on $\chi \times \mathbb{R}^N$ with output z is also observable, then properties (a)–(c) become:

(a') *$\alpha(k) \in [L(k), U(k)]$;*

(b') $\|[L(k + 1), U(k + 1)]\| \le \|[L(k), U(k)]\|$;
(c') $L(k) \to \alpha(k)$ and $U(k) \to \alpha(k)$ as $k \to \infty$

Proof. The proof proceeds in two steps. In the first step we show that Assumptions (i)–(iii) imply that

$$\text{for all } w \in [L(k + 1), U(k + 1)], \text{ there exists } x \in [L(k), U(k)] : w = \tilde{f}(x) \quad (3)$$

$$\text{for all } x \in [L(k), U(k)], \ x \in A_y(k). \quad (4)$$

In the second step we show that properties (3) and (4) together with Assumption (iv) imply property (c), (a) and (b).

Step 1. Property (4) can be proved directly using the definition of $L(k)$ and $U(k)$ given in expressions (1) and (2). In fact if $x \in [L(k), U(k)]$ then $x \le U(k)$ and by (2) we have $x \le \bigvee A_y(k)$. Also $x \ge L(k)$, which by (1) implies $x \ge \bigwedge A_y(k)$.

To prove (3) we first show that $\tilde{f}$ is an order isomorphism on each sub-lattice of $A_y(k)$, then we notice that $[L(k), U(k)]$ is a sublattice of $A_y(k)$, and therefore property (3) is a direct consequence of the definition of order isomorphic maps. Let $\bar{A}_y(k) = [\bar{l}_y, \bar{u}_y]$ for some $\bar{l}_y \in A_y(k)$ and $\bar{u}_y \in A_y(k)$. Clearly $\bar{A}_y(k) \subseteq A_y(k)$, and $\bar{A}_y(k)$ is a lattice. Therefore $\tilde{f} : \bar{A}_y(k) \to \tilde{f}(\bar{A}_y(k))$ is a lattice isomorphism since $\tilde{f}$ is an isomorphism on $A_y(k)$. We now show that $\tilde{f}(\bar{A}_y(k)) = [f(\bar{l}_y), f(\bar{u}_y)]$. To prove this equality we need to show that each element of the first set is contained in the second set, and *viceversa*. For any $z \in \tilde{f}(\bar{A}_y(k))$ we have $z \in [\bigwedge \tilde{f}(\bar{A}_y(k)), \bigvee \tilde{f}(\bar{A}_y(k))]$. Since $\tilde{f} : \bar{A}_y(k) \to \tilde{f}(\bar{A}_y(k))$ is a lattice isomorphism, by Lemma 1 $\tilde{f}(\bigwedge \bar{A}_y(k)) = \bigwedge \tilde{f}(\bar{A}_y(k))$ and $\tilde{f}(\bigvee \bar{A}_y(k)) = \bigvee \tilde{f}(\bar{A}_y(k))$. Then, since $\bar{l}_y = \bigwedge \tilde{f}(\bar{A}_y(k))$ and $\bar{u}_y = \bigvee \tilde{f}(\bar{A}_y(k))$, we have $z \in [\tilde{f}(\bar{l}_y), \tilde{f}(\bar{u}_y)]$. We now show that for any $z \in [\bigwedge \tilde{f}(\bar{A}_y(k)), \bigvee \tilde{f}(\bar{A}_y(k))]$ we also have $z \in \tilde{f}(\bar{A}_y(k))$. Since $\bigvee \bar{A}_y(k) \in A_y(k)$, and $\bigwedge \bar{A}_y(k) \in A_y(k)$, we have that $\tilde{f}(\bigvee \bar{A}_y(k)) \in \tilde{f}(A_y(k))$, and $\tilde{f}(\bigwedge \bar{A}_y(k)) \in \tilde{f}(A_y(k))$. This in turn implies that $\tilde{f}(\bigwedge A_y(k)) \le \tilde{f}(\bigwedge \bar{A}_y(k)) \le z \le \tilde{f}(\bigvee \bar{A}_y(k)) \le \tilde{f}(\bigvee A_y(k))$, so that $z \in f(A_y(k))$. Since $z \in f(A_y(k))$, there exist $x \in A_y(k)$ such that $z = \tilde{f}(x)$. Since $\tilde{f} : A_y \to f(A_y(k))$ is order embedding we have that $\tilde{f}(\bigwedge \bar{A}_y(k)) \le z = \tilde{f}(x) \le \tilde{f}(\bigvee \bar{A}_y(k))$ implies $\bigwedge \bar{A}_y(k) \le x \le \bigvee \bar{A}_y(k)$, which in turn implies that $x \in \bar{A}_y(k)$, and therefore $z \in \tilde{f}(\bar{A}_y(k))$.

Step 2. Let us prove (a) first (correctness). We show this by induction on the step k. Initially $\alpha \in [L(0), U(0)] = [l_y, u_y]$. For the induction step assume that $\alpha(k) \in [L(k), U(k)]$, let us show that $\alpha(k + 1) \in [L(k + 1), U(k + 1)]$. This can be shown by using the fact that $\tilde{f}$ is order preserving. In fact $L(k) \le \alpha(k) \le U(k)$ implies $\tilde{f}(L(k)) \le \tilde{f}(\alpha(k)) \le \tilde{f}(U(k))$. Also $\alpha(k + 1) = \tilde{f}(\alpha(k)) \in [l_y(k + 1), u_y(k + 1)]$ therefore $\alpha(k+1) \le (\tilde{f}(U(k)) \wedge u_y(k+1)) = U(k+1)$, and $\alpha(k+1) \ge (\tilde{f}(L(k)) \vee l_y(k+1)) = L(k+1)$.

To prove (b) we can directly use property (3). In fact by (3) we have that for each $w \in [L(k + 1), U(k + 1)]$ there is a $x \in [L(k), U(k)]$ such that $w = \tilde{f}(x)$. This in turn implies that $\|[L(k + 1), U(k + 1)]\| \le \|[L(k), U(k)]\|$.

To prove (c) notice that by properties (3), (4), and the fact that $\mathcal{U}$ is invariant with respect to $\tilde{f}$, we have that for each $x' \in [L(k+1), U(k+1)] \cap \mathcal{U}$ there is $x \in [L(k), U(k)] \cap \mathcal{U}$, such that $x' = f(x)$, and $x \in A_y(k)$. This in turn implies that the sequence $\{x(k), y(k)\}_{k \in \mathbb{N}}$

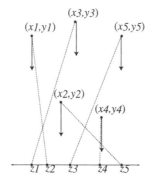

Fig. 2. Example of the RoboFloag Drill for 5 robots. Here $\alpha = \{3, 1, 5, 4, 2\}$ and the dashed lines indicate these assignments. The attackers are moving down along y direction as indicated by the arrows.

corresponds to an execution σ of system Σ, that is $x(k) = \sigma(k)(x)$. Therefore for any $x, w \in [L(k), U(k)] \cap \mathcal{U}$, there are sequences $\{x(k), y(k)\}_{k \in \mathbb{N}}$ and $\{w(k), y(k)\}_{k \in \mathbb{N}}$ corresponding to executions σ_1 and σ_2 of Σ, where $x(k) = \sigma_1(k)(x)$, $w(k) = \sigma_1(k)(w)$, and $\sigma_1(k)(y) = \sigma_2(k)(y) = y(k)$ for all k. Since the system is observable, the two executions must coincide, that is $x(k) = w(k)$. Therefore there exist a k_0 such that for all $k \geq k_0$ we have that $|[L(k), U(k)] \cap \mathcal{U}| = 1$. This together with (a) proves (c). $\quad\blacksquare$

We then refer to the system in equations (1) and (2) as an observer for Σ.

4   An Example: The RoboFlag Drill

In this section we consider a simplified version of the RoboFlag Drill system described in [8] that is similar to "capture the flag", only for robots. We do not propose to devise a strategy that addresses the full complexity of the game. Instead we examine the following very simple *drill* or exercise. Some number of blue robots with positions $(z_i, 0) \in \mathbb{R}^2$ must defend their zone $\{(x, y) \in \mathbb{R}^2 \mid y \leq 0\}$ from an equal number of incoming red robots. The positions of the red robots are $(x_i, y_i) \in \mathbb{R}^2$. An example for 5 robots is illustrated in Figure 2. The red robots move straight toward the blue defensive zone. The blue robots are assigned each to a red robot and they coordinate to intercept the red robots. Let N represent the number of robots in each team. The robots start with a random (bijective) assignment $\alpha : \{1, ..., N\}$ into $\{1, ..., N\}$. At each step, each blue robot communicates with its neighbors and decides to either switch assignments with its left or right neighbor or keep its assignment. It is possible to show that the α assignment reaches the equilibrium value $[1, ..., N]$ (see [8] for details). We consider the problem of estimating the current assignment α given the motions of the blue robots – which might be of interest to, for example, the red robots in that they may use such information to determine a better strategy of attack. We do not consider the problem of how they would change their strategy in this paper.

The system can be described with a guarded command program. Such programs are constituted by a set of clauses. Each clause is of the form *guard* : *rule*, where *guard* is the guard, and *rule* is the rule. When a guard becomes true the corresponding rule is executed (for more details see [7]). The description here is similar to the one in [8]). The red robot dynamics Σ_{Red} are described by the N clauses

$$y_i \quad \delta > 0 : y_i' = y_i \quad \delta$$

for $i \in \{1, ..., N\}$. These state simply that the red robots move a distance δ toward the defensive zone at each step. The blue robot dynamics Σ_{Blue} are described by the $3N$ clauses

$$z_i < x_{\alpha_i} : z_i' = z_i + \delta , \quad z_i > x_{\alpha_i} : z_i' = z_i \quad \delta, \quad z_i = x_{\alpha_i} : z_i' = z_i \qquad (5)$$

for $i \in \{1, ..., N\}$. For the blue robots we assume that initially $z_i \in [z_{min}, z_{max}]$ and $z_i < z_{i+1}$ and that $x_i \leq z_i \leq x_{i+1}$ for all time. We define $x = (x_1, ..., x_N)$, $z = (z_1, ..., z_N)$, $\alpha = (\alpha_1, ..., \alpha_N)$. The assignment protocol dynamics Σ_{Assign} is defined by

$$x_{\alpha_i} \geq z_{i+1} \wedge x_{\alpha_{i+1}} \leq z_{i+1} : (\alpha_i', \alpha_{i+1}') = (\alpha_{i+1}, \alpha_i) , \qquad (6)$$

which is a modification of the protocol presented in [8], since two adjacent robots switch assignments only if they are moving one against the other. The complete RoboFalg specification is then given by $\Sigma_{RF} := \Sigma_{Red} \cup \Sigma_{Blue} \cup \Sigma_{Assign}$. In particular the clauses in (5), representing Σ_{Blue}, model the function h that updates the continuous variables, and the clauses in (6), representing Σ_{Assign}, model the function f that updates the discrete variables.

RoboFlag Drill Observation Problem: Given initial values for x and y and the values of z corresponding to an execution of $\Sigma_{Blue} \cup \Sigma_{Assign}$, determine the value of α during that execution.

5   Observer Construction for the RoboFlag Drill System

In this section we first show that the RoboFalg Drill is observable, and then we show how Theorem 1 can be applied to construct the observer in equations (1- 2).

5.1   Observability

Lemma 2. *The system Σ represented by the guarded command program (5) and (6) with measurable variables z is observable.*

Proof. Since we are interested in the observability of the α trajectories, for proving observability we show that any two executions of $\Sigma_{Blue} \cup \Sigma_{Assign}$, σ_1 and σ_2, with $\{\alpha_1(k)\}_{k \in \mathbb{N}} \neq \{\alpha_2(k)\}_{k \in \mathbb{N}}$ have different output sequences. For output we consider the vector of directions of motion of the z_i. Since the measurable variables are the z_i's, also their direction of motion is measurable; let $g(\sigma(k)) = (g_1(\sigma(k)), ..., g_N(\sigma(k)))$ denote the vector of directions at step k for the execution σ. From equations (5) it is clear that the direction of motion depends only on α and not on z, therefore $g(\sigma) = g(\alpha)$. Note that every α trajectory reaches the equilibrium value $[1, ..., N]$, and therefore there is a step k

at which $f(\alpha_1(k)) = f(\alpha_2(k))$ and $\alpha_1(k) \neq \alpha_2(k)$. Therefore it is enough to prove that for any $\alpha_1 \neq \alpha_2$ we have $g(\alpha_1) = g(\alpha_2) \implies f(\alpha_1) \neq f(\alpha_2)$. $g(\alpha_1) = g(\alpha_2)$ by (5) implies that (1) $z_{i,1} < x_{\alpha_{i,1}} \iff z_{i,2} < x_{\alpha_{i,2}}$ and (2) $z_{i,1} \geq x_{\alpha_{i,1}} \iff z_{i,2} \geq x_{\alpha_{i,2}}$. This implies that $x_{\alpha_{i,1}} \geq z_{i+1,1} \wedge x_{\alpha_{i+1,1}} \leq z_{i+1,1} \iff x_{\alpha_{i,2}} \geq z_{i+1,2} \wedge x_{\alpha_{i+1,2}} \leq z_{i+1,2}$. By letting $\alpha' = f(\alpha)$, we thus have that $(\alpha'_{i,1}, \alpha'_{i+1,1}) = (\alpha_{i+1,1}, \alpha_{i,1}) \iff (\alpha'_{i,2}, \alpha'_{i+1,2}) = (\alpha_{i+1,2}, \alpha_{i,2})$. Hence if there exists an i such that $\alpha_{i,1} \neq \alpha_{i,2}$, then there exists a j such that $\alpha'_{j,1} \neq \alpha'_{j,2}$, and therefore $f(\alpha_1) \neq f(\alpha_2)$.

5.2 Lattice Structure

We now construct a lattice χ and extensions of f and h such that assumptions (i)–(iii) of Theorem 1 are verified.

We choose as χ the set of vectors in $\mathbb{N}^N$ with coordinates $x_i \in [1, .., N]$, that is

$$\chi = \{x \in \mathbb{N}^N : x_i \in [1, ..., N]\} .$$

The partial order that we choose on such a set is given by

$$\forall x, w \in \chi, \ x \leq w \text{ if } x_i \leq w_i \ \forall i . \tag{7}$$

We define join and meet in the following way:

$$\forall x, w \in \chi, \ v = x \vee w \text{ if } v_i = \max\{x_i, w_i\}$$
$$\forall x, w \in \chi, \ v = x \wedge w \text{ if } v_i = \min\{x_i, w_i\} .$$

In this way we have for example $\bigvee \chi = [N, ..., N]$ and $\bigwedge \chi = [1, ..., 1]$, and the set χ with the order defined in (7) is clearly a lattice. The set $\mathcal{U}$ is the set of all permutations of N elements and it is a subset of χ. All the elements in $\mathcal{U}$ form an anti-chain of the lattice, that is any two elements in $\mathcal{U}$ in χ are not related by the order defined in (7). In the sequel we will denote by w the variables with type χ not specifying if the type is $\mathcal{U}$, and we will always denote by α the variables with type $\mathcal{U}$.

The function h can be naturally extended in the following way

$$z_i < x_{w_i} : z'_i = z_i + \delta , \quad z_i > x_{w_i} : z'_i = z_i \quad \delta, \quad z_i = x_{w_i} : z'_i = z_i \tag{8}$$

for $w \in \chi$. Then the clauses (8) model the function $\tilde{h}$. In analogous way f is extended as

$$x_{w_i} \geq z_{i+1} \wedge x_{w_{i+1}} \leq z_{i+1} : (w'_i, w'_{i+1}) = (w_{i+1}, w_i) , \tag{9}$$

for $w \in \chi$. Then the clauses (9) model the function $\tilde{f}$. As a consequence we have two new functions $\tilde{h} : \mathbb{R}^N \times \chi \to \mathbb{R}^N$ and $\tilde{f} : \mathbb{R}^N \times \chi \to \chi$, such that $\tilde{f}|_{\mathbb{R}^N \times \mathcal{U}} = f$ and $\tilde{h}|_{\mathbb{R}^N \times \mathcal{U}} = h$.

5.3 Properties of the Extended Functions

We analyze in this section the properties of the extensions $\tilde{f}$ and $\tilde{h}$ proposed in the previous section. In particular we show that properties (ii) and (iii) of Theorem 1 hold.

Lemma 3. *Property (ii) of Theorem 1 holds with the lattice structure chosen in Section 5.2.*

Proof. We need to show that

$$A_y(k) = \{w \in \chi : y(k+1) = \tilde{h}(y(k), w)\} = [\bigwedge A_y(k), \bigvee A_y(k)],$$

where $y = z$. By (8) we have that $\{w \in \chi : z(k+1) = \tilde{h}(z(k), w)\} = \{w | x_{w_i} > z_i,\}$ if $z_i(k+1) = z_i(k) + \delta$, $\{w \in \chi : z(k+1) = \tilde{h}(z(k), w)\} = \{w | x_{w_i} < z_i,\}$ if $z_i(k+1) = z_i(k)$ δ, and $\{w \in \chi : z(k+1) = \tilde{h}(z(k), w)\} = \{w | x_{w_i} = z_i,\}$ if $z_i(k+1) = z_i(k)$. By assuming $x_i \le z_i \le x_{i+1}$ for all time, we have $x_{w_i} > z_i$ if and only if $w_i > i$ and $x_{w_i} < z_i$ if and only if $w_i < i$. Therefore

$$A_y(k) = \{w \in \chi : [(w_i > i) \wedge (z_i(k+1) = z_i(k) + \delta)]$$
$$\vee [(w_i < i) \wedge (z_i(k+1) = z_i(k) \delta)]$$
$$\vee [(w_i = i) \wedge (z_i(k+1) = z_i(k))]\}$$

Since also $w \in \chi$ we have that $1 \le w_i \le N$, and therefore there exist $l_y(k) \in \chi$ and $u_y(k) \in \chi$ such that $A_y(k) = \{w \in \chi : w \ge l_y(k) \wedge w \le u_y(k)\}$, so that (ii) of Theorem 1 holds.

Lemma 4. *Property (iii) of Theorem 1 holds with the lattice structure chosen in Section 5.2.*

Proof. We need to show that $\tilde{f} : A_y(k) \to [\tilde{f}(l_y(k)), \tilde{f}(u_y(k))]$ is an order isomorphism we need to show: a) that it is onto; b) that it is order embedding.

a) To show that it is onto, we show directly that $f(A_y) = [\tilde{f}(l_y), \tilde{f}(u_y)]$. We omit the dependence on k to simplify notation. Our arguments relay on the coordinates structure of the sets A_y and $\tilde{f}(A_y)$. In particular from equations (9) we deduce that $A_y = (A_{y,1}, ..., A_{y,N})$, i.e. the set A_y is a vector of sets whose elements are in $\mathbb{N}$, and in particular $A_{y,i} \in \{[1, i], [i+1, N], [i, i]\}$. Denote by $\tilde{f}(A_y)_i$ the ith coordinate set of $\tilde{f}(A_y)$. By equations (9) we derive that $\tilde{f}(A_y)_i \in \{A_{y,i}, A_{y,i}\ _1, A_{y,i}\ _1\}$. We consider the case where $\tilde{f}(A_y)_i = A_{y,i}\ _1$, the other cases can be treated in analogous way. If $\tilde{f}(A_y)_i = A_{y,i}\ _1$ then $\tilde{f}(A_y)_i\ _1 = A_{y,i}$. Then we have that

$$(i)\ \tilde{f}(A_y)_i = A_{y,i}\ _1 \text{ and } \tilde{f}(A_y)_i\ _1 = A_{y,i} \implies$$

$$(ii)\ \forall x \in A_{y,i} \text{ we have } x \le i, \text{ and } \forall z \in A_{y,i}\ _1 \text{ we have } z \ge i,$$

which implies $(iii)\ u_{y,i} \le i$, $l_{y,i} \le i$ and $u_{y,i}\ _1 \ge i$, $l_{y,i}\ _1 \ge i$. This last expression finally implies that

$$(iv)\ \tilde{f}(l_y)_i = l_{y,i}\ _1, \ \tilde{f}(u_y)_i = u_{y,i}\ _1, \text{ and } \tilde{f}(l_y)_i\ _1 = l_{y,i}, \ \tilde{f}(u_y)_i\ _1 = u_{y,i}.$$

Since for any i we have that $A_{y,i} = [\bigwedge A_{y,i}, \bigvee A_{y,i}] = [l_{y,i}, u_{y,i}]$, (i) and (iv) imply that $\tilde{f}(A_y)_i = [\tilde{f}(l_y)_i, \tilde{f}(u_y)_i]$. The same reasoning holds for any $\tilde{f}(A_y)_i \in \{A_{y,i}, A_{y,i}\ _1, A_{y,i}\ _1\}$, and for any i, therefore $f(A_y) = [\tilde{f}(l_y), \tilde{f}(u_y)]$.

b) To show that it is order embedding it is enough to note again that $\tilde{f}(A_y)$ is obtained by switching $A_{y,i}$ with $A_{y,i+1}, A_{y,i}\ _1$, or leaving it to $A_{y,i}$. Therefore if $w \le v$ for $w, v \in A_y$ then $f(w) \le f(v)$ since coordinate-wise we will compare the same numbers. By the same reasoning the reverse is also true, that is if $f(w) \le f(v)$ then $w \le v$.

The construction of system in equations (1-2) is straightforward, since we need to "copy" the dynamics reported in (9) and compute a join and a meet. Then write lower and upper bounds L and U coordinate-wise as $U = (U_1, ..., U_N)$ and $L = (L_1, ..., L_N)$ and initialize $L = \bigwedge \chi$ and $U = \bigvee \chi$, so that $L_i = 1$ and $U_i = N$. Then the guarded command program which implements the observer in (1-2) is given by

$$x_{L_i} \geq z_{i+1} \wedge x_{L_{i+1}} \leq z_{i+1} :$$
$$\{[(z_i' = z_i + \delta) \Rightarrow (l_{y,i}' = i + 1)] \vee [(z_i' = z_i \quad \delta) \Rightarrow (l_{y,i}' = 1)]\}$$
$$\wedge \{[(z_{i+1}' = z_{i+1} + \delta) \Rightarrow (l_{y,i+1}' = i + 2)] \vee [(z_{i+1}' = z_{i+1} \quad \delta) \Rightarrow (l_{y,i+1}' = 1)]\}$$
$$\wedge (L_i', L_{i+1}') = (\max\{L_{i+1}, l_{y,i}'\}, \max\{L_i, l_{y,i+1}'\}) \tag{10}$$

$$x_{U_i} \geq z_{i+1} \wedge x_{U_{i+1}} \leq z_{i+1} :$$
$$\{[(z_i' = z_i + \delta) \Rightarrow (u_{y,i}' = N)] \vee [(z_i' = z_i \quad \delta) \Rightarrow (u_{y,i}' = i)]\}$$
$$\wedge \{[(z_{i+1}' = z_{i+1} + \delta) \Rightarrow (u_{y,i+1}' = N)] \vee [(z_{i+1}' = z_{i+1} \quad \delta) \Rightarrow (u_{y,i+1}' = i + 1)]\}$$
$$\wedge (U_i', U_{i+1}') = (\min\{U_{i+1}, u_{y,i}'\}, \min\{U_i, u_{y,i+1}'\}) \tag{11}$$

Since we have shown that (i)-(iv) of Theorem 1 are verified, then the sequences $L(k)$ and $U(k)$ have the properties (a)–(c) given by Theorem 1. Note that properties (a')–(c') do not hold since we can prove that the extended system $\tilde{\Sigma} = (\tilde{f}, \tilde{h})$, with measurable variables V_C is not observable.

5.4   Complexity Considerations

The amount of computation required for updating L and U according to (10) and (11) is proportional to the amount of computation required for updating the variables α in system Σ. In fact we have $2N$ clauses, $2N$ variables, and $2N$ computations of "max" and "min" between values in $\mathbb{N}$. Therefore we can roughly say that the complexity of the algorithm that generates the sequences $L(k)$ and $U(k)$ is about twice the complexity of the algorithm that generates the α trajectories. Also note that the clauses in (10) and (11) are obtained by "copying" the clauses in (9) and correcting them by means of the output information, according to how the observer is constructed for dynamical systems (see [9] for details).

By Theorem 1 we have that the function of k $|[L(k), U(k)] \cap \mathcal{U} \quad \alpha(k)|$ tends to zero and it is non increasing. This function is useful for analysis purposes, but it is not necessary to compute it at any point in the algorithm proposed in equation (10) and (11). However, since the sequence $L(k)$ is not converging to the sequence $U(k)$, once the algorithm has converged, i.e. $|[L(k), U(k)] \cap \mathcal{U}| = 1$, we cannot recover α from the values of $U(k)$ and $L(k)$ directly. Instead of computing directly $[L(k), U(k)] \cap \mathcal{U}$, we carry out a simple algorithm, that in the case of the RoboFlag Drill example takes at most $(N^2 + N)/2$ steps and takes as inputs $L(k)$ and $U(k)$ and gives as output $\alpha(k)$ if the algorithm has converged. This is formally explained in the following paragraph.

Refinement Algorithm. Let $c_i = [L_i, U_i]$. Then the algorithm

$$(m_1, ..., m_N) = Refine(c_1, ..., c_N),$$

which takes assignment sets $c_1, ..., c_N$ and produces assignment sets $m_1, ..., m_N$, is such that If $m_i = \{k\}$ then $k \notin m_j$ for any $j \neq i$.

For such an algorithm we have the properties shown in the following lemmas.

Lemma 5. *When the set* $[L(k), U(k)] \cap \mathcal{U}$ *has converged to* $\alpha(k)$*, the refinement algorithm is such that* $(m_1(k), ..., m_N(k)) = \alpha(k)$*.*

Proof. When $[L(k), U(k)] \cap \mathcal{U}$ has converged to α, we have that $[L(k), U(k)] \cap \mathcal{U}$ is of the form $\{\alpha(k)$, elements not in $\mathcal{U}\}$. Denote with c_i the sets $[L_i, U_i]$ before the refinement has occurred, and denote with m_i the refined version of c_i's. Then we show that among the sets $[L_i(k), U_i(k)]$ there is at least one i for which $L_i(k) = U_i(k)$, and therefore we have at least one singleton to take out from the other coordinates. Then the proof proceeds by iteration on N.

To indicate that $\mathcal{U}$ is the set of permutations of N elements, we will write $\mathcal{U}_N$. To show that when $[L(k), U(k)] \cap \mathcal{U}_N$ has converged to $\alpha(k)$ at least for one i $L_i(k) = U_i(k)$ (c_i is a singleton), it is sufficient to notice that if this were not the case we would have more than one possible $\alpha \in \mathcal{U}_N$ in $[L(k), U(k)]$. Without loss in generality assume that such i is equal to N. Then take out that singleton from all the other sets c_j for $j < N$ to obtain new sets m_j whose elements take values in a set of possible N 1 natural numbers. Still there is only one $\beta \in \mathcal{U}_{N\ 1}$ such that $\beta \in (m_1, ..., m_{N\ 1})$. Then we can apply again the reasoning that for this to be true there must exist at least one singleton among the sets m_j, for $j \in [1, N$ 1]. Proceeding iteratively, we get the result.

We can also show that the sum of the cardinalities of the m_i sets is not increasing along the time step k. This is formally shown in the following lemma:

Lemma 6. *Let* $c_i(k) = [L_i(k), U_i(k)]$*, and denote by* $m_i(k)$ *the sets obtained with the refinement algorithm. Then*

$$\sum_{i=1}^{N} |m_i(k+1)| \leq \sum_{i=1}^{N} |m_i(k)|$$

Proof. Let us denote with primed variables the variables at step $k+1$ and with unprimed variables the variables at step k. The proof proceeds by showing that for each j there exist a k such that $m'_j \subseteq m_k$. By equations (10) and (11) we deduce that we can have one of the following cases for each i: (a) $c'_i \subseteq c_{i+1} \wedge c'_{i+1} \subseteq c_i$, (b) $c'_i \subseteq c_i$, (c) $c'_i \subseteq c_{i\ 1} \wedge c'_{i\ 1} \subseteq c_i$. Let us consider case (a), the other cases can be treated in analogous way. Let c_j be a singleton. In the refinement process it is deleted from any other set, so that we have $c_{i+1} = m_{i+1}$ c_j and $c_i = m_i$ c_j for all i. Assume that in the first refinement iteration no new singletons are created. We have one of the following situations: $c'_j \subseteq c_{j+1} \wedge c_{j+1} \subseteq c_j, c'_j \subseteq c_j, c'_j \subseteq c_{j\ 1} \wedge c'_{j\ 1} \subseteq c_j$. This implies that one of the c'_i is equal to the singleton c_j. The sets m'_i are created removing such singleton for all the other sets, so that we obtain $m'_i + c_j = c'_i \subseteq c_{i+1} = m_{i+1} + c_j$ and $m'_{i+1} + c_j = c'_{i+1} \subseteq c_i = m_i + c_j$. This in turn implies that $m'_i \subseteq m_{i+1}$ and $m'_{i+1} \subseteq m_i$. This holds for all of the cases (a),(b), (c), and for each i. Thus $\sum_{i=1}^{N} |m'_i| \leq \sum_{i=1}^{N} |m_i|$.

The same kind of reasoning can be applied if the first refinement iteration of the c_i creates new singletons.

It is easy to show that the refinement algorithm can be executed in at most $(N^2 + N)/2$ steps.

6 Simulation Results

The RoboFlag Drill system represented in equations (5) and (6) has been implemented in MATLAB together with the observer reported in equations (10) and (11). Figure 3 (left) shows the behavior of the quantity

$$V(k) = |[L(k), U(k)] \cap \mathcal{U}|$$

and

$$E(k) = \frac{1}{N} \sum_{i=1}^{N} |\alpha_i(k) - i|.$$

$V(k)$ represents the the cardinality of the set of all possible assignments at each step. This quantity gives an idea of the convergence rate of the observer. $E(k)$ is a function of α, and it is not increasing along the executions of the system $\Sigma_{Assign} \cup \Sigma_{Blue}$. This quantity is showing the rate of convergence of the α assignment to its equilibrium $[1, ..., N]$. In

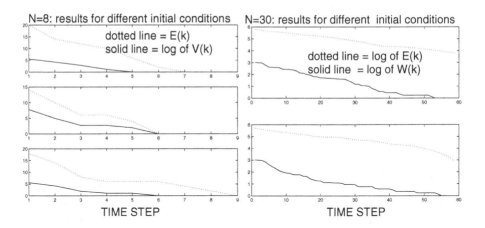

Fig. 3. (Left) Example with N=8: note that the function $\log(V(k))$ is always non-increasing and it is converging to zero. (Right) Example with N=30: note that the function $W(k)$ is always non-increasing and its logarithm is converging to zero.

Figure 3 (right) we show the results for $N = 30$ robots per team. In particular we report the log of $E(k)$ and the log of $W(k)$ defined as

$$W(k) = \frac{1}{N} \sum_{i=1}^{N} |m_i(k)|,$$

which by virtue of Lemmas 5 and 6 is non increasing and converging to one, that is the sets $(m_1(k), ..., m_N(k))$ converge to $\alpha(k) = (\alpha_1(k), ..., \alpha_N(k))$. In the same figure we notice that when $W(k)$ converges to one, $E(k)$ has not converged to zero yet. This suggests that the observer is much faster than the dynamics of the system under study. We cannot explain such a good performance formally yet, and the observer speed issue will be addressed in future work.

7   Conclusions

We have proposed a way for estimating discrete variables in a class of hybrid systems where the continuous variables are measured. The observer is constructed on a lattice structure and it updates the least element and the greatest element of the set of all discrete variables values compatible with the observed output sequence. These ideas are applied to a multi-robot example: The RoboFlag Drill. This approach is promising for reducing the computational effort of the observer since it updates a "cheap" representation of a set rather than the set itself.

More work is needed to establish how general the conditions listed in Theorem 1 are, and what is the compromise between generality and complexity. Also more investigation is needed to understand when the extended system is still observable. Computing the intersection $[L(k), U(k)] \cap \mathcal{U}$ is needed once the observer has converged for recovering the α value. The complexity of this computation is smaller than $(N^2 + N)/2$ for the RoboFlag Drill system with N robots, but the general case needs more investigation. A question to be still addressed is concerned with the speed of convergence; the simulation results are encouraging to this regard and a formal analysis needs to be developed.

Acknowledgments.
This work was supported in part by the ONR grant N00014-10-1-0890 under the MURI program, and the NSF Center for Neuromorphic Systems Engineering. We would like to thank Professor Eric Klavins for his contribution to our knowledge on computer science related subjects and for his insightful comments.

References

1. A. Balluchi, L. Benvenuti, M. D. Di Benedetto, and A. Sangiovanni-Vincentelli. Design of observers for hybrid systems. *Lecture Notes in Computer Science 2289,C. J. Tomlin and M. R. Greensreet Eds. Springer*, pages 76–89, 2002.
2. A. Bemporad, G. Ferrari-Trecate, and M. Morari. Observability and controllability of piecewise affine and hybrid systems. *IEEE Transactions on Automatic Control*, 45:1864–1876, 1999.
3. P. E. Caines. Classical and logic-based dynamic observers for finite automata. *IMA J. of Mathematical Control and Information*, pages 45–80, 1991.
4. A. R. Cassandra, L. P. Kaelbling, and M. L Littman. Acting optimally in partially observable stochastic domains. In *Proc. 12th Conference on Artificial Intelligence*, pages 1023–1028, Seattle, WA, 1994.

5. B. A. Davey and H. A. Priesteley. *Introduction to Lattices and Order.* Cambridge University Press, 2002.
6. C. M. Özveren and A. S. Willsky. Observability of discrete event dynamic systems. *IEEE Transactions on Automatic Control*, 35(7):797–806, 19.
7. E. W. Dijkstra. Guarded commands, non-determinacy and a calculus for the derivation of programs. In *Proceedings of the international conference on Reliable software*, pages 2 – 2.13, Los Angeles, California, 1975. http://portal.acm.org.
8. E. Klavins. A formal model of a multi-robot control and communication task. In *Conference on Decision and Control*, Hawaii, 2003.
9. David G. Luenberger. An introduction to observers. *IEEE Transactions on Automatic Control*, AC-16:6:596–602, 1971.
10. Z. Manna and A. Pnueli. *The Temporal Logic of Reactive and Concur- rent Systems: Speci- cation.* Springer-Verlag, 1992.
11. P. J. Ramadge. Observability of discrete event systems. In *Proc. 25th Conference on Decision and Control*, pages 1108–1112, Athens, Greece, 1986.
12. D. Del Vecchio and E. Klavins. Observation of guarded command programs. In *Conference on Decision and Control*, Hawaii, 2003.

Benchmarks for Hybrid Systems Verification*

Ansgar Fehnker[1] and Franjo Ivančić[2]

[1] Carnegie Mellon University,5000 Forbes Ave, Pittsburgh, PA 15213 (USA)
ansgar@cmu.edu
[2] NEC Laboratories America Inc.,4 Independence Way, Princeton, NJ 08540 (USA)
ivancic@nec-labs.com

Abstract. There are numerous application examples for hybrid systems verification in recent literature. Most of them were introduced to illustrate a new approach to hybrid systems verification, and are therefore of a limited size. Others are case studies that serve to prove that an approach can be applied to real world problems. Verification of these typically requires a lot of domain experience to obtain a tractable, verifiable model. Verification of a case study yields a singular result that is hard to compare and time-consuming to reproduce.
This paper introduces three benchmarks for hybrid systems verification. These benchmarks are independent from a particular approach to verification, they have a limited domain, and have a simple basic structure. Nevertheless, these benchmarks can be scaled to arbitrary complexity, and offer the possibility to inject phenomena that are known to be problematic in hybrid verification. This paper presents result for a first set of instances, as an example of how these benchmark can be used to compare different tools and approaches.

1 Introduction

Recently, it has been questioned whether Hybrid System verification is scalable and applicable to real world applications. There have been a number of case studies, but these are either fairly small and serve mainly to illustrate a concept, or they are very specific and hard to compare and reproduce. This paper introduces some problems that we propose as benchmarks for evaluating and comparing tools for hybrid system design and verification.

The primary purpose of benchmarks is to compare different methods, and to provide a means to record future advances. In the area of hybrid verification this means that different verification methods are applied to the same benchmark

---

* This research was supported by the Defense Advanced Research Project Agency (DARPA) MoBIES project under contracts no. F3361500C1701 and F33615-02-C-0429, by the Army Research Office (ARO) under contract no. DAAD19-01-1-0485, by the National Science Foundation (NSF) under grants no. CCR-0121547 and CCR-0098072, by the Office of Naval Research (ONR) under contract no. N00014-95-1-0520. The views and conclusions in this document are those of the authors and should not be interpreted as representing the official policies, either expressed or implied, of DARPA, ARO, ONR, NSF, the U.S. Government or any other entity.

R. Alur and G.J. Pappas (Eds.): HSCC 2004, LNCS 2993, pp. 326–341, 2004.
© Springer-Verlag Berlin Heidelberg 2004

problems. For each method this can then reveal the limits of a certain method. A useful benchmark should be scalable in different dimensions. In hybrid verification important dimensions include the number of discrete control locations, the number of continuous variables, and type of the dynamic behavior – timed, rectangular, linear, or non-linear.

Benchmarks help to determine the limits of a certain method, and these can then be compared to the limits of other methods. But equally important, knowing these limits helps to determine whether a certain method is suitable for a certain problem at all. Or vice versa, when a certain method has to be used, knowing its limitations determines how a model needs to be modified.

Especially in verification of hybrid systems it is quite common that a system can only be verified after tweaking the model and the verification parameters. Obtaining a verifiable model is often the most work in this area, and results depend often on particular smart choices, so that it becomes difficult to determine whether the particular method solved the problem or the experienced user. Having multiple instances of similar benchmarks may reduce these effects for the following reason. Tweaking model and method is inherently tedious and difficult, and a good choice of verification parameters for one instance, may not be a proper choice for another instance. When a method performed well on a range of instances, one can assume that the method mattered, rather than the experienced user finding a proper setup.

An important part in verification is, as mentioned before, the process of obtaining a model. Some methods even rely on a particular modelling framework. Benchmarks can be used for comparison of different frameworks. The benchmarks will be defined in general terms, informal but precise. Part of the benchmark problem is then to provide a formal model, and one can thus compare for example different methods for composition and synchronization.

A number of application examples and case studies have been used in the literature to evaluate tools. The generalized railway crossing example was put forward by Heitmeyer in [HJL93] as a benchmark to evaluate approaches to specify and verify real-time systems. This benchmark was for example used to illustrate the capabilities of HyTech in [HHWT95], of STeP in [BMSU97] and of the ESTEREL toolkit in [JPO95]. Bérad and Sierra use this benchmark in [BS00] to compare quantitatively the performance of the model checkers HyTech [HHWT95], UPPAAL [LPY97] and KRONOS [Yov97]. They use a scalable model of the railway crossing example, very much like the benchmarks presented in this paper, except that this benchmark remains in the realm of timed automata.

A qualitative assessment of different algorithmic approaches in hybrid verification is given in [SSKE01]. This paper used a batch reactor system proposed in [SKPT98] to compare features, such as the interface, the logic used for specification, and the expressiveness of the modelling framework, of a number of verification tools. Since the performance of the tools was not subject of this paper, there was no need for a scalable model of the batch reactor system.

Stauner et al. presented an automotive level control system in [SMF97] as a hybrid automaton with linear dynamics. They provided an abstraction of the system and verified the system with HyTech. Alternative approaches to hybrid

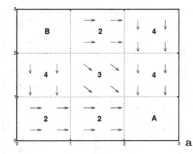 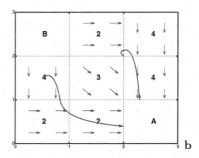

Fig. 1. a. The map determines the desired velocity of the moving object, depending on the position of the object. **b.** Two trajectories of objects moving in the plane. Both objects eventually reach cell **A**.

verification were applied by [Feh98,BM99,EB99] to the same problem. These papers use the automotive level control system to prove a concept, and consider therefore only a single instance. Comparison of the results is hindered by the fact that all papers use slight modifications, simplifications or additional assumptions to obtain the result.

There are numerous other application examples, but most of them share that they are either not scalable, fairly particular to a certain framework, or that results are hard to compare and reproduce. The next section presents three benchmark problems for hybrid systems that tackle these problems. The first considers a moving object, the second leaking valves in a network of pressurized pipelines, and the last a house with a limited number of heaters. The benchmarks are scalable, and to offer the possibility to inject phenomena that are known be problematic for verification. Section 3 discusses the different problem dimensions and characteristics of the benchmarks. Section 4 presents first results for one of the benchmarks. Finally, Section 5 concludes the paper by giving a few guidelines on how to use these benchmarks.

2   Benchmarks

2.1   Navigation Benchmark

The first benchmark deals with an object[1] that moves in the $\mathbb{R}^2$ plane. The desired velocity $\mathbf{v}_d$ is determined by the position of the object in an $n \times m$ grid, and the desired velocities may take values $(\sin(i * \pi/4), \cos(i * \pi/4))$, for $i = 0, \ldots, 7$. We assume that the length and the width of a cell is 1, and that the lower left corner of the grid is the origin. An example of a 3×3 grid is depicted in Figure 1.a, where the label i in each cell refers to the desired velocity. In addition, the grid contains cells labelled **A** that have to be reached and cells labelled **B** that ought to be avoided.

---

[1] This object can be thought of as a vehicle, though the dynamics are not exactly vehicle dynamics

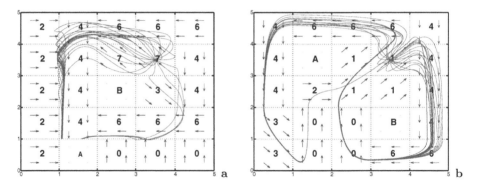

Fig. 2. A number of different trajectories for the two instances of the navigation benchmark.

Given $\mathbf{v}_d$ the behavior of the actual velocity $\mathbf{v}$ is determined by the differential equation $\dot{\mathbf{v}} = A(\mathbf{v} - \mathbf{v}_d)$, where $A \in \mathbb{R}^{2 \times 2}$ is assumed to have eigenvalues with strictly negative real part. This guarantees that the velocity will converge to the desired velocity. Figure 1.b shows two trajectories, with $A = \begin{pmatrix} -1.2 & 0.1 \\ 0.1 & -1.2 \end{pmatrix}$. Both satisfy the property that $\mathbf{A}$ should be reached, and $\mathbf{B}$ avoided.

If the trajectory leaves the grid, the desired velocity $\mathbf{v}_d$ is the velocity of the closest cell. Hence, the outer cells are assumed to be unbounded in the direction of the border of the map. For example, the desired velocity in Figure 1 is $(\sin(4 * \pi/4), \cos(4 * \pi/4))$ for all $\mathbf{x} = (x_1, x_2)^T$ with $x_1 >= 2$ and $x_2 >= 1$

An instance of this benchmark is characterized by the initial condition on $\mathbf{x}$ and $\mathbf{v}$, by matrix A in the differential equation for $\mathbf{v}$ and by the map of the grid, which can be represented as $n \times m$ matrix with elements from $\{0, \dots, 7\} \cup \{\mathbf{A}, \mathbf{B}\}$. For the example in Figure 1 this matrix is

$$
\begin{array}{ccc}
\mathbf{B} & 2 & 4 \\
4 & 3 & 4 \\
2 & 2 & \mathbf{A}
\end{array}
\tag{1}
$$

We will refer to this matrix as the map of an instance.

The map and the matrix A determines mainly the size and complexity of an instance. Proper choices are used to stress a certain aspect in hybrid verification. Figure 2.a shows a few trajectories for an instance with a 5×5 map. For this instance we chose $A = \begin{pmatrix} -0.8 & -0.2 \\ -0.1 & -0.8 \end{pmatrix}$. This instance satisfies the requirements, but a few trajectories are getting close to cell $\mathbf{B}$; this instance thus puts an emphasis on numerical accuracy of a method. Figure 2.b shows trajectories for another instance with the same initial conditions, but a different map and with $A = \begin{pmatrix} -1.2 & 0.1 \\ 0.2 & -1.2 \end{pmatrix}$. None of the trajectories in Figure 2.b reaches $\mathbf{A}$, but all of them avoid $\mathbf{B}$. This instance is an example of a hybrid systems with behaviors of infinite length.

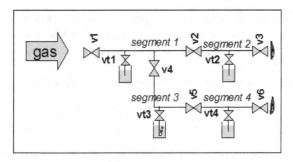

Fig. 3. A simple network with four segments

2.2 Leak Test Procedure

The next benchmark is inspired by earlier work presented in [TPP97], but it differs from it in that we define the dynamics as ordinary differential equations. The benchmark deals with the detection of leaks in a pressurized network. The network is a tree, with a source of gas (methane) at the root, and burners at the leaves of the tree. Figure 3 depicts an example of such a network. Each segment is connected via a tap valve to a trickle device. This device is nothing more than a cup of water with an incomming pipe. If the tap valve is open, bubbles indicate that the pressure in the segment is above a certain threshold.

Leaking valves in the network can lead to flammable clouds during shutdown periods. A leak test procedure checks for leaks across the network, to reduce the risk of explosions. The leak test procedure first pressurizes the network. It then closes all valves, and tests segment by segment, starting with the segments close to the burners.

For each segment the test is performed as follows: First, wait for a certain amount of time, then open the tap valve. Absence of bubbling indicates that a downstream valve is leaking and has to be replaced. Note that segments, such as segment 1 in the Figure 3, can have more than one downstream valve. When the bubbling does start, wait for it to stop. If it does not stop within a given time, a leak in the upstream valve is assumed. When bubbling does stop, the test for this segment is completed.

The leak test procedure starts with the leaf-segments of the network. The other segments are tested as soon as the tests for all downstream segments are completed. This means for the network in Figure 3, that the procedure starts with segments 4 and 2, as soon as the network is pressurized. When the test for segment 4 is completed successfully, the test for segment 3 will begin. As soon as the tests for segment 2 and 3 are completed, the test for segment 1 will begin. If a leak is detected at any time during the procedure the complete procedure aborts.

The pressure in a segment depends on the pressure in adjacent segments, it depends on what valves are open or closed, and it depends on whether the tap valve is open or closed. For each segment i we model the pressure by a state variable x_i. We refer for simplicity to pressure at the source of the gas as x_0 and to the pressure in the environment as x_{n+1}. For the source of gas and the environment we assume that the pressure is either constant, or can take any value in a given interval.

For a segment i_0 with adjacent segments $i_1, \ldots, i_k$ we have

$$\dot{x}_{i_0} = \sum_{j=1,\ldots,k} c_j f(x_{i_0}, x_{i_k}) + dg(x_{i_0}) \tag{2}$$

The constants c_j depend on whether the valve between segment i_0 and segment i_j is open, and the constant d depends on whether the tap valve of segment i_0 is open. The functions f and g are defined as follows.

$$f(x, y) = \begin{cases} -\sqrt{x - y} & \text{if } x \geq y \\ \sqrt{y - x} & \text{otherwise} \end{cases} \tag{3}$$

$$g(x) = \begin{cases} -\sqrt{x - z_{off}} & \text{if } x \geq z_{off} \\ 0 & \text{otherwise} \end{cases} \tag{4}$$

with z_{off} a constant that determines at what pressure bubbling starts.

Segment 3 in Figure 3 for example is connected to valves **v4** and **v5** and tap valve **vt3**. This leads to eight possible combinations of open and closed valves. Assumed that the rate is for an open valve 1, for a closed valve 0.01, and for the tap valve 0.1. Supposed that that the tap valve **vt3** and **v5** are open and valve **v4** is closed, we then obtain for (2):

$$x_3 = f(x_3, x_4) + 0.01 \, f(x_3, x_1) + 0.1 \, g(x_3) \tag{5}$$

Supposed that the valves **vt3** and **v5** are closed and valve **v4** is open we obtain:

$$x_3 = 0.01 \, f(x_3, x_4) + f(x_3, x_1) \tag{6}$$

The verification problem is to show that leaking valves are detected properly. We require the following for each segment:

1. If a segment is tested and if **none** of its upstream valves leaks, then the bubbling should start.
2. If a segment is tested, and if an upstream valve leaks, then the bubbling should not start. We assume that the model is deadlock free, and that time can pass.
3. If the root segment is tested, the test should detect correctly whether or not the downstream valve leaks.

Suppose for example that valve **v5** leaks. The requirement for segment 3 is satisfied, if the test detects an upstream leak, or if the test for this segment is not performed. The latter will be the case if the test of segment 4 will detect a leak, either in valve **v5** or **v6**. If a leak is detected, the procedure is terminated, and segment 3 will not be tested.

An instance of the benchmark is defined by the topology of the network, the waiting times of the procedure per segment, the constants for open and

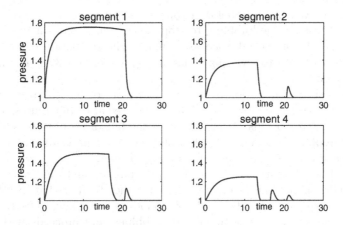

Fig. 4. The leak test procedure starts with segments 2 and 4. In this simulation it correctly finds that no leaks are present.

closed valves and the thresholds for bubbling. Each valve in the network has a unique upstream segment, and each segment has a unique upstream valve. The network with n segments and m valves is defined by an n-tuple, that defines for each segment the upstream valve, and an m-tuple, that defines for each valve the upstream segment. The root valve has as upstream node 0. The network in Figure 3 has four segments and six valves. The connections from segments to upstream valves are encoded as $\texttt{seg2val} = (1, 2, 4, 5)$ and the connection of valves to upstream segments as $\texttt{val2seg} = (0, 1, 2, 1, 3, 4)$.

Given the network, we define the initial pressure either by an n-tuple, whose elements are scalars or intervals. The pressure in the environment and at the gas source is given as either a constant or constraint to an interval. In the latter case the pressure may change arbitrarily within this interval. The simulation result in Figure 4 uses for the pressure at the source and in the environment $x_0 = 2$, and $x_5 = 1$, respectively, and as the pressure of the segments $i = 1, \ldots, 4$ at time zero $x_i(0) = 1$.

For each valve we have to define the flow rate c_i in (2). For each instance we define two m-tuples. The first defines the rate for open valves, the second defines it for closed valves. Elements of these tuples can be intervals as well. In this case the rate takes a constant value in that interval, i.e. it is an uncertain parameter of the problem. The simulation shown in Figure 4 uses for the open valves $c_{open} = (1, 1, 1, 1, 1, 1)$, for the closed valves $c_{closed} = (0.01, 0.01, 0.01, 0.01, 0.01, 0.01)$. In addition, we have to indicate which valves are leaking. In the instance we assume that none is leaking. The constant b in (2) for the tap valve, and the threshold z when bubbling starts is the same for all segments. The simulation in Figure 4 uses $d = 0.1$ and $z_{off} = 1.1$. There is no flow and thus no bubbling when the tap valve is closed.

Finally, one has to define the durations that determine the leak test procedure. This is the initialization time, which in the example is $t_{init} = 10$, and for each segment waiting time before it opens its tap valve, and finally the time it waits at most for the bubbling to stop. These times may vary from segment to segment, and they are defined as n-tuples. The simulation in Figure 4 uses $t_{wait} = (3, 3, 3, 3)$ for the waiting times and $t_{test} = (3, 3, 3, 3)$ as maximal duration of the bubbling.

Figure 4 shows simulation result for an instance of the leak test problem. In the initial phase all valves are open. They are closed after 10 minutes, and testing of segment 2 and 4 begins. After 3 minutes the tap valves of these segments are opened. Bubbling starts in both segments since pressure is above 1.1 bar. Thus none of the downstream valves is found to be leaking.

After about 2 minutes segment 4 stops bubbling, and the procedure starts with segment 3. Bubbling stops in segment 2 shortly after that. Neither of the upstream valves of segment 2 and 4 is found to be leaking. The test for segment 3 opens the tap valve, it detects bubbling, and proceeds with the test. When bubbling in segment 2 and 3 stops, segment 1 is tested. This test also completes successfully. Note that the pressure rises in segment 2, 3 and 4, when the downstream valve of segment 1 is opened.

2.3   Room Heating Benchmark

This last benchmark deals with a house with a number of rooms that are heated by a limited number of heaters. The temperature in each room depends on the temperature of the adjacent rooms, on the outside temperature, and on whether a heater is in the room. The number of heaters is assumed to be smaller than the number of rooms, and each room may have at most one heater. The heater is controlled by a typical thermostat, i.e. it is switched on if the temperature is below a certain threshold, and off if it is beyond another (higher) threshold.

When the temperature in a room falls below a certain level, it may get a heater from one of the adjacent rooms, provided that the temperature in this room is significantly higher. In this way the heaters are shared by the different rooms to maintain some minimum temperature in all rooms.

Let x_i be the temperature in room i, u the outside temperature, and h_i a boolean variable that is 1 when there is a heater in the room and switched on, and 0 otherwise. The temperature of a room depends linearly on the difference of the temperature with the other rooms, the difference with the outside temperature, and on whether the heater is present and switched on or off. The system dynamics are given by

$$\dot{x}_i = c_i h_i + b_i(u - x_i) + \sum_{i \neq j} a_{i,j}(x_j - x_i) \tag{7}$$

with constants $a_{i,j}, b_i, c_i$. We assume that the heat exchange is symmetric, i.e. $a_{i,j} = a_{j,i}$, and that all heaters are identical. We say that rooms i and j are adjacent if $a_{i,j} > 0$.

Each heater has a thermostat that switches the heater on if the temperature in a room is below a certain threshold, and off when the temperature reaches a

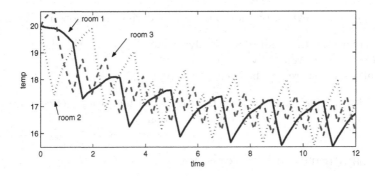

Fig. 5. Simulink simulation of the temperature of three rooms, that are heated by two heaters.

higher temperature. For each room we define thresholds on_i and off_i; the heater in room i is on if $x_i \leq on_i$ and off if $x_i \geq off_i$.

A heater is moved from room j to an adjacent room i if the following holds

- room i has no heater
- room j has a heater
- temperature $x_i \leq get_i$
- the difference $x_j - x_i \geq dif_i$

The constants get_i and dif_i may differ for each room. When two or more heaters can be moved, the choice is made non-deterministically.

An instance is defined by the number of rooms n, the number of heaters m, the coefficients $a_{i,j}, b_i, c_i$, and the thresholds $on_i, off_i, get_i, dif_i$. In addition, one needs to know how the heaters are initially distributed over the different rooms.

Figure 5 shows simulation results for an instance of the room heating benchmark. Let x be the vector of temperatures, h be a boolean vector that denotes whether a heater is on or off. The continuous behavior is then governed by

$$\dot{x} = \begin{pmatrix} -0.9 & 0.5 & 0 \\ 0.5 & -1.3 & 0.5 \\ 0 & 0.5 & -0.9 \end{pmatrix} x + \begin{pmatrix} 0.4 \\ 0.3 \\ 0.4 \end{pmatrix} u + diag(6,7,8)\, h \qquad (8)$$

The outside temperature is constantly $u = 4$. We assume initially $x(0) = (20, 20, 20)^T$ and $h(0) = (1, 1, 0)^T$. The thresholds for the heaters are $off = (21, 21, 21)^T$ and $on = (20, 20, 20)^T$. The control strategy is determined by $get = (18, 18, 18)^T$ and $dif = (1, 1, 1)^T$.

Figure 5 shows the simulation results for this instance. Even though the initial condition is a single point, the simulation does not cover the complete behavior. The control strategy includes non-deterministic choices, and the simulation shows just one possible path. At time 1 the temperature in room 2 is below 18. The differences $x_1 - x_2$ and $x_3 - x_2$ are both greater than 1, and the controller has to make non-deterministic choice from which room to move the heater to room 2. In this simulation room 1 is chosen.

For the room heating problem we are considering the following requirements:

- The temperature in all rooms is always above a given threshold.
- All rooms get eventually a heater.
- In all rooms there will be eventually no heater.

The last two requirements ensure that each room has at least once a heater, and shares the heater at least once with other rooms.

3   Benchmark Characteristics

The benchmarks that were presented in the pervious section can be used to examine different aspects of hybrid system verification. All benchmarks were chosen such that they are scalable in different problem dimensions.

The most constraining problem dimensions in hybrid verification are the number of continuous state variables and the number of discrete locations and transitions.

Each instance of the navigation benchmark has 4 continuous state variables, and linear dynamics. The navigation benchmark can be modelled with just 10 discrete states, 8 for each possible commanded direction and one for the cells labelled **A** and **B**, respectively. The number of transitions typically increases with a larger map, independent of how the cells are mapped to locations in the model. However, the number of transitions is bounded by four outgoing transitions per cell - namely to the neighboring cells of the grid map.

Given that the number of state variables is fixed, but the number of transitions (and probably also of the locations) increases with the size of the map, this benchmark is suitable to determine the influence of the complexity of the switching logic on the performance of a method.

All instances of the leak test benchmark have one continuous state variable for each segment to model the pressure. The different branches are tested concurrently, and for each branch an additional continuous state variable is necessary to time the steps of the procedure. Testing the different branches concurrently may also introduce interleavings and branching, but since the procedure contains no loops, each discrete control location can be visited at most once. This yields a rather simple discrete control structure for the leak test benchmark. This benchmark is therefore aimed to investigate the influence of an increasing complexity in the continuous part on the performance of a verification method.

Given an instance of the room heating benchmark with h heaters and r rooms where $1 \leq h \leq r$, there are $\binom{r}{h}$ many ways to distribute the h heaters across the r rooms. In addition, in each of these configurations, each heater may either be turned on or turned off, which brings the total to $\binom{r}{h} \cdot 2^h$ many configurations. The dynamics can be different in each of these cases, and thus introduce an additional control location. The number of transitions from each location is, in worst case, $h + h(r - h)$. This number is derived from the fact that each heater can switch from on to off (or vice versa), and that each heater can move to its adjacent empty rooms, in worst case $r - h$ many. This benchmark is to be

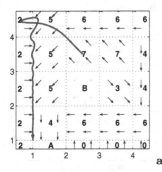 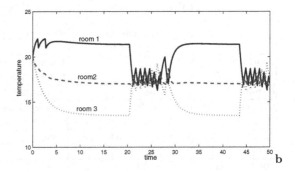

Fig. 6. a. Instance of the navigation benchmark that can exhibit chattering close to $x = 1$. **b.** Simulation result for an instance of the heating benchmark. The system changes periodically between an almost stable state and and a period of fast switching.

expected to grow fastest in complexity, when rooms and heaters are added. Most current hybrid systems verification tools require to flatten the model a priori. We expect that verification of large benchmark instances will only become feasible when the modularity in the model is exploited.

Whether an approach to verification can be used for a certain problem often depends on the kinds of dynamics. Some approaches assume e.g. that the dynamics are linear. An approach to deal with nonlinear system is then to use abstractions with simplified dynamics. The navigation benchmark and the heating benchmark both have linear dynamics. The leak test benchmark has, as mentioned before, non-linear dynamics, due to the square root in (3) and (4). But since the functions f and g are continuous and monotonic, we expect that finding suitable abstractions should be possible, if it is necessary at all.

Besides the number of continuous variables, the number of discrete locations transitions and the kind of dynamics, an instance may exhibit other characteristics that may make it hard to analyze. A first example are hybrid systems that chatter, i.e. they take many discrete transitions in a short amount of time. A particular problem can be caused by Zeno behavior, i.e. that an infinite number of transitions are taken in a finite amount of time. Figure 6.a shows an instance of the navigation benchmark that chatters around $x = 1$. Even though it is not Zeno, it may cause problems during analysis.

The opposite effect can be observed when an instance includes (stable) equilibrium points. In this case the system can stay in the equilibrium forever, without taking any further discrete transition. Figure 6.b shows simulation results for an instance with one heater for three rooms. When the heater is in room 1 and switched on, then there is a stable equilibrium just below the 17 degrees threshold for room 2. When the temperature drops below 17 degrees, it may obtain the heater from room 1. In this case this threshold is eventually reached and we observe long periods with no switching, interspersed with periods of fast switching.

Table 1. Characteristics of the different benchmarks.

	navigation benchmark	leak test benchmark	room heating benchmark
continuous variables	4	1 per segment (plus 1 per branch)	1 for each room
dynamics	linear	non-linear	linear
discrete locations	at least 10	at least 3 per segment	$\binom{r}{h}2^h$ for h heaters and r rooms
chattering / Zeno behavior	some instances	none	none
convergence to equibrium	none	none	some instances
non-deterministic switching	none	none	some instances
sampled transitions	none	some instances	none

The instances of benchmarks can exemplify different kinds of switching. The heating example has non-deterministic switching, as already noted in the previous section. Any model of the heating instances should capture this non-determinism. Some approaches to verification benefit if transitions can only happen at sampling times [SK01]. The analysis can treat these transitions differently, such that it is not necessary to include the continuous state variables to time the steps of the procedure. The leaking procedure for example waits for a certain time before it tests for bubbling. Autonomous switching in contrast can happen at any point in time.

4   Benchmark Results

In the following, a few experimental results will be presented that have been obtained for instances of the navigation benchmark. These result serve as example of how benchmarks can be used to compare tools, and how they can be used to examine the impact of characteristics of an instance on the result

The set of instances in Table 2 tests the effects of varying initial conditions. The variation is in the set of initial conditions for the velocity of the object. The instances are both run using the d/dt tool [Dan99] as well as the predicate abstraction based verifier [ADI02] of the CHARON toolkit [AGH+00].

The model of these benchmark instances has been differs slightly from the description given in Section 2.1. It is assumed that the width of each cell is $1+2\epsilon$ for $0 \leq \epsilon < 0.5$, and that the lower left corner of the grid is located at $(-\epsilon, -\epsilon)^T$. The square grid cells are arranged such that neighboring cells overlap for 2ϵ. First consider the case that $\epsilon = 0$. Then each cell can be described by its lower left corner at some $(j, k)^T \in \mathbb{R}^2$ and its upper right corner at $(j+1, k+1)^T$ for $j, k \in \mathbb{N}$. However, if each cell has width $1 + 2\epsilon$ and overlaps as described above, then it can be described by having its lower left corner at $(j - \epsilon, k - \epsilon)^T \in \mathbb{R}^2$

Table 2. Varying initial conditions on the velocity of the moving object

Instance	Initial Conditions
NAV01	$\mathbf{x}_0 \in [-0.3, 0.3], \mathbf{v}_0 \in [-0.3, 0]$
NAV02	$\mathbf{x}_0 \in [-0.3, 0.3], \mathbf{v}_0 \in [-0.3, 0.3]$
NAV03	$\mathbf{x}_0 \in [-0.4, 0.4], \mathbf{v}_0 \in [-0.4, 0.4]$

and its upper right corner at $(j + 1 + \epsilon, k + 1 + \epsilon)^T$. In fact, in certain regions of the grid three and even four cells may overlap. This introduces non-determinism and improves numerical stability of various analyses, since determining the exact time of the switch of the moving object between the cells may be numerically hard to compute. At the same time this model is an abstraction of the instance, in the sense that all behaviors of the instance will be contained in the model. A script has been developed that produces a CHARON model from a short textual description of an instance of this benchmark.

The instance uses the map and the matrix given in Figure 1, but uses different initial conditions. The initial position of the object is the grid cell just above the attracting cell labelled **A**, with different sets of initial velocities. The set of initial conditions are described in Table 2. We choose $\epsilon = 0.1$ for the overlap. The first instance NAV01 described in Table 2 is an easily verifiable instance of the benchmark model, since the object has an initial starting velocity pointing towards the attracting cell. However, the second and third instance are of somewhat higher complexity since the object may start off with an initial velocity that is pointing away from the attracting cell directly towards the bad cell.

The experiments were performed both with the CHARON based verifier and the d/dt tool. The latter supplies some library functions to the predicate abstraction based verification tool of CHARON. As expected, both tools were able to verify instance NAV01 without any significant user-guidance in a few seconds. In fact, it turned out that for this instance, the d/dt tool outperformed the predicate abstraction based method of the CHARON tool with respect to the computation time. This is mainly due to the fact that certain initialization steps of the CHARON based tool are not needed by d/dt.

When trying to verify instance NAV02, both tools were able to complete the verification task and prove safety (avoidance of the bad cell). However, during the verification of this instance several verification parameters needed to be adjusted in both tools to complete the task. The verification of instance NAV03, however, was proven in the CHARON based verifier with the same set of parameters, while the d/dt tool was not able to complete the verification task. Either, the time-step was too large, and safety could not be proven, or the verification task was not completed due to a memory overflow.

In this section we showed how to use instances of a benchmark to compare different approaches to hybrid verification. It became also clear that a proper setup of the verification algorithm is important, too. More results on this benchmark, and on verification results for some instances of the room heating benchmark can be found in [Iva03]. The considered set of instances of the navigation benchmark

Table 3. Textual description of the first instance of the navigation benchmark. See Figure 1 and Table 2

```
MAP=[B 2 4; 2 3 4; 2 2 A]
MatA = [ -1.2 0.1;0.1 -1.2]
x0 in [2,3]x[1,2]
v0 in [-0.3,0.3]x[-0.3,0]
```

tests the CHARON based verifier with respect to its adaptiveness to verification tasks where the number of locations grows substantially. It also provides more background to the approaches used in this section.

5 Conclusions

This paper presents three benchmarks for hybrid verification. These benchmarks are scalable in the number of continuous variables and the number of discrete locations. This helps to asses how different approaches deal with increasing complexity. Furthermore, instances can be chosen to exhibit certain characteristics that maybe problematic for certain approaches.

These benchmarks are aimed at all methods for hybrid verification. This includes methods for computer aided verification that require user-interaction. A successful application of a verification approach should be able to prove or disprove the properties for a number of benchmark instances.

We will provide for each benchmark 30 instances. A valid model of an instance should include all behaviors of an instance. This means that a model of a room heating instance has to maintain the non-deterministic choice, rather than resolving the non-determinism. On the other hand, it does include abstractions (or over-approximations) that preserve the behavior of the instance. In Subsection 4 we present a model for the navigation benchmark that extends each cell by ϵ in each direction, and thus contains all behaviors described in the benchmark.

The instances and the description of the benchmarks will be maintained on a web-page (http://www.ece.cmu.edu/~ansgar/benchmark/). Each instance of this benchmark is given by a brief textual description as depicted in Table 3. On this web-page we will also put a Simulink models of a number of instances. These models, however, should not be used as baseline for verification, but just as auxiliary to gain some insight into a benchmark. The Simulink models are just particular implementations of benchmark instances, and in some cases -due to limitations in Simulink's modelling framework - just approximation of a proper implementation.

Acknowledgement. The authors thank Rajeev Alur and Bruce Krogh for their input and feedback on defining the scope and purpose of the benchmarks presented in this paper.

References

[ADI02]   R. Alur, T. Dang, and F. Ivančić, *Reachability analysis of hybrid systems via predicate abstraction*, 5th Int. Workshop on Hybrid Systems: Computation and Control, LNCS 2289, Springer, 2002, pp. 35–48.

[AGH+00]   R. Alur, R. Grosu, Y. Hur, V. Kumar, and I. Lee, *Modular specification of hybrid systems in charon*, 3rd Int. Workshop on Hybrid Systems: Computation and Control, LNCS 1790, Springer, 2000.

[BM99]   A. Bemporad and M. Morari, *Verification of hybrid systems via mathematical programming*, 2nd Int. Workshop on Hybrid Systems: Computation and Control, LNCS 1569, Springer, 1999.

[BMSU97]   N. Bjorner, Z. Manna, H. Sipma, and T. Uribe, *Deductive verification of real-time systems using STeP*, 4th Int. AMAST Workshop on Real-time Systems, LNCS 1231, Springer, 1997.

[BS00]   B. Bérad and L. Sierra, *Comparing verification with HyTech, Kronos and Uppaal on the railroad crossing example*, Tech. Report LSV-00-2, CNRS & ENS de Chachan, France, 2000.

[Dan99]   T. Dang, *Vérification et synthèse des systémes hybrides*, Ph.D. thesis, Verimag, Grenoble, 1999.

[EB99]   N. Elia and B. Brandin, *Verification of an automotive active leveler*, Proc. of the 1999 American Control Conference, 1999.

[Feh98]   A. Fehnker, *Automotive control revisited – Linear inequalities as approximation of reachable sets*, Int. Workshop on Hybrid Systems: Computation and Control, LNCS 1386, Springer, 1998.

[HHWT95]   T.A. Henzinger, P.H. Ho, and H. Wong-Toi, *HyTech: The next generation*, IEEE Real-Time Systems Symposium, 1995.

[HJL93]   C.L. Heitmeyer, R.D. Jeffords, and B.G. Labaw, *A benchmark for comparing different approaches for specifying and verifying real-time systems*, 10th IEEE Workshop on Real-Time Operating Systems and Software, IEEE Computer Society Press, 1993.

[Iva03]   F. Ivančić, *Modeling and analysis of hybrid systems*, Ph.D. thesis, School of Engineering and Applied Science, University of Pennsylvania, 2003.

[JPO95]   L.J. Jagadeesan, C. Puchol, and J.E. Von Olnhausen, *Safety property verification of Esterel programs and applications to telecommunications software*, 7th Int. Conference On Computer Aided Verification, LNCS 939, Springer Verlag, 1995.

[LPY97]   K.G. Larsen, P. Pettersson, and W. Yi, UPPAAL *in a Nutshell*, Int. Journal on Software Tools for Technology Transfer **1** (1997), no. 1–2, 134–152.

[SK01]   B.I. Silva and B.H. Krogh, *Modeling and verification of hybrid system with clocked and unclocked events*, 40th Conference on Decision and Control, 2001.

[SKPT98]   O. Stursberg, S. Kowalewski, J. Preussig, and H. Treseler, *Block-diagram based modelling and analysis of hybrid processes under discrete control*, J. Europeen des Syst. Automatises **32** (1998), no. 9-10, 1097–1118.

[SMF97]   T. Stauner, O. Müller, and M. Fuchs, *Using HyTech to verify an automotive control system*, Int. Workshop on Hybrid and Real-Time Systems, LNCS 1201, Springer, 1997.

[SSKE01]   B.I. Silva, O. Stursberg, B. Krogh, and S. Engell, *An assessment of the current status of algorithmic approaches to the verification of hybrid systems*, 40th IEEE Conf. on Decision and Control, 2001, pp. 2867–2874.

[TPP97]   A. Turk, S. Probst, and G. Powers, *Verification of a chemical process leak test procedure*, 9th Int. Conference On Computer Aided Verification, LNCS 1254, Springer, 1997.

[Yov97]   S. Yovine., *Kronos: A verification tool for real-time systems*, Int. Journal of Software Tools for Technology Transfer **1** (1997), no. 1/2,.

On the Optimal Control of
Switch-Mode DC-DC Converters

Tobias Geyer, Georgios Papafotiou, and Manfred Morari

Automatic Control Laboratory, Swiss Federal Institute of Technology (ETH)
CH-8092 Zurich, Switzerland,
{geyer,papafotiou,morari}@control.ee.ethz.ch

Abstract. This paper presents a new solution approach to the optimal
control problem of fixed frequency switch-mode DC-DC converters using
hybrid systems methodologies. In particular, the notion of the N-step
model is introduced to capture the hybrid nature of these systems, and
an optimal control problem is formulated and solved online, which allows
one to easily incorporate in the controller design safety constraints such
as current limiting. Simulation results are provided that demonstrate
the prospect of this approach.

Keywords: Power Electronics, DC-DC Converters, Model Predictive
Control, Hybrid Systems

1 Introduction

Switch-mode DC-DC converters are power electronic circuits that are used in
a large variety of applications due to their light weight, compact size and high
efficiency and reliability. They constitute the enabling technology in computer
power supplies, battery chargers, sensitive and demanding aerospace and medical
applications, and variable speed DC motor drives.

Their analysis and design both in the open and the closed loop have attracted a wide research interest, and the quest for efficient control techniques is
of interest for both the research and the industrial community. Because the DC
voltage at the input is unregulated (consider for example the result of an AC
rectification) and the output power demand changes significantly over time constituting a time-varying load, the scope is to achieve output voltage regulation
in the presence of input voltage and output load variations. The difficulties in
controlling DC-DC converters arise from their hybrid nature. In general, these
converters feature three different modes of operation, where each mode has an
associated linear continuous-time dynamic. Furthermore, constraints are present
which result from the converter topology. In particular, the manipulated variable (duty cycle) is bounded between zero and one, and in the discontinuous
current mode a state (inductor current) is constrained to be nonnegative. Additional constraints are imposed as safety measures, such as current limiting or
soft-starting, where the latter constitutes a constraint on the maximal derivative
of the current during start-up. The control problem is further complicated by

R. Alur and G.J. Pappas (Eds.): HSCC 2004, LNCS 2993, pp. 342–356, 2004.
© Springer-Verlag Berlin Heidelberg 2004

gross operating point changes due to input voltage and output load variations, and model uncertainties.

Fixed-frequency switch-mode DC-DC converters are switched circuits that transfer power from a DC input to a load. Using a semiconductor switch that is periodically switched on and off and a low-pass filtering stage with an inductor and a capacitor, a DC voltage with a small ripple is produced at the output. The switch is driven by a pulse sequence that has a constant frequency (period), the *switching frequency* f_s (*switching period* T_s), which characterizes the operation of the converter. The DC component of the output voltage can be regulated through the duty cycle d that is defined by $d = \frac{t_{on}}{T_s}$, where t_{on} represents the interval within the switching period during which the switch is in conduction.

The main approach to model DC-DC converters is the method of state-space averaging [19,4]. In order to bypass the difficulties posed by the hybrid nature of the system, an averaged continuous-time model is obtained that uses the duty cycle as an input and describes the system's slow dynamics. The result of this procedure is still a nonlinear model due to the presence of multiplicative terms involving the state variables and the duty cycle. The controller design is carried out using linear control techniques for a model linearized around a specific operating point. Apart from the limitations of this approximation, the averaging procedure hides all information about the fast dynamics of the system, and fast instabilities like subharmonic oscillations are not captured. A more rigorous approach is to describe the system with discrete-time models that map the state variables from the beginning to the end of the switching period [11,14]. These methods successfully describe many aspects of the complex DC-DC converters' dynamics and are very suitable for analyzing phenomena like subharmonic and chaotic oscillations that have been observed when DC-DC converters operate in closed loop [8]. Nevertheless, for design purposes they still carry the basic disadvantage of being nonlinear with respect to the duty cycle, and therefore do not always offer a systematic approach to the controller design problem.

The main control objective for DC-DC converters is to drive the semiconductor switch with a duty cycle such that the DC component of the output voltage is equal to its reference. This regulation needs to be maintained despite variations in the load or the input voltage. The basic concept that is currently used for the control of DC-DC converters is the Pulse Width Modulation (PWM): The switch is turned on at the beginning of each switching period, and it is turned off by the controller when a certain condition is fulfilled. A latch keeps the switch turned off until the beginning of the next period. With this formulation, the control problem is to decide at which instant within the switching period the switch should be turned off.

In practice a variety of different control strategies are used, categorized in voltage and current mode control schemes [20]. They are all PI-type controllers tuned based on the above linearized average models. Simple rules, such as selecting a cross-over frequency an order of magnitude smaller than the switching frequency and a phase margin in the range of 45 to 60 degrees are used. Depending on the converter topology and the control strategy selected, these tuning guidelines result in step responses with typical overshoots of up to five percent and settling times in the range of 5 − 30 switching periods.

In the literature a wide range of different strategies has been proposed for improved controller design. The methods introduced vary from Fuzzy Logic [7] to Linear Quadratic Regulators (LQR) [15,16,5], and from non-linear control techniques [21,22,9] to feedforward control [12,13]. The common element in all these approaches is the use of simplified models for the description of the dynamic behavior of switch-mode DC-DC converters. It is obvious that approximations like the use of averaged or locally linearized models do not allow to capture the complex dynamics that stem from the hybrid nature of DC-DC converters, and unavoidably narrow the space of the explored phenomena producing results of limited validity. In particular, for the LQR design in [15,16] discrete-time models linearized around an operating point are used, and for the nonlinear design in [21, 22,9] the hybrid nature of the DC-DC converters is bypassed by using an averaged model for the controller design. Furthermore, none of the proposed controllers allows to address the issue of constraints in the design procedure. In more recent work, the hybrid nature of DC-DC converters is addressed for modelling and controller design [23,17].

Motivated by these difficulties, we present in this paper a novel approach to the modelling and controller design problem for DC-DC converters, using a synchronous step-down DC-DC converter as an illustrative example. The converter is modelled as a hybrid system using the Mixed Logic Dynamic (MLD) [2] framework. This leads to a model that is valid for the whole operating regime and captures the evolution of the state variables within the period. Based on the MLD model, we formulate and solve a finite time optimal control problem. This results in a systematic controller design that achieves the objective of regulating the output voltage to the reference despite input voltage and output load variations while satisfying the constraints. In particular, the control performance does not degrade for changing operating points.

The paper is organized in the following way: In Section 2, the synchronous step-down converter is modelled in the MLD framework by introducing the notion of the N-step model. In Section 3, an optimal control problem incorporating the above mentioned control objectives is formulated. Simulation results illustrating various aspects of the system's behavior are given in Section 4. Finally, conclusions and further research directions are discussed in Section 5.

2   Modelling the Synchronous Converter

We start by modelling the synchronous step-down converter in continuous-time, and derive for each mode of operation the state-space equations. The model incorporates the parasitic elements, in particular the internal resistance of the inductor and the Equivalent Series Resistance (ESR) of the capacitor.

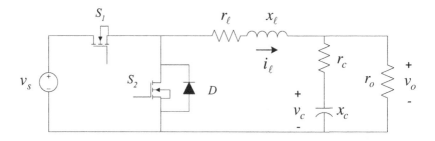

Fig. 1. Topology of the step-down synchronous converter

2.1   Continuous-Time Model

The circuit topology of the synchronous step-down converter is shown in Fig. 1. Using normalized quantities, r_o denotes the output load which we assume to be ohmic, r_c the ESR of the capacitor, r_ℓ is the internal resistance of the inductor, x_ℓ and x_c represent the inductance and the capacitance of the low-pass filtering stage, and v_s denotes the input voltage. For every period k, a duty cycle $d(k)$ which is bounded between zero and one is chosen by the controller. For the time interval $kT_s \leqslant t < (k + d(k))T_s$ the switch S_1 is conducting and power is transferred from the input directly to the load. While S_1 is on, the switch S_2 is off and the diode D is reversed biased. At the end of this interval, S_1 is turned off and kept off until the beginning of the next cycle. The switch S_2, which operates dually with respect to S_1, is turned on for $(k+d(k))T_s \leqslant t < (k+1)T_s$. Together with the diode D, the switch S_2 provides a path for the inductor's current i_ℓ regardless whether the latter is positive or negative.

Defining $x(t) = [i_\ell(t) \ v_c(t)]^T$ as the state vector, where $i_\ell(t)$ is the inductor current and $v_c(t)$ the capacitor voltage, and given the duty cycle $d(k)$ during the k-th period, the system is described by the following set of affine continuous-time state-space equations. While S_1 is conducting, they amount to

$$\dot{x}(t) = Fx(t) + fv_s, \quad kT_s \leqslant t < (k + d(k))T_s, \tag{1}$$

and if S_1 is off, the system evolves autonomously, i.e.

$$\dot{x}(t) = Fx(t), \quad (k + d(k))T_s \leqslant t < (k + 1)T_s. \tag{2}$$

where the matrices F and f are given by

$$F = \begin{bmatrix} -\frac{1}{x_\ell}\left(r_\ell + \frac{r_o r_c}{r_o+r_c}\right) & -\frac{1}{x_\ell}\frac{r_o}{r_o+r_c} \\ \frac{1}{x_c}\frac{r_o}{r_o+r_c} & -\frac{1}{x_c}\frac{1}{r_o+r_c} \end{bmatrix}, \quad f = \begin{bmatrix} \frac{1}{x_\ell} \\ 0 \end{bmatrix}. \tag{3}$$

The output voltage $v_o(t)$ across the load r_o is expressed as a function of the states through

$$v_o(t) = g^T x(t) \tag{4}$$

with

$$g = \left[\begin{array}{cc} \frac{r_o r_c}{r_o + r_c} & \frac{r_o}{r_o + r_c} \end{array} \right]^T. \tag{5}$$

The output variable which is of main interest from a control point of view, however, is the output voltage error which is obtained by integrating the difference between the output voltage and its reference over the k-th switching period, i.e.

$$v_{o,err}(k) = \int_{kTs}^{(k+1)Ts} \left(v_o(t) - v_{o,ref} \right) dt, \tag{6}$$

where $v_{o,ref}$ denotes the reference of the output voltage.

Summing up, the synchronous converter features two operation modes with two different affine dynamics. Both modes differ only in the affine expression and have the same output function. At the beginning of each period, always the first mode with (1) is active. The duty cycle $d(k)$ determines the transition time from the first to the second mode which evolves according to (2).

It is important to note that in current practice the inductor current $i_\ell(k)$ and the output voltage $v_o(k)$ can be directly measured. Based on these two measurements, the second state $v_c(k)$ can be easily computed. Alternatively, given the fact that the capacitor's ESR is very small, assuming that the capacitor voltage $v_c(k)$ is equal to the output voltage $v_o(k)$ at the sampling instants k introduces only a small error. Variations in the input voltage v_s are also considered to be measurable in accordance with common practice [20].

The constraints that are present in the converter model come from two different sources. By definition, the duty cycle $d(k)$ is constrained between zero and one. The fact that the semiconductor devices and the load can physically handle only a certain maximal current poses an additional upper bound on the inductor current, given by $i_\ell(t) < i_{\ell,max}$. This constraint is known as the current limit and is application specific.

2.2   N-Step Discrete-Time Hybrid Model

The goal of this section is to derive a model of the synchronous step-down converter that is suitable as a prediction model for the optimal control problem which we will formulate in the Section 3. This model should include the following properties. First, it is natural to formulate the model and the controller in the discrete-time domain, as the manipulated variable given by the duty cycle is constant within a period T_s and changes only at every time-instant kT_s, $k \in \mathbb{N}$. Second, it would be beneficial to capture the evolution of the states also within one period, as this would enable us to impose constraints not only on the states at time-instants kT_s but also on intermediate values. This is particularly important for the inductor current which can vary drastically within one period and would allow us to keep its peaks below the current limit. Third, the model needs to yield an approximation of the output voltage error. Most important, as the converter is intrinsically hybrid in nature, we aim to retain the structure of the two operation modes and account for the hybrid character.

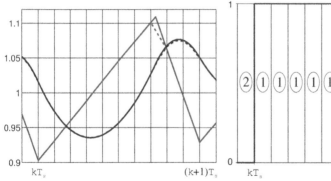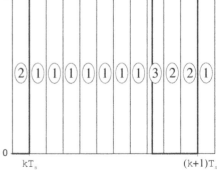

(a) Evolution of the states

(b) Position of the switch S_1 and the number of the mode which is active in the respective subperiod

Fig. 2. The N-step modelling approach visualized for the k-th period. The evolution of the states of the continuous-time nonlinear model (solid lines) is compared with the sequence of states of the discrete-time hybrid model (dashed lines) using $N = 10$ subperiods, where the saw tooth shaped line represents i_ℓ and the smooth curve is v_c.

Motivated by these considerations, we introduce the N-step modelling approach that accounts for all the above requested properties by dividing the period of length T_s into N *subperiods* of length $\tau_s = T_s/N$ with $N \in \mathbb{N}$, $N \geq 2$. This concept is illustrated in Fig 2. We denote the states within a subperiod sampled with τ_s by $\xi(n)$, and we refer to the discrete time-instants of the subperiods by n, where $n \in \{0, 1, \ldots, N-1\}$. Furthermore, by definition, $\xi(0) = x(k)$ and $x(k+1) = \xi(N-1)$ hold.

Next, we introduce N binary variables

$$\sigma_n = \text{true} \iff d(k) \geq \frac{n}{N}, \qquad n = 0, \ldots, N-1 \tag{7}$$

which represent the sampled switch position of S_1 at time-instants $n\tau_s$. Recall that the switch S_2 is dually operated with respect to S_1.

For each subperiod, we introduce the two modes discussed above (switch closed and open, respectively) plus an additional third mode that captures the transition from mode 1 to 2. More specifically, the modes are (i) the switch S_1 remains closed for the whole subperiod, (ii) the switch S_1 is open for the whole subperiod, and (iii) the switch S_1 is opening within the subperiod. Hence, for the n-th subperiod, the state-update equations amount to

$$\xi(n+1) = \begin{cases} \Phi\, \xi(n) + \Psi, & \text{if } \sigma_n \wedge \sigma_{n+1}, \\ \Phi\, \xi(n), & \text{if } \bar{\sigma}_n, \\ \Phi\, \xi(n) + \Psi(Nd(k) - n), & \text{if } \sigma_n \wedge \bar{\sigma}_{n+1}, \end{cases} \tag{8}$$

where Φ and Ψ are the discrete-time representations of F and f as defined in (3) with sampling time τ_s. The third (auxiliary) mode refers to the mode transition where the switch S_1 opens within a subperiod. Note that if we are in the third mode, i.e. $\sigma_n \wedge \bar{\sigma}_{n+1}$ holds, $Nd(k) - n$ is bounded by zero and one. Thus, the third mode constitutes a weighted average of modes one and two. The error introduced by averaging can be made arbitrarily small by increasing N.

Using the sampled output voltage given by

$$v_o(n) = g^T \, \xi(n), \tag{9}$$

we approximate the voltage error integral (6) for the k-th period in the following way.

$$v_{o,err}(k) = \sum_{n=0}^{N-2} \frac{v_o(n) + v_o(n+1)}{2(N-1)} - v_{o,ref} \tag{10}$$

In summary, the N-step modelling approach provides a description of the state evolution within one period. In particular, the discrete-time sequence of $\xi(n)$, $n = 0, \ldots, N-1$ is an accurate sampled representation of the continuous-time evolution of $x(t)$ for $t \in [kT_s, (k+1)T_s]$. The only approximation that has been introduced appears in the third mode of (8) when the switch S_1 is turned off.

2.3   MLD Framework

The three operation modes of the N-step model call for appropriate modelling using hybrid methodologies. As basically all discrete-time hybrid modelling schemes can be transformed into each other, we employ the Mixed Logical Dynamic (MLD) framework as it allows for convenient modelling using HYSDEL (HYbrid System DEscription Language) [24], and it is well-suited for optimal control, namely Model Predictive Control (MPC) computations. In particular, efficient conversion tools are available [6] to transform MLD models into piecewise affine (PWA) models. A PWA representation will be needed at a later stage to precompute offline the MPC feedback law for the whole state space that renders the optimal controller applicable for online implementations with sampling times in the range of several μs [3].

The general MLD form of a hybrid system introduced in [2] is

$$x(k+1) = Ax(k) + B_1u(k) + B_2\delta(k) + B_3z(k) \tag{11a}$$

$$y(k) = Cx(k) + D_1u(k) + D_2\delta(k) + D_3z(k) \tag{11b}$$

$$E_2\delta(k) + E_3z(k) \leq E_4x(k) + E_1u(k) + E_5, \tag{11c}$$

where $k \in \mathbb{N}$ is again the discrete time-instant, and $x \in \mathbb{R}^{n_c} \times \{0,1\}^{n_\ell}$ denotes the states, $u \in \mathbb{R}^{m_c} \times \{0,1\}^{m_\ell}$ the inputs and $y \in \mathbb{R}^{p_c} \times \{0,1\}^{p_\ell}$ the outputs, with both continuous and binary components. Furthermore, $\delta \in \{0,1\}^{r_\ell}$ and $z \in \mathbb{R}^{r_c}$ represent binary and auxiliary continuous variables, respectively. These variables are introduced when translating propositional logic or PWA functions into linear inequalities. All constraints on states, inputs and auxiliary variables are summarized in the inequality (11c). Note that the equations (11a) and (11b) are linear; the nonlinearity is hidden in the integrality constraints over the binary variables. We consider MLD systems that are *completely well-posed* [2], i.e. for given $x(k)$ and $u(k)$, the values of $\delta(k)$ and $z(k)$ are uniquely defined by the inequality (11c). This assumption is not restrictive and is always satisfied when real plants are described in the MLD form [2].

The above procedure yields an MLD system with two states, $7N + 3$ z-variables, N δ-variables and $24N + 18$ inequality constraints. The derivation of the MLD system is performed by the compiler HYSDEL generating the matrices of the MLD system starting from a high-level description of the system.

3 Optimal Control

3.1 Model Predictive Control

Model Predictive Control (MPC) has been used successfully for a long time in the process industry and recently also for hybrid systems. As shown in [2], MPC is well suited for the control of hybrid systems described in the MLD framework. The control action is obtained by minimizing an objective function over a finite or infinite horizon subject to the mixed-integer linear inequality constraints of the MLD model (11) and the physical constraints on the manipulated variables. Depending on the norm used in the objective function, this minimization problem amounts to solving a *Mixed-Integer Linear Program* (MILP) or *Mixed-Integer Quadratic Program* (MIQP).

The major advantage of MPC is its straight-forward design procedure. Given a (linear or hybrid) model of the system, one only needs to set up an objective function that incorporates the control objectives. Additional hard (physical) constraints can be easily dealt with by adding them as inequality constraints, whereas soft constraints can be accounted for in the objective function using penalties. For details concerning the set up of the MPC formulation in connection with MLD models, the reader is referred to [2] and [1]. Details about MPC can be found in [18].

3.2 Optimal Control Problem

The control objectives are to regulate the average output voltage to its reference as fast and with as little overshoot as possible, or equivalently, to minimize the output voltage error $v_{o,err}(k)$, despite changes in the input voltage v_s or changes in the load resistance r_o, and to respect the constraint on the inductor current. Let

$$\Delta d(k) = d(k) - d(k-1) \tag{12}$$

denote the difference between two consecutive duty cycles. To allow for aggressive control moves when the voltage error is large but to force the controller to act cautiously if the output voltage is close to the reference and the voltage error is small, we penalize a saturated version of $\Delta d(k)$ using the variable

$$\varepsilon_d(k) = \begin{cases} \Delta d(k), & \text{if } |\Delta d(k)| \leq \Delta d_{max}, \\ \Delta d_{max}, & \text{else} \end{cases} \tag{13}$$

rather than $\Delta d(k)$ directly. To account for the bound $i_{\ell,max}$ on the inductor current, we introduce the variable $\varepsilon_i(k)$ that describes the degree of the violation of this constraint.

$$\varepsilon_i(k) = \begin{cases} 0, & \text{if } i_\ell(k) \leq i_{\ell,max}, \\ i_\ell(k) - i_{\ell,max}, & \text{else} \end{cases} \tag{14}$$

By associating a large penalty weight with $\varepsilon_i(k)$, the upper bound on the inductor current is modelled as a soft constraint. Note that for (14) an additional binary variable is not needed as it can be represented by a slack variable.

Define the penalty matrix $Q = \text{diag}(q_1, q_2, q_3)$ with $q_1, q_2, q_3 \in \mathbb{R}^+$ and the vector $\varepsilon(k) = [v_{o,err}(k),\ \varepsilon_d(k),\ \varepsilon_i(k)]^T$, with $v_{o,err}(k)$ as defined in (10). Consider the objective function

$$J(D(k), x(k), d(k-1)) = \sum_{\ell=0}^{L-1} \|Q \, \varepsilon(k + \ell|k)\|_1 \tag{15}$$

which penalizes the predicted evolution of $\varepsilon(k + \ell|k)$ from time-instant k on over the finite horizon L using the 1-norm. The control law at time-instant k is then obtained by minimizing the objective function (15) over the sequence of control moves $D(k) = [d(k), \ldots, d(k + L - 1)]^T$ subject to the mixed-integer linear inequality constraints of the MLD model (11), the physical constraint on the duty cycle $d(k) \in [0, 1]$, and the expressions (12)-(14). As we are using the 1-norm, this minimization problem is a *Mixed-Integer Linear Program* (MILP) for which efficient solvers exist.

4   Simulation Results

In this section, simulation results demonstrating the potential advantages of the proposed control methodology are presented. The circuit parameters used in the simulations were chosen to represent a realistic problem set-up, describing for example a 48 V to 32 V, 100 W step-down DC-DC converter. Expressed in the per unit system, they are given by $x_c = 600$ p.u., $x_\ell = 3$ p.u., $r_c = 0.005$ p.u. and $r_\ell = 0.05$ p.u. If not otherwise stated, the output resistance is given by $r_o = 1$ p.u. and the output voltage reference is $v_{o,ref} = 1$.

The four cases included here represent different scenarios that are of interest in practical applications and pose performance challenges for any control scheme. In all cases, the current limit for the converter has been set to $i_{\ell,max} = 8$ p.u. The penalty matrix is chosen to be $Q = \text{diag}(5, 1, 1000)$, putting a rather small weight on the changes of the manipulated variable and a very large penalty

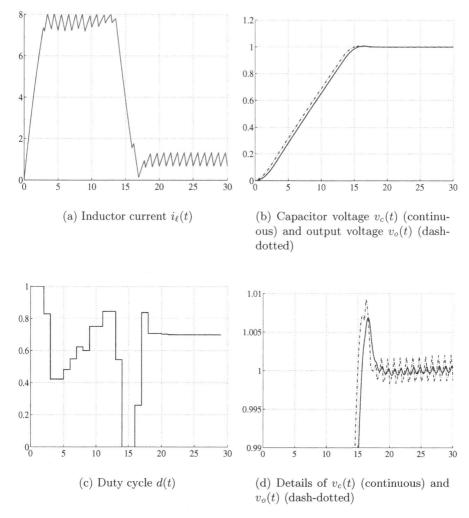

(a) Inductor current $i_\ell(t)$

(b) Capacitor voltage $v_c(t)$ (continuous) and output voltage $v_o(t)$ (dash-dotted)

(c) Duty cycle $d(t)$

(d) Details of $v_c(t)$ (continuous) and $v_o(t)$ (dash-dotted)

Fig. 3. Step response of the converter in nominal operation

on the violation of the current limit. Furthermore, the saturation limit for the maximal cost on the changes in the control moves is chosen as $\Delta d_{max} = 0.02$. The prediction horizon in all cases is $L = 4$. Although even 10 subperiods yield very accurate results, $N = 20$ subperiods are chosen for the N-step model to very accurately model the nonlinear dynamics. All the simulation results presented in the following figures are normalized, including the time scale where one time unit is equal to one switching period.

The first case presented in Fig. 3 shows the step response of the converter in nominal operation during start-up. The initial state is given by $x(0) = [0,\ 0]^T$, the input voltage is $v_s = 1.5\,\text{p.u.}$ and the reference for the output is $v_{o,ref} = 1\,\text{p.u.}$ The current constraint is respected by the peaks of the inductor current during

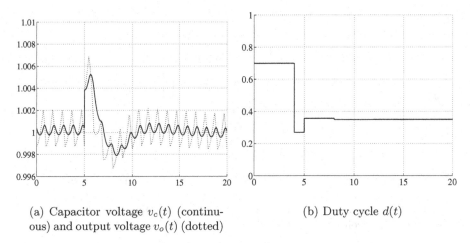

(a) Capacitor voltage $v_c(t)$ (continuous) and output voltage $v_o(t)$ (dotted)

(b) Duty cycle $d(t)$

Fig. 4. Response of the converter to a step change in the input voltage from $v_s = 1.5$ p.u. to $v_s = 3$ p.u. at time-instant $k = 4$

start-up, and the output voltage reaches its steady state within 15 switching periods with practically no overshoot. As mentioned in the introduction, settling times of up to 30 periods and overshoots of 5 percent are commonly encountered when using PI-type controllers. The difference between the ripples of the capacitor and the input voltages is due to the presence of the ESR of the capacitor and is an inherent characteristic of switch-mode DC-DC converters. This also holds for the ripple that is observed in the inductor current.

In the second case, the converter is initially at steady state when a step change in the input voltage from $v_s = 1.5$ p.u. to $v_s = 3$ p.u. is applied at time-instant $k = 4$. As can be seen from Fig. 4, the output voltage remains practically unaffected and the controller finds the new steady state duty cycle very quickly. This new duty cycle is also responsible, due to the open-loop characteristics of the converter, for a larger ripple in the inductor current. For such a rapid response to be possible, the input voltage v_s is considered to be measurable and fed to the controller. This technique is also used in current practice, where v_s is measured and used in feed-forward schemes in order to achieve faster output voltage regulation with respect to input voltage changes [20].

In the following two cases, the response of the converter to output load changes is addressed. The load resistance r_o can vary significantly over time, featuring both slow changes and step changes. Since the controller is designed through a model-based approach, it is important that some estimation procedure is employed in order to update the model used for the online optimization. The basic concept of such a scheme is briefly outlined here.

Given the measured states at time-instants $k - 1$ and k, and the duty cycle at time $k - 1$, we observe the following. Firstly, for a given combination of states $x(k - 1)$, duty cycle $d(k - 1)$ and load resistance $r_o(k - 1)$ at time-instant $k - 1$, computing the states at time-instants k is straightforward and involves only

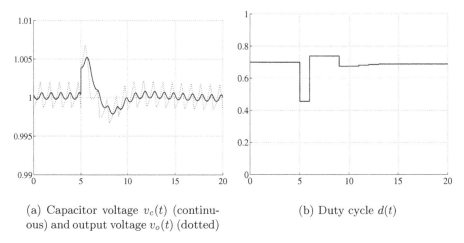

(a) Capacitor voltage $v_c(t)$ (continuous) and output voltage $v_o(t)$ (dotted)

(b) Duty cycle $d(t)$

Fig. 5. Response of the converter to a step change in the load resistance from $r_o = 1$ p.u. to $r_o = 1.5$ p.u. at time-instant $k = 4$

matrix multiplications. We refer to these states as *predicted* states $\hat{x}(k|k-1)$ using $r_o(k-1)$. Secondly, it can be shown that, when varying $r_o(k-1)$, the 2-norm of the difference between the measured and the predicted states

$$||x(k) - \hat{x}(k|k-1)||_2 \tag{16}$$

is quasi-convex in $r_o(k-1)$. Thus we can employ standard bisection optimization techniques to minimize (16). This yields at time-instant k the estimate $\hat{r}_o(k-1)$ of the load resistance. Such an estimator scheme works well if the measurement noise and the model uncertainties are negligible as is the case here. In general, however, the load resistor estimates need to be further processed and smoothed (for example by a low-pass filter) making the use of an extended Kalman filter preferable [10].

Employing the above described estimation scheme, the response of the converter to a step change in the output load is presented in Fig. 5. Starting from the steady state, the load steps up at time-instant $k = 4$ from $r_o = 1$ p.u. to $r_o = 1.5$ p.u. The new parameter for the output resistance is estimated within one switching period after the step change, and the model used for the optimal control problem is updated accordingly. As can be seen from both the current and the voltage responses, this disturbance is rejected very effectively by the controller, and the output voltage is quickly restored to the reference.

In the last case, we examine a crucial aspect of the controller operation, namely the system's protection against excessive load currents. The load drops at $k = 4$ from its nominal value to a very small one (namely to $r_o = 0.05$), almost creating a short circuit at the output. The simulation results in Fig. 6 show that the controller respects the current limit and forces the output voltage to drop to the level that is needed in order to keep the current bounded.

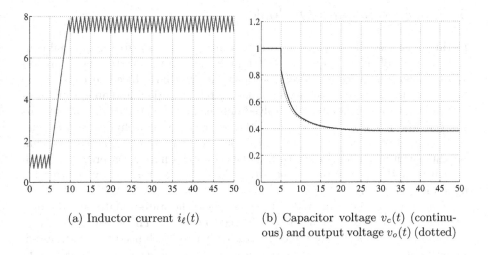

(a) Inductor current $i_\ell(t)$

(b) Capacitor voltage $v_c(t)$ (continuous) and output voltage $v_o(t)$ (dotted)

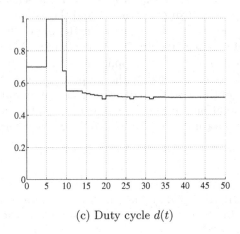

(c) Duty cycle $d(t)$

Fig. 6. Response of the converter to a step change in the load resistance from $r_o = 1$ p.u. to $r_o = 0.05$ p.u. at time-instant $k = 4$

This example shows that the two control objectives *minimize the output voltage error* and *respect the constraint on the inductor current* are potentially contradicting each other. By putting a very large penalty on the violation of the soft constraint, we have prioritized these objectives making sure that the latter objective is always fulfilled and the converter is not destroyed by excessive current. Such a feature is utilized in all practical applications through various protection schemes, but is usually not considered as part of the controller design.

5   Conclusions and Outlook

In this paper, we have presented a new solution approach to the optimal control problem of fixed frequency switch-mode DC-DC converters using hybrid systems methodologies. A novel N-step model was introduced to capture the hybrid nature of these systems within one switching period, and an optimal control problem was formulated and solved online. The use of MPC has allowed us to explicitly take into account during the controller design physical constraints, such as the restriction of the duty cycle between zero and one, and safety constraints, such as current limiting. Simulation results have been provided which demonstrate that this approach leads to a closed-loop system with very favorable dynamical properties.

This study has been limited to the case where the state-updates and the proposed load estimation scheme are considered to be ideal. These assumptions represent shortcomings that in the course of further research need to be addressed. In particular, the robustness of the proposed control scheme with respect to model uncertainties and measurement noise, and the asymptotic stability of the closed-loop system need to be investigated. Furthermore, the online solution of the optimal control problem requires computation times that are well above the sampling times used in real-life applications. Therefore, the experimental verification of the foreseen benefits of the proposed approach also requires the computation of the optimal state-feedback control law parameterized over the state space. This operation reduces the online optimization involving MILPs to a simple search in a look-up table requiring only matrix multiplications.

References

1. A. Bemporad, F. Borrelli, and M. Morari. Piecewise linear optimal controllers for hybrid systems. In *Proceedings American Control Conference*, pages 1190–1194, Chicago, IL, June 2000.
2. A. Bemporad and M. Morari. Control of systems integrating logic, dynamics, and constraints. *Automatica*, 35(3):407–427, March 1999.
3. F. Borrelli. *Constrained Optimal Control of Linear and Hybrid Systems*, volume 290 of *Lecture Notes in Control and Information Sciences*. Springer, 2003.
4. R.W. Erickson, S. Čuk, and R. D. Middlebrook. Large signal modeling and analysis of switching regulators. In *IEEE Power Electronics Specialists Conference Records*, pages 240–250, 1982.
5. F. Garofalo, P. Marino, S. Scala, and F. Vasca. Control of DC/DC converters with linear optimal feedback and nonlinear feedforward. *IEEE Transactions on Power Electronics*, 9(6):607–615, November 1994.
6. T. Geyer, F. D. Torrisi, and M. Morari. Efficient mode enumeration of compositional hybrid systems. In A. Pnueli and O. Maler, editors, *Hybrid Systems: Computation and Control*, volume 2623 of *Lecture Notes in Computer Science*, pages 216–232. Springer-Verlag, 2003.
7. T. Gupta, R. R. Boudreaux, R. M. Nelms, and J. Y. Hung. Implementation of a fuzzy controller for DC-DC converters using an inexpensive 8-b microcontroller. *IEEE Transactions on Industrial Electronics*, 44(5):661–669, October 1997.

8. D. C. Hamill, J. H. B. Deane, and D. Jefferies. Modeling of chaotic DC-DC converters by iterated nonlinear mappings. *IEEE Transactions on Power Electronics*, 7(1):25–36, January 1992.

9. S. Hiti and D. Borojevic. Robust nonlinear control for the boost converter. *IEEE Transactions on Power Electronics*, 10(6):651–658, November 1995.

10. A. H. Jazwinski. *Stochastic Processes and Filtering Theory*. Academic Press, 1970.

11. J.G. Kassakian, M.F. Schlecht, and G.C. Verghese. *Principles of Power Electronics*. Addison-Wesley, 1991.

12. M. K. Kazimierczuk and A. Massarini. Feedforward control dynamic of DC/DC PWM boost converter. *IEEE Transactions on Circuits and Systems-I: Fundamental Theory and Applications*, 44(2):143–149, February 1997.

13. M. K. Kazimierczuk and L. A. Starman. Dynamic performance of PWM DC/DC boost converter with input voltage feedforward control. *IEEE Transactions on Circuits and Systems-I: Fundamental Theory and Applications*, 46(12):1473–1481, December 1999.

14. G.Th. Kostakis, S.N. Manias, and N.I. Margaris. A generalized method for calculating the RMS values of switching power converters. *IEEE Transactions on Power Electronics*, 15(4):616–625, July 2000.

15. F. H. F. Leung, P. K. S. Tam, and C. K. Li. The control of switching DC-DC converters – a general LQR problem. *IEEE Transactions on Industrial Electronics*, 38(1):65–71, February 1991.

16. F. H. F. Leung, P. K. S. Tam, and C. K. Li. An improved LQR-based controller for switching DC-DC converters. *IEEE Transactions on Industrial Electronics*, 40(5):521–528, October 1993.

17. B. Lincoln. *Dynamic Programming and Time-Varying Delay Systems*. PhD thesis, Department of Automatic Control, Lund Institute of Technology, Sweden, 2003.

18. J.M. Maciejowski. *Predictive Control*. Prentice Hall, 2002.

19. R. D. Middlebrook and S. Čuk. A general unified approach to modeling switching power converter stages. In *IEEE Power Electronics Specialists Conference Records*, pages 18–34, 1976.

20. N. Mohan, T. M. Undeland, and W. P. Robbins. *Power Electronics: Converters, Applications and Design*. Wiley, 1989.

21. H. S. Ramirez. Nonlinear P-I controller design for switchmode DC-to-DC power converters. 38(4):410–417, April 1991.

22. S. R. Sanders and G. C. Verghese. Lyapunov-based control for switched power converters. *IEEE Transactions on Power Electronics*, 7(1):17–23, January 1992.

23. M. Senesky, G. Eirea, and T. J. Koo. Hybrid modelling and control of power electronics. In A. Pnueli and O. Maler, editors, *Hybrid Systems: Computation and Control*, volume 2623 of *Lecture Notes in Computer Science*, pages 450–465. Springer-Verlag, 2003.

24. F.D. Torrisi and A. Bemporad. Hysdel — a tool for generating computational hybrid models for analysis and synthesis problems. Technical Report AUT02-03, Automatic Control Laboratory ETH Zurich, http://control.ee.ethz.ch/, 2002. To appear in IEEE Transactions on Control Systems Technology.

Event-Driven Programming
with Logical Execution Times*

Arkadeb Ghosal, Thomas A. Henzinger, Christoph M. Kirsch, and
Marco A.A. Sanvido

University of California, Berkeley
{arkadeb,tah,cm,msanvido}@eecs.berkeley.edu

Abstract. We present a new high-level programming language, called xGIOTTO, for programming applications with hard real-time constraints. Like its predecessor, xGIOTTO is based on the LET (logical execution time) assumption: the programmer specifies when the outputs of a task become available, and the compiler checks if the specification can be implemented on a given platform. However, while the predecessor language GIOTTO was purely time-triggered, xGIOTTO accommodates also asynchronous events. Indeed, through a mechanism called event scoping, events are the main structuring principle of the new language. The xGIOTTO compiler and run-time system implement event scoping through a tree-based event filter. The compiler also checks programs for determinism (absence of race conditions).

1 Introduction

One of the key issues in real-time software is the development of high-level programming languages. On one hand, a real-time programming language should be sufficiently abstract as to support the automatic verification of programs against mathematical models such as hybrid automata or Simulink, which are commonly used in practice. On the other hand, the language should be sufficiently concrete as to support the automatic compilation of a program into efficient code. While some tools generate code directly from mathematical models (Real-Time Workshop, dSpace), the resulting code is useful for rapid prototyping but, especially on distributed platforms, it is neither sufficiently efficient nor sufficiently reliable to be used in safety-critical products. By contrast, we envision a future where hard real-time properties are guaranteed by a compiler that produces code of sufficient quality such that, as with current optimizing compilers for conventional (non-real-time) programming languages, manual code tweaking is rarely (if ever) necessary or desirable.

Previous attempts to define real-time languages fall mostly into two categories. The first approach uses *priorities* to specify (indirectly) the relative deadlines of software tasks [1]. This approach supports efficient code generation based on scheduling theory [2]. The resulting run-time behavior of a program, however, is highly nondeterministic; for example, varying execution times of tasks cause race conditions. This makes

* This research is supported by the AFOSR MURI grant F49620-00-1-0327, the DARPA SEC grant F33615-C-98-3614, the MARCO GSRC grant 98-DT-660, and the NSF grants CCR-0208875 and CCR-0225610.

R. Alur and G.J. Pappas (Eds.): HSCC 2004, LNCS 2993, pp. 357–371, 2004.
© Springer-Verlag Berlin Heidelberg 2004

program verification difficult. The second approach is based on the *synchrony* assumption [3], which postulates that the execution platform is sufficiently fast as to complete all computation before the next environment event arrives. This approach leads to deterministic behavior and supports formal verification. It is, however, nontrivial to compile synchronous programs if either non-negligible execution times or distributed execution platforms are involved [4,5]. We submit that the priority-based approach, which sacrifices determinacy in order to accommodate varying physical task execution times, is insufficiently abstract; and that the strictly synchronous approach, which sacrifices non-negligible task execution times in order to recover determinacy, is insufficiently realistic about the physical platform.

We propose an intermediate approach, which is based on the LET (logical execution time) assumption. Using LET, the programmer specifies with every task invocation the logical execution time of the task, that is, the time (or event) at which the task provides its outputs. The compiler makes sure that, on a specified platform, the outputs are computed in time. If the outputs are ready early, then they are made visible only when the specified logical execution time expires. This buffering of outputs achieves determinacy in both timing (no jitter) and functionality (no race conditions). LET programming, therefore, trades code efficiency in favor of code predictability when compared with traditional task scheduling, which makes all outputs visible as soon as they become available. We have demonstrated, however, that the loss in efficiency is insignificant even in high-performance control applications, such as helicopter flight control [6]. When compared with the synchrony assumption, LET programming trades mathematical expressiveness in favor of computational realities: it accommodates tasks with varying execution times, but in order to avoid fixpoint issues, all logical execution times are assumed to be strictly positive.

Previously, we have proposed and implemented a LET-based language for time-triggered programming, called GIOTTO [7]. In this paper we generalize GIOTTO to accommodate also asynchronous events. Indeed, through a mechanism called event scoping, events are the main structuring principle of the new language, which is called xGIOTTO. Event scoping admits a variety of ways for handling events within a hierarchical block structure: an out-of-scope event may either be ignored, or it may be postponed until the event comes back into scope, or it may cause the current scope to terminate as soon as all currently active tasks are terminated. The xGIOTTO compiler and run-time system implement event scoping through a tree-based event filter. The xGIOTTO compiler also checks programs for determinism (absence of race conditions caused by multiple tasks terminating at the same time). Finally, we show how the compiler could check for time safety (schedulability within logical execution times). This has not yet been implemented in the current compiler prototype.

2   The xGiotto Language

xGIOTTO is an event-driven real-time programming language that is built around the notion of software tasks with logical execution times. A *LET task* is sequential code operating on memory that is assigned to the task upon its release and which is not accessible to any other tasks. The memory holds the input and output as well as possible

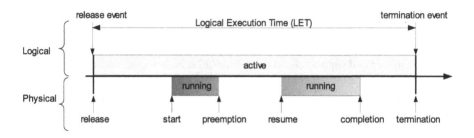

Fig. 1. Logical and physical execution of a task

state information of the task. In xGIOTTO, the same task may be instantiated on different memory at the same time. This task model is more general than GIOTTO tasks [7], which consist of both code and memory (i.e., fixed input and output ports).

Figure 1 shows that the logical execution of a LET task begins with the *release* of the task and ends with the *termination* of the task. The release as well as the termination of a LET task are triggered by events such as clock ticks or sensor interrupts. This is a generalization of GIOTTO tasks, which can be released and terminated only at clock ticks. From the release event to the termination event, the task is called *active*. A LET task is *time-safe* on some given hardware if the task *completes* execution on that hardware before the termination event occurs. The output of a time-safe LET task is made accessible to other tasks and to actuators only when the termination event occurs, even if the task completes its physical execution earlier. Similarly, the input of a LET task is written into its assigned memory when the release event occurs, not when the task actually *starts* executing. As a consequence, a LET task always exhibits the same behavior in the value and time domain on different hardware as long as the task is time-safe. Note that proving time safety is usually impossible if unconstrained events are used as release or termination events for LET tasks. For example, an unconstrained event may occur immediately after a LET task is released. This problem could be solved by an *explicit* environment assumption on the minimal inter-arrival time between events. With xGIOTTO, however, we propose a new approach based on the notion of *event scoping*, which allows us to encode an *implicit* environment assumption in xGIOTTO programs. Event scoping temporarily disables event monitoring for a subset of the observed events. In this way, the environment assumption is reflected by the control structure of the program itself.

xGIOTTO has three important programming constructs. The statement `react {b} until [e]` is a *reaction block*, with a body b of xGIOTTO statements and an *until event* e, which determines when the reaction block, and the tasks that are released within the block, are terminated. The statements in b are executed logically in zero time but possibly at different time instants, if the reaction block contains nested reaction blocks. Even if all statements in b have been executed, the reaction block waits for the until event e to occur. During the wait, released tasks may be executed by the system scheduler. The second type of statement, `release t(in)(out)` first allocates memory for a new instance of the task t, then loads data stored in the list `in` of input ports into the allocated memory, and finally releases t to the system scheduler for execution. When the enclosing reaction terminates, the task is assumed to be complete and its output is made available in the list

out of output ports, which can be used as input for other tasks. Third, the statement when
[e] r enables the *reaction* r, which is a parallel composition of reaction blocks, to be
invoked when the *when event* e occurs. If two sequential when statements share the same
event e, then the corresponding reactions are invoked by two different occurrences of e.
If, however, the two when [e] statements are nested, then the corresponding reactions
are invoked by the same occurrence of e.

A reaction block in xGIOTTO defines the event scope for the statements in its body.
An *event scope* consists of the until event of the reaction block and the when events of
the when statements in the body of the reaction block. Upon invoking the reaction of one
of the when statements, the current event scope is pushed onto a stack (i.e., it becomes
passive) and a new event scope is created and becomes the *active* scope. In general, a
reaction is a parallel composition of reaction blocks. If two or more reaction blocks are
invoked in parallel, then the scope of the parent block is pushed onto the stack and the
scopes of all parallel blocks become active. Therefore we have a tree of scopes with the
root of the tree being the initial scope, and the leaves of the tree being the active scopes.
There are two ways for parallel reaction blocks to terminate. If the parallel reaction
blocks are invoked with wait-parallelism, then the until event of one of the blocks will
close the corresponding leaf of the tree. Consequently, the entire reaction consisting of
wait-parallel reaction blocks terminates once all until events have occurred, and then
the parent scope is resumed. In contrast, if the parallel reaction blocks are invoked with
asap-parallelism, then the until event of any one of the reaction blocks disables the
sibling blocks. Disabling a reaction block does not cause its immediate termination, but
it implies that no new activity (e.g., task releases) will happen until the until event of the
reaction block occurs: all when events are erased from the disabled event scope, leaving
only its until events active.

An event of an active scope either, in the case of a when event, invokes a reaction, or
in the case of an until event, terminates the corresponding scope. If an event e of an active
scope can both invoke a reaction as well as terminate the scope, then the termination
action has precedence. An event of a passive scope can be handled in the following
three ways: it may be ignored (keyword forget); or it may be postponed until its scope
becomes active again, once all descendent blocks have terminated (keyword remember);
or it may disable all descendent blocks, thus speeding up their termination (keyword
asap). Note that only active until events can terminate active tasks; in particular, active
tasks cannot be prematurely terminated, neither by the termination of asap-parallel
reaction blocks nor by passive asap events.

Since xGIOTTO is a generalization of the GIOTTO language [7], consider first the
two GIOTTO program fragments on the left of Figure 2. A GIOTTO mode specifies a set
of periodic tasks. The mode m shown here contains a task t1 with a period of 20 ms
and a task t2 with a period of 10 ms. The LET of a GIOTTO task is equal to its period.
At 0 ms, both tasks load input (code not shown here) into their memory and are then
released to execute concurrently. At 10 ms, the result of task t2 is made accessible to
actuators and to other tasks. However, task t1 may load new input only at 20 ms, even
if t1 has not had the chance to start before 10 ms. On the other hand, t2 now loads
new input such as sensor data, but does not yet have access to the output of t1, even if
t1 has already completed execution. For now, t2 is released to execute a second time,
logically in parallel with t1. At 20 ms, the results of both tasks are made accessible,

```
mode m() period 20 {
   taskfreq 1 do t1();
   taskfreq 2 do t2();
}

mode n() period 60 {
   taskfreq 3 do t1();
   taskfreq 2 do t2();
}
```

```
react {
   release t1()();
   begin
      react {
         release t2()();
      } until [10];
      react {
         release t2()();
      } until [10];
   end
} until [20];
```

```
react {
   whenever [20]
      react {
         release t1()();
      } until [20];
} until [60] ||
react {
   whenever [30]
      react {
         release t2()();
      } until [30];
} until [60];
```

Fig. 2. GIOTTO and xGIOTTO code fragments

possibly to each other, and a new round of mode m begins. The xGIOTTO fragment in the middle of Figure 2 implements exactly the behavior of one round of mode m. For simplicity, we have omitted the input and output ports of tasks. The code is a sequence of two reaction blocks. Initially the code releases task t1 and executes the first inner block, which releases task t2. We write 10 (resp. 20) for the event that recurs every 10 ms (resp. 20 ms). The termination of a task is defined by the until event of the surrounding reaction block, and therefore t1 and t2 terminate at 20 ms and 10 ms, respectively. At 10 ms, the second inner block is entered. Now, task t2 is released a second time and terminated at 20 ms.

The right column of Figure 2 implements, in xGIOTTO, one round of the GIOTTO mode n with two nonharmonic tasks: task t1 has again a period of 20 ms but task t2 has now a period of 30 ms. For this, the xGIOTTO program uses a reaction that consists of two parallel reaction blocks. The first reaction block releases the task t1 every 20 ms: the whenever [20] statement invokes its reaction every 20 ms, i.e., at 0 ms, 20 ms, and 40 ms, respectively. The second reaction block releases the t2 task every 30 ms. Both parallel blocks terminate at 60 ms, implementing one round of the nonharmonic GIOTTO mode n.

```
react {
   when remember [async]
      react {
         release ta()();
      } until [1];
   release t1()();
   begin
      react {
         release t2()();
      } until [10];
      react {
         release t2()();
      } until [10];
   end
} until [20];
```

```
react {
   release t1()();
   begin
      react {
         when [async] react {
            release ta()();
         } until [1];
         release t2()();
      } until [10];
      react {
         when [async] react {
            release ta()();
         } until [1];
         release t2()();
      } until [10]
   end
} until [20];
```

```
react {
   when asap [async]
      react {
         release ta()();
      } until [1];
   release t1()();
   begin
      react {
         when [asyncb] react {
            release tb()();
         } until [1];
         release t2()();
      } until [10];
   end
} until [20];
```

Fig. 3. xGIOTTO code fragments with asynchronous event handling

In the middle code fragment of Figure 2, we add an asynchronous event `async`, which instantiates a task `ta` with a LET of 1 ms. This cannot be done in GIOTTO. We use the hierarchical structure of xGIOTTO to constrain the times at which the asynchronous event may cause the release of a new task instance. First consider the left column of Figure 3. Since the event `async` is remembered, if it occurs between 0 ms and 10 ms, during the first inner reaction block, then task `ta` is released at 10 ms and terminated at 11 ms. Since the event `10` is also remembered (by default), the second inner reaction block is invoked at 11 ms, releasing task `t2` a second time, and terminated at 20 ms. If `async` occurs, instead, between 10 ms and 20 ms, then task `ta` is never released, because until events —i.e., block termination (at 20 ms)— have precedence over when events. If the event `async` would have been specified as `forget` instead of `remember`, then task `ta` would never be released, because we assume that no two unrelated events can happen at exactly the same time (e.g., `async` cannot happen at exactly 10 ms). Now consider the middle column of Figure 3. Here, the event `async` may be serviced twice, once between 10 ms and 20 ms, and a second time between 10 ms and 20 ms. While our default specification of an event is `remember`, note that in this case, it does not matter if `async` is specified as `forget` or `remember`. The third column of Figure 3 shows the use of an asap event. In this example an occurrence of the `async` event between 0 ms and 10 ms disables the reaction to the `asyncb` event and releases task `ta` at 10 ms.

3   Syntax

We refer to the language manual [8] for a full definition of the language. Here we introduce only the syntax necessary for understanding the most important xGIOTTO concepts:

```
Program  = "program" Ident '{' [ConstDecl] [TypeDecl] [PortDecl] [EventDecl]
           {ReactionDecl | TaskDecl} ReactionBody '}'.

ConstDecl = "const" {Ident "=" Number ";"}.
TypeDecl = "type" {TypeId (("array" Number "of" TypeId) |
           ("record" '{' {TypeId Ident ';' } '}'))';'}.
PortDecl = "port" {TypeId Ident [InitPort] ';'}.
EventDecl = "event" {TypeId Ident ["at" Ident] ';' }.

TaskDecl = "task" Ident Pars "output" Pars ["var" Pars] Body.
Body = '{' StatSeq '}'.
StatSeq = Statement {";" Statement }.
Pars = '(' [TypeId Ident {',' TypeId Ident }] ')'.

ReactionDecl = "react" Ident ReactionBody "until" '[' TypeId Ident ']'.
ReactionBody = '{' Triggers Releases [("begin" | "loop") RStatSeq "end" ";"] '}'.
Triggers = { [Condition] ("when" | "whenever") Event Reaction ";" }.
Releases = { [Condition] "release" Ident ParsRef ParsRef ";"}.
RStatSeq = Reaction {";" Reaction }.
Reaction = ReactionBlock { ('||' | '&&' ) ReactionBlock }.
ReactionBlock = "react" ((Ident) | ReactionBody) "until" Event.
ParsRef = '(' [Ident {',' Ident }] ')'.
Event = ["asap" | "remember" | "forget"] '[' [Number] Ident ']'.
Condition = '(' BoolExpression ')'.
```

Constant, type, port, and event declarations. Constant declarations allow to associate a name with a value. Type declarations associate a name with a structured data type.

Each port has a fixed type and can be initialized, if an initial value different from a type-dependent default value is desired. Similarly, each event has as a fixed type, the value being assigned by the interrupt generating the event. The events `time` and `now` are predefined. The integer event `time` is bound to the system clock. The event `now` is a placeholder for the current event and can be used in `when` statements only (not in `whenever` and `until` statements). Events are structured hierarchically in a tree, e.g., the event 20 occurs at every other occurrence of the event 10. Logically, no two *unrelated* events (i.e., neither one is a descendent of the other in the event tree) can happen simultaneously, as they are sequenced by the interrupt handler.

Task declarations. A task header specifies a task name, formal input parameters, formal output parameters, and local variables. The task body is a standard sequential program without reference to events (we omit the exact syntax). The input parameters are passed by value, i.e., they are local ports to which the actual parameters are assigned as initial values upon release of a task instance. The output parameters are passed by value-reference, i.e., they are local ports with the actual parameters as initial values, but their values are instantaneously copied back to the actual parameters at termination of the task instance.

Reaction block declarations. A header specifies the name of the reaction block and a formal until-event parameter. The body of the reaction block contains three parts: (1) conditional `when` and `whenever` statements called *trigger* statements, (2) conditional `release` statements, and (3) sequential reaction statements. The trigger statements whose condition is true specify the active events of the reaction block (in addition to the until event, which is also active) and the corresponding reactions. The occurrence of an active event is processed in the order in which the trigger statements are declared. The events can be specified as `forget`, `remember`, or `asap`. A `whenever` statement corresponds to a `when` statement that reenables itself immediately after its event occurs, until the surrounding reaction block is terminated. The reenabled active event will be processed after all the other previously enabled events are processed. The `release` statements whose condition is true hand task instances to the system scheduler. The sequential reaction statements can be declared either as a one-time sequence or as a loop of reaction statements. Each reaction statement is an `asap`-parallel (defined by `&&`) or a `wait`-parallel (defined by `||`) composition of reaction blocks. Each reaction invocation renders the active events passive. When the until event of the reaction block is active and arrives, the scope and all tasks released in its scope are terminated, and control is returned to the invoking reaction block, reenabling its active events. The trigger and `release` statements are executed instantaneously (in logical zero time), but time passes between events; in particular, time passes during the execution of a `react` statement, between the trigger and `release` statements of the reaction block, and the until event of the block.

Core-xGIOTTO. The syntax of xGIOTTO given by the above grammar is used in all program examples in this paper. However, the corresponding formal semantics is provided only for a fully expressive fragment called core-xGIOTTO. Each xGIOTTO program can be transformed into a core-xGIOTTO by replacing each call to a named reaction block with the code of the reaction block, and by removing from each reaction block all sequential reaction statements as follows: each one-time sequence of reaction statements is replaced by a set of when trigger statements; each loop, by a set of whenever trigger statements. xGIOTTO programs with recursive (cyclic) calls of reaction blocks are considered illegal, because they represent infinite core-xGIOTTO programs. Note that in core-xGIOTTO, a reaction block consists of a sequence of trigger statements, a set of release statements, and an until event.

Example of a control program. Figure 4 shows a program for controlling a one-dimensional system with an actuator u, a position sensor p, and a velocity sensor v. The controller is a cascaded controller combining a proportional velocity controller in the inner loop, and a proportional position controller in the outer loop. The proportional controllers are used for simplicity; more advanced controller algorithms can easily replace the task code of Pos and Vel. The velocity controller updates the actuator every 2 time units, whereas the position controller updates the target velocity every 3 time units. The target of the position controller is a position point stored in the position array p. When the position is reached, the next target position is chosen from p. If the last position in p is reached, the system stabilizes at the actual position. The system will follow the trajectory stored in p until the last point of the trajectory is reached. In addition to the two periodic tasks, we introduce an asynchronous task, which computes an array of target position points for a given set of way-points. The asynchronous task is triggered by an external event, such as an operator input. We limit the number of asynchronous way-point updates to one every 6 time units.

4   Semantics

The execution of an xGIOTTO program yields a possibly infinite sequence of configurations. Each configuration consists of the values of all program variables (*ports*) and a tree of scopes. Each *scope* corresponds to a reaction block of the program; it contains a termination event, a trigger queue, and a ready set. The active scopes are the leaves. The *trigger queue* contains the enabled reactions, each associated with an invocation event: if the invocation event for an enabled reaction of an active scope arrives, then the first such reaction is invoked, and for each of its parallel reaction blocks, a new scope is added as a child to the present scope, rendering that scope passive. The *ready set* of a scope contains the tasks that have been released in the scope; their termination event is the termination event of the scope. Each when and whenever statement of a reaction block adds an event-reaction pair to the trigger queue; each release statement adds a task to the ready set. The termination event of an active scope removes that scope.

In the following, we make this formal by defining a state-transition graph whose states are the program configurations, and whose transitions correspond to the occurrence of a new event, the termination of a scope, and the invocation of a core-xGIOTTO reaction. When a new event arrives, first an *event transition* records the event occurrence in all scopes, then a sequence of *termination transitions* removes (possibly nested) scopes that have terminated, and finally a sequence of *reaction transitions* adds (possibly nested) new scopes by invoking enabled reaction blocks. If no more reaction blocks can be invoked, the configuration is called *waiting*, and the arrival of the next event is awaited. All transitions take place in logical zero time; time advances only in waiting configurations. No two unrelated events arrive at the same time.

```
program CascadedAsyncController {

 const Kp = 0.8;

 type
  waypoint array 10  of real;
  points   array 100 of real;

 port
  real p; real v; /*sensor values*/
  /* destination values */
  points dp; int ip; real dv;
  real u; /* actuator */

 event
  waypoint A;
  bool start; bool stop;

 task Waypoints2Pos (waypoint wp)
  output (points dp, int ip) {
  ip = 0; /* reset start point*/
  /* compute a spline */
  dp = spline(wp);
 }

 task Pos(points dp, int ip, real p)
  output (int newip, real u)
  var (real error) {
  if ((error > 1) | (ip == 9))
   newip = ip;
  else
   newip = ip+1;
  error = dp[newip] - p;
  u = Kp*error;
 }
```

```
 task Vel(real dv, real v)
  output (real u) var (real error) {
  error = dv - v;
  u = Kp*error;
 }

 react computePos {
  release Waypoints2Pos(A)(dp, ip);
 } until [int c]

 react mode {
  whenever remember [6time]
   react {
    release Vel(dv, v)(u);
    whenever [2time]
     react {
      release Vel(dv, v)(u);
     } until [2time];
   } until [6time]
  || react {
      release Pos(dp,ip,p)(ip,dv);
      whenever [3time]
       react {
        release Pos(dp,ip,p)(ip,dv);
       } until [3time];
    } until [6time]
  || react {
      when [A]
       react computePos until [1time];
     } until [6time];
  } until [bool b]

 { whenever [start]
    react mode until asap [stop];
 }
}
```

Fig. 4. xGIOTTO program for a cascaded controller

Configurations. Consider an xGIOTTO program with ports P, events E, task addresses T, and reaction addresses R. A *configuration* is a pair (Σ, Δ), where Σ is a function from the port set P to values, and Δ is a labeled tree —each node is labeled by a scope. A *scope* is a tuple (U, Q, S, α), where U specifies the termination event instance, Q is a queue of triggers, S is a set of task instances, and $\alpha \in \{\texttt{asap}, \texttt{wait}\}$ specifies the parallelism for (the siblings of) the scope. An *event instance* is a tuple (e, n, β), where $e \in E, n \in \mathbb{N}$, and $\beta \in \{\texttt{A}, \texttt{R}, \texttt{F}\}$, denoting asap, remember, and forget, respectively; the tuple implies that the required action (terminating a scope, or invoking a reaction) happens when the event e occurs n number of times. A *trigger* is a tuple (I, m, r), where I specifies the invoking event instance, $m \in \mathbb{N} \cup \{\bot\}$ records if the trigger is registered by a when ($m = \bot$) or whenever ($m \in \mathbb{N}$) statement, and $r \in R$ is the invoked reaction. A *task instance* is a tuple (t, p_i, s_i, p_o), where $t \in T$ and $p_i, p_o \subseteq P$, and s_i is a function from p_i to values. At task termination the output ports p_o are updated to the values computed by the task t, given that the input ports p_i had the values s_i when the task was released.

In the *initial* configuration, all ports have their initial values, and the scope tree has a single node labeled by the scope of the main reaction block. A scope is *terminating* if it is a leaf scope and its terminating event instance has the form $(e, 0, \beta)$. A scope is *reacting* if it is a leaf scope and its trigger queue contains a trigger with an invoking event instance of the form $(e, 0, \beta)$; this is called an *invoked* trigger. A configuration is *waiting* if all its scopes are neither terminating nor reacting.

Event transitions. For each waiting configuration (Σ, Δ) and event $e' \in E$, an event successor is obtained by replacing each event instance (e, n, β) in Δ with $(e, n - 1, \beta)$ if $n > 0$ and $e = e'$ and either (1) $\beta \in \{\text{A}, \text{R}\}$ or (2) $\beta = \text{F}$ and the event instance occurs in a leaf scope. Moreover, if the terminating event instance of a scope is replaced by $(e', 0, \text{A})$, then the trigger queues of all descendent scopes are emptied.

Termination transitions. For each configuration (Σ, Δ) which has a terminating scope, a termination successor is obtained by removing the leaf with the terminating scope. Second, for each task instance (t, p_i, s_i, p_o) of the removed scope, the port values of p_o in Σ are updated by applying task t to the port values s_i of p_i. Third, if the removed scope is asap-parallel, then the trigger queues of all sibling scopes and their descendents are emptied. If the program is free of race conditions (see next section), then each sequence of termination transitions leads, independent of their order, to a unique configuration without terminating scopes.

Reaction transitions. For each configuration (Σ, Δ) which has no terminating scope but a reacting scope, if the first invoked trigger in the queue is $g = ((e, 0, \beta), m, r)$, then a reaction successor is obtained by adding to the node with the reacting scope a set of children —one for each reaction block of r. Moreover, the trigger g is removed from the queue, and if $m \neq \bot$, then the new trigger $((e, m, \beta), m, r)$ is appended at the end of the queue. The scope of each new node is computed by executing the corresponding reaction block: the termination event instance of the new scope is determined by the until event of the reaction block; the trigger queue of the new scope contains one trigger for each when and whenever statement whose condition is true in Σ, in the order of the statements; the ready set of the new scope contains one task instance for each release statement whose condition is true in Σ, where the values of the task input ports are taken from Σ; and the parallelism of the new scope is determined by whether the reaction block is composed with asap- or wait-parallelism. It is not difficult to see that each sequence of reaction transitions leads, independent of their order, to a unique waiting configuration.

5   Program Analysis

The xGIOTTO compiler performs several program analyses. First, it does a conservative check and rejects programs whose execution may encounter a race condition. A race occurs when two tasks that are terminated by the same event write to the same port; in this case, the port value is not predictable. By contrast, for a given event sequence, programs without race conditions are executed deterministically. Second, since the memory of embedded systems is often constrained, the xGIOTTO compiler computes a conservative estimate for the memory requirements of a program. Third, we show how the compiler could check for time safety (schedulability) of a program on a given platform. The platform is specified through WCETs (worst-case execution times) for all tasks.

Race detection. A program trace is a sequence of transitions starting from the initial configuration. A trace contains a *race* if it has two termination transitions that update the same port without an interspersed event transition. The absence of races can be checked precisely by a traversal of the exponential configuration graph. The compiler performs a less precise, but conservative polynomial-time check on the program text. It associates with every reaction block b a set $T(b)$ of *potential termination events*: the set $T(b)$ contains the until event of b, and if the until event of b has type `remember` or `asap`, then $T(b)$ contains also all potential termination events of the immediate subblocks of b. If for any two distinct `release` statements s and s' that have an output port in common, the potential termination events of the reaction blocks containing s and s' are disjoint, then all program traces are race-free. A less conservative analysis might consider the configuration graph, but with all port values abstracted.

Resource requirements. In order to allocate sufficient memory, the compiler computes from conservative bounds on the size of the scope tree, trigger queues, and ready sets of an xGIOTTO program (the computation of exact bounds would again require a traversal of the configuration graph). As the reaction block structure of a program is nonrecursive, the size of the scope tree is bounded. An upper bound on the tree size for a reaction block is 1 plus the maximum of the tree sizes for the contained reactions, and for each reaction, it is the sum of the tree sizes for the contained reaction blocks. The length of the trigger queue of a reaction block is bounded by the number of `when` and `whenever` statements of the block, and the size of the ready set of a reaction block is bounded by the number of `release` statements.

Time-safety (schedulability) analysis. The execution of an xGIOTTO program is *time-safe* if each active task instance completes before its termination event. Time safety, of course, depends not only on the program but also on the execution platform. In particular, for time-safety analysis, the xGIOTTO compiler needs WCET information. For example, if there is a single task instance, then the program is time-safe if the WCET is less than the LET. In general, there may be concurrent active task instances and time-safety checking requires a schedulability analysis. The xGIOTTO compiler uses discrete time. The WCET for each task is assumed to be a positive integer, and scheduling decisions (i.e., task preemptions) are taken only at integer times. For this purpose, we assume there is a periodic event called `tick`. In every waiting configuration, the scheduler assigns to the CPU one of the tasks that have been released but not completed. Scheduling decisions take effect only if the subsequent event is a `tick` event. Then, an integer counter that keeps the task execution time is decremented. At task release the counter is initialized to the WCET, and if the termination event arrives before the counter is 0, then a *time-safety violation* occurs.

Formally, the schedulability of an xGIOTTO program (on a single CPU) is defined as a two-player safety game. The game graph is an extended configuration graph, where each configuration is extended with execution-time counters for all active tasks, and in addition to event, termination, and reaction transitions, there are *scheduling transitions*. An *extended configuration* is a triple (c, ν, b), where $c = (\Sigma, \Delta)$ is a configuration, ν is a function that assigns a positive integer to each task instance in the ready set for each node of Δ, and b is a bit. The function ν indicates for each task instance the remaining (worst-case) execution time. The bit b indicates which player moves next in the

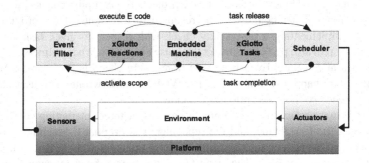

Fig. 5. The system architecture

scheduling game: if $b = 0$, then the environment chooses an event or the system performs a termination or reaction transition; if $b = 1$, then the scheduler chooses a task to be executed. The transitions between extended configurations are: if (c, c') is a transition other than an event transition on $\texttt{tick}$, then $((c, \nu, 0), (c', \nu, 0))$ is the corresponding extended transition; if (c, c') is an event transition on $\texttt{tick}$, then $((c, \nu, 0), (c', \nu, 1))$ is the corresponding extended transition; and $((c, \nu, 1), (c, \nu', 0))$ is a *scheduling transition* if either (1) the scheduler does not schedule any task and $\nu' = \nu$, or (2) the scheduler schedules a task instance i of c and $\nu'(\texttt{i}) = \nu(\texttt{i}) - 1$, and $\nu'(\texttt{i}') = \nu(\texttt{i}')$ for all task instances i' different from i.

Player 1 is the system and its environment; they choose event, termination, and reaction transitions. Player 2 is the scheduler; it chooses scheduling transitions, i.e., it determines the task whose execution-time counter is to be decremented (while the execution-time counters of all other tasks stay unchanged). The program is *time-safe* with respect to a given WCET mapping (which maps each task to a WCET) if in this game player 2 —the scheduler— has a strategy to avoid time-safety violations forever. Safety games can be solved in linear time in the size of the game graph. Since the extended configuration graph is exponential (even if port values are abstracted), in theory the schedulability problem for xGIOTTO is complete for EXPTIME. It is an interesting question to look for restrictions on the program structure which make the problem tractable in practice, at least if ports values are abstracted. For example, in GIOTTO (which is a special case of xGIOTTO) the schedulability check can be done by a simple utilization test [10].

6 Implementation

The prototype implementation of the xGIOTTO system consists of a compiler and a run-time environment. The run-time environment is shown in the upper part of Figure 5 and executes the code generated by the xGIOTTO compiler. The generated code is divided into two parts, *reaction code* and *task code*. Reaction code is essentially E code (the instruction set of the E Machine [9]), whereas task code is similar to Java byte-code. This can be any platform-native code, but we chose to interpret the task code in our prototype and generate native code in a later stage of the project. The compiler checks race conditions and determines upper bounds on the resource requirements of the program. We are currently implementing a time-safety check with respect to given task WCETs. The run-time system also performs checks that raise exceptions when a time-safety violation is detected at run time. Even if a static time-safety check is performed a time-safety violation may happen at run time if the WCET data is wrong. The user can specify, again in xGIOTTO, how exceptions are handled.

The xGIOTTO run-time environment consists of three interacting components: the event filter, the E Machine, and the scheduler. The original E Machine is insufficient to implement event scoping; therefore we have augmented the architecture presented in [11] with an event filter. The *event filter* implements the event-scoping mechanism and presents the filtered events to the E Machine. The implementation of the event filter is tree-based, where each node of the tree is the event scope of a reaction block. The leaves of the tree are the active event scopes. An event scope is composed of the trigger events (from the when and whenever statements), the until event of the reaction block, and the set of released tasks. At run-time, the occurrence of an event is processed by the event filter. The event filter computes the event transition and the termination transitions on the tree of event scopes and gives to the E Machine a set of E code addresses, which correspond to the invoked reaction blocks. The E Machine interprets the E code, thus performing the reaction transitions. The E code instructions may release new tasks to the scheduler and enable new triggers. When all invoked reactions are processed by the E Machine, the system scheduler chooses a task to execute from the ready set of the active event scopes, and whenever such a task completes, the E Machine is notified. In addition, the E Machine monitors the running tasks by detecting task overruns (time-safety violations). If a task overrun is detected (i.e., if a task termination event arrives before the task completes), a run-time exception is generated.

The lower part of Figure 5 shows the execution environment. The platform interacts with the environment through actuators and sensors. The actuators are driven by the task outputs and the sensors generate *raw* events (interrupts), which are handled by the event filter. The prototype system is implemented in Java and is able to run any xGIOTTO program on any Java virtual machine (JVM). The E Machine is available on several platforms, including JVM, POSIX, HelyOS, and KURT-Linux, and we are in the process of porting the xGIOTTO system to these platforms.

7   Related Work

xGIOTTO has been inspired by the GIOTTO [7] language. The GIOTTO programmer's model is restricted to time-triggered task release and termination, and therefore well-suited for control applications with a periodic task structure. The interest in investigating a LET-based programmer's model that can handle also asynchronous events and aperiodic tasks has been the main driver for the xGIOTTO language project. *Timed multitasking* (TM) [12] is based on a computational model similar to the LET assumption. However, in TM the execution time of each parallel task is logically fixed only by time, and not by general, dynamically scoped events as in xGIOTTO.

The zero-time execution of xGIOTTO statements is inspired by synchronous reactive languages, such as Esterel [13] and Lustre [14]. In synchronous reactive languages all computations are assumed to take zero logical time, as opposed to xGIOTTO, where all task computations have a strictly positive logical execution time. xGIOTTO, therefore, on one hand restricts the theoretical expressiveness of synchronous reactive languages, and on the other hand integrates them with scheduling theory. Esterel allows the parallel execution of tasks in a way similar to xGIOTTO. A parallel task can be started by the exec statement, and at its completion a signal is raised. While Esterel can stop the task execution, it cannot specify its termination point; it has no notion of LET. Moreover, event scoping would have to be explicitly coded into an Esterel program. Recent work in the synchronous language community has been aimed at relating logical (synchronous) time and physical (real) time. For example, Taxys [15] relaxes the zero-delay assumption with real-time constraints by merging the Esterel language and the Kronos real-time constraint verifier, and an extension to Lustre with a relaxed zero-delay assumption has been proposed as well [16].

nesC [17] is a programming language especially targeted to small, networked sensor devices. The goal of nesC is very similar to xGIOTTO. Both compilers check for race conditions. Interestingly, xGIOTTO task instantiation can be specified in nesC by using the post command, which releases a computation, but without explicitly giving a termination requirement. The main difference between nesC and xGIOTTO is the absence of the concept of time, and therefore no hard-real time constraints can be guaranteed by the nesC compiler. Also, the nesC programmer's model is platform-independent but not value-deterministic. In particular, the same program running on different platforms with the same input events may produce different results. Erlang [18] is a functional language for real-time embedded systems, specifically for the telecommunication domain. Erlang, like xGIOTTO, generates code for a virtual machine, and is therefore easily portable to different platforms. Erlang features the execution of parallel tasks but, like nesC, does not explicitly address real-time requirements apart from timeouts and the handling of run-time exceptions.

Real-Time Euclid [19] is a language designed specifically to address reliability and schedulability issues in time-constrained environments. The language definition forces every construct in the language to be time- and space-bounded. These restrictions make it easier to estimate the execution time of the program, and they facilitate scheduling to meet all deadlines. Therefore, RT-Euclid programs can always be analyzed for schedulability. However, RT-Euclid does not have any notion of event reaction and is therefore lacking an important aspect of embedded-systems programming. The programming language Flex [20] extends C++ by introducing explicit real-time constraints. In Flex, timing constraints can be specified for each section of code. The run-time mechanism of Flex ensures that the timing constraints are satisfied, or else the block is aborted and an exception handler is invoked. In Flex timing constrains are guaranteed at run-time and no schedulability analysis is performed at compile-time. However, like xGIOTTO, both Flex and Real-Time Euclid define a platform-independent logical execution model for real-time programs, which makes them predictable.

References

1. Burns, A., Wellings, A.: Real-Time Systems and Programming Languages. Addison-Wesley (2001)
2. Buttazzo, G.: Hard Real-Time Computing Systems. Kluwer (1997)
3. Halbwachs, N.: Synchronous Programming of Reactive Systems. Kluwer (1993)
4. Girault, A., Ménier, C.: Automatic production of globally asynchronous, locally synchronous systems. In: Embedded Software. LNCS 2491. Springer (2002) 266–281
5. Girault, A., Nicollin, X.: Clock-driven automatic distribution of Lustre programs. In: Embedded Software. LNCS 2855. Springer (2003) 206–222
6. Henzinger, T.A., Kirsch, C.M., Sanvido, M.A.A., Pree, W.: From control models to real-time code using GIOTTO. IEEE Control Systems Magazine 23 (2003) 50–64
7. Henzinger, T.A., Horowitz, B., Kirsch, C.M.: GIOTTO: a time-triggered language for embedded programming. Proc. IEEE 91 (2003) 84–99
8. Sanvido, M.A.A., Ghosal, A., Henzinger, T.A.: xGIOTTO language report. Technical Report UCB//CSD-03-1261, UC Berkeley (2003)
9. Henzinger, T.A., Kirsch, C.M.: The Embedded Machine: predictable, portable real-time code. In: Proc. Programming Language Design and Implementation, ACM (2002) 315–326
10. Henzinger, T.A., Kirsch, C.M., Majumdar, R., Matic, S.: Time-safety checking for embedded programs. In: Embedded Software. LNCS 2491. Springer (2002) 76–92
11. Kirsch, C.M., Henzinger, T.A., Sanvido, M.A.A.: A programmable microkernel for real-time systems. Technical Report UCB/CSD-03-1250, UC Berkeley (2003)
12. Liu, J., Lee, E.A.: Timed multitasking for real-time embedded software. IEEE Control Systems Magazine 23 (2003) 65–75
13. Boussinot, F., de Simone, R.: The Esterel language. Proc. IEEE 79 (1991) 1293–1304
14. Halbwachs, N., Caspi, P., Raymond, P., Pilaud, D.: The synchronous data-flow programming language Lustre. Proc. IEEE 79 (1991) 1305–1320
15. Bertin, V., Closse, E., Poize, M., Pulou, J., Sifakis, J., Venier, P., Weil, D., Yovine, S.: Taxys = Esterel + Kronos. A tool for verifying real-time properties of embedded systems. In: Proc. Decision and Control, IEEE 3 (2001) 2875–2880
16. Caspi, P., Curic, A., Maignan, A., Sofronis, C., Tripakis, S., Niebert, P.: From Simulink to Scade/Lustre to TTA: a layered approach for distributed embedded applications. In: Proc. Languages, Compilers, and Tools for Embedded Systems, ACM (2003) 153–162
17. Gay, D., Levis, P., von Behren, R., Welsh, M., Brewer, E., Culler, D.: The nesC language: a holistic approach to networked embedded systems. In: Proc. Programming Languages Design and Implementation, ACM (2003) 1–11
18. Armstrong, J., Virding, R., Wikström, C., Williams, M.: Concurrent Programming in Erlang. Prentice-Hall (1992)
19. Kligerman, E., Stoyenko, A.: Real-time Euclid: a language for reliable real-time systems. IEEE Trans. Software Engineering 12 (1986) 941–949
20. Kenny, K., Lin, K.J.: Building flexible real-time systems using the Flex language. IEEE Computer 24 (1991) 70–78

A Stochastic Hybrid Model for Air Traffic Control Simulation

William Glover[1] and John Lygeros[2]

[1] Department of Engineering
University of Cambridge, Cambridge, CB2 1PZ, U.K.
wg214@eng.cam.ac.uk
[2] Department of Electrical and Computer Engineering
University of Patras, Patras, GR26500, Greece,
lygeros@ee.upatras.gr

Abstract. A method for modelling the evolution of multiple flights from the point of view of an air traffic controller is developed. The model is multi-agent, hybrid and stochastic. It consists of many instances of flights, each with different aircraft dynamics, flight plan and flight management system. The motions of different flights are coupled through the effect of the wind, which is modelled as a random field. Estimates of the statistical properties of the wind field (variance and spatio-temporal correlation structure) are extracted from publicly available weather data. The model is coded in Java, so that it can be simulated to generate realistic data for validating conflict detection and resolution algorithms.

1 Introduction

1.1 Air Traffic Management Context

The Air Traffic Management (ATM) system has operated reliably in its present form for many years. The increasing demand for air travel is stressing it to its limits, however. Projections of air traffic levels range from an increase of 50% to 200% over the next 10 years [5]. This increase could lead to both safety and performance degradation in the near future, and place an additional burden on the already overloaded human operators. It is believed, for example, that it is one of the major causes that contributed to a 33% increase in air traffic controller error over the period 1996-2000 [1].

One of the most promising solutions for this problem is increasing the level of automation. It is believed that by doing this, the efficiency of ATM can be improved and the tasks of human operators can be simplified. This may allow them to handle the increased demand in air traffic in a more reliable way, enhancing the level of safety over the current system. A number of different approaches to increasing the level of automation in the ATM process have been proposed in the literature (see, for example, [7,14,2,8,17,9,10]).

Separation assurance forms a major part of the current Air Traffic Control (ATC) workload. If the level of automation in the ATM process increases, some

R. Alur and G.J. Pappas (Eds.): HSCC 2004, LNCS 2993, pp. 372–386, 2004.
© Springer-Verlag Berlin Heidelberg 2004

of the separation assurance tasks can be transferred to the automated system. One approach for doing this is to rely on Conflict Detection and Resolution (CDR) strategies to assist ATC. CDR strategies try to predict the trajectory of aircraft within the managed airspace, analyse these trajectories to decide if there is a substantial possibility of loss of separation (conflict detection) and, if there is, issue advisories to the ATC and/or pilots on how to resolve the problem (conflict resolution).

1.2   Model Based CDR

Models of the ATM process are needed in different phases of the development of CDR strategies.

Conflict Prediction. Models are needed to predict the "future" of an encounter to determine whether it is likely to lead to a conflict or not.

Conflict Resolution. Models are also useful for conflict resolution. In the simplest case, possible resolution manoeuvres can be analysed in an "if-then" manner, with the model being used to predict the implications of each one. Moreover, most of the conflict resolution strategies based on control theoretic and path planning methods rely on an underlying model to generate the manoeuvres and analyse their performance.

Validation. Validation is a crucial step in the development of CDR algorithms. Eventually the algorithms will have to be validated in *field trials* involving air traffic controllers. This type of validation is likely to be very costly and time consuming. An alternative may be to try to validate the algorithms on *real data*. This approach is appealing, but suffers from a number of drawbacks. For example, flight track data is difficult to obtain (usually proprietary); conflict data is of course particularly sensitive! Moreover, conflict situations are (thankfully) extremely rare. Track data includes implicitly the actions of the air traffic controllers, whose job is precisely to prevent conflicts from occurring. To validate our algorithms, on the other hand, we would like to identify situations that would result in a conflict *if ATC were to take no action*. We would then notify ATC if one of these situations arises to ensure that *they do take action*.

A promising alternative is to validate the algorithms on *synthetic data*. The idea here is to simulate a realistic model of the aircraft and weather conditions and use the data generated by the model as the "real world". This approach does not suffer from any of the disadvantages listed above. However, it requires one to develop and tune a realistic model of how aircraft fly (from the point of view of ATC) as well as the uncertainty that enters into the process (due to a large extend to wind, but possibly also to under-modelling and other factors).

In this paper we take a first step in this direction. We develop a multi-aircraft model that allows us to capture

- Continuous dynamics, arising from the physical motion of the aircraft.
- Discrete dynamics, arising mainly because of the flight plan and the logic embedded in the Flight Management System (FMS).

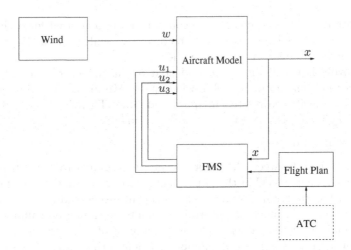

Fig. 1. Block diagram of multi-aircraft model components

– Stochastic dynamics, arising primarily because of the effect of wind on the aircraft tracks[1].

The model described here was implemented in a Java based object oriented simulator. To demonstrate possible applications of this work, we use Monte-Carlo simulation to perform a numerical study of the effect of the spatio-temporal correlation of wind on the probability of conflict. Other possible applications of the model include randomized conflict detection algorithms based on particle filter methods (as outlined, for example, in [19]).

1.3 Model Overview

Our main aim is to develop a model that does not necessarily reproduce exactly the systems used in commercial aircraft, but adequately simulates their behaviour from the point of view of an Air Traffic Controller (ATC), while maintaining a workable degree of simplicity. Our model is, however, intended to be more accurate than the simplified models used by most conflict detection and resolution approaches to predict the future motion of aircraft.

The model allows one to capture many flights taking place at the same time. In the simulation, each flight is represented by an instance of the class *Aircraft*. With each *Aircraft* we associate the following model components:

– The flight plan.
– The aircraft dynamics.
– The flight management system.

---

[1] The model also allows one to include uncertainty about some of the actions of the air traffic controller, for example the time at which they order an aircraft to begin its final descent. The air traffic controller is not modelled in detail however; for work in this direction see [6] and the references therein.

A separate instance of each of these components is generated for each *Aircraft*. In the notation used in this report, however, we will drop the dependence of these components on *Aircraft* for simplicity.

The evolution of flights is also affected by the weather. The only element of weather present in our model is wind speed. We model the wind speed as a stochastic quantity, correlated in space and time. Therefore, the evolutions of different flights are coupled to one another through

− The wind model.

The relations between these components are summarised in Figure 1. The component labelled ATC in the figure is not part of our model. Our model only provides a few functions to allow one to capture some rudimentary aspects of controller behaviour, such as uncertainty about the timing of commands.

Our multi-aircraft model contains a number of parameters, such as the masses of aircraft, their aerodynamic coefficients, the gains of the controllers used to model the FMS, the variance and spatio-temporal correlation of the wind, etc. We obtain typical values for many of these parameters (aircraft masses, aerodynamic coefficients) from Eurocontrol's Base of Aircraft Data (BADA) database [4]. We also use flight plans based on real flight data provided by Eurocontrol's Central Flow Management Unit (CFMU). For the remaining parameters (FMS gains, wind statistics), one would ideally like to determine values through formal system identification experiments. However, for reasons highlighted in [3] (unavailability of data, multiple time scales, etc.), this approach may be unrealistic. Instead we adopt a more heuristic approach. We first estimate the wind statistics from publicly available weather data. We then run Monte-Carlo simulations of our multi-aircraft model driven by random wind with the computed statistics, compare the results to earlier studies on the deviation of aircraft from their flight plan, and tune the values of the FMS gains to get the results of the simulations to match the observations in these studies.

1.4   Paper Overview

The rest of this paper provides some details of the models developed for each one of the components listed in Figure 1 and clarifies the nature of the interactions between them. The flight plan is discussed in Section 2, the model for the aircraft dynamics in Section 3, the model for the FMS in Section 4 and the basics of the model for the wind in Section 5. Section 6 presents the tuning of the model parameters, based on publicly available weather data and Monte-Carlo simulation of the model itself. Section 7 describes a numerical case study on the effect of wind correlation on the probability of conflict carried out using the simulator presented in this paper.

2   Flight Plan

The flight plan consists of a sequence of way-points, $\{O(i)\}_{i=0}^{M}$ in three dimensions, $O(i) \in \mathbb{R}^3$. Each way-point is time stamped with an expected time of

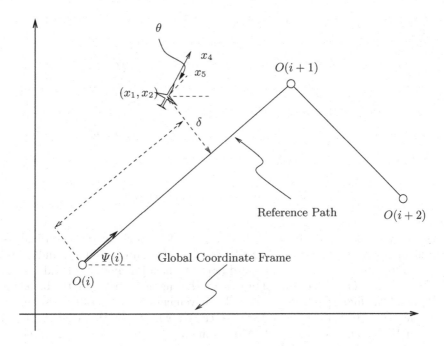

Fig. 2. Top view of a typical flight plan showing way-points and angles

arrival, $\{t(i)\}_{i=0}^{M}$. The way point data used in our simulations corresponds to real flights and comes from Eurocontrol's CFMU.

The sequence of way points defines a sequence of straight lines joining each way point to the next. We refer to this sequence of straight lines as the *reference path*. For each way point, $O(i)$, we also define the *reference heading*, $\Psi(i)$, as the angle that the line segment joining $O(i)$ to $O(i+1)$ makes with the X-axis of the frame in which the way point coordinates are given (Figure 2).

In our implementation the expected times of arrival are ignored. Instead we assume that the speed when flying between two way-points is dictated by the speed profiles provided by BADA. This approach is sometimes referred to as a *3D way-point model*. An alternative to our approach would be a *4D way-point model*. This would require one to add a system for either assigning different speeds depending on the arrival times, or assigning different climb and descent profiles, e.g. staying longer at high altitude and then descending faster to produce a faster but less efficient flight path. [18] provides an example of trajectory synthesis using the 4D approach.

3   Aircraft Dynamics

From the point of view of ATC an aircraft can be adequately modelled using a Point Mass Model (PMM), which can be easily derived from basic aerodynamics (Figure 3). After some simplifying assumptions (appropriate for airliners which

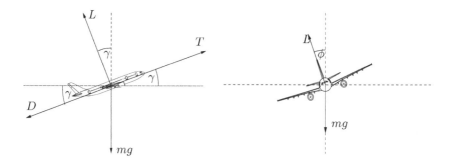

Fig. 3. Forces acting on an aircraft.

normally execute only benign manoeuvres) the model can be described as a control system with six states: the horizontal position (x_1 and x_2) and altitude (x_3) of the aircraft, the true airspeed (x_4), the heading angle (x_5) and the mass of the aircraft (x_6). The control inputs are the engine thrust (u_1), the bank angle (u_2) and the flight path angle (u_3). The movement of the aircraft is also affected by the wind, which acts as a disturbance. We will model the wind through its speed $W = (w_1, w_2, w_3) \in \mathbb{R}^3$. After some algebra (omitted in the interest of space), the equations simplify to

$$\dot{x} = \begin{bmatrix} x_4 \cos(x_5) \cos(u_3) + w_1 \\ x_4 \sin(x_5) \cos(u_3) + w_2 \\ x_4 \sin(u_3) + w_3 \\ -\frac{C_D S \rho(x_3)}{2} \frac{x_4^2}{x_6} - g \sin(u_3) + \frac{1}{x_6} u_1 \\ \frac{C_L S \rho(x_3)}{2} \frac{x_4}{x_6} \sin(u_2) \\ -\eta u_1 \end{bmatrix}. \tag{1}$$

Here C_L and C_D are aerodynamic lift and drag coefficients, S is the total wing surface area, $\rho(x_3)$ is air density and η is a coefficient relating thrust to fuel consumption.

In addition to its continuous state, each *Aircraft* has associated with it a discrete aircraft type (e.g. Airbus A330, Boeing 737, etc.) We use a discrete parameter *Aircraft_Type* to store this; the (many) possible values that the parameter *Aircraft_Type* can take are listed in the BADA documentation. In our simulator *Aircraft_Type* is used to retrieve values from the BADA database for parameters such as drag coefficients, bounds on the mass, bounds on speed, etc.

4   Flight Management System

4.1   Continuous Control

The FMS can be thought of as a controller that measures the state of the aircraft dynamics, x, and uses it together with the flight plan information to determine the values for the inputs, u.

In our model we assume that aircraft control their horizontal position using exclusively the bank angle input (u_2). This is done by first controlling the heading angle (x_5) through the equation

$$\dot{x}_5 = \frac{C_L S \rho(x_3)}{2} \frac{x_4}{x_6} \sin(u_2).$$

x_5 can then be used to control the horizontal position of the aircraft (x_1, x_2) through the equations[2]

$$\dot{x}_1 = x_4 \cos(x_5) \cos(u_3) + w_1$$
$$\dot{x}_2 = x_4 \sin(x_5) \cos(u_3) + w_2.$$

Our model assumes that the FMS sets the bank angle based on the heading error and the cross track deviation from the reference path (Figure 2). The controller operates in continuous time and consists of a linear feedback part

$$\phi_1(t) = k_1 \delta(t) + k_2 \theta(t).$$

followed by non-linearities to ensure that the behaviour is reasonable even with extreme inputs. Such extreme inputs may arise in sharp turns dictated by the flight plan, especially in the interactive version of the simulator, where the operator can move the way points at will. Methods for setting the values of the gains k_1 and k_2 are discussed in subsequent sections; for more details see [11].

The thrust u_1 and flight path angle u_3 are used to set the speed and the Rate of Climb/Descent (ROCD). At the moment, our model assumes that the FMS always tries to track a desired speed, V_{nom}. V_{nom} depends on altitude and aircraft type and is set according to a lookup table, based on data contained in BADA. When cruising at a constant altitude, the FMS sets the flight path angle to zero, hence achieving zero ROCD. The thrust is then used to control the speed through the equation

$$\dot{x}_4 = -\frac{C_D S \rho(x_3)}{2} \frac{x_4^2}{x_6} + \frac{1}{x_6} u_1. \tag{2}$$

When climbing or descending, on the other hand, the thrust is set to a fixed value. The flight path angle is then adjusted to control the speed through equation (2). The FMS accepts whatever ROCD is obtained from

$$\dot{x}_3 = x_4 \sin(u_3) + w_3.$$

---

[2] Notice that the other two inputs (thrust u_1 and flight path angle u_3) also affect horizontal position, either directly (u_3 also appears in the above equations) or indirectly (through the speed, x_4). The direct effect of u_3 is clearly small: it enters through $\cos(u_3)$ which is second order in u_3 and positive for realistic values of u_3. The effect of x_4 can be substantial; it appears, however, that with 3D FMS (the current standard, see also Section 2) x_4 is set independently of the aircraft's horizontal position. This is clearly something that will have to be changed in our model if 4D FMS become more common in the future.

This procedure for setting the thrust and flight path angle appears to be the most commonly used, because it allows for efficient climbs and descents. An alternative procedure where ROCD is explicitly controlled is usually only invoked by the instruction of ATC. For landing controlled ROCD may have to be used to make sure the aircraft hits the runway.

4.2   Discrete State

In our model, the values of the inputs u are determined to some extent by conventional, continuous controllers. However, the parameters and set points of this controller depend on a fairly complicated, logic based, decision making process. We refer to the discrete quantities used in this decision making as the *discrete state* of the FMS.

The discrete state of the FMS can be represented by 8 discrete variables: flight level (FL), way-point index (WP), acceleration mode (AM), climb mode (CM), speed hold mode (SHM), flight phase (FP), reduced power mode (RPM) and troposphere mode (TrM). In the interest of space, we only provide some details on the four most important discrete variables: flight level (FL), way-point index (WP), acceleration mode (AM), climb mode (CM).

Flight Level. The discrete variable representing the flight level takes on values representing the following altitude discretisation

$$\{0ft, 500ft, 1000ft, 1500ft, 2000ft, 3000ft, 6000ft, 10000ft, 14000ft\}$$

The value of FL is updated based exclusively on the continuous state x_3. Among other things, FL is used to set the nominal speed, V_{nom}; V_{nom} in turn determines the settings for the trust through the discrete state AM. the discretization levels of FL reflect the quantization of the lookup table used for setting V_{nom}.

Way Point Index. The discrete variable representing the way point index takes integer values reflecting the number of waypoints in the flight plan,

$$WP \in \{0, 1, \ldots, M\}.$$

$WP = i$ implies that the aircraft is on its way between the ith way-point at position $O(i) \in \mathbb{R}^3$ and the $(i+1)^{st}$ way point at position $O(i+1) \in \mathbb{R}^3$.

The value of the way point is updated based on the horizontal position of the aircraft, x_1 and x_2; the dynamics are summarised in Figure 4.2. To determine the domain and guard of the automaton we assume that the aircraft performs "fly-by" turns, i.e. turns from one segment of the flight plan to the next without passing directly over the waypoint. We assume that the aircraft turns at constant speed and at a fixed bank angle. A simple geometric calculation leads to a linear condition for when the aircraft should begin its turn.

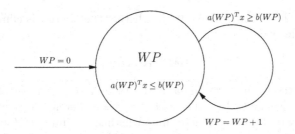

Fig. 4. Finite State Machine for WP. $a(WP)$ is a matrix and $b(WP)$ is a vector and together they determine the linear condition for where an aircraft should begin its turn.

Acceleration Mode. The discrete variable for the acceleration mode reflects whether the aircraft is accelerating, decelerating or cruising at constant speed,

$$AM \in \{A, D, C\}.$$

The value is reset whenever the desired speed of the aircraft changes. This may be the case, for example, when the aircraft changes flight level, or the climb mode state changes. The state returns to C when the aircraft reaches the desired speed. A buffer of $1ms^{-1}$ is introduced to prevent chattering.

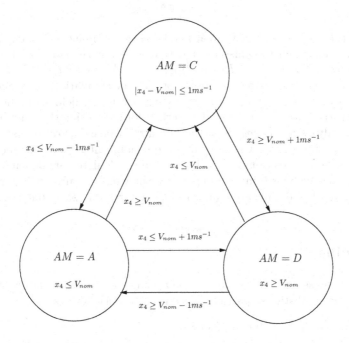

Fig. 5. Finite State Machine for AM.

Climb Mode. The climb mode reflects whether the aircraft is climbing, descending or flying level

$$CM \in \{C, D, L\}.$$

The value is reset whenever the aircraft starts a new segment of the reference path. If $WP = i$ and $O(i + 1) = (x, y, z)$ the difference between the present altitude, x_3 and z is used to determine whether to climb ($CM = C$) or descent ($CM = D$). The state returns to L when the aircraft reaches its desired altitude, z. A buffer of $1m$ is introduced to prevent chattering. The state diagram for CM is very similar to that of AM.

CM and AM together are used to set the thrust input, as discussed in the previous section.

5   Wind Model

The wind is modelled as the sum of two components, nominal and stochastic. The nominal wind will eventually be modelled as a look-up table, similar in temporal and spatial resolution to meteorological data available to air traffic controllers. At the moment, however, the nominal wind is assumed to be zero and all wind is considered to be stochastic.

The stochastic wind component is modelled as a random field:

$$w : \mathbb{R} \times \mathbb{R}^3 \to \mathbb{R}^3$$

where $w(t, P)$ represents the wind at point $P \in \mathbb{R}^3$ at time $t \in \mathbb{R}$. We assume that the wind field is jointly Gaussian, and that we know the correlation structure, i.e. we know $R(t, P, t', P') = E[w(t, P)]E[w(t', P')]^T$, for all $t, t' \in \mathbb{R}$, $P, P' \in \mathbb{R}^3$.

The main problem from the point of view of simulation is to find a computationally efficient method for generating a random field with the required statistical structure. We developed a method for computing the wind in discrete time and only at the positions of the aircraft[3], a *model-directed synthesis*. The algorithm is similar to a Cholesky decomposition, but is implemented progressively because the positions at which the wind is calculated are dependent on the aircraft positions, which in turn depend on the wind the aircraft experienced at earlier times. The details are omitted in the interest of space, but can be found in [11].

6   Tuning

The model presented above needs to be tuned to ensure that the trajectories it generates are realistic. In particular, we need to select values for

- The control parameters k_1 and k_2

---

[3] The alternative of gridding both in space and in time would be much more expensive computationally.

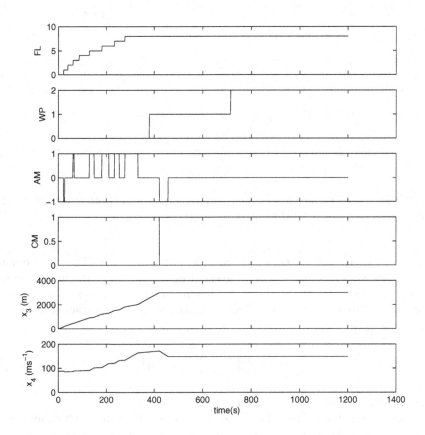

Fig. 6. Selected discrete and continuous variables from the simulation of a simple 20 minute flight plan.

- The wind parameters (mean, variance, covariance function).

To tune these parameters we made use of two sources of information:

- Experimental statistics of aircraft deviations from their flight plans [15,13, 16,12]
- Wind field data from Rapid Update Cycle (RUC).

To gain some insight into the correlation structure for the stochastic component we started with the RUC wind data. This data is used in the USA and is freely available over the Internet. First we found the mean and variance of the wind from the RUCdata and verified that the along track aircraft deviation statistics is consistent with these findings. We then estimated the values of k_1

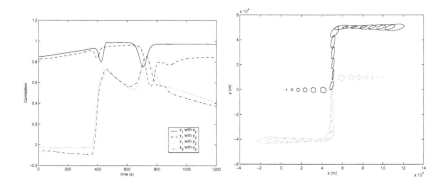

Fig. 7. Plot of correlation between the position components of both aircraft (left) and error ellipses for the simulated flight-plan (right).

and k_2 which give the correct cross-track deviation statistics. This can be done using Monte-Carlo methods. Alternatively, if we assume that the wind is roughly constant over periods of the order of a few minutes, we can derive an analytic expression. If we assume the standard deviation of the cross track deviation is $2nmi$, $\sigma = 8ms^{-1}$ and $v = 250ms^{-1}$ then

$$\frac{k_2}{k_1} \simeq E(y_\infty^2) \left(\frac{v}{w_y}\right)^2 = 115000m \tag{3}$$

Here y_∞ denotes the steady state cross track error.

More systematic methods for tuning the model (e.g. using techniques developed for random field identification) are a subject of ongoing work.

7   Simulation

The model presented here was coded in a Java object oriented simulator. A graphical user interface was developed to allow visualizing the results and running the simulation in interactive mode (where the used can change flight plans on-line, more or less as an air traffic controller would). Figure 6 shows the simulation of a simple 20 min, 4 waypoint flightplan.

To demonstrate possible uses of the model developed here we have conducted a numerical study of the effect of correlation in the wind on the probability that aircraft will come dangerously close to one another (conflict probability). This is a topic of contention among researchers and practitioners in the field of air traffic management. Some authors believe that correlation is important and must be accounted for, while others believe that correlation is unimportant and can be ignored; both classes provide heuristic arguments that support their view!

Our simulator can be used to quantify this effect. We conducted a number of simulations of a pair of aircraft both following a simple flight plan. We find

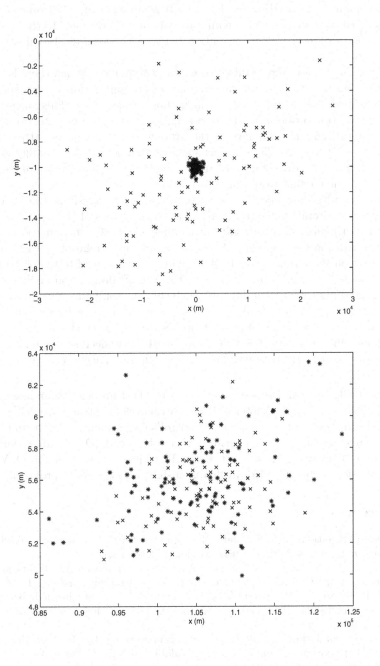

Fig. 8. Scatter plots of aircraft positions after twenty minutes. The first shows difference in aircraft position, the second shows average aircraft position. In both plots "×" denotes simulations with correlation, "＊" simulations without correlation.

the probability distribution of the aircraft separation after 20 min. This will give an idea of the chance of the aircraft coming into conflict. In the first set of simulations we do not have correlation between the aircraft. In the second we do.

Figures 7, 8 show the results of the two experiments. When there is correlation between the two aircraft the variance of the separation is very small (the standard deviation is 305m vs 5000m without separation). This suggests that conflict detection probes that ignore correlation would be too conservative in this case. Interestingly, the variance of the average position is larger (the standard deviation is 7120m vs 5250m). This suggests that although a conflict could be predicted more accurately if correlation is included, the prediction of the actual position of the conflict would be more variable.

These results allow one to draw some interesting conclusions. Clearly correlation between aircraft makes a difference to the statistics of the positions of each aircraft and hence the probability of conflict. Generally speaking the variance of the separation between aircraft will be less with correlation, although this is dependent on the geometry of the flightplans. This will lead to the probability of conflict being lower for situations where the aircraft do not nominally come into conflict, and higher for situations in which they do nominally come into conflict. The fact that the position of conflict is less well known will not make a large difference to the accuracy of conflict probes. In summary the effect of ignoring correlation in conflict probes will be to create an unnecessary number of false alerts, so it is important to develop methods that can account for correlation.

Acknowledgement. Research supported by the European Commission under HYBRIDGE, IST-2001-32460 and Eurocontrol under contract C20051E/BM/03. The authors would like to thank Eurocontrol's Experimental Centre and Central Flow Management Unit for providing access to the BADA database and flight plan data. They are grateful to H. Blom, R. Irvine, A. Lecchini and O. Watkins for discussions that provided invaluable insight into the ATM problem.

References

1. Federal Aviation Authority. Safer skies [online]. 2001. Available from World Wide Web: http://www.faa.gov/apa/safer_skies/saftoc.htm.
2. K. Blin. Stochastic conflict detection for air traffic management. Technical report, Eurocontrol Experimental Centre, BP 15, 91222 Brétigny-sur-Orge, France, 2000.
3. M. L. Bujorianu, W. Glover, J. Lygeros, and G. Pola. A stochastic hybrid process modelling framework. Technical Report WP1, Deliverable D1.2, HYBRIDGE, May 29, 2003.
4. Eurocontrol Experimental Centre. User manual for the base of aircraft data (BADA) revision 3.3 [online]. 2002. Available from World Wide Web: http://www.eurocontrol.fr/projects/bada/.
5. U.K. Department of Transport. Air traffic forecasts for the United Kingdom 1997. Technical report, U.K. Governement, Department of Transport, 1997. Available from World Wide Web: http://www.aviation.dft.gov.uk/aed/air/aircont.htm.

6. M.D. di Benedetto and G. Pola. Inventory of error evolution control problems in air traffic management. Technical Report WP7, Deliverable D7.1, HYBRIDGE, November 4, 2002.

7. Heinz Erzberger, Thomas J. Davis, and Steven Green. Design of Center-TRACON automation system. In *Proceedings of the AGARD Guidance and Control Syposium on Machine Intelligence in Air Traffic Management*, pages 11.1–11.12, 1993.

8. J. M. Hoekstra et al. Overview of NLR free flight project 1997-1999. Technical report, National Aerospace Laboratory, NLR, 2000.

9. Eurocontrol. Aircraft in the future air traffic management system. Technical report, Eurocontrol, 2001.

10. Defence Evaluation and Research Agency (UK). The more autonomous - aircraft in the future air traffic management system. Technical report, DERA, 2000.

11. W. Glover and J. Lygeros. A multi-aircraft model for conflict detection and resolution algorithm validation. Technical Report WP1, Deliverable D1.3, HYBRIDGE, July 23, 2003.

12. D. Harrison and G. Moek. European studies to investigate the feasability of using 1000 ft vertical seperation minima above FL290, part ii. precision radar data analysis and collision risk assessment. *Journal of Navigation*, 45:91, 1992.

13. D.A. Hsu. Long-tailed distributions for position errors in navigation. *Applied Statistics*, 28:62–72, 1979.

14. C. Meckiff and P. Gibbs. PHARE highly interactive problem solver. Technical Report EEC 273/94, Eurocontrol Experimental Centre, BP 15, 91222 Brétigny-sur-Orge, France, November 1994.

15. R. A. Paielli. Empirical test of conflict probability estimation. Technical report, NASA Ames Research Centre, Moffett Field CA 94035-1000, U.S.A., 1998.

16. H.J. Rome and V. Krishnan. Causal probabilistic model for evalutating future transoceanic airlane seperations. *IEEE Tr. Aerospace and Electronic Systems*, 26:804–817, 1990.

17. Conflict Detection RTCA Special Committee 186, Working Group-1 and Resolution Subgroup. Application of airborne conflict management: Detection, prevention and resolution. Technical report, RTCA, 2000.

18. R. Slattery and Y. Zhao. Trajectory synthesis for air traffic automation. *Journal of Guidance, Control and Dynamics*, 20:232–238, 1997.

19. O. Watkins and J. Lygeros. Stochastic reachability for discrete time systems: An application to aircraft collision avoidance. In *IEEE Conference on Decision and Control (CDC03)*, Hawaii, USA, December 9-12 2003. To appear.

Stochastic Hybrid Systems: Application to Communication Networks⋆

João P. Hespanha

Dept. of Electrical and Computer Eng.,
Univ. of California, Santa Barbara, CA 92106-9560

Abstract. We propose a model for Stochastic Hybrid Systems (SHSs) where transitions between discrete modes are triggered by stochastic events much like transitions between states of a continuous-time Markov chains. However, the rate at which transitions occur is allowed to depend both on the continuous and the discrete states of the SHS. Based on results available for Piecewise-Deterministic Markov Process (PDPs), we provide a formula for the extended generator of the SHS, which can be used to compute expectations and the overall distribution of the state. As an application, we construct a stochastic model for on-off TCP flows that considers both the congestion-avoidance and slow-start modes and takes directly into account the distribution of the number of bytes transmitted. Using the tools derived for SHSs, we model the dynamics of the moments of the sending rate by an infinite system of ODEs, which can be truncated to obtain an approximate finite-dimensional model.

1 Introduction

One of the more general formal models for stochastic hybrid systems was proposed by [15], where the deterministic differential equations for the continuous flows are replaced by their stochastic counterparts, and the reset maps are generalized to (state-dependent) distributions that define the probability density of the state after a discrete transition. However, in this model transitions are always triggered by deterministic conditions (guards) on the state.

In the model proposed in this paper for SHSs, transitions between modes are triggered by stochastic events, much like the transitions between states of a continuous-time Markov chains. However, the probability that a transition occurs in a given interval of time depends both on the continuous and discrete components of the current SHS's state. The state of the SHS so defined is a Piecewise-Deterministic Markov Process (PDPs) in the sense of [9]. Based on this observation, we provide a formula for the extended generator of the SHS, which can be used to compute expectations and probability distributions/densities of its discrete/continuous states.

⋆ This material is based upon work supported by the National Science Foundation under Grants No. CCR-0311084, ANI-0322476.

R. Alur and G.J. Pappas (Eds.): HSCC 2004, LNCS 2993, pp. 387–401, 2004.

The basic model proposed is (i) limited to a deterministic evolution of the continuous state inside each discrete mode and (ii) it does not allow for transitions triggered by deterministic conditions on the state (e.g., guards being crossed). The first restriction is only introduced for simplicity of presentation and it is shown how the model can be generalized to allow for continuous evolutions driven by stochastic differential equations. The rationale for disallowing transitions triggered by guard-crossings is that this allows us to exclude Zeno phenomena [18]. However, we show how one can approximate systems with guards (and potentially prone to Zeno phenomena) by a sequence of Zeno-free SHSs.

The model proposed is inspired by piecewise deterministic jump systems (PDJSs), where the evolution of the continuous state in each mode is modeled by a deterministic differential equation and transitions between modes are governed by a continuous-time Markov process [8,3,31,11,10]. In general, the transitions rates in PDJs are assumed independent of the continuous state, which is too restrictive for our applications. The work of [11] is a notable exception but requires a time-scale separation between the (purely deterministic) continuous dynamics and the discrete jump dynamics. In switched diffusion processes (SDPs), as defined by [12], the evolution of the continuous state in each mode is modeled by a stochastic differential equation and transitions between modes are controlled by a continuous-time Markov process. The transition rates of the Markov process can depend on the state but transitions do not generate jumps on the continuous state (i.e., no resets). The reader is referred to [28] for a comparison of the models in [9,12,15]. The SHSs considered here can be viewed as special cases of general jump-diffusion processes [17]. In fact, Theorem 1 can be viewed as an Itô rule for SHSs. However, in the application of interest, we are faced with the technical difficulty that jump-intensities are not bounded and moreover the jump-distributions do not have compact support.

Our SHS model was inspired by the need to obtain accurate models for TCP congestion control in communication networks. The use of hybrid models to characterize the behavior of congestion control was proposed by [14] and further pursued in [5,6]. In these models, packet drops trigger transitions between different "modes" for the evolution of TCP's congestion window size. The drop models in [14,5] were completely deterministic but, as noted in [6], their use is limited to simple network topologies.

There is an extensive literature on models that describe the behavior of TCP congestion control for long-lived flows, i.e., flows that have an infinite amount of data to transmit. A great deal of effort has been placed in characterizing the steady-state behavior of these flows [26,23,24,27,30]. In particular, in studying the relationship between the average transmission rate μ, the average round-trip time RTT, and the per-packet drop rate p_{drop} for a single TCP flow. In most of this work, μ and p_{drop} should be understood as *time-averages for a single TCP flow*. This type of approach was also pursued in [27,29,22,19,20, 21] to derive dynamic models for the congestion avoidance stage of long-lived TCP flows. However, these single-flow models are only valid over time scales much longer than the round-trip time for one packet. To avoid averaging over long time intervals, [25] utilized *ensemble averages* to construct models for the dynamics of long-lived flows. [29] also used stochastic aggregation to reduce the time-scales over which a single-flow model is valid.

We pursue here a stochastic analysis of the hybrid models proposed in [6]. As in [25] time averaging is done over intervals of roughly one round-trip time to obtain continuously varying sending rates, and we then investigate the dynamics of ensemble averages. However, here we consider ensembles of *on-off* TCP flows. The off-periods are assumed exponentially distributed whereas the on-periods are determined by the amount of data being transfered. We take as given the probability distribution of the transfer-sizes, which implicitly determines the distribution for the on-periods. The model takes into account the correlation between the (variable) sending rate and the duration of the (also variable) on-periods. Not surprisingly, the ensemble behavior of on-off TCP flows varies very significantly with the probability distribution of the transfer sizes. By feeding our models with realistic distributions reported in the literature, we conclude that the dynamics of the sending rate is dominated by high-order statistics, exhibiting much larger standard deviations than the average value. Moreover, the packet drop rate seems to have a surprisingly small effect on the average drop rate but provides a strong control on its standard deviation. This has significant implications for the design of congestion control mechanisms.

Notation. By a *piecewise continuous signal* it is meant a function $x : [0, \infty) \to \mathbb{R}^n$ that is right-continuous and has left-limit at every point. We denote by $x^-(t)$ the left-limit of $x(\tau)$ as $\tau \uparrow t$. A signal x is called *piecewise constant* if it is piece-continuous and it is constant on every interval where it is continuous. Given a *measurable space* $(\Omega, \mathfrak{F})$ and *probability measure* $\mathrm{P} : \mathfrak{F} \to [0, 1]$, vector-valued random variables $\boldsymbol{\alpha} : \Omega \to \mathbb{R}^n$ and stochastic processes $\mathbf{x} : \Omega \times [0, \infty) \to \mathcal{X} \subset \mathbb{R}^n$ are denoted in **boldface**. A stochastic process with piecewise constant sample paths is called a *jump process*. When a jump process takes values on the set $\mathbb{N}$ of nonnegative integers it is called a *stochastic counter*.

2   Stochastic Hybrid Systems

A *stochastic hybrid system (SHS)* is defined by a differential equation

$$\dot{\mathbf{x}} = f(\mathbf{q}, \mathbf{x}, t), \qquad f : \mathcal{Q} \times \mathbb{R}^n \times [0, \infty) \to \mathbb{R}^n, \tag{1}$$

a family of m *discrete transition/reset maps*

$$(\mathbf{q}, \mathbf{x}) = \phi_\ell(\mathbf{q}^-, \mathbf{x}^-, t), \quad \phi_\ell : \mathcal{Q} \times \mathbb{R}^n \to \mathcal{Q} \times \mathbb{R}^n \times [0, \infty), \, \ell \in \{1, \dots, m\}, \tag{2}$$

and a family of m *transition intensities*

$$\lambda_\ell(\mathbf{q}, \mathbf{x}, t), \qquad \lambda_\ell : \mathcal{Q} \times \mathbb{R}^n \times [0, \infty) \to [0, \infty), \, \ell \in \{1, \dots, m\}, \tag{3}$$

where $\mathcal{Q}$ denotes a (typically finite) set with no particular topological structure. A SHS characterizes a jump process $\mathbf{q} : \Omega \times [0, \infty) \to \mathcal{Q}$ called the *discrete state*; a stochastic process $\mathbf{x} : \Omega \times [0, \infty) \to \mathbb{R}^n$ with piecewise continuous sample paths called the *continuous state*; and m stochastic counters $\mathbf{N}_\ell : \Omega \times [0, \infty) \to \mathbb{N}$ called the *transition counters*.

In essence, between transition counter increments the discrete state remains constant whereas the continuous state flows according to (1); and at transition times the continuous and discrete states are reset according to (2). Each transition counter $\mathbf{N}_\ell$ counts the number of times that the corresponding discrete transition/reset map ϕ_ℓ is "activated." The frequency at which this occurs is determined by the transition intensities (3). In particular, the probability that the counter $\mathbf{N}_\ell$ will increment and therefore that the corresponding transition takes place in an "elementary interval" $(t, t + dt]$ is given by $\lambda_\ell(\mathbf{q}(t), \mathbf{x}(t), t)dt$. In practice, one can think of the intensity of a transition as the instantaneous rate at which that transition occurs. We will shortly make these statements mathematically precise.

It is often convenient to represent SHSs by a directed graph as in Figure 1, where each vertex corresponds to a discrete mode and each edge to a transition between discrete modes. The vertices are labeled with the corresponding discrete mode and the vector fields that determines the evolution of the continuous state in that particular mode. The source of each edge is labeled with the probability that the transition will take place in an elementary interval $(t, t + dt]$ and the destination is labeled with the corresponding reset-map.

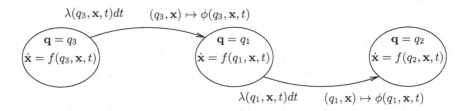

Fig. 1. Graphical representation of a stochastic hybrid system

2.1 Construction of the Stochastic Processes

We now provide the formal procedure to construct the sample paths of the discrete state, continuous state, and transition counters and show that it is indeed consistent with the intuition given above. Aside from its theoretical interest, this construction is useful to run Monte Carlo simulations of SHSs. It is inspired by the one used in [9, Chapter 2] to define Piecewise-Deterministic Markov Processes (PDPs). The following regularity assumption on the vector field f is required for the SHS to be well defined:

Assumption 1. *For every* $(q_0, x_0, t_0) \in \mathcal{Q} \times \mathbb{R}^n \times [0, \infty)$ *there exists a unique global solution* $\varphi(\cdot; t_0, q_0, x_0) : [t_0, \infty) \to \mathbb{R}^n$ *to* (1) *with initial condition* $\mathbf{x}(t_0) = x_0$ *and* $\mathbf{q}(t_0) = q_0$. $\qquad\qquad\square$

In what follows, the $\boldsymbol{\mu}_k^\ell$, $\ell \in \{1, \ldots, m\}$, $k \in \mathbb{N}$ denote independent random variables all uniformly distributed in the interval $[0, 1]$. We will call these *transition triggers*. Consider an initial condition $(q_0, x_0, t_0) \in \mathcal{Q} \times \mathbb{R}^n \times [0, \infty)$. For a given $\omega \in \Omega$, the sample paths of $\mathbf{q}(\omega, \cdot) : [t_0, \infty) \to \mathcal{Q}$, $\mathbf{x}(\omega, \cdot) : [t_0, \infty) \to \mathbb{R}^n$, and all the $\mathbf{N}_\ell(\omega, \cdot) : [t_0, \infty) \to \mathbb{N}$ can be constructed as follows:

1. Set $\mathbf{t}_0(\omega) = t_0$, $\mathbf{q}(\omega, 0) = q_0$, $\mathbf{x}(\omega, 0) = x_0$, $\mathbf{N}_\ell(\omega, 0) = 0$, $\forall \ell$.
2. Let $\mathbf{t}_1(\omega)$ be the largest time on $(\mathbf{t}_0(\omega), \infty]$ for which

$$e^{-\int_{\mathbf{t}_0(\omega)}^t \lambda_\ell(\mathbf{q}(\omega, \mathbf{t}_0(\omega)), \varphi(s; \mathbf{t}_0(\omega), \mathbf{q}(\omega, \mathbf{t}_0(\omega)), \mathbf{x}(\omega, \mathbf{t}_0(\omega))), s) ds} > \boldsymbol{\mu}_0^\ell(\omega), \qquad (4)$$

$\forall t \in [\mathbf{t}_0(\omega), \mathbf{t}_1(\omega))$, $\ell \in \{1, \ldots, m\}$.
3. On the interval $[\mathbf{t}_0(\omega), \mathbf{t}_1(\omega))$, the sample paths of $\mathbf{q}(\omega, \cdot)$ and all the counters $\mathbf{N}_\ell(\omega, \cdot)$ remain constant, whereas the sample path of $\mathbf{x}(\omega, \cdot)$ equals $\varphi(\cdot; \mathbf{t}_0(\omega), \mathbf{q}(\omega, \mathbf{t}_0(\omega)), \mathbf{x}(\omega, \mathbf{t}_0(\omega)))$.
4. Denoting by $\boldsymbol{\ell}_1(\omega) \in \{1, 2, \ldots, m\}$ the index for which (4) is violated at time $t = \mathbf{t}_1(\omega)$, the counter $\mathbf{N}_{\boldsymbol{\ell}_1(\omega)}(\omega)$ is incremented by one and

$$\big(\mathbf{q}(\omega, \mathbf{t}_1(\omega)), \mathbf{x}(\omega, \mathbf{t}_1(\omega))\big) = \phi_{\boldsymbol{\ell}_1(\omega)}\big(\mathbf{q}^-(\omega, \mathbf{t}_1(\omega)), \mathbf{x}^-(\omega, \mathbf{t}_1), \mathbf{t}_1(\omega)\big).$$

5. In case $\mathbf{t}_1(\omega) < \infty$, repeat the construction from the step 2 above with $\mathbf{t}_0(\omega)$, $\boldsymbol{\mu}_0^\ell(\omega)$, $\mathbf{t}_1(\omega)$, $\boldsymbol{\ell}_1(\omega)$ replaced by $\mathbf{t}_k(\omega)$, $\boldsymbol{\mu}_k^\ell(\omega)$, $\mathbf{t}_{k+1}(\omega)$, $\boldsymbol{\ell}_{k+1}(\omega)$, respectively, for $k = 1, 2, \ldots$
The random variables $\mathbf{t}_k$ defined by (4) are called *transition times*.

The stochastic processes so defined depend on the initial condition for the SHS. To emphasize this dependence we sometimes use P_{z_0} and E_{z_0} to denote the probability measure and expected value corresponding to the initial condition $z_0 := (q_0, x_0, t_0) \in \mathcal{Q} \times \mathbb{R}^n \times [0, \infty)$.

Step 1 provides the initialization for all the stochastic processes. Step 3 guarantees that the discrete state remains constant and the continuous state flows according to (1) between transitions. Step 4 enforces that the continuous and discrete states are reset according to (2) at transition times. The frequency at which these occur is determined by Step 2. In fact, one can derive from (4) [13] that

$$\lim_{dt \downarrow 0} \frac{P\left(\mathbf{N}_\ell(t + dt) > \mathbf{N}_\ell(t)\right)}{dt} = \lim_{dt \downarrow 0} E\left[\frac{1}{dt} \int_t^{t+dt} \lambda_\ell(\mathbf{q}(t), \varphi(s; t, \mathbf{q}(t), \mathbf{x}(t)), s) ds\right],$$

$$(5)$$

which shows that the probability $P\left(\mathbf{N}_\ell(t + dt) > \mathbf{N}_\ell(t)\right)$ that the transition ϕ_ℓ will occur in an (arbitrarily) small interval $(t, t+dt]$ is proportional to the length of the interval with the proportionality constant given by the right-hand-side of (5). This equation specifies the precise meaning of the observation made above to the extent that "the probability that the counter $\mathbf{N}_\ell$ will increment in an elementary interval $(t, t + dt]$ is given by $\lambda_\ell(\mathbf{q}(t), \mathbf{x}(t), t)dt$." Note that when λ_ℓ is continuous, the right-hand-side of (5) is precisely equal to $\mathrm{E}[\lambda_\ell(\mathbf{q}(t), \mathbf{x}(t), t)]$.

The above construction guarantees that the sample-paths are indeed right-continuous and have left-limits at every point with probability one. However, without further assumptions there is no guarantee that the sample path are defined globally on $[0, \infty)$. We will return to this issue later.

2.2   Generalizations

The model for stochastic hybrid systems presented above is more general than it may appear at first. We discuss next some of the generalizations possible and refer the reader to [13] for a discussion of their implication on the results in Sect. 3.

The model allows for transitions where the *next state is chosen according to a given distribution*. For example, suppose one would like the intensity $\lambda(\mathbf{q}, \mathbf{x}, t)$ to trigger transitions to the discrete-states q_1 or q_2 with probabilities p_1 or $1 - p_1$, respectively. This could be achieved by considering two transitions with intensities $p_1\lambda(\mathbf{q}, \mathbf{x}, t)$ and $(1 - p_1)\lambda(\mathbf{q}, \mathbf{x}, t)$, respectively, and reset maps $\phi_1(q, x, t) = (q_1, \varphi_1(x, t), t)$ and $\phi_2(q, x, t) = (q_2, \varphi_2(x, t), t)$, respectively, where the φ_i denote (possibly distinct) continuous-state resets.

The above model does not directly consider differential equations *driven by stochastic processes*. However, many important classes of stochastic processes can be obtained as the limit of jump processes that can be modeled by SHSs. For example, the stochastic differential equation

$$\dot{\mathbf{x}} = a\mathbf{x} + b\dot{\mathbf{w}} \qquad . \qquad (6)$$

where $\mathbf{w}$ denotes Brownian motion, can be regarded as the limit as $\epsilon \downarrow 0$ of the jump system with continuous dynamics $\dot{\mathbf{x}} = a\mathbf{x}$ and resets $\mathbf{x} \mapsto \mathbf{x} + b\sqrt{\epsilon}$ and $\mathbf{x} \mapsto \mathbf{x} - b\sqrt{\epsilon}$ both triggered with fixed intensity $\frac{1}{2\epsilon}$. We can therefore model continuous evolutions of the form (6) as limits to a sequences of SHSs.

The basic model also does not directly consider *discrete transitions triggered by deterministic conditions of the state*, e.g., a guard being crossed. However, this behavior can also be obtained as the limiting solution to a sequence of SHSs. Consider for example the well known bouncing-ball single-mode deterministic hybrid system with dynamics $\ddot{x} = -g$, $g > 0$ and state reset $(x, \dot{x}) \mapsto (0, -c\dot{x})$, $c \in (0, 1)$ triggered by the condition $\dot{x} < 0$ and $x \leq 0$. We could approximate this system by a sequence of SHSs for which the resets are triggered with intensities given by a "barrier function" of the form

$$\lambda_k(x) := \begin{cases} \epsilon e^{-x/\epsilon} & \dot{x} < 0 \\ 0 & \dot{x} > 0, \end{cases} \qquad \epsilon > 0. \qquad (7)$$

As $\epsilon \downarrow 0$, transitions will occur in a small neighborhood of $x = 0$ with increasingly higher probability. Figure 2 shows confidence intervals for the sample-paths of three SHSs that approximate with increased accuracy the deterministic bouncing-ball. It is important to emphasize that, for any $\epsilon > 0$, the sample paths of the SHSs are globally defined with probability one. This approach may in fact be a promising technique to overcome difficulties posed by the Zeno phenomena that occur for the deterministic bouncing-ball system [18].

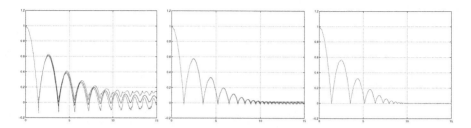

Fig. 2. 95% confidence intervals for the **x** sample paths of three SHS that approximate the bouncing-ball deterministic system with Zeno time equal to 10. The transition intensities of the SHSs are given by (7) with $\epsilon = 10^{-2}$, 10^{-3}, 10^{-4} from left to right. These results were obtained via Monte Carlo simulations.

3   Generator for SHSs

In this section we provide a result to compute expectations on the state of a SHS. The following assumptions are needed:

Assumption 2.   *(i)   The transition intensities $\lambda_\ell : \mathcal{Q} \times \mathbb{R}^n \times [0, \infty) \to [0, \infty)$, $\ell \in \{1, \dots, m\}$ are measurable functions (e.g., continuous).*
(ii) For every initial condition $z_0 := (q_0, x_0, t_0) \in \mathcal{Q} \times \mathbb{R}^n$ there exists a continuous functions $\alpha_{z_0} : [0, \infty) \to [0, \infty)$ such that the sample-paths are defined globally and $\|\mathbf{x}(t)\| \leq \alpha_{z_0}(t)$, $\forall t \geq t_0$ with probability one with respect to P_{z_0}. ☐

Assumption 2(ii) may be difficult to check, but we will shortly provide conditions that are more friendly to verify. We are now ready to state the main result of this section. Due to space limitations, we refer the reader to [13] for its proof.

Theorem 1. *Suppose that Assumptions 1 and 2 hold. For every initial condition $z_0 := (q_0, x_0, t_0) \in \mathcal{Q} \times \mathbb{R}^n \times [0, \infty)$ and every function $\psi : \mathcal{Q} \times \mathbb{R}^n \times [0, \infty) \to \mathbb{R}$ that is continuously differentiable with respect to its second and third arguments, we have that*

$$\mathrm{E}_{z_0}[\psi(\mathbf{q}(t), \mathbf{x}(t), t)] = \psi(q_0, x_0, t_0) + \mathrm{E}_{z_0}\left[\int_{t_0}^{t} (L\psi)(\mathbf{q}(s), \mathbf{x}(s), s)ds\right], \quad (8)$$

where $\forall (q, x, t) \in \mathcal{Q} \times \mathbb{R}^n \times [0, \infty)$

$$(L\psi)(q,x,t) := \frac{\partial\psi(q,x,t)}{\partial x}f(q,x,t) + \frac{\partial\psi(q,x,t)}{\partial t} +$$

$$+ \sum_{\ell=1}^{m}\Big(\psi\big(\phi_\ell(q,x,t),t\big) - \psi(q,x,t)\Big)\lambda_\ell(q,x,t), \quad (9)$$

and $\frac{\partial\psi(q,x,t)}{\partial x}$ and $\frac{\partial\psi(q,x,t)}{\partial t}$ denote the gradient of $\psi(q,x,t)$ with respect to x and the partial derivative of $\psi(q,x,t)$ with respect to t, respectively. □

Following [9], we call the operator $\psi \mapsto L\psi$ defined by (9) the *extended generator* of the SHS. It is often convenient to write (8) in the following differential form[1]

$$\frac{\partial \mathrm{E}[\psi(\mathbf{q}(t),\mathbf{x}(t),t)]}{\partial t} = \mathrm{E}[(L\psi)(\mathbf{q}(t),\mathbf{x}(t),t)].$$

Assumption 2(ii) rules out finite escape time almost surely. Although this is a mild requirement, it may be difficult to verify directly. The following lemma provides a condition that is more restrictive but easily checkable:

Lemma 1. *[13] Let $\phi_\ell^x : \mathcal{Q} \times \mathbb{R}^n \times [0,\infty) \to \mathbb{R}^n$, $\ell \in \{1,\dots,m\}$ denote the projection of ϕ_ℓ into $\mathbb{R}^n$ [i.e., $\phi_\ell^x(q,x,t) = \bar{x}$ where $(\bar{q},\bar{x}) = \phi_\ell(q,x,t)$]. Assumptions 2(ii) holds, if there exists a continuous function $\gamma_f : [0,\infty) \to [0,\infty)$ and constants c_f, c_ϕ such that*

$$\|f(q,x,t)\| \le \max\{\gamma_f(t)\|x\|, c_f\}, \qquad \|\phi_\ell^x(q,x,t)\| \le \max\{\|x\|, c_\phi\},$$

$\forall q \in \mathcal{Q}, x \in \mathbb{R}^n, t \ge 0, \ell \in \{1,\dots,m\}$. □

This lemma essentially requires f and the ϕ_ℓ to have linear growth in x over $\mathbb{R}^n$. Moreover, the growth constant of the ϕ_ℓ must not be larger than one. This is a strong requirement and one might be tempted to think that it could be replaced by a local condition if one would restrict one's attention to a finite time interval $[0,T]$, $T < \infty$. It turns out that in general this is not true, as shown in [13] by counter example.

4   A Stochastic Model for TCP Flows

In this section we present a SHSs model for a single-user on-off TCP flow based on the hybrid modeling framework proposed by [6]. The model is represented graphically in Figure 3. It has two continuous states—TCP's congestion window size $\mathbf{w}$ and the cumulative number of packets sent in a particular connection $\mathbf{s}$—and three discrete states $\{off, ss, ca\}$. During the *off* mode the flow is inactive and no packets are transmitted. The *ss* mode corresponds to TCP's slow-start and during this mode the window size $\mathbf{w}$ increases exponentially. The *ca* mode corresponds to TCP's congestion-avoidance and during this mode $\mathbf{w}$ increases linearly. In any of the active modes, $\mathbf{w}$ packets are sent each round-trip time RTT, leading to a packet transmission rate $\dot{\mathbf{s}} = \mathbf{r} := \frac{\mathbf{w}}{RTT}$. The reader is referred to [13] for further details. The transitions between modes occur as follows:

---

[1] Recall that all signals are right-continuous with probability one and derivatives should be understood as right-limits.

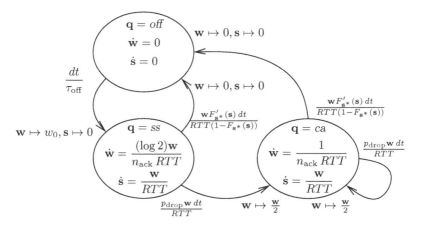

Fig. 3. Stochastic hybrid model for a TCP flow, where n_{ack} denotes the number of data packets acknowledged per each ACK packet received and $w_0 := .693$ when $n_{ack} = 1$ or $w_0 := 1.428$ when $n_{ack} = 2$.

1. Drops occurrences—which correspond to transitions from the ss or the ca modes to the ca mode—occur at a rate $p_{drop}\mathbf{r}$, where p_{drop} denotes the per-packet drop probability and $\mathbf{r} := \frac{\mathbf{w}}{RTT}$ the packet sending rate.
2. The start of new flows—which correspond to the transitions from the off to the ss mode—occur at a rate $\frac{1}{\tau_{off}}$. This is consistent with an exponentially distributed duration of the off periods with average τ_{off}.
3. The termination of flows—which correspond to transitions from the ss and ca modes to the off mode—occur at a rate $\frac{\mathbf{r}F'_{\mathbf{s}^*}(\mathbf{s})}{1-F_{\mathbf{s}^*}(\mathbf{s})}$. This is consistent with a distribution $F_{\mathbf{s}^*} : [0, \infty) \to [0, 1]$ for the number $\mathbf{s}^*$ of packets sent in each TCP session [13].

We focus our attention on two specific instances of the general model in Figure 3:

Exponential sizes. This model is obtained by assuming that the number of packets to transmit is exponentially distributed with mean k, i.e., $F_{\mathbf{s}^*}(s) = 1 - e^{-\frac{s}{k}}, \forall s \geq 0$.

Mixed-exponential sizes. It has been observed that modeling the distribution of transfer-sizes as an exponential is an over-simplification. For example, it has been observed that heavy-tail models are more fitting to experimental data (cf., e.g., [1,2]). An alternative that turns out to be computationally attractive and still fits reasonably well with experimental data is a mixture of exponentials. According to this model, transfer-sizes are sampled from a family of M exponential random variables $\mathbf{s}_i$, $i \in \{1, 2, \ldots, M\}$ by selecting a sample from the ith random variable $\mathbf{s}_i$ with probability p_i. Each $\mathbf{s}_i$ corresponds to a distinct mean transfer-size k_i. To model this as a SHS, we consider M alternative $\{ss_i, ca_i : i = 1, 2, \ldots, M\}$ modes, each corresponding to a specific exponential distribution for the transfer-sizes. The transition from the inactive mode *off* to the slow-start mode ss_i corresponding to a mean transfer-size of k_i occurs with probability p_i.

4.1   Analysis of the TCP SHS Models

To investigate the dynamics of the moments of the sending rate $\mathbf{r}(t) = \frac{\mathbf{w}(t)}{RTT(t)}$ for the mixed-exponentials TCP model, $\forall n \geq 0$, $q_0 \in \mathcal{Q}$ let

$$\mu_{q_0,n}(t) := \mathrm{E}\left[\psi_{q_0,n}(\mathbf{q}(t), \mathbf{w}(t), t)\right], \quad \psi_{q_0,n}(q, w, t) := \begin{cases} \frac{w^n}{RTT(t)^n} & q = q_0 \\ 0 & \text{otherwise.} \end{cases}$$

The following result can be obtained by directly applying Theorem 1 to the SHS TCP model. Details of the computations can be found in [13].

Theorem 2 (Full-order models). *For the mixed-exponentials model in Sect. 4 we have*[2]

$$\dot{\mu}_{\mathrm{off},0} = -\frac{\mu_{\mathrm{off},0}}{\tau_{\mathrm{off}}} + \sum_{j=1}^{M} k_j^{-1}(\mu_{ss_j,1} + \mu_{ca_j,1}) \tag{10}$$

$$\dot{\mu}_{ss_i,n} = \frac{p_i w_0^n \mu_{\mathrm{off},0}}{\tau_{\mathrm{off}} RTT^n} + n \frac{(\log 2) - n_{\mathrm{ack}} \dot{RTT}}{n_{\mathrm{ack}} RTT} \mu_{ss_i,n} - (p_{\mathrm{drop}} + k_i^{-1})\mu_{ss_i,n+1} \tag{11}$$

$$\dot{\mu}_{ca_i,n} = \frac{n \mu_{ca_i,n-1}}{n_{\mathrm{ack}} RTT^2} - \frac{n \dot{RTT} \mu_{ca_i,n}}{RTT} - (p_{\mathrm{drop}} + k_i^{-1})\mu_{ca_i,n+1}$$
$$+ \frac{p_{\mathrm{drop}}}{2^n}(\mu_{ss_i,n+1} + \mu_{ca_i,n+1}). \tag{12}$$

4.2   Reduced-Order Model

The system of infinitely many differential equations that appear in Theorem 2 describes exactly the evolution of the moments of the sending rate $\mathbf{r}$ but finding the exact solution to these equations does not appear to be simple. However, as noted by [4], Monte Carlo simulations reveal that the steady-state distribution of the sending rate is often well approximated by a Log-Normal distribution. Assuming that on each mode the sending rate $\mathbf{r}$ approximately obeys a Log-Normal distribution even during transients, we can truncate the systems of infinitely many differential equations that appear in Theorem 2. We recall that, if the random variable $\mathbf{x}$ has a Log-Normal distribution then $\mathrm{E}[\mathbf{x}^3] = \frac{\mathrm{E}[\mathbf{x}^2]^3}{\mathrm{E}[\mathbf{x}]^3}$. Therefore if $\mathbf{r}$ is approximately Log-Normal distributed in the mode $q \in \mathcal{Q}$, we have that

$$\mu_{q,3} = \mu_{q,0} \mathrm{E}[\mathbf{r}^3 \mid \mathbf{q} = q] \approx \mu_{q,0} \frac{\mathrm{E}[\mathbf{r}^2 \mid \mathbf{q} = q]^3}{\mathrm{E}[\mathbf{r} \mid \mathbf{q} = q]^3} = \frac{\mu_{q,0} \mu_{q,2}^3}{\mu_{q,1}^3}, \tag{13}$$

---

[2] To simplify the notation, we omit the time-dependence of RTT and p_{drop}.

where we used the fact that

$$\mu_{q,n} = P(\mathbf{q} = q) \, E[\mathbf{r}^n \mid \mathbf{q} = q] = \mu_{q,0} \, E[\mathbf{r}^n \mid \mathbf{q} = q].$$

Using (13) in (10)–(12), we can eliminate any terms $\mu_{q_0,n}$, $n \geq 3$ in the equations for $\dot{\mu}_{q_0,n}$, $n \leq 2$, thus can constructing a finite-dimensional model to approximately describe the dynamics of the first two moments of the sending rate. We present next simulations of this reduced model for a few representative parameter values.

Figure 4 corresponds to a transfer-size distribution that results from the mixture of two exponentials ($M = 2$) with parameters

$$p_1 = 88.87\%, \qquad k_1 = 3.5\text{KB}, \qquad p_2 = 11.13\%, \qquad k_2 = 246\text{KB}. \qquad (14)$$

The first exponential corresponds to small "mice" transfers (3.5KB average) and the second to "elephant" mid-size transfers (246KB average). The small transfers are assumed more common (88.87%). These parameters result in a distribution with an average transfer-size of 30.58KB and for which 11.13% of the transfers account for 89.7% of the total volume transfered. This is consistent with the file distribution observed in the UNIX file system [16]. However, it does not accurately capture the tail of the distribution (it lacks the "mammoth" files that will be considered later). The results obtained with the reduced model match reasonably well those obtained from Monte Carlo simulations of the full SHS model, especially taking into account the very large standard deviations. It is worth it to point out that the simulation of the reduced model takes just a few seconds, whereas each Monte Carlo simulation takes several hours of CPU.

Two somewhat surprising conclusions can be drawn from Figure 4 for this distribution of transfer-sizes and off-times:

1. The *average total sending rate varies very little with the drop rate* (at least up to the drop rate of 33% shown in the plots), with most of the packets transmitted belonging to "elephant" mid-size transfers.
2. The *dynamics of TCP are completely dominated by second order moments.* In Figure 4, the standard deviation is 5 to 20 times larger than the average sending rate, which is very accurately predicted by the reduced model.

This behavior is completely different from the one observed for TCP flows that are always on, for which it has been shown that the steady-state average sending rate is approximately given by $\frac{c}{RTT\sqrt{p_{\text{drop}}}}$, where RTT denotes the average round-trip time, p_{drop} the per-packet drop rate, and c a constant ranging from 1.225 to 1.310 depending on the method used to derive the equation [26,23,24, 14,5].

We considered next a transfer-size distribution that results from a mixture of three exponentials ($M = 3$) with parameters

$$p_1 = 98\%, \ k_1 = 6\text{KB}, \ p_2 = 1.7\%, \ k_2 = 400\text{KB}, \ p_3 = .02\%, \ k_3 = 10\text{MB}. \quad (15)$$

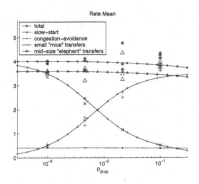 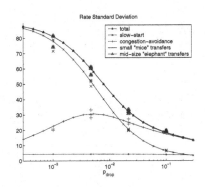

Fig. 4. Steady-state values for the average (left) and standard deviation (right) of the sending rate as a function of the drop probability. The solid lines were obtained from the reduced model whereas the (larger) symbols were obtained from Monte Carlo simulations, with $RTT = 50$ms, $n_{ack} = 1$, a transfer-size distribution resulting from the mixture of two exponentials with parameters in (14), and mean off-time $\tau_{off} = 5$sec.

The first exponential corresponds to small "mice" transfers, the second to mid-size "elephant" transfers, and the third to large "mammoth" transfers. The resulting distribution approximates the one reported by [1] obtained from monitoring transfers from a world-wide web proxy within an Internet Service Provider. This distribution has a much heavier tail than the one considered before.

Figure 5 contains results obtained from the reduced model. We do not present Monte Carlo results because the simulation times needed to capture the tails of the transfer-size distribution are prohibitively large. It turns out that the main conclusions drawn before still hold: the average sending rate varies relatively little with the drop rate and the dynamics of TCP are completely dominated by second order moments. The mid-size "elephants" still dominate followed by the small "mice." The large "mammoth" transfers occur at a rate that is not sufficiently large to have a significant impact on the average sending rate.

5   Conclusions

This paper presents a new model for SHSs where transitions between discrete modes are triggered by stochastic events, which occur at rates that are allowed to depend on both the continuous and the discrete states of the SHS. Based on results available for Piecewise-Deterministic Markov Process (PDPs), we provide a formula for the extended generator of the SHS.

As an illustration, we presented a SHS model for on-off TCP flows that considers both slow-start and congestion avoidance. One important observation that stems from this work is that for realistic transfer-size distributions high-order statistical moments seem to dominate the dynamics of TCP. Also, the probability of drop appears to have a much larger effect on the standard deviation of the sending rate than on its mean value. We are currently investigating the

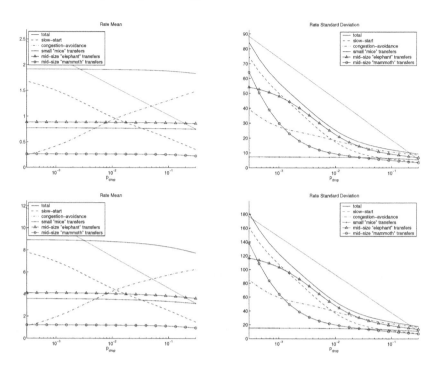

Fig. 5. Steady-state values for the average (left) and standard deviation (right) of the sending rate as a function of the drop probability. These results were obtained from the reduced model, with $RTT = 50$ms, $n_{\text{ack}} = 1$, and a transfer-size distribution resulting from the mixture of three exponentials with the parameters in (15). The mean off time was set to $\tau_{\text{off}} = 5$sec (top) and 1sec (bottom).

impact of this observation on the stability and performance of congestion control mechanisms.

This work opens several avenues for future research. We would like to determine conditions under which Assumption 2(ii) holds, milder than those required by Lemma 1. It is also worth to investigate how solutions to deterministic hybrid systems that exist only in a finite interval due to Zeno phenomena can be globally extended using SHSs. Finally, one needs to develop general tools to approximate the dynamics of SHSs by finite-dimensional systems of ODEs, as was done for the TCP example.

Acknowledgments. The author would like to thank Roger Brockett for providing a preprint of [7]; Martin Arlitt for making available the processed data regarding the transfer-size distribution reported in [1]; Sanjoy Mitter and John Lygeros for provided several relevant references; and Stephan Bohacek, Yonggang Xu, Guillaume Bonnet, and the anonymous reviewers for insightful comments.

References

[1] M. Arlitt, R. Friedrich, and T. Jin. Workload characterization of a web proxy in a cable modem environment. Technical Report HPL-1999-48, Hwelett-Packard Laroratories, Palo Alto, CA, Apr. 1999.

[2] P. Barford, A. Bestavros, A. Bradley, and M. Crovella. Changes in web client access patterns. *World Wide Web,* Special Issue on Characterization and Performance Evaluation, 2(1–2):15–28, 1999.

[3] K. Benjelloun and E. K. Boukas. Mean square stochastic stability of linear time-delay system with Markovian jumping parameters. *IEEE Trans. on Automat. Contr.,* 43(10):1456–1460, Oct. 1998.

[4] S. Bohacek. A stochastic model of TCP and fair video transmission. In *Proc. of the IEEE INFOCOM,* 2003.

[5] S. Bohacek, J. P. Hespanha, J. Lee, and K. Obraczka. Analysis of a TCP hybrid model. In *Proc. of the 39th Annual Allerton Conf. on Comm., Contr., and Computing,* Oct. 2001.

[6] S. Bohacek, J. P. Hespanha, J. Lee, and K. Obraczka. A hybrid systems modeling framework for fast and accurate simulation of data communication networks. In *Proc. of the ACM Int. Conf. on Measurements and Modeling of Computer Systems (SIGMETRICS),* June 2003.

[7] R. Brockett. Lecture notes on stochastic control. Provided by the author, 2002.

[8] O. L. V. Costa and M. D. Fragoso. Stability results for discrete-time linear systems with Markovian jumping parameters. *J. Mathematical Anal. and Applications,* 179:154–178, 1993.

[9] M. H. A. Davis. *Markov models and optimization.* Monographs on statistics and applied probability. Chapman & Hall, London, UK, 1993.

[10] Y. Fang and K. A. Loparo. Stabilization of continuous-time jump linear systems. *IEEE Trans. on Automat. Contr.,* 47(10):1590–1603, Oct. 2002.

[11] J. A. Filar, V. Gaitsgory, and A. B. Haurie. Control of singularly perturbed hybrid stochastic systems. *IEEE Trans. on Automat. Contr.,* 46(2):179–190, Feb. 2001.

[12] M. K. Ghosh, A. Arapostathis, and S. Marcus. Ergodic control of switching diffusions. *SIAM J. Contr. Optimization,* 35(6):1952–1988, Nov. 1997.

[13] J. P. Hespanha. Stochastic hybrid systems: Application to communication networks (extended version). Technical report, Dept. of Electrical and Computer Eng., University of California, Santa Barbara, Jan. 2004.

[14] J. P. Hespanha, S. Bohacek, K. Obraczka, and J. Lee. Hybrid modeling of TCP congestion control. In M. D. D. Benedetto and A. Sangiovanni-Vincentelli, editors, *Hybrid Systems: Computation and Control,* number 2034 in Lect. Notes in Comput. Science, pages 291–304. Springer-Verlag, Berlin, Mar. 2001.

[15] J. Hu, J. Lygeros, and S. Sastry. Towards a theory of stochastic hybrid systems. In N. A. Lynch and B. H. Krogh, editors, *Hybrid Systems: Computation and Control,* volume 1790 of *Lect. Notes in Comput. Science,* pages 160–173. Springer, 2000.

[16] G. Irlam. Unix file size survey – 1993. Available at http://www.base.com/gordoni/ufs93.html, Nov. 1994.

[17] J. Jacod and A. N. Shiriaev. *Limit Theorems for Stochastic Processes.* Springer Verlag, 2nd edition, 2002.

[18] K. H. Johansson, M. Egerstedt, J. Lygeros, and S. Sastry. On the regularization of Zeno hybrid automata. *Syst. & Contr. Lett.,* 38:141–150, 1999.

[19] S. Kunniyur and R. Srikant. Analysis and design of an adaptive virtual queue (AVQ) algorithm for active queue management. In *Proc. of the ACM SIGCOMM,* San Diego, California, USA, 8 2001.

[20] A. Lakshmikantha, C. Beck, and R. Srikant. Robustness of real and virtual queue based active queue management schemes. In *Proc. of the 2003 Amer. Contr. Conf.*, pages 266–271, June 2003.

[21] S. H. Low. A duality model of TCP and queue management algorithms. *IEEE/ACM Trans. on Networking*, Oct. 2003. To appear.

[22] S. H. Low, F. Paganini, and J. C. Doyle. Internet congestion control. *IEEE Contr. Syst. Mag.*, 22(1):28–43, Feb. 2002.

[23] J. Mahdavi and S. Floyd. TCP-friendly unicast rate-based flow control. Technical note sent to the end2end-interest mailing list, Jan. 1997.

[24] M. Mathis, J. Semke, J. Mahdavi, and T. Ott. The macroscopic behavior of the TCP congestion avoidance algorithm. *ACM Comput. Comm. Review*, 27(3), July 1997.

[25] V. Misra, W. Gong, and D. Towsley. Stochastic differential equation modeling and analysis of TCP-windowsize behavior. In *Proc. of PERFORMANCE'99*, Istanbul, Turkey, 1999.

[26] T. Ott, J. H. B. Kemperman, and M. Mathis. Window size behavior in TCP/IP with constant loss probability. In *Proc. of the DIMACS Workshop on Performance of Realtime Applications on the Internet*, Nov. 1996.

[27] J. Padhye, V. Firoiu, D. Towsley, and J. Kurose. Modeling TCP Reno performance: A simple model and its empirical validation. *IEEE/ACM Trans. on Networking*, 8(2):133–145, Apr. 2000.

[28] G. Pola, M. L. Bujorianu, J. Lygeros, and M. D. D. Benedetto. Stochastic hybrid models: An overview. In *Proc. of the IFAC Conf .on Anal. and Design of Hybrid Syst.*, June 2003.

[29] S. Shakkottai and R. Srikant. How good are deterministic fluid models of Internet congestion control? In *Proc. of the IEEE INFOCOM*, June 2002.

[30] B. Sikdar, S. Kalyanaraman, and K. Vastola. Analytic models for the latency and steady-state throughput of TCP Tahoe, Reno and SACK. In *Proc. of the IEEE GLOBECOM*, pages 25–29, 2001.

[31] L. Xiao and A. H. J. P. How. Control with random communication delays via a discrete-time jump system approach. In *Proc. of the 2000 Amer. Contr. Conf.*, volume 3, pages 2199–2204, June 2000.

Rigorous Modeling of Hybrid Systems Using Interval Arithmetic Constraints

Timothy J. Hickey and David K. Wittenberg

Computer Science Department, Brandeis University
{tim,dkw}@cs.brandeis.edu

Abstract. We provide a rigorous approach to modeling, simulating, and analyzing hybrid systems using CLP(F) (Constraint Logic Programming (Functions)) [14], a system which combines CLP (Constraint Language Programming) [21] with interval arithmetic [30]. We have implemented this system, and provide timing information. Because hybrid systems are often used to prove safety properties, it is critical to have a rigorous analysis. By using intervals throughout the system, we make it easier to include measurement errors in our models and to prove safety properties.

1 Introduction

We wish to rigorously model hybrid systems. Because models of hybrid systems are often used in safety-critical applications, it is crucial to get accurate results with explicit limits on the errors in the model and calculations. This requires a rigorous approach. Any technique to model these systems which does not account for rounding error or error in the approximation to the solution of the ODEs governing the problem is not rigorous. We use interval arithmetic to provide an explicit limit on rounding errors and on the ODE solution errors.

Interval arithmetic [30][2] is an obvious choice for modeling hybrid systems, as the interface between the analog and the digital part involves imperfect hardware whose description must include error bars. Intervals are a very clear way of explicitly expressing error bars. Because constraint logic programming (CLP) [21] provides constraints on the range of values that each variable can take on, it is well suited to describing intervals and to proving safety properties.

We use CLP(F) [14], a CLP language with explicit support for interval arithmetic and function variables, to model hybrid systems. Our approach has a formal model (inherited from the formal semantics of CLP) so the results generated by our system can be thought of as theorems about the behavior of the underlying mathematical model of the hybrid system. These theorems can also be used as lemmas in proofs about safety properties of real hybrid systems.

To demonstrate the CLP(F) approach to hybrid system modeling, we consider the hybrid system of two interacting water tanks described by Stursberg *et al.* [33] and later studied by Henzinger *et al.* [13]. We provide a one page CLP(F) program for simulating and analyzing the two tanks problem.

R. Alur and G.J. Pappas (Eds.): HSCC 2004, LNCS 2993, pp. 402–416, 2004.

2   Related Work

In this paper we describe a practical tool for modeling and analyzing hybrid systems. Our tool has a simple formal logical semantics and is based on interval arithmetic and constraint logic programming. This paper represents the first attempt to combine these approaches to build a practical tool for rigorously proving properties of hybrid systems governed by non-linear ODEs as well as digital logic. In this section we describe the related work on which this paper builds. These foundations are in three separate areas: Hybrid systems, constraint logic programming, and interval arithmetic.

2.1   Formal Models of Hybrid Systems

There has been considerable research on developing formal models of hybrid systems. Among others, Davoren and Nerode developed logics [4], Maler *et al.* [28], Lynch *et al.* [27] [26], Henzinger *et al.* [11], and Alur *et al.* [1] developed formal models. From our point of view, a limitation of these models is the difficulty in applying them to real systems, and the amount of overhead that must be relied on to trust the results.

Another major research push has been in the development of practical tools for modeling and analyzing realistic hybrid systems. For example, Kowalewski *et al.* [23] describe eight such systems (Matlab, Simulink, gPROMS, Shift, Dymola, BASIP, SMV, HyTech) that can be applied to model and/or analyze fairly complex hybrid systems. All of these systems sacrifice some degree of rigor in order to handle moderately complex hybrid systems. For example, HyTech does not allow the physical system to be governed by ODEs, the other systems that do allow ODEs use some form of approximation that introduces errors which are then ignored. The simulation based systems rely on the user to correctly identify the worst case when there is a non-deterministic choice.

2.2   CLP Approaches to Hybrid Systems

Constraint Logic Programming (CLP) grew from a merger of logic programming and constraint solving. In CLP, everything (including i/o, queries, and answers) is a constraint. CLP uses backtracking to provide all the sets of values which satisfy a query. Jaffar and Maher's [21] survey provides an excellent introduction to CLP.

We are not the first to use constraint logic programming to model and analyze hybrid systems. Gupta *et al.* [10][9] introduced a ground breaking approach called "hybrid cc" which allowed one to formally describe hybrid systems using a logic programming language with constraints. The resulting models automatically inherit a formal logical semantics from the underlying language thereby allowing program results to be interpreted as formal theorems. The main disadvantage of their approach is that they were restricted to hybrid systems with linear ODEs.

Urbina [34] has pioneered another approach using CLP($\mathcal{R}$) to model and analyze hybrid systems. This approach also suffers from a lack of rigor in the handling of the underlying dynamic systems (the CLP($\mathcal{R}$) system uses floating point arithmetic and does not account for roundoff error, moreover, it can only directly solve linear constraints).

Delzanno and Podelski [6][7] have explored analyzing hybrid systems using CLP(Q,R) [18], a system which handles linear constraints with real and/or rational coefficients, as well as Boolean constraints. Their approach is to define a translator from Shankar's guarded command language [31] to CLP(Q,R). The system is not able to handle general non-linear ODEs rigorously.

2.3   Interval Arithmetic

The standard method of describing non-integer numbers on a computer is to use a finite set of floating point numbers to model an infinite set of real numbers. Floating point numbers [22] do not have the nice properties (associativity, commutativity ...) that we learned in third grade that all numbers have. This introduces a class of round-off errors in which mathematically equivalent operations give different results. One approach to these problems is interval arithmetic. Interval arithmetic [30] uses an interval (X_{min}, X_{max}) to represent each real number X. The true value of X is within the interval representing X. Hickey, Ju, and van Emden [17] have shown that by careful use of IEEE 754 [19] rounding directives, it is possible to soundly perform arithmetic operations on intervals with floating point numbers as end points. Edalat and Heckmann [8] use "linear fractional transformations", in which they use infinite precision rationals as the end points of intervals, and calculate as much precision as is needed. This is a sort of lazy evaluation.

We are not the first to apply interval arithmetic techniques to the problem of rigorously modeling hybrid systems. HyperTech [13] take a major step towards reliability of their results by using interval arithmetic ODE solving as a tool to add rigor to the very successful HyTech system. This system merges, for the first time, the rigor of the formal model approaches and the practicality of the more engineering-based approaches by employing validated ODE solving.

HyperTech does standard hybrid automata calculations while using intervals in the calculations, rather than as the fundamental unit. This is partially because HyperTech grew out of HyTech [12] which does all its calculations with infinite precision rationals.

3   Benefits of an Interval Arithmetic Constraints Approach

Our approach can be thought of as combining Henzinger *et al.*'s innovation in using interval arithmetic and Urbina's [34] and Gupta *et al.*'s [9] use of constraint systems with the semantic elegance of the logic programming approach.

In addition, this combination yields some new and potentially useful capabilities, which we highlight in this paper. We use an interval arithmetic ODE constraint solver that automatically and rigorously accounts for the sources of error which other systems often do not handle (choice of case for non-deterministic systems, round-off error, approximation error for the ODEs, ...) and is able to handle highly non-linear ODEs with full mathematical rigor. We use intervals for all calculations (to provide over-approximations to deal with rounding error) and for all measurements (to model the inevitable error-bars of instruments). We avoid the "modeling error" of other interval arithmetic based ODE approaches by explicitly expressing the ODE as a constraint on function variables. We do this by modeling the system declaratively as a CLP(F) [15] program in which the differential equations appear directly as constraints in the program. The underlying constraint solver allows function variables which may be constrained by non-linear ODEs to generate interval results. The system makes careful use of the IEEE 754 [19] floating point rounding directives to obtain provably correct numeric results from standard processors. The resulting CLP(F) program has the property that the results computed using the CLP(F) system are guaranteed to contain all solutions of the ODEs modeled by the constraints. This soundness property is inherited from CLP [20][21].

One of the major benefits of this approach is that the problem of analyzing the hybrid system is transformed into the problem of analyzing the corresponding CLP(F) program. In principle, one should be able to apply well understood program analysis techniques [32][16][5] to this program and directly infer provable properties of the corresponding hybrid system. Also the constraint language for specifying ODEs is very expressive and quite close to standard mathematical notation. Here we describe only the simpler types of analysis that one can do by directly solving CLP(F) constraints related to the hybrid system.

A further advantage of our approach is that the system is quite simple, and the programs remarkably simple. We provide the complete program for analyzing the two tanks problem as Figure 1 and Figure 2. The code fits on one page. This makes the argument for the correctness of a result from the system less complex to state. By making the argument for correctness of the system simpler (because the system itself is simpler), we make it less likely that there will be an error in the proof of correctness.

4   CLP(F)

The language CLP(F) [14] is a constraint logic programming language [20][21] in which the constraints specify arithmetic and analytic relations among real and function variables. CLP(F) is related to QSIM [24] in that each attempts to find an over approximation of the possible states of a system of ODEs (QSIM uses the term "qualitative behaviours") .

4.1   Analytic Constraints in CLP(F)

In CLP(F) the constraint domain allows one to declare variables representing various analytic values including:

- *real numbers, X*
- *infinitely differentiable functions, F, on a finite interval [a,b]*
- *vectors of numbers, functions, or vectors*

A full description of the language is available [15] [14]. In this section, we provide a brief overview of the language, its semantics, its implementation, and its use.

As is common in CLP languages, the constraints are enclosed in curly braces "{}". The different types of variables are declared using the **type** predicate. The CLP(F) interpreter provides answers to queries in the form of a sequence of solution sets, where each solution set provides a real interval for each of the constraint variables. The soundness property of CLP implies that every correct solution to the query must be contained in one of the solution sets (assuming that the program eventually terminates). On the other hand, not every element of the solution set is guaranteed to be a solution (and indeed, there may not be any actual solutions in any particular solution set returned by the interpreter).

Rigorous Numeric Constraint Solving. The CLP(F) constraint language allows one to express any algebraic or trigonometric equality or inequality constraint among real variables. For example,

```
| ?- {X^2=2,X>0}.
X = 1.41421356237309... ? ;
no
| ?-
```

The CLP(F) interpreter represents the interval for X in a compact form. The ellipsis "..." indicates that all shown digits are correct and hence X must lie in the interval:

```
[1.41421356237309,
 1.41421356237310)
```

Also, note that the user entered a semi-colon after the solution and the interpreter responded with "no" which indicates that there are no more solutions.

Multiple Solutions and Non-determinism. Sometimes there maybe more than one solution to a given constraint. The constraint solver will indicate this by returning an interval that contains all solutions:

```
| ?- {X^2=2}.
X = [-1.4142135623730953675192267837,
     1.4142135623730953675192267837] ?
no
| ?-
```

Here, to find the discrete set of solutions one must explicitly apply a divide-and-conquer approach where one divides the interval into subintervals and searches for solutions in each one. This is done using the "queue" method of the `solve_clip` solver and typing a semicolon after each solution that it finds:

```
| ?- {X^2=2},solve_clip(queue,[X],0.000001).
X = 1.41421356237309... ? ;
X = -1.41421356237309... ?
(10 ms) no
| ?-
```

The "no" at the end indicates that there are no more solutions to that query.

4.2 Analytic Constraints and ODEs

CLP(F) also allows one to constrain functions and real variables by equations involving derivatives and arithmetic, trigonometric, or exponential functions. In addition, one can constrain a function to take specific values at specific points and to have a range that lies within an interval.

Consider the following mathematical constraint Q on the function variable F and real variables A and E:

$$Q(F, A, E) \equiv$$
$$(F \in \mathcal{H}([0,1]), F' = F, F([0,1]) \subseteq [-100, 100], F(0) = 1, F(A) = 2, F(1) = E)$$

Q can be represented and solved by presenting the following constraint to the CLP(F) interpreter:

```
| ?- type([F],function(0,1)), {[ ddt(F,1)=F,    F in [-100,100],
         eval(F,0)=1,eval(F,A)=2, eval(F,1)=E ]}.
```

where the `type` predicate indicates that $F \in \mathcal{H}([0,1])$, i.e., F is an analytic function in some open neighborhood of the interval $[0,1]$. The output given by CLP(F) after 0.3 seconds is (All timings given in this paper were measured on a 500 MHz Pentium 2, running Linux 2.2.19.):

```
A = .6931471...    E = 2.7182818...
```

which represents the following answer constraint:

$$C(F, A, E) \equiv (A \in [0.6931471, 0.6931472) \wedge E \in [2.7182818, 2.7182819))$$

The soundness of the CLP(F) interpreter implies that it has proven a theorem about the query and its solution constraint:

$$\forall F, A, E \quad Q(F, A, E) \Rightarrow C(F, A, E)$$

In other words, if F, A, and E represent a solution to Q, then they must satisfy the answer constraint C. Note that one cannot infer from this theorem that Q has any solutions at all. In this particular case, Q clearly does have a solution

$$F(t) = \exp(t), \quad A = \ln(2), \quad E = e$$

which of course satisfies the answer constraint C.

The CLP(F) system solves analytic constraints by soundly approximating analytic functions by power series and introducing arithmetic constraints among the Taylor coefficients of the functions at the endpoints, at points in the interval, and over the entire range. A more thorough description of CLP(F) is in [14].

4.3   Programs

CLP(F) programs are Prolog programs in which the bodies of rules may contain CLP(F) constraints. CLP(F) provides the full power of Prolog in addition to the power of the underlying constraint solver and both are combined within a single logical semantics. Moreover, by the soundness and completeness of CLP [21] semantics, if a CLP interpreter returns N solutions sets $C_1, \ldots, C_n$ for a query $Q(X, F)$ and then halts, then every solution of the query $Q(X, F)$ consisting of a real vector X and a vector F of real-valued functions, is contained in the union of the solution sets C_i.

The logical semantics of CLP(F) programs can be summarized in the following theorem [14].

Theorem 1. *Let P be a CLP(F) program, $Q(x)$ a CLP(F) query where x is a tuple of real variables, and assume the interpreter returns N answer constraints $\{x \in I_j\}$ for tuples of intervals $I_1, \ldots, I_N$. Let P^* be the first order theory obtained from a logic reading of P (by Clark's Completion Semantics [3][25]), and let T be the first order theory of the domain F of analytic functions on real intervals. Then one can infer that*

$$P^* \cup T \vdash \forall x \left(Q(x) \Rightarrow x \in \bigcup_j I_j \right)$$

Theorem 2. *Notation as in the previous theorem. If the interpreter halts with no answer constraints (i.e., N=0), then one can infer*

$$P^* \cup T \vdash \neg \exists x \, Q(x)$$

i.e., the query is not satisfiable.

This theorem allows one to infer correctness of a CLP(F) simulator for a hybrid system as well as safety properties of the system directly from the corresponding CLP(F) program. We now illustrate this using the two tanks example.

5   Two Tanks in CLP

5.1   Description of the Two Tanks Problems

The "two tanks" problem is a system consisting of two water tanks. There is a flow of water in to the higher tank, and a horizontal pipe from the bottom of the higher tank to some point in the side of the lower tank. There is an outflow pipe at the bottom of the lower tank. In some versions of the problem, there are valves controlling some or all of the input flow, the flow in the pipe between the two tanks, and the output flow. The obvious questions to ask are "Is there an equilibrium given a set of flow rates?", "Does either tank overflow before equilibrium is achieved?", and, in the case where the model has valves, "Does some particular program have a specified safety property?"

Kowalewski *et al.* [23] use 6 methods to model a realistic version of this two tanks problem previously studied by the same group (Stursberg *et al.* [33]). Later, Henzinger *et al.* [13] provided another technique for studying a simplified version of this problem. Here, we consider the simplified version with no valves.

Mathematics of the Two Tanks Problem. The precise problem we study can be described as follows. There are two tanks, an upper tank and a lower tank. The height of the water in the upper tank at time t is given by $f_1(t)$ and the height in the lower tank is $f_2(t)$. The heights f_1 and f_2 are measured from the bottom of their respective tanks. There is a constant inflow of water into the upper tank (where the flow rate is given by a constant k_1, and a flow rate out of the bottom tank given by $k_4\sqrt{f_2}$. The bottom of the upper tank is k_3 meters above the bottom of the lower tank and there is a horizontal pipe connecting the bottom of the upper tank to the lower tank. The flow through the pipe is governed by an ODE in the constant k_2 and the water heights in the two tanks. The heights $f_1(t)$ and $f_2(t)$ are governed by a pair of ODEs. One member of the pair holds when the water in the lower tank is below the level of the connecting pipe ($f_2(t) \leq k_3$), the other member of the pair holds when the water level is above the connecting pipe ($f_2(t) > k_3$). When the water level is equal to the height of the connecting pipe, the ODEs are the same, so we choose one arbitrarily.

These ODEs are:

$$f_1' = \begin{cases} k_1 - k_2\sqrt{f_1 - f_2 + k_3} & f_2 > k_3 \\ k_1 - k_2\sqrt{(f_1)} & f_2 \leq k_3 \end{cases}$$

$$f_2' = \begin{cases} k_2\sqrt{f_1 - f_2 + k_3} - k_4\sqrt{f_2} & f_2 > k_3 \\ k_2\sqrt{(f_1)} - k_4\sqrt{(f_2)} & f_2 \leq k_3 \end{cases}$$

6   Rigorous Simulation of Hybrid Systems

In this section, we give the complete CLP(F) program describing the two tanks problem, and show how it can be used to rigorously model the behavior of this system.

```
twotank(case1,X10,X20,T0,X11,X21,T1,[K1,K2,K3,K4]) :-
        decls([X1,X2],function(T0,T1)),
    {[  ddt(X1,1) = K1 - K2*psqrt(X1-X2+K3),
        ddt(X2,1) = K2*psqrt(X1-X2+K3) - K4*psqrt(X2),
        eval(X1,T0)=X10,    eval(X1,T1)=X11,
        eval(X2,T0)=X20,    eval(X2,T1)=X21,
        X1 in [E,1000],         X2 in [K3,1000], E=0.0000001
    ]}.


twotank(case2,X10,X20,T0,X11,X21,T1,[K1,K2,K3,K4]) :-
decls([X1,X2],function(T0,T1)),
    {[  ddt(X1,1) = K1 - K2*psqrt(X1),
        ddt(X2,1) = K2*psqrt(X1) - K4*psqrt(X2),
        eval(X1,T0)=X10,    eval(X1,T1)=X11,
        eval(X2,T0)=X20,    eval(X2,T1)=X21,
        X1 in [E,1000],     X2 in [E,K3]
    ]}.

twotank(case12,X10,X20,T0,X11,X21,T1,Ks) :-
    {T0=<Ta, Ta<T1},Ks=[_,_,K3,_],{X2a=K3},
    twotank(case1,X10,X20,T0,X1a,X2a,Ta,Ks),
    nl,nl,print(case12(X1a,X2a,Ta)),nl,nl,
    twotank(case2,X1a,X2a,Ta,X11,X21,T1,Ks).

twotank(case21,X10,X20,T0,X11,X21,T1,Ks) :-
    {T0=<Ta, Ta<T1},    Ks=[_,_,K3,_],{X2a=K3},
    twotank(case2,X10,X20,T0,X1a,X2a,Ta,Ks),
    nl,nl,print(case21(X1a,X2a,Ta)),nl,nl,
    twotank(case1,X1a,X2a,Ta,X11,X21,T1,Ks).

% equilibrium is at  X10=0.625,  X20=0.5625,
ks([K1,K2,K3,K4]) :-   K2=1, K4=1, % sqrt(meters)/second
                       K3= 1/2, % meters
                       K1= 3/4. % meters/sec
```

Fig. 1. CLP(F) code for Case1, Case2, and transitions between them

The program consists of two parts. The first part (Figure 1) describes the relation between the heights of the waters in the two tanks at two times t_0 and t_1. There are four cases considered

- case 1: the lower tank's water level is above the pipe throughout the interval $[t_0, t_1]$
- case 2: the lower tank's water level is below the pipe throughout the interval $[t_0, t_1]$
- case 12: the lower tank's water level is above the pipe at time t_0 and stays above until some point t_2, at which it is equal to the height of the lower pipe, and then remains below the pipe until time t_1.

```
iterate(N,_DT,X10,X20,T0,X10,X20,T0,_Ks) :-   {N<0},fail.
iterate(N,_DT,X10,X20,T0,X10,X20,T0,_Ks) :-   {N=0}.
iterate(N,DT,X10,X20,T0,X11,X21,T1,Ks) :-   {T1a=T0+DT,   N1=N-1},
  contract_vars([X1a,X2a,T1a], twotank(_Case,X10,X20,T0,X1a,X2a,T1a,Ks)),
  iterate(N1,DT,X1a,X2a,T1a,X11,X21,T1,Ks).
```

Fig. 2. CLP(F) code for iterating to find a fixpoint

- case 21: the symmetric case, where the water level rises from t_0 to t_1 and is equal to the height of the pipe at exactly one time t_2.

The code in the figure is a straightforward representation of these cases. For example, we use the range constraints X2 in [K2,1000] to specify that the height of the water in the second tank is always above K2. The upper bound for the height of the water is specified to be 1000 for performance reasons. Providing a finite upper bound speeds some calculations greatly. Note that the problem of finding the transition point t_2 is automatically handled by the underlying CLP(F) system by simply adding the constraint X2a=K3 in case12.

The second part of the program is an iterator (Figure 2) that repeatedly steps through the time domain applying the appropriate case (or when nondeterminism is present, cases) to compute the current water levels in the two tanks. This program makes the assumption that the water level does not cross the height of the pipe more than once in any DT interval. We could handle this by making the program a little more complex, but for presentation purposes we stick to this simple case for now. (We would need to use an adaptive step size when switching from case 1 to case 2 or back). The contract_vars call is used as a space optimization to minimize the size of the constraint set.

This program can now be executed by loading it into the CLP(F) interpreter and posing queries. For example, in Figure 3 we show the (slightly edited) output results of a query that rigorously follows the water levels over a period of two seconds with 0.1 second steps. Note that it finds the transition point from case 2 to case 1 automatically. The calculation took 53.5 seconds.

7   Rigorous Analysis of Hybrid Systems

The same program can be used to prove properties of the two tanks system. In this section we show how to prove the following safety property, which states that if the tank levels are ever sufficiently close to an "equilibrium" point, then they stay relatively near that point forever, more precisely:

If the tank levels X_0 for the upper tank and Y_0 for the lower tank satisfy

$$0.62 \leq X_0 \leq 0.63 \;\land\; 0.558 \leq Y_0 \leq 0.567$$

at time 0, then for all times t in the future the tank levels X and Y satisfy

$$0.61922 \leq X \leq 0.63083 \land 0.55674 \leq Y \leq 0.56815$$

```
| ?- reset_clip, ks(Ks),iterate(N,0.1,0.75,0.375,0,  X,Y,T, Ks).

N = 0   X = 0.75   Y = 0.375 ? ;
N = 1   X = .738726862085376...   Y = .399047107506... ? ;
N = 2   X = .7280907797217...     Y = .420650585576... ? ;
N = 3   X = .7180600004968...     Y = .44006784395... ? ;
N = 4   X = .7086039345668...     Y = .45752125423... ? ;
N = 5   X = .69969315162...       Y = .47320505137... ? ;
N = 6   X = .691299373883...      Y = .4872904076... ? ;
N = 7   X = .6833954653...        Y = .4999292640... ? ;


case21(.68335011672...,   .50000000, T = .7005915275...)

N = 8   X = .67628864233...       Y = .5109318083... ? ;
N = 9   X = .6702047371...        Y = .5202036733... ? ;
N = 10  X = .664998108...         Y = .52800756... ? ;
N = 11  X = .660542112...         Y = .534567665... ? ;
N = 12  X = .656727105...         Y = .540075051... ? ;
N = 13  X = .6534585...           Y = .54469235... ? ;
N = 14  X = .6506551...           Y = .54855781... ? ;
N = 15  X = .6482472...           Y = .5517887... ? ;
N = 16  X = .646175...            Y = .5544847... ? ;
N = 17  X = .644388...            Y = .5567299... ? ;
N = 18  X = .642844...            Y = .558595... ? ;
N = 19  X = .64150...             Y = .560142... ? ;
N = 20  X = .6403...              Y = .561420... ?
```

Fig. 3. CLP(F) results showing transition between cases

We prove this in two steps. First we prove that if the tank levels are in the initial interval $[0.62, 0.63] \times [0.558, 0.567]$ at time 0, then they are also in that interval at time 0.1. This implies that they are in that interval at time $N * 0.1$ for all integers N. Next we prove (Fig. 6) that if they start in the given interval at time 0, then they are in the second stated interval at all times t with $0 \le t \le 0.1$. This proves the safety property.

The first part can be proved directly by using the "solve_clip" solver which provides increasingly more precise bounds on the answer constraint as shown in Figure 4. This corresponds to the standard interval arithmetic ODE solving approach. In our system, it takes about 4 minutes to prove this directly.

Another approach to proving the first part is to use constraints and try to find an initial point (X, Y) such that after 0.1 seconds it is "out of the box". This is specified by the query in Figure 5. As can be seen, this returns with a "no" answer, which means no such point exists and hence all such (X, Y) must end up inside the "box". The calculation takes about 1.3 seconds and is more elegant than the direct approach.

```
| ?-{X0 = [0.62,0.63],Y0=[0.558,0.567]},
       ks(Ks), twotank(case1,X0,Y0,0.0,X,Y,0.1,Ks),
       solve_clip(fwchk,[X,Y],N).


N = 0  X = [.61931, .63069]      Y = [.55697, .56802]
N = 1  X = [.61964, .63035]      Y = [.55758, .56741]
N = 2  X = [.61985, .63013]      Y = [.55796, .56703]
N = 3  X = [.61995, .63004]      Y = [.55812, .56687]
N = 4  X = [.62000, .62999]      Y = [.55819, .56680]

(214510 ms) yes
| ?-
```

Fig. 4. IA direct proof of safety property

```
| ?- {X10 = [0.62,0.63],X20=[0.558,0.567]},
     ks(Ks), twotank(case1,X10,X20,0.0,X11,X21,0.1,Ks),
  ({X11<0.62} ; {X11>0.63}; {X21<0.558}; {X21>0.567}).

(1330 ms) no
| ?-
```

Fig. 5. Safety Property Proof via negative answer

```
?- {T = [0,0.1]}, {X10 = [0.62,0.63],X20=[0.558,0.567]},
    ks(Ks), twotank(case1,X10,X20,0.0,X,Y,T,Ks).

T = (0,0.10000000000000001942890293094)
X = [.61924, .63076]
Y = [.55697, .56802] ?

(900 ms) yes
```

Fig. 6. Computation of range over $[0, 1]$ in Safety analysis

The second part of the proof, involves computing the range of possible values of (X, Y) over the interval $[0, 0.1]$ assuming they start in the specified box. This is done by making the query in Figure 6 in just under one second.

8   Advantages of Our Approach

There are several advantages to using CLP(F):

- The paradigm allows simpler proofs. We can prove convergence by splitting a region into areas, and showing that each of those areas eventually leads to a loop.
- The system can rigorously handle non-linear ODEs.
- The semantics of CLP(F) are close to the ODEs describing the problem. The problem specification is translated trivially into a program.
- By making the argument for correctness of the system simpler (because the system itself is simpler), we make it less likely that there will be an error in the proof of correctness.
- While CLP(F) is limited to analytic functions, it can handle points at which a function is not analytic, as long as the function is continuous (or nearly so) at all points. One simply writes one function for values above the non-analytic point and another for values below that point.

9   Limitations of CLP(F)

The primary disadvantage of this approach is that it is very resource intensive and hence can not currently model systems over a long modeling period. The wrapping problem [29] is that in multi-dimensional interval arithmetic, the interval is always an n-dimensional rectangle (a hyper-cube). This rectangle is often much larger than the minimum volume shape to cover all possible values. This excessive over-approximation can make true statements unprovable. CLP(F) makes no attempt to handle the wrapping problem, other than the simple minded solution technique of dividing each rectangle into smaller pieces, exacerbating the performance problems.

Acknowledgements. We thank the anonymous referees for pointing out the work of Edalat, Kuipers, and their respective groups to us.

References

1. R. Alur, C. Courcoubetis, N. Halbwachs, T. A. Henzinger, P.-H. Ho, X. Nicollin, A. Olivero, J. Sifakis, and S. Yovine. The algorithmic analysis of hybrid systems. *Theoretical Computer Science*, 138:3–34, 1995.
2. F. Benhamou and W. J. Older. Applying interval arithmetic to real, integer, and boolean constraints. *Journal of Logic Programming*, 32(1):1–24, Jul 1997.
3. K. Clark. Negation as failure. In H. Gallaire and J. Minker, editors, *Logic and Databases*, pages 293–322. Plenum Press, New York, NY, 1978.
4. J. Davoren and A. Nerode. Logics for hybrid systems. *Proceedings of the IEEE*, 88(7):985–1010, Jul 2000.

5. S. Debray and T. J. Hickey. Constraint-based termination analysis for cyclic rule activation in active databases. In *Proceedings of DOOD 2000: Sixth International Conference on Rules and Objects in Databases*, volume 1861 of *LNAI*, pages 1121–1136. Springer Verlag, Jul 2000.

6. G. Delzanno and A. Podelski. Model checking in CLP. In R. Cleaveland, editor, *Proceedings of the Fifth International Conference on Tools and Algorithms for the Construction and Analysis of Systems (TACAS '99)*, volume 1579 of *LNCS*, pages 223–239. Springer Verlag, 1999.

7. G. Delzanno and A. Podelski. Constraint-based deductive model checking. *International Journal on Software Tools for Technology Transfer (STTT)*, 3(3), 2001.

8. A. Edalat and R. Heckmann. Computing with real numbers: (i)LFT approach to real computation, (ii) domain-theoretic model of computational geometry. In G. Barthe, P. Dybjer, L. Pinto, and J. Saraiva, editors, *Applied Semantics: International summer school, APPSEM 2000*, volume 2395 of *LNCS*. Springer Verlag, 2002.

9. V. Gupta, R. Jagadeesan, and V. Saraswat. Hybrid cc, hybrid automata and program verification. In R. Alur, T. A. Henzinger, and E. D. Sontag, editors, *Hybrid Systems III: Verification and Control*, volume 1066 of *LNCS*, pages 52–63. Springer Verlag, 1996.

10. V. Gupta, R. Jagadeesan, V. Saraswat, and D. G. Bobrow. Programming in hybrid constraint languages. In P. Antsaklis, W. Kohn, A. Nerode, and S. Sastry, editors, *Hybrid Systems II*, volume 999 of *LNCS*, pages 226–251. Springer Verlag, 1995.

11. T. A. Henzinger. The theory of hybrid automata. In *Proceedings, 11th Symposium on Logic in Computer Science (LICS '96)*, pages 278–292. IEEE Computer Society Press, 1996.

12. T. A. Henzinger, P.-H. Ho, and H. Wong-Toi. HYTECH: A model checker for hybrid systems. *Software Tools for Technology Transfer*, 1(?):110–122, 1997.

13. T. A. Henzinger, B. Horowitz, R. Majumdar, and H. Wong-Toi. Beyond HYTECH: Hybrid systems analyis using interval numerical methods. In N. Lynch and B. H. Krogh, editors, *Hybrid Systems: Computation and Control (HSCC 2000)*, volume 1790 of *LNCS*, pages 130–144. Springer Verlag, 2000.

14. T. J. Hickey. Analytic constraint solving and interval arithmetic. In *POPL'00 ACM SIGPLAN-SIGACT Symposium on Principles of Programming Languages*, pages 338–351, 2000. published as vol. 27 of SIGPLAN notices.

15. T. J. Hickey. Metalevel interval arithmetic and verifiable constraint solving. *Journal of Functional and Logic Programming*, 2001(7), October 2001. http://danae.uni-muenster.de/lehre/kuchen/JFLP/articles/2001/S01-02/JFLP-A01-07.pdf.

16. T. J. Hickey and J. Cohen. Automating program analysis. *JACM*, 35(1):185–220, 1988.

17. T. J. Hickey, Q. Ju, and M. H. van Emden. Interval arithmetic: from principles to implementation. *JACM*, 48(5):1038–1068, Sep 2001.

18. C. Holzbaur. *OFAI CLP(Q,R) Manual*. Austrian Research Institute for Artificial Intelligence, Vienna, 1.3.3 edition, 1995. TR-95-05.

19. IEEE. IEEE standard 754-1985 for binary floating-point arithmetic. *SIGPLAN*, 22(2):9–25, 1985.

20. J. Jaffar and J. Lassez. Constraint logic programming. In *Proceedings 14th ACM Symposium on the Principles of Programming Languages*, pages 111–119, 1987.

21. J. Jaffar and M. J. Maher. Constraint logic programming: A survey. *Journal of Logic Programming*, 19/20:503–581, 1994.

22. W. Kahan. Lecture notes on the status of IEEE standard 754 for binary floating-point arithmetic. Technical report, EECS, University of California, Berkeley, 1996.
23. S. Kowalewski, O. Stursberg, M. Fritz, H. Graf, I. Hoffman, J. Preußig, M. Remelhe, S. Simon, and H. Treseler. A case study in tool-aided analysis of discretely controlled continuous systems: The two tanks problem. In P. Antsaklis, W. Kohn, M. Lemmon, A. Nerode, and S. Sastry, editors, *Hybrid Systems V*, volume 1567 of *LNCS*, pages 163–185. Springer Verlag, 1999.
24. B. J. Kuipers. Qualitative simulation: Then and now. *Artificial Intelligence*, 59:133–140, 1993.
25. J. W. Lloyd. *Foundations of Logic Programming*. Springer Verlag, second, expanded edition, 1987.
26. N. Lynch, R. Segala, and F. Vaandrager. Hybrid I/O automata revisited. In M. D. D. Benedetto and A. Sangiovanni-Vincentelli, editors, *Hybrid Systems: Communication and Control*, volume 2034 of *LNCS*, pages 403–417. Springer Verlag, 2001.
27. N. Lynch, R. Segala, F. W. Vaandrager, and H. Weinberg. Hybrid I/O automata. Technical Report CSI-R9907, Computing Science Institue Nijmegen; Faculty of Mathematics and Informatics; Catholic University of Nijmegen, Toernooivveld 1; 6525 ED Nijmegen; The Netherlands, Apr 1999.
28. O. Maler, Z. Manna, and A. Pnueli. From timed to hybrid systems. In J. de Bakker, C. Huizing, W. de Roever, and G. Rozenberg, editors, *Real-Time: Theory in Practice*, volume 600 of *LNCS*, pages 447–484, Mook, The Netherlands, Jun 1991. Rex Workshop, Springer Verlag.
29. S. Markov and R. Angelov. An interval method for systems of ODE. In K. Nickel, editor, *Interval Mathematics 1985*, volume 212 of *LNCS*, pages 103–108. Springer Verlag, 1985.
30. R. E. Moore. *Interval Analysis*. Prentice-Hall, 1966.
31. A. U. Shankar. An introduction to assertional reasoning for concurrent systems. *ACM Computing Surveys*, 25(3):225–262, Sep 1993.
32. D. A. Smith and T. J. Hickey. Partial evaluation of a CLP language. In S. Debray and M. Hermenegildo, editors, *Proceedings of the 1990 North American Conference in Logic Programming*, pages 119–138, 1990.
33. O. Stursberg, S. Kowalewski, I. Hoffman, and J. Preußig. Comparing timed and hybrid automata as approximations of continuous systems. In P. Antsaklis, W. Kohn, A. Nerode, and S. Sastry, editors, *Hybrid Systems IV*, volume 1273 of *LNCS*, pages 361–377. Springer Verlag, 1997.
34. L. Urbina. Analysis of hybrid systems in CLP($\mathcal{R}$). In E. C. Freuder, editor, *Principles and Practice of Constraint Programming – CP96*, volume 1118 of *LNCS*, pages 451–467. Springer Verlag, Aug 1996.

Modeling Subtilin Production in *Bacillus subtilis* Using Stochastic Hybrid Systems*

Jianghai Hu, Wei-Chung Wu, and Shankar Sastry

Department of Electrical Engineering and Computer Sciences
University of California at Berkeley - Berkeley CA 94720, USA
{jianghai,wcwu,sastry}@eecs.berkeley.edu

Abstract. The genetic network regulating the biosynthesis of subtilin in *Bacillus subtilis* is modeled as a stochastic hybrid system. The continuous state of the hybrid system is the concentrations of subtilin and various regulating proteins, whose productions are controlled by switches in the genetic network that are in turn modeled as Markov chains. Some preliminary results are given by both analysis and simulations.

1 Background of Subtilin Production

In order to survive, bacteria develop a number of strategies to cope with harsh environmental conditions. One of the survival strategies employed by bacteria is the release of antibiotics to eliminate competing microbial species in the same ecosystem [15]. It is observed that the production of antibiotics in the cells is affected by not only the environmental stimuli (*e.g.* nutrient levels, aeration, *etc.*) but also the local population density of their own species [12]. Therefore, the physiological states of the cell and the external signals both contribute to the regulation of antibiotic synthesis. Our study focuses on the subtilin, an antibiotic produced by *Bacillus subtilis* ATCC 6633, because the genetics of subtilin is known and its biosynthetic pathways are well characterized [2,7,11].

We briefly describe the production process of subtilin in *B. subtilis*. It is shown in [19] that the production is controlled by two independent mechanisms. When the foods are abundant, the population proliferates and the cells produce very little amount (non-lethal dose) of subtilin. However, when the foods become scarce, the production of subtilin picks up as follows. First, sigma-H (SigH), a sigma factor that regulates gene expression, enables the production of SpaRK (SpaR and SpaK) proteins by binding to the promoter regions of their genes (*spaR* and *spaK*). The membrane-bound SpaK protein senses the extracellular subtilin accumulating in the environment as the cell colony becomes large, and activates the SpaR protein. The activated SpaR (SpaR$\sim$p) in turn directs the productions of the subtilin structural peptide SpaS, the biosynthesis complex SpaBTC which modifies SpaS to yield the final product subtilin, and the immunity machinery SpaIFEG which protects the cell against the killing effect of

---

* This research is partially supported by the National Science Foundation under Grant No. EIA-0122599.

R. Alur and G.J. Pappas (Eds.): HSCC 2004, LNCS 2993, pp. 417–431, 2004.

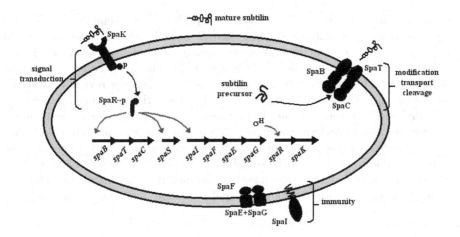

Fig. 1. Schematic representation of subtilin biosynthesis, immunity, and regulation in *Bacillus subtilis*. Subtilin prepeptide SpaS is modified, cleaved, and translocated across the cell membrane by the subtilin synthetase complex SpaBTC. The genes of subtilin are organized in an operon-like structure (*spaBTC, spaS, spaIFEG,* and *spaRK*) so that each functional unit is transcribed together. The extra-cellular subtilin functions as pheromone that regulates its own synthesis via an autoinduction feedback pathway.

subtilin. See Fig. 1 for a schematic representation of the biosynthesis process of subtilin in *B. subtilis*. In this work, a simplified version of the production process is adopted for ease of study. Namely, we ignore the dynamics in the post-translational processing of SpaS by SpaBTC to form mature subtilin and the signal transduction between SpaK and SpaR. Hence, the amount of SpaS is assumed to be equivalent to the amount of subtilin released by the cell and the SpaK and SpaR proteins are considered as one protein species.

From the above description, a dynamical model of subtilin production consists of two parts: discrete events and continuous dynamics. The discrete events include the initiations and terminations of transcriptions of various genes due to the binding and unbinding of their transcription regulators to their promoter regions, while the continuous dynamics include the accumulations and degradations of the protein species after the expressions of their genes are being switched on and off, respectively. Thus, hybrid systems can be a suitable choice for such a model.

Furthermore, in cellular networks involving coupled genetic and biochemical reactions, the expressions of genes are intrinsically non-deterministic, as is evidenced by the random fluctuations (noises) in the concentrations of protein species in the cell population, even in an isogenic culture [6]. One reason for the stochasticity in gene expressions is the small copy number of interacting molecular species (*e.g.* regulatory proteins and genes) in the relatively large cell volume [13,14,16], since in a chemical system with extremely low concentrations of reacting species, a reaction (collision of the reacting molecules) occurs in a short time interval and is best viewed as a probabilistic event [9]. This is also the case in our example, as an individual *B. subtilis* cell has only one copy of each *spa* gene for the corresponding *spa* protein. Techniques such as stochastic differential equations and Monte Carlo algorithms are often used to model and simulate such biological systems with noises (see [17] for a review). Although stochastic algorithms are computationally involved, they produce a more realistic and complete description of the time-dependent behavior of biochemical systems than deterministic algorithms. In this paper, we adopt such a stochastic point of view and propose a stochastic hybrid systems approach to analyze the dynamics of the *spa* genes in the subtilin system. We also present simulation results of the subtilin regulatory network to demonstrate the distinctive behaviors of the systems using the deterministic and stochastic modeling formalisms.

2 Stochastic Hybrid Systems

A framework first proposed by the engineering community to model systems that exhibit both continuous dynamics and discrete state changes, hybrid systems have in recent years found increasingly wide applications in many practical fields. In particular, applications of hybrid systems in modeling of biological systems can be found in [8,1], to name a few. However, most of the models proposed in the literature so far are deterministic, and are not suitable to model system with inherent randomness. This is the case, for example, in cellular processes modeling, especially when the number of participating cells is not large enough and random fluctuations within single cells cannot be ignored. Hence one needs to extend the framework to a more general class of hybrid systems with built-in randomness, namely, stochastic hybrid systems.

There have already been some work on stochastic hybrid systems (see, for example, [10,3]). In this section we shall present a simple model suitable for our main example, the production of subtilin, to be given in the next section. Basically, the state of the stochastic hybrid system consists of two parts, a continuous one and a discrete one. The discrete state has a finite number of possible values, and evolves randomly according to a Markov chain. The continuous state, on the other hand, takes value in a certain Euclidean space, and evolves deterministically according to some ordinary differential equations. The dynamics of the discrete and the continuous states are coupled in the following sense: on one hand, the transition probabilities of the Markov chain for the discrete state depend on the value of the continuous state at the moment of jump; on the other hand, the differential equations governing the evolution of the continuous state are different when the discrete state takes on different values.

More formally, we consider the following model of a stochastic hybrid system. Its state (q, x) consists of a discrete part (mode) q taking values in a finite set Q and a continuous part x taking values in a Euclidean space $\mathbb{R}^n$, $n \geq 1$. Both q and x are functions of time t and their dynamics are specified in the following.

- (*Discrete Dynamics*) The discrete state q follows a Markov chain that jumps at epochs $t = 0, \Delta, 2\Delta, \ldots$ of constant interval $\Delta > 0$ with transition probabilities

$$p_{ij}(z) \triangleq P\{q(t^+) = j | q(t^-) = i, x(t^-) = z\}, \quad \forall i, j \in Q. \tag{1}$$

Here $q(t^-)$ and $q(t^+)$ denote the values of the discrete state immediately before and after the jump at time t, respectively. Note that the transition probabilities as defined in (1) depend on the value of the continuous state at the moment of the jump.

- (*Continuous Dynamics*) For each $i \in Q$, let f_i be a vector field on $\mathbb{R}^n$. Then the dynamics of the continuous state x follows

$$\dot{x}(t) = f_i(x(t)) \tag{2}$$

in any open time interval where $q \equiv i$. Here we assume that solutions to equation (2) starting from an arbitrary initial position are well defined on all time intervals. This is automatically satisfied if each f_i is Lipschitz continuous in x.

- (*Reset Condition*) We assume that the continuous state is reset trivially at any moment t of discrete state jump, namely, $x(t^-) = x(t^+)$ for all $t = 0, \Delta, 2\Delta, \ldots$. Thus we shall simply denote them by $x(t)$.

It is obvious from the definition that solutions (or *executions*) $(q(t), x(t))$ of the stochastic hybrid system exist and are stochastic processes with continuous $x(t)$ and piecewise constant $q(t)$.

Remark 1. Instead of a discrete Markov chain jumping at fixed time intervals, we can alternatively model the discrete dynamics as a continuous Markov chain with generator $[r_{ij}(z)]_{i,j \in Q}$ satisfying $r_{ij}(z) \geq 0$ for $i \neq j$ and $\sum_{j \in Q} r_{ij}(z) = 0$, $\forall i \in Q$. Therefore, given that $x(t) = z$ and $q(t^+) = i$ right after the time t of jump, the discrete state will remain in i for a random time of exponential distribution with parameter $-r_{ii}(z)$, and then jump to a new state $j \neq i$ with probability $r_{ij}(z) / \sum_{j \neq i} r_{ij}(z)$.

3   Model of Subtilin Production

3.1   Population Growth Model

Denote by D the size of *B. subtilis* population, and by X the total amount of nutrient available in the environment, both properly normalized. The growth of *B. subtilis* population can be modeled by the logistic equation:

$$\frac{dD}{dt} = rD\left(1 - \frac{D}{D_\infty}\right). \tag{3}$$

Here D_∞ represents the equilibrium population size that can be sustained in the long term given the amount X of available nutrient. Solutions to equation (3) with a fixed D_∞ are

$$D(t) = \frac{D_\infty}{1 + \left(\frac{1}{D(0)} - 1\right)e^{-rt}}, \tag{4}$$

which, starting from any initial value $D(0) > 0$, converge to D_∞ as $t \to \infty$. In our model D_∞ changes with X, the amount of available nutrient, in the following way:

$$D_\infty = \min\{X/X_0, D_{max}\} \tag{5}$$

for some constant X_0. Thus D_∞ increases linearly with the increase of X before it saturates at a fixed level D_{max} due to space limit and competition within the population. With a time-varying X, so is D_∞, and solutions to equation (3) do not have a simple expression as in (4).

The dynamics of X is given by

$$\frac{dX}{dt} = -k_1 D + k_2 \overline{[\text{SpaS}]}, \tag{6}$$

for some constants k_1 and k_2. By equation (6), there are two factors affecting the dynamics of X: the nutrient is consumed at a rate proportional to the population size (the first term); and it is replenished at a rate proportional to the average concentration of SpaS protein in the population due to the elimination of competitors caused by SpaS in the environment. The bar over [SpaS] indicates that it is a population level average, not for a particular cell.

3.2   Single Cell Model

Within each *B. subtilis* cell, there are several modulating proteins affecting the concentration level of SpaS. In this section we shall present models of their dynamics.

First of all, SigH is a sigma factor whose production is switched on if and only if the food level X is below a certain threshold ηD_{max} for some $\eta > 0$. Its production rate is assumed to be $k_3 > 0$ when it is being produced and negligible when it is not. Thus the dynamics of its concentration [SigH] can be modeled as

$$\frac{d[\text{SigH}]}{dt} = \begin{cases} -\lambda_1[\text{SigH}] & X \geq \eta D_{max}, \\ k_3 - \lambda_1[\text{SigH}] & X < \eta D_{max}, \end{cases} \tag{7}$$

where λ_1 is the natural decaying rate of SigH.

The production of the protein SpaRK is controlled by a switch S_1 in the following way. The switch has two states 1 (on) and 0 (off), corresponding to the cases where SigH is bound and unbound to the promoter region of the gene *spaRK*, respectively. SpaRK is produced at a constant rate k_4 when the switch is on, and at a negligible rate when the switch is off. Taking into consideration its natural decaying rate of λ_2, the dynamics of [SpaRK] is given by

$$\frac{d[\text{SpaRK}]}{dt} = \begin{cases} -\lambda_2[\text{SpaRK}] & \text{if } S_1 \text{ is off,} \\ k_4 - \lambda_2[\text{SpaRK}] & \text{if } S_1 \text{ is on.} \end{cases} \tag{8}$$

The switch S_1 is modeled as evolving randomly at constant time interval $\Delta > 0$ according to a Markov chain with a probability transition matrix dependent on the concentration level of SigH as follows:

$$A([\text{SigH}]) = \begin{pmatrix} 1 - a_0([\text{SigH}]) & a_0([\text{SigH}]) \\ a_1([\text{SigH}]) & 1 - a_1([\text{SigH}]) \end{pmatrix}. \tag{9}$$

Here $a_0([\text{SigH}])$ and $a_1([\text{SigH}])$ denote the probabilities that S_1 switches from off to on and from on to off, respectively. In practice one may not know exactly the statistics of the random time interval between successive switchings of S_1. However, by choosing sufficiently small Δ and proper $A([\text{SigH}])$, one can approximate the random time interval probabilistically, as long as it has an exponential distribution.

The choice of the transition matrix in (9) should, nevertheless, satisfy the following inherent biochemical constraint. Denote by p_{rk} the probability of S_1 switching on in the equilibrium distribution. Then one should have [18]

$$p_{rk} = \frac{e^{-\Delta G_{rk}/RT}[\text{SigH}]}{1 + e^{-\Delta G_{rk}/RT}[\text{SigH}]}, \tag{10}$$

where ΔG_{rk} is the Gibbs free energy of the molecular configuration when the switch is on (the Gibbs free energy is 0 if the switch is off), T is the temperature in Kelvin (K), and $R = 1.99$ cal/mol/K is the gas constant. A simple calculation shows that for transition matrix (9), the equilibrium probability of S_1 switching on is

$$\frac{a_0([\text{SigH}])}{a_0([\text{SigH}]) + a_1([\text{SigH}])}.$$

Thus we must have

$$\frac{a_0([\text{SigH}])}{a_0([\text{SigH}]) + a_1([\text{SigH}])} = \frac{e^{-\Delta G_{rk}/RT}[\text{SigH}]}{1 + e^{-\Delta G_{rk}/RT}[\text{SigH}]}. \tag{11}$$

The set of $a_0([\text{SigH}])$ and $a_1([\text{SigH}])$ satisfying condition (11) is characterized exactly by the following family:

$$a_0([\text{SigH}]) = \mu, \quad a_1([\text{SigH}]) = \mu e^{\Delta G_{rk}/RT}[\text{SigH}]^{-1}, \tag{12}$$

for all $0 < \mu < \min\{1, e^{-\Delta G_{rk}/RT}[\text{SigH}]\}$. The difference between these choices is that they result in different frequencies of actual switchings for the Markov chain S_1. Indeed, starting from the on (respectively, off) state, it takes an expected time of $\Delta\mu^{-1}e^{-\Delta G_{rk}/RT}[\text{SigH}]$ (respectively, $\Delta\mu^{-1}$) for S_1 to switch to the other state, provided that $[\text{SigH}]$ is kept constant. Thus μ (together with Δ) is a parameter controlling the switching frequency of S_1.

A particular choice in (12) is

$$a_0([\text{SigH}]) = \frac{e^{-\Delta G_{rk}/RT}[\text{SigH}]}{1 + e^{-\Delta G_{rk}/RT}[\text{SigH}]},$$

$$a_1([\text{SigH}]) = \frac{1}{1 + e^{-\Delta G_{rk}/RT}[\text{SigH}]}. \tag{13}$$

This results in a Markov chain (9) that can be verified to be *reversible* [5]. Reversible Markov chains (or random walks on graphs) find many applications in diverse fields of physics, such as the Ising model [4]. Thus they may be particularly relevant in modeling S_1 in the thermal equilibrium state.

The dynamics of the concentration of the third protein, SpaS, is similar to that of [SpaRK]. There is a switch S_2 with two states 1 (on) and 0 (off), corresponding to the cases where activated SpaR is bound and unbound to the promoter region of the gene *spaS*, respectively. SpaS is being produced at a constant rate k_5 whenever S_2 is on, and at a negligible rate whenever S_2 is off. In other words,

$$\frac{d[\text{SpaS}]}{dt} = \begin{cases} -\lambda_3[\text{SpaS}] & \text{if } S_2 \text{ is off,} \\ k_5 - \lambda_3[\text{SpaS}] & \text{if } S_2 \text{ is on,} \end{cases} \tag{14}$$

where λ_3 is the natural decaying rate of SpaS. Moreover, S_2 switches randomly at constant time interval Δ according to a Markov chain with a probability transition matrix dependent on [SpaRK]:

$$B([\text{SpaRK}]) = \begin{pmatrix} 1 - b_0([\text{SpaRK}]) & b_0([\text{SpaRK}]) \\ b_1([\text{SpaRK}]) & 1 - b_1([\text{SpaRK}]) \end{pmatrix}. \tag{15}$$

It is required that the equilibrium probability of S_2 switching on be ([18])

$$p_s = \frac{e^{-\Delta G_s/RT}[\text{SpaRK}]}{1 + e^{-\Delta G_s/RT}[\text{SpaRK}]}, \tag{16}$$

where ΔG_s is the Gibbs free energy of the molecular configuration when the switch S_2 is on.

A family of $b_0([\text{SpaRK}])$ and $b_1([\text{SpaRK}])$ satisfying constraint (16) is

$$b_0([\text{SpaRK}]) = \nu, \qquad b_1([\text{SpaRK}]) = \nu e^{\Delta G_s/RT}[\text{SpaRK}]^{-1},$$

where $0 < \nu < \min\{1, e^{-\Delta G_s/RT}[\text{SpaRK}]\}$ is a parameter controlling the actual switching frequency of S_2. In particular, if we choose

$$b_0([\text{SpaRK}]) = \frac{e^{-\Delta G_s/RT}[\text{SpaRK}]}{1 + e^{-\Delta G_{rk}/RT}[\text{SpaRK}]},$$

$$b_1([\text{SpaRK}]) = \frac{1}{1 + e^{-\Delta G_s/RT}[\text{SpaRK}]}, \tag{17}$$

then the corresponding Markov chain S_2 is reversible.

3.3   Stochastic Hybrid Systems Model

To sum up, each individual $B.$ $subtilis$ cell can be modeled as a stochastic hybrid system. Its discrete state is $(S_1, S_2) \in \{0,1\} \times \{0,1\}$, where $(S_1, S_2) = (0,1)$ corresponds to the case when the switch S_1 is off and the switch S_2 is on, $etc.$ So there are four possible discrete states in total. Its continuous state is $([\text{SigH}], [\text{SpaRK}], [\text{SpaS}]) \in \mathbb{R}^3$ with dynamics given by equations (7), (8), and (14). The discrete state changes mode randomly every Δ time according to a Markov chain whose probability transition matrix can be obtained from $A([\text{SigH}])$ in (9) and $B([\text{SpaRK}])$ in (15) (in fact, it is the tensor product $A([\text{SigH}]) \otimes B([\text{SpaRK}]))$, and depends on the values of $[\text{SigH}]$ and $[\text{SpaRK}]$ at the moment of transition. The food level X appearing in the continuous dynamics in (7) is a population level quantity and can be thought of as an external input to the stochastic hybrid system.

One way to study a population of $B.$ $subtilis$ is to model it as a collection of such stochastic hybrid systems evolving independently from one another. However, this is difficult to implement in practice, since the population size D is changing according to (3). Thus the number of individual stochastic hybrid systems is time varying. To overcome this difficulty, one can replace the differential equation (3) by a birth-and-death Markov chain D on $\mathbb{N}$ with properly chosen transition probabilities, with D being the (integer) number of cells in the population. One keeps track of the state of each cell, from its birth to its death, and $\overline{[\text{SpaS}]}$ is the average of $[\text{SpaS}]$ of the currently living cells. This approach will be pursued in future work. In this paper we adopt a simplified version by assuming that $\overline{[\text{SpaS}]} = \xi[\text{SpaS}]$ for some constant ξ. Although simulation results under this assumption tend to exaggerate the random fluctuations of $\overline{[\text{SpaS}]}$, insights can still be gained on how individual $B.$ $subtilis$ cell modulates its production of subtilin at different growth stages of the population.

Intuitively, the $B.$ $subtilis$ population as a whole reacts to the food level signal X in a way similar to a feedback control system. For example, when X drops below the threshold ηD_{max}, SigH starts to be produced according to (7). An increased $[\text{SigH}]$ then makes it more likely for S_1 to switch on, thus resulting in an increased $[\text{SpaRK}]$. In turn, $[\text{SpaS}]$ will increase due to a higher probability of S_2 switching on. As this occurs for the cells in the population, more foods will be made available by equation (6), offsetting the decrease in X. Exactly the opposite happens when X is above the threshold ηD_{max}. So it is reasonable to expect that some equilibrium state will be reached eventually for the overall system, as will be illustrated in the next two sections by analysis and simulations, respectively.

4   Analysis

In this section, we focus on a single cell, and study how the concentrations of its various proteins evolve over time, i.e., the continuous dynamics of the stochastic hybrid system modeling the cell as described in Section 3.

We first observe that the dynamics of [SpaS] is affected indirectly through S_2 by [SpaRK], and in turn the dynamics of [SpaRK] is affected indirectly through S_1 by [SigH]. Moreover, [SigH] is relatively slow-varying compared with [SpaRK] and [SpaS]. Therefore, we shall focus on two sub-problems: the evolution of [SpaRK] under a fixed [SigH] and the evolution of [SpaS] under a fixed [SpaRK].

Suppose that [SigH] is fixed. Then it is easy to see that

Proposition 1. ([SpaRK], S_1) *at the time* $0, \Delta, 2\Delta, \ldots$ *is a Markov process.*

Indeed, S_1 follows a Markov chain with probability transition matrix (9), and according to (8), [SpaRK] transits as follows:

$$[\text{SpaRK}]_{(n+1)\Delta} = \begin{cases} e^{-\lambda_2 \Delta}[\text{SpaRK}]_{n\Delta} & \text{if } S_1 \text{ is off,} \\ \frac{k_4}{\lambda_2} + e^{-\lambda_2 \Delta}\{[\text{SpaRK}]_{n\Delta} - \frac{k_4}{\lambda_2}\} & \text{if } S_1 \text{ is on,} \end{cases} \tag{18}$$

for all $n = 0, 1, \ldots$ Here $[\text{SpaRK}]_{n\Delta}$ denotes the value of [SpaRK] at the time epoch $n\Delta$. Note that $([\text{SpaRK}], S_1)_{n\Delta}$ is not a Markov chain in the conventional sense since [SpaRK] takes values in the uncountable set $\mathbb{R}$.

Note that S_1 evolves independently from [SpaRK], and its state distribution at time $n\Delta$ will converge to the stationary distribution as $n \to \infty$, namely, S_1 will open with probability p_{rk} given in (10), and close with probability $1 - p_{rk}$.

Proposition 2. *Suppose that* S_1 *has reached its stationary distribution. Then* $[\text{SpaRK}]_{n\Delta}$, $n = 0, 1, \ldots$, *is a Markov process with transition probabilities*

$$P\{[\text{SpaRK}]_{(n+1)\Delta} = y | [\text{SpaRK}]_{n\Delta} = x\}$$
$$= \begin{cases} 1 - p_{rk} & \text{if } y = e^{-\lambda_2 \Delta}x, \\ p_{rk} & \text{if } y = \frac{k_4}{\lambda_2} + e^{-\lambda_2 \Delta}\{x - \frac{k_4}{\lambda_2}\}. \end{cases}$$

In other words, $[\text{SpaRK}]_{n\Delta}$ is a random walk on $\mathbb{R}$ that in one time step either jumps towards 0 or towards k_4/λ_2 by a fixed proportion $e^{-\lambda_2 \Delta}$ with constant probabilities. Thus one can expect that it will eventually achieve an equilibrium distribution on the interval $[0, k_4/\lambda_2]$. Depending on whether $p_{rk} < 0.5$ or $p_{rk} > 0.5$, the equilibrium distribution will concentrate more on the left (or right) half of the interval. Moreover, the smaller $e^{-\lambda_2 \Delta}$ is, the further $[\text{SpaRK}]_{n\Delta}$ will jump towards either 0 or k_4/λ_2, hence the larger the variance of $[\text{SpaRK}]_{n\Delta}$ (normalized by k_4/λ_2) in the equilibrium distribution.

Remark 2. The exact expression of the equilibrium distribution of $[\text{SpaRK}]_{n\Delta}$ can be complicated. For example, assuming $k_4/\lambda_2 = 1$, if $e^{-\lambda_2 \Delta}$ is rational and [SpaRK] starts from a rational number, then $[\text{SpaRK}]_{n\Delta}$ can only jump to rational numbers. In this case, $[\text{SpaRK}]_{n\Delta}$ is a random walk on $\mathbb{Q}$ instead of on $\mathbb{R}$. In particular, let us take the example of $e^{-\lambda_2 \Delta} = 1/m$ for some integer $m \geq 2$. If $[\text{SpaRK}]_{n\Delta}$ has an m-nary expression $0.\gamma_1\gamma_2\ldots$ where $\gamma_1, \gamma_2, \ldots \in \{0, \ldots, m-1\}$, then by Proposition 3, $[\text{SpaRK}]_{(n+1)\Delta}$ will have an m-nary expression $0.\gamma_0\gamma_1\gamma_2\ldots$, where $\gamma_0 = m-1$ with probability p_{rk} and $\gamma_0 = 0$ with probability $1 - p_{rk}$. From this it is easy to see that the equilibrium distribution of $[\text{SpaRK}]_{n\Delta}$ as $n \to \infty$ is characterized by $0.\gamma_1\gamma_2\ldots$ where

$\gamma_1, \gamma_2, \ldots$ are a sequence of i.i.d. random variables that take the value $m - 1$ with probability p_{rk} and the value 0 with probability $1 - p_{rk}$. Note that in this characterization $0.\gamma_1\gamma_2\ldots$ must represent a rational number, i.e., we want the resulting distribution to be restricted on $\mathbb{Q}$ since we have assumed that [SpaRK] starts from a rational number. Unless $m = 2$, this equilibrium distribution is concentrated only on a subset of $\mathbb{Q}$.

Suppose now that [SpaRK] is fixed. Then the dynamics of [SpaS] as given by (14) can be analyzed in a similar way to obtain

Proposition 3. $([\text{SpaS}], S_2)$ *at the time* $0, \Delta, 2\Delta, \ldots$ *is a Markov process.*

Proposition 4. *Suppose that* S_2 *has reached its stationary distribution. Then* $[\text{SpaS}]_{n\Delta}$, $n = 0, 1, \ldots$, *is a Markov process with transition probabilities*

$$P\{[\text{SpaS}]_{(n+1)\Delta} = y | [\text{SpaS}]_{n\Delta} = x\}$$
$$= \begin{cases} 1 - p_s & \text{if } y = e^{-\lambda_3 \Delta} x, \\ p_s & \text{if } y = \frac{k_5}{\lambda_3} + e^{-\lambda_3 \Delta}\{x - \frac{k_5}{\lambda_3}\}. \end{cases}$$

The equilibrium distribution of $[\text{SpaS}]_{n\Delta}$ concentrates on the interval $[0, k_5/\lambda_3]$, and has more weight on the left half interval or the right half interval depending on whether $p_s < 0.5$ or $p_s > 0.5$. In addition, the smaller $e^{-\lambda_3 \Delta}$ is, the larger the variance of $[\text{SpaS}]_{n\Delta}$ (normalized by k_5/λ_3) in the equilibrium distribution.

Instead of the above Markov process analysis, one can adopt the following deterministic approximation procedure. Suppose that [SigH] is kept constant, and that the Markov chain S_1 is in its equilibrium distribution. Then by averaging the dynamics of [SpaRK] in (8) in the two cases using the equilibrium probabilities of S_1, one obtains the "averaged dynamics" of [SpaRK]:

$$\frac{d}{dt}[\text{SpaRK}] = \frac{\alpha_1 [\text{SigH}]}{1 + \alpha_2 [\text{SigH}]} - \lambda_2 [\text{SpaRK}], \tag{19}$$

where $\alpha_1 = k_4 e^{-\Delta G_{rk}/RT}$ and $\alpha_2 = e^{-\Delta G_{rk}/RT}$. This practice of obtaining deterministic dynamics through averaging the random dynamics is often used in the biological literature. Similarly, the averaged dynamics of SpaS can be obtained from (14) as

$$\frac{d}{dt}[\text{SpaS}] = \frac{\beta_1 [\text{SpaRK}]}{1 + \beta_2 [\text{SpaRK}]} - \lambda_3 [\text{SpaS}], \tag{20}$$

where $\beta_1 = k_5 e^{-\Delta G_s/RT}$ and $\beta_2 = e^{-\Delta G_s/RT}$.

Equations (19) and (20), together with equations (3), (6) and (7), form a deterministic differential system whose solutions approximate the solutions to the original stochastic hybrid system in the average sense. Simulation results of both approaches will be compared in the next section.

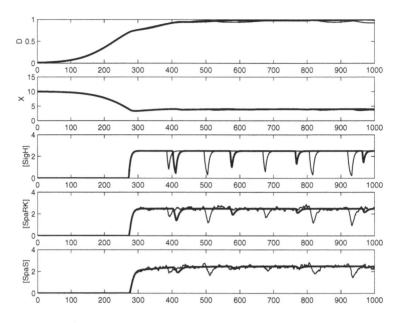

Fig. 2. A typical solution of the stochastic hybrid system model.

5   Simulation Results

In this section, we present the simulation results for the stochastic hybrid system model introduced in Section 3, which consists of equations (3), (6), (7), (8), and (14). We also compare the results with those obtained using the deterministic model consisting of equations (3), (6), (7), (19), and (20). Unless otherwise stated, the parameters are chosen as follows: $r = 0.02$, $D_{max} = 1$, $k_1 = 0.1$, $k_2 = 0.4$, $k_3 = 0.5$, $k_4 = 1$, $k_5 = 1$, $\xi = 0.1$, $\lambda_1 = \lambda_2 = \lambda_3 = 0.2$, $\eta = 4$, $X_0 = 4$, $e^{-\Delta G_{rk}/RT} = 0.4$, and $e^{-\Delta G_s/RT} = 0.4$. The initial conditions are $D(0) = 0.01$, $X(0) = 10$, and $[\text{SigH}]_0 = [\text{SpaRK}]_0 = [\text{SpaS}]_0 = 0$.

Fig. 2 plots one typical realization of the continuous state trajectories of the stochastic hybrid system in thin solid lines. Simulation results of the deterministic model are plotted in the same figure in thick solid lines. As expected, the continuous state tends to some equilibrium position eventually. In particular, the population density D grows from 0.01 to some value slightly below the maximal density D_{max}, while the food level X drops from 10 to around $\eta D_{max} = 4$. The continuous states that exhibit the most random fluctuations are [SpaRK] and [SpaS], both of which fluctuate around the values predicted by the deterministic model. On the other hand, there is a visible discrepancy between the values of [SigH] in the two models.

In order to examine the population density-dependent behavior of subtilin production in the cell, we simulate our models by varying the maximum density D_{max} (carrying capacity of the incubating medium) at which a cell culture can grow to. Fig. 3 shows the results obtained by using the stochastic model (left)

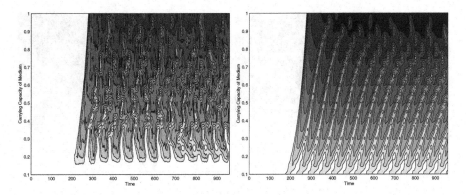

Fig. 3. Simulation results of the stochastic (left) and deterministic (right) models under different carrying capacity of medium D_{max}.

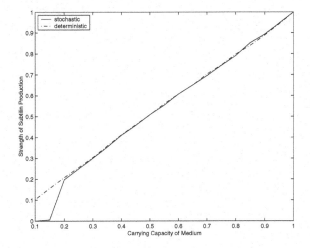

Fig. 4. Average subtilin production strength vs. carrying capacity of medium.

and the deterministic model (right), respectively. In both plots the vertical axis represents D_{max}, the horizontal axis represents the time, and the gray level at each point represents the concentration level of SpaS. Thus, each horizontal slice is one simulation run of [SpaS] with a particular D_{max}. The contours of [SpaS] are also plotted in both cases. It can be seen that a cell exhibits greater variations in the strength of subtilin production at lower cell densities in the stochastic case than in the deterministic case. From a biological perspective, these variations may be attributed to uncertainty in the signal transduction pathway (between the SpaK and SpaR proteins) under the condition of low level of external stimuli (*i.e.* extracellular subtilin) and are captured by the stochastic formalism of our model. In addition, as shown in Fig. 4 where the average subtilin production strength at equilibrium condition is plotted at different D_{max}, results of the

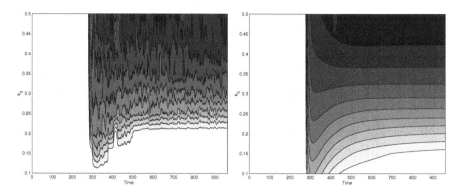

Fig. 5. Simulation results of the stochastic (left) and deterministic (right) models under different values of k_3.

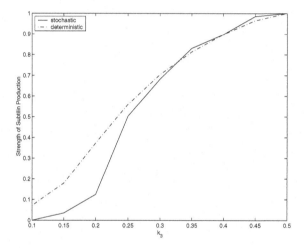

Fig. 6. Average subtilin production strength vs. k_3.

stochastic model reveals that there is a threshold for D_{max} below which the cell can not be induced to produce subtilin (the concentration of subtilin in the medium is too dilute due to the sparse population to induce subtilin production in individual cells) and that the production level exhibits a linear response to the extracellular subtilin concentration if the maximum population density is above this value, as is observed experimentally in [12]. The deterministic model of subtilin production, in contrast, shows a linear response over the entire range of the carrying capacity of the medium.

We also examine the level of subtilin production in the cell in response to intracellular signals (*i.e.* SigH). We obtain different average concentrations of SigH at equilibrium condition by varying the parameter k_3 (larger k_3 implies larger average [SigH] at steady state) and simulate the corresponding subtilin production process. The results are shown in Fig. 5 for the stochastic model (left) and the deterministic model (right). Similar to the previous case, the "noises" in the SpaS protein synthesis due to low level of the activating signals inside the cell can be better reflected by using the Markov chain formalism. In addition, Fig. 6 suggests that the SpaS protein synthesis seems to exhibit a switching behavior in response to the increasing concentration of the activating SigH in the cell. Again, such a switching behavior is more obvious in the stochastic case than in the deterministic case. This finding, along with the simulation of varying D_{max}, supports the hypothesis that a threshold mechanism exists for the subtilin production in *B. subtilis*.

6   Conclusion and Future Directions

In this paper a stochastic hybrid system model and a deterministic model of the subtilin synthesis process for *B. subtilis* cells are constructed. Although simulations of the two models generate results similar in the average sense, the stochastic model may be better suited to explain the intrinsic random fluctuations in gene expressions under the condition of a small number of participating players (*i.e.* low concentrations of regulatory proteins intracellularly and a small cell population extracellularly). The stochastic model also demonstrates the cell density-dependent, sigmoid-like switching behavior of subtilin production in *B. subtilis*.

This work can be extended in several directions. For example, more regulating proteins such as SpaB, SpaT, and SpaC could be incorporated into the models; the population size D could be modeled as a birth-and-death Markov chain instead of as the solution to the logistic equation, as is pointed out in Section 3.3; and experiments on *B. subtilis* could be performed and the data collected to validate the proposed models and the simulation results.

Acknowledgment. The authors would like to thank D. M. Wolf for helpful discussions and pointers to the relevant literatures.

References

1. K. Amonlirdviman, R. Ghosh, J. D. Axelrod, and C. Tomlin. A hybrid systems approach to modeling and analyzing planar cell polarity. In *Proc. 3rd Int. Conf. on Systems Biology*, Stockholm, Sweden, December 2002.
2. S. Banerjee and J. N. Hansen. Structure and expression of a gene encoding the precursor of subtilin, a small protein antibiotic. *J. Biol. Chem.*, 263(19):9508–9514, 1988.
3. M. L. Bujorianu and J. Lygeros. Reachability questions in piecewise deterministic markov processes. In O. Maler and A. Pnueli, editors, *Hybrid Systems: Computation and Control, 6th International Workshop, Prague, Czech Republic*, volume 2623 of *Lecture Notes in Computer Science*, pages 126–140. Springer-Verlag, 2003.
4. B. A. Cipra. An introduction to the Ising model. *Amer. Math. Monthly*, 94:937–959, 1987.

5. R. Durrett. *Probability: Theory and Examples.* Duxbury Press, second edition, 1996.

6. M. B. Elowitz, A. J. Levine, E. D. Siggia, and P. S. Swain. Stochastic gene expression in a single cell. *Science,* 297:1183–1186, 2002.

7. K. D. Entian and W. M. de Vos. Genetics of subtilin and nisin biosyntheses: biosynthesis of lantibiotics. *Antonie van Leeuwenhoek,* 69:109–117, 1996.

8. R. Ghosh and C. Tomlin. Lateral inhibition through delta-notch signaling: A piecewise affine hybrid model. In M. D. di Benedetto and A. L. Sangiovanni-Vincentelli, editors, *Hybrid Systems: Computation and Control, 4th International Workshop, Rome, Italy,* volume 2034 of *Lecture Notes in Computer Science,* pages 232–246. Springer-Verlag, 2001.

9. D. T. Gillespie. Exact stochastic simulation of coupled chemical reactions. *J. of Phys. Chem.,* 81(25):2340–2361, 1977.

10. J. Hu, J. Lygeros, and S. Sastry. Towards a theory of stochastic hybrid systems. In N. Lynch and B.H. Krogh, editors, *Hybrid Systems: Computation and Control, 3rd International Workshop, Pittsburgh, PA,* volume 1790 of *Lecture Notes in Computer Science,* pages 160–173. Springer-Verlag, 2000.

11. P. Kiesau, U. Eikmanns, Z. G. Eckel, S. Weber, M. Hammelmann, and K. D. Entian. Evidence for a multimeric subtilin synthetase complex. *J. of Bacteriology,* 179(5):1475–1481, 1997.

12. M. Kleerebezem and L. E. Quadri. Peptide pheromone-dependent regulation of antimicrobial peptide production in gram-positive bacteria: a case of multicellular behavior. *Peptides,* 22:1579–1596, 2001.

13. H. H. McAdams and A. Arkin. Stochastic mechanisms in gene expression. *Proc. Natl. Acad. Sci.,* 94:814–819, 1997.

14. H. H. McAdams and A. Arkin. It's a noisy bussiness! genetic regulation at the nanomolar scale. *TIG,* 15(2):65–69, 1999.

15. T. Msadek. When the going gets tough: survival strategies and environmental signaling networks in Bacillus subtilis. *Trends in Microbiology,* 7(5):201–207, 1999.

16. E. M. Ozbudak, M. Thattai, I. Kurtser, A. D. Grossman, and A. van Oudenaarden. Regulation of noise in the expression of a single gene. *Nature Genetics,* 31:69–73, 2002.

17. C. V. Rao, D. M. Wolf, and A. P. Arkin. Control, exploitation and tolerance of intracellular noise. *Nature,* 402:231–237, 2002.

18. M. A. Shea and G. K. Ackers. The O_R control system of bacteriophage lambda. A physical-chemical model for gene regulation. *J. Mol. Biol.,* 181:211–230, 1985.

19. T. Stein, S. Borchert, P. Kiesau, S. Heinzmann, S. Kloss, C. Klein, M. Helfrich, and K. D. Entian. Dual control of subtilin biosynthesis and immunity in Bacillus subtilis. *Molecular Microbiology,* 44(2):403–416, 2002.

Sound Code Generation from Communicating Hybrid Models

Yerang Hur[1], Jesung Kim[1], Insup Lee[1], and Jin-Young Choi[2]

[1] Department of Computer and Information Science
University of Pennsylvania, Philadelphia, PA, USA
[2] Department of Computer Science and Engineering
Korea University, Seoul, Korea

Abstract. Precise translation from hybrid models to code is difficult because models are defined in the continuous-time domain whereas code executes on digital computers in a discrete fashion. Traditional approach is to associate the model with a sampling rate before code generation, and rely on an approximate algorithm that computes the next state numerically. Depending on the choice of the sampling rate and the algorithm, the behavior of the code may vary significantly due to numerical errors, but the discrepancy has been addressed informally, making the analysis results at the model level less meaningful for implementation. Formal relationship between the model and the code becomes even more unclear when components of the code execute concurrently. In this paper, we propose a formal framework that addresses the issue of soundness of concurrent programs generated from communicating hybrid models. The motivation is that concurrent programs executing in different rates may cause an erroneous transition when transition conditions are evaluated using values from different time instances. The essence of our technique is to refine the model by tightening transition conditions according to the maximum errors due to different sampling rates. We claim that the generated code has a trace of discrete transitions that is equivalent to one of the traces observable from the model, and that the values of variables are bounded. Our framework demonstrates how hybrid models defined in the continuous time domain are translated into discretized models with or without consideration of errors due to asynchronous sampling, and finally into executable code with real-time scheduling.

1   Introduction

A model-based approach is an emerging paradigm for developing robust software, and has been the focus of increasing research effort. Models are used during the design phase to ensure systems under consideration have desired properties. Benefits of high-level modeling can be significantly improved if the code is generated automatically from the model. However, precise translation from models to code is difficult especially when the model is based on hybrid systems. Hybrid models combine continuous state change specified by differential equations with discrete state transition specified by the finite state machine. Formally, a

R. Alur and G.J. Pappas (Eds.): HSCC 2004, LNCS 2993, pp. 432–447, 2004.

hybrid model consists of a vector $x = (x_1, x_2, \ldots, x_n)$ of (continuously updated) variables, a finite set of discrete states P that associates x with a differential equation $\dot{x} = f_p(x)$ for each $p \in P$, a set of transitions $E \subseteq P \times P$, a guard set $G((p, p')) \subseteq \mathbb{R}^n$ for each $(p, p') \in E$ specifying the condition that the transition (p, p') can be taken, and an invariant set $I(p) \subseteq \mathbb{R}^n$ for each $p \in P$ specifying the condition that x follows $\dot{x} = f_p(x)$. Hypothetically, precise implementation of a hybrid model would be possible if there exists a program that computes valuation $x(t)$ of x at time $t \in \mathbb{R}$ according to the dynamics $\dot{x} = f_p(x)$ defined at the current discrete state p, and decides the next state p' according to the invariant set $I(p)$ and the guard set $G((p, p'))$, all in infinitesimal time. Of course, such a program is not feasible in digital computers, since it requires indefinite computation power and precision.

A traditional approach to automatic code generation from hybrid models is to associate the model with a sampling rate, and generate code that computes the state of the model at the given rate approximately by using a numerical method (e.g., Runge-Kutta method). Depending on the choice of the sampling rate and the numerical method, the behavior of the synthesized code may vary significantly. However, reasoning on the discrepancy between the model and the code is oftentimes left to the designer's intuition and/or ad hoc experiments. In the case of the code generated from a model consisting of multiple components with different sampling rates, the issue of formal relationship between the model and the code becomes even more unclear. Thus, analysis results obtained at the model level is less useful to the generated code. The desire to bridge this gap motivates our research.

Formally, we can define a discrete-time abstraction of a given hybrid model A over a discrete time domain $T = \{t_i | t_i \in \mathbb{R}, i = 0, 1, 2, \ldots, t_i < t_{i+1}\}$, denoted by A/T, as an extended finite state machine with an equivalent set of variables x_T and discrete states P_T, and $x_T(t_{i+1}) = x_T(t_i) + \int_{t_i}^{t_{i+1}} f_p(x_T)\, dt$. A/T abstracts A, that is, $x_T(t) = x(t)$ for all $t \in T$, provided that A satisfies $x(t') \in I(p_i)$ for all $t' \in [t_i, t_{i+1}]$ for all $i \geq 0$. An implementation $\text{prog}(A/T)$ of A/T, then, is a program that computes $x(t_{i+1})$ based on a routine $\text{prog}(f_p)$ that solves the equation $x(t_{i+1}) = x(t_i) + \int_{t_i}^{t_{i+1}} f_p(x)\, dt$ numerically, and determines the next discrete state p', on or before time t_{i+1}. $\text{prog}(A/T)$ is a precise implementation of A/T if (1) a precise algorithm $\text{prog}(f_p)$ to solve $\int_{t_i}^{t_{i+1}} f_p(x)\, dt$ is provided, and (2) execution of the algorithm and decision of the next discrete state can be done within the time constraint $(t_{i+1} - t_i)$. The latter requirement is a classic real-time computing problem. In a special case where $t_{i+1} - t_i = h$ for all $i \geq 0$, $\text{prog}(A/T)$ can easily be mapped to a periodic task of the RTOS with a period h. On the other hand, the former requirement can be satisfied only for a limited class of differential equations (e.g., zero-order differential equations) and a sampling rate carefully selected to avoid floating-point errors. The effect of numerical errors in hybrid models can be significant since discrete transitions based on erroneous values may lead to entirely different trajectory.

When the model consists of multiple components and the code is generated such that components are mapped to concurrent tasks, in addition to the aforementioned requirements, tasks need to be synchronized with each other. That is, given a composite hybrid model $A = A_1 \| A_2 \| \ldots \| A_n$, $\mathrm{prog}(A/T)$ would consist of concurrent programs $\mathrm{prog}(A_1/T), \mathrm{prog}(A_2/T), \ldots, \mathrm{prog}(A_n/T)$ such that each program $\mathrm{prog}(A_l/T)$ executes (1) a numerical algorithm to solve $x_{A_l}(t_{i+1}) = x_{A_l}(t_i) + \int_{t_i}^{t_{i+1}} f_{p_{A_l}}(x_{A_l}) \, dt$ where x_{A_l} is a vector of variables whose dynamics is constrained by A_l, (2) wait for A_m for all $m \neq l$ to finish computation of $x_{A_m}(t_{i+1})$, and (3) decides the next discrete state. This requirement may be costly if the programs are executed in a distributed system where communication is an expensive operation. Moreover, formal relationship between the model and the code is not obvious when the concurrent tasks are executing at different rates. Modern modeling tools such as SIMULINK, for example, support code generation with different sampling rates (assuming they are harmonic) for different components of a single model to improve the CPU utilization, but there have been no formalism on the semantic relationship between the implementation and the model. In general, a set of concurrent programs $\mathrm{prog}(A_1/T_1), \mathrm{prog}(A_2/T_2), \ldots, \mathrm{prog}(A_n/T_n)$ for $A = A_1 \| A_2 \| \ldots \| A_n$, does not implement A/T precisely for any T if $T_l \neq T_m$ for some m, l. The reason is that, to evaluate a guard set $G(p, p')$ of A_l at time t, valuation $x_m(t)$ should be available for all $1 \leq m \leq n$, which is true only when $T_1 = T_2 = \ldots = T_n$. Evaluation of guard sets based on valuation from different time instances may lead to an erroneous discrete transition that is not allowed in the hybrid model. For example, suppose a hybrid model consisting of two variables x_1, x_2 and the code that is generated such that the two variables are updated at different rates. At time t, the generated code may have valuation $x_1(t)$ of x_1 at time t, but, for x_2, only valuation $x_2(t')$ at time $t' < t$ may be available. Suppose again, that $(x_1(t), x_2(t')) \in G((p, p'))$ for some p' where p is the discrete state at time t. In this case, the generated code may take the transition (p, p') since it *appears* to be enabled. However, if the hybrid model indicates $x(t) = (x_1(t), x_2(t)) \notin G((p, p'))$, the transition should not be taken at time t, implying the generated code is not consistent to the model. We call this type of errors *synchronization errors*.

In this paper, we propose a framework aiming at sound code generation from Communicating hybrid models that prevents synchronization errors. Our approach is based on a model refinement technique that we call *instrumentation*. Instrumentation replaces the guard set and the invariant set with their subsets to exclude valuations that may potentially lead to an erroneous discrete transition due to different valuation times of variables. Note that a model obtained by instrumentation is subsumed by the original hybrid model, that is, every possible behavior of the instrumented model is also a valid behavior of the original hybrid model. This comes from the semantics of hybrid automata where transitions *may* be taken when the associated enabling condition (i.e., *guard*) is true (that is, the transition condition is an enabler, rather than a trigger). Therefore, the behavior observed from the code generated from the instrumented model is guaranteed to belong to (a discrete-time abstraction of) the original hybrid model.

Figure 1 shows overall flow of our framework. We start with Communicating Hybrid Automata defined in the continuous time domain. Associating a discrete time domain to Communicating Hybrid Automata defines *Discretized Communicating Hybrid Automata*. States of Discretized Communicating Hybrid Automata are defined only at the time instances belonging to the given time domain. Discretized Communicating Hybrid Automata generate exact snapshots of Communicating Hybrid Automata in a discrete fashion, under a condition that will be explained in Section 3. *Instrumented Communicating Hybrid Automata* allows heterogeneous discrete time domains between components. States of Instrumented Communicating Hybrid Automata are defined at the time instances belonging to the union of all the discrete time domains of the components. We claim that, for every trace of discrete transitions of Instrumented Communicating Hybrid Automata, there exists an equivalent trace of discrete transitions in Communicating Hybrid Automata. We also claim that the deviation of valuation at every discrete transition is bounded.

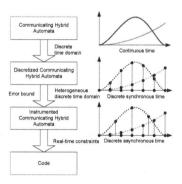

Fig. 1. Design flow.

The remainder of the paper is organized as follows. The next section gives a formal description of Communicating Hybrid Automata and the semantics. In the next, we present Discretized Communicating Hybrid Automata and their relationship with Communicating Hybrid Automata. The following is a detailed description of Instrumented Communicating Hybrid Automata with a motivational example. Additional issues that need to be considered when the instrumented model is converted into code are described in the next section. Finally, concluding remarks are given in the last section.

2   Communicating Hybrid Automata

This section defines Communicating Hybrid Automaton (*CHA*) as an extension of the timed automaton [1] to include shared variable-based communication. To simplify discussion, we limit our attention to Communicating Hybrid Automata with independent dynamics and guard/invariant sets specified by intervals.

Definition 1. *(CHA). A Communicating Hybrid Automaton, CHA, is a tuple*
$A = (P, VC, SV, p_0, F, E, I, G, R, INIT)$, *where*

- P *is a finite set of distinct positions,*
- VC *is a finite set of continuous real variables, where* $|VC| = n$,
- $SV \subseteq VC$ *is a non-empty finite set of shared variables which are partitioned into input* $SV|_{in}$ *and output* $SV|_{out}$,
- $p_0 \in P$ *is the initial position,*
- $F: P \to \mathcal{F}$ *assigns to* $p \in P$ *a function* $F_p \in \mathcal{F}: \mathbb{R}^n \to \mathbb{R}^n$, *which defines ordinary differential equations satisfying the assumptions for existence and uniqueness of solutions for all variables in* $VC - SV|_{in}$,
- $E \subseteq P \times P$ *is a finite set of discrete transitions,*
- $I: P \to (2^{\mathbb{R}})^n$ *assigns the invariant interval to* $p \in P$ *such that* $I(p) \in (2^{\mathbb{R}})^n$ *and, for all* $x \in VC$, *we denote the invariant interval of* x *at the position* p *by* $I_x(p)$,
- $G: E \to (2^{\mathbb{R}})^n$ *assigns to* $(p_1, p_2) \in E$ *the guard interval such that for all* $x \in VC$, $G_x((p_1, p_2)) \cap I_x(p_1) \neq \emptyset$, *where* $G_x((p_1, p_2))$ *denotes the guard interval of* x,
- $R: E \times VC \to \mathbb{R}$ *assigns a reset value* $R((p_1, p_2), x) \in I_x(p_2)$ *to a pair* $(p_1, p_2) \in E$ *and* $x \in VC - SV|_{in}$, *and*
- $INIT: VC \to \mathbb{R}$ *assigns to a variable the initial value satisfying* $INIT(x) \in I_x(p_0)$, *for all* $x \in VC - SV|_{in}$. □

In the rest of the paper, we denote P of A by P_A. Likewise, we use VC_A, p_0^A, F_A, E_A, I_A, G_A, R_A, and $INIT_A$ to denote VC, p_0, F, E, I, G, R, and $INIT$ of A, respectively. For all $x \in VC_A$, the invariant and the guard intervals of x are denoted by $I_{A,x}$ and $G_{A,x}$, respectively. When it is clear, we omit A.

Definition 2. *(State of a CHA). Given a CHA A, a (time-stamped) state* $s = (p, u, t)$ *is an element of* $P_A \times \mathbb{R}^n \times \mathbb{R}$ *satisfying the following condition: at time t, for all* $x \in VC$, $u(x) \in I_x(p)$, *where* $u(x)$ *is the valuation of* x. □

A state (p, u, t) means that at time t the system is at the position p with the valuation u. When a state $s_i = (p_i, u_i, t_i)$ is given, we use $s_i|_p, s_i|_u, s_i|_t$ to denote p_i, u_i, t_i, respectively. In addition, we use $u \in I_A(p)$ if $u(x) \in I_{A,x}(p)$ for all $x \in VC$, and $u \in G_A((p_1, p_2))$ if $u(x) \in G_{A,x}((p_1, p_2))$ for all $x \in VC$.

Definition 3. *(Discrete transition step of a CHA). Given a CHA A, a pair of states* (s_i, s_j) *is called a discrete transition step if the following conditions are satisfied:*

- $s_i|_t = s_j|_t$,
- $(s_i|_p, s_j|_p) \in E_A$,
- $s_i|_u \in G_A((s_i|_p, s_j|_p))$, *and*
- $s_j|_u(x) = R_A((s_i|_p, s_j|_p), x)$, *for all* $x \in VC - SV|_{in}$. □

The value of input variable is defined later in Definition 7. Note that a discrete transition is of the form (p_m, p_n), where $p_m, p_n \in P$, i.e., a directed edge from the node p_m to the node p_n, whereas a discrete transition step is (s_i, s_j), where s_i and s_j are states defined in Definition 2.

Definition 4. *(Continuous transition step of a CHA). Given a CHA A, a pair of states (s_i, s_j) is called a continuous transition step if the following conditions are satisfied:*

- $s_i|_t < s_j|_t$,
- $s_i|_p = s_j|_p$,
- *for all $t \in [s_i|_t, s_j|_t]$, $x(t) \in I_x(s_i|_p)$, for all $x \in VC$, and*
- *for all $t \in [s_i|_t, s_j|_t]$, $dx(t)/dt$ is the same as the dynamics defined by $F_{s_i|_p}$, for all $x \in VC - SV|_{in}$.*   □

The value of input variable is defined later in Definition 8. The continuous transition step corresponds to the continuous flow at the position p with the dynamics specified by F_p from time t_i to time t_j.

Definition 5. *(System of Communicating Hybrid Automata). Given a finite set of CHAs $\{(A_0, SV_0), \dots, (A_i, SV_i), \dots, (A_n, SV_n)\}$, a System of Communicating Hybrid Automata denoted by SCHA C is a tuple $((A_0, SV_0), \dots, (A_i, SV_i), \dots, (A_n, SV_n))$, such that*

- $\cup_i SV_i|_{in} \subseteq \cup_i SV_i|_{out}$ *and*
- $SV_i|_{out} \cap SV_j|_{out} = \emptyset$, *for all $0 \le i \ne j \le n$.*   □

We will denote C as $(A_0, A_1, \dots, A_n, SV)$, where $SV = \bigcup_i SV_i|_{out}$. Note that the shared variables in SV are write-exclusive.

Definition 6. *(State of an SCHA). Given an SCHA $C = (A_0, A_1, \dots, A_n, SV)$, a state s is defined as $((p^{A_0}, u^{A_0}), \dots, (p^{A_n}, u^{A_n}), t)$, where (p^{A_i}, u^{A_i}, t) is a state of CHA A at time t satisfying that $u^{A_i}(x) = u^{A_j}(x)$ if $x \in SV_i|_{in} \cap SV_j|_{out}$.*   □

Note that $s|_{A_i}$ denotes (p^{A_i}, u^{A_i}, t), and that $s|_t$ denotes the time t. We will use $s|_{A_i,p}$, $s|_{A_i,u}$, and $s|_{A_i,t}$ to denote p^{A_i}, u^{A_i}, and t, respectively.

Definition 7. *(Discrete transition step of an SCHA). Given an SCHA C, a pair of states (s_i, s_j) is called a discrete transition step if there exists A_m such that $(s_i|_{A_m}, s_j|_{A_m})$ is a discrete transition step in A_m, and for all A_k where $(s_i|_{A_k}, s_j|_{A_k})$ is not a discrete transition step in A_k, if the following is satisfied:*

$$s_i|_{A_k,t} = s_j|_{A_k,t}, \ s_i|_{A_k,p} = s_j|_{A_k,p}, \ and$$

$$s_j|_{A_k,u}(x) = \begin{cases} s_j|_{A_l,u}(x) \ if \ x \in SV_k|_{in} \cap SV_l|_{out} \ for \ some \ A_l, \\ s_j|_{A_k,u}(x) \ otherwise. \end{cases}$$ □

Definition 8. *(Continuous transition step of an SCHA). Given an SCHA C, a pair of states (s_i, s_j) is called a continuous transition step if the following is satisfied:*

- $s_i|_t < s_j|_t$,
- $(s_i|_{A_k}, s_j|_{A_k})$ *is a continuous transition step for all $k \in \{0, 1, \dots, n\}$, and*
- $s_j|_{A_k,u}(x) = s_j|_{A_l,u}(x)$, *for all $x \in SV_k|_{in} \cap SV_l|_{out}$.*   □

Definition 9. *(Run of an SCHA). A run of an SCHA $C = (A_0, A_1, \ldots, A_n, SV)$ is a (possibly infinite) sequence of states $\langle s_0, s_1, \ldots, s_i, s_{i+1}, \ldots \rangle$, where*

- *$s_0 = ((p_0^{A_0}, INIT_{A_0}), (p_0^{A_1}, INIT_{A_1}), \ldots, (p_0^{A_n}, INIT_{A_n}), 0)$, and*
- *(s_i, s_{i+1}) is either a discrete transition step or a continuous transition step for all $i \geq 0$.*

A run is called an alternating run if discrete transition steps and continuous transition steps occurs alternately, i.e., if (s_i, s_{i+1}) is a continuous transition step, then (s_{i+1}, s_{i+2}) is a discrete transition step, and vice versa. □

3   Discretized Communicating Hybrid Automata

We now give a formal definition of Discretized Communicating Hybrid Automata as the first step towards the generated code. A Discretized Communicating Hybrid Automaton is a discrete-time abstraction of a given Communicating Hybrid Automaton over a discrete time domain.

Definition 10. *(DCHA) A Discretized Communicating Hybrid Automaton, DCHA, is a tuple $H = (A, T)$, where*

- *A is a Communicating Hybrid Automaton,*
- *$T = \{t_0, t_1, t_2, \ldots\}$ is a discrete time domain, where $t_i \in \mathbb{R}$ and $t_{i+1} > t_i$ for all i.* □

Definition 11. *(State of DCHA). Given a DCHA H, a (time-stamped) state $s = (p, u, t)$ is an element of $P_A \times \mathbb{R}^n \times \mathbb{R}$ satisfying the following condition: $t \in T$, and s is a state of A.* □

Note that states of DCHA are defined only at time instances belonging to the given discrete time domain T. The following defines a continuous transition step of DCHA over T. A discrete transition step is defined similarly.

Definition 12. *(Continuous transition step of DCHA). Given a DCHA H, a pair of states (s_i, s_j) is called a unit continuous transition step if the following conditions are satisfied:*

- *$s_i|_t = t_m$ and $s_j|_t = t_{m+1}$ for some $t_m, t_{m+1} \in T$,*
- *$s_i|_p = s_j|_p$,*
- *$s_i|_u, s_j|_u \in I_A(s_i|_p)$, and*
- *for all $x \in VC - SV|_{in}$, $s_j|_u(x) = s_i|_u(x) + \int_{t_m}^{t_{m+1}} F_p(x)\, dt$*

When $\langle (s_i, s_{i+1}), (s_{i+1}, s_{i+2}), \ldots, (s_{j-1}, s_j) \rangle$ is a sequence of unit continuous transition step, we say that (s_i, s_j) is a continuous transition step. When it is clear, a unit continuous transition step is also called a continuous transition step. □

Note that a pair (s_i, s_j) of states of CHA is a continuous transition step of DCHA if (s_i, s_j) is a continuous transition step of CHA and $s_i|_t = t_m$, $s_j|_t = t_{m+1}$ for some $t_m, t_{m+1} \in T$. However, the contrary is not always true. That is, a pair of states constituting a continuous transition step of DCHA is not necessarily a continuous transition step of CHA. This is because that a continuous transition step of CHA requires that for all $t \in [s_i|_t, s_j|_t]$, $x(t) \in I_x(s_i|_p)$, whereas a continuous transition step of DCHA only requires $s_i|_u, s_j|_u \in I(s_i|_p)$. Thus, DCHA does not represent CHA faithfully when the dynamics changes rapidly during a short time interval such that invariant violation may occur even if the states at the endpoints of the interval satisfy the invariant. The following definition formalizes such a condition. (See [2,3] for more general discussion on event detection problems of hybrid systems.)

Definition 13. *(h-insensitivity). Given a CHA A, the invariant $I_x(p)$ is said h-insensitive if, for all $x \in VC - SV|_{in}$, $x(t) \in I_x(p)$ and $x(t + h) = x(t) + \int_t^{t+h} F_p(x)\,dt \in I_x(p)$ implies $x(t + \delta) = x(t) + \int_t^{t+\delta} F_p(x)\,dt \in I_x(p)$ for all $\delta \in [0, h]$, where $x(t)$ denotes valuation of x at time t. When all invariants in A are h-insensitive, A is said h-insensitive. We say that SCHA C is h-insensitive when all CHA A_k of C is h-insensitive.* □

Now we give a definition of discretized SCHA.

Definition 14. *(discretized SCHA). Given an SCHA $C = (A_0, A_1, \ldots, A_n, SV)$ and a discrete time domain T, a discretized SCHA, denoted by DSCHA, is a tuple $(H_0, H_1, \ldots, H_n, SV)$, where $H_i = (A_i, T)$.* □

Note that the components of DSCHA shares the same discrete time domain. That is, we are defining a *discretized* system of CHA, rather than a *system* of discretized CHA. This issue will become clear in Section 4 when we define SICHA that allows heterogeneous time domains. Given that, a state of DSCHA and a run of DSCHA can be defined similar to the case of SCHA. The following lemma states the relation between DSCHA and SCHA.

Lemma 1. *Every run of DSCHA has an equivalent run in the originating SCHA, if SCHA is h-insensitive, where $h = \max(t_{m+1} - t_m), t_m, t_{m+1} \in T$.* □

4 Instrumented Communicating Hybrid Automata

In this section, we present the effect of accumulated numerical errors and synchronization errors in code generated from an SCHA. To formalize the effect of accumulated numerical errors and synchronization errors of an SCHA, we propose the formalism called a System of Instrumented Communicating Hybrid Automata (SICHA). We show that a run of the SICHA is always included in that of the SCHA. Thus, the SICHA provides correct execution results with regard to runs of the original model. The essence of our idea is to reflect the effect of the errors to the invariants and the guards of each position so that the resulting instrumented hybrid automata will produce a sound trace on discrete transition steps. This paper focuses on instrumenting an SCHA considering the effect of asynchrony due to discretization of a model. For the details of the effect of accumulated numerical errors, refer to the the the paper [4].

Motivating example. Figure 2 describes the effect of a synchronization error. Let a shared variable $y \in SV|_{in}^{A_0} \cap SV|_{out}^{A_1}$ be read by A_0 and written by A_1, where the integration stepsizes of A_0 and A_1 are 0.001 and 0.002, respectively (namely, $h_{A_0} = 0.001$ and $h_{A_1} = 0.002$). In this case, y is updated by A_1 at time 0, 0.002, 0.004, ..., and read by A_0 at time 0, 0.001, 0.002, 0.003, 0.004, ... In Figure 2, A_0 needs to decide whether or not it will take a *discrete transition step* at time $0.001 \times (2n+1)$ with a computation result using the value of y produced at time $0.001 \times 2n$, where n is a non-negative integer. For example, at time 0.003 A_0 will evaluate the transition condition with the value of y produced at time 0.002. We need to decide which approximated value of y A_0 will use in evaluating the state of A_0. It relies on the effect of discrepancy between the correct value and the approximated value different from the correct one due to numerical errors and synchronization errors.

Now consider an example of an SCHA. Figure 3 illustrates SCHA `foo` composed of Communicating Hybrid Automata A_0 and A_1.

Table 1 shows that an unexpected trace occurs during simulation of an SCHA `foo` even if we do not consider the effect of numerical errors. If we use the execution stepsize $1.0 \cdot 10^{-3}$ and $2.0 \cdot 10^{-3}$ for A_0 and A_1, respectively, the value of y, $u(y)$ read by A_0 at time 2.000 becomes 50.000000. At time 2.001, A_0 uses

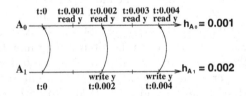

Fig. 2. The Effect of Synchronization Errors

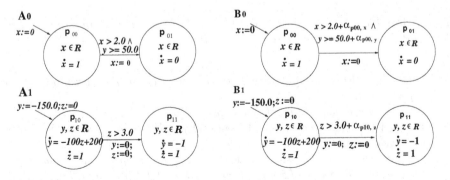

Fig. 3. SCHA `foo`   **Fig. 4.** Instrumented `foo`

Table 1. The Effect of Synchronization Errors of SCHA `foo`

t	y	$y_{simulation}$
...	...	...
1.998	49.999980	49.999980
1.999	49.999995	49.999980
2.000	50.000000	50.000000
2.001	49.999995	50.000000
...	...	...

the value produced at time 2.000, thus *discrete transition* from p_{00} to p_{01} is enabled. In `foo`, however, the transition (p_{00}, p_{01}) must not occur, as the value of y is always less than 50.000000, where $x \in (2.000, \infty)$.

We denote the bound of that discrepancy at position p by $\gamma_{p_j,y}$ and will compute $\gamma_{p_j,y}$ statically using Equation (1). Note that we allow only *exclusive-write/multiple-read* shared variables.

Given an SCHA $C = ((A_0, SV_0), \ldots, (A_n, SV_n))$ and a shared variable $y \in SV_j|_{in} \cap SV_k|_{out}$, the bound of discrepancy due to synchronization error denoted by $\gamma_{p_j,y}$ at position p_j is computed as follows:

$$\gamma_{p_j,y} = \begin{cases} |f(t,y) \cdot h(p_k)|_{max} & \text{if } h(p_k) \geq h(p_j), \\ |f(t,y) \cdot h(p_j)|_{max} & \text{if } h(p_k) < h(p_j), \\ \text{where } f(t,y) \text{ is the derivative of } y \text{ at time } t, \ p_k \in P_{A_k}, \text{ and } p_j \in P_{A_j}. \end{cases}$$
$$(1)$$

To formalize the effect of that asynchronous integration effect in code execution, we propose the formalism called System of Instrumented Communicating Hybrid Automata (SICHA). First, we define ICHA as a correspondent of CHA followed by definition of SICHA and then, we show that the alternating run of the SICHA is always included in that of the SCHA. Thus, the SICHA provides sound execution results with regard to the alternating run of the original model.

In the rest of the paper, given an interval b, we use $l(b)$ and $r(b)$ to denote the lower and the upper bounds of b, respectively. An interval b can be open on either or both sides; so, b can be $(l(b), r(b)), (l(b), r(b)], [l(b), r(b)),$ or $[l(b), r(b)]$. For arithmetic operations with $l(b)$ and $r(b)$, we assume that $\infty \pm x = \infty$ for any real x.

Definition 15. *(ICHA). Given a CHA A, an Instrumented Communicating Hybrid Automaton of A, called ICHA, is defined as a tuple $B = (A, N, h, \beta, \gamma)$, where*

- $N: P_A \to PROG$ *assigns to $p \in P_A$ a numerical method program with a stepsize $h(p)$,*
- $h: P_A \to \mathbb{R}^+$ *assigns to $p \in P_A$ a stepsize $h(p)$,*
- $\beta: P_A \times VC \to \mathbb{R}$ *assigns to $x \in VC$ at each $p \in P_A$, a maximum accumulated numerical error to calculate x denoted by $\beta_{p,x}$,*
- $\gamma: P_A \times SV|_{in} \to \mathbb{R}$ *assigns to $x \in SV|_{in}$ at each $p \in P_A$, a maximum difference of the value of x from time t to time $t + h(p)$ denoted by $\gamma_{p,x}$,*
- *for each $p \in P_A$ and the invariant interval $I_{A,x}(p)$, $l(I_{B,x}(p)) = l(I_{A,x}(p)) + \alpha_{p,x}$, $r(I_{B,x}(p)) = r(I_{A,x}(p)) - \alpha_{p,x}$, for all $x \in VC_A$, and*

- *for each* $e \in E_A$ *and the guard interval* $G_{A,x}(e)$, $l(G_{B,x}(e)) = l(G_{A,x}(e)) + \alpha_{p,x}$, $r(G_{B,x}(e)) = r(G_{A,x}(e)) - \alpha_{p,x}$, *for all* $x \in VC_A$,

where

$$\alpha_{p,x} = \begin{cases} \beta_{p,x} & \text{if variable } x \notin SV|_{in} \text{ at position } p \\ \beta_{p,x} + \gamma_{p,x} & \text{otherwise.} \end{cases} \qquad \square$$

We will use α or α_x instead of $\alpha_{p,x}$ when clear. The definition of *state* and *discrete transition step* for ICHA are the same as the definitions in Section 2.

Definition 16. *(Continuous transition step of an ICHA). Given an ICHA B, a pair of states* (s_i, s_j) *is called a unit continuous transition step if the following conditions are satisfied:*

- $s_j|_t = s_i|_t + h(s_i|_p)$,
- $s_i|_p = s_j|_p$,
- *for all* i, j, $s_i|_u, s_j|_u \in I_A(s_i|_p)$, *and*
- *for all* $x \in VC - SV_i|_{in}$, $s_j|_u(x)$ *is computed with* $N(s_j|_p), h(s_j|_p)$, *and* $s_i|_u(x)$. $\qquad \square$

The value of input variable is defined later in Definition 19 and Definition 20.

Definition 17. *(System of Instrumented Communicating Hybrid Automata). Let* $C = (A_0, A_1, \ldots, A_n, SV)$ *be an SCHA. A System of ICHA (SICHA) D of an SCHA C is defined by a tuple* $(B_0, B_1, \ldots, B_n, SV)$ *where* B_i *is an ICHA of* A_i. $\qquad \square$

Definition 18. *(State of an SICHA). Given an SICHA* $D = (B_0, B_1, \ldots, B_n, SV)$ *of SCHA C, a state* s *at time* t *is defined as* $((p^{B_0}, u^{B_0}, t^{B_0}), (p^{B_1}, u^{B_1}, t^{B_1}), \ldots, (p^{B_n}, u^{B_n}, t^{B_n}))$, *letting* $s|_t$, $s|_{B_i}$, $s|_{B_i,p}$, $s|_{B_i,u}$, *and* $s|_{B_i,t}$ *be* t, $(p^{B_i}, u^{B_i}, t^{B_i})$, p^{B_i}, u^{B_i}, *and* t^{B_i}, *respectively, where*

- *for every* i, $s|_{B_i}$ *is a state of ICHA* B_i,
- *for every* i, $s|_{B_i,t} \leq s|_t$,
- *for some* i, $s|_{B_i,t} = s|_t$,
- *for every* i, $s|_t - s|_{B_i,t} < h(s|_{B_i,p})$, *and*
- *if* $x \in SV_{A_i}|_{in} \cap SV_{A_j}|_{out}$ *and* $s|_{B_j,t} < s|_{B_i,t}$ *then* $s|_{B_i,u}(x) = s|_{B_j,u}(x)$. $\qquad \square$

Definition 19. *(Discrete transition step of an SICHA). Given an SICHA D, a pair of states* (s_i, s_j) *is called a discrete transition step at time* t, *if the followings are satisfied:*

- $s_i|_{B_k,t} = s_j|_{B_k,t}$ *for every ICHA* B_k *in* D,
- *there exists some non-empty set* $K \subseteq \{0, 1, \ldots, n\}$, *satisfying the following:*
  - *if* $k \in K$ *then* $(s_i|_{B_k}, s_j|_{B_k})$ *is a discrete transition step of* B_k *at time* $s_i|_t$, *(that is,* $s_i|_{B_k,t} = s_j|_{B_k,t} = s_i|_t$*), and*

$$s_j|_{B_k,u}(x) = \begin{cases} s_j|_{B_l,u}(x) & \text{if } x \in SV_k|_{in} \cap SV_l|_{out} \\ R((s_i|_{B_k,p}, s_j|_{B_k,p}), x) & \text{otherwise,} \end{cases}$$

- if $k \notin K$ then $s_i|_{B_k,t} = s_j|_{B_k,t}$, $s_i|_{B_k,p} = s_j|_{B_k,p}$, and $s_i|_{B_k,u}(x) = s_j|_{B_k,u}(x)$ for all $x \in VC_{B_k}$. □

Definition 20. *(Continuous transition step of an SICHA). Given an SICHA D, a pair of states (s_i, s_j) is called a unit continuous transition step if the following conditions are satisfied:*

- $s_i|_t < s_j|_t$,
- *there exists a unique non-empty set $K \subseteq \{0, 1, \dots, n\}$ such that*
  - *for $k \in K$, $(s_i|_{B_k}, s_j|_{B_k})$ is a continuous transition step of B_k such that $s_j|_t = s_i|_{B_k,t} + h(s_i|_{B_k,p})$, and $s_j|_{B_k,u}(x) = s_i|_{B_l,u}(x)$, if $x \in SV_k|_{in} \cap SV_l|_{out}$, and*
  - *for $k \notin K$, $s_i|_{B_k,t} + h(s_i|_{B_k,p}) > s_j|_t$ and $s_i|_{B_k,t} = s_j|_{B_k,t}$, $s_i|_{B_k,p} = s_j|_{B_k,p}$, and $s_i|_{B_k,u}(x) = s_j|_{B_k,u}(x)$ for all $x \in VC_{B_k}$.* □

Definition 21. *(Run of an SICHA). A run of an SICHA $D = (B_0, B_1, \dots, B_n, SV)$ is a sequence of states $\langle s_0, s_1, \dots, \rangle$ such that*

- $s_0 = ((p_0^{B_0}, INIT_{B_0}), (p_0^{B_1}, INIT_{B_1}), \dots, (p_0^{B_n}, INIT_{B_n}), 0)$,
- *if $s_i|_t = s_{i+1}|_t$, (s_i, s_{i+1}) is a discrete transition step at time $s_i|_t$, and*
- *if $s_i|_t < s_{i+1}|_t$, (s_i, s_{i+1}) is a unit continuous transition step.*

The alternating run of an SICHA is defined similarly to that of an SCHA. A run of an SICHA D is called an alternating run of D, if the discrete transition step and the continuous transition step occurs in D alternately. □

Let A be an HA and B be its instrumented correspondent. In this paper, we assume that A is h_B-insensitive, where $h_B = h_B(p)_{max}, p \in P_B$. Then, given an HA A its IHA B always produces safe alternating runs. The claim is stated formally in Theorem 1 and its proof is given in [4]. Also, the proofs of Lemma 2 and Lemma 3 are presented in [5].

Theorem 1. *Given an HA A, let $B = (A, N, h, \beta, \gamma)$ be an IHA such that A is h_B-insensitive. Then, for every alternating run $\langle s_0^B, \dots, s_i^B, \dots, \rangle$, there exists an alternating run $\langle s_0^A, \dots, s_i^A, \dots, \rangle$ of A such that*

- $s_i^A|_p = s_i^B|_p$,
- $s_i^A|_u(x) \in [s_i^B|_u(x) - \beta_x, s_i^B|_u(x) + \beta_x]$ *for all $x \in VC_A - SV|_{in}$, and*
- $s_i^A|_t = s_i^B|_t$. □

Lemma 2. *Given an SCHA $C = (A_0, A_1, \dots, A_n, SV)$, let $D = (B_0, B_1, \dots, B_n, SV)$ be its SICHA and let s^C and s^D be states in C and D, respectively, satisfying the following conditions:*

- $s^C|_t = s^D|_t$,
- $s^C|_{A_i,p} = s^D|_{B_i,p}$ *for all $i, 0 \le i \le n$, and*
- $s^C|_{A_i,u}(x) \in [s^D|_{B_i,u}(x) - \alpha_x, s^D|_{B_i,u}(x) + \alpha_x]$ *for all $x \in VC_{A_i}$ and for all $i, 0 \le i \le n$.*

Suppose A_i is h_{B_i}-insensitive and, for some state s'^D of D if (s^D, s'^D) is a unit continuous transition step with respect to K, then there exists a continuous transition step (s^C, s'^C) for some state s'^C in C and it satisfies followings:

1. $s'^C|_{A_i,p} = s'^D|_{B_i,p}$ *for every i,*
2. $s'^C|_{A_i,u}(x) \in \begin{cases} [s'^D|_{B_i,u}(x) - \beta_x, s'^D|_{B_i,u}(x) + \beta_x] & \text{if } i \in K \text{ and } x \notin SV_{A_i}|_{in} \\ [s'^D|_{B_i,u}(x) - \alpha_x, s'^D|_{B_i,u}(x) + \alpha_x] & \text{otherwise,} \end{cases}$
3. $s'^C|_t = s'^D|_t$, *and*
4. $s'^C|_{A_i,u}(x) \in I_{A_i,x}(s'^C|_{A_i,p})$ *for all $x \in VC_{A_i}$ and for all i.* $\qquad\square$

Lemma 3. *Given an SCHA $C = (A_0, A_1, \ldots, A_n, SV)$, let $D = (B_0, B_1, \ldots, B_n, SV)$ be its SICHA and let s^C and s^D be its states satisfying the conditions for some $K \subseteq \{0, 1, \ldots, n\}$,*

- $s^C|_{A_i,p} = s^D|_{B_i,p}$, *for all i, $0 \le i \le n$,*
- $s^C|_{A_i,u}(x) \in [s^D|_{B_i,u}(x) - \alpha_x, s^D|_{B_i,u}(x) + \alpha_x]$, *for all $x \in SV_{A_i}$ and for all i, $0 \le i \le n$,*
- $s^C|_t = s^D|_t$, *and*
- $s^D|_{B_j,u}(x) \in G_x(s^D|_{B_j,p})$, *if $j \in K$.*

Then, for some state s'^B of B, if (s^B, s'^B) is a discrete transition step with respect to K then there exists a discrete transition step (s^C, s'^C) with respect to K for some state s'^C in C satisfying followings:

1. $s'^C|_{A_i,p} = s'^D|_{B_i,p}$, *for all $i, 0 \le i \le n$,*
2. $s'^C|_{A_i,u}(x) = s'^D|_{B_i,u}(x)$, *if $i \in K$ and $x \notin SV_{A_i}|_{in}$,*
3. $s'^C|_{A_i,u}(x) \in [s'^D|_{B_i,u}(x) - \alpha_x, s'^D|_{B_i,u}(x) + \alpha_x]$, *if $i \notin K$ or $x \in SV_{A_i}|_{in}$,*
4. $s'^C|_t = s'^D|_t$, *and*
5. $s'^C|_{A_i,u}(x) \in I_x(s'^C|_{A_i,p})$, *for all $x \in SV_{A_i}$ and for all $i \in K$.* $\qquad\square$

Theorem 2. *Let C and D be an SCHA, $(A_0, \ldots, A_j, \ldots, A_n, SV)$, and its SICHA, $(B_0, \ldots, B_j, \ldots, B_n, SV)$, respectively. Suppose A_j is h_{B_j}-insensitive, then, for every alternating run $\langle s_0^D, s_1^D \ldots, s_i^D, \ldots, \rangle$ in D, there exists an alternating run $\langle s_0^C, s_1^C \ldots, s_i^C, \ldots, \rangle$ in C such that*

- $s_i^C|_{A_i,p} = s_i^D|_{B_i,p}$,
- $s_i^C|_{A_i,u}(x) \in [s_i^D|_{A_i,u}(x) - \alpha_x, s_i^D|_{B_i,u}(x) + \alpha_x]$, *and*
- $s_i^C|_t = s_i^D|_t$.

Proof. Immediately followed by lemma 2 and lemma 3. $\qquad\square$

Example revisited. Figure 4 depicts the instrumented version of the SCHA `foo` described in Figure 3 to exclude the unexpected execution trace from `foo`. As the stepsize of A_0 and A_1 are $1.0 \cdot 10^{-3}$ and $2.0 \cdot 10^{-3}$, respectively, $\gamma_{p00,y}$ is $0.002 \cdot 100.0 = 0.2$. If we instrument the guard at position p_{00} of A_0 with $\gamma_{p00,y}$, then the unexpected trace disappears.

5   Executable Code

We have implemented a code generator that produces C++ code implementing SICHA. The generated code needs to be associated with a real-time scheduler to satisfy timely computation. Each ICHA B_i of an SICHA can be mapped to a periodic task with the period and the deadline equal to $\min(h_{B_i}(p))$. In addition, a scheduling policy that guarantees the condition of a valid state of an SICHA (Definition 18) should be chosen. That is, for every state s of an SICHA, the condition $s|_t - s|_{B_i,t} < h(s|_{B_i,p})$ should be satisfied for all B_i. This implies that the task for B_i should be scheduled earlier than the task for B_j if $s|_{B_i,t} + h(s|_{B_i,p}) < s|_{B_j,t} + h(s|_{B_j,p})$. Note that this requirement is equivalent to the well-known EDF scheduling policy. (The RM scheduling policy can satisfy the requirement only when the periods are harmonic.)

Moreover, it is also required that the task for B_i should be blocked even when the system is idle if the task for B_k such that $s|_{B_k} + h(s|_{B_k,p}) < s|_{B_i} + h(s|_{B_i,p})$ is not ready (i.e., $t < s|_{B_k,t}$, where t is the real time). This wastes the CPU utilization and may affect schedulability, similarly to the problem of scheduling of tasks with dependency. This problem can be addressed in two ways. First, the execution result of a task can be buffered and emitted later to avoid blocking of such tasks (see [6,7], for example). Second, the model can be instrumented to tolerate the errors due to scheduling of such tasks, in the same way as we do for models with different rates. Our approach has the advantage of avoiding possible overhead of buffering.

Another important issue is how to resolve non-determinism of discrete transitions. The non-determinism comes from two sources. First, a discrete transition may or may not be taken when the associated guard is enabled. Second, there may be more than one transition whose guard is enabled. Depending on the decision, different behaviors may arise. The set of behaviors are acceptable as long as they do not violate the invariant condition. Note that our framework guarantees that every behavior of SICHA is also found in the hybrid model (within bounded deviation) up to the point before the invariant is violated whatever a decision is made on non-deterministic discrete transitions.

In the case where the code detects violation of the invariant, it means either (1) the hybrid model also has an equivalent run that ends with invariant violation, or (2) the code missed an outgoing transition before the invariant is violated due to discretized guard checking. The former issue is the matter of the validity of the model, rather than code generation. That is, such a case can be prevented by refining the model such that the states outside of the invariant set are unreachable. (See [8,9,10] for systematic approaches.) On the other hand, the latter case is an artifact of code generation. Instrumentation may additionally cause such an artifact that should not otherwise occur, because it reduces the guard set and the invariant set, and thus gives a better chance of transition misses. Assuming that the hybrid model is valid (i.e., the invariant set is unreachable), transition misses can be prevented if the guard set and the invariant set overlap for a duration of time longer than the step size, and the code employs an *urgent transition* policy (i.e., transition is taken as soon as it is detected enabled). For detailed description, see [11].

6 Conclusion

In this paper, we have proposed a code generation framework for hybrid models that focuses on soundness of synthesized code. The idea behind the sound code generation is to refine the hybrid model such that it is robust to erroneous values. In this paper, we have focused on the effect of synchronization errors that occur when components of a hybrid model are synthesized into concurrent programs having different rates. We have proved that every possible behavior of the model instrumented with maximum possible errors is a valid behavior of the original hybrid model. We have also explained the issue of scheduling and non-determinism when the instrumented hybrid automata are finally converted into executable code.

We implemented our idea in the context of the hybrid systems modeling language CHARON [12]. Previous implementation of the code generator [11,13] has been extended to allow instrumentation of the guard and the invariant. We have also performed preliminary experiments with Sony's robot dog AIBO to avoid erroneous behavior that is not consistent to the model.

Our work can be extended further in many ways. First, a more systematic way of model instrumentation may be possible if model checking techniques are employed. The predicate abstraction-based model checking tool developed for CHARON [14] can be used for this purpose. We expect that model checking based instrumentation leads to more tightly instrumented code. Second, we can also include controller synthesis techniques [8,9,10] to our framework to allow automatic refinement of the model such that the generated code is guaranteed to satisfy the invariant condition.

Acknowledgement. This research was supported in part by NSF CCR-9988409, NSF CCR-0086147, NSF CCR-0209024, ARO DAAD19-01-1-0473, and DARPA ITO MOBIES F33615-00-C-1707.

References

1. Alur, R., Dill, D.L.: A theory of timed automata. Theoretical Computer Science **126** (1994) 183–235
2. Esposito, J., Kumar, V., Pappas, G.: Accurate event detection for simulating hybrid systems. In: Proceedings of HSCC. LNCS 2034 (2001) 204–217
3. Park, T., Barton, P.: State event location in differential-algebraic models. ACM Transactions on Modeling and Computer Simulation **6** (1996) 137–165
4. Choi, J.Y., Hur, Y., Lee, I.: IHA: Ensuring sound numerical simulation of hybrid automata. Technical Report MS-CIS-03-06, University of Pennsylvania (2003)
5. Choi, J.Y., Hur, Y., Kim, J., Lee, I.: Sound synchronization of communicating hybrid automata. Technical Report MS-CIS-03-30, University of Pennsylvania. (2003)

6. Henzinger, T., Horowitz, B., Kirsch, C.: Giotto: A time-triggered language for embedded programming. In: Proceedings of EMSOFT. (2001) 166–184
7. Kodase, S., Wang, S., Gu, Z., Shin, K.G.: Improving scalability of task allocation and scheduling in large distributed real-time systems using shared buffers. In: Proceedings of RTAS. (2003) 181–188
8. Wong-Toi, H.: The synthesis of discrete controllers for linear hybrid automata. In: Proceedings of CDC. (1997) 4607–4612
9. Altisen, K., Gößler, G., Pnueli, A., , Sifakis, J., Yovine, Y.: A framework for scheduler synthesis. In: Proceedings of RTSS. (1999) 154–163
10. Altisen, K., Gößler, G., Sifakis, J.: A methodology for the construction of scheduled systems. In: Proceedings of FTRTFT. (2000) 106–120
11. Alur, R., Ivančić, F., Kim, J., Lee, I., Sokolsky, O.: Generating embedded software from hierarchial hybrid models. In: Proceedings of LCTES. (2003) 171–182
12. Alur, R., Dang, T., Esposito, J., Hur, Y., Ivančić, F., Kumar, V., Lee, I., Mishra, P., Pappas, G., Sokolsky, O.: Hierarchical modeling and analysis of embedded systems. Proceedings of the IEEE **91** (2003) 11–28
13. Kim, J., Lee, I.: Modular code generation from hybrid automata based on data dependency. In: Proceedings of RTAS. (2003) 160–168
14. Alur, R., Dang, T., Ivančić, F.: Reachability analysis of hybrid systems via predicate abstraction. In: Proceedings of HSCC. LNCS 2289 (2002) 35–48

Multi-Parametric Toolbox (MPT)

Michal Kvasnica, Pascal Grieder, Mato Baotić, and Manfred Morari

Automatic Control Laboratory, Swiss Federal Institute of Technology (ETH)
CH-8092 Zurich, Switzerland,
{kvasnica,grieder,baotic,morari}@control.ee.ethz.ch

Abstract. A Multi-Parametric Toolbox (MPT) for computing optimal or suboptimal feedback controllers for constrained linear and piecewise affine systems is under development at ETH. The toolbox offers a broad spectrum of algorithms compiled in a user friendly and accessible format: starting from different performance objectives (linear, quadratic, minimum time) to the handling of systems with persistent additive disturbances and polytopic uncertainties. The algorithms included in the toolbox are a collection of results from recent publications in the field of constrained optimal control of linear and piecewise affine systems [10,13, 4,9,16,17,15,14,7].

1 Introduction

Optimal control of constrained linear and piecewise affine (PWA) systems has garnered great interest in the research community due to the ease with which complex problems can be stated and solved. The aim of the *Multi-Parametric Toolbox* (MPT) is to provide efficient computational means to obtain feedback controllers for these types of constrained optimal control problems in a MATLAB programming environment. By multi-parametric programming a linear or quadratic optimal control problem is solved off-line as a function of the initial state as a parameter. The associated solution takes the form of a PWA state feedback law. In particular, the state-space is partitioned into polyhedral sets and for each of those sets the optimal control law is given as one affine function of the state. In the on-line implementation of such controllers, computation of the controller action reduces to a simple set-membership test, which is one of the reasons why this method has attracted so much interest in the research community.

As shown first for quadratic [8] and then for linear [4] objectives, a feedback controller may be obtained for constrained linear systems by applying multi-parametric quadratic and linear programming techniques, respectively. The multi-parametric algorithms for constrained finite time optimal control (CFTOC) of linear systems contained in the MPT are based on [1] and are similar to [29]. Both [1] and [29] give algorithms that are significantly more efficient than the original procedure proposed in [8].

It is current practice to approximate the constrained infinite time optimal control (CITOC) by receding horizon control (RHC) - a strategy where the

R. Alur and G.J. Pappas (Eds.): HSCC 2004, LNCS 2993, pp. 448–462, 2004.
© Springer-Verlag Berlin Heidelberg 2004

CFTOC problem is solved at each time step, and then only the initial value of the optimal input sequence is applied to the plant. The main problem of RHC is that it does not, in general, guarantee stability or constraint satisfaction. In order to obtain these properties, certain conditions have to be added to the original problem [25]. The extensions to guarantee these properties are a part of the MPT. It is furthermore possible to impose a minimax optimization objective which allows for the computation of robust controllers for linear systems subject to polytopic uncertainties and additive disturbances [6,20]. As an alternative to computing suboptimal stabilizing controllers, the procedures to compute the infinite time optimal solution for constrained linear systems [13] are also provided.

Optimal control of piecewise affine systems has received great interest in the research community since PWA systems represent a powerful tool for approximating non-linear systems and because of their equivalence to hybrid systems [18]. The algorithms for computing the feedback controllers for constrained PWA systems were presented for quadratic and linear objectives in [10] and [3] respectively, and are also included in this toolbox. Instead of computing the feedback controllers which minimize a finite time cost objective, it is also possible to obtain the infinite time optimal solution for PWA systems [2].

Even though the multi-parametric approaches rely on off-line computation of a feedback law, the computation can quickly become prohibitive for larger problems. This is not only due to the high complexity of the multi-parametric programs involved, but mainly because of the exponential number of transitions between regions which can occur when a controller is computed in a dynamic programming fashion [10,21]. The MPT therefore also includes schemes to obtain sub-optimal controllers of low complexity for linear and PWA systems as presented in [16,14,15,17].

In addition to control tools, the toolbox also provides extensive functionality for polytope manipulation [31]: convex hulls, convex unions and envelopes, Minkowski sums, Pontryagin differences, as well as many other operations can be performed efficiently by MPT. Most of the functionality supports both single polytopes and non-convex unions thereof. Other commercial software, such as the Geometric Bounding Toolbox (GBT) [30], provides similar functionality on the level of polytope manipulation. MPT explicitly takes advantage of object-oriented programming to provide a transparent and easy to use interface. The toolbox is provided free and is based on state of the art optimization packages (compatibility with CPLEX [19], NAG [26], SeDuMi [28], CDD [11] and more).

2 Problem Description and Properties

Polytopic (or, more general, polyhedral) sets are an integral part of multi-parametric programming. For this reason we give some definitions and fundamental operations with polytopes. For more details we refer reader to [31].

Definition 1 (polyhedron). *A convex set $Q \subseteq \mathbb{R}^n$ given as an intersection of a finite number of closed half-spaces $Q = \{x \in \mathbb{R}^n \mid Q^x x \leq Q^c\}$, is called* polyhedron.

Definition 2 (polytope). *A bounded polyhedron* $\mathcal{P} \subset \mathbb{R}^n$

$$\mathcal{P} = \{x \in \mathbb{R}^n \mid P^x x \leq P^c\}, \tag{1}$$

is called polytope.

It follows from the above definitions that every polytope represents a convex, compact (i.e., bounded and closed) set. We say that a polytope $\mathcal{P} \subset \mathbb{R}^n$, $\mathcal{P} = \{x \in \mathbb{R}^n \mid P^x x \leq P^c\}$ is *full dimensional* if $\exists x \in \mathbb{R}^n : P^x x < P^c$. Furthermore, if $\|(P^x)_i\| = 1$, where $(P^x)_i$ denotes i-th row of a matrix P^x, we say that the polytope $\mathcal{P}$ is *normalized*. One of the fundamental properties of a polytope is that it can also be described by its vertices

$$\mathcal{P} = \{x \in \mathbb{R}^n \mid x = \sum_{i=1}^{v_P} \alpha_i V_P^{(i)}, \ 0 \leq \alpha_i \leq 1, \ \sum_{i=1}^{v_P} \alpha_i = 1\}, \tag{2}$$

where $V_P^{(i)}$ denotes the i-th vertex of $\mathcal{P}$, and v_P is the total number of vertices of $\mathcal{P}$. We will henceforth refer to the half-space representation (1) and vertex representation (2) as $\mathcal{H}$ and $\mathcal{V}$ representation respectively.

Definition 3 (face). *Linear inequality* $a'x \leq b$ *is called* valid *for a polyhedron* $\mathcal{P}$ *if* $a'x \leq b$ *holds for all* $x \in \mathcal{P}$. *A subset* $\mathcal{F}$ *of a polyhedron is called a* face *of* $\mathcal{P}$ *if it is represented as* $\mathcal{F} = \mathcal{P} \cap \{x \in \mathbb{R}^n \mid a'x = b\}$, *for some valid inequality* $a'x \leq b$. *The faces of polyhedron* $\mathcal{P}$ *of dimension* 0, 1, $(n-2)$ *and* $(n-1)$ *are called vertices, edges, ridges and facets, respectively.*

We say that a polytope $\mathcal{P} \subset \mathbb{R}^n$, $\mathcal{P} = \{x \in \mathbb{R}^n \mid P^x x \leq P^c\}$ is in a *minimal representation* if the removal of any of the rows in $P^x x \leq P^c$ would change it (i.e., there are no redundant halfspaces). It is straightforward to see that a normalized, full dimensional polytope $\mathcal{P}$ has a *unique* minimal representation. This fact is very useful in practice. Normalized, full dimensional polytopes in minimal representation allow us to avoid any ambiguity when comparing them and very often speed-up other polytope manipulations. We will now define some of the basic manipulations on polytopes.

2.1   Polytope Manipulation

The Set-Difference of two polytopes $\mathcal{P}$ and $\mathcal{Q}$ is a union of polytopes $\mathcal{R} = \bigcup_i \mathcal{R}_i$

$$\mathcal{R} = \mathcal{P} \setminus \mathcal{Q} := \{x \in \mathbb{R}^n \mid x \in \mathcal{P}, x \notin \mathcal{Q}\}. \tag{3}$$

The Pontryagin-Difference of two polytopes $\mathcal{P}$ and $\mathcal{W}$ is a polytope

$$\mathcal{P} \ominus \mathcal{W} := \{x \in \mathbb{R}^n \mid x + w \in \mathcal{P}, \ \forall w \in \mathcal{W}\}. \tag{4}$$

The Minkowski addition of two polytopes $\mathcal{P}$ and $\mathcal{W}$ is a polytope

$$\mathcal{P} \oplus \mathcal{W} := \{x + w \in \mathbb{R}^n \mid x \in \mathcal{P}, \ w \in \mathcal{W}\}. \tag{5}$$

The convex hull of a union of polytopes $\mathcal{P}_i \subset \mathbb{R}^n$, $i = 1, \ldots, p$, is a polytope

$$\text{hull}\left(\bigcup_{i=1}^{p} \mathcal{P}_i\right) := \{x \in \mathbb{R}^n \mid x = \sum_{i=1}^{p} \alpha_i x_i, \ x_i \in \mathcal{P}_i, \ 0 \le \alpha_i \le 1, \ \sum_{i=1}^{p} \alpha_i = 1\}. \tag{6}$$

The envelope of two $\mathcal{H}$-polyhedra $\mathcal{P} = \{x \in \mathbb{R}^n \mid P^x x \le P^c\}$ and $\mathcal{Q} = \{x \in \mathbb{R}^n \mid Q^x x \le Q^c\}$ is an $\mathcal{H}$-polyhedron

$$\text{env}(\mathcal{P}, \mathcal{Q}) = \{x \in \mathbb{R}^n \mid \bar{P}^x x \le \bar{P}^c, \ \bar{Q}^x x \le \bar{Q}^c\}, \tag{7}$$

where $\bar{P}^x x \le \bar{P}^c$ is the subsystem of $P^x x \le P^c$ obtained by removing all the inequalities not valid for the polyhedron $\mathcal{Q}$, and $\bar{Q}^x x \le \bar{Q}^c$ are defined in the similar way with respect to $Q^x x \le Q^c$ and $\mathcal{P}$ [7].

2.2 Multi-parametric Programming

This section first covers some of the fundamentals of multi-parametric programming for linear systems before restating results for PWA systems. Consider a discrete-time linear time-invariant system

$$x(t+1) = Ax(t) + Bu(t) \tag{8a}$$
$$y(t) = Cx(t) + Du(t) \tag{8b}$$

with $A \in \mathbb{R}^{n \times n}$ and $B \in \mathbb{R}^{n \times m}$. Let $x(t)$ denote the state at time t and $x_{t+k|t}$ denote the predicted state at time $t + k$ given the state at time t. For brevity we denote $x_{k|0}$ as x_k. Let u_k be the computed input for time k, given $x(0)$. Assume now that the states and the inputs of the system in (8) are subject to the following constraints

$$x \in \mathbb{X} \subset \mathbb{R}^n, \qquad u \in \mathbb{U} \subset \mathbb{R}^m \tag{9}$$

where $\mathbb{X}$ and $\mathbb{U}$ are compact polyhedral sets containing the origin in their interior, and consider the constrained finite-time optimal control (CFTOC) problem

$$J_N^*(x(0)) = \min_{u_0, \ldots, u_{N-1}} \|Q_f x_N\|_\ell + \sum_{k=0}^{N-1} \|R u_k\|_\ell + \|Q x_k\|_\ell \tag{10a}$$

$$\text{subj. to} \quad x_k \in \mathbb{X}, \ u_{k-1} \in \mathbb{U}, \qquad \forall k \in \{1, \ldots, N\}, \tag{10b}$$

$$x_N \in \mathcal{X}_{set}, \tag{10c}$$

$$x_0 = x(0), \ x_{k+1} = Ax_k + Bu_k, \ \forall k \in \{0, \ldots, N-1\}, \tag{10d}$$

$$\text{if } \ell = 2, \text{then } Q = Q' \succeq 0, \ Q_f = Q_f' \succeq 0, \ R = R' \succ 0 \tag{10e}$$

where (10c) is a user defined set-constraint on the final state which may be chosen such that stability of the closed-loop system is guaranteed [25]. The cost (10a) may be linear (e.g., $\ell \in \{1, \infty\}$) [4] or quadratic (e.g., $\ell = 2$) [8] whereby the matrices Q, R and Q_f represent user-defined weights on the states and inputs.

Definition 4. *We define the N-step feasible set* $\mathcal{X}_f^N \subseteq \mathbb{R}^n$ *as the set of initial states* $x(0)$ *for which the CFTOC problem (10) is feasible, i.e.*

$$\mathcal{X}_f^N = \{x(0) \in \mathbb{R}^n \mid \exists (u_0, \dots , u_{N-1}) \in \mathbb{R}^{Nm},$$
$$x_k \in \mathbb{X}, \ u_{k-1} \in \mathbb{U}, \ \forall k \in \{1, \dots , N\}\}. \tag{11}$$

For a given initial state $x(0)$, problem (10) can be solved as an LP or QP for linear or quadratic cost objectives respectively. However, this type of on-line optimization may be prohibitive for control of fast processes. As shown in [8,4, 9], problem (10) can be solved for all parameters $x(0) \in \mathcal{X}_f^N$ to obtain a feedback solution with the following properties,

Theorem 1. *[8,9] Consider the CFTOC problem (10). Then, the set of feasible parameters* $\mathcal{X}_f^N$ *is convex, the optimizer* $U_N^* : \mathcal{X}_f^N \to \mathbb{R}^{Nm}$ *is continuous and piecewise affine (PWA), i.e.*

$$U_N^*(x(0)) = F_r x(0) + G_r \quad if \quad x(0) \in \mathcal{P}_r = \{x \in \mathbb{R}^n | H_r x \le K_r\}, \ r = 1, \dots , R \tag{12}$$

and the optimal cost $J_N^* : \mathcal{X}_f^N \to \mathbb{R}$ *is continuous, convex and piecewise quadratic* $(\ell = 2)$ *or piecewise linear* $(\ell \in \{1, \infty\})$.

According to Theorem 1, the feasible state space $\mathcal{X}_f^N$ is partitioned into R polytopic regions, i.e., $\mathcal{X}_f^N = \{\mathcal{P}_r\}_{r=1}^R$. An approach was presented in [8], but more efficient algorithms for the computation are given in [1,29]. With sufficiently large horizons or appropriate terminal set constraints (10c) the closed-loop system is guaranteed to be stabilizing for receding horizon control [13,25]. However, no robustness guarantees can be given. This issue is addressed in [20,6] where the authors present minimax methods which are able to cope with additive disturbances

$$x(t+1) = A(\lambda)x(t) + B(\lambda)u(t) + w(t), \quad w(t) \in \mathcal{W}, \tag{13}$$

where $\mathcal{W}$ is a polytope with the origin in its interior. The minimax approach can be applied also when there is polytopic uncertainty in the system dynamics,

$$\Omega := \text{conv}\{[A^{(1)}|B^{(1)}], [A^{(2)}|B^{(2)}], \dots , [A^{(L)}|B^{(L)}]\}, \quad [A(\lambda)|B(\lambda)] \in \Omega, \tag{14}$$

i.e., there exist L nonnegative coefficients $\lambda_l \in \mathbb{R}$ $(l = 1, \dots , L)$ such that

$$\sum_{l=1}^L \lambda_l = 1 , \qquad [A(\lambda)|B(\lambda)] = \sum_{l=1}^L \lambda_l [A^{(l)}|B^{(l)}]. \tag{15}$$

The set of admissible λ can be written as $\Lambda := \{x \in [0,1]^L \mid ||x||_1 = 1\}$. In order to guarantee robust stability of the closed loop system, the objective (10a) is modified such that the feedback law which minimizes the worst case is computed, hence the name *minimax* control.

The results in [8] were extended in [5,10,3] to compute the optimal explicit feedback controller for PWA systems of the form

$$x(k + 1) = A_i x(k) + B_i u(k) + f_i, \tag{16a}$$
$$\text{s.t. } L_i x(k) + E_i u(k) \le W_i, \quad i \in I \tag{16b}$$
$$\text{if } [x'(k) \ u'(k)]' \in \mathcal{D}_i \tag{16c}$$

whereby the dynamics (16a) with the associated constraints (16b) are valid in the polyhedral set $\mathcal{D}_i$ in (16c). The set $I \subset \mathbb{N}$, $I = \{1, \dots, d\}$ represents all possible dynamics, and d denotes the number of different dynamics. Henceforth, we will abbreviate (16a) and (16c) with $x(k + 1) = f_{PWA}(x(k), u(k))$. Note that we do not require $x(k + 1) = f_{PWA}(x(k), u(k))$ to be continuous. The optimization problem considered here is then given by (10) whereby the dynamics (10d) and constraints in (9) are replaced by (16).

For PWA systems, the constraint (10c) is user-specified and imposed on the terminal state in order to guarantee stability [24,14,9]. As an alternative, the infinite horizon optimal controller for PWA systems guarantees stability as well [2]. In order to robustify controllers with respect to additive disturbances, a minimax approach is taken [21] which is identical to what was proposed for linear systems [20,9].

All multi-parametric programming methods suffer from the curse of dimensionality. As the prediction horizon N increases, the number of partitions R ($\mathcal{X}_f^N = \{\mathcal{P}_r\}_{r=1}^R$) grows exponentially making the computation and application of the solution intractable. Therefore, there is a clear need to reduce the complexity of the solution. This was tackled in [15,16,14] where the authors present two methods for obtaining feedback solutions of low complexity for constrained linear and PWA systems. The first controller drives the state in minimum time into a convex set $\mathcal{X}_{set}$, where the cost-optimal feedback law is applied [16,14]. This is achieved by iteratively solving one-step multi-parametric optimization problems. Instead of solving one problem of size N, the algorithm solves N problems of size 1, thus the decrease in both on-line and off-line complexity. This scheme guarantees closed-loop stability. If a linear system is considered, an even simpler controller may be obtained by computing a controller for prediction horizon $N = 1$, with the additional constraint that $x_1 \in \mathcal{X}_f^N$ [16,17]. In order to guarantee stability of this closed-loop system, an LMI analysis is performed which aims at constructing a Lyapunov function [15,17].

3   MPT Content

3.1   References

Aside from standard polytopic-manipulation functions, at this stage the toolbox contains the algorithms presented in the following references. Additions will be made in the future to cover a wider spectrum of the literature.

- Set difference computation and convexity recognition of the union of polyhedra [7].

- Multi-parametric solvers for quadratic objectives for constrained linear [1] and PWA [10] systems.
- Invariant set computation of linear [12] and PWA systems [15].
- Computation of invariant sets for linear [22] and PWA systems [27] subject to bounded disturbances.
- Stability analysis of PWA systems through LMIs [15].
- Robust stability analysis of PWA systems through LMIs [17].
- Multi-parametric computation of robust feedback controllers for constrained linear systems [6].
- Multi-parametric computation of low complexity controllers for constrained linear [16] and PWA [14] systems.

In order to utilize the full functionality of MPT, an LMI solver is needed therefore. The SDP solver interface Yalmip [23] is included in MPT and we recommend to its use in combination with SeDuMi [28], though other LMI solvers are compatible as well (see [23] for details). In order to perform certain polytopic manipulations (e.g., vertex-enumeration, Minkowski-Addition) in dimensions larger than 3, it is necessary to have CDD [11] installed. CDD [11] is also included in MPT. The MPT furthermore supports different LP and QP solvers, namely MATLAB's linprog and quadprog, the LP and QP solvers of the Numerical Algorithms Group (NAG) as well as the CPLEX, GLPK and CDD solvers. If the user wishes to utilize another LP or QP solver, a simple modification to the functions mpt_solveLP and mpt_solveQP will do.

3.2   Classes and Basic Polytope Manipulations

The toolbox defines a new class polytope inside the MATLAB programming environment along with overloaded operators which are presented [1] in Table 1. The functions for polytope manipulations are given in Table 2. All functions take either polytopes or unions thereof as an input argument which is illustrated in the following example:

Example 1.

```
>> P=polytope([eye(2);-eye(2)],[1 1 1 1]');        %Create Polytope P
>> W=polytope([eye(2);-eye(2)],0.1*[1 1 1 1]');    %Create Polytope W
>> DIF=P-W;                                         %Pontryagin difference P-W
>> ADD=P+W;                                         %Minkowski addition P+W
>> plot(ADD, P, DIF, W);                            %Plot polytopes
```

The resulting plot is depicted in Figure 1(a). When a polytope object is created, the constructor automatically normalizes its representation and removes all redundant constraints. Note that all elements of the polytope class are private and can only be accessed as described in the tables. Furthermore, all information on a polytope is stored in the internal polytope structure. In this way unnecessary

---

[1] Please note that Tables 1-3 list only a part of the functions available in the toolbox. Check the MPT manual for more details.

Table 1. Short overview of overloaded operators for the class `polytope`.

P=polytope(Px,Pc)	Constructor for creating the polytope $P = \{x \in \mathbb{R}^n \mid P^x x \leq P^c\}$.
[,]	Concatenation of polytopes into a (non-convex) union.
P == Q, P ∼= Q	Check if two polytopes are equal $(P = Q)$,
	or not-equal $(P \neq Q)$, respectively.
P > Q, P < Q	Check if $P \supset Q$ or $P \subset Q$, respectively.
P & Q	Intersection of two polytopes, $P \cap Q$.
P | Q	Convex union of polytopes, $P \cup Q$.
P + Q, P - Q	Minkowski sum, $P \oplus Q$ and Pontryagin difference, $P \ominus Q$.
P \ Q	Set difference operator.

Table 2. Functions defined for class `polytope`.

V=extreme(P)	Computes extreme points (vertices) of a polytope P.
E=envelope(P,Q)	Computes envelope E of two polytopes P and Q.
P=hull(PA)	Computes hull of a polytope array PA
P=hull(V)	or hull of an array of vertices V.
plot(P)	Plots a given polytope or polytope array in 2D or 3D.
P=range(Q,A,f)	Affine transformation of a polytope.
	$P = \{Ax + f \in \mathbb{R}^n \mid x \in Q\}$
P=domain(Q,A,f)	Compute polytope that is mapped to Q.
	$P = \{x \in \mathbb{R}^n \mid Ax + f \in Q\}$

repetitions of the computations during polytopic manipulations in the future can be avoided. More functions on polytopes are given in Table 2 and are illustrated in the following example.

Example 2.

```
>> P=polytope([eye(2);-eye(2)],[1 1 1 1]');      %Create Polytope P
>> Q=polytope([eye(2);-eye(2)],0.1*[1 1 1 1]'); %Create Polytope Q
>> D=P\Q;                         %Compute set difference between P and Q
>> U=D|Q;                         %Compute union of D and Q
>> U==P                           %Check if two polytopes are equal
   ans=1
```

The polytopes P and Q are depicted in Figures 1(b) and 1(c). The `hull` function is overloaded such that it takes both elements of the `polytope` class as well as matrices of points as input arguments.

3.3 Control Functions

This subsection will give a brief overview of the main control functions which are provided with the MPT. All functions may be called by using the accessor function

```
[ctrlStruct]=mpt_Control(sysStruct,probStruct,Options)
```

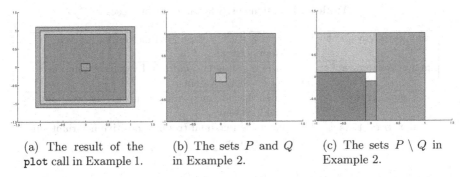

(a) The result of the plot call in Example 1.

(b) The sets P and Q in Example 2.

(c) The sets $P \setminus Q$ in Example 2.

Fig. 1. Results obtained for Examples 1 and 2.

which takes the structures defined in Section 3.5 as parameters and automatically calls one of the functions described below depending on the parameters which were passed. Every function returns a controller structure ctrlStruct which contains the regions over which the feedback law is unique, i.e. $u = F_i x + G_i$ if $x \in P(i)$. The different functions for obtaining these solutions are:

[ctrlStruct]=mpt_optControl(sysStruct,probStruct,Options):
  This function solves a constrained optimal control problem as defined in (10) for linear and quadratic cost objectives for linear systems with the method proposed in [1,4].

[ctrlStruct]=mpt_optInfControl(sysStruct,probStruct,Options):
  This function computes a solution to the constrained infinite-time optimal control problem for linear systems and quadratic cost objectives using the algorithm described in [13].

[ctrlStruct]=mpt_iterative(sysStruct,probStruct,Options):
  This function applies the minimum time computation scheme described in [16]. The function returns the stabilizing minimum time controller as well as the controller obtained at the final iteration. The final controller guarantees feasibility for all time, but stability still needs to be checked with mpt_getPWQLyapFunction (see Section 3.4). This scheme can also be used to obtain robust solutions by setting the appropriate flags [15].

[ctrlStruct]=mpt_iterativePWA(sysStruct,probStruct,Options):
  This function applies the minimum time computation scheme described in [14]. The function returns the stabilizing controller represented by the controller structure ctrlStruct. This scheme can also be used to obtain robust solutions for PWA systems affected by additive disturbance by setting the appropriate flags [21].

3.4   Analysis Functions

Various scripts which serve to plot the obtained results as well as analysis functions are included in the toolbox. Some of these function are vital in obtaining stability and feasibility properties for the low complexity controllers [16,15,14]. The corresponding functions are given in Table 3.

Table 3. Functions used for analysis purposes.

mpt_getPWQLyapFct	Computes a PWQ Lyapunov function for a given closed-loop system.
mpt_getCommonLyapFct	Computes a common quadratic Lyapunov function for a set of linear systems.
mpt_infset	Calculates the maximal (robust) positively invariant set for an LTI system
mpt_infsetPWA	Computes the maximal (robust) positive invariant subset for PWA systems

3.5 Structures and Objects

As indicated in the previous sections, the toolbox utilizes three main structures: the system structure sysStruct, the problem structure probStruct, and the controller structure ctrlStruct. The details of these structures are given in Tables 4, 5, and 6. System structure describes dynamics of the system and input/output constraints. The problem structure serves to state properties of a problem the user wants to solve. Finally, the controller structure encapsulates results of the calculation and can be later used to evaluate control actions.

Table 4. Fields of the system (sysStruct) structure.

A, B, C, D, f, g	State-space dynamic martices in (8) and (16a). Set elements to empty if they do not apply.
umin, umax	Bounds on inputs $\texttt{umin} \leq u(t) \leq \texttt{umax}$.
dumin, dumax	Bounds on $\texttt{dumin} \leq u(t)\text{-}u(t\text{-}1) \leq \texttt{dumax}$.
ymin, ymax	Constraints on the outputs $\texttt{ymin} \leq y(t) \leq \texttt{ymax}$.
noise	A polytope bounding the additive disturbance, i.e. noise=$\mathcal{W}$ in (13).
Aunc, Bunc	Cell arrays containing the vertices of the polytopic uncertainty (14).
guardX, guardU, guardC	Polytope cell array defining where the dynamics are active (for PWA systems). $\mathcal{D}_i = \{(x,u) \mid \texttt{guardXi}\ x + \texttt{guardUi}\ u \leq \texttt{guardCi}\}$.

3.6 Examples

In order to obtain a feedback controller, it is necessary to specify both a system as well as the problem. We demonstrate the procedure on a simple second-order double integrator, with bounded input $|u| \leq 1$ and output $||y(k)||_\infty \leq 5$:

Example 3.

```
>> sysStruct.A=[1 1; 0 1];      %x(k+1)=Ax(k)+Bu(k)
>> sysStruct.B=[0 1];           %x(k+1)=Ax(k)+Bu(k)
>> sysStruct.C=[1 0; 0 1];      %y(k)=Cx(k)+Du(k)
>> sysStruct.D=[0;0];           %y(k)=Cx(k)+Du(k)
```

Table 5. Fields of the problem (`probStruct`) structure.

Q, R	Weighting matrices in the cost function.
N	Prediction horizon. Values: 1,2,3, ...
norm	1/2/inf norm solution. Values: 1/2/inf. Default 2.
subopt_lev	Which level of sub-optimality to use (0 = optimal solution, 1 = minimum-time solution, 2 = sub-optimal solution). Default 0.
x0bounds	Impose constraints also on x_0? Values: 1 (yes)/0 (no). Default 0.
Tconstraint	Which terminal constraint to use (0 = no, 1 = LQR invariant set, 2 = user defined terminal set). Default 1.
P_N	Terminal cost $(x'_N P_N x_N)$. Only applies if Tconstraint$\neq$ 1.
Tset	A polytope defining the terminal set $(x_N \in$ Tset$)$. Only applies if Tconstraint = 2.

Table 6. Fields of the controller structure (`ctrlStruct`).

Pn	Polyhedral partition over which the control law is defined.
Fi,Gi	Cell arrays containing the PWA control law, i.e. U = Fi{m} x + Gi{m}
Ai,Bi,Ci	Cell arrays containing value function 1/2 x'Ai{m}x + Bi{m}x + Ci{m}
Pfinal	The maximum controllable set as a polytope object.
details	More details about the solution

```
>> sysStruct.umin=-1;        %Input constraints umin<=u(k)
>> sysStruct.umax=1;         %Input constraints u(k)<=umax
>> sysStruct.ymin=[-5 -5]';  %Output constraints ymin<=y(k)
>> sysStruct.ymax=[5 5]';    %Output constraints y(k)<=ymax
```

For this system we will now formulate the problem with quadratic cost objective in (10) and a prediction horizon of $N = 5$:

```
>> probStruct.norm=2;        %Quadratic Objective
>> probStruct.Q=eye(2);      %Objective: min_U J=sum x'Qx + u'Ru...
>> probStruct.R=1;           %Objective: min_U J=sum x'Qx + u'Ru...
>> probStruct.N=5;           %...over the prediction horizon 5
>> probStruct.subopt_lev=0;  %Compute optimal solution
```

If we now call

```
%Compute feedback controller
>> [ctrlStruct]=mpt_Control(sysStruct,probStruct);
>> mpt_plotPartition(ctrlStruct)
```

the controller[2] for the given problem is returned and plotted (see Figure 2(a)). If we wish to compute a low complexity solution, we can run the following:

```
>> probStruct.subopt_lev=2;   %Compute low complexity solution.
>> [ctrlStruct]=mpt_Control(sysStruct,probStruct);
```

---

[2] Calculated in 1.2 seconds on a 2.4 GHz Pentium 4 machine using Matlab R12.1

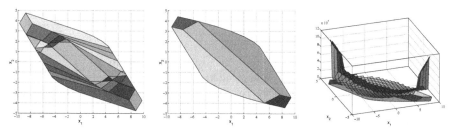

(a) The $N = 5$ step optimal feedback solution.   (b) The iterative low complexity solution for the double integrator.   (c) Lyapunov function for the low complexity solution.

Fig. 2. Results obtained for Example 3.

```
>> [Q,L,C,feasible]=mpt_getPWQLyapFct(ctrlStruct);
>> feasible
      ans=1
>> mpt_plotPartition(ctrlStruct)
>> mpt_plotPWQ(ctrlStruct.Pn,Q,L,C)
```

The resulting partition[3] and Lyapunov function is depicted in Figures 2(b) and 2(c) respectively. In the following we will solve the PWA problem introduced in [24] by defining two different dynamics which are defined in the left- and right half-plane of the state space respectively.

Example 4.

```
%Polytopic state constraints Hx(k)<=K
>> H=[-1 1; -3 -1; 0.2 1; -1 0; 1 0; 0 -1];
>> K=[  15;   25;    9;    6;   8;   10];

%System Dynamics 1/2: x(k+1)=Ax(k)+Bu(k)+f
>> syst.A{1} = [1 0.2; 0 1]; syst.B{1} = [0; 1]; syst.f{1} = [0; 0];
>> syst.A{2} = [0.5 0.2; 0 1]; syst.B{2} = [0; 1]; syst.f{2} = [0.5; 0];

%System Dynamics 1/2: y(k)=Cx(k)+Du(k)+g
>> syst.C{1} = [1 0]; syst.D{1} = [0]; syst.g{1} = [0];
>> syst.C{2} = [1 0]; syst.D{2} = [0]; syst.g{2} = [0];

%Dynamics 1/2 defined in guardA x <= guardC
>> syst.guardA{1} = [1 0; H]; syst.guardC{1} = [  1; K];
>> syst.guardA{2} = [-1 0; H]; syst.guardC{2} = [  -1; K];

%Input/Output constraints for dynamic 1 and 2
>> syst.umin = -1; syst.umax = 1; syst.ymin = -10; syst.ymax = 10;
```

---

[3] Calculated in 1.9 seconds on a 2.4 GHz Pentium 4 machine using Matlab R12.1

we can now compute the low complexity feedback controller by defining the problem as follows:

```
>> probl.norm=2;              %Quadratic Objective
>> probl.Q=eye(2);            %Objective: min_U J=sum x'Qx + u'Ru...
>> probl.R=0.1;               %Objective: min_U J=sum x'Qx + u'Ru...
>> probl.subopt_lev=1;        %Compute low complexity controller.
```

and calling the control function,

```
>> [ctrlStruct]=mpt_Control(syst,probl);
>> mpt_plotPartition(ctrlStruct)
```

The result[4] is depicted in Figure 3.

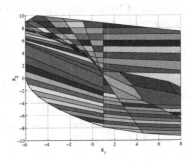

Fig. 3. Controller partition obtained for Example 4.

4   Outlook

The version of MPT presented here is an initial release which we hope to continually extend as new advances in the field of optimal control are made. We encourage all researchers which are active in related fields to contribute code to the toolbox such that the community as a whole has access to the latest developments. Details on how to contribute as well as the latest versions of MPT and a more detailed manual can be obtained from:

http://control.ee.ethz.ch/~hybrid/mpt/

Acknowledgment. We would like to thank all contributors to the toolbox which are not in the authors list. Specifically (in alphabetical order): Alberto Bemporad, Francesco Borrelli, Frank J. Christophersen, Eric Kerrigan, Marco

---

[4] Obtained after 24.9 seconds on a 2.4 GHz Pentium 4 machine using Matlab R12.1

Lüthi, Saša V. Raković, Fabio Torrisi and Kari Unneland. A special thanks goes to Komei Fukuda (cdd) and Johan Löfberg (Yalmip) for allowing us to include their respective packages in the distribution. Thanks to their help MPT truly is an 'unpack-and-use' toolbox.

References

1. M. Baotić. An efficient algorithm for multi-parametric quadratic programming. Technical Report AUT02-04, Automatic Control Laboratory, ETH Zurich, Switzerland, February 2002.
2. M. Baotić, F. J. Christophersen, and M. Morari. Infinite time optimal control of hybrid systems with a linear performance index. In *Proc. of the Conf. on Decision and Control, Maui, Hawaii, USA*, December 2003.
3. M. Baotić, F.J. Christophersen, and M. Morari. A new Algorithm for Constrained Finite Time Optimal Control of Hybrid Systems with a Linear Performance Index. In *European Control Conference*, Cambridge, UK, September 2003.
4. A. Bemporad, F. Borrelli, and M. Morari. Explicit solution of LP-based model predictive control. In *Proc. 39th IEEE Conf. on Decision and Control*, Sydney, Australia, December 2000.
5. A. Bemporad, F. Borrelli, and M. Morari. Optimal controllers for hybrid systems: Stability and piecewise linear explicit form. In *Proc. 39th IEEE Conf. on Decision and Control*, Sydney, Australia, December 2000.
6. A. Bemporad, F. Borrelli, and M. Morari. Min-max control of constrained uncertain discrete-time linear systems. *IEEE Trans. Automatic Control*, 48(9):1600–1606, 2003.
7. A. Bemporad, K. Fukuda, and F.D. Torrisi. Convexity recognition of the union of polyhedra. *Computational Geometry*, 18:141–154, April 2001.
8. A. Bemporad, M. Morari, V. Dua, and E.N. Pistikopoulos. The explicit linear quadratic regulator for constrained systems. *Automatica*, 38(1):3–20, January 2002.
9. F. Borrelli. *Constrained Optimal Control Of Linear And Hybrid Systems*, volume 290 of *Lecture Notes in Control and Information Sciences*. Springer, 2003.
10. F. Borrelli, M. Baotić, A. Bemporad, and M. Morari. An efficient algorithm for computing the state feedback optimal control law for discrete time hybrid systems. In *Proc. 2003 American Control Conference*, Denver, Colorado, USA, June 2003.
11. K. Fukuda. *Cdd/cdd+ Reference Manual*, December 1997. www.cs.mcgill.ca/~fukuda/soft/cdd_home/cdd.html.
12. E. G. Gilbert and K. Tin Tan. Linear systems with state and control constraints: the theory and applications of maximal output admissible sets. *IEEE Trans. Automatic Control*, 36(9):1008–1020, 1991.
13. P. Grieder, F. Borrelli, F.D. Torrisi, and M. Morari. Computation of the constrained infinite time linear quadratic regulator. In *Proc. 2003 American Control Conference*, Denver, Colorado, USA, June 2003.
14. P. Grieder, M. Kvasnica, M. Baotić, and M. Morari. Low complexity control of piecewise affine systems with stability guarantee. *Submitted*, 2003.
15. P. Grieder, M. Lüthi, P. Parillo, and M. Morari. Stability & feasibility of receding horizon control. In *European Control Conference*, Cambridge, UK, September 2003.
16. P. Grieder and M. Morari. Complexity reduction of receding horizon control. In *Proc. 42nd IEEE Conf. on Decision and Control*, Maui, Hawaii, USA, December 2003.

17. P. Grieder, P. Parillo, and M. Morari. Robustness of receding horizon control. In *Proc. 42nd IEEE Conf. on Decision and Control*, Maui, Hawaii, USA, December 2003.
18. W.P.M.H. Heemels, B. De Schutter, and A. Bemporad. Equivalence of hybrid dynamical models. *Automatica*, 37(7):1085–1091, July 2001.
19. ILOG, Inc. *CPLEX 7.0 User Manual*. Gentilly Cedex, France, 2000.
20. E. C. Kerrigan and J. M. Maciejowski. Robustly stable feedback min-max model predictive control. In *Proc. 2003 American Control Conference*, Denver, Colorado, USA, June 2003.
21. E. C. Kerrigan and D. Q. Mayne. Optimal control of constrained, piecewise affine systems with bounded disturbances. In *Proc. 41st IEEE Conference on Decision and Control*, Las Vegas, Nevada, USA, dec 2002.
22. I. Kolmanovsky and E. G. Gilbert. Theory and computation of disturbance invariant sets for discrete-time linear systems. *Mathematical Problems in Egineering*, 4:317–367, 1998.
23. J. Löfberg. *Yalmip*. http://www.control.isy.liu.se/~johanl/yalmip.html.
24. D. Q. Mayne and S. Raković. Model predictive control of constrained piecewise affine discrete-time systems. *Int. J. of Robust and Nonlinear Control*, 13(3):261–279, April 2003.
25. D. Q. Mayne, J.B. Rawlings, C.V. Rao, and P.O.M. Scokaert. Constrained model predictive control: Stability and optimality. *Automatica*, 36(6):789–814, June 2000.
26. Numerical Algorithms Group, Ltd. *NAG Foundation Toolbox for MATLAB 6*. Oxford, UK, 2002.
27. S. Raković, P. Grieder, M. Kvasnica, D. Q. Mayne, and M. Morari. Computation of invariant sets for piecewise affine discrete time systems subject to bounded disturbances. 2003. Submitted.
28. J.F. Sturm. Using SeDuMi 1.02, a MATLAB toolbox for optimization over symmetric cones. *Optimization Methods and Software*, pages 625–653, October 1999.
29. P. Tøndel, T.A. Johansen, and A. Bemporad. An algorithm for multi-parametric quadratic programming and explicit MPC solutions. In *Proc. 40th IEEE Conf. on Decision and Control*, December 2001.
30. S. M. Veres. Geometric Bounding Toolbox (GBT) for MATLAB, 2003.
31. G. M. Ziegler. *Lectures on Polytopes*. Springer, 1994.

Dynamic Partitioning of Large Discrete Event Biological Systems for Hybrid Simulation and Analysis

Natasha A. Neogi

Department of Aerospace Engineering, University of Illinois,
Urbana-Champaign, Champaign, IL 61820
neogi@uiuc.edu

Abstract. Biological systems involving genetic reactions are large discrete event systems, and often contain certain species that occur in small quantities, and others that occur in large quantities, leading to a difficulty in modelling and simulation. Small populations inhibit the usefulness of utilizing differential equations to represent the system, while the large populations cause stochastic discrete event simulation to become computationally intensive. This paper presents an algorithmic approach for the dynamic partitioning and stochastic hybrid simulation of biological systems. The algorithm uses a Poisson approximation for discrete event generation and a Langevin approximation for continuous behaviour. The populations are dynamically partitioned so that some populations are simulated in a discrete stochastic fashion, while others are simulated by continuous differential equations, and this partition between discrete and continuous behaviour is updated at regular intervals. The hybrid model of a simple biological toggle switch yields promising results, and a more complex example is explored.

1 Introduction

The advancement of experimental techniques and rapid accumulation of genetic information have opened a new frontier in biomedical engineering. The ability to engineer artificial gene regulatory networks with sophisticated computational and functional abilities grows ever closer due to the availability of well-characterized components from natural gene networks. Hence, the construction, analysis and interpretation of qualitative and quantitative models acts to drive the field forward [3]. There are several complementary approaches involving discrete and stochastic simulation that can be used to model gene networks, which are surveyed in this paper. The goal is to use such descriptions to accurately predict the properties and function of modules connected into networks, and to make *in silico* suggestions for optimal design strategies prior to implementation *in vivo*. However, as the models become progressively complex, the algorithms become computationally expensive [2].

For systems with species fluctuating by varying orders of magnitude, the largest fluctuating species require the most time to simulate stochastically because exact stochastic simulation techniques scale with the number of reaction events [8]. The use of stochastic partitioning, whereby the state of the reaction is modelled using extents of reactions rather than molecules of species, thereby leading to the ability to separate the state into subsets of fast and slow reactions, allows for the reduction in the computational burden

R. Alur and G.J. Pappas (Eds.): HSCC 2004, LNCS 2993, pp. 463–476, 2004.

for simulation. The fast reactions can then be approximated deterministically as ordinary differential equations or stochastically by the Langevin Equations, while the slow reactions can be treated as stochastic events with time varying reaction rates. However, the partition must be evaluated periodically, as reactions can change their behaviour as time progresses.

In the next section, an informal discussion of the hybrid nature of large, discrete event biological systems is conducted. A survey of simulation and analysis techniques to date is performed, and the potential limitations of these methods are discussed. Section 3 focuses on the various modelling techniques used to encapsulate biological systems. Deterministic differential equations, the Langevin approximation and discrete stochastic simulation models are developed. A Poisson process is used to define the discrete reaction rate for continuous mass action models in Section 4. Section 5 discusses several strategies to partition reactions in subsets which can be modelled continuously or discretely. A method for sampling from a non-homogeneous Poisson process in order to determine the next reaction and time to next reaction is outlined in Section 6. Section 7 contains the discussion of two examples, the first of which is a model of a toggle switch that is simulated using dynamic partitioning of a stochastic hybrid model, and the second of which is a yeast Glucose-Galactose reaction.

2   Problems with Large Discrete Event Biological Systems

In many systems, the probability of occurrence of any event in an infinitesimal time interval dt will only depend on the number of individuals at time t and on parameters that might depend on t, that is, the future evolution of the system only depends on its present state, and not on the system's history. Such processes are referred to being Markov processes [10]. These systems are memoryless, and do not need to keep a state history to determine their evolution.

Systems which are Markov in nature and have exponential event distributions can be modelled using Monte Carlo simulation. The notion of Monte Carlo simulation comes from the solution of the inverse problem where differential equations are approximated by stochastic jumps obtained by the Monte Carlo method. These simulations are simple realizations of the Markov process, and is often called the Feller process [9].

If the population size is large, then in the limiting case, the fractions of the total population represented by each species are the relevant quantities to be considered. This notion is called the Mass-Action Law, and is commonly accepted in physical chemistry [11].

2.1   Current Simulation and Analysis Techniques

Solutions to the stochastic formulation of coupled chemical reactions can be computed using the Monte Carlo procedure specified by Gillespie [13]. The algorithm calculates a stochastic description of the temporal behaviour of the coupled reactions which can be shown to have a more rigorous physical basis than conventional kinetic equation formulations based on the assumption that changes in the chemical reaction system over time are both continuous and deterministic. This assumption is invalid for low concentrations of reactant species or slow enough reactant rates. The Direct and First

Reaction methods [13], outlined by Gillespie, are simulation algorithms that calculate the probabilistic outcome of each discrete chemical event and the resulting changes in the number of each molecular species. It should be noted that, in the limit of large numbers of reactant molecules, these methods are entirely equivalent to the solution of the traditional kinetic differential equations derived from the Law of Mass Action [10].

As models become progressively more complex, however, these algorithms often become expensive computationally. Several techniques have been employed to reduce the computational burden. Employing a deterministic equilibrium assumption on polymerization reaction kinetics has yielded a decrease in computational complexity, as shown by He, Zhang, Chen and Yang [15]. Gibson and Bruck have refined Gillespie's First Reaction algorithm to reduce the required number of random numbers, a technique that works best for systems in which some reactions occur much more frequently than others [7]. Rao and Arkin have demonstrated how to numerically simulate systems reduced by the quasi-steady-state assumption [16]. This work expands upon ideas by Janssen [17] and Vlad and Pop [18], who examined the adiabatic elimination of fast relaxing variables in stochastic chemical kinetics. Resat, Wiley and Dixon address systems with reaction rates varying by several orders of magnitude by applying a probability-weighted Monte Carlo approach, but this method increases error in species fluctuations [20]. Haseltine and Rawlings [18] expand upon the idea of a partitioned system and simulation via Gillespie's direct method to construct approximations that reduce the computational burden for simulation. This work sets up the framework for partitioning a system into discrete and continuous reactions but, only addresses static partitioning.

Recently, an approximation to stochastic population dynamics based on almost independent Poisson processes whose parameters obey a set of coupled ordinary differential equations was developed by Solari *et al.* [4,5,6]. Error bounds for the moment generating function have been developed. For large populations, the Poisson approximation becomes a discrete integration of the Langevin approximation [14]. A implementation of this simulation method has been outlined, and several improvements to improve its efficiency are discussed in relevant literature [4].

Unfortunately, for large scale biological systems which have complex macromolecules (i.e. proteins), long and short time scales, and interactions of several different molecule types, no one approach has yet to yield satisfactory results in all the arenas of accuracy, computational complexity, scalability and coverage.

3   Modelling

A coupled system of p biochemical reactions can be modelled by equations of the form:

$$\sum_i R_i^k \rightarrow \sum_j S_j^k \tag{1}$$

where one molecule each of n different reactants react to form one molecule each of m different products P_i, $k = 1 \ldots p$. If it is assumed that enough molecules of each species is present such that the number of molecules can be approximated as a continuous quantity that varies deterministically over time, the concentration of each species can be written in terms of the concentrations $[R_i]$, $[P_i]$ of all other species via a set of differential equations. However, when the concentrations of certain species drop below a given level, the assumption that the number of molecules can be approximated as a continuously varying deterministic function is no longer valid.

Alternatively, it can be assumed that non-reactive collisions occur far more often than reactive collisions and thus the fast dynamics of motion can be neglected [7]. Thus, the system may be represented best using the number of each kind of molecule. Using this approach, it can be concluded that the probability that a certain reaction μ will take place in the next instant of time dt is given by $a_\mu dt + o(dt)$, where a_μ is independent of dt and $o(dt)$ represents terms that are negligible for small dt. However, a_μ may depend on μ, the current number of molecules of each kind, and the current time. Furthermore, a_μ depends on quantities such as temperature and volume, which may change with time. The state of the system in the stochastic framework is defined by the number of molecules of each species and changes discretely whenever one of the reactions occurs. Formally, we can define the probability that the state S of a system changes to S' via the occurrence of the reaction μ as being [7]:

$$P(S', t + dt \mid S, t) = a_\mu dt + o(dt). \tag{2}$$

Note that since a_μ, and thus the transition probability is dependent on only the current state and not on previous states, the underlying process is Markov in nature. If an individual probability variable is created for each possible state of the system, then Equation 2 can be used to write out the system of coupled differential equations that defines the system, such as:

$$\frac{d}{dt} P(S_j, t + dt \mid S_i, t) = f(a_{\mu_{ij}}, P(S_i, t)) \tag{3}$$

for all reactions μ_{ij} which bring the system state from S_i to S_j. This set of differential equations has probabilities as variables and is referred to as a *Master Equation*. It is a direct consequence of the probabilities satisfying the forward Kolmogorov equation [12]. For systems with very few states, the entire set of Master Equations may be written out and explicitly solved. For large systems, however, this approach quickly becomes intractable [7].

The Master Equation, can, however, be approximated by the stochastic Langevin equations, which are differential equations, and therefore scale more easily with respect to population size. If the characteristic size of the system is defined by Ω, the Master Equation is recast in terms of intensive variables (concentrations), and a Kramers-Moyal expansion is performed, the Master equation results in a system size expansion in Ω. In the limit as Ω becomes large, the discrete Master Equation can be approximated by its first two differential moments with the continuous Fokker-Planck equation, and has Ito solution of the form [7]:

$$d[\mu_i] = b_i(\mu)dt + \sqrt{b_i(\mu)}dW_i \tag{4}$$

where:

$$b_i(\mu) = \sum_{i=0}^{all\ \mu} a_i P(S, t) \tag{5}$$

and dW_i is a Weiner process. This is a stochastic differential equation that specifies the evolution of the trajectories of the system state [7]. The error induced by this approximation is directly related to the size of the system Ω. Even if the system size Ω is large, the Langevin approximation will most likely only be valid for a subset of the reactions [12].

We wish to create a process model for the large, discrete event system which, in the limiting case of large population sizes, captures the Langevin equations, and in the case of small population sizes, can be represented using stochastic discrete interactions.

4   Poisson Processes for Mass-Action Models

Intuitively, the mass action law formalizes the notion that if the size of a system (both in populations and the environment) increases, then the rate of actions also increases. Mathematically, if the rate of the ith reaction is $\lambda_i(X)$, which is a function of the population size X, then the mass action law enforces the limiting property [10]:

$$\lim_{X \to \infty} \lambda_i(X) = k\lambda_i \left(\frac{X}{k} \right). \tag{6}$$

More specifically, in the context of chemical reactions, the mass action law states that the rate of actions is proportional to the product of the concentration of the dependent populations. Consider a system with M substances (populations), in which r reactions occur. Let $X_i, i = 1, 2, 3 \ldots M$ be the quantities of each substance. Each of the r reactions are represented as follows:

$$R_r = \sum_{i=1}^{M} \alpha_{i,r} X_i \to \sum_{i=1}^{M} \beta_{i,r} X_i \tag{7}$$

where is k_r the kinetic reaction constant associated with each reaction.

This system can then be modelled using a Continuous Time Markov Chain (CTMC), where each state $\vec{X} = (X_i = val \mid i = 1 \ldots M, val \in R)$ corresponds to a distinct valuation for each X_i. In a state $\vec{X}$, each reaction potentially fires according to a Poisson process, that is, it fires after an exponentially distributed random delay whose rate is given by:

$$\lambda_r(X) = \frac{k_r}{V \sum_{i=1}^{M} (\alpha_{i,r} - 1)} \left[\prod_{i=1}^{M} \frac{X_i!}{(X_i - \alpha_{i,r})!} \right]. \tag{8}$$

As the population size increases, that is, $X_i \to \infty, i = 1 \ldots M$, the limiting behaviour of the above CTMC can be described by the following differential equations:

$$\lim_{X_i, \ldots X_M \to \infty} \frac{dX_i}{dt} = \sum_r (\beta_{i,r} - \alpha_{i,r}) k_r \left(\prod_{i=1}^{M} [X_i]^{\alpha_{i,r}} \right) \tag{9}$$

where:

$$[X_i] = \frac{X_i}{V} \tag{10}$$

and $[X_i]$ is the concentration of the substance X_i in the limit. A first order correction for stochastic departure can be introduce to arrive at the corresponding Langevin Equations.

Between the event-by-event realizations of the Monte-Carlo simulation method and the large population, sufficient event per unit time limit of the Langevin approximation, there is a need for a method which meshes the advantages of this approach in order to address both large and small population sizes.

5   Partitioning Techniques: Continuous versus Discrete Behaviour

Our basic approach is to partition the set R of reactions into a set of *continuous* reactions and a set of *discrete* reactions. The continuous reactions evolve using the differential equations, while the discrete reactions evolve using standard CTMC simulation. During the occurrence of two consecutive discrete reactions, the system state changes due to the continuous reactions. Since these continuous reactions could change the quantities of substances on which the rates of the discrete reactions depend, the discrete reactions have to be represented by non-homogeneous Poisson processes (rate is time varying). Between two consecutive discrete events, progress of the continuous reactions is simulated using standard differential equations simulation.

5.1   Dynamic Partitioning

Although the determination of which reactions exhibit deterministic behaviour versus which exhibit stochastic behaviour could be done statically, more flexibility (and accuracy) can be obtained by deciding the partition after each state change due to a discrete event (Figure 1). The partition is based on the rates of reaction (as given by Equation 8 and 9). The approaches to perform such a partitioning are given below. They each have their advantages and their problems. Note that the dynamic partitioning described here is performed after a state change due to a discrete event. This ensures that all continuous variables will be updated by the effects of the discrete event instantaneously. True dynamism would involve re-partitioning as and when needed i.e. even between discrete events. This true dynamism has not yet been implemented, and is the subject of future work.

5.1.1   Population Partitioning
In the population partitioning approach, the basic idea is to partition the various populations X_i in the system into a set of continuous populations, and a set of discrete populations. Let $P = X_i \mid i = 1 \ldots M$ be the set of populations in the system. For some state $\vec{X}, C(\vec{X}) \subset P$ is the set of continuous populations, and $D(\vec{X}) = P - C(\vec{X})$ is the set of discrete populations. The set of reactions R is also partitioned into two sets; those which modify any discrete population, and those that do not.

After the occurrence of each event, we reconstruct $C(\vec{X})$ and $D(\vec{X})$ if needed using the rule: if $X_i > k$ then $X_i \in C(\vec{X})$ for some threshold k. Initially, the threshold k would be a user definable parameter based on experimental determination of the magnitude at which the discrete behaviour of the species in question is reasonably approximated by continuous equations for the given environmental conditions. If the performance of the simulation algorithm is sensitive to disturbances in k, it becomes necessary to define an

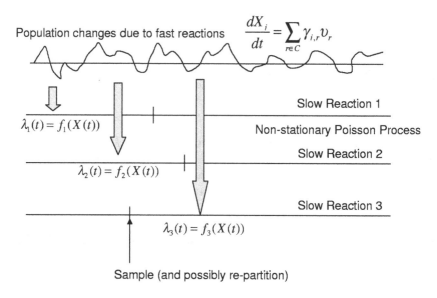

Population changes due to fast reactions $\quad \dfrac{dX_i}{dt} = \displaystyle\sum_{r \in C} \gamma_{i,r} \upsilon_r$

$\lambda_1(t) = f_1(X(t))$

Slow Reaction 1

Non-stationary Poisson Process

Slow Reaction 2

$\lambda_2(t) = f_2(X(t))$

Slow Reaction 3

$\lambda_3(t) = f_3(X(t))$

Sample (and possibly re-partition)

Fig. 1. Partitioning of State Variables into Continuous and Discrete Classes for Simulation

error bound on k, and to reformulate the algorithm so that it adaptively selects k to be the lowest value that gives a bounded error for any propagation of the simulation within one discrete time step. This technique is similar to the technique used by adaptive meshing algorithms that are used to pick the step size in the numerical solution of differential equations [12]. The error bounds derived on the simulation of non-homogeneous Poisson processes [4] would be useful in this process to limit the highest value selected for k.

Partitioning based on population size is intuitive and reactions may change from discrete to continuous only at discrete events, while reactions may change from continuous to discrete at any point the population size drops below the threshold k. However, only those reactions that do not modify any discrete populations can be simulated using differential equations. The remaining reactions must be simulated using CTMC simulation. The examples in Section 7 utilize this method.

5.1.2 Action Partitioning

In this hypothetical approach, the reactions are partitioned directly without partitioning the populations as well. This partitioning is done strictly based on the rate of reaction. Hence, some limiting condition that provides an estimate of the error between the stochastic model and the deterministic model for a reaction with a given rate must be derived to act as an upper bound. It is unclear at present what exact metric will best serve this purpose. All fast reactions can then be simulated using differential equations, resulting in a great computational savings, thereby greatly increasing the size of system which can be modelled. However, reactions may change from discrete to continuous at any time, and hence the partitions may have to be updated at every differential equation time step. Stochastically simulating reactions which depend on both continuous and discrete variables is more computationally intensive, due to the increase in Poisson parameters λ_i in the stochastic process. All the populations can change between two discrete events. Hence the number of continuous parameters to the continuous Poisson process increases, thus decreasing its efficiency. At this point, it is unclear how to exactly implement this approach, and it will be investigated more thoroughly in future work.

6   Sampling from a Non-homogeneous Poisson Process

Using the partitioning approaches described in Section 5, the simulation problem reduces to one of simulating a non-homogeneous Poisson process, i.e. one in which the rate changes continuously with time. Such a process can be simulated using the technique of *thinning* [9]. Thinning is essentially a uniformization technique, whereby the variable rate of the Poisson process is uniformized using a constant rate λ_{max} that upper bounds the varying rate of the process between updates. An exponentially distributed random number with rate λ_{max} is then generated to represent a tentative next arrival time for the non homogeneous Poisson process. Let the current time be t and the tentative next arrival time be Δt. The actual rate $\lambda(t + \Delta t)$ of the non-homogeneous Poisson process is computed at time $t + \Delta t$. Then, the tentative arrival time is accepted as the next arrival time of the non-homogeneous Poisson process with probability (Figure 2):

$$\frac{\lambda(t + \Delta t)}{\lambda_{max}} \tag{11}$$

and rejected with probability

$$1 - \frac{\lambda(t + \Delta t)}{\lambda_{max}}. \tag{12}$$

If the arrival time is rejected, the process of generating tentative arrival times can be repeated with the current time set to $t + \Delta t$, due to the memoryless nature of the Poisson process, until an arrival time is finally accepted. Let the random variable N represent the number of arrival events (all but the last one being tentative) that need to be generated to simulate one discrete event. If Δt_i is the ith tentative arrival time, then the probabilistic moment function for N is given by:

$$P[N = n] = \prod_{i=1}^{n-1} \left(1 - \frac{\lambda\left(t + \sum_{j=1}^{i} \Delta t_j\right)}{\lambda_{max}} \right) \left(\frac{\lambda\left(t + \sum_{j=1}^{n} \Delta t_j\right)}{\lambda_{max}} \right). \tag{13}$$

Let:

$$0 \le r(i) = \frac{\lambda\left(t + \sum_{j=1}^{i} \Delta t_j\right)}{\lambda_{max}} \le 1 \tag{14}$$

be the acceptance probability for the ith sample, and let:

$$r_{max} = max(r(i)) \tag{15}$$

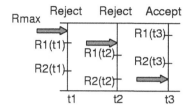

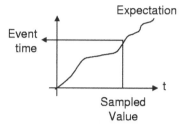

(a) Accept/Reject Process for Next Event   (b) Expected Value of Next Event Time

Fig. 2. (a) Next Event Generation: Arrow Represents the Maximum Rate for the Reactions R1 and R2 (b) "Time to Next Event" Process Generation

be the maximum possible value for $r(n)$. Then, the average value of N can be upper bounded by the average value of a geometric random variable with success probability r_{max}. That is:

$$E(N) \leq \frac{1}{r_{max}} \tag{16}$$

Clearly, bringing this ratio as close to 1 as possible will result in the generation of fewer event arrival time and improve the running time of the algorithm. Two techniques can be used to do this task. First, using the memoryless nature of the Poisson process, we can make more informed estimates of λ_{max} at the time of each tentative event rejection. Such a technique is similar to adaptive uniformization. The second technique is to use the law of conservation of mass to compute an upper limit. However, this approach is clearly conservative because the law of conservation of mass provides an upper limit on the amount of substance that can ever be generated in the given system. A better approach might be to optimistically assume a smaller upper bound $\lambda_{max}(optimistic)$, relying on the fact that most of the generated arrival times will not be too far away. Then, while integrating, if the actual rates ever become higher than $\lambda_{max}(optimistic)$, then we redo the computation from the last event with a larger $\lambda_{max}(optimistic)$. The efficiency of this computation can be calculated based on the exponential distribution function. Clearly, the more number of times we have to recompute, the less gains we obtain. Also, it is possible that this technique biases the arrival rate distribution.

7   Example Simulations and Difficulties

Gardner et al. [23] describe a genetic switch that toggles between stable transcription from either of two promoters in response to external signals. It is constructed from two promoters and their cognate repressors, arranged so that each promoter can be inhibited by the repressor transcribed by the other promoter. The circuit has two stable states: the "high" state with the promoter P2 on, and the "low" state with the promoter P1 on, given comparable promoter kinetics. Gardner et al. [23] demonstrate how this inherently bistable relation can be engineered by using the *IPTG* inducable *lac* promoter (*Plac*), and the thermally unstable *CI* repressor, whereby the state of the switch is sensed using

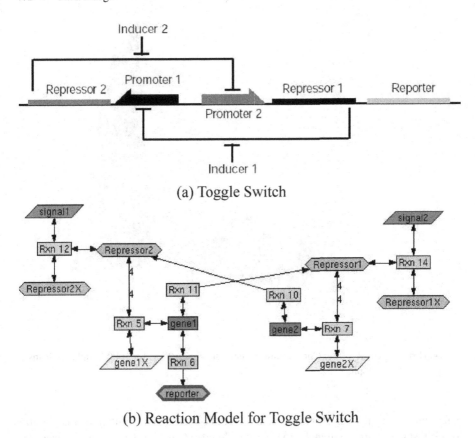

(a) Toggle Switch

(b) Reaction Model for Toggle Switch

Fig. 3. Toggle Switch Model (a) Promoter-Repressor-Inducer Reactions [23] (b) Model for Reaction Equations (Equation 17) [25]

a reporter gene coding for green fluorescent protein (*GFP*) directly downstream from the *CI* gene. The "high" state occurs with the introduction of inducer 1 (I1), *IPTG*, which turns the promoter P2 (*Plac*) on, and produces repressor 2 (R2) *TetR* and the reporter *GFP*. The "low" state occurs when inducer 2 (I2), *aTc*, is introduced, and the promoter P1, *Ptet*, is turned on, and *LacCI* is made (Figure 3). Gardner et al. found that all cells grown in colonies for six hours in the presence of IPTG under conditions for CI stability remained in the P2 on state after the removal of IPTG. Transiently increasing the temperature so that CI was unstable for 7 hours resulted in the toggling of the system state to P1 on.

For the purpose of simulation, using Poisson event generation for CTMC processes and the Langevin approximation, the reporter distribution was simulated for an initial setting of the toggle switch as being in the "high" state, that is, the IPTG inducer signal (30 ng/ml) is present, and Plac is expressed. Then, the signal is removed at 500 seconds, and the aTc inducer signal (30 ng/ml) is applied at 3000 seconds. The kinetic reaction parameters are taken from the literature [23,24]. The concentration of the reporter dis-

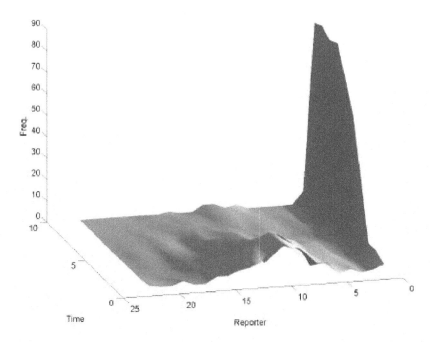

Fig. 4. Histogram of Reporter Concentration Distribution over Time for 1000 Simulation Runs for Toggle Switch Example

tribution with time over 1000 runs is shown in Figure 4. The simulation concentration of GFP starts at approximately 15 ng/ml, and ends at an average of 0 ng/ml over 1000 runs.

The main equations that govern this system can be expressed (Figure 3):

$$
\begin{aligned}
IPTG + TetRX &\leftrightarrow TetR \\
4TetR + LacX &\leftrightarrow Lac + GPF + LacCI \\
aTc + LacCIX &\leftrightarrow LacCI \\
4LacCI + TetX &\leftrightarrow Tet + TetR
\end{aligned}
\tag{17}
$$

where *geneX* is the unexpressed form of the promoter or repressor *gene*. Dynamic partitioning via population was performed, and thresholds for continuous behaviour were set for concentrations at 0.75 of the predicted normalized final value. Thus, the first two reactions in (17) start as continuous reactions, and the latter are simulated discretely. At approximately 6000 seconds, the first two equations are reclassified as discrete, and by 8000 seconds the latter two equations become continuous in simulation. The results compare favourably with those found in experimental literature, in that the behaviour is correct [24]. The computation time taken for this example is marginally better than that achieved by statically partitioned hybrid simulation [24,8]. It is hoped that greater computational saving will be evinced in the simulation of a more complex example, such as the yeast Glucose-Galactose system.

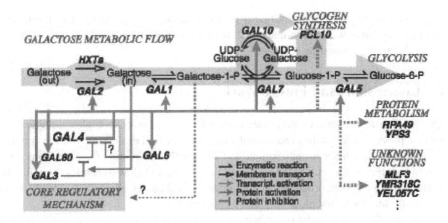

Fig. 5. Yeast Glucose-Galactose Model [21]

Presently, the simulation of the yeast Glucose-Galactose switch, a larger example, which possesses a signal transduction mechanism and a single metabolic pathway with Protein-Protein interactions and regulated gene expression is being attempted. This system has been extensively described [21,22] and possesses a large number of mutants and phenotypes, as seen in Figure 5. Unfortunately, upon simulation, the results did not properly match the experimental findings. An elementary analysis, in which an invariant regarding the mass conservation law was formulated to check the maximal concentration values of all reactants, revealed the unregulated overproduction of a single product in the early stages of the simulation results, leading to the discovery of a mistake in the entry of a reaction in the simulation model using a single simulation run. This allowed for the debugging of the model (which consists of numerous reactions) in an online fashion, at a comparatively cheap computational cost, as usually the simulation would be forced to completion (generally hundreds of runs) before the results would be synthesized and a conclusion made.

Even after the model was extensively debugged, the results were still inaccurate, and the major divergence between experimental and simulated results occurred in the overproduction of glucose. For a large number of simultaneously occurring biological reactions which have common products and reactants, such as the yeast Glucose-Galactose switch, even if the reactions can be abstracted into a class of fast and slow reactions, experimentally the fast reactions often reach a bottleneck. This may be due in part to the coupled nature of the reactions: the slow reactions may not produce enough products, or release enough catalytic converters (such as UDP, see Figure 5) to enable some of the fast reactions to remain fast [8]. The bottleneck can lead to an aperiodic switching of reactions between the set of fast reactions and the set of slow reactions. Certain reactions then play a key role in system dynamics: the reactants behave according to their original partitioning, until some limiting resource is encountered, whereby a subset of the fast reactions is then suddenly inhibited, until the resource becomes plentiful once again. It is postulated that certain driving reactions play a critical role in complex, coupled systems. The critical reactants/products and enabling catalysts which drive the entire process forwards must be identified *a priori*. This would help to identify the kinetic reaction constants which dominate each reaction regime, that would in turn lead to a better dynamic partitioning scheme.

8 Conclusions and Future Work

Quantitative models and simulation techniques for the analysis of complex biological and genetic processes are indispensable in the construction and evaluation of these systems. The ability to dynamically approximate and allocate the behaviour of fast reactions using continuous dynamics such as the Langevin Equations, and slow dynamics through non-homogeneous Poisson processes in continuous time Markov chains has proved to be a successful technique for modelling these systems,

Future efforts will focus on creating a hierarchical representation of the biological models which will enable the user to ascertain whether the model has all of the correct reactions entered. As well, this will hopefully aid in the identification of key reactions, that, in complex models, may create bottlenecks in efficiency in the dynamic partitioning of fast and slow reactants, thereby allowing for more complex examples to be accurately simulated.

References

[1] McAdams, Harley H., and Adam Arkin, "Stochastic Mechanisms in Gene Expression", Biochemistry, Proc. Natl. Acad. Sci., Vol. 94, pp. 814-819, February 1997.

[2] Kastner, Jason, Solomon, Jerry, and Scott Fraser, "Modeling a Hox Gene Network in Silico Using a Stochastic Simulation Algorithm, Developmental Biology, 246, Elsevier Science, pp. 122-131, 2002

[3] Kaern, Mads, Blake, William J., and J.J. Collins, "The Engineering of Gene Regulatory Networks", Annu. Rev. Biomed. Eng., 2003, 5:179-206.

[4] Solari, H.G., and M.A. Natiello, "Poisson Approximation to Density Dependent Stochastic Processes: A Numerical Implementation and Test", Physical Review, 2003, *in press.*

[5] Solari, H.G., and M.A. Natiello, "Stochastic Population Dynamics: the Poisson Approximation", Physical Review E, 67:031918, 2003

[6] Aparicio, Juan P., and H. G. Solari, "Population Dynamics: Poisson Approximation and Its Relation to the Langevin Process", Physical Review Letter, Vol. 86, No. 18, April 30, 2001.

[7] Gibson, M.A., and J. Bruck, "Efficient Exact Stochastic Simulation of Chemical Systems with Many Species and Many Channels", J. Phys. Chem. A 2000, 104, pp.1876-1889.

[8] Haseltine, E. L., and J.B. Rawlings, "Approximate Simulation of Coupled Fast and Slow Reactions for Stochastic Chemical Kinetics", Journal of Chemical Physics, Vol. 117, No. 15, pp. 6959-6969, October 15, 2002.

[9] Gardiner, C.W., *Handbook of Stochastic Methods for Physics, Chemistry and the Natural Sciences,* 2nd ed., Springer-Verlag, Berlin, 1990.

[10] Gillespie, D.T., *Markov Processes: An Introduction for Physical Scientists*, Academic, New York, 1992.

[11] Gard, T.C., *Introduction to Stochastic Differential Equations*, Marcel Dekker, New York, 1998.

[12] Gibson, M.S., Mjolsness, E, *Computational Methods for Modelling Biochemical Networks*, Bower, J, Bolouri, H., eds., MIT Press, Cambridge, MA, *in press*

[13] Gillespie, D.T., "Exact Stochastic Simulation of Coupled Chemical Reactions", Journal of Physical Chemistry, 81:2340-2361, 1977.

[14] Kurtz, G.T., "Approximation of Discontinuous Processes by Continuous Processes", in L. Arnold and R. Lefever, eds., Stochastic Nonlinear Systems in Physics, Chemistry and Biology, Springer-Verlag, Berlin, 1981

[15] He, J., Zhang, H., Chen, J., and Y. Yang, Macromolecules **30**, 8010, 1997.

[16] Rao, C., and A. Arkin, Journal Chem. Phys. *submitted*.

[17] Janssen, J.A.M., Journal of Statistical Physics, **57**, 171, 1989.

[18] Vlad, M.O., and A. Pop, Physica A **155**, 276, 1989.

[19] Gillespie, D.T., Physica A **188**, 404, 1992.

[20] Resat, H, H.S. Wiley, and D.A. Dixon, Journal of Physical Chemistry B **105**, 11026, 2001.

[21] Idaker, T., Science, 2001.

[22] Ostergaard, S., National Biotechnical Journal, 2000.

[23] Gardner, T.J., Cantor, C.R, Collins, J.J., Construction of a Genetic Toggle Switch in Escherichia Coli, Nature, 2000.403.339-342.

[24] Goss & Peccoud, Proc. Nat. Acad. Sci., 1998.

Safety Verification of Hybrid Systems Using Barrier Certificates

Stephen Prajna[1]* and Ali Jadbabaie[2]

[1] Control and Dynamical Systems, California Institute of Technology,
Pasadena, CA 91125 - USA,
prajna@cds.caltech.edu
[2] Department of Electrical and Systems Engineering, University of Pennsylvania,
Philadelphia, PA 19104 - USA,
jadbabai@seas.upenn.edu

Abstract. This paper presents a novel methodology for safety verification of hybrid systems. For proving that all trajectories of a hybrid system do not enter an unsafe region, the proposed method uses a function of state termed a barrier certificate. The zero level set of a barrier certificate separates the unsafe region from all possible trajectories starting from a given set of initial conditions, hence providing an exact proof of system safety. No explicit computation of reachable sets is required in the construction of barrier certificates, which makes nonlinearity, uncertainty, and constraints can be handled directly within this framework. The method is also computationally tractable, since barrier certificates can be constructed using the sum of squares decomposition and semidefinite programming. Some examples are provided to illustrate the use of the method.

1 Introduction

Much research effort has been devoted to the development of hybrid systems theory in the recent years. This is partly due to the ubiquity of engineering and physical systems that are best modelled as hybrid systems. One important example is the class of embedded systems [16], whose dynamics involve interaction between digital control software and analog plants via sensors and actuators.

Complex behaviors that can be exhibited by hybrid systems make the safety verification of such systems both critical and challenging. In principle, safety verification or reachability analysis aims to show that starting at some initial conditions, a system cannot evolve to some unsafe region in the state space. Verification of purely discrete systems using temporal logic [10] as well as verification of continuous systems within the framework of robust control theory [26] are mature areas with many success stories. Unfortunately, neither of them is adequate for handling hybrid systems.

---

* The work of the first author was supported by funding from AFOSR.

R. Alur and G.J. Pappas (Eds.): HSCC 2004, LNCS 2993, pp. 477–492, 2004.

For verification of hybrid systems, several methods have since been proposed. Explicit computation of either exact or approximate reachable sets corresponding to the continuous dynamics is crucial for virtually all of these methods. For linear systems with certain eigenstructures and semialgebraic initial sets, exact reachability set calculation using quantifier elimination has been addressed in [14,3]. It has been extended to approximate analysis of linear systems with almost arbitrary eigenstructures in [22]. Recently, a scalable method based on geometric programming relaxations has been proposed by [25] for linear systems with polytopic sets. In another vein, several other techniques have also been developed for approximate reachability analysis. Such techniques rely on numerical methods for solving the Hamilton Jacobi equations [23], ellipsoidal calculus [13, 6], flow-pipe approximations [9], and polygonal approximations [5,4,2].

In this paper, we present a new method for safety verification that is different from the above approaches as it does not require computation of reachable sets, but instead relies on what we term barrier certificates, which were previously used in the context of nonlinear model validation [19]. For a continuous system, a barrier certificate is a function of state satisfying a set of inequalities on both the function itself and its time derivative along the flow of the system (cf. Theorem 1). In the state space, the zero level set of a barrier certificate separates an unsafe region from all system trajectories starting from a given set of initial conditions, and therefore the existence of such a function provides an exact certificate/proof of system safety. Similar to the Lyapunov stability results, the main idea is to study properties of the system (reachability in this case) without the need to compute the flow explicitly. Although an over-approximation of the reachable set may also be a witness for safety, a barrier certificate can be much easier to compute when the system is nonlinear and uncertain, and the latter is notably more exact when the safety is to be verified for infinite time horizon.

The method described in the previous paragraph can be easily extended to handle hybrid systems. In this case, a barrier certificate is constructed from a set of functions of continuous state indexed by the system location. Instead of satisfying the aforementioned inequalities in the whole continuous state space, each function needs to satisfy the inequalities only within the invariant set of its location. Functions corresponding to different locations are linked via appropriate conditions that must be satisfied during discrete transitions between the locations. The idea here is again analogous to using multiple Lyapunov-like functions [8,11] for stability analysis of hybrid systems.

With this methodology, we are able to treat a large class of hybrid systems, including those with nonlinear continuous dynamics, uncertain inputs, uncertain parameters, and constraints (even dynamic constraints such as integral quadratic constraints [15], a tool of robust control which can be used to represent e.g. unmodelled system dynamics). When the vector fields of the system are polynomials and the sets in the system description are semialgebraic (i.e., described by polynomial equalities and inequalities), a tractable computational method using the sum of squares decomposition [18] and semidefinite programming [24] can be utilized for constructing a polynomial barrier certificate, e.g., using the software [20]. While the computational cost of this construction depends on the degrees of the vector fields and the barrier certificate in addition to the dimension of the continuous state, for fixed degrees the complexity grows polynomially with respect to the state dimension. Hence we expect our method to be more scalable than many other existing methods.

This paper is organized as follows. Section 2 describes the hybrid modelling framework that we use in this paper. In Section 3, safety verification of continuous and hybrid systems using barrier certificates is addressed. We present two sets of convex and non-convex conditions for barrier certificates, either of which guarantees the safety of the system. Later in the same section we incorporate constraints, in particular integral constraints, into the framework. In Section 4, we first show how a barrier certificate satisfying the convex conditions can be computed by convex optimization, and then we present an iterative scheme for handling the non-convex conditions, which potentially yield a less conservative barrier certificate. Section 5 contains detailed examples illustrating the use of the methodology. Finally, we end the paper by conclusions in Section 6.

2   Preliminaries

Throughout the paper, we adopt the hybrid modelling framework that was first proposed in [1]; see also [2] for a more detailed explanation and example. A hybrid system is a tuple $H = (\mathcal{X}, L, X_0, I, F, T)$ with the following components:

- $\mathcal{X} \subseteq \mathbb{R}^n$ is the continuous state space.
- L is a finite set of locations. The overall state space of the system is $X = L \times \mathcal{X}$, and a state of the system is denoted by $(l, x) \in L \times \mathcal{X}$.
- $X_0 \subseteq X$ is the set of initial states.
- $I : L \to 2^{\mathcal{X}}$ is the invariant, which assigns to each location l an invariant set $I(l) \subseteq \mathcal{X}$ that contains all possible continuous states while at location l.
- $F : X \to 2^{\mathbb{R}^n}$ is a set of vector fields. F assigns to each $(l, x) \in X$ a set $F(l, x) \subseteq \mathbb{R}^n$ which constrains the evolution of the continuous state according to the differential inclusion $\dot{x} \in F(l, x)$.
- $T \subseteq X \times X$ is a relation capturing discrete transitions between two locations. Here a transition $((l, x), (l', x')) \in T$ indicates that from the state (l, x) the system can undergo a discrete jump to the state (l', x').

Trajectories of the hybrid system H start from some initial state $(l_0, x_0) \in X_0$ and are concatenations of a sequence of continuous flows and discrete transitions. During a continuous flow, the discrete location l is maintained and the continuous state evolves according to the differential inclusion $\dot{x} \in F(l, x)$, as long as x remains inside the invariant set $I(l)$. At a state (l_1, x_1), a discrete transition to (l_2, x_2) can occur if $((l_1, x_1), (l_2, x_2)) \in T$. Given a hybrid system H and a set of unsafe states $X_u \subseteq X$, the safety verification problem is concerned with proving that all trajectories of the hybrid system H cannot enter the unsafe region X_u.

For computational purposes, we will assume that the uncertainty in the continuous flow is caused by some disturbance inputs in the following manner:

$$F(l, x) = \{\dot{x} \in \mathbb{R}^n : \dot{x} = f_l(x, d), \text{ for some } d \in D(l)\},$$

where $f_l(x, d)$ is a vector field that governs the flow of the system at location l, and d is a vector of disturbance inputs that takes value in the set $D(l) \subset \mathbb{R}^m$. In addition, for each location $l \in L$, we define the set of initial and unsafe continuous states as $\text{Init}(l) = \{x \in \mathcal{X} : (l, x) \in X_0\}$ and $\text{Unsafe}(l) = \{x \in \mathcal{X} : (l, x) \in X_u\}$. To each tuple $(l, l') \in L \times L$ with $l \neq l'$, we associate a guard set $\text{Guard}(l, l') = \{x \in \mathcal{X} : ((l, x), (l', x')) \in T \text{ for some } x' \in \mathcal{X}\}$, and a (possibly set valued) reset map $\text{Reset}(l, l') : x \mapsto \{x' \in \mathcal{X} : ((l, x), (l', x')) \in T\}$, whose domain is $\text{Guard}(l, l')$. Obviously, if no discrete transition from location l to location l' is possible, then the set $\text{Guard}(l, l')$ will be regarded as empty, and the associated reset map needs not be defined.

Although not explicitly stated, it is assumed that the description of the hybrid system given above is well-posed. For example, $(l, x) \in X_0$ automatically implies that $x \in I(l)$, and $((l, x), (l', x')) \in T$ implies that $x \in I(l)$ and $x' \in I(l')$.

3   Safety Verification Using Barrier Certificates

3.1   Continuous Systems

In this subsection we address the safety verification of continuous systems, to establish a foundation for the subsequent results. Consider a continuous system

$$\dot{x} = f(x, d), \tag{1}$$

where $x \in \mathcal{X}$ is the state of the system, and $d \in D$ is a collection of uncertain disturbance inputs. We assume that the system trajectories start at $x(0) \in X_0$. Analogous to the notation described in Section 2, the unsafe region here is denoted by $\mathcal{X}_u$.

Our method for verifying safety relies on the existence of barrier certificates [19]. As mentioned in the introduction, a barrier certificate is a function of state satisfying some conditions on both the function itself and its time derivative along the flow of the system. It proves that a given system is safe by depicting a 'barrier' between possible system trajectories and the given unsafe region (cf. Section 5.1 for a visual illustration). In achieving this, no explicit computation of system flows nor reachable sets is required. The following theorem states the conditions that must be satisfied by a barrier certificate.

Theorem 1. *Let the system (1) and the sets $\mathcal{X}$, D, $\mathcal{X}_0$ and $\mathcal{X}_u$ be given. Suppose there exists a barrier certificate, namely a function $B : \mathcal{X} \to \mathbb{R}$ that is differentiable with respect to its argument and satisfies the following conditions:*

$$B(x) > 0 \quad \forall (x) \in \mathcal{X}_u, \tag{2}$$

$$B(x) \leq 0 \quad \forall (x) \in \mathcal{X}_0, \tag{3}$$

$$\frac{\partial B}{\partial x}(x) f(x, d) \leq 0 \quad \forall (x, d) \in \mathcal{X} \times D \text{ such that } B(x) = 0, \tag{4}$$

then the safety of the system (1) is guaranteed. That is, there exists no trajectory of the system (1) contained in $\mathcal{X}$ that starts from an initial state in $\mathcal{X}_0$ and reaches another state in $\mathcal{X}_u$.

Proof. Assume that a barrier certificate satisfying the above conditions can be found. Take any trajectory $x(t)$ in $\mathcal{X}$ that starts at some $x_0 \in \mathcal{X}_0$ and consider the evolution of $B(x(t))$ along this trajectory. Condition (3) asserts that $B(x_0) \leq 0$. Together with (4) this implies that along the flow of the system $B(x(t))$ cannot become positive. Consequently, any such trajectory can never reach an unsafe state $x_u \in \mathcal{X}_u$, whose $B(x_u)$ is positive according to (2). We conclude that the safety of the system is guaranteed.

In the above theorem we have assumed that the unknown disturbance input can vary arbitrarily fast. If it is known that the variation of the disturbance input is bounded (e.g. when there are uncertain parameters, which can be regarded as time-invariant disturbance), then a less conservative verification can be performed by considering a barrier certificate $B(x, d)$ that also depends on the instantaneous value of the disturbance and modifying (2)–(4) accordingly. For example, in condition (4) we need to take into account the extra derivative term $\frac{\partial B}{\partial d}(x, d)\dot{d}$, with $\dot{d}$ taking its value in some bounded set.

At this point, we would like to note that the set of barrier certificates satisfying (2)–(4) is unfortunately non-convex, due to the restriction $B(x) = 0$ in (4). As a consequence, the construction of such barrier certificates cannot be performed using convex optimization, even though in Section 4 we will present an iterative method that can be used to search for a barrier certificate in this set. Nevertheless, it is useful to know that alternative conditions defining a convex set of barrier certificates can be derived. They are given in Proposition 1 below.

Proposition 1. *Let the system (1) and the sets $\mathcal{X}$, D, $\mathcal{X}_0$ and $\mathcal{X}_u$ be given. Suppose there exists a barrier certificate $B : \mathcal{X} \to \mathbb{R}$ that is differentiable with respect to the first argument and satisfies the conditions (2)–(3) and*

$$\frac{\partial B}{\partial x}(x)f(x, d) \leq 0 \quad \forall (x, d) \in \mathcal{X} \times D.$$

Then the safety of the system (1) is guaranteed. Moreover, the set of barrier certificates that satisfy the above conditions is a convex set.

Proof. It can be directly seen that a barrier certificate satisfying the above conditions also satisfies (2)–(4) because of the set inclusion $\{x \in \mathcal{X} : B(x) = 0\} \subset \mathcal{X}$, and thus the system safety is guaranteed. The fact that the set of barrier certificates is convex can be established by taking arbitrary $B_1(x)$ and $B_2(x)$ satisfying the above conditions and showing that for $\alpha \in [0, 1]$, $B(x) = \alpha B_1(x) + (1 - \alpha)B_2(x)$ satisfies the conditions as well.

The conditions in the above proposition are obviously more restrictive than those in Theorem 1 and therefore the conclusion that we can draw is generally also more conservative. However, a barrier certificate satisfying the convex conditions can be sought directly using convex optimization. As we will see later, this will be useful for initializing the iterative search for a better barrier certificate in the non-convex set.

3.2 Hybrid Systems

Verification of hybrid systems requires the use of a barrier certificate that not only is a function of the continuous state, but also depends on the discrete location. For this purpose, we construct a barrier certificate from a set of functions of continuous state, where each function corresponds to a discrete location of the system. Since in each location the continuous state can only take value within the invariant of the location, each function only needs to satisfy inequalities similar to (2)–(4) in the invariant set associated to it. Functions corresponding to different locations are linked via appropriate conditions that take care of possible discrete transitions between the locations. We state the conditions that must be satisfied by the barrier certificate in the following theorem.

Theorem 2. *Let the hybrid system $H = (\mathcal{X}, L, X_0, I, F, T)$ and the unsafe set X_u be given. Suppose there exists a barrier certificate, i.e., a collection of differentiable functions $B_l(x)$ which, for each $l \in L$ and $(l, l') \in L^2$, $l' \neq l$, satisfy*

$$B_l(x) > 0 \quad \forall x \in \text{Unsafe}(l), \tag{5}$$

$$B_l(x) \leq 0 \quad \forall x \in \text{Init}(l), \tag{6}$$

$$\frac{\partial B_l}{\partial x}(x) f_l(x, d) \leq 0 \quad \forall (x, d) \in I(l) \times D(l) \text{ such that } B_l(x) = 0, \tag{7}$$

$$B_{l'}(x') \leq 0 \quad \forall x' \in \text{Reset}(l, l')(x), \text{ for all } x \in \text{Guard}(l, l') \text{ s.t. } B_l(x) \leq 0. \tag{8}$$

Then the safety of the hybrid system H is guaranteed.

Proof. Assume that a barrier certificate $\{B_l(x)\}$ satisfying the above conditions can be found. Take any trajectory of the hybrid system that starts at arbitrary $(l_0, x_0) \in X_0$, and consider the evolution of $B_{l(t)}(x(t))$ along this trajectory. The condition (6) asserts that $B_{l_0}(x_0) \leq 0$. Next, (7) implies that during a segment of continuous flow $B_{l(t)}(x(t))$ cannot become positive, while (8) guarantees that during a discrete transition $B_{l(t)}(x(t))$ cannot jump to a positive value. Consequently, any such trajectory can never reach an unsafe state $(l_u, x_u) \in X_u$, whose $B_{l_u}(x_u)$ is positive according to (5). We conclude that the safety of the system is guaranteed.

Similar to what we encounter in the continuous case, the conditions (7)–(8) in the above theorem define a non-convex set of barrier certificates. Conditions defining a convex set of barrier certificates are given in the following proposition.

Proposition 2. *Let the hybrid system $H = (\mathcal{X}, L, X_0, I, F, T)$, the unsafe set X_u, and some fixed nonnegative constants $\sigma_{l,l'}$ be given. Suppose there exists a barrier certificate, i.e., a collection $\{B_l(x)\}$ of differentiable functions $B_l(x)$ which, for each $l \in L$ and $(l, l') \in L^2$, $l' \neq l$, satisfy (5)–(6) and*

$$\frac{\partial B_l}{\partial x}(x) f_l(x, d) \leq 0 \quad \forall (x, d) \in I(l) \times D(l),$$

$$B_{l'}(x') - \sigma_{l,l'} B_l(x) \leq 0 \quad \forall x' \in \text{Reset}(l, l')(x), \ x \in \text{Guard}(l, l').$$

Then the safety of the hybrid system H is guaranteed. Moreover, all barrier certificates that satisfy the above conditions form a convex set.

Proof. Analogous to the proof of Proposition 1.

Remark 1. Two possible choices for $\sigma_{l,l'}$ are 0 and 1. The choice $\sigma_{l,l'} = 0$ corresponds to modifying (8) to

$$B_{l'}(x') \leq 0 \quad \forall x' \in \text{Reset}(l, l')(x), \text{ for some } l \in L \text{ and } x \in \text{Guard}(l, l'),$$

and in this case a successful verification will actually prove that the system is safe even if during a transition from location l to l' the continuous state is allowed to jump to any continuous state x' in the image of the reset map. On the other hand, choosing $\sigma_{l,l'} = 1$ is useful for handling integral constraints, as we will shortly see.

3.3 Incorporating Constraints

In the remainder of this section we will briefly discuss how constraints can be handled within this framework. There are three kinds of constraints that can be incorporated: algebraic equality, algebraic inequality, and integral constraints; see [19] for a more thorough discussion. Here we will focus on integral constraints, as no existing methods can explicitly compute reachable sets when such constraints exist. Instead of assuming that the disturbance d is confined in $D(l)$, let us now assume that d and the continuous state x is constrained via

$$\int_0^T \phi(x(t), d(t))dt \geq 0, \quad \forall T > 0. \tag{9}$$

Constraints like this usually arise in systems analysis in the form of integral quadratic constraints [15] and are useful e.g. for describing a set of norm-bounded operators (cf. the example in Section 5.3), which may represent unmodelled continuous dynamics. Conditions guaranteeing safety when an integral constraint is present are given in the following theorem.

Theorem 3. *Let the hybrid system $H = (\mathcal{X}, L, X_0, I, F, T)$, the unsafe set X_u, and the constraint (9) be given. Suppose there exist a nonnegative constant multiplier σ and a collection $\{B_l(x)\}$ of differentiable functions $B_l(x)$ that satisfy*

$$B_l(x) > 0 \quad \forall x \in \text{Unsafe}(l), \tag{10}$$

$$B_l(x) \leq 0 \quad \forall x \in \text{Init}(l), \tag{11}$$

$$\frac{\partial B_l}{\partial x}(x)f_l(x, d) + \sigma\phi(x, d) \leq 0 \quad \forall (x, d) \in I(l) \times \mathbb{R}^m, \tag{12}$$

$$B_{l'}(x') \leq B_l(x) \quad \forall x' \in \text{Reset}(l, l')(x), \ x \in \text{Guard}(l, l') \tag{13}$$

for each $l \in L$ and $(l, l') \in L^2$, $l' \neq l$. Then $\{B_l(x)\}$ is a barrier certificate proving the safety of the system.

Proof. Assume that a barrier certificate satisfying the above conditions can be found. Consider any trajectory of the hybrid system on the time interval $[0, T]$ that starts at arbitrary $(l_0, x_0) \in X_0$. Assume that discrete transitions for this trajectory occur at time $t_1, t_2, ..., t_N$ where the system switches to location l_1,

$l_2, ..., l_N$. Denote the continuous states before and after the i-th transition by x_i^- and x_i^+, respectively. Then from (12) we obtain

$$B_{l_0}(x_1^-) - B_{l_0}(x_0) + B_{l_1}(x_2^-) - B_{l_1}(x_1^+) + ... + B_{l_N}(x(T)) - B_{l_N}(x_N^+)$$

$$= \int_0^{t_1^-} \frac{\partial B_{l_0}}{\partial x}(.)f_{l_0}(.)dt + \int_{t_1^+}^{t_2^-} \frac{\partial B_{l_1}}{\partial x}(.)f_{l_1}(.)dt + ... + \int_{t_N^+}^{T} \frac{\partial B_{l_N}}{\partial x}(.)f_{l_N}(.)dt$$

$$\leq -\sigma \int_0^T \phi(x,d)dt \leq 0.$$

Now, (13) guarantees that $B_{l_i}(x_i^+) - B_{l_{i-1}}(x_i^-) \leq 0$ for $i = 1, ..., N$, and hence it follows from the above inequality that $B_{l_N}(x(T)) \leq B_{l_0}(x_0)$. By (10)–(11) we conclude that $x(T)$ is outside the unsafe region. The safety of the system is thus guaranteed, since both the trajectory and the final time T are arbitrary.

4   Computational Method

Construction of barrier certificates is generally not easy, as is the case with Lyapunov function synthesis. However, for systems whose vector fields are polynomial and whose set descriptions are semialgebraic (i.e., described by polynomial equalities and inequalities), a tractable computational method exists if we also postulate the barrier certificate to be polynomial. The method uses the sum of squares decomposition of multivariate polynomials [18] and semidefinite programming [24], which we will describe now.

A multivariate polynomial $f(x)$ is a sum of squares if there exist polynomials $f_1(x), ..., f_m(x)$ such that $f(x) = \sum_{i=1}^m f_i^2(x)$. This is equivalent to the existence of a quadratic form $f(x) = Z^T(x)QZ(x)$ for some positive semidefinite matrix Q and vector of monomials $Z(x)$. A sum of squares decomposition for $f(x)$ can be computed using semidefinite programming, since it accounts to searching for an element Q in the intersection of the cone of positive semidefinite matrices and a set defined by some affine constraints. Together they provide a polynomial-time computational relaxation for proving global nonnegativity of multivariate polynomials [21,18] (since $f(x)$ is obviously nonnegative if it can be decomposed as a sum of squares), which belongs to the class of NP-hard problems. They have also been exploited for algorithmically constructing Lyapunov functions for nonlinear systems [18,17].

The same technique can be used in the computation of barrier certificates. Real coefficients $c_1, ..., c_m$ are used to parameterize a set of candidate barrier certificates in an affine manner, e.g., $\mathcal{B}_l = \{B_l(x) : B_l(x) = b_{0,l}(x) + \sum_{i=1}^m c_{i,l}b_{i,l}(x)\}$, for each $l \in L$, where the $b_{i,l}(x)$'s are some monomials in x. For example, one could arbitrarily determine an upper bound on the degree of the barrier certificate and then include all monomials whose degrees are less than or equal to the bound. The search for a barrier certificate $\{B_l(x) \in \mathcal{B}_l\}$, or equivalently coefficients $c_{i,l}$'s, such that the conditions in Theorems 2–3 or Proposition 2 are satisfied can be formulated as a sum of squares problem. In the case of Proposition 2 or Theorem 3, the resulting sum of squares problem can be solved directly using semidefinite programming (cf. Section 4.1), while in the other case it can be solved by an iterative method, which we will describe in Section 4.2.

Even though the computational approach discussed in this section assumes that the system is described by polynomials, non-polynomial descriptions can be handled (although possibly with some conservatism) and non-polynomial barrier certificates can be constructed by recasting of variables as proposed in [17], or by over-approximating the system by one that has polynomial vector fields and semialgebraic set descriptions.

4.1   Sum of Squares Formulation

Let us now consider a concrete example of a hybrid system $H = (\mathcal{X}, L, X_0, I, F, T)$ whose vector fields $f_l(x, d)$ are polynomial for each $l \in L$, and assume that the invariant sets $I(l)$ are described as $I(l) = \{x \in \mathbb{R}^n : g_{I(l)}(x) \geq 0\}$. In these set descriptions, the g's are vectors of polynomials, and the inequalities are satisfied entry-wise. For example, when $I(l)$ is the n-dimensional hypercube $[\underline{x_1}, \overline{x_1}] \times \ldots \times [\underline{x_n}, \overline{x_n}]$, we may define

$$g_{I(l)}(x) = \begin{bmatrix} (x_1 - \underline{x_1})(\overline{x_1} - x_1) \\ \vdots \\ (x_n - \underline{x_n})(\overline{x_n} - x_n) \end{bmatrix}.$$

Similarly, define the sets $D(l)$, $\text{Init}(l)$, $\text{Unsafe}(l)$, and $\text{Guard}(l, l')$ by the inequalities $g_{D(l)}(d) \geq 0$, $g_{\text{Init}(l)}(x) \geq 0$, $g_{\text{Unsafe}(l)}(x) \geq 0$, and $g_{\text{Guard}(l,l')}(x) \geq 0$. Finally, let the value of the reset map $\text{Reset}(l, l')$ evaluated at $x \in \text{Guard}(l, l')$ also be defined as $\text{Reset}(l, l')(x) = \{x' \in \mathbb{R}^n : g_{\text{Reset}(l,l')}(x, x') \geq 0\}$.

For this system, the search for a barrier certificate can be formulated as the sum of squares optimization problem given in the following proposition.

Proposition 3. *Let the hybrid system H and the descriptions of all the sets $I(l)$, $D(l)$, $\text{Init}(l)$, $\text{Unsafe}(l)$, $\text{Guard}(l, l')$, and $\text{Reset}(l, l')(x)$ be given. Suppose there exist polynomials $B_l(x)$ and $\lambda_{B_l}(x, d)$, a positive number ϵ, and vectors of sums of squares $\sigma_{\text{Unsafe}(l)}(x)$, $\sigma_{\text{Init}(l)}(x)$, $\sigma_{I(l)}(x, d)$, $\sigma_{D(l)}(x, d)$, $\sigma_{\text{Guard}(l,l')}(x, x')$, $\sigma_{\text{Reset}(l,l')}(x, x')$, and $\sigma_{l,l'}(x, x')$, such that the following expressions:*

$$B_l(x) - \epsilon - \sigma_{\text{Unsafe}(l)}^T(x) g_{\text{Unsafe}(l)}(x) \tag{14}$$

$$- B_l(x) - \sigma_{\text{Init}(l)}^T(x) g_{\text{Init}(l)}(x) \tag{15}$$

$$- \frac{\partial B_l}{\partial x}(x) f_l(x, d) - \sigma_{D(l)}^T(x, d) g_{D(l)}(d) - \sigma_{I(l)}^T(x, d) g_{I(l)}(x) - \lambda_{B_l}(x, d) B_l(x) \tag{16}$$

$$- B_{l'}(x') + \sigma_{l,l'}(x, x') B_l(x) - \sigma_{\text{Guard}(l,l')}^T(x, x') g_{\text{Guard}(l,l')}(x)\ldots$$
$$- \sigma_{\text{Reset}(l,l')}^T(x, x') g_{\text{Reset}(l,l')}(x, x') \tag{17}$$

are sums of squares for each $l \in L$ *and* $(l, l') \in L^2$, $l' \neq l$. *Then* $\{B_l(x)\}$ *satisfies the conditions in Theorem 2, and therefore the safety of the system is guaranteed.*

Proof. First notice that the expressions (14)–(17) are nonnegative, since they are sums of squares. Now take any $x \in \text{Unsafe}(l)$. For any such x the last term in (14) are nonpositive, and therefore it follows that $B_l(x) - \epsilon \geq 0$. Since ϵ is positive, condition (5) is immediately satisfied. Applying the same argument to the second, third, and fourth expressions, it is straightforward to show that (6)–(8) are satisfied by $B_l(x)$ for each $l \in L$, and thus we conclude that the collection $\{B_l(x)\}$ is a barrier certificate.

Remark 2. If the reset map $\text{Reset}(l, l')$ actually maps $x \in \text{Guard}(l, l')$ to a single-ton, e.g., if $\text{Reset}(l, l') : x \mapsto g_{\text{Reset}(l,l')}(x)$ for some polynomial vector $g_{\text{Reset}(l,l')}$, then (17) can be simplified to

$$- B_{l'}(g_{\text{Reset}(l,l')}(x)) + \sigma_{l,l'}(x) B_l(x) - \sigma_{\text{Guard}(l,l')}^T(x) g_{\text{Guard}(l,l')}(x),$$

where $\sigma_{l,l'}(x)$ and the entries of $\sigma_{\text{Guard}(l,l')}^T(x)$ are sums of squares.

Remark 3. The conditions (14)–(17) can be regarded as a generalization of the S-procedure [7], which verifies the nonnegativity of a quadratic form $x^T Q x$ on the set $\mathcal{Q} = \{x : x^T Q_i x \geq 0, \text{ for } i = 1, ..., n\}$ by finding nonnegative scalar multipliers σ_i, $i = 1, ..., n$ such that the matrix $Q - \sum_{i=1}^n \sigma_i Q_i$ is positive semidefinite. They are a special case of *positivstellensatz*, a central result in real algebraic geometry for proving emptiness of semialgebraic sets, which also provides a nested family of less conservative tests for nonnegativity. See [18] for details.

The sum of squares problem stated in Proposition 3 can be solved using semidefinite programming, if either the barrier certificate $\{B_l(x)\}$ or the multipliers $\lambda_{B_l}(x, d)$ and $\sigma_{l,l'}(x, x')$ are fixed in advance. By fixing either of them, we eliminate the products between unknown coefficients in the multipliers and the $B_l(x)$'s; this results in all the unknown coefficients being constrained in an affine manner, which is necessary for converting the problem to a semidefinite program. For example, the convex conditions in Proposition 2 are formulated in terms of a sum of squares problem similar to the one stated above, with the multipliers $\lambda_{B_l}(x, d)$ set equal to zero and $\sigma_{l,l'}(x, x')$ set equal to some nonnegative constants $\sigma_{l,l'}$ (cf. also Remark 1). In this case, a barrier certificate $\{B_l(x)\}$ can be searched directly using semidefinite programming, e.g. with the help of the software [20]. While the computational cost of this search depends on both the degrees of (14)–(17) and the dimension of (x, d), for fixed degrees the required computations grow polynomially with respect to the dimension of (x, d).

4.2   Iterative Approach

Fixing multipliers as explained in the previous subsection yields a barrier certificate that lies in the convex set defined by the conditions in Proposition 2. We will now present an iterative method for searching a barrier certificate that is not necessarily in the above set, but nevertheless still lies in the non-convex set of Theorem 2.

The reason to search for a barrier certificate in the non-convex set is that such a barrier certificate is generally less conservative than a barrier certificate in the convex set. For instance, the former may prove safety for larger disturbance sets, guard sets, unsafe sets, etc. Thus in the iteration we may start with some sufficiently small sets, and increase their sizes as the iteration progresses.

Algorithm 1

1. **Initialization:** Start with sufficiently small $D(l)$, $\text{Guard}(l, l')$ etc. Specify $\lambda_{B_l}(x, d)$ and $\sigma_{l,l'}(x, x')$ in advance, e.g., by choosing $\lambda_{B_l}(x) = 0$ and $\sigma_{l,l'}(x, x') = 0$ or 1. Search for $B_l(x)$ and the remaining multipliers.
2. **Fixing the barrier certificate:** Fix the $B_l(x)$ obtained from the previous step. Enlarge $D(l)$, $\text{Guard}(l, l')$, etc. Search for $\lambda_{B_l}(x, d)$, $\sigma_{l,l'}(x, x')$, and the remaining multipliers.
3. **Fixing the multipliers:** Fix the $\lambda_{B_l}(x, d)$ and $\sigma_{l,l'}(x, x')$ obtained from the previous step. Enlarge $D(l)$, $\text{Guard}(l, l')$, etc. Search for $B_l(x)$ and the remaining multipliers. Repeat to Step 2.

For an example illustrating the benefit of using this method, we refer the reader to Section 5.2. It should be noted, however, that solving a non-convex optimization problem by an iteration like this is not guaranteed to yield the globally optimal solution, as the iteration may actually converge to a local optimum. In our case, the barrier certificate we obtain at the end of our iteration may not be a barrier certificate that is able to prove safety for the maximum possible disturbance sets etc.

5   Examples

5.1   Example 1

Consider the two-dimensional system (taken from [12, page 180]) $\dot{x}_1 = x_2$, $\dot{x}_2 = -x_1 + \frac{p}{3}x_1^3 - x_2$, where the uncertain time-invariant parameter p lies in the interval $[0.9, 1.1]$. We want to verify that for any p in the above interval, all trajectories of the system starting at $\mathcal{X}_0 = \{x \in \mathbb{R}^2 : (x_1 - 1.5)^2 + x_2^2 \leq 0.25\}$ will never reach the unsafe set $\mathcal{X}_u = \{x \in \mathbb{R}^2 : (x_1 + 1)^2 + (x_2 + 1)^2 \leq 0.16\}$. Using the computational method described in Section 4, we are able to find a quartic barrier certificate $B(x, p)$, linearly parameterized by p, that satisfies the conditions in Proposition 1. Hence the safety of the system is verified. In fact, this barrier certificate proves that all trajectories starting from the zero sublevel set of $B(x, p)$ cannot reach any state for which $B(x, p) > 0$.

For $p = 1$, the phase portrait of the system and the zero level set of the barrier certificate are shown in Figure 1. The system has a stable focus at the origin, and two saddle points at $(\pm\sqrt{3}, 0)$. The zero level set of the barrier certificate separates $\mathcal{X}_u$ from all trajectories starting at $\mathcal{X}_0$. Note that since $\mathcal{X}_0$ contains a

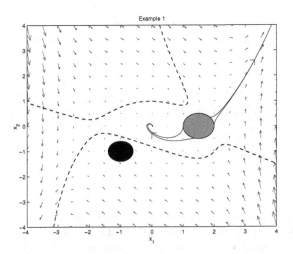

Fig. 1. Phase portrait of the system in Example 1. Solid patches are (from the left) $\mathcal{X}_u$ and $\mathcal{X}_0$, respectively. Dashed curves are the zero level set of $B(x,p)$, whereas solid curves are some trajectories of the system.

part of the unstable manifold corresponding to the equilibrium $(\sqrt{3}, 0)$, the safety of this system cannot be verified exactly by computation of forward reachable sets in a finite time horizon.

5.2 Example 2

Consider a hybrid system whose discrete transition diagram is depicted in Figure 2. The system starts in location 1 (NO CONTROL mode), with its continuous state initialized at $\{x \in \mathbb{R}^3 : x_1^2 + x_2^2 + x_3^2 \le 0.01\}$. In this location, the continuous state evolves according to $\dot{x} = f_1(x, d)$, until it reaches some point in the guard set $\text{Guard}(1,2) = \{x \in \mathbb{R}^3 : 0.99 \le x_1^2 + 0.01x_2^2 + 0.01x_3^2 \le 1.01\}$, at which instance a controller whose objective is to prevent $|x_1|$ from getting too big will be turned on, and the system jumps to location 2 (CONTROL mode). In location 2, the continuous dynamics is described by $\dot{x} = f_2(x, d)$. The system will remain in this location until the continuous state enters the second guard set $\text{Guard}(2,1) = \{x \in \mathbb{R}^3 : 0.03 \le x_1^2 + x_2^2 + x_3^2 \le 0.05\}$, where the controller will be turned off and the system jumps to location 1. We assume nondeterminism in the jump from location 1 to location 2 and vice versa. The invariant sets of both locations are shown in Figure 2, and the vector fields are given by

$$f_1(x, d) = \begin{bmatrix} x_2 \\ -x_1 + x_3 \\ x_1 + (2x_2 + 3x_3)(1 + x_3^2) + d \end{bmatrix}, \ f_2(x, d) = \begin{bmatrix} x_2 \\ -x_1 + x_3 \\ -x_1 - 2x_2 - 3x_3 + d \end{bmatrix}.$$

Our task in this example is to verify that $|x_1|$ never gets bigger than 5, if the instantaneous magnitude of the disturbance d is bounded by 1. We define our unsafe sets as $\text{Unsafe}(1) = \emptyset$, $\text{Unsafe}(2) = \{x \in \mathbb{R}^3 : 5 \le x_1 \le 5.1\} \cup \{x \in$

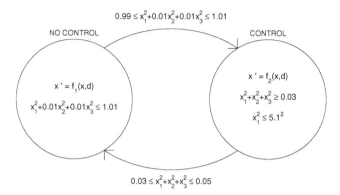

Fig. 2. Discrete transition diagram of the system in Example 2. This system has two discrete locations: NO CONTROL and CONTROL, with the vector field and the invariant of each location depicted inside the corresponding circle. The text labelling the transition between locations describes the guard set.

Table 1. Description and results of the iterative method used in Example 2. The third column indicates the disturbance range for which safety is verified.

Iteration	Description	Verified
1	Set $\lambda_{B_l}(x,d) = 0$, find $B_l(x)$.	$-0.005 \le d \le 0.005$
2	Fix $B_l(x)$, find $\lambda_{B_l}(x,d)$.	$-0.625 \le d \le 0.625$
3	Fix $\lambda_{B_l}(x,d)$, find $B_l(x)$.	$-1 \le d \le 1$

$\mathbb{R}^3 : -5.1 \le x_1 \le -5\}$, and compute a quartic barrier certificate satisfying the conditions in Theorem 2. Using the iterative method described in Section 4 to enlarge the verifiable disturbance set, we obtain the results shown in Table 1. At the third iteration, we are able to prove the safety of the system.

5.3   Example 3

In this example, we analyze the reachability of a linear system in feedback interconnection with a relay. The block diagram of the system is shown in Figure 3, with the matrices A, B, C, and D given by

$$A = \begin{bmatrix} 0 & 1 & 0 \\ 0 & 0 & 1 \\ -0.2 & -0.3 & -1 \end{bmatrix}, \quad B = \begin{bmatrix} 0 \\ 0 \\ 0.1 \end{bmatrix}, \quad C = \begin{bmatrix} 1 \\ 0 \\ 0 \end{bmatrix}^T, \quad D = 0,$$

and the relay element having the following characteristic: $w = 10$ if $y \ge 0$, and $w = -10$ if $y < 0$. For the sets $\mathcal{X} = \{x \in \mathbb{R}^3 : x_1^2 + x_2^2 + x_3^2 \le 4^2\}$, $\mathcal{X}_0 = \{x \in \mathbb{R}^3 : (x_1+2)^2 + x_2^2 + x_3^2 \le 0.1^2\}$, and $\mathcal{X}_u = \{x \in \mathbb{R}^3 : (x_1-2)^2 + x_2^2 + x_3^2 \le 0.1^2\}$, we pose the following question: is it possible to design a controller K (possibly nonlinear and time-varying) with the L_2-gain no greater than one, which is connected to the system in the way shown in Figure 2, such that the system can be steered from $\mathcal{X}_0$ to $\mathcal{X}_u$ while maintaining the state in $\mathcal{X}$?

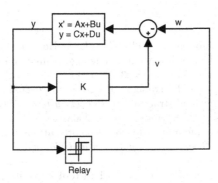

Fig. 3. Block diagram of the system in Example 3. We ask if it is possible to design a controller K that steers the system from an initial set $\mathcal{X}_0$ to a destination set $\mathcal{X}_u$, subject to some other specifications.

The requirement that the L_2-gain of the controller is no greater than one can be equivalently formulated as an integral quadratic constraint (IQC) [15] $\int_0^T [y^2(t) - v^2(t)]dt \geq 0, \forall T > 0$. This specification introduces dynamic uncertainty to the problem, and consequently the reachable sets cannot be computed explicitly with existing methods. Nevertheless, we can perform reachability analysis by adjoining the above IQC using a nonnegative constant multiplier to the conditions on the time derivative of barrier certificates (cf. Theorem 3). For this example, a quartic barrier certificate that satisfies the required conditions can be found. Hence we conclude that the given specification is impossible to meet.

6   Conclusions

In this paper, we presented a novel approach for reachability refutation of uncertain hybrid systems with nonlinear continuous dynamics. Our approach is based on the construction of a barrier certificate, whose zero level set separates all trajectories emanating from a set of initial conditions from some given unsafe set. Contrary to most existing techniques, our method does not require computing the flow of the system. Rather, we utilize a Lyapunov-like formalism to construct a safety proof.

Our approach is suitable for hybrid systems whose continuous dynamics are described by polynomial vector fields and whose invariant sets, guard sets, etc are described by polynomial equalities and inequalities. By formulating the conditions for barrier certificates as sum of squares problems and using semidefinite programming to solve them, it is possible to search for barrier certificates in a computationally tractable fashion. We demonstrated the efficacy of our approach by some examples of nonlinear and uncertain hybrid systems. Higher dimensional problems can also be handled by our method, since the computational cost of constructing barrier certificates grows polynomially with respect to the state dimension.

References

1. R. Alur, C. Courcoubetis, N. Halbwachs, T. A. Henzinger, P.-H. Ho, X. Nicollin, A. Oliviero, J. Sifakis, and S. Yovine. The algorithmic analysis of hybrid systems. *Theoretical Computer Science*, 138:3–34, 1995.
2. R. Alur, T. Dang, and F. Ivancic. Progress on reachability analysis of hybrid systems using predicate abstraction. In *Hybrid Systems: Computation and Control, LNCS 2623*, pages 4–19. Springer-Verlag, 2003.
3. H. Anai and V. Weispfenning. Reach set computations using real quantifier elimination. In *Hybrid Systems: Computation and Control, LNCS 2034*, pages 63–76. Springer-Verlag, 2001.
4. E. Asarin, T. Dang, and O. Maler. The d/dt tool for verification of hybrid systems. In *Computer Aided Verification, LNCS 2404*, pages 365–370. Springer-Verlag, 2002.
5. A. Bemporad, F. D. Torrisi, and M. Morari. Optimization-based verification and stability characterization of piecewise affine and hybrid systems. In *Hybrid Systems: Computation and Control, LNCS 1790*, pages 45–58. Springer-Verlag, 2000.
6. O. Botchkarev and S. Tripakis. Verification of hybrid systems with linear differential inclusions using ellipsoidal approximations. In *Hybrid Systems: Computation and Control, LNCS 1790*, pages 73–88. Springer-Verlag, 2000.
7. S. Boyd, L. El Ghaoui, E. Feron, and V. Balakrishnan. *Linear Matrix Inequalities in System and Control Theory*. SIAM, Philadelphia, PA, 1994.
8. M. S. Branicky. Multiple Lyapunov functions and other analysis tools for switched and hybrid systems. *IEEE Trans. Automatic Control*, 43(4):475–482, 1998.
9. A. Chutinan and B. H. Krogh. Computational techniques for hybrid system verification. *IEEE Trans. Automatic Control*, 48(1):64–75, 2003.
10. E. M. Clarke and R. P. Kurshan. Computer-aided verification. *IEEE Spectrum*, 33(6):61–67, 1996.
11. M. Johansson and A. Rantzer. Computation of piecewise quadratic Lyapunov functions for hybrid systems. *IEEE Trans. Automat. Control*, 43(4):555–559, 1998.
12. H. K. Khalil. *Nonlinear Systems*. Prentice-Hall, Inc., Upper Saddle River, NJ, second edition, 1996.
13. A. Kurzhanski and P. Varaiya. Ellipsoidal techniques for reachability analysis. In *Hybrid Systems: Computation and Control, LNCS 1790*, pages 203–213. Springer-Verlag, 2000.
14. G. Lafferriere, G. J. Pappas, and S. Yovine. Symbolic reachability computations for families of linear vector fields. *J. Symbolic Computation*, 32(3):231–253, 2001.
15. A. Megretski and A. Rantzer. System analysis via integral quadratic constraints. *IEEE Trans. Automatic Control*, 42(6):819–830, 1997.
16. R. M. Murray (Ed.). *Control in an Information Rich World: Report of the Panel on Future Directions in Control, Dynamics, and Systems*. SIAM, Philadelphia, PA, 2003. Available at http://www.cds.caltech.edu/~murray/cdspanel.
17. A. Papachristodoulou and S. Prajna. On the construction of Lyapunov functions using the sum of squares decomposition. In *Proceedings IEEE CDC*, 2002.
18. P. A. Parrilo. *Structured Semidefinite Programs and Semialgebraic Geometry Methods in Robustness and Optimization*. PhD thesis, Caltech, Pasadena, CA, 2000.
19. S. Prajna. Barrier certificates for nonlinear model validation. In *Proceedings IEEE Conference on Decision and Control*, 2003.
20. S. Prajna, A. Papachristodoulou, and P. A. Parrilo. Introducing SOSTOOLS: A general purpose sum of squares programming solver. In *Proceedings IEEE CDC*, 2002. Available at http://www.cds.caltech.edu/sostools and http://www.aut.ee.ethz.ch/~parrilo/sostools.

21. N. Z. Shor. Class of global minimum bounds of polynomial functions. *Cybernetics*, 23(6):731–734, 1987.
22. A. Tiwari. Approximate reachability for linear systems. In *Hybrid Systems: Computation and Control, LNCS 2623*, pages 514–525. Springer-Verlag, 2003.
23. C. J. Tomlin, I. Mitchell, A. M. Bayen, and M. Oishi. Computational techniques for the verification of hybrid systems. *Proc. of the IEEE*, 91(7):986–1001, 2003.
24. L. Vandenberghe and S. Boyd. Semidefinite programming. *SIAM Review*, 38(1):49–95, 1996.
25. H. Yazarel and G. Pappas. Geometric programming relaxations for linear systems reachability. Submitted to the American Control Conference, 2004.
26. K. Zhou, J. C. Doyle, and K. Glover. *Robust and Optimal Control*. Prentice-Hall, Inc., Upper Saddle River, NJ, 1996.

Piecewise-Linear Output-Error Methods for Parameter Estimation in Direction-Dependent Processes

Fredrik Rosenqvist and Anders Karlstöm

Department of Signals and Systems
Chalmers University of Technology, SE-412 96 Göteborg, Sweden
fr@s2.chalmers.se

Abstract. In direction-dependent processes, the dynamic responses depend on the direction of the system input. The parameter estimation of these processes under noisy conditions can be somewhat problematic in terms of predictor choice and asymptotic behaviour. For parameter estimation, a convenient way to model direction dependence is to use a piecewise-linear model formulation, whose switching depends on the input direction. This paper analyses a prediction-error minimisation method for direction-dependent processes in terms of piecewise-linear dynamics. In particular, the asymptotic convergence properties are investigated and relevant conditions for the utilisation of the estimation method are given. Further, it is demonstrated that a piecewise-linear output-error predictor is preferable in situations where the impact of disturbances is predominant. The main reason for this is that it separates the disturbances from the process model.

1   Introduction

In a direction-dependent process, the dynamics in terms of time constants and gains depend on the system direction [6]. In this case, the direction should be interpreted as the sign of the input change — or of the input derivative for the continuous-time counterpart. These odd-symmetry characteristics [13] can be represented as hybrid systems whose switching rules depend on the input direction. Unfortunately, there is a shortage of analytical results for direction-dependent processes, despite their frequently being encountered in industry, in chemical reactors [6], gas turbines and nuclear reactors [7], distillation columns [14,21], automotive suspensions [20] and thermo-mechanical pulping processes [15] for example. The work that has been performed on direction-dependent processes has focused on system identification. One approach has been to use the cross-correlation function to trace direction dependence by applying different kinds of maximum-length binary signals to the process [1,6,7,20]. Other approaches have considered parameter estimation using different model structures, such as neural networks [21] or Wiener models [1].

Direction-dependent processes are apparently nonlinear and require adequate model systems. One convenient way to model direction-dependent dynamics is to extract the direction dependence, using a piecewise-linear (*PWL*) model formulation, whose switching depends on the input direction. By regarding the process as a system from the input change to the output change, the input change becomes the input signal to the *PWL* model and it is also the signal that governs the switching in this hybrid process. Further, the *PWL*

R. Alur and G.J. Pappas (Eds.): HSCC 2004, LNCS 2993, pp. 493–507, 2004.

form is suitable when it comes to the parameter estimation of these processes, as it is considerably simpler in its structure than a more comprehensive physical (first-principle) model of the pertinent process. To achieve a satisfactory parameter estimation in spite of the hybrid character of the process, traditional concepts, such as predictor models and asymptotic convergence, must be analysed in the light of the *PWL* representation.

In the next section, the modelling principles of direction-dependent processes in terms of *PWL* systems are reviewed [16,17] and, in Section 3, the former work on the parameter estimation of piecewise-linear output-error (*PWOE*) predictors is continued. Proposition 3, which is an extension of the convergence properties for linear time-invariant (*LTI*) systems, is one of the main results of this paper. The other main result is in Section 4, where the properties of the *PWOE* predictor for direction-dependent processes are compiled and put into a more general framework; ways of carrying out the parameter estimation of direction-dependent processes in practice, using the existing results, are discussed.

2   Direction-Dependent Processes

Nonlinear dynamic processes can display many complex characteristics and, if the main nonlinearity is the direction dependence, an *LTI* approximation is not sufficient. The approach here is to approximate the process using a *PWL* system from the input change to the output change. If the system input is $u(k) \in \mathcal{U} \subseteq \mathbb{R}$ and the output signal is $y(k) \in \mathcal{Y} \subseteq \mathbb{R}$, the process from the input change $u_\Delta(k) = u(k) - u(k-1)$ to the output change $y_\Delta(k) = y(k) - y(k-1)$ becomes

$$\begin{aligned} \xi(k) &= A_{\sigma(k-1)}\xi(k-1) + B_{\sigma(k-1)}u_\Delta(k-1) \\ y_\Delta(k) &= C_{\sigma(k)}\xi(k) \end{aligned} \tag{1}$$

where $k \in \{1, 2, ...N\}$ is the discrete time, $\xi(k) \subseteq \mathbb{R}^n$ is the state vector and the switching function $\sigma(k) : \mathcal{U}_\Delta \to \{1, 2\}$ is defined as

$$\sigma(k) = \begin{cases} 1, & u_\Delta(k) < 0 \\ 2, & u_\Delta(k) > 0 \\ \sigma(k-1), & u_\Delta(k) = 0 \end{cases} \tag{2}$$

As different dynamic responses to increasing and decreasing input signals are obtained, there are two reasons why it is advantageous to use a piecewise-linear dynamic description from u_Δ to y_Δ to represent direction-dependent processes. Firstly, the switching function, σ, depends on the sign of the input change and, secondly, different gains in different directions can be favourably represented by such linear submodels. The signal values of $y(k)$ are computed as the sum of the changes added to the value of y at the initial time K_0

$$y(k) = y(K_0) + \sum_{i=K_0+1}^{k} y_\Delta(i) \tag{3}$$

In order to represent the direction-dependent process as a system from the input signal, $u \in \mathcal{U} \subseteq \mathbb{R}$, to the output signal, $y \in \mathcal{Y} \subseteq \mathbb{R}$, two additional states are introduced

$$v(k) = u(k-1)$$
$$z(k) = y(k-1) \tag{4}$$

and, using these two augmented states, Eq.(1) can be represented as

$$\begin{aligned}
\xi(k) &= A_{\sigma(k-1)}\xi(k-1)+ \\
&\quad + B_{\sigma(k-1)}(u(k-1) - v(k-1)) \\
z(k) &= C_{\sigma(k-1)}\xi(k-1) + z(k-1) \\
y(k) &= C_{\sigma(k)}\xi(k) + z(k)
\end{aligned} \tag{5}$$

By introducing an augmented state vector

$$w(k) = \left[\, v(k)\ \xi^T(k)\ z(k)\,\right]^T \tag{6}$$

Eq.(5) can be written as

$$\begin{aligned}
w(k) &= F_\sigma w(k-1) + G_\sigma u(k-1) \\
y(k) &= H_\sigma w(k)
\end{aligned} \tag{7}$$

where

$$F_\sigma = \begin{bmatrix} 0 & 0 & 0 \\ -B_{\sigma(k-1)} & A_{\sigma(k-1)} & 0 \\ 0 & C_{\sigma(k-1)} & 1 \end{bmatrix} \qquad \begin{aligned} G_\sigma &= \left[1\ B_{\sigma(k-1)}^T\ 0\right]^T \\ H_\sigma &= \left[0\ C_{\sigma(k)}\ 1\right] \end{aligned} \tag{8}$$

Direction-dependent dynamic systems, as described in Eq.(7),(8), do not exhibit unique stationary levels. As demonstrated in Fig.1, a positive step in the input signal, u, is followed by a negative step back to the original level, whereas the output signal, y, levels off at a different level than where it originated. Because u_Δ and y_Δ equal nought when u and y are constant, the process representation in Eq.(1) provides an opportunity to describe all stationary points at $\xi = 0$, as long as A_σ is invertible for $\sigma \in \{1, 2\}$.

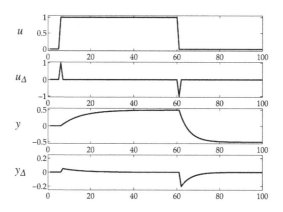

Fig. 1. Step response — positive and negative respectively — of a direction-dependent process. A simulation with the sample time $T_S = 1s$ is performed, where $A_\sigma \in \{0.8, 0.9\}$, $B_\sigma \in \{0.2, 0.05\}$ and $C_\sigma = 1$ are scalars. The linear submodels thus correspond to first-order dynamics.

To estimate a parametric model of a direction-dependent process from input/output (I/O) data, it is preferable to consider the input and output changes (u_Δ, y_Δ) as in Eq.1. The I/O form of direction-dependent processes is commonly represented in terms of piecewise-linear dynamics [2,5,17]

$$y_\Delta(k) = \frac{\sum_{j=1}^{n_b} b_{j,\sigma} q^{-j}}{1 + \sum_{i=1}^{n_a} a_{i,\sigma} q^{-i}} u_\Delta(k) \qquad (9)$$

where the inverse shift operator, q^{-1}, is defined such that $q^{-1}x(k) = x(k-1)$. The parameter $\sigma(k) : \mathcal{U}_\Delta \to \{1,2\}$ depends on $u_\Delta(k)$, as described in Eq.(2). However, it is not obvious which k determines the active sub-model for a given parameter [17]. In the literature, the common interpretation is that $\sigma = \sigma(k-1)$ for all the parameters in Eq.(9) [2,3,5].

A direction-dependent process given in the piecewise-linear state-space form cannot generally not be converted into an I/O model in which each parameter belongs only to one mode. There are, however, cases where this is possible.

Proposition 1. *[17] If the direction-dependent state-space model in Eq.(1) is represented in the form*

$$A_{\sigma(k)} = \begin{bmatrix} -a_{1,\sigma(k)} & \cdots & -a_{n-1,\sigma(k)} & -a_{n,\sigma(k)} \\ 1 & \cdots & 0 & 0 \\ \vdots & \ddots & \vdots & \vdots \\ 0 & \cdots & 1 & 0 \end{bmatrix} \qquad \begin{aligned} B_{\sigma(k)} &= \begin{bmatrix} 1 \ldots 0 \ 0 \end{bmatrix}^T \\ C_{\sigma(k)} &= \begin{bmatrix} b_{1,\sigma(k)} & \cdots & b_{n-1,\sigma(k)} & b_{n,\sigma(k)} \end{bmatrix} \end{aligned}$$

there is a corresponding I/O model, in which each parameter is associated with only one mode

$$y_\Delta(k) = \frac{\sum_{j=1}^{n} b_{j,\sigma(k-1)} q^{-j}}{1 + \sum_{i=1}^{n} a_{i,\sigma(k-1)} q^{-i}} u_\Delta(k) \qquad (10)$$

Moreover, if the state-space model is in the form

$$A_{\sigma(k)} = \begin{bmatrix} -a_{1,\sigma(k)} & 1 \ldots 0 \\ \vdots & \vdots \ddots \vdots \\ -a_{n-1,\sigma(k)} & 0 \ldots 1 \\ -a_{n,\sigma(k)} & 0 \ldots 0 \end{bmatrix} \qquad \begin{aligned} B_{\sigma(k)} &= \begin{bmatrix} b_{1,\sigma(k)} & \cdots & b_{n-1,\sigma(k)} & b_{n,\sigma(k)} \end{bmatrix}^T \\ C_{\sigma(k)} &= \begin{bmatrix} 1 \ 0 \ldots 0 \end{bmatrix} \end{aligned}$$

there is a corresponding I/O model, in which each parameter is associated with only one mode

$$y_\Delta(k) = \frac{\sum_{j=1}^{n} b_{j,\sigma(k-j)} q^{-j}}{1 + \sum_{i=1}^{n} a_{i,\sigma(k-i)} q^{-i}} u_\Delta(k) \qquad (11)$$

The I/O model in Eq.(10) will be called the *instant* switching model, as all the parameters switch simultaneously, which can be observed by considering how the updates of the b_j's and a_i's depend on $\sigma = \sigma(k-1)$. The I/O model in Eq.(11) will be called the *delayed* switching model, as the parameter switches are delayed for the higher order parameters, which can be observed by considering how the updates of b_j's and a_i's depend on the time instants $\sigma = \sigma(k-j)$ and $\sigma = \sigma(k-i)$ respectively.

3   Parameter Estimation — Fundamentals

To identify the above parameters, piecewise-linear *PWARX* predictors for instant-switching systems have been derived [2,5]. However, if the perturbations are assumed to be independent of the different sub-models, a piecewise-linear output-error (*PWOE*) predictor which adds the perturbation directly to the output would be more natural [17]. A predictor for a direction-dependent process can be written in the general form

$$\hat{y}_\Delta(k, \Theta) = \Theta^T \Phi(k) \tag{12}$$

Regardless of the predictor type, the parameter vector, Θ, for the system is an array consisting of the parameter vectors of all sub-models

$$\Theta = \begin{bmatrix} \theta_1 \\ \theta_2 \end{bmatrix} ; \theta_p = \begin{bmatrix} a_{1,p} \dots a_{n_a,p} \, b_{1,p} \dots b_{n_b,p} \end{bmatrix}^T \tag{13}$$

and the regression vector consists of one vector, $\phi(k)$, for each sub-model, where two non-zero entries at corresponding positions are not possible

$$\Phi(k) = \begin{bmatrix} \phi(k) * \bar{\delta}_{\sigma 1}(k) \\ \phi(k) * \bar{\delta}_{\sigma 2}(k) \end{bmatrix} \tag{14}$$

where $\delta_{\sigma p}(k)$ is the Kronecker delta function and the multiplication, $*$, in Eq.(14) is scalar if $\bar{\delta}_{\sigma 1}(k) = \bar{\delta}_{\sigma 1}^I(k)$ and entrywise if $\bar{\delta}_{\sigma 1}(k) = \bar{\delta}_{\sigma 1}^D(k)$.

The *PWARX* and *PWOE* predictors differ in $\phi(k)$

$$\phi_{PWARX}(k) = \begin{bmatrix} -y_\Delta(k-1) \dots -y_\Delta(k-n_a) \, u_\Delta(k-1) \dots u_\Delta(k-n_b) \end{bmatrix}^T$$
$$\phi_{PWOE}(k) = \begin{bmatrix} -\hat{y}_\Delta(k-1) \dots -\hat{y}_\Delta(k-n_a) \, u_\Delta(k-1) \dots u_\Delta(k-n_b) \end{bmatrix}^T \tag{15}$$

The instant (*I*) and delayed (*D*) switching models differ in $\bar{\delta}_{\sigma p}(k)$

$$\bar{\delta}_{\sigma p}^I(k) = \delta_{\sigma p}(k-1)$$
$$\bar{\delta}_{\sigma p}^D(k) = \begin{bmatrix} \delta_{\sigma p}(k-1) \dots \delta_{\sigma p}(k-n_a) \, \delta_{\sigma p}(k-1) \dots \delta_{\sigma p}(k-n_b) \end{bmatrix}^T \tag{16}$$

The parameters of the direction-dependent output-error predictor in Eq.(12), i.e. $\hat{y}_\Delta(k, \Theta) = \Theta^T \Phi_{PWOE}(k)$, are to be estimated using input-output data from a presumably direction-dependent process. To find parameters, Θ, such that the predicted values, $\hat{y}_\Delta(k, \Theta)$, correspond to the measured values, $y_\Delta(k)$, satisfactorily, the prediction error method (*PEM*)[10] is utilised. This method is based on the minimisation of a norm criterion that penalises the residuals

$$\epsilon(k, \Theta) = y_\Delta(k) - \hat{y}_\Delta(k, \Theta)$$
$$k = \{1, 2, \dots, N\} \tag{17}$$

The hypothetical norm $\bar{V}(\Theta, Z^\infty)$, whose minimisation gives the argument $\bar{\Theta}$, is based on a infinitely large data set

$$Z^\infty = Z^N, N \to \infty$$
$$Z^N = \{u_\Delta(1), y_\Delta(1), \dots, u_\Delta(N), y_\Delta(N)\} \tag{18}$$

This norm is defined as

$$\bar{V}(\Theta, Z^\infty) = \lim_{N \to \infty} \frac{1}{N} \sum_{k=1}^{N} E[v(\epsilon(k, \Theta))] \tag{19}$$

where $v(\epsilon(k, \Theta))$, $\mathbb{R} \to [0, \infty)$ is a non-decreasing function of ϵ. The goal is to find parameters, $\bar{\Theta}$, in a certain parameter set, Θ_S, such that $\bar{V}(\Theta)$ is minimised.

$$\bar{\Theta} = \arg \min_{\Theta \in \Theta_S} \bar{V}(\Theta, Z^\infty) \tag{20}$$

where $\bar{\Theta} \in \Theta_S$ is a parameter set that ideally reduces to include only one element. As it is non-trivial to compute the norm $\bar{V}(\theta, Z^\infty)$, a time-averaged norm

$$V_N(\Theta, Z^N) = \frac{1}{N} \sum_{k=1}^{N} v(\epsilon(k, \Theta)) \tag{21}$$

is regarded as an approximation of $\bar{V}(\Theta, Z^\infty)$. As a result, the approximate estimate of the parameters becomes

$$\hat{\Theta}_N = \arg \min_{\Theta \in \Theta_S} V_N(\Theta, Z^N) \tag{22}$$

A very common and useful choice of norm is to square the residuals, i.e. $v(\epsilon) = \epsilon^2$, which becomes a least-square problem when the predictor is linear in the parameters, Θ, e.g. the *PWARX* case. However, when the predictor is a nonlinear function of the parameters, such as in the *PWOE* case, an iterative procedure is required.

For the *PWOE* predictor, the algorithm for finding the parameter estimate must be iterative, as the cost function to be minimised is a function of the parameter vector itself. The search algorithm used here is a Newton method

$$\hat{\Theta}_{i+1} = \hat{\Theta}_i - \mu_i R_i^{-1} \frac{\partial}{\partial \Theta} V_N(\hat{\Theta}_i) \tag{23}$$

where i is the iteration step, μ_i is the step size and R_i is the Hessian which, together with the gradient, $\frac{\partial}{\partial \Theta} V_N$, determines the search direction [19]. The Hessian is calculated as

$$R_i = \frac{1}{N} \sum_{k=1}^{N} \Psi(\Phi(k), \hat{\Theta}_i) \Psi^T(\Phi(k), \hat{\Theta}_i) \tag{24}$$

where

$$\Psi(\Phi(k), \Theta) = \frac{\partial}{\partial \Theta} \hat{y}_\Delta(k) \tag{25}$$

Further,

$$\frac{\partial}{\partial \Theta} V_N(\hat{\Theta}_i) = -\frac{1}{N} \sum_{k=1}^{N} \Psi(\Phi(k), \hat{\Theta}) \epsilon(k, \hat{\Theta}) \tag{26}$$

The step size, μ_i, is optimised through a line search, where the value of the cost function for the next iteration is minimised, given the current value and the search direction.

Because the predictor is a function of previous predictions, the model becomes recurrent [11,19]. This property does not affect the iterative algorithm itself, but some extra computational effort is required to approximate Eq.(24).

Proposition 2. *[17] Given a PWOE predictor in Eq.(12-16), its differentiation with respect to the parameter vector can be computed as*

$$(1 + \sum_{h=1}^{n_a} a_{h,\sigma(k-h^*)} q^{-h}) \Psi = \Phi \tag{27}$$

where

$$k - h^* = \begin{cases} k & \text{if } (\Psi, \Phi) = (\Psi^I, \Phi^I) \\ k - h & \text{if } (\Psi, \Phi) = (\Psi^D, \Phi^D) \end{cases} \tag{28}$$

As it is the empirical values of the prediction error rather than its expected values that are considered, when minimising the squared sum, it might not be true that the minimising argument in Eq.(22) coincides with the one in Eq.(20). A convergence analysis is required to ensure that the time-averaged cost function in Eq.(21) asymptotically behaves like the norm in Eq.(19)

$$\sup_{\Theta \in \Theta_S} |V_N(\Theta, Z^N) - \bar{V}(\Theta)| \to 0 \text{ w.p.1 as } N \to \infty \tag{29}$$

Given the squared residual norm together with the expression for $\bar{V}(\Theta)$ in Eq.(20), the expression in Eq.(29) is equivalent to

$$\sup_{\Theta \in \Theta_S} \frac{1}{N} \left| \sum_{k=1}^{N} \epsilon^2(k, \Theta) - \sum_{k=1}^{N} E[\epsilon^2(k, \Theta)] \right| \to 0 \text{ w.p.1 as } N \to \infty \tag{30}$$

This convergence is proven to be fulfilled in certain conditions for linear [10] and more general systems [8,9]. In the case of piecewise-linear systems, whose switching schemes depend solely on the input signal, the convergence analysis can be carried out in the framework of linear time-varying (*LTV*) systems [18], as long as the identification is carried out in open loop.

Assume that the hypothetical *I/O* data (Z^∞) are generated by an uniformly bounded-input bounded-output (*BIBO*) system, whose output, y_Δ, includes a disturbance, $v(k)$

$$y_\Delta(k) = \sum_{\tau=1}^{\infty} G(k, \tau) u_\Delta(k - \tau) + v(k) \tag{31}$$

The uniform *BIBO* condition means that any unit-pulse response is bounded [18], i.e.

$$\sum_{\tau=1}^{\infty} |G(k, \tau)| < K_G < \infty, \quad \forall k \tag{32}$$

Further, it is assumed that the disturbance, $v(k)$, is generated by a white-noise driven *LTI* filter

$$v(k) = \sum_{\tau=1}^{\infty} H(\tau) e(k - \tau) \tag{33}$$

where $\{e(k)\}$ is an independently distributed random signal with the properties: $E[e(k)] = 0$, $E[e^2(k)] = \lambda_k$ and $E[e^4(k)] < \infty$. The *LTI* filter $H(\tau)$ is assumed to be uniformly *BIBO*

$$\sum_{\tau=1}^{\infty} |H(\tau)| < K_H < \infty \tag{34}$$

The *BIBO* condition on $G(k, \tau)$ is a slight generalisation of the stability conditions for *LTI* systems, whereas the *BIBO* condition on the noise model, $H(\tau)$, falls within the framework of the stability conditions for *LTI* systems [10].

According to Proposition 1, the predictor, $\hat{y}_\Delta(k)$, can be stated in the state-space form

$$\begin{aligned} \xi(k) &= A_{\sigma(k-1)}\xi(k-1) + B_{\sigma(k-1)}u_\Delta(k-1) \\ \hat{y}_\Delta(k) &= C_{\sigma(k)}\xi(k) \end{aligned} \tag{35}$$

and, as $\{u_\Delta(k)\}$ is a part of the *I/O* data, the switching sequence for a certain data set, Z^∞, is given. Consequently, in the case of open-loop data acquisition, the system matrices can be described as a function of the time, k

$$\{A_{\sigma(k)}, B_{\sigma(k)}, C_{\sigma(k)}\} = \{A(k), B(k), C(k)\} \tag{36}$$

The input/output realisation of the predictor can thus be written as an *LTV* filter

$$\begin{aligned} \hat{y}_\Delta(k) &= \sum_{\tau=1}^{\infty} C(k)T(k, k-\tau)B(k-\tau)u_\Delta(k-\tau) \\ T(k, k-\tau) &= A(k)A(k-1)\ldots A(k-\tau) \end{aligned} \tag{37}$$

The residual in Eq.(17) can now be described in terms of Eq.(31) and Eq.(37).

$$\begin{aligned} \epsilon(k, \Theta) &= \sum_{\tau=1}^{\infty} \left(G(k, \tau) - C(k)T(k, k-\tau)B(k-\tau)\right) u_\Delta(k-\tau) + \\ &\quad + \sum_{\tau=1}^{\infty} H(\tau)e(k-\tau) \end{aligned} \tag{38}$$

The first term in Eq.(38) is an *LTV* filter, whereas the second term — which handles the process disturbances — is an *LTI* filter.

Proposition 3. *Given the data set Z^∞, the predictor, $\hat{y}_\Delta(k, \Theta)$, and the parameter set Θ_S such that $\Theta \in \Theta_S$ and the signal $\epsilon(k, \Theta)$ as described as in Eq.(38); then, under the following assumptions:*

- *the filter $C(k)T(k, k-\tau)B(k-\tau)$ is uniformly BIBO for all $\Theta \in \Theta_S$,*
- *$u_\Delta(k) < K_u < \infty$ $\forall k$, and*
- *$E[e(k)] = 0$, $E[e^2(k)] = \lambda_e$, $E[e^4(k)] < \infty$,*

the strong uniform convergence according to Eq.(30) is ensured.

Before proving Proposition 3, the following lemma is stated and proven.

Lemma 1. *Let the filter $Q_\Theta(k, \tau)$ be BIBO, then, under the conditions in Proposition 3,*

$$E\left[\sup_\Theta |\sum_{k=r}^{N}\sum_{\tau=0}^{\infty} Q_\Theta(k, \tau)u_\Delta(k-\tau)e(k-\kappa)|\right]^2 \leq K(N-r) \tag{39}$$

Proof. Consider

$$S = \sum_{k=r}^{N}\sum_{\tau=0}^{\infty} Q_\Theta(k,\tau)u_\Delta(k-\tau)e(k-\kappa)$$

and its square

$$S^2 = \sum_{k=r}^{N}\sum_{l=r}^{N}\sum_{\tau_1=0}^{\infty}\sum_{\tau_2=0}^{\infty} Q_\Theta(k,\tau_1)u_\Delta(k-\tau_1)e(k-\kappa)\times$$
$$\times Q_\Theta(k,\tau_2)u_\Delta(k-\tau_2)e(k-\kappa)$$

Observing the fact that

$$\left(\sup_\Theta |S|\right)^2 = \sup_\Theta S^2$$

the following inequality can be stated

$$E\left[\sup_\Theta |S|\right]^2 \leq \left\{\Theta_M \in \Theta : S^2 = \max_\Theta S^2\right\}$$

$$E\left[\sum_{k=r}^{N}\sum_{l=r}^{N}\sum_{\tau_1=0}^{\infty} Q_{\Theta_M}(k,\tau_1)u_\Delta(k-\tau_1)\sum_{\tau_2=0}^{\infty} Q_{\Theta_M}(l,\tau_2)u_\Delta(l-\tau_2)e(k-\kappa)e(l-\kappa)\right]$$

Due to the fact that the deterministic filter $Q(k,\tau)$ is *BIBO* and that $e(k)$ is an independently distributed random signal, the expected value can be upper bounded as

$$E\left[\sup_\Theta |S|\right]^2 \leq K_Q^2 \sum_{k=r}^{N} E\left[e(k-\kappa)\right]^2 \leq K_Q^2\lambda_e(N-r)$$

This proves the lemma.

Proof. (Proposition 3) Consider

$$R_\Theta(N,r) = \sum_{k=r}^{N}(\epsilon^2(k,\tau) - E\left[\epsilon^2(k,\tau)\right]) \tag{40}$$

It has been proven [10] that the strong uniform convergence is valid, provided that

$$E\left[\sup_\Theta |R_\Theta(N,r)|\right]^2 \leq K(N-r) \tag{41}$$

Rewrite $\epsilon(k,\Theta)$ in Eq.(38) to simplify the notation

$$\epsilon(k,\Theta) = \sum_{\tau=1}^{\infty} (Q_\Theta(k,\tau))\, u_\Delta(k-\tau) + \sum_{\tau=1}^{\infty} H(\tau)e(k-\tau) \tag{42}$$

where $Q_\Theta(k,\tau) = G(k,\tau) - C(k)T(k,k-\tau)B(k-\tau)$ is an *LTV* filter that is *BIBO*, as both terms are bounded according to the assumptions, i.e.

$$\sum_{\tau=1}^{\infty} |Q_\Theta(k,\tau)| < \infty, \quad \forall k$$

Eq.(40) can now be evaluated as follows:

$$R_\Theta(N,r) = \sum_{k=r}^{N}\sum_{\tau=0}^{\infty}\sum_{\kappa=0}^{\infty} H(\tau)H(\kappa)\left[e(k-\tau)e(k-\kappa) - E\left[e(k-\tau)e(k-\kappa)\right]\right] +$$
$$+ 2\sum_{k=r}^{N}\sum_{\tau=0}^{\infty}\sum_{\kappa=0}^{\infty} Q_\Theta(k,\tau)u_\Delta(k-\tau)H(\kappa)e(k-\kappa)$$

$$(43)$$

An upper bound of the absolute value can be derived using the Chauchy-Schwarz and the triangle inequalities. Note that the second term is multiplied by an infinite sum of value unity.

$$|R_\Theta(N,r)| \le$$
$$\le \sum_{\tau=0}^{\infty}\sum_{\kappa=0}^{\infty} |H(\tau)|\,|H(\kappa)| \underbrace{\left|\sum_{k=r}^{N}\left[e(k-\tau)e(k-\kappa) - E\left[e(k-\tau)e(k-\kappa)\right]\right]\right|}_{S_1(\tau,\kappa)} +$$

$$(44)$$

$$+2\sum_{\kappa=0}^{\infty}|H(\kappa)| \underbrace{\left|\sum_{k=r}^{N}\sum_{\tau=0}^{\infty} Q_\Theta(k,\tau)u_\Delta(k-\tau)e(k-\kappa)\right|}_{S_2(\kappa)} \underbrace{\sum_{\tilde\tau=0}^{\infty}F(\tilde\tau)}_{=1}$$

where

$$F(\tilde\tau) > 0 \quad \forall\tilde\tau$$

Consequently, after reorganising the τ-indices, the supremum over the parameter set can be written as

$$\sup_\Theta |R_\Theta(N,r)| \le$$
$$\le \sum_{\tau^*=0}^{\infty}\sum_{\kappa=0}^{\infty}\underbrace{\left[|H(\tau^*)|\,|H(\kappa)| \;\; 2F(\tau^*)|H(\kappa)|\right]}_{\alpha(\tau^*,\kappa)}\underbrace{\left[S_1(\tau^*,\kappa) \;\; \tilde S_2(\kappa)\right]^T}_{S^T(\tau^*,\kappa)}$$

$$(45)$$

where $\tilde S_2(\kappa) = \sup_\Theta S_2(\kappa)$. According to Eq.(41), the expected value of the square of Eq.(45) is of interest. Note that only $S(\tau^*,\kappa)$ contains stochastic elements

$$E\left[\sup_\Theta |R_\Theta(N,r)|\right]^2 \le$$

$$\le \sum_{\tau_1^*=0}^{\infty}\sum_{\tau_2^*=0}^{\infty}\sum_{\kappa_1=0}^{\infty}\sum_{\kappa_2=0}^{\infty} \mathrm{tr}\left[\alpha(\tau_1^*,\kappa_1)E\left[S(\tau_1^*,\kappa_1)S^T(\tau_2^*,\kappa_2)\right]\alpha^T(\tau_2^*,\kappa_2)\right] \le$$

$$\le \sum_{\tau_1^*=0}^{\infty}\sum_{\tau_2^*=0}^{\infty}\sum_{\kappa_1=0}^{\infty}\sum_{\kappa_2=0}^{\infty} ||\alpha(\tau_1^*,\kappa_1)||E\,\mathrm{tr}\left[S(\tau_1^*,\kappa_1)S^T(\tau_2^*,\kappa_2)\right]||\alpha^T(\tau_2^*,\kappa_2)||$$

$$(46)$$

Consider the stochastic part of Eq.(46), where Chauchy-Schwarz inequality can be applied

$$E\left[\text{tr}S(\tau_1^*,\kappa_1)S^T(\tau_2^*,\kappa_2)\right] = E\left[S_1(\tau_1^*,\kappa_1)S_1(\tau_2^*,\kappa_2) + \tilde{S}_2(\kappa_1)\tilde{S}_2(\kappa_2)\right] \leq$$
$$\leq \sqrt{E\left[S_1^2(\tau_1^*,\kappa_1)\right]E\left[S_1^2(\tau_2^*,\kappa_2)\right]} + \sqrt{E\left[\tilde{S}_2^2(\kappa_1)\right]E\left[\tilde{S}_2^2(\kappa_2)\right]} = \tag{47}$$
$$= E\left[S_1^2(\tau,\kappa)\right] + E\left[\tilde{S}_2^2(\kappa)\right]$$

As, both $S_1(\tau,\kappa)$ [10] and $S_2(\kappa)$ (see Lemma 1) are bounded as

$$E\left[S_1^2\right] \leq K_1(N-r)$$
$$E\left[\tilde{S}_2^2\right] \leq K_2(N-r)$$

Eq.(47) can, with $K = K_1 + K_2$, be written as

$$E\left[\text{tr}S(\tau_1^*,\kappa_1)S^T(\tau_2^*,\kappa_2)\right] \leq E\left[S_1^2(\tau,\kappa)\right] + E\left[\tilde{S}_2^2(\kappa)\right] \leq (K_1+K_2)(N-r) \tag{48}$$

As a result, the inequality of Eq.(46) can be derived as

$$E\left[\sup_{\Theta}|R_{\Theta}(N,r)|\right]^2 \leq K(N-r)\sum_{\tau_1^*=0}^{\infty}\sum_{\kappa_1=0}^{\infty}\|\alpha(\tau_1^*,\kappa_1)\|\sum_{\tau_2^*=0}^{\infty}\sum_{\kappa_2=0}^{\infty}\|\alpha(\tau_2^*,\kappa_2)\|$$
$$\tag{49}$$

At this point, the bounds on the double summations have to be validated

$$\sum_{\tau=0}^{\infty}\sum_{\kappa=0}^{\infty}\|\alpha(\tau,\kappa)\| \leq \sum_{\kappa=0}^{\infty}|H(\kappa)|\sum_{\tau=0}^{\infty}\left\|\left[|H(\tau)| \quad 2F(\tau)\right]\right\| \leq$$
$$\leq K_H\sum_{\tau=0}^{\infty}2(|H(\tau)| + 2F(\tau)) \leq 2K_H(K_H + 2)$$

This means that Eq.(41) holds under the given assumptions and that Proposition 3 is proven.

Proposition 3 guarantees the strong uniform convergence for the norm, V_N. This is required in order to conclude anything about the parameter convergence, Θ_N [8,9]

$$\hat{\Theta}_N \to \bar{\Theta} \text{ w.p.1 as } N \to \infty \tag{50}$$

As long as the minimising argument, $\bar{\Theta}$, includes only one element, the interpretation is clear. On the contrary, $\bar{\Theta}$ could be a set of minimisers, which means that Θ_N asymptotically approaches this set, but there is no convergence within the set.

4   Parameter Estimation — Implementation

The procedure of estimating the parameters of a presumably direction-dependent process is generally similar to the parameter estimation in the *LTI* case. The parameter set, Θ_S, i.e. the available parameter vectors, must fulfil the conditions of Proposition 3 and there should be a parameter set, $\bar{\Theta} \in \Theta_S$, which minimises the norm, as in Eq.(20). According to Proposition 3, a sufficiently large data set, Z^N, will return a parameter estimate, $\hat{\Theta}_N$, that is sufficiently near to $\bar{\Theta}$, as illustrated in Fig. 2.

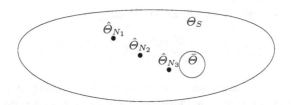

Fig. 2. Asymptotic convergence within a parameter set, Θ_S. Consider the data sets $\{Z^{N_1}, Z^{N_2}, Z^{N_3}\}$, where $N_1 < N_2 < N_3$. The estimate, $\hat{\Theta}_{N_i}$, then approaches $\bar{\Theta}$ as N_i increases.

The dimension of $\bar{\Theta}$ leads the parameter estimation procedure into the consideration of identifiability aspects. Preferably, the dimension is unity, which implies that only one parameter vector minimises the cost function. In the event of higher dimensions, there are traditionally two causes of this: the experimental conditions are not optimal or the model parameterisation could be improved. The experimental conditions generally refer to the design of the input signal, which should have sufficient energy at those frequencies that excite the process. The parameterisation issue deals with the choice of parametric model, as well as the number of parameters in the model.

The identifiability aspects of the direction-dependent predictors extend those of the *LTI* predictors. As the process is nonlinear, it is not obvious which input frequencies excite the process. However, step-response analysis, for example, reveals how fast the system is in either direction. Another issue that is more specific for the direction-dependent parameter estimation is the fraction between the increasing mode and the decreasing mode. Either direction should, therefore, correspond to a significant fraction of the total time, N.

As the direction-dependent predictor has twice as many parameters, compared with its linear counterpart, the algorithm becomes more complex. Further, the Hessian, which is the output of a nonlinear filter as described in Proposition 2, slows down the computation of the parameter estimates. Consequently, it is even more important to keep the number of parameters low. In noisy environments in particular, the number of data points, N, must be substantially larger than the number of parameters to avoid models that attempt to parameterise the noise.

Additionally, the family of parameter sets available for the estimation algorithm must be in the set Θ_S, according to Proposition 3. This means that any $\Theta \in \Theta_S$ must give rise to a *BIBO* predictor. A parameter vector whose corresponding state-space representation, according to Proposition 1, is uniformly exponentially stable, results in a *BIBO* predictor [18]. Consequently, there is a necessary condition for Θ to be an element of Θ_S.

The uniform exponential stability for a system in state-space form, Eq.(1), can be proven if the matrices, B_σ and C_σ, are bounded and the autonomous systems described by A_1 and A_2 have a common Lyaponov function.

Proposition 4. *[4] The state-space representation of a direction-dependent system as described in Eq.(1) is uniformly BIBO for arbitrary switching if*

$$B_\sigma \leq K_B < \infty \,, \quad C_\sigma \leq K_C < \infty \,, \quad \sigma \in \{1, 2\} \tag{51}$$

and if there exists a positive definite matrix P such that

$$A_1^T P A_1 - P < 0$$
$$A_2^T P A_2 - P < 0 \tag{52}$$

The *BIBO* analysis of the parameter vector is thus transferred into a linear matrix inequality [4], which is a convex optimisation problem, and it can be effectively solved by standard procedures.

One conservative aspect of Proposition 4 is that it allows arbitrary switching; in the event of frequent sampling, there may exist a least number of samples, l, between the switches, which would allow a larger set of *BIBO* predictors. Another stability condition based on the spectral radius, ρ, can then be applied. Uniform exponential stability, which implies *BIBO*, is ensured if [12]

$$\rho(A_1^l A_2^l) < 1 \tag{53}$$

Unfortunately, this condition is conservative for low l's, so Proposition 4 is to be used for arbitrary switching.

Stability tests should be carried out for the initial values of the iterative algorithm. As the optimisation is non-convex, one suitable approach is to apply a number of sophisticated initial-value guesses and disregard those that are not *BIBO*. With the remaining ones, the minimising arguments, $\hat{\Theta}_N$, are pursued and, of those $\hat{\Theta}_N$ that are stable, the one corresponding to the smallest norm, $V_N(\hat{\Theta})$, is chosen. Finally, the parameter estimate is validated using a different data set, which is the standard procedure in parameter estimation [10].

Example 1. Let the true system be a parametric model from $u(k)$ to $y(k)$, as described in Eq.(7),(8), where band-limited white noise, $e(k)$, with variance $\lambda_e \approx 1$ is added to the output, $y(k)$. The system matrices are

$$A_1 = \begin{bmatrix} 0.5 & 1 \\ 0 & 0.5 \end{bmatrix} \quad A_2 = \begin{bmatrix} 1.2 & 1 \\ -0.2 & 0.4 \end{bmatrix}$$
$$B = \begin{bmatrix} 0 & 1 \end{bmatrix}^T \quad C = \begin{bmatrix} 1 & 0 \end{bmatrix} \tag{54}$$

The system is in a form which is not transferable to the *I/O* representation and the residuals will therefore consist of variance error as well as bias.

The parameter estimation was carried out as described above, using one data set for identification and one for validation respectively. Both data sets had the size $N = 1000$. Further, the data were differentiated into $\{y_\Delta(k), u_\Delta(k)\}$ to agree with the representation of the predictors. The suggested model structures for these data were second-order *PWARX* and *PWOE*; in all four different structures, *PWARX2I*, *PWARX2D*, *PWOE2I* and *PWOE2D*, as there are both instant, I, and delayed, D, switching realisations. The *PWARX* models were estimated, partly for comparison and partly for use as an initial value candidate. The other candidates were linear estimates using the same model in both directions.

The estimated model was evaluated with respect to validation data. In addition, the norm $V(\hat{\Theta})$ was computed and the *PWOE* models produced significantly better

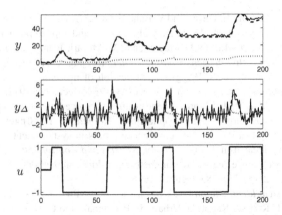

Fig. 3. Validation data. For the upper and middle plots, the thin, solid lines correspond to y and y_Δ respectively, the dashed lines correspond to the *PWOE2D* model and the dotted lines correspond to the *PWARX2D* model.

results, $V_{PWOE2I} = 1.99$ and $V_{PWOE2D} = 1.96$, whereas the *PWARX* models were unsatisfactory, $V \approx 4$. Fig.3 shows the first 200 samples of the validation data, compared with the corresponding *PWOE* and *PWARX* models.

5 Conclusions

The finding of satisfactory parametric estimates of direction-dependent processes under noisy conditions can be somewhat problematic in terms of predictor choice and asymptotic behaviour. The way the choice of predictor affects the final estimate has been discussed in this paper and *PWOE* predictors in particular are analysed. The advantage of the *PWOE* predictor is that the disturbances are completely separated from the process dynamics. In contrast, the *PWARX* model implies a predictor whose noise partly shares the process dynamics and, consequently, the noise dynamics depend on $\sigma(u_\Delta(k))$, which seems awkward, as the disturbance is generally independent of the input signal. The drawback of the *PWOE* predictors is, however, that — as in the case of linear output-error predictors — they must be stable (*BIBO*). Nonetheless, this stability condition can be handled by effective methods, which means that the *PWOE* algorithm is available when needed.

References

1. H.A. Barker, A.H. Tan, and K.R. Godfrey. Wiener models of direction-dependent dynamic systems. *Automatica*, 39(1):127–133, 2003.
2. A. Bemporad, J. Roll, and L. Ljung. Identification of hybrid systems via mixed-integer programming. In *Conference on Descision and Control*, pages 786–792, 2001.
3. S.A. Billings and W.S.F. Voon. Piecewise linear identification of non-linear systems. *International Journal of Control*, 46:215–235, 1987.

4. S. Boyd, L. El Ghaoui, E. Feron, and V. Balakrishnan. *Linear Matrix Inequalities in System and Control Theory*, volume 15. Society of industrial and applied mathematics, 1994.
5. G. Ferrari-Trecate, M. Muselli, D. Liberati, and M. Morari. Identification of piecewise affine and hybrid systems. In *American Control Conference*, pages 3521–3526, 2001.
6. K. R. Godfrey and P. A. N. Briggs. Identification of processes with direction-dependent dynamic responses. *IEE Proceedings*, 119:1733–1739, December 1972.
7. K. R. Godfrey and D. J. Moore. Identification of processes having direction-dependent responses, with gas-turbine engine applications. *Automatica*, 10(10):469–481, 1974.
8. T.A. Johansen and E. Weyer. On convergence proofs in system identification — a general principle using ideas from learning theory. *Systems and Control Letters*, 34:85–92, 1998.
9. L. Ljung. Convergence analysis of parametric identification methods. *Transactions on Automatic Control*, 23(5):770–783, October 1978.
10. L. Ljung. *System Identification — Theory for the User*. Prentice Hall, 1999.
11. O. Nerrand, P. Roussel-Ragot, D. Urbani, L. Personnaz, and G. Dreyfus. Training recurrent neural networks: why and how? an illustration in dynamical process modeling. *Transactions on Neural Networks*, 5(2):178 – 184, March 1994.
12. J. Oh and D. S. Bernstein. Modeling and identification of rate-dependent hysteresis using a semilinear duhem model. In *Symposium on System Identification*, pages 1578–1583, Rotterdam, the Netherlands, August 2003. IFAC.
13. R. K. Pearson. Selecting nonlinear model structures for computer control. *Journal of process control*, 13:1–26, 2003.
14. G. Ravi Sriniwas, Y. Arkun, I-Lung Chien, and B. A. Ogunnaike. Nonlinear identification and control of a high-purity distillation column: a case study. *Journal of Process Control*, 5(3):149–162, 1995.
15. F. Rosenqvist, K. Eriksson, and A. Karlström. Modelling a thermomechanical wood-chip refiner. In *IASTED Modelling, Identification and Control*, pages 763–768, Innsbruck, Austria, 2001.
16. F. Rosenqvist and A. Karlström. Controllability of direction-dependent processes. In *Conference of Decision and Control*, December 2003.
17. F. Rosenqvist and A. Karlström. Piecewise-linear output-error models. In *IFAC Symposium on System Identification*, Rotterdam, August 2003. IFAC.
18. J. R. Rugh. *Linear System Theory*. Prentice-Hall, Inc., Upper Saddle River, NJ, USA, 2nd edition, 1996.
19. J. Sjöberg, Q. Zhang, L. Ljung, A. Benveniste, B. Delyon, P-Y. Glorennec, H. Hjalmarsson, and A. Juditsky. Nonlinear black-box modeling in system identification: a unified overview. *Automatica*, 31(12):1691–1724, 1995.
20. A.H. Tan and K.R. Godfrey. Identification of processes with direction-dependent dynamics. *IEE Control theory applications*, 148(5):362–369, September 2001.
21. P. Turner, G. Montague, and J. Morris. Nonlinear and direction-dependent dynamic process modelling using neural networks. *IEE Control theory applications*, 143(1):44–48, 1996.

A Spatial Logic for the Hybrid π-Calculus

William C. Rounds*

CSE Division, University of Michigan, Ann Arbor, MI 48109, USA
University of Cambridge Computer Laboratory
Cambridge, CB3 0FD, UK

Abstract. We present a formal logic for stating properties of systems expressed in the hybrid π-calculus, or Φ-calculus. It is a very expressive logic, subsuming many standard logics like CTL and the modal μ-calculus. Because the π-calculus and the Φ-calculus allow passing of names to achieve reconfigurability of hybrid systems, and because we must abstract over these names, the logic (a hybrid extension of a logic by Caires and Cardelli for the π-calculus) uses a new method of defining abstractions – FM set theory – for expressing syntax and semantics of Φ-calculus models, and for expressing the semantics of spatial logic. We provide several new constructions for this logic, including an assume-guarantee principle, and illustrate many of the semantic features using an extended example of a robotic parts feeder and parts carrier in a minifactory.

1 Introduction

The Φ-calculus [7] is a hybrid extension of Milner's powerful π-calculus, designed so that concurrent and reconfigurable programs can interact with a (concurrent) continuous environment in the sense in which ordinary hybrid automata do so. This paper presents a logic expressing properties of systems defined in this language. One of the difficulties involved here is that not many logics have been proposed for reasoning about properties of π-calculus programs themselves. The difficulty has to do with the subtleties of *name-passing*, and even more, the subtleties of *fresh name generation*. These mechanisms are crucial in the π-calculus for expressing *mobility* (more properly, reconfigurability), and *protection*, which is the ability to create modular subsystems not subject to outside interference.

A recent paper by Caires and Cardelli [2] introduces their *spatial logic for concurrency*, a general logic intended not just as an assertion language for the π-calculus, but for possibly other process-algebraic models which deal with reconfigurability and with protection. Their logic has several attractive features. It has a propositional connective |, so that the formula $\phi \mid \psi$ is satisfied only by a parallel composition of systems $P \mid Q$ in which P satisfies ϕ and Q satisfies ψ. (This is the source of the word "spatial"; the connective | refers to a structural property of systems satisfying it.) This connective has a so-called *adjoint* $\phi \triangleright \psi$, which provides the crucial property of *assume-guarantee* reasoning [4]. A system

---

* Research supported by US NSF Grant 0233960.

R. Alur and G.J. Pappas (Eds.): HSCC 2004, LNCS 2993, pp. 508–522, 2004.
© Springer-Verlag Berlin Heidelberg 2004

P satisfies $\phi \triangleright \psi$ if for any system Q, if Q satisfies ϕ (assume), then $P \mid Q$ satisfies ψ (guarantee). The Caires-Cardelli logic also features a "fresh name" quantifier $\mathsf{N}x$, read "for some/all fresh names x," which allows for reasoning both about reconfigurability and protection. This quantifier appears in a paper by Gabbay and Pitts [3], who work with *Fraenkel-Mostowski* techniques, a novel and important set-theoretic approach to the problems arising from changing bound variable names in programs which abstract over these variables.

The issues involved in extending the C&C logic to the hybrid π-calculus include (i) finding one or more connectives for dealing with continuous flows over time; (ii) dealing with the passing of continuous names and creation of fresh continuous names; (iii) reformulating the hybrid structural operational semantics within FM set theory (with which the axiom of choice is inconsistent), and (iv) giving a concise Tarski-style semantics for the new logic. We are able to overcome these problems by reformulating the syntax and semantics of C&C logic directly in FM set theory. We get around issue (iii) because of the way the hybrid π-calculus treats the continuous environment – as a separate component of what we termed an *embedded system* in [7]. Our connective for continuous flows refers only to the continuous part of the system, with the result that any properties of the continuous system itself that we may need (stability, attractors, etc.), which follow from standard theorems on dynamical systems, can still be assumed to hold even in the new set theory.

The C&C logic, and our extension of it, is really a modal logic. Standard interpretations of modal calculi use the idea of Kripke structures; C&C's logic uses a space of "Psets" as a kind of Kripke structure. We elide the interpretation of our formulas in Kripke structures, and instead perform a direct translation of our formulas into formal assertions of FM set theory. The idea comes from the well-known [1] *standard translation* of modal logic into first-order logic of Kripke structures. Our translation of the modal logic directly into *ZFA* – the formal language of FM set theory – provides a much simpler semantics than in C&C, while affording a tailor-made extension to the hybrid setting.

Our logic is quite expressive. It subsumes Caires and Cardelli's logic, which already subsumes the modal μ-calculus [5]. As an example of expressiveness, we show that for a given program, we can construct a formula satisfied by all those hybrid states reachable from a given initial continuous state and with initial discrete state equal to the initial state of the program. The technique of expressing our semantics in *ZFA* makes such constructions completely natural. As mentioned, the logic includes a capacity for defining "assume-guarantee" reasoning. All of this attests to expressiveness; one can of course argue that the logic is *too* expressive, in that model-checking will be a very undecidable problem. We concede that this is the case, but we think that the connectives and the quantifiers we introduce can form the material for schematizing classes of special formulas for which model-checking is a viable enterprise.

In the present paper, we work in a sublanguage of the Φ-calculus, the *physical* Φ-calculus. This omits the passing of channel names, but allows the passing of continuous names. It is well able to specify physically reconfigurable systems, and it makes our presentation of formalities much simpler. We organize the paper into 4 sections. Section 2 reviews the physical Φ-calculus. Section 3.1 deals briefly with expressing the structural operational semantics (SOS) of the Φ-calculus in ZFA. In section 3.2 we introduce our logic and give its model theory. In 3.3 we give an extended example of a spatial formula satisfied by the robotics part carrier. In 3.4 we discuss fixpoint formulas, and show how to define reachability. Section 4 is a short conclusion.

2 The Physical Φ-Calculus

2.1 Syntax

Let $\mathcal{A}$ be a countable set of *names* a; put $\overline{\mathcal{A}} = \{\overline{a} \mid a \in \mathcal{A}\}$, and $\mathcal{L} = \mathcal{A} \cup \overline{\mathcal{A}}$. These names correspond to the "named actions" of an ordinary finite automaton; the overlined names allow participation in *reactions* (see below). We also have the *silent action* τ, which represents uncontrollable "internal choice."

Let $\mathcal{X}$ be a countable set of *environment variable names* disjoint from $\mathcal{A}$ and let $\dot{\mathcal{X}} = \{\dot{x} \mid x \in \mathcal{X}\}$ be the "dotted versions" (formal variables for differential equations.) The names in $\mathcal{X}$ can be "received" or "sent" from one process to another, and they carry real values. In the grammar below, receiving actions are of type (i) and sending actions are of type (ii). The names a are used as "channels" over which continuous names are sent.

The continuous evolution of a Φ-calculus process takes place in an "active environment" . This environment consists of three components: (i) a current **state**: a vector in some $\mathbb{R}^n$; (ii) a **flow law**: a differential equation (vector field); and (iii) a set of **invariant predicates**, all of which must be true in order for time to progress. Interaction with this environment takes place via **environmental actions**, which correspond to the guards and resets of hybrid automata. Formally, an *environmental action* is a syntactic form $\alpha = [\psi \to d; G; \phi]$, where the formula ψ is called a *guard*, and G and ϕ tell how to reset the state, flow law, and invariant set respectively. Any one or more of these entities, including the guard, can be omitted.

The following grammar defines "sums", "processes", "abstractions", and "concretions" in the Φ-calculus. Sums allow the possibility of choice of next actions; abstractions and concretions are formal constructions providing bound variable abstraction and application of these abstractions to specific arguments.

Definition 1 *P ranges over processes, F over abstractions, C over concretions, M over sums, α over environmental actions EnvAct, a over $\mathcal{A}$, x, z over $\mathcal{X}$ in the following grammar:*

$$P ::= M \mid 0 \mid (P \mid P) \mid !P \mid \nu(a)P \mid \nu(x)P$$
$$M ::= \tau.P \mid \alpha.P \mid aF \mid \overline{a}C \mid M + M$$
$$F ::= P \mid (x)F$$
$$C ::= P \mid \langle z \rangle C$$

A term of this grammar is a P, F, M, or C (process, sum, abstraction, or concretion).

The syntax for processes in this grammar specify that the can be sums, parallel combinations of processes, a replicated process, or a process in which a fresh (new) restricted name is generated, either a *pi*-name or a new continuous name. The latter construction is the way protected new continuous variables enter the environment.

2.2   Dynamics

We define an *embedded system* to be a pair (E, P), where E is an environment, and P is a process expression. Such a system can evolve in three ways. The first is via a discrete transition involving only the process expression. The second is that the continuous environment can flow on its own according to its current vector field. Finally, via environmental actions, a process expression can remove its action prefix and update the environment all in one step. with We present the rules defining discrete process transitions. These are given in the standard form of transition inference rules, embodying the method of *structural operational semantics*. A full discussion of them can be found in [7].

Definition 2 (Transitions in Φ_P) *In these rules,* $b \in \mathcal{A} \cup \overline{\mathcal{A}}$, *and* μ *is a* b, *or* τ, *or an environmental action* α; $g \in F$, $k \in C$, *and* $H \in F \cup C$. *Finally, we have elided the symmetric rules* $R - par$ *and* $R - react$.

$$Act - \pi : (E, bH) \overset{b}{\to} (E, H)$$

$$Act - \alpha : (E, \alpha.P) \overset{\alpha}{\to} ((E \uparrow \alpha, P) \; \text{if} \; \alpha.guard(E.state) \; \text{is true;}$$

$$Sum : \frac{(E, M) \overset{\mu}{\to} (E', M')}{(e, M + N) \overset{\mu}{\to} (E', M')}$$

$$L - React : \frac{(E, P) \overset{b}{\to} (E, G) \qquad (E, Q) \overset{\overline{b}}{\to} (E, K)}{(e, P \mid Q) \overset{\tau}{\to} (E, G@K)}$$

$$L - par : \frac{(E, P) \overset{\mu}{\to} (E', H)}{(e, P \mid Q) \overset{\mu}{\to} (E', H \mid Q)}$$

$$Rep : \frac{(E, P \mid !P) \overset{\mu}{\to} (E', Q)}{(E, !P) \overset{\mu}{\to} (E', Q)}$$

$$Res - pi : \frac{(E, P) \overset{\mu}{\to} (E', H)}{(E, \nu a P) \overset{\mu}{\to} (E', \nu a H)} \quad \text{if} \; \mu \notin \{a, \overline{a}\}$$

$$Res - x : \frac{(E, P) \overset{\mu}{\to} (E', Q)}{(E, \nu x P) \overset{\mu}{\to} (E', \nu x Q)} \quad \text{if} \; \mu \; \text{is not an} \; x\text{-action}$$

$$Env : (E, \nu x P) \overset{\tau}{\to} (E, P[w/x])$$

$$(w \in \mathcal{X}, \; w \; \text{not mentioned in} \; E \; \text{and not free in} \; P.)$$

In the rule Act-α, the notations $E \uparrow \alpha$ and $\alpha.guard(E.state)$ refer to the guard of the action α and to the updating of the state, flow law, and invariant by means of the actions spelled out in the body of α. In the rule *L-React*, we use the notion of an abstraction G applied to a concretion K ($G@K$). We need abstractions and concretions, because environments may flow in a parameterized way, with differing variables participating in a flow at different times. (The robotic feeder-carrier in Example 1, below, illustrates this.) We include the relevant definitions:

Definition 3 *(i)* Φ_P*-abstractions are of the form* $F = (\boldsymbol{w}).P$ *($\boldsymbol{w}$ an ordered list of variables over $\mathcal{X}$). (ii)* Φ*-concretions are of the form* $K = \langle \boldsymbol{y} \rangle.P$*, where $\boldsymbol{y}$ is over $\mathcal{X}$. (iii) The application* $F@K$ *of a ϕ-abstraction and concretion is defined as follows:*

$$((\boldsymbol{w})P)@\langle \boldsymbol{y} \rangle.Q =_{\text{def}} (\{\boldsymbol{w} \leftarrow \boldsymbol{y}\}P \mid Q)$$

where $\boldsymbol{y}$ and $\boldsymbol{w}$ have the same length.

In (iii), $\{\boldsymbol{w} \leftarrow \boldsymbol{y}\}$ denotes the simultaneous substitution of the variables y_i for the (bound) variables w_i in P. This is a crucial definition, as it allows names to migrate from one process to another, achieving reconfigurability, and we must pay careful attention to it, because substitutions must avoid the problem of "accidental capture" of a name inside a binding prefix. This is one of the reasons we use the FM techniques mentioned in the introduction, and explained briefly in the next section.

An embedded system – in particular, the environment component – can evolve over time. This involves *flow transition* rules. In the next formal definition, we regard states as valuations: maps from a finite set $\mathcal{V}$ of continuous names to $\mathbb{R}$, and we regard a differential equation as a mapping assigning a C^1 function to each "dotted variable" in the finite set $\dot{\mathcal{V}}$.

Definition 4 (Flow transitions) *Let $c \in [\mathcal{V} \to \mathbb{R}]$, and suppose that the differential equation $F \in [\dot{\mathcal{V}} \to C^1[\mathbb{R}^{\mathcal{U}}]]$ is closed, i.e., $\mathcal{U} = \mathcal{V}$. Then the flow $\xi(t,c)$ of the equation will be defined in some time-interval $J = [0, u)$ of $\mathbb{R}$. We then have the following flow transitions:*

$$\text{Sum:} \ (\{c, F, I\}, \Sigma_i \mu_i P_i) \xrightarrow{t} (\{\xi(t,c), F, I\}, \Sigma_i \mu_i P_i) \tag{1}$$

provided that for all $0 \le s < t$: (i) $\xi(s,c)$ is defined and satisfies all constraints in I ; and (ii) no μ_i is an environmental action $\psi \to (d; G; \phi)$ with $\psi(s)$ true.

Flow transitions are extended to other Φ-expressions by

$$\text{Par:} \ \frac{(E, P) \xrightarrow{t} (E', P) \qquad (E, Q) \xrightarrow{t} (E', Q)}{(E, P \mid Q) \xrightarrow{t} (E', P \mid Q)} \tag{2}$$

$$\text{Res:} \ \frac{(E, P) \xrightarrow{t} (E', P)}{(E, \nu a P) \xrightarrow{t} (E', \nu a P)} \tag{3}$$

Note that we have "amalgamated" the summands in the Sum rule for brevity.

Example 1. A *parts feeder* can be modelled using recursion and the ν operator. The task of this feeder is to produce a never-ending stream of different parts in a factory. The feeder operates by proximity; a robot with position r, $0 < r < 2$, is approaching 0 along the x-axis. The parts feeder waits for r to be within some small ϵ of 0, and then produces a new part for the robot. It sends this part out along a channel *feed* to a controller for both the robot r and the part. We call this recursive process PF. It is actually defined using recursion, though we use a familiar syntactic sugaring for this in place of the official replication operator (for details see [6]).

$$PF ::= [r \leq \epsilon].\nu p\big([p : \epsilon; \dot{p} : 0].\overline{feed}\langle p \rangle.[\dot{r} > 0].PF \big).$$

The test $r \leq \epsilon$ in this process becomes true when the robot gets to exactly ϵ distance of the parts feeder. This triggers a call of the localizing operator νp. This in turn creates a fresh part name, using bound variable conversion to avoid clashes with part names in the environment when the "new" process "decays" at an *Env* "reaction". The name of the part is sent to the robot along channel pf. An extra guard $[\dot{r} > 0]$ is set instantaneously to prevent infinite iteration of the call to PF. Parts start with 0 velocity at position ϵ.

The robot moving left along the x-axis is operating under a control law that will slow its velocity to almost zero at $x = \epsilon$. We assume the robot starts at this position. It initializes a (one-dimensional) controller $\dot{r} = f_L(r)$ for this purpose. After picking up the current part, it moves right using another controller which moves it (and the part) back to position $r = 2 - \epsilon$, where it drops the part. The code for these two robot motions is

$$LEFT ::= [\dot{r} : f_L(r); \{2 - \epsilon \geq r > \epsilon\}].RIGHT$$
$$RIGHT ::= feed(p).[(\dot{p}, \dot{r} : f_R(p, r); \{\epsilon \leq r < 2 - \epsilon\}][\dot{p} \doteq 0].LEFT$$

The whole system can be started in the environment $E = \begin{pmatrix} r : 0.5 \\ \dot{r} : f_L(r) \\ \{2 - \epsilon \geq r > \epsilon\} \end{pmatrix}$,

and the resulting embedded system is $(E, LEFT \mid PF)$. The system can evolve, e.g., to $(E', LEFT|PF)$, where

$$E' = \begin{pmatrix} (r : 2 - \epsilon : p_1 : 2 - \epsilon; p_2 : 2 - \epsilon) \\ (\dot{p}_1 : 0, \dot{p}_2 : 0, \dot{r} : f_L(r)) \\ \{2 - \epsilon \geq r > \epsilon\} \end{pmatrix}.$$

We will use this system to illustrate our spatial logic.

3   Spatial Logic

3.1   The FM Universe

The semantics of our logic uses the formal vocabulary of Gabbay-Pitts-Fraenkel-Mostowski set theory. (We call this theory *ZFA*.) It is standard ZF set theory, without the axiom of choice, and where an infinite set of *individual names* is added, intuitively to represent those names which can be bound in an expression[1]. We give the semantics of our spatial fomulas via a syntactic, recursive

---

[1] We actually have two sets $\mathcal{X}$ and $\mathcal{A}$ of (bindable) atoms, the first for continuous names and the second for discrete names.

translation into formulas of *ZFA*, which then receive a model-theoretic interpretation in the *FM universe*. The sets in this universe can be standard ZF sets, or they can contain atoms (urelements). All of the sets in the universe are constructed so that they involve only finitely many atoms, and so that permuting the atoms in a set of the universe gives another set in the universe. The *support* of a set is the finite set of atoms involved in its construction. The set of atoms is required to be infinite, so that all objects satisfy the *freshness* property: for each object, there is a (fresh) atom not involved in its construction.

This notion of freshness can be codified in the language *ZFA*, the formal language of FM set theory. Let $\phi(a)$ be a formula of *ZFA*, where a is a formal variable ranging over atoms. Then $\mathsf{N}a\phi$ (read "for some/all fresh atom(s) a, $\phi(a)$") says that the set $\{a \in \mathcal{A} \mid \phi(a)\}$ is cofinite; i.e., there is always a new atom available to make the formula ϕ true. The reason that we can say "all new atoms" is the "equivariance property": if a formula $\phi(a)$ holds, then if we interchange a with another atom b uniformly in the formula ϕ, the resulting formula still holds [3, Lemma 4.7].

We apply these ideas in several ways. First, we represent terms of the ϕ-calculus (the syntactic objects) as sets in the FM universe. The support of a term is the set of free names in it. Next, we do the same for environments. Here we make full use of the fact that all of dynamic system theory can be represented in ordinary ZF, and therefore also in the FM universe, as this includes the standard von Neumann universe. The state, the flow law, and the finite collection of invariant predicates all do involve atoms. For example, the state is officially represented as a valuation from a finite set of atoms into $\mathbb{R}$, but this is an object of finite support. Similar remarks apply to the invariants and to the flow law.

Finally, the transition relations and the flow relations, defined via structural induction, have also to be representable in the FM universe. We do not have the space to give a full account of this representation. Briefly, though, one considers each structural rule in turn, and considers an arbitrary instance of the rule. Take any permutation of the atoms, and show that applying the permutation uniformly to the objects in the antecedents and the consequent of the rule gives another valid instance of the rule. If this obtains for all rules involved, say, for the flow relations, then the (fixedpoint) of the recursive construction will in fact be definable as a relation in the FM universe. (This is again a consequence of the equivariance property mentioned above.)

3.2 Syntax and Semantics of Spatial Logic

We first need to make a distinction between individual atoms (names) and variables ranging over these names, because we wish in our spatial logic to quantify over names. Thus, variables over $\mathcal{X}, \mathcal{A}$ will be in $\mathcal{V}_X, \mathcal{V}_A$ respectively. We will continue to use, however, the symbols $a, b, x, y, \dots$ for these variables, as implicitly these symbols are formal variables over atoms in *ZFA* anyway. When we refer to individual names, we will subscript these symbols as a_0, x_1, etc. $X, Y \in \mathcal{V}_P$ will be used for variables whose values are (finitely supported) sets of processes.

$$A, B ::=$$

ff	(False)
ϕ_b	(Base continuous formula)
$A \wedge B$	(Conjunction)
$\neg A$	(Negation)
$\mathbf{0}$	(Void)
$A \mid B$	(Tensor)
$A \triangleright B$	(Assume-guarantee)
$\nu\{x, a\} A$	(Revelation of continuous or discrete name)
$A \oslash \{x, a\}$	(Hiding continuous or discrete name)
$a\langle x \rangle A$	(Message)
$\alpha.A$	(Environmental action)
$\forall\{x, a\}.A$	(Universal quantifying over names)
$\text{И}\{x, a\}.A$	(Fresh name quantification)
Δ	(Invariant violation)
$\Diamond A$	(Can react)
$\langle \rightsquigarrow \rangle A$	(Can flow)
X	(PSet variable)
S	(ES set variable)
$\forall X.A$	(Universal PSet quantification)
$\forall S.A$	(Universal ES quantification)

Fig. 1. Formulas of hybrid spatial logic. The expression $\{x, a\}$ means that the relevant operator can occur with either a continuous name or a discrete name. A name constant can of course be substituted for any free occurrence of a name variable. A Pset is just a set of processes, and ES refers to the set of embedded systems.

We define "modal" formulas which will be satisfied by embedded systems (E, P). The syntax appears in Figure 1. The semantics, given in Figure 2, is a recursive translation into formulas of *ZFA* having two free variables e and p.

Some remarks are in order about our syntax and semantics.

- The syntax includes new types of variables: over environments and over continuous names Each of these types is well-defined in *ZFA* by what we have said in Section 2.
- The base logic has formulas ϕ_b, typically Boolean combinations of open formulas involving inequalities on variables for continuous names and over specific continuous names themselves. An unusual consequence of our rules is that a formula $\exists x(x \leq 1)$, where x is a variable over continuous names, does not quantify over real values of the variable x, because x varies over names. This formula then states that there is a name in the environment whose current value is ≤ 1. This formula would be true in an environment where $y_0 = 1$, where y_0 is a particular name. One could of course quantify over the values of these particular names in the usual way, but we have chosen to omit this here.
- $\langle \rightsquigarrow \rangle A$ indicates that the environment can flow for some positive amount of time until the formula A becomes true in the new environment. It is because this modal operator is the only one referencing the actual flow of a differential equation that we can ensure that no contradictions arise with the Axiom of

$$\mathtt{ff}^*(e,p) = \mathtt{ff};$$
$$\phi_b(e,p) = \phi_b(e.state)$$
$$(A \wedge B)^*(e,p) = A^*(e,p) \wedge B^*(e,p);$$
$$(\neg A)^*(e,p) = (e,p) \in ES) \wedge \neg A^*(e,p)$$
$$0^*(e,p) = (p = 0);$$
$$(A \mid B)^*(e,p) = \exists q, r.(p = (q \mid r) \wedge A^*(e,q) \wedge B^*(e,r));$$
$$(A \triangleright B)^*(e,p) = \forall q.(A^*(e,q) \rightarrow B^*(e,p \mid q));$$
$$(\nu a A)^*(e,p) = \exists q.(p = \nu a q \wedge A^*(e,q)) \text{ (similar for } \nu x A);$$
$$(A \oslash a)^*(e,p) = A^*(e,\nu a p) \text{ (similar for } A \oslash x);$$
$$(\overline{a}\langle x \rangle A)^*(e,p) = \exists q.(p = \overline{a}\langle x \rangle.q \wedge A^*(e,q));$$
$$(\alpha.A)^*(e,p) = \exists q.(p = \alpha.q \wedge (\psi(e.state) \wedge A^*(e \uparrow \alpha, q)));$$
$$(\mathsf{V} x.A)^*(e,p) = \mathsf{V} x.A^*(e,p) \text{ (similar for } \mathsf{V} a.A);$$
$$(\forall x.A)^*(e,p) = \forall x.A^*(e,p) \text{ (similar for } \forall a.A);$$
$$\Delta^*(e,p) = \neg(e.state \models e.inv);$$
$$(\Diamond A)^*(e,p) = \exists q.(p \xrightarrow{\tau} q \wedge A^*(e,q));$$
$$((\leadsto)A)^*(e,p) = \exists e', t > 0.((e,p) \xrightarrow{t} (e',p) \wedge A^*(e',p));$$
$$(X)^*(e,p) = X \in \mathsf{pow}P \wedge p \in X;$$
$$S^*(e,p) = (e,p) \in S \wedge S \in \mathsf{pow}ES;$$
$$(\forall X.A)^*(e,p) = (\forall X \in \mathsf{pow}P)A^*(e,p);$$
$$(\forall S.A)^*(e,p) = (\forall S \in \mathsf{pow}ES)A^*(e,p).$$

Fig. 2. Translation of Φ-formulas into *ZFA*. p ranges over the process set P and e over environments. *ES* is the set of embedded systems.

Choice in our logic. Because the flows of an equation with given variables are definable in pure set theory without atoms, any results proved for them will continue to hold in the setting of *ZFA*.

- The formula Δ indicates in a particular environment that the boundary of an invariant region (there could be several, as the invariant is a set of predicates) has been reached.
- Notice that $\exists$ and V quantifications bind names in both the environment and in the process.

We present an extended example of the logic in the next subsection. This example uses the *Env* commitment rule, and also uses "input-prefixing". These will be common examples, so we propose two new derived syntactic forms to account for their effects:

- In the case of the *Env* commitment rule

$$(e, \nu x p) \xrightarrow{\tau} (e, p[w/x]) \quad (w \in \mathcal{X}, w \text{ not mentioned in } e \text{ and not free in } p)$$

we propose a new "generate" quantifier

$$\mathsf{G}x.A = \mathsf{V}x.(\Diamond A).$$

This says that a fresh name (both in environment and process) can be generated, and then the system can silently evolve to one satisfying A.

– We define a derived "input prefix" connective

$$a(x).A = \mathsf{V}x\forall X.(\overline{a}\langle x \rangle.X \rhd \Diamond(A \mid X)).$$

This holds of a process P (and environment E) if for any name x and any process which is willing to output a fresh x on channel a and have a continuation Q satisfying an arbitrary X, then there is a reaction after which $P \mid Q$ (and environment E) satisfies $A \mid X$.

3.3   An Extended Example: The Robot Carrier

First recall Example 1:

$$PF ::= [r \le \epsilon].\nu p\big([p : \epsilon; \dot{p} : 0].\overline{feed}\langle p \rangle.[\dot{r} > 0].PF \big);$$
$$LEFT ::= [\dot{r} \doteq f_L(r); \{2 - \epsilon \ge r > \epsilon\}].RIGHT$$
$$RIGHT ::= feed(p).[(\dot{p}, \dot{r}) \doteq f_R(p, r); \{\epsilon \le r < 2 - \epsilon\}][r \ge 2 - \epsilon \to \dot{p} \doteq 0].LEFT$$

We truncate this system so that the robot makes only a pass to the left and then a pass to the right, and then terminates. We also truncate the parts feeder so that it generates just one part. This is because we want to ignore recursion and fixpoints, in order to illustrate the other constructions. Thus we redefine

$$PF ::= [r \le \epsilon].\nu p\big(\alpha2(p).\overline{feed}\langle p \rangle[\dot{r} > 0].PF \big);$$
$$LEFT ::= \alpha4.RIGHT;$$
$$RIGHT ::= feed(p).\alpha5(p).\alpha6(p).0$$

where

$$\alpha2(p) = [p \doteq \epsilon; \dot{p} \doteq 0];$$
$$\alpha4 = [\dot{r} \doteq f_L(r); I_L];$$
$$\alpha5(p) = [(\dot{p}, \dot{r}) \doteq f_R(p, r); I_R];$$
$$\alpha6(p) = [r \ge 2 - \epsilon \to \dot{p} \doteq 0].$$

Here I_L and I_R denote the two invariants $\{2 - \epsilon \ge r > \epsilon\}$ and $\{\epsilon \le r < 2 - \epsilon\}$ respectively.

The evolution of the system starting from $(E_0, LEFT \mid PF)$, where E_0 is the initial environment

$$\begin{pmatrix} r : 0.5 \\ \dot{r} : f_L(r) \\ I_L \end{pmatrix},$$

is displayed in the following table.

$$(E_0, LEFT \mid PF) \quad \overset{\alpha 4}{\to} \quad \left(\begin{matrix} r : 0.5 \\ \dot{r} : f_L(r) \\ I_L \end{matrix} \right), RIGHT \mid PF)$$

$$\overset{t_1}{\to} \qquad (E_1, RIGHT \mid PF) \qquad\qquad \text{where } E_1 = \left(\begin{matrix} r : \epsilon \\ \dot{r} : f_L(r) \\ I_L \end{matrix} \right)$$

$$\overset{[r \le \epsilon]}{\to} \qquad (E_1, RIGHT \mid \nu p(\, \alpha 2.\overline{feed}\langle p \rangle.[\dot{r} > 0].0 \,)) \qquad \text{by definition of } PF$$

$$\overset{\tau}{\to} \qquad (E_1, RIGHT \mid \alpha 2(w_1).\overline{feed}\langle w_1 \rangle.[\dot{r} > 0].0) \qquad \text{by } Env$$

$$\overset{\alpha 2(w_1)}{\to} \quad (E_2, feed(p).\alpha 5(p).\alpha 6(p).0 \mid \overline{feed}\langle w_1 \rangle.[\dot{r} > 0].0) \quad \text{where } E_2 = \left(\begin{matrix} w_1 : \epsilon, r : \epsilon \\ \dot{w}_1 : 0, \dot{r} : f_L(r) \\ I_R \end{matrix} \right)$$

$$\overset{\tau}{\to} \qquad (E_2, \alpha 5(w_1).e6(w_1).0 \mid [\dot{r} > 0].0) \qquad\qquad \text{by } React$$

$$\overset{\alpha 5(w_1)}{\to} \qquad (E_3, \alpha 6(w_1).0 \mid [\dot{r} > 0].0) \qquad\qquad \text{where } E_3 = \left(\begin{matrix} w_1 : \epsilon; r : \epsilon \\ (\dot{w}_1, \dot{r}) : f_R(w_1, r) \\ I_R \end{matrix} \right))$$

$$\overset{[\dot{r} \ge 0]}{\to} \qquad (E_3, \alpha 6(w_1).0 \mid 0) \qquad\qquad \text{(now the test } [\dot{r} > 0] \text{ is true)}$$

$$\overset{t_2}{\to} \qquad (E_4, \alpha 6(w_1).0 \mid 0) \qquad\qquad \text{where } E_4 = \left(\begin{matrix} w_1 : 2 - \epsilon; r : 2 - \epsilon \\ (\dot{w}_1, \dot{r}) : f_R(w_1, r) \\ I_R \end{matrix} \right)$$

$$\overset{\alpha 6(w_1)}{\to} \qquad \left(\left(\begin{matrix} w_1 : 2 - \epsilon; r : 2 - \epsilon \\ \dot{w}_1 : 0, \dot{r} : f_R(r) \\ I_R \end{matrix} \right), 0 \right)$$

We now write a spatial formula A which is true of $(E_0, LEFT \mid PF)$ where E_0 is the initial environment

$$\left(\begin{matrix} r : 0.5 \\ \dot{r} : f_L(r) \\ I_L \end{matrix} \right).$$

The formula looks remarkably like the system itself, illustrating the spatiality idea.

$$A = A_{LEFT} \mid A_{PF};$$
$$A_{LEFT} = \alpha 4.\langle\leadsto\rangle A_{RIGHT};$$
$$A_{RIGHT} = feed(p)(\alpha 5(p).\langle\leadsto\rangle \alpha 6(p).0)$$
$$= \Lambda p.\forall X.(\overline{feed}\langle p \rangle.X \rhd \Diamond(\alpha 5(p)\langle\leadsto\rangle \alpha 6(p).0 \mid X));$$
$$A_{PF} = \langle\leadsto\rangle[r \le \epsilon].\mathsf{G}p.(\alpha 2(p).\overline{feed}\langle p \rangle.[\dot{r} > 0].0)$$

Now we are going to show that $(E_0, LEFT \mid PF)$ satisfies the formula A; in other words, that this particular embedded system model-checks. The work is displayed in the next table, which was constructed from the bottom row upwards.

Looking at the top line of the table, we see that the initial embedded system satisfies

$$A_{LEFT} \mid A_{PF} = A.$$

Some remarks are in order about the two lines containing τ-transitions. The first line corresponds to the generation of the fresh name w_1, according to the Env

Transition	New Embedded System	Formula Satisfied
$(E_0, LEFT \mid PF) \overset{\alpha 4}{\rightarrow}$	$\left(\begin{pmatrix} r : 0.5 \\ \dot{r} : f_L(r) \\ I_L \end{pmatrix}, RIGHT \mid PF \right)$	$\langle\leadsto\rangle A_{RIGHT} \mid A_{PF}$
$\overset{t_1}{\rightarrow}$	$(E_1, RIGHT \mid PF)$	$A_{RIGHT} \mid [r \leq \epsilon].Gp.\alpha 2(p).\overline{feed}\langle p \rangle [\dot{r} > 0].0$
$[r \leq \epsilon]$	$(E_1, RIGHT \mid \nu p(\, \alpha 2(p).\overline{feed}\langle p \rangle.[\dot{r} > 0].0 \,))$	$A_{RIGHT} \mid Gp.\alpha 2(p).\overline{feed}\langle p \rangle [\dot{r} > 0].0$
$\overset{\tau}{\rightarrow}$	$(E_1, RIGHT \mid \alpha 2(w_1).\overline{feed}\langle w_1 \rangle.[\dot{r} > 0].0)$	$A_{RIGHT} \mid \alpha 2(w_1).\overline{feed}\langle w_1 \rangle [\dot{r} > 0].0$
$\alpha 2(w_1)$	$(E_2, RIGHT \mid \overline{feed}\langle w_1 \rangle.[\dot{r} > 0].0)$	$A_{RIGHT} \mid \overline{feed}\langle w_1 \rangle [\dot{r} > 0].0$
$\overset{\tau}{\rightarrow}$	$(E_2, \alpha 5(w_1).\alpha 6(w_1).0 \mid [\dot{r} > 0].0)$	$\alpha 5(w_1).\langle\leadsto\rangle(\alpha 6(w_1).0) \mid [\dot{r} > 0].0$
$\alpha 5(w_1)$	$(E_3, \alpha 6(w_1).0 \mid [\dot{r} > 0].0)$	$\langle\leadsto\rangle(\alpha 6(w_1).0) \mid [\dot{r} > 0].0$
$[\dot{r} > 0]$	$(E_3, \alpha 6(w_1).0 \mid 0)$	$\langle\leadsto\rangle(\alpha 6(w_1).0) \mid 0$
$\overset{t_2}{\rightarrow}$	$(E_4, \alpha 6(w_1).0 \mid 0)$	$(\alpha 6(w_1).0) \mid 0$
$\alpha 6(w_1)$	$\left(\begin{pmatrix} w_1 : 2 - \epsilon; r : 2 - \epsilon \\ \dot{w}_1 : 0, \dot{r} : f_R(r) \\ I_R \end{pmatrix}, 0 \mid 0 \right)$	$0 \mid 0$

rule. We know (even by inspection) that $(E_1, \alpha 2(w_1).\overline{feed}\langle w_1 \rangle.[\dot{r} > 0].0)$ satisfies $\alpha 2(w_1).\overline{feed}\langle w_1 \rangle [\dot{r} > 0].0$, and therefore that $(E_1, \nu p(\, \alpha 2(p).\overline{feed}\langle p \rangle.[\dot{r} > 0].0 \,))$ satisfies $\Diamond(\alpha 2(w_1).\overline{feed}\langle w_1 \rangle [\dot{r} > 0].0)$, where w_1 is fresh in both E_1 and the restricted process. Therefore E_1 together with the restricted process satisfy $Gp.\alpha 2(p).\overline{feed}\langle p \rangle.[\dot{r} > 0].0$, and this justifies the right hand side of the spatial formula displayed on the line just before the first τ-transition.

The second τ-transition corresponds to a reaction. Consider the line just before, where we claim that

$$\left(E_2, RIGHT \mid \overline{feed}\langle w_1 \rangle.[\dot{r} > 0].0\right)$$

satisfies

$$A_{RIGHT} \mid \overline{feed}\langle w_1 \rangle [\dot{r} > 0].0.$$

Writing out A_{RIGHT} in full, we have the formula

$$\textrm{И} p.\forall X.(\overline{feed}\langle p \rangle.X \rhd \Diamond(\alpha 5(p)\langle\leadsto\rangle\alpha 6(p).0 \mid X)) \mid \overline{feed}\langle w_1 \rangle [\dot{r} > 0].0.$$

This is a good example of assume-guarantee reasoning. First, the environment does not play a role in this argument until the end, so we drop mention of it until then. Second, we know from the *React* rule that any process of the form $feed(p).Q(p)$, when combined in parallel with a process of the form $\overline{feed}\langle w_1 \rangle R$, will satisfy $\Diamond(A \mid X)$ for any formula A and any actual (definable) set of processes X_0, provided there is a fresh w_1 such that $Q\{p \leftarrow w_1\}$ satisfies A and R is in X_0. Writing out the process $RIGHT = feed(p).\alpha 5(p).\alpha 6(p).0$, we take $Q(p)$ in this instance to be $\alpha 5(p).\alpha 6(p).0$. We then choose X_0 to be the set of processes satisfying $[\dot{r} > 0].0$ in the current environment E_2. (These will be all processes (structurally congruent to) the form $[\dot{r} > 0].0$, because this test is not met in E_2.) This implies that $\overline{feed}\langle w_1 \rangle [\dot{r} > 0].0$ is a valid instance of the "assume" part $\overline{feed}\langle p \rangle.X$ of the $\rhd$ operator, so that we have guaranteed $Q(w_1) \mid [\dot{r} > 0].0$, as claimed.

3.4   Recursive Formulas

Our translation of spatial logic into *ZFA*-formulas has the advantage of enabling easy proofs of desired properties of our logic, because we can use the full expressive power of the formal theory of *ZFA*. We consider, for example, the existence of least fixpoints for set-valued formulas. Call a free occurrence of the set variable X *positive* if occurs under the scope of an even number of negations, and *negative* if it occurs under the scope of an odd number (it may do both; treat $A \triangleright B$ as $\neg A \vee B$ for this purpose). Then, by a standard inductive proof on the structure of formulas, as in Caires and Cardelli [2, Proposition 6.5], that a formula where the variable X occurs only positively is monotonic in X. More formally,

Theorem 5. *Let A be a formula, and v an assignment of sets to the (free) variables of A^*. Let M and $N \in \mathrm{pow}P$ with $M \subseteq N$.*

1. *If X occurs only positively in A then $A^* v[X \leftarrow M] \subseteq A^* v[X \leftarrow N]$.*
2. *If X occurs only negatively in A then $A^* v[X \leftarrow M] \supseteq A^* v[X \leftarrow N]$.*

It is worth noting that the inductive step of the proof of the above theorem for the case $\Pi x.A$ follows trivially from monotonicity of the Π quantifier in *ZFA*; see Gabbay-Pitts, Corollary 4.11.

We suppress the $*$ on the translation of a formula A, and regard A as syntactic sugar for its translation. As an example, we may speak of fixing all the free variables of A except for the variable X. Then A defines a function on $\mathrm{pow}P$ which under condition (1) of the above theorem, is monotonic in X.

Theorem 6 (Knaster-Tarski). *Any (ZFA-definable) monotonic function $F : \mathrm{pow}P \to \mathrm{pow}P$ has a greatest and least fixed point.*

Proof. The collection of sets

$$\mathcal{M} = \{M \in \mathrm{pow}P \mid M \subseteq F(M)\}$$

is definable, and by the formal Union axiom the set $\nu F = \bigcup \mathcal{M}$ is definable as well. The standard argument shows that νF is the greatest fixpoint of F. The proof for the least fixpoint μF is just as easy:

$$\mu F = \{p \mid \forall Y.(F(Y) \subseteq Y \to p \in Y)\}.$$

Because of these two theorems, we are justified in adding the formulae $\nu X A$ (greatest fixpoint) and $\mu X A$ (least fixpoint) to our collection, provided X occurs positively in A.

We now add recursion to the carrier system formula A, thus getting a formula satisfied by the original parts feeder. We define $A_{LEFT}(S)$ and $A_{PF}(T)$, where S and T are embedded system set variables, as follows:

$$A_{LEFT}(S) = \alpha 4.\langle \leadsto \rangle.feed(p)(\alpha 5(p).\langle \leadsto \rangle \alpha 6(p).S)$$
$$A_{PF}(T) = \langle \leadsto \rangle [r \le \epsilon].\mathrm{G}p.\alpha 2(p).\overline{feed}\langle p \rangle.[\dot{r} > 0]\langle \leadsto \rangle T.$$

Then we put

$$A = (\nu S)(\nu T)(A_{LEFT}(S) \mid A_{PF}(T)).$$

Remark 1. We use a greatest fixpoint formula here, because in effect we are giving a *coinductive specification*. The specification guarantees that our carrier system will continue forever, instead of saying that a state will be reached, or that a set of states will not be reached. (See below for a use of least fixpoint formulas in defining reachability.)

The above formula does not mention the status of the parts drop at the end of the robot cycle. We redefine $A_{PF}(T)$ by introducing base formulas into refer to the environment:

$$A_{PF}(T) = \langle\leadsto\rangle[r \leq \epsilon].\mathsf{G}p.\alpha2(p).\overline{feed}\langle\,p\,\rangle.[\dot{r} > 0]\langle\leadsto\rangle(p = 2 - \epsilon \wedge \dot{p} = 0 \wedge T).$$

The name p is bound in the base formulas by $\mathsf{G}p$. This means that on unfolding the recursive formula, the next generated p will be a fresh one; the formula thus expresses that more and more parts accumulate in the drop.

We conclude the paper by using recursion to express the important property of reachability. The formula expressing this is a least fixpoint one over an embedded system set variable S:

$$Reach(e,p) = \mu S.(S \vee (\diamond S) \vee (\langle\leadsto\rangle S) \vee \exists\alpha.(\psi_\alpha(e.state) \wedge \alpha.S))$$

where α has guard ψ_α.

This formula says (recursively) that a state is reachable if it occurs now, or there is a silent transition to a reachable state (i.e., the result of a reaction), or there is a flow transition to a reachable state, or there is an enabled environmental action, the result of which is a reachable state. The formula is temporarily outside of our present logic, because we have not allowed the quantification $\exists\alpha$ over environmental actions. We can circumvent the problem, though, if we can tailor a specification formula to a given process expression; in that case, there are only finitely many environmental actions mentioned in the expression, so we can replace the existential quantification $\exists\alpha$ with a finite disjunction of formulas in each of which there is a particular α mentioned.

4 Conclusion

The challenge for further research into logics for reconfigurable hybrid systems is to provide assistance with automatic verification of system properties. We are looking into modifications of existing model checking software which will accommodate limited kinds of reconfigurability, such as as the physical Φ-calculus employs. We also need to isolate tractable sublogics of the full spatial logic, perhaps corresponding to CTL, yet still dealing with name passing and name generation. This is already a challenge for the purely discrete case; we expect that solutions found for that case will generalize to the hybrid setting.

Acknowledgement. I would like to thank Jamie Gabbay, Robin Milner, Andy Pitts, and Hosung Song for conversations and suggestions for this paper.

References

1. Patrick Blackburn, Maarten de Rijke, and Yde Venema. *Modal Logic*, volume 53 of *Cambridge Tracts in Theoretical Computer Science*. Cambridge University Press, 2001.
2. Luis Caires and Luca Cardelli. A spatial logic for concurrency (part I). In *Proceedings, Theoretical Aspects of Computer Software; 4th International Symposium, Sendai, Japan*, 2001. To appear in I & C special issue on TACS'01.
3. M. J. Gabbay and A. M. Pitts. A new approach to abstract syntax with variable binding. *Formal Aspects of Computing*, 13:341–363, 2001.
4. Thomas A. Henzinger, Shaz Qadeer, and Sriram K. Rajamani. Decomposing refinement proofs using assume-guarantee reasoning. In *Proceedings of the International Conference on Computer-Aided Design (ICCAD)*, pages 245–252. IEEE Computer Society Press, 2000.
5. D. Kozen. Results on the propositional mu-calculus. *Theoretical Computer Science*, 27, 1983.
6. Robin Milner. *Communicating and Mobile Systems: the π-calculus*. Cambridge University Press, 1999.
7. W. Rounds and H. Song. The Φ-calculus - a language for distributed control of reconfigurable embedded systems. In *Hybrid Systems: Computation and control*, LNCS 2263, pages 435–449, Prague, Czech Republic, 2003. Springer-Verlag.

Full Paper Sheet Control Using Hybrid Automata

Rene Sanchez, Roberto Horowitz, Masayoshi Tomizuka, and Slobodan N. Simić

University of California at Berkeley

Abstract. Some high speed color printers require that the sheets be accurately controlled in order to achieve a precise alignment of colors. To accomplish this goal a steerable nips mechanism has been proposed as the actuator. This steerable nips mechanism allows the sheet to be precisely controlled in longitudinal, lateral and skew directions. In this paper we develop a control strategy based on hybrid automata that precisely controls the position of the sheet. This hybrid control law has four finite states among which the system switches during the trajectories tracking process. Switching from one state to another is necessary since the normal control mode cannot be used when the trajectory being tracked requires the wheels to have zero angular velocity. The proposed controller is able to move the sheet from an initial position at rest to an arbitrary final position also at rest. The system model is nonlinear and subject to four nonholonomic constraints. Two of these constraints come from the fact that the velocities perpendicular to the wheels must be zero, and the other two constraints are due to the no-slip condition.

1   Introduction

Some high speed color printers require that sheets be accurately positioned so that colors can be accurately placed on the sheet. This is a challenge especially at high speeds. In this paper we propose a solution to this problem using hybrid automata.

Hybrid automata are dynamical systems which involve the interaction of continuous and discrete dynamics. Systems of this type naturally arise in a number of engineering applications. For example, they have been successfully used in air traffic control [1], automotive control [2], bioengineering [3], process control [4,5], highway systems [6,7], and manufacturing [8]. The particular needs of these applications have sparked the development of theoretical and computational tools for modeling, simulation, analysis, verification, and controller synthesis for hybrid systems.

To accomplish our goal of accurately positioning sheets in a color printer, a steerable nips mechanism has been proposed as the actuator. It is schematically depicted in Figure 1. The problem of controlling paper trajectories with steerable nips is similar to a two wheel robot, such as the one studied in [9]. However, the proposed control law of [9] fails to account for singularities that arise when the steering angle of the wheels approach zero. Also, in the case of the two-wheel

R. Alur and G.J. Pappas (Eds.): HSCC 2004, LNCS 2993, pp. 523–538, 2004.

robot, three inputs are needed to follow the reference trajectories. Similar to the two-wheel robot, the steerable nips mechanism is a nonholonomic system. These systems have been extensively studied. Analytic work related to this subject can be found at [10], [11].

The control objective considered here is to move the sheet on the plane from an initial position $(x(0), y(0), \phi(0), \delta(0))$ at rest, to a final position $(0,0,0,0)$. The generalized coordinates x, y, ϕ are the position of paper in longitudinal $\underline{i}_u$, lateral $\underline{j}_u$, and skew $\underline{k}_u$ directions. The generalize coordinate δ represents the change in length of the line that connects point 1 and 2 along the sheet, i.e. the amount of buckling or stretching of the sheet ($\delta = 0$ for a flat sheet). Hybrid automata are used to control the position of a sheet. This control strategy uses both steerable and non-steerable nips to track the paper trajectories. Steerable nips permit a more swift correction of lateral errors. Non-steerable nips can only indirectly correct lateral errors through the steering of the media.

Also, the paper can neither be stretched nor compressed, for this reason the proposed controller tracks to zero the velocity, $\dot{\delta}$, and the change in length of the line that connects point 1 and 2 along the sheet, δ. This can be seen in Figure 3. The system model has four inputs, inputs one and two rotate wheels one and two respectively. Inputs three and four steer wheels one and two respectively.

To move the sheet from rest to any other position, the proposed hybrid controller has four discrete control modes. During normal control operation both wheels are driven and steered to move the paper toward its final position while enforcing the constraints. The second control mode is needed because of the fact that the normal control fails when either velocity of the wheel approaches zero. For this case, an alternative control law is derived. In this control mode the longitudinal position, x, and the change in length of the line that connects point 1 and 2 along the sheet, i.e. the amount of buckling or stretching of the sheet, δ, are the only outputs being tracked. The third and fourth control modes are used at the beginning and at the end of the controlled motion. During these times the angles of the wheels are zero.

Results obtained in this paper show that by using hybrid automata it is possible to drive the paper from rest to any other position. This was accomplished while satisfying the nonholonomic constraints at all times.

The remainder of this paper is organized as follows. In §2 will derive that nonholonomic constraints, kinematic model, and dynamic model of the steerable nips mechanism. The control modes of the system will be derived in §3. The proposed hybrid automaton will be presented in §4. Results will be shown in §5. Finally, we draw some conclusions in §6.

2   Kinematic and Dynamic Model of the Steerable Nips Mechanism

The steerable nips and a sheet are shown in Figs. 2-3. The sheet moves on a flat surface. Figure 2 represents a sheet position while it is being tracked. The left corner of the sheet, point C is tracked to a desired trajectory. The angular

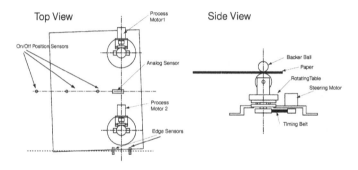

Fig. 1. Steerable Nips Shematic

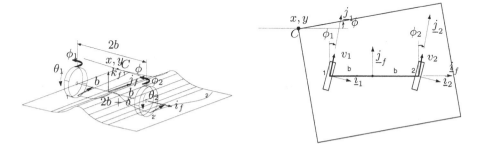

Fig. 2. Steerable Nips with Paper Buckled

Fig. 3. Coordinate System of Steerable Nips

orientation of the sheet is also tracked. It is know that a sheet can be easily buckled but can not stretched.

2.1   Notation

Figure 3 shows a schematic representation of the modeling variables of the steerable nips system. This system has two independently steering wheels, located at points 1 and 2 respectively. These steerable wheels are separated by a distance $2b$.

Three coordinate frames are defined to describe the position and orientation of the paper. The coordinate frame with $(\underline{i}_f, \underline{j}_f, \underline{k}_f)$ represents the global coordinates. The other two sets of coordinates, $(\underline{i}_1, \underline{j}_1, \underline{k}_1)$, and $(\underline{i}_2, \underline{j}_2, \underline{k}_2)$ are local and are attached to wheel 1 and 2 respectively. The generalized coordinates of the system are $(x, y, \phi, \delta, \theta_1, \theta_2, \phi_1, \phi_2)$. Generalized coordinates x, y will be used to respectably represent the lateral and longitudinal position of the left corner of the sheet, the generalized coordinate ϕ represents the angular position of the sheet and the generalized coordinate δ represents the change in length of the line that connects point 1 and 2 along the sheet, i.e. the amount of buckling or stretching of the sheet ($\delta = 0$ for a flat sheet). Generalized coordinates θ_1 and ϕ_1 will be used to respectably describe the angular position of wheel 1 in the directions parallel and perpendicular to the sheet. Likewise, θ_2 and ϕ_2 will respectably describe the angular position of wheel 2 in the directions parallel and perpendicular to the sheet.

2.2 Velocities

The velocities of the paper at points 1 and 2 in global coordinates are

$$\underline{v}_1 = (\dot{x} + \dot{\phi}y)\underline{i}_f + (\dot{y} - \dot{\phi}(x + b))\underline{j}_f \tag{1}$$

$$\underline{v}_2 = (\dot{x} + \dot{\phi}y)\underline{i}_f + (\dot{y} + \dot{\phi}(-x + b + \delta))\underline{j}_f \tag{2}$$

Invoking the non-slip condition, they can also be written in terms of the angular speed of the wheels in its local coordinates

$$\underline{v}_1 = r\dot{\theta}_1\underline{i}_1 \tag{3}$$

$$\underline{v}_2 = r\dot{\theta}_2\underline{i}_2 \tag{4}$$

where r is the radius of the wheels.

2.3 Constraint Equations

Four constraint equations can be obtained by writing Eq. (1) and Eq. (2) in terms of the local coordinates. The velocities at 1 and 2 in local coordinates are:

$$\underline{v}_1 = ((\dot{x} + \dot{\phi}y)\cos\phi_1 - (\dot{y} - \dot{\phi}(x + b)\sin\phi_1))\underline{i}_1$$
$$+((\dot{x} + \dot{\phi}y)\sin\phi_1 + (\dot{y} - \dot{\phi}(x + b)\cos\phi_1))\underline{j}_1 \tag{5}$$

$$\underline{v}_2 = ((\dot{x} + \dot{\phi}y)\cos\phi_2 - (\dot{y} + \dot{\phi}(-x + b + \delta)\sin\phi_2))\underline{i}_2$$
$$+((\dot{x} + \dot{\phi}y)\sin\phi_2 + (\dot{y} + \dot{\phi}(-x + b + \delta)\cos\phi_2))\underline{j}_2 \tag{6}$$

This gives us four nonholonomic constraints. Two come from the fact that the velocities perpendicular to the wheels at point 1 and 2 are zero. This means that the velocity at 1 in the direction $\underline{i}_1$ must be zero. The same must be true at 2. Thus, its velocity in the direction $\underline{i}_2$ must also be zero.

$$(\dot{x} + \dot{\phi}y)\cos\phi_1 - (\dot{y} - \dot{\phi}(x + b)\sin\phi_1) = 0 \tag{7}$$

$$(\dot{x} + \dot{\phi}y)\cos\phi_2 - (\dot{y} + \dot{\phi}(-x + b + \delta)\sin\phi_2) = 0 \tag{8}$$

The other two constraints are due to the non-slip condition.

$$(\dot{x} + \dot{\phi}y)\sin\phi_1 + (\dot{y} - \dot{\phi}(x + b)\cos\phi_1) = r\dot{\theta}_1 \tag{9}$$

$$(\dot{x} + \dot{\phi}y)\sin\phi_2 + (\dot{y} + \dot{\phi}(-x + b + \delta))\cos\phi_2 = r\dot{\theta}_2 \tag{10}$$

Using the previously defined generalized coordinate $p = \begin{bmatrix} x\ y\ \phi\ \delta\ \theta_1\ \theta_2\ \phi_1\ \phi_2 \end{bmatrix}^T$, each constraint can be written as

$$a_i(p)\dot{p} = 0 \quad i = 1, ..., 4 \quad p \in \mathbb{R}^8$$

For our system the constraints can be written in matrix form as

$$A(p)\dot{p} = 0 \tag{11}$$

where $A(p)$ is the 4×8 matrix defined below.

$$A(p) = \begin{bmatrix} \cos\phi_1 & -\sin\phi_1 & y\cos\phi_1 + (x + b)\sin\phi_1 & 0 & 0 & 0 & 0 & 0 \\ \sin\phi_1 & \cos\phi_1 & y\sin\phi_1 - (x + b)\cos\phi_1 & 0 & -r & 0 & 0 & 0 \\ \cos\phi_2 & -\sin\phi_2 & y\cos\phi_2 - (-x + b + \delta)\sin\phi_2 & \cos\phi_2 & 0 & 0 & 0 & 0 \\ \sin\phi_2 & \cos\phi_2 & y\sin\phi_2 + (-x + b + \delta)\cos\phi_2 & \sin\phi_2 & 0 & -r & 0 & 0 \end{bmatrix}$$

Equation (11) is refered to as the Pfaffian constraint [12]. The constraint Eq.(11) is nonholonomic and therefore it cannot be integrated.

2.4   Kinematic Model

The kinematic model represents the kinematic relation of the system in the direction that it can move. These are the directions of motion where the non-holonomic constraints are satisfied at all times. As detailed in [12] this is given by a basis of the right null space of the constraints, which will be denoted by $g_j(p) \in \mathbb{R}^n$, $j = 1, ..., n - k = m$. By construction, this basis satisfies

$$a_i(p)g_j(p) = 0 \quad i = 1, ..., k \quad j = 1, ..., n - k \quad p \in \mathbb{R}^n$$

and all allowable trajectories of the system can thus be written as the possible solutions of the system

$$\dot{p} = g_1(p)u_1 + ... + g_m(p)u_m. \tag{12}$$

That is, $p(t)$ is a feasible trajectory of the system if and only if $p(t)$ satisfies Eq. (12) for a choice of control $u(t) \in \mathbb{R}^m$.

For our system this basis can be obtained by casting equations (3) and (4) in terms of the global coordinates and equating them to (1) and (2) respectively. The velocities at 1 and 2 are respectively given by

$$r\dot{\theta}_1(\sin\phi_1 \underline{i}_f + \cos\phi_1 \underline{j}_f) = (\dot{x} + \dot{\phi}y)\underline{i}_f + (\dot{y} - \dot{\phi}(x + b))\underline{j}_f \tag{13}$$

$$r\dot{\theta}_2(\sin\phi_2 \underline{i}_f + \cos\phi_2 \underline{j}_f) = (\dot{x} + \dot{\phi}y)\underline{i}_f + (\dot{y} + \dot{\phi}(-x + b + \delta))\underline{j}_f \tag{14}$$

From Eq. (13) and Eq. (14) the following relations are obtained

$$\dot{x} = (r \sin \phi_1 + \frac{yr}{2b+\delta} \cos \phi_1)\dot{\theta}_1 - \frac{yr}{2b+\delta} \cos \phi_2 \dot{\theta}_2 \tag{15}$$

$$\dot{y} = (r \cos \phi_1 - \frac{(x+b)r}{2b+\delta} \cos \phi_1)\dot{\theta}_1 + \frac{(x+b)r}{2b+\delta} \cos \phi_2 \dot{\theta}_2 \tag{16}$$

$$\dot{\phi} = \frac{r}{2b+\delta}(\cos \phi_2 \dot{\theta}_2 - \cos \phi_1 \dot{\theta}_1) \tag{17}$$

$$\dot{\delta} = r \sin \phi_2 \dot{\theta}_2 - r \sin \phi_1 \dot{\theta}_1 \tag{18}$$

The above equations are the kinematic equations of our system. They can be written in the following form

$$\underline{\dot{p}} = G(\underline{p})\underline{\dot{\eta}} \tag{19}$$

where

$$\underline{p} = \begin{bmatrix} \dot{x} \\ \dot{y} \\ \dot{\phi} \\ \dot{\delta} \\ \dot{\theta}_1 \\ \dot{\theta}_2 \\ \dot{\phi}_1 \\ \dot{\phi}_2 \end{bmatrix}, G(\underline{p}) = \begin{bmatrix} r \sin \phi_1 + \frac{yr}{2b+\delta} \cos \phi_1 & -\frac{yr}{2b+\delta} \cos \phi_2 & 0 & 0 \\ r \cos \phi_1 - \frac{(x+b)r}{2b+\delta} \cos \phi_1 & \frac{(x+b)r}{2b+\delta} \cos \phi_2 & 0 & 0 \\ -\frac{r}{2b+\delta} \cos \phi_1 & \frac{r}{2b+\delta} \cos \phi_2 & 0 & 0 \\ -r \sin \phi_1 & r \sin \phi_2 & 0 & 0 \\ 1 & 0 & 0 & 0 \\ 0 & 1 & 0 & 0 \\ 0 & 0 & 1 & 0 \\ 0 & 0 & 0 & 1 \end{bmatrix}, \underline{\dot{\eta}} = \begin{bmatrix} \dot{\theta}_1 \\ \dot{\theta}_2 \\ \dot{\phi}_1 \\ \dot{\phi}_2 \end{bmatrix}$$

In the above equation $\underline{\dot{\eta}} \in \mathbb{R}^4$ is a vector of independent velocities. Note that in general $\underline{\dot{\eta}}$ can be a function that is smooth in $\underline{p}$, and linear in $\underline{\dot{p}}$, $\underline{\dot{\eta}}(\underline{p},\underline{\dot{p}})$ [10]. The above equation indicates that velocities $\dot{\theta}_1, \dot{\theta}_2, \dot{\phi}_1, \dot{\phi}_2$ are sufficient to determine the instantaneous velocities of all generalized coordinates of the system. Also, note that the velocities calculated with Eq.(19) satisfy the nonholonomic constraints, since $G(\underline{p}) = [g_1(\underline{p}) \quad g_2(\underline{p}) \quad g_3(\underline{p}) \quad g_4(\underline{p})]$ is the right null space of the constraints. That is

$$A(\underline{p})g_j(\underline{p}) = 0$$

Equation(19) is referred as the *kinematic state-model* [13].

2.5   Dynamic Model

A dynamic model of the system is obtained by only considering the dynamics of the actuators. The dynamics due to the mass of the paper has been neglected since it is small. For the normal mode of operation we consider the kinematical model derived in section § 2.4. This system has a two-wheel driven, and two-wheel steered system. Each wheel can turn freely around its horizontal and vertical axis. The contact points between each of the wheels and the paper must satisfy pure rolling and non-slip conditions. The kinematical model of this system is described by Eq. (15), Eq. (16), Eq. (17) and Eq. (18). To get the dynamic model of the system we start by differentiating the kinematic equations, Eq. (15), Eq. (16), Eq. (17) and Eq. (18). For simplicity, we consider actuator dynamics of the following form

$$\ddot{\theta}_1 = u_1, \ddot{\theta}_2 = u_2, \ddot{\phi}_1 = u_3, \ddot{\phi}_2 = u_4.$$

This gives us the following dynamical system

$$\underline{\dot{x}} = \underline{f}_1(\underline{x}) + \underline{B}_1(\underline{x})\underline{u}_1, \tag{20}$$

where

$$\underline{x} = [x \quad \dot{x} \quad y \quad \dot{y} \quad \phi \quad \dot{\phi} \quad \delta \quad \dot{\delta} \quad \theta_1 \quad \dot{\theta}_1 \quad \theta_2 \quad \dot{\theta}_2 \quad \phi_1 \quad \dot{\phi}_2]^T,$$

$$\underline{f}_1(\underline{x}) = \begin{bmatrix} f1_1 \\ f1_2 \\ f1_3 \\ f1_4 \\ f1_5 \\ f1_6 \\ 0 \\ f1_8 \\ 0 \\ f1_9 \\ 0 \\ 0 \\ 0 \\ 0 \end{bmatrix}, \underline{B}_1(\underline{x}) = \begin{bmatrix} 0 & 0 & 0 & 0 \\ b1_{21} & b1_{22} & b1_{23} & b1_{24} \\ 0 & 0 & 0 & 0 \\ b1_{41} & b1_{42} & b1_{43} & b1_{44} \\ 0 & 0 & 0 & 0 \\ b1_{61} & b1_{62} & b1_{63} & b1_{64} \\ 0 & 0 & 0 & 0 \\ b1_{81} & b1_{82} & b1_{83} & b1_{84} \\ 0 & 0 & 0 & 0 \\ 1 & 0 & 0 & 0 \\ 0 & 0 & 0 & 0 \\ 0 & 1 & 0 & 0 \\ 0 & 0 & 1 & 0 \\ 0 & 0 & 0 & 1 \end{bmatrix}, \underline{u}_1 = \begin{bmatrix} u_1 \\ u_2 \\ u_3 \\ u_4 \end{bmatrix} = \begin{bmatrix} \ddot{\theta}_1 \\ \ddot{\theta}_2 \\ \ddot{\phi}_1 \\ \ddot{\phi}_2 \end{bmatrix}.$$

with
$f1_1 = \dot{x}$, $f1_2 = -\dot{\phi}\dot{y} + \frac{y\dot{\delta}\dot{\phi}}{2b+\delta}$, $f1_3 = \dot{y}$, $f1_4 = \dot{\phi}\dot{x} - \frac{(x+b)\dot{\delta}\dot{\phi}}{2b+\delta}$, $f1_5 = \dot{\phi}$, $f1_6 = -\frac{\dot{\delta}\dot{\phi}}{2b+\delta}$,
$f1_7 = \dot{\delta}$, $f1_9 = \dot{\theta}_1$, $f1_{11} = \dot{\theta}_2$, $b1_{21} = \frac{yr}{2b+\delta}\cos\phi_1 + r\sin\phi_1$, $b1_{22} = -\frac{yr}{2b+\delta}\cos\phi_2$,
$b1_{23} = r\cos\phi_1\dot{\theta}_1 - \frac{yr}{2b+\delta}\sin\phi_1\dot{\theta}_1$, $b1_{24} = +\frac{yr}{2b+\delta}\sin\phi_2\dot{\theta}_2$, $b1_{41} = r\cos\phi_1 - \frac{(x+b)r}{2b+\delta}\cos\phi_1$,
$b1_{42} = \frac{(x+b)r}{2b+\delta}\cos\phi_2$, $b1_{43} = -r\sin\phi_1\dot{\theta}_1 + \frac{(x+b)r}{2b+\delta}\sin\phi_1\dot{\theta}_1$, $b1_{44} = -\frac{(x+b)r}{2b+\delta}\sin\phi_2\dot{\theta}_2$,
$b1_{61} = -\frac{r}{2b+\delta}\cos\phi_1$, $b1_{62} = \frac{r}{2b+\delta}\cos\phi_2$, $b1_{63} = \frac{r}{2b+\delta}\sin\phi_1\dot{\theta}_1$, $b1_{64} = -\frac{r}{2b+\delta}\sin\phi_2\dot{\theta}_2$,
$b1_{81} = -r\sin\phi_1$, $b1_{82} = r\sin\phi_2$, $b1_{83} = -r\cos\phi_1\dot{\theta}_1$, $b1_{84} = r\cos\phi_2\dot{\theta}$.

3   Control Modes

3.1   Normal Feedback Control

In this section we derive the control law for normal operation. During the derivation of the feedback dynamic system we will obtain conditions for mode changes.

In this mode we want to control the position of the paper and satisfy $\delta = 0$ at all time. This means that states (x, y, ϕ, δ) have to be controlled at all times, therefore the output vector function is

$$\underline{y} = h(\underline{x}) = \begin{bmatrix} x & y & \phi & \delta \end{bmatrix}^T. \tag{21}$$

The above system is a square Multi-Input Multi-Output(MIMO) system. It is called square because it has as many inputs as outputs. This MIMO system can be linearized by static state feedback. This is accomplished by differentiating the j_{th} output with respect to time, see [15] for details. After differentiating, the following equation is obtained

$$\ddot{\underline{y}} = \begin{bmatrix} \ddot{x} & \ddot{y} & \ddot{\phi} & \dot{\delta} \end{bmatrix}^T = \underline{C}_1(\underline{x}) + \underline{E}_1(\underline{x})\underline{u}_1, \tag{22}$$

where

$$\underline{C}_1(\underline{x}) = \begin{bmatrix} c l_1 \\ c l_2 \\ c l_3 \\ 0 \end{bmatrix}, \underline{E}_1(\underline{x}) = \begin{bmatrix} e l_{11} & e l_{12} & e l_{13} & e l_{14} \\ e l_{21} & e l_{22} & e l_{23} & e l_{24} \\ e l_{31} & e l_{32} & e l_{33} & e l_{34} \\ e l_{41} & e l_{42} & e l_{43} & e l_{44} \end{bmatrix},$$

with
$cl_1 = -\dot{\phi}\dot{y} + \frac{y\delta\dot{\phi}}{2b+\delta}$, $cl_2 = \dot{\phi}\dot{x} - \frac{(x+b)\delta\dot{\phi}}{2b+\delta}$, $cl_3 = -\frac{\delta\dot{\phi}}{2b+\delta}$, $el_{11} = \frac{yr}{2b+\delta}\cos\phi_1 + r\sin\phi_1$, $el_{12} = -\frac{yr}{2b+\delta}\cos\phi_2$, $el_{13} = r\cos\phi_1\dot{\theta}_1 - \frac{yr}{2b+\delta}\sin\phi_1\dot{\theta}_1$, $el_{14} = \frac{yr}{2b+\delta}\sin\phi_2\dot{\theta}_2$, $el_{21} = r\cos\phi_1 - \frac{(x+b)r}{2b+\delta}\cos\phi_1$, $el_{22} = \frac{(x+b)r}{2b+\delta}\cos\phi_2$, $el_{23} = -r\sin\phi_1\dot{\theta}_1 + \frac{(x+b)r}{2b+\delta}\sin\phi_1\dot{\theta}_1$, $el_{24} = -\frac{(x+b)r}{2b+\delta}\sin\phi_2\dot{\theta}_2$, $el_{31} = -\frac{r}{2b+\delta}\cos\phi_1$, $el_{32} = \frac{r}{2b+\delta}\cos\phi_2$, $el_{33} = \frac{r}{2b+\delta}\sin\phi_1\dot{\theta}_1$, $el_{34} = -\frac{r}{2b+\delta}\sin\phi_2\dot{\theta}_2$, $el_{41} = -r\sin\phi_1$, $el_{42} = r\sin\phi_2$, $el_{43} = -r\cos\phi_1\dot{\theta}_1$, $el_{44} = r\cos\phi_2\dot{\theta}_2$.
Then, choose the following state feedback law:

$$\underline{u}_1 = \underline{E}_1^{-1}(\underline{x})(\underline{v}_1 - \underline{C}_1(\underline{x})), \tag{23}$$

where

$$\underline{E}_1^{-1}(\underline{x}) = \begin{bmatrix} i e_{11} & i e_{12} & i e_{13} & i e_{14} \\ i e_{21} & i e_{22} & i e_{23} & i e_{24} \\ i e_{31} & i e_{32} & i e_{33} & i e_{34} \\ i e_{41} & i e_{42} & i e_{43} & i e_{44} \end{bmatrix}$$

with
$ie_{11} = \frac{\cos\phi_1\sin\phi_1}{r\cos\phi_1}$, $ie_{12} = \frac{1-\sin\phi_1^2}{r\cos\phi_1}$, $ie_{13} = \frac{-b-x-\sin\phi_1(-y\cos\phi_1-(b+x)\sin\phi_1)}{r\cos\phi_1}$, $ie_{21} = \frac{\cos\phi_2\sin\phi_2}{r\cos\phi_2}$, $ie_{22} = \frac{\cos\phi_2^2}{r\cos\phi_2}$, $ie_{23} = \frac{\cos\phi_2((b-x+\delta)\cos\phi_2+y\sin\phi_2)}{r\cos\phi_2}$, $ie_{24} = \frac{\cos\phi_2\sin\phi_2}{r\cos\phi_2}$, $ie_{31} = \frac{\cos\phi_1}{r\dot{\theta}_1}$, $ie_{32} = \frac{-\sin\phi_1}{r\dot{\theta}_1}$, $ie_{33} = \frac{y\cos\phi_1+(b+x)\sin\phi_1}{r\dot{\theta}_1}$, $ie_{41} = \frac{y\cos\phi_2}{r\dot{\theta}_2}$, $ie_{42} = -\frac{\sin\phi_2}{r\dot{\theta}_2}$, $ie_{43} = \frac{y\cos\phi_2-(b-x+\delta)\sin\phi_2}{r\dot{\theta}_2}$, $ie_{44} = \frac{\cos\phi_2}{r\dot{\theta}_2}$.
This yields the linear closed loop system

$$\begin{bmatrix} \ddot{x} & \ddot{y} & \ddot{\phi} & \dot{\delta} \end{bmatrix}^T = \begin{bmatrix} v_1 & v_2 & v_3 & v_4 \end{bmatrix}^T. \tag{24}$$

At this point we have four decoupled equations. This means that v_1, v_2, v_3 and v_4 only affect the outputs x, y, ϕ and δ respectably. Choose $v_1 = \ddot{x}_d + k_1\tilde{x} + q_1\tilde{x}$,

$v_2 = \ddot{y}_d + k_2\dot{\tilde{y}} + q_2\tilde{y}$, $v_3 = \ddot{\phi}_d + k_3\dot{\tilde{\phi}} + q_3\tilde{\phi}$ and $v_4 = \ddot{\delta}_d + k_4\dot{\tilde{\delta}} + q_4\tilde{\delta}$ where $\tilde{x} = x_d - x$, $\tilde{y} = y_d - y$, $\tilde{\phi} = \phi_d - \phi$, $\tilde{\delta} = \delta_d - \delta$, and k_1, k_2, k_3, k_4, q_1, q_2, q_3, q_4 are positive constants. The choice of v_i with positive constants for k_i, q_i give exponentially decaying errors. The differential equation of these errors will be $\ddot{\tilde{x}}_i + k_1\dot{\tilde{x}} + q_1\tilde{x} = 0$, $\ddot{\tilde{y}}_i + k_2\dot{\tilde{x}} + q_2\tilde{x} = 0$, $\ddot{\tilde{\phi}}_i + k_3\dot{\tilde{\phi}} + q_3\tilde{\phi} = 0$ and $\ddot{\tilde{\delta}}_i + k_4\dot{\tilde{\delta}} + q_4\tilde{\delta} = 0$.

Note that this control law, $\underline{u}_1$, has terms with $\dot{\theta}_1$ and $\dot{\theta}_2$ in the denominator. This means that this matrix will be ill conditioned if either $\dot{\theta}_1$ or $\dot{\theta}_2$ is zero. This makes this control law unusable when $\dot{\theta}_1$ or $\dot{\theta}_2$ are close or equal to zero. Based on the above discussion we introduce the first discrete control mode q_1:

q_1: Trajectory tracking $\begin{bmatrix} x_{ref} & y_{ref} & \phi_{ref} & \delta_{ref} \end{bmatrix}^T$. This mode is conditioned on $\dot{\theta}_1 \geq \dot{\theta}_{min} \wedge \dot{\theta}_2 \geq \dot{\theta}_{min}$.

3.2   Feedback Control to Overcome Wheel Velocity Singularity

It was shown above that the normal feedback control fails when the velocity of either wheel is zero (angular velocity of the wheels in the direction parallel to the sheet). This comes from the fact the lateral error cannot be corrected unless the media is moving. For this case we derive another control law. We choose to track the longitudinal position and the change in nominal distance of point 1 and 2 along the sheet (x, δ). Also, during the tracking of x and δ we will maintain the orientation of the wheels fixed therefore $\dot{\phi}_1$ and $\dot{\phi}_2$ will be zero. For this mode the state space equation and the output function are

$$\dot{\underline{x}} = \underline{f}_2(\underline{x}) + \underline{B}_2(\underline{x})\underline{u}_2, \tag{25}$$

$$\underline{y} = h(\underline{x}) = \begin{bmatrix} x & \delta \end{bmatrix}^T \tag{26}$$

where

$$\underline{f}_2(\underline{x}) = \begin{bmatrix} f2_1 & f2_2 & f2_3 & f2_4 & f2_5 & f2_6 & f2_7 & 0 & f2_9 & 0 & f2_{11} & 0 & 0 & 0 \end{bmatrix}^T,$$

$$\underline{B}_2 = \begin{bmatrix} 0 & b2_{12} & 0 & b2_{14} & 0 & b2_{16} & 0 & b2_{18} & 0 & 1 & 0 & 0 & 0 & 0 \\ 0 & b2_{22} & 0 & b2_{44} & 0 & b2_{26} & 0 & b2_{28} & 0 & 0 & 1 & 0 & 0 & 0 \end{bmatrix}^T, \underline{u}_2 = \begin{bmatrix} u_1 \\ u_2 \end{bmatrix} = \begin{bmatrix} \ddot{\theta}_1 \\ \ddot{\theta}_2 \end{bmatrix}$$

with

$f2_1 = \dot{x}$, $f2_2 = -\dot{\phi}\dot{y} + \frac{y\dot{\delta}\dot{\phi}}{2b+\delta}$, $f2_3 = \dot{y}$, $f2_4 = \dot{\phi}\dot{x} - \frac{(x+b)\dot{\delta}\dot{\phi}}{2b+\delta}$, $f2_5 = \dot{\phi}$, $f2_6 = -\frac{\dot{\delta}\dot{\phi}}{2b+\delta}$, $f2_7 = \dot{\delta}$, $f2_9 = \dot{\theta}_1$, $f2_{11} = \dot{\theta}_2$, $b2_{12} = \frac{yr}{2b+\delta}\cos\phi_1 + r\sin\phi_1$, $b2_{22} = -\frac{yr}{2b+\delta}\cos\phi_2$, $b2_{14} = r\cos\phi_1 - \frac{(x+b)r}{2b+\delta}\cos\phi_1$, $b2_{24} = \frac{(x+b)r}{2b+\delta}\cos\phi_2$, $b2_{16} = -\frac{r}{2b+\delta}\cos\phi_1$, $b2_{26} = \frac{r}{2b+\delta}\cos\phi_2$, $b2_{18} = -r\sin\phi_1$, $b2_{28} = r\sin\phi_2$.

Again differentiating the output until one of the inputs appears and cancelling the terms that have $\dot{\phi}_1$ and $\dot{\phi}_2$, we get the following output equation:

$$\underline{y} = \begin{bmatrix} \ddot{x} & \ddot{\delta} \end{bmatrix}^T = \underline{C}_2(\underline{x}) + \underline{E}_2(\underline{x})\underline{u}_2, \tag{27}$$

where

$$\underline{C}_2(\underline{x}) = \begin{bmatrix} -\dot{\phi}\dot{y} + \frac{y\dot{\delta}\dot{\phi}}{2b+\delta} \\ 0 \end{bmatrix}, \underline{E}_2(\underline{x}) = \begin{bmatrix} \frac{yr}{2b+\delta}\cos\phi_1 + r\sin\phi_1 & -\frac{yr}{2b+\delta}\cos\phi_2 \\ -r\sin\phi_1 & r\sin\phi_2 \end{bmatrix}.$$

The state feedback control law for this system is

$$\underline{u}_2 = \underline{E}_2^{-1}(\underline{x})(\underline{v}_2 - \underline{C}_2(\underline{x})), \tag{28}$$

where

$$\underline{E}_2^{-1}(\underline{x}) = \begin{bmatrix} \frac{(2b+\delta)\sin\phi_2}{d_2} & \frac{y\cos\phi_2}{d_2} \\ \frac{(2b+\delta)\sin\phi_1}{d_2} & \frac{y\cos\phi_1+(2b+\delta)\sin\phi_1}{d_2} \end{bmatrix}.$$

with

$$d_2 = r(-y\cos\phi_2\sin\phi_1 + (y\cos\phi_1 + (2b+\delta)\sin\phi_1)\sin\phi_2).$$

The above state feedback yields the following linear closed loop system

$$\ddot{\underline{y}} = \begin{bmatrix} \ddot{x} & \ddot{\delta} \end{bmatrix}^T = \begin{bmatrix} v_1 & v_2 \end{bmatrix}^T. \tag{29}$$

For this system we have two decoupled equations. This means that v_i only affects the output y_i, for $i = 1, 2$. Choosing $v_1 = \ddot{x}_d + k_1\dot{\tilde{x}} + q_1\tilde{x}$ and $v_2 = \ddot{\delta}_d + k_2\dot{\tilde{\delta}} + q_2\tilde{\delta}$ where $\tilde{x} = x_d - x$, $\tilde{\delta} = \delta_d - \delta$, k_1, k_2, q_1, and q_2 are positive constants, we get errors that are exponentially decaying. The differential equations of these errors will be $\ddot{\tilde{x}} + k_1\dot{\tilde{x}} + q_1\tilde{x} = 0$ and $\ddot{\tilde{\delta}} + k_2\dot{\tilde{\delta}} + q_2\tilde{\delta} = 0$. Note that the matrix in the control law (28) will be ill conditioned if $\phi_1 = \phi_2 = 0$. Therefore, this control law cannot be used under these conditions. This case occurs when the lateral errors have been corrected. Based on the above discussion the second discrete control mode is as follows:

q_2: Trajectory tracking $\begin{bmatrix} x_{ref} & \delta_{ref} \end{bmatrix}^T$. This mode is condition on $(\dot{\theta}_1 \leq \dot{\theta}_{min} \vee \dot{\theta}_2 \leq \dot{\theta}_{min}) \wedge (\phi_1 \neq \phi_2 \neq 0)$.

3.3   Feedback Control with No Steering

The two wheels will have a zero steering angle when the lateral error has been corrected or at initial operation when the wheels are starting to move. This takes us to the third and fourth discrete control modes. In these modes of operation the wheels have zero steering angle. The control law used in these cases was developed by Kanayama [16]. Kanayama proposed a control law that makes use of reference velocities and current posture of the vehicle to control the vehicle position. Note that this problem is similar to the one of moving paper with fixed wheels. This control rule uses the linear and rotational reference velocities of the paper to correct for the position errors and follow a given trajectory. The kinematic model for this system is

$$\begin{bmatrix} \dot{x} \\ \dot{y} \\ \dot{\phi} \end{bmatrix} = \begin{bmatrix} \cos(\phi) & 0 \\ \sin(\phi) & 0 \\ 0 & 1 \end{bmatrix} \begin{bmatrix} \nu \\ \omega \end{bmatrix}, \begin{bmatrix} \nu \\ \omega \end{bmatrix} = \begin{bmatrix} \frac{r}{2} & \frac{r}{2} \\ \frac{r}{2b} & -\frac{r}{2b} \end{bmatrix} \begin{bmatrix} \dot{\theta}_1 \\ \dot{\theta}_2 \end{bmatrix}. \tag{30}$$

The nonholonomic constraints of this system is

$$\dot{x}\sin(\phi) - \dot{y}\cos(\phi) = 0. \tag{31}$$

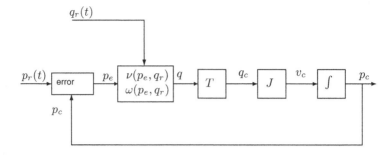

Fig. 4. Tracking Controller Block Diagram for Unsteerable Wheels

The error posture used by the controller is defined as

$$p_e = \begin{bmatrix} \dot{x}_e \\ \dot{y}_e \\ \dot{\phi}_e \end{bmatrix} = \begin{bmatrix} \cos(\phi) & \sin(\phi) & 0 \\ -\sin(\phi) & \cos(\phi) & 0 \\ 0 & 0 & 1 \end{bmatrix} (p_r - p), \tag{32}$$

where p_r is the reference posture. The block diagram of this controller is shown in Figure 4. The law for the velocities is as follows:

$$q = \begin{bmatrix} \nu \\ \omega \end{bmatrix} = \begin{bmatrix} \nu(p_e, q_r) \\ \omega(p_e, q_r) \end{bmatrix} = \begin{bmatrix} \nu_r \cos(\phi_e) + K_x x_e \\ \omega_r + \nu_r (K_y y_e + K_\phi \sin(\phi_e)) \end{bmatrix}, \tag{33}$$

where K_x, K_y and K_ϕ are positive constants, and ν_r and ω_r are the reference velocities. A proof of the stability of this control law can be found in [16]. The following Lyapounov function candidate (34) was used to show that the control law is asymptotically stable.

$$V = \frac{1}{2}(x_e^2 + y_e^2) + (1 - \cos(\phi_e))/K_y. \tag{34}$$

Based on the above discussion the third and fourth discrete control mode correspond to the case when the lateral errors have been corrected and when the wheels are starting to move from rest. They are respectively:

q_3: Trajectory tracking $\begin{bmatrix} x_{ref} & y_{ref} & \phi_{ref} \end{bmatrix}^T$. This mode is conditioned on $(\dot{\theta}_1 \leq \dot{\theta}_{min} \vee \dot{\theta}_2 \leq \dot{\theta}_{min}) \wedge (\phi_1 = \phi_2 = 0)$.

q_4: Trajectory tracking $\begin{bmatrix} x_{ref} & y_{ref} & \phi_{ref} \end{bmatrix}^T$. This mode is conditioned on $(\phi_1 = \phi_2 = 0) \wedge y \leq y_{min}$.

4   Control Using Hybrid Automata

In this section we construct a switched mode feedback controller which provides global finite-time convergence of the continuous time states to the origin. The switched mode feedback controller is constructed as a hybrid system comprising

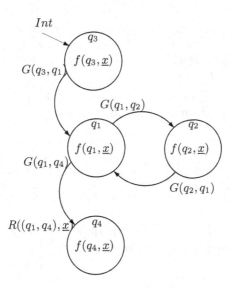

Fig. 5. Hybrid Automaton for a Steerable Nips System

of states at which the system will switch to during the tracking of the trajectories. A hybrid automaton of the steerable nips is shown in Figure 5. There are four discrete states in which the system can be at a given time. The state q_3 represents the initial state. In this state the velocity of the sheet is the only thing being tracked. The reason for tracking only the speed is that, at the start, the velocities of the wheels are zero. The full steerable nips system cannot be used since the control law requires that the speeds of the wheels are nonzero. Once both wheels have reached the minimum speed, $\dot{\theta}_{min}$, the normal control law, q_1, can be used. During the normal control mode the controller will track the references. Longitudinally, the paper will track a sinusoidal reference with a given magnitude. The lateral and angular references are zero. The reason to track a sinusoidal reference is that we want to oscillate between the final longitudinal position while the lateral and angular errors are being corrected. Tracking the sinusoidal reference means that at a given point the wheel velocities have to be zero. This is the point at which the second control mode, q_2, will be used. Finally, once the lateral errors have been corrected, the control mode will be switched from q_1 to q_4. At this point the lateral errors and angular errors have been corrected and the system needs to be driven to its final longitudinal positon $x = 0$. The hybrid automaton of this system is defined based on [17], that is,

- $Q = \{q_1, q_2, q_3, q_4\}$
- $X : \underline{x} = \begin{bmatrix} x & \dot{x} & y & \dot{y} & \phi & \dot{\phi} & \delta & \dot{\delta} & \theta_1 & \dot{\theta}_1 & \theta_2 & \dot{\theta}_2 & \phi_1 & \phi_2 \end{bmatrix}$
- $Int = \{q\} \times \{\underline{x} \in \mathbb{R}^{14} : \dot{x} = \dot{y} = \dot{\phi} = \delta = \dot{\delta} = \theta_1 = \dot{\theta}_1 = \theta_2 = \dot{\theta}_2 = \phi_1 = \phi_2 = 0\}$
- $f(q_1, \underline{x}, \underline{u}_1) = f_1(\underline{x}) + B_1 \underline{u}_1$
- $\begin{bmatrix} \ddot{x} & \ddot{y} & \ddot{\phi} & \ddot{\delta} \end{bmatrix}^T = \underline{C}_1(\underline{x}) + \underline{E}_1(\underline{x}) \underline{u}_1$
- $\underline{u}_1 = \underline{E}_1^{-1}(\underline{x})(\underline{v}_1 - \underline{C}_1(\underline{x}))$, $v_{11} = \ddot{x}_d + k_1 \dot{\tilde{x}} + q_1 \tilde{x}$, $v_{12} = \ddot{y}_d + k_2 \dot{\tilde{y}} + q_2 \tilde{y}$,

$v_{13} = \ddot{\phi}_d + k_3\dot{\tilde{\phi}} + q_3\tilde{\phi}$, $v_{14} = \ddot{\delta}_d + k_4\dot{\tilde{\delta}} + q_4\tilde{\delta}$, where $\tilde{x} = x_d - x$, $\tilde{y} = y_d - y$, $\tilde{\phi} = \phi_d - \phi$, $\tilde{\delta} = \delta_d - \delta$ and $k_1, k_2, k_3, k_4, q_1, q_2, q_3, q_4 \in \mathbb{R}_+$

- $f(q_2, \underline{x}, \underline{u}_2) = f_2(\underline{x}) + \underline{B}_2\underline{u}_2$
- $[\ddot{x} \quad \ddot{\delta}]^T = \underline{C}_2(\underline{x}) + \underline{E}_2(\underline{x})\underline{u}_2$
- $\underline{u}_2 = \underline{E}_2^{-1}(\underline{x})(\underline{v}_2 - \underline{C}_2(\underline{x}))$, $v_{21} = \ddot{x}_d + k_1\dot{\tilde{x}} + q_1\tilde{x}$, $v_{22} = \ddot{\delta}_d + k_4\dot{\tilde{\delta}} + q_4\tilde{\delta}$ where $\tilde{x} = x_d - x$, $\tilde{\delta} = \delta_d - \delta$ and $k_1, k_4, q_1, q_4 \in \mathbb{R}+$
- $f(q_3, \underline{x}, \underline{u}_3)$ such   that

$$\begin{bmatrix} \dot{x} \\ \dot{y} \\ \dot{\phi} \end{bmatrix} = \begin{bmatrix} \cos(\phi) & 0 \\ \sin(\phi) & 0 \\ 0 & 1 \end{bmatrix} \begin{bmatrix} \nu \\ \omega \end{bmatrix}, \begin{bmatrix} \nu \\ \omega \end{bmatrix} = \begin{bmatrix} \frac{r}{2} & \frac{r}{2} \\ \frac{r}{2b} & -\frac{r}{2b} \end{bmatrix} \begin{bmatrix} \dot{\theta}_1 \\ \dot{\theta}_2 \end{bmatrix}, \begin{bmatrix} \ddot{\theta}_1 \\ \ddot{\theta}_2 \end{bmatrix} = \begin{bmatrix} u_1 \\ u_2 \end{bmatrix}$$

$$p_e = \begin{bmatrix} \dot{x}_e \\ \dot{y}_e \\ \dot{\phi}_e \end{bmatrix} = \begin{bmatrix} \cos(\phi) & \sin(\phi) & 0 \\ -\sin(\phi) & \cos(\phi) & 0 \\ 0 & 0 & 1 \end{bmatrix} \begin{bmatrix} x_{ref} - x \\ y_{ref} - y \\ \phi_{ref} - \phi \end{bmatrix}$$

$$q = \begin{bmatrix} \nu \\ \omega \end{bmatrix} = \begin{bmatrix} \nu(p_e, q_r) \\ \omega(p_e, q_r) \end{bmatrix} = \begin{bmatrix} \nu_r \cos(\phi_e) + K_x x_e \\ \omega_r + \nu_r(K_y y_e + K_\phi \sin(\phi_e)) \end{bmatrix}$$

with $x_{ref}(t) = At$, $A \in \mathbb{R}+$, $\nu_{ref} = \nu_{min}$, $\omega_{ref} = 0$.
- $f(q_4, \underline{x}, \underline{u}_4) = f(q_3, \underline{x}, \underline{u}_3)$
  with $x_{ref} = 0$, $\nu_{ref} = 0$, $\omega_{ref} = 0$.
- $D(q_1) = \{\underline{x} \in \mathbb{X} : \dot{\theta}_1 \geq \dot{\theta}_{min} \wedge \dot{\theta}_2 \geq \dot{\theta}_{min}\}$, $D(q_2) = \{\underline{x} \in \mathbb{X} : \dot{\theta}_1 \leq \dot{\theta}_{min} \vee \dot{\theta}_2 \leq \dot{\theta}_{min} \wedge (\phi_1 \neq \phi_2 \neq 0)\}$, $D(q_3) = \{\underline{x} \in \mathbb{X} : \dot{\theta}_1 \leq \dot{\theta}_{min} \vee \dot{\theta}_2 \leq \dot{\theta}_{min} \wedge (\phi_1 = \phi_2 = 0)\}$, $D(q_4) = \{(\phi_1 = \phi_2 = 0) \wedge y \leq y_{min}\}$
- $E = \{(q_1, q_2), (q_2, q_1), (q_2, q_4), (q_3, q_2)\}$
- $G(q_1, q_2) = \{\underline{x} \in \mathbb{X} : \dot{\theta}_1 \leq \dot{\theta}_{min} \vee \dot{\theta}_2 \leq \dot{\theta}_{min} \wedge (\phi_1 \neq \phi_2 \neq 0)\}$, $G(q_2, q_1) = \{\underline{x} \in \mathbb{X} : \dot{\theta}_1 \geq \dot{\theta}_{min} \wedge \dot{\theta}_2 \geq \dot{\theta}_{min}\}$, $G(q_3, q_1) = \{\underline{x} \in \mathbb{X} : \dot{\theta}_1 \geq \dot{\theta}_{min} \wedge \dot{\theta}_2 \geq \dot{\theta}_{min}\}$, $G(q_1, q_4) = \{y \leq y_{min}\}$
- $R((q_1, q_2), \underline{x}) = R((q_2, q_1), \underline{x}) = R((q_3, q_1), \underline{x}) = \underline{x}$, $R((q_1, q_4), \underline{x}) = (x, \dot{x}, y, \dot{y}, \phi, \dot{\phi}, \delta, \dot{\delta}, \theta_1, \dot{\theta}_1, \theta_2, \dot{\theta}_2, 0, 0)$

5   Simulation Results

The model was simulated for the following initial conditions. $x_0 = -10mm$, $y_0 = 10mm$, $\phi = 4^o$. Simulation results are shown in Figs. 6 - 9. Figure 6 shows the trajectory of the paper as it goes from its initial position at $(x, y, \phi, \delta) = (-10mm, 10mm, 4^o, 0)$ to its final position at $(x,y,\phi,\delta)=(0,0,0,0)$. Figure 7 shows the position of the paper and control modes used during the simulation. As shown the initial control mode, q_3 is used for less that 0.001 second. The reason is that the normal feedback control can be used only when the velocity of the wheels are non zero. This happens almost instantaneously. Also note that the normal feedback control q_1 is used most of the time during the correction of lateral

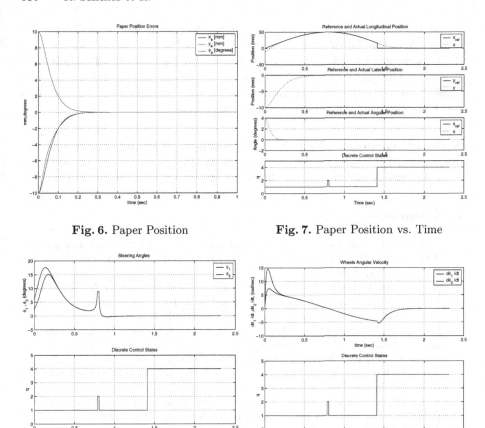

Fig. 6. Paper Position

Fig. 7. Paper Position vs. Time

Fig. 8. Wheels Steering Angle vs. Time

Fig. 9. Angular velocities of the Wheels vs. Time

displacement. The steering angles of both wheels are shown in Figure 8 and the velocity of both wheels are shown in Figure 9. The initial steering angles of the wheels are zero. They are steered immediately once the normal control mode is in use, this action will correct the lateral errors. The steering angle will become zero once the lateral errors have been corrected, and at this point the control mode switches from q_1 to q_4.

6   Conclusion

In this paper we have successfully used hybrid automata to fully control the position of a sheet. The use of hybrid automata was necessary to overcome singularities of the normal control action law. This singularity was due to the fact that the control law matrix has elements with angular velocities in the denominator. For this matrix not to be ill conditioned the angular velocities of the wheels cannot be zero. During the actuation of the paper the velocity of the wheels are zero. This happens at the beginning since the sheet starts at rest. Also, the longitudinal reference is sinusoidal with zero mean; therefore the velocity will be zero at one point during the actuation. Results obtained in this paper have shown that by using hybrid automata it is possible to drive the paper from rest to any other position also at rest. This can be accomplished by satisfying the nonholonomic constraints at all time.

Acknowledgements This work was support by the National Science Fundation under Award ID 0301719. The authors thank Gabriel Gomes for his numerous critical remarks and suggestions during the preparation of this manuscript.

References

1. C. Tomlin, G. Pappas, and S. Sastry. Conflict resolution for air traffic management: A study in multiagent hybrid systems. *IEEE Transactions on Automatic Control*, 43(4):509–521, 1998.
2. A. Balluchi, L. Benvenutti, M. Di Benedetto, C. Pinello, , and A. Sangiovanni-Vincentelli. Automotive engine control and hybrid systems: Challenges and opportunities. *Proceedings of the IEEE*, 7:888–912, July 2000.
3. R. W. Brockett. Hybrid models for motion control systems. In H. Trentelman and J. Willems, editors, *Essays in Control: Perspectives in the Theory and Its Applications*, pages 29–53. Birkhäuser, Boston, 1993.
4. B. Lennartsson, M. Tittus, B. Egardt, and S. Pettersson. Hybrid systems in process control. *Control Systems Magazine*, 16(5):45–56, 1996.
5. S. Engell, S. Kowalewski, C. Schultz, and O. Strusbe rg. Continuous-discrete interactions in chemical process plan ts. *Proceedings of the IEEE*, 7:1050–1068, July 2000.
6. P. Varaiya. Smart cars on smart roads: Problems of control. *IEEE Transactions on Automatic Control*, 38(2):195–207, 1993.
7. R. Horowitz and P. Varaiya. Control design of an automated highway system. *Proceedings of the IEEE*, 88(7):913–925, July 2000.
8. D.L. Pepyne and C.G. Cassandras. Optimal control of hybrid systems in manufacturing. *Proceedings of the IEEE*, 7:1108–1123, July 2000.
9. Xiaoping Yun and N. Sarkar. Dynamic feedback control of vehicles with two steerable wheels. In *1996 IEEE International Conference on Robotics and Automation*, pages 3105–3110, 1996.
10. G. Campion, B. d'Andrea Novel, and G. Bastin. Modelling and state feedback control of nonholonomic mechanical systems. In *Proceedings of the 30th IEEE Conference on Decision and Control*, pages 1184–1189, Brighton, England, December 1991.
11. B. d'Andrea Novel, G. Bastin, and G. Campion. Modelling and control of nonholonomic wheeled mobile robots. In *Proceedings of the 1991 IEEE Conference on Robotics and Automation*, pages 1130 –1135, Sacramento, CA, April 1991.
12. Richard M. Murray, Zexiang Li, and Shankar S. Sastry. *A Mathematical Introduction to Robotic Manipulation*. CRC Press, 1993.
13. G. Campion, d'Andrea Novel, and G. Bastin. Controllability and state feedback stabilisability of nonholonomic mechanical systems. In *Advanced robot control : proceedings of the International Workshop on Nonlinear and Adaptive Control: Issues in Robotics*, pages 106 –124, Grenoble, November 1990.

14. R. W. Brockett. Asymptotic stability and feedback stabilization. In R. W. Brockett, R. S. Milman, and H. J. Sussmann, editors, *Differential Geometric Control Theory*. Birkhauser, Boston, 1983.

15. S. S. Sastry. *Nonlinear Systems : Analysis, Stability, and Control*. Springer, 1999.

16. Y. Kanayama, Y. Kimura, F. Miyazaki, and T. Noguchi. A stable tracking control method for an autonomous mobile robot. In *Proceedings of the IEEE International Conference on Robotics and Automation*, pages 384–389, 1990.

17. J. Lygeros, K.H. Johansson, S.N. Simić, J. Zhang, and S.S. Sastry. Dynamical properties of hybrid automata. *IEEE Transactions on Automatic Control*, 48:2–17, 2003.

Constructing Invariants for Hybrid Systems

Sriram Sankaranarayanan, Henny B. Sipma, and Zohar Manna*

Computer Science Department
Stanford University
Stanford, CA 94305-9045
{srirams,sipma,zm}@theory.stanford.edu

Abstract. An invariant of a system is a predicate that holds for every reachable state. In this paper, we present techniques to generate invariants for hybrid systems. This is achieved by reducing the invariant generation problem to a constraint solving problem using methods from the theory of ideals over polynomial rings. We extend our previous work on the generation of algebraic invariants for discrete transition systems in order to generate algebraic invariants for hybrid systems. In doing so, we present a new technique to handle consecution across continuous differential equations. The techniques we present allow a trade-off between the complexity of the invariant generation process and the strength of the resulting invariants.

1 Introduction

Hybrid Systems are reactive systems that combine discrete mode changes with the continuous evolution of the system variables, specified in the form of differential equations. The analysis of hybrid systems is an important problem that has been studied extensively both by the control theory, and the formal verification community for over a decade. The most important analysis questions for hybrid systems are those of *safety*, i.e, deciding whether a given property ψ holds in all the reachable states, and the dual problem of *reachability*, i.e, deciding if a state satisfying the given property ψ is reachable. Both these problems are computationally hard — intractable even for the simplest of cases, and undecidable for most practical cases.

In this paper, we provide techniques to generate invariants for hybrid systems. An *invariant* of a hybrid system is a property ψ that holds in all the reachable states of the system. An *inductive assertion* of a hybrid system is an assertion ψ that holds at the initial state of the system, and is preserved by all discrete and continuous state changes of the system. Therefore, any inductive assertion being true of all the reachable states is also an invariant assertion. Furthermore, the standard technique for proving a given assertion φ invariant is to generate an

---

* This research was supported in part by NSF grants CCR-01-21403, CCR-02-20134 and CCR-02-09237, by ARO grant DAAD19-01-1-0723, by ARPA/AF contracts F33615-00-C-1693 and F33615-99-C-3014, and by NAVY/ONR contract N00014-03-1-0939.

R. Alur and G.J. Pappas (Eds.): HSCC 2004, LNCS 2993, pp. 539–554, 2004.

inductive assertion ψ that implies φ. The advantage of an inductive assertion is that it can be checked easily [15]. Therefore, the problem of invariant generation is one of inductive assertion generation. This problem has received wide attention in the program analysis community [13,6,7,19,17,5,2]. The generation of linear inductive assertions for the special case of linear hybrid systems has also been studied [10]. Many other approaches that compute the exact or the approximate reach-set of a given hybrid system, can also be shown to compute reach-sets that are inductive assertions [11,18,14].

In this paper, we extend our previous work on non-linear inductive assertion generation [17] for discrete systems, by adapting it to generate invariants for hybrid systems. We use the theory of ideals over polynomials and standard computational techniques in algebraic geometry involving Gröbner bases to provide a technique for computing inductive assertions for a given hybrid system. The key idea behind our technique is that given a template assertion, i.e, a polynomial of bounded degree in the system variables with unknown coefficients, we derive constraints on the unknown coefficients so that any solution to these constraints is an inductive assertion. In order to keep these constraints tractable, however, we consider several restrictions on the nature of an invariant. In particular, we consider stronger conditions for inductiveness than the traditional requirements [15]. Also, we provide conceptually simple techniques to handle the continuous evolution; these techniques require neither a closed form solution to the differential equations nor an approximation thereof.

The key advantage of our technique is that it can construct inductive assertions using less time and space than traditional techniques. Depending on the nature of the consecution condition chosen, our constraint generation technique is linear in the number of modes and discrete transitions, and polynomial in the number of system variables. Furthermore, the constraints generated can range in complexity from the more intractable non-linear constraints requiring quantifier elimination to simple constraints involving only linear equalities. Of course, the more complex constraints can potentially yield stronger invariants than the simpler constraints. This trade-off is useful in practice, and contributes to making the method scale.

The rest of the paper is organized as follows: Section 2 presents our computational model and the basic theory behind ideals and Gröbner bases. Section 3 presents the constraint generation process. The nature of these constraints and their solution techniques are discussed in Section 4. In Section 5, we present some examples demonstrating the application of our techniques. Section 6 concludes with a discussion of the pros and cons.

2   Preliminaries

To model hybrid systems we use hybrid automata [12].

2.1   Computational Model: Hybrid Automata

Definition 1 (Hybrid System) A *hybrid system* Ψ: $\langle V, \mathcal{L}, \mathcal{T}, \Theta, \mathcal{D}, \mathcal{I}, \ell_0 \rangle$ consists of the following components:

- V, a set of real-valued system *variables*. The number of variables($|V|$) is called the *dimensionality* of the system;
- $\mathcal{L}$, a finite set of locations;
- $\mathcal{T}$, a set of (discrete) transitions. Each transition $\tau : \langle \ell_1, \ell_2, \rho_\tau \rangle \in \mathcal{T}$ consists of a prelocation $\ell_1 \in \mathcal{L}$, a postlocation $\ell_2 \in \mathcal{L}$, and an assertion ρ_τ over $V \cup V'$, representing the next-state relation, where V' denotes the values of V in the next state;
- Θ, an assertion specifying the *initial* condition;
- $\mathcal{D}$, a map that maps each location $\ell \in \mathcal{L}$ to a *differential rule* $\mathcal{D}(\ell)$, an assertion over $V \cup \{\dot{v} \mid v \in V\}$. The differential rule at a location specifies how the system variables evolve in that location;
- $\mathcal{I}$, a map that maps each location $\ell \in \mathcal{L}$ to a *location condition (location invariant)*, $\mathcal{I}(\ell)$, an assertion over V;
- $\ell_0 \in \mathcal{L}$, the *initial location*.

Definition 2 (Computation) A computation of a hybrid automaton is an infinite sequence of states $\langle l, \boldsymbol{x} \rangle \in \mathcal{L} \times \mathcal{R}^{|V|}$ of the form

$$\langle l_0, \boldsymbol{x}_0 \rangle, \langle l_1, \boldsymbol{x}_1 \rangle, \langle l_2, \boldsymbol{x}_2 \rangle, \dots$$

such that the *initiation* condition $l_0 = \ell_0$ and $\boldsymbol{x}_0 \models \Theta$ holds, and for each consecutive state pair $\langle l_i, \boldsymbol{x}_i \rangle$, $\langle l_{i+1}, \boldsymbol{x}_{i+1} \rangle$, one of the two *consecution* conditions below is satisfied.

Discrete Consecution: there exists a transition $\tau : \langle \ell_1, \ell_2, \rho_\tau \rangle \in \mathcal{T}$ such that $l_i = \ell_1$, $l_{i+1} = \ell_2$, and $\langle \boldsymbol{x}_i, \boldsymbol{x}_{i+1} \rangle \models \rho_\tau$, or

Continuous Consecution: $l_i = l_{i+1} = \ell$, and there exists a time interval $\delta \geq 0$, and a continuous and differentiable function $f : [0, \delta] \mapsto \mathcal{R}^n$, such that f evolves from $\boldsymbol{x}_i$ to $\boldsymbol{x}_{i+1}$ according to the differential rule at location ℓ, while satisfying the location condition $\mathcal{I}(\ell)$. Formally,

1. $f(0) = \boldsymbol{x_1}$, $f(\delta) = \boldsymbol{x_2}$, and $(\forall t \in [0, \delta])$, $f(t) \models \mathcal{I}(\ell)$,
2. $(\forall t \in [0, \delta))$, $\left\langle f(t), \dot{f}(t) \right\rangle \models \mathcal{D}(\ell)$.

Example 1 (Bouncing Ball). Figure 1 shows a graphical representation of the following hybrid system, representing a ball bouncing on a soft floor ($y = 0$):

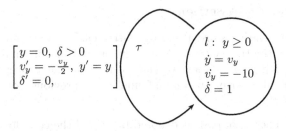

Fig. 1. The hybrid automaton for a bouncing ball

$$V = \{y, v_y, \delta\}$$
$$\mathcal{L} = \{l\},$$
$$\mathcal{T} = \{\tau\}, where, \ \tau = \left\langle l, l, \begin{bmatrix} \delta > 0 \ \wedge \ y = 0 \ \wedge \ y' = y \ \wedge \\ v'_y = -\frac{v_y}{2} \ \wedge \ \delta' = 0 \end{bmatrix} \right\rangle$$
$$\Theta = (y = 0 \ \wedge \ v_y = 16 \ \wedge \ \delta = 0)$$
$$\mathcal{D}(l) = \left(\dot{y} = v_y \ \wedge \ \dot{v}_y = -10 \ \wedge \ \dot{\delta} = 1 \right)$$
$$\mathcal{I}(l) = (y \geq 0)$$

The variable y represents the position of the ball, v_y represents its velocity, and δ denotes the time elapsed since its last bounce. A bounce is modelled by the transition τ, in which the velocity v_y of the ball is halved and the ball reverses direction.

Definition 3 (Invariant) An *invariant* of a hybrid system Ψ at a location l is an assertion ψ such that for any reachable state $\langle l, x \rangle$ of Ψ, $x \models \psi$.

Definition 4 (Inductive Assertion Map) An *inductive assertion map* η is a map that associates with each location $l \in \mathcal{L}$ an assertion $\eta(l)$, satisfying the following requirements:

Initiation. $\Theta \models \eta(l_0)$,

Discrete Consecution. For each discrete transition $\tau : \langle l_1, l_2, \rho \rangle$, starting from a state satisfying $\eta(l_1)$, ρ_τ establishes $\eta(l_2)$:

$$\eta(l_1) \ \wedge \ \rho_\tau \models \eta(l_2)'$$

Continuous Consecution. For every location $l \in \mathcal{L}$, and states $\langle l, x_1 \rangle$, $\langle l, x_2 \rangle$ such that x_2 evolves from x_1 according to the differential rule $\mathcal{D}(l)$ at l, if $x_1 \models \eta(l)$ then $x_2 \models \eta(l)$.

An assertion φ is *inductive* if the assertion map that maps each location to φ is an inductive assertion map. It is easy to see that an inductive assertion is an invariant. However, an invariant assertion is not necessarily inductive.

Example 2. For the hybrid system in Example 1, the assertion $y = v_y \delta - 5\delta^2$ is an inductive invariant assertion. On the other hand, the assertion $v_y \leq 16$ is an invariant but not inductive.

2.2   Algebraic Assertions

Our target invariants are algebraic assertions. The invariant generation method is based on the theory of ideals in polynomial rings and makes use of Gröbner bases. We will give a brief overview of the relevant concepts in this theory. A more detailed description can be found in our previous work [17] or in standard textbooks [8,16,1].

Notation. The set of reals is denoted by $\mathcal{R}$ and the complex numbers by $\mathcal{C}$. The set of polynomials over variables $x_1, \dots, x_n$, with coefficients in the field K is denoted by $K[x_1, \dots, x_n]$ or $K[\boldsymbol{x}]$.

Definition 5 (Algebraic Assertion) An *algebraic assertion* over $\mathcal{R}[x_1, \dots, x_n]$ is an assertion of the form $\bigwedge_{i=1}^m (p_i(\boldsymbol{x}) = 0)$, where each polynomial $p_i \in \mathcal{R}[\boldsymbol{x}]$ for $1 \leq i \leq m$. The same algebraic assertion can alternatively be described by the polynomial set $\{p_1, \dots, p_m\}$.

Definition 6 (Algebraic Hybrid Systems) An *algebraic hybrid system* is a hybrid system $\Psi : \langle V, \mathcal{L}, \mathcal{T}, \Theta, \mathcal{D}, \mathcal{I}, \ell_0 \rangle$, where, for each transition $\tau : \langle \ell_1, \ell_2, \rho_\tau \rangle \in \mathcal{T}$, the relation ρ_τ is an algebraic assertion, and the initial condition Θ, and the location conditions $\mathcal{I}(\ell)$ are algebraic assertions. Furthermore each rule $\mathcal{D}(\ell)$ is an algebraic assertion of the form $\bigwedge_i \dot{x}_i = p_i(x_1, \dots, x_n)$.

Definition 7 (Ideal) An *ideal* $I \subseteq \mathcal{R}[x_1, \dots, x_n]$ is a set of polynomials with the following properties:

- $0 \in I$,
- If $p_1, p_2 \in I$ then $p_1 + p_2 \in I$,
- If $p \in I$ and $q \in \mathcal{R}[\boldsymbol{x}]$ then $pq \in I$.

The ideal generated by a set $P = \{p_1, \dots, p_m\} \subseteq \mathcal{R}[\boldsymbol{x}]$, $n \geq 0$, of polynomials is written as

$$\langle P \rangle = \{g_1 p_1 + \dots + g_m p_m \mid p_1, \dots, p_m \in P, \ g_1, \dots, g_m \in \mathcal{R}[\boldsymbol{x}]\}$$

Ideal I is finitely generated if $I = \langle P \rangle$ for some finite set P, called the *basis* of I. It can be shown that any ideal in $\mathcal{R}[x_1, \dots, x_n]$ is finitely generated.

An ideal can be viewed as representing the polynomial consequences of a finite set of polynomials. It contains all polynomials whose zeroes are a superset of the common zeroes of the polynomials in the basis set.

Theorem 1. *Let I be an ideal generated by the basis $\{p_1, \dots, p_m\}$. Then for any polynomial p, if $p \in I$ then $\{p_1 = 0, \dots, p_m = 0\} \models (p = 0)$.*

Proof. Since $p \in I$, $p = g_1 p_1 + \dots g_m p_m$ for some $g_1, \dots, g_m$. Therefore, if for some $z \in \mathcal{C}^n$, $p_1(z) = 0 \wedge \dots \wedge p_m(z) = 0$ then $p(z) = 0$.

Theorem 1 states that in order to establish the entailment $\varphi \models (p = 0)$, it is sufficient to test membership of p in the ideal generated by φ. In the remainder of this section we will describe a method for testing ideal membership. The converse also holds (under some restrictions), known as *Hilbert's Nullstellensatz* [8], but is not relevant to the soundness of our method.

Let $X = \{x_1, \ldots, x_n\}$ be a set of variables. A *monomial* over X is of the form $x_1^{r_1} x_2^{r_2} \cdots x_n^{r_n}$, where each $r_i \in N$. A *term* is of the form $c \cdot p$ where $c \in \mathcal{R}$ and p is a monomial. Our technique assumes the presence of a linear ordering among terms that satisfies certain criteria. An example of such an ordering is the *lexicographic ordering*. Given a linear ordering $\prec$ on the variables in X ($x_1 \succ x_2 \succ \cdots \succ x_n$), the lexicographic extension $\prec_{lex}$ is the lexicographic ordering on the tuple $\langle r_1, \ldots, r_n \rangle$ corresponding to a term $x_1^{r_1} \cdots x_n^{r_n}$. Given a polynomial g, we define its *lead term* (denoted $\mathrm{LT}(g)$) to be the largest among all its terms w.r.t. a given term-ordering.

Definition 8 (Reduction) Let f, g be polynomials, with a term-ordering $<$. The reduction relation over polynomials, $\xrightarrow{g}$ is defined as: $f \xrightarrow{g} f'$ iff there exists term p in f s.t. $\mathrm{LT}(g)$ divides p, where, $f' = f - \frac{p}{\mathrm{LT}(g)} g$

The reduction cancels out the term p that was selected. If no such reduction can be made, then f is said to be a normal-form w.r.t. $\xrightarrow{g}$, denoted $g \in \mathrm{NF}_P(f)$. For a finite set P of polynomials, $f \xrightarrow{P} f'$ iff $(\exists g \in P)\ f \xrightarrow{g} f'$. The transitive closure of $\xrightarrow{P}$ is denoted $\xrightarrow{P}\!\!\!\twoheadrightarrow$. The reduction $\xrightarrow{P}$ can be shown to be terminating for all P. The reduction is *confluent* if every polynomial can be shown to reduce to a unique normal form [1].

Theorem 2 (Ideal Membership). *Let $I = \langle P \rangle$ be an ideal and f be a polynomial. If $f \xrightarrow{P}\!\!\!\twoheadrightarrow 0$ then $f \in I$.*

Example 3. Assume a set of variables x, y, z with ordering $x > y > z$. Let $I = \langle f : x^2 - y,\ g : y - z,\ h : x + z \rangle$ and $p = x^2 - y^2$. The lead term in the polynomial $f : x^2 - z$ is x^2, which divides the term $t : x^2$ in p. Thus, $p \xrightarrow{f} p'$, where

$$p' = \underbrace{(x^2 - y^2)}_{p} - \underbrace{\frac{x^2}{x^2}}_{\substack{t \\ \mathrm{LT}(f)}} \underbrace{(x^2 - y)}_{f} = (-y^2 + y)$$

The following sequence of reductions shows the membership of p in I

$$p \xrightarrow{h} -zx - y^2 \xrightarrow{h} z^2 - y^2 \xrightarrow{g} -yz + z^2 \xrightarrow{g} -z^2 + z^2 \equiv 0$$

thus $p \xrightarrow{I}\!\!\!\twoheadrightarrow 0$ and hence $p \in I$. However, the reduction sequence

$$p \xrightarrow{f} -y^2 + y \xrightarrow{g} -yz + y \xrightarrow{g} -z^2 + y \xrightarrow{g} -z^2 + z$$

reaches a normal-form without showing the ideal membership.

For an arbitrary ideal basis P, the reduction relation $\xrightarrow{P}$ may not be confluent, and hence, may not provide a decision procedure for ideal membership. However, given an ideal I, there is a special basis G, called the Gröbner basis, such that $I = \langle G \rangle$, and the reduction relation $\xrightarrow{G}$ is confluent.

Theorem 3 (Gröbner Basis). *Let $I = \langle P \rangle$ be an ideal and f be a polynomial. Let G be the Gröbner basis of I. Then $f \xrightarrow{G} 0$ iff $f \in I$.*

A proof of this theorem can be found in any standard text or survey on this topic [8,16]. The standard algorithm for computing the Gröbner basis of an ideal is known as the *Buchberger algorithm* with numerous implementations [20].

Example 4. Consider again the ideal $I = \langle x^2 - y, \ y - z, \ x + z \rangle$ from Example 3. The Gröbner basis for I is $G = \langle z^2 - z, \ y - z, \ x + z \rangle$. With this basis, every reduction of $p : \ x^2 - y^2$ will yield a normal form 0.

2.3 Algebraic Templates

Our technique for invariant generation aims to find polynomials that satisfy certain properties, namely the conditions for invariance. The method starts with a candidate invariant that is a generic polynomial template with coefficients that are linear expressions over a set of template variables. Satisfaction of the desired properties then imposes constraints on the template variables, and the solution to these constraints provides the coefficients of the target invariant.

We give a brief overview how to extend the theory of ideals over polynomial rings to templates. A more detailed description can be found in [17].

Definition 9 (Template) Let A be a set of *template variables* and $\mathcal{L}(A)$ be the domain of all *linear expressions* over variables in A of the form $c_0 + c_1 a_1 + \ldots + c_n a_n$, $c_i \in \mathcal{R}$. A *template* over A, X is a polynomial in $\mathcal{L}(A)[x]$. An A-*environment* is a map α that assigns a real value to each variable in A, and by extension, maps each expression in $\mathcal{L}(A)$ to a real value, and each template in $\mathcal{L}(A)[x_1, \ldots, x_n]$ to a polynomial in $\mathcal{R}[x_1, \ldots, x_n]$.

Example 5. Let $A = \{a_1, a_2, a_3\}$, hence $\mathcal{L}(A) = \{c_0 + c_1 a_1 + c_2 a_2 + c_3 a_3 \ | \ c_0, \ldots, c_3 \in \mathcal{R}\}$. An example template is $(2a_2 + 3)x_1 x_2^2 + (3a_3)x_2 + (4a_3 + a_1 + 10)$. The environment $\alpha \equiv \langle a_1 = 0, a_2 = 1, a_3 = 2 \rangle$, maps this template to the polynomial $5x_1 x_2^2 + 6x_2 + 18$.

The reduction $\xrightarrow{g}$ for polynomials can be extended to templates as follows:

Definition 10 (Reduction of Templates) Let p be a polynomial in $\mathcal{R}[x_1, \ldots, x_n]$ and f, f' be templates over A and $\{x_1, \ldots, x_n\}$. The reduction relation is defined as: $f \xrightarrow{p} f'$ iff the lead term $\text{LT}(p)$ divides a term $c(a_0, \ldots, a_m) \cdot t$ in f and $f' = f - \frac{c \cdot t}{\text{LT}(p)} p$

Example 6. Let p be the polynomial $x^2 - y$, with $\text{LT}(p) = x^2$. Consider the template $f : ax^2 + by^2 + cz^2 + dz + e$. The lead-term of p ($\text{LT}(p)$) divides the term ax^2 in f. Therefore, $f \xrightarrow{p} f'$, where

$$f' : (ax^2 + by^2 + cz^2 + dz + e) - \frac{ax^2}{x^2}(x^2 - y) = by^2 + cz^2 + dz + e + ay$$

In [17] it is shown that confluence of the reduction relation w.r.t. Gröbner bases extends to templates in the natural way.

The heart of our invariant generation method is to establish the conditions on the template variables that identify all A-environments for which the corresponding template instance belongs to a given ideal. Recall that a polynomial p belongs to an ideal I iff its normal form w.r.t. a Gröbner basis for I is identically zero.

Theorem 4. *A polynomial $p(x_1, \ldots, x_n)$ is zero for all the possible values of $x_1, \ldots, x_n$ iff all its coefficients are identically zero.*

Thus given a template f and an ideal I with Gröbner basis G all instances of the template belong to I if the coefficients of all terms in the normal from of f are zero.

Example 7. Consider the template $f = a_1 x^2 + a_2 y^2 + a_3 xy + a_4 y$ and the ideal I given by the Gröbner basis $\langle x^2 - 2y, y^2 \rangle$. The normal form of f is $\text{NF}_G = (2a_1 + a_4)y + a_3 xy$. Thus for all A-environments for which $2a_1 + a_4 = 0$ and $a_3 = 0$ the corresponding template instance belongs to $\mathcal{I}$.

3   Constraint-Generation

Our invariant generation algorithm consists of the following steps:

1. fix a template map for the candidate invariant;
2. encode the conditions for invariance as an ideal-membership question;
3. derive the constraints on the template variables that guarantee the appropriate ideal-membership from (2);
4. solve the constraints to obtain the desired class of invariants.

In this section we describe and illustrate the the first three steps; the last step is presented in section 4.

3.1   Template Map

The first step in our method is to fix the shape of the desired invariants. Let $A = \{a_1, a_2, \ldots\}$ be a set of template variables and let Ψ be an algebraic hybrid system with location set $\mathcal{L} = \{\ell_1, \ldots, \ell_m\}$ and variables $V = \{x_1, \ldots, x_n\}$. A generic degree-k template over A and V is the sum of all monomials of degree k or less, written as

$$\sum_{i_1 + \cdots + i_n \leq k} a_{\langle i_1, i_2, \ldots, i_n \rangle} x_1^{i_1} \cdots x_n^{i_n}$$

with a total of $\binom{n+k}{k}$ terms, and as many template variables. For example, a degree-2 template for 5 variables has 21 terms.

A *template map* η associates each location ℓ with a template. For maximum generality, the template variables in the templates should be all different. However, templates for different locations may have different degree.

Example 8. For the system introduced in Example 1 we fix the template map η as follows:

$$\eta(l) = a_1 y^2 + a_2 v_y^2 + a_3 \delta^2 + a_4 y v_y + a_5 v_y \delta + a_6 y \delta + a_7 y + a_8 v_y + a_9 \delta + a_{10}$$

with the objective to identify the values of the coefficients $a_1 \ldots a_{10}$ for which the assertion

$$a_1 y^2 + a_2 v_y^2 + a_3 \delta^2 + a_4 y v_y + a_5 v_y \delta + a_6 y \delta + a_7 y + a_8 v_y + a_9 \delta + a_{10} = 0$$

is an invariant at location l.

3.2   Encoding Invariance Conditions

The second step in our technique is the encoding of the conditions for invariance as an ideal membership statement. The idea is, given a template $\eta(\ell)$, to recast the invariance conditions in the form

$$\eta(\ell) \in \langle p_1, \ldots, p_k \rangle$$

where $p_1, \ldots, p_k$ are appropriate polynomials representing the condition. This is equivalent to $\mathrm{NF}_G(\eta(\ell)) \equiv 0$, where G is the Gröbner basis of $\langle p_1, \ldots, p_k \rangle$.

Initiation: The initiation condition, $\Theta \models (\eta(\ell_0) = 0)$, is encoded by $\eta(\ell_0) \in \langle \Theta \rangle$, that is, the template must belong to the ideal generated by the initial condition, and thus $\mathrm{NF}_\Theta(\eta(\ell_0)) \equiv 0$.

Example 9. The initial condition for the bouncing ball example (Example 1) is $(y = 0,\ v_y = 16,\ \delta = 0)$. Taking the template from Example 8 the normal form w.r.t. Θ is $\mathrm{NF}(\eta(l_0)) = a_{10} + 256a_2 + 16a_8$. Hence the constraint corresponding to initiation is $a_{10} + 256a_2 + 16a_8 = 0$.

Discrete Consecution: The consecution condition states that the invariant map must be preserved by all transitions, that is, for each transition $\langle \ell_1, \ell_2, \rho \rangle$, $(\eta(\ell_1) = 0) \wedge \rho \models (\eta(\ell_2)' = 0)$ must hold. Encoding this exactly would require the reduction of one template $(\eta(\ell_2))$ w.r.t. to another template $(\eta(\ell_1))$. As noted in our previous work [17], this leads to complex constraints which are hard to solve in general. As an alternative we propose to use stronger conditions for consecution that imply the original consecution condition, but avoid the template in the antecedent. It is easily shown that this is sound [17]. However, it may sacrifice completeness, because some invariant may satisfy the general condition of consecution but not the stronger condition.

Name	Condition	Encoding
Local (LC)	$\rho \models (\eta(l_2)' = 0)$	$\mathrm{NF}_\rho(\eta(l_2)') \equiv 0$
Constant-Value(CV)	$\rho \models (\eta(l_1) = \eta(l_2)')$	$\mathrm{NF}_\rho(\eta(l_1) - \eta(l_2)') \equiv 0$
Constant-Scale(CS)	$(\exists\, \lambda)\, \rho \models (\eta(l_2)' = \lambda\eta(l_1))$	$(\exists\lambda)\, \mathrm{NF}_\rho(\eta(l_2)' - \lambda\eta(l_1)) \equiv 0$
Polynomial-Scale(PS)	$(\exists\, f)\, \rho \models (\eta(l_2)' = f \cdot \eta(l_1))$	

Fig. 2. Consecution Conditions for Algebraic Templates

Figure 2 shows the different consecution conditions together with their encodings. The first condition (LC) states that the transition simply establishes the invariant at the post location, without any assumptions on the precondition. Invariants that can be established in this way are also known as *local* invariants or *reaffirmed* invariants. The constant-value (CV) condition states that the value of the polynomial at the prelocation ($\eta(\ell_1)$) and post location ($\eta(\ell_2)$) is not changed by the transition. Hence, if it is zero before the transition, then it will be zero after the transition, thus preserving the invariant map. The constant-scale condition states that the value of the polynomial may only change by a constant factor, λ. The last condition states that the transition may change the value of the polynomial by a polynomial factor. In all these cases, if the value of the polynomial is zero before the transition is taken, it will be zero after-wards. In the last two cases new unknowns, namely λ and f are added to the constraint solving problem, generally rendering the constraint problem non-linear, as we will see in the next section.

The encodings for the consecution conditions involve the system variables and the primed system variables. To ensure that the primed variables are eliminated as much as possible, a variable ordering must be chosen such that $V' > V$.

Example 10. The transition relation for the discrete transition τ in Example 1 is

$$\left[\delta > 0 \,\wedge\, y = 0 \,\wedge\, y' = y \,\wedge\, v'_y = -\tfrac{v_y}{2} \,\wedge\, \delta' = 0 \right]$$

Omitting the conjunct $\delta > 0$ to make the transition relation algebraic (note that it is sound to weaken the antecedent), the reduction of the template given in Example 8 according to local consecution yields a normal form

$$\mathrm{NF}_\rho(\eta'(\ell)) \;=\; \frac{a_2}{4}v_y^2 - \frac{a_8}{2}v_y + a_{10}$$

Reduction of the same template according to the constant scale consecution condition leads to the normal form

$$\mathrm{NF}_\rho(\eta'(\ell) - \lambda\eta(\ell)) \;=\; \frac{4a_2\lambda - a_2}{4}v_y^2 - a_5\lambda v_y\delta - \frac{2a_8\lambda + a_8}{2}v_y - a_3\lambda\delta^2 - a_9\lambda\delta$$
$$-a_{10}(\lambda - 1)$$

Continuous Consecution: The continuous consecution condition states that if the invariant holds at some state $\langle \ell, \boldsymbol{x_1} \rangle$ then it must hold at any state $\langle \ell, \boldsymbol{x_2} \rangle$ where $\boldsymbol{x_2}$ can be reached from $\boldsymbol{x_1}$ according to the differential rule $\mathcal{D}(\ell)$, while

Name	Condition	Encoding
Constant Value (CV)	$\mathcal{I}(\ell) \models \dot{\eta}(\ell) = 0$	$\mathrm{NF}_{\mathcal{I}(\ell)}(\dot{\eta}(\ell)) \equiv 0$
Constant Scale (CS)	$(\exists\, \lambda)\ \mathcal{I}(\ell) \models \dot{\eta}(\ell) - \lambda\eta(\ell) = 0$	$(\exists\lambda)\mathrm{NF}_{\mathcal{I}(\ell)}(\dot{\eta}(\ell) - \lambda\eta(\ell)) \equiv 0$

Fig. 3. Continuous consecution conditions

satisfying $\mathcal{I}(\ell)$. As in the discrete case, encoding this exactly is not practical, and therefore we impose stronger conditions, shown in Figure 3.

The first condition states that the value of the polynomial is constant throughout the continuous move, expressed by the condition that the derivative of the template invariant with respect to time is zero, thus guaranteeing that the assertion is preserved. Noting that the system variables are functions of time only, the derivative of the template can be obtained by the chain rule as follows:

$$\dot{\eta}(\ell) = \sum_i \left(\frac{\partial \eta(\ell)}{\partial x_i} \dot{x}_i \right)$$

Recall that in algebraic hybrid systems the differential rule is a conjunction of the form $\bigwedge_i \dot{x}_i = p_i(x_1, \dots, x_n)$, yielding the following template for $\dot{\eta}(\ell)$:

$$\dot{\eta}(\ell) = \sum_i \left(\frac{\partial \eta(\ell)}{\partial x_i} p_i(x_1, \dots, x_n) \right)$$

The second condition, CS, makes use of the fact that the value of the polynomial is zero, resulting in the more general condition that requires only that the difference between the derivative and a constant factor times the invariant itself be zero.

The encodings are similar to those for the discrete case. In both cases we compute the normal form with respect to the location invariant and equate the result to zero to obtain the constraints.

Example 11. Returning to the bouncing-ball system from Example 1, and the template from Example 8, the derivative of the template is

$$\dot{\eta}(l) = \begin{pmatrix} (2a_1y + a_4v_y + a_6\delta + a_7)\ \dot{y}\ + \\ (2a_2v_y + a_4y + a_5\delta + a_8)\ \dot{v}_y\ + \\ (2a_3\delta + a_5v_y + a_6y + a_9)\ \dot{\delta} \end{pmatrix}$$

which, with $\mathcal{D}(l): \dot{y} = v_y \ \wedge\ \dot{v}_y = -10 \ \wedge\ \dot{\delta} = 1$ gives

$$\dot{\eta}(l) = \begin{pmatrix} a_4v_y^2 + 2a_1yv_y + a_6\delta v_y + (-20a_2 + a_5 + a_7)v_y + \\ (2a_3 - 10a_5)\delta + (-10a_4 + a_6)y + (a_9 - 10a_8) \end{pmatrix}$$

For this system the location condition $\mathcal{I}(l)$ does not have any algebraic conjuncts and therefore $\mathrm{NF}_{\mathcal{I}(l)}(\dot{\eta}(l)) = \dot{\eta}(l)$.

3.3   Deriving the Constraints

The constraints on the template coefficients $a_1, \ldots, a_n$ are derived by equating to zero the coefficients of the normal forms of the template w.r.t. the initial condition, and the consecution conditions for all discrete transitions and continuous moves. By Theorem 4 the solutions to these constraints provide all combinations of values of the template coefficients for which the corresponding assertion satisfies the imposed conditions.

Example 12. Consider again the system presented in Example 1 and the template of Example 8. From above we have that the normal forms representing the initial condition, discrete consecution (LC) of τ and continuous consecution (CV) at location ℓ are

$$
\begin{aligned}
\text{NF}(\eta(l_0)) &= a_{10} + 256a_2 + 16a_8 \\
\text{NF}_\rho(\eta'(\ell)) &= \tfrac{a_2}{4}v_y^2 - \tfrac{a_8}{2}v_y + a_{10} \\
\text{NF}_{\mathcal{I}(\ell)}(\eta(\dot{l})) &= \begin{pmatrix} a_4 v_y^2 + 2a_1 y v_y + a_6 \delta v_y + (-20a_2 + a_5 + a_7)v_y + \\ (2a_3 - 10a_5)\delta + (-10a_4 + a_6)y + (a_9 - 10a_8) \end{pmatrix}
\end{aligned}
$$

yielding the set of constraints

$$
\begin{aligned}
a_{10} + 256a_2 + 16a_8 &= 0, \quad a_2 = a_8 = a_{10} = a_4 = a_1 = a_6 = 0 \\
-20a_2 + a_5 + a_7 &= 0, \quad a_3 - 5a_5 = 0, \quad a_6 - 10a_4 = 0, \quad a_9 - 10a_8 = 0
\end{aligned}
$$

A solution to this set of constraints is presented in the next section.

4   Solving Constraints

The encodings presented in the previous section can generate several types of constraints. Figure 4 shows the different types obtained for the various conditions and encodings. Solution techniques for linear inequalities are well understood and tend to be computationally inexpensive. For example Gaussian elimination can be done efficiently in polynomial time. The set of solutions is finitely generated by a set of basis vectors. On the other hand, techniques for solving non-linear equalities are complex, either requiring specialized techniques as in the case of eigenproblems, or generic elimination techniques such as quantifier elimination over complex or real numbers [3].

Condition	Restriction	Constraint types
Initiation		linear equalities
	Local (LC)	linear equalities
Consecution	Constant Value (CV)	linear equalities
	Constant Scale (CS)	eigenvalue problems
	Polynomial Scale (PS)	non-linear algebraic

Fig. 4. Constraints obtained from different conditions for inductive assertions

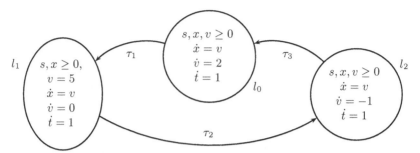

Fig. 5. Hybrid Automaton for the Train System

The non-linearities in the constraints are due to the use of scale parameters (λ) or parametric polynomials (in PS consecution). The constraints corresponding to constant scale (CS) consecution yield a generalized eigenvalue problem of the form $A\boldsymbol{x} = \lambda B\boldsymbol{x}$. Solution techniques to these problems may be numerical or symbolic. Numerical solution techniques are faster and more easily implemented. However errors in numerical computation may create errors in the final result, and plugging in an inaccurate value for λ will yield only the trivial solution. On the other hand symbolic techniques depend on polynomial root solving techniques which work only in special cases. In our experience the use of numerical techniques are adequate provided the values obtained for λ are rational or algebraic of a low degree.

General non-linear constraints are much harder to solve than linear constraints. For small to medium size systems these constraints can be handled using a combination of simplification and quantifier elimination, with the help of a tool suited to low degree polynomials such as REDLOG[9]. For higher-degree polynomials generic quantifier elimination techniques over the reals are required, which have been shown to be successful for small sized problems [4].

Example 13. The generator of the solutions to the linear equality constraints derived in example 12 is given by

$$a_5 = 1, a_3 = 5, a_7 = -1, a_1 = a_2 = a_4 = a_6 = a_8 = a_9 = a_{10} = 0$$

corresponding to the inductive assertion $-y + 5\delta^2 + v_y\delta = 0$.

5   Applications

We demonstrate the results of our technique on some application examples.

Train System: Figure 5 shows a hybrid automaton modeling a train accelerating (location l_0), travelling at constant speed (l_1), and decelerating (l_2). The system has three continuous variables: x, the position of the train, v, the train's velocity, and t, a masterclock. The system has one discrete variablem s, representing the number of stops made so far. The initial condition is given by

$x = s = t = v = 0$. There are three discrete transitions, τ_1, τ_2, and τ_3, with transition relations

$$\rho_{\tau_1} : v = 5$$
$$\rho_{\tau_2} : true$$
$$\rho_{\tau_3} : v = 0 \land s' = s + 1 \land t' = t + 2$$

Application of our technique resulted in the following assertion map:

$$\eta(l_0) : v^2 - 4x - 10v + 115s - 20t = 0$$
$$\eta(l_1) : 5v^2 + 4xv + 115vs - 20vt = 0$$
$$\eta(l_2) : 2v^2 + 4x - 20v + 115s - 20t + 75 = 0$$

With $v = 5$ at l_1 the assertion $\eta(l_1)$ can be simplified to $4x + 115s - 20t + 25 = 0$.

An analytic argument for the assertion $\eta(l_0)$ is as follows. Consider the system at the state $\langle l_0, \langle s, v, x, t \rangle \rangle$. Each stop s consists of accelerating from 0 to 5 in l_0 and decelerating from 5 to 0 in l_2. The distance covered in these two modes is $\frac{25}{4}$ and $\frac{25}{2}$ respectively. Furthermore, accelerating from 0 to v in l_0 advances the position another $\frac{v^2}{4}$. Hence the total distance travelled is given by $x = s(\frac{25}{4} + \frac{25}{2}) + \frac{v^2}{4} + 5t_{l_1}$, where t_{l_1}, the time spent in location l_1 is given by $t - t_{l_0} - t_{l_2} = t - (v/2 + s(\frac{5}{2})) - (\frac{5}{1}s + 2s)$. Substituting, we obtain the inductive assertion $4x = v^2 - 115s + 20t - 10v$. Similar arguments can be provided for the other locations.

Looping the Loop: Consider a heavy particle on a circular path of radius 2 with an initial angular velocity $\omega = \omega_0$ starting at $x = 2, y = 0$. The differential equation for its motion is given by

$$\dot{x} = r(\cos \theta) = -r(\sin \theta)\dot{\theta} = -y\omega$$
$$\dot{y} = r(\sin \theta) = xw$$
$$\dot{\omega} = -\frac{g \sin \theta}{r} = -\frac{5}{2}x$$

Using CV consecution, the quadratic invariants obtained were $x^2 + y^2 = 4$ and $\omega^2 + 5y = \omega_0^2$. The former invariant is a result of our modelling (though not explicitly posed as a location invariant) and the latter is the energy conservation equation. This invariant also establishes that unless $\omega_0 \geq \sqrt{10}$, the particle will be unable to complete a full circle.

6   Conclusion

We have presented a constraint-based technique for generating inductive assertions of hybrid systems. One of the main features of this technique is that it generates constraints without solving the differential equations. These differential equations may be hard to solve symbolically in practice, and may also involve exponentials lying outside the chosen assertion domain. We also avoid the use of over-approximations to these equations, relying instead on the conceptually simpler constant value and constant scale consecutions.

The technique is not guaranteed to generate the exact solution to the reachability problem, because of the relaxations made to maintain tractability. It also requires a degree bound to be specified a priori, the choice of which may be arbitrary. We are investigating strategies for guessing optimal degree bounds. A more serious shortcoming is that, at present, the technique does not handle inequalities. Inequalities frequently occur in the guards and location conditions, and not being able to use them in the constraint generation process may weaken the resulting invariants considerably. However, preliminary investigations indicate that a relatively simple extension may be sufficient to incorporate inequalities.

References

1. BAADER, F., AND NIPKOW, T. *Term Rewriting and* All That. Cambridge University Press, 1998.
2. BENSALEM, S., BOZGA, M., FERNANDEZ, J.-C., GHIRVU, L., AND LAKHNECH, Y. A transformational approach for generating non-linear invariants. In *Static Analysis Symposium* (June 2000), vol. 1824 of *LNCS*, Springer Verlag.
3. BOCKMAYR, A., AND WEISPFENNING, V. Solving numerical constraints. In *Handbook of Automated Reasoning*, A. Robinson and A. Voronkov, Eds., vol. I. Elsevier Science, 2001, ch. 12, pp. 751–842.
4. COLLINS, G. E., AND HONG, H. Partial cylindrical algebraic decomposition for quantifier elimination. *Journal of Symbolic Computation 12*, 3 (sep 1991), 299–328.
5. COLÓN, M., SANKARANARAYANAN, S., AND SIPMA, H. Linear invariant generation using non-linear constraint solving. In *Computer Aided Verification* (July 2003), F. Somenzi and W. H. Jr, Eds., vol. 2725 of *LNCS*, Springer Verlag, pp. 420–433.
6. COUSOT, P., AND COUSOT, R. Abstract Interpretation: A unified lattice model for static analysis of programs by construction or approximation of fixpoints. In *ACM Principles of Programming Languages* (1977), pp. 238–252.
7. COUSOT, P., AND HALBWACHS, N. Automatic discovery of linear restraints among the variables of a program. In *ACM Principles of Programming Languages* (Jan. 1978), pp. 84–97.
8. COX, D., LITTLE, J., AND O'SHEA, D. *Ideals, Varieties and Algorithms: An Introduction to Computational Algebraic Geometry and Commutative Algebra.* Springer, 1991.
9. DOLZMANN, A., AND STURM, T. REDLOG: Computer algebra meets computer logic. *ACM SIGSAM Bulletin 31*, 2 (June 1997), 2–9.
10. HALBWACHS, N., PROY, Y., AND ROUMANOFF, P. Verification of real-time systems using linear relation analysis. *Formal Methods in System Design 11*, 2 (1997), 157–185.
11. HENZINGER, T., AND HO, P.-H. Algorithmic analysis of nonlinear hybrid systems. In *Computer-Aided Verification*, P. Wolper, Ed., LNCS 939. 1995, pp. 225–238.
12. HENZINGER, T. A. The theory of hybrid automata. In *Logic In Computer Science (LICS 1996)* (1996), IEEE Computer Society Press, pp. 278–292.
13. KARR, M. Affine relationships among variables of a program. *Acta Inf. 6* (1976), 133–151.
14. LAFFERRIERE, G., PAPPAS, G., AND YOVINE, S. Symbolic reachability computation for families of linear vector fields. *J. Symbolic Computation 32* (2001), 231–253.

15. MANNA, Z., AND PNUELI, A. *Temporal Verification of Reactive Systems: Safety.* Springer-Verlag, New York, 1995.
16. MISHRA, B., AND YAP, C. Notes on Gröbner bases. *Information Sciences 48* (1989), 219–252.
17. SANKARANARAYANAN, S., SIPMA, H., AND MANNA, Z. Non-linear loop invariant generation using Gröbner bases. In *ACM Principles of Programming Languages (POPL), to appear* (2004).
18. TIWARI, A. Approximate reachability for linear systems. In *Hybrid Systems: Computation and Control HSCC* (2003), vol. 2623 of *LNCS*, pp. 514–525.
19. TIWARI, A., RUESS, H., SAÏDI, H., AND SHANKAR, N. A technique for invariant generation. In *TACAS 2001* (2001), vol. 2031 of *LNCS*, pp. 113–127.
20. WINDSTEIGER, W., AND BUCHBERGER, B. Gröbner: A library for computing Gröbner bases based on saclib. Tech. rep., RISC-Linz, 1993.

Bisimulation of Dynamical Systems

Arjan van der Schaft[*]

Department of Applied Mathematics, University of Twente
P.O. Box 217, 7500AE Enschede, The Netherlands
`a.j.vanderschaft@math.utwente.nl`

Abstract. A general notion of bisimulation is studied for dynamical systems. An algebraic characterization of bisimulation together with an algorithm for computing the maximal bisimulation relation is derived using geometric control theory. Bisimulation of dynamical systems is shown to be a concept which unifies the system-theoretic concepts of state space equivalence and state space reduction, and which allows to study equivalence of systems with non-minimal state space dimension. The notion of bisimulation is especially powerful for 'non-deterministic' dynamical systems, and leads in this case to a notion of equivalence which is finer than equality of external behavior. Furthermore, by merging bisimulation of dynamical systems with bisimulation of concurrent processes a notion of structural bisimulation is developed for hybrid systems with continuous input and output variables.

1 Introduction

A crucial notion in the theory of concurrent processes and model-checking is the concept of *bisimulation*. This notion expresses when a (sub-) process can be considered to be externally equivalent to another process. At the same time, classical notions in systems and control theory are *state space equivalence*, and *reduction* of an input-state-output system to an equivalent system with minimal state space dimension. These notions have been instrumental in e.g. linking input-output models to state space models, and in studying the properties of interconnected systems.

Developments in both areas have been rather independent, one of the reasons being that the mathematical formalisms for describing both types of systems (discrete processes on the one hand, and continuous dynamical systems on the other hand) are rather different. However, with the rise of interest in *hybrid systems*, there is a clear need to bring these theories together.

The aim of this paper is to make a further step in the reapproachment between the theory of concurrent processes and mathematical systems theory by defining and characterizing a notion of *bisimulation for continuous dynamical systems*, and to relate it to system-theoretic notions of state space equivalence and state space reduction. Furthermore, by *merging* the notion of bisimulation of continuous dynamical systems with the established notion of bisimulation for

---

[*] Research partially supported by the EU-project HYBRIDGE, IST-2001-32460.

concurrent processes we give a definition of structural bisimulation for hybrid systems with continuous communication variables.

Extensions of the notion of bisimulation to continuous dynamical systems have been explored before in a series of innovative papers by Pappas and co-authors [6,7,1,10,11,12,3,17], and the present paper is very much inspired by this work. A main difference is that while in [10,11,12,17] the focus is on characterizing bisimulation of a dynamical system by a "projected" dynamical system with lower state space dimension ("an abstraction"), the present paper (see also [15]) deals with a general notion of bisimulation between two continuous dynamical systems and gives algebraic conditions when two systems are bisimilar. (Note that the abstract definition of bisimulation relations for dynamical systems has been given before in a general context in [3].) Furthermore, the present paper as well as [15] makes precise the relations with system-theoretic notions of state space equivalence and state space reduction.

The continuous dynamical systems that we study are of the form

$$\dot{x} = Ax + Bu + Gd, \, x \in \mathbb{R}^n, u \in \mathbb{R}^m, d \in \mathbb{R}^s$$
$$y = Cx, \qquad\qquad y \in \mathbb{R}^p \tag{1}$$

where x are the state variables, u are the input variables, y are the output variables, while d are additional input variables, which can be thought of as *disturbances*. Thus we restrict to *linear input-state-output systems* although most of the theory can be generalized to the nonlinear case, cf. [15]; see also [17] in the case of abstraction. The basic problem of bisimulation we address is when two systems of the form (1) can be considered to be externally *equivalent*, in the sense that for all time instants t_0 the solution trajectories for $t \geq t_0$ of one system are mimicked by the other in such a way that the input and output trajectories $u(t)$ and $y(t)$ of both systems are the same for $t \geq t_0$, *without* imposing any relation between the values of their disturbance variables d.

In case the disturbance variables d are absent this problem comes down to the usual system-theoretic notion of *state space equivalence*, if *additionally* the systems have *minimal state space dimension*. Furthermore, it will become clear that the notion of bisimulation of continuous dynamical systems and its algebraic characterization is closely linked to the notion of *controlled invariance*, as introduced in linear systems in [19,2]. This last connection was already explored by Pappas and co-authors [11,10,12,17] in the more restricted context when a system is bisimilar to an "abstraction" of itself, and [15] makes explicit how these previously obtained results fit within the framework of the present paper. (Note that in [10,11,17] the input term Bu plays the same role as the disturbance term Gd in our setting.)

The notion of bisimulation for concurrent processes as introduced in [8,13]) is especially powerful for concurrent processes which are *non-deterministic* in the sense that branching in the (discrete) state may occur while the traces generated by the transition system are the same. In fact, the existence of a bisimulation relation between two *deterministic* processes is equivalent to equality of their external behaviors (the set of traces or the language generated by the process), and in this case bisimulation provides an efficient way to check equality of external behavior. For non-deterministic processes, however, bisimulation provides a finer equivalence than equality of external behavior, and, for example, also captures the *deadlock behavior* of concurrent processes.

A similar picture appears to arise for bisimulation of continuous dynamical systems (1). First, a type of "non-determinism" is present in systems (1) if we consider u and y as the external variables of the system (analogously to the labels of the discrete transitions of a process), while d denotes a disturbance generator in the evolution of the state x. If d is absent then (1) reduces to an ordinary "deterministic" system, and bisimulation can be shown (cf. [15]) to be equivalent to equality of external behavior, while generalizing the notion of state space equivalence to systems with non-minimal state space dimension. On the other hand, for *non-deterministic* systems bisimulation will be a stronger (finer) type of equivalence than equality of external behavior.

By *combining* the characterization of bisimulation of continuous dynamical systems with the usual notion of bisimulation for concurrent processes we will propose a notion of structural bisimulation for hybrid systems with continuous communication variables, which lends itself to algebraic characterizations. Indeed, in [14] this has been worked out in the special case of switching linear systems without invariants and guards, including an algorithm for computing the maximal bisimulation relation. The general proposed notion of structural hybrid bisimulation makes use of the definition of hybrid automata with continuous communication variables as recently provided in [16].

The structure of the paper is as follows. In Section 2 a linear-algebraic characterization of bisimulation is given, based on geometric control theory. The maximal bisimulation relation is computed in Section 3, and reduction of dynamical systems is treated using the notion of a bisimulation relation between the system and itself. In Section 4 a notion of structural bisimulation for hybrid system automata with continuous input and output variables is provided. Finally, Section 5 contains the conclusions and questions for further research.

2   Bisimilar Linear Dynamical Systems

Consider two dynamical systems of the form (1):

$$\Sigma_i : \quad \begin{aligned} \dot{x}_i &= A_i x_i + B_i u_i + G_i d_i, \quad x_i \in \mathcal{X}_i, u_i \in \mathcal{U}, d_i \in \mathcal{D}_i \\ y_i &= C_i x_i, \qquad\qquad\qquad\quad y_i \in \mathcal{Y} \quad i = 1, 2 \end{aligned} \qquad (2)$$

with $\mathcal{X}_i, \mathcal{D}_i, \mathcal{U}, \mathcal{Y}$ finite-dimensional linear spaces (over $\mathbb{R}$).

Before defining bisimulation we need to specify the solution trajectories of the systems (the *"semantics"*). That is, we have to specify the function classes of admissible input functions $u : [0, \infty) \to \mathcal{U}$ and admissible disturbance functions $d : [0, \infty) \to \mathcal{D}$, together with compatible function classes of state and output solutions $x : [0, \infty) \to \mathcal{X}$ and $y : [0, \infty) \to \mathcal{Y}$. For compactness of notation we usually denote these time-functions respectively by $u(\cdot), d(\cdot), x(\cdot)$ and $y(\cdot)$. The exact class from which the functions are chosen is not very important. For example, we can take all functions to be C^∞ although in some cases it may be natural/advantageous to require the property that if $d_1(\cdot)$ and $d_2(\cdot)$ are admissible disturbance functions then for every $\tau \geq 0$ also the function $d_3(\cdot)$ defined by $d_3(\cdot) = d_1(\cdot)(0 \leq t < \tau)$ and $d_3(\cdot) = d_2(\cdot)(t \geq \tau)$ is admissible.

Definition 1. *A (linear) bisimulation relation between Σ_1 and Σ_2 is a linear subspace $\mathcal{R} \subset \mathcal{X}_1 \times \mathcal{X}_2$ with the following property. Take any $(x_{10}, x_{20}) \in \mathcal{R}$ and any joint input function $u_1(\cdot) = u_2(\cdot)$. Then for every disturbance function $d_1(\cdot)$ there should exist a disturbance function $d_2(\cdot)$ such that the resulting state solution trajectories $x_1(\cdot)$, with $x_1(0) = x_{10}$, and $x_2(\cdot)$, with $x_2(0) = x_{20}$, satisfy*

$$(i) \quad (x_1(t), x_2(t)) \in \mathcal{R}, \quad \textit{for all } t \geq 0 \tag{3}$$

$$(ii) \quad C_1 x_1(t) = C_2 x_2(t), \quad \textit{for all } t \geq 0 \tag{4}$$

(or more precisely, for all $t \geq 0$ for which the trajectories are defined). Conversely, for every disturbance function $d_2(\cdot)$ there should exist a disturbance function $d_1(\cdot)$ such that again the resulting state trajectories $x_1(\cdot)$ and $x_2(\cdot)$ satisfy (3) and (4).

Hence for every pair $(x_{10}, x_{20}) \in \mathcal{R}$ all possible trajectories $x_1(\cdot)$ with $x_1(0) = x_{10}$ can be "simulated" by a trajectory $x_2(\cdot)$ with $x_2(\cdot) = x_{20}$ in the sense of giving the same input-output data for all future times while $(x_1(t), x_2(t)) \in \mathcal{R}$ for all $t \geq 0$, and conversely.

Remark 1. A similar definition (for the case that u_i is absent) has been given before in a general context in [3].

We shall only deal with *linear* bisimulation relations, that is, $\mathcal{R}$ is throughout assumed to be a linear subspace of $\mathcal{X}_1 \times \mathcal{X}_2$. Hence we will drop the adjective "linear", and simply call $\mathcal{R}$ a *bisimulation relation*. (See [15] for a treatment of bisimulation of nonlinear systems.)

Definition 2. *Two systems Σ_1 and Σ_2 as in (2) are* bisimilar *if there exists a bisimulation relation $\mathcal{R} \subset \mathcal{X}_1 \times \mathcal{X}_2$ with the property that*

$$\pi_1(\mathcal{R}) = \mathcal{X}_1, \quad \pi_2(\mathcal{R}) = \mathcal{X}_2 \tag{5}$$

where $\pi_i : \mathcal{X}_1 \times \mathcal{X}_2 \to \mathcal{X}_i$, $i = 1, 2$, denote the canonical projections.

Remark 2. Definition 2 constitutes a slight departure from the definition of bisimulation relation as usually given for discrete processes [8,13], by imposing the extra requirement (5). The reason is that in computer science discrete processes are usually defined with respect to a *fixed* initial state (or, a subset of initial conditions). In our setting we consider the behavior of the systems Σ_i for *arbitrary* initial states. Hence for every initial condition x_{10} of Σ_1 there should exist an initial condition x_{20} of Σ_2 with $(x_{10}, x_{20}) \in \mathcal{R}$ and vice versa; thus implying (5). The generalization to *subsets* of initial conditions $\mathcal{X}_{i0} \subset \mathcal{X}_i$ obviously can be done by relaxing (5) to $\pi_i(\mathcal{R}) = \mathcal{X}_{i0}, i = 1, 2$.

Remark 3. For $G_1 = G_2 = 0$ the above notion of bisimilarity is close to the usual notion of *state space equivalence* of two input-state-output systems

$$\Sigma_i : \begin{aligned} \dot{x}_i &= A_i x_i + B_i u_i, \; x_i \in \mathcal{X}_i, u_i \in \mathcal{U}, y_i \in \mathcal{Y} \\ y_i &= C_i x_i \qquad\quad i = 1, 2 \end{aligned} \tag{6}$$

Indeed, in this case one usually starts with a linear equivalence *mapping* $S : \mathcal{X}_1 \to \mathcal{X}_2$,
which is assumed to be invertible (implying that dim $\mathcal{X}_1 = $ dim $\mathcal{X}_2$) with the property that

$$Sx_1(t) = x_2(t), \; \text{for all } t \geq 0 \tag{7}$$

$$Cx_1(t) = Cx_2(t), \; \text{for all } t \geq 0 \tag{8}$$

for all state trajectories $x_1(\cdot)$ and $x_2(\cdot)$ resulting from initial conditions x_{10} and x_{20} related by $Sx_{10} = x_{20}$ and all input-functions $u_1(\cdot) = u_2(\cdot)$. Defining the linear subspace

$$\mathcal{R} = \{(x_1, x_2) \in \mathcal{X}_1 \times \mathcal{X}_2 \mid x_2 = Sx_1\} \tag{9}$$

(i.e., the graph of the mapping S) it is easily seen that $\mathcal{R}$ is a bisimulation relation which satisfies $\pi_1(\mathcal{R}) = \mathcal{X}_1$ trivially and $\pi_2(\mathcal{R}) = \mathcal{X}_2$ because of invertibility of S.

Clearly, by allowing $\mathcal{R}$ to be a *relation* instead of the graph of a mapping, the notion of bisimilarity even in the case $G_1 = G_2 = 0$ is more general than state space equivalence. In particular, we may allow $\mathcal{X}_1$ and $\mathcal{X}_2$ to be of *different dimension*. Furthermore, by doing so we incorporate in the notion of bisimilarity the notion of *reduction* of an input-state-output system to a lower-dimensional input-state-output system, and especially the reduction to a *minimal* input-state-output system. This is worked out in [15].

Using well-known ideas from state space equivalence of linear dynamical systems and especially from the theory of controlled invariance, see e.g. [19,2], it is easy to derive an algebraic characterization of the notion of a bisimulation relation.

Proposition 1. *A subspace $R \subset \mathcal{X}_1 \times \mathcal{X}_2$ is a bisimulation relation between Σ_1 and Σ_2 if and only if for all $(x_1, x_2) \in R$ and all $u \in \mathcal{U}$ the following properties hold:*

(i) For all $d_1 \in \mathcal{D}_1$ there should exist a $d_2 \in \mathcal{D}_2$ such that

$$(A_1 x_1 + B_1 u + G_1 d_1, A_2 x_2 + B_2 u + G_2 d_2) \in \mathcal{R}, \tag{10}$$

and conversely for every $d_2 \in \mathcal{D}_2$ there should exist a $d_1 \in \mathcal{D}_1$ such that (10) holds.
(ii)

$$C_1 x_1 = C_2 x_2 \tag{11}$$

Proof. Consider (3). Then by differentiating $x_1(t)$ and $x_2(t)$ with respect to t and evaluating at any t we obtain (10), with $x_1 = x_1(t), x_2 = x_2(t), u = u_1(t) = u_2(t), d_1 = d_1(t), d_2 = d_2(t)$. Conversely, if (10) holds then $(\dot{x}_1(t), \dot{x}_2(t)) \in \mathcal{R}$ for all $t \geq 0$, thus implying (3). Equivalence of (4) and (11) is obvious.

A main theorem proved in [15] is the following.

Theorem 1. *A subspace* $\mathcal{R} \subset \mathcal{X}_1 \times \mathcal{X}_2$ *is a bisimulation relation between* Σ_1 *and* Σ_2 *if and only if*

$$(a) \; \mathcal{R} + \mathrm{im} \begin{bmatrix} G_1 \\ 0 \end{bmatrix} = \mathcal{R} + \mathrm{im} \begin{bmatrix} 0 \\ G_2 \end{bmatrix} =: \mathcal{R}_e$$

$$(b) \; \begin{bmatrix} A_1 & 0 \\ 0 & A_2 \end{bmatrix} \mathcal{R} \subset \mathcal{R}_e$$

$$(c) \; \mathrm{im} \begin{bmatrix} B_1 \\ B_2 \end{bmatrix} \subset \mathcal{R}_e$$

$$(d) \; \mathcal{R} \subset \ker \begin{bmatrix} C_1 \vdots -C_2 \end{bmatrix}$$

(12)

Remark 4. Note that a subspace $\mathcal{R} \subset \mathcal{X}_1 \times \mathcal{X}_2$ satisfies properties (12a,b) if and only if the mapping F (from subspaces $\mathcal{S} \subset \mathcal{X}_1 \times \mathcal{X}_2$ to subspaces $F(\mathcal{S}) \subset \mathcal{X}_1 \times \mathcal{X}_2$) defined by

$$\mathcal{S} \overset{F}{\mapsto} \{ z \in \mathcal{X}_1 \times \mathcal{X}_2 \mid \begin{bmatrix} A_1 & 0 \\ 0 & A_2 \end{bmatrix} z + \mathrm{im} \begin{bmatrix} G_1 \\ 0 \end{bmatrix} \subset \mathcal{S} + \mathrm{im} \begin{bmatrix} 0 \\ G_2 \end{bmatrix},$$
$$\begin{bmatrix} A_1 & 0 \\ 0 & A_2 \end{bmatrix} z + \mathrm{im} \begin{bmatrix} 0 \\ G_2 \end{bmatrix} \subset \mathcal{S} + \mathrm{im} \begin{bmatrix} G_1 \\ 0 \end{bmatrix} \}$$

satisfies $\mathcal{R} \subset F(\mathcal{R})$. This will be instrumental to compute the maximal bisimulation relation, see Algorithm 2; in fact, the maximal bisimulation relation turns out to be a *fixed-point* of this mapping. (This is well-known in the theory of bisimulation for concurrent processes [8].)

Bisimilarity is easily seen to imply *equality of external behavior.* Consider two systems $\Sigma_i, i = 1, 2$, as in (2), with external behavior $\mathcal{B}_i$ defined as

$$\mathcal{B}_i := \{ (u_i(\cdot), y_i(\cdot)) \mid \exists x_i(\cdot), d_i(\cdot) \text{ such that (2) is satisfied} \} \qquad (13)$$

Proposition 2. *Let* $\Sigma_i, i = 1, 2$, *be bisimilar. Then their external behaviors* $\mathcal{B}_i$ *are equal.*

However, in the case of non-deterministic systems, that is, d_i is present, systems may have the same external behavior, while *not* being bisimilar. This is illustrated by the following example.

Example 1. Consider the two systems

$$\Sigma_1 : \begin{aligned} \dot{x}^1 &= x^2 \\ \dot{x}^2 &= d_1 \\ y_1 &= x^1 \end{aligned} \tag{14}$$

and

$$\Sigma_2 : \begin{aligned} \dot{z} &= d_2 \\ y_2 &= z \end{aligned} \tag{15}$$

It can be readily seen that there does not exist any bisimulation relation between Σ_1 and Σ_2 (consider condition (12a)). On the other hand, if we restrict e.g. to C^∞ external behaviors then obviously $\mathcal{B}_1 = \mathcal{B}_2$. (Note the different logical quantifiers in the definition of bisimilarity and in equality of external behavior. For bisimilarity there should exist for every x^1, x^2 a z such that for every d_1 there exists a d_2 with equal external trajectories and conversely, while for equality of external behavior there should exist for every x^1, x^2, d_1 a pair z, d_2 with equal external trajectories, and conversely.)

An *interpretation* of the fact that Σ_1 and Σ_2 are not bisimilar can be given as follows. Suppose we "test" the system Σ_1 at some time instant $t = t_0$ in the sense of observing one of its possible external trajectories $y_1(t), t \geq t_0$. At $t = t_0$ the system Σ_1 is in a given, but unknown, initial state $(x^1(t_0), x^2(t_0))$. Hence, all possible runs $y_1(t), t \geq t_0$, starting from this fixed initial state will have a *fixed* time-derivative $\dot{y}_1(t_0) = x^2(t_0)$ at $t = t_0$. On the other hand, for Σ_2 the possible runs $y_2(t), t \geq t_0$, can have arbitrary time-derivative at $t = t_0$. Hence, Σ_1 and Σ_2 can be considered to be externally *different*.

For deterministic systems (d_i void) it is shown in [15] that equality of external behavior *does* imply bisimilarity, and how the bisimulation relation can be easily derived.

3   Maximal Bisimulation Relation and Reduction

In this section we first show how to compute the *maximal* bisimulation relation $R \subset \mathcal{X}_1 \times \mathcal{X}_2$ for two linear dynamical systems Σ_1 and Σ_2. The way to do this is very similar to the computation of the maximal controlled invariant subspace contained in a given subspace, which is the central algorithm in linear geometric control theory [19]. Furthermore, structurally the algorithm is the same as the existing algorithms to compute the maximal bisimulation relation for two discrete processes, see e.g. [5]. For details we refer to [15].

First we remark that the *maximal* bisimulation relation exists if there exists at least one bisimulation relation (contrary to e.g. the *minimal* bisimulation relation). The argument is similar to the argument showing the existence of a maximal controlled invariant subspace, and is based on the following simple observations.

Proposition 3. *Let $\mathcal{R}_a \subset \mathcal{X}_1 \times \mathcal{X}_2$ and $\mathcal{R}_b \subset \mathcal{X}_1 \times \mathcal{X}_2$ be bisimulation relations. Then also $\mathcal{R}_a + \mathcal{R}_b \subset \mathcal{X}_1 \times \mathcal{X}_2$ is a bisimulation relation.*

Proof. Since $\mathcal{R}_a, \mathcal{R}_b$ are bisimulation relations they satisfy properties (12). It follows that also $\mathcal{R}_a + \mathcal{R}_b$ satisfies (12), and thus is a bisimulation relation.

Proposition 4. *Given Σ_1 and Σ_2 and suppose there exists a bisimulation relation between Σ_1 and Σ_2. Then the* maximal *bisimulation relation exists.*

Proof. Suppose there exists a bisimulation relation. Let $\mathcal{R}^{max}$ be a bisimulation relation of *maximal dimension*. Take any other bisimulation relation $\mathcal{R}$. Then $\mathcal{R} \subset \mathcal{R}^{max}$, since otherwise dim $(\mathcal{R} + \mathcal{R}^{max}) >$ dim $\mathcal{R}^{max}$ while also $\mathcal{R} + \mathcal{R}^{max}$ is a bisimulation relation; a contradiction with the maximality of dimension of $\mathcal{R}^{max}$.

The maximal bisimulation relation $\mathcal{R}^{max}$ can be computed in the following way, similarly to the algorithm to compute the maximal controlled invariant subspace [19]. For notational convenience define

$$A^\times := \begin{bmatrix} A_1 & 0 \\ 0 & A_2 \end{bmatrix}, \quad G_1^\times := \begin{bmatrix} G_1 \\ 0 \end{bmatrix}, \quad G_2^\times := \begin{bmatrix} 0 \\ G_2 \end{bmatrix}, \quad C^\times := \begin{bmatrix} C_1 \vdots -C_2 \end{bmatrix} \quad (16)$$

Algorithm 2. *Given two dynamical systems Σ_1 and Σ_2. Define the following sequence $\mathcal{R}^j, j = 0, 1, 2, \cdots$ of linear subspaces of $\mathcal{X}_1 \times \mathcal{X}_2$*

$$\mathcal{R}^0 = \mathcal{X}_1 \times \mathcal{X}_2$$

$$\mathcal{R}^1 = \{z \in \mathcal{R}^0 \mid z \in \ker C^\times\}$$

$$\mathcal{R}^2 = \{z \in \mathcal{R}^1 \mid A^\times z + \operatorname{im} G_1^\times \subset \mathcal{R}^1 + \operatorname{im} G_2^\times, A^\times z + \operatorname{im} G_2^\times \subset \mathcal{R}^1 + \operatorname{im} G_1^\times\}$$

$$\vdots$$

$$\mathcal{R}^{j+1} = \{z \in \mathcal{R}^j \mid A^\times z + \operatorname{im} G_1^\times \subset \mathcal{R}^j + \operatorname{im} G_2^\times, A^\times z + \operatorname{im} G_2^\times \subset \mathcal{R}^j + \operatorname{im} G_1^\times\}$$
$$(17)$$

Assumption 3 *Assume that the subspaces $\mathcal{R}^j$ in (17) are non-empty.*

Theorem 4. *Let Assumption 3 be satisfied. The sequence of subspaces $\mathcal{R}^j$ satisfies the following properties.*

1. *$\mathcal{R}^0 \supset \mathcal{R}^1 \supset \mathcal{R}^2 \cdots \supset \mathcal{R}^j \supset \mathcal{R}^{j+1} \supset \cdots$*
2. *There exists a finite k such that $\mathcal{R}^k = \mathcal{R}^{k+1} =: \mathcal{R}^*$ and then $\mathcal{R}^j = \mathcal{R}^*$ for all $j \geq k$.*
3. *$\mathcal{R}^*$ is the maximal subspace of $\mathcal{X}_1 \times \mathcal{X}_2$ satisfying properties (12a,b,d) of Proposition 1.*

The proof is very similar to the proof of the corresponding properties of the algorithm for computing the maximal controlled invariant subspace [19], and is given in [15].

If $\mathcal{R}^*$ as obtained from Algorithm 2 satisfies property (12c), then it follows that $\mathcal{R}^*$ equals the *maximal bisimulation relation* $\mathcal{R}^{max}$ between Σ_1 and Σ_2, while if $\mathcal{R}^*$ does *not* satisfy property (12c) then there does *not* exist any bisimulation relation between Σ_1 and Σ_2. With regard to bisimilarity (Definition 2), we have the following immediate consequence.

Corollary 1. *Σ_1 and Σ_2 are bisimilar if and only if Assumption 3 is satisfied and $\mathcal{R}^*$ satisfies Property (12c) and Equation (5).*

In the rest of this section we study the question how to *reduce* a linear dynamical system to a system with *lower state space dimension*, which is *bisimilar* to the original system, and in particular how to reduce the system to a bisimilar system with *minimal* state space dimension. This is achieved by considering bisimulation relations between the system and *a copy of itself*. Furthermore, the reduction to a bisimilar system with minimal state space dimension can be performed by using the same algorithm as given in the previous section for computing the maximal bisimulation relation. Actually, this idea is well-known in the context of concurrent processes, see e.g. [5]. Consider a linear dynamical system as in (1)

$$\Sigma: \quad \begin{aligned} \dot{x} &= Ax + Bu + Gd, \quad x \in \mathcal{X}, u \in \mathcal{U}, d \in \mathcal{D} \\ y &= Cx, \qquad\qquad\quad y \in \mathcal{Y} \end{aligned} \tag{18}$$

with $\mathcal{X}, \mathcal{U}, \mathcal{Y}$ and $\mathcal{D}$ finite-dimensional linear spaces. Now consider a bisimulation relation between Σ and itself, that is, in view of Theorem 1, subspaces $\mathcal{R} \subset \mathcal{X} \times \mathcal{X}$ satisfying

$$(a) \ \mathcal{R} + \mathrm{im} \begin{bmatrix} G \\ 0 \end{bmatrix} = \mathcal{R} + \mathrm{im} \begin{bmatrix} 0 \\ G \end{bmatrix} =: \mathcal{R}_e$$

$$(b) \ \begin{bmatrix} A & 0 \\ 0 & A \end{bmatrix} \mathcal{R} \subset \mathcal{R}_e$$

$$(c) \ \mathrm{im} \begin{bmatrix} B \\ B \end{bmatrix} \subset \mathcal{R}_e \tag{19}$$

$$(d) \ \mathcal{R} \subset \ker \begin{bmatrix} C \vdots - C \end{bmatrix}$$

Every $\mathcal{R} \subset \mathcal{X} \times \mathcal{X}$ defines a *relation* on $\mathcal{X}$ by saying that $x_a, x_b \in \mathcal{X}$ are related by $\mathcal{R}$ if and only if $(x_a, x_b) \in \mathcal{R}$. For reduction we should restrict attention to $\mathcal{R} \subset \mathcal{X} \times \mathcal{X}$ such that the corresponding relation on $\mathcal{X}$ is an *equivalence* relation, i.e., $\mathcal{R}$ is reflexive ($(x, x) \in \mathcal{R}$ for all $x \in \mathcal{X}$), symmetric ($(x_a, x_b) \in \mathcal{R} \iff (x_b, x_a) \in \mathcal{R}$), and transitive ($(x_a, x_b) \in \mathcal{R}, (x_b, x_c) \in \mathcal{R} \Rightarrow (x_a, x_c) \in \mathcal{R}$). This can be done without loss of generality. Indeed, by Proposition 3 we may always add to any bisimulation relation $\mathcal{R}$ the identity bisimulation relation $\mathcal{R}_{id} := \{(x, x) \mid x \in \mathcal{X}\}$, thus enforcing reflexivity. Furthermore, let $\mathcal{R}$ satisfy (19), then also the inverse relation $\mathcal{R}^{-1} := \{(x_a, x_b) \mid (x_b, x_a) \in \mathcal{R}\}$ satisfies

(19), implying that the symmetric closure $\mathcal{R} + \mathcal{R}^{-1}$ satisfies (19). Finally, for *linear* relations reflexivity and symmetry already *implies* transitivity: if $(x_a, x_b), (x_b, x_c) \in \mathcal{R}$, then $(x_a - x_c, 0) = (x_a, x_b) - (x_c, x_b) \in \mathcal{R}$, and thus $(x_a, x_c) = (x_a - x_c, 0) + (x_c, x_c) \in \mathcal{R}$. Any equivalence relation $\mathcal{R} \subset \mathcal{X} \times \mathcal{X}$ can be uniquely associated with a linear subspace $\bar{\mathcal{R}} \subset \mathcal{X}$ as follows:

$$\bar{\mathcal{R}} := \{x_a - x_b \mid (x_a, x_b) \in \mathcal{R}\} \tag{20}$$

Indeed, $\bar{\mathcal{R}}$ defined by (20) is a *linear space* if and only if $\mathcal{R}$ is reflexive and symmetric (and therefore an equivalence relation). In terms of $\bar{\mathcal{R}}$ conditions (19) reduce as follows.

Theorem 5. *Let $\mathcal{R} \subset \mathcal{X} \times \mathcal{X}$ be an equivalence relation, and define $\bar{\mathcal{R}} \subset \mathcal{X}$ as in (19). Conditions (19a,b,c,d) for $\mathcal{R}$ are equivalent to*

$$A\bar{\mathcal{R}} \subset \bar{\mathcal{R}} + \operatorname{im} G$$
$$\tag{21}$$
$$\bar{\mathcal{R}} \subset \ker C$$

Proof. It is readily seen that (19b,d) are equivalent to (21). Satisfaction of (19a,c) follows from reflexivity of $\mathcal{R}$.

A subspace $\bar{\mathcal{R}}$ satisfying the first line of (21) is called in geometric control theory a *controlled invariant subspace* , cf.[2,19]. Thus there is a one-to-one correspondence between *bisimulation equivalence relations* $\mathcal{R}$ and *controlled invariant subspaces* $\bar{\mathcal{R}}$ which are contained in $\ker C$.

The *maximal* bisimulation $\mathcal{R}^{max} = \mathcal{R}^*$ between Σ and itself always exists, since it contains $\mathcal{R}_{id}$. Hence $\mathcal{R}^*$ is reflexive, while by symmetry of the data it follows that the symmetric closure of $\mathcal{R}^*$ (adjoining (x_b, x_a) if $(x_a, x_b) \in \mathcal{R}^*$) also satisfies (19a,b,d), and hence $\mathcal{R}^*$ is symmetric. Thus the maximal bisimulation relation $\mathcal{R}^*$ is an equivalence relation. The corresponding subspace $\bar{\mathcal{R}}^* \subset \mathcal{X}$ is precisely the *maximal* controlled invariant subspace contained in $\ker C$, and can be computed in this way, cf. [19,2].

It is now clear how to reduce Σ to a lower-dimensional system that is bisimilar to Σ. Let R be a bisimulation equivalence relation. Define the reduced state space

$$\mathcal{X}_\mathcal{R} := \mathcal{X}/\bar{\mathcal{R}} \tag{22}$$

with canonical projection $\Pi_\mathcal{R} : \mathcal{X} \to \mathcal{X}/\bar{\mathcal{R}}$. By the first line of (21) there exists a "feedback" map K such that

$$(A + GK)\bar{\mathcal{R}} \subset \bar{\mathcal{R}} \tag{23}$$

and thus $A + GK$ projects to a linear map $A_\mathcal{R} : \mathcal{X}_\mathcal{R} \to \mathcal{X}_\mathcal{R}$ satisfying $A_\mathcal{R}\Pi_\mathcal{R} = \Pi_\mathcal{R}(A + GK)$. Furthermore, define $G_\mathcal{R} := \Pi_\mathcal{R}G$, $B_\mathcal{R} := \Pi_\mathcal{R}B$, and by the second line of (21) we may define $C_R : \mathcal{X}_\mathcal{R} \to \mathcal{Y}$ such that $C_R\Pi_\mathcal{R} = C$. Together this defines a reduced system

$$\Sigma_\mathcal{R} : \quad \begin{aligned} \dot{x}_\mathcal{R} &= A_\mathcal{R}x_\mathcal{R} + B_\mathcal{R}u + G_\mathcal{R}d \\ y &= C_\mathcal{R}x_\mathcal{R} \end{aligned} \tag{24}$$

Proposition 5. *(See [15] for the proof.) Let $\mathcal{R}$ be a bisimulation equivalence relation between Σ and itself, and construct $\Sigma_{\mathcal{R}}$ as above. Then $\Sigma_{\mathcal{R}}$ is bisimilar to Σ. Furthermore, let $\mathcal{R}^*$ denote the maximal bisimulation relation between Σ and itself. Then $\Sigma_{\mathcal{R}^*}$ is the smallest system that is bisimilar by reduction to Σ.*

4   Structural Bisimulation of Hybrid Systems with Continuous Input-Output Behavior

Aim of this section is to characterize bisimulation for hybrid systems with discrete *and* continuous external variables. The discrete external variables are the actions corresponding to the discrete transitions, while the continuous external variables are the continuous inputs and outputs as before. The bisimulation relation should thus respect the *total* external behavior of the hybrid system, that is, with respect to the actions, *as well as* with respect to the continuous external variables. The inclusion of continuous external variables makes the setting different from previous notions of bisimulation of hybrid systems, which only involve the *discrete* external behavior, see e.g. [4,1,6,7,18].

We start from the definition of a hybrid automaton with continuous external variables as given in [16].

Definition 3 (Hybrid automaton). *A hybrid automaton is described by a six-tuple $\Sigma^{hyb} := (\mathcal{L}, \mathcal{X}, \mathcal{A}, \mathcal{W}, E, F)$, where the symbols have the following meanings.*

- *$\mathcal{L}$ is a finite set, called the set of discrete states or locations.*
- *$\mathcal{X}$ is a finite-dimensional manifold called the continuous state space.*
- *$\mathcal{A}$ is a finite set of symbols called the set of discrete communication variables, or actions.*
- *$\mathcal{W}$ is a finite-dimensional linear space called the space of continuous communication variables. In the sequel the vector $w \in \mathcal{W}$ will be often partitioned into an input vector u and an output vector y.*
- *E is a subset of $\mathcal{L} \times \mathcal{L} \times \mathcal{A} \times \mathcal{X} \times \mathcal{X}$; a typical element of this set is denoted by (l^-, l^+, a, x^-, x^+).*
- *F is a subset $\mathcal{L} \times T\mathcal{X} \times \mathcal{W}$, where $T\mathcal{X}$ denotes the tangent bundle of $\mathcal{X}$; a typical element of this set is denoted by $(l, x, \dot{x}, w)$.*

A hybrid trajectory or *run* of the hybrid system Σ^{hyb} on the time-interval $[0, T]$ consists of the following ingredients. First such a trajectory involves a discrete set $\mathcal{E} \subset [0, T]$ denoting the *event times* $t \in [0, T]$ associated with the trajectory. Secondly, there is a function $l : [0, T] \to \mathcal{L}$ which is constant on every subinterval between subsequent event times $t_a, t_b \in \mathcal{E}$, and which specifies the location of the hybrid system for $t \in (t_a, t_b)$. Thirdly, the trajectory involves admissible time-functions $x : [0, T] \to \mathcal{X}$, $w : [0, T] \to \mathcal{W}$, satisfying for all $t \notin \mathcal{E}$ the dynamics

$$(l, x(t), \dot{x}(t), w(t)) \in F \qquad (25)$$

with l the location between subsequent event times $t_a, t_b \in \mathcal{E}$. Finally, the trajectory includes a discrete function $a : \mathcal{E} \to \mathcal{A}$ such that for all $t \in \mathcal{E}$

$$(l(t^-), l(t^+), a(t), x(t^-), x(t^+)) \in E \qquad (26)$$

Here, of course, $x(t^-)$ and $x(t^+)$ denote the limit values of the variables x when approaching t from the left, respectively from the right, and the same for $l(t^-)$ and $l(t^+)$. (Hence we throughout assume that the class of admissible functions x is chosen in such a way that these left and right limits are defined.) Thus a hybrid run is specified by a five-tuple

$$r = (\mathcal{E}, l, x, a, w) \qquad (27)$$

Note that the subset F (the *flow* conditions) specifies the continuous dynamics of the hybrid system depending on the location the system is in, and this continuous dynamics remains the same between subsequent event times. On the other hand, E (the *event* conditions) stands for the event behavior at the event times, entailing the discrete state variables $l \in \mathcal{L}$ and the discrete communication variables $a \in \mathcal{A}$, together with a reset of the continuous state variables x. In [16] it is discussed how the flow conditions F incorporate the notion of *location invariant*, while the event conditions E include the notion of *guard*.

Remark 5. Much more can be said about the possible semantics of the hybrid automaton defined above. In particular, additional requirements can be imposed on the set $\mathcal{E} \subset [0, T]$ of event times, while on the other hand the notion of a trajectory can be further generalized by allowing for *multiple events* at the same event time. For a discussion of these issues we refer to [16].

In terms of the hybrid runs a natural definition of hybrid bisimulation is given as follows:

Definition 4 (Hybrid bisimulation relation). *Consider two hybrid automata $\Sigma_i^{hyb} = (\mathcal{L}_i, \mathcal{X}_i, \mathcal{A}_i, \mathcal{W}_i, E_i, F_i), i = 1, 2$, as above. A hybrid bisimulation between Σ_1^{hyb} and Σ_2^{hyb} is a subset*

$$\mathcal{R} \subset (\mathcal{L}_1 \times \mathcal{X}_1) \times (\mathcal{L}_2 \times \mathcal{X}_2)$$

with the following property. Take any $(l_{10}, x_{10}, l_{20}, x_{20}) \in \mathcal{R}$. Then for every hybrid run $r_1 = (\mathcal{E}_1, l_1, x_1, a_1, w_1)$ of Σ_1^{hyb} with $(l_1(0), x_1(0)) = (l_{10}, x_{10})$ there should exist a hybrid run $r_2 = (\mathcal{E}_2, l_2, x_2, a_2, w_2)$ of Σ_1^{hyb} with $(l_2(0), x_2(0)) = (l_{20}, x_{20})$ such that for all times t for which the hybrid run r_1 is defined

- $\mathcal{E}_1 = \mathcal{E}_2 =: \mathcal{E}$

- $w_1(t) = w_2(t)$ *for all $t \geq 0$ with $t \notin \mathcal{E}$*

- $a_1(t) = a_2(t)$ *for all $t \geq 0$ with $t \in \mathcal{E}$*

- $(l_1(t), x_1(t), l_2(t), x_2(t)) \in \mathcal{R}$ *for all $t \geq 0$ with $t \notin \mathcal{E}$,*

and conversely for every hybrid run r_2 of Σ_2^{hyb} there should exist a hybrid run r_1 of Σ_1^{hyb} with the same properties.

A more checkable version of hybrid bisimulation is obtained by merging the previous type of algebraic characterization of bisimulation relations for dynamical systems with the common notion of bisimulation for concurrent processes. Hereto we throughout assume that the continuous state space parts of the bisimulation relation $\mathcal{R}$, namely all sets

$$\mathcal{R}_{l_1 l_2} := \{(x_1, x_2) \mid (l_1, x_1, l_2, x_2) \in \mathcal{R}\} \subset \mathcal{X}_1 \times \mathcal{X}_2 \tag{28}$$

are submanifolds.

Definition 5 (Structural hybrid bisimulation relation). *Consider two hybrid automata* $\Sigma_i^{hyb} = (\mathcal{L}_i, \mathcal{X}_i, \mathcal{A}_i, \mathcal{W}_i, E_i, F_i), i = 1, 2$, *as above. A structural hybrid bisimulation relation between* Σ_1^{hyb} *and* Σ_2^{hyb} *is a subset*

$$\mathcal{R} \subset (\mathcal{L}_1 \times \mathcal{X}_1) \times (\mathcal{L}_2 \times \mathcal{X}_2)$$

such that all sets $\mathcal{R}_{l_1 l_2}$ *are submanifolds and have the following property. Take any* $(l_1^-, x_1^-, l_2^-, x_2^-) \in \mathcal{R}$. *Then for every* l_1^+, x_1^+, a *for which*

$$(l_1^-, l_1^+, a, x_1^-, x_1^+) \in E_1,$$

there should exist l_2^+, x_2^+ *such that*

$$(l_2^-, l_2^+, a, x_2^-, x_2^+) \in E_2$$

while $(l_1^+, x_1^+, l_2^+, x_2^+) \in \mathcal{R}$, *and conversely.*
Furthermore, take any $(l_1, x_1, l_2, x_2) \in \mathcal{R}$. *Then for every* $\dot{x}_1, w$ *for which*

$$(l_1, x_1, \dot{x}_1, w) \in F_1$$

there should exist $\dot{x}_2$ *such that*

$$(l_2, x_2, \dot{x}_2, w) \in F_2$$

while $(\dot{x}_1, \dot{x}_2) \in T_{(x_1, x_2)} \mathcal{R}_{l_1 l_2}$, *and conversely.*

It is easily seen that any structural hybrid bisimulation relation is a hybrid bisimulation relation in the sense of Definition 4. The basic observation is that the infinitesimal invariance condition $(\dot{x}_1(t), \dot{x}_2(t)) \in T_{(x_1, x_2)} \mathcal{R}_{l_1 l_2}$ implies that the trajectory $(l_1, l_2, x_1(t), x_2(t))$ remains in $\mathcal{R}$.

Definition 5 provides a checkable condition for bisimulation once we have derived algebraic conditions for $\mathcal{R}$ being a structural hybrid bisimulation relation. In particular, let $\mathcal{X}_1, \mathcal{X}_2$ be *linear* spaces with *linear* subspaces $\mathcal{R}_{l_1 l_2} \subset \mathcal{X}_1 \times \mathcal{X}_2$, while the flow conditions F assign to every $l \in \mathcal{L}$ a linear non-deterministic input-state-output system

$$\dot{x} = A^l x + B^l u + G^l d, x \in \mathcal{X}, u \in \mathcal{U}, d \in \mathcal{D}$$

$$y = C^l x, \qquad y \in \mathcal{Y} \tag{29}$$

with $w = (u, y) \in \mathcal{W} := \mathcal{U} \times \mathcal{Y}$ and d as before a disturbance generator. Then we may use Theorem 1 to characterize the continuous part of the bisimulation.

For the important special case of *switching linear systems*, where the discrete dynamics is independent of the continuous dynamics (no invariants nor guards, reset map is the identity map) and all discrete transitions have the same action label, this has been worked out in [14]. This paper also shows how to compute in this case the *maximal bisimulation relation*, based on Algorithm 2 and the underlying discrete dynamics.

5   Conclusions and Outlook

We have studied a notion of bisimulation for continuous dynamical systems, motivated by the theory of bisimulation for concurrent processes and by previously obtained results on abstraction by Pappas and co-authors. The notion of bisimulation appears to be a notion which *unifies* the concepts of state space equivalence and state space reduction, and which allows to study equivalence of systems with non-minimal state space dimension, cf. [15].

Compared with classical systems theory a new twist to the problem is given by the idea of considering *non-deterministic* continuous dynamical systems. For concurrent discrete processes the advantages of allowing non-determinism are clear [8,5]. Apart from abstraction we believe that there are other good reasons to allow some type of "non-determinism" in continuous dynamical systems. Indeed, it would be interesting to investigate if uncertainty and robustness issues can be fruitfully cast in this framework.

We have provided a notion of *structural hybrid bisimulation* for hybrid systems. Main difference with existing notions is that we consider hybrid systems which interact with the environment not only via their discrete actions but also via their continuous (input-output) behavior. Next step is to give an algorithm for computing the maximal structural hybrid bisimulation relation, extending the results obtained in [14] for switching linear systems without invariants and guards. Secondly, it is important to relate the proposed notion of structural hybrid bisimulation with previously proposed notions of bisimulation for hybrid systems without (or with 'abstracted') continuous external behavior, see e.g. [4, 1,6,7,18,11,3].

Acknowledgements. Initial discussions with George Pappas and Paulo Tabuada (University of Pennsylvania) and ongoing conversations with Jan Willem Polderman, Rom Langerak, Agung Julius and Stefan Strubbe (all University of Twente) are gratefully acknowledged.

References

1. R. Alur, T.A. Henzinger, G. Lafferriere, G.J. Pappas, Discrete abstractions of hybrid systems, *Proceedings of the IEEE, vol. 88*, pp. 971–984, 2000.

2. G. Basile, G. Marro, *Controlled and conditioned invariants in linear system theory*, Prentice Hall, Englewood Cliffs, 1992.

3. E. Haghverdi, P. Tabuada, G.J. Pappas, Unifying bisimulation relations for discrete and continuous systems, *Category Theory and Computer Science, Electronic Notes in Theoretical Computer Science*, August 2002.

4. T.A. Henzinger, "Hybrid automata with finite bisimulations", in ICIALP 95: Automata, Languages, and programming, eds. Z. Fulop, F. Gecseg, Lecture Notes in Computer Science 944, pp. 324–335, Springer, New York, 1995

5. H. Hermanns, *Interactive Markov Chains*, Lecture Notes in Computer Science 2428, Springer, 2002.

6. G. Lafferriere, G.J. Pappas, S. Sastry, "Hybrid systems with finite bisimulations", in *Hybrid Systems V*, eds. P. Antsaklis, W. Kohn, M. Lemmon, A. Nerode, S. Sastry, Lecture Notes in Computer Science, Springer, 1998.

7. G. Lafferriere, G.J. Pappas, S. Sastry, "O-minimal hybrid systems", *Math. Contr. Signals, Syst.*, vol. 13, pp. 1-21, 2000.

8. R. Milner, *Communication and Concurrency*, Prentice Hall International Series in Computer Science, 1989.

9. R. Milner, *Communication and Mobile Systems: the π- Calculus*, Cambridge University Press, Cambridge, UK, 1999.

10. G.J. Pappas, G. Lafferriere, S. Sastry, Hierarchically consistent control systems, *IEEE Transactions on Automatic Control, 45(6)*, pp. 1144–1160, 2000.

11. G.J. Pappas, Bisimilar linear systems, *Automatica, 39*, pp. 2035–2047, 2003.

12. G.J. Pappas, S. Simic, Consistent abstractions of affine control systems, *IEEE Transactions on Automatic Control, 47*, pp. 745–756, 2002.

13. D. Park, Concurrency and automata on infinite sequences. In P. Deussen, Editor, *Fifth GI Conference on Theoretical Computer Science*, vol. 104 of *Lecture Notes in Computer Science*, Springer, 1981.

14. G. Pola, A.J. van der Schaft, M.D. Di Benedetto, Bisimulation theory for switching linear systems, in preparation.

15. A.J. van der Schaft, "Equivalence of dynamical systems by bisimulation", Technical Report Department of Applied Mathematics, University of Twente, October 2003, submitted for publication.

16. A.J. van der Schaft, J.M. Schumacher, *An Introduction to Hybrid Dynamical Systems*, Springer Lecture Notes in Control and Information Sciences, Vol.251, Springer-Verlag, London, 2000. Second revised edition to appear in *Communications and Control Engineering Series*, Springer, London, 2004.

17. P. Tabuada, G.J. Pappas, "Bisimilar control affine systems", *Systems and Control Letters*, to appear.

18. P. Tabuada, G.J. Pappas, P. Lima, "Composing abstractions of hybrid systems", in *Hybrid Systems: Computation and Control*, eds. C. Tomlin, M.R. Greenstreet, Lecture Notes in Computer Science, pp. 436–450, Springer, 2002.

19. W.M. Wonham, *Linear multivariable control: a geometric approach*, Springer, New York, Third Edition, 1985.

Control Design for a Hybrid Dynamic System: A NASA Life Support System

Dharmashankar Subramanian, Kartik Ariyur, Nitin Lamba,
Ranjana Deshpande, and Sonja Glavaski

Honeywell Labs
3660 Technology Drive, Minneapolis, MN 55418
dharmashankar.subramanian@honeywell.com

Abstract. We consider the control problem of a Variable Configuration CO_2 Removal system (VCCR), which exhibits a hybrid dynamical character due to the various configurations/modes in which one could operate the system. The VCCR is part of an overall Air Recovery System of an intended human life-support system for space exploration. The objective of the control problem is to track a desired concentration profile of CO_2 in a crew cabin while also ensuring safety in terms of keeping the CO_2 and O_2 concentrations in the crew cabin within permissible bounds. We present a mathematical programming based control synthesis formulation, as well as a simulation-based hybrid feedback controller. We exploit the problem structure and map the hybrid optimization problem onto a continuous nonlinear program with the aid of an appropriate representation of time and set definitions. We also discuss case studies showing the performance of these controllers during off-nominal and failure conditions.

1 Introduction

Hybrid dynamic models describe hierarchical processes, which evolve according to different sets of lower level dynamic components (differential or difference equations) depending on the upper level logical/discrete mode that characterizes the system, at any given point in time. Hybrid systems have many applications and there are many approaches to developing control schemes for them. The goal of this work is to investigate approaches that may be of practical use to a broad class of hybrid problems. The specific application domain for this work is advanced life support systems that are used for manned space exploration missions. In particular, we consider the control problem of a Variable Configuration CO_2 Removal system (VCCR), which exhibits a hybrid dynamical character due the various configurations/modes in which one could operate the system. The VCCR is part of an overall Air Recovery System ([1],[6]), which in turn is part of an intended human life-support system for space exploration.

The paper is organized as follows: Section 2 presents the configuration and hybrid dynamic model of the VCCR system, Sections 3 and 4 present a nonlinear programming approach to control design, and design of a hybrid feedback controller respectively, and Section 5 presents simulation results.

R. Alur and G.J. Pappas (Eds.): HSCC 2004, LNCS 2993, pp. 570–584, 2004.
© Springer-Verlag Berlin Heidelberg 2004

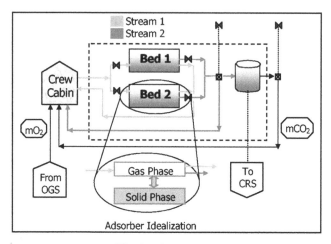

Fig. 1. VCCR Model

2 Variable Configuration Carbon Dioxide Removal

Adsorption is a process that uses adsorbents to remove substances from gaseous/liquid mixtures. In the adsorption step, we have selective mass transfer of the removable substance from the mixture onto the adsorbent. In the desorption step, we recover the removable substance from the adsorbent. The basic functions of the VCCR system include recovery of CO_2 from the crew cabin by adsorption into one of two adsorber beds, which operate in a sequence of 'half-cycles' (defined below). It also includes desorbing the accumulated CO_2 and sending it to a buffer for downstream CO_2 Removal System (CRS).

In this study, we look at a physical idealization of the VCCR system (the configuration of which was obtained from Metrica Traclabs) that consists only of the crew cabin, two adsorber beds, and the CO_2 buffer, without the CRS system. The schematic of this physical system is shown in Figure 1.

The physical configuration of the system is such that when one of the adsorber beds is connected to the crew cabin, and is undergoing CO_2 uptake via adsorption, the other bed is undergoing desorption. In this context, we use the term 'half-cycle' to denote the following definition of synchronized operation of the two beds. During the time interval corresponding to a 'half-cycle', the adsorbing bed returns CO_2-lean air back into the cabin, while the desorbing bed involves two modes of operation in sequence - the Air-Save mode and the CO_2-desorb mode. In Air-save mode, the desorbing bed recycles CO_2-lean air back into the cabin from its gas phase. For the remainder of the 'half-cycle', it operates in the CO_2-desorb mode in which it delivers CO_2 that is released from the solid phase. This CO_2 can either be vented, or be accumulated into the CO_2 buffer. The buffer can be used to supply make-up CO_2 into the cabin, if needed. The adsorber beds have a saturation capacity beyond which they cannot adsorb any more CO_2. As a result, after every half-cycle, the beds change their roles and the adsorbing bed starts desorption while the re-generated bed is connected

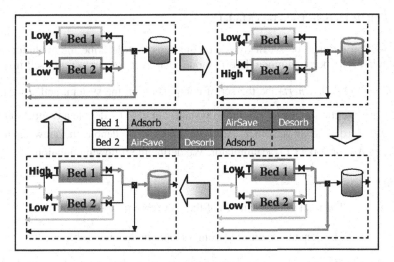

Fig. 2. Hybrid Modes of Operation

to the cabin for adsorption. Lastly, the overall system has an oxygen generation system (OGS), which can send make-up O_2 into the cabin, if required. Therefore, the system is operated in a cyclical pattern of operation. At any given point in time, the system can exist in any of four different hybrid modes (see figure 2):

- *Mode 1*: Bed 1 in Adsorb mode, and Bed 2 in Air-Save mode
- *Mode 2*: Bed 1 in Adsorb mode, and Bed 2 in Desorb mode
- *Mode 3*: Bed 2 in Adsorb mode, and Bed 1 in Air-Save mode
- *Mode 4*: Bed 2 in Adsorb mode, and Bed 1 in Desorb mode

The dynamic equations that describe the state evolution in the adsorber beds, crew cabin, and the CO_2 buffer are different, depending on what mode of operation applies to the system. The decisions that need to be made over any choice of the horizon include (1) the operating modes of the two beds, and the corresponding lengths of the adsorption/desorption 'half-cycles' with the possibility that the 'half-cycle' duration varies from step to step; (2) the fraction of each cycle that the desorbing bed spends in the Air-Save mode (or equivalently, the CO_2 -desorb mode); and (3) the flow rates of each stream in the system.

2.1 Model Assumptions

We assume each adsorber operates at its constant average adsorb/desorb rate. We also assume that only CO_2 is adsorbed/desorbed from the beds (in the appropriate operating modes) and that during Air-save, the solid phase is frozen (i.e. no gas escapes from the adsorber bed). We further assume a cyclical pattern of bed operation i.e. when one bed undergoes CO_2 adsorption, the other necessarily undergoes air-save followed by desorption during that time. Finally, we assume the accumulator to contain only pure CO_2 and define component mass balances for all three components in the VCCR system, namely O_2, CO_2 and inert.

2.2 VCCR Hybrid Dynamic Model

This section defines the set of dynamic equations that describe the evolution of the system in each operating mode (hybrid mode) that the system can find itself in.

Let $C = \{CO_2, O_2, inert\}$ be the set of components in the system, and $J = \{1,2\}$ be the set representing the two beds in the system. Let $c \in C$ denote a component in air and $j \in J$ denote an adsorber. Also, let subscript C denote the crew cabin, and subscript A denote the CO_2 accumulator. We define the following notation:

Cabin

V_C The total volume (in m³) of the crew cabin.

$\rho_C(c)$ The density (in g/m³) of component c in the crew cabin.

$r_C(c)$ The rate of generation (in g/hr) of component c in the crew cabin.

$\dot{m}(c)$ The mass flow (in g/hr) of component c into the cabin, make-up stream.

Note that $r_C(c)$ and $\dot{m}(c)$ are nonzero for O_2 and CO_2 only.

Adsorbers

V_j The total volume (in m³) of adsorber j.

$\rho(c, j)$ The density (in g/m³) of component c in fluid phase of adsorber j.

$Q(c, j)$ The mass (in g) of component c present in solid phase of adsorber j.

$r_{ads}(j,c)$ The rate of adsorption (in g/hr) of component c in adsorber j.

$r_{des}(j,c)$ The rate of desorption (in g/hr) of component c in adsorber j.

Note that $Q(c, j)$, $r_{ads}(j,c)$ and $r_{des}(j,c)$ are nonzero for CO_2 only.

Other

$Q_A(c)$ The mass (in g) of component c present in accumulator.

v_1 (Stream 1)   Volumetric flow rate from the cabin to the bed in Adsorb mode

v_2 (Stream 2)   Volumetric flow rate from the bed in Air-Save or Desorb mode.

For the different modes of operation that are relevant to the system at any given point in time, the dynamic equations for adsorbers and accumulator take the following form.

Modes 1, 3: Adsorber j Is Adsorbing, Adsorber $j' \neq j$ Is in AirSave

In these modes, adsorber j is connected to the cabin and CO_2 from the cabin gets accumulated at the corresponding rate of adsorption. Stream 1 from the adsorber bed into the cabin, is the only outflow from the adsorber bed. There is another inlet flow into the cabin because adsorber j' is sending air back since it is in Air-save mode. Hence, the component mass balance equation of the cabin becomes:

$$V_C \dot{\rho}_C(c) = v_1 \rho(c,j) - v_1 \rho_C(c) + v_2 \rho(c,j') + r_C(c) + \dot{m}(c) \tag{1}$$

The generation rate $r_C(c)$ is positive for CO_2, negative for O_2 and zero for inert.

For adsorber j, the component balance becomes:

$$V_j \dot{\rho}(c,j) = v_1 \rho_C(c) - v_1 \rho(c,j) - r_{ads}(j,c) \tag{2}$$

$$\dot{Q}(c,j) = r_{ads}(j,c) \tag{3}$$

Similarly, the component mass balances for adsorber j' become:

$$V_{j'} \dot{\rho}(c,j') = -v_2 \rho(c,j') \tag{4}$$

$$\dot{Q}(c,j') = 0 \tag{5}$$

Since there is no O_2 and inerts in the accumulator, its mass balance takes the form:

$$\dot{Q}_A(c) = -\dot{m}(c) \tag{6}$$

The negative sign indicates that the CO_2 make-up stream is an outlet from the accumulator and hence reduces the mass inside it.

Modes 2, 4: Adsorber j Is Adsorbing, Adsorber $j' \neq j$ Is Desorbing:

In these modes, Stream 2 does not have any flow into the cabin so v_2 term in (1) disappears and the equation for cabin takes the following form:

$$V_C \dot{\rho}_C(c) = v_1 \rho(c,j) - v_1 \rho_C(c) + r_C(c) + \dot{m}(c) \tag{7}$$

The dynamics of adsorber j remains the same in this mode. However, adsorber j' starts to desorb CO_2 and mass balance becomes:

$$V_{j'} \dot{\rho}(c,j') = -v_2 \rho(c,j') + r_{des}(j,c) \tag{8}$$

$$\dot{Q}(c,j') = -r_{des}(j,c) \quad c \in \{CO_2\} \tag{9}$$

Now that the outlet of adsorber j' is connected to the accumulator, its mass balance modifies to the following:

$$\dot{Q}_A(c) = v_2 \rho(c, j') - \dot{m}(c) \quad c \in \{CO_2\} \tag{10}$$

All permissible combinations of the above sets of dynamic equations (modes) can be taken to fully describe all possible mode-dependent dynamics of the VCCR system. With two adsorber beds, this leads to a total of four possible states that the system can find itself in. As seen from the above descriptions, this overall system provides a fairly complex and rich set of interesting scenarios to model, simulate and control. The control issues include:

- Maintain O_2 concentration in the cabin within specified upper and lower bounds

- Maintain CO_2 concentration in the cabin within specified upper and lower bounds

- Maintain acceptable operations under the following degraded conditions:

  - Bed contamination resulting in decreased bed adsorption/desorption capacity

  - Reduction in adsorption or desorption rates

  - Single side operations

3   A Nonlinear Programming (NLP) Based Control Synthesis

Controller synthesis with mathematical programming is based on the so-called receding horizon philosophy. A sequence of future control actions is chosen according to a model-based prediction of the future evolution of the system, and applied to the plant until new measurements are available. Then, a new sequence is determined which replaces the previous one. Each sequence is evaluated by means of a mathematical programming based optimization formulation whose primary objective is to track a desired state trajectory, also known as the reference trajectory, while ensuring the satisfaction of all stipulated operating constraints. The Mixed Logical Dynamical form was introduced for the control of linear hybrid systems by Bemporad and Morari [3], and is based on well-established mathematical programming notions of transforming propositional logic relations into mixed-integer linear inequalities. Our formulation is closest in spirit to the MLD form, in that it results in a single set of algebraic equations and inequalities. The differences are that we have a nonlinear system, and we introduce a transformation of the hybrid control problem onto a continuous nonlinear program without any discrete variables by exploiting the problem structure and using a judicious modeling of time along with careful set definitions over the time representation. The formulation also presents itself in a very natural format for moving horizon optimal control and model predictive control (MPC) that have been widely adapted for tracking problems of systems subject to constraints (Lee and Cooley [4]).

3.1 Time Representation and Modeling

The cyclical mode of operation is best described by the following schematic:

Bed 1	Adsorb	Adsorb	Air-Save	Desorb
Bed 2	Air-Save	Desorb	Adsorb	Adsorb

The schematic shows an illustration of one full-cycle that the two beds undergo. The time duration corresponding to the Adsorb mode of either bed is split into two contiguous time slots that align with the other bed's Air-Save mode and Desorb mode respectively. The full-cycle can now be interpreted as a sequence of four quarter-cycles. The actual time duration corresponding to each quarter-cycle can be chosen independently, and this could vary across subsequent full-cycles.

Firstly, the time axis is modeled into a specified number of quarter-cycles along with some careful set definitions that exploit the problem structure. Let $I = \{0,1,2,...,M\}$, where M is the number of quarter-cycles under consideration. Without loss of generality, we may assume that Bed 1 starts with two quarter-cycles in the Adsorb mode. Further, consider the following set definitions (for subsets of set I) motivated by the cyclical pattern of operation in the problem structure.

$$B_{A,1} = \{i \mid i \in I \text{ and } ((i = 4p - 3) \text{ or } (i = 4p - 2))\}, \text{where } p \in \left\{1,2,...,\frac{M+3}{4}\right\}$$

This corresponds to quarter-cycles of Bed 1 in the Adsorb mode. Similarly, we judiciously identify the following subsets of set I: Set $B_{A,2}$ that corresponds to quarter-cycles of Bed 2 in the Adsorb mode, Set $B_{AS,1}$ that corresponds to quarter-cycles of Bed 1 in the Air-Save mode, Set $B_{AS,2}$ that corresponds to quarter-cycles of Bed 2 in the Air-Save mode, Set $B_{D,1}$ that corresponds to quarter-cycles of Bed 1 in the Desorb mode, and Set $B_{D,2}$ that corresponds to quarter-cycles of Bed 2 in the Desorb mode. For notational convenience in describing the mathematical program, let the following definitions hold:

$$B_A = \{(i,j) \mid i \in I \text{ and } (j = 1 \text{ and } i \in B_{A,1}) \text{ or } (j = 2 \text{ and } i \in B_{A,2})\}$$

$$B_{AS} = \{(i,j) \mid i \in I \text{ and } (j = 1 \text{ and } i \in B_{AS,1}) \text{ or } (j = 2 \text{ and } i \in B_{AS,2})\}$$

$$B_D = \{(i,j) \mid i \in I \text{ and } (j = 1 \text{ and } i \in B_{D,1}) \text{ or } (j = 2 \text{ and } i \in B_{D,2})\}$$

Lastly, let $K = \{0,1,2,...N_D\}$ be the set representing time points within each quarter-cycle's time duration, for the purposes of discretizing the differential equations. The above representation of time is used in the NLP formulation that is described next. For a given number of full-cycles under consideration, the control inputs to be decided include the following for each quarter cycle: Volumetric flow rate, v_1, Volumetric flow rate, v_2, Time duration of each quarter cycle, Mass flow rate of CO_2 from the accumulator to the cabin, and Mass flow rate of O_2 from the OGS to the cabin.

3.2 NLP Formulation

In this section we describe a nonlinear programming model for controller synthesis based on the above time representation. In the following formulation, the discretized variables are indexed as follows: index c refers to the component, index i refers to the quarter-cycle time slot, index j refers to the bed identity, and index k refers to the discretization point. For (differential) state variables that are only indexed with time index i (without any further discretization point), the time instant corresponds to the end of the quarter-cycle time slot, i. We define only newly appearing symbols below. The remaining symbols correspond to the continuous dynamic model.

$\rho_{end}(c,i,j)$ Fluid phase concentration of component c, in bed, j, at the end of quarter-cycle time slot, i, in grams/m³.

$\rho_{C,end}(c,i)$ Concentration of component c, in the crew cabin, at the end of quarter-cycle time slot, i, in grams/m³.

$T(i)$ Time duration of quarter-cycle time slot, i, in hrs.

$y_C(c,i,k)$ Mass fraction of component c, in the crew cabin, at discretization point k, within quarter-cycle time slot, i.

The set of quarter cycles that correspond to hybrid Modes 1 and 3, (Adsorber j is adsorbing, Adsorber $j' \neq j$ is in Airsave) is given by

$$I_1 = \left\{ i \in I \middle| \exists (i,j,j') \middle| (j \neq j', \& (i,j) \in B_A, \& (i,j') \in B_{AS}) \right\}$$

Similarly, we define set I_2, of quarter cycles that correspond to hybrid Modes 2 and 4, (Adsorber j is adsorbing, Adsorber $j' \neq j$ is in Desorb). It is clear that $I = I_1 \cup I_2$, and $I_1 \cap I_2 = \phi$. These sets allow us to write a monolithic set of discretized algebraic equations to describe the entire hybrid dynamics over the above time representation without involving any discrete variables, as follows:

Dynamics for Modes 1 and 3

The hybrid dynamics of Modes 1 and 3 take the following algebraic discretized form:

$$V_C(\rho_C(c,i,k+1)-\rho_C(c,i,k))=\frac{T(i)}{N_D}\left[\begin{array}{l}v_1(i)(\rho(c,i,j,k)-\rho_C(c,i,k))\\+r_C(c)+v_2(i)\rho(c,i,j',k)+\dot{m}(i,c)\end{array}\right] \quad (11)$$

$$\forall i \in I_1, k < N_D, \; c \in C.$$

$$V_j(\rho(c,i,j,k+1)-\rho(c,i,j,k))=\frac{T(i)}{N_D}\left[\begin{array}{l}v_1(i)(\rho_C(c,i,k)-\rho(c,i,j,k))\\-r_{ads}(j,c)\end{array}\right] \quad (12)$$

$$\forall i \in I_1, k < N_D, \; c \in C, \; \& \; (i,j) \in B_A$$

$$Q(c,i,j)-Q(c,i-1,j)=T(i)r_{ads}(j,c), \quad \forall i \in I_1, \; c \in C, \& \; (i,j) \in B_A \quad (13)$$

$$V_j(\rho(c,i,j,k+1)-\rho(c,i,j,k))=\frac{T(i)}{N_D}\left[-v_2(i)\rho(c,i,j,k)\right] \quad (14)$$

$$\forall i \in I_1, k < N_D, \; c \in C, \& \; (i,j) \in B_{AS}$$

$$Q(c,i,j)-Q(c,i-1,j)=0, \quad \forall i \in I_1, \; c \in C, \& \; (i,j) \in B_{AS} \quad (15)$$

$$Q_A(c,i)-Q_A(c,i-1)=-T(i)\dot{m}(i,c), \; for \; c=CO_2, \forall i \in I_1 | \exists j, s.t. (i,j) \in B_{AS} \quad (16)$$

Dynamics for Modes 2 and 4

Similarly, the hybrid dynamics of Mode 2 take the following form. The dynamics of the adsorbing bed (Equations (11) and (12)) apply for $i \in I_2$, as they stay the same in Modes 1(and 3) and 2 (and 4), and these are not repeated below.

$$Q(c,i,j)-Q(c,i-1,j)=T(i)r_{ads}(j,c), \quad \forall i \in I_2, \; c \in C, \& \; (i,j) \in B_A \quad (17)$$

$$V_j(\rho(c,i,j,k+1)-\rho(c,i,j,k))=\frac{T(i)}{N_D}\left[-v_2(i)\rho(c,i,j,k)+r_{des}(j,c)\right] \quad (18)$$

$$\forall i \in I_2, k < N_D, \; c \in C, \; \& \; (i,j) \in B_D$$

$$Q(c,i,j)-Q(c,i-1,j)=-T(i)r_{des}(j,c), \quad \forall i \in I_2, \; c \in C, \& \; (i,j) \in B_D \quad (19)$$

$$Q_A(c,i) - Q_A(c,i-1) = -T(i)\dot{m}(i,c) + \sum_{k=0}^{N_D-1} \frac{T(i)}{N_D}[v_2(i)\rho(c,i,j,k)],$$

$$for\ c = CO_2, \forall i \in I_2, \&\ (i,j) \in B_D \tag{20}$$

Equations (11) through (20) capture the entire dynamics of the hybrid system in the form of one monolithic equation set involving only continuous variables. As a result, we are able to transform the hybrid optimization problem onto a continuous optimization problem. Further, the mass fraction of every component in the crew cabin is defined with the following constraint:

$$y_C(c,i,k)\sum_{c' \in C} \rho_C(c',i,k) = \rho_C(c,i,k), \forall i > 0, k, c \in C \tag{21}$$

The constraints that model the continuity conditions across the quarter-cycle time slots in the discretized model are as follows:

$$\rho_{C,end}(c,i) = \rho_C(c,i,N_D),\ \forall i > 0, c \in C$$

$$\rho_C(c,i,0) = \rho_{C,end}(c,i-1), \forall i > 0, c \in C$$

$$\rho_{end}(c,i,j) = \rho(c,i,j,N_D), \forall i > 0, c \in C \tag{22}$$

$$\rho(c,i,j,0) = \rho_{end}(c,i-1,j), \forall i > 0, c \in C$$

The objective function for determining the optimal control actions is expressed as a weighted sum of three measures. The first measure pertains to CO_2 concentration control, and is the sum of the squares of the differences between the crew cabin CO_2 mass fraction, and the desired CO_2 mass fraction set point, the difference being summed over the set of discretized time points. Similarly, the second measure pertains to O_2 concentration control. The third measure seeks to maximize the full-cycle times, and is intended to prevent chattering control solutions in which the adsorber beds switch modes too rapidly. $\alpha, \beta,$ and γ are the three weights. The NLP is summarized as follows. $y_C^*(CO_2)$ and $y_C^*(O_2)$ are the desired set points.

$$Minimize\ \alpha\sum_{i=1}^{M}\sum_{k=0}^{N_D-1}\left(y_C(CO_2,i,k) - y_C^*(CO_2)\right)^2$$

$$+ \beta\sum_{i=1}^{M}\sum_{k=0}^{N_D-1}\left(y_C(O_2,i,k) - y_C^*(O_2)\right)^2 - \gamma\sum_{i=1}^{M}T(i) \tag{23}$$

Subject to: Equations (11) to (22), and variable bounds and parameter values. The physical restrictions of the system define system parameters and limits on the control and manipulated variables. Together, they define the feasible space for the controller.

The multi-objective function described above requires tuning of the weights for the three terms. The tuning exercise was carried out in two steps: first, taking into account the typical magnitudes of the contributions of the three terms to the objective, and then, factoring the relative importance of these goals. The CO_2 concentration control was chosen as the most important, and controller chattering was chosen as the least important goal. The performance of the controller with the tuned weights has been studied in a case study with a nominal initial condition of the system. The tuned values of the weights along with model parameters, nominal and off-nominal initial conditions, and numerical details of the case studies that are described below can be found in [2]. The NLP optimization formulation was modeled using GAMS [5] and solved using CONOPT[1]. The formulation had 2014 constraints, 2112 variables, 10055 non-zero elements in the constraint matrix, and a non-linearity complexity score of 8230 (GAMS [5]). The formulation solves in ~3 minutes on a Dell Precision 330 Workstation (1400 MHz, 2 GB RAM).

4   Dynamic Simulator and Hybrid Feedback Controller

This section describes a dynamic simulation platform for the life support system and a simple hybrid feedback controller in regulating the levels of O_2 and CO_2 in the crew cabin under different scenarios. The platform attempts to model comprehensively the various subsystems and their interactions for the purpose of designing and validating feedback controllers. The model considers only mass conservation in the overall system.

All of the governing differential equations, (1) – (10), are of the form – mass accumulation rate in subsystem equals rate of mass input into the subsystem less the rate of mass output and mass consumption in it. The hybrid nature of the system comes in through the fact that the rates of accretion and depletion are different in different discrete states of the subsystems. The physical limits of bed saturation and the physical requirement of non-negative concentrations are incorporated as saturation limits in the integrators in the dynamic simulation model implemented in SIMULINK® and MATLAB®[2]. We simulate a cabin connected to two adsorption beds. In the simulation study of a hybrid feedback controller presented here, we use model parameters and initial conditions corresponding to those used in the NLP-based control design of the previous section.

4.1 Feedback Controller

We have implemented a feedback controller for regulating/stabilizing the levels of O_2 and CO_2 in the cabin to standard atmospheric levels (mass fractions of 23% and 0.76% respectively at atmospheric pressure, under varying operating conditions). The controller is designed to reject disturbances to cabin O_2 and CO_2 concentrations caused

---

[1] CONOPT is a solver for large-scale nonlinear optimization (NLP) developed and maintained by ARKI Consulting & Development A/S in Bagsvaerd, Denmark.

[2] MATLAB® and SIMULINK® are registered trademarks of The MathWorks, Inc.

by variations of crew metabolism in the cabin, and also to be robust to degradation of the adsorbent zeolites in the beds, i.e., reduction in bed capacity.

Sensing

The controller uses the following measurements – the densities ($\rho_C(c)$) in the cabin and bed fluid phase ($\rho(c,j)$) of CO_2, O_2 and inert gases (assumed to be completely nitrogen in our calculations). The level of CO_2 accumulation in the bed solid phase $Q(CO_2,j)$ is also measured. This is justified from the use of gas chromatographs to measure mass fractions in the fluid phase of the cabin and beds. The monitoring of the bed weight can be performed online, and the mass fractions along with knowledge of the volume of cabin and beds will give us the densities.

Actuation and Control Laws

Our control law actuates the compensatory supply of O_2 from the OGS, and compensates for CO_2 level in the cabin through a classical proportional-integral-derivative (PID) control law:

$$\dot{m}(O_2) = \left(k_P + \frac{k_I}{s} + k_D s \right) \left[\rho_C(O_2) - \rho_{C,ref}(O_2) \right]$$

$$\dot{m}(CO_2) = \left(k_P + \frac{k_I}{s} + k_D s \right) \left[\rho_C(CO_2) - \rho_{C,ref}(CO_2) \right],$$

$$(24)$$

where the proportional gain, $k_P = 8$ integral gain, $k_I = 9.0001$, and the derivative gain $k_D = 1$. The integrator states have appropriate lower and upper saturation limits. Integral control is the natural option to track the movement of an unknown variable (slowly varying) with the integrator state and regulate its level. The proportional and derivative actions help to improve disturbance rejection and convergence. We have designed the speeds of the control action such that the control laws are not sensitive to the periodic sudden fluctuations of gas concentrations caused by the beds switching from adsorb to airsave to desorb. The adsorption and desorption volume flow rates (in effect the control of blower speed for adsorption and pump speed for desorption) are controlled by 'proportional' feedback, where $k_P^{ads} = 0.1$, and $k_P^{des} = 5$.

$$\dot{v}_j^{ads} = \max\left\{ 0, \dot{v}_{j,nom}^{ads} + k_P^{ads} \left(\rho_C(CO_2) - \rho_{C,ref}(CO_2) \right) \right\}$$

$$\dot{v}_j^{des} = k_P^{des} \rho(CO_2,j)$$

$$(25)$$

The rationale for the proportional control is to keep the blowing/pumping effort proportional to the quantity of CO_2 in the fluid phase, and thus keep our efforts economical. Finally, the switching of adsorption from one bed to another is governed by:

$$
S_k = \begin{cases}
1 & \text{if } S_{k-1} = 1, \quad Q(CO_2,1) < Q_{\max}(CO_2,1), \quad \text{and } Q(CO_2,2) > 0. \\
2 & \text{if } S_{k-1} = 1, \quad Q(CO_2,1) = Q_{\max}(CO_2,1), \quad \text{or } Q(CO_2,2) = 0. \\
2 & \text{if } S_{k-1} = 2, \quad Q(CO_2,2) < Q_{\max}(CO_2,2), \quad \text{and } Q(CO_2,1) > 0. \\
1 & \text{if } S_{k-1} = 2, \quad Q(CO_2,2) = Q_{\max}(CO_2,2), \quad \text{or } Q(CO_2,1) = 0.
\end{cases} \tag{26}
$$

where $S_k = 1$ implies adsorption into bed 1 and $S_k = 2$ implies adsorption into bed 2. The switching law simply covers all possible cases and ensures that energy is not spent in trying to adsorb more into a saturated bed, or to desorb more CO_2 away from an empty bed. The above simple switching law is adequate for a bed with constant adsorption and desorption rates. When the rates of adsorption and desorption are state-dependent, we will need to use more information in the switching rule.

5 Simulation Study

For the purpose of comparing performance of the feedback controller with the NLP-based controller, simulation results of the controlled system are shown for the case of high initial CO_2 (Figure 3), and for single bed operation (Figure 4). The figures show the time traces of cabin mass fractions of O_2 and CO_2 for a constant crew size. We note here that the traces for the NLP-based controller are much shorter as they are only plotted for a single optimization horizon. In Figure 3, both controllers regulate the cabin CO_2 concentration to standard atmospheric level, while also maintaining the O_2 concentration at atmospheric level. Both controllers are also able to keep the gaseous concentrations within safe operating limits. While the feedback controller produces a slightly oscillatory transient before converging to the set-point, the NLP-based controller has a more monotone behavior though its periodic sampling can result in sharp jumps as seen at the end of the O_2 concentration trace. In Figure 4, where one of the beds has failed, both controllers are able to maintain operation within safe operating limits for some time (3 hours for the NLP-based controller, and 4 hours for the feedback controller within which critical action needs to be taken) before the CO_2 level goes beyond the bounds (dash-dot lines).

In this case, the feedback control actions lead to oscillations in the cabin concentration levels: the CO_2 concentration falls when the good bed is adsorbing and rises when it has to desorb. It should be noted that the greater the number of beds, the closer the operation is to continuous operation (smaller oscillations due to switching). In both cases, the closed loop (with measurement based feedback control inputs) control seeks to maintain the mass fraction of O_2 at around the atmospheric level of 23% and the mass fraction of CO_2 at the atmospheric level of 0.76%. Finally, we note that the success of the hybrid control designs is due in part to the system being over-designed; future work will address control design for a system operating at its limits (resulting in considerable weight-saving for the manned mission).

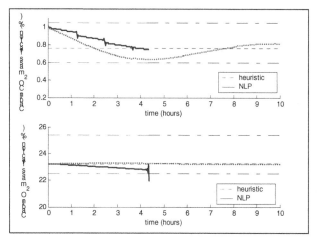

Fig. 3. Variation of Cabin CO_2 and O_2 with Time: High Initial CO_2 Concentration

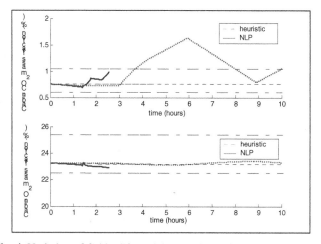

Fig. 4. Variation of Cabin CO_2 and O_2 with Time: Single Bed Operation

6   Conclusions and Future Work

A hybrid dynamic model has been developed to capture the dynamics of the NASA VCCR system. Two methodologies have been applied to design hybrid controllers for the system. First, a receding horizon control strategy has been implemented with three weighted objectives in the form a multi-objective nonlinear program. A careful representation of time, along with appropriate set definitions of time indices, allows us to transform the hybrid optimization problem onto a continuous optimization problem. Second, an online hybrid feedback controller has been designed using classical PID combined with a switching rule. Our case studies for comparing the two strategies include the off-nominal conditions of very high initial cabin carbon dioxide concentration in the cabin, and the failure mode of a single-bed operation. Work on improving the model to incorporate state-dependent adsorption and desorption rates, and development of an analytic framework for proving closed loop stability is in progress. This will give us guarantees of performance over a large set of operating conditions, without the need for extensive simulation studies or experimentation.

Acknowledgements. This research has been funded by NASA Ames Research Center, under Contract # NAS2-01067. We thank Dr. Robert Morris for his support and Metrica Traclabs for providing system physical parameters.

References

1. Finn, C.: "Documentation of the BIO-Plex Baseline Simulation Model", NASA Ames Research Center, January 20, 1999
2. Glavaski, S., Subramanian, D., Ariyur, K., Lamba, N., Deshpande, R.: "Automatically Synthesizing Guaranteed Hybrid Controllers For Adaptive Autonomous Systems (ASHC)", Annual Report submitted to NASA-Ames Research Center under Contract Number NAS2-01067, June 2003
3. Bemporad, A., Morari, M.: "Control of Systems integrating logic, dynamics, and constraints", Automatica, 35, 407-427, 1999.
4. Lee, J. H., Cooley, B.: "Recent Advances in Model Predictive Control", Chemical Process Control – V, AIChe Sympo. Ser. New York, Vol. 93, No. 316, 201-216b, 1997.
5. Brooke, A., Kendrick, D., Meeraus, A.,Raman, R.: GAMS, A User's Guide, GAMS Development Corporation, 1998.
6. Malin, J., Kowing, J., Schreckenghost, D.,Bonasso, P., Nieten, J., Graham, J., Fleming, L., MacMahon, M., Thronesbery, C.: "Multi-Agent Diagnosis and Control of an Air Revitalization System for Life Support in Space", IEEE Aerospace, 2000.

Non-concurrent Error Detection and Correction in Switched Linear Controllers

Shreyas Sundaram and Christoforos N. Hadjicostis

University of Illinois at Urbana-Champaign

Abstract. In this paper, we consider protection schemes for linear time-invariant (LTI) controllers in switched systems. These controllers are often digital in nature and, as such, are subject to internal hardware malfunctions (faults). A discrete-time (DT) LTI system is usually protected against faults by embedding the state-space of the original system into the state-space of a higher dimensional redundant system. These embeddings preserve the state evolution of the original system in some encoded form, but enable error detection and correction through *concurrent* parity checks (i.e., parity checks that are performed at the end of each time step). In this paper, we present a systematic method of constructing linear embeddings for protecting switched DT LTI controllers. These methodologies allow an external mechanism to detect and identify transient state-transition faults through *non-concurrent* (e.g., periodic) parity checks. The resulting error detection and correction procedures can then be performed periodically, thereby relaxing the requirements on the reliability of the checking mechanism.

1 Introduction

The concept of *switching* in the design of control systems has been the subject of recent intensive research, partially due to its applicability to a wide range of problems [1,2,3,4,5]. For instance, when facing modeling uncertainty, switching controllers provide performance that is not obtainable through a single controller (e.g., *nonholonomic systems* cannot be asymptotically stabilized through the use of a continuous feedback law, making switched control an attractive option [5]).

In switched control, one obtains the desired behavior from a plant by using logic-based decisions to dynamically switch between controllers in the control loop. Figure 1 shows the block diagram for a system with switched control. Such schemes have been studied extensively, aiming to ensure that desirable system properties such as stability, reachability and controllability are maintained [6, 7,8,9]. The controllers and control strategies in these systems often arise in an inherently discrete-time setting, as in the case where micro-controllers are used to regulate continuous plants [10].

As systems become more complex, the issue of *fault tolerance* becomes important. For example, it has been demonstrated that harsh conditions, such as lightning and electromagnetic radiation, are a source of upsets in digital flight control systems [11,12]. Recent research has investigated methods of estimating

R. Alur and G.J. Pappas (Eds.): HSCC 2004, LNCS 2993, pp. 585–599, 2004.

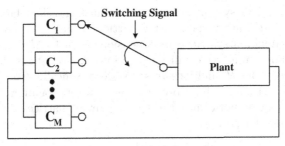

Fig. 1. Switched Control

the state of a system in the presence of intermittent sensor or measurement failures [13,14]. In this paper, we broadly define fault tolerance as the ability of a system to detect and rectify internal faults which cause the system to be in an incorrect state. In particular, we are interested in protecting against internal faults in discrete-time switched control mechanisms. A traditional approach to fault tolerance has been to use *modular redundancy*, i.e., replicate fault-prone components in the system and use a voting scheme to determine the correct state or behavior [15]. In an effort to find more efficient methods for fault tolerance, the use of arithmetic codes [16] and algorithm-based fault tolerance (ABFT) schemes [17] have also been studied extensively in the context of computing systems. In addition, for discrete-time systems, researchers have developed techniques that map the state-space of the system to a higher-dimensional state-space of a redundant system. This mapping is constructed in a way that preserves the state evolution of the original system, but with the added capability to perform error detection and correction. These techniques typically require *concurrent* checks (i.e., checks at the end of each discrete-time step).

A method for performing *non-concurrent* checks (e.g., periodic checks) was presented in [18] for discrete-time linear time-invariant (DT LTI) dynamic systems. Here, we extend the concepts presented in that paper to the realm of switched DT LTI systems. The proposed scheme for protecting switched discrete-time systems allows for periodic checking for errors in the family of controllers, thereby providing increased reliability and requiring relatively low overhead.

This paper is organized as follows. Section 2 provides mathematical background on our systems of interest. Section 3 describes how to design a switched system with non-concurrent fault detection and correction capabilities. We provide an example of our method in Sect. 4 and conclude in Sect. 5 with a summary of our results and directions for future work.

2   Background

Consider a DT LTI system in the form

$$x[k+1] = Ax[k] + Bu[k] \ , \tag{1}$$

where $x[k] \in \mathbb{R}^n$ is the state vector at time step k, $u[k] \in \mathbb{R}^m$ is the input at time step k, and A and B are constant real-valued matrices of appropriate dimensions.

In [19], a DT LTI system is protected against transient faults that corrupt one or more of its state variables at a particular time step t by embedding it into a larger redundant system $\mathcal{H}$ of dimension $\eta = n + d, d > 0$. The embedding is such that under fault-free conditions, all information about the initial system can be retrieved from $\mathcal{H}$, and vice-versa. More specifically, if $x[k]$ represents the state vector in (1), and $x_h[k]$ represents the state vector in $\mathcal{H}$, *linear* decoding and encoding can be performed through a pair of matrices $\mathbf{L}$ and $\mathbf{G}$ that are chosen to satisfy (for all k)

$$x[k] = \mathbf{L}x_h[k] \ , \tag{2}$$
$$x_h[k] = \mathbf{G}x[k] \ , \tag{3}$$

at least under proper initialization and fault-free conditions. In other words, the state evolution of the redundant system $\mathcal{H}$ is captured by

$$x_h[k+1] = \mathcal{A}x_h[k] + \mathcal{B}u[k] \ , \tag{4}$$

where $\mathcal{A}$ and $\mathcal{B}$ are chosen so that (2) and (3) are satisfied.

The above approach was extended in [18] to allow non-concurrent error detection and correction in DT LTI dynamic systems. Assuming (without loss of generality) that the system starts operation at time step 0, this paper presented a method to perform the first error check at some time step N. Specifically, [18] showed that matrices $\mathcal{A}$ and $\mathcal{B}$ in (4) can be chosen so that if a total of D transient faults take place between time steps 0 and $N - 1$, and affect state variables $i_1, i_2, \ldots, i_D$ by initial additive errors of $v_1, v_2, \ldots, v_D$ respectively, an error check that depends only on the corrupted state at time step N is sufficient to determine which states were corrupted, and to obtain the time step and error value by which they were affected.

This work is further extended in this paper to protect switched DT LTI systems.

3   Application to Switched Systems

3.1   Notation and Preliminaries

Consider a DT LTI switched system $\mathcal{S}$ in the form

$$x[k+1] = \mathbf{A}_{\sigma[k]}x[k] + \mathbf{B}_{\sigma[k]}u[k] \ , \tag{5}$$

where $\sigma[k] \in \Omega = \{1, 2, \ldots, M\}$ represents the switching path among the M systems, $x[k] \in \mathbb{R}^n$ is the state vector at time step k, and $u[k] \in \mathbb{R}^m$ is the input at time step k. At any given time step k, the $(\mathbf{A}_{\sigma[k]}, \mathbf{B}_{\sigma[k]})$ matrices are taken to be constant real-valued matrices of appropriate dimensions.

If the system is allowed to run for N time steps, the state at the end of time step $N - 1$ (beginning of time step N) is easily calculated to be

$$x[N] = \left(\prod_{i=0}^{N-1} \mathbf{A}_{\sigma[i]} \right) x[0] + \left(\prod_{i=1}^{N-1} \mathbf{A}_{\sigma[i]} \right) \mathbf{B}_{\sigma[0]}u[0] + \cdots$$
$$\cdots + \mathbf{A}_{\sigma[N-1]}\mathbf{B}_{\sigma[N-2]}u[N-2] + \mathbf{B}_{\sigma[N-1]}u[N-1] \ . \tag{6}$$

3.2   Embeddings of Switched Systems

We start with the switched system $\mathcal{S}$ in (5). To protect against transient state-transition faults, we will map the n-dimensional state-space of $\mathcal{S}$ into a larger state-space of dimension $\eta = n + d, d > 0$. This system, denoted by $\mathcal{H}$, will be given by

$$x_h[k + 1] = \mathcal{A}_{\sigma[k]} x_h[k] + \mathcal{B}_{\sigma[k]} u[k], \quad \sigma[k] \in \Omega = \{1, 2, \ldots, M\} , \tag{7}$$

where the initial state $x_h[0]$, and all $\eta \times \eta$ transition matrices $\mathcal{A}_{\sigma[k]}$ and $\eta \times m$ input matrices $\mathcal{B}_{\sigma[k]}$ will be chosen such that, under fault-free conditions, $\mathcal{H}$ provides complete information about the original system $\mathcal{S}$, and vice-versa. As in the single system case described in the previous section, we restrict ourselves to linear encoding and decoding mappings, i.e., we require that there exist matrices $\mathbf{L}$ and $\mathbf{G}$ such that, when $x_h[0] = \mathbf{G}x[0]$ and under fault-free conditions, we have $x[k] = \mathbf{L}x_h[k]$ and $x_h[k] = \mathbf{G}x[k]$ for all k. Faults that cause the state $x_h[k]$ to lie outside the column space of $\mathbf{G}$ can be detected through the use of a *parity check* of the form $\mathbf{s}[k] \equiv \mathbf{P}x_h[k]$, where $\mathbf{P}$ is an appropriate parity check matrix of dimension $d \times \eta$. More specifically, by selecting $\mathbf{P}$ to be full row-rank and satisfy $\mathbf{PG} = 0$, we can check for errors in $x_h[k]$ by performing the calculation $\mathbf{P}x_h[k]$ and ensuring that it is identically zero.

Theorem 1. *In the setting described above, the switched system $\mathcal{H}$ in (7) is a redundant implementation for the switched system $\mathcal{S}$ in (5) (i.e., it satisfies (2) and (3) for all time steps k) if and only if there exists an $\eta \times \eta$ transformation matrix $\mathcal{T}$ and a standard redundant switched system $\mathcal{H}_r$ with state evolution given by*

$$x_r[k + 1] = \mathcal{A}_{r_{\sigma[k]}} x_r[k] + \mathcal{B}_{r_{\sigma[k]}} u[k], \quad \sigma[k] \in \Omega = \{1, 2, \ldots, M\} , \tag{8}$$

where

$$\mathcal{T}^{-1} \mathcal{A}_{\sigma[k]} \mathcal{T} = \begin{bmatrix} \mathbf{A}_{\sigma[k]} & \mathbf{A}_{12_{\sigma[k]}} \\ 0 & \mathbf{A}_{22_{\sigma[k]}} \end{bmatrix} \equiv \mathcal{A}_{r_{\sigma[k]}} , \tag{9}$$

$$\mathcal{T}^{-1} \mathcal{B}_{\sigma[k]} = \begin{bmatrix} \mathbf{B}_{\sigma[k]} \\ 0 \end{bmatrix} \equiv \mathcal{B}_{r_{\sigma[k]}} , \tag{10}$$

$$\mathbf{L}\mathcal{T} = \begin{bmatrix} \mathbf{I}_n & 0 \end{bmatrix} \equiv \mathbf{L}_r , \tag{11}$$

$$\mathcal{T}^{-1} \mathbf{G} = \begin{bmatrix} \mathbf{I}_n \\ 0 \end{bmatrix} \equiv \mathbf{G}_r , \tag{12}$$

$$\mathbf{P}\mathcal{T} = \begin{bmatrix} 0 & \mathbf{I}_d \end{bmatrix} \equiv \mathbf{P}_r . \tag{13}$$

In the above theorem, $\mathbf{A}_{\sigma[k]}$ and $\mathbf{B}_{\sigma[k]}$ are the matrices from the original system $\mathcal{S}$, and $\mathcal{A}_{\sigma[k]}$ and $\mathcal{B}_{\sigma[k]}$ are the matrices from the redundant implementation $\mathcal{H}$. The $d \times d$ matrices $\mathbf{A}_{22_{\sigma[k]}}$ describe the added redundant dynamics associated with the system that is active at time step k. The $n \times d$ matrices $\mathbf{A}_{12_{\sigma[k]}}$

describe the coupling between the redundant and original states at time step k. Associated with this standard redundant system $\mathcal{H}_r$, we have the decoding, encoding and parity check matrices given by $\mathbf{L}_r$, $\mathbf{G}_r$ and $\mathbf{P}_r$ respectively.

The proof of Theorem 1 is similar to the proof for the single system case given in [19], and is omitted here. Note that we are completely free to choose matrices $\mathbf{A}_{12_{\sigma[k]}}$ and $\mathbf{A}_{22_{\sigma[k]}}$; thus, there are many redundant implementations of $\mathcal{S}$ for a given $\mathbf{L}$ and $\mathbf{G}$. Later in this paper, we will discuss how to choose $\mathbf{A}_{22_{\sigma[k]}}$ to allow non-concurrent error detection and correction.

3.3 Transient State-Transition Faults and Error Propagation

As mentioned earlier, our goal is to design a redundant switched system $\mathcal{H}$ so that we can protect the original switched system $\mathcal{S}$ against transient state-transition faults. For now, we assume that a transient fault during the calculation of the next state at time step $k - 1$ causes an error in exactly one of the state variables in the next state vector. It will become clear from our discussion that this assumption can be relaxed, but we adopt it now for pedagogical purposes.

Assume (without loss of generality) that our system begins operation with $x_h[0] = \mathbf{G}x[0]$ and that the first non-concurrent check is performed at the end of time step $N - 1$ (i.e., at the beginning of time step N). If a single error occurs in our system at time step $k = N - t - 1$, $0 \le t \le N - 1$, and affects the ith state variable by an additive error value v, the erroneous state vector at the beginning of time step $k = N - t$ will be given by

$$x_f[N - t] = x_h[N - t] + ve_i , \tag{14}$$

where $x_h[N - t]$ is the state that $\mathcal{H}$ would be in at the beginning of time step $N - t$ under fault-free conditions, and e_i is an η-dimensional vector with a "1" as its ith entry and "0" everywhere else. Note that through an appropriate choice of v and e_i, this additive error model can be used to handle any fault that corrupts a single state variable.

If we were to perform a (concurrent) parity check at the end of time step $N - t - 1$ (beginning of time step $N - t$), we would get the syndrome

$$\mathbf{s}[N - t] \equiv \mathbf{P}x_f[N - t] = \mathbf{P}ve_i = v\mathbf{P}(:, i) ,$$

where $\mathbf{P}(:, i)$ denotes the ith column of the parity check matrix $\mathbf{P}$. In the above expansion, we have used the fact that $\mathbf{P}x_h[k] = \mathbf{P}\mathbf{G}x[k] = 0$ for all k. Assuming that no further errors occur in the interval $[N - t, N - 1]$, we can use (6) to obtain the erroneous state of system $\mathcal{H}$ at the end of time step $N - 1$:

$$x_f[N] = \left(\prod_{i=N-t}^{N-1} \mathcal{A}_{\sigma[i]} \right) x_f[N - t] + \left(\prod_{i=N-t+1}^{N-1} \mathcal{A}_{\sigma[i]} \right) \mathcal{B}_{\sigma[N-t]}u[N - t] + \cdots$$
$$\cdots + \mathcal{A}_{\sigma[N-1]}\mathcal{B}_{\sigma[N-2]}u[N - 2] + \mathcal{B}_{\sigma[N-1]}u[N - 1] .$$

Substituting our expression for the erroneous state variable from (14) into the above equation, we obtain

$$x_f[N] = x_h[N] + v \left(\prod_{i=N-t}^{N-1} \mathcal{A}_{\sigma[i]} \right) e_i \; ,$$

where $x_h[N]$ is the error-free state that $\mathcal{H}$ would have been in at the beginning of time step N, had there been no fault. Clearly, the parity check that is performed at the end of time step $N-1$ will yield the syndrome

$$\mathbf{s}[N] \equiv \mathbf{P} x_f[N] = v\mathbf{P} \left(\prod_{i=N-t}^{N-1} \mathcal{A}_{\sigma[i]} \right) e_i \qquad (15)$$

because $\mathbf{P} x_h[N] = \mathbf{P} \mathbf{G} x[N] = 0$.

Theorem 2. *Let switched system $\mathcal{S}$ have a redundant implementation $\mathcal{H}$, whose corresponding standard redundant switched system $\mathcal{H}_r$ satisfies*

$$\mathcal{T}^{-1} \mathcal{A}_{\sigma[k]} \mathcal{T} = \begin{bmatrix} \mathbf{A}_{\sigma[k]} & \mathbf{A}_{12_{\sigma[k]}} \\ 0 & \mathbf{A}_{22_{\sigma[k]}} \end{bmatrix} \equiv \mathcal{A}_{r_{\sigma[k]}}$$

for all $\sigma[k] \in \Omega = \{1, 2, \ldots, M\}$. The non-concurrent syndrome $\mathbf{s}[N]$ due to a single transient state-transition fault that occurs during the execution of time step $N - t - 1$ and corrupts the ith state variable by an additive value v is equal to

$$\mathbf{s}[N] \equiv \mathbf{P} x_f[N] = v \left(\prod_{i=N-t}^{N-1} \mathbf{A}_{22_{\sigma[i]}} \right) \mathbf{P} e_i \; .$$

Proof. From (15), the syndrome $\mathbf{s}[N]$ will be given by

$$\mathbf{s}[N] = v\mathbf{P} \left(\prod_{i=N-t}^{N-1} \mathcal{A}_{\sigma[i]} \right) e_i$$

$$= v\mathbf{P} \left(\prod_{i=N-t}^{N-1} \mathcal{T} \mathcal{A}_{r_{\sigma[i]}} \mathcal{T}^{-1} \right) e_i$$

$$= v\mathbf{P}\mathcal{T} \left(\prod_{i=N-t}^{N-1} \mathcal{A}_{r_{\sigma[i]}} \right) \mathcal{T}^{-1} e_i$$

$$= v\mathbf{P}\mathcal{T} \begin{bmatrix} * & * \\ 0 & \prod_{i=N-t}^{N-1} \mathbf{A}_{22_{\sigma[i]}} \end{bmatrix} \mathcal{T}^{-1} e_i$$

$$= v\mathbf{P}_r \begin{bmatrix} * & * \\ 0 & \prod_{i=N-t}^{N-1} \mathbf{A}_{22_{\sigma[i]}} \end{bmatrix} \mathcal{T}^{-1} e_i \qquad \text{(from (13))}$$

$$= v \left(\prod_{i=N-t}^{N-1} \mathbf{A}_{22_{\sigma[i]}} \right) \begin{bmatrix} 0 & \mathbf{I}_d \end{bmatrix} \mathcal{T}^{-1} e_i$$

$$= v \left(\prod_{i=N-t}^{N-1} \mathbf{A}_{22_{\sigma[i]}} \right) \mathbf{P} e_i \ . \qquad \text{(from (13))}$$

In the above calculations, the symbol $*$ stands for arbitrary matrices of appropriate dimensions. We have made use of the fact that all matrices $\mathcal{A}_{r_{\sigma[k]}}$ are upper-triangular, so their product is also an upper-triangular matrix. The bottom d rows of this product only depend on the matrices $\mathbf{A}_{22_{\sigma[k]}}$, which describe the redundant dynamics in the standard implementation $\mathcal{H}_r$ associated with $\mathcal{H}$. □

Notice that if all $\mathbf{A}_{22_{\sigma[k]}}$ are chosen to be identical (i.e., some constant matrix $\mathbf{A}_{22}$) then the syndrome at time step N will be

$$\mathbf{s}[N] \equiv \mathbf{P} x_f[N] = v \mathbf{A}_{22}^t \mathbf{P} e_i \ ,$$

which is independent of the switching sequence.

We can now generalize the above results to the case of multiple faults within the interval $[0, N-1]$. We assume that a total of D transient faults occur at time steps $N - t_1 - 1, N - t_2 - 1, \ldots, N - t_D - 1$, originally corrupting state variables $i_1, i_2, \ldots, i_D$ by initial additive errors of $v_1, v_2, \ldots, v_D$ respectively. We also assume (without loss of generality) that $0 \leq t_D \leq t_{D-1} \leq \cdots \leq t_1 \leq N-1$. The erroneous state at the end of time step $N - t_2 - 1$ will be

$$x_f[N - t_2] = x_h[N - t_2] + v_1 \left(\prod_{i=N-t_1}^{N-t_2-1} \mathcal{A}_{\sigma[i]} \right) e_{i_1} + v_2 e_{i_2} \ .$$

Similarly, the state at the end of time step $N - t_3 - 1$ will be

$$x_f[N - t_3] = x_h[N - t_3] + v_1 \left(\prod_{i=N-t_1}^{N-t_3-1} \mathcal{A}_{\sigma[i]} \right) e_{i_1} + v_2 \left(\prod_{i=N-t_2}^{N-t_3-1} \mathcal{A}_{\sigma[i]} \right) e_{i_2} + v_3 e_{i_3} \ .$$

Continuing in this manner for the rest of the errors, we obtain the following expression for the erroneous state at the end of time step $N - 1$:

$$x_f[N] = x_h[N] + v_1 \left(\prod_{i=N-t_1}^{N-1} \mathcal{A}_{\sigma[i]} \right) e_{i_1} + v_2 \left(\prod_{i=N-t_2}^{N-1} \mathcal{A}_{\sigma[i]} \right) e_{i_2} + \ldots$$

$$\cdots + v_D \left(\prod_{i=N-t_D}^{N-1} \mathcal{A}_{\sigma[i]} \right) e_{i_D}$$

$$= x_h[N] + \sum_{j=1}^{D} \left\{ v_j \left(\prod_{i=N-t_j}^{N-1} \mathcal{A}_{\sigma[i]} \right) e_{i_j} \right\} \ .$$

This leads us to the following generalization of Theorem 2.

Theorem 3. *Let switched system $\mathcal{S}$ have a redundant implementation $\mathcal{H}$, whose corresponding standard redundant switched system $\mathcal{H}_r$ satisfies*

$$\mathcal{T}^{-1}\mathbf{A}_{\sigma[k]}\mathcal{T} = \begin{bmatrix} \mathbf{A}_{\sigma[k]} & \mathbf{A}_{12_{\sigma[k]}} \\ 0 & \mathbf{A}_{22_{\sigma[k]}} \end{bmatrix} \equiv \mathcal{A}_{r_{\sigma[k]}}$$

for all $\sigma[k] \in \Omega = \{1, 2, \ldots, M\}$. The non-concurrent syndrome $\mathbf{s}[N]$ due to D transient state-transition faults that occur during time steps $N - t_1 - 1, N - t_2 - 1, \ldots, N - t_D - 1$, and corrupt state variables $i_1, i_2, \ldots, i_D$ by initial additive errors of $v_1, v_2, \ldots, v_D$ respectively is equal to

$$\mathbf{s}[N] \equiv \mathbf{P}x_f[N] = \sum_{j=1}^{D} \left\{ v_j \left(\prod_{i=N-t_j}^{N-1} \mathbf{A}_{22_{\sigma[i]}} \right) \mathbf{P}e_{i_j} \right\} .$$

Notice that if all $\mathbf{A}_{22_{\sigma[k]}}$ are chosen to be identical (i.e., some constant matrix $\mathbf{A}_{22}$) then the syndrome at time step N will be

$$\mathbf{s}[N] \equiv \mathbf{P}x_f[N] = \sum_{j=1}^{D} \left\{ v_j \mathbf{A}_{22}^{t_j} \mathbf{P}e_{i_j} \right\} , \tag{16}$$

which is independent of the switching sequence.

The proof of Theorem 3 mirrors the earlier proof, and is omitted here.

3.4   Multiple Error Detection, Identification, and Correction

We now present a method to construct a redundant implementation $\mathcal{H}$ of the switched system $\mathcal{S}$ given by (5) so that we can perform non-concurrent error detection, identification and correction of multiple errors. For simplicity, we will choose $\mathbf{A}_{22_{\sigma[k]}} = \mathbf{A}_{22}$ for all $\sigma[k] \in \Omega = \{1, 2, \ldots, M\}$, where $\mathbf{A}_{22}$ is a constant $d \times d$ matrix to be determined.

From (16), we can see that if D transient state-transition faults occur at time steps $0 \le N - t_1 - 1 \le N - t_2 - 1 \le \cdots \le N - t_D - 1 \le N - 1$, and corrupt state variables $i_1, i_2, \ldots, i_D$ by initial additive errors of $v_1, v_2, \ldots, v_D$ respectively, then the syndrome at the end of time step $N - 1$ will be a linear combination of D columns of the $d \times N\eta$ syndrome matrix

$$\mathbf{S} = \begin{bmatrix} \mathbf{P} & \mathbf{A}_{22}\mathbf{P} & \mathbf{A}_{22}^2\mathbf{P} & \cdots & \mathbf{A}_{22}^{N-1}\mathbf{P} \end{bmatrix} . \tag{17}$$

In order to detect D or less errors in the interval $[0, N - 1]$, we need all linear combinations of any subset of D columns of $\mathbf{S}$ to be nonzero. To be able to uniquely identify the originally affected variables $(i_1, i_2, \ldots, i_D)$, the values by which they were initially corrupted $(v_1, v_2, \ldots, v_D)$, and the time steps during which the errors took place $(N - t_1 - 1, N - t_2 - 1, \ldots, N - t_D - 1)$, we need all linear combinations of any subset of D columns of $\mathbf{S}$ to be different from a linear combination of any other subset of D columns of $\mathbf{S}$. To see why this condition is required, assume that we have two different subsets of D columns of $\mathbf{S}$, $\{s_{l_1}, s_{l_2}, \ldots, s_{l_D}\}$ and $\{s'_{l_1}, s'_{l_2}, \ldots, s'_{l_D}\}$, such that $\sum_{j=1}^{D} \alpha_j s_{l_j} = \sum_{j=1}^{D} \beta_j s'_{l_j}$. In this case, the corresponding two sets of errors cannot be distinguished by the syndrome $\mathbf{s}[N]$.

Later on we describe how the redundant system can be constructed so that detection and identification of D (or less) errors is possible; for now, assuming that the system is constructed in this way, the following procedure describes how errors can be detected, identified and eventually corrected.

1. At the end of time step $N-1$, calculate $\mathbf{s}[N] = \mathbf{P}x_f[N]$.
2. Find the unique linear combination of D' ($D' \leq D$) columns of the syndrome matrix $\mathbf{S}$ that results in $\mathbf{s}[N] = \sum_{i=1}^{D'} \alpha_j \mathbf{S}(:, l_j)$. It is possible to use a modified version of the Peterson-Gorestein-Zeigler (PGZ) decoding algorithm to efficiently determine the D' errors based on the syndrome $\mathbf{s}[N]$, without resorting to an exhaustive search. The details are presented in [18], and are omitted here. We can now identify the unique combination of errors of the form v_j, e_{i_j}, and t_j, $j \in \{1, 2, \ldots, D'\}$ (the jth error takes place during time step $N - t_j - 1$ and originally affects the (i_j)th state variable by an initial value v_j), such that $\mathbf{s}[N] = \sum_{j=1}^{D'} v_j \mathbf{A}_{22}^{t_j} \mathbf{P}e_{i_j}$ as follows:

$$v_j = \alpha_j \ , \quad i_j = 1 + [(l_j - 1) \stackrel{.}{\mod} \eta] \ , \quad t_j = \frac{l_j - i_j}{\eta} \ .$$

3. Declare that D' errors have taken place in the interval $[0, N-1]$.
4. If the switching sequence over the last N cycles is known, we can perform error correction by setting

$$x_h[N] = x_f[N] - \sum_{j=1}^{D'} \left\{ v_j \left(\prod_{i=N-t_j}^{N-1} \mathcal{A}_{\sigma[i]} \right) e_{i_j} \right\} \ ,$$

where $x_f[N]$ is the current erroneous state at time step N. In the specific case where the switching pattern $\sigma[k]$ is periodic (as in [9], for example) of period N, this error correction can be done by precomputing the $N-1$ matrices

$$\left\{ \mathcal{A}_{\sigma[N-1]} \ , \quad \mathcal{A}_{\sigma[N-1]} \mathcal{A}_{\sigma[N-2]} \ , \quad \cdots \ , \quad \prod_{j=1}^{N-1} \mathcal{A}_{\sigma[j]} \right\} \ ,$$

and selecting the appropriate ones to use in the correction step.

Due to the fact that the syndrome matrix in (17) is the same as the one in [18], we can adapt the construction given there to this case. More specifically, we would like to choose the matrices $\mathbf{A}_{22}$ and $\mathbf{P}$ in such a way that the syndrome matrix $\mathbf{S}$ has the rank properties required for error detection and identification (namely, for correction of up to D errors, any subset of $2D$ columns of $\mathbf{S}$ are linearly independent). We start by recalling the definition of the Vandermonde matrix.

Definition 1. *Let* $\mathbf{V}(w_1, w_2, \ldots, w_\rho)$ *denote the* $2D \times \rho$ *matrix*

$$\mathbf{V}(w_1, w_2, \ldots, w_\rho) = \begin{bmatrix} w_1 & w_2 & \cdots & w_\rho \\ w_1^2 & w_2^2 & \cdots & w_\rho^2 \\ \vdots & \vdots & \ddots & \vdots \\ w_1^{2D-1} & w_2^{2D-1} & \cdots & w_\rho^{2D-1} \\ w_1^{2D} & w_2^{2D} & \cdots & w_\rho^{2D} \end{bmatrix} .$$

It is well-known that Vandermonde matrices of the form $\mathbf{V}(w_1, w_2, \ldots, w_{2D})$ are invertible if and only if $w_i \neq 0$ for $1 \leq i \leq 2D$ and $w_i \neq w_j$ for $1 \leq i < j \leq 2D$. We are now in position to prove the following theorem.

Theorem 4. *Let switched system* $\mathcal{S}$ *have a redundant implementation* $\mathcal{H}$, *whose corresponding standard redundant switched system* $\mathcal{H}_r$ *satisfies (for all* $\sigma[k] \in \Omega = \{1, 2, \ldots, M\}$)

$$\mathcal{T}^{-1} \mathcal{A}_{\sigma[k]} \mathcal{T} = \begin{bmatrix} \mathbf{A}_{\sigma[k]} & \mathbf{A}_{12_{\sigma[k]}} \\ 0 & \mathbf{A}_{22} \end{bmatrix} \equiv \mathcal{A}_{r_{\sigma[k]}}$$

for a constant matrix $\mathbf{A}_{22}$. *Any* D *or less errors due to transient faults in the interval* $[0, N-1]$ *will be detected and identified by a parity check at the end of time step* $N-1$ *if the following conditions are satisfied:*

1. *The corresponding standard redundant switched system (as given in (8)-(13) of Theorem 1) satisfies the following conditions:*
   a) *The number of additional state variables is* $d = 2D$.
   b) *The* $2D \times 2D$ *matrix* $\mathbf{A}_{22}$ *is of the form*

$$\mathbf{A}_{22} = \mathbf{M}^{-1} \Lambda \mathbf{M} ,$$

   where (i) $\Lambda = \operatorname{diag}(w, w^2, w^3, \ldots, w^{2D-1}, w^{2D})$ *is a* $2D \times 2D$ *diagonal matrix and (ii)* $\mathbf{M} = \mathbf{V}(w_{n+1}, w_{n+2}, \ldots, w_\eta)$ *is a* $2D \times 2D$ *Vandermonde matrix.*
2. *The* $\eta \times \eta$ *transformation matrix* $\mathcal{T}$ *that is used to transform from the standard redundant switched system* $\mathcal{H}_r$ *to the redundant switched system* $\mathcal{H}$ *is given by*

$$\mathcal{T} = \begin{bmatrix} \mathbf{I}_n & 0 \\ \mathbf{C} & \mathbf{I}_{2D} \end{bmatrix} ,$$

   where the $2D \times n$ *matrix* $\mathbf{C}$ *is chosen so that*

$$\mathbf{C} = -\mathbf{M}^{-1} \mathbf{V}(w_1, w_2, \ldots, w_n) .$$

3. *The real numbers* w *and* $w_1, w_2, \ldots, w_\eta$ *are chosen so that*
   a) $w_i \neq 0$ *for* $1 \leq i \leq \eta$;
   b) $w_i \neq w_j$ *for* $1 \leq i < j \leq \eta$;
   c) $w^t w_i \neq w^{t'} w_j$ *for* $1 \leq i, j \leq \eta$ *and* $0 \leq t < t' \leq N-1$.

Proof. We start with the standard redundant switched system $\mathcal{H}_r$ given by (8)-(13), and set $x_h[k] = \mathcal{T}x_r[k]$, where $\mathcal{T} = \begin{bmatrix} \mathbf{I}_n & \mathbf{0} \\ \mathbf{C} & \mathbf{I}_{2D} \end{bmatrix}$. This yields a redundant implementation with the following state evolution:

$$x_h[k+1] = \underbrace{\left[\begin{array}{c|c} \mathbf{A}_{\sigma[k]} - \mathbf{A}_{12_{\sigma[k]}}\mathbf{C} & \mathbf{A}_{12_{\sigma[k]}} \\ \hline \mathbf{CA}_{\sigma[k]} - \mathbf{CA}_{12_{\sigma[k]}}\mathbf{C} - \mathbf{A}_{22}\mathbf{C} & \mathbf{CA}_{12_{\sigma[k]}} + \mathbf{A}_{22} \end{array}\right]}_{\mathcal{A}_{\sigma[k]} = \mathcal{T}\mathcal{A}_{r_{\sigma[k]}}\mathcal{T}^{-1}} x_h[k]$$

$$+ \underbrace{\left[\begin{array}{c} \mathbf{B}_{\sigma[k]} \\ \hline \mathbf{CB}_{\sigma[k]} \end{array}\right]}_{\mathcal{B}_{\sigma[k]} = \mathcal{T}\mathcal{B}_{r_{\sigma[k]}}} u[k] \ . \tag{18}$$

Note that the parity check matrix for $\mathcal{H}$ is given by $\mathbf{P} = \mathbf{P}_r\mathcal{T}^{-1} = \begin{bmatrix} -\mathbf{C} & \mathbf{I}_{2D} \end{bmatrix}$, where $\mathbf{C} = -\mathbf{M}^{-1}\mathbf{V}(w_1, w_2, \ldots, w_n)$. The syndrome matrix $\mathbf{S}$ in (17) consists of submatrices of the form $\mathbf{A}_{22}^t\mathbf{P}$. With the choice of $\mathbf{P}$ and $\mathbf{A}_{22}$ from the theorem, it is shown in [18] that

$$\mathbf{A}_{22}^t\mathbf{P} = \mathbf{M}^{-1}\mathbf{V}(w_1 w^t, w_2 w^t, \ldots, w_\eta w^t) \ , \tag{19}$$

so that the syndrome matrix $\mathbf{S}$ can be expressed as

$$\mathbf{S} = \mathbf{M}^{-1}\mathbf{V}(w_1, \ldots, w_\eta, w_1 w, \ldots, w_\eta w, \ldots, w_1 w^{N-1}, \ldots, w_\eta w^{N-1}) \ .$$

Note that all the parameters in the above syndrome matrix are unique, due to the restrictions on parameters $w, w_1, w_2, \ldots, w_\eta$ as given in Condition 3 of the theorem. This guarantees that any $2D$ or less columns are independent, which implies that we can detect and identify any combination of D' $(D' \leq D)$ errors in the interval $[0, N-1]$. The same approach can also detect, but not necessarily identify, $2D$ or less errors in the interval $[0, N-1]$. □

4   Example

Consider a switched system $\mathcal{S}$ of the form given in (5), which switches between two linear systems, described by matrix pairs $(\mathbf{A}_1, \mathbf{B}_1)$ and $(\mathbf{A}_2, \mathbf{B}_2)$, and a switching path $\sigma[k] \in \Omega = \{1, 2\}$, $k \geq 0$. The system has $n = 3$ state variables and $m = 1$ input (i.e., $x[k] \in \mathbb{R}^3$, $u[k] \in \mathbb{R}$), and the two pairs of matrices are given by

$$\mathbf{A}_1 = \begin{bmatrix} -1/2 & 1 & 0 \\ 1/4 & 0 & 1 \\ 1/5 & 0 & 0 \end{bmatrix}, \quad \mathbf{B}_1 = \begin{bmatrix} 1 \\ 0 \\ 1 \end{bmatrix};$$

$$\mathbf{A}_2 = \begin{bmatrix} -1/5 & 1 & 0 \\ 1/3 & 0 & 1 \\ 1/9 & 0 & 0 \end{bmatrix}, \quad \mathbf{B}_2 = \begin{bmatrix} 1.5 \\ 1 \\ 0 \end{bmatrix}.$$

We wish to protect the system $\mathcal{S}$ in a way that allows us to detect and identify two or less transient state-transition faults in the interval $[0, 9]$ (i.e., $D = 2$ and

$N = 10$). According to Theorem 4, we need $d = 2D = 4$ extra state variables to provide such protection, giving us a total of $\eta = n + d = 3 + 4 = 7$ state variables. We choose the parameters w_i, $1 \leq i \leq 7$, to be

$$\{w_1, w_2, w_3, w_4, w_5, w_6, w_7\} = \{-1, 1, -3, 3, -5, 5, 7\} \ ,$$

and set $w = \frac{1}{2}$. Note that this choice of parameters satisfies Condition 3 of Theorem 4. With these parameters, the Vandermonde matrix $\mathbf{M}$ and the diagonal matrix Λ are

$$\mathbf{M} = \mathbf{V}(w_4, w_5, w_6, w_7) = \begin{bmatrix} 3 & -5 & 5 & -7 \\ 9 & 25 & 25 & 49 \\ 27 & -125 & 125 & -343 \\ 81 & 625 & 625 & 2401 \end{bmatrix} \ ,$$

$$\Lambda = \mathrm{diag}(w, w^2, w^3, w^4) = \begin{bmatrix} 1/2 & 0 & 0 & 0 \\ 0 & 1/4 & 0 & 0 \\ 0 & 0 & 1/8 & 0 \\ 0 & 0 & 0 & 1/16 \end{bmatrix} \ .$$

Matrix $\mathbf{C}$ is set to

$$\mathbf{C} = -\mathbf{M}^{-1}\mathbf{V}(w_1, w_2, w_3) = \begin{bmatrix} 0.3000 & -0.4000 & 0.4000 \\ -0.1800 & 0.0800 & -0.7200 \\ -0.0800 & 0.0800 & -0.1200 \\ 0.0571 & -0.0286 & 0.1714 \end{bmatrix} \ .$$

The transformation matrix $\mathcal{T}$ is

$$\mathcal{T} = \begin{bmatrix} \mathbf{I}_n & \mathbf{0} \\ \hline \mathbf{C} & \mathbf{I}_{2D} \end{bmatrix} = \left[\begin{array}{ccc|cccc} 1 & 0 & 0 & 0 & 0 & 0 & 0 \\ 0 & 1 & 0 & 0 & 0 & 0 & 0 \\ 0 & 0 & 1 & 0 & 0 & 0 & 0 \\ \hline 0.3000 & -0.4000 & 0.4000 & 1 & 0 & 0 & 0 \\ -0.1800 & 0.0800 & -0.7200 & 0 & 1 & 0 & 0 \\ -0.0800 & 0.0800 & -0.1200 & 0 & 0 & 1 & 0 \\ 0.0571 & -0.0286 & 0.1714 & 0 & 0 & 0 & 1 \end{array} \right] \ ,$$

and is used to obtain the parity check matrix given by (13):

$$\mathbf{P} = \begin{bmatrix} \mathbf{0} | \mathbf{I}_4 \end{bmatrix} \mathcal{T}^{-1} = \begin{bmatrix} -\mathbf{C} | \mathbf{I}_4 \end{bmatrix} = \left[\begin{array}{ccc|cccc} -0.3000 & 0.4000 & -0.4000 & 1 & 0 & 0 & 0 \\ 0.1800 & -0.0800 & 0.7200 & 0 & 1 & 0 & 0 \\ 0.0800 & -0.0800 & 0.1200 & 0 & 0 & 1 & 0 \\ -0.0571 & 0.0286 & -0.1714 & 0 & 0 & 0 & 1 \end{array} \right] \ .$$

We are now ready to construct the standard redundant transition matrices given by equations (9)-(10). We choose the coupling matrices $\mathbf{A}_{12_{\sigma[k]}} = \mathbf{0}$ for all $\sigma[k] \in \Omega$, and keep the redundant matrix $\mathbf{A}_{22_{\sigma[k]}} = \mathbf{A}_{22}$ for all $\sigma[k] \in \Omega$. Following the construction in Theorem 4, the $\mathbf{A}_{22}$ matrix is given by

$$\mathbf{A}_{22} = \mathbf{M}^{-1}\Lambda\mathbf{M} = \begin{bmatrix} 0.6043 & -0.4395 & 0.9277 & -0.3254 \\ -0.0837 & 0.5801 & -0.0371 & 0.8460 \\ -0.1036 & 0.1289 & -0.0742 & 0.0995 \\ 0.0305 & -0.1535 & 0.0140 & -0.1727 \end{bmatrix} \ .$$

The transition matrices of the redundant implementation are given by (18) and are shown below:

$$
\mathcal{A}_1 = \begin{bmatrix}
-0.5000 & 1 & 0 & 0 & 0 & 0 & 0 \\
0.2500 & 0 & 1 & 0 & 0 & 0 & 0 \\
0.2000 & 0 & 0 & 0 & 0 & 0 & 0 \\
-0.3376 & 0.4934 & -0.7910 & 0.6043 & -0.4395 & 0.9277 & -0.3254 \\
0.0442 & -0.2327 & 0.3816 & -0.0837 & 0.5801 & -0.0371 & 0.8460 \\
0.0787 & -0.1230 & 0.1883 & -0.1036 & 0.1289 & -0.0742 & 0.0995 \\
-0.0272 & 0.0756 & -0.1200 & 0.0305 & -0.1535 & 0.0140 & -0.1727
\end{bmatrix} ,
$$

$$
\mathcal{A}_2 = \begin{bmatrix}
-0.2000 & 1 & 0 & 0 & 0 & 0 & 0 \\
0.3333 & 0 & 1 & 0 & 0 & 0 & 0 \\
0.1111 & 0 & 0 & 0 & 0 & 0 & 0 \\
-0.3165 & 0.4934 & -0.7910 & 0.6043 & -0.4395 & 0.9277 & -0.3254 \\
0.0609 & -0.2327 & 0.3816 & -0.0837 & 0.5801 & -0.0371 & 0.8460 \\
0.0720 & -0.1230 & 0.1883 & -0.1036 & 0.1289 & -0.0742 & 0.0995 \\
-0.0277 & 0.0756 & -0.1200 & 0.0305 & -0.1535 & 0.0140 & -0.1727
\end{bmatrix} ,
$$

$$
\mathcal{B}_1 = \begin{bmatrix} 1 & 0 & 1 & | & 0.7000 & -0.9000 & -0.2000 & 0.2286 \end{bmatrix}^T ,
$$

$$
\mathcal{B}_2 = \begin{bmatrix} 1.5 & 1 & 0 & | & 0.0500 & -0.1900 & -0.0400 & 0.0571 \end{bmatrix}^T .
$$

From (17) and (19), the syndrome matrix for non-concurrent error detection and correction in this system is given by

$$
\mathbf{S} = \mathbf{M}^{-1} \begin{bmatrix} \mathbf{S}_0 & \mathbf{S}_1 & \mathbf{S}_2 & \cdots & \mathbf{S}_9 \end{bmatrix} ,
$$

where $\mathbf{S}_t = \mathbf{V}(-w^t, w^t, -3w^t, 3w^t, -5w^t, 5w^t, 7w^t)$, $w = \frac{1}{2}$. The modified syndrome matrix is given by

$$
\mathbf{S}' = \mathbf{M}\mathbf{S} = \begin{bmatrix} \mathbf{S}_0 & \mathbf{S}_1 & \mathbf{S}_2 & \cdots & \mathbf{S}_9 \end{bmatrix} .
$$

Once the redundant system is constructed, let us assume it is operating under some switching sequence $\sigma[k] \in \Omega$, and some input $u[k]$. Let us also assume that two transient faults take place in the interval $[0, 9]$ as follows.

1. Fault 1 takes place during time step 1, and corrupts the fifth state variable with an additive initial error of value 0.4.
2. Fault 2 takes place during time step 7, and corrupts the fourth state variable with an additive initial error of value 0.95.

The syndrome at the end of time step 9 (beginning of time step 10) is given by

$$
\mathbf{s}[10] = \mathbf{P}x_f[10] = \begin{bmatrix} 0.2783 & -0.0650 & -0.0588 & 0.0230 \end{bmatrix}^T
$$

and the modified syndrome is given by

$$\mathbf{s}'[10] = \mathbf{Ms}[10] = \begin{bmatrix} 0.7047 & 0.5345 & 0.4008 & 0.3006 \end{bmatrix}^T .$$

Note that the syndrome does not depend on the actual input *or* switching sequence that is applied to the system, as long as the faults take place at the same time steps and originally affect the same state variables by the same initial additive errors. The only way we can write our modified syndrome as a linear combination of at most two columns of $\mathbf{S}'$ is given by

$$\mathbf{s}'[10] = 0.4\mathbf{S}_8(:,5) + 0.95\mathbf{S}_2(:,4) .$$

Therefore, we conclude that there have been two faults: one affecting the fifth state variable at time step $1 (= 10 - 8 - 1)$ by an additive error of 0.4, and one affecting the fourth state variable at time step $7 (= 10 - 2 - 1)$ by an additive error of 0.95. A systematic method of determining the above linear combination is presented in [18].

5   Conclusions

In this paper, we have presented a methodology for providing fault tolerance to discrete-time controllers in switched LTI systems through non-concurrent (e.g., periodic) error detection and correction. Specifically, we showed how to embed the state-space of the controllers into a larger redundant state-space, so that all information about the initial system is preserved, but with the added capability to detect and identify transient faults that affect state variables. The ability to perform error detection non-concurrently allows the reliability constraints of the error-checking mechanism to be relaxed.

There are a number of interesting directions for future research in this area:

1. How can we make use of the flexibility in the coupling dynamics between the original and redundant state variables (given by matrix $\mathbf{A}_{12_{\sigma[k]}}$ in Theorem 1)?
2. How can we design systems that are optimal in terms of minimizing the number of redundant arithmetic operations that are performed (instead of minimizing the number of redundant state variables)?
3. When working in the realm of real numbers, finite-precision issues must be considered during the design of the redundant system. How can we choose redundant dynamics in our system to provide robustness in the face of these issues?

Furthermore, it will be interesting to study various methods of mapping this system into hardware.

References

1. Morse, A.S., ed.: Control Using Logic-Based Switching. Springer-Verlag (1997)
2. Zefran, M., Burdick, J.: Design of switching controllers for systems with changing dynamics. In: Proc. 37th IEEE Conf. on Decision and Control. Volume 2. (1998) 2113–2118
3. Hespanha, J., Liberzon, D., Morse, A.: Logic-based switching control of a nonholonomic system with parametric modeling uncertainty. Systems and Control Letters, Special Issue on Hybrid Systems **38** (1999) 167–177
4. Hespanha, J.: Logic-Based Switching Algorithms in Control. PhD thesis, Yale University (1998)
5. Liberzon, D.: Switching in Systems and Control. Birkhauser (2003)
6. Ge, S.S., Sun, Z., Lee, T.H.: Reachability and controllability of switched linear discrete-time systems. IEEE Transactions on Automatic Control **46** (2001) 1437–1441
7. Liberzon, D., Morse, A.: Basic problems in stability and design of switched systems. IEEE Control Systems Magazine **19** (1999) 59–70
8. Xie, G., Zheng, D., Wang, L.: Controllability of switched linear systems. IEEE Transactions on Automatic Control **47** (2002) 1401–1405
9. Ezzine, J., Haddad, A.H.: Controllability and observability of hybrid systems. International Journal of Control **49** (1989) 2045–2055
10. Sangiovanni-Vincentelli, A.: Embedded system design and hybrid systems. In Morse, A.S., ed.: Control Using Logic-Based Switching. Springer-Verlag (1997) 17–38
11. Gray, W.S., Gonzalez, O.R., Dogan, M.: Stability analysis of digital linear flight controllers subject to electromagnetic disturbances. IEEE Transactions on Aerospace and Electronic Systems **36** (2000) 1204–1218
12. Gray, W.S., Patilkulkarni, S., Gonzalez, O.R.: Towards hybrid models of recoverable computer control systems. In: Proc. 2002 Digital Avionics Systems Conference. (2002) 13.C.2–1–9
13. Babaali, M., Egerstedt, M., Kamen, E.W.: An observer for linear systems with randomly-switching measurement equations. In: Proc. 2003 American Control Conference. (2003) 1879–1884
14. Smith, S.C., Seiler, P.: Optimal pseudo-steady-state estimators for systems with Markovian intermittent measurements. In: Proc. 2002 American Control Conference. (2002) 3021–3027
15. von Neumann, J.: Probabilistic Logics and the Synthesis of Reliable Organisms from Unreliable Components. Princeton, NJ: Princeton Univ. Press (1956)
16. Rao, T.R.N., Fujiwara, E.: Error-Control Coding for Computer Systems. Englewood Cliffs, NJ:Prentice-Hall (1989)
17. Huang, K.H., Abraham, J.A.: Algorithm-based fault tolerance for matrix operations. IEEE Transactions on Computers **33** (1984) 518–528
18. Hadjicostis, C.N.: Non-concurrent error detection and correction in fault-tolerant discrete-time LTI dynamic systems. IEEE Transactions on Circuits and Systems **50** (2003) 45–55
19. Hadjicostis, C.N., Verghese, G.: Structured redundancy for fault tolerance in LTI state-space models and Petri nets. Kybernetika **35** (1999) 39–55

Nonlinear Systems: Approximating Reach Sets*

Ashish Tiwari[1] and Gaurav Khanna[2,3]

[1] SRI International, 333 Ravenswood Ave, Menlo Park, CA, U.S.A
Tel:+1.650.859.4774, Fax:+1.650.859.2844, tiwari@csl.sri.com
[2] Theoretical and Computational Studies Group
Long Island University, Southampton NY 11968,
gkhanna@liu.edu
[3] Department of Physics, U. of Massachusetts, Dartmouth, MA 02747

Abstract. We describe techniques to generate useful reachability information for nonlinear dynamical systems. These techniques can be automated for polynomial systems using algorithms from computational algebraic geometry. The generated information can be incorporated into other approaches for doing reachability computation. It can also be used when abstracting hybrid systems that contain modes with nonlinear dynamics. These techniques are most naturally embedded in the hybrid qualitative abstraction approach proposed by the authors previously. They also show that the formal qualitative abstraction approach is well suited for dealing with nonlinear systems.

1 Introduction

Computing the set of states reachable from the initial states is central to the problem of proving that a system is safe, that is, it does not enter a "bad" region. Exact reachability set computation is, however, elusive for both discrete transition systems and continuous dynamical systems. Hybrid systems combine these two formalisms and inherit their complexities. For purposes of proving safety, though, the exact reachability set is not required and suitable over approximations of this set suffice. The approaches for computation of (over approximations of) the reachability set can be broadly be classified into two categories: (i) methods based on explicit computation of the reachability set by forward simulating the system and widening [7,16,6], and (ii) methods based on abstraction [1,13,26]. In this paper, we present analytical results on computing over approximations of the set of reachable states, which can be integrated with both these methods. Despite their generality, these results are best motivated in the context of our hybrid qualitative abstraction approach.

* Research of the first author was supported in part by the National Science Foundation under grant CCR-0311348, NASA Langley Research Center contract NAS1-00108 to Rannoch Corporation, and DARPA BioSpice contract DE-AC03-765F00098 to Lawrence Berkeley Laboratory. Second author was supported in part by the National Science Foundation under grant PHY-0140236.

R. Alur and G.J. Pappas (Eds.): HSCC 2004, LNCS 2993, pp. 600–614, 2004.

Our approach to analyzing hybrid system is based on constructing sound discrete abstractions of the hybrid system [26]. The abstraction methodology combines predicate abstraction technique [10], for abstracting the discrete component of the hybrid system, and qualitative abstraction [26,15], for handling the continuous dynamics.

The effectiveness of our abstraction method, as with all approaches based on abstraction, depends on the choice of abstraction predicates. The discrete component of a hybrid system is "simpler", in this respect, than the continuous component. This is because the guard conditions, state invariants, and reset assignments immediately suggest what predicates are important for the discrete logic. And in most real world problems, the discrete logic is simple enough that this choice is adequate. The choice of predicates for constructing good (qualitative) abstractions of the continuous components is not always so obvious. When we first described the hybrid abstraction algorithm [26], we proposed the use of first, second, and higher-order derivatives of the expressions that occur in the guards, property, and initialization. For example, if the dynamics is given by $\dot{x} = 100 - x$, and interest is in the value of x, then clearly $100 - x$ is a good candidate expression to monitor. But this does not work always. For example, in the two-dimensional linear system $\dot{x} = -2x + y$, $\dot{y} = x - 2y$, say initially $x = 5$ and $y = 0$, and we are interested in proving that $y \leq 5$ always, given the state invariant $x \geq 0$. The (higher-order) derivatives of $y - 5$ or x do not help much. However, if we look at the function $x + y$, then we immediately notice that $(x + y) = -(x + y)$ and we can (just using qualitative reasoning) get to the desired conclusion.

The above observation suggests that concepts, such as Lyapunov functions, from linear and nonlinear systems theory can yield useful reachability information too. In a previous article [25], we considered linear systems and suggested the use of left eigenvectors for generating useful functions for the process of qualitative abstraction. In this paper, we present some initial results for nonlinear systems.

In the case of linear systems, using simple linear algebra, we can always get *linear* functions $V : \Re^n \mapsto \Re$ that are either (i) exponentially changing ($\dot{V} = \lambda V$), (ii) oscillating ($\ddot{V} = \lambda V$), or (iii) oscillating with exponentially decaying amplitude ($\ddot{V} = a\dot{V} + bV$.) The *exact* reach set is computable (in some cases) when there are enough (different) functions V of the first kind [19,18]. In [25], we showed that even when there do not exist sufficiently many such V's, useful *partial* reachability information can be obtained.

The functions V can be interpreted as representing the total "energy" of the system (though V can be increasing in our case). In this paper, we are interested in computing linear and nonlinear functions V for nonlinear systems. Such functions are used in the process of abstracting the continuous dynamics inside a mode of a hybrid system. Whenever possible, we shall explicitly show the resulting over approximation of the reach set. We also present methods for computing these functions whenever the function itself is a polynomial and the nonlinear system too is described using polynomials.

Unlike linear systems, there are no standard concepts, like eigenvectors, that can be used for nonlinear systems. The functions V satisfying (i), (ii), or (iii) need not be linear, in fact they need not even be polynomials. But we introduce some new concepts such as *exact-ideal*, a subset of a polynomial ideal, to compute polynomial V's whenever they exist.

1.1 Preliminaries

A (nonlinear) dynamical system S consists of a finite set $x_1, x_2, \ldots, x_n$ of real valued variables, a set of differential equations $dx_1/dt = p_1(x_1, x_2, \ldots, x_n), dx_2/dt = p_2(x_1, x_2, \ldots, x_n), \ldots, dx_n/dt = p_n(x_1, x_2, \ldots, x_n)$, a set $Init \subseteq \Re^n$ of initial states, and a set $Inv \subseteq \Re^n$ of the invariant region. We use matrix notation to represent the dynamics. The n variables are represented as a $n \times 1$ column vector $\boldsymbol{x}$ and the $n \times 1$ column vector consisting of the functions $p_1, p_2, \ldots, p_n$ is called a *vector field* and is denoted by $\boldsymbol{p}$. In short, the dynamics are written as $\dot{\boldsymbol{x}} = \boldsymbol{p}$. We often assume that the p_i's are polynomials over the n variables $x_1, x_2, \ldots, x_n$.

The invariant region Inv is specified as a formula ϕ with free variables $x_1, \ldots, x_n$ in the theory of reals. We assume no particular representation for the set of initial states $Init$. The theory of reals, and the set of all reals, are both denoted by $\Re$ – the intention is disambiguated by the context. The notation $\Re \vdash \psi$ means that the formula ψ (universally quantified) is valid in the theory $\Re$, that is, it is true for all real valuations of the variables. For example, $\Re \vdash (x_1^2 + x_2^2 \geq 0)$.

The semantics $[[S]]$ of a dynamical system S, with dynamics $\dot{\boldsymbol{x}} = \boldsymbol{p}$, initial states $Init$ and invariant Inv, over an interval $I = [t_0, t_1] \subseteq \mathbb{R}$ is a collection of mappings $\boldsymbol{x} : I \mapsto \mathbf{X}$ satisfying (i) the initial condition: $\boldsymbol{x}(t_0) \in Init$, (ii) the continuous dynamics: for all $t \in [t_0, t_1]$, $\dot{\boldsymbol{x}}(t) = \boldsymbol{p}(t)$, and (iii) the invariant: for all $t \in (t_0, t_1)$, $\boldsymbol{x}(t) \in Inv$. In case the interval I is left unspecified, it is assumed to be the interval $[0, \infty)$. The motivation for the invariant region Inv comes from hybrid systems and informally, the semantics is given such that only those trajectories of the dynamical system are valid which do not take the system out of the set Inv. We say that a state $\boldsymbol{s} \in \Re^n$ is *reachable* in the system S if there exists a function $\boldsymbol{x} \in [[S]]$ such that $\boldsymbol{s} = \boldsymbol{x}(t)$ for some $t \in I$. The reach set, $Reach(S)$, is defined as the set of all reachable states of the system S.

We are interested in smooth functions $V : \Re^n \mapsto \Re$ satisfying certain nice properties. A $1 \times n$ row vector of such functions will be called a **1-form**. If V is a function, then the notation $\boldsymbol{dV}$ denotes the 1-form consisting of partial derivatives of V with respect to the n variables, that is, $\boldsymbol{dV} = [\partial V/\partial x_1, \partial V/\partial x_2, \ldots, \partial V/\partial x_n]$. In matrix notation, a 1-form is denoted by $\boldsymbol{q}^T$. We use some differential geometry terminology in this paper, but it is always backed up with detailed expansions, and hence the presentation may appear verbose to an expert reader.

2   Linear Invariants

We consider (time invariant) polynomial nonlinear dynamical systems, that is, in the dynamics $\dot{x} = p$, each component of the vector field p is specified by a (possibly nonlinear) polynomial $p_i(x_1, \ldots, x_n)$ over the variables $x_1, \ldots, x_n$ in x. We will separate out the nonlinear component from the linear component and represent such a dynamical system as

$$\dot{x} = Ax + By$$

where y is the vector of non-linear power-products of state variables in x. Here A is an $n \times n$ matrix, B is an $n \times m$ matrix, x is a $n \times 1$ vector, and y is a $m \times 1$ vector. In the case of linear systems, $m = 0$. Example 1 gives a simple illustration of this notation.

Let c be a real eigenvector of A^T which is also in the *kernel* of B^T (that is, the linear subspace of zeros of B^T), that is,

$$A^T c = \lambda c \qquad B^T c = 0,$$

where the components of c are reals.

The transpose c^T of the vector c is a 1-form. Consider the linear function $V = c^T x$.

$$\dot{V} = c^T \dot{x} = c^T(Ax + By) = (A^T c)^T x + (B^T c)^T y = (\lambda c)^T x + 0 = \lambda V.$$

The value of the function V will either (i) monotonically increase or decrease while remaining sign-invariant (if $\lambda > 0$), or (ii) asymptotically converge to 0 (if $\lambda < 0$), or (iii) remain constant (if $\lambda = 0$). Thus, $c^T x$ can be used to generate useful invariants of the dynamical system and give bounds on the reach sets of such systems as summarized in the following theorem.

Theorem 1. *Let $\dot{x} = Ax + By$ be a nonlinear dynamical system with initial states Init. Let λ be a real eigenvalue of the matrix A^T, $c = [c_1, c_2, \ldots, c_n]^T$ be a corresponding eigenvector (of A^T), and $V = c_1 x_1 + c_2 x_2 + \cdots + c_n x_n = c^T x$ be the corresponding linear function. Suppose that c is also in the kernel of B^T.*

If d_{min} and d_{max} denote, respectively, the minimum and maximum values in the set $\{c^T x(0) : x(0) \in Init\}$, then the formula ϕ, as defined below, is an over approximation of the reach set of the nonlinear system:
(i) Case $\lambda > 0$: if $d_{min} > 0$, then ϕ is $V \geq d_{min}$, if $d_{max} < 0$, then ϕ is $V \leq d_{max}$, and if $d_{min} = d_{max} = 0$, then ϕ is $V = 0$;
(ii) Case $\lambda < 0$: ϕ is defined as $min\{0, d_{min}\} \leq V \wedge V \leq max\{0, d_{max}\}$; and
(iii) Case $\lambda = 0$: ϕ is defined as $V = V(x(0))$.

We illustrate the above technique from an example from the sporulation initiation network of the bacteria *B.Subtilis* [32,27].

Example 1. The proteins $(SinI)$ and $(SinR)$ are known to be crucial in the decision for committing to sporulation. High concentration of $(SinR)$ inhibits sporulation. Under conditions of stress, the production of $(SinI)$ increases, $(SinI)$

binds with $(SinR)$, thus reducing the concentration of free $(SinR)$, and thus promoting sporulation. The dynamics of these two protein concentrations is given by:

$$(\dot{SinI}) = \Delta_{(SinI)} - \lambda(SinI) - k(SinI)(SinR)$$

$$(\dot{SinR}) = \Delta_{(SinR)} - \lambda(SinR) - k(SinI)(SinR)$$

where $\Delta_{(SinI)}$ and $\Delta_{(SinR)}$ are determined by the corresponding transcription and translation rates and k is the rate of reaction that binds $(SinI)$ to $(SinR)$. In a *hybrid* model of the network, the dynamics of the values of $\Delta_{(SinI)}$ and $\Delta_{(SinR)}$ are captured through *discrete* mode transitions. In any given mode, the values of $\Delta_{(SinI)}$ and $\Delta_{(SinR)}$ can be assumed constants.

In matrix notation, let $x = [(SinI), (SinR), z]^T$, and let $y = [(SinI)(SinR)]$, we have $\dot{x} = Ax + By$, where

$$A = \begin{bmatrix} -\lambda & 0 & \Delta_{(SinI)} \\ 0 & -\lambda & \Delta_{(SinR)} \\ 0 & 0 & 0 \end{bmatrix} \qquad B = \begin{bmatrix} -k \\ -k \\ 0 \end{bmatrix}$$

Consider $c = [-\lambda, \lambda, \Delta_{(SinI)} - \Delta_{(SinR)}]^T$. This vector is an eigenvector of A^T with corresponding eigenvalue $-\lambda$ and it is also in the kernel of B^T.

Define $V = c^T x$. Assume that in the "stressed" mode, $\Delta_{(SinI)} = \Delta_{(SinR)}$. In this mode, if the cell goes into the state where $(SinI) \geq (SinR)$, then (in all subsequently reachable states) it will always be the case that $(SinI) \geq (SinR)$. Thus $(SinI) \geq (SinR)$ would be a stable region.

The above method can be implemented since it only involves computing eigenvectors and testing if an eigenvector is in the kernel of another matrix. This can be efficiently done when the eigenvalue λ is a rational (as in the above example). If not, then we will need to represent and compute with algebraic numbers.

This method can be effectively used on most of the hybrid models that result from modeling of genetic regulatory networks. However, for other more general classes of systems, it is not quite as effective, since it can only generate *linear* functions V. We next discuss approaches to discover nonlinear functions V.

3   Polynomial Invariants

We are interested in polynomial invariants of nonlinear systems. We generate such invariants using various computational techniques from the field of algebraic geometry, most notably Gröbner bases and Syzygy bases computations [5], and the Frobenius theorem [30].

Consider the dynamics given by $\dot{x} = p$, where p is a vector field. The syzygies, Syz, of the vector field p is defined as the set of all 1-forms h^T s.t. $h^T p = 0$:

$$Syz(p) := \{h^T : h^T p = 0\}$$

A 1-form h^T is *exact* if there exists a smooth function (polynomial, in our case) V such that $h^T = dV$.

Suppose there is a syzygy q^T of the vector field p which is also exact. Consequently, there is a polynomial V such that

$$\partial V/\partial x_1 = q_1, \ \partial V/\partial x_2 = q_2, \ \ldots, \ \partial V/\partial x_n = q_n \text{ and}$$
$$q_1 p_1 + q_2 p_2 + \cdots + q_n p_n = 0$$

Under these assumptions, it is easy to note that the Lie derivative of V with respect to the vector field p vanishes, that is,

$$\frac{dV}{dt} = dVp = \frac{\partial V}{\partial x_1}\frac{dx_1}{dt} + \frac{\partial V}{\partial x_2}\frac{dx_2}{dt} + \cdots + \frac{\partial V}{\partial x_n}\frac{dx_n}{dt}$$
$$= q_1 p_1 + q_2 p_2 + \cdots + q_n p_n = 0$$

Hence, the value of the expression $V(x_1, x_2, \ldots, x_n)$ remains invariant through the time evolution of the nonlinear system.

Theorem 2. *Let $\dot{x} = p$ be a nonlinear dynamical system. Suppose the 1-form h^T is a syzygy of p and is exact such that $h^T = dV$.*

If $x(0)$ is some initial state, then the formula $V = V(x(0))$ denotes an over approximation of the set of states reachable from $x(0)$.

Given a polynomial vector field p, the set of generators for the set $Syz(p)$ is computable using well-known techniques from computational algebraic geometry. Frobenius theorem can be used to check if a given syzygy is exact.

Example 2. Consider the nonlinear dynamical system:

$$\dot{x}_1 = x_1 x_2 \qquad \dot{x}_2 = -x_1$$

It is the case that $1x_1 x_2 + x_2(-x_1) = 0$ and hence $(1, x_2)$ is a syzygy of the polynomials $x_1 x_2, -x_1$. A solution for V that satisfies both $\partial V/\partial x_1 = 1$ and $\partial V/\partial x_2 = x_2$, is $V = x_1 + x_2^2/2$. It is easily observed that $\dot{V} = 0$ and hence V is an invariant of the above dynamical system.

Example 3. Consider the rotational motion of a rigid body in three-dimensional space. In the absence of external torques, the motion can be described by

$$\dot{x}_1 = a x_2 x_3 \qquad \dot{x}_2 = -b x_1 x_3 \qquad \dot{x}_3 = c x_1 x_2$$

in a suitably chosen coordinate axes. A syzygy for the vector field $p = [a x_2 x_2, -b x_1 x_3, c x_1 x_2]^T$ is $[a' x_1, b' x_2, c' x_3]$ whenever $a'a - b'b + c'c = 0$. Thus, we are constrained to find a V such that $\partial V/\partial x_1 = a' x_1$, $\partial V/\partial x_2 = b' x_2$, and $\partial V/\partial x_3 = c' x_3$. By Frobenius theorem, we know these constraints are satisfiable and indeed $V = a' x_1^2/2 + b' x_2^2/2 + c' x_3^2/2$ is the desired invariant function.

Details of the computability issues are postponed to a later section. We move on to more general forms of polynomial invariants[1].

---

[1] Polynomial functions V such that $\dot{V} = 0$, discussed in this subsection, are also known as "constants of motion" or "first integral" in the theory of dynamical systems.

3.1   Exponentially Changing Functions

A set of functions that we have successfully used for computing approximate reachability for linear systems are polynomials V such that $dV/dt = \lambda V$, for some real constant λ. In the case of linear systems, it is known that the exact reachability set is *computable* whenever n such linear functions exist [18]. In [25], we showed that approximate reachability sets can be computed in the case when fewer than n such functions exist. Computation of such (linear) functions for linear systems reduces to eigenvector computation.

For a system with dynamics $\dot{x} = p$, it is the case that

$$\frac{dV}{dt} = \lambda V \qquad \text{iff} \qquad dVp = \lambda V$$

Define the ideal, $Ideal(p)$, generated by a polynomial vector field p as

$$Ideal(p) := \{r : r = q^T p, q^T \text{ is any polynomial 1-form}\}$$

The statement $dVp = \lambda V$ is equivalent to saying that (i) $V \in Ideal(p)$, that is, there exists a polynomial 1-form q^T such that $V = q^T p$ and (ii) $dV = \lambda^{-1} q^T$.

Ideal membership is efficiently decided by Gröbner basis computation [5]. The details of computability are relegated to a later section. If we have computed a polynomial V and constant λ satisfying the above two conditions, then we immediately get the following upper-bound on the set of reachable states of the nonlinear system.

Theorem 3. *Let $\dot{x} = p$ be a nonlinear dynamical system and Init denote the set of initial states of the system. Suppose V is a (nonlinear) polynomial such that*

– *$V \in Ideal(p)$, that is, $V = q^T p$, and*
– *$dV = \lambda^{-1} q^T$.*

If d_{min} and d_{max} denote, respectively, the minimum and maximum values in the set $\{V(x(0)) : x(0) \in Init\}$, then the formula ϕ, as defined below, is always an over approximation of the set of reachable states of the system:
(i) Case $\lambda > 0$: if $d_{min} > 0$, then ϕ is $V \geq d_{min}$, if $d_{max} < 0$, then ϕ is $V \leq d_{max}$, and if $d_{min} = d_{max} = 0$, then ϕ is $V = 0$;
(ii) Case $\lambda < 0$: ϕ is $min\{0, d_{min}\} \leq V \wedge V \leq max\{0, d_{max}\}$; and
(iii) Case $\lambda = 0$: ϕ is $V = V(x(0))$.

Proof. The Lie derivative of the function V with respect to the vector field p is λV, and hence $V(x(t)) = V(x(0))e^{\lambda t}$. The conclusions follow.

We note here that for linear systems, the 1-form q^T can be chosen to be the left eigenvector of the A matrix [25] and hence such q^T's can be easily computed. For nonlinear systems, q^T can be seen as a suitable generalization of the concept of an (left) eigenvector, but computing such an q^T is not as easy, see Section 4.

3.2   Nondecreasing Functions

Theorem 3 makes strong assumptions which restrict its applicability. We weaken the conditions by noticing that λ need not be a constant, it can be any nonpositive or nonnegative definite function. We say that a function r (from $\Re^n$ to $\Re$) is *nonnegative definite relative to* ψ if it is the case that the formula ψ implies $r \geq 0$ in the theory of reals, that is, $\Re \vdash \psi \Rightarrow r \geq 0$. The formula ψ would represent the state invariant of the mode of the hybrid system whose dynamics are being studied.

A minor variant of the method of Section 3.1 considers functions V such that the Lie derivative of V with respect to the vector field $\boldsymbol{p}$ of the nonlinear system is (relatively) nonnegative definite. In other words, the function V satisfies the equation $dV/dt = r$, where the polynomial r is nonnegative definite (relative to the state invariant). Note that even when no state invariant is given (that is, ψ is just *True*), we can still have nontrivial p's which are nonnegative definite. In particular, these will be sums of squares of polynomials.

Theorem 4. *Let* $\dot{\boldsymbol{x}} = \boldsymbol{p}$ *be a nonlinear dynamical system with initial states Init and state invariant* ψ. *If* r *is nonnegative definite relative to* ψ *and such that*

- $r \in Ideal(\boldsymbol{p})$, *that is,* $r = \boldsymbol{q}^T\boldsymbol{p}$, *and*
- *the 1-form* $\boldsymbol{q}^T$ *is exact, that is,* $d V = \boldsymbol{q}^T$,

then the formula $V \geq d_{min}$ *is an over approximation of the set of reachable states of the system, where* $d_{min} = min\{V(\boldsymbol{x}(0)) : \boldsymbol{x}(0) \in Init\}$.

We can weaken the conditions of Theorem 4 and require the polynomial function r to be nonnegative definite relative to either $\psi \wedge V > 0$ or $\psi \wedge V < 0$. The conclusion is correspondingly weakened.

Corollary 1. *Let* $\dot{\boldsymbol{x}} = \boldsymbol{p}$ *be a nonlinear dynamical system with initial states Init and state invariant* ψ. *Let* r *and* V *be such that*

- $r = d V \boldsymbol{p}$ *and*
- r *is nonnegative definite relative to* $\psi \wedge V > 0$ *(alternatively, relative to* $\psi \wedge V < 0$).

Define $d_{min} = min\{V(\boldsymbol{x}(0)) : \boldsymbol{x}(0) \in Init\}$. *If* $d_{min} > 0$ *(alternatively,* $d_{min} < 0$), *then the formula* $V \geq d_{min}$ *is an over approximation of the set of reachable states of the system.*

Proof. If V and r are defined as above, then $\dot{V} = d V \boldsymbol{p} = r$ and $\Re \vdash \psi \wedge V > 0 \Rightarrow r > 0$. If $d_{min} > 0$, then in all initial states, $r \geq 0$, and hence the value of V is always nondecreasing, and hence $V \geq d_{min}$.

Alternatively, consider the case when $\Re \vdash \psi \wedge V < 0 \Rightarrow r \geq 0$. In this case, whenever the value of the function V drops below zero, its derivative r becomes nonnegative. In particular, when $V = d_{min} < 0$, then $\dot{V} \geq 0$, and hence $V \geq d_{min}$ always.

We illustrate the two results by some examples.

Example 4. Consider the following nonlinear system

$$\dot{x}_1 = x_2 + x_1 x_2^2 \qquad \dot{x}_2 = -x_1 + x_1^2 x_2$$

Let us assume that we are given $x_1 \geq 0 \wedge x_2 \geq 0$ as the state invariant. Gröbner basis computation reveals that $x_1 x_2 \in Ideal(p_1, p_2)$ and we get $x_1 \dot{x}_1 - x_2 \dot{x}_2 = 2x_1 x_2 = r$. A suitable function V such that $r = dVp$ is $x_1^2/2 - x_2^2/2$. Clearly, by construction, $\dot{V} = 2x_1 x_2$ and $r \geq 0$ whenever $x_1 \geq 0$ and $x_2 \geq 0$. Hence, we conclude that V is always nondecreasing. In particular, this means that if $x_1 > x_2$ initially, then $x_1 > x_2$ always.

Example 5. Consider the nonlinear system

$$\dot{x}_1 = x_1 - x_2 + x_1 x_2 \qquad \dot{x}_2 = -x_2 - x_2^2.$$

The nonnegative definite polynomial x_2^2 is in the ideal generated by $x_1 - x_2 + x_1 x_2$ and $-x_2 - x_2^2$ and we correspondingly have $x_2^2 = -x_2(x_1 - x_2 + x_1 x_2) - x_1(-x_2 - x_2^2)$. Now, we notice that $\partial(-x_2)/\partial x_2 = \partial(-x_1)/\partial x_1 = -1$ and we get the corresponding V as $-x_1 x_2$. In all, we conclude that $d/dt(-x_1 x_2) = x_2^2$. Since $x_2^2 \geq 0$ is always true, we can infer that the value of $-x_1 x_2$ is nondecreasing (Theorem 4).

Example 6. Consider another nonlinear system

$$\dot{x}_1 = x_1 + 2x_2 + x_1 x_2^2 \qquad \dot{x}_2 = 2x_1 + x_2 - x_1^2 x_2$$

Assume that we are given the state invariant $x_1 \geq 0$ and $x_2 \geq 0$.

We note that the polynomial $r = (x_1 + x_2)^2 + 2x_1 x_2$ is in the ideal of the two polynomials above and that $dVp = r$ for $V = x_1^2/2 + x_2^2/2$. Now, r is nonnegative definite relative to the state invariant $x_1 \geq 0 \wedge x_2 \geq 0$. Hence, we conclude that V is nondecreasing.

A different choice of r in the ideal is $r = x_1^2 - x_2^2 + 2x_1^2 x_2^2$, where $r = dVp$ for $V = x_1^2/2 - x_2^2/2$. The polynomial r can be expressed as $2V + 2x_1^2 x_2^2$ and hence $\Re \vdash V > 0 \Rightarrow r \geq 0$. Thus, if $V > 0$ in the initial states of the system, then $V > 0$ always subsequently. Note that we do not need the state invariant in this case.

New tools for effective sum of squares decomposition of polynomials are now available, which can be used to determine if a particular polynomial is positive or negative definite [23].

3.3   Oscillating Functions

Another useful class of functions that yield interesting reachability information are functions V whose value oscillates as the dynamical system evolves. If the frequency of oscillation was a constant, then such a V would satisfy the equation

$$\ddot{V} = -kV$$

But the frequency of oscillation is often not a constant and hence, finding V that satisfies the above property usually ends in failure. However, oscillating functions satisfy another very interesting property, which can be used to detect such behavior.

Let p be a vector field. Consider a set $V = \{V_1, V_2, \ldots, V_k\}$ of k (polynomial) functions. Define the *extended monoid* of a V as the minimal set $Mon(V)$ such that (i) $V \subset Mon(V)$, (ii) $V_1 V_2 \in Mon(V)$ whenever $V_1, V_2 \in Mon(V)$, and (iii) $rV_1 \in Mon(V)$ whenever $V_1 \in Mon(V)$ and r is nonpositive or nonnegative definite. In other words, the set $Mon(V)$ is the monoid over V *and* all nonpositive and nonnegative definite functions.

We say that a set of (polynomial) functions $V_1, V_2, \ldots, V_k$ is *closed under Lie derivative computation with respect to p upto multiplication* if for every function V_i, the Lie derivative of V_i w.r.t p is in $Mon(V)$. An important property of any such set is that if the signs $(+, -, 0)$ of $V_1, \ldots, V_k$ are known at any state, then the signs of their Lie derivatives are also known at that state.

For a given dynamical system $\dot{x} = p$, any set of functions that is closed under Lie derivative computation w.r.t p can provide useful information about oscillation or divergence of the system. We cannot state a formal theorem since the exact reachable sets depend on how the Lie derivatives are related, but we illustrate the method with a few examples.

Example 7. The Volterra predator-prey model [30] is given by

$$\dot{x}_1 = -x_1 + x_1 x_2 \qquad \dot{x}_2 = x_2 - x_1 x_2$$

where x_1 indicates the number of predators and x_2 indicates the number of prey. It is an easy exercise to note that the set of four polynomials $V = \{x_1, x_2, (x_2 - 1), (x_1 - 1)\}$ is closed under Lie derivative computation. To see this, just factor the polynomials in the vector field p as follows:

$$\dot{x}_1 = x_1(x_2 - 1) \qquad \dot{x}_2 = -x_2(x_1 - 1)$$

The qualitative abstraction of this model [26] over the four polynomials in V shows the possible oscillatory behavior of the systems. Another choice of a closed set is $\{x_1 + x_2, x_2 - x_1, x_1 + x_2 - 2x_1 x_2, 1 - 2x_1 x_2\}$ and this can be used to refine the above abstraction [26].

Example 8. Consider the pendulum equations

$$\dot{x}_1 = x_2 \qquad \dot{x}_2 = -x_1 + x_1^3/6$$

Factoring the polynomial $-x_1 + x_1^3/6$ as $x_1(-1 + x_1^2/6)$, we note that the derivative of the factor $-1 + x_1^2/6$ is $2x_1 x_2$, which is a product of x_1 and x_2. Hence, the set $V = \{x_1, x_2, -1 + x_1^2/6\}$ is closed under Lie derivative computation. A qualitative abstraction over these three polynomials exhibits oscillatory behavior [26].

Example 7 also shows a weakness of the polynomial-based qualitative abstraction approach. *If* we only use polynomials, then *any* qualitative abstraction of the system in Example 7 would have trajectories that allow the dynamics to collapse onto one of the axes ($x_1 = 0$ or $x_2 = 0$) even if the initial state has $x_1 \neq 0$ and $x_2 \neq 0$. In this example, we really need nonpolynomial functions (in particular, $\ln(x_1) - x_1 + \ln(x_2) - x_2$) to show that the system oscillates. Note that Theorem 2 can be used to determine such nonpolynomial invariants, but the computability issues are a challenge.

4 Computability Issues

The real value of the results presented in the preceding sections arises from the fact that the interesting functions V can be computed in the domain of polynomials. We describe some techniques that can be used for this purpose. Gröbner bases is a canonical representation for the ideal generated by a set of polynomials. They are also used for computing the bases for the set of syzygies of a set of polynomials.

4.1 Gröbner Bases Computation

Given a set $p_1, p_2, \ldots, p_n$ of polynomials, Gröbner basis computation algorithms [5] work by generating new polynomials p in the ideal of these n polynomials by repeatedly eliminating highest degree power-product terms from the polynomials $p_1, p_2, \ldots, p_n$. For example, if p_1 is $x_2 + x_1 x_2^2$ and p_2 is $-x_1 + x_1^2 x_2$ (see Example 4), then Gröbner basis computation generates the polynomial $p_3 = x_1 p_1 - x_2 p_2$ because this way the highest power-products in p_1 and p_2 are canceled. The new polynomial $p_3 = 2x_1 x_2$ is added to the original set of polynomials $\{p_1, p_2\}$. The new polynomial can be used to delete p_1 from this set and replace it by $p_1 - x_2 p_3/2 = x_2$. Similarly, p_2 can be replaced by x_1. The polynomial x_2 can be used to delete p_3. Thus, the set $\{x_1, x_2\}$ is a Gröbner basis of $\{p_1, p_2\}$. It is routine to generate the 1-form q^T s.t. $q^T p$ is equal to the polynomials generated in this procedure. For example, $x_2 = (-x_1 x_2/2 + 1)p_1 - x_2 p_2$.

We are interested in $r \in Ideal(p)$ s.t. if $r = q^T p$, then the 1-form q^T is exact. The polynomials r in the final Gröbner basis need not satisfy this condition. But each of the intermediate polynomials generated during the computation of a Gröbner basis can be tested. In the above example, the 1-form corresponding to the intermediate polynomial p_3 is indeed exact. This is the form used in Example 4. It is also observed that all the polynomials used in other examples in this paper can be similarly generated.

It should be emphasized that the method outlined above is not *complete*, that is, there could be elements in $Ideal(p)$ which correspond to exact 1-forms which are not tested by the procedure. It is a very interesting problem for future work to determine if the set of ideal members generated by exact 1-forms is computable. Define

$$ExactIdeal(p) = \{q^T p : q^T \text{ is exact}\}$$

As far as the authors know, computability of this set is open. But as in several other practically useful real algebraic geometry computational procedures, polynomials of bounded degree in $ExactIdeal(\boldsymbol{p})$ can be generated and used.

4.2   Syzygy Computation

In our methods, interest was in syzygies which were also exact. The Gröbner basis method can be used to construct a basis for the set of syzygies for polynomials $p_1, p_2, \ldots, p_n$ as follows: the polynomials $p_1, \ldots, p_n$ are partitioned into two disjoint sets, say $\{p_1\}$ and $\{p_2, \ldots, p_n\}$. Next, Gröbner basis is computed for the set $\{p_1(1-Y), p_2Y, p_3Y, \ldots, p_nY\}$ where Y is a new variable. Any polynomial p in the Gröbner basis *that does not contain* Y gives a syzygy. By repeating this process with $\{p_2, \ldots, p_n\}$, we can get the generators for the set of syzygies for $p_1, \ldots, p_n$ [5].

Each of the syzygies generated needs to be tested for being exact. This test can be done using the Frobenius theorem. The corresponding polynomial can then be easily generated by simple symbolic integration routines. Again note that the method described here is not complete. Just as in the case of Gröbner basis, we can define the set $ExactSyzygy(\boldsymbol{p})$ and a challenge for future work is to determine if this set is computable.

4.3   Linear Constraint Solver

A second technique for generating the functions V with the required properties is to assume that V is of a bounded degree, say it is quadratic with unknown coefficients. The properties required to be satisfied by V impose *linear constraints* on the unknown coefficient variables. Using a linear arithmetic solver, these constraints can be tested for satisfiability. Note that this method, though attractive, cannot be used for the techniques in Section 3.2 because they additionally involve unknown positive or negative definite functions.

Example 9. Consider the four-dimensional nonlinear system

$$\dot{x}_1 = x_2 \qquad \dot{x}_2 = -x_1/2 - x_2$$
$$\dot{x}_3 = x_4 \qquad \dot{x}_4 = -x_3 + 2x_1x_2 - 2x_2^2$$

If we guess that a function V of the form $x_1^2 + bx_1x_3 + cx_1 + dx_3$ satisfies the equation $\ddot{V} = \lambda V$, then we get the following constraint:

$$\begin{aligned} \ddot{F} &= 2x_1(-x_1/2 - x_2) + 2x_2^2 + 2bx_2x_4 + bx_1(-x_3 + 2x_1x_2 - 2x_2^2) + \\ &\quad bx_3(-x_1/2 - x_2) + c(-x_1/2 - x_2) + d(-x_3 + 2x_1x_2 - 2x_2^2) \\ &= \lambda F \end{aligned}$$

This gives rise to the following linear constraints over the variables a, b, c, d and λ.

$$\begin{array}{cccc} -1 = \lambda & -2 + 2d = 0 & 2 - 2d = 0 & 2b = 0 \\ -b - b/2 = 0 & & 2b = 0 & -2b = 0 & -b = 0 \\ -c/2 = \lambda c & & c = 0 & -d = \lambda d \end{array}$$

A satisfying assignment is $\lambda = -1$, $d = 1$, and $b = c = 0$. Thus, $x_1^2 + x_3$ is the required function.

5 Related Work and Conclusion

There is a lot of work in the theory of nonlinear systems [30,24]. Energy functions are used to get analytical descriptions of trajectories and provide arguments for stability or periodicity. However, the problem of generating these functions and issues about computability have not been addressed. Moreover, such functions have not been used to get over approximations of the reach sets. These features distinguish this work from the well established theory of nonlinear systems.

Techniques from algebraic geometry, mainly Gröbner basis methods, have been used for generating switching surfaces [31], and generating constraints on parameters and bounds for determining Lyapunov functions for *local* stability regions [9,8]. In most of these applications, Gröbner basis is used as a quantifier elimination procedure – a simpler alternative to quantifier elimination in the theory of reals [4].

This paper presents some first results on computing interesting polynomial functions for nonlinear systems. The use of these functions can be integrated within other methods: the functions can be used directly as predicates in an abstraction framework to generate good abstractions, such as in [2,26], or they can be used as invariants to strengthen the reach sets computed by other reachability computing tools such as [14,13]. For example, approximate reach sets are computed for nonlinear hybrid systems by computing reach sets for conservative linear hybrid automata approximations [12,13] or timed automata approximations [11] of the original nonlinear system. The building of the approximation can be made more effective using invariants generated by our approach.

This work opens several interesting directions for future work. On the theoretical side, one can ask the question if we can get decidability of reachability for certain classes of nonlinear systems, whenever sufficiently many such energy functions V's exist. In the linear case, we know the answer is positive [19]. Furthermore, as in the linear case, can we extend the computational methods to richer decidable theories than the theory of reals? These decidability results can then be used to get newer classes of hybrid systems with decidable reachability problem [18,17,3]. In the field of computational algebraic geometry, the challenge is to find if the sets exact-ideal and exact-syzygy are computable.

The theory outlined in this paper is useful even when the answers to the above questions are unknown. Construction of useful polynomial functions can be automated using bounded degree approximations as described in this paper. And it can be made more powerful using other existing tools, such as the sum of squares tool [23], which also shows how incomplete techniques can still be very effective in solving real and challenging problems [22,21].

References

[1] R. Alur, T. Dang, and F. Ivancic. Reachability analysis of hybrid systems via predicate abstraction. In Tomlin and Greenstreet [28].

[2] R. Alur, T. Dang, and F. Ivancic. Progress on reachability analysis of hybrid systems using predicate abstraction. In Maler and Pnueli [20].

[3] R. Alur, T. Henzinger, G. Lafferriere, and G. J. Pappas. Discrete abstractions of hybrid systems. *Proceedings of the IEEE*, 88(2):971–984, July 2000.

[4] H. Anai and V. Weispfenning. Reach set computations using real quantifier elimination. In M. D. Di Benedetto and A. L. Sangiovanni-Vincentelli, editors, *HSCC*, volume 2034 of *Lecture Notes in Computer Science*, pages 63–76. Springer, 2001.

[5] T. Becker and V. Weispfenning. *Gröbner bases: a computational approach to commutative algebra*. Springer-Verlag, Berlin, 1993.

[6] A. Chutinan and B. H. Krogh. Verification of polyhedral-invariant hybrid automata using polygonal flow pipe approximations. In Vaandrager and van Schuppen [29], pages 76–90.

[7] T. Dang and O. Maler. Reachability analysis via face lifting. In T. A. Henzinger and S. Sastry, editors, *HSCC*, volume 1386 of *LNCS*, pages 96–109. Springer, 1998.

[8] K. Forsman. Construction of Lyapunov functions using Gröbner bases. In *30th CDC*. IEEE, 1991.

[9] K. Forsman and T. Glad. Constructive algebraic geometry in nonlinear control. In *29th CDC*, volume 5, pages 2825–2827. IEEE, 1990.

[10] S. Graf and H. Saïdi. Construction of abstract state graphs with PVS. In O. Grumberg, editor, *Proc. of 9th Conference on Computer-Aided Verification (CAV'97)*, volume 1254, pages 72–83. Springer Verlag, 1997.

[11] T. A. Henzinger and P.-H. Ho. Algorithmic analysis of nonlinear hybrid systems. In P. Wolper, editor, *Computer Aided Verification, Proc. of the 7th Intl. Conf., CAV '95*, volume 939 of *LNCS*, pages 225–238. Springer, 1995.

[12] T. A. Henzinger and H. Wong-Toi. Linear phase-portrait approximations for nonlinear systems. In R. Alur, T. Henzinger, and E. D. Sontag (eds.), editors, *Hybrid Systems III*, volume 1066 of *LNCS*, pages 377–388, Berlin, 1996. Springer-Verlag.

[13] Thomas A. Henzinger, Pei-Hsin Ho, and Howard Wong-Toi. Algorithmic analysis of nonlinear hybrid systems. *IEEE Transactions on Automatic Control*, 43:540–554, 1998.

[14] B. H. Krogh and O. Stursberg. On efficient representation and computation of reachable sets for hybrid systems. In Maler and Pnueli [20].

[15] B. J. Kuipers. *Qualitative reasoning: Modeling and simulation with incomplete knowledge*. MIT Press, Cambridge, MA, 1994.

[16] A. B. Kurzhanski and P. Varaiya. Ellipsoidal techniques for reachability analysis. In N. A. Lynch and B. H. Krogh, editors, *HSCC*, volume 1790 of *LNCS*, pages 202–214. Springer, 2000.

[17] G. Lafferriere, G. J. Pappas, and S. Sastry. O-minimal hybrid systems. *Mathematics of Control, Signals, and Systems*, 13(1):1–21, 2000.

[18] G. Lafferriere, G. J. Pappas, and S. Yovine. A new class of decidable hybrid systems. In Vaandrager and van Schuppen [29], pages 137–151.

[19] G. Lafferriere, G. J. Pappas, and S. Yovine. Symbolic reachability computations for families of linear vector fields. *J. Symbolic Computation*, 32(3):231–253, 2001.

[20] O. Maler and A. Pnueli, editors. *Hybrid Systems: Computation and Control, 6th International Workshop, HSCC 2003*, volume 2623 of *LNCS*. Springer, April 2003.

[21] P. A. Parrilo. *Structured semidefinite programs and semialgebraic geometric methods in robustness and optimization*. PhD thesis, California Institute of Technology, Pasadena, 2000.

[22] P. A. Parrilo and B. Sturmfels. Minimizing polynomial functions. In *Algorithmic and quantitative real algebraic geometry*, volume 60 of *DIMACS series in discrete mathematics and theoretical computer science*, pages 83–99, 2003. http://www/arxiv.org/abs/math.OC/0103170.

[23] S. Prajna, A. Papachristodoulou, and P. A. Parrilo. *SOSTOOLS: Sum of square optimization toolbox for MATLAB*, 2002.

[24] S. Sastry. *Nonlinear systems:Analysis, stability, and control*. Springer, 1999.

[25] A. Tiwari. Approximate reachability for linear systems. In Maler and Pnueli [20], pages 514–525.

[26] A. Tiwari and G. Khanna. Series of abstractions for hybrid automata. In Tomlin and Greenstreet [28], pages 465–478.

[27] A. Tiwari, D. Wolf, A. Arkin, and P. Lincoln. Hybrid modeling and analysis of genetic regulatory networks: Sporulation initiation in bacillus subtilis, 2003. In preparation.

[28] C. Tomlin and M. R. Greenstreet, editors. *Hybrid Systems: Computation and Control, 5th International Workshop, HSCC 2002, Proceedings*, volume 2289 of *Lecture Notes in Computer Science*. Springer, 2002.

[29] F. W. Vaandrager and J. H. van Schuppen, editors. *Hybrid Systems: Computation and Control, Second International Workshop, HSCC'99, Proceedings*, volume 1569 of *Lecture Notes in Computer Science*. Springer, 1999.

[30] M. Vidyasagar. *Nonlinear systems analysis*. Prentice Hall, 1993.

[31] U. Walther, T. Georgiou, and A. Tannenbaum. On the computation of switching surfaces in optimal control:A Gröbner basis approach. *IEEE Transactions on Automatic Control*, 46(4), 2001.

[32] D. Wolf and A. Arkin. Survival strategy selection as an emergent property of uber-network topology, 2003. Unpublished manuscript, Lawrence Berkeley Laboratory, Berkeley.

On Practical Stability and Stabilization of Hybrid and Switched Systems

Xuping Xu[1] and Guisheng Zhai[2]

[1] Department of Electrical and Computer Engineering,
Penn State Erie, Erie, PA 16563, USA
Xuping-Xu@psu.edu
[2] Department of Opto-Mechatronics,
Wakayama University, Sakaedani, Wakayama 640-8510, JAPAN
zhai@sys.wakayama-u.ac.jp

Abstract. In this paper, practical stability and stabilization problems for hybrid and switched systems are studied. We formally introduce the notions of ϵ-practical stability and practical stabilizability. The main results of the paper include a direct method for the ϵ-practical stability analysis of hybrid systems and sufficient conditions for the practical stabilizability of switched systems. Moreover, we construct an ϵ-practically stabilizing switching law in the proof of the stabilizability results and apply it to a tracking problem to show its effectiveness.

1 Introduction

Recently, it has been noticed that, under appropriate switching laws, hybrid and switched systems whose subsystems have no common equilibrium may still exhibit interesting behaviors similar to those of a conventional stable system near an equilibrium. These behaviors are formally defined as practical stability in [11,12,13,14]. Such practical stability notions are extensions of the traditional concepts on practical stability [3,4] and finite time stability [7,8,10], which are concerned with bringing the system trajectories to be within given bounds. Similar boundedness behaviors have also been observed by other researchers. For example, Lin and Antsaklis in [6] study the ultimate boundedness problem for switched linear systems with uncertainties.

In this paper, we study practical stability analysis and practical stabilization design problems for hybrid and switched systems within a unified framework. In particular, we focus on practical stability and stabilization problems of infinite time horizon. The notions of ϵ-practical stability and practical stabilizability are formally introduced. Extensions of previous results [13,14] on practical stability analysis using a direct method are proposed in the paper. The direct method uses ϵ-practical Lyapunov-like functions and provides us with sufficient conditions for the ϵ-practical stability of hybrid systems. Besides the practical stability analysis, we also propose sufficient conditions for the practical stabilizability of switched systems with time-varying subsystems. Such stabilizability results are extensions of our previous results for switched systems with integrator and

R. Alur and G.J. Pappas (Eds.): HSCC 2004, LNCS 2993, pp. 615–630, 2004.

time-invariant subsystems [11,12]. In the proof of the stabilizability results, we explicitly construct a valid switching law under which the system is ϵ-practically stable. As an example, we then apply the proposed switching law to solve an interesting and challenging tracking problem.

It should be noted that, unlike the available literature results which usually study either the practical stability problem or the practical stabilization problem, here we present results for both problems within a unified framework. As opposed to the many special classes of hybrid systems (e.g., systems with time-invariant or linear subsystems) in the literature, our results here apply to more general hybrid and switched systems with time-varying subsystems. Such systems are quite useful. For example, many interesting tracking problems by switched systems, such as the one presented in this paper, are concerning time-varying subsystems. We expect that our results in the present paper can stimulate more interest in the new research direction of practical stability of hybrid systems, and will relate hybrid and switched systems to more useful applications.

In the following, we introduce the models of hybrid and switched systems in Section 2. The results for ϵ-practical stability are presented in Section 3. In Section 4, we present the results for practical stabilizability. Section 5 concludes.

2   Hybrid and Switched Systems

In this paper, we consider hybrid systems consisting of subsystems[1]

$$\dot{x} = f_i(x,t), \quad i \in I \triangleq \{1, 2, \cdots, M\}. \tag{1}$$

The active subsystem at each time instant is orchestrated by a switching law. Given any initial time t_0 and state $x_0 = x(t_0)$, the switching law will generate a switching sequence $\sigma = \big((t_0, i_0), (t_1, i_1), \cdots, (t_k, i_k), \cdots\big)$ $(t_0 \leq t_1 \leq \cdots \leq t_k \leq \cdots, i_k \in I)$ which indicates that subsystem i_k is active in $[t_k, t_{k+1})$. For a hybrid system to be well-behaved, we only consider **nonZeno** sequences which switch at most a finite number of times in any finite time interval.

For hybrid system (1), there is a discontinuous state jump described by

$$x(t_k) = g_{i_{k-1}, i_k}\big(x(t_k^-), t_k\big) \tag{2}$$

when it switches from subsystem i_{k-1} to i_k at time instant t_k. In (2), each function $g_{i,j}$ $(i, j \in I, i \neq j)$ characterizes the jump between subsystem i and j.

Remark 1. In the sequel, we simply call the abovementioned hybrid system by system (1)-(2). If there is no state jump at the switching instants, we call such system a **switched system**. It will then be denoted by switched system (1). In this paper, we assume that $f_i(x,t)$ is locally Lipschitz continuous in both x and t. And we assume that for every (x_0, t_0) and σ, the hybrid system we are studying possesses a unique solution for $t \geq t_0$.   □

---

[1] The term 'subsystem' is widely used in switched systems literatures (e.g., [5]), although 'mode' might be better than 'subsystem' here as the system dynamics can be different but the state variables remain the same.

The following definition specifies more clearly what we mean by a switching law which has been mentioned above.

Definition 1 (Switching Law). *For system (1)-(2), a switching law $\mathcal{S}$ is defined to be a mapping $\mathcal{S} : \mathbb{R}^n \times \mathbb{R} \to \bigcup_{t_0} \Sigma_{[t_0,\infty)}$ which specifies a switching sequence $\sigma = \sigma(x_0, t_0) \in \Sigma_{[t_0,\infty)}$ for any initial (x_0, t_0). Here $\Sigma_{[t_0,\infty)} \triangleq \{$switching sequence σ starting at time $t_0\}$.* □

In the sequel, when we say that a switching law is *valid*, we mean that it generates a nonZeno switching sequence for every pair (x_0, t_0).

Remark 2. $\mathcal{S}$ is often described by some rules or algorithms, which describe how to generate a switching sequence given (x_0, t_0), rather than mathematical formulae. In this paper, we specify switching laws using such descriptions.   □

3   Practical Stability

3.1   Motivation

In most of the literature results on stability analysis and stabilization of hybrid and switched systems, it is assumed that a common equilibrium exists for all subsystems. However, this assumption may not be true and may limit the applicability of hybrid systems. In fact, when subsystems have different equilibria or no equilibrium, a system can still exhibit interesting behaviors around a given point under appropriate switching laws. The behaviors are similar to those of a conventional stable system near an equilibrium. The following example illustrates such behaviors.

Example 1. Consider a switched system consisting of: subsystem 1: $\dot{x} = [-3, 2.5]^T$; subsystem 2: $\dot{x} = [-2.5, -3]^T$; subsystem 3: $\dot{x} = [3, -2.5]^T$; subsystem 4: $\dot{x} = [2.5, 3]^T$. If we apply the switching rule which makes subsystem 1 active in quadrant I, subsystem 2 active in quadrant II, subsystem 3 active in quadrant III, and subsystem 4 active in quadrant IV, the system will exhibit "convergent behaviors" around the origin. Figure 1 shows a trajectory from $x_0 = [2, 1]^T$ under this switching rule in a finite time duration.   □

In Example 3.1, under the given switching rule, the origin exhibits behaviors similar to those of an asymptotically stable system. However, as the trajectory becomes closer and closer to the origin, the system needs to switch faster and faster. This violates the nonZenoness requirement for switching sequences. In practice, a lower bound for the time between switchings can be imposed to prevent Zenoness. Such a lower bound is called a *minimum dwell time* [2] and its value may be different given different application objectives. If we incorporate a minimum dwell time into the switching rule in Example 3.1, trajectories starting from any point in $\mathbb{R}^2$ will be attracted toward the origin and eventually oscillate near the origin within certain bound.

The concept of keeping the trajectory to be within a given bound is useful in practice. For example, in temperature control systems, usually we are more

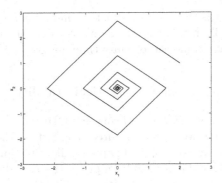

Fig. 1. A sample trajectory starting from $x_0 = [2, \ 1]^T$ for Example 3.1.

interested in keeping the temperature within certain bounds, rather than stabilizing the system asymptotically to a fixed point. In fact, such concept has been formally termed practical stability in [3,4] for ordinary differential equations. In the following, we extend such practical stability notion to hybrid system (1)-(2).

3.2   The Notion of Practical Stability

Now we introduce the notion of practical stability for system (1)-(2). Without loss of generality, we only discuss the case of the origin and consider the initial time $t_0 \geq 0$. In the following, the vector (and matrix) norm $\| \cdot \|$ denotes the 2-norm, and $B[x, r]$ denotes the closed ball $\{y \in \mathbb{R}^n \| \|y - x\| \leq r\}$.

Definition 2 (ϵ-Practical Stability). *Assume that a valid switching law S is given for hybrid system (1)-(2). Given an $\epsilon > 0$, the system is said to be ϵ-practically stable around the origin under S if, for any $t_0 \geq 0$, there exists a $\delta = \delta(\epsilon, t_0) > 0$ such that $x(t) \in B[0, \epsilon]$, $\forall t \geq t_0$, whenever $x_0 = x(t_0) \in B[0, \delta]$. If δ is independent of t_0, i.e., if $\delta = \delta(\epsilon)$, then the system is said to be* uniformly *ϵ-practically stable around the origin under S.*   □

Remark 3. Note the following differences between Definition 2 and the classical definition of stability. First, unlike the classical stability concept, here we do not assume that $f_i(0, t) = 0$, $\forall i \in I$, i.e., the origin does not have to be a common equilibrium for system (1)-(2). Actually, it does not even have to be an equilibrium for any subsystem. Second, unlike the classical definition which is based on the existence of δ for any ϵ, here the ϵ is given and hence does not vary (this is why we term it ϵ-practical stability). Given a switching law S, it can be true that for one given ϵ, δ exists; while for another ϵ value, δ does not exist. □

Remark 4. Unlike the practical stability definition in [13] which assumes that both ϵ and δ are given, here we consider practical stability in which only ϵ is given. This is due to our interest in practical stabilization in the next section. Usually, we are interested in keeping the system trajectory to be within a given

ϵ bound. However, it is the designer's task to find a bound δ for the initial state. Moreover, unlike [13], in this paper, we only consider the behaviors of a system for infinite time horizon instead of finite time horizon.   □

3.3 Sufficient Conditions for Practical Stability

As in the case of classic stability theory for ODEs (see, e.g., [9]) and hybrid systems (see, e.g., [1]), we develop a direct method for the ϵ-practical stability of system (1)-(2) using ϵ-practical Lyapunov-like functions in this subsection. However, note that these functions have properties that differ significantly from the usual Lyapunov functions in classical stability theory.

Definition 3 (ϵ-Practical Lyapunov-like Function). *Given a switching law $\mathcal{S}$, a continuously differentiable real-valued function $V(x,t)$ satisfying $V(0,t) = 0, \forall t \geq 0$ is said to be an ϵ-practical Lyapunov-like function under $\mathcal{S}$ if there exist a Lebesgue integrable function $\phi(x,t)$, a positive constant μ, and a positive real-valued function $\gamma(t_0)$ (a function of t_0), such that for any state trajectory $x(t)$ generated by $\mathcal{S}$ which starts from x_0 at t_0 and its corresponding switching sequence $\sigma = \big((t_0, i_0), (t_1, i_1), \cdots, (t_k, i_k), \cdots \big)$, the following conditions hold*

(a). $\dot{V}\big(x(t),t\big) \leq \phi\big(x(t),t\big)$ for almost every $t \geq t_0$; and

(b). $V\Big(g_{i_{k-1},i_k}\big(x(t_k^-),t_k\big),t_k\Big) \leq \mu V\big(x(t_k^-),t_k\big)$ at any switching instant t_k; and

(c). $\int_{t_0}^{t} \mu^{N(\tau,t)} \phi\big(x(\tau),\tau\big)\, d\tau < \inf_{x \notin B[0,\epsilon]} V(x,t) - \mu^{N(t_0,t)} \cdot \gamma(t_0), \forall t \geq t_0.$

Here in (a), $\dot{V}\big(x(t),t\big)$ denotes the derivative of $V(x,t)$ along the trajectory $x(t)$, i.e., $\dot{V}\big(x(t),t\big) = V_x\big(x(t),t\big) f_{i(t)}\big(x(t),t\big) + V_t\big(x(t),t\big)$ where $i(t)$ corresponds to the index of the active subsystem at time instant t. In (c), $N(a,b)$ denotes the number of switchings during the time interval (a,b).   □

Remark 5. The real-valued Lyapunov-like function V in the above definition is not a Lyapunov function in the usual sense since we do not require any particular definiteness condition concerning it or its derivatives. We use the term "Lyapunov-like function" since, similarly to the classical Lyapunov theory, this function serves as an auxiliary function in a direct method.   □

Theorem 1. *Given a valid switching law $\mathcal{S}$, system (1)-(2) is ϵ-practically stable around the origin under $\mathcal{S}$, if there exists an ϵ-practical Lyapunov-like function $V(x,t)$ under $\mathcal{S}$.*

Proof: For any given (x_0, t_0), let $x(t)$ be the corresponding trajectory of system (1)-(2) under the switching law $\mathcal{S}$. Due to the continuity of V, we can choose a $\delta = \delta(\epsilon, t_0)$ such that $0 < \delta < \epsilon$ and $\sup_{x \in B[0,\delta]} V(x,t_0) \leq \gamma(t_0)$. We can then show that $x(t) \in B[0,\epsilon], \forall t \geq t_0$ if $x_0 \in B[0,\delta]$. The proof is by contradiction. Assume that there exists a $\bar{t} \geq t_0$ at which the trajectory intersects the ϵ-sphere for the first time. Let $t_1, \cdots, t_K$ denote the switching instants before $\bar{t}$. Then, since V satisfies condition (a) in Definition 3, we have

$$V\big(x(\bar{t}), \bar{t}\big) = V\big(x(t_K), t_K\big) + \int_{t_K}^{\bar{t}} \dot{V}\big(x(\tau), \tau\big) \, d\tau$$

$$\leq V\big(x(t_K), t_K\big) + \int_{t_K}^{\bar{t}} \phi\big(x(\tau), \tau\big) \, d\tau \qquad (3)$$

and

$$V\big(x(t_k^-), t_k\big) = V\big(x(t_{k-1}), t_{k-1}\big) + \int_{t_{k-1}}^{t_k} \dot{V}\big(x(\tau), \tau\big) \, d\tau$$

$$\leq V\big(x(t_{k-1}), t_{k-1}\big) + \int_{t_{k-1}}^{t_k} \phi\big(x(\tau), \tau\big) \, d\tau \qquad (4)$$

for $k = K, \cdots, 1$.

Due to condition (b) in Definition 3, we have

$$V\big(x(t_k), t_k\big) = V\Big(g_{i_{k-1}, i_k}\big(x(t_k^-), t_k\big), t_k\Big) \leq \mu V\big(x(t_k^-), t_k\big), \ \ k = K, \cdots, 1. \quad (5)$$

Combining (5) with (3) and (4), we then obtain

$$V\big(x(\bar{t}), \bar{t}\big) \leq \mu^{N(t_0, \bar{t})} V\big(x(t_0), t_0\big) + \int_{t_0}^{\bar{t}} \mu^{N(\tau, \bar{t})} \phi\big(x(\tau), \tau\big) \, d\tau \qquad (6)$$

In view of condition (c) in Definition 3 and our choice of δ, we have

$$V\big(x(\bar{t}), \bar{t}\big) \leq \mu^{N(t_0, \bar{t})} \sup_{x \in B[0, \delta]} V(x, t_0) + \int_{t_0}^{\bar{t}} \mu^{N(\tau, \bar{t})} \phi\big(x(\tau), \tau\big) \, d\tau$$

$$\leq \mu^{N(t_0, \bar{t})} \cdot \gamma(t_0) + \int_{t_0}^{\bar{t}} \mu^{N(\tau, \bar{t})} \phi\big(x(\tau), \tau\big) \, d\tau < \inf_{x \notin B[0, \epsilon]} V(x, \bar{t}) \quad (7)$$

which implies that $x(\bar{t})$ must be in the interior of $B[0, \epsilon]$. This leads to a contradiction to the original assumption. Therefore, there does not exist a $\bar{t} \geq t_0$ as asserted above, and thus $x(t)$ is in the interior of $B[0, \epsilon]$, $\forall t \geq t_0$. This completes the proof. $\qquad \square$

Remark 6. In fact, in order to lead to the conclusion of Theorem 1, weaker conditions for (a) and (b) in Definition 3 can be posed as follows.

(a). $\dot{V}\big(x(t), t\big) \leq \phi\big(x(t), t\big)$ for almost every $t \geq t_0$ at which $x(t) \in B[0, \epsilon]$; and

(b). $V\Big(g_{i_{k-1}, i_k}\big(x(t_k^-), t_k\big), t_k\Big) \leq \mu V\big(x(t_k^-), t_k\big)$ at any switching instant t_k at which $x(t_k^-) \in B[0, \epsilon]$. $\qquad \square$

Remark 7. A stronger condition than the existence of $\phi(x,t)$ can be posed in Definition 3. Assume that there exists a Lebesgue integrable function $\psi(t)$ such that conditions (a) and (c) in Definition 3 can be modified as

(a). $\dot{V}\big(x(t),t\big) \leq \psi(t)$ for almost every $t \geq t_0$; and

(c). $\int_{t_0}^{t} \mu^{N(\tau,t)} \psi(\tau)\, d\tau < \inf_{x \notin B[0,\epsilon]} V\big(x,t\big) - \mu^{N(t_0,t)} \cdot \gamma(t_0), \forall t \geq t_0$.

The condition is then stronger since ψ does not depend on x here. Such stronger conditions have been adopted in [13,14]. □

A real-valued function $V(x,t) : \mathbb{R}^n \times \mathbb{R} \to \mathbb{R}$ is said to be *decrescent* if there exists a positive definite function $W(x) : \mathbb{R}^n \to \mathbb{R}$ such that $|V(x,t)| \leq W(x)$, $\forall t \geq 0$. If the V in Theorem 1 is decrescent, then we have the following theorem.

Theorem 2. *Given a valid switching law $\mathcal{S}$, system (1)-(2) is uniformly ϵ-practically stable around the origin under $\mathcal{S}$, if there exists a decrescent ϵ-practical Lyapunov-like function $V(x,t)$ under $\mathcal{S}$ and the $\gamma(t_0)$ corresponding to $V(x,t)$ can be chosen to be a constant $\gamma > 0$.*

Proof: Since V is decrescent, we have $|V(x,t)| \leq W(x), \forall x \in \mathbb{R}^n$ for some positive definite function $W(x)$. The proof is similar to that of Theorem 1 except that now we can choose $\delta = \delta(\epsilon)$ such that $0 < \delta < \epsilon$ and $\sup_{x \in B[0,\delta]} W(x) \leq \gamma$. □

Example 2. Consider a hybrid system (1)-(2) where $f_i(x,t) = A_i(t)x(t) + b_i(t)$, $i \in I$ and $g_{i,j}\big(x(t^-),t\big) = \Theta_{i,j}(t)x(t^-), i,j \in I, i \neq j$. Here $A_i(t) \in \mathbb{R}^{n \times n}$, $b_i(t) \in \mathbb{R}^n$ and $\Theta_{i,j}(t) \in \mathbb{R}^{n \times n}$. Consider a switching law $\mathcal{S}$ which depends only on time and specifies a fixed switching sequence $\sigma = \big((t_0,i_0),(t_1,i_1),\cdots,(t_k,i_k),\cdots\big)$. Note here the origin may not be an equilibrium of the system. Hence we may not be able to study the stability of the system. However, we can still study the practical stability of the system.

Let $V(x,t) = \sqrt{x^T x} = \|x\|$ and $Q_i(t) = \frac{1}{2}\big(A_i(t) + A_i^T(t)\big), i \in I$. Let $\hat{\lambda}_i(t)$ denote the maximum instantaneous eigenvalue of $Q_i(t)$. Then, on any time interval $[t_k,t_{k+1})$,

$$\dot{V}\big(x(t),t\big) = \frac{x^T(t)Q_{i_k}(t)x(t) + x^T(t)b_{i_k}(t)}{\sqrt{x^T(t)x(t)}} \leq \frac{\hat{\lambda}_{i_k}(t)\|x(t)\|^2 + \|x(t)\| \cdot \|b_{i_k}(t)\|}{\|x(t)\|}$$

$$= \hat{\lambda}_{i_k}(t)\|x(t)\| + \|b_{i_k}(t)\|. \tag{8}$$

If we choose $\phi(x,t) = \epsilon\hat{\lambda}(t) + \|b(t)\|$ where $\hat{\lambda}(t) = \hat{\lambda}_{i_k}(t)$ and $b(t) = b_{i_k}(t)$ when $t \in [t_k,t_{k+1})$ and if $\|\Theta_{i,j}(t)\| \leq 1, \forall i,j \in I, i \neq j, \forall t \geq 0$, then conditions (a) and (b) in the form as in Remark 6 are satisfied (here $\mu = 1$). According to Theorem 2, the system is uniformly ϵ-practically stable around the origin under $\mathcal{S}$ if there exists a $0 < \gamma < \epsilon$ such that

$$\int_{t_1}^{t_2} \hat{\lambda}(\tau) + \|b(\tau)\|\, d\tau < \epsilon - \gamma, \forall 0 \leq t_1 < t_2 < \infty. \tag{9}$$

Note that given the $A_i(t)$'s and the disturbance $b_i(t)$'s, (9) may be satisfied for ϵ values that are large enough. However, we may not be able to reduce the value of ϵ as small as possible and still guarantee the ϵ-practical stability. □

4   Practical Stabilization

In the ϵ-practical stability analysis in Section 3, we explicitly assume that a bound ϵ and a switching law are given. However, in practice, we are sometimes interested in knowing if there exists a switching law such that the system is ϵ-practically stable for a given $\epsilon > 0$. This leads us into the topic on practical stabilization design.

4.1   The Notion of Practical Stabilizability

Definition 4 (Practical Stabilizability). *Hybrid system (1)-(2) is said to be (locally) practically stabilizable around the origin if for any $\epsilon > 0$, there exists a switching law $S = S(\epsilon)$ such that the system is ϵ-practically stable around the origin under S.*   □

Remark 8. In the definition of practical stabilizability, ϵ can be varied as opposed to the fixed ϵ in Definition 2. Hence a practically stabilizable system has the property that, for any given $B[0, \epsilon]$, a valid switching law can be found that keeps the system trajectories, whose initial states are in $B[0, \delta]$, in $B[0, \epsilon]$. Such a definition provides us with the flexibility in design, since in design problems, the bound ϵ will vary depending on the specific task we are facing.   □

In general, conditions for practical stabilizability and design of ϵ-practically stabilizing switching laws for hybrid systems are difficult to derive and are still under extensive research. However, for switched system (1), there has already been some results on sufficient conditions for practical stabilizability and design of switching laws [11,12]. In the following, we report extensions of the results in [11,12] to switched system (1) with time-varying subsystems.

4.2   Sufficient Conditions for Practical Stabilizability

Now we focus on the practical stabilizability and the design of ϵ-practical stabilizing switching laws for switched system (1). We will present sufficient regularity conditions (Theorem 3) for the practical stabilizability of such systems. Since the direct method presented in Section 3 establishes practical stability analysis for certain ϵ, we have to use it for stabilizability problem by changing the ϵ with trial and error. To avoid such a drawback, we propose a more effective method which is not based on the direct method. The proof of Theorem 3 is constructive, i.e., for any given $\epsilon > 0$, we actually construct a switching law which achieves the ϵ-practical stability of switched system (1) around the origin.

Definition 5 (Regularity Conditions). *In the sequel, we call the following conditions regularity conditions for the vector fields $f_i(x,t)$'s:*

(a). $f_i(0,t) \neq 0$, $\forall t \geq 0, \forall i \in I$.

(b). There exists a $G_1 > 0$ such that for any $t \geq 0$, every $x \in B[0,1]$ can be expressed as

$$x = \sum_{i=1}^{M} \gamma_i(t) f_i(0,t) \tag{10}$$

where the $\gamma_i(t)$'s satisfy $\gamma_i(t) \leq 0$, $i \in I$ and

$$\sum_{i=1}^{M} |\gamma_i(t)| \leq G_1. \tag{11}$$

(c). There exists a $G_2 > 0$ such that $\|f_i(0,t)\| \leq G_2$, $\forall t \geq 0, \forall i \in I$.
(d). $f_i(x,t)$'s satisfy the local Lipschitz condition in x around the origin, i.e., $\exists L_1 > 0$ such that

$$\|f_i(x_1,t) - f_i(x_2,t)\| \leq L_1 \|x_1 - x_2\| \tag{12}$$

for any x_1, x_2 in some neighborhood $B[0,r]$ and $\forall t \geq 0, \forall i \in I$.
(e). $f_i(x,t)$'s satisfy the global Lipschitz condition in t, i.e., $\exists L_2 > 0$ such that

$$\|f_i(x,t_1) - f_i(x,t_2)\| \leq L_2 |t_1 - t_2| \tag{13}$$

for any $t_1, t_2 \geq 0$ and $\forall x \in \mathbb{R}^n, \forall i \in I$.   □

Theorem 3. *Switched system (1) in $\mathbb{R}^n$ is practically stabilizable if it satisfies the regularity conditions (a), (b), (c), (d), and (e).*

Before proving Theorem 3, let us first introduce the idea of the proof and some preliminary results that will be used in the proof. First of all, we note that given a time interval $[T_k, T_{k+1}]$, a trajectory $x(t)$ starting from $x(T_k)$ can be decomposed into two parts $x_a(t)$ and $x_b(t)$, i.e., $x(t) = x_a(t) + x_b(t)$ for $t \in [T_k, T_{k+1}]$. Here $x_a(t)$ corresponds to the trajectory generated by an integrator switched system consisting of subsystems

$$\dot{x}_a(t) = f_i(0, T_k), \ i \in I \tag{14}$$

for $t \in [T_k, T_{k+1}]$, under the same switching sequence as that corresponds to $x(t)$, and with the initial condition $x_a(T_k) = x(T_k)$. And $x_b(t)$ corresponds to the trajectory generated by a switched system consisting of subsystems

$$\dot{x}_b(t) = f_i(x,t) - f_i(0, T_k) \stackrel{\triangle}{=} \Delta f_i(x,t,T_k), \ i \in I \tag{15}$$

for $t \in [T_k, T_{k+1}]$, under the same switching sequence as that corresponds to $x(t)$, and with the initial condition $x_b(T_k) = 0$.

The idea of the proof is as follows. We will partition the whole time range $[t_0, \infty)$ into time interval $[T_k, T_{k+1}]$'s, $k = 0, 1, 2, \cdots$, and on each interval decompose the state trajectory $x(t)$ into $x_a(t)$, $x_b(t)$ as mentioned above. We will construct a switching law $\mathcal{S}(\epsilon)$ for any given $\epsilon > 0$, such that $\exists 0 < \delta \le \frac{\epsilon}{2}$ so that $x(t_0) \in B[0, \delta]$ implies that $\|x_a(t)\| \le \frac{\epsilon}{2}$ and $\|x_b(t)\| \le \delta < \frac{\epsilon}{2}$, $\forall t \ge t_0$. In this way, we can conclude that $\|x(t)\| \le \|x_a(t)\| + \|x_b(t)\| \le \frac{\epsilon}{2} + \delta < \epsilon$, $\forall t \ge t_0$. Moreover, the time intervals are actually generated by $\mathcal{S}(\epsilon)$.

Let us first consider the switched system whose dynamics is (14). Note that this system corresponds to an integrator switched system during each time interval $[T_k, T_{k+1}]$. The following switching law can be applied to the switched system (14) to generate a nonZeno switching sequence for initial $x(t_0) \in B[0, 1]$.

Switching Law A (for integrator switched system (14) with $x_a(t_0) = x(t_0) \in \overline{B[0, 1]}$):

(1). Assume that the system trajectory starts from $x_a(t_0) \in B[0, 1]$ at time t_0. Set $k = 0$, $T_k = t_0$ and the current state $x_a(T_k) = x_a(t_0)$.

(2). Obtain the expression of the current state $x_a(T_k) = \sum_{i=1}^{M} \gamma_i(T_k) f_i(0, T_k)$ as in (10). First switch to subsystem 1 and stay for time $|\gamma_1(T_k)|$, then switch to subsystem 2 and stay for time $|\gamma_2(T_k)|$ and so on. In other words, we obtain a switching sequence $((T_k, 1), (T_k + |\gamma_1(T_k)|, 2), (T_k + |\gamma_1(T_k)| + |\gamma_2(T_k)|, 3), \cdots, (T_k + |\gamma_1(T_k)| + \cdots + |\gamma_{M-1}(T_k)|, M))$ from time T_k to $\tilde{T}_k \overset{\triangle}{=} T_k + \sum_{i=1}^{M} |\gamma_i(T_k)|$.

(3). From time $\tilde{T}_k$ on, we let subsystem M be active until the state trajectory intersects the unit sphere.

(4). When the state intersects the unit sphere, set $k = k+1$ and denote T_k to be the time instant of intersection (note that $x_a(T_k)$ is the intersecting point). Go back to step (2).   □

Under Switching Law A, note that $x_a(\tilde{T}_k) = 0$, $\forall k \ge 0$. Since for any $x_a(T_k)$ on the unit sphere, to drive the state to the origin, no switching law will take less than the time duration $\frac{1}{\max_{1 \le i \le M} \|f_i(0, T_k)\|}$, we conclude that it takes no less than time $\frac{1}{G_2}$ and no more than M switchings to complete one iteration of steps (2), (3), and (4) in Switching Law A (for any $x(T_k)$ on the unit sphere). Therefore, using Switching Law A, we obtain a nonZeno switching sequence for initial state $x_a(t_0) \in B[0, 1]$. Moreover, for any $x_a(t_0) \in B[0, 1]$, we can show that under Switching Law A, there exists a $G > 1$ such that the trajectory $x_a(t) \in B[0, G]$ for any $t \ge t_0 = T_0$. The G can be chosen as follows. Consider any $T_0 \le t \le \tilde{T}_0$, we have

$$\|x_a(t)\| \le \|x_a(T_0)\| + \sum_{i=1}^{M} |\gamma_i(T_0)| \cdot \max_{1 \le i \le M} \|f_i(0, T_0)\| \le 1 + G_1 G_2 \qquad (16)$$

Defining $G \overset{\triangle}{=} 1 + G_1 G_2$, we then have $G > 1$ and $\|x_a(t)\| \le G$ for $t \in [T_0, \tilde{T}_0]$. For $t \in [\tilde{T}_0, T_1]$ where $T_1 = \tilde{T}_0 + \frac{1}{\|f_M(0, T_0)\|}$, by Switching Law A, the trajectory $x_a(t) \in B[0, 1]$ and hence is in $B[0, G]$. Similarly, such arguments can be applied to any time interval $[T_k, T_{k+1}]$ to establish the validity of $x_a(t) \in B[0, G]$, $\forall t \ge t_0$.

Corollary 1. *If* $f_i(x,t)$*'s satisfy the regularity condition (b), then for any given* $\epsilon_1 > 0$*, any* $x \in B[0, \frac{\epsilon_1}{2G}]$ *can be expressed as* $x = \sum_{i=1}^{M} \hat{\gamma}_i(t) f_i(0,t)$ *where* $\hat{\gamma}_i(t) \le 0$ *for* $1 \le i \le M$ *and* $\sum_{i=1}^{M} |\hat{\gamma}_i(t)| \le \frac{\epsilon_1 G_1}{2G}$.

Proof: For every $x \in B[0, \frac{\epsilon_1}{2G}]$, we have $\frac{2G}{\epsilon_1} x \in B[0,1]$ and can be expressed as $\frac{2G}{\epsilon_1} x = \sum_{i=1}^{M} \gamma_i(t) f_i(0,t)$ due to the regularity condition (b). The conclusion of the corollary then follows by defining $\hat{\gamma}_i(t) \stackrel{\triangle}{=} \frac{\epsilon_1}{2G} \gamma_i(t)$. $\qquad\square$

Remark 9. Substituting $\gamma_i(T_k)$'s by $\hat{\gamma}_i(T_k)$'s, and the unit sphere by the $\frac{\epsilon_1}{2G}$-sphere in Switching Law A, a similar law can be developed for system (14) with $x_a(t_0) \in B[0, \frac{\epsilon_1}{2G}]$ such that $x_a(\tilde{T}_k) = 0$, $\forall k \ge 0$, and $\|x_a(t)\| \le \frac{\epsilon_1}{2}$, $\forall t \ge t_0$. $\qquad\square$

In the following, we define $\delta \stackrel{\triangle}{=} \frac{\epsilon_1}{2G}$. The following law is a modification of Switching Law A and is suitable for switched system (1) with $x(t_0) \in B[0, \delta]$.

Switching Law B (for switched system (1) with $x(t_0) \in B[0, \delta]$):

(1). Assume that the system trajectory starts from $x(t_0) \in B[0, \delta]$ at time t_0. Set $k = 0$, $T_k = t_0$ and the current state $x(T_k) = x(t_0)$.

(2). Obtain the expression of the current state $x(T_k) = \sum_{i=1}^{M} \hat{\gamma}_i(T_k) f_i(0, T_k)$. First switch to subsystem 1 and stay for time $|\hat{\gamma}_1(T_k)|$, then switch to subsystem 2 and stay for time $|\hat{\gamma}_2(T_k)|$ and so on. In other words, we obtain a switching sequence $\big((T_k, 1), (T_k + |\hat{\gamma}_1(T_k)|, 2), (T_k + |\hat{\gamma}_1(T_k)| + |\hat{\gamma}_2(T_k)|, 3), \cdots, (T_k + |\hat{\gamma}_1(T_k)| + \cdots + |\hat{\gamma}_{M-1}(T_k)|, M)\big)$ from time T_k to $\tilde{T}_k \stackrel{\triangle}{=} T_k + \sum_{i=1}^{M} |\hat{\gamma}_i(T_k)|$.

(3). From time $\tilde{T}_k$ on, we let subsystem M be active until the state trajectory intersects the δ-sphere.

(4). When the state intersects the δ-sphere, set $k = k + 1$ and denote T_k to be the time instant of intersection (note that $x(T_k)$ is the intersecting point). Go back to step (2). $\qquad\square$

Equipped with Corollary 1 and Switching Law B, we are now ready to present the proof of Theorem 3. The proof is based on the application of Switching Law B to switched system (1). Before proceeding, a remark is in order.

Remark 10. Note that at each T_k, $x(t)$ can be decomposed into $x_a(T_k) = x(T_k)$ and $x_b(T_k) = 0$. Thus when Switching Law B is applied to switched system (1), we have $x_a(\tilde{T}_k) = 0$ and $\|x_a(t)\| \le \frac{\epsilon_1}{2G} \cdot G = \frac{\epsilon_1}{2}$ (see Remark 9). However, $x(\tilde{T}_k)$ may not be equal to 0, and $x(T_{k+1})$ may not even exist (since it is possible that after certain $\tilde{T}_k$, the trajectory generated by step (3) may never intersect the δ-sphere). Of course, if T_{k+1} does exist, we must have $\|x(T_{k+1})\| = \delta$. Also, in order to carry out step (3), we need to justify that $x(\tilde{T}_k) \in B[0, \delta]$. This will be shown to be true in our proof of Theorem 3 in the following. $\qquad\square$

Proof of Theorem 3: Consider $x_b(t)$ for the switched system (15) under the switching sequence generated by Switching Law B. First note that during $[T_0, \tilde{T}_0]$, $x_b(t)$ can be expressed as $x_b(t) = \int_{T_0}^{t} \Delta f_{i(\tau)}\big(x(\tau), \tau, T_0\big) \, d\tau$ where $i(\tau)$ indicates the active subsystem at time instant τ (also note that $x_b(T_0) = 0$). Assume that $x(t) \in B[0, \epsilon_1]$ for any $t \in [T_0, \tilde{T}_0]$. Under this assumption, we have $\|x_b(t)\| \leq \max_{i \in I, x \in B[0, \epsilon_1]} \|\Delta f_i(x, t, T_0)\| \cdot (t - T_0)$ for any $t \in [T_0, \tilde{T}_0]$.

Now note that

$$\|\Delta f_i(x, t, T_0)\| = \|f_i(x, t) - f_i(0, T_0)\| \leq \|f_i(x, t) - f_i(0, t)\| + \|f_i(0, t)$$
$$- f_i(0, T_0)\| \leq L_1 \|x\| + L_2 |t - T_0| \leq L_1 \epsilon_1 + L_2(\tilde{T}_0 - T_0) \quad (17)$$

for $\forall x \in B[0, \epsilon_1] \subseteq B[0, r]$, $\forall t \in [T_0, \tilde{T}_0]$. From (17) and Corollary 1, we note that if ϵ_1 is small enough, we have

$$\|x_b(t)\| \leq \max_{i \in I, x \in B[0; \epsilon_1]} \|\Delta f_i(x, t, T_0)\| \cdot (t - T_0)$$
$$\leq \max_{i \in I, x \in B[0; \epsilon_1]} \|\Delta f_i(x, t, T_0)\| \cdot (\tilde{T}_0 - T_0)$$
$$\leq (L_1 \epsilon_1 + L_2 \sum_{i=1}^{M} |\hat{\gamma}_i(T_0)|) \sum_{i=1}^{M} |\hat{\gamma}_i(T_0)| \leq (L_1 + L_2 \frac{G_1}{2G}) \frac{G_1}{2G} \epsilon_1^2. \quad (18)$$

From (18), we conclude that if $0 < \epsilon_1 < \min\{\frac{1}{(L_1 + L_2 \frac{G_1}{2G})G_1}, r\}$, we have

$$\|x_b(t)\| \leq (L_1 + L_2 \frac{G_1}{2G}) \frac{G_1}{2G} \epsilon_1^2 \leq \frac{\epsilon_1}{2G} = \delta < \frac{\epsilon_1}{2}. \quad (19)$$

To completely justify the validity of (19), we need to verify that our assumption $x(t) \in B[0, \epsilon_1]$ is true for any $t \in [T_0, \tilde{T}_0]$. We prove its validity by contradiction. Assume that there exists a $t_1 \in [T_0, \tilde{T}_0]$ at which the state trajectory intersects the ϵ_1-sphere for the first time. For such a t_1, we must have

$$\|x(t_1)\| = \|x_a(t_1) + x_b(t_1)\| \leq \|x_a(t_1)\| + \|x_b(t_1)\|$$
$$\leq \frac{\epsilon_1}{2} + \max_{i \in I, x \in B[0, \epsilon_1]} \|\Delta f_i(x, t, T_0)\| \cdot (t_1 - T_0)$$
$$\leq \frac{\epsilon_1}{2} + (L_1 \epsilon_1 + L_2 \sum_{i=1}^{M} |\hat{\gamma}_i(T_0)|) \sum_{i=1}^{M} |\hat{\gamma}_i(T_0)|$$
$$\leq \frac{\epsilon_1}{2} + (L_1 + L_2 \frac{G_1}{2G}) \frac{G_1}{2G} \epsilon_1^2 \leq \frac{\epsilon_1}{2} + \frac{\epsilon_1}{2G} < \frac{\epsilon_1}{2} + \frac{\epsilon_1}{2} = \epsilon_1 \quad (20)$$

which is a contradiction to $\|x(t_1)\| = \epsilon_1$. Hence we conclude that if $x_0 \in B[0, \delta]$, then $x(t) \in B[0, \epsilon_1]$ for any $t \in [T_0, \tilde{T}_0]$. In particular, at $t = \tilde{T}_0$, we have $x_a(\tilde{T}_0) = 0$ and $x_b(\tilde{T}_0) \in B[0, \delta]$; hence $x(\tilde{T}_0) \in B[0, \delta]$. For any $t \in [\tilde{T}_0, T_1]$, due to step (3) in Switching Law B, we have $x(t) \in B[0, \delta] \subset B[0, \epsilon_1]$. Using a similar argument as the above, we can then prove that $x(t) \in B[0, \epsilon_1]$ for $t \in [T_1, T_2]$ and $t \in [T_2, T_3]$ and so on, which consequently establishes that $x(t) \in B[0, \epsilon_1]$ for any $t \geq t_0$.

Finally, for any given $\epsilon > 0$, we can choose an ϵ_1 satisfying $0 < \epsilon_1 \leq \epsilon_0 \triangleq \min\{\epsilon, \frac{1}{(L_1 + L_2 \frac{G_1}{2G})G_1}, r\}$, and then choose $\delta = \frac{\epsilon_1}{2G}$. In this way, whenever $x(t_0) \in B[0, \delta]$, we have $x(t) \in B[0, \epsilon_1]$ and hence $x(t) \in B[0, \epsilon]$, $\forall t \geq t_0$. $\qquad \square$

Remark 11. From the proof of Theorem 3, we note that even if $\epsilon > 0$ is given, we usually need to choose $\epsilon_1 \leq \epsilon_0$ in order to determine δ. If the given $\epsilon > \epsilon_0$, we can see that the trajectory $x(t)$ will actually be in $B[0, \epsilon_0]$; hence ϵ will be an overestimate of the trajectory bound. However, it may not be possible in this case to relax δ by a small amount so as to make ϵ a tight bound. This is because if $x(t_0)$ deviates from 0 too much, it may then be impossible to keep the trajectory in $B[0, \epsilon]$. This explains why the result is local in nature.   □

Remark 12. From the proof of Theorem 3, we note that our choice of δ does not depend on t_0. Therefore, Switching Law B actually renders the switched system uniformly ϵ-practically stable.   □

Remark 13. In order to apply Theorem 3, we need to verify the validity of the regularity condition (b). Below is a way to check the condition without exhaustively checking it for every $x \in B[0, 1]$. Consider the unit vectors $e_1, \cdots, e_n$ in $\mathbb{R}^n$ and their negatives $-e_1, \cdots, -e_n$. We denote them as $\hat{e}_1 = e_1, \cdots, \hat{e}_n = e_n$, $\hat{e}_{n+1} = -e_1, \cdots, \hat{e}_{2n} = -e_n$. In order to check the validity of the regularity condition (b), we only need to check if there exist constants $G_{k,i} > 0$ ($1 \leq k \leq 2n$, $i \in I$) such that every $\hat{e}_k$ can be expressed as $\hat{e}_k = \sum_{i=1}^{M} \lambda_{k,i}(t) f_i(0, t)$ where $0 \leq \lambda_{k,i}(t) \leq G_{k,i}$, $\forall t \geq 0$. If such $G_{k,i}$'s exist, then since every vector $x \in B[0, 1]$ can be represented as $x = \sum_{k=1}^{n} \alpha_k e_k$ where $\alpha_k \in \mathbb{R}$, $\sum_{k=1}^{n} \alpha_k^2 \leq 1$, we can represent x as $x = \sum_{k=1}^{2n} \beta_k \hat{e}_k$ where $\beta_k = \begin{cases} \alpha_k, & \text{if } \alpha_k \leq 0 \\ 0, & \text{if } \alpha_k > 0 \end{cases}$ for $1 \leq k \leq n$ and $\beta_k = \begin{cases} -\alpha_{k-n}, & \text{if } \alpha_{k-n} > 0 \\ 0, & \text{if } \alpha_{k-n} \leq 0 \end{cases}$ for $n+1 \leq k \leq 2n$. Note that every $\beta_k \leq 0$ and $\sum_{k=1}^{2n} \beta_k^2 = \sum_{k=1}^{n} \alpha_k^2 \leq 1$.

From the expression of x in $\hat{e}_k$'s, we then have $x = \sum_{k=1}^{2n} \beta_k \left(\sum_{i=1}^{M} \lambda_{k,i}(t) \cdot f_i(0, t) \right) = \sum_{i=1}^{M} \left(\sum_{k=1}^{2n} \beta_k \lambda_{k,i}(t) \right) f_i(0, t) = \sum_{i=1}^{M} \gamma_i(t) f_i(0, t)$ where $\gamma_i(t) \triangleq \sum_{k=1}^{2n} \beta_k \lambda_{k,i}(t) \leq 0$, $\forall i \in I$ and $\sum_{i=1}^{M} |\gamma_i(t)| \leq \sum_{i=1}^{M} \left(\left(\sum_{k=1}^{2n} \beta_k^2 \right)^{\frac{1}{2}} \cdot \left(\sum_{k=1}^{2n} \lambda_{k,i}^2(t) \right)^{\frac{1}{2}} \right) \leq \sum_{i=1}^{M} \left(\sum_{k=1}^{2n} \lambda_{k,i}^2(t) \right)^{\frac{1}{2}} \leq \sum_{i=1}^{M} \left(\sum_{k=1}^{2n} G_{k,i}^2 \right)^{\frac{1}{2}} \triangleq G_1$.   □

Remark 14. For switched systems with time-invariant subsystem $f_i(x)$'s, due to Remark 13, the regularity condition (b) is equivalent to the existence of nonnegative constants $\lambda_{k,i}$'s such that $\hat{e}_k = \sum_{i=1}^{M} \lambda_{k,i} f_i(0)$, $k = 1, 2, \cdots, 2n$. Moreover, it can be shown that such a condition is equivalent to the condition $C = \mathbb{R}^n$ where C is the convex cone $C = \{\sum_{i=1}^{M} \lambda_i f_i(0) | \lambda_1 \geq 0, \cdots, \lambda_M \geq 0\}$. This shows us that the result in [12] is a special case of our result in this paper.   □

4.3   A Tracking Problem Example

Now we apply Switching Law B proposed above to a tracking problem example.

Example 3. Consider a switched system in $\mathbb{R}^2$ which consists of 4 subsystems

$$\dot{y} = A_i y + b_i, \quad i = 1, 2, 3, 4 \tag{21}$$

where $A_1 = A_2 = \begin{bmatrix} -0.1 & 0 \\ 0 & -0.1 \end{bmatrix}$, $A_3 = A_4 = \begin{bmatrix} -0.2 & 0 \\ 0 & -0.2 \end{bmatrix}$, $b_1 = \begin{bmatrix} 0.5 \\ 0.5 \end{bmatrix}$, $b_2 = \begin{bmatrix} -0.5 \\ 0.5 \end{bmatrix}$, $b_3 = \begin{bmatrix} -0.5 \\ -0.5 \end{bmatrix}$, and $b_4 = \begin{bmatrix} 0.5 \\ -0.5 \end{bmatrix}$. We want to develop a switching law such that the switched system state $y(t)$ would approximately track the state trajectory of the dynamical system

$$\dot{z} = Az = \begin{bmatrix} -0.1 & 0 \\ 0 & -0.2 \end{bmatrix} z \tag{22}$$

in the sense that $\|y(t) - z(t)\| \le \epsilon$ (ϵ is a prespecified tolerance level) for $t \ge 0$. Here we assume that $y(0) = z(0) = [0.2, \ 0.2]^T$.

We transform the above tracking problem into a practical stabilization problem by defining $x(t) \overset{\triangle}{=} y(t) - z(t)$ and considering the following switched system

$$\dot{x} = f_i(x, t) = A_i x + b_i + (A_i - A)e^{At} z(0), \quad i = 1, 2, 3, 4 \tag{23}$$

(which comes from the subtraction of (22) from the subsystems in (21)). To solve the tracking problem, we only need to design a switching law under which the switched system (23) becomes ϵ-practical stable around the origin.

Note here $f_1(0, t) = b_1 + (A_1 - A)e^{At} z(0) = [0.5, \ 0.5 + 0.02e^{-0.2t}]^T$, $f_2(0, t) = b_2 + (A_2 - A)e^{At} z(0) = [-0.5, \ 0.5 + 0.02e^{-0.2t}]^T$, $f_3(0, t) = b_3 + (A_3 - A)e^{At} z(0) = [-0.5 - 0.02e^{-0.1t}, \ -0.5]^T$, and $f_4(0, t) = b_4 + (A_4 - A)e^{At} z(0) = [0.5 - 0.02e^{-0.1t}, \ -0.5]^T$. So the regularity conditions (a) and (c) are satisfied. In fact, G_2 can be chosen to be $G_2 = \sqrt{0.5^2 + 0.5^2} = 0.7214$. To check the validity of the regularity condition (b), we use the method in Remark 13. We can express $\hat{e}_k, k = 1, 2, 3, 4$ as $\sum_{i=1}^{4} \lambda_{k,i}(t) f_i(0, t)$ where the $\lambda_{k,i}(t)$'s can be chosen to be $\lambda_{1,1}(t) = 0.5/(0.5 - 0.01e^{-0.1t} + 0.01e^{-0.2t} - 0.0004e^{-0.3t})$, $\lambda_{1,2}(t) = \lambda_{1,3}(t) = 0$, $\lambda_{1,4}(t) = (0.5 + 0.02e^{-0.2t})/(0.5 - 0.01e^{-0.1t} + 0.01e^{-0.2t} - 0.0004e^{-0.3t})$, $\lambda_{2,1}(t) = \lambda_{2,2}(t) = 1/(1 + 0.04e^{-0.2t})$, $\lambda_{2,3}(t) = \lambda_{2,4} = 0$, $\lambda_{3,1}(t) = 0$, $\lambda_{3,2}(t) = 0.5/(0.5 + 0.01e^{-0.1t} + 0.01e^{-0.2t} + 0.0004e^{-0.3t})$, $\lambda_{3,3}(t) = (0.5 + 0.02e^{-0.2t})/(0.5 + 0.01e^{-0.1t} + 0.01e^{-0.2t} + 0.0004e^{-0.3t})$, $\lambda_{3,4}(t) = 0$, $\lambda_{4,1}(t) = \lambda_{4,2}(t) = 0$, $\lambda_{4,3}(t) = 1 - 0.04e^{-0.1t}$, $\lambda_{4,4}(t) = 1 + 0.04e^{-0.1t}$. Hence we can choose $G_{k,i}$'s and consequently choose $G_1 = 5.7728$. The regularity conditions (d) and (e) are also satisfied by $f_i(x, t)$'s. We can choose $L_1 = \max_{1 \le i \le 4} \|A_i\| = 0.2$ and $L_2 = 0.02 \cdot 0.2e^0 = 0.004$.

Since all the regularity conditions are satisfied, we can apply Switching Law B to the system (23) to render it ϵ-practically stable around the origin. Assume that we are given $\epsilon = 0.05$, we can simply choose $\epsilon_1 = \min\{\epsilon, \frac{1}{(L_1+L_2\frac{G_1}{2G})G_1}\} = \min\{0.05, 0.8566\} = 0.05$ and consequently $\delta = \frac{\epsilon_1}{2G} = \frac{\epsilon_1}{2(1+G_1G_2)} = 0.0048$. Once we have ϵ_1 and δ, Switching Law B can readily be applied. The $x(t)$ thus obtained can then be reinterpreted into $y(t)$. Figure 2(a) shows the desired trajectory $z(t)$ to be tracked and Figure 2(b) shows the trajectory $y(t)$ for a finite time duration. It can be seen that $y(t)$ approximately tracks $z(t)$ and satisfies $\|y(t) - z(t)\| \le 0.05$. A closer look into a portion of the trajectories $y(t)$ and $z(t)$ is shown in Figure 3. $\qquad\square$

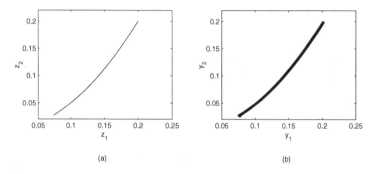

(a)   (b)

Fig. 2. (a). The trajectory $z(t)$ with $z(0) = [0.2,\ 0.2]^T$ for $t \in [0, 10]$. (b). The trajectory $y(t)$ (under Switching Law B) with $y(0) = [0.2,\ 0.2]^T$ for $t \in [0, 10]$.

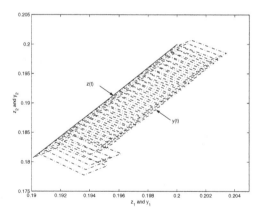

Fig. 3. The trajectory $z(t)$ (solid curve) and $y(t)$ (dashdot curve) with $y(0) = z(0) = [0.2,\ 0.2]^T$ for $t \in [0, 0.5]$.

5   Conclusion

This paper reports some results on practical stability analysis and practical stabilization of hybrid and switched systems with time-varying subsystems. A direct method for the ϵ-practical stability analysis of hybrid systems was proposed and sufficient conditions for the practical stabilizability of switched systems were proved. Moreover, a switching law for ϵ-practical stability was constructed. The switching law can easily be implemented. The research in this paper is a continuation of our previous studies in [11,12,13,14]. Future research includes derivations of more relaxed sufficient conditions for ϵ-practical stability and practical stabilizability, and extensions of the practical stabilization results to hybrid systems with discontinuous state jumps.

References

1. M.S. Branicky. Multiple Lyapunov functions and other analysis tools for switched and hybrid systems. *IEEE Trans. on Automatic Contr.*, 43(4): 475-482, April 1998.
2. J.P. Hespanha. *Logic-Based Switching Algorithms in Control.* Ph.D. Thesis, Yale University, 1998.
3. V. Lakshmikantham, S. Leela, and A.A. Martynyuk. *Practical Stability of Nonlinear Systems.* World Scientific, 1990.
4. J.P. LaSalle and S. Lefschetz. *Stability by Lyapunov's Direct Method with Applications.* Academic Press, New York, 1961.
5. D. Liberzon and A.S. Morse. Basic problems in stability and design of switched systems. *IEEE Control Systems Magazine*, 19(5):59-70, October 1999.
6. H. Lin and P.J. Antsaklis. Uniformly ultimate boundedness control for uncertain switched linear systems. ISIS Technical Report, ISIS-2003-004, University of Notre Dame, August 2003, available at: http://www.nd.edu/~isis/tech.html
7. A.N. Michel. Quantitative analysis of simple and interconnected systems: stability, boundedness and trajectory behavior. *IEEE Trans. on Cir. The.*, 17: 292-301, 1970.
8. A.N. Michel. Analysis of discontinuous large-scale systems: stability, transient behavior and trajectory bounds. *Int. J. Sys. Sci.*, 2: 77-95, 1971.
9. R.K. Miller and A.N. Michel. *Ordinary Differential Equations.* Academic Press, New York, 1982.
10. L. Weiss and E.F. Infante. Finite time stability under perturbing forces and on product spaces. *IEEE Trans. on Automatic Contr.*, 12: 54-59, 1967.
11. X. Xu and P.J. Antsaklis. Practical stabilization of integrator switched systems. In *Proceedings of the 2003 American Control Conference*, pp. 2767-2772, 2003.
12. X. Xu. Practical stabilizability of a class of switched systems. *The 2004 American Control Conference*, submitted, 2003.
13. G. Zhai and A.N. Michel. On practical stability of switched systems. In *Proceedings of the 41st IEEE Conference on Decision and Control*, pp. 3488-3493, 2002.
14. G. Zhai and A.N. Michel. Generalized practical stability analysis of discontinuous dynamical systems. In *Proceedings of the 42nd IEEE Conference on Decision and Control*, pp. 1663-1668, 2003.

A Numerical Technique for Stability Analysis of Linear Switched Systems

Christos A. Yfoulis and Robert Shorten

Hamilton Institute, NUI, Maynooth, Ireland,
`Christos.Yfoulis@may.ie`

Abstract. In this paper the *ray-gridding approach*, a new numerical technique for the stability analysis of linear switched systems is presented. It is based on uniform partitions of the state-space in terms of ray directions which allow refinable families of polytopes of adjustable complexity to be examined for invariance. In this framework the existence of a *polyhedral Lyapunov function* that is common to a family of asymptotically stable subsystems can be checked efficiently via simple iterative algorithms. The technique can be used to prove the stability of switched linear systems, classes of linear time-varying systems and Linear Differential Inclusions. We also present preliminary results on another related problem; namely, the construction of *multiple polyhedral Lyapunov functions* for specifying the existence of *stabilising switching sequences*.

1 Introduction

Recent years has seen enormous interest in switching systems. While many important issues have been resolved, many issues related to the stability of such systems remain open. In this context two very important questions remain unresolved; namely, if a given switching system remains stable under arbitrary switching sequences, or if this is impossible to identify the switching domains in the state-space and/or switching frequencies which result in stable behavior.

Lyapunov theory provides a convenient starting point for the study of continuous time and discrete-time linear and nonlinear systems. While most of the available results pertain to the existence of *quadratic* Lyapunov functions, recently derived converse theorems, suggest that while such a function always exists for stable switching systems, the associated Lyapunov function may not be quadratic. In this context interest has grown in the study of non-quadratic, and in particular, *piecewise linear* (PL) Lyapunov functions (LFs). PL LFs have been considered in a number of papers for establishing the stability of nonlinear time-varying systems and numerical techniques for the calculation of such functions have been developed. Although the class of PL LFs appears powerful in theory, the computational requirements necessary to establish their existence represents a serious bottleneck in practice. The main reason is that a complex representation (with a large number of parameters and conditions) is usually

R. Alur and G.J. Pappas (Eds.): HSCC 2004, LNCS 2993, pp. 631–645, 2004.
© Springer-Verlag Berlin Heidelberg 2004

required for a solution to be found rendering the techniques applicable to low-dimensional problems only.

In this work we develop a new numerical technique for the calculation of *polyhedral* Lyapunov functions (PLFs) for switched linear systems. The existence of a polyhedral LF is equivalent to the existence of a polytope which is invariant under the dynamical flow of a set of Linear Time Invariant (LTI) systems. The *ray-gridding* technique developed for the problem of calculating controllable and recoverable regions in [1] is applied here for the stability analysis problem of linear switched systems. It is shown that the calculation of invariant polytopes is significantly simplified resulting in a noteworthy reduction in the computational burden. Although the technique is conceived for linear switched systems, it can be also applied to nonlinear systems represented in the form of LDIs or in an absolute stability framework. The suitability of the technique to other related problems in stability of switched systems has been also investigated. More specifically, the technique has been applied to the calculation of *multiple* polyhedral Lyapunov functions specifying families of stabilising switching sequences for stable subsystems. Preliminary results on another related problem, namely the existence of *stabilising switching sequences* for a switched system constructed from a family of *unstable* linear subsystems are also reported in [2].

Notation :   In this paper, $\mathbb{R}$ denotes the real numbers and $\mathbb{R}^n$ is the vector space of n-dimensional real vectors. All vectors are assumed to be column vectors, $\boldsymbol{x}^T$ denotes the transpose and and x_i the i-th component of vector $\boldsymbol{x}$. For a polytope P, $vert\{P\}$ denotes the set of vertices of P and $conv\{V\}$ denotes the convex hull of a set of vectors V. The inequality symbols $>, \geq, <, \leq$ for vectors are understood componentwise.

2   Mathematical Results and Preliminaries

We are interested in *switched linear systems* of the form

$$\dot{\boldsymbol{x}} = \boldsymbol{A}(t)\boldsymbol{x} \quad , \quad \boldsymbol{A}(t) \in \{\boldsymbol{A}_1, \boldsymbol{A}_2, \dots, \boldsymbol{A}_p\}, \boldsymbol{A}_i \in \mathbb{R}^{n \times n} \ , \ i = 1, 2, \dots, p \quad (1)$$

where all the individual subsystems $\boldsymbol{A}_i$ are linear continuous-time invariant systems and switching between them occurs according to a rule which may be unknown or even random, or it is a matter of the control engineer's or the system designer's choice. The linear subsystems in (1) may be stable or unstable. It might be the case that system (1) remains stable for any switching strategy, hence appropriate methods for investigating whether this is true are important. If Lyapunov theory is to be used, proving asymptotic stability is equivalent to the existence of a *common* Lyapunov function for all subsystems. We consider the following problem [3]:

Problem 1. Check the existence of a common Lyapunov function for each individual linear subsystem of (1), which guarantees that system (1) is stable or asymptotically stable for any switching signal.

A similar problem in the literature is checking asymptotic stability of an LDI (Linear Differential Inclusion). Again, the problem of finding a Lyapunov function proving stability is equivalent to finding a simultaneous Lyapunov function for all subsystems $\dot{\boldsymbol{x}} = \boldsymbol{A}_i \boldsymbol{x}$, $i = 1, \ldots, p$ [4]. Moreover, the classical *absolute stability* problem with a fixed linear part and one or more nonlinearities satisfying sector conditions in the feedback loop can be easily transformed again into a differential inclusion.

It is obvious that a necessary condition for the asymptotic stability of (1) is that all individual subsystems are asymptotically stable. From now on, when focusing to Problem 1 we will assume that all linear systems $\dot{\boldsymbol{x}} = \boldsymbol{A}_i \boldsymbol{x}$, $i = 1, \ldots, p$ are asymptotically stable, i.e. that all matrices $\boldsymbol{A}_i$ are Hurwitz. For a solution to Problem 1, we restrict our attention to the class of *polyhedral* Lyapunov functions (PLFs), a special class of piecewise linear Lyapunov functions. PLFs are *set-induced* PL functions

$$V_P(\boldsymbol{x}) = \max_{1 \leq i \leq s} \{\boldsymbol{f}_i^T \cdot \boldsymbol{x}\} \tag{2}$$

induced by a *polyhedral* set of the form

$$P = \{\boldsymbol{x} \in \mathbb{R}^n : \boldsymbol{f}_i^T \cdot \boldsymbol{x} \leq 1 \, , \, i = 1, \ldots, s\} \tag{3}$$

which is compact and contains the origin in its interior. Such functions can be shown to be proper and locally Lipschitz [5] and decompose the state-space into a number of convex cones $\mathcal{C}_i = \{\boldsymbol{x} \in \mathbb{R}^n : V(\boldsymbol{x}) = \boldsymbol{f}_i^T \cdot \boldsymbol{x}\}$ with disjoint relative interiors $ri\{\mathcal{C}_i\} \cap ri\{\boldsymbol{C}_j\} = \emptyset$, $i \neq j$. Note that now P can be expressed as $P = \{\boldsymbol{x} \in \mathbb{R}^n : V_P(\boldsymbol{x}) \leq 1\}$. The linear functions $\boldsymbol{f}_i^T \cdot \boldsymbol{x}$ are called the *generators* of the PL function $V_P(\boldsymbol{x})$.

If the polyhedron P is bounded and centrally symmetric, then it is a *polytope* and V_P can be expressed as

$$V_P(\boldsymbol{x}) = \|F \cdot \boldsymbol{x}\|_\infty = \max_{1 \leq i \leq m} \{|\boldsymbol{f}_i^T \cdot \boldsymbol{x}|\} \, , \, F \in \mathbb{R}^{m \times n}, m \geq n \tag{4}$$

where $\|\cdot\|_\infty$ the infinity vector norm in $\mathbb{R}^n$. The positive invariance principle and the use of positively invariant sets is vital in the construction of set-induced PLFs. A complete survey of their properties and usage for a series of problems in control theory can be found in [6]. A set P is called *positively invariant* with respect to the trajectories of a dynamical system if for all $\boldsymbol{x}(0) \in P$ the solution $\boldsymbol{x}(t) \in P$ for $t > 0$. Invariance for a polytope P implies stability which can be shown with its set-induced PLF (2).

In a number of theoretical works, several authors [7], [4], [8] have considered the problem of absolute stability of an LDI and proved that the class of PLFs is *universal*, i.e. absolute stability of an LDI and existence of a common PLF function are equivalent. More recently the authors in [9] have studied the problem of the existence of a Lyapunov function for exponentially stable switching systems, and proved that a non-quadratic common Lyapunov function always exists.

A number of attempts have also been made to develop numerical techniques for the construction of such Lyapunov functions by Brayton and Tong [10], Barabanov [11] , Ohta et al. [5], Blanchini [12] and more recently Julian et. al. [13],

Polanski [14] and Yfoulis et. al. [1]. Although powerful in theory, PLFs suffer from high computational complexity in practice, when numerical techniques are applied for their computation. Computationally demanding convex hull computations and/or large-scale linear programs are highly responsible for exponential increase in computational time and computer memory requirements, restricting their applicability to planar and classes of three-dimensional systems.

3   Main Results

Efficient construction of PLFs for solving Problem 1 is based on flexible search for invariant polytopes for all linear subsystems involved. For this purpose, uniform partitions of the state space which can be easily refined to an adjustable degree of complexity in the search for a solution are vital. For PL systems the partition is usually imposed by the PL system description. For nonlinear systems approximated as PL or linear uncertain a typical choice is a uniform gridding of the state space and use of more general PL functions than polyhedral [13].

As an alternative to standard gridding, *ray-gridding* of the state-space has been proposed in [1] in an attempt to build up a framework where families of polytopes of adjustable complexity and flexible representation could be used as invariant polytope candidates. These families of polytopes generated by ray-gridding and the corresponding set-induced polyhedral functions are suitable for linear switched systems. The *ray-gridding* technique operates in terms of rays.

3.1   Definitions

We begin with the following definitions:

Definition 1. *A* **ray partition** *in* $\mathbb{R}^n$ *is a set* $\mathcal{R} = \{r_i \, , \; i = 1, 2, \ldots, N\}$ *of rays, where* $r_i = \{x \in \mathbb{R}^n \; : \; x = \lambda_i \cdot e_i \, , \; \lambda_i \geq 0 \, , \; e_i \in \mathbb{R}^n, e_i \neq 0\}$. *The vectors* e_i *which specify the rays are termed* **ray vectors** *and then any point on the ray* r_i *is uniquely determined by the non-negative scalar* λ_i, *referred to herein as its* **scaling factor**. *The number* N *of the rays in* $\{r_i\}$ *is the* **order** *of the ray partition. The* **scaling vector** $\lambda = [\lambda_1, \ldots, \lambda_N]^T$ *is the collection of all scaling factors.*

Definition 2. *A ray-partition is* **proper** *when all its rays* r_i *are disjoint, or* $r_1 \cap r_2 \cap \ldots \cap r_N = \{0\}$, *i.e. they only intersect at the origin. Otherwise it is called* **improper**. *A ray-partition is called* **unit** *if and only if all its ray vectors are unit vectors, i.e. their magnitude is equal to 1, and* **constrained** *when all its scaling factors are bounded, i.e. there exist upper limits* $\overline{\lambda}_i$ *such that* $0 \leq \lambda_i \leq \overline{\lambda}_i$. *A constrained ray partition is called* **normalized** *if and only if all its scaling factors are bounded by 1, i.e.* $\overline{\lambda}_i = 1$, $\forall i$. *A ray partition is also termed* **symmetric** *if and only if for every ray* r_i *there exists another ray* r_j *such that* $\forall x \in r_i \, , \; -x \in r_j$.

Definition 3. *A* **ray-polytope** *induced by a proper ray-partition* $\mathcal{R} = \{r_i, i = 1, \dots, N\}$ *is a polytope* $R = conv\{v_1, v_2, \dots, v_M\}$ *with non-empty interior whose vertices* $v_j \in vert\{R\}, j = 1, \dots, M$ *belong to one and only one of the rays in* $\mathcal{R}$, *i.e.* $N = M$ *and* $\forall i = 1, \dots N \ \exists j = 1, \dots, M \ s.t. \ v_j = \lambda_i e_i$. *Conversely, any polytope* R *induces a ray partition* $\mathcal{R}$ *with ray directions defined by the vertices of* R.

Let us consider an n-dimensional convex polytope $P \in \mathbb{R}^n$. Then there always exists a *ray-polytope* R with a corresponding appropriately selected ray-partition and scaling factors λ_i, $i = 1, \dots, N$, such that P and R coincide. Moreover, the ray partition $\{r_i\}$ specifies a whole family of polytopes $R(\lambda) = conv\{x_i = \lambda_i e_i$, $i = 1, \dots, N\}$ with vertices on the rays and variable scaling factors $\lambda = [\lambda_1, \dots, \lambda_N]^T$. For different selections for the scaling vector λ new scaled versions of $R(\overline{\lambda})$, $\overline{\lambda} = [\overline{\lambda}_1, \dots, \overline{\lambda}_N]^T$ are produced. For sufficiently large N and uniform coverage of the whole state-space any shape can be approximated with arbitrary accuracy. With candidates from the class of the ray-polytopes $R(\lambda)$, $0 < \lambda \leq \overline{\lambda}$ the search for invariant polytopes can be done very efficiently due to simplicity in the invariance conditions. For linear switched systems, *centrally symmetric* polytopes P, $\mathbf{0} \in ri\{P\}$ are a suitable choice, since $\forall x : x \in vert\{P\}$, $-x \in vert\{P\}$, hence the invariance conditions need to be checked for half of the vertices only.

3.2 The Ray-Gridding Approach

Inspired by the family of *regular* polygons in the planar case –which ensure a uniform coverage of the phase plane by approximating uniformly the unit circle– we would like to consider similar families $R(\lambda)$ of ray-polytopes which correspond to *uniform simplicial* partitions of the unit n-sphere $S_n = \{x \in \mathbb{R}^n : \|x\| = 1\}$. Strictly speaking, uniform partitions of the unit n-sphere cannot be achieved in the same sense as in $\mathbb{R}^2$, since there are only few regular polytopes in $\mathbb{R}^n$. However, nearly uniform simplicial subdivisions of the unit n-sphere with corresponding refinable ray-partitions can be generated.

For our families of ray-polytopes $R(\lambda)$ in $\mathbb{R}^n$ a decision has been made to work with *simplicial* polytopes, because this simplifies the facial structure and permits easier handling of the geometric objects formed. If $x_0, x_1, \dots, x_n$ are $(n+1)$ points in $\mathbb{R}^n$, a *simplex* $S(x_0, \dots, x_n)$ is their convex combination $S(x_0, \dots, x_n) = \{x : x = \sum_{i=0}^{n} \mu_i x_i, \ 0 \leq \mu_i \leq 1, \ \sum_{i=0}^{n} \mu_i = 1\}$. It is called *proper* iff it cannot be contained in an (n-1)-dimensional hyperplane $H = \{x : n^T x = c\}$, where c a constant.

Systematic simplicial subdivisions of n-dimensional rectangular domains have a long history in the circuits community, see e.g. Julian [13] and references therein. The procedure consists of a tessellation into small rectangles–producing a grid of points and regions– followed by a canonical decomposition of each region into simplices. This approach is useful for piecewise linear modelling and the parametrization of PL LFs, as shown in [13]. However, it is not useful, as it is, for our purpose of checking invariance on (n-1)-dimensional boundaries of candidate ray-polytopes. We propose another technique for generating nearly uniform simplicial subdivisions on (n-1)-dimensional boundaries :

Step 1 : Start from an initial symmetric rectangular domain $D_n(L)$ in $\mathbb{R}^n$
$D_n(L) = \{x : -L \cdot \mathbf{1} \le x \le L \cdot \mathbf{1}\}$, $\mathbf{1} = [1, \dots, 1]^T \in \mathbb{R}^n$, $L \in \mathbb{Z}^+$ which corresponds to carving up the state-space with hyperplanes parallel to the main axes $x_i = c_i$, $c_i = -L, \dots, 0, \dots, L$ into $N(L) = (2 \cdot L)^n$ unit hypercubes with vertices $V = \{x : x_i = c_i\}$.

Step 2 : Apply a "lifting" map $L : \mathbb{R}^{n-1} \to \mathbb{R}^n$

$$x = [x_1 \, x_2 \dots x_{n-1}]^T \longrightarrow \pm \hat{x} = \frac{1}{L} \cdot \left[x_1 \, x_2 \dots x_{n-1} \pm (L - \max_i |x_i|) \right]^T \quad (5)$$

which "lifts" all points from the rectangular grid to the boundary of a crosspolytope $C_n^\Delta = \{x \in \mathbb{R}^n : \sum_i |x_i| \le 1\} \in \mathbb{R}^n$ –the equivalent of an octahedron in $\mathbb{R}^3$ or a rhombus in $\mathbb{R}^2-$.

Step 3 : Map all points from the boundary ∂C_n^Δ to the boundary of the unit n-sphere forming a nearly uniform simplicial subdivision, provided that the grid size is sufficiently small. The "lifting" procedure is illustrated in Figure 1 for $n = 2$ and $n = 3$.

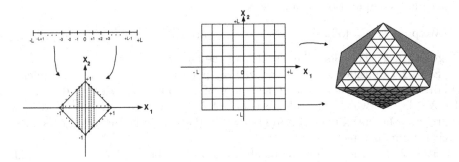

Fig. 1. The lifting procedure for $n = 2$ and $n = 3$.

A number of results from [2] are presented next with only brief sketches of the proofs, due to space limitations.

Proposition 1. *A necessary and sufficient condition for the existence of an invariant ray-polytope $R(\lambda)$, $\lambda \in \mathbb{R}^{N \times 1}$ under the dynamical flow of system (1) in $\mathbb{R}^n$ is the existence of positive scaling factors $\lambda_r > 0$, $r = 1, \dots, N$ s.t. the following set of conditions is satisfied*

$$\sum_{k=1}^n \delta_k^{(i)} \cdot \lambda_{k_1^{(i)}} \lambda_{k_2^{(i)}} \dots \lambda_{k_{n-1}^{(i)}} \le 0 \quad (6)$$

where $\delta_k^{(i)}$, $i = 1, \dots, p$, $k = 1, \dots, n$ appropriate coefficients and $k_j^{(i)}$ (with $k_j^{(i)} \ne k_l^{(i)}$ for $j \ne l$, $j, l = 1, \dots, n-1$) determine the rays $r_{k_j^{(i)}}$ which specify *the active conic sector (simplex) which contains the velocity vector for all points on the current ray for the linear subsystem $\dot{\boldsymbol{x}} = \boldsymbol{A}_i \cdot \boldsymbol{x}$ of (1).*

Proof. We consider a simplex S in $\mathbb{R}^n$ formed by the origin and n linearly independent points $\boldsymbol{x}_i = \lambda_i \cdot \boldsymbol{e}_i$, $i = 1, ..., n$ on distinct rays r_i with corresponding ray vectors $\boldsymbol{e}_i$. Assuming that the simplex S considered is the *active* simplex for the linear system $\dot{\boldsymbol{x}} = \boldsymbol{A}\boldsymbol{x}$, i.e the velocity vector $\dot{\boldsymbol{x}}$ for points on ray r_1 points to S, the invariance condition takes the form $\boldsymbol{n}^T \cdot \dot{\boldsymbol{x}}_1 \leq 0$ where $\boldsymbol{n}$ the vector normal to the $(n-1)$-dimensional hyperplane defined by $\boldsymbol{n}^T \cdot \boldsymbol{x} = 1$ and containing the n vertices $\boldsymbol{x}_i$. Let $\boldsymbol{X} = [\boldsymbol{x}_1 \boldsymbol{x}_2 \ldots \boldsymbol{x}_n] \in \mathbb{R}^{n \times n}$ and $\boldsymbol{E} = [\boldsymbol{e}_1 \boldsymbol{e}_2 \ldots \boldsymbol{e}_n] \in \mathbb{R}^{n \times n}$. Then the normal $\boldsymbol{n}$ can be found as $\boldsymbol{n} = (\boldsymbol{X}^T)^{-1} \cdot \boldsymbol{1}$ and can be directly related to $\boldsymbol{E}^{-1}$ and the scaling factors λ_i , $i = 1, \ldots, n$. Further manipulations yield $\sum_{k=1}^{n} \delta_k \cdot \lambda_{k_1} \lambda_{k_2} \ldots \lambda_{k_{n-1}} \leq 0$ and $\lambda_1 \leq -\frac{\delta_1 \cdot \lambda_2 \ldots \lambda_n}{\sum_{k=2}^{n} \delta_k \cdot \lambda_{k_1} \lambda_{k_2} \ldots \lambda_{k_{n-2}}}$, $k_1 \neq k_2 \ldots \neq k_{n-2} \neq 1$. For the linear switched dynamics (1) a number of linear subsystems $\dot{\boldsymbol{x}} = \boldsymbol{A}_i \boldsymbol{x}$ are involved, hence we arrive at (6), where $\delta_k^{(i)}$, $i = 1, \ldots, p$, $k = 1, \ldots, n$ the coefficients obtained for all individual subsystems. It is obvious that the scaling factor upper bound is determined by the scaling factors of incident rays in the same simplex in terms of a linear inequality (6), which offers simplicity and efficiency in the implementation of the technique. The use of linear programs or convex hull computations is not necessary.

We propose the following iterative algorithm :

Algorithm 2. The algorithm consists of the following steps :

Step 1 : Consider a unit normalized ray-partition $\mathcal{R}$ induced by a simplicial subdivision and the corresponding family of ray-polytopes $R(\boldsymbol{\lambda})$, $\boldsymbol{0} < \boldsymbol{\lambda} \leq \boldsymbol{1}$, $\boldsymbol{\lambda} \in \mathbb{R}^{N \times 1}$, which are scaled versions of $R(\boldsymbol{1})$, $\boldsymbol{1} = [1, 1, \ldots, 1]^T \in \mathbb{R}^{N \times 1}$. Start from the initial polytope $R(\boldsymbol{1})$ in which the scaling factors of all rays have their maximum value $\lambda_i = 1$.

Step 2 : Consider all rays one after another in their ordered sequence and update their scaling factors. Visit ray r_k , $k = 1, \ldots, N$ and modify its scaling factor to a new value $\hat{\lambda}_k$ s.t. all corresponding conditions (6) for all subsystems involved are satisfied. Note that (6) is a linear inequality which can be solved very efficiently to find $\hat{\lambda}_k$.

Step 3 : After visiting all rays in Step 2, the values of some scaling factors may have been reduced, thus (6) is not necessarily satisfied for all rays. Check whether all conditions (6) are satisfied for the new updated values $\hat{\lambda}_k$. If they are satisfied, stop. If not, continue in a number of iterations, i.e. return to Step 2 and update all scaling factors again until they converge.

Step 4 : Since there is a lower limit ($=0$) for the scaling factors, when the algorithm stops the scaling factors have converged either to fixed positive values or to zero. In the first case a solution is found, while in the second infeasibility is concluded.

Proposition 2. *Algorithm 2 converges to an optimal solution $R(\boldsymbol{\lambda}^*)$ iff an invariant polytope from the family $R(\boldsymbol{\lambda})$, $\boldsymbol{0} < \boldsymbol{\lambda} \leq \boldsymbol{1}$, $\boldsymbol{\lambda} \in \mathbb{R}^{N \times 1}$ exists.*

Proof. Necessity : Suppose there exists an invariant polytope from the family $R(\boldsymbol{\lambda})$, $0 < \boldsymbol{\lambda} \leq 1$, $\boldsymbol{\lambda} \in \mathbb{R}^{N \times 1}$ for some $\boldsymbol{\lambda}^* > 0$. Algorithm 1 starts from the upper bound $\boldsymbol{\lambda} = \overline{\boldsymbol{\lambda}} = 1$ and progressively reduces some of the scaling factors when this is found necessary in order to satisfy conditions (6). Since these are not only sufficient but also necessary for invariance, the steps followed by Algorithm 1 are also necessary for a solution. Algorithm 1 is a means for "scanning" the interior of the unit circle with scaled versions of ray-polytopes exhaustively, and therefore, it cannot miss to find $R(\boldsymbol{\lambda}^*)$ or a polytope arbitrarily close to $R(\boldsymbol{\lambda}^*)$. *Sufficiency* : When Algorithm 1 finds a solution this obviously proves the existence of an invariant ray-polytope. The solution is also *optimal* in size, since a ray-polytope with maximal scaling factors for all rays is obviously found. This is true because the algorithm starts from the upper bound and reduces the scaling factors when this is necessary. Note that restriction of the polytope families considered in the interior of the unit n-sphere (which is selected as our working domain) does not restrict the applicability of the technique. For linear systems, if an invariant polytope not included in the unit circle exists, there always exists a scaled version of it in our working domain.

The iterative algorithm described has been implemented to a number of examples in dimensions 2 and 3. Planar examples can be tackled very efficiently, even for very large populations of rays, as reported in many examples in [2]. Implementation in three-dimensional problems has also shown very good results in terms of computational efficiency, and a significant improvement compared to previous techniques, as evidenced by the next example.

Example 1. [absolute stability] Absolute stability of the following LDI in $\mathbb{R}^3$

$$
A_1 = \begin{bmatrix} -10 & -10\,\alpha & -10\,\alpha \\ 1 & 0 & 0 \\ 0 & 1 & 0 \end{bmatrix} , \quad A_2 = \begin{bmatrix} -10 & -10\,\beta & -10\,\beta \\ 1 & 0 & 0 \\ 0 & 1 & 0 \end{bmatrix} \tag{7}
$$

has been considered in [14], where α has been assigned a fixed value $\alpha = 0.2$. A solution to the problem of finding the maximum value of β for absolute stability using a PLF gave the result $\beta = 1.00$ in [14] with a polytope constructed with 40 layers. Note that the circle criterion (quadratic Lyapunov function) gives $\beta = 0.5467$. This example is appropriate for testing the efficiency of the ray-gridding technique. The results in [14] reveal that the implementation using a compact matrix formulation with linear programming suffers from high computational complexity. Indeed, experiments with more than 40 layers fail due to high memory requirements, since –although being sparse– extremely large matrices are required. Implementation of the ray-gridding technique in this example revealed its superiority both in terms of computational time and complexity of the polytope structures. The ray-gridding technique is much faster and polytopes with up to $L = 250$ layers (with 2×125001 vertices) can be dealt with, although the computational time increases significantly compared to smaller values for L. The results found for different values for L and β are shown in Table 1 [1]. For

---

[1] The computational times shown have been obtained from experiments with Matlab v.6.5 running on a Pentium 4, 1.8 GHZ personal computer

Table 1. Implementation results of the ray-gridding technique for the absolute stability of the LDI with vertex matrices (7) for $\alpha = 0.2$ and changing values for β and L.

Description of the ray-polytope R		Result of applying the algorithm			
No. of layers $2L =$	No. of vertices $2N =$	Succeeded for $\beta =$	Time (mins)	Failed for $\beta =$	Time (mins)
2×50	2×5101	1.0	2.18	1.5	3.5
2×100	2×20001	1.2	30	1.5	55
2×150	2×45001	1.5	213	1.7	256
2×200	2×80001	1.55	675	1.6	610
2×200	2×80001	1.57	620	1.5	580
2×250	2×125001	1.5	1560	2.0	2200

$\alpha = 0.2$, $\beta = 0.6$ and $L = 15$ layers the polytope found is depicted in Figure 2. The maximal value found with $L = 200$ layers is $\beta = 1.57$ with a two digit accuracy. The polytope found is shown in Figure 3. The value $L = 200$ has been found a good choice for checking absolute stability, resulting in a reasonable trade-off between computational complexity and efficiency in finding solutions.

We observe significant improvement in the maximum value found for β. Although partitions with $L = 200$ layers correspond to polytopes with a very complex structure (2×80001 vertices), such polytopes can be found in relatively reasonable computational times. This implies that the technique suggested can provide complete solutions in dimension $n = 3$ even in very demanding cases and problems, such as absolute stability. Application of the technique in higher dimensions $n = 4$ or $n = 5$ can be carried out for medium and small-sized problems, i.e. those that can be resolved with a reduced number of layers and corresponding polytopes of limited complexity.

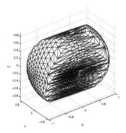

Fig. 2. An invariant polytope (after computing the convex hull) with 15 layers corresponding to the LDI (7) with $\alpha = 0.2, \beta = 0.6$.

Fig. 3. An invariant polytope (after computing the convex hull) with 200 layers corresponding to the LDI (7) with $\alpha = 0.2, \beta = 1.57$.

4 Calculation of Multiple Lyapunov Functions for Linear Switched Systems with Stable Subsystems

The methodology proposed in [15] for finding stabilising switching control laws is based on the assumption that each individual subsystem i admits a PL LF $V_i(\boldsymbol{x})$. Then a multiple Lyapunov function is defined by $V(\boldsymbol{x}) = V_i(\boldsymbol{x})$ for the time interval for which subsystem $\boldsymbol{A}_i$ is active. If for any switching from subsystem $\boldsymbol{A}_i$ to subsystem $\boldsymbol{A}_j$ the inequality

$$V_j(\boldsymbol{x}) \le V_i(\boldsymbol{x}) \tag{8}$$

is satisfied then the switching system is stable. Identification of all conic domains for which the previous inequality is satisfied specifies the switching law proposed. When the state reaches a region in which (8) is satisfied then obviously switching from $\boldsymbol{A}_i$ to $\boldsymbol{A}_j$ is safe and produces a stabilising switching sequence. Switching laws based on (8) for all subsystems involved are easily specified. An algorithm is proposed to compute the domains

$$\Omega_i^j = \{\boldsymbol{x} \in \mathbb{R}^n : V_j(\boldsymbol{x}) \le V_i(\boldsymbol{x})\} \tag{9}$$

as unions of polyhedral cones. The cones are the regions defined by the ray partitions of the invariant polytopes which correspond to the PL LFs of the individual subsystems. Since, in general, a different ray-partition for each subsystem is selected, the algorithm has to construct a new composite ray-partition which is the union of the individual ray-partitions and iterate through all conic sectors of the composite partition to specify subsets of them that satisfy (8) for all pairs of indexes i, j. The regions Ω_i^j in (9) are then specified as unions of conic subsectors.

Although this methodology is simple and can pave the way for future work in the area, its applicability is limited by a number of issues that need to be addressed. The applicability of the technique depends on the size and shape of the invariant polytopes specified. Appropriate normalisation (scaling) is required so that the algorithm can find non-trivial results. The technique is not robust, since for different scaling and different initial polytopes different results are found. Methods for specifying optimal, suboptimal or refined choices of individual Lyapunov functions that can specify larger classes of stabilising switching laws are not proposed. Moreover, for each conic sector specified, switching to a *single* linear system is only allowed, although situations in local regions in which arbitrary switching between two or more subsystems can result in stable trajectories are usual, e.g. stable chattering motion with finite or infinite frequency. The following example reveals some of the issues mentioned above :

Example 2. We consider the example used in [15], a switched continuous-time system $\dot{\boldsymbol{x}} = \boldsymbol{A}_p \cdot \boldsymbol{x}$, $p \in \{1, 2\}$, where

$$\boldsymbol{A}_1 = \begin{bmatrix} 1.7 & 1.8 \\ -4.5 & -3.7 \end{bmatrix} \quad , \quad \boldsymbol{A}_2 = \begin{bmatrix} 0.7 & -1 \\ 1.6 & -1.7 \end{bmatrix} \tag{10}$$

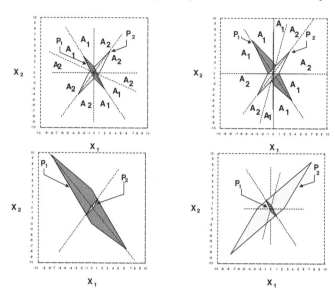

Fig. 4. The results returned by the technique in [15] for system (10) for $P_1 \cap P_2 \neq \emptyset$ without scaling (upper left), with scaling (upper right), $P_2 \subset P_1$ (lower left) and $P_1 \subset P_2$ (lower right).

Both subsystems admit PLFs with a minimal number of generators ($m = 2$ in (4)). The PLF functions used in [15] are $V_1(\boldsymbol{x}) = \max\{|x_1 + x_2|, |2x_1 + x_2|\}$ and $V_2(\boldsymbol{x}) = \max\{|-x_1 + x_2|, |2x_1 - 0.5x_2|\}$. In Figure 4 (upper left) the invariant polytopes P_1, P_2, $P_1 \cap P_2 \neq \emptyset$ corresponding to $V_1(\boldsymbol{x})$, $V_2(\boldsymbol{x})$ and the result returned by the technique are shown. The conic partition and the number of the subsystem–to which we can safely switch–specified at each region are also shown. If instead of P_1 a scaled version $2 \cdot P_1$ is used, a different result is obtained (upper right picture). For scaled versions of P_1 or P_2 for which one of the polytopes is included in the interior of the other, a trivial result is returned. In the lower left picture of Figure 4 switching to subsystem 1 is only possible (since $V_1(\boldsymbol{x}) < V_2(\boldsymbol{x}) \;\; \forall \boldsymbol{x}$), while in the lower right picture the opposite is true.

Application of the ray-gridding technique for the calculation of the multiple LFs (8) and the regions (9) can provide solutions to many of the aforementioned problematic issues.

Example 3. We consider again the system used in Example 2 and apply the ray-gridding technique. After selecting a uniform ray-partition $\mathcal{R}$, a PLF $V_k(\boldsymbol{x})$ from the induced polytope family $R(\boldsymbol{\lambda})$ is found for each linear subsystem $\boldsymbol{A}_k$. Before applying the multiple LF technique, an attempt to find a common PLF for the two subsystems has been made, which failed to find a solution. Hence, there exist destabilising switching laws. The results obtained for progressively refined uniform ray-partitions with 16,32,64 and 128 rays are shown in Figure 5. The conic sectors and the number of the subsystem (to which we can safely

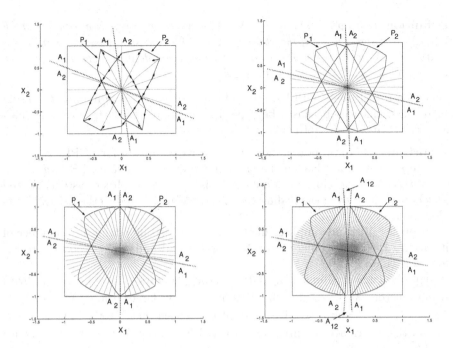

Fig. 5. The results returned by the ray-gridding technique for system (10) with 16,32,64 and 128 rays.

switch) are also marked. We observe that as the ray-partition is progressively refined larger sectors are found which converge to the sector shown in Figure 5 for 128 rays. The sufficiently dense ray-partition in Figure 5 revealed a small sector (marked with A_{12}) in which the two polytopes P_1, P_2 coincide. This implies that in this sector $V_1 = V_2$ and thus arbitrary switching to any subsystem guarantees stability. Switching from A_1 to A_2 and conversely will result in a chattering motion (the two subsystems are of opposite direction, A_1 is clockwise and A_2 is anticlockwise). Infinite frequency switching will produce a sliding mode, which is proved to be stable since $V_1 = V_2$ in A_{12}. If sliding modes are undesirable, the analysis informs us that infinite switching in A_{12} should be avoided.

In Example 3 we observe that the ability of the ray-gridding to refine allows the identification of larger sectors and also additional subsectors in which switching to more than one subsystems is possible. However, a shortcoming of this multiple Lyapunov Function technique is that it is largely dependent on the initial conditions. Indeed, observe the sectors found in Figure 4.

A further step for improving the multiple Lyapunov function technique introduced in [15] is next described. Since *global* common PLFs do not exist, the main idea is to investigate the possibility for the existence of *local* common PLFs. For the sake of simplicity assume that a linear switched system (1) with two subsystems A_1, A_2 is considered.

Definition 4. *Two linear systems $A_1, A_2 \in \mathbb{R}^{n \times n}$ admit a local common PLF $V(x)$ if for some subset of the state space $\Omega \in \mathbb{R}^n$ we have positive definiteness $V(0) = 0$, $V(x) > 0 \ \forall x \neq 0 \in \Omega$, and negative definite derivative for both systems $\dot{V}(x) = \frac{\partial V(x)}{\partial x} \cdot A_i x \leq 0$, $i = 1, 2$*

Local common PLFs (LCPLFs) are useful for our purposes of finding stabilising switching sequences because they specify regions of the state-space in which arbitrary switching to both subsystems is safe.

Algorithm 3. We propose a modified iterative algorithm for LCPLFs:

Step 1 : Assume that on the basis of a ray-partition $\mathcal{R}$ a PLF $V_i(x)$, $i = 1, 2$ with a corresponding invariant set P_i is found for each subsystem. To find LCPLFs we start from the scaling vectors λ_1, λ_2 associated to the invariant sets P_i , $i = 1, 2$.

Step 2 : Visit all simplices in the simplicial decomposition in a number of iterations, keep the scaling vector λ_2 constant and update λ_1 according to the following rule :

For the current simplex S_i and its associated rays r_j , $j = 1, \ldots, n$ with scaling factors λ_j search for the existence of new larger scaling factors $\hat{\lambda}_j \geq \lambda_j$, $j = 1, \ldots, n$ and a positive constant $k > 0$ such that $\hat{V}_1(x) = k V_2(x)$, $x \in S_i$ and the invariance conditions (6) are satisfied. $\hat{V}_1(x)$ is the PLF $V_1(x)$ with modified scaling factors $\hat{\lambda}_j$ in the current simplex. If there exist $\hat{\lambda}_j \geq \lambda_j$ these constitute the new updated scaling factors.

Step 3 : Check whether any modifications have been made during the last iteration. If yes returns to Step 2, otherwise convergence has occurred to a new modified scaling vector $\hat{\lambda}_1$.

Step 4 : Steps 2 and 3 are repeated with a changing role for the two scaling vectors and corresponding LFs. Keep the initial scaling vector λ_1 constant and update the scaling vector λ_2 to a modified $\hat{\lambda}_2$ using the same rule as in Step 2.

Proposition 3. *The convergence of Algorithm 3 to new invariant polytopes corresponding to LPCLFs is guaranteed, iff LPCLFs exist.*

Proof. Algorithm 3 in Steps 2 and 4 starts from an initial choice which corresponds to an invariant polytope and aims at approximating a target polytope in as many sectors as possible. The algorithm converges since it operates by specifying monotonically increasing sequences of one of the scaling vectors while there is an upper bound determined by the other scaling vector. It converges to new invariant polytopes since it starts from an invariant polytope and at each step an increase of some scaling factors is performed such that the invariance conditions are satisfied. Note that increase of some scaling factors does not affect the invariance of neighboring rays and simplices, thus there is no need to check other neighboring invariance conditions.

Example 4. Algorithm 3 has been applied successfully to the polytopes P_1, P_2 in Figure 5 with 64 rays and the result is depicted in Figure 6. Two new invariant polytopes W_1, W_2 with 64 rays are found which specify two conic sectors

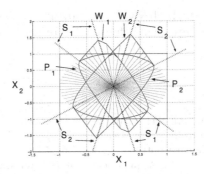

Fig. 6. The LCPLFs returned by the ray-gridding technique for system (10) with 64 rays.

S_1, S_2 corresponding to LCPLFs. This result provides more information on the local properties of the two vector fields and specifies a larger class of stabilising switching sequences. In the sectors S_1, S_2 arbitrary switching between the two subsystems is possible. Since the two subsystems are of opposite directions, the result of switching in S_1, S_2 will be chattering. Infinitely fast switching will result in sliding modes, which, however, can be proved to be stable using the LCPLFs found. If undesirable, they can be avoided by keeping the frequency of switching low. Outside the sector $S_1 \cup S_2$ switching to one of the subsystems is only allowed. These rules specify a larger class of different stabilising switching laws, and stability can be proved using the same multiple Lyapunov function arguments and an appropriate selection of any scaled versions of polytopes P_1, P_2, W_1, W_2, depending on the switching strategy chosen. Algorithm 3 can be extended to more than two linear subsystems or can be applied to different pairs of subsystems.

5   Concluding Remarks

In this paper the ray-gridding approach, a new framework for stability analysis of linear switched systems has been presented. It is supported by simple and efficient numerical iterative algorithms that have been shown to provide solutions to different problems related to stability analysis. The main problem considered was the computation of common polyhedral Lyapunov functions that guarantee stability of arbitrary switching between stable subsystems. Improved results in terms of computational complexity have been found. The same framework has been used to improve the calculation of multiple Lyapunov functions for linear switched systems proposed in [15].

Acknowledgements. This work was supported by Science Foundation Ireland grant 00/PI.1/C067 and by the European Union funded research training network *Multi-Agent Control*, HPRN-CT-1999-00107[2]. Neither the European Union or Enterprise Ireland is responsible for any use of data appearing in this publication.

References

1. Yfoulis, C., Muir, A., P.E.Wellstead: A new approach for estimating controllable and recoverable regions for systems with state and control constraints. Int. Journal of Robust and Nonlinear Control **12** (2002) 561–589
2. Yfoulis, C.A., Shorten, R.: A numerical technique for stability analysis of linear switched systems. Technical Report NUIM/SS/2003/04, Hamilton Institute, NUI Maynooth, Ireland (2003)
3. Liberzon, D., Morse, A.: Basic problems in stability and design of switched systems. IEEE Control Systems Magazine (1999) 59–70
4. Molchanov, A., Pyatnitskiy, Y.: Criteria of asymptotic stability of differential and difference inclusions encountered in control theory. Systems and Control Letters **13** (1989) 59–64
5. Ohta, Y., Imanishi, H., Haneda, H.: Computer Generated Lyapunov Functions for a Class of Nonlinear Systems. IEEE Transactions on Circuits and Systems **40** (1993) 343–353
6. Blanchini, F.: Set invariance in control. Automatica **35** (1999) 1747–1767
7. Molchanov, A., Pyatnitskii, E.: Lyapunov functions that specify Necessary and Sufficient Conditions of Absolute Stability of Nonlinear Nonstationary Control Systems. III. Automation and Remote Control (1986) 38–49
8. Pyatnitskiy, Y., Rapoport, B.: Criteria of Asymptotic Stability of Differential Inclusions and Periodic Motions of Time-Varying Nonlinear Control Systems. IEEE Transactions on Circuits and Systems **43** (1996) 219–229
9. Dayawansa, W., Martin, C.: A Converse Lyapunov Theorem for a Class of Dynamical Systems which Undergo Switching. IEEE Transactions on Automatic Control **44** (1999) 751–760
10. Brayton, R.K., Tong, C.H.: Constructive stability and asymptotic stability of dynamical systems. IEEE Transactions on Circuits and Systems (1980) 1121–1130
11. Barabanov, N.: Method for the Computation of the Lyapunov exponent of a Differential Inclusion. Automation and Remote Control (1989) 53–58
12. Blanchini, F.: Nonquadratic Lyapunov functions for Robust Control. Automatica **31** (1995) 451–461
13. Julian, P., Guivant, J., Desages, A.: A parametrization of piecewise linear lyapunov functions via linear programming. Int. Journal of Control **72** (1999) 702–715
14. Polanski, A.: On absolute stability analysis by polyhedral Lyapunov functions. Automatica **36** (2000) 573–578
15. Koutsoukos, X.D., Antsaklis, P.J.: Design of stabilizing switching control laws for discrete and continuous-time linear systems using piecewise-linear lyapunov functions. Int. Journal of Control **75** (2002) 932–945

---

[2] This work is the sole responsibility of the authors and does not reflect the European Union's opinion

Asymptotic Stability and Boundedness of Delay Switching Diffusions[*]

Chenggui Yuan[1] and John Lygeros[2]

[1] Department of Engineering,
University of Cambridge,
Cambridge CB2 1PZ, U.K.
cy222@eng.cam.ac.uk

[2] Department of Electrical and Computer Engineering,
University of Patras, Patras, GR 26500, Greece
lygeros@ee.upatras.gr

Abstract. Multiple Lyapunov functions are used to establish sufficient conditions for locating the limit sets of switching diffusions. The conditions lead to a number of useful results on stochastic asymptotic stability and boundedness for this class of stochastic hybrid systems.

Keywords: Itô formula; Switching diffusions; Lyapunov function; Stochastic asymptotic stability.

1 Introduction

Questions of stability of equilibria and invariant sets for switched and hybrid systems have attracted considerable attention in recent year. Most of the effort in this direction has been towards extensions of Lyapunov's Direct Method to the hybrid domain [1,2,3]. The work of [4] provided effective computational tools, based on linear matrix inequalities, for applying these results to a class of piecewise linear systems. For an overview of the literature in this area the reader is referred to [5,6].

This paper deals with extensions of Lyapunov based results to switching diffusions. Switching diffusions are one of many different classes of stochastic hybrid processes that have been studied in the stochastic processes literature; for a brief overview of this and other classes the reader is referred to [7]. The state of a switching diffusion has two components, $x(t)$ and $r(t)$. $x(t)$ takes values in Euclidean space, while $r(t)$ can take a finite number of values; abusing the terminology somewhat, x is referred to as the state while r is regarded as the mode. The evolution of x is governed by a stochastic differential equation which depends on the value of r. r, on the other hand, changes discretely, very much like a Markov chain with transition rates that depend on x. The basic properties of this class of stochastic hybrid systems have been thoroughly studied in the

---

[*] Research supported by the European Commission under COLUMBUS, IST-2001-38314.

R. Alur and G.J. Pappas (Eds.): HSCC 2004, LNCS 2993, pp. 646–659, 2004.

stochastic processes literature (see, for example, [11]). The stability and control of switching diffusions have also received a lot of attention recently, see, for example, [8,13,23,25,26,30] and the references therein.

Stochastic stability of stochastic systems was an active area of research from the late 1950's to the early 1970's (see, for example, [14]). The most often used concept of stochastic stability is that of existence of an invariant measure. In this paper we restrict attention to almost sure convergence of the state process to the zero value. Control engineering intuition suggests that time-delays are common in practical systems and are often the cause of instability and/or poor performance. Moreover, it is usually difficult to obtain accurate values for the delay and conservative estimates often have to be used. The importance of time delay has already motivated several studies on the stability of switching diffusions with time delay, see, for example, [9,10,12,21,27].

Most of the existing results on stochastic stability for switching diffusions rely on the existence of a single Lyapunov function. Examples from the hybrid systems literature, however, suggest that even in the deterministic case one can find systems for which a single Lyapunov function does not exist; the systems can nontheless be shown to be stable if one considers multiple Lyapunov functions. Motivated by this observation, in this paper we study the stability of delayed switching diffusions using multiple Lyapunov functions in the spirit of [28,15, 1,2,3,22], i.e. besides the Lyapunov functions $V(x, t, i), i \in S$, there is another Lyapunov function $U(x, t)$ (see Theorem 1 and Theorem 2), which is different from [9,29]. On a more technical note, our new asymptotic stability criteria do not require the diffusion operator associated with the underlying stochastic differential equations to be negative definite, as is the case with most of the existing results.

2   Background on Switching Diffusions

Let $(\Omega, \mathcal{F}, \mathcal{F}_t, P)$ be a complete probability space with a filtration $(\mathcal{F}_t$ which is right continuous and $\mathcal{F}_0$ contains all P-null sets. Let $B(t) = (B_t^1, \ldots, B_t^m)^T$ be an m-dimensional Brownian motion defined on this probability space. Let $|\cdot|$ denote the Euclidean norm for vectors and the trace norm for matrices. Let $\tau > 0$ and $C([-\tau, 0]; \mathbb{R}^n)$ denote the family of all continuous $\mathbb{R}^n$-valued functions on $[-\tau, 0]$. Let $C^b_{\mathcal{F}_0}([-\tau, 0]; \mathbb{R}^n)$ be the family of all $\mathcal{F}_0$-measurable bounded $C([-\tau, 0]; \mathbb{R}^n)$-valued random variables $\xi = \{\xi(\theta) : -\tau \leq \theta \leq 0\}$. If K is a subset of $\mathbb{R}^n$ and $x \in \mathbb{R}^n$, denote the distance from x to K by $d(x, K) = \inf_{y \in K} |x - y|$. Let $\mathcal{K}$ denote the class of continuous increasing functions α from $\mathbb{R}_+ \to \mathbb{R}_+$ with $\alpha(0) = 0$. We also denote by $L^1(\mathbb{R}_+; \mathbb{R}_+)$ the family of all functions $\lambda : \mathbb{R}_+ \to \mathbb{R}_+$ such that $\int_0^\infty \lambda(t)dt < \infty$ while denote by $\mathcal{D}(\mathbb{R}_+; \mathbb{R}_+)$ the family of all continuous functions $\eta : \mathbb{R}_+ \to \mathbb{R}_+$ such that $\int_0^\infty \eta(t)dt = \infty$.

Switching diffusions are a class of stochastic hybrid systems that arises in numerous applications of systems with multiple modes; examples include fault-tolerant control systems, multiple target tracking, flexible manufacturing systems, etc. The state of the system at time t is given by two components

$(x(t), r(t)) \in \mathbb{R}^n \times S$, $S = \{1, 2, \dots, N\}$. For simplicity, our attention is limited to one delay, the result can be extended to multiple delays. The evolution of the process $(x(t), r(t))$ is governed by the following equations:

$$dx(t) = f(x(t), x(t - \tau), t, r(t))dt + g(x(t), x(t - \tau), t, r(t))dB(t) \qquad (2.1)$$

$$P\{r(t + \Delta) = j | r(t) = i\} = \begin{cases} \gamma_{ij}(x(t))\Delta + o(\Delta) & \text{if } i \neq j, \\ 1 + \gamma_{ii}(x(t))\Delta + o(\Delta) & \text{if } i = j, \end{cases} \qquad (2.2)$$

on $t \geq 0$ with initial value $x(\theta) = \xi$, $-\tau \leq \theta \leq 0$ and $r(0) = i_0$, where $\Delta > 0$, $f : \mathbb{R}^n \times \mathbb{R}^n \times \mathbb{R}_+ \times S \to \mathbb{R}^n$ and $g : \mathbb{R}^n \times \mathbb{R}^n \times \mathbb{R}_+ \times S \to \mathbb{R}^{n \times m}$. If $i \neq j$, $\gamma_{ij} \geq 0$ is transition rate from i to j, while

$$\gamma_{ii} = -\sum_{i \neq j} \gamma_{ij}.$$

$r(t), t \geq 0$ is a right-continuous Markov chain on the probability space taking values in a finite state space $S = \{1, 2, \dots, N\}$. Recall that a continuous time Markov chain $r(t)$ with generator $\Gamma = \{\gamma_{ij}\}_{N \times N}$ can be represented as a stochastic integral with respect to a Poisson random measure (cf. [8,11]). Indeed, let Δ_{ij} be consecutive, left closed, right open intervals of the real line each having length γ_{ij} such that

$$\Delta_{12}(x) = [0, \gamma_{12}(x)),$$
$$\Delta_{13}(x) = [\gamma_{12}(x), \gamma_{12}(x) + \gamma_{13}(x)),$$
$$\vdots$$
$$\Delta_{1N}(x) = [\sum_{j=2}^{N-1} \gamma_{1j}(x), \sum_{j=2}^{N} \gamma_{1j}(x)),$$
$$\Delta_{21}(x) = [\sum_{j=2}^{N} \gamma_{1j}(x), \sum_{j=2}^{N} \gamma_{1j}(x) + \gamma_{21}(x)),$$
$$\Delta_{23}(x) = [\sum_{j=2}^{N} \gamma_{1j}(x) + \gamma_{21}(x), \sum_{j=2}^{N} \gamma_{1j}(x) + \gamma_{21}(x) + \gamma_{23}(x)),$$
$$\vdots$$
$$\Delta_{2N}(x) = [\sum_{j=2}^{N} \gamma_{1j}(x) + \sum_{j=1, j\neq 2}^{N-1} \gamma_{2j}(x), \sum_{j=2}^{N} \gamma_{1j}(x) + \sum_{j=1, j\neq 2}^{N} \gamma_{2j}(x)),$$

and so on. Define a function $h : S \times \mathbb{R} \to \mathbb{R}$ by

$$h(x, i, y) = \begin{cases} j - i & : \quad \text{if } y \in \Delta_{ij}(x), \\ 0 & : \quad \text{otherwise.} \end{cases}$$

Then

$$dr(t) = \int_{\mathbb{R}} h(x(t), r(t-), y)\nu(dt, dy), \tag{2.3}$$

where $\nu(dt, dy)$ is a Poisson random measure with intensity $dt \times m(dy)$, in which m is the Lebesgue measure on $\mathbb{R}$.

We assume that

(H) *Both f and g satisfy a local Lipschitz condition and a linear growth condition. That is, for each $k = 1, 2, \ldots$, there is an $h_k > 0$ such that*

$$|f(x, y, t, i) - f(\bar{x}, \bar{y}, t, i)| + |g(x, y, t, i) - g(\bar{x}, \bar{y}, t, i)|$$
$$\leq h_k(|x - \bar{x}| + |y - \bar{y}|)$$

for all $i \in S, t \geq 0$ and those $x, y \in \mathbb{R}^n$ with $|x| \vee |y| \vee |\bar{x}| \vee |\bar{y}| \leq k$; and there is an $h > 0$ such that

$$|f(x, y, t, i)| + |g(x, y, t, i)| \leq h(1 + |x| + |y|)$$

for all $x, y \in \mathbb{R}^n$ and $i \in S, t \geq 0$. $\gamma_{ij}(x)$ are Lipschitz, i.e. for any $x \in \mathbb{R}^n$, there is a $\bar{\gamma} > 0$ such that

$$|\gamma_{ij}(x) - \gamma_{ij}(y)| \leq \bar{\gamma}|x - y|.$$

Moreover, $\nu(\cdot, \cdot)$ and $B(\cdot)$ are independent.

Under this hypothesis and from [11,21,31,24], Eq. (2.1) and (2.3) has a unique continuous solution $(x(t), r(t))$ on $t \geq 0$. We shall omit the proof here and report it elsewhere.

Let $C^{2,1}(\mathbb{R}^n \times \mathbb{R}_+ \times S; \mathbb{R}_+)$ denote the family of all non-negative functions $V(x, t, i) : \mathbb{R}^n \times \mathbb{R}_+ \times S \to \mathbb{R}_+$ which are continuously differentiable twice in x and once in t. For $V \in C^{2,1}(\mathbb{R}^n \times \mathbb{R}_+ \times S; \mathbb{R}_+)$, define the operator $LV : \mathbb{R}^n \times \mathbb{R}^n \times \mathbb{R}_+ \times S \to \mathbb{R}$ by

$$LV(x, y, t, i) = V_t(x, t, i) + V_x(x, t, i)f(x, y, t, i) + \sum_{j=1}^{N} \gamma_{ij}V(x, t, j)$$

$$+ \frac{1}{2}\text{trace}[g^T(x, y, t, i)V_{xx}(x, t, i)g(x, y, t, i)], \tag{2.4}$$

where

$$V_t(x, t, i) = \frac{\partial V(x, t, i)}{\partial t}, \quad V_x(x, t, i) = \left(\frac{\partial V(x, t, i)}{\partial x_1}, \ldots, \frac{\partial V(x, t, i)}{\partial x_n}\right)$$

and

$$V_{xx}(x, t, i) = \left(\frac{\partial^2 V(x, t, i)}{\partial x_i \partial x_j}\right)_{n \times n}.$$

Fix any ξ and i_0 and write $x(t; \xi, i_0) = x(t)$ for simplicity.

For the convenience of the reader we also cite the generalized Itô formula for this class of stochastic hybrid processes (cf. [11,31]). If $V \in C^{2,1}(\mathbb{R}^n \times \mathbb{R}_+ \times S; \mathbb{R}_+)$, then for any $t \geq 0$

$$V(x(t), t, r(t)) = V(x(0), 0, r(0)) + \int_0^t LV(x(s), x(s - \tau), s, r(s))ds$$

$$+ \int_0^t V_x(x(s), s, r(s))g(x(s), x(s - \tau), s, r(s))dB(s)$$

$$+ \int_0^t \int_{\mathbb{R}} (V(x(s), s, i_0 + h(r(s), l)) - V(x(s), s, r(s)))\mu(ds, dl), \qquad (2.5)$$

where $\mu(ds, dl) = \nu(ds, dl) - m(dl)ds$ is a martingale measure. Since $r(t)$ can be written by a stochastic integral, the value of the term $i_0 + h$ will be in the range of S.

3   Main Results

In this paper we show the following two results.

Theorem 1. *Assume that there are functions $V \in C^{2,1}(\mathbb{R}^n \times \mathbb{R}_+ \times S; \mathbb{R}_+)$, $\lambda \in L^1(\mathbb{R}_+; \mathbb{R}_+)$, $U \in C(\mathbb{R}^n \times [-\tau, \infty); \mathbb{R}_+)$, $\eta \in \mathcal{D}(\mathbb{R}_+; \mathbb{R}_+)$ and $w \in C(\mathbb{R}_+; \mathbb{R}_+)$, such that*

$$\lambda(t) - LV(x, y, t, i) - U(x, t) + U(y, t - \tau)$$

$$\geq \max\{0, \eta(t)w(x) - |V_x(x, t, i)g(x, y, t, i)|^2\} \qquad (3.1)$$

for all $(x, y, t, i) \in \mathbb{R}^n \times \mathbb{R}^n \times \mathbb{R}_+ \times S$ and

$$\lim_{|x| \to \infty} \left[\inf_{t \geq 0, i \in S} V(x, t, i) \right] = \infty. \qquad (3.2)$$

Then $D_\omega = \{x \in \mathbb{R}^n : w(x) = 0\} \neq \emptyset$ and, moreover, for every initial data $\xi \in C^b_{\mathcal{F}_0}([-\tau, 0]; \mathbb{R}^n)$, $i_0 \in S$

$$\liminf_{t \to \infty} d(x(t; \xi, i_0), D_\omega) = 0 \quad a.s. \qquad (3.3)$$

Theorem 1 shows that the solutions of equations (2.1) and (2.2) will visit the neighborhood of D_ω infinitely many times with probability 1. In other words, D_ω attracts the solutions infinitely many times so we many say that D_ω is a weak attractor for the solutions. However, the theorem does not guarantee that the solution will be attracted by D_ω eventually. For this stronger property, we need to impose additional conditions.

Theorem 2. *In addition to the conditions of Theorem 1 assume*

(i) *For some constants $\delta > 0$ and $p \geq 1$*

$$
\begin{aligned}
\lambda(t) - LV(x,y,t,i) - U(x,t) + U(y,t-\tau) \\
+ |V_x(x,t,i)g(x,t,i)|^2 \geq \delta U^p(x,t)
\end{aligned}
\tag{3.4}
$$

holds for all $(x,y,t,i) \in \mathbb{R}^n \times \mathbb{R}^n \times \mathbb{R}_+ \times S$.

(ii) *$D_\omega = \cup_{l \in \imath} F_l$, where $\imath$ is an index set which may be finite or countably infinite while F_l is a closed subset of $\mathbb{R}^n$ and F_l's are mutually disjoint. For each $l \in \imath$ there is an open neighborhood G_l of F_l and two functions $\alpha_l, \beta_l \in \mathcal{K}$ and constants c_l such that*

$$
\lim_{t \to \infty} V(x,t,i) = c_l \quad \text{uniformly in } (x,i) \in F_l \times S
\tag{3.5}
$$

while

$$
\alpha_l(d(x,F_l)) \leq |V(x,t,i) - c_l| \leq \beta_l(d(x,F_l)),
\tag{3.6}
$$

for $(x,t,i) \in (G_l - F_l) \times \mathbb{R}_+ \times S$.

Then

$$
\lim_{t \to \infty} d(x(t;\xi,i_0), D_\omega) = 0 \quad a.s.
\tag{3.7}
$$

The proofs make use of the nonnegative semi-martingale convergence theorem [19].

Lemma 1. *Let $A_1(t)$ and $A_2(t)$ be two continuous adapted increasing processes on $t \geq 0$ with $A_1(0) = A_2(0) = 0$ a.s. Let $M(t)$ be a real-valued continuous local martingale with $M(0) = 0$ a.s. Let ζ be a nonnegative $\mathcal{F}_0$-measurable random variable such that $E\zeta < \infty$. Define*

$$
X(t) = \zeta + A_1(t) - A_2(t) + M(t) \text{ for } t \geq 0.
$$

If $X(t)$ is nonnegative, then

$$
\left\{ \lim_{t \to \infty} A_1(t) < \infty \right\} \subset \left\{ \lim_{t \to \infty} X(t) < \infty \right\} \cap \left\{ \lim_{t \to \infty} A_2(t) < \infty \right\} \quad a.s.
$$

where $C \subset D$ a.s. means $P(C \cap D^c) = 0$. In particular, if $\lim_{t \to \infty} A_1(t) < \infty$ a.s., then for almost all $\omega \in \Omega$, $\lim_{t \to \infty} X(t) < \infty$, $\lim_{t \to \infty} A_2(t) < \infty$ and $-\infty < \lim_{t \to \infty} M(t,\omega) < \infty$. That is, all of the three processes $X(t), A_2(t)$ and $M(t)$ converge to finite random variables.

The following lemma also plays a key role in the proofs.

Lemma 2. *Assume that there are functions $V \in C^{2,1}(\mathbb{R}^n \times \mathbb{R}_+ \times S; \mathbb{R}_+)$, $\lambda \in \Gamma(\mathbb{R}_+; \mathbb{R}_+)$ and $U \in C(\mathbb{R}^n \times [-\tau, \infty); \mathbb{R}_+)$ such that*

$$
LV(x,y,t,i) \leq \lambda(t) - U(x,t) + U(y,t-\tau)
\tag{3.8}
$$

for all $(x, y, t, i) \in \mathbb{R}^n \times \mathbb{R}^n \times \mathbb{R}_+ \times S$. *Then, for every initial value* $\xi \in C^b_{\mathcal{F}_0}([-\tau, 0]; \mathbb{R}_+)$, $i_0 \in S$, *the solution* $x(t) = x(t; \xi, i_0)$ *of equations (2.1) and (2.2) has the properties that*

$$\lim_{t \to \infty} \left[V(x(t), t, r(t)) + \int_{t-\tau}^t U(x(s), s) ds \right] < \infty \quad a.s. \tag{3.9}$$

$$\int_0^\infty [\lambda(t) - LV(x(t), x(t - \tau), t, r(t))$$
$$- U(x(s), s) + U(x(s - \tau), s - \tau)$$
$$+ |V_x(x(t), t, r(t)) g(x(t), x(t - \tau), t, r(t))|^2] dt < \infty \quad a.s. \tag{3.10}$$

Proof: By the Itô formula

$$V(x(t), t, r(t)) = V(x(0), 0, r(0)) + \int_0^t LV(x(s), x(s - \tau), s, r(s)) ds$$

$$+ \int_0^t V_x(x(s), s, r(s)) g(x(s), x(s - \tau), s, r(s)) dB(s)$$

$$+ \int_0^t \int_{\mathbb{R}} (V(x(s), s, i_0 + h(x(s), r(s), l)) - V(x(s), s, r(s))) \mu(ds, dl).$$

Noting that

$$\int_{t-\tau}^t U(x(s), s) = \int_{-\tau}^0 U(x(s), s) ds + \int_0^t (U(x(s), s) - U(x(s - \tau), s - \tau)) ds.$$

So

$$V(x(t), t, r(t)) + \int_{t-\tau}^t U(x(s), s) ds$$

$$= V(x(0), 0, r(0)) + \int_{-\tau}^0 U(\xi(\theta), \theta) d\theta + \int_0^t \lambda(s) ds$$

$$- \int_0^t [\lambda(s) - LV(x(s), x(s - \tau), s, r(s)) - U(x(s), s)$$
$$+ U(x(s - \tau), s - \tau)] ds$$

$$+ \int_0^t V_x(x(s), s, r(s)) g(x(s), x(s - \tau), s, r(s)) dB(s)$$

$$+ \int_0^t \int_{\mathbb{R}} (V(x(s), s, i_0 + h(x(s), r(s), l)) - V(x(s), s, r(s))) \mu(ds, dl).$$

Noting that $\int_0^t \lambda(s) ds < \infty$ a.s. and (3.8), we can apply Lemma 1 to get the assertions (3.9) and

$$\int_0^\infty [\lambda(s) - LV(x(s), x(s - \tau), s, r(s))$$
$$- U(x(s), s) + U(x(s - \tau), s - \tau)] ds < \infty \quad a.s.$$

Moreover

$$-\infty < \lim_{t \to \infty} M(t) < \infty \quad a.s., \tag{3.11}$$

where

$$M(t) = \int_0^t V_x(x(s), s, r(s))g(x(s), x(s-\tau), s, r(s))dB(s)$$

$$+ \int_0^t \int_{\mathbb{R}} (V(x(s), s, i_0 + h(r(s), l)) - V(x(s), s, r(s)))\mu(ds, dl)$$

$$=: M_1(t) + M_2(t).$$

For every integer $N \geq 1$, define the stopping time

$$\tau_N = \inf\{t \geq 0 : |M(t)| \geq N\},$$

where here and throughout this paper we set $\inf \emptyset = \infty$. Obviously τ_N is increasing. In particular, by (3.11), there is a subset Ω_1 of Ω with $P(\Omega_1) = 1$ such that for every $\omega \in \Omega_1$ there is a finite number $N(\omega)$ such that $\tau_N(\omega) = \infty$ for all $N \geq N(\omega)$. On the other hand, since $M_1(t)$ is continuous martingale and $M_1(t)$ is discontinuous martingale, we have, for any $t > 0$, $E[M_1(t \wedge \tau_N)M_2(t \wedge \tau_N)] = 0$. Therefore

$$N^2 \geq E|M(t \wedge \tau_N)|^2 = E|M_1(t \wedge \tau_N) + M_2(t \wedge \tau_N)|^2$$

$$= E|M_1(t \wedge \tau_N)|^2 + E|M_2(t \wedge \tau_N)|^2 \geq E|M_1(t \wedge \tau_N)|^2$$

$$= E \int_0^{t \wedge \tau_N} |V_x(x(s), s, r(s))g(x(s), x(s-\tau), s, r(s))|^2 ds.$$

Letting $t \to \infty$ yields

$$E \int_0^{\tau_N} |V_x(x(s), s, r(s))g(x(s), x(s-\tau), s, r(s))|^2 ds \leq N^2,$$

which implies that

$$\int_0^{\tau_N} |V_x(x(s), s, r(s))g(x(s), x(s-\tau), s, r(s))|^2 ds < \infty \tag{3.12}$$

holds with probability 1. Hence there is another subset Ω_2 of Ω with $P(\Omega_2) = 1$ such that if $\omega \in \Omega_2$, (3.12) holds for every $N \geq 1$. Therefore, for any $\omega \in \Omega_1 \cap \Omega_2$, we have

$$\int_0^{\infty} |V_x(x(s), s, r(s))g(x(s), x(s-\tau), s, r(s))|^2 ds$$

$$= \int_0^{\tau_{N(\omega)}(\omega)} |V_x(x(s), s, r(s))g(x(s), x(s-\tau), s, r(s))|^2 ds < \infty.$$

Since $P(\Omega_1 \cap \Omega_2) = 1$, we must have (3.10).   ∎

Proof of Theorem 1: Write $x(t; \xi, i_0) = x(t)$. By Lemma 2 and (3.1) we observe that there is a subset $\bar{\Omega}$ of Ω with $P(\bar{\Omega}) = 1$ such that for every $\omega \in \bar{\Omega}$

$$\limsup_{t \to \infty} \min_{i \in S} V(x(t, \omega), t, i) < \infty \tag{3.13}$$

while

$$\int_0^\infty \eta(t) w(x(t, \omega))) dt < \infty \tag{3.14}$$

Noting (3.2) and (3.13), we know that $\{x(t, \omega) : t \geq 0\}$ is bounded, moreover, since $\eta \in \mathcal{D}(\mathbb{R}_+, \mathbb{R}_+)$, (3.14) derives that

$$\liminf_{t \to \infty} w(x(t, \omega)) = 0.$$

So there exists a divergent sequence t_k such that

$$\lim_{k \to \infty} w(x(t_k, \omega)) = 0.$$

But, due to the boundedness of $\{x(t_k, \omega)\}$, there must be a convergent subsequence $\{x(t_{\bar{k}}, \omega)\}$ that convergences to $\bar{x} \in \mathbb{R}^n$. Since w is continuous, we must have

$$w(\bar{x}) = \lim_{\bar{k} \to \infty} w(x(t_{\bar{k}}, \omega) = 0.$$

In other words, $\bar{x} \in D_\omega$ so $D_\omega \neq \emptyset$ and the required assertion (3.3) follows, as required. ∎

Proof of Theorem 2: Write $x(t; \xi, i_0) = x(t)$. By (3.10) and (3.4), there exists a subset $\bar{\Omega}$ of Ω with $P(\bar{\Omega}) = 1$ such that for every $\omega \in \bar{\Omega}$ such that

$$\int_0^\infty U^p(x(t, \omega), t, r(t)) dt < \infty,$$

this implies

$$\lim_{t \to \infty} \int_{t-\tau}^t U^p(x(s, \omega), s, r(s)) ds = 0.$$

Using the Hölder inequality,

$$\limsup_{t \to \infty} \int_{t-\tau}^t U(x(s, \omega), s, r(s)) ds = 0.$$

This, together with (3.9), yields

$$\lim_{t \to \infty} V(x(t, \omega), t, r(t)) < \infty. \tag{3.15}$$

As in the proof of Theorem 1, there exists a sequence $\{x(t_k)\}$ and a vector $\bar{x} \in D_\omega$, say $\bar{x} \in F_l$ for some $l \in \imath$, such that

$$\lim_{k \to \infty} x(t_k, \omega) = \bar{x}. \tag{3.16}$$

Using the standard method of the proof of Theorem 2.2 in [22], leads to

$$\lim_{t \to \infty} d(x(t, \omega), F_l) = 0. \tag{3.17}$$

The required assertion (3.7) follows. ∎

4   Implications for Boundedness and Stability

The results of Section 3 can be used to establish sufficient criteria for the boundedness and the almost sure stability of switching diffusions. From the proof of Theorem 1, the following result is almost immediate.

Corollary 3. *Under the assumptions of Theorem 1, the solutions of equations (2.1) and (2.2) are bounded in the sense that*

$$\sup_{-\tau \leq t < \infty} |x(t; \xi)| < \infty \quad a.s.$$

Moreover, one can also show the following.

Corollary 4. *Assume (3.1), (3.2) and (3.4) hold and D_ω is bounded, i.e.*

$$\sup_{x \in D_\omega} |x| \leq K < \infty.$$

Then for any initial data $\xi \in C^b_{\mathcal{F}_0}([-\tau, 0]; \mathbb{R}^n)$, $i_0 \in S$, the solution of equations (2.1) and (2.2) has the property that

$$\limsup_{t \to \infty} |x(t; \xi, i_0)| \leq K \quad a.s.$$

Proof: Since D_ω is bounded, there exists a sequence $\{y_l : l \in \imath\}$ which is dense in D_ω. By (3.15) we know that for each $i \in \imath$, there is an open neighborhood G_l of y_l, c_l, α_l and β_l such that (3.6) holds. Therefore, we must have

$$\lim_{t \to 0} d(x(t; \xi, i_0), D_\omega) = 0.$$

The required assertions follows.   ■

Corollary 5. *If (3.1), (3.2) and (3.4) hold and $D_\omega = \{0\}$ and, moreover, there is an open neighborhood G of the origin and two functions $\alpha, \beta \in \mathcal{K}$ such that*

$$\alpha(|x|) \leq V(x, t, i) \leq \beta(|x|) \quad (x, t, i) \in G \times \mathbb{R}_+ \times S.$$

Then for any initial data $\xi \in C^b_{\mathcal{F}_0}([-\tau, 0]; \mathbb{R}^n)$, $i_0 \in S$, the solution of equations (2.1) and (2.2) has the property that

$$\lim_{t \to \infty} x(t; \xi, i_0) = 0 \quad a.s. \tag{4.1}$$

5   An Example

To illustrate the results listed in the previous sections we consider a simple example with a one dimensional continuous state. Let $B(t)$ be a scalar Brownian motion and $r(t)$ be a right-continuous Markov chain taking values in $S = \{1, 2\}$ with generator

$$\Gamma = (\gamma_{ij})_{2\times 2} = \begin{pmatrix} -1 & 1 \\ 2 & -2 \end{pmatrix}.$$

Assume that $B(t)$ and $r(t)$ are independent. Consider a one-dimensional stochastic differential delay equation with Markov switching of the form

$$dx(t) = [-a(t, r(t))x(t) + b(t, r(t))x(t - \tau)]dt + \sigma(t, r(t))x(t)dB(t) \quad (5.1)$$

on $t \geq 0$ with initial data $\xi \in C^b_{\mathcal{F}_0}([-\tau, 0]; \mathbb{R})$ and $r(0) = i_0$. Assume $a(t, i), b(t, i), \sigma(t, i)$ are all bounded continuous functions and $\sigma = \inf_{t \geq 0, i \in S} \sigma(t, i) > 0$ and

$$4a(t, 1) + 1 - \sigma^2(t, 1) \geq 2b(t, 1) + 2b(t - \tau, 1),$$
$$2a(t, 2) - 2 - \sigma^2(t, 2) \geq b(t, 2) + b(t - \tau, 2).$$

Define

$$V(x, t, i) = \beta_i x^2, \quad w(x) = x^2,$$

with $\beta_2 = 1$ and $\beta_1 = 2$. It is easy to show that the operator LV from $\mathbb{R} \times \mathbb{R} \times \mathbb{R}_+ \times S$ to $\mathbb{R}$ has the form

$$LV(x, y, t, i) = 2\beta_i x[-a(t, i)x + b(t, i)y] + \beta_i \sigma^2(t, i)x^2$$
$$+ (\gamma_{i1}\beta + \gamma_{i2})|x|^2 + (\gamma_{i1}\beta + \gamma_{i2})|x|^2.$$

Computing, by the conditions, we then have

$$LV(x, y, t, 1) \leq -[4a(t, 1) - 2b(t, 1) + 1 - 2\sigma^2(t, 1)]|x|^2 + 2b(t, 1)y^2$$
$$\leq -2b(t - \tau, 1)w(x) + 2b(t, 1)w(y)$$

and

$$LV(x, y, t, 2) \leq -[2a(t, 2) - b(t, 2) - 2 - \sigma^2(t, 2)]|x|^2 + b(t, 2)y^2$$
$$\leq -b(t - \tau, 2)w(x) + b(t, 2)w(y).$$

On the other hand

$$|v_x(x, t, i)\sigma(t, i)x|^2 = 4\beta_i^2 \sigma^2(t, i)x^4 \geq 4\sigma^2 w^2(x).$$

Therefore, by the conditions, we must have

$$-LV(x, y, t, 1) - 2b(t - \tau, 1)w(x) + 2b(t, 1)w(y)$$
$$\geq 0 \geq 4\sigma^2 w^2(x) - |v_x(x, t, 1)\sigma(t, 1)x|^2 \quad (5.2)$$

and

$$-LV(x, y, t, 2) - b(t - \tau, 2)w(x) + b(t, 2)w(y)$$
$$\geq 0 \geq 4\sigma^2 w^2(x) - |v_x(x, t, 2)\sigma(t, 2)x|^2. \quad (5.3)$$

By Lemma 2, (5.2) and (5.3), we have

$$\lim_{t\to\infty}\left[V(x(t),t,r(t))+\int_{t-\tau}^{t}b(s,r(s))w(x(s))\right]ds<\infty\quad a.s.\qquad(5.4)$$

and

$$\int_{0}^{\infty}w^{2}(x(s))ds<\infty\quad a.s.\qquad(5.5)$$

By the Hölder inequality and the boundedness of $b(t,i)$ we obtain

$$\int_{t-\tau}^{t}b(s,r(s))w(x(s))ds<\infty\quad a.s.$$

This, together with (5.4) and (5.5), yields

$$\lim_{t\to\infty}x^{2}(t)<\infty\quad\text{and}\quad\int_{0}^{\infty}x^{4}(t)dt<\infty.$$

So we must have

$$\lim_{t\to\infty}x(t)=0.$$

6   Conclusion

The logic next step is to study the ergodic control of delay switching diffusion. The existence of a stable, nonrandomized Markov policy which almost surely minimizes the pathwise long-run average cost could be established.

Acknowledgements. The authors would like to thank the associate editors and the referees for their very useful suggestions and detailed comments.

References

1. H. Ye, A. Michel, and L. Hou, *Stability theory for hybrid dynamical systems* IEEE Transactions on Automatic Control, vol. 43, no. 4, pp. 461–474, 1998.
2. M.S. Branicky, *Multiple Lyapunov functions and other analysis tools for switched and hybrid systems*, IEEE Transactions on Automatic Control, vol. 43, no. 4, pp. 475–482, 1998.
3. A.N. Michel and B. Hu, *Towards a stability theory for hybrid dynamical systems*, Automatica, vol. 35, pp. 371–384, 1999.
4. M. Johansson and A. Rantzer, *Computation of piecewise quadratic Lyapunov functions for hybrid systems*, IEEE Transactions on Automatic Control, vol. 43, no. 4, pp. 555–559, 1998.
5. R. De Carlo, M. Branicky, S. Pettersson, and B. Lennarston, *Perspectives and results on the stability and stabilizability of hybrid systems*, Proceedings of the IEEE, vol. 88, no. 7, pp. 1069–1082, July 2000.

6. D. Liberzon and A.S. Morse, *Basic problems in stability and design of switched systems*, IEEE Control Systems Magazine, vol. 19, pp. 59–70, October 1999.
7. G. Pola, M. Bujorianu, J. Lygeros, and M.D. Di Benedetto, *Stochastic hybrid models: An overview*, in IFAC Conference on Analysis and Design of Hybrid Systems ADHS03, pp. 52–57, Saint Malo, France, June 16-18 2003.
8. G. K. Basak, A. Bisi and M. K. Ghosh, *Stability of a random diffusion with linear drift*, J. Math. Anal. Appl. 202 (1996), 604–622.
9. E. K. Boukas and Z. K. Liu, *Robust H_∞ Control of discrete-dime Markovian jump linear system with mode-dependent time-delays*, IEEE Trans. Automat. Control 46(2001), 1981-1924.
10. Y. Y. Cao, Y. X. Sun and J. Lam, *delay-dependent robust H_∞ control for uncertain systems with time-varying delays*. IEEE Proceeding- Control Theory and Applications, 145, 338-344.
11. M. K. Ghosh, A. Arapostahis and S. I. Marcus, *Optimal control of switching diffusions with applications to flexible manufacturing systems*, SIAM J. Control Optim. 31(1993), 1183-1204.
12. E.T. Jeung, J. H. Kim and H. B. Park, *H_∞ output feedback controller design for linear systems with time-varying delayed state*. IEEE Trans. Automat. Control 43 (1998), 971-974.
13. Y. Ji and H. J. Chizeck, *Controllability, stabilizability and continuous-time Markovian jump linear quadratic control*, IEEE Trans. Automat. Control 35 (1990), 777–788.
14. R. Z. Khas'minskii, *Stochastic Stability of Differential Equations*, Sijthoff and Noordhoff, 1981.
15. G. S. Ladde, and V. Lakshmikantham, *Random Differential Inequalities*, Academic Press, 1980.
16. V. Lakshmikantham, S. Leeda and A. Martynyu, *Stability Analysis of Nonlinear Systems*, Academic Press, 1980.
17. V. Lakshmikantham, V. M. Matrosov and S. Sivasundaram, *Vector Lyapunov Functions and Stability Analysis of Nonlinear Systems*, Kluwer Academic Publishers, 1991.
18. J. P. Lasalle, *Stability theory of ordinary differential equations*, J. Differential Equations 4(1968), 57-65.
19. R. Sh. Liptser and A. N. Shiryayev, *Theory of Martingales*, Kluwer Academic Publishers, 1989.
20. X. Mao, *Stochastic Differential Equations and Applications*, Horwood, 1997.
21. X. Mao, A. Matasov and A. B. Piunovskiy, *Stochastic differential delay equations with Markovian switching*, Bernoulli 6 (2000), 73–90.
22. X. Mao, *Some contributions to stochastic asymptotic stability and boundedness via multiple Lyapunov functions*, J. Math. Ana. Appl. 260(2001), 325-340.
23. M. Mariton, *Jump Linear Systems in Automatic Control*, Marcel Dekker, New York, 1990.
24. S.-E. A. Mohammed, *Stochastic Functional Differential Equations*, Longman, Harlow/New York, 1984.
25. P. V. Pakshin, *Robust stability and stabilization of family of jumping stochastic systems*, Nonlinear Analysis 30(1997), 2855-2866.
26. G. Pan and Y. Bar-Shalom, *Stabilization of jump linear Gaussian systems without mode observations*, Int. J. Contr. 64 (1996), 631–661.
27. P. Park, *A delay-dependent stability criterion for systems with uncertain linear systems*. IEEE Trans. Automat. Control 44(1999).

28. L. Salvadori, *Some contributions to asymptotic stability theory*, Ann. Soc. Sci. Bruxelles 88(1974), 183-194.

29. P. Seiler and R. Sengupta, *A Bounded Real Lemma for Jump Systems.* IEEE Trans. Automat. Control 48(2003), 1651-1654.

30. L. Shaikhet, *Stability of stochastic hereditary systems with Markov switching*, Theory of Stochastic Processes 2 (1996) 180–184.

31. A. V. Skorohod, *Asymptotic Methods in the Theory of Stochastic Differential Equations*, American Mathematical Society, Providence, 1989.

Author Index

Printed in the United States
By Bookmasters